PIMLICO

403

CHURCHILL
A Life

Martin Gilbert was born in London in 1936. After two years' National Service he read Modern History at Magdalen College, Oxford. In 1962 he was elected to a Fellowship at Merton College, Oxford, and in the same year became one of the research assistants to Randolph Churchill, then writing the first two volumes of his father's official biography. On Randolph's death in 1968, Gilbert was asked to complete the biography. The eighth and final volume was published in 1988. In addition to these narrative volumes, Gilbert has continued to edit the multi-volume documentary series of Churchill's letters and documents. He has also published, as part of the biography, *Churchill: A Photographic Portrait* (also available in Pimlico).

In addition to his Churchill work, Gilbert has been a pioneer in the design and publication of historical atlases, and has written a general history of the Holocaust, one-volume histories of the First and the Second World War, and a three-volume history of the twentieth century. He was knighted in 1995.

CHURCHILL
A Life

Martin Gilbert

PIMLICO

Published by Pimlico 2000

6 8 10 9 7

First published in Great Britain by
William Heinemann Ltd 1991

Pimlico edition 2000

Pimlico
Random House, 20 Vauxhall Bridge Road,
London SW1V 2SA

Random House Australia (Pty) Limited
20 Alfred Street, Milsons Point, Sydney,
New South Wales 2061, Australia

Random House New Zealand Limited
18 Poland Road, Glenfield,
Auckland 10, New Zealand

Random House (Pty) Limited
Endulini, 5a Jubilee Road, Parktown 2193, South Africa

Random House Group Limited Reg. No. 954009
www.randomhouse.co.uk

A CIP catalogue record for this book
is available from the British Library

ISBN 0-7126-6725-3

Papers used by Random House are natural,
recyclable products made from wood grown in sustainable forests.
The manufacturing processes conform to the environmental
regulations of the country of origin

Printed and bound in Great Britain by
Mackays of Chatham plc, Chatham, Kent

For Natalie, David and Joshua

Contents

Illustrations

Section Two

Section Four

List of Maps

Author's Note to the Second Edition

A year after the publication of this book in 1991, an abridged version was issued which inevitably conveyed less in its 662 pages than the full picture which I tried to present within these 959 pages. The bringing back into print of this fuller version will enable readers once more to range in detail over the full span of Churchill's career, his thoughts, aspirations and actions.

Martin Gilbert
7 January 2000

Preface

It is my aim in these pages to give a full and rounded picture of Churchill's life, both in its personal and political aspects. His career has been the subject of countless books and essays, in which he has sometimes been cavalierly, sometimes harshly, judged. I have sought to give a balanced appraisal, based on his actual thoughts, actions, achievements and beliefs, as opposed to the many misconceptions that exist.

The record of Churchill's life is a particularly full one, for which a vast mass of contemporary material survives. It is therefore possible, for almost every incident in which he was involved, to present his own words and arguments, his thinking, his true intentions, and his precise actions.

My own researches began in October 1962, when I started work as the junior member of Randolph Churchill's research team, a year after he had been asked by his father to undertake the writing of a multi-volume biography, and edition of supporting documents. At the time of his death in 1968, Randolph Churchill had taken his father's story up to the outbreak of war in 1914. I was asked to continue his work. My own final volume, the eighth in the series, ended with Churchill's death at the age of ninety.

The official biography, as it has become known, set out in detail the story of Churchill's life based upon five main sources, each of which I have returned to for this one-volume account; from these sources I have also drawn much new material, particularly for Churchill's earlier years, up to the First World War.

The first of these sources is Churchill's own enormous personal archive of political, Ministerial, literary and personal correspondence, now at Churchill College Cambridge. This contains private and public correspondence spanning the whole of his ninety years.

The second source is his wife Clementine's papers, including the many hundreds of letters which her husband wrote to her from the time of their marriage in 1908 until his last years. This is under the custody of Churchill's daughter, Lady Soames, and gives a remarkable picture of every aspect of Churchill's personality.

The third source is the Government archive of Churchill's two Premierships, and of his official Ministerial work, which began in December 1905, and continued until his retirement from public life in April 1955. This archive, located at the Public Record Office at Kew, contains all the War Cabinet and Chiefs of Staff discussions for the Second World War, as well as the papers of his eleven Ministries during those years, and of the War Council on which he served in 1914 and 1915.

The fourth source is the private archives, some of them substantial, others fragmentary, of his friends, colleagues and opponents; those who had been in contact with him at different times throughout his life. These materials are to be found in many archives, libraries and private collections, in Britain and abroad. They show how he struck his contemporaries: what they said about him among themselves; how some detested him, and how others, from his earliest years, saw him as a person of exceptional qualities, and as a future Prime Minister.

The fifth source, which I myself built up during thirty years, is the personal recollections of Churchill's family, his friends and his contemporaries. These recollections come from people in all walks of life, among others from the pilots who taught him to fly before the First World War and the officers and men who served with him on the Western Front in 1916. I was fortunate to meet, and to get to know, his literary assistants of the pre- and postwar years, including Maurice Ashley, Sir William Deakin and Denis Kelly; his Private Secretaries, among them Sir Herbert Creedy, who was with him in 1919, and members of his Second World War Private Office, including Sir John Martin, Sir John Peck and Sir John Colville; also Anthony Montague Browne, who was with him from 1953 to 1965.

As Churchill's biographer, I was particularly fortunate to have been able to see him from the perspective of his secretaries, among them Kathleen Hill, who joined him in 1936, Elizabeth Layton and Marian Holmes, who worked with him during the Second World War, and Elizabeth Gilliatt, Lady Onslow, Jane Portal and Doreen Pugh, who were with him in his later years. So much of Churchill's life was spent at Chartwell; Grace Hamblin, who worked there since 1932, has been a guide to those years.

Several million words drawn from these five sources are edited and annotated in the volumes of documents published (and still being published) for each of the volumes of the multi-volume biography.

I have set out to provide enough material in this single volume for readers to judge for themselves Churchill's actions and abilities during his remarkably long career. It was a career often marked by controversy and dogged by antagonism; for he was always outspoken and independent, and expressed his views without prevarication, criticising those whom he thought were wrong with a powerful armoury of knowledge, and with vivid, adept and penetrating language.

Churchill's involvement in public life spanned more than fifty years. He had held eight Cabinet posts before he became Prime Minister. When he resigned from his second Premiership in 1955 he had been a Parliamentarian for fifty-five years. The range of his activities and experiences was extraordinary. He received his Army commission during the reign of Queen Victoria, and took part in the cavalry charge at Omdurman. He was closely involved in the early development of aviation, learning to fly before the First World War, and establishing the Royal Naval Air Service. He was closely involved in the inception of the tank. He was a pioneer in the development of anti-aircraft defence, and in the evolution of aerial warfare. He foresaw the building of weapons of mass destruction, and in his last speech to Parliament proposed using the existence of the hydrogen bomb, and its deterrent power, as the basis for world disarmament.

From his early years, Churchill had an uncanny understanding and vision of the future unfolding of events. He had a strong faith in his own ability to contribute to the survival of civilisation, and the improvement of the material well-being of mankind. His military training, and his natural inventiveness, gave him great insight into the nature of war and society. He was also a man whose personal courage, whether on the battlefields of Empire at the turn of the century, on the Western Front in 1916, or in Athens in 1944, was matched with a deep understanding of the horrors of war and the devastation of battle.

Both in his Liberal and Conservative years, Churchill was a radical; a believer in the need for the State to take an active part, both by legislation and finance, in ensuring minimum standards of life, labour and social well-being for all citizens. Among the areas of social reform in which he took a leading part, including drafting substantial legislation, were prison reform, unemployment insurance, State-aided pensions for widows and orphans, a permanent arbitration machinery for labour disputes, State assistance for those in search of employment, shorter hours of work, and improved conditions on the shop and factory floor. He was also an advocate of a National Health Service, of wider access to education, of the taxation of excess profits, and of profit-sharing by employees. In his first public speech, in 1897, three years before he entered Parliament, he looked forward to the day when the labourer would become 'a shareholder in the business in which he worked'.

At times of national stress, Churchill was a persistent advocate of conciliation, even of coalition; he shunned the paths of division and unnecessary confrontation. In international affairs he consistently sought the settlement of the grievances of those who had been defeated, and the building up of meaningful associations for the reconciliation of former enemies. After two world wars he argued in favour of maintaining the strength of the victors in order to redress the grievances of the vanquished, and to preserve peace. It was he who first used the word 'summit' for a meeting of the leaders of the Western and Communist worlds, and did his utmost to set up such meetings to end the dangerous confrontations of the Cold War. Among the agreements that he negotiated, with patience and understanding, were the constitutional settlements in South Africa and Ireland, and the war debt repayment schemes after the First World War.

A perceptive, shrewd commentator on the events taking place around him, Churchill was always an advocate of bold, farsighted courses of action. One of his greatest gifts, seen in several thousand public speeches, as well as heard in his many broadcasts, was his ability to use his exceptional mastery of words, and love of language, to convey detailed arguments and essential truths; to inform, to convince, and to inspire. He was a man of great humour and warmth, of magnanimity; a consistent and life-long liberal in outlook; a man often turned to by successive Prime Ministers for his skill as a conciliator. His dislike of unfairness, of victimisation, and of bullying – whether at home or abroad – was the foundation-stone of much of his thinking.

Churchill's public work touched every aspect of British domestic and foreign policy, from the struggle for social reform before the First World War to the search for a summit conference after the Second. It involved Britain's relations with France, Germany, the United States, and the Soviet Union, each at their most testing time. His finest hour was the leadership of Britain when it was most isolated, most threatened and most weak; when his own courage, determination and belief in democracy became at one with the nation.

Martin Gilbert,
Merton College,
Oxford

23 January 1991

ACKNOWLEDGEMENTS

I am grateful to all those who, over the past thirty years, have given me their recollections of Churchill. Those who are quoted in this volume were generous both with their time and their memories. I should like to thank Valentin Berezhkov, Harold J. Bourne, Sir John Colville, Ivon Courtney, Sir William Deakin, Sir Donald MacDougall, Robert Fox, Eve Gibson, Elizabeth Gilliatt, Grace Hamblin, Pamela Harriman, Kathleen Hill, Marian Holmes, Patrick Kinna, Elizabeth Layton, James Lees-Milne, Brigadier Maurice Lush, John J. McCloy, Jock McDavid, Malcolm MacDonald, Viscount Margesson, Sir John Martin, Trevor Martin, Anthony Montague Browne, Field Marshal Viscount Montgomery of Alamein, Sir John Peck, Captain Sir Richard Pim, Doreen Pugh and Lady Williams of Elvel (Jane Portal).

My most grateful thanks, for both insights and material over many years, are to Churchill's children; Sarah Lady Audley, Lady Soames, and Randolph Churchill, my predecessor as biographer.

In addition to those who helped me with recollections, I am grateful to all who answered my historical queries for this volume, or who provided me with extra documentary material. My thanks for this help go to Patricia Ackerman, Archivist, Churchill College Archives Centre; J. Albrecht, Ligue Suisse pour la Protection de la Nature; Larry Arnn, Claremont Institute for the Study of Statesmanship and Political Philosophy; Jeanne Berkeley; Alan S. Baxendale; Dr David Butler; Julian Challis; Robert Craig; Henry E. Crooks; Michael Diamond; Dr Michael Dunnill; Felicity Dwyer, Researcher, *Daily Express*; Nicholas P. Eadon; Linda Greenlick, Chief Librarian, *Jewish Chronicle*; Irene Morrison, Scottish Tourist Board; David Parry, Department of Photographs, Imperial War Museum; Gordon Ramsey; Andrew Roberts; James Rusbridger; Matthew Spalding; Ken Stone, Metropolitan Police Historical Museum; Jonathan de Souza; Lord Taylor of Hadfield; Professor Vladimir Trukhanovsky; Mrs

M.E.Vinall, Personnel and Administration Manager, *Evening Standard;* Frank Whelan, researcher, *Sunday Call-Chronicle;* and Benedict K.Zobrist, Director, Harry S.Truman Library, Independence, Missouri.

I am also grateful, for the use of previously unpublished Churchill material, to the British Library Manuscript Collections, Christie's Auction Rooms, the Hollinger Corporation, A. Rosenthal, Chas W Sawyer, John R. Smethurst, *The Times* Archive, Blenheim Palace Archive, and the National Trust Collection.

For copyright permission to reproduce the photographs, I should like to thank World Wide Photos Inc (number 5); the Radio Times Hulton Picture Library (numbers 6, 12, 21, 30, 63, 64, 72, 73, 74, 75, 88 and 136); Odhams Press (9); J. Bowers, Pretoria, (11); the Bettman Archive (14); Longmans Green (16); Syndication International, Photo Division, *Daily Mirror* (24, 25, 57, 60 and 81); *Die Woche* (28); Elliot and Fry (29), The Press Association (33, 36, 40, 55, 56, 77 and 129); *Daily Sketch* (37); *Tatler* (38 and 83); London News Agency Photo (41, 58); Major-General Sir Edmund Hakewill-Smith (43); Imperial War Museum (44, 45, 91, 92, 93, 96, 97, 98, 99, 100, 103, 104, 112, 113, 118, 121, 122, 123, 126 and 127); The Trustees of the Low Estate (49 and 89); Central Press Photos, Ltd (53); G. M. Georgoulas (51); Keystone Press (59, 90, 94, 102, 128, 130 and 140); The Topical Press Agency Ltd (61); Times Newspapers Ltd (62); Associated Press Ltd (65, 68, 70 and 84); Stefan Lorant (71); Fox Photos (76 and 85); *Daily Express* (79); *Punch* (80); H. Roger Viollet (87); United Press International (95, 106 and 141); J.J.Moss (105); War Office Photograph, photographer Captain Horton (114); Thomas Dalby (116); Viscount Montgomery Collection (117 and 125); Donald Wiedenmayer (119); Earl Alexander Collection (120, 132 and 133); Signal Corps Photo (131); Photo Heminger (134): Life Photo, photographer N.R. Farbman (135); Emery Reves (142). The remaining photographs are from the Broadwater Collection at Churchill College, Cambridge.

For their help in scrutinising the text and making important suggestions as to its content, I am exceptionally grateful to Sir David Hunt, Adam O'Riordan and Edward Thomas, each of whom has given me the benefit of his wide knowledge and critical scrutiny. Helen Fraser, Laura Beadle and the many others involved at William Heinemann in publishing this book, have always been helpful and encouraging, at the different and at times difficult stages of production; the copyediting and proofreading were expertly done by Lisa Glass and Arthur Neuhauser; Rachelle Gryn assisted in the discovery of important facts; Kay Thomson carried out myriad secretarial duties.

As with all my previous Churchill work, I am indebted to my wife Susie, for her contribution at every stage, and to every page.

1

Childhood

Winston Churchill was born in 1874, half way through the Victorian Era. That November, his mother, Lady Randolph Churchill, then less than seven months pregnant, had slipped and fallen while walking with a shooting party at Blenheim Palace. A few days later, while riding in a pony carriage over rough ground, labour began. She was rushed back to the Palace, where, in the early hours of November 30, her son was born.

The magnificent palace at Blenheim was the home of the baby's grandfather, the 7th Duke of Marlborough. On his father's side he was a child of the British aristocracy, descended both from the 1st Earl Spencer and from the distinguished soldier John Churchill, 1st Duke of Marlborough, commander of the coalition of armies that had defeated France at the beginning of the eighteenth century. On his mother's side he had an entirely American lineage; her father, Leonard Jerome, then living in New York, was a successful stockbroker, financier and newspaper proprietor. A century earlier his ancestors had fought in Washington's armies for the independence of the American Colonies.

Almost a year before Churchill's birth, his father, Lord Randolph Churchill, had been elected to the House of Commons as Member of Parliament for Woodstock. This small borough, of which Blenheim was a part, had scarcely more than a thousand electors; it had long been accustomed to send members of the Ducal family, or their nominees, to Westminster. In January 1877 Churchill's grandfather, the 7th Duke of Marlborough, was appointed Viceroy of Ireland, with Lord Randolph as his private secretary. The two-year-old boy travelled with his parents to Dublin, together with his nanny, Mrs Everest.

When Churchill was four, Ireland suffered a severe potato famine, and an upsurge of nationalist ferment led by the Fenians. 'My nurse, Mrs Everest, was nervous about the Fenians,' he later wrote. 'I gathered these were wicked people and there was no end to what they would do if they had their way.' One day, when Churchill was out riding on his donkey, Mrs Everest thought that she saw a Fenian procession approaching. 'I am sure now,' he later reflected, 'that it must have been the Rifle Brigade out for a route march. But we were all very much alarmed, particularly the donkey, who expressed his anxiety by kicking. I was thrown off and had concussion of the brain. This was my first introduction to Irish politics!'

As well as his nanny, the young boy acquired a governess while in Dublin. Her task was to teach him reading and mathematics. 'These complications,' he later wrote, 'cast a steadily gathering shadow over my daily life. They took one away from all the interesting things one wanted to do in the nursery or the garden.' He also recalled that although his mother took 'no part in these impositions', she had given him to understand that she approved of them, and 'sided with the governess almost always'.

Fifty years later Churchill wrote of his mother: 'She shone for me like the Evening Star. I loved her dearly – but at a distance.' It was with his nanny that he found the affection which his parents did not provide. 'My nurse was my confidante,' he later wrote. 'Mrs Everest it was who looked after me and tended all my wants. It was to her I poured out my many troubles.'

In February 1880 Churchill's brother Jack was born. 'I remember my father coming into my bedroom at Vice-Regal Lodge in Dublin & telling me (aged 5) "You have a little brother",' he recalled sixty-five years later. Shortly after Jack's birth the family returned to London, to 29 St James's Place. There, Churchill was aware of the final illness of Disraeli, the former Conservative Prime Minister. 'I was always sure Lord Beaconsfield was going to die,' he later wrote, 'and at last the day came when all the people I saw went about with very sad faces because, as they said, a great and splendid Statesman who loved our country and defied the Russians, had died of a broken heart because of the ingratitude with which he had been treated by the Radicals.' Benjamin Disraeli, 1st Earl of Beaconsfield, died when Churchill was six years old.

At Christmas 1881, just after his seventh birthday, Churchill was at Blenheim. It was from there that his first surviving letter was written, posted on 4 January 1882. 'My dear Mamma,' he wrote, 'I hope you are quite well. I thank you very very much for the beautiful presents those Soldiers and Flags and Castle they are so nice it was so kind of you and dear Papa I send you my love and a great many kisses Your loving Winston.' That spring Churchill returned to Blenheim for two months. 'It is so nice being in the country,' he wrote to his mother that April. 'The gardens and the park are so much nicer to walk in than the Green Park or Hyde Park.' But he missed his parents, and when his grandmother went to London, he wrote to his father, 'I wish I was with her that I might give you a kiss.'

It was Mrs Everest who looked after the two brothers at Blenheim. 'When we were out on Friday near the cascade,' Churchill wrote to his mother shortly before Easter, 'we saw a snake crawling about in the grass. I wanted to kill it but Everest would not let me.' That Easter Mrs Everest took the two boys to the Isle of Wight, where her brother-in-law was a senior warder at Parkhurst prison. They stayed at his cottage at Ventnor, overlooking the sea. From Ventnor, Churchill wrote to his mother, 'We had a Picnic we went to Sandown took our dinner on the Beach and we went to see the Forts & Guns at Sandown there were some enormous 18 ton Guns.'

That autumn Churchill was told that he was to be sent to boarding school. 'I was,' he later wrote, 'what grown-up people in their off-hand way called "a troublesome boy". It appeared that I was to go away from home for many weeks at a stretch in order to do lessons under masters.' He was not 'troublesome' to everyone, however; Lady Randolph's sister Leonie found him 'full of fun and quite unselfconscious' when he stayed with her.

The boarding school was St George's, near Ascot. Churchill was sent there four weeks before his eighth birthday. Term was already half over; his mother took him there that first afternoon. The two of them had tea with the headmaster. 'I was preoccupied', he recalled nearly fifty years later, 'with the fear of spilling my cup and so making "a bad start". I was also miserable at the idea of being left alone among all these strangers in this great, fierce, formidable place.'

Unhappiness at school began from the first days. 'After all,' Churchill later wrote, 'I was only seven, and I had been so happy with all my toys. I had such wonderful toys: a real steam engine, a magic lantern, and a collection of soldiers already nearly a thousand strong. Now it was to be all lessons.' Severity, and at times brutality, were part of life at St George's. 'Flogging with the birch in accordance with the Eton fashion,' Churchill later wrote, 'was a great feature of the curriculum. But I am sure no Eton boy, and certainly no Harrow boy of my day,' – Churchill was at Harrow from 1888 to 1892 – 'ever received such a cruel flogging as this Headmaster was accustomed to inflict upon the little boys who were in his care and power. They exceeded in severity anything that would be tolerated in any of the Reformatories under the Home Office.'

Among the boys who witnessed these floggings was Roger Fry. 'The swishing was given with the master's full strength,' he later wrote, 'and it took only two or three strokes for drops of blood to form everywhere and it continued for 15 or 20 strokes when the wretched boy's bottom was a mass of blood.' Churchill himself was later to recall how during the floggings the rest of the boys 'sat quaking, listening to their screams'.

'How I hated this school,' he later wrote, 'and what a life of anxiety I lived for more than two years. I made very little progress at my lessons, and none at all at games. I counted the days and the hours to the end of every term, when I should return home from this hateful servitude and range my soldiers in line of battle on the nursery floor.'

Churchill's first holiday from St George's, after a month and a half at school, was at Christmas 1882. Home was now another house in London, 2 Connaught Place, on the north side of Hyde Park, where his parents were to live for the next ten years. 'As to Winston's improvement,' his mother wrote to his father on December 26, 'I am sorry to say I see none. Perhaps there has not been time enough. He can read very well, but that is all, and the first two days he came home he was terribly slangy and loud. Altogether I am disappointed. But Everest was told down there that next term they mean to be more strict with him.' Lady Randolph also told her husband that their elder son 'teases the baby more than ever'; to remedy this 'I shall take him in hand'. She ended her reference to her eight-year-old son, 'It appears that he is afraid of me.'

Churchill's first school report was a poor one. His place in the form of eleven boys was eleventh. Under Grammar it read, 'He has made a start,' and under Diligence, 'He will do well, but must treat his work in general, more seriously next term.' The report ended with a note by the Headmaster, 'Very truthful, but a regular "pickle" in many ways at present – has not fallen into school ways yet but this could hardly be expected.'

Anxiety at school went hand in hand with ill-health, which was another cause of concern to his parents. 'I'm sorry poor little Winston has not been well,' Lord Randolph wrote to his wife from the South of France on New Year's Day 1883, 'but I don't make out what is the matter with him. It seems we are a sickly family & cannot get rid of the doctors.' Four days later he wrote again: 'I am so glad to hear Winny is right again. Give him a kiss from me.' To cure whatever was wrong with the boy, the doctor advised a week by the sea, at Herne Bay.

Back at St George's, Churchill repeatedly and unsuccessfully asked his mother to visit him. Before term ended there was sports day. 'Please do let Everest and Jack come down to see the athletics,' he wrote, 'and come down your self dear. I shall expect to see you and Jack & Everest.' Lady Randolph did not take up her son's invitation, but there was a consolation. 'My dear Mamma,' he wrote to her when the sports day was over, 'It was so kind of you to let Everest come down here. I think she enjoyed her-self very much,' and he added, 'Only 18 more days.'

In Churchill's report that term there was praise for his History, Geography, Translation and General Conduct. The rest of the report was less complimentary: Composition was 'very feeble', Writing 'good – but so

terribly slow', Spelling 'about as bad as it well can be'. Under Diligence was
written; 'Does not quite understand the meaning of hard work – must
make up his mind to do so next term.' His place in the Division of nine
boys was ninth; his place in the Set of thirteen was thirteenth.

That summer, while Churchill was at school, his grandfather, the 7th
Duke of Marlborough, died. In deep mourning, Lord Randolph sought
solace in travel. As Churchill himself was later to write, in his biography
of his father, 'Lord Randolph hurried away with his wife and son to
Gastein.' This visit, to one of the most fashionable spas of the Austro-
Hungarian Empire, was Churchill's first visit to Europe. On the way there,
father and son passed through Paris. 'We drove along together through
the Place de la Concorde,' he told the citizens of Metz sixty-three years
later. 'Being an observant child I noticed that one of the monuments was
covered with wreaths and crêpe and I at once asked him why. He replied,
"These are monuments of the Provinces of France. Two of them, Alsace
and Lorraine, have been taken from France by the Germans in the last
war. The French are very unhappy about it and hope some day to get them
back." I remember quite distinctly thinking to myself, "I hope they will get
them back".'

After he returned to St George's, the quality of Churchill's work was in
contrast with his conduct. 'Began term well,' his report read, 'but latterly
has been *very* naughty! – on the whole he has made progress.' According
to the next term's report, History and Geography were 'sometimes exceedingly good'. The headmaster commented, 'He is, I hope, beginning to
realize that school means work and discipline,' and he added, 'He is rather
greedy at meals.'

In February 1884 Lord Randolph announced his intention of standing for
Parliament for Birmingham, as Woodstock was among the hundreds of
family boroughs about to be abolished. By going to an overwhelmingly
radical area, he was intent on showing that 'Tory Democracy' was more
than a slogan. In March the headmaster's wife visited the Midlands. 'And
she heard,' Churchill wrote to his mother, 'that they were betting two to
one that Papa would get in for Birmingham.' This was the first of
Churchill's letters in which politics appears. The rest of the letter was about
a school outing: 'We all went to a sand pit the other day and played a very
exciting game. As the sides are about 24 feet high, and a great struggle,
those who got out first kept a fierce struggle with the rest.'

Churchill's next school report showed that, while he was certainly clever,
he was also extremely unhappy. History and Geography were both 'very
good, especially History'. But Conduct was described as 'exceedingly bad.
He is not to be trusted to do any one thing', and his lateness for morning

school, twenty times in the forty day term, was described as 'very disgraceful'. The pages of the report-card reveal Churchill's torment, 'Is a constant trouble to everybody and is always in some scrape or other,' and, 'He cannot be trusted to behave himself anywhere.' But even the headmaster of St George's could not fail to notice that the nine-year-old boy had 'very good abilities'.

The following term Churchill's letters to his mother show how lonely he felt in that predominantly hostile world. 'It is very unkind of you,' he wrote early in June, 'not to write to me before this, I have only had one letter from you this term.' That summer term his school work was again praised; Grammar, Music and French were all 'good', History and Geography were 'very good'. His General Conduct was described as 'better – but still troublesome'. The headmaster commented, 'He has no ambition – if he were really to exert himself he might yet be first at the end of Term.'

When Churchill was nine and a half, his father gave him Robert Louis Stevenson's *Treasure Island*. 'I remember the delight with which I devoured it,' he later wrote. 'My teachers saw me at once backward and precocious, reading books beyond my years and yet at the bottom of the form. They were offended. They had large resources of compulsion at their disposal, but I was stubborn.' His school report that summer also gave evidence of continual problems with regard to discipline, commenting under Diligence: 'Fair on the whole. Occasionally gives a great deal of trouble.'

What that trouble was, the report did not say, but another St George's boy, Maurice Baring, who arrived at the school shortly after Churchill left, wrote in his memoirs that Churchill had been flogged 'for taking sugar from the pantry, and so far from being penitent, he had taken the Headmaster's sacred straw hat from where it hung over the door and kicked it to pieces'. This defiance had already become a legend.

That autumn Churchill suffered from yet another bout of ill-health. The Churchill family doctor, Robson Roose, who practised both in London and in Brighton, suggested that his health would improve if he went to a school by the sea; he suggested the school in Brighton at which his own son was a pupil. Roose offered to keep a watching eye on the boy. 'As I was now supposed to be very delicate,' Churchill later recalled, 'it was thought desirable that I should be under his constant care.' The new boarding school was run by the two Thomson sisters at 29 and 39 Brunswick Road, Brighton. Term began in September 1884. 'I am very happy here,' he wrote to his mother at the end of October. Two days later he wrote again, 'I have been very extravagant, I have bought a lovely stamp-book and stamps, will you please send a little more money.'

On November 30 Churchill celebrated his tenth birthday. Three days later his father left England for India, where he stayed until March 1885, absorbing himself in the problems of the sub-continent; he expected to be made Secretary of State for India if the Conservatives returned to power. His family saw him off. 'I should like to be with you on that beautiful ship,' Churchill wrote after his return to school. 'We went and had some hotel soup after you went, so we did not do amiss. We saw your big ship steaming out of harbour as we were in the train.'

That winter Lady Randolph's sister Clara wrote to the boy's American grandmother, 'Winston has grown to be such a nice, charming boy.' From his new school, however, his mother was sent in mid-December an alarming letter written by one of the Thomson sisters, Charlotte. She had just been called to see Churchill, who, she wrote, 'was in a trouble that might have proved very serious'. Charlotte Thomson went on to explain: 'He was at work in a drawing examination, and some dispute seems to have arisen between him and the boy sitting next to him about a knife the tutor had lent them for their work. The whole affair passed in a moment, but Winston received a blow inflicting a slight wound in the chest.'

Dr Roose was able to assure Miss Thomson that the boy 'is not much hurt, but that he might have been'. This was not the first time, Miss Thomson added, that complaint had been made of the other boy, who had a passionate temper. His parents would be asked to take him away from the school. Writing about the stabbing to her husband, Lady Randolph commented rather unsympathetically, 'I have no doubt Winston teased the boy dreadfully – & it ought to be a lesson to him.' Churchill returned to London for a few days with Dr Roose. It was then that Lady Randolph learned that the penknife with which her son had been stabbed 'went in about a quarter of an inch', but, she added in her letter to Lord Randolph, 'of course, as I thought, he began by pulling the other boy's ear'.

'What adventures Winston does have,' Lord Randolph wrote to his wife from Bombay. 'It is a great mercy he was no worse injured.'

The first term at Brighton ended a week before Christmas. No doubt in part because of the disruption caused by the stabbing incident, Churchill did not do too well, coming bottom of the class in French, English and Mathematics. The report noted, however, that he had shown 'decided improvement in attention to work towards the latter part of the term'. Churchill later wrote: 'This was a smaller school than the one I had left. It was also cheaper and less pretentious. But there was an element of kindness and of sympathy which I had found conspicuously lacking in my first experiences.'

Churchill spent the Christmas holidays of 1884 in London. His mother found it difficult to cope with him. 'I shall have Jack back before Christmas,' she had written to her sister Clara shortly before the holiday, 'as I could not undertake to manage Winston without Everest – I am afraid even she can't do it'. Churchill returned to Brighton on 20 January 1885, writing to his mother on the following day: 'You must be happy without me, no screams from Jack or complaints. It must be heaven on earth.' Three days later he told her of a school success, 'I have been out riding today and rode without the leading rein and we cantered.'

As at Ascot, so now at Brighton, Churchill was eager for his mother to visit him. One opportunity was the school play. 'I shall expect to see you,' he wrote at the end of January, 'and shall be very disappointed indeed if I do not see you, so do come.' Lady Randolph did go, taking the five-year-old Jack with her. 'They were so happy together,' she wrote to her husband on the following day, '& Winny was wildly excited but I thought he looked very pale & delicate. What a care the boy is.' Her letter continued, 'He told me that he was very happy, & I think he likes the school.'

That term's report spoke of 'very satisfactory progress'. In English, French and Classics, in the class of ten, Churchill had come fourth. Under Conduct, however, he was placed twenty-ninth out of twenty-nine. Back at school after the holiday, there were many reminders of Lord Randolph's growing fame. 'I have been out riding with a gentleman,' Churchill wrote to his father that May, 'who thinks that Gladstone is a brute and thinks that "the one with the curly moustache ought to be Premier".' The driver of the electric railway that ran along the sea front had gone so far as to say 'that Lord R. Churchill would be Prime Minister'.

Churchill was learning to swim, he wrote to his mother that month, and 'getting on capitally'. He was also enjoying riding. As to study, 'I am getting on with my French and Latin but am rather backward with Greek.' He was, however, hoping to go on to school at Winchester, 'so I will try and work it up'.

The ten-year-old boy was excited that summer when he read an article about his father in the *Graphic*. It was, he informed his mother, 'very good indeed'. There was a photograph 'of Papa in the library with all the photographs and the ink-stand'. Six days later the Liberal Government was defeated in the House of Commons and Gladstone resigned. A new government was formed by the Conservative Leader, Lord Salisbury; Churchill's father was appointed Secretary of State for India.

Churchill's third term at Brighton came to an end that July. Although under Conduct he still came bottom of his class, thirtieth out of thirty, his position in the academic subjects was high. He was first in the Classics class of nine, and third in French. 'Very marked progress during the term,' Charlotte Thomson wrote. 'If he continues to improve in steadiness and application, as during this term, he will do very well indeed.' That summer

Churchill and his brother spent their holiday at Cromer by the North Sea. Their parents were again on holiday elsewhere. 'Do come and see us soon,' Churchill wrote to his mother in mid-August. Six days later he wrote again, 'Will you come and see me?'

Lady Randolph did not respond to her son's appeal, but she did arrange for a governess to give him lessons during the holidays. This was not to his liking. 'I am not enjoying myself much as the lessons always tie me down,' he wrote to his mother on August 25. Eight days later he wrote again: 'The weather is fine. But, I am not enjoying myself very much. The governess is very unkind, so strict and stiff, I can't enjoy myself at all.' The only solace was that in a few days' time his mother would come down for ten days. 'Then I shall be able to tell you all my troubles.' Ill-health had marred the holiday. At first, a rash on his legs had forced him to go about in a donkey-carriage. Most recently, he explained, his temper had been 'not of the most amiable, but I think it is due to the liver as I have had a bilious attack which thoroughly upset me, my temperature was 100 once instead of 98 & 2/5 which is normal'.

Back at Brighton for the autumn term, Churchill read in the local newspaper that his father had made a speech in the town. 'I cannot think why you did not come to see me, while you were in Brighton,' he wrote. 'I was very disappointed but I suppose you were too busy to come.' As Secretary of State for India, Lord Randolph had authorised a military expedition against King Theebaw of Burma, who, having long refused to halt attacks on British traders and merchant ships, had imposed a Customs fine on a British trading company. Within ten days Mandalay had been occupied and the King taken prisoner. The future of Burma had now to be determined in the Cabinet room at 10 Downing Street. Lord Randolph, his son later wrote, 'was for annexation simple and direct'. Despite Lord Salisbury's hesitations, Lord Randolph's view prevailed; on 1 January 1886, as what he called 'a New Year's present to the Queen', Burma was annexed to the British Empire.

The Conservative Government was defeated in the Commons on 26 January 1886. The subsequent General Election, while securing Lord Randolph a seat in Parliament, gave the Irish Nationalists the balance of power at Westminister. Gladstone, nailing the Liberal flag to the mast of Irish Home Rule, formed a Government with Irish Nationalist support. The young Churchill, his finances once more in difficulties, is said to have remarked, '*We're* out of office, and they're economising on *me*.'

That March, pneumonia brought the eleven-year-old Churchill almost to death's door. His temperature rose to 104. Lady Randolph hurried to Brighton, followed by her husband. 'I am in the next room,' Dr Roose wrote to Lord Randolph on the evening of Sunday March 14, 'and shall watch the patient during the night – for I am anxious.' At midnight that Sunday the continued high temperature alarmed the doctor, 'indicating exhaustion' he told Lord Randolph at six on the following morning. 'I used stimulants, by the mouth and rectum, with the result that at 2.15 a.m. the temp had fallen to 101, and now to 100, thank God!' Roose added, 'I shall give up my London work and stay by the boy today.'

By midday on Monday March 15 Churchill's temperature had risen again. 'We are still fighting the battle for your boy,' Roose wrote to Lord Randolph at one o'clock that afternoon. 'His temperature is 103 now but he is taking his nourishment *better* and there is no increase of lung mischief. As long as I can fight the temp and keep it under 105 I shall not feel anxious.' The crisis continued but Roose was confident that the danger could be averted. 'Nourishment, stimulants and close watching will save your boy,' he wrote in his 1 p.m. bulletin, and he added, 'I am sanguine of this.'

At eleven that evening Roose sent Lord Randolph another note: 'Your boy, in my opinion, on his perilous path is holding his own well! The temp is 103.5 at which I am satisfied, as I had anticipated 104!' There would be no immediate cause for anxiety for at least twelve hours, 'so *please* have a good night, as we are armed at all points!' The danger was not over. 'We have had a very anxious night,' Roose reported on the following morning, 'but have managed to hold our own.' The boy's pulse still showed 'good power, and the delirium I hope may soon cease and natural sleep occur'. The left lung was still uninvolved. They could expect another twenty-four hours of 'this critical condition'. Roose added in a postscript, 'I have given you a statement of fact, your boy is making a wonderful fight and I do feel please God he will recover.'

By the morning of Wednesday March 17 Churchill was through the worst. 'Winston has had *6 hours quiet sleep,*' Roose reported. 'Delirium has now ceased. Temp: 99, Pulse 92, Respiration 28. He sends you and her ladyship his love.' Churchill was also eager to see Mrs Everest, who was waiting for the first opportunity to be with him. The doctor advised against this, however. 'Forgive my troubling you with these lines,' he wrote to Lady Randolph later on March 17, 'to impress upon you the absolute necessity of quiet and sleep for Winston and that Mrs Everest should not be allowed in the sick room today – even the excitement of pleasure at seeing her might do harm! and I am so fearful of relapse knowing that we are not quite out of the wood yet.'

Learning that the worst was over, Lady Randolph's brother-in-law Moreton Frewen wrote to her on March 17: 'Poor dear Winny, & I hope it will leave no troublesome after effects, but even if it leaves him delicate for a long time to come you will make the more of him after being given back to you from the very threshold of the unknown.'

Slowly the boy recovered. His father went to Brighton twice to see him, once in March with grapes, and again in April when he brought him a toy steam engine. It was a time of considerable controversy for Lord Randolph. Gladstone had pledged the Liberal Government to introduce a Home Rule Bill, aimed at setting up a Parliament in Ireland with power to transact all exclusively Irish business. Lord Randolph's efforts were devoted to attacking and preventing the Bill, stressing the unease of the Irish Protestants at what would be a predominantly Catholic administration. On May 8 *The Times* printed a letter which he had written to a member of the Liberal Party in Glasgow, in which Lord Randolph declared that if the Liberal Government were to impose Home Rule on the Protestants of Ireland, 'Ulster will fight; Ulster will be right.' This phrase became a rallying-cry of the Protestants in the North.

By July Churchill was well enough to return to school. He was excited by the coming General Election. 'I hope the Conservatives will get in,' he wrote to his mother, 'do you think they will?' His father had already faced the electors, on July 2. 'I am very glad Papa got in for South Paddington by so great a majority. I think that was a victory!' Lord Randolph had polled 2,576 votes, as against 769 cast for his opponent. The election result centred upon the part to be played by Joseph Chamberlain, and his seventy-seven fellow breakaway Liberals, who, opposing Home Rule for Ireland, called themselves Liberal Unionists and supported the Conservatives. With that alliance Lord Salisbury formed his second administration. A new political party, the Conservative and Unionist Party, was in the making; fifty-three years later Churchill was to become its Leader.

Lord Randolph, who had greatly encouraged the Liberal Unionist breakaway, became Chancellor of the Exchequer. He was thirty-seven years old. Churchill, who had closely followed the election and its aftermath, was proud of his father's achievement. He was also happy at Brighton. 'I got gradually much stronger in that bracing air and gentle surroundings,' he later wrote. 'I was allowed to learn things which interested me: French, History, lots of Poetry by heart, and above all Riding and Swimming. The impression of those years makes a pleasant picture in my mind, in contrast to my earlier schoolday memories.'

Looking back at his Brighton days six years later, while he was a schoolboy at Harrow, Churchill's reflections were more prosaic. 'I have often thought of Miss Thomsons,' he wrote to a fellow-pupil, '& have arrived at the conclusion that many of the rules & most of the food were utterly damnable. Far be it for me however to speak ill of either Miss

Kate or Miss C. as I have always "cherished the most affectionate remembrances of both" – still, half a sausage – ugh!!!'

In one of his letters in the summer of 1886 Churchill told his mother, 'I am very sorry to say that I am bankrupt and a little cash would be welcome.' This was not his first appeal for money, nor was it to be his last; indeed, as his requests for more money began to proliferate, his mother's letters filled with complaints about his financial extravagance. He was also becoming more and more interested in the world outside school; that September he told his mother of the Brighton municipality's expenditure of £19,000 to enlarge the Parade, 'I think it is a great waste of money.' In the money values of 1990, it was £750,000.

Churchill's letter about excessive public spending was written four days before Lord Randolph, speaking at Dartford in Kent, pledged himself to reduce Government expenditure. He was also working that autumn on plans to alter the basis of taxation in order, his son later wrote, to apply 'much more closely than his predecessors that fundamental principle of democratic finance – the adjusting of taxation to the citizen's ability to pay'.

That winter the son's need for his father's love was again disappointed. On November 10, three weeks before his twelfth birthday, he wrote to him, 'You never came to see me on Sunday when you were in Brighton.' This was the second time his father had been in Brighton but had not gone to see him.

In preparing his first budget, Lord Randolph sought to persuade both the First Lord of the Admiralty and the Secretary of State for War to reduce their spending for the coming year, in order to further the cause of a more equitable taxation system, and to frustrate what his son was later to call 'an ambitious foreign policy supported by growing armaments'. On December 20, when it became clear that the two Service Ministers were unwilling to cut their respective departmental spending, Lord Randolph wrote to Lord Salisbury, 'I do not want to be wrangling and quarrelling in the Cabinet, and therefore must request to be allowed to give up my office and retire from the Government.' As soon as Salisbury received this letter, he treated it as a letter of resignation and accepted it. Lord Randolph was devastated. He had intended his letter as a warning shot, perhaps the decisive shot, in his battle against the Admiralty and the War Office, not as a letter of resignation abruptly ending his career.

The deed was done; Lord Randolph was no longer Chancellor of the Exchequer. He was never to present a budget nor return to the Cabinet. Twenty years later Churchill published a detailed account of his father's resignation. 'Of course he hoped the others would give way,' he wrote. 'Undoubtedly he expected to prevail.' His father's mistake was to have 'overlooked the anger and jealousy that his sudden rise to power had excited'.

The twelve-year-old boy was soon to experience that mood of public anger. As Lady Randolph explained in February 1887 to her husband, who was then in Morocco, 'Winston was taken to a pantomime at Brighton where they hissed a sketch of you – he burst into tears – & then turned furiously on a man – who was hissing behind him – & said "Stop that row you snub nosed Radical" !!!' Lord Randolph was so delighted at his son's loyalty that he arranged for him to be given a gold sovereign. 'We all of course looked forward to his reconquest of power,' Churchill later wrote. 'We saw as children the passers-by take off their hats in the streets and the workmen grin when they saw his big moustache.'

That summer Churchill fought a valiant battle to be allowed to go to London at the time of Queen Victoria's Jubilee. It took him three letters to his mother to achieve his object. This was the first:

My dear Mamma,

Miss Thomson doesn't want me to go home for the Jubilee and because she says that I shall have no place in Westminster Abbey and so it is not worth going. Also that you will be very busy and unable to be with me much.

Now you know that this is not the case. I want to see Buffalo Bill & the Play as you promised me. I shall be very disappointed, disappointed is not the word I shall be miserable, after you have promised me, and all, I shall never trust your promises again. But I know that Mummy loves her Winny much too much for that.

Write to Miss Thomson and say that you have promised me and you want to have me home. Jack entreats you daily I know to let me come and there are seven weeks after the Jubilee before I come home. Don't disappoint me. If you write to Miss Thomson she will not resist you. I could come home on Saturday to stay till Wednesday. I have got a lot of things, pleasant and unpleasant to tell you. Remember for my sake. I am quite well but in a torment about coming home, it would upset me entirely if you were to stop me.

This letter was posted from Brighton on June 11. A second letter followed within twenty-four hours, 'I hope you will not disappoint me. Uncertainty is at all times perplexing. Write to me by return post please!!!' Churchill now enclosed a draft which he had prepared of the letter he wanted his mother to send Miss Thomson. 'Could you allow Winston to come up to London on Saturday the 18th for the Jubilee,' it read. 'I should like him to see the procession very much, and I also promised him that he should come up for the Jubilee.'

Churchill's draft letter made no mention of Buffalo Bill. But in his letter to his mother, he reminded her again of this aspect of his return to London. The show was to be at Earls Court, presented by Buffalo Bill Cody himself, with large numbers of Indians, cowboys, scouts, settlers and Mexicans. His second letter ended, 'For Heavens sake Remember!!!' His third letter, sent on June 15, was shorter: 'I am nearly mad with suspense. Miss Thomson says that she will let me go if you write to ask for me. For my sake write before it is too late. Write to Miss Thomson by return post please!!!'

Churchill's persistence was rewarded. Lady Randolph did as her son wished, and he went up to London, to celebrate the fiftieth year of Queen Victoria's accession to the throne. It was clearly a boisterous visit. 'I hope you will soon forget my bad behaviour while at home,' he wrote to his mother on the day after his return to Brighton, 'and not to make it alter any pleasure in my summer Holidays.' He went on to point out that two other boys who had gone up to London returned even later than he had. As for his work: 'I am getting on capitally in Euclid. I and another boy are top of the school.' Four days later he reported that he was also getting on 'capitally' in Greek and Latin. In a letter on July 5 he reported the opinion of one master 'that I am getting on much better in my Greek'. This was important as 'Greek is my weak point & I cannot get into Winchester without it, so I am very glad I have made a start'.

Churchill hoped to spend his summer holidays in Paris 'or somewhere on the continent'. He suspected that his mother had an extra plan for him. 'My darling,' he wrote to her three weeks before the holidays were to begin, 'I hope you don't intend to make my Holidays miserable by having a Tutor.' She did; the tutor was to be his Greek master, the twenty-four-year-old James Best. Churchill was somewhat assuaged. 'Now as he is a Master here,' he wrote to his mother, 'and I like him pretty well I shall not mind him at all, on one condition viz. "Not to do any work". I give up all other conditions except this one.' Churchill added: 'I never have done work in my holidays and I will not begin now. I will be very good if this is not forced upon me and I am not bothered about it.'

Lady Randolph was determined her son should study during the holidays. But he was becoming skilled at putting his own point of view. 'I promise you I will be a very good boy indeed in the Holidays,' he wrote on July 14. 'Only do let me off the work because I am working hard this term & I shall find quite enough to do in the holidays. I am never at a loss for anything to do while I am in the country for I shall be occupied with "Butterflying" all day (I was last year). Do let me try it for a week.' Even if the tutoring was only for one hour a day, he told his mother, 'I shall feel that I have got to be back at a certain time and it would hang like a dark shadow over my pleasure'.

But tutoring there was to be, though part of Churchill's holiday that summer was again spent with Jack and Mrs Everest on the Isle of Wight. On his return to Brighton he learned that his parents were to send him, not to Winchester, for which he had been preparing, but to Harrow. His earlier ill-health made Harrow more attractive, as it was on a hill. That autumn the headmaster, Dr Welldon, wrote to Lord Randolph, 'You may rely upon my placing him in a House where his health will be carefully watched.'

Churchill was pleased by the decision. 'I am very glad to hear that I am going to Harrow & not to Winchester,' he wrote to his father. 'I think I shall pass the entrance examination, which is not so hard as Winchester.' In Arithmetic, 'we are doing "Square Root" and have quite mastered Decimal fractions & Rule of three'. He was learning a second group of Greek verbs. At the end of term he would be playing Martine in Molière's *Médecin Malgré Lui*. He was also learning his part in an extract from a Greek play, *The Knights* by Aristophanes, 'in which there are only two characters one of whom is myself'.

In preparation for the preliminary examination for Harrow, Churchill persevered with his Greek verbs, making steady progress. On his own initiative he wrote for advice to a boy who had been with him at Brighton and had gone on to Harrow. 'He wrote back & told me all about it,' Churchill informed his mother. As the examination drew near, his spirits rose, 'I am hoping to have the success that is due to a long term of hard work.' Jack and Mrs Everest were at Brighton, which also raised his spirits. The result was remarkable: in the first six papers he took, he came first in four, English History, Algebra, Ancient History and Bible History, and second in Geography. Two weeks later he came second in Arithmetic.

As the examinations continued, Lord Randolph went down to Brighton and took his son out to tea. His thirteen-year-old son was already planning his Christmas entertainment. 'We will not have a Christmas tree this year,' he wrote to his mother on December 13. 'But I think a good 3 guinea Conjuror and a Tea and amusements and games after tea would answer better.' For three guineas, Churchill pointed out, the conjuror 'gives ventriloquism and an hours good conjuring'. He would get 'a lot of addresses this time' of boys to invite.

On the following day Churchill's Christmas party plans came to nought. His parents were leaving for Russia in five days' time and would be away until February. 'I am very disappointed that I must spend my holidays without you,' he wrote to his mother on hearing the news from Miss Thomson, 'But I am trying to make the "Best of a bad job". We shall not be able to have a party of course.' Returning to London, he spent his Christmas holidays without his parents. 'It is very dull without you,' he wrote to his mother on December 26. He also told her that he had won two school prizes, for English and for Scripture.

That Christmas, Mrs Everest was taken ill with diphtheria. 'It is very hard to bear,' Churchill wrote to his mother on December 30, 'we feel so destitute.' He and Jack had left Connaught Place and were being looked after by Dr Roose at 45 Hill Street, off Berkeley Square. Four days later the two boys were taken to Blenheim, where they stayed for a week. 'It has done them good,' their grandmother, the dowager Duchess, wrote to Lord Randolph on 8 January 1888, '& I keep Winston in good order as I know you like it. He is a clever Boy & really not naughty but he wants a firm hand. Jack requires no keeping in order.'

From Blenheim, the two boys returned to London, to stay with the Duchess at 46 Grosvenor Square. They were taken to see the new Gilbert and Sullivan, *HMS Pinafore* and to the pantomime *Puss in Boots*. But a governess was in attendance from ten till seven each day, and the Duchess discouraged too many evening outings. 'I fear Winston thinks me very strict,' she wrote to Lord Randolph on January 19, 'but I really think he goes out too much & I do object to late parties for him. He is so excitable. But he goes back to school on Monday. Meantime he is affectionate & not naughty.' He was also much concerned about Mrs Everest, 'Woomany' as he called her. 'It might have been so much worse if Woomany had died,' he wrote to his mother, who was still in Russia.

In a letter written to await his mother in London, Churchill asked for 'a good Latin-English & a good English-Latin dictionary'. A week later he asked for a Greek Lexicon. He had begun Virgil, 'which I like', and also Herodotus in the original Greek. He was confident he would do well in the Harrow entrance examination. 'I hear that Algebra is an extra subject and so I hope to score in that, as I am very fond of it.' By the end of term he would know the first book of Euclid 'perfectly, which will be more than I shall want. They only require Arithmetic, Vulgar Fractions & Decimal fractions & Simple & Compound Interest, which I know.' He had also made further progress in languages: 'I have learnt some Greek irregular verbs & a lot of French. I do so want to get in.'

In February, Churchill wrote to his mother, 'I am working hard for Harrow.' He was 'not very good at Latin verse but it is of little importance, prose being the chief thing in which I am rapidly improving'. He was learning the geography of the United States. 'When I come home you must question me.' He was also reading novels; when Rider Haggard sent him a copy of his latest book, *Allan Quatermain*, Churchill wrote back that he liked it better than *King Solomon's Mines*. 'It is more amusing,' he explained.

Nine days before the Harrow entrance examination, Churchill told his father he was 'getting through the 2nd Book of Virgil's *Aeneid* all-right, I like that better than anything else'. He had finished another group of Greek verbs: 'I hope I shall pass. I think I shall.'

Churchill's confidence was not misplaced. On March 15 he sat, and passed, the Harrow entrance examination. But it had been a nerve-racking experience. When Churchill left Harrow by train for London, Charlotte Thomson informed Lord Randolph, he had 'a severe attack of sickness'. She had been worried about the effect of his 'nervous excitement' on his work and her fears had been realised. 'He has only just scraped through,' she wrote, having been 'terribly upset' after the morning examinations. It was the Latin translation that had been the problem; Churchill assured Miss Thomson 'over and over again', she told Lord Randolph, 'that he had never translated Latin into English so of course he could not do the piece of prose set on the paper. As I knew that he had for more than a year been translating Virgil and for much longer Caesar, I was rather surprised by the assertion but of course I did not contradict him.'

'I have passed,' Churchill wrote to his mother from Brighton on March 16, 'but it was far harder than I expected.' The Latin translation had been 'very, very hard' as was the Greek translation. There had been no Greek Grammar 'in which I had hoped to score' and no French. He was 'very tired now but that does not matter now that I know I have passed. I am longing to go to Harrow, it is such a nice place – beautiful view – beautiful situation – good swimming bath – a good gymnasium – & a carpentering shop & many other attractions.' There was yet another attraction to Harrow, 'You will often be able to come & see me in the summer, it is so near to London you can drive from Victoria in an hour & 15 minutes or so.'

Churchill's last month at Brighton was filled with thoughts of going home. 'I want to have Easter with you, tremendously,' he wrote on March 27. But that Easter his mother was again away from home; in vain he pleaded with her, 'Do come home soon.'

2

Harrow

Churchill entered Harrow School in April 1888. As at St George's and at Brighton he was a boarder, seeing his parents only in the holidays, if then. 'I like everything immensely,' was his comment in his first letter home, written three days after his arrival. In his second letter, written the next day, he was proud that one of the masters had told him his entrance paper in Arithmetic was 'the best'.

During his first month at Harrow, Churchill joined the school cadet force, and, he told his mother, 'attended my drills punctually'. He also went with the cadet force to Rickmansworth, where there was a mock battle with Haileybury School. 'As I had not got a uniform I only carried cartridges,' he wrote home. 'I carried 100 rounds to give away in the thick of the fight, consequently my business enabled me to get a good view of the field. It was most exciting, you could see through the smoke the enemy getting nearer & nearer.' The Harrow boys were beaten, however, '& forced to retire'.

In his first essay at Harrow, Churchill wrote about Palestine in the time of John the Baptist, when the land 'lay at the feet of the Roman, who was then at the apex of his glory'. Of the Zealots, he wrote that they were 'always ready for a rebellion, ready to risk their lives, their homes, their all for their country's freedom'. As to the Pharisees: 'Their faults were many. Whose faults are few? For let him with all the advantages of Christianity avouch that they are more wicked than himself, he commits the same crime of which he is just denouncing them.'

Churchill was learning to shoot with the Martini-Henry rifle, the one used by the army. He was also learning a thousand lines of Macaulay for a form prize. 'Anyone who likes to take the trouble to learn them can get one,' he explained to his father, 'as there is no limit to the prizes.' On this occasion it was a thousand lines of *The Lays of Ancient Rome* which secured him a prize.

Churchill still yearned for his mother's visits, but sometimes they led to unhappiness of their own. 'Don't be cross with me any more,' he wrote at the end of June. 'I will try and work, but you were so cross to me you made me feel quite dull. I have kept my room quite tidy since you came.' And he added: 'Do come down Mamma on Saturday. I am not lazy & untidy but careless & forgetful.'

Lady Randolph did not visit her son that Saturday. He expected her to do so a week later, however, when he was singing in the school choir as a treble. 'I rank as one of the prominent trebles,' he explained, '& am in what is called the nucleus of the choir. Of course I am so young that my voice has not yet broken and as trebles are rare I am one of the few.' Despite this attraction Lady Randolph did not go down for Speech Day. Churchill had to be content with a visit from his aunt Lady Fanny Marjoribanks, whose son was also at Harrow and whose husband was a rising star on the Liberal benches.

The school songs Churchill sang on Speech Day roused his enthusiam. 'The stirring patriotism these verses evoked,' his son Randolph later wrote, 'abided with him forever and was the mainspring of his political conduct.' When, at the height of the Blitz in 1940, Randolph accompanied his father to Harrow for the annual school songs, Churchill told him, 'Listening to those boys singing all those well-remembered songs I could see myself fifty years before singing those tales of great deeds and of great men and wondering with intensity how I could ever do something glorious for my country.'

Churchill himself was later to recall, in a speech to the boys at Harrow in October 1945, how he had also been 'much attracted' by the kettle-drum. Again and again he thought, 'If only I could get hold of this on one of these fine evenings.' But he was never allowed that opportunity. 'So I gave up that ambition and transferred my aspirations to another part of the orchestra. I thought, "If I cannot have the kettle-drum I might try to be the conductor". There was a great deal in the gestures, at any rate.' That could not be arranged either, while he was at Harrow, 'but eventually, after a great deal of perseverance, I rose to be conductor of quite a considerable band. It was a very large band and it played with very strange and formidable instruments, and the roar and thunder of its music resounded throughout the world.'

As part of the regular allowance of breaks, Churchill looked forward to going home for a weekend in July. But he was forced to stay at school. It was not that he was 'in any way wilfully troublesome', Henry Davidson, the assistant master, explained to Lady Randolph, 'but his forgetfulness, carelessness, unpunctuality, and irregularity in every way, have really been so serious, that I write to ask you, when he is at home to speak very gravely to him on the subject'.

There were further complaints to come. 'Winston, I am sorry to say, has, if anything got worse as the term passed,' Davidson explained. 'Constantly late for school, losing his books, and papers and various other things into which I need not enter – he is so regular in his irregularity that I really don't know what to do; and sometimes think he cannot help it.' If he was not able to 'conquer this slovenliness', Davidson warned, 'he will never make a success of a public school'. It was very serious indeed that he had acquired 'such phenomenal slovenliness'. He had 'such good abilities' but these would be 'made useless by habitual negligence'. And yet, Davidson added, 'I ought not to close without telling you that I am very much pleased with some history work he has done for me.' That term Churchill was awarded a form prize for English History.

A new challenge in the autumn term was a school prize for reciting a thousand lines of Shakespeare. Churchill's letters to his parents show how eager he was to win it, but he lost it by only twenty-seven marks, telling them, 'I was rather astonished as I beat some twenty boys who were much older than I.' Then, just before his fourteenth birthday, he wrote with pride of winning a history prize for the second term running. He had also come top in Roman History and was doing well at Greek and Latin.

At home over the Christmas and New Year, Churchill's throat was swollen and his liver 'still bad', he wrote to his mother, who was again travelling during his holiday. Medicine six times a day, he added, 'is a horrible nuisance'. As he recovered he was told by Dr Roose that he must go to the seaside to recuperate fully. Once more he went to the Isle of Wight with Mrs Everest. Back at school, however, illness continued to impede his progress. In March he told his mother he was 'far from well & am in bed because I can hardly stand'. His solace was a visit from Mrs Everest. 'I do not know how the day would have passed but for Woomany,' he told his mother.

Churchill's qualities did not go unnoticed. In April, Welldon decided to take him into his own House, writing to Lord Randolph, 'He has some great gifts and is, I think, making progress in his work.' Lord Randolph had sent his son a bicycle. 'I rode eight miles with it,' he wrote to his father in May, 'it is a beautiful little machine.' He enjoyed his new House, telling his mother, 'All the boys are so kind and nice.' But illness again intervened when he fell off the bicycle and was concussed; he had to spend a week in bed. Once more Mrs Everest hurried down to Harrow, but Churchill wanted his mother to be with him. 'Can't you come instead?' he asked. 'I was rather disappointed at not seeing you as I fully expected to.' The fall had been a serious one. 'I am very tender all over my body,' he told his mother, 'but feel cheery and not a bit dull, the time passes very quickly. Especially when I can have visitors.' His best piece of news was that the hospital nurse had gone 'and so I am alone with Woomany'.

As he recovered from his concussion, Churchill asked his father to come down for Speech Day. 'I don't think that you will be asked to make a speech,' he sought to reassure him. 'In fact I should think it will be very improbable.' Churchill added, 'You have never been to see me & so everything will be new to you.' It was more than a year since Churchill had entered Harrow. Lord Randolph did at last go down; while he was there he told Welldon he wanted his son to go into the Army Class, instead of the regular classes. Because the Army Class entailed extra lessons on the military subjects needed to enter a military academy, Churchill would have no opportunity to continue with those subjects taken by boys who wished to go to university, as he already hoped to do.

Churchill's results that term were such that there was no reason he should not eventually pass the University entrance examination. But Lord Randolph was emphatic that his son go into the Army, and therefore into the Army Class. Many years later Churchill reflected on his father's decision, recalling a visit of inspection which he had made one holiday to see his son's collection of nearly fifteen hundred toy soldiers. 'All the troops were arranged in the correct formation of attack. He spent twenty minutes studying the scene – which was really impressive – with a keen and captivating smile. At the end he asked me if I would like to go into the army. I thought it would be splendid to command an army, so I said "Yes" at once: and immediately I was taken at my word.'

Churchill added, wryly: 'For years I thought my father with his experience and flair had discerned in me the qualities of military genius. But I was told later that he had only come to the conclusion that I was not clever enough to go to the Bar.' Welldon arranged for Churchill to take the Army Class examination. He did badly in mathematics, making it difficult for him to contemplate going on to Woolwich, the academy for cadets seeking commissions in the Royal Artillery or Royal Engineers. Instead he would have to prepare for Sandhurst, the academy for would-be infantry and cavalry officers. 'I have joined the "Army class",' he wrote to his mother at the end of September. 'It is rather a "bore" as it spoils your half Holiday: however we do French & Geometrical drawing which are the two things which are most necessary for the army.'

As Churchill began the extra work which being in the Army Class entailed, he urged his mother to write to him. 'It is more than a fortnight since I heard from you,' he complained at the beginning of October. 'In fact I have only had one letter this term. It is not very kind darling Mummy to forget all about me, not answer my epistles.' One of Churchill's letters

to his mother, a month before his fifteenth birthday, was dictated to a
school friend. 'Milbanke is writing this for me,' he explained, 'as I am
having a bath.' Many years later other shorthand writers were to take
dictation while Churchill the Prime Minister was in his bath.

Milbanke, who was killed in action in 1915 at Gallipoli, during the
landing at Suvla Bay, was nearly two years Churchill's senior. 'When my
father came down to see me,' Churchill later recalled, 'he used to take us
both to luncheon at the King's Head Hotel. I was thrilled to hear them talk,
as if they were equals, with the easy assurance of one man of the world to
another. I envied him so much. How I should have loved to have that sort
of relationship with my father! But alas I was only a backward schoolboy
and my incursions into the conversation were nearly always awkward or
foolish.'

Alone with his friends Churchill was far from inhibited or overwhelmed. 'Like other boys at Harrow,' another older boy, Murland Evans,
later recalled, 'I was greatly attracted by this extraordinary boy. His
commanding intelligence, his bravery, charm, and indifference to ugly
surroundings, vivid imagination, descriptive powers, general knowledge
of the world and of history – gained no one knew how, but never disputed
– and above all that magnetism and sympathy which shone in his eyes, and
radiated from a personality which – even under the severe repression of
our public school system – dominated great numbers around him, many
of whom were his superiors in age and prowess.'

Speaking of his future, Churchill told his aunt Lady Rodney, 'If I had
two lives I would be a soldier and a politician. But as there will be no war
in my time I shall have to be a politician.' He had become a voracious
reader. One boy, finding him curled up in a chair reading, asked to see
the book. It was Carlyle's *French Revolution*. But from his father there
seemed little encouragement; Churchill's cousin Shane Leslie later recalled that when the boys staged plays at home Lord Randolph would
remark, 'I shall preserve a stony and acid silence.'

That winter Churchill was put on 'report' by Welldon; each week his
masters had to give an account of his progress. Even when it became clear
that his progress was satisfactory and that the masters had 'no complaint'
Welldon kept him on report. 'It is a most shameful thing that he should
keep me on like this,' Churchill wrote to his mother, urging her to come
down and speak to the headmaster direct. 'Please don't be afraid of him,
because he always promises fair & acts in a very different way. You must
stick up for me because, if you don't nobody else will.'

A week after his fifteenth birthday Churchill wrote proudly to his
mother, 'I am working very hard.' So hard, in fact, that despite the extra
work of the Army Class, he got his Remove into a higher division of the

fourth form. 'We were delighted to hear you had your remove,' his mother wrote on the eve of leaving for Europe yet again, '& do hope you will continue to work. You ought to feel much encouraged & full of ambition.'

Churchill had begun to study English under a master who taught it with enthusiasm and skill, breathing life into the normally dull topic of sentence construction. The master was Robert Somervell, 'a most delightful man', Churchill later wrote, 'to whom my debt is great'. Somervell's method, Churchill recalled, was to divide up a long sentence into its component clauses 'by means of black, red, blue and green inks', and teaching it almost daily as 'a kind of drill'; by this method 'I got into my bones the essential structure of the ordinary British sentence – which is a noble thing'.

'I am getting on capitally in my new form,' Churchill reported to his mother in January 1890. 'Papa said he thought singing was a waste of time, so I left the singing class and commenced drawing.' He studied drawing for an extra hour each week, in the evening, telling his mother that he had been drawing 'little landscapes & bridges & those sort of things' and was about to begin shading in sepia. An unexpected letter of encouragement came from his grandmother Duchess Fanny, who wrote: 'Am pleased to see you are beginning to be ambitious! You have a great example of industry in your dear father & of thoroughness in work.'

The Army Class, Churchill complained to his father that spring, 'takes me away from all the interesting work of my form & altogether spoils my term'. Nine-tenths of the boys in the Army Class would in any case go to a crammer before their Army Exam. All of them disliked the Army Class because 'it made them come out low in their form'. Harrow was 'a charming place but Harrow & the Army Class don't agree'. His protest was of no avail.

In May, Churchill began learning German. 'Ugh,' he wrote to his mother. 'Still I hope to be able to "Sprechen ze Deutche" one of these days.' This hope was never to be realised.   16

Half way through the summer term of 1890, Churchill was confronted by parental anger. His father had sent him five pounds, and had not received a thank-you letter until a week later. His half-term school report was also disappointing. These two facts combined to produce a formidable letter from his mother. 'You work in such a fitful inharmonious way,' she wrote, 'that you are bound to come out last – look at your place in the form!' Her letter continued: 'Dearest Winston you make me very unhappy – I had built up such hopes about you & felt so proud of you – & now all is gone. My only consolation is that your conduct is good & that you are an affectionate son – but your work is an insult to your intelligence. If you would only trace out a plan of action for yourself & carry it out & be determined to do so – I am sure you could accomplish anything you wished.' There was more advice to come. 'The next year or two,' she warned, '& the use you make of them, will affect your whole life – stop and think it out for yourself & take a good pull before it is too late.'

Churchill made an effort to defend himself. The thank-you letter to his father had been written that same evening, he explained, but because of the lateness of the hour he had been forced to give it to someone else to post. 'He I suppose forgot & did not post it until several days had elapsed.' As to his bad report: 'I will not try to excuse myself for not working hard, because I know that what with one thing and another I have been rather lazy. Consequently when the month ended the crash came I got a bad report & got put on report etc, etc. that is more than 3 weeks ago, and in the coming month I am bound to get a good report.' There was plenty of time until the end of term 'and I will do my very best in what remains'.

The crisis passed; Churchill's work improved and his parents' anger was assuaged. That autumn he began to smoke, provoking further criticism. 'Darling Winston,' his mother wrote in September, 'I hope you will try & not smoke. If only you knew how foolish & how silly you look doing it you would give it up, at least for a few years.' There was to be an inducement to giving up smoking, 'I will get Papa to get you a gun & a pony.' Churchill deferred to his mother's advice. He would give up smoking 'at any rate for six months'. That September Duchess Fanny had further advice: 'Take care of yourself & work well & keep out of scrapes & don't flare up so easily!!!'

As Churchill approached his sixteenth birthday, he followed with alarm the spread of an influenza epidemic that, after ravaging much of Europe and Asia, spread, briefly, to Britain. The epidemic became the subject of a poem he wrote, in twelve verses, that was published in the *Harrovian* magazine. One verse read,

> *O'er miles of bleak Siberia's plains*
> *Where Russian exiles toil in chains*
> *It moved with noiseless tread,*
> *And as it slowly glided by*
> *There followed it across the sky*
> *The spirits of the dead.*

Another verse referred to the two German provinces he had visited with his father seven years earlier,

> *Fair Alsace and forlorn Lorraine,*
> *The cause of bitterness and pain*
> *In many a Gallic breast,*

Receive the vile, insatiate scourge,
And from their towns with it emerge
And never stay nor rest.

The final verse rejoiced that Britain had not been as terribly affected as the Continents, and expressed his pride in the British Empire,

God shield our Empire from the might
Of war or famine, plague or blight
And all the power of Hell,
And keep it ever in the hands
Of those who fought 'gainst other lands,
Who fought and conquered well.

As his sixteenth birthday approached, Churchill worked on his Army preliminary examination. Curiously insensitive to the strains of such work, his mother let it be known that she was not satisfied with his progress. 'I hear that you are greatly incensed against me!' he wrote. 'I am very sorry. But I am very hard at work & I am afraid some enemy hath sown tares in your mind.' He had already explained that his earlier problems had arisen 'on account of my being put under a master whom I hated & who returned that hate'. He was now being taught 'by masters who take the greatest interest in me & who say that I have been working very well. If you will take my word of honour to the effect that I am working my very best, well & good, if not – I cannot do anything more than try.'

It was from one of his mother's friends, Lady Wilton, who signed her letters to him 'your deputy mother', that Churchill now received words of affection and encouragement. 'I'm sorry you have so much hard work before you,' she wrote ten days before his sixteenth birthday, 'but – if you face it – it will gradually appear less hard – & I'm sure you'll pass well.' The examination was to take place on December 10. 'I expect you will distinguish yourself,' Lady Wilton wrote in a second letter, adding, 'I will rejoice in it'.

In Geography, Churchill would have to answer questions about one particular country; which country, none of the boys knew. On the night before the exam he wrote the names of each of the twenty-five possible countries on scraps of paper, put them into his hat, closed his eyes, and drew one out. 'New Zealand was the one,' he wrote to his mother, 'and New Zealand was the first question on the paper.' This good luck, combined with Churchill's hard work over many months, was effective. He passed the examination in all subjects. 'I am very pleased to hear the good news,' Duchess Fanny wrote to him when the results were known. 'I hope it will encourage you to continue to exert & distinguish yourself & make us all proud of you.'

Churchill and Jack spent the New Year of 1891 at Banstead, a house which Lord Randolph had rented near Newmarket racecourse. As their parents were yet again abroad, Mrs Everest looked after them. 'We have slaughtered many rabbits,' Churchill reported to his mother. 'About eleven brace altogether. Tomorrow we slay the rats.' His main effort at Banstead with Jack was to build a 'Den', a hut made of mud and planks, with a straw floor. Surrounded by a ditch which served as a moat, the Den was defended with a home-made elastic catapault that fired apples at any would-be intruder. Churchill took charge of the defences, using his brother Jack, and his two cousins, the five-year-old Shane Leslie and the six-year-old Hugh Frewen, sometimes as allies to be drilled and defended, sometimes as enemies to be repulsed.

Back at Harrow, Churchill continued to be troubled by ill-health, writing to his mother in May of how he had strained his abdomen, felt considerable pain, and was 'frightened'. His teeth were also giving him trouble. 'Poor old man,' Mrs Everest wrote, 'have you tried the heroin I got you – get a bottle of Elliman's embrocation & rub your face when you go to bed & tie your sock up over your face, after rubbing for a 1/4 of an hour, try it I am sure it will do you good.' To his mother Churchill signed himself, 'Your tooth-tormented – but affectionate son.' Her advice was that he should brush his teeth more often. From Mrs Everest came a warning about not going swimming in the Harrow pool as 'the wind is still east & treacherous'. Her kindly advice was continuous. 'Be sure,' she wrote that summer, 'you don't attempt to get into the train after it moves off dear. I always feel uneasy about that because you stand at the Book Stall reading & forget your train. Do be careful there's a dear boy.'

That May, Churchill also told his mother he had been in the 'deuce of a row' at school. To his father, who was in South Africa, he explained how he and four other boys, while out walking, had discovered a disused factory. 'Everything was in ruin and decay but some windows yet remained unbroken; we facilitated the progress of time with regard to these, with the result that the watchman complained to Welldon, who having made enquiries and discoveries, "swished" us.' It was not this episode, however, but another fault, that led to a further parental complaint. 'Mamma is in despair about your spending so much money,' Mrs Everest wrote in the second week of June. 'She is greatly troubled about it, she says you are always asking her for more money.' In his defence Churchill explained to his mother that he had to pay his repeated dentist bills and taxi fares to the dentist, as well as 'an old bicycle debt' and the 'window smashing stupidity'.

Churchill had been made a Lance Corporal in the school cadet force. There had been a 'sham fight' which he had enjoyed immensely, he told his father. 'I took the opera glasses you gave me and through them scrutinised the foe.' He was suffering that summer from pain in his gums. 'I am not able to go out,' he wrote to his father, 'as I am tormented with toothache which has now turned to an abscess, so my face is swelled to twice its normal size.' From Mrs Everest came advice about his teeth, 'Don't eat too many of those nasty pickles, they are poisonous things.' One tooth would have to go; it was finally extracted in London under the supervision of a leading authority on the use of anaesthetics in dental surgery. 'I remembered nothing,' Churchill told his mother, 'but went to sleep & snored throughout the whole performance.'

Churchill hoped to spend a week that summer at Banstead, in his Den. But Mrs Everest explained that 'the reason Mamma cannot have you home is the house is to be full of visitors for the race week'. He went instead to London, staying with Duchess Fanny at 50 Grosvenor Square. While he was in London his mother's friend Count Kinsky took him to the Crystal Palace, where they saw a fire-brigade drill specially performed in the presence of the German Emperor, William II. 'There were nearly 2,000 firemen & 100 engines,' Churchill told his brother. The Emperor wore a helmet 'of bright brass surmounted by a white eagle nearly six inches high, a polished steel cuirass & a perfectly white uniform with high boots'. After the march-past, Kinsky took Churchill out to dine. 'Very tolerable dinner,' he told Jack. 'Lots of champagne which pleased your loving brother very much.'

Welldon had suggested that Churchill go to France to improve his French for the Army examination. Churchill begged his mother to let him stay in England. 'I shouldn't see Jack nor you, nor Everest at all.' As for the examination: 'Really I feel less keen about the Army every day. I think the Church would suit me much better.' After much correspondence and heated argument it was agreed that he would not have to go to France; a governess would suffice. 'I can't tell you how happy I am that I am not to go abroad for the holidays,' he wrote to his mother. From Banstead came a letter from Jack; the Den was 'very hard to approach for huge thistles & stinging nettles are all round about, and the ditch is empty of water'. His French lessons over, Churchill set to work to clear the Den and make it defensible again. 'Here I am at Banstead,' he wrote to his father at the end of August, 'leading what to me is an almost ideal existence.'

The two brothers 'have been happy as kings riding and shooting', Lady Randolph wrote to her husband in mid-September, 'and lately they have had great fun building a house. We had tea there today'. Shortly before he had to return to school for the autumn term, Churchill had a bilious attack, and remained in London for two extra days. Welldon demanded a letter of explanation. 'Don't say anything about the theatre,' Churchill warned his mother, 'or that would make him rampant. Merely say I looked tired & pale from the journey (as indeed I did) & that, combined with the fact that you wanted me to see a doctor induced you to "Keep me back".'

That term Churchill dropped German and began Chemistry. 'It is very interesting,' he told his brother, '& when I come home I will show you many wonders.' His mother was anxious to find a tutor who would travel abroad with him in the next holidays. 'On the whole he has been a very good boy,' she explained to Lord Randolph, 'but honestly he is getting a bit too old for a woman to manage. After all he will be seventeen in two months and he really requires to be with a man.'

The 'woman' was Mrs Everest, to whom Churchill was as devoted as she to him. 'Fancy having a room all to yourself,' she wrote at the end of September, 'but my dearest Boy do let me impress it upon you to be careful of your fire & candle at night. Don't go to sleep and leave it burning by your bedside.' He should work hard that term, she advised, not only to please his parents but to 'disappoint some of your relations who prophesy a future of profligacy for you'.

Churchill did not depend only on his mother for his luxuries. 'I am going to sell my bicycle for a bulldog,' he wrote to her that term. 'I have known him some time & he is very tame & affectionate.' His father had told him he used to have a bulldog at Eton, 'so why not I at Harrow?'

Work that term went well. 'Mr Welldon told me since his return he has worked very hard,' Lady Randolph told her husband in October. But from Mrs Everest came a protest. 'I think you are awfully extravagant to have spent 15/- in one week,' she wrote, 'some families of six or seven people have to live upon 12/- a week. You squander it away & the more you have the more you want & spend.' Her letter ended: 'My poor sweet old precious lamb how I am longing for a hug – although you are not perfect I do love you so very much & I do so want you to have more discretion & judgment about spending your money. You do everything at random my Pet without thinking & it is a growing evil & unless you try & cure yourself of it you will have to suffer severely later on.'

That term Churchill had his first letter published; a two-sentence appeal for more convenient opening hours for the school library, it appeared in the school magazine, the *Harrovian*, on 8 October 1891. Six weeks later, in a much longer letter, he urged that greater use be made of the school gymnasium for special events. 'It is time there should be a change,' he wrote, 'and I rely on your influential columns to work that change.'

A week before his seventeenth birthday, Churchill went to London for the day. A postscript to his next letter home contained a reference to the opposite sex. 'It was awfully bad luck having to go,' he wrote to his mother, 'just as I was making an impression on the pretty Miss Weaslet. Another 10 minutes and . . . !?'

During that day in London, Churchill learned that Mrs Everest was to leave Lady Randolph's employ. Jack was now eleven and a nanny was no longer needed. 'I do not feel very happy & cannot sleep,' Mrs Everest wrote to Churchill. 'But I suppose there must be something to bring us to our end.' He must remember, she added, to wear a coat 'this wet weather'. As for his younger brother: 'Please don't tell Jackie about my going away he will be so unhappy poor darling. What a cruel world this is.' Distressed at Mrs Everest's imminent departure, Churchill protested vigorously on Jack's behalf. It was eventually arranged that she would work for their grandmother, Duchess Fanny, at Grosvenor Square, where the two boys would still see her.

A week after his seventeenth birthday, Churchill wrote to his mother to say that he once more refused to go to France, this time during the Christmas holidays to learn French with a family in Rouen. The family had been chosen by Welldon. If he went, he explained, he would miss his father's homecoming from South Africa. If forced to go, 'I will do as little as I can and the holidays will be one continual battle.' Lady Randolph was not pleased by this threat. 'My dear boy,' she replied, 'I feel for you in every way & can quite understand your anxiety & desire to be at home for Xmas, but quite apart from other considerations, the tone of your letter is not calculated to make one over lenient. When one wants something in this world, it is not by delivering ultimatums that one is likely to get it. I tell you frankly that I am going to decide not you.'

Churchill did not give up the argument. 'You say that "You tell me frankly", very well Mamma I only told you frankly my intentions. You say it is for you to decide. I am required to give up my holidays – not you, I am forced to go to people who bore me excessively – not you.' He was 'very much surprised and pained to think that both you & Papa should treat me so, as a machine. I should like to know if Papa was asked to "give up his holidays" when he was at Eton.'

Towards the end of his letter, which covered three pages, Churchill wrote: 'I am more unhappy than I can possibly say. Your unkindness has relieved me however from all feelings of duty.' Lady Randolph was now much angered. 'I have only read one page of your letter,' she replied, 'and I send it back to you – as its style does not please me.' Upset, Churchill answered that he would never again write her a letter 'of any length, as in my letter's length I can perceive a reason for your not reading it'. He added: 'I expect you were too busy with your parties and arrangements for Christmas. I comfort myself by this.'

Both Welldon and Lady Randolph were emphatic that Churchill should study French in France that holiday. It was arranged that the recently appointed Modern Languages master at Harrow, Bernard Minssen, would accompany him, and that he would stay with Minssen's parents at Versailles. 'Mr Minssen will do everything for him, if he is docile and industrious,' Welldon wrote to Lady Randolph, 'but he will not let him waste his time and, if he is idle, he must be sent home.' Churchill would be allowed to accept only three social invitations a week, and Minssen would supply 'such pocket money as is necessary'.

Churchill stayed at Versailles for a month. 'The food is very queer,' he wrote to his mother in his first letter. 'But there is plenty, & on the whole it is good.' Minssen's parents were being 'very kind' to him. 'Of course,' he added, 'I would give much to return, if you wish it I will come tomorrow – but considering all things I am prepared to stay my month.' From Mrs Everest came a letter of encouragement: 'Cheer up old Boy, enjoy yourself & try to feel contented. You have very much to be thankful for, if only you consider, & fancy how nice it will be to be able to parlez vous francais.'

Life at Versailles did not prove too burdensome. Three of Lady Randolph's friends invited Churchill to meals; one of them, the Austro-Hungarian railway magnate Baron Maurice de Hirsch, took him to the morgue under one of the bridges over the Seine, to see the corpses which had been dragged out of the river that day. 'Only 3 Macabres – not a good bag,' Churchill reported to his mother.

As his month at Versailles came to an end Churchill hoped to persuade his parents to let him have a week off school, in order to be with his father, whom he had not seen for more than eight months. But it was not to be. 'The loss of a week now,' his father wrote from London in mid-January, 'means your not passing, which I am sure you will admit would be very discreditable & disadvantageous.' Father and son would still have 'a few days together' before school began, Lord Randolph noted, and after that the Easter holidays 'will soon be upon us, tho I must say I hope you will work like a little dray horse right up to the summer examination, only about four months off.'

Churchill worked extremely hard throughout the early months of 1892. He also began preparing for the school fencing cup. Money problems continued to beset him. 'I am getting terribly low in my finances,' he wrote to his mother in February. 'You say I never write for love but always for money. I think you are right but remember that you are my banker and who else have I to write to?'

In March, Lady Randolph went to Monte Carlo. 'I am very sick with you for going away like that,' Churchill wrote. He was only a few days away from the fencing competition. He was even more 'terrified', he told her, to learn that she had been robbed of her purse at the Casino, 'for at the same moment I must put in a request for "un peu plus d'argent" '. He also had good news to impart: 'I have won the fencing. A very fine cup. I was far and away first. Absolutely untouched in the finals.'

Churchill was now preparing for the Public Schools fencing championship, but when he asked his father to come to Aldershot to watch him, Lord Randolph replied, 'It is Sandown races which I must go to.' As to Churchill's continual requests for money, 'If you were a millionaire,' his father complained that March, 'you could not be more extravagant.' Were he to get into the Army 'six months of it will see you in the Bankruptcy Court'. In his defence, Churchill pointed out that he had to pay each week for his own teas and breakfasts, for fruit, and for Saturday night biscuits; these alone used up his parents' allowance of a pound a week. This explanation, accurate in itself, did not entirely assuage his mother. 'Your wants are many,' she wrote at the beginning of May, '& you seem a perfect sieve as regards money.'

That month Churchill won the Public Schools fencing championship. 'His success,' wrote the *Harrovian*, 'was chiefly due to his quick and dashing attack, which quite took his opponents by surprise.' Preparation for the Army exam was now continuous. 'I am working awfully hard,' he told his mother, 'without rotting I have done at least 10 hours today.' But the work was in vain; when he took the Sandhurst entrance examination that July he failed. The minimum marks needed to enter the Cavalry were 6,457; Churchill obtained 5,100. Of the 693 candidates he came 390th. The results were not entirely discouraging; in English History he was eighteenth out of more than four hundred candidates who took the paper. 'I think your marks & place very creditable for your first try,' wrote his Army Class tutor, Louis Moriarty.

Churchill would have to take the examination again. 'If he fails again,' Lord Randolph wrote to Duchess Fanny, 'I shall think about putting him in business.' Using his Rothschild connection 'I could get him something very good.'

In the summer of 1892 Lord Salisbury's Conservative Government was defeated, and Gladstone once more became Prime Minister. Although Lord Randolph had long been excluded from Conservative counsels, it was thought, Churchill later recalled, that in opposition he would regain his Parliamentary ascendancy: 'No one cherished these hopes more ardently than I.' Such hopes were illusions. 'Although in the past little had been said in my hearing,' Churchill later wrote, 'one could not grow up in my father's house, and still less among his mother and sisters, without understanding that there had been a great political disaster.'

That August, at Banstead, Churchill startled his father by firing a double-barrelled gun at a rabbit which had appeared on the lawn right under his window. 'He had been very angry and disturbed,' Churchill recalled. 'Understanding at once that I was distressed, he took occasion to reassure me. I then had one of the three or four long intimate conversations with him which are all I can boast.' Lord Randolph explained to his son that older people, absorbed in their own affairs, were not always considerate towards the young 'and might speak roughly in sudden annoyance'. He then began to talk 'in the most wonderful and captivating manner about school and going into the Army and the grown-up life which lay beyond. I listened spellbound to this sudden complete departure from his usual reserve, amazed at his intimate comprehension of all my affairs. Then at the end he said, "Do remember things do not always go right with me. My every action is misjudged and every word distorted. So make some allowances." '

That autumn Jack joined his brother at Harrow, as he worked to take the Army exam again. 'I suppose,' wrote Lady Randolph that September, 'I have made too much fuss over you & made you out a sort of paragon. However it will be all right if you put your shoulder to the wheel this time.' Even the headmaster was helping. 'Welldon is very nice,' Churchill told his mother. 'He makes me do proses for him every evening and looks over them himself with me; a thing hitherto unheard of, as he of course is very pressed for time.'

The examination was to take place at the end of November, a day before Churchill's eighteenth birthday. 'His work this term has been excellent,' Welldon told Lord Randolph. 'He understands now the need of taking trouble, and the way to take it, and, whatever happens to him, I shall consider that in the last twelve months he has learned a lesson of life-long value.' Welldon added, 'It is due to him to say that of late he has done all that could be asked of him.'

When the results were announced Churchill was devastated to learn that he had failed again. All his marks had improved, but not sufficiently; he had obtained 6,106, only 351 short of the pass mark. In Chemistry he had come eighth out of 134 candidates. As Welldon had warned Lord Randolph, the standard, because of a rise in the permitted age of admission, was 'likely to be very high'. From his mathematics tutor, C.H.P. Mayo, came words of encouragement, 'A gain of 900 marks in so short a time is very pleasing and must make you feel confident about the examination in June.'

That November, Lord Randolph's elder brother Blandford, 8th Duke of Marlborough, died suddenly at Blenheim, at the age of forty-eight. Blandford's son, Churchill's cousin Sunny, was now Duke of

Marlborough. He was not quite twenty-one. Were Sunny to die before having a son, Lord Randolph would become Duke of Marlborough, and Churchill, as the heir to the Dukedom, would be Marquess of Blandford.

Churchill was now eighteen. He still had to pass a third examination if he was to enter the Army. He was to take this third exam, not at school, but at a special crammers. His nine years as a schoolboy and a boarder at St George's, Brighton and Harrow had been a predominantly unhappy time, 'a sombre grey patch on the chart of my journey', he later called it. 'It was an unending spell of worries that did not then seem petty, and of toil uncheered by fruition; a time of discomfort, restriction and purposeless monotony.' All his contemporaries, he later wrote, and even younger boys, 'seemed in every way better adapted to the condition of our little world. They were far better at both games and at the lessons. It is not pleasant to feel oneself so completely outclassed and left behind at the very beginning of the race.'

'I am all for the Public schools,' was Churchill's comment in 1930, 'but I do not want to go there again.'

3

Towards the Army:
'A fresh start'

On 11 January 1893, diligent readers of *The Times* learned, from a small news item, that the elder son of Lord and Lady Randolph Churchill had 'met with an accident' on the previous afternoon. 'No bones were broken,' the newspaper reported, 'but he was very much shaken and bruised.' He had in fact fractured his thigh, though in the year before the first use of X-rays this was not known; indeed, it did not become known for seventy years, when this same thigh was X-rayed after a fall in Monte Carlo in 1963.

While seeking to evade his brother and a cousin during a holiday chase on his grandmother's estate in Bournemouth, Churchill, trapped on a bridge over a chine, and looking for a way to evade capture, had seen the slender top of a fir tree and jumped on to it. His grip failed him and he plunged down the ravine. It had been a twenty-nine-foot fall, on hard ground. For three days he lay unconscious. Then, in considerable pain, he was taken up to London. 'The doctors say I shall not be cured for two months yet,' he wrote to Jack in the first week of February. 'I pass the greater part of my time in bed.'

For the last month of his recuperation Churchill went back to the south coast, this time to Brighton, to the house of the 8th Duke of Marlborough's widow, Duchess Lily. She was 'kindness personified' he wrote to his father. While at Brighton he befriended a young Army officer, Hugh Wyllie; twenty-three years later Wyllie, then serving on the Western Front, was killed by a shell on the Menin road.

At the beginning of March, Churchill began work at Captain James's, a crammers in Lexham Gardens, in West London. 'I have issued orders,' James wrote to Lord Randolph, 'for your son to be kept at work and that in future he is to do the full hours. I had to speak to him the other day about his casual manner. I think the boy means well but he is distinctly inclined to be inattentive and to think too much of his abilities.' Churchill had been 'rather too much inclined up to the present,' James wrote, 'to teach his instructors instead of endeavouring to learn from them, and this is not the frame of mind conducive to success.' James had been particularly annoyed when his new pupil 'suggested to me that his knowledge of history was such that he did not want any more teaching in it! The boy has very many good points in him but what he wants is very firm handling.'

That Easter, Churchill returned to Brighton. 'I am very glad to have Winston with me,' Duchess Lily wrote to Lord Randolph, 'for I have grown really fond of the boy. He has lots of good in him – and only needs sometimes to be corrected, which he always takes so smartly and well.'

While at Brighton, Churchill had sent a telegram to his father warning of an outbreak of fever at Harrow. He was worried that his brother might be in danger of catching it. 'Papa was so angry with you for telegraphing to him in that stupid way,' Lady Randolph wrote in rebuke. '*Of course* we all know about the fever from Jack & from Mr Welldon – & in any case to write was quite enough. You take too much on yourself young man, & write in such a pompous style. I'm afraid you are becoming a prig!'

Among Duchess Lily's dinner guests while Churchill was at Brighton was A.J. Balfour, the future Conservative Prime Minister. Lady Randolph was somewhat nervous of her son's social life. 'I don't want to preach dear boy, but mind you are quiet & don't talk too much & don't drink too much.' Churchill now followed his father's own speeches carefully, later recalling with sadness that 'he seemed to be hardly holding his own'. He hoped the time would eventually come when he would be able 'come to his aid', and he encouraged his father with enthusiastic comments on his speeches. 'If you will let me say so,' he wrote after reading the text of one such speech in *The Times*, 'I thought it better than anything you have done so far.' He also became a frequent visitor to the House of Commons, always able because of his father to find a place in the Distinguished Strangers' Gallery.

At lunch and dinner parties given by his parents in the spring of 1893, Churchill met two future Liberal Prime Ministers, Lord Rosebery and H.H. Asquith. On April 21 he was in the Gallery when Gladstone wound up the second reading of the Home Rule Bill. 'The Grand Old Man,' he later recalled, 'looked like a great white eagle at once fierce and splendid. His sentences rolled forth majestically and everyone hung upon his lips and gestures, eager to cheer or to deride.'

After a dinner at Grosvenor Square at the end of May, Churchill's uncle Edward Marjoribanks, then Liberal Chief Whip, spent half an hour explaining to him how the Liberals would overcome the opposition of the House of Lords. 'I wish you had been there to answer him,' Churchill wrote to his father, who was at a public meeting in Bradford, 'as I am sure there was an answer though I could not think of it.' The Liberals were in fact unable to find a means of overcoming the Peers, who defeated the Home Rule Bill by 419 votes to 41. 'Overcoming the Peers' was to be Churchill's own battle cry fifteen years later.

A newly elected Conservative MP, Edward Carson, invited Churchill to dine with him in the House of Commons. Churchill asked his father if he could break off his work at the crammers to do so. That week Churchill was Carson's guest at a Home Rule debate. Twenty-one years later, when Carson himself took Lord Randolph's cry 'Ulster will fight, Ulster will be right' to the streets, Churchill was not only his opponent, but was prepared to use force against Carson's Ulster Volunteers.

At the end of July, Churchill took his third Sandhurst examination. On August 3, before the results were known, he prepared to leave London for Switzerland and Italy with his brother Jack and a tutor, John Little. They met at the station, where, to Churchill's surprise, Little congratulated him on his success. It was the first he knew of it. 'I looked in the paper', he told his father, '& found this to be true.' He was at last a soldier.

Churchill had raised his marks by 163, to 6,309. This was not quite good enough, by only eighteen marks, to get him into the infantry, but he came fourth on the cavalry list. From Dover, just before crossing the Channel, he sent telegrams announcing his success to his parents, his relations and his former headmaster. 'I was *so* pleased to get your wire today and to know you had "got in" !! ' Duchess Lily replied that same day. 'Never mind the infantry: you will love the cavalry, and when Papa comes back we will get the charger.' She added, '*Don't* tumble down another precipice and hurt any more of your organs – for I will not be there to take care of you.'

'I cannot help saying how much I rejoice in your success,' wrote Welldon, 'and how keenly I feel that you have deserved it.'

As he travelled through Switzerland, Churchill sent his father two accounts of the holiday. In the first week of August he was at a hotel in Lucerne with 'lifts, electric light & fireworks (every Saturday)'. On the fourth day of the holiday Mr Little wrote to Lord Randolph, 'We have all got on very well together; although Winston is inclined to be extravagant.' On August 8 Churchill wrote to his father, 'I am looking forward to going to Sandhurst very much, & am very thankful I was lucky enough to get in.' Three days later he promised his father he would 'try & do well there, from the first'.

On August 14, when he was in Milan, Churchill received a letter from his father about the Sandhurst results. It was a letter neither of congratulation nor of praise. Unknown to his son, Lord Randolph was beset by an illness, diagnosed by his doctors as syphilis, that was undermining his health and his sanity. He could share none of the pleasure of Duchess Lily or Dr Welldon at his son's success. 'I am rather surprised,' he wrote, 'at your tone of exultation over your inclusion in the Sandhurst list. There are two ways of winning in an examination, one creditable, the other the reverse. You have unfortunately chosen the latter method, and appear to be much pleased with your success.' In the failure to get into the infantry, Lord Randolph continued, 'is demonstrated beyond refutation your slovenly happy-go-lucky harum scarum style of work for which you have always been distinguished at your various schools. Never have I received a really good report of your conduct in your work from any master or tutor you had from time to time to do with.'

Showing all the anger that was to characterize the gradual collapse of his nervous system, Lord Randolph continued, 'With all the advantages you had, with all the abilities which you foolishly think yourself to possess & which some of your relations claim for you, with all the efforts that have been made to make your life easy & agreeable & your work neither oppressive nor distasteful, this is the grand result that you come up among the 2nd rate & 3rd rate class who are only good for commissions in a cavalry regiment.' There was more anger to come, the sign of a mind that was becoming slowly deranged, although the young Churchill had no idea of this. 'Now it is a good thing,' Lord Randolph continued, 'to put this business very plainly before you. Do not think I am going to take the trouble of writing you long letters after every folly & failure you commit & undergo. I shall not write again on these matters & you need not trouble to write any answer to this part of my letter, because I no longer attach the slightest weight to anything you may say about your own achievements & exploits.'

The next paragraph of Lord Randolph's letter was the harshest. 'Make this position indelibly impressed on your mind,' he wrote, 'that if your conduct and action at Sandhurst is similar to what it has been in the other establishments in which it has been sought vainly to impart to you some education, then my responsibility for you is over. I shall leave you to depend on yourself, giving you merely such assistance as may be necessary to permit of a respectable life. Because I am certain that if you cannot prevent yourself from leading the idle useless unprofitable life you have had during your schooldays & later months, you will become a mere social wastrel, one of the hundreds of the public school failures, and you will degenerate into a shabby unhappy & futile existence. If that is so you will have to bear all the blame for such misfortunes yourself. Your own conscience will enable you to recall & enumerate all the efforts that have been made to give you the best of chances which you were entitled to by your position, & how you have practically neglected them all.'

Lord Randolph had sent a similarly disturbed letter to Duchess Fanny, in which he wrote that the 'whole result' of the family's kindnesses to the young boy 'had been either at Harrow or Eton to prove his total worthlessness as a scholar or a conscientious worker'. Churchill had of course never been to Eton; his father was already losing his grip on reality. Unaware of the cause, Churchill was crushed by his father's rebuke. 'When he showed me your letter,' Mr Little wrote to Lord Randolph, 'we had a long talk and he told me a good deal about his views of man and things. He was a good deal depressed.' Mr Little tried to help Churchill overcome the shock of his father's letter, pointing out that in going to Sandhurst he would begin what was 'practically a new page in his life', and that such opportunities for a new start occurred 'at most, but once or twice in a lifetime'.

'I am very sorry indeed that you are displeased with me,' the unhappy Churchill wrote to his father from Milan. 'As however you tell me not to refer to the part of your letter about the Examination I will not do so, but will try to modify your opinion of me by my work & conduct at Sandhurst during the time I shall be there.' Churchill sought to assure him, 'My extremely low place in passing in will have no effect whatever on my chance there.' To his mother he wrote that same day of what a disappointment it was to find that his father was 'not satisfied', and he added, 'After slaving away at Harrow & James' for this Exam, & trying, as far as I could, to make up for the time I had wasted, I was only too delighted to find that I had at length got in.' At Sandhurst he would begin with new subjects, 'in which I shall not be handicapped by past illness'.

'If I had failed,' Churchill told his mother, 'there would have been an end of all my chances. As it is, my fate is in my own hands & I have a fresh start.'

The holiday continued, with swimming in the baths at Milan and a visit to the cathedral. Then the trio went north to Baveno for an expedition in a rowing boat on Lake Maggiore. Then they went back to Switzerland, to Zermatt, before returning to England. Churchill was pleased that as a result of a number of last-minute vacancies he could go into the infantry after all. Lord Randolph had in fact used his influence to obtain a special commission for his son in the infantry, in the 60th Rifles. 'The future now is in your hands,' Lady Randolph wrote that September, 'to make or to mar it. I have trust in you to make it a success.'

Churchill's first letters from the Royal Military College, Sandhurst, reveal his determination to make the best of his new career. 'Of course it is very uncomfortable,' he wrote to his father about his room: 'No carpet or curtains. No ornamentation or adornments of any kind. No hot water and very little cold.' The discipline was 'far stricter than Harrow. Hardly any law is given to juniors on joining. No excuse is ever taken – not even with a plea of "don't know" – after the first few hours, and of course no such thing as unpunctuality or untidiness is tolerated.' There was, however, Churchill wrote, 'something very exhilarating in the military manner in which everything works; and I think that I shall like my life here during the next 18 months very much'.

Churchill quickly became absorbed in the professional world of the soldier. 'The work is very interesting and extremely practical,' he wrote to his father on his tenth day, 'Shot and shell of all kinds – bridges, guns, field and siege, mapping, keeping regimental savings bank accounts, inspecting meat etc', as well as the parades and drills. There were five subjects of study; fortification, tactics, topography, military law, and military administration.

Lord Randolph remained cantankerous, complaining on several occasions about the style of his son's letters to him. 'I am awfully sorry that Papa does not approve of my letters,' Churchill wrote to his mother. 'I take a great deal of pains over them & often re-write entire pages. If I write a descriptive account of my life here, I receive a hint from you that my style is too sententious & stilted. If on the other hand I write a plain and excessively simple letter – it is put down as slovenly. I never can do anything right.' Thus far, Churchill added: 'I have been extremely good. Neither late nor lazy, & have always had five minutes to wait before each parade or study.'

Churchill's letters to his parents were full of enthusiasm. 'Today,' he wrote to his father on September 20, 'we learnt to make all kinds of knots and to lash beams together. We have also been out making, or learning to make sketch maps.' He was shooting with both revolver and rifle. 'On Monday we have to go and fire with a new 12 pounder gun, which has just been issued to the Artillery.' After a month he wrote proudly to his mother, 'So far I have not been late for anything (& there are at least six engagements per diem).' From Mrs Everest came the same caring counsel he had received from her while he was at Harrow, 'Don't expose youself to the sun this hot weather dear', and 'Don't run into debt or keep bad company.'

Ill-health was still a burden and a worry; that October, after a three-quarter of a mile run with 'rifles & accoutrements', Churchill had to be helped off the parade ground and, he told his mother, 'have been bad ever since'. He had seen the doctor, who said there was nothing wrong 'except that my heart does not seem very strong'.

That autumn Churchill's relationship with his father improved, as did Lord Randolph's health, though this was only a temporary remission. 'I think Papa seems much better for his rest,' Churchill wrote to his mother, '& much less nervous.' He had been 'very pleased to see me and talked to me for quite a long time about his speeches & my prospects'. Churchill was pleased when his father, in a renewed burst of political vigour, lashed into

Asquith during a speech at Yarmouth, calling Asquith's speeches 'a laby-
rinth of nonsense'. The Yarmouth speech, he told his father, was 'very
good'. The relationship between father and son was closer than it had ever
been. His son was 'much smartened up', Lord Randolph wrote to Duchess
Fanny; at Lord Rothschild's house at Tring the guests 'took a great deal
of notice of him' and yet he was 'very quiet & nice mannered'.

  'What a comfortable house this is,' was Churchill's comment to his
mother on Tring, comparing it with Sandhurst's 'dilapidated & tobacco-
smelling rooms'. Lord Randolph now gave his son some extra money to
pay his bills, and sent him two boxes of his best cigarettes. He also took him
to the Empire Theatre and to the homes of his racing friends. Yet even at
this time of closeness all was not well. 'If ever I began to show the slightest
idea of comradeship,' Churchill later recalled, 'he was immediately offended; and when once I suggested that I might help his private secretary
to write some of his letters, he froze me into stone.'

  That winter Lady Randolph told her son that Duchess Fanny, who two
years earlier had taken on Mrs Everest after Lady Randolph had no longer
needed her, decided she would have to leave. She was to be dismissed by
letter. 'If I allowed Mrs Everest to be cut adrift without protest in the
manner which is proposed,' Churchill wrote, 'I should be extremely ungrateful – besides I should be very sorry not to have her at Grosvenor
Square because she is in my mind associated more than anything else with
home.' Mrs Everest was 'an old woman', he pointed out. She had been in
Lady Randolph's employ for nearly twenty years. 'She is more fond of Jack
and me than any other people in the world & to be packed off in the way
the duchess suggests would possibly, if not probably break her down
altogether.'

  As intended, Mrs Everest was dismissed by letter. 'I think such proceedings cruel & rather mean,' Churchill wrote; she should not be sent away
until she had found 'a good place' elsewhere; 'Dearest Mamma, I know
you are angry with me for writing. I am very sorry but I cannot bear to
think of Everest not coming back, much less being got rid of in such a
manner.' His appeal was in vain; Mrs Everest left the family employ.

  From Lady Randolph came a complaint; his father did not like him
smoking cigars. 'I will not do so any more,' he promised. 'I am not fond
enough of them in having any difficulty in leaving them off.' To his father,
Churchill promised not to smoke 'more than one or two a day – and very
rarely that'.

  Churchill's time at Sandhurst was one of learning and comradeship. 'In
contrast with my school days,' he wrote thirty-five years later, 'I had made
many friends, three or four of whom still survive.' The fate of the others
was to become a cause of sorrowful reflection. 'The South African War

accounted for a large proportion not only of my friends but of my company,' he explained, 'and the Great War killed almost all the others. The few that survived have been pierced through thigh or breast or face by the bullets of the enemy. I salute them all.'

On 30 November 1893 Churchill celebrated his nineteenth birthday. Ten days later he took his first Sandhurst examination in all five subjects. 'I have caught a cold in my teeth on both sides,' he told his father, '& have got a very bad toothache – which has made me lose a few marks in the examination.' He passed, however, with 1,198 marks out of 1,500. The tactics paper proved his best; he received 278 marks out of 300. That Christmas he stayed at Blenheim. His cousin Sunny and his American wife Consuelo, the Vanderbilt heiress, were 'very kind to me', he told his father on Christmas Day, while to his mother he confided a day later, 'I am enjoying myself here very much – though there is plenty of divine service.' He had been smitten while in London by 'the beautiful Polly Hacket'; the thought of seeing her again, he told his mother, was consolation for leaving Blenheim.

'Polly Hacket came for a walk this morning,' Churchill wrote to Jack on the last day of January 1894, '& we went and strolled Bond Street way.' Later that day he received a note from Miss Hacket herself. 'Did you really mean to leave all those lovely sweets for me,' she asked. 'It was too, too kind of you.'

That February, Churchill had a riding accident. 'Winston is very sorry for himself,' Lady Randolph wrote to Jack, 'he makes a great fuss over his "scraped tail" but he will have plenty of rest from riding when he gets back to Sandhurst.'

Back at Sandhurst, Churchill was taken more seriously ill. From his father came a sympathetic letter. 'That influenza was most unlucky,' he wrote. There was also paternal advice, 'Keep down smoking, keep down the drink & go to bed as early as you can.' Lord Randolph hoped his son would get good reports and positions. 'Well I have written you a regular lecture but it is all sound. The better you do the more I shall be inclined to help you.'

'Such a kind letter from Papa,' Churchill told his mother, to whom he wrote a few days later to report that he had been put head of the riding class. 'It was quite worth while getting up early and taking those lessons', he wrote to his father. Lord Randolph was so pleased that he sent his son a pound each for the men who had looked after him at the barracks. When, later that week, he told his father that Saturday and Sunday were 'terrible' days at Sandhurst, with nothing at all to do, his father replied: 'Why don't you read books on Saturday & Sunday – I will send you some.'

From Mrs Everest, now living at Crouch End in North London, came words of guidance, 'Take plenty of open air exercise & you will not require medicine.' As to character: 'Be a good Gentleman, upright, honest, just, kind & altogether lovely. My sweet old darling, how I do love you, be good for my sake.' That April, Churchill went to see her. 'I hope you will be kept from all evil & bad companions,' she wrote after his return to Sandhurst, '& not go to the Empire & stay out at night, its too awful to think of, it can only lead to wickedness & everything bad. I cannot bear to think of you being led astray like that.'

A week after this appeal Churchill did go to the Empire Theatre for an evening of fun before returning to the routine of riding and map-making. He also joined a voluntary signalling class. There was trouble, however, after he sent a letter to his father announcing his next visit to London. 'If you are always running up to town every week on some pretext or other,' Lord Randolph wrote, 'your mind is distracted from your work besides being an unnecessary expenditure of money.' Lord Randolph added, 'You are 20 & in November 21, & you must remember always that you are a military cadet and not a Harrow schoolboy.' In fact Churchill was nineteen, and would be twenty in November; the lapse was in keeping with Lord Randolph's recurring and now worsening illness. That April a Parliamentary commentator described him as 'bowed down with physical and mental suffering'. He could no longer finish his speeches; while speaking, his voice would become slurred and he would lose his train of thought.

Churchill was now so afraid of upsetting his father that, when he accidentally dropped his watch into a stream near a deep pool at Sandhurst, he at once took off his clothes and dived for it. He had cause to be concerned; it was a gold watch with the Churchill family arms in enamel on the back, which to his father's distress he earlier dropped on the pavement, denting the case. So now he plunged into the pool to retrieve it; but the bottom was so uneven and the water so cold that he could only stay in for ten minutes, and failed to find it. The next day he arranged to have the pool dredged, but without result. He then borrowed twenty-three soldiers from an infantry detachment, paid them to dig a new course for the stream, borrowed the College fire engine and pumped the pool dry. The watch was found. Churchill sent it at once to his father's London watchmaker, Mr Dent, for repair. By an unfortunate coincidence, Lord Randolph went to Dent that week and was told of the new damage to the watch. His anger was intense. 'I have written a letter to Winston he won't forget,' he told Lady Randolph.

Knowing nothing of the saga of how his son had retrieved the watch, Lord Randolph wrote: 'I would not believe you could be such a young stupid. It is clear that you are not to be trusted with a valuable watch & when I get it from Mr Dent I shall not give it to you back.' The irate father went on to point out that Churchill's brother 'has had the watch I gave him longer than you have had yours'. In all 'qualities of steadiness, taking care of his things & never doing stupid things, Jack is vastly your superior'.

In reply, Churchill sent his father a full account of the search for the watch. 'I tell you all this,' he wrote, 'to show you that I appreciated fully the value of the watch and that I did not treat the accident in a casual way. The labour of the men cost me over £3.' Everything else his father had ever given him, he added, 'is in as good repair as when you gave it first. Please don't judge me entirely on the strength of the watch.' Lord Randolph gave the watch to Jack, who kept it all his life; but his health had again taken a turn for the worse, and within two weeks of his angry letter about the watch, he was advised by Dr Roose to give up public life 'at least for a while', as his nervous symptoms required rest. Churchill was also unwell again. 'Extraordinary headaches all week', he explained to his mother, had forced him to stay in the Sandhurst hospital. As soon as he was well enough, he went up to London. 'I went back and got a very good room at the corner of Jermyn Street,' he wrote to his brother on June 5, 'had an excellent dinner at the Berkeley, and then went on to the Empire.' He had lunched the next day with Polly Hacket, and intended to bring her down to Harrow to see him. He would also go to the Derby, 'However I am not going to bet.' On June 24 he wrote again: 'I had a very pleasant week at Ascot and saw all the races. I backed a couple of winners and a lot of Stiff uns but altogether paid my way.' So much for his intentions not to bet! He had also dined two nights in succession with Lord Wolverton, a Lord-in-Waiting, at Windsor, 'and rode in the Queen Anne's drive and back fourteen miles after dinner'.

Lord Randolph now prepared to travel round the world accompanied by his wife and also by a doctor, George Keith. Before his parents left England, Churchill applied for leave to go to London to see them off. As it was mid-week, his application was refused as a matter of routine. Lord Randolph at once telegraphed to the Secretary of State for War, Sir Henry Campbell-Bannerman, pointing out it was his 'last day in England'. Permission was granted, but Churchill was not at Sandhurst when it arrived. He was making a road map on Chobham Common.

A messenger cycled at once from Sandhurst with an order for Churchill 'to proceed at once to London'. On the following day Lord Randolph was ready to leave. Lord Rosebery, then Prime Minister, was among those at the station to see him off. Churchill later recalled the leave-taking: 'In spite of the great beard which he had grown during his South African journey four years before, his face looked terribly haggard and worn with mental pain. He patted me on the knee in a gesture which however simple was perfectly informing. Then followed his long journey around the world. I never saw him again, except as a swiftly-fading shadow.' Churchill had no idea how ill his father was. 'If Papa comes back all right,' he wrote to his mother in mid-July, 'I shall not regret your going away.'

With his parents in distant lands, Churchill sent Mrs Everest regular reports of his mishaps. 'I have heard from Winny,' she wrote to Jack, 'he says he is better & going about. I hope he is not going to do much of that sort of thing, falling off his horse he may easily be a cripple for life or even get killed poor dear old Boy he is so reckless.' In another letter, after she had seen Churchill in London, she wrote to Jack: 'Poor old boy he was not at all well, he had two boils on his hind quarters which were very painful he could hardly walk, also bad toothe ache, altogether out of sorts. He went back to Sandhurst in spite of his ailments though I waited with him till he left.' The problem, in Mrs Everest's view, was London, 'the late hours & late dinners & so on & no fresh air or exercise, it is utterly impossible to do without that.' A few days later she wrote again: 'Fancy Winny coming up to London every week. He seems to enjoy himself there.'

That August, Churchill again travelled in Europe with Jack and Mr Little. In Belgium, they visited the battlefield of Waterloo. At Antwerp they saw an American warship, the *Chicago*, and 'examined it', Churchill wrote to his mother, 'as closely as the authorities would let us'. On reaching Switzerland they went to Zermatt, where Churchill climbed Monte Rosa. 'More than sixteen hours of continual walking,' he told his mother. 'I was very proud & pleased to find I was able to do it and to come down very fresh.'

From Zermatt, Churchill, his brother and Mr Little went to Ouchy, below Lausanne. On the third day there Churchill went rowing on the lake with Jack, and, from the boat, they swam. As they did so, a strong breeze caught the red awning over the stern seats, blowing the boat away from them. In vain did Churchill, a good swimmer, try to reach the boat. Again and again, just as he thought he had succeeded, the boat was blown further away. Meanwhile, he later recalled, 'the breeze was freshening', and he and Jack, especially Jack, began to be tired. 'Up to this point no idea of danger had crossed my mind. The sun played upon the sparkling blue waters; the wonderful panorama of mountains and valleys, the gay hotels and villas still smiled. But now I saw Death as near I believe as I have ever seen him. He was swimming in the water at our side, whispering from time to time in the rising wind which continued to carry the boat away from us at about the same speed we could swim.'

Twice more Churchill nearly reached the boat. Each time, however, a gust of wind caught the awning and blew the boat further off. Then 'by a supreme effort I caught hold of its side in the nick of time before a still stronger gust bulged the red awning again'. Churchill quickly rowed back

for Jack who, he later wrote, 'though tired, had not apparently realized
the dull yellow glare of mortal peril that had so suddenly played around
us'.

Returning to Sandhurst, Churchill prepared for the final examination.
Riding, at which he had become most skilled, was now his passion and joy.
But when he wrote to his father asking to be allowed to go into the cavalry,
Lord Randolph replied from California, 'You had better put that out of
your head altogether at any rate during my lifetime during which you will
be dependent on me.' The extra cost of the horses was the barrier. 'I still
have hopes,' Churchill wrote to his mother that September, 'that when he
sees how anxious I am, he will not force me into the infantry against my
inclination.'

Lord and Lady Randolph had reached Japan, where Randolph's condition began to deteriorate. In London, Churchill was making his first
foray into public controversy, joining the protests at the move to close the
Empire Theatre because of the gathering of young people who, he later
recalled, 'not only conversed together during the performance and its
intervals, but also from time to time refreshed themselves with alcoholic
liquors'. The foyer was also a favourite haunt of the 'Ladies of the Empire'.

In a letter to the *Westminster Gazette*, signed with his initials 'WLSC',
Churchill argued that 'the improvement in the standard of public decency
is due rather to improved social conditions and to the spread of education
than to the prowling of the prudes'. He also wrote, quite unaware of the
nature of his father's illness and its cause: 'Nature metes out great and
terrible punishments to the "roué and libertine"–far greater punishments
than it is in the power of any civilised State to award. These penalties have
been exacted since the world was young, and yet immorality is still common. State intervention, whether in the form of a Statute or by the decision
of licensing committees, will never eradicate the evil.'

Churchill accepted that both disputants at the Empire were anxious to
see England 'better and more moral' but went on to stress that 'whereas
the Vigilante Societies wish to abolish sin by Act of Parliament, and are
willing to sacrifice much of the liberty of the subject into the bargain, the
"anti-prudes" prefer a less coercive and more moderate procedure'. To
try to improve things by repressive measures was 'a dangerous method,
usually leading to reaction'.

This letter was published on October 18. On November 3 Churchill
made a last effort to rally the anti-prude forces. 'Did you see the papers
about the riot at the Empire last Saturday,' he wrote to his brother. 'It was
I who led the rioters – and made a speech to the crowd.' His battle-cry that
night was 'Ladies of the Empire, I stand for Liberty!' and he told his

fellow-protesters: 'You have seen us tear down these barricades tonight. See that you pull down those who are responsible for them at the coming election.' The battle, however, was lost, and the theatre was closed down. 'I don't quite know what your opinion on the subject might be,' Churchill wrote to his father, 'but I am sure you will disapprove of so coercive and futile a measure.'

Churchill's father was on his way from Hong Kong to India; a telegram from Dr Keith in the first week of November revealed that he was suffering fleeting delusions, and unable to speak properly. Much alarmed, Churchill persuaded Dr Roose to tell him how serious his father's condition was; he was told the symptoms but not their cause. 'I had never realized how ill Papa had been,' he wrote at once to his mother, 'and had never until now believed that there was anything serious the matter.'

Churchill now made every effort to ensure that the news was kept from his grandmother, who had already been shown several alarming bulletins. 'I would advise, if I might,' he wrote to his mother, 'that you and Keith would write nothing but good to the Duchess.' Bad news upset her greatly. 'She lives, thinks, and cares for nothing else in the world but to see Papa again – and has a week of misery after anything like an unsatisfactory report.'

At the end of November, when Lord Randolph was at Madras, Dr Keith telegraphed to Dr Roose with the terrible news that his patient had only 'about six months' to live. Roose showed this telegram to Churchill, who wanted to leave at once for India. 'I do not know how far distant the end of Papa's illness may be,' he wrote to his mother, 'but I am determined that I will come out and see him again.' He also suggested that his parents should return as quickly as possible to Egypt, or to the French Riviera, where he and Jack could join them. 'It must be awful for you,' he wrote to his mother, 'but it is almost as bad for me. You at least are there – on the spot & near him.'

Lady Randolph decided that her husband, increasingly delirious and incoherent, should be brought back to the South of France. On November 29, the day before his twentieth birthday, Churchill wrote to Jack: 'Papa & Mamma are coming home and will be at Monte Carlo by the end of December – so we shall be able to go out there and see them. The doctors think that if he keeps *perfectly* quiet he may yet get well – though he will never be able to go into Politics again.'

Churchill's time at Sandhurst was even then coming to an end. To his delight he came second in the Riding examination, out of 127 cadets. 'I hope you will be pleased,' he wrote to his father. But Lord Randolph was no longer able to take in what was happening around him; on reaching

Colombo he had to be put into a strait-jacket. From there he was taken to Cairo, and, too ill to seek recuperation in the South of France, he was brought back to London.

On December 24 Lord Randolph was back at Grosvenor Square. A few days later he was in such terrible pain that his family thought he was about to die. Alarmed by this news, the Prince of Wales asked his own doctor, Sir Richard Quain, to ask Lord Randolph's neurologist, Dr Buzzard the nature of the disease. Buzzard replied: 'Lord Randolph is affected with "General Paralysis" the early symptoms of which, in the form of tremor of the tongue & slurring articulation of words were evident to me at an interview two years ago. I had not seen him for a long while – a year or two, I think – previously, so that it is impossible to say how long he has been affected with the disease.' In layman's language 'General Paralysis' is a manifestation of syphilis that usually occurs ten to twenty years after primary infection.

At this distance in time it is never possible to be absolutely certain of the diagnosis, but Buzzard was a widely respected neurologist with great experience of the disease. His letter continued, 'You well know how much such cases vary as regards particular symptoms although they usually agree in leading to a fatal termination in the course of three or four years.'

Buzzard was not entirely without hope, telling Quain: 'Under regular feeding & rest his Lordship has greatly recuperated and can now converse – recognise persons & the room in which he lies and shews a fair amount of memory of past events. His articulation, however, makes it at times difficult to understand a word that he says. He has no delusions. The condition is rather one of mental feebleness. It is quite possible, I think, that his mental condition may become still clearer if his life be spared. But just as there have been successive assaults of paralysis on different parts so he may at any time, experience others, & the occurrence of one in a vital situation might produce sudden death. His heart is very weak. Or it is possible that he may sink into a state of increasing dementia with its accompanying physical troubles – slowly ending in death.'

'Physically he is better,' Lady Randolph wrote to her sister Leonie on 3 January 1895, 'but mentally he is 1,000 times worse. Even his mother wishes now that he had died the other day.' A few days later, waking from a deep sleep, Lord Randolph asked those around him when they would be leaving for Monte Carlo. He was told that they would start the next day. 'That's all right,' he said, then saw his son and asked him when and how he had passed the Sandhurst examination. Churchill had passed out twentieth in a class of 130.

Lord Randolph died on the morning of January 24, three weeks before his forty-sixth birthday. Three days later he was buried in the churchyard at Bladon, just beyond the walls of Blenheim. 'Over the landscape brilliant with sunshine,' Churchill later recalled, 'snow had spread a glittering pall.'

Unaware of the terrible cause of his father's death, Churchill believed it was yet further proof that the Churchills died young. Both he and Jack had been premature. At Jack's birth it was thought he was dead. Three of Lord Randolph's brothers had died in infancy, a fourth brother, the 8th Duke, had died in his forties, like Lord Randolph. Churchill's own health had always been poor.

These were frightening facts; Churchill was not only driven forward to defend his father's memory and prove to himself that he was not the wastrel his father had accused him of being; he was also haunted by the prospect that he too might die young. 'Is it forty and finished?' he was to ask twenty years later. Never having seen Buzzard's letter to Quain, a letter first found and published by his son Randolph in 1967, Churchill never knew that his fear of dying young through hereditary weakness was misplaced.

In the summer of 1895, six months after his father's death, Churchill went back to Bladon to see the grave.' The service in the little church was going on,' he wrote to his mother, 'and the voices of the children singing all added to the beauty and restfulness of the spot. The hot sun of the last few days has dried up the grass a little – but the rose bushes are in full bloom and make the churchyard very bright. I was so struck by the sense of quietness & peace as well as by the old world air of the place – that my sadness was not unmixed with solace. It is the spot of all others he would have chosen. I think it would make you happier to see it.'

4

Second Lieutenant: 'I cannot sit still'

On 20 February 1895, four weeks after his father's death, Churchill entered the cavalry, being gazetted a Second Lieutenant with the 4th Hussars, then stationed at Aldershot. His commission was made out, according to custom, from Queen Victoria to 'Our Trusty and well beloved Winston Leonard Spencer Churchill, Gentleman', and was signed by the Secretary of State for War, Campbell-Bannerman, who less than eleven years later was to give Churchill his first Ministerial office, as Under-Secretary of State for the Colonies.

The routine at Aldershot was not severe; it began at 7.45., Churchill wrote to his brother during his first week there, with 'Breakfast in bed'. For one hour a day he was in charge of a squad of thirty men 'and have to see the horses groomed, watered, fed & the men's rooms clean etc'. There was also two hours' riding school each morning, and a drill in the afternoon 'mostly spent in drilling the men myself'. This was followed by 'hot baths', dinner, billiards and bezique. 'I play a great deal of whist in the evenings,' he told his mother a few days later. He had also been to London, where his aunt, Duchess Lily, had agreed to pay for his horse.

After Churchill had been only two weeks at Aldershot, the electors of the Barnesbury constituency asked the twenty-year-old subaltern to address them. It was his first invitation to give a political speech, 'but after much communing with myself,' he told his brother, 'I wrote them that the honour was too great – or words to that effect.'

Accidents still beset the young man; in March he wrote to his mother: 'I have had the misfortune to smash myself up while trying a horse on the steeplechase course. The animal refused and swerved – I tried to cram him in – and he took the wings. Very nearly did I break my leg – but as it is I am only bruised and stiff.' He had struck his knee a 'resounding blow', he told Jack, 'but am now better and can hobble about on sticks'.

Having assured his mother that he would not take any further risks by steeplechasing, Churchill entered a Cavalry Brigade steeplechase under the name 'Mr Spencer'. The race in which he rode was the 4th Hussars Subalterns' Challenge Cup. 'It was very exciting and there is no doubt about it being dangerous,' he told Jack. 'I had never jumped a regulation fence before and they are pretty big things as you know.' His horse came third. Later there was a scandal when it emerged that the winner might not have been the horse it was stated to be; the race was declared null and void and all the horses which had taken part in it, including the one Churchill had ridden, were perpetually disqualified from further racing. All five subalterns were under suspicion of having participated in the deception, which, a year later, was violently denounced in the radical magazine *Truth*.

There was another unfortunate episode that spring, only three weeks after the steeplechase affair. A recently commissioned officer, Alan Bruce, who was about to join the 4th Hussars, and had been at Sandhurst with Churchill, was so unpopular with his fellow subalterns that, at a dinner to which five of them, including Churchill, specially invited him, he was told that he ought to leave the regiment. A year later this episode was also denounced in *Truth*, which called it a 'gross cavalry scandal'. According to the editor, the Radical MP Henry Labouchere, it was Churchill who, 'acting apparently as spokesman of the junior officers of the regiment', had informed Bruce he was 'not wanted'. Not long afterwards Bruce was asked officially to leave, and did so.

In two of his letters to his mother Churchill referred to this aspect of Army life, though not to his own involvement. 'When I see how some fellows who are disliked are treated,' he wrote that April, 'I feel very thankful I have been so fortunate as to make my own friends and generally find my footing.' Three months later he told her, 'If you aren't liked you have to go & that means going through life with an unpleasant stigma.'

At the end of April, Churchill was in London for the wedding of his widowed aunt, Duchess Lily, to Lord William Beresford. 'A most excellent breakfast which must have cost a great deal,' he wrote to his mother, 'and crowds to eat it, were the chief feature.' From London he went to the races at Newmarket, where the Prince of Wales had spoken to him. 'The whole world' had been in the stand, 'all most civil & agreeable'. Polo, too, was now at the forefront of his interests. 'It is the finest game in the world,' he wrote to his mother at the end of May, 'and I should almost be content to give up any ambition to play it well and often. But that will no doubt cease to be my view in a short time.'

In June, Churchill's friend Polly Hacket married Edward Wilson. Churchill had already befriended Wilson's sister Muriel, who was his guest at Aldershot for the Queen's Birthday Parade. That month he joined the Bachelors' Club in London. 'I have had a great many invitations,' he told his mother, '& could go to a ball every night did I wish to – but field days & drills make me more eager for bed than anything else.' That June, Nasrulla Khan, son of the Emir of Afghanistan, visited England; when he inspected the troops at Aldershot, Churchill was chosen to be part of the escort of the Duke of Connaught. 'I was seven hours on horseback without dismounting or taking off my busby,' he told his mother, '& two more hours after lunch – but it was a great honour to have been selected.'

In the early evening of July 2 Churchill received a telegram at Aldershot announcing that Mrs Everest's condition was 'critical'. He set off at once for her house at 15 Crouch Hill, in North London. 'She knew she was in danger,' he later recalled, 'but her only anxiety was for me. There had been a heavy shower of rain. My jacket was wet. When she felt it with her hands she was greatly alarmed for fear I should catch cold. The jacket had to be taken off and thoroughly dried before she was calm again.'

From North London, Churchill hurried to the centre of town to engage a nurse and to see Dr Keith, who agreed at once to go to Mrs Everest's bedside. Churchill then took the midnight train back to Aldershot so as not to miss the early morning parade. As soon as the parade was over he returned to London, to Mrs Everest's side. But despite hopes that she might rally 'she only sank into a stupor,' Churchill told his mother, 'which gave place to death at 2.15 this morning'. The nurse had arrived only for the end. 'It was very sad & her death was shocking to see – but I do not think she suffered much pain.'

It was still early morning; Churchill took the train from London to Harrow to tell Jack the news, wanting to spare him the anguish of a telegram. 'He was awfully shocked,' Churchill told his mother, 'but tried not to show it.' Returning to London he made the necessary arrangements for Mrs Everest's funeral. He also ordered a wreath in his mother's name, as 'I thought you would like to send one'. As to Mrs Everest, he told her, 'I shall never know such a friend again.'

Mrs Everest was buried at the City of London Cemetery in East London on July 5. 'The coffin was covered in wreaths,' Churchill wrote to his mother that night, '& everything was as it should be.' The funeral over, he returned to Aldershot. 'Well my dearest Mummy,' he wrote that evening, 'I am very tired as I have been knocking about for two nights & have done all my duty here at the same time. I feel very low – and find that I never realized how much poor old Woom was to me.' Later he arranged for a stone to be put on her grave; the inscription states that it had been erected 'by Winston Spencer Churchill and John Spencer Churchill'.

'I felt very despondent and sad,' Churchill told his mother. 'It is indeed another link with the past gone, & I look back with regret to the old days at Connaught Place when fortune still smiled.' Lady Randolph did not even have a home of her own now; she was living in hotels and with relatives. 'I am longing for the day when you will be able to have a little house of your own,' Churchill wrote, 'and when I can really feel that there is such a place as home.' For him, Aldershot was home. 'I have a great many friends,' he told his mother, '& I know my ground.' There was much to do and see. On July 23 the Duke and Duchess of York, later King George V and Queen Mary, were present at the field day '& I was asked to meet them at dinner'. He also had 'quite a long talk with the Duke of Connaught about the Election'.

It was the first General Election for nearly thirty years in which Gladstone was not the Liberal leader. 'For my part,' Churchill told his mother at the height of the campaign, 'I attribute the ruin of the radical party entirely to the absence of Mr Gladstone's sustaining power. Ever since '86 when the great split took place they have steadily declined – but his personality imparted to them a fictitious strength – just as fever animates a sick man. As soon as this departed the collapse ensued.'

Rosebery and the Liberals were defeated, and Salisbury became Prime Minister, at the head of a Conservative and Unionist administration. Leading places were given to Joseph Chamberlain and other Liberal stalwarts of a decade earlier. As to the defeated Gladstonian Liberals, 'a more disappointed & broken down party was never seen', Churchill told his mother. The Unionists, by contrast, 'come in with nearly every able man in both Houses in their Cabinet – with the House of Commons at their feet – & the Lords at their back – supported by all sections of the nation – unfettered by promises or hampered by pledges'. No Party had ever had 'such a chance'; it remained to be seen 'what use they will make of it'. But he ended his letter with a warning about the new Government's staying power: 'To my mind they are too strong – too brilliant altogether. They are just the sort of Government to split on the question of Protection. Like a huge ship with powerful engines they will require careful steering – because any collision means destruction.'

Protection, the Unionist demand for a tariff system to protect Imperial trade against foreign competition, was indeed to split the Party and bring it down. In this future political convulsion, Churchill, then a young Conservative MP, was to achieve political prominence as a leading opponent of tariffs.

At Aldershot, Churchill's life was still dominated by riding. 'We are now in the midst of manoeuvres,' he wrote to his mother that August. 'Eight hours in the saddle every day – then two hours stables and then to polo indefatigably.' And yet, he told her, politics already lured him: 'It is a fine game to play – the game of politics, and it is well worth waiting for a good hand – before really plunging. At any rate, four years of healthy and pleasant existence, combined with both responsibility & discipline, can do no harm to me – but rather good.' The more he saw of soldiering, 'the more I like it – but the more I feel convinced that it is not my *metier*. Well, we shall see.'

A week later Churchill told his mother that Army life was leading to a state of mental stagnation 'quite in accordance' with the spirit of the Army. 'From this "slough of Despond" I try to raise myself by reading & re-reading Papa's speeches – many of which I almost know by heart.' If he were to be quartered in London he was thinking of taking a tutor for one or two hours a week to study Economics or Modern History: 'I need someone to point out some specific subject & to direct my reading in that subject. The desultory reading I have so far indulged in has only resulted in a jumble of disconnected & ill-assorted facts.'

Lady Randolph, who did not entirely understand what her son had in mind, suggested he should make a study of the 'supply of army horses'. This, he replied, was a subject which, while having much to commend it to a cavalry officer, was 'more calculated to narrow and groove one's mind than to expand it'. Something 'more literary and less material would be the sort of mental medicine I need'. All his life, he explained, first at Harrow, then at Sandhurst and finally at James's, he had received a 'purely technical' education aimed at passing some approaching examination. 'As a result my mind has never received that polish which for instance Oxford or Cambridge gives. At these places one studies questions and sciences with a rather higher object than mere practical utility. One receives in fact a liberal education.'

Three months before his twenty-first birthday Churchill embarked upon a self-taught course of just such a liberal education. Although he was a cavalry officer with plenty of duties and riding commitments, and pleasures, he became a private undergraduate at his own university. The first of his teachers was Fawcett's *Manual of Political Economy*, published thirty years earlier. It was a book, he told his mother, 'essentially devoted to "first principles" – and one which would leave at least a clear knowledge of the framework of the subject behind – and would be of use even if the subject were not persevered in'. After Fawcett, he planned to read Gibbon's *Decline and Fall of the Roman Empire* and Lecky's *European Morals from Augustus to Charlemagne*. 'These will be tasks more agreeable than the mere piling up of shoppy statistics.'

In the autumn of 1895 Lady Randolph acquired a London house, 35a Great Cumberland Place. If he were to be stationed nearer the capital,

Churchill wrote to his mother, 'I could live with you at 35 and soldier on a season ticket.' His letter continued: 'I do so look forward to having a house once more. It will be too delightful to ring the door bell of one's own front door again. Poor old Everest – how she would have loved to see us ensconced in a house again. She looked forward to it so much.'

In October 1895 Churchill decided to go with a friend, Reginald Barnes, to Cuba, where Spanish forces were trying to crush a rebellion of the islanders. To his mother, who was hesitant about his journey, he wrote, 'The fact is that I have decided to go.' Lady Randolph replied at once: 'Considering that I provide the funds, I think that instead of saying "I *have* decided to go" it may have been nicer & perhaps wiser to have begun by consulting me.' She would not put any obstacle in his way, 'But I suppose experience of life will in time teach you that tact is a very essential ingredient in all things.'

While preparing for the journey, Churchill went to see Field Marshal Lord Wolseley, Commander-in-Chief of the British Army. With Wolseley's approval he and Barnes saw the Director of Military Intelligence, General Chapman, who gave them maps and information. For their part, Churchill told his mother, they had been asked to collect information and statistics on various points, '& particularly as to the effect of the new bullet – its penetration and striking power'. This request, he added, 'invests our mission with an almost official character & cannot fail to help one in the future'. There was also a less official side to the journey. 'I shall bring back a great many Havana cigars,' he told his mother, 'some of which can be "laid down" in the cellars of 35 Great Cumberland Place.' Before leaving he persuaded the *Daily Graphic*, for which his father had written while in South Africa, to let him send regular reports from the scene of the insurrection.

Churchill left England a month before his twenty-first birthday, on board the Cunard Royal Mail Steamship *Etruria*. It was his first transatlantic crossing. Proudly he told his mother that he and Barnes were never seasick and never missed a meal. But, he added, 'I do not contemplate ever taking a sea voyage for pleasure & I shall always look upon journeys by sea as necessary evils, which have to be undergone in the carrying out of any definite plan.' The shipboard concert, he wrote, was the occasion when 'all the stupid people among the passengers intend to perform and the stupider ones to applaud'.

New York was a delight to Churchill. 'Everybody is very civil and we have engagements for every meal for the next few days about three deep,' he told his mother. Her own cousins were all most helpful and friendly; one of them had engaged 'an excellent valet' for the two travellers. They visited the American Army headquarters of the Atlantic Military District, and also West Point, the Sandhurst of the United States. The young Sandhurst graduate was horrified by the discipline at West Point. 'They are not allowed to smoke or have any money in their possession,' he told his brother, 'nor are they given any leave except two months after the first two years.' This was a 'positively disgraceful' state of affairs. 'Young men of 24 or 25 who would resign their personal liberty to such an extent can never make good citizens or fine soldiers. A child who rebels against that sort of control should be whipped – so should a man who does not rebel.'

While in New York, Churchill visited an American warship, the cruiser *New York* . The American sailors interested him more than the ship itself, 'for while any nation can build a battleship, it is the monopoly of the Anglo-Saxon race to breed good seamen', he wrote to his Aunt Leonie. 'What an extraordinary people the Americans are!' he exclaimed to his mother. 'Their hospitality is a revelation to me and they make you feel at home and at ease in a way that I have never before experienced.' On the other hand, he wrote, 'their press and their currency impress me very unfavourably'. The paper dollar with which he paid his fare across Brooklyn Bridge was possibly 'the most disreputable "coin" the world has ever seen', he told Leonie; he had reflected for some time on 'how to reconcile the magnificent system of communication with the abominable currency'. Paper money was a shock to him until he found the solution, 'The communication of New York is due to private enterprise while the State is responsible for the currency: and hence I come to the conclusion that the first class men of America are in the counting houses and the less brilliant ones in the government.'

'This is a very great country my dear Jack,' Churchill wrote to his brother on his fifth day in New York. 'Not pretty or romantic but great and utilitarian, there seems to be no such thing as reverence for tradition. Everything is eminently practical and things are judged from a matter of fact standpoint.' In a courtroom to which he had been invited to sit on the bench, the judge had been discussing the evidence with Churchill 'as it was given' and 'generally making himself socially agreeable – & all the while a pale miserable man was fighting for his life'. There had been 'no robes or wigs or uniformed ushers. Nothing but a lot of men in black coats & tweed suits. Judge, prisoner, jury, counsel & warders all indiscriminately mixed. But they manage to hang a man all the same, and that after all is the great thing.'

There was much to stimulate Churchill during his short visit; the essence of American journalism, he told his brother, was 'vulgarity divested of truth', but he did not wish to be over-censorious: 'I think, mind you, that vulgarity is a sign of strength. A great, crude, strong, young people are the Americans – like a boisterous healthy boy among enervated but well bred ladies and gentlemen.' Enthusiastically he concluded, 'Picture to yourself the American people as a great lusty youth – who treads on all your sensibilities, perpetrates every possible horror of ill manners – whom neither age nor just tradition inspire with reverence – but who moves about his affairs with a good hearted freshness which may well be the envy of older nations of the earth.'

After a week in New York, Churchill and Barnes went by train to Florida. Their New York host, Bourke Cockran, in whose apartment they had stayed, obtained a private room for them in the train. As a result, their thirty-six-hour journey south was not 'as unpleasant', Churchill told his mother, 'as if we had had to travel in a regular compartment'. At Key West they took ship to Havana, where the British Consul-General introduced them to the Spanish military governor, who in turn telegraphed to the Spanish commander-in-chief that they had arrived.

On November 21 Churchill and Barnes left Havana by train to join the Spanish troops in the field. 'Our luck has been almost uncanny,' Churchill told his mother. 'We missed two trains that were both smashed up by the rebels by about half an hour. We went into a town in which every sort of dreadful disease was spreading, and finally, if without any particular reason I had not changed my position about one yard to the right, I should infallibly have been shot.' Added to all this 'I left a fiver to be put on "The Rush" at 8 to 1 and it simply romped home. So you see my dear Mamma – there *is* a sweet little cherub.'

Churchill's five despatches to the *Daily Graphic* were headed 'Letters from the Front' and signed with the initials 'WSC'. There was no doubt, he wrote in the first letter, written while he was still on the way to the front, that the Cuban insurgents 'possess the sympathy of the entire population, and hence have constant and accurate intelligence. On the other hand Spain is equally determined to crush them, and is even now pouring in fresh troops by the thousand. How it will end it is impossible to say, but whoever wins, and whatever may be the results, the suffering and misery of the entire community are certain.'

On November 23 Churchill reached the centre of the island. 'The more I see of Cuba,' he wrote that day, 'the more I feel sure that the demand for independence is national and unanimous. The insurgent forces contain the best blood in the island, and can by no perversion of the truth be classed as banditti. In fact, it is a war, not a rebellion.' On the following day a military column of about 2,700 men was formed by General Valdez to escort supplies through the mountains to the various Spanish garrisons. 'The General gave us horses and servants,' Churchill told his mother when he was back in Havana two weeks later, 'and we lived with his personal staff.'

November 30 was Churchill's twenty-first birthday. That day General Valdez led his force in search of the main rebel army. Churchill and Barnes went with him, camping that night in the open. On the following day, after marching to a new camp, the two Englishmen persuaded two Spanish officers 'to come with us and bathe in the river'. Their swim over, the four men were dressing on the bank when 'suddenly', as Churchill reported in his next despatch, 'we heard a shot fired. Another and another followed; then came a volley. The bullets whistled over our heads. It was evident that an attack of some sort was in progress.' Quickly dressing, one of the Spanish officers ran to collect fifty men, who drove off the attackers.

Churchill and Barnes returned to Valdez's headquarters half a mile away, where a larger skirmish was taking place. It too was repulsed. Then, just before midnight, Churchill reported, 'they came back and fired at us for about an hour'. Several Spanish soldiers were killed. 'One bullet came through the thatch of the hut in which we were sleeping and another wounded an orderly just outside.'

On the following day, December 2, which a year later Churchill was to call 'the most remarkable anniversary in my own life', the Spanish troops started off at first light. The mist, he wrote in his despatch to the *Daily Graphic*, 'gave cover to the rebel marksmen, who saluted us as soon as we got across the river with a well-directed fire'. Later that morning the column was forced to come to a halt as Spanish infantrymen moved forward. During the halt 'the enemy's bullets whizzed over our heads or cut into the soft ground underfoot'. The cavalry column moved forward. 'We attacked the enemy's positions,' Churchill told his mother, 'and advanced right across open ground under heavy fire.' Unfortunately, General Valdez, 'a very brave man in a white and gold uniform on a grey horse – drew a great deal of fire on to us and I heard enough bullets whistle and hum to satisfy me for some time to come'.

'There was a sound in the air,' Churchill wrote in his despatch, 'sometimes like a sigh, sometimes like a whistle, and at others like the buzz of an offended hornet.' Churchill and Barnes stayed close to the General throughout the action, with the result, Churchill explained to his mother, that they were 'in the most dangerous place in the field'. The Spaniards, he believed, were lucky not to lose more men than they did, 'but as a rule the rebels shot very high'. After ten minutes' heavy firing, the rebels retreated. No pursuit was attempted and the Spaniards then withdrew. 'Here you have a General of Division,' Churchill wrote in his fifth and final despatch, 'and two thousand of the best troops in the island, out for over ten days in search of the enemy, overcoming all sorts of difficulties, undergoing all kinds of hardships, and then being quite contented with taking thirty or forty rebels and taking a low grass hill which was destitute of the slightest importance.' At this rate of progress 'it would take the Emperor William, with the German Army, twenty years to crush the revolt'.

In this final despatch Churchill reflected on the justice of the rebel struggle. Cuba had been 'overtaxed in a monstrous manner for a considerable period'. So much money was taken from the country by Spain that 'industries are paralysed and development is impossible'. Bribery and corruption pervaded the administration 'on a scale almost Chinese'. The entire Spanish administration was corrupt. 'A national and justifiable revolt is the only possible result of such a system.' Yet the rebel methods were the tactics of 'incendiarists and brigands – burning canefields, shooting from behind hedges, firing into sleeping camps, destroying property, wrecking trains, and throwing dynamite'. These, Churchill concluded, were 'perfectly legitimate in war, no doubt, but they are not acts on which States are founded'.

It was widely rumoured in Cuba, one British journalist wrote to Churchill, 'that your sympathies went over to the rebels'. This rumour was offset by the fact that Churchill and Barnes had accepted a Spanish military decoration, the Red Cross. Yet Churchill was certain, as he wrote in his final despatch for the *Daily Graphic*, that the Cubans would never be driven from vast areas of the countryside; what was needed was a Cuba 'free and prosperous, under just laws and a patriotic administration, throwing open her ports to the commerce of the world, sending her ponies to Hurlingham and her cricketers to Lord's, exchanging the cigars of Havana for the cottons of Lancashire, and the sugars of Matanzas for the cutlery of Sheffield. At least let us hope so.'

A year after his visit to Cuba, Churchill wrote to his mother: 'I reproach myself somewhat for having written a little uncandidly and for having perhaps done injustice to the insurgents. I rather tried to make out, and in some measure succeeded in making out, a case for Spain. It was politic, and did not expose me to the charge of being ungrateful to my hosts, but I am not quite clear whether it was right.'

In the second week of December Churchill left Cuba for the United States and home. Speaking in New York to an interviewer from the *New York World*, he remarked, about the Spanish troops, 'I make no reflections on their courage, but they are well versed in the art of retreat.' As to the future, 'I think that the upshot of it will be that the United States will intervene as a peacemaker.' In the event, the United States was soon to go to war with Spain, defeating the Spaniards on the island, leading to an independent Cuba in 1901.

'I am going to bring over excellent coffee, cigars and guava jelly to stock the cellars of 35a,' Churchill had written to his mother in his last letter from

Havana. He was true to his word, but on his return to England, the many satisfactions of his adventures were overshadowed by the widely-publicised accusation that while at Sandhurst he had committed 'acts of gross immorality of the Oscar Wilde type'. The accusation was made by A.C. Bruce-Pryce, the father of the officer-cadet who had earlier accused Churchill and his friends of having forced him to leave the regiment. Bruce-Pryce senior also alleged that another officer had been flogged by his fellow-subalterns for having committed a gross act of indecency with Churchill.

Churchill brought an action against Bruce-Pryce in the High Court. Within a month the father formally withdrew his accusation and paid £400 damages, the equivalent of more than £15,000 in 1990. The whole affair, Churchill's commanding officer, Colonel Brabazon, wrote to him, 'only shows to what lengths mendacity and malice will go'. The case of Bruce-Pryce's son did not go away so easily, however, being raised repeatedly by *Truth*, which also continued to fulminate about the steeple-chase episode of a year earlier.

Churchill's social life flourished; at Lord Rothschild's house at Tring, Asquith and Balfour were among the guests. 'Altogether, as you may imagine,' Churchill told his mother, 'I appreciate meeting such clever people and listening to their conversation very much indeed.' There was much talk about South Africa. In a recent speech the Colonial Secretary, Joseph Chamberlain, had said that it was only an 'anomaly' that the majority of the population of the Transvaal paid nine-tenths of the taxes but had no representation in the Boer Parliament. Churchill commented, 'It was for such an "anomaly" that America rebelled from England & a similar "anomaly" was the prime cause of the French Revolution.'

In February 1896 the United States began to press Spain to give up Cuba. 'I hope,' Churchill wrote to Bourke Cockran, 'the United States will not force Spain to give up Cuba – unless you are prepared to accept responsiblity for the results of such action.' If the United States were to annex Cuba, however, 'though this would be very hard on Spain, it would be the best and most expedient course for both the island and the world in general'. But he would consider it 'monstrous' if all America did was to 'procure the establishment of another South American Republic' without maintaining 'any sort of control over its behaviour'. Above all, Churchill told Cockran, Britain and the United States must avoid a quarrel. 'Do please be pacific,' he wrote, 'and don't go dragging the 4th Hussars over to Canada in an insane and criminal struggle.'

Cockran had been angered by the British Government's arrest of a number of Irishmen found in possession of dynamite. 'I had the opportunity of talking to Mr Asquith on this subject,' Churchill told him, 'and I said I would have released them in deference to the opinion of the Irish people.' Much impressed by Churchill, Cockran urged him to study sociology and political economy. 'With your remarkable talent for lucid and attractive expression,' he wrote, 'you would be able to make great use of the information to be acquired by study of these branches. Indeed I firmly believe you would take a commanding position in public life at the first opportunity which arose.'

That February the *Saturday Review* published an article by Churchill on Cuba. Lady Randolph sent a copy to Joseph Chamberlain, who was struck by what he called 'the best short account I have seen of the problems with which the Spaniards have to deal, & agrees with my own conclusions'. Chamberlain added, 'It is evident that Mr Winston kept his eyes open.'

In the summer of 1896 Churchill decided to go to Egypt, hoping 'to be a galloper' to the British commander-in-chief, General Sir Herbert Kitchener, in the struggle to retake the Sudan. When this scheme failed he asked the *Daily Chronicle* if he could go as their special correspondent to Crete, where the Greeks of the island were struggling for independence against Turkish rule. He also asked his mother to use her influence with the Secretary of State for War, Lord Lansdowne, to help him go to South Africa to join the forces then suppressing the native uprising in Matabeleland.

Not only was Lansdowne unable to help, but he warned Lady Randolph 'as a friend' that in view of the enquiry which was now to take place into the charges made against him by *Truth*, it might not be 'wise on Winston's part to leave England at this moment'. Lansdowne added, 'There are plenty of ill-natured people about, and it is just conceivable that an attempt might be made to misrepresent his action.' A month after Lansdowne's letter Churchill was still trying to get permission to go to Matabeleland. Although his own regiment was due to leave soon for India, the 9th Lancers were to go to Matabeleland at the end of August. 'This we will talk over on Friday,' he wrote to his mother at the beginning of the month, 'but my dear Mamma you cannot think how I would like to sail in a few days to scenes of adventure and excitement – to places where I could gain experience and derive advantage – rather than to the tedious land of India – where I shall be equally out of the pleasures of peace and the chances of war.'

Going to India with his 'unfortunate regiment', Churchill told his mother, was an 'utterly unattractive' prospect. Not to go to the war in Matabeleland was to let 'the golden opportunity' go by. By failing in that 'I feel that I am guilty of an indolent folly that I shall regret all my life'. A few months in Matabeleland would earn him the South Africa Medal and 'in all probability' the British South Africa Company's Star. 'Thence hot foot to Egypt, to return with two more decorations in a year or two – and beat my sword into an iron despatch box.' Both Matabeleland and Egypt were 'within the bounds of possibility and yet here I am out of both. I cannot believe that, with all the influential friends you possess, and all those who would do something for me for my father's sake, I could not be allowed to go, were those influences properly exerted.'

Churchill begged his mother to use her influence: 'It is useless to preach the gospel of patience to me. Others as young are making the running now and what chance have I of ever catching up? I put it down here – definitely on paper – that you really ought to leave no stone unturned to help me at such a period. Years may pass before such chances occur again.' His frustration was intense; still only twenty-one, he feared that his whole Army service might be spent in barracks and far from any action. 'You can't realise how furiously intolerable this life is to me,' he told his mother, 'when so much is going on a month away from here.'

Matabeleland it was not to be; on September 11 Churchill sailed for India with the 4th Hussars, disappointed that his hope of action had failed. On October 1 he reached Bombay; three days later he was at camp in Poona. 'I have engaged a capital Indian servant,' he told his mother, 'who is indefatigable in looking after me and who has a very good character for honesty.' From Poona he went to Bangalore, where he was to remain for more than six months. The city, three thousand feet above sea level, was noted for its healthy climate. Churchill shared a spacious bungalow with two friends, Reginald Barnes and Hugo Baring. It was, he told his mother, 'a magnificent pink and white stucco palace in the middle of a large and beautiful garden'.

For servants, Churchill, Barnes and Baring each had a butler whose duties were 'to wait at table, to manage the household and to supervise the stables', a First Dressing Boy as valet, a Second Dressing Boy as his assistant, and a groom for every horse or pony. In addition, the three young officers shared the services of two gardeners, four washermen and a watchman. 'Such,' Churchill told his mother, 'is our menage.' His first letter also contained several requests; he wanted his mother to send him a card table, 'any books (very welcome)', his bicycle, a dozen shirts, and various items for butterflying – collecting-boxes, setting boards, a net, a box of pins and a 'killing tin'. As to his own 'indulgences', he wrote, 'I am teetotaller and practically non-smoker till sundown – drinking lemon squash – or occasionally – *beer* – which after all is but a temperance prescription.'

India was 'in every respect the exact contrast' of the United States, Churchill wrote to Jack. 'The obsequious native servants replace the uncivil "freeborn citizens". Labour here is cheap and plentiful. Existence costs but little and luxury can be easily obtained.' His own garden, he added, was full of butterflies, 'Purple Emperors, White Admirals & Swallowtails and many other beautiful and rare insects. I shall be able to make a fine collection – with very little trouble – and much amusement.' In advising Jack, who was still at Harrow, to 'try and get hold of a certain amount of knowledge', Churchill confided: 'I only wish I had worked more. There are great pleasures in life – to those who know the Latin or the Greek tongues well. Of course at school one only sees the seamy and unattractive side of classics, the grammar & prosody – instead of the manners and customs.'

While he was at Bangalore, an article Churchill had written about Sandhurst was published in the *Pall Mall Magazine*. 'For those who enter the college direct from Eton or Harrow,' he wrote, 'or any of our public schools, the life at Sandhurst is a pleasing emancipation, profitable to experience, agreeable to recall. It is a time of merriment and sport, a time of high hopes and good friends, of many pleasures and of insignificant worries – a period of gratified ambitions and of attained ideals.'

From Churchill's former headmaster, Dr Welldon, came words of advice, 'There is no reason why you should not learn Latin (so far as it is unknown to you) or even Greek.' But it was not only study that concerned Welldon. 'Above all, my dear Churchill, think more of others than yourself, be ready to learn from those that are below you and keep your conscience as restful as you can.' The recent accusations which *Truth* was continuing to publish, had upset Welldon. 'I implore you,' he wrote, 'not to let your wild spirits carry you away to any action that may bring dishonour on your school or your name.' It was impossible, he added, 'that I should not hear of your follies and impertinences if you are guilty of them, and you will recognise that you put a severe strain upon my friendship if you ask me to treat you as a friend when other people speak of you with indignation or contempt'.

Angered that the hostile articles in *Truth* were continuing, Churchill wrote to his mother: 'It seems indeed hard that when we are away in a foreign land and unable to answer or even read immediately any misstatement he may make – such attacks should go on – and that the public should swallow all of them greedily. I enclose a letter from Mr Welldon, which evidently refers to this affair. He has apparently mingled with those – and I daresay they are not few – who have accepted Labouchere's version of the whole story.'

Life at Bangalore continued at a leisurely pace. Early breakfast, Churchill explained to his mother, was at five; parade at six; second breakfast, bath and 'such papers as there are' at eight, followed by an hour of stables; then 'no other engagement until polo at 4.15'. Then there was an interval which he filled 'by sleeping, writing, reading or pursuing butterflies', followed by dinner and bed. But this pleasant life was disturbed when another of Labouchere's articles arrived, 'vicious and insulting' Churchill told his mother. The new article insinuated that the War Office had only been prevented from taking action against Churchill by pressure exerted on his behalf. 'The young officer who assumed the part of ringleader in the conspiracy to eject Mr Bruce from the 4th Hussars,' wrote *Truth*, 'belongs to an influential family, and all the influence at his back has been used to prevent an opening of the case.'

'A more mischievous suggestion it is hard to invent,' Churchill commented, 'and after our experience of what that influence was worth in another direction, it seems ironical.'

Since his earliest days, Churchill had been troubled by the inability to pronounce the letter 's', which he spoke with a slur, pronouncing it more like 'sh'. Before leaving London he had consulted Felix Semon, a leading physician for diseases of the throat. Semon's report reached him in India. 'He is sanguine,' Churchill told his mother, 'that practice and perseverance are alone necessary and that no organic defect exists.'

India, Churchill told his mother, was a 'godless land of snobs and bores'. But at the beginning of November, while playing polo at Secunderabad, he met Pamela Plowden, daughter of the British Resident in Hyderabad. 'I must say she is the most beautiful girl I have ever seen,' he told his mother. 'We are going to try to do the City of Hyderabad together – on an elephant. You dare not walk or the natives spit at Europeans – which provokes retaliation leading to riots.'

The ride on the elephant duly took place, and a life-long friendship began. Fifty-five years later Churchill was to write to Pamela, 'I cherish your signal across the years, from the days when I was a freak – always that – but much hated & ruled out, but there was one who saw some qualities.'

While at Bangalore, an article which Churchill was sent about his father's abilities as an administrator gave him, he told his mother, 'a delightful morning's occupation and has made me equally low and despondent this evening'. A week earlier he had learned of a vacancy in the East Bradford constituency, scene of one of his father's great speeches a decade earlier. 'Had I been in England,' he wrote to his mother, 'I might have contested it and should have won – almost to a certainty. Instead of being an insignificant subaltern I should have had opportunities of learning those things which will be of value to me in the future.' Perhaps it was 'just as well that I am condemned to wait, though I will not disguise from you that life out here is stupid, dull & uninteresting'.

Churchill could not banish British political life from his mind. 'What a pity I was not home for East Bradford,' he told his mother. 'I see a soldier got in.' The soldier, a Unionist, had beaten his Liberal opponent by just under four hundred votes. Had he come to India as a Member of Parliament, Churchill reflected, 'however young & foolish, I could have had access to all who know and can convey. As a soldier, my intelligent interests are supposed to stop short at polo, racing & Orderly Officer. I vegetate – even reading is an effort & I am still in Gibbon.' In another letter to his mother from Bangalore he again forecast that the power of the Unionist Party would be shattered when the 'landed interest (after all the most powerful element on the Conservative side) force Salisbury to raise the question of Protection!' The Liberal Unionists would then say to their Conservative partners, and 'rightly' in his view, that they could not follow the Party 'into the land of Protection'.

Churchill told his mother that the result of such a split in the Conservative and Unionist ranks would be the creation of a new Party led by Joseph Chamberlain and Lord Rosebery. Both men, he felt, would be 'worthy leaders of the Tory Democracy'. The extremes of both parties would be left in the cold, and the 'solid remnants' of the Conservative Party, 'peers, property, publicans, parsons & turnips', would lose their power. When the split did come seven years later, Churchill was quickly to emerge as a leading Free Trader in the Conservative ranks; he even tried to persuade Rosebery to return to active politics at the head of a centre party, but in vain. As for Chamberlain, far from leading the Free Trade forces as Churchill forecast, it was his advocacy of Protection that gave the Free Traders, Churchill among them, their main opponent.

Yet another article in *Truth* now plagued the young officer. Referring to the steeplechase race and naming Churchill, it alleged that he and the other four subalterns had deliberately conspired to obtain money by malpractice on the Turf. Churchill at once reminded his mother that the National Hunt Committee had long ago written to the War Office, 'expressly vindicating us from any charge of dishonesty or of dishonourable behaviour'. If these continuing allegations were not rebutted, he wrote, 'it would be fatal for any future in public life for me', and he wanted to take legal action. He would probably be exposed to attacks, he told his mother, 'even on the grounds of having helped to turn Bruce out', but the racing matter was 'more serious'. Until something was done to contradict it, 'I appear in a very unpleasant light.'

On November 30 Churchill was twenty-two. As action still eluded him he begged his mother to try to get him sent to Kitchener's Army in Egypt. 'I hear it is decided,' he wrote, 'to make a further advance this year'. Lady Randolph's task was to write direct to Kitchener. 'Two years in Egypt,'

Churchill told her three weeks later, 'with a campaign thrown in, would I think qualify me to be allowed to beat my sword into a paper cutter & my sabretache into an election address.'

Meanwhile, from Bangalore, Churchill told Jack that his roses had flourished; he now had 250 rose trees, 'so that every morning I can cut about three great basins full of the most beautiful flowers which nature produces'. But his much-prized butterfly collection, which included 'upward of 65 different sorts', had been destroyed 'by the malevolence of a rat who crawled into the cabinet and devoured all the specimens. I have however caught the brute and had him killed by "Winston" the terrier – and have begun again perseveringly.'

Unusually for a young soldier eager to see military action, Churchill deprecated increased military expenditure by the Government, writing to his mother, of a proposal by Lansdowne to spend more on the Army, that the strain of the taxation involved 'is not without its effect on the prosperity and happiness of the nation'. What Britain needed, in Churchill's view, was a fleet 'strong enough to render us superior to a combination of any two powers, & with an ample margin for accidents'. He would support taxation 'to almost any extent' to attain that end. Given Britain's 'unquestioned command of the sea' there was no part of the Empire 'which our present army could not protect – and without such command there is no part which two such armies could maintain'.

That December Churchill travelled to Calcutta, a five-day train journey, to play polo. 'I shall meet many people who will be amiable,' he wrote to his mother, 'and some who may be useful.' But when he reached Calcutta he found it 'full of supremely uninteresting people'. There had been a ball at Viceregal Lodge, but 'as you know, I do not shine on the parquet', so he had not gone. Each time he met the British residents of India, 'I immediately desire to fly the country. It is only in my comfortable bungalow, among my roses, polo ponies & butterflies, that I feel that philosophical composure which alone can make residence in India endurable.' Calcutta was 'bitterly cold after dark' and he had caught a chill. But he was glad to have seen the city 'for the same reason Papa gave for being glad to have seen Lisbon, namely "that it will be unnecessary ever to see it again" '.

Jack was now thinking of going to university. 'I shall envy you the enjoyment of a classical education,' Churchill wrote, 'and of the power to appreciate the classical works.' His own reading continued without interruption. Lady Randolph had sent him a twelve-volume set of Macaulay's works, which 'I shall shortly begin to read'. He had been 'lured' from completing Gibbon by Plato's *Republic* and Winwood Reade's *Martyrdom of Man.* 'If only I knew Latin & Greek,' he wrote to his mother, 'I think I would leave the army and try and take my degree in History, Philosophy & Economics. But I cannot face parsing & Latin prose again.'

Winwood Reade had argued that in the world of reason, Christianity was no longer needed. 'One of these days, perhaps,' Churchill commented, 'the cold bright light of science & reason will shine through the cathedral windows & we shall go out into the fields to seek God for ourselves. The great laws of Nature will be understood – our destiny and our past will be clear. We shall then be able to dispense with the religious toys that have agreeably fostered the development of mankind. Until then, anyone who deprives us of our illusions – our pleasant, hopeful illusions – is a wicked man & should (I quote my Plato) "be refused a chorus".'

In February 1897 Churchill was made Brigade Major, 'a most important duty', he explained to his mother, 'and one which in England could never have been obtained under fourteen or fifteen years' service'. He was becoming 'a very "correct soldier". Full of zeal etc.', and he added, 'Even in homoeopathic doses Responsibility is an exhilarating drink.' The Colonel of the regiment was consulting him 'on nearly all points', he wrote a week later. 'Though all is of course on a small scale, I cannot disguise from myself that it is an excellent training.' He had now been in the Army for two years. Of one thing he was 'certain', he told his mother, 'that unless a good opportunity presents itself of my obtaining a seat in the House of Commons, I should continue in the army for two years more'. Meanwhile, his reading included Hallam's *Constitutional History* and Adam Smith's *Wealth of Nations.*

That February, the Greeks on the island of Crete raised the standard of revolt against their Turkish rulers. Britain supported the Turks, Lord Salisbury's government sending British warships to the Mediterranean, to stop help reaching Crete from Greece. Churchill's sympathies were with the Cretan insurgents, as they had been with the Cuban insurgents just over a year earlier. When his mother argued that it was right to help the Turkish authorities, he replied, 'We are doing a very wicked thing in firing on the Cretan insurgents & in blockading Greece so that she cannot succour them.' He admitted that 'the material arguments' were rather on the other side; that was 'bound to be the case', but there was more to it than material advantage. 'I look on this question from the point of view of right & wrong: Lord Salisbury from that of profit and loss.'

Salisbury's real purpose, Churchill told Lady Randolph, was to preserve the Turkish Empire so as to prevent the Russians taking Constantinople. 'The Turkish Empire he is determined to maintain. He does not care a row of buttons for the sufferings of those who are oppressed by that

Empire.' As to the Turkish capital, he argued, 'as surely as night follows day, the Russians are bound to get Constantinople. We could never stop them even if we wished. Nor ought we to wish for anything that could impede the expulsion from Europe of the filthy Oriental.' Russia's desire for Constantinople was 'the just aspiration of a mighty people. I would sooner face an avalanche. Seventy millions of people without a warm water port. Is it rational?'

Russia's presence in Crete, however, disturbed Churchill. 'I do not trust her. Such rectitude would not be human. She cannot be acting in good faith.' It was 'inconceivable' that Russia was acting disinterestedly. 'Never will I believe it.'

Churchill told his mother if he were in Parliament there were no lengths to which he would not go in opposing Salisbury's Government, 'I am a Liberal in all but name.' His views already excited the 'pious horror' of his fellow-officers. Were it not for Home Rule, 'to which I will never consent, I would enter Parliament as a Liberal.' He then outlined to his mother what was essentially a Liberal programme at home; extension of the franchise to every adult male, universal education, the establishment of all religions, and a progressive income tax. 'I will vote for them all.' In foreign affairs he advocated non-intervention in Europe, 'keep absolutely unembroiled – isolated if you like'. Defend the colonies with 'a mighty navy'. Create a system of Imperial defence. East of Suez, however, 'democratic reins are impossible. India must be governed on old principles.' And he added: 'There! That is the creed of Tory Democracy. Peace & power abroad – prosperity and progress at home.'

Churchill decided to return to England for a month's leave, but his mother's reaction stunned him. It was 'wild talk', she wrote, and 'absolutely out of the question, not only on account of money, but for the sake of your reputation.' She went on to explain: 'They will say & with some reason that you can't stick to anything. You have only been out six months & it is on the cards that you may be called to Egypt. There is plenty for you to do in India. I confess I am quite disheartened about you. You seem to have no real purpose in life & won't realise at the age of twenty-two that for a man life means work, & hard work if you mean to succeed.'

Many men at Churchill's age, Lady Randolph added, 'have to work for a living & support their mothers. It is useless my saying more – we have been over this ground before – it is not a pleasant one. I will only repeat that I cannot help you any more & if you have any grit in you & are worth your salt you will try & live within your income & cut down your expenses in order to do it. You cannot but feel ashamed of yourself under the present circumstances.' Unaware of the imminent arrival of this rebuke,

Churchill wrote to his mother, 'So far as I know I am in favour with God and man, but there are days when I feel I cannot sit still.'

Thanks to the further despatch of books from his mother, Churchill had begun reading the *Annual Register of World Events*, beginning with 1880. As he read, he annotated the Register's summaries of Parliamentary debates with thoughts and interventions of his own. The method he pursued, he told his mother, was not to read any particular debate 'until I have recorded my own opinion of the subject on paper, having regard only to general principles. After reading I reconsider and finally write', setting out in pencil, on small pieces of paper, his own views on each subject, which he then pasted into the volumes. He hoped by this method 'to build up a scaffolding of logical and consistent views, which will perhaps tend to the creation of a logical and consistent mind'. The facts of the *Annual Register*, he told his mother, would 'arm me with a sharp sword'. Macaulay, Gibbon, Plato and others 'must train the muscles to wield that sword to the greatest effect'.

One topic in the notes which he pasted into the *Annual Register* was education, on which he wrote, 'The object of Governments should be the equal education of the whole people, not the advantage of any one sect.' Nor should religious instruction be entrusted to the hands of any one sect. 'All are partisan. The Church of England equally with the others. I am in favour of secular instructors appointed by Government.' The campaign to give women the vote, however, was 'a ridiculous movement'. Votes for women should be avoided. 'Once you give the vote to vast numbers of women who form the majority of the community,' he warned, 'all power passes to their hands.'

In response to his mother's financial problems, the result of her own considerable extravagance, Churchill was sending her his horse Firefly, in the hope that she would be able to sell him. 'He is a great pet,' Churchill wrote, '& prefers above all things bread & butter or a biscuit.' Lady Randolph was still opposed to her son's plans to return, instead of staying in India '& showing that you can work & do something'. She so wanted to help him; if only she had some money she would do so. 'I am so proud of you,' she wrote, '& of all your great & endearing qualities. I feel sure that if you live you will make a name for yourself, but I know to do it you have to be made of sterner stuff, & not mind sacrifice & self denial.'

Churchill remained in India; that spring, while sitting in the rifle butts in charge of the markers at a rifle practice, he had a near escape, telling his mother how 'a bullet struck the iron edge of the target, flew into splinters & rebounded all over me'. One of the fragments struck his left hand just below his thumb, penetrating more than an inch. 'It is to the mercy of God, as some would say, or to the workings of chance or the doctrine of averages, as others prefer, that I was not hit in the eye; in this case I should have been blinded infallibly.' After an 'abominable twenty minutes' of probing by the doctor, the splinter was extracted, '& since then I have had a bad time every morning when the wound has to be syringed. Knowing as you do my keen aversion to physical pain or even discomfort, I am sure you will sympathise with me.' Ever resourceful, and plucky, he played polo with the reins strapped to his wrist.

In mid-April, Turkey declared war on Greece. Churchill now had a new goal; he would go to the front as a correspondent. His mother must find a newspaper that wanted his reports. 'Lord Rothschild would be the person to arrange this for me,' he told her, 'as he knows everyone.' But to which side he should go: 'This my dearest Mamma must depend on you. Of course my sympathies are entirely with the Greeks, but on the other hand the Turks are bound to win – are in enormous strength & will be on the offensive the whole time. If I go on this side it will be less glorious but much more safe & as I have no wish to be involved in the confusion of a defeated army my idea is that they would be more suitable. You must decide. If you can get me good letters to the Turks – to the Turks I will go. If to the Greeks – to the Greeks.'

While awaiting his mother's answer, Churchill sailed from Bombay, hoping when he reached Italy to find that his mother had arranged everything. He expected the war to be 'short and sharp'. Very likely 'I shall be too late'. He was indeed too late; the Turks defeated the Greeks before his ship reached Italy. He therefore continued to London where, at Conservative Central Office, he asked the Party organizers to arrange some speaking engagements for him while he was on leave. This they did, with the result that on June 26 he made his first political speech, to a Primrose League meeting just outside Bath. It was his father who had founded the League, in order to perpetuate the memory of Disraeli and the values of Tory Democracy.

If it were 'pardonable in any speaker', the local newspaper reported Churchill as saying, 'to begin with the well-worn and time-honoured apology, "unaccustomed as I am to public speaking", it would be pardonable in his case, for the honour he was enjoying at that moment of addressing an audience of his fellow-countrymen and women was the first honour of the kind he had ever received'. He went on to praise the Government's Workmen's Compensation Bill, designed to protect workmen in dangerous trades from poverty if they were injured in the service of their employer. The Bill, he said, 'removed the question from the shifting sands of charity and placed it on the firm bedrock of law'.

The twenty-two-year-old speaker had been introduced to his audience as the son of Lord Randolph. In his speech he spoke enthusiastically of

Tory Democracy. The British workman had 'more to hope for from the rising tide of Tory Democracy than from the dried-up drain-pipe of Radicalism'. He hoped the labourer would ultimately become 'a shareholder in the business in which he worked', making him willing to stand the pressure of a bad year 'because he shared some of the profits of a good one'.

Turning to Imperial affairs, Churchill spoke of those who, even in the Jubilee year of 1897, said that the British Empire had reached the height of its glory and power 'and that now we should begin to decline, as Babylon, Carthage and Rome had declined'. Do not believe these croakers, he said, 'but give the lie to their dismal croaking by showing by our actions that the vigour and vitality of our race is unimpaired and that our determination is to uphold the Empire that we have inherited from our fathers as Englishmen' – here he was interrupted by cheers – 'that our flag shall fly high upon the sea, our voice be heard in the councils of Europe, our Sovereign supported by the love of her subjects, then we shall continue to pursue that course marked out for us by an all-wise hand and carry out our mission of bearing peace, civilisation and good government to the uttermost ends of the earth'.

'My speech went off all right,' Churchill wrote to his brother. 'The *Morning Post* had a very good report & everyone seems pleased.' From Bath he went to Goodwood for the races. 'I was on the lawns at Goodwood,' he later recalled, 'in lovely weather and winning my money, when the revolt of the Pathan tribesmen on the Indian frontier began.' He read in the newspapers that a Field Force of three brigades was being formed to fight the uprising. It was to be headed by General Sir Bindon Blood, who, when Churchill had met him at Duchess Lily's house, promised that if he ever commanded another frontier expedition he would let Churchill go with him. He at once telegraphed to the General to remind him of his promise. Then, before receiving a reply, he left London by train for Brindisi, where he joined the Indian mail boat *Rome*. As the ship neared Aden he wrote to his mother, asking her to send out his polo sticks, and also the collected speeches of Gladstone and Disraeli.

Three weeks after his speech at Bath, Churchill was back at Bangalore. His speech at Bath, he told his mother, 'is much appreciated out here. Everybody reading the *Morning Post*'. He added, 'One more favour. Indulge my vanity by sending me any favourable opinions you may hear.' While in England, he had outlined to his mother the plot of a novel which he had decided to write. 'I have been writing my novel every day,' he wrote to her from Bangalore on August 24. 'It is far and away the best thing I have ever done.' He had already written eighty pages; it was a political romance set in a hypothetical republic. 'I am quite enthusiastic about it.

All my philosophy is put into the mouth of the hero.' Churchill's letter to his mother crossed with one from Sir Bindon Blood, stating that his personal staff was filled, but advising Churchill to come up to the North-West Frontier as a Press correspondent, 'and when you are here I shall put you on the strength on the first opportunity'. One of Churchill's friends had done just this, the General explained; he was now attached to the force in place of an officer killed in action.

Churchill at once telegraphed to his mother to find a British newspaper willing to make him its correspondent. He then obtained 'with much difficulty' a month's leave, put aside his novel, asked his mother to send out the first volume of Gibbon's collected correspondence, and prepared for the five-day journey northward, with his horses. If he were stopped on the train, he told his mother, he would ride to the scene of the fighting. 'I have considered everything,' he told her as he began a train journey of more than two thousand miles, 'and I feel that the fact of having seen service with British troops while still a young man must give me more weight politically – must add to my claims to be listened to, and may perhaps improve my prospects of gaining popularity with the country.'

This letter was written late on the evening of August 29. On the following day Churchill's commanding officer at Bangalore wrote to Lady Randolph, 'I thought perhaps that you would like a line as your son started last night for the frontier.'

5

In Action

Churchill was on his way to a scene of violent confrontation. Almost all the 'fierce wild warlike tribes of Afghan stock are in revolt', he explained to his brother on 31 August 1897, in a letter written in the train going north. More than 50,000 British and Indian soldiers had been massed against them. It was impossible, he added, for the British Government 'to be content with repelling an injury – it must be avenged. So we in our turn are to invade Afridis & Orakzais and others who have dared to violate the Pax Britannica.'

Behind Churchill, in the Bangalore region, less than five hundred British troops guarded an area inhabited by more than twelve million Indians, most of them Muslims sympathetic to the Afridis. Crossing an area of India almost as far in miles as America was from England, Churchill told his brother: 'It is a proud reflection that all this vast expanse of fertile, populous country is ruled and administered by Englishmen. It is all the prouder when we reflect how complete and minute is the ruling – and how few are the rulers.'

In the first week of September, Churchill reached the North-West Frontier at Malakand. There he learned that his mother had persuaded the influential *Daily Telegraph* to publish his letters from the war. She must decide whether or not they were to be signed with his name. 'I am myself very much in favour of signing,' he told her, 'as otherwise I get no credit for the letters. It may help me politically to come before the public in this way.'

Churchill had also persuaded the *Allahabad Pioneer*, for which Kipling had once written, to let him send them a three-hundred-word telegram every day from the frontier; it was this commission which made it possible for him to proceed to Sir Bindon Blood's headquarters. 'As to fighting,' he told his mother on September 5, 'we march tomorrow.' Before the week was over there would be a battle, 'the biggest yet fought on the frontier this year'. For himself, 'I have faith in my star – that I am intended to do something in this world. If I am mistaken – what does it matter? My life has been a pleasant one and though I should regret to leave it, it would be a regret that perhaps I should never know.'

While awaiting the start of the fighting Churchill sent his first nine letters to the *Daily Telegraph,* describing the situation on the frontier. They were published without his name, as being by 'a young officer'. In the confrontation on the North-West Frontier, he wrote in his letter of September 12, 'civilisation is face to face with militant Mohammedanism'. Given the 'moral and material forces' arrayed against each other, 'there need be no fear of the ultimate issue, but the longer the policy of half measures is adhered to the more distant the end of the struggle will be'.

Churchill now rode through the Mohmand valley to Nawagai. Eager to arrive 'in time for an action', he later explained to his mother, he rode on by himself ahead of a cavalry detachment 'and was met by nearly fifty armed tribesmen. Luckily they turned out to be friendlies – and were much amazed at my galloping wildly through them, pistol in hand. But how could I tell? I was so close on them that there was nothing for it but a dash.'

Having reached Nawagai without further incident, Churchill wrote to Reggie Barnes, 'The Mohmands need a lesson – and there is no doubt we are a very cruel people.' At Malakand, he explained, the Sikhs 'put a wounded man into the cinerator & burned him alive. This was hushed up.' Churchill added: 'I feel rather a vulture. The only excuse is that I might myself become the carrion.'

On the day after he wrote this letter Churchill was attached, at General Blood's request, to the second brigade of the Malakand Field Force, which had just been ordered into action. The temporary journalist was again a serving officer. On September 16, the day after his attachment to the Field Force, he saw the action he sought. It was near the frontier village of Markhanai. He began the day at half past six, riding forward with 1,300 cavalry and, he told his mother, 'saw the first shot fired'. After an hour of skirmishing he rode forward on his pony along a spur of the hillside with a Sikh infantry regiment, the 35th, 'until firing got so hot that my grey pony was unsafe'. He continued on foot. Then the order was given to retire down the spur. 'I remained till the last. The retirement was an awful rout in which the wounded were left to be cut up by these wild beasts.'

Two British officers standing near Churchill, Lieutenants Cassells and Hughes, were hit by Afridi rifle fire. Then an Afridi soldier, coming up to Hughes, tried to cut up his body. Churchill fired at him from thirty yards. 'He dropped but came on again.' Hughes was killed; Cassells survived. Together with a third subaltern, Churchill then carried a wounded Sikh soldier back towards the retreating troops, 'and might, had there been any gallery, have received some notice,' he told his mother. 'My pants are still stained with the man's blood.'

The Afridis came on to within forty yards. As Churchill and another young officer fired their pistols, the Afridis threw stones at them. Then they opened fire again. 'It was a horrible business. For there was no help for the man that went down. I felt no excitement and very little fear. All the excitement went out when things became really deadly.' For more than an hour Churchill was in danger as the Afridis renewed their attack. 'So close and critical did affairs become,' he told his grandmother, 'that I was forced to fire my revolver nine times in self-defence.' At one moment he replaced his pistol with a rifle dropped by a wounded man, and, he told Reggie Barnes, 'fired 40 rounds with some effect at close quarters. I cannot be certain, but I think I hit 4 men. At any rate they fell.'

The action ended and skirmishing resumed. After what he had just been through, Churchill told his mother, the skirmishing 'did not even excite me, though the young officers of this regiment were highly delighted at a few bullets that whistled about or kicked up the dust close by, and considered each a tremendous escape'. Altogether, Churchill told Lord William Beresford, 'it was a lively day. I was personally under fire from 7.30 a.m. to 8.30 p.m. without a stop, though of course it varied.'

Reflecting three days later on what he had done during the fight, in which fifty of the 1,300 British and Sikh soldiers had been killed, and a hundred wounded, Churchill wrote to his mother that no one could speak against him as far as courage was concerned. 'I rode on my grey pony all along the skirmish line when everyone else was lying down in cover. Foolish perhaps, but I play for high stakes and given an audience there is no act too daring or too noble.' During the retirement down the spur his pony, and hence its rider, had been noticed by the British commanding officer of the 35th Sikhs who, in his report of the action, recommended that Churchill be mentioned in despatches. The Brigadier endorsed this recommendation, writing to Churchill four months later, 'You were in several warm corners with my Brigade, and I dare say it will be some time before you are so hotly engaged again.'

After the action of September 16, Sir Bindon Blood appointed Churchill his orderly officer. As a result, Churchill explained to his mother, 'I shall get a medal and perhaps a couple of clasps.' Twice more that week he was in action, first at Domadola and then, on September 23, at Zagai, when he again rode his grey pony along the skirmish line. He then applied to transfer to another expedition, on its way to the Tirah, 'as that', he told his mother, 'would mean another clasp to my medal'.

'I have had some dangerous hours,' Churchill wrote to his mother on September 27, 'but feel sure my luck is good enough to pull me through.'

Three days later an Indian infantry regiment, the 31st Punjabis, was badly mauled in action. Bindon Blood at once attached Churchill to the regiment to fill the vacancy of some of the officers killed; 'I have put him in,' he explained to Colonel Brabazon, 'as he was the only spare officer within reach, and he is working away equal to two ordinary subalterns.'

On September 30 the 31st Punjabi Regiment was in action at Agrah, where sixty men were killed or wounded. 'To my intense mortification,' Churchill told Beresford, 'I saw the British infantry run and leave their officer on the ground, though this last I was too far off to notice.' The British regiment was the Royal West Kents. 'Thus,' Churchill added, 'in my short experience I have seen both black and white on the run.' Some months later Churchill told his mother, 'I cried when I met the Royal West Kents on the 30th September and saw the men really unsteady under the fire and tired of the game, and that poor young Browne-Clayton, literally cut in pieces on a stretcher – through his men not having stood by him.' Lieutenant Browne-Clayton was just one year older than Churchill at the time of his death.

He had been under fire at Agrah for five hours, Churchill wrote to his mother shortly after the action, 'but did not get into the hottest corners'. Nevertheless, although he did not tell her till later, he had ridden his grey pony along the skirmish line for the third time. When he was next in action he hoped to be commanding a hundred men. Then he would have 'some other motive for taking chances than merely love of adventure'.

Churchill wrote this letter on October 2, at General Blood's headquarters at Inayat Kila. He had a fever; '103 and an awful head' he told his mother, and went on to confide in her that it was a war without quarter. 'They kill and mutilate everyone they catch and we do not hesitate to finish their wounded off. I have seen several things which have not been very pretty since I have been up here – but as you will believe I have not soiled my hands with any dirty work – though I recognize the necessity of some things.'

From his tent on the frontier, Churchill was eager to have his brother's view of his speech at Bath. 'Let me have your candid opinion, if it is a good opinion,' he wrote. 'I don't want any adverse criticism. Criticism ceases to be of value to the criticised when it is hostile. And oh – wait till you see my novel!'

In the following ten days Churchill was under fire several times. 'If he gets a chance,' Sir Bindon Blood wrote to Colonel Brabazon, 'he will have the VC or the DSO', to which Brabazon commented, 'I am sure there's grit in that boy'. On October 12 Churchill told his mother that in the previous four weeks he had been under fire fifteen times since his first frontier action, 'Quite a foundation for political life.' He was contemplating writing a book about the Malakand Field Force, in which he would combine descriptions of the action with his comments and criticisms of Government policy. 'I know the ground, the men and the facts,' he told his mother, and he added, 'I have earned my medal and clasp. Blood says not one in a hundred have seen as much fighting as I have – and mind you – not from the staff or a distance but from the last company of the rearguard every time.'

Writing to his grandmother about the fighting, Churchill confided: 'The tribesmen torture the wounded & mutilate the dead. The troops never spare a single man who falls into their hands – whether he be wounded or not.' The field hospitals and the sick convoys were the 'special target' of the tribesmen. In response the British not only destroyed the water tanks by which alone the frontier tribes could get water for the summer, but 'employ against them a bullet', the new Dum Dum bullet, 'the shattering effects of which are simply appalling'. Churchill added: 'I believe no such bullet has ever been used on human beings before but only on game – stags, tigers etc. The picture is a terrible one, and naturally it has a side to which one does not allude in print. I wish I could come to the conclusion that all this barbarity – all these losses – all this expenditure – had resulted in a permanent settlement being obtained. I do not think however that anything has been done, that will not have to be done again.'

Churchill later told Beresford that on his very last day on the frontier 'I was nearer killed – by a subaltern who forgot his pistol was loaded – than at any other time. It would have been an irony of fate.'

In the third week of October, Churchill was ordered back to Bangalore. His time on the frontier, he wrote to his mother, had been 'the most glorious and delightful that my life has yet contained. But the possibility was always in view that it might be abruptly terminated. I saw a great many people killed and wounded and heard many bullets strike all round or whistle by – so many that if I had counted them you would not perhaps believe me.' No bullet had come 'nearer than a foot – in a former letter I said a yard, but since then the interval has decreased. My luck was throughout extraordinarily good.' So was Churchill's coolness under fire; as well as receiving the campaign medal for participating in the action, he was mentioned in despatches for 'courage and resolution', having, as the citation read, 'made himself useful at a critical moment'.

Churchill's pride at being mentioned in despatches was considerable. 'I am more ambitious for a reputation for personal courage,' he wrote to his mother, 'than anything else in the world.' To his brother he wrote: 'Being in many ways a coward – particularly at school – there is no ambition I cherish so keenly as to gain a reputation of personal courage.' As to deserving such an honour, 'I feel that I took every chance,' he told his mother, 'and displayed myself with ostentation wherever there was danger, but I had no military command and could not expect to receive credit for what should after all be merely the behaviour of a philosopher – who is also a gentleman.' Perhaps, he told Jack, 'my good grey pony caught the speaker's eye'.

Churchill now waited while his letters to the *Daily Telegraph* were published. In them he not only described the action, but set out his view of the folly of the Government's policy in allowing the tribesmen to control the buffer zone between British India and Afghanistan. This buffer zone, he argued, ought to be annexed as soon as possible. Then the raids would cease. Annexation was a word the British public 'will have, ultimately, to swallow, and the sooner they do it, the sooner things will begin to mend'. In the end Britain would probably be compelled to absorb even Afghanistan 'right up to the Russian frontier'. The safest frontier line was a political one, 'red & yellow posts fifty yards apart and sentries, as between Austria & Russia. There is no room for doubt as to what is meant. To cross that is war. These "buffer state" policies are only temporary affairs and lead to more trouble than anything else.'

To Churchill's chagrin, although his letters were published in the *Daily Telegraph*, they continued to appear without his name. 'I had written them with design,' he told his mother, 'a design which took form as the correspondence advanced, of bringing my personality before the electorate. I had hoped that some political advantage might have accrued.' Eager to enable her son to enter politics, Lady Randolph made sure that as many influential people as possible knew he was the author of the articles. But he was still not content. 'Though I value the opinion of your friends in London,' he wrote, 'that narrow circle is not the audience to whom I had meant to appeal.'

While in Bangalore, Churchill missed a political opportunity. 'I see there has been a vacancy in Lancashire which might have suited me,' he wrote to his mother that October. 'But I was better employed.' That same day he wrote to his grandmother, 'If I live, I intend to stand for Parliament at the General Election – so that my sojourn abroad will not be indefinitely prolonged.' But there was one more scene of military action to which he wanted to be sent. 'I must now go to Egypt,' he told his mother, 'and you should endeavour to stimulate the Prince into writing to Kitchener on the subject.' His life in India was 'not big enough' to hold him. 'I want to be up and doing and cannot bear inaction or routine.' Even polo 'has lost half its charm and no longer satisfies me'. His aim now was 'Khartoum next year'. He would enter the Dervish capital with its conquerors.

From Bangalore, Churchill sent his mother an article he had written on rhetoric, propounding the view that true rhetoric was 'the key to the hearts of men', for her to place somewhere for publication. 'It will make me enemies,' he wrote, 'but they are inevitable in any case'. Meanwhile he wanted to see action wherever it was taking place. 'You should be able to get me sent from one place to another,' he told his mother, explaining that he had hoped to go to Abyssinia with a British mission. It would have been 'the very thing', but nothing had come of it. Joseph Chamberlain might have arranged it 'with a word', he told his mother reproachfully, adding, 'I feel plenty of confidence in myself now, and am certain I shall do something in the world – if physical injury does not befall me.'

While at Bangalore, Churchill continued to work on his novel. Nine chapters were written by the beginning of November. But within a few weeks he set it aside to write about the Malakand Field Force. He enlisted his mother to send him published material from England, as well as the opinions of 'prominent actors' in the political aspects of the campaign. Two years earlier, he told her, Colonel Younghusband had made 'a large sum of money' by his book on the Chitral campaign. 'I do not see why I should not make an account of the much more severe fighting we experienced equally interesting.' He had already written to 'all the Colonels and knowledgeable people' he had met on the frontier to ask them for information. 'I do not doubt I shall receive volumes by return of post. Such is the modesty of the age. Few people are above saying what really happened from their point of view. Of course I shall have to discriminate.'

Churchill was working on his book six hours a day, 'and quite a hole is worn in my second finger by it', he told his mother. Writing was far from easy; 'Everything is worked out by hard labour and frequent polishing.' He was ambitious of something 'better than the railway bookstalls. However I daresay I take an inflated view of everything.' To Jack he wrote about his 'affection' for reading about the past. 'A good knowledge of history is a quiver full of arrows in debate.' A good knowledge of French would be of 'the greatest service in life'; when he left the Army he hoped to go to Paris for a few months to improve his French. He hoped Jack too would travel, to see something 'of this great Empire of ours – to the maintenance of which I shall devote my life'.

As he reached his twenty-third birthday, Churchill's mind was set on entering the House of Commons. He had decided that if there was a vacancy in the Paddington constituency, once his father's, he would sail back to England at once, and asked his mother to persuade the existing member, who was over sixty, to stand down. 'I have been hotting up Fardell,' she wrote on December 10, 'but he is not prepared to resign as yet!' Nor did he resign until 1910. Churchill was later to remark, in appreciation of his mother's efforts in entertaining so widely on his behalf, 'She left no stone unturned, she left no cutlet uncooked.'

Lady Randolph had expressed her displeasure at her son's account of his courage on the frontier. As to his boasting, he replied, 'I only unburden to my friends. They understand & forgive my vanity.' To ride a grey pony along the skirmish line 'is not a common experience. But I had to play for high stakes and have been lucky to win.' Bullets, 'to a philosopher my dear Mamma', were not worth considering. 'Besides I am so conceited I do not believe the Gods would create so potent a being as myself for so prosaic an ending.'

That December, Churchill again asked his mother to write to Kitchener on his behalf, 'Strike while the iron is hot & the ink wet.' It would be much safer in Egypt than on the Indian frontier he tried to assure her. During the action on September 16 'we lost 150 out of 1,000. We call it an action.' At Firket in Egypt 'they lost 45 out of 10,000. They call it a battle. It must have been more like a slum fight.'

On the last day of 1897, Churchill sent his mother the manuscript of his book *The Story of the Malakand Field Force*. Arthur Balfour, to whom she had already mentioned the book, had promised to help find a good publisher. He did so by introducing her to his publishing 'broker', the literary agent A.P. Watt, who was much impressed by the 'conspicuous ability' of Churchill's letters to the *Daily Telegraph*, and within a week had placed the book with a publisher. 'Perhaps the book may be a financial success,' Churchill wrote to his mother. 'Mind you write and say nice things to me about it. Tell me what parts you like. I love praise. It is delicious.'

Churchill had excluded all personal matters from the book; the only reference to himself was a footnote to say where he was serving at the time of the action. It was a narrative of events based not only on his own experiences but on wide reading and correspondence with those involved. His own feelings about the campaign were outspoken. 'The whole expedition was a mistake,' he told his mother, 'because its success depended on the tribesmen giving in when their country was invaded & their property destroyed. This they have not done. We have done them all the harm possible and many of them are still defiant.' It was because Britain had 'no real means, except by prolonged occupation, of putting the screw on these tribesmen & making them give in', he argued, that it was 'a great mistake to make the attempt'.

'Oh how I wish I could work you up over Egypt!' Churchill wrote to his mother in mid-January. 'I know you could do it with all your influence, and the people you know. It is a pushing age and we must shove with the rest.' After the Tirah campaign, to which he still hoped to be sent, and then Egypt, he would 'turn from war to peace & politics. If, that is I get through all right. I think myself I shall, but of course one has only to look at Nature and see how very little store she sets by life. Its sanctity is entirely a human idea. You may think of a beautiful butterfly – 12 million feathers on his wing, 16,000 lenses in his eye – a mouthful for a bird. Let us laugh at fate. It might please her.'

Two of Churchill's friends had also been war correspondents on the Indian frontier. One, Lord Fincastle, had won the Victoria Cross. The other, Lieutenant R.T. Greaves, had been killed in action. 'A very little luck,' Churchill told his mother, 'might have carried me to the highest of all prizes or have ended the game.'

6

To Omdurman and Beyond

In January 1898 Churchill went to Calcutta, where he stayed with the Viceroy, Lord Elgin, dined with the Commander-in-Chief, Sir George White, and 'moved in high and exalted circles generally', as he told Jack. A mere eight years later he was to serve under Elgin at the Colonial office, his first ministerial appointment. Nor was political life ever absent from his plans even then; that month he sent Conservative Central Office, at its suggestion, an election address, in case the seat at Paddington fell vacant, or a General Election was called unexpectedly. 'In politics,' he wrote to his mother from Bangalore at the end of the month, 'a man, I take it, gets on not so much by what he does, as by what he is. It is not so much a question of brains as of character & originality.' It was for these reasons 'that I would not allow others to suggest ideas and that I am somewhat impatient of advice as to my beginning in politics'.

Introductions, connections, powerful friends, a name, good advice well-followed, 'all these things count', Churchill told his mother, 'but they only lead to a certain point. As it were, they may ensure admission to the scales. Ultimately every man has to be weighed, and if found wanting, nothing can procure him the public confidence.' If he was not good enough, others were welcome to take his place. 'I should never care to bolster up a sham reputation and hold my position by disguising my personality. Of course – as you have known for some time – I believe in myself. If I did not, I might perhaps take other views.'

Throughout these months in India, Churchill was beset by financial worries. He was angered by what he considered his mother's extravagance in clothes, travelling and entertaining. 'Speaking quite frankly on the subject,' he wrote to her from Bangalore, 'there is no doubt we are both – you & I – equally thoughtless – spendthrift and extravagant. We both know what is good, and we both like to have it.' Two days later he wrote again: 'In the three years from my father's death you have spent a quarter of our entire fortune in the world. I have also been extravagant: but my extravagances are a very small matter besides yours.'

For Churchill a new source of funds now opened up; for *The Story of the Malakand Field Force* he would receive £50, the equivalent in 1990 of £2,000. In addition he would get £100 for every two thousand copies sold. The book was published in London on March 14, 'the most noteworthy act of my life', he told his mother, 'up to date (of course)'. Two thousand copies were printed, followed within ten months by a further 4,500, bringing him an extra £250. It had become clear to him that he could earn a living by writing. Proudly, he informed his grandmother that the *Daily Telegraph* had paid him £100 for his frontier letters, and the *Allahabad Pioneer* £25 for his telegrams.

The attitude of senior officers, Lady Randolph told her son that summer, was that whereas he was the most 'promising youngster out', nevertheless 'you wrote too well to remain in the army, where your talents would be wasted & where your writings would sooner or later get you into trouble.' That winter the Prince of Wales wrote to him: 'You have great facility in writing, which is a great advantage. I only hope you will be prudent in your remarks & shun all acrid criticisms which would be resented by the authorities.' Churchill commented to his mother that he was 'Tory enough' to regard this letter as 'a great honour'. As to his military aspirations, he had been befriended by Captain Aylmer Haldane, who arranged for him to be attached to the Tirah Expeditionary Force, then based at Peshawar. 'My reputation, for what it is worth, has interested him,' Churchill told his mother.

As Churchill hurried northward it seemed he was to be cheated of action. 'There can be no doubt that the most ferocious savages in Asia have had enough,' he told his mother. Yet even without being in combat he would get an extra clasp on his frontier medal. 'It counts in my record of service and as an extra campaign,' he explained. But the chief value of going to the Tirah lay elsewhere. 'I now know all the generals who are likely to have commands in the next few years.'

At Peshawar, Churchill waited for orders to move to the Tirah. 'Of course I hope for a fight,' he told his mother, 'but I do not delude myself. Both sides are sick of it.' At the end of March, in a letter to a friend which was published a month later in *The Times*, Churchill defended the British Army on the North-West Frontier. India, ruled as it was by only a few thousand Englishmen, provided what he called 'an accurate measure of the distance through which development, aided by civilisation, has carried the human species'. Yet there had long existed in England a prejudice 'often latent, never absent' against both the civil and military public servants employed 'in this far-off land'.

Now everyone was searching for a scapegoat for the failure to suppress the frontier tribes, but, Churchill wrote, in mountain warfare 'there are no general actions on a great scale, no brilliant successes, no important surrenders, no chance for *coups de théâtre*. It is just a rough, hard job, which must be carried through.' And he went on to point out that at the very moment that the Army in India 'receives the humble submission of the most ferocious savages in Asia, we are assailed by the taunts and re-proaches of our countrymen at home'.

This letter, Churchill confided to his mother, would establish his posi-tion with the Indian military authorities 'on unshakeable foundations'. Those authorities were 'extraordinarily sensitive of Press criticism and welcome the slightest favourable comment'. If 'properly boomed', he told his uncle Moreton Frewen, his letter 'might just make a stir – and will be very acceptable to my superiors in India. It is also just.'

The campaign in the Tirah for which Churchill had hoped did not take place. After a final skirmish, the one remaining warring tribe made their peace. 'They bear but little malice,' Churchill told his mother, 'would kill you if they could, but otherwise perfectly friendly. I confess I like them. I saw a lot of them in Jamrud this last month – ever with a cheery grin in spite of the terrible destruction we wrought in their valleys.' To a journalist friend, Hubert Howard, Churchill wrote: 'I had very little fighting with the Tirah force, only a few sniper & picket affairs. To be honest I only heard one bullet – and that was fired by an enthusiastic Irishman. Still it was interesting and counts as another show.'

At the request of the *United Services Magazine* Churchill wrote an article on the ethics of the frontier policy. For the *Harmsworth Magazine* he wrote a short story, 'Man Overboard, An Episode of the Red Sea'. He was also completing his novel, 'a wild and daring book', he told his mother, 'tilting recklessly here and there and written with no purpose whatever, but to amuse. This I believe it will do. I have faith in my pen. I believe the thoughts I can put on paper will interest & be popular with the public.' He contemplated writing a life of Garibaldi, and a 'short & dramatic' history of the American Civil War. He was also tempted by a publisher's offer to write both a life of his illustrious military ancestor, John Churchill, 1st Duke of Marlborough, and a biography of his father. If he ever attempted a life of Lord Randolph, he told his mother, 'I should make it the labour of years.'

Churchill's life of his father was to be published within eight years of this letter, his life of Marlborough in the 1930s, and his history of the American Civil War, as part of a four-volume History of the English-Speaking Peoples, in the 1950s. Garibaldi was never attempted. Mean-while, his literary earnings grew steadily; that May the *Allahabad Pioneer* published five letters from him on the recent American invasion of Cuba. These would pay his mess bill for at least a month, he told his mother, 'and were written straight off without recopying'.

To his Aunt Leonie, who had heard rumours of the novel, Churchill wrote from Bangalore: 'You ask why! I should reply "*il faut vivre*". I hope later on to produce something really good. You know I have unbounded faith in myself.' His thoughts were on the Sudan: 'I hope to be in at the death this winter at Khartoum. You must try and stimulate any tame generals you may know on my behalf.'

Worried about money, Churchill had begun a legal action to prevent his mother from passing on his portion of his inheritance to a second husband, should she remarry. 'I felt a horrid, sordid beast to do what I did,' he told his Aunt Leonie, 'but I had to contemplate the possibility of Mamma marrying perhaps a poor man that I disliked, some wanderer. I have withdrawn the conditions now – but only because I have confidence in my ability to keep myself from squalor by journalism in the ultimate issue.' He was worried nevertheless about his mother's extravagance: 'Indeed the picture is very black. I can never afford to go into politics – after the properties are so reduced. Fancy *half* is spent. But then with the prospects of an autumn campaign it is unphilosophical to despair. I may find the answer to all one's puzzles awaiting me, in a compendious form.'

'Am I extravagant!' Churchill asked his aunt rhetorically, and went on to deny it: 'I neither race nor drink nor gamble nor squander my money on concubines. Only I don't worry over accounts and small details, and hence pay about twice as much as I need for the little pleasure there is in this crossgrained existence.'

To his mother, Churchill wrote from Bangalore that May about what he called his one 'mental flaw', telling her, with startling frankness: 'I do not care so much for the principles I advocate as for the impression which my words produce & the reputation they give me. This sounds very terrible. But you must remember that we do not live in the days of Great Causes.' He often yielded, he confessed, 'to the temptation of adapting my facts to my phrases. But Macaulay is the arch-offender in this respect. I think a keen sense of necessity or of burning wrong or injustice would make me sincere, but I very rarely detect genuine emotion in myself.' An exception to this was during the action of September 30 in the Malakand, when he had wept, 'So I believe that *au fond* I am genuine. But in most matters my head or my wits would direct, and my heart would lend a little emotion whichever way was required. It is a philosophic virtue, not a human one.'

Reflecting on the American war with Spain and invasion of Cuba, Churchill told his mother: 'I am sorry for Spain. America certainly presents its unattractive side to the world. But they are right, and deep down in the heart of a great democracy there is a very noble spirit.' As a 'representative of both sides', he found the idea of an Anglo-American rapprochement 'very pleasant. One of the principles of my politics will always be to promote the good understanding between the English-speaking communities'. The Americans should be admired for their action in Cuba, Churchill argued, 'though as a nation in a diplomatic sense their manners are odious. They always contrive to disgust polite people. Yet their heart is honest.'

There was a call that summer for firm British action, even war, against Russia, whose troops were fighting in China. Churchill opposed any such action. 'We cannot harm Russia,' he told his mother. But Russia could force Britain to mobilize 100,000 soldiers on the Indian frontier and do sufficient harm to Britain's sea-borne trade 'to give the filthy Germans a chance of finally gaining the commercial supremacy of the world'.

Churchill realized that in opposing an anti-Russian policy his views would not be popular in 'a jingo age'. It was the fault of all 'booms of sentiment', he told his mother, that they carried men too far and led to reactions. 'Militarism degenerates into brutality. Loyalty promotes tyranny and sycophancy. Humanitarianism becomes maudlin and ridiculous. Patriotism shades into cant. Imperialism sinks to jingoism.'

At the beginning of June, Churchill prepared to go on leave, asking his mother to arrange two or three political meetings for him, particularly at Bradford where he hoped one day to stand for Parliament. He wanted one 'real big meeting of at least 2,000 men', and he told her: 'Compel them to come in. I am sure I can hold them. I have got lots of good material for at least three speeches, all carefully written out and docketed.' Lady Randolph did as she was asked. Her son meanwhile sailed from Bombay, left his Indian servant and campaigning kit, including tents and saddles in Egypt, in the hope of being able soon to return there, and returned to London.

Churchill reached London on July 2. Twelve days later he spoke at Bradford, where he was thrilled by his reception. 'I was listened to with the greatest attention for fifty-five minutes,' he told his mother, 'at the end of which time there were loud & general cries of "Go on". Five or six times they applauded for about two minutes without stopping.' When he finished 'many people mounted their chairs and there was really a very great deal of enthusiasm'. To his cousin Sunny, Churchill wrote that 'Bradford was the greatest pleasure of my life. I hope to have more.'

Churchill now made every effort to be attached to Kitchener's army in the Sudan. The Prime Minister, Lord Salisbury, had just read *The Story of the Malakand Field Force* and asked his Private Secretary to arrange a meeting with the young author, the son of his former colleague. Thus it was that Churchill entered 10 Downing Street for the first time. 'I remember well,' he later wrote, 'the old-world courtesy with which he met me at the door and with a charming gesture of welcome and salute conducted me to a seat on a small sofa in the midst of his vast room.'

Salisbury told Churchill that he had been able 'to form a truer picture of the kind of fighting that has been going on in these frontier valleys from your writings than from any other documents which it has been my duty to read'. When after twenty minutes Churchill rose to leave, the Prime Minister kept him for another ten, then told him, as he conducted him to the door: 'I hope you will allow me to say how much you remind me of your father, with whom such important days of my political life were lived. If there is anything at any time that I could do which would be of assistance to you, pray do not fail to let me know.'

Encouraged by this interest, Churchill asked Salisbury's Private Secretary if he could send a telegram to Kitchener, requesting him to consider Churchill for the Expeditionary Force. Salisbury agreed to do so, but Kitchener's reply was cool. He already had sufficient officers and if a vacancy did occur there were others with better claims than Churchill to take their place. Undeterred, Churchill went to see Lord Cromer, who promised to write direct to Kitchener. Lady Randolph also wrote direct to the commander-in-chief, as did her friend Lady Jeune, who telegraphed boldly: 'Hope you will take Churchill. Guarantee he won't write.'

Lady Jeune's assurance did not impress Kitchener. But she was also a close friend of Sir Evelyn Wood, the Army's Adjutant General, who at a private dinner party had expressed unease at Kitchener's reluctance to accept War Office nominees. On learning this, Churchill urged her to tell Wood of the Prime Minister's interest in his own nomination. She did so, and Wood telegraphed to Kitchener on Churchill's behalf. Two days later he learned that he was to go to Egypt at once, to the 21st Lancers. 'I had very great difficulty in getting out here,' he wrote to a friend two weeks later, from the Nile, '& indeed had not two young officers died I doubt very much whether I should have succeeded.' Lady Jeune had also played her part.

While still in London, Churchill contacted a family friend, Oliver Borthwick, a newspaper proprietor, who commissioned him to write 'as opportunity served' a series of letters for the *Morning Post* at £15 a column. His journalistic commission secured, he left London on the morning of July 27. Three days later he boarded ship at Marseilles. The vessel, he told his mother, was 'a filthy tramp, manned by these detestable French sailors'. He was worried that he might receive a telegram from Bangalore to say that his leave was at an end. 'However,' he informed his mother, 'I was glad not to have received a telegram of recall so far. My having started makes my case much stronger.' Reaching Egypt on the evening of August 2, he went at once to the 21st Lancers' barracks. 'They were very civil,' he told his mother, 'and had had an official communication attaching me to them.' Of the nine officers in his squadron, six were friends from Harrow and Bangalore, so that '*this* time I shall not be among strangers as in the Mohmand valley'.

Churchill had reached Cairo just in time. On the following day his squadron left by boat up the Nile. 'It is a very strange transformation scene that the last eight days have worked,' he wrote to his mother from Luxor on August 5, 'when I think of the London streets, dinners, balls etc, and then look at the khaki soldiers – the great lumbering barge full of horses – the muddy river, and behind and beyond the palm trees and the sails of the dahabiahs.' Even more complete was the change 'in my own mind'. The anticipations of Parliament, of speeches and of political life generally 'have faded before more vivid possibilities and prospects, and my thoughts are more concerned with swords, lances, pistols – & soft-nosed bullets – than with Bills, Acts & by-elections'.

Among those on the boat was Churchill's friend Hubert Howard, who had been commissioned by *The Times* to report on the campaign. Five days later, still going up river, Churchill sent his mother the first two letters for the *Morning Post*. 'They will act as foundations and as scaffolding for my book,' he told her. While on the Nile, Churchill reflected on the advice given by two of his cousins, Sunny Marlborough and Ivor Guest, that he was 'too good for this sort of work'. He was satisfied, he told his mother, that what he had done was 'wise and worthy of a man'. He was not 'careless of the possible results, for I want as you know to live and to accomplish much, but I do not fear them nor shall I complain'. Beside these 'fortifying, philosophic reflections', he confided, 'I have a keen aboriginal desire to kill several of these odious Dervishes & drive the rest of the pestiferous breed to Orcus, and I anticipate enjoying this exercise very much. I should like to begin tomorrow.'

Even as he travelled towards the Dervish army, Churchill asked his mother to fix up 'really big & well-boomed' political meetings for him on his return, 'one at Bradford and the other, I think, at Birmingham'. He also asked Captain Haldane to send him 'a little slip of the ribbon' to which he was entitled as a result of the Malakand. 'I am possessed of a keen desire,' he explained, 'to mount the ribbon on my breast while I face the Dervishes here.' He was hoping for action soon, he told Haldane on August 11. 'But it would be a very great nuisance to be killed and I hope I shall avoid the great revelation for the present.'

Three days later, the 21st Lancers reached Atbara where they camped, then rode forward along the bank of the Nile. One night Churchill missed his way while trying to catch up with the column, and, as he told his mother, in telegraphese, 'Spent miserable night and day without food or water in desert. Stars were all clouded up. Luckily had sense to wait till sunrise without watering horse – and made for river and thus, after nearly seventy miles of meandering, found convoy again.' Churchill rejoined his fellow-Lancers. By August 24 they were only sixty miles from Omdurman. Within ten days, he told his mother, 'there will be a general action – perhaps a very severe one. I may be killed. I do not think so. But if I am you must avail yourself of the consolations of philosophy and reflect on the utter insignificance of all human beings.' He wanted to come back, and hoped all would be well. 'But I can assure you I do not flinch – though I do not accept the Christian or any other form of religious belief.'

'Nothing,' Churchill continued, 'not even the certain knowledge of approaching destruction, would make me turn back now, even if I could with honour. But I shall come back afterwards the wiser and the stronger for my gamble. And then we will think of other and wider spheres of action. I have plenty of faith – in what I do not know – that I shall not be hurt.' After all, he added, 'there will be nothing hotter than the 16th September of last year, and I am sure that of the next world we may say – if any – then better'. If he were severely wounded, he wrote in a postscript, 'you would do well to come out and help me back'.

On August 26, as Kitchener's army of 25,000 men drew closer to Omdurman, Churchill made a last minute effort to transfer from the Lancers to the Egyptian Cavalry, as, he explained to his mother, 'tho' more dangerous, it is a much better business as far as chances of distinction go'. The Colonel commanding the Egyptian Cavalry had asked for him, but his own Colonel did not want to let him go. 'He is quite right,' Churchill admitted, 'but it is a pity, as I should have stood a much better chance of getting something out of the business with the Egyptians.'

Churchill learned that day that Kitchener had spoken critically of him, saying that he thought he 'was not going to stay in the Army – was only making a convenience of it', and that he disapproved of him coming in place of others 'whose professions were at stake'. And yet, Churchill told his mother, Kitchener had also said 'that I was quite right to try my best'. Kitchener did not wish to meet the young lieutenant. 'If I live,' Churchill wrote, 'he will recognise that it might have been worth while to impress me with his ideas on Egypt & the Sudan. As it is I shall form my own.'

It was at Omdurman, across the river from Khartoum, that the Dervishes decided to attack. At midday on September 1 it seemed as if their army, moving rapidly out of Omdurman, might come into collision with the main British force before nightfall. Churchill, whose squadron was with the other cavalry in front of the main Expeditionary Force, was told by his cavalry commander to ascertain the scale of the Dervish advance and report back to Kitchener. 'I climbed the black hill of Surgham,' he later wrote, 'and looked around. The great army of the Dervishes was dwarfed by the size of the landscape to mere dark smears and smudges on the brown plain. Looking east, another army was now visible – the British and Egyptian army.'

Neither force could see the other, Churchill recalled, 'though but five miles divided them. I looked alternately at each array. That of the enemy was, without doubt, both longer and deeper. Yet there seemed a superior strength in the solid battalions, whose lines were so straight that they might have been drawn with a ruler.' The Dervish forces were advancing. Churchill hurried back on his grey pony towards the main British camp to report what he had seen. As he approached the camp he saw Kitchener – the Sirdar – and a dozen Staff officers riding in his direction. They were themselves on their way to Surgham Hill to see what was happening. Thus the General and the subaltern, who sixteen years later were to serve in the War Cabinet together, met for the first time.

Although Kitchener was on his way to the hill, Churchill wrote, he nevertheless 'invited me to describe the situation as seen from the advanced squadrons. This I did.' Kitchener listened without speaking, 'our horses crunching the sand as we rode forward side by side'.

'You say the Dervish army is advancing,' Kitchener commented. 'How long do you think I've got?'

'You have got at least an hour,' Churchill replied, 'probably an hour and a half, sir, even if they come on at their present rate.'

'The Sirdar was very calm,' Churchill recalled. 'His confidence had been communicated to his staff. "We want nothing better", they said. "Here is a good field of fire. They may as well come today as tomorrow"'.

The Dervish army halted before it reached the British positions, leaving Surgham Hill between the two armies. Churchill and his fellow-Lancers now joined the main body of Kitchener's army, on the flank nearest the Nile. Having served on the North-West Frontier of India, Churchill scorned the British officers of the Egyptian Army who spoke always of 'battles'; in the perspective of those like himself who had fought in India, these 'battles' were no more than 'actions'. In any case, Churchill was to recall after the First World War, 'to the great mass of those who took part in the little wars of Britain in those vanished light-hearted days', death in action was 'only a sporting element in a splendid game'.

Most of those who fought in India or in the Sudan 'were fated', Churchill later wrote, to see a war, the First World War, in which 'the hazards were reversed, where death was the general expectation and severe wounds were counted as lucky escapes, where whole brigades were shorn away under the steel flail of artillery and machine-guns, where the survivors of one tornado knew that they would certainly be consumed in the next or the next after that'. Everything depended upon the scale of events. 'We young men who lay down to sleep that night within three miles of 60,000 well-armed fanatical Dervishes, expecting every moment their violent onset or inrush and sure of fighting at latest with the dawn – we may perhaps be pardoned if we thought we were at grips with real war.'

During the night, Surgham Hill was occupied by a unit of the Egyptian Cavalry. At sunrise, other cavalry patrols rode out to reconnoitre. Churchill went with one of them. His task, and that of the seven Lancers with him, was to return to Surgham Hill, then called Heliograph Hill by the British, and report on the Dervish strength and positions. 'We galloped forward,' he later wrote, 'and as we did not know that the Egyptian squadron and its officer had already looked over the ridge, we enjoyed all the excitement without any of the danger, and were elated by the thought that we were the first to see what lay beyond.'

What lay beyond was impressive and formidable. Not until he wrote his book about the reconquest of the Sudan did Churchill know that other cavalrymen had been on the hill before him. Two weeks later he wrote to an army friend, Ian Hamilton, that he had been, 'I think, the first to see the enemy – certainly the first to hear their bullets.' His letter continued: 'Never shall I see such a sight again. At the very least there were 40,000 men – five miles long in lines with great humps and squares at intervals – and I can assure you that when I heard them all shouting their war songs from my coign of vantage on the ridge of Heliograph Hill I and my little patrol felt very lonely.' Although he 'never doubted the issue', Churchill added, 'I was in great awe'.

It was a quarter to six. Churchill immediately wrote out, in pencil, a message for Kitchener: 'Dervish Army, strength unchanged, occupies last night's position with their left well extended. Their patrols have reported the advance and loud cheering is going on.' There were no Dervish troops within three miles of Kitchener's camp, but as the light grew stronger Churchill saw that the Dervish force was in fact advancing. Their leader, the Khalifa, had decided to throw back the oncoming army. In a second pencilled note, timed at 6.20, Churchill reported this move to Kitchener. Most of the Dervish cavalry, he noted, were accompanying the advancing force.

Churchill remained on the hill. 'Their cavalry patrols,' he told Hamilton two weeks later, 'which consisted of five or six horsemen each made no attempt to drive me back, and I waited until one great brigade of perhaps 2,000 men got to within 400 yards. I didn't realize they could shoot and thought they were all spearmen.' For a quarter of an hour the Dervishes seemed to pay no attention at all to Churchill and his seven Lancers, treating them 'with complete disdain'. Then, however, he told Hamilton, 'Foolishly I dismounted 4 and opened magazine into the brown of them. Thereat they sent out 20 riflemen and began to make very close practice. Finally I had to gallop and as we did so I did not hear less than 30 bullets.' It was a dangerous moment. 'Luckily – (you know how capricious Fortune is) – we never had a man touched. If we had it would have meant others.'

Churchill sent his seven Lancers behind the hill for safety, 'and went to the top myself '. There he dismounted, but his grey pony remained a target, 'and it got too hot for me to stay although the scene was worth looking at. Various frantic people, Adjutant, trumpeters etc, then arrived and brought me back to my Squadron. But I assumed so very lofty a position – pointing out that no one was even hurt (and they admitted the value of the information) that I was allowed to go off again.' On this second patrol, Churchill and his men proceeded and returned without incident. 'I attributed the fact that we had no casualties to my "experience",' he told Hamilton. 'It was really due to the Almighty's amiability. For candidly the fire was for the time being as hot as anything I have seen – barring only those 10 minutes with the 35th Sikhs' – a year earlier.

As the Dervish advance came within rifle shot of the British lines Kitchener ordered his infantry into action. The cavalry squadrons were sent back to the camp. There, Churchill told his friend, 'we listened for an hour to 20,000 rifles, near sixty guns and twenty Maxims without seeing much'. The horses were watered and fed. There were 'a few bullets', but all of them were high, as the cavalrymen and their horses were in good cover by the river bank. At half past eight the Dervish attack weakened. The cavalry were at once 'bustled out' of the camp to take their place on the left flank of the British lines. 'We halted on the old ridge,' Churchill told Hamilton, 'and messed about with carbines for a quarter of an hour. Beyond the ridge, thousands of Dervishes could be seen, as I thought fugitives – "meet to be cut up".' At that moment the apparently beaten Dervishes seemed to Churchill to be the victims of 'supine apathy'.

At 8.40 the cavalry mounted their horses 'and rode slowly towards these crowds'. It was Churchill's first cavalry charge in action. He was 'confident', he told Hamilton, 'that we should spear them till we could not sit on our horses. But between us and the distant fugitives was a single line of 150 men.' It seemed to the cavalry officers that these 150 Dervishes were spearmen. They let the British horsemen get within 250 yards of them. 'We proposed,' Churchill told Hamilton, 'at least I think this was the idea, to move round their flank and slip a squadron at them, and then on to better things beyond.'

The cavalrymen rode across the front of the 150 Dervishes from right to left, looking for a point to turn and spear them. But these were not in fact spearmen caught in an isolated line, but riflemen. As the British troops rode past them, they got down on their knees and began to open fire. 'There was a loud, brisk crackle of musketry,' Churchill wrote. 'The distance was too short for it to be harmless on so big a target.'

Two courses were open to the surprised cavalrymen. One was to wheel left into line and gallop off, 'coming back for the wounded – a bad business'. The other was to right wheel and charge the Dervish line. 'I think everybody made his own decision,' Churchill told his friend. 'At any rate while the trumpet was still jerking we were all at the gallop towards them. The fire was too hot to allow of second lines – flank squadrons or anything like that – being arranged. The only order given was "Right Wheel into Line". "Gallop" and "Charge" were understood.'

The twenty-three-year-old Churchill was taking part in a cavalry charge, not, as expected, against demoralized spearmen, but against riflemen determined not to yield. As he rode the first hundred yards towards the Dervishes, he looked repeatedly over his left shoulder to see what effect their fire was having on his men. 'It seemed small. Then I drew my Mauser pistol – a ripper – and cocked it. Then I looked to my front. Instead of the 150 riflemen who were still blazing, I saw a line nearly (in the middle) 12 deep, and a little less than our own front, of closely jammed spearmen.'

These hitherto unseen forces were in a ravine with steep sloping sides six feet deep and twenty feet broad. It was a totally unforeseen hazard. But after his experiences on the North-West Frontier, Churchill told Hamilton, 'I thought – capital – the more the merrier.' His troop then struck at the Dervishes diagonally, not jumping across the ravine, but galloping through it.

'Opposite me they were about 4 deep. But they all fell knocked AOT' – 'arse over tip' – 'and we passed through without any sort of shock. One man in my troop fell. He was cut to pieces. Five or six horses were wounded by backhanders etc. But otherwise unscathed.'

The cavalry charge was over and the troop dispersed. 'It was, I suppose, the most dangerous 2 minutes I shall live to see,' Churchill told Hamilton. Of the 310 officers and men in the charge, one officer and twenty men had been killed, and four officers and forty-five men wounded. 'All this in 120 seconds!' Churchill commented. He had fired 'exactly 10 shots' and had emptied his pistol, 'but without a hair of my horse or a stitch of my clothing being touched. Very few can say the same.'

Around the scene of the charge Churchill could now see 'scattered men and personal combats'. He at once 'pulled into a trot and rode up to individuals, firing my pistol in their faces and killing several – three for certain – two doubtful – one very doubtful. Then I looked round and saw the Dervish mass reforming. The charge had passed through, knocking over nearly half. They were getting on their legs again and their Emirs were trying to collect them into a lump again.' As Churchill, on horseback, watched the Dervishes regroup, he realized that this mass of men was a mere twenty yards away. 'I looked at them stupidly for what may have been two seconds. Then I saw two men get down on their knees and take aim with rifles – and for the first time the danger & peril came home to me.'

Turning away from the Dervishes, Churchill determined to gallop back to his men. As he turned, the two riflemen fired at him. 'At that close range I was grievously anxious,' he told Hamilton, 'but I heard none of their bullets – which went Heaven knows where. So I pulled into a canter and rejoined my troop.' A few moments later a Dervish suddenly sprang up in the midst of the troop. 'How he got there,' Churchill later wrote, 'I do not know. He must have leapt out of some scrub or hole. All the troopers turned upon him with their lances: but he darted to and fro causing for the moment a frantic commotion. Wounded several times, he staggered towards me raising his spear. I shot him at less than a yard. He fell on the sand and lay there dead.'

Churchill re-formed his troop, collecting fifteen of them. They might, he told them, have to charge again, and perhaps once more after that. Hearing this, one of them called out, 'All right Sir – we're ready – as many times as you like.' When Churchill asked a sergeant 'if he had enjoyed himself' the man replied, 'Well, I don't exactly say I enjoyed it Sir, but I think I'll get more used to it next time.' Reflecting two weeks later on these comments, Churchill told Hamilton, 'My faith in our race & blood was much strengthened.' As for himself, 'I did not distinguish myself in any way, although as my composure was undisturbed, my vanity is of course increased.'

It was 9.15. The Dervish forces were in retreat. Churchill was anxious for the Regiment to charge again. 'Never were soldiers more willing,' he wrote to his mother two weeks later. 'I told my troop they were the finest men in the world and I am sure they would have followed me as far as I would have gone, and that – I may tell you and you only – was a very long way – for my soul becomes very high in such moments.' Churchill tried to persuade the adjutant to order a second charge. 'Another fifty or sixty casualties would have made the performance historic,' he told his mother. But as the discussion about a second charge continued, he later wrote, there came from the direction of the continuing infantry struggle, 'a succession of grisly apparitions; horses spouting blood, struggling on three legs, men bleeding from terrible wounds, fish-hook spears stuck right through them, arms and faces cut to pieces, bowels protruding, men gasping, crying, collapsing, expiring'. There was to be no further cavalry charge. 'The blood of our leaders had cooled,' he told his mother, 'and the regiment was handled with rare caution for the rest of the day.'

Churchill still felt that more action ought to have been ordered. A renewed charge, he told Hamilton, 'would have been a very fine performance and men and officers could easily have done it while they were warm. But the dismounted fire was more useful, though I would have liked the charge – "*pour la gloire*" – and to buck up British cavalry.' But even his own ardour diminished. 'We all got a little cold an hour afterwards,' he told Hamilton, 'and I was quite relieved to see that "heroics" were "off" for the day at least.'

The Lancers now rode forward to a spot where they could dismount and fire their rifles at the Dervish flank. After a few minutes of intense firing the Dervish troops withdrew. The Lancers then returned to the very ravine into which they had earlier charged. Here they halted for breakfast. In the ravine, Churchill later recalled, were thirty or forty Dervish dead. 'Among these lay the bodies of over twenty Lancers, so hacked and mutilated as to be mostly unrecognisable.'

That morning, as the infantry advanced in triumph towards Khartoum, thousands of wounded Dervishes were killed by the victorious troops. Churchill took no part in this destruction, and was appalled by it. 'The victory at Omdurman,' he later told his mother, 'was disgraced by the inhuman slaughter of the wounded', and that 'Kitchener was responsible'.

From Khartoum, Churchill was able to send a three-word telegram to his mother, 'All right. Winston.' That same evening an officer friend of his mother telegraphed to her: 'Big fight. Fine sight. Winston well.' In a letter to his mother two days after the cavalry charge, Churchill wrote, 'I never felt the slightest nervousness and felt as cool as I do now.' The charge itself 'was nothing like as alarming as the retirement on the 16th of Sept last year. It passed like a dream and some part I cannot quite recall. The Dervishes showed no fear of cavalry and would not move unless you knocked them over with the horse. They tried to hamstring the horses, to cut the bridles, reins – slashed and stabbed in all directions and fired rifles at a few feet range. Nothing touched me. I destroyed those who molested me and so passed out without any disturbance of body or mind.'

Robert Grenfell, whom Churchill had befriended on the journey from Cairo, was the one officer killed in the charge. 'This,' Churchill told his mother, 'took the pleasure and exultation out of the whole affair, as far as I was concerned.' Two other friends had been wounded. Hubert Howard had been killed. 'He had ridden out our charge unhurt and it was indeed the irony of fate to kill him with a friendly shell.' These things had made

him 'anxious and worried' during the night of September 2, 'and I specu-
lated on the shoddiness of war. You cannot gild it. The raw comes
through.'

That night, realising that with Howard killed and a second correspondent wounded *The Times* had no one to report on the battle, Churchill went
to Army Headquarters and asked a friend there, Colonel Wingate, if he
could send a telegram. Wingate agreed, whereupon Churchill wrote out,
in the name of the correspondent of *The Times* in Cairo, a long descriptive
telegram on the action and the cavalry charge. Although the telegram was
passed by the censor, Kitchener refused to allow it to be sent. 'No doubt,'
Churchill wrote to the editor of *The Times* two weeks later, Kitchener
'would have refused to allow any military officer to act as a newspaper
correspondent – but no military officer with more satisfaction than myself.'

Two days after the battle Churchill rode from Khartoum to the battlefield. 'I hope to get some spears etc,' he wrote to his mother, and he added,
'I shall write a history of this war.' His battlefield visit proved a searing
experience. More than ten thousand Dervishes had been killed, and a
further fifteen thousand wounded. The badly wounded Dervishes had
been left on the battlefield to die. The scenes were horrific; Churchill saw
hundreds of badly wounded men who had crawled for three days to the
banks of the Nile, and then died at the water's edge, or lay desperately
wounded in the scrub. After describing the scenes in his book *The River
War*, he wrote: 'It may be that the Gods forbad vengeance to man because
they reserved for themselves so intoxicating a drink. But the cup should
not be drained to the bottom. The dregs are often filthy-tasting.'

In his book Churchill was particularly outspoken in his criticism of
Kitchener. With regard to the killing of wounded Dervish soldiers, he
wrote, 'The stern and unpitying spirit of the commander was communicated to his troops, and the victories which marked the progress of the
River War were accompanied by acts of barbarity not always justified even
by the harsh customs of savage conflicts or the fierce and treacherous
nature of the Dervish.' While in Khartoum, Churchill visited the ruins of
its most sacred building, the Mahdi's Tomb. 'By Sir H. Kitchener's orders,'
he wrote in *The River War*, 'the Tomb has been profaned and razed to the
ground. The corpse of the Mahdi was dug up. The head was separated
from the body, and, to quote the official explanation, "preserved for
future disposal" – a phrase which must in this case be understood to mean,
that it was passed from hand to hand till it reached Cairo.'

In a passage that was greatly to anger Kitchener, Churchill added: 'If
the people of the Sudan cared no more for the Mahdi, then it was an act
of vandalism and folly to destroy the only fine building which might attract

the traveller and interest the historian. It is a gloomy augury for the future of the Sudan that the first action of its civilised conquerors and present ruler should have been to level the one pinnacle which rose above the mud houses. If, on the other hand, the people of the Sudan still venerated the memory of the Mahdi – and more than 50,000 had fought hard only a week before to assert their respect and belief – then I shall not hesitate to declare that to destroy what was sacred and holy to them was a wicked act, of which the true Christian, no less than the philosopher, must express his abhorrence.'

Churchill's outspokenness was to gain him enemies at every stage of his career, but his character had made a favourable impression on one of his fellow-officers, Captain Frank Henry Eadon, who wrote in a letter home that week, 'He is a nice cheery lad and I like him a good deal and I think he has inherited some of his father's abilities.'

As he prepared to leave Khartoum, Churchill learned that a badly wounded fellow-officer, Richard Molyneux, was in urgent need of a skin graft. He immediately offered a piece of his own skin, which was cut from his chest. 'It hurt like the devil,' he later recalled. Forty-seven years later Molyneux wrote to Churchill, who was then Prime Minister, 'I never mention and always conceal it, for fear people might think I was bucking.' Churchill replied: 'Thank you so much dear Dick. I often think of those old days, and I should like to feel that you showed that bit of pelt. I have frequently shown the gap from which it was taken.'

Impatient to get back to London, Churchill was angered, he told his mother, that in a show of 'petty spite' Kitchener instructed him to take transport back 'by long slow marches' to Atbara. He then reflected: 'What does it matter? It is enough to be alive and to have the game of life before one.' Travelling southward, he was handed a telegram from the editor of *The Times*, asking him to act as correspondent for the paper 'at the front'. It was now too late, he replied, but he was 'sensible of the compliment you have paid me'. On the journey south he also read of an imminent British naval action off Crete, where several hundred Greek Christians had been massacred by the Turks. Once again he thought of altering his plans in order to witness, and report from, the new scene of action. 'When Fortune is in the giving mood,' he told his mother, 'one must back one's luck.'

It was the death of Hubert Howard that provoked Churchill's most solemn reflections in his letters home. Howard had been such a 'hard looking, veteran type,' he wrote to Lady Randolph. 'I can see him without much effort of imagination giving you the full details of the death of your – very youthful looking son.' Churchill added: '*Au revoir* my dearest. The picture is better as it is, better for you & for me, and who shall say it shall not be better for the Empire.'

The Crete crisis passed, as it had done earlier, too quickly for Churchill to take advantage of it. He returned to London. 'I cannot help feeling,' wrote the Prince of Wales, 'that Parliamentary & literary life is what would suit you best, as the monotony of military life in an Indian station can have no attraction for you.' After his return Churchill spoke in public at Rotherhithe in London, and then at Dover. He had one moment at Dover, he told his mother, 'when I lost my train of thought – but I remained silent until I found it again – and I don't think it mattered'. The newspapers gave full and friendly reports of what he had said.

Churchill's finances were also improving; the *Morning Post* paid him £220 for his letters from the Sudan and he was offered £100 for the serialisation of his novel. 'Only the successful novels are serialised,' he told his mother proudly. These two sums were the equivalent of more than £13,000 in 1990.

Rumours of Churchill's imminent entry into politics abounded. At the beginning of November an article in the *World* stated that he was leaving the Army to become secretary to the Under-Secretary of State for War, George Wyndham, and would 'come into Parliament as soon as he can'. The article continued, 'He is sure to do well; he has great ambition, great aplomb, and an unlimited amount of energy; and he has a great deal of his father's ability, besides being a good speaker.'

Churchill had now to return to India, to his regiment. Before leaving he saw a certain amount of Pamela Plowden, the girl who had so attracted him in Hyderabad. She was right, he wrote to her at the end of November, to warn him that he made 'unnecessary enemies'. But she was wrong to say that he was 'incapable of affection', and he continued: 'I love one above all others. And I shall be constant. I am no fickle gallant, capriciously following the fancy of the hour. My love is deep and strong. Nothing will ever change it. I might it is true divide it. But the greater part would remain true – will remain true till death.' Who, he went on to ask, was 'this that I love? Listen – as the French say – over the page I will tell you.' And over the page he wrote, 'Yours very sincerely, Winston S. Churchill'.

Immediately after his twenty-fourth birthday Churchill left London for India. 'I hated the Channel passage worse than a flogging,' he told his mother, 'and was ill & wretched.' Crossing Europe by train, he boarded ship at Brindisi. 'The *Osiris* does not sail till midnight,' he wrote to his Aunt Leonie on December 2, 'but I fear that I shall be ill shortly afterwards. I hate the sea and have a constitutional aversion to travel. Hence my fate'. Once the *Osiris* was on its way he wrote to Jack: 'The ship is a witch. Even the captain was sick. Never will I leave England on a sentimental cruise again.'

Churchill had decided to leave the Army within six months and to enter politics. 'I wonder whether Aylesbury would have suited,' he wrote to his mother from Bangalore. 'They asked me to address their annual dinner this month.' He was spending most of his time writing his new book. It would be in two volumes. 'I am rather low spirited today,' he wrote to his mother on December 29, 'having worked all the morning and made no progress at all. However it comes by fits and starts – though I continually persevere.' He added: 'I do not feel as vigorous here as in England. A great stagnation of thought – a diminution of energy oppresses me.' In its account of Kitchener's part, he told his mother, the book 'grows rather in bitterness'. His former Commander-in-Chief, he added, was 'a vulgar common man, without much of the non-brutal elements in his composition.'

Writing a book, Churchill told his cousin Ivor Guest, was like living 'in a strange world bounded on the north by the Preface and on the south by the Appendix & whose natural features consist of chapters & paragraphs'. He did not think the book would bring him many friends, but, he reflected, 'friends of the cheap & worthless every-day variety are not of very great importance. And after all, in writing the great thing is to be honest.'

Churchill went on to warn his cousin not to become too closely identified, as he seemed to be, with the anti-Catholic and 'anti-ritual' forces in religion. 'I deprecate all Romish practices,' he explained, 'and prefer those of Protestantism, because I believe that the Reformed Church is less deeply sunk in the mire of dogma than the Oriental Establishment.' Protestantism was 'at any rate, a step nearer Reason'. But at the same time, Churchill added: 'I can see a poor parish – working men living their lives in ugly white-washed factories, toiling day after day amid scenes & surroundings destitute of the element of beauty. I can sympathise with them for their aching longing for something not infected by the general squalor & something to gratify their love of the mystic, something a little nearer to the "all-beautiful" – and I find it hard to rob their lives of this one ennobling aspiration – even though it finds expression in the burning of incense, the wearing of certain robes and other superstitious practices.'

Churchill went on to warn his cousin 'that people who think much of the next world rarely prosper in this: that men must use their minds and not kill their doubts by sensuous pleasures: that superstitious faith in nations rarely promotes their industry; that, in a phrase, Catholicism – all religion if you like, but particularly Catholicism – is a delicious narcotic. It may soothe our pains and chase our worries, but it checks our growth and saps our strength. And since the improvement of the British breed is my political aim in life, I would not permit too great indulgence if I could prevent it without assailing another great principle – Liberty'.

From India, at the beginning of 1899, Churchill sent his mother a copy of a passage which he had written for his new book. It was about the Dervish leader, the Mahdi, who had been left an orphan while still young. 'Solitary trees,' Churchill wrote, 'if they grow at all, grow strong: and a boy deprived of a father's care often develops, if he escape the perils of youth, an independence and a vigour of thought which may restore in after life the heavy loss of early years.'

Churchill also wrote to his mother about British politics. After telling her that Chamberlain was 'losing ground a good deal' he added: 'I feel it instinctively. I know I am right. I have got instinct in these things. Inherited probably.' That February he received a letter from Robert Ascroft, the Member of Parliament for Oldham, a constituency that returned two members to Westminster. Ascroft asked Churchill to stand with him at the next General Election in place of the other Conservative member, who was expected to retire through ill-health. Churchill accepted. His ambition to enter Parliament was a step nearer fulfilment. A month later he fulfilled his final Indian ambition, playing in the Inter-Regimental Polo Tournament, and doing so with a dislocated shoulder which had to be strapped to his side for each of the matches.

Churchill's team won; of its four members, Albert Savory was to be killed in action in the Boer War, Reginald Barnes was to reach the rank of General, and Reginald Hoare that of Brigadier, both of them living to see Churchill become Prime Minister.

In the third week of March, Churchill left India for London, never again to set foot on the sub-continent. He was confident that he had done the right thing in giving up soldiering. 'Had the army been a source of income to me instead of a channel of expenditure,' he wrote to his Marlborough grandmother on the voyage home, 'I might have felt compelled to stick to it. But I can live cheaper & earn more as a writer, special correspondent or journalist: and this work is moreover more congenial and more likely to assist me in pursuing the larger ends of life.' It had nevertheless been 'a great wrench' and he was 'very sorry to leave all my friends & put on my uniform & medals for the last time'.

On his way back to England, Churchill stopped for two weeks in Egypt, working on his book and talking to those who could help him with facts and background. The opportunity of making the book 'a standard work on the war, instead of a breezy and satirical criticism', he told his mother, 'is too good to be passed over'. While he was in Cairo the British Agent, Lord Cromer, had three long talks with him, each lasting for more than an hour and a half, guiding him with regard to events going back to the loss of the Sudan and the death of Gordon. He also introduced Churchill to the Khedive of Egypt, Abbas Hilmi, *'de jure* ruler of Egypt', whose attitude, Churchill told his mother, 'reminded me of a school-boy who is brought to see another school-boy in the presence of the headmaster.'

The letters which Churchill sent his mother from Cairo that April were dictated. 'I rather like these dictated letters,' he told her in a handwritten postscript: 'They are very simple & natural and I think it is good practice in talking fluently. I gave this to a stenographer as fast as she could take it down and it runs quite smoothly.'

In mid-April Churchill was back in London. Shortly after his return, his Marlborough grandmother died. But he did not allow the period of family mourning to impede his new-found political activities. 'I do not consider myself prevented from attending public meetings next month,' he wrote to Robert Ascroft at Oldham a week after the Dowager Duchess's death. Not only did Churchill speak at Oldham but also at Paddington and Cardiff. On May 2, at a private dinner where both Asquith and Balfour were present, Balfour, Churchill told his mother, 'was markedly civil to me, I thought – agreed with and paid great attention to everything I said'.

Churchill expected to stand for Oldham at the next General Election, presumably in a year or more's time. But on June 19 Ascroft died and a by-election was called. Six days later Churchill issued his election address. He was, he said, a Conservative and also a Tory Democrat. 'I regard the improvement of the condition of the British people as the main end of modern government.' If elected he would promote legislation which, 'without impairing that tremendous energy of production on which the wealth of the nation and the good of the people depend, may yet raise the standard of comfort and happiness in English homes'. He would seek 'better provision for the aged poor' through legislation 'as wide and generous as possible'. He would oppose Home Rule, 'that odious measure'. As to the liquor traffic, while he supported 'voluntary temperance', he was opposed to 'compulsory abstinence' through the withholding of public house licences. In foreign policy he would follow Salisbury's lead in maintaining 'command of the seas' and preserving the frontiers of Empire from aggression.

Electioneering was hectic, 'I am getting on very well,' Churchill wrote to his cousin Sunny early in the campaign, 'and scoring off all the people who ask me questions.' However Radical the audience 'I am always received with the greatest enthusiasm, but at the same time, the tide is running strongly against the Tory Party and my private impression is that we shall be beaten.' Conservative Central Office, he told his mother, 'sent stupid, bad speakers from London and the Liberals are much better at placarding & pushing their propaganda'.

In the last week of the campaign Churchill spoke up to eight times a day. 'I now make speeches involuntarily,' he told Pamela Plowden. Whatever the result might be 'I shall never forget the succession of great halls packed with excited people until there was not room for one single person more – speech after speech – meeting after meeting – three even four in one night – intermittent flashes of Heat & Light & enthusiasm – with cold air and the rattle of a carriage in between.' His speeches improved every time he spoke, Churchill told Pamela. 'I have hardly repeated myself at all. And at each meeting I am conscious of growing powers – and facilities of speech.' It was in this that he would find consolation should the result be, 'as is probable – unfortunate'.

The votes were counted on July 6. 'As for Mr Churchill,' the *Manchester Courier* reported, 'he looked upon the process of counting with amusement. A smile lit up his features, and the result of the election did not disturb him.' Churchill and his fellow-Conservative had been defeated, but the result had been particularly close. The two Liberal candidates received 12,976 and 12,770 votes respectively. Churchill won 11,477 and his running mate, a local trade unionist, 11,449. His attempt to enter Parliament had been watched by all those at the centre of British politics. 'Winston made a splendid fight, but the Borough bears a bad name for fickleness,' the Prime Minister, Lord Salisbury wrote to Lady Randolph, who also received a letter from Asquith, the Liberal under whom her son was to reach high office. 'Winston's good fight at Oldham,' he wrote, 'gives him his spurs.'

Balfour, Churchill's future Party leader, and later opponent, wrote to him of how much he had looked forward to seeing him in the House 'where your father & I fought many a good battle side by side in days gone by'. Balfour added, 'Never mind – it will all come right; and this small reverse will have no permanent ill-effect upon your political fortunes.' Defeat was not without one positive result. 'I speak now however quite easily without preparation,' Churchill told a friend, 'which is a new weapon that will not wear out.'

That autumn Lord Salisbury agreed to allow Churchill to dedicate his new book to him. 'I have not forgotten your kindness,' Churchill wrote, 'in helping me to take part in the final campaign.' When he wrote this letter, on August 9, Churchill had no further fighting in prospect. But a month later, in a letter to a Birmingham politician who had asked him to speak in the city, he wrote, 'I expect there will be war in the Transvaal in November and if so I shall go as a special correspondent.' This letter was dated September 13. Five days later Churchill received a telegram from the *Daily Mail* asking him to go as their correspondent to South Africa. He at once sent a telegram of his own to his friend Oliver Borthwick at the *Morning Post*, telling him of the *Daily Mail* offer and offering his services to the *Morning Post* for four months for £1,000 'from shore to shore' with all expenses paid, the equivalent of more than £40,000 in the money values of 1990. His terms were accepted.

Chamberlain agreed to give Churchill a letter of introduction to Sir Alfred Milner, British High Commissioner at the Cape, who was determined to end the independence of the two Boer Republics, the Transvaal and the Orange Free State. Negotiations between Milner and the Republics dragged on with no sign of compromise on either side; war between Briton and Boer seemed imminent. On October 2 Churchill wrote to his mother, 'my time is busy with preparations for departure'. One extraordinarily innovative plan he had was to take to South Africa a film camera and its operator, and to make a film of the war. For that he estimated £700 would be needed. A young MP, Murray Guthrie, a relative by marriage, was willing to put up half the sum.

On October 6, Churchill drafted a formal application to join a British Yeomanry Regiment. In a covering letter he asked for his application to be 'pushed through as quickly as possible, as I sail for South Africa on the 14th and it is of some importance to me to have the status of an officer before the war begins'. In the event he did not send this letter, having learned that it would be easier to obtain a yeomanry commission in South Africa itself, where one of his father's friends was Adjutant of the 9th Yeomanry Brigade. But he was first to see action there, not as an officer but as a journalist. That same day, October 6, he paid for the repair of his telescope and field-glasses, and bought a compass. He also arranged for the despatch to the boat of eighteen bottles of whisky and twelve bottles of lime juice.

A Boer ultimatum to Britain, to withdraw all British troops from the territory of the two Republics, was sent on October 9. It expired, unanswered, two days later. The first shots of the war were fired on October 12. That day Churchill travelled to Oldham for a last public meeting. His aim was still to defeat the two Liberal MPs at the next election, whenever that election might be. Back in London two days later he learned that an American film company had already sent out a film camera to South Africa. Later that day he left by train for Southampton. During the train journey he wrote to Guthrie that he still had hopes about their film scheme. 'I have no doubt that, barring accidents, I can obtain some very strange pictures.' But the American competition proved too great a commercial risk, Churchill's fear being, he told Guthrie, that 'all the theatres will be pledged to the American company'.

Early that evening, accompanied by his father's former manservant, Thomas Walden, Churchill sailed from Southampton for Cape Town. His third war in scarcely more than two years was about to begin.

7

South Africa : Adventure, Capture, Escape

The *Dunottar Castle*, with General Buller and his Staff on board, as well as the newspaper correspondents, reached Cape Town on 31 October 1899, ~ 25 after a seventeen-day voyage. On arrival, Churchill went to see the British High Commissioner, Sir Alfred Milner, who told him that the Boers had put into the field 'far greater numbers than were expected', and that the whole of Cape Colony was 'trembling on the verge of rebellion'.

That evening Churchill took the night train from Cape Town with a fellow-correspondent, John Atkins. Their aim was to get, by train, ship and train, to Ladysmith, then under threat of capture by the Boers. On reaching Beaufort West the next day they learned of the surrender near Ladysmith of 1,200 British soldiers. This made speed all the more urgent; on reaching De Aar they caught the very last train to leave the town for East London on the Indian Ocean. The Boer advance towards De Aar had just begun; at one point on their journey Churchill learned that the Boers were only twenty-five miles away.

'We have greatly underestimated the strength and spirit of the Boers,' Churchill wrote to his mother on November 3 as the train drew near to East London. But he was in good spirits, telling her that as a result of catching the last train from De Aar 'we have gained four days on all other correspondents'. Churchill added, 'I believe I am to be preserved for future things.'

As soon as their train reached East London, Churchill and Atkins made haste to get as quickly as possible to Durban, intent on proceeding from Durban to Ladysmith by rail. 'We joined a tiny coastal vessel and had a gruelling passage,' Atkins later recalled, 'both of us being very sick.' Reaching Durban at midnight on November 4, Churchill was shocked to find Reginald Barnes on board a hospital ship, having been shot through

the groin in one of the first battles. He also learned at Durban that
Ladysmith was cut off, that Sir George White and his troops were inside
the town, and that General Buller, although ordered to relieve Ladysmith
as soon as possible, would not reach Durban for three days.

Buller would need several more days before all his stores would be ready
for the move up the railway line. Churchill and Atkins decided to proceed
alone. Their first step, on the morning of November 5, was to take the
morning train to Pietermaritzburg, sixty miles and four hours away.
There, however, they found that the line northward was no longer operating. Ever resourceful, Churchill hired a special train and instructed its
driver to proceed as near to Ladysmith as possible. On reaching Colenso,
a few miles short of Ladysmith on the south bank of the Tugela River, they
found that the railway line to the north was cut. 'The Boers were across it,'
Atkins later recalled. Ladysmith was besieged.

'We scurried out of Colenso,' Churchill wrote to Sir Evelyn Wood,
'cornered by a 12-pounder gun.' The correspondents then returned to
Estcourt, a station further down the line, guarded by two battalions of
British troops in what Churchill described to Wood as 'an untenable cup
in the hills'.

'We pitched our tents in the railway yard at Estcourt,' Atkins wrote. 'We
had found a good cook and we had some good wine. We entertained
friends every evening, to our pleasure and professional advantage and,
we believed, to their satisfaction.' Churchill was critical of the British
military authorities in South Africa. 'It is astonishing how we have under-
rated these people,' he wrote to Sir Evelyn Wood from Estcourt. He was
also critical of the British forces engaged in the fighting. The Boers had
captured twice as many soldiers as they had hit, 'not a very pretty proportion. I think we ought to punish people who surrender troops under their
command.'

On November 6 *The River War* was published in London. Two days later
Churchill returned to the outskirts of Colenso, travelling as a passenger
on a special armoured train which the Army had devised. The train was
made up, from front to back, of a gun truck, with a nine-inch naval gun
and sailors to operate it, an armoured truck with troops, an engine, a
tender, two further armoured trucks with troops, and a breakdown gang
truck with a platelaying gang to repair any destroyed rails.

Reaching Chieveley, those on the train could see the balloon which the
soldiers besieged in Ladysmith had put up in order to spot any Boer attack.
The train then continued to within half a mile of Colenso, where, on foot,
Churchill followed an officer and a sergeant to the deserted British
trenches on the outskirts of the town, and then into the town itself. There
were no Boers anywhere. At one end of the town, Churchill wrote in his

despatch to the *Morning Post* that evening, a few natives, 'alarmed at the aspect of the train, waved a white rag on a stick steadily to and fro'. The train continued a little way further northward, to where, as it approached the bridge over the Tugela, the line had been cut. It then returned to Estcourt without incident.

On November 9, not by the train but riding with the British troops, Churchill returned to the outskirts of Colenso. He and Atkins then rode to a hilltop to look across the Tugela. As they stood silhouetted against the skyline, they were surrounded by armed horsemen. 'Got you, I think,' said one of them; fortunately he was a British sergeant. The journalists produced their passes and the crisis was over. 'The sergeant looked disappointed,' Churchill reported to the *Morning Post*, 'but was appeased by being photographed "for the London papers".'

After riding back to Estcourt, Churchill wrote to Evelyn Wood, 'I have been afraid to ride through the lines, although it has been done – so I down my heels pending the arrival of an army to clear the way.' Ladysmith was 'blocked completely' and the British cavalry shut up inside it. Even the railway line was vulnerable. If the Boer General, Joubert, decided to leave the security of the Boer line on the Tugela River and advance on Estcourt, 'we must fly'.

The officer commanding the troops at Estcourt, fearing he could not hold the position there in the event of a Boer attack, decided to pull his troops back towards Pietermaritzburg. On the night of the planned withdrawal he was dining with Churchill and Atkins in their tent while, Atkins later recalled, 'the clang of field guns being loaded into trucks went on unceasingly'. Churchill was convinced that no withdrawal was necessary. 'As dinner proceeded,' Atkins wrote, 'Winston, with an assurance which I partly envied and partly deprecated, argued that Joubert was probably too cautious to advance yet; that he was no doubt delighted with the security of the Tugela River; that it would be a pity to point the way to Maritzburg, and so on.'

The dinner came to an end and the officer left. Shortly afterwards, Atkins noted, 'the clanging in the trucks, which had ceased, began again. The trucks were being unloaded. Winston gleamed. "I did that!" he said; but added gracefully, "*We* did that!" Whether he did it or not we shall never know. The officer may have acted on fresh information. At least Winston's effort was singular for persuasive reasoning.'

On his ninth day at Estcourt, Churchill's friend from the Indian frontier, Captain Aylmer Haldane, was ordered to take the train out at first light on November 15 to reconnoitre once more in the direction of Colenso. In his official report, Haldane wrote that, on receiving his orders and leaving the military office, 'I noticed Churchill, who, as well as some other correspondents, was hanging about to pick up such crumbs of information for his newspaper as might be available.' Haldane told Churchill what he had been ordered to do and 'aware that he had been out in the train and knew something of the country through which it was wont to travel, suggested that he might care to accompany me the next day'.

Churchill hesitated at first. He had made that particular journey twice already, but in the end he agreed to go. It was to be one of the most fateful days of his life. The armoured train, with 150 men on board, left Estcourt at 5.10 in the morning, in the direction of Colenso. An hour and ten minutes later it reached Frere station. 'No enemy had been seen,' Haldane reported back to Estcourt. After a fifteen-minute halt, therefore, he ordered the train to proceed to Chieveley, which it reached at 7.10. There it was learned that Boer troops had been in Chieveley during the night.

A message from Estcourt now warned Haldane that about fifty Boers had been seen to the west of the railway, moving south. He was therefore to 'remain at Frere in observation, watching your safe retreat'. He at once reversed the train out of Chieveley towards Frere. Then, as he later wrote, 'on rounding the spur of a hill which commanded the line, the enemy opened on us at 600 yards with artillery, one shell striking the leading truck'.

The engine driver, Charles Wagner, hoping to run past the ambush, put on full steam. The train ran down the gradient at full speed. Three quarters of a mile from Frere, as it reached level ground, the breakdown gang truck and the two armoured trucks, which were now in front of the engine, were derailed. A large stone had been placed on the line by the Boers after the train had passed by on its way to Chieveley.

As a result of the derailment, one of the armoured trucks now straddled the line. Churchill, who was with Haldane in the armoured truck next to the gun truck, 'immediately offered me his services,' Haldane wrote, 'and knowing how thoroughly I could rely on him, I gladly accepted them, and undertook to keep down the enemy's fire while he endeavoured to clear the line.'

Leaving the armoured truck, Churchill went to the three derailed trucks and began to organise the men to push them off the track. This was done with the help of the engine-driver, whom Churchill instructed to move the engine to and fro along the track, butting at the wreckage and gradually pushing it clear. Then Wagner was wounded in the head by a shell fragment. Later he was to tell Churchill's valet, Walden, that on being hit he turned to Churchill with the words, 'I'm finished,' to which Churchill replied, 'Buck u₁ bit, I will stick to you.'

'I feared he would not work his engine any more,' Churchill wrote to the Prince of Wales two weeks later. 'But when I promised him that if he did so, he should be mentioned for distinguished gallantry in action, he pulled himself together and under my directions returned to his post.' As Churchill, the engine-driver and the soldiers worked at their difficult task, the British naval gun opened fire on the Boers. After firing four rounds it was struck by a Boer shell and knocked over. Haldane then ordered the gun crew into the safety of the armoured truck, from where, he reported, 'a continuous fire was kept up on the enemy's guns, considerably disconcerting their aim'.

Two Boers were killed by the fire from the armoured truck. Meanwhile, at the track, Churchill continued to direct efforts to right the three derailed wagons, as rifle, artillery and Maxim-gun fire was directed against him, the engine and the soldiers. Four soldiers were killed and thirty wounded. Churchill later learned from the commandant of the Boer artillery that the three heavy artillery guns averaged thirty rounds per gun per minute. 'When you reflect,' he told the Prince of Wales in his letter of two weeks later, 'that the range was only 900 & 1,300 yards, you may imagine the pounding we had and what an astonishing din the great projectiles exploding and crashing among the iron trucks made.'

'For an hour,' Haldane wrote in his official report, 'efforts to clear the line were unsuccessful, as the trucks were heavy and jammed together, and the break-down gang could not be found,' but Churchill 'with indomitable perseverance, continued his difficult task'. He was the man 'mainly responsible' for trying to get the engine clear of the derailed trucks. While working at this task 'he was frequently exposed to the full fire of the enemy. I cannot speak too highly of his gallant conduct'.

One of the soldiers with the armoured train, Private Walls, wrote a month later to his sister, who sent the letter to Lady Randolph: 'Churchill is a splendid fellow. He walked about in it all as coolly as if nothing was going on, & called for volunteers to give him a hand to get the truck out of the road. His presence and way of going on were as much good as fifty men would have been.'

Churchill's efforts were successful. At about 8.30 a.m. the engine was able to force its way past the obstructing truck, which, however, then fell forward again some inches across the line. The engine was past the obstruction. Churchill thereupon directed Wagner to steam back to the rear trucks which were still on the line, intending to hook them on to the engine and take the majority of the men back to Frere. But the coupling had been damaged by a Boer shell and could not be used. Churchill then 'threw off his revolver and field glasses', Wagner reported, 'and helped the engine-driver pick twenty wounded up and put them on the tender of the engine'. Wagner watched as Churchill brought the wounded to the engine. 'He was as cool as anything,' he told Churchill's valet a few days later, 'and worked like a nigger, and how he escaped he doesn't know, as about fifty shells hit the engine.'

Once the wounded were on the engine Churchill directed Wagner, whom later he was to recommend for an Albert Medal, to drive the engine and its tender slowly towards Frere. As they proceeded, several more wounded men were seen. Churchill managed to get them on board. His conduct, one officer told the *Natal Witness* two days later, was that 'of as brave a man as could be found'.

With its cab and tender crowded with the wounded, the engine returned towards Frere. Churchill went with it. 'After the engine got clear,' Private Walls told his sister, 'he came about half a mile on it and then coolly got off & walked back to help the others.' Having assured himself that Wagner and the other wounded men would be taken care of, Churchill returned on foot in the direction of the scene of the derailment, to 'look after Captain Haldane', Walden told Lady Randolph. Haldane, meanwhile, was hoping to get his fifty men to a nearby farmhouse and to continue fighting the Boers from there. But even as he gave the order, two British soldiers standing two hundred yards from the train held up white handkerchiefs. At this signal of surrender the Boers stopped firing and rode up.

It was 8.50 in the morning. Haldane had no option but to surrender with his men. At that moment Churchill was still walking back along the line to the scene of the derailment. He was never to reach it. After walking about two hundred yards he thought he saw two of the platelayers. He was wrong, the two men were Boers, who immediately pointed their rifles at him. He turned and ran back along the railway line towards the engine, 'the two Boers firing', he later recalled, 'as I ran between the metals. Their bullets, sucking to right and left, seemed to miss only by inches'.

Churchill was in a cutting some six foot deep. Its banks gave him no cover. The two Boers were aiming their rifles again. 'Movement seemed the only chance. Again I darted forward: again two soft kisses sucked in the air; but nothing struck me.' He tried to leave the cutting, clambered up the bank, and crawled through the wire fence at the top. There, he found a tiny hollow, and crouched for cover, 'struggling to get my breath again'. Looking up, he saw that he was only two hundred yards from a deep river gorge. 'There was plenty of cover there,' he later recalled. He therefore rose from his hollow, determined to make a dash for the gorge. Suddenly he saw a horseman galloping 'furiously' towards him.

When the mounted Boer and the crouching Briton were forty yards apart, the Boer, Field Cornet Oosthuizen, reined in his horse and shouted something Churchill did not understand. 'I thought I would kill this man,' he later recalled, 'and after the treatment I had received I earnestly desired to do so.'

Churchill put his hand to his belt, feeling for his pistol. It was not there. In his effort to help the engine-driver after the derailment he had taken it off and put it on the engine. It was now back at Frere. The Boer horseman was now pointing his rifle at him, looking at him through the sights. Churchill held up his hands. He was a prisoner.

Those soldiers who were safe at Frere spoke warmly in praise of Churchill, whose bravery at the scene of the derailment made headlines everywhere. Cartoonists vied with each other in portraying how he had helped to right the engine. Many newspapers suggested that he would be recommended for the Victoria Cross. From Pietermaritzburg, Walden wrote to Lady Randolph, 'I am sorry to say Mr Churchill is a prisoner, but I am almost certain he is not wounded.' Walden was in Pietermaritzburg, he explained, 'to bring all his kit until Mr Winston gets free'. Every officer in Estcourt, he added, 'thinks Mr C and the engine-driver will get the VC.'

It was not yet ten in the morning. At the scene of the derailment the prisoners were rounded up 'like cattle!' Churchill later told Atkins. 'The greatest indignity of my life!' He was then led, he wrote in one of his newspaper articles five months later, 'a miserable captive, casting longing eyes at the Ladysmith balloon, and vigilantly guarded by the Boer mounted escort'. The prisoners were marched for two days across country to Modderspruit, a small station on the railway to Pretoria. While waiting for a train, Churchill handed over his credentials as a Press correspondent and asked that they might be forwarded 'to the proper authority'. He was then locked in the ticket office.

The train journey to Pretoria took nearly twenty-four hours. Once in the Boer capital the officers were taken to the States Model School building near the centre of the town, which had been requisitioned to serve as a prisoner-of-war camp. 'As I was quite unarmed and in possession of my full credentials as a Press correspondent,' Churchill wrote to his mother from the prison three days after his capture, 'I do not imagine they will keep me.' He was wrong; the Boers had no intention of letting him go. General Joubert, in a telegram to the Boer State Secretary, pointed out that although Churchill claimed he was 'only a newspaper correspondent', yet from the newspaper accounts of the action 'it appears entirely otherwise and it is for this reason that I urge you that he must be guarded and watched as dangerous for our war; otherwise he can still do us a lot of harm. In other words he must not be released during the war. It is through his active part that one section of the armoured train got away.'

Particularly galling for the Boers was their failure to capture the engine, for they had none of their own running south of Ladysmith.

After three days as a prisoner, Churchill pressed the Boer authorities to let him go, writing direct to the Secretary for War, Louis de Souza. He also sought help from home. 'I trust you will do all in your power to procure my release,' he wrote to his mother from Pretoria on November 18, commenting on his captivity, 'this is a new experience – as was the heavy shell fire'. Having received no reply to his formal request for release, on November 21 he wrote again to de Souza to ask what course was to be taken 'with regard to setting me at liberty'. He was 'naturally anxious to continue my journalistic work and I have already been detained for six days'. Surely the Boers would welcome the war being chronicled 'by one who has had the opportunity of being well treated by its citizens'.

Five days later Churchill wrote a third letter to de Souza. Once more he denied having taken an active part in the defence of the train, though 'I naturally did all I could to escape from so perilous a situation and to save my life. Indeed in this aspect my conduct was precisely that of the civilian platelayers & railway servants, who have since been released by your Government.' He offered, if released, to give 'any parole that the Transvaal Government may require'. Even though he wanted to continue his journalistic work, he would agree, if asked to do so, 'to withdraw altogether from South Africa during the war'.

No reply was made to this offer; Captain Theron, a Boer officer who was present at the action at Frere, opposed Churchill's release, telling de Souza that during the action 'Churchill called for volunteers and led them at a time when the officers were in confusion.' According to Press reports, 'he now claims that he took no part in the battle. That is all lies. He also refused to stand still until Field Cornet Oosthuizen warned him to surrender. He surrendered only when he aimed his gun at him.' Theron added that in his view Churchill was 'one of the most dangerous prisoners in our hands', not least because the Natal newspapers 'are making a big hero out of him'.

Among the members of the official board of the prison was one who took particular pleasure in insulting and goading the prisoners, Churchill included. Churchill went up to him one day and after reminding him 'that in war either side may win', asked if he was wise to place himself in a separate category 'as regards behaviour to prisoners'.

'Why?' asked the man.

'Because it might be convenient to the British Government to be able to make one or two examples,' Churchill replied. Neither he nor the others were troubled by the man again.

November 30 was Churchill's twenty-fifth birthday. He spent it in the States Model School prison, writing letters. One was to the Prince of Wales, in which he noted that the prisoners-of-war had been allowed to become members of the Transvaal State Library 'so that now, although it is irritating to be out of everything while so much is doing, I have a secure refuge and I shall hope, philosophically, to improve my education'. His thoughts, he wrote that day to Bourke Cockran, were on the 'vast combinations of capital' against which many Americans railed. Capitalism in the form of trusts and cartels, Churchill told his American friend, 'has reached a pitch of power which the old economists never contemplated and which excites my most lively terror'. Merchant princes were 'all very well, but if I have anything to say to it, their kingdom shall not be of this world'.

The new century, Churchill told Cockran, 'will witness the great war for the existence of the Individual'. Prison was 'damnably prosaic'. His body was penned up 'and all the while great matters are being settled and history made – the history, mind you, I was to have recorded. I am 25 today. It is terrible to think how little time remains!' Almost five years had passed since his father's death; the fear of dying young through some hereditary fault could not be shaken off. On December 8 he again wrote to de Souza, stressing: 'I did not fight against the Boer forces, but only assisted in clearing the line from the debris.' This was precisely what the civilian platelayers and railway staff had done. 'They have since been released.'

In this letter Churchill again offered, if released, 'to give any parole that may be required not to serve against the Republican forces or to give any information affecting the military situation'. He received no reply. Two days later he asked Haldane if he could join him in an escape plan whereby Haldane, and Sergeant-Major Brockie, who came from Johannesburg and spoke Dutch, would climb over the wall next to the latrine, into the garden of the private house behind the wall, and then leave Pretoria, hiding by day and travelling by night, walking the three hundred miles to the border of Portuguese Mozambique.

Brockie was reluctant to add a third person to the escape plan, especially one whose absence would be noticed, but Haldane agreed that Churchill should go 'as he served me so well at Chieveley'. The night chosen for the escape was December 11. That day Haldane noted in his diary, 'Churchill is in a great state of excitement and letting everyone know that he means going tonight.' During the day, news of two British military defeats seemed to give urgency to the escape. 'I passed the afternoon in positive terror,' Churchill wrote eleven days later, in his first account of that dramatic moment. 'Nothing, since my schooldays, has ever disturbed me so much as this.'

That afternoon Churchill tried to read but could not concentrate. Then he played chess 'and was hopelessly beaten'. Finally it grew dark, and at ten minutes to seven he and Haldane crossed the back yard of the building to the latrine. Brockie followed a few minutes later. The sentries, however, 'gave us no chance,' Churchill wrote. 'They did not walk about. One of them stood exactly opposite the only practicable part of the wall. We waited for two hours but the attempt was plainly impossible, and so, with a most unsatisfactory feeling of relief, to bed.'

On December 12 there was more bad news from the battlefield. 'As you remember,' Churchill wrote to Haldane nine months later, 'I was for making a desperate venture and risking the chance of detection, while you were in favour of patience and waiting night after night until the best opportunity could be secured.' During the day, Churchill told Brockie that he thought he could have got over the wall the previous night.

'Why the hell didn't you?' Brockie asked.

'Where should I have been,' Churchill replied, 'if I had got over and you had found it impossible to follow?'

'If you will ever get over,' Brockie retorted, 'we will follow all right, don't be afraid of that.'

That afternoon the tension between the three would-be escapees was considerable. Haldane wrote in his diary: 'Churchill, whose excited condition as he strode up and down the backyard was evident to his fellow-prisoners, said to me, "We must go tonight". I answered, "There are three of us to go, and we will certainly do so if the chance is favourable".'

'I was insistent,' Churchill wrote in a private account twelve years later, 'that at whatever risk, we should force the thing through that night.' The previous day he had written his fifth letter to de Souza, which he now placed under his pillow. 'I do not consider your Government was justified in holding me, a press correspondent and a non combatant, and I have therefore resolved to escape,' the letter began. In it he wrote of his 'admiration of the chivalrous and humane character of the Republican forces', and expressed the hope 'that when this most grievous and unhappy war shall have come to an end, a state of affairs may be created which shall preserve at once the national pride of the Boers and the security of the British, and put a final stop to the rivalry and enmity of both races.' His letter ended, 'Regretting that circumstances have not permitted me to bid you a personal farewell, believe me, yours very sincerely, Winston S. Churchill.'

As soon as it got dark, but before the moon had risen, Haldane and Churchill again walked over to the latrine. There, Churchill later recalled, the two men 'waited for a chance of climbing over; but after much hesitation we could not make up our minds to it, we thought it too dangerous; and came back to the verandah again'. On the verandah sat Brockie. 'He jeered,' wrote Haldane in his diary, 'and said that we were afraid and that he could go any night. I said to him, "Then go and see for yourself" '. Brockie crossed the yard to the latrine. After quite some time, as he had not emerged, Churchill said to Haldane, 'I am going across, follow me presently.' Crossing the yard, Churchill reached the entrance to the latrine. As he did so he met Brockie coming out, but, he later wrote, 'we dared not speak to each other in the presence of the sentry, and though he muttered something as he went by, I did not hear what it was'.

Churchill entered the latrine. 'I had come to the conclusion,' he later recalled, 'that we should waste the whole night in hesitations unless the matter were clinched once and for all; and as the sentry turned to light his pipe, I jumped on the ledge of the wall and in a few seconds had dropped into the garden safely on the other side. Here I crouched down and waited for the others to come.' In later years Churchill was insistent that he had expected Haldane and Brockie to come over the wall after him. 'According to our agreement, which was that I should go first and wait for the others,' he wrote to Haldane nine months later, 'I waited for half an hour and began to get very anxious.'

Waiting was agonising; 'I expected them to come every minute,' Churchill later wrote. 'My position in the garden was a very anxious one, because I had only a few small and leafless bushes to hide behind, and people kept passing to and fro, and the lights of the house were burning.' Twice, as he waited for Haldane and Brockie to join him, a man from the house came out into the garden and walked along a path within seven or eight yards of where he was crouching.

After fifteen minutes it became clear to Churchill that something had gone wrong. In fact, Haldane and Brockie had gone to the dining-room, where the evening meal had begun. In an attempt to contact them, he managed to attract the attention 'by tapping gently' of an officer who had come into the latrine, and told him to tell Haldane 'that I had succeeded in getting over, and that he must come and make the attempt to join me as soon as he could'.

After another fifteen minutes Haldane and Brockie came to the latrine. Haldane then tried to climb the wall, but at the very moment his shoulders were level with the top, the sentry turned round, challenged him, and levelled his rifle at him. Haldane was ordered back to the main building. The sentry did not suspect that an escape attempt was in progress.

Alone in the garden, Churchill waited; he had no compass, no map, no money and no medicine. He was also dependent on Brockie to be able to communicate with anyone they might meet during their three-hundred-mile walk through the Transvaal. An hour passed. Then Churchill heard tapping. It was Haldane, 'who had come to tell me that he had made his attempt and been stopped by the sentry; that the position of the sentry now made it quite impossible for him or Brockie to follow that night'.

Churchill now thought of climbing back, but as the wall on the garden side was higher than on the latrine side, and had no ledge, he could not do it without considerable noise. To walk round the front of the building and give himself up would only lead to an enquiry, and the closing of the 'loophole of escape' for the future. Still whispering to Haldane, he spoke of his position as hopeless. He would never reach the frontier undetected. 'Haldane and I discussed the situation in whispers through the chinks in the corrugated iron fence,' he later wrote. 'He quite agreed with me that it was impossible to come back, and that I must go on alone. It was a great disappointment to him to be left behind.'

'If I remember rightly,' Churchill wrote to Haldane nine months after the event, 'you offered to throw your compass over to me, but I declined, thinking it would make a noise, so you bade me good-bye.'

Churchill decided that he could never succeed on foot, alone, over such a great distance. Instead he would to try to reach the railway line that ran from Pretoria to the Portuguese port of Lourenço Marques, on the Indian Ocean, and make the journey hidden on a goods train. Leaving his hiding-place in the garden he walked straight out of the gate into the road, passing a sentry who stood in the roadway scarcely three yards from him. In bright moonlight, with electric street lights at regular intervals, he walked down the middle of the street in the direction by which he believed he could most quickly reach the railway line. Luckily, he was wearing a brown civilian jacket and trousers. 'There were many people passing in the street to and fro,' he wrote, 'but nobody spoke to me.'

Humming a tune, Churchill reached the railway line. There, he calculated that his best chance of jumping on a train would be about two hundred yards out of the station, before it had gathered speed, on an uphill gradient when it would be slowing down, and on an outward curve when he would be hidden from the view both of the engine-driver and the guard. When the train came he jumped on the coupling between two wagons. Then he clambered on to a wagon full of empty coal bags. The train moved slowly eastward through the night. Just before dawn, afraid that he might somehow be discovered once it was daylight, he jumped down from the wagon on to the ground. He was near Witbank, a small mining community sixty miles east of Pretoria. There he waited, at the side of the railway track, intent on clambering on to a train the following night and continuing to the coast. 'My sole companion,' he later wrote, 'was a gigantic vulture, who manifested an extravagant interest in my condition, and made hideous and ominous gurglings from time to time.'

As Churchill hid by the railway at Witbank, his escape was discovered in Pretoria and a considerable search was begun in the hope of catching him. His picture was circulated throughout the Transvaal together with the description, 'Englishman 25 years old, about 5 ft 8 inches tall, average build, walks with a slight stoop, pale appearance, red brown hair, almost invisible small moustache, speaks through the nose, cannot pronounce the letter "s", cannot speak Dutch, has last been seen in a brown suit of clothes.'

That night, hungry and thirsty, Churchill made his way from the railway line towards some lights, which he thought came from a native kraal which might befriend him. The lights, however, were those of a coal mine. Fearful that the man who came to the door might be hostile, Churchill asked him, 'Are you an Englishman?' The man, worried lest the stranger was a Boer spy, kept him covered with a pistol, and without answering Churchill's question, asked who he was. 'I am Dr Bentinck,' Churchill replied, 'I have fallen off the train and lost my way.'

The man ordered Churchill inside, into his dining-room, and, still covering him with the pistol, urged him to tell the truth. Hesitating at first, Churchill suddenly declared, 'I am Winston Churchill.' To his good fortune the man to whom he revealed his secret was an Englishman, John Howard, the manager of the mine. 'Thank God you have come here!' Howard exclaimed. 'It is the only house for twenty miles where you would not have been handed over, but we are all British here, and we will see you through.' That night Howard let four other men into the secret, among them his mine engineer, Dan Dewsnap. It was agreed to hide Churchill in the mine. As he was being hidden, Dewsnap, who was from Oldham, pressed his hands with the words, 'They'll all vote for you next time.'

On December 14 a two-word Reuter news agency telegram reached London, 'Churchill escaped.' In sending a copy to Lady Randolph, Oliver Borthwick wrote that 'knowing his practical turn of mind, I have no doubt that he knows what he is about, and will turn up with an extra chapter of his book finished in a few days time at some English encampment'.

Churchill remained hidden at the mine at Witbank. The Boers were searching for him everywhere and had posted a reward of £25 alive or dead. For three days he stayed deep underground in a stable recently built for the underground pit ponies. 'The mine was infested with white rats,' Howard later recalled. 'On one occasion when I paid him a surreptitious visit, I found him in absolute darkness, for the rats had commandeered his candle.' On another occasion Churchill, who had been smoking a cigar, was discovered by an African mine boy. 'When the native got the whiff,' Howard later recalled, 'he trailed it down into the stable, but as soon as he saw Mr Churchill he bolted and told the other boys there was a spook in that part of the mine. For a long time afterwards we could not get any of the boys to move in that vicinity at all.'

After three days underground, in virtual solitary confinement, Churchill was taken ill. A doctor, James Gillespie, was let into the secret, and advised that he be brought up to the surface, as he had become 'very nervy'. He was taken to a store-room on the surface, given a key and locked in. Then, on the evening of December 19, with Howard's connivance and that of a second Englishman, Charles Burnham, he left the colliery and was hidden in some bales of wool in a railway wagon Burnham was loading for despatch to the coast. With him he took a revolver, two roast chickens, some slices of cold meat, a loaf of bread, a melon and three bottles of cold tea. The revolver, a semi-automatic German Mauser, was a gift from his mining friends.

The wagon in which Churchill hid was shunted by the colliery engine, with six other wagons, from the coal mine to Witbank station. There it was linked to a train going to the coast. Burnham, who travelled on the train, was relieved to be told at one station on the route, 'Oh yes, Churchill passed here two days ago, dressed as a Roman Catholic priest.'

Churchill stayed hidden among the bales of wool as the train reached the Transvaal side of the Portuguese border. There it was shunted on to a siding for eighteen hours. At one moment some men approached the wagon in which Churchill was hiding and began to search it. 'I heard the tarpaulin rustle as they pulled at it,' he later wrote, 'but luckily they did not search deep enough.' The train then continued on its way through Portuguese East Africa. Churchill, who had memorized the names of the stations, emerged from his bales of wool as soon as he saw the first station name on the Portuguese side of the border, and, he later recalled, 'sang and shouted and crowed at the top of my voice'.

So carried away was Churchill with 'thankfulness and delight', he later wrote, 'that I fired my revolver two or three times in the air'. On reaching the goods yard at Lourenço Marques he jumped down 'black as a sweep', Burnham later recalled, 'by reason of the coal dust which was in the bottom of the truck'. It was four in the afternoon of December 21. Churchill went at once to the British Consulate, where the consul telegraphed to Milner, 'Please inform relations that Winston Churchill arrived today.'

At the Consulate, Churchill found 'a hot bath, clean clothes, an excellent dinner, means of telegraphing – all I could want'. Among the telegrams he sent that afternoon was one to Louis de Souza in Pretoria, in which he assured him, 'Escape not due to any fault of your guards'. This was a magnanimous gesture, intended to protect the sentries from undue punishment.

Reading the newspapers which the consul gave him, Churchill saw for the first time the full extent of the recent British defeats, greater than any since the Crimean War nearly half a century earlier. Among those beaten in the field had been General Buller, forced back from Colenso when he tried to cross the Tugela and lift the siege of Ladysmith. Eager to return to the front, Churchill decided to leave that very night by steamer for Durban. There were fears, however, that Boer sympathisers in Lourenço Marques might try to kidnap him and take him back to Pretoria. To prevent this, a group of Englishmen living in the town gathered in the Consulate garden, fully armed, escorted him to the quayside, and, four hours after his arrival, saw him safely on board ship.

'It is from the cabin of this little vessel as she coasts along the sandy shores of Africa,' Churchill informed the *Morning Post*, 'that I write the concluding lines of this letter, and the reader will perhaps understand why I write them with a feeling of triumph, and better than triumph, a feeling of pure joy.'

Reaching Durban on the afternoon of December 23, Churchill was amazed to find a large and enthusiastic crowd at the quayside. Cheering and excited, they escorted him to the steps of the Town Hall, where he told them of his escape and spoke with confidence of the outcome of the war. 'After an hour of turmoil,' he wrote, 'which I frankly admit I enjoyed extremely, I escaped to the train.' Eager to return to the front, he travelled back on the very railway line on which he had been captured a month earlier, to Pietermaritzburg, to link up with the British forces.

That night Churchill was the guest of the Governor of Natal. On the following day he continued by rail to Buller's headquarters. To his surprise, the General's headquarters were virtually at the same spot as the ambush of the armoured train. It was Christmas Eve. Churchill spent it in the platelayers' hut a few hundred yards from where he had been captured thirty-six days earlier. 'Winston Churchill turned up here yesterday escaped from Pretoria,' Buller wrote to a friend on December 26. 'He really is a fine fellow and I must say I admire him greatly. I wish he was leading irregular troops instead of writing for a rotten paper. We are very short of good men, as he appears to be, out here.'

At a bad time for the war Churchill's escape provided a gratifying moment of excitement and success. It made him known throughout Britain, ensuring that his subsequent reports to the *Morning Post* were widely read. In the words of a popular music hall song that month:

> *You've heard of Brimstone Chapel,*
> *So of course I needn't say*
> *He's the latest and the greatest*
> *Correspondent of the day.*

On 3 January 1900 the British newspapers announced that on the previous day Churchill had accepted a commission in the South African Light Horse. He was once again a soldier, and yet, he wrote to his mother on

January 6, Buller had given him a lieutenancy 'without requiring me to abandon my status of correspondent so that I am evidently in very high favour'. To Pamela Plowden, however, he commented in a letter on January 10 that Buller himself was worth 'very little'. There was 'only one great General, but the War Office will not consider him – Sir Bindon Blood – so what is the use of crabbing the man at the wheel'. Churchill also urged Miss Plowden to be 'brave and confident' about the outcome of the conflict, 'and do not let the incidents of war obscure the general trend of events'. The Boer Republics, he added, 'are wearing thin'.

The Boer determination to resist was, however, formidable. When, in the second week of January, Buller crossed the Tugela, Churchill wrote of the battle in his report to the *Morning Post*, 'I have often seen dead men, killed in war – thousands at Omdurman, scores elsewhere, black and white, but the Boer dead aroused the most painful emotions.' He then described a man in his sixties, 'with firm aquiline features and a short beard' who had refused all suggestions of surrender and who, when his left leg was smashed by a bullet, continued to load his rifle until he bled to death. Next to him was a boy of about seventeen, shot through the heart. And a little further on lay 'our own two poor riflemen with their heads smashed like egg-shells'. Churchill added, 'Ah, horrible war, amazing medley of the glorious and squalid, the pitiful and the sublime, if modern men of light and leading saw your face closer, simple folk would see it hardly ever.'

Across the Tugela, Churchill saw many further examples of war's severity. 'The scenes on Spion Kop were among the strangest and most terrible I have ever witnessed,' he wrote to Pamela Plowden on January 28. The battle had been a 'serious reverse' with the loss of seventy officers and 1,500 men 'to little purpose'. He had just gone through 'five very dangerous days continually under shell & rifle fire and once the feather in my hat was cut through by a bullet'. Even if he were only a journalist he would not come home now. 'For good or ill I am committed and I am content. I do not know whether I shall see the end or not, but I am quite certain that I will not leave Africa until the matter is settled.'

Two weeks earlier Churchill had declined an appeal from the Conservative electors of Southport to be their candidate at the next General Election.

On January 28, Lady Randolph arrived at Durban, in charge of the hospital ship *Maine*, which she had helped to organise and equip. Churchill hurried back to Durban to meet her, and to take back with him to the Tugela front his brother Jack, now an officer in the Territorials, who had come out with her. From his cousin Hugh Frewen, who had written about the bad mood at home, Churchill wrote on February 5, from the Tugela: 'You must not allow your mother and friends to be despondent about this war. It is the duty of some British citizens to shoot straight, but of all to remain cheerfully determined.'

'We are going to make a general attack this afternoon or tomorrow morning, upon the Boer positions beyond the Tugela,' Churchill told Frewen, 'and I hope and pray that you may soon have some good news of victory.' In the action that followed, Jack was wounded in the calf; he was sent back to Durban and to his mother's hospital ship. 'Poor Jack,' Churchill wrote to Pamela Plowden. 'Here is an instance of Fortune's caprice. There was a very hot fire, bullets hitting the ground or whizzing by in dozens. Jack, whose luck was fresh, was lying down. I was walking about without any cover – I who have tempted Fortune so often. Jack was hit.'

Churchill was again in the midst of action on February 25. 'I was very nearly killed two hours ago by a shrapnel,' he wrote to Miss Plowden that day. 'But though I was in the full burst of it God preserved me. Eight men were wounded by it.' He wondered now 'whether we shall get through it, and whether I shall live to see the end'. There was 'a continual stream of wounded flowing by' to the hospitals, nearly a thousand in the previous two days. 'The war is very bitter, but I trust we shall not show ourselves less determined than the enemy.' His letter ended on a personal note, 'My nerves were never better, and I think I care less for bullets every day.'

On February 28, Lord Dundonald, with two cavalry squadrons, prepared to enter Ladysmith. He invited Churchill to ride with him. Also on that historic ride was Ronald Brooke, one of Churchill's soldier friends, whose brother Alan was to become Chief of the Imperial General Staff in the Second World War. 'Never shall I forget that ride,' Churchill wrote in the *Morning Post*. 'The evening was deliciously cool. My horse was strong and fresh, for I had changed him at midday. The ground was rough with many stones, but we cared little for that.' As the cavalry rode forward, they could hear British artillery still firing. 'What was happening? Never mind, we were nearly through the dangerous ground. Brigadier, staff and troops let their horses go.' Suddenly there was a challenge; it was an armed picket.

'Halt, who goes there?'

'The Ladysmith relief column,' came the answer.

Then, wrote Churchill, 'from out of trenches and rifle pits artfully concealed in the scrub a score of tattered men came running, cheering feebly, and some were crying. In the half light they looked ghastly pale and thin. A poor, white-faced officer waved his helmet to and fro, and laughed foolishly, and the tall, strong colonial horsemen, standing up in their stirrups, raised a loud resounding cheer, for then we knew we had reached the Ladysmith picket line.'

The siege of Ladysmith was over; that night Churchill dined there with the town's defender, Sir George White. Next to him at dinner sat another of the defenders, his friend Ian Hamilton. 'Never before have I sat in such brave company,' he later wrote, 'nor stood so close to a great event.' His account of the entry into Ladysmith, appearing in the *Morning Post*, was widely read and appreciated. As well as describing the excitement of the ending of the siege, he wrote of his conviction that, in England itself, once the war was won, 'the people of England must devote themselves to stimulating and sustaining the spirit of the people by measures of social improvement and reform'.

Among those reading Churchill's reports from South Africa was Joseph Chamberlain, who wrote to him of how 'amiable and graphic' they were, and wished him 'continued success and distinction'. Also from England came news that his novel *Savrola* had been published. Many of the reviewers had praised its scenes of action; the *Manchester Courier* called them 'brilliant in the extreme'. Many phrases in the novel were singled out for favourable comment, among them his description of a degenerate imperialism, 'Our morals will be gone, but our Maxims will remain.'

On the day after the relief of Ladysmith, Churchill sent the *Morning Post* a telegram describing the victory parade. 'It was a procession of lions. And presently when the two battalions of Devons met – both full of honours – and old friends breaking from the ranks gripped each other's hands and shouted, everyone was carried away, and I waved my feathered hat, and cheered and cheered until I could cheer no longer for joy that I had lived to see the day.'

Churchill's reports were widely appreciated; one officer, Captain Skipwith, after writing critically in a private letter about the lack of any real experience on the part of the many journalists then in South Africa, added, 'Winston Churchill is the one exception to the lot – he does go and see things with his own eyes and not through a long-range telescope, or through his ears.' While he was still in Ladysmith, Churchill received a letter from an American lecture agent, Major James Pond, offering to set up a lecture tour for him throughout the United States. He at once wrote to his mother, 'Now please don't let this thing be thrown away,' and instructed her to find out if the agent concerned was 'the biggest man, and if not who is'.

Full of inventiveness, Churchill also decided to write a play about the Boer War, telling Pamela Plowden that he wanted the play to be performed in London in the autumn, at Her Majesty's Theatre. 'It will be perfectly true to life in every respect, and the scenic effects should be of such a novel and startling character that the audience will imagine themselves under fire.' The play would have to be 'largely spectacular', he added, 'but I believe that with my name, and a good deal of assistance from a skilful playwright, a great success might be obtained'. He would need help with the plot, but was confident, he told her, that 'I can make the people talk and act as they would do in real war.'

On a personal note Churchill commiserated with Pamela that so many of her friends had been killed in the war. 'I trust I shall not fulfil the general rule.' To a correspondent who urged him to take care of himself, he replied: 'I do not think the Boers are taking any especial pains to kill me. If they are, I cannot so far congratulate them on their skill, for they have had plenty of opportunity and as yet, I thank God, no success.'

Many of those who now came across Churchill realised that he was a person of remarkable quality. 'I am very proud to have met you,' wrote the naval gunnery expert, Captain Percy Scott, then Military Commandant of Durban, 'because without any luck you have made a wonderful career.' Scott felt 'certain that I shall some day shake hands with you as Prime Minister of England, you possess the two necessary qualifications, genius and plod. Combined, I believe nothing can keep them back.'

While in Ladysmith, Churchill had been shocked at the violence of popular feeling against the Boers. 'I would treat the Boers with all generosity and tolerance,' he wrote to one correspondent on March 22, 'even to providing for those crippled in the war and for the destitute women and children.' To last, a peace would have to be honourable. 'We do not seek vengeance,' he wrote to the *Natal Witness* on March 29, even from the 'load of shame' of the early defeats. The aim of the war had been 'to win peace for ourselves, not to give others their deserts'. Nothing should be done to prevent the attainment of peace. 'While we continue to prosecute the war with tireless energy,' he wrote, 'and remorselessly beat down all who resist – to the last man if necessary – we must also make it easy for the enemy to accept defeat. We must tempt as well as compel.'

Churchill then set out a general rule for the last phase of the conflict: 'Beware of driving men to desperation. Even a cornered rat is dangerous. We desire a speedy peace and the last thing we want is that this war should enter upon a guerrilla phase. Those who demand "an eye for an eye and a tooth for a tooth" should ask themselves whether such barren spoils are worth five years of bloody partisan warfare and the consequent impoverishment of South Africa.'

There had to be 'fusion and concord' between the Dutch and the British, Churchill wrote. Nothing should be done that would enable it to be said of the people of Natal that they had fought well 'but they were drunk with racial animosity', that they were brave in battle 'but they are spiteful in victory'. The reaction to this call for moderation, and to similar calls in his telegrams to the *Morning Post*, was hostile. 'Winston is being severely criticised about his peaceful telegrams,' Jack, who was also then in Ladysmith, wrote to their mother at the beginning of April, 'and everyone here in Natal is going against his views.'

That week, learning that Haldane had escaped from Pretoria by tunnelling out of the States Model School, Churchill wrote to congratulate him. He also noted that the episode of the armoured train in which they had both been captured 'has become rather famous in the story of the war'.

Churchill now asked permission to join Ian Hamilton's column in its advance through the Orange Free State, to the Transvaal and Pretoria. Later he learned that Lord Roberts had not wanted him to go to the Orange Free State as a correspondent on the grounds that his presence there, he told his mother, 'would probably be obnoxious to Lord Kitchener in consequence of *The River War*'. But Roberts deferred to Churchill's fame and now, in April, he was on his way to a new campaign, travelling by train from Ladysmith to Durban, past the scene of the ambush of the armoured train and the wreck of the train itself, 'still lying', he wrote to the *Morning Post*, 'where we had dragged it with such labour and peril, just clear of the line'.

From Durban, Churchill set sail for East London, then took the train to Cape Town, then travelled inland again by train, to Bloemfontein and the front. There, at Dewetsdorp, as he had promised his friend Angus McNeill a few days earlier, he joined McNeill's Scouts for the day. It was April 22; their task that day was to cut off a Boer commando from the crest of a hill. Forty or fifty Scouts, Churchill with them, rode towards the crest, but the Boers had got there first. McNeill ordered his men back. At that very moment the Boers opened fire with their rifles. Churchill, who had dismounted, put his foot in the stirrup. 'The horse, terrified at the firing, plunged wildly. I tried to spring into the saddle; it turned under the animal's belly. He broke away, and galloped madly off.'

Most of the Scouts were already two hundred yards away. Churchill was alone, dismounted, within close range of the Boers, and a mile at least from cover of any kind. 'One consolation I had – my pistol. I could not be hunted down unarmed in the open as I had before. But a disabling wound was the brightest prospect.' He turned and, as he had done in the railway cutting five months earlier, ran for his life on foot from the Boer marksmen. As he ran, he thought to himself, 'Here at last I take it.'

Suddenly one of McNeill's Scouts rode past him. Churchill shouted out to him, 'Give me a stirrup.' The Scout stopped and Churchill jumped up behind him. 'Then we rode. I put my arms round him to catch a grip of the mane. My hand became soaked with blood. The horse was hard hit;

but, gallant beast, he extended himself nobly. The pursuing bullets piped and whistled – for the range was growing longer – overhead.'

'Don't be frightened,' Churchill's rescuer called out to him, then cried out: 'My poor horse, oh, my poor horse; shot with an explosive bullet. The devils! But their hour will come. Oh, my poor horse!'

'Never mind,' said Churchill, 'you've saved my life.'

'Ah,' rejoined the soldier, 'but it's the horse I'm thinking about.'

A few moments later Churchill was safe, and unscathed. 'I had thrown double sixes again,' was his comment when he telegraphed the story to the *Morning Post*, in which he also noted that Trooper Charles Roberts, the horseman who had saved his life, had been mentioned as a possible recipient of the Victoria Cross for his bravery. Roberts received no award of any sort, however. It was not until 1906, when Churchill was Under-Secretary of State for the Colonies, that he was able to persuade the authorities to award him the Distinguished Conduct Medal.

Churchill was aware of his good fortune at Dewetsdorp. 'Indeed,' he wrote to his mother, 'I do not think I have ever been so near destruction.' Together with his cousin Sunny, and a new friend, 'Bendor' Duke of Westminster, Churchill now rode with General Hamilton's column towards Pretoria. As they advanced, several of his closest soldiering friends were killed. Churchill wrote to his mother of how George Brasier-Creagh, her friend as well as his, after being shot in the stomach, 'died in great pain, and all alone at a farm-house'.

Another of Churchill's friends, Ronald Brooke's brother Victor, had just had his left hand smashed. 'He is such a nice, bright, clever fellow,' Churchill told his mother, 'very good-looking, very brave.' She should ask him to lunch 'and treat him kindly for my sake', and 'do him a service' by asking one or two important Generals of her acquaintance to meet him. Fourteen years later, Victor Brooke was to be killed in action in France in the opening months of the First World War.

As Churchill rode with Hamilton's army on its long march through the Orange Free State, witnessing each engagement at close quarters, he decided to accept the repeated pleas of the Oldham Conservatives to stand again at the next General Election. Several other constituencies had asked for him, but Oldham it would be. 'They have implored me not to desert them,' he told his mother on May 1.

'I have had so many adventures,' Churchill wrote to his Aunt Leonie two weeks later, 'that I shall be glad of a little peace and security. I have been under fire now in forty separate affairs in this country alone, and one cannot help wondering how long good luck will hold.' As to himself, 'I stand the wear and tear pretty well, and indeed my health, nerve and spirits were never better than now, at the end of seven months of war.'

On May 15, while Churchill was riding with Hamilton towards Pretoria, his fourth book was published in London. Based on the first twenty-two reports he had sent to the *Morning Post*, it was given the title *London to Ladysmith via Pretoria.* Two weeks after its publication he had another adventure. Hamilton was then south of Johannesburg, and Lord Roberts west of the town, which the Boers had not yet fully evacuated. Wanting to send the *Morning Post* his account of the most recent battle by the quickest means possible, Churchill decided to risk going through Johannesburg in order to send it from Roberts's headquarters. Hamilton, impressed by Churchill's daring, gave him his own official account of the battle, to be handed to Roberts. A Frenchman, Lautré by name, who worked in one of the nearby gold mines, warned that the journey on horseback through Johannesburg would be dangerous, as the Boers would surely arrest any horseman riding through the town. It could, however, he believed, be done by bicycle by someone wearing civilian clothes.

Lautré offered to go with him. 'I doffed my khaki,' Churchill told his readers in his next report, 'and put on a suit of plain clothes which I had in my valise, and exchanged my slouch hat for a soft cap.' Thus disguised he cycled with Lautré into Johannesburg. 'If they stop us,' Lautré told him, 'speak French.' The two men cycled on. 'Groups of moody-looking people chatted at street corners,' Churchill wrote, 'and eyed us suspiciously.' At one point an armed Boer, on horseback, rode up alongside them. 'I looked at his face and our eyes met. Then he turned away carelessly. Presently he set his spurs to his horse and cantered on.'

Cycling out of the town, Churchill was accosted by three British soldiers. They were looking for something to eat. Churchill warned them that there were still armed Boers roaming the streets. The soldiers turned back, accompanying the two cyclists to the British lines. Churchill was safe again. He was also able to report to Roberts's headquarters that the Boers had all but evacuated Johannesburg. That night, after he had sent his telegram to the *Morning Post* and delivered Hamilton's despatch, he was invited in by Roberts himself. 'How did you get through?' asked the Commander-in-Chief. Churchill told him. 'His eyes twinkled,' Churchill wrote. They 'twinkled brightly with pleasure or amusement or approbation, or, at any rate, something friendly'.

Johannesburg was occupied, and the British advance to Pretoria continued. On June 4 the Boer forces were defeated outside their capital. On the following morning, before the main body of British troops entered the town, Churchill set off with a large group of officers, overtaking at one point the General who was advancing on the railway station. As they rode forward, the officers were stopped by the closed gates of a level crossing. 'Quite slowly,' Churchill later recalled, 'there now steamed past before our eyes a long train drawn by two engines and crammed with armed Boers whose rifles bristled from every window. We gazed at each other dumb-founded at three yards' distance. A single shot would have precipitated a horrible carnage on both sides. Although sorry that the train should escape, it was with unfeigned relief that we saw the last carriage glide slowly past our noses.'

Churchill's path was to the new building where the British soldiers were now being held captive. That morning, fifty Boer sentries in and around the prison were guarding 150 British officers and thirty men. One of the prisoners, Melville Goodacre, wrote in his diary of how, at about nine o'clock, 'suddenly Winston Churchill came galloping over the hill and tore down the Boer flag, and hoisted ours amid cheers'.

'I raised my hat and cheered,' Churchill wrote. 'The cry was instantly answered from within.' Among those who saw Churchill's hat raised was Lieutenant Frankland, who had been captured with him on the armoured train. 'There was a wild rush across the enclosure,' Frankland later wrote; 'hoarse discordant yells, and the prisoners tore like madmen to welcome the first of their deliverers. Who should I see on reaching the gate but Churchill.' In the First World War, Frankland was to be killed at Gallipoli, one of the first British officers to land on the Peninsula.

Five hours after the release of the prisoners, Roberts entered Pretoria, where he took the salute of his victorious troops. Now that Pretoria was taken, Churchill wrote to his mother on June 9, 'I propose to come home. Politics, Pamela, finances and books all need my attention.' He also advised his brother, who was still serving with the forces in Natal, to return to England, 'Indeed, when I reflect upon the unguarded condition of our island home, I strongly recommend you to volunteer for service in London.'

Churchill continued with Hamilton's army to Diamond Hill. There, on June 11, he was in the midst of a violent battle, a 'rat trap' of rifle and artillery fire he called it in his telegram to the *Morning Post*. What he did not write was anything about his own action on that occasion, nor did he even refer to his own action in his memoirs thirty years later. Forty-four years after the battle, however, Hamilton published a full account of what he called Churchill's 'conspicuous gallantry (the phrase often used in recommendations for the VC) for which he has never received full credit'.

Hamilton's troops lay below a high mound, the crest of which was held by the Boers. The key to the battlefield, Hamilton wrote, lay on the summit, 'but nobody knew it until Winston, who had been attached to my column by the High Command, somehow managed to give me the slip and climb this mountain, most of it being dead ground to the Boers lining the crestline, as they had to keep their heads down owing to our heavy gunfire. He climbed this mountain as our scouts were trained to climb on the Indian frontier, and ensconced himself in a niche not much more than a pistol shot directly below the Boer commandos – no mean feat of arms in broad daylight.' It was also a feat, Hamilton reflected, which showed 'a fine trust' on Churchill's part in the accuracy of the British artillery firing at the crest.

Had even half a dozen of the Boers 'run twenty yards over the brow', Hamilton wrote, 'they could have knocked him off his perch with a volley of stones. Thus it was that from his lofty perch Winston had the nerve to signal me, if I remember right, with his handkerchief on a stick, that if I could only manage to gallop up at the head of my mounted infantry, we ought to be able to rush this summit.'

That was what Hamilton did; the battle, which ensured that the Boers could not recapture Pretoria, was in Hamilton's opinion 'the turning point of the war'. That night the Boers retreated. Watching the victorious British troops march past Lord Roberts, Churchill, who made no reference to his own part in the battle, described them as 'weary of war, but cheered by the hopes of peace, and quite determined to see the matter out. May they all come safely home.'

From Diamond Hill, Churchill returned to Pretoria. He was there on June 16 when 3,000 copies of his book *London to Ladysmith via Pretoria* were published in the United States. Four days later he took the train for Cape Town; a hundred miles south of Johannesburg, after the train had gone through Kopjes Station, it stopped suddenly. Churchill got out. Then to his horror a Boer shell burst almost at his feet, 'with a startling bang' he later recalled, 'throwing up clods from the embankment'. A hundred yards ahead, a wooden bridge was in flames. The train was crowded with soldiers being sent south, or home. 'No one was in command. The soldiers began to get out of the carriages in confusion. I saw no officers.'

Churchill now took charge. Fearing an ambush like that of the armoured train at Frere, he ran along the track to the engine, 'climbed into the cab, and ordered the engine-driver to blow his whistle to make the men get back into the train, and steam back instantly to Kopjes Station'. The engine-driver obeyed. 'While I was standing on the footplate to make sure the soldiers had got back into the train,' Churchill later recalled, 'I saw, less than a hundred yards away in the dry watercourse under the burning bridge, a cluster of dark figures. These were the last Boers I was to see as enemies. I fitted the wooden stock to the Mauser pistol and fired six or seven times at them. They scattered without firing back. Then the engine started and we were soon all safely within the entrenchment at Kopjes Station.'

'What an escape he must have had,' Jack wrote to his mother.

At Kopjes Station it was learned that a fierce action was proceeding only a few miles further down the line, where the train before Churchill's was even then being attacked by a large Boer guerrilla force complete with artillery. More than fifty of the soldiers on the train were killed or wounded. The line to Cape Town thus being cut, Churchill borrowed a horse to continue his journey homeward. 'I thought for many years,' he wrote in 1930, 'that the 2-inch Creusot shell which had burst so near us on the embankment was the last projectile I should ever see fired in anger.'

Back in Cape Town, Churchill had a third talk with Milner, who was hopeful of obtaining the help of the Boer moderates against the extremists. 'I spoke very freely of my ideas as to the future,' Milner wrote to him on the following day, 'because I see your interest and want your help.' While in Cape Town, Churchill learned of the considerable success of *London to Ladysmith via Pretoria*: it had sold 11,000 copies in less than six weeks. This, he explained to his brother, 'means £720 to me'. The income from his other books, skilfully invested by his father's friend Sir Ernest Cassel, had brought in a further £427. The *Morning Post* telegrams had earned him a total of £2,050, the highest sum yet paid to a journalist for such work, and the equivalent of £88,000 in 1990. The money worries of a year before were over.

Churchill left South Africa on July 7. He was never to see it again.

8

Into Parliament

On 10 July 1900, as Churchill's ship was bringing him home from South Africa, the magazine *Vanity Fair* published a cartoon of him by Spy, and a character sketch. 'He is a clever fellow, who has the courage of his convictions,' the magazine reported. 'He can write and he can fight.' He had 'hankered after politics since he was a small boy, and it is probable that his every effort, military or literary, has been made with political bent'. He was something of a sportsman, and 'prides himself on being practical rather than a dandy; he is ambitious; he means to get on, and he loves his country. But he can hardly be the slave of any Party.'

On July 20 Churchill landed at Southampton. Then, on July 25, he went to Oldham, where he was adopted as the prospective candidate for the General Election. He was confident he could reverse the defeat of the previous year. During his visit, he told his brother, he was given 'a most extraordinary reception. Over 10,000 people turned out in the streets with flags and drums beating and shouted themselves hoarse for two hours, and, although it was twelve o'clock before I left the Conservative Club, the streets were still crowded with people.'

On the following day, at the Theatre Royal, Oldham, Churchill described his escape to an ecstatic audience. 'As our forces had now occupied the Witbank colliery district,' he later recalled, 'and those who had aided me were safe under British protection, I was free for the first time to tell the whole story. When I mentioned the name of Mr Dewsnap, the Oldham engineer who had wound me down the mine, the audience shouted "His wife's in the gallery". There was general jubilation.'

Churchill's mother had not been at Southampton to meet him, as he had hoped; she was about to marry an Army officer, Captain George Cornwallis-West, who was a mere sixteen days older than her son and twenty years younger than herself. The marriage took place on July 27. 'Everything went off very well,' Churchill told Jack. 'The whole of the

Churchill family from Sunny downwards was drawn in a solid phalanx and their approval ratified the business.'

Three days after his mother's wedding, Churchill was the guest of George Wyndham in the House of Commons. 'I was treated with great civility by many people,' he told Jack. He was entertained on the terrace 'and all sorts of members from Mr Chamberlain downwards, came up and generally gave me a very flattering reception'. His political future seemed assured. 'The newspapers all give me paragraphs whenever I make a speech,' he told his brother, 'and a great many of the country newspapers write leading articles upon it. There are large piles of Press cuttings coming in, and generally speaking, one has no reason to be dissatisfied with the progress made.'

That August, Churchill spoke not only at Oldham, but in a dozen other towns. 'These speeches take a great deal from me,' he told his mother. At Plymouth he spoke of the weakness of the British Army should there be a European war. *The Times* reported his words extensively, filling almost a whole column: 'Few made very elaborate preparations against, as they thought, such a remote contingency,' Churchill said. But both the Government and the Opposition were agreed that the powers of Europe, 'armed to the teeth, viewed us with no friendly eye, and that our arrangements for military defence were not such that we could contemplate the situation without anxiety'.

For seven years he had been trained in the theory and practice of modern war, Churchill told his Plymouth audience. 'Heaven forbid that he should pose as an expert, but he knew enough to tell them that there were very few things in military adminstration which a business man of common sense and little imagination could not understand if he turned his attention to the subject; and anyone who told them to the contrary was nothing better than a humbug.' The courage of the British soldier was the same as in the days of old, 'but that was no reason why his weapon should be of an ancient pattern'. The Government should accelerate the supply of war stores.

Reading the full account of this speech in *The Times*, under the heading 'Mr Churchill on Army Reform', Churchill hastened to thank both the Managing Director and the editor, writing on August 20 to Charles Moberly Bell: 'I am really much obliged to you, and to Mr Buckle, for the very excellent report of my speech at Plymouth which appeared in Saturday's issue of *The Times*. It is extremely kind of you to help me in this way.' Fourteen years earlier, Buckle had sought, but too late, to dissuade Churchill's father from sending in his letter of resignation to Lord Salisbury.

Churchill was slowly mastering every aspect of the art of speech-making. 'I flattened out all the interrupters in the end,' he wrote to his mother after

one pre-election effort, 'to the delight of the audience.' He also spoke that
autumn at the annual dinner of the Institute of Journalists. It was 'an
opportunity not to be missed', he told his mother, 'to speak before an
audience which represents practically the whole Press, all the editors, all
the writers of Great Britain'. Politicians hastened to have him as their
guest. Lord Rosebery, with whom he dined, urged him to take elocution
lessons, but Churchill told him, 'I fear I shall never learn to pronounce an
"s" properly'. Nor did he, though he eventually learned to make the 'sh'
sound that he made instead seem a little less conspicuous. Muriel Wilson
later recalled walking with him up and down the drive of her parents'
home, Tranby Croft, as he practised the lines, 'The Spanish ships I cannot
see, for they are not in sight.'

That August, Churchill's cousin Sunny rented him a bachelor flat in
Mayfair, at 105 Mount Street. For the next six years this was to be his home
and office. He was his own taskmaster; when his mother invited him to
Scotland that August he declined. Oldham was where he had to be, and to
stay. 'It would be so foolish,' he told her, 'to throw away any chance of
winning the seat for the purpose of pleasure or relaxation.'

On September 19 Churchill set up his campaign headquarters in a
house just outside Oldham. He was worried, he told his mother, that the
constituency organisation was 'far from perfect, as they will insist on
managing it themselves, not allowing an expert or paid agent to do the
work properly'. His own activities helped redress this weakness. He was
able to persuade Chamberlain to speak for him, a considerable feather in
his cap. John Hulme, a writer who watched him as he campaigned, wrote
in *Temple Magazine*: 'Under ordinary circumstances, he uses carefully
prepared notes properly arranged according to the effect intended. His
temperament is highly nervous, which may explain his tendency to over
gesticulate. A favourite platform attitude, used whenever he has made a
point, is to place both hands on his hips, at which time he beams the smile
of satisfaction. At other times, when excited, he seems to be hammering
home his words with both hands raised aloft.'

Polling at Oldham took place on October 1. It was one of the very first
seats to be fought in an election where polling was spread over three weeks.
Churchill was successful, but only just. In the two-member constituency,
the largest number of votes, 12,947, went to the first of his Liberal
challengers, who was duly elected. Churchill, with only sixteen less votes,
was also a victor. The second Liberal candidate, a mere 221 votes behind
Churchill, was defeated, as was the second Conservative, Churchill's co-
challenger, with 187 fewer votes. It had been an exceptionally close result.

In an unusual lapse *The Times* reported that Churchill had been defeated. It corrected this error on the following day, and in a leading article

welcomed his arrival at Westminster. 'I have been returned to Parliament,' Churchill told Bourke Cockran, 'as representative of almost the greatest constituency in England, containing 30,000 thriving working men electors; and this victory, happening to come at the outset of the general contest, was of great use and value to the Conservative Party, as it gave them a lead and started a movement.'

At Balfour's urgent request, Churchill had not even returned from Oldham to London, but, after a messenger boarded his train, went instead to Manchester to speak in Balfour's constituency, where polling had not yet taken place. He later recalled how, when he reached the hall, and Balfour was already speaking, 'the whole meeting rose and shouted at my entry'. That night he travelled with Balfour to Stockport to help wind up Balfour's campaign. 'I have suddenly become one of the two or three most popular speakers in this election,' he told Cockran, 'and am now engaged on a fighting tour, of the kind you know – great audiences (five and six thousand people) twice & even three times a day, bands, crowds and enthusiasm of all kinds.'

Churchill's extra effort was appreciated. 'You have worked well for the Party,' Chamberlain wrote to him, 'and it will be counted to you in the future.' Still only twenty-five, Churchill was now a Member of Parliament. 'It is the starting point,' wrote Lord Curzon from Viceregal Lodge at Simla, 'of great possibilities, infinite excitement, & dangerous vicissitudes. I doubt not that you will triumph over all these.'

'No man who ever got into Parliament,' wrote St John Brodrick, the new Secretary of State for War, 'has done more than you have done in the last two years to entitle him to represent a constituency.' His 'only regret', Brodrick added, with what was to prove unerring perspicacity, 'is that to all appearances you will not be in Opposition, for your artillery will inevitably be directed against us!'

On October 12, twelve days after his election to Parliament, Churchill published another book, based on the thirteen telegraphic reports he had sent to the *Morning Post* between Bloemfontein and Diamond Hill, and entitled *Ian Hamilton's March*. 'This too,' he told his brother, 'should have a good sale.' It did, 8,000 copies by the end of the year, with a further 1,500 copies in the United States. He was now the author of five books, each earning him money. By the age of twenty-five, he would later remark with a chuckle, he had written 'as many books as Moses'.

Churchill was about to embark on yet another career, that of paid lecturer. A tour had been arranged by a professional lecture agent which would enable him, for a percentage of the gate money, to tell the story of the Boer War to audiences all over Britain. The tour began at Harrow. 'This is my first attempt to lecture,' he wrote to his former schoolmaster

Henry Davidson, 'and I fear it will not be a great success.' The lectures were in fact a remarkable success, drawing large numbers to hear them. Between October 25 and his twenty-sixth birthday a month later he gave thirty lectures, travelling as far north as Dundee, and crossing the Irish Sea to speak in Belfast and Dublin. He also spoke at both Oxford and Cambridge. His topic was 'The war as I saw it.' When he spoke at the St James's Hall in London, the Commander-in-Chief, Lord Wolseley, was in the chair. 'It says not a little for his qualities as a lecturer,' *The Times* reported, 'that for an hour and a half he was able to hold fast the attention of every one in that very spacious auditorium.'

The London meeting obtained Churchill £265, a year's salary for a young man in one of the professions. He at once agreed to put his earnings into a quick profit-making scheme proposed by his fellow Conservative candidate at Oldham, Charles Crisp, to whom he wrote on October 30: 'Yes please make some profit for me if you can. I have got a thousand pounds now in hand, which I was about to invest in something tolerably solid, but there is no reason why it should not have a gallop first. I don't understand your prospectus but I shall be very much obliged if you will make me some money.'

Churchill's largest audience that November was at Liverpool, where his share of the takings was £273. On November 30, his twenty-sixth birthday, he lectured at Cheltenham where he made £220. When the lecture tour was over, he had earned £3,782, the equivalent of more than five years' income for a professional man of his age. But that was not the end; on December 1, a day after his Cheltenham lecture, he sailed for the United States. An even more strenuous lecture tour was about to begin. 'You must not drag me about too much,' he had written to his American lecture agent, James Pond, 'and I don't want to wear myself out by talking to two-penny-half-penny meetings in out of the way places.' Nor did he want 'to be dragged to any social functions of any kind nor shall I think of talking about my experiences to anybody except when I am paid for doing so'.

Reaching New York on December 8, Churchill began his lectures at once. He was introduced to his first audience by Mark Twain, who declared, 'Mr Churchill by his father is an Englishman, by his mother he is an American, no doubt a blend that makes the perfect man.' After the lecture, Churchill persuaded Twain to sign each volume of a twenty-five-volume set of his collected writings. In volume one Twain wrote a personal inscription, 'To be good is noble; to teach others how to be good is nobler, & no trouble.'

In Washington, Churchill met President McKinley, with whom, he told his mother, 'I was considerably impressed'. In Albany he met the recently elected Vice-President, Theodore Roosevelt, who within a year was to become President following McKinley's assassination. In many cities the lecture tour was marred by the pro-Boer sentiment of his audiences, but the *Westminster Gazette* reported of his lecture in New York that 'the lecture was so moderate in tone, so generous in its tribute to the beaten enemy, so loyal, so vivid in narrative, so effective in proportion and perspective, as to win the entire sympathy of a very brilliant and very critical audience.'

After his financial success in England, Churchill was disappointed with the American result. His total transatlantic earnings were £1,600, much less than he had hoped for, partly because his lecture agent took more than three-quarters of the receipts. Even so it was a formidable sum. On a personal note also Churchill was unhappy. 'A certain amount of nervousness in starting my tour,' he told his mother, 'and the hard work attendant on it, together with a chill I think I must have got travelling in these stuffy trains, alternately too drafty to sit in and too hot to live in, brought on an attack of fever.' When he lectured in Washington he had a temperature of 102.

From the United States, Churchill went to Canada, speaking to large and enthusiastic audiences in Toronto, Montreal and Ottawa. While in Ottawa he was the guest of the Governor-General at Government House. Another of the guests was Pamela Plowden. Their romance was now over. 'We had no painful discussions,' Churchill told his mother, 'but there is no doubt in my mind that she is the only woman I could ever live happily with.' Turning to his finances, and to his literary and lecture earnings, Churchill told his mother: 'I am very proud of the fact that there is not one person in a million who at my age could have earned £10,000 without any capital in less than two years. But sometimes it is very unpleasant work. For instance last week, I arrived to lecture in an American town & found Pond had not arranged any public lecture, but that I was hired out for £40 to perform at an evening party in a private house – like a conjuror.' Several time he had spoken in local theatres to 'almost empty benches'.

While in Ottawa, Churchill arranged for those who had sheltered him in the mine at Witbank, after his escape from Pretoria, to be sent gold watches, with engraved inscriptions of thanks. 'I do not think it would be too much to spend £30 or £40 on this,' he told his mother. He also sent her, a short time afterwards, a gift of £300 for the Princess of Wales Fund for the wives of soldiers serving in South Africa. He had raised the money at a special charity lecture. 'In a certain sense it belongs to you,' he wrote, 'for I could never have earned it had you not transmitted to me the wit and energy which are necessary.'

Articles, like lectures, took time and effort to prepare. 'I write very rarely,' Churchill explained to his mother in reply to a request for an article, 'and when I do I like to get a very wide circulation, and to produce some little effect upon the opinion of the country.'

On 22 January 1901, while Churchill was still in Canada, lecturing in Winnipeg, he learned that Queen Victoria had died. Ten days later, on the day of the Queen's funeral, he sailed for England, having first asked his mother to send 'complete files' of *The Times* and various weekly papers to be waiting for him at the quayside. On February 14 he took his seat in Parliament. Henceforth his life was to be spent before the public eye. Every speech he made in Parliament and outside it was to be reported in the newspapers, and to be the subject of Press and public comment. Even his maiden speech in the House of Commons, on February 28, was listened to, the *Morning Post* noted, by an audience 'which very few new members have commanded', including two senior Liberal politicians, Campbell-Bannerman and Asquith. Also present, in the Ladies' Gallery, were his mother, and four of his father's sisters, Lady Wimborne, Lady Tweedmouth, Lady Howe and Lady de Ramsey: his aunts Cornelia, Fanny, Georgiana and Rosamond.

When, during his speech, Churchill told the House, 'If I were a Boer I hope I should be fighting in the field,' the Irish Nationalist members cheered, and Chamberlain muttered to his neighbour, 'That's the way to throw away seats.' But Churchill quickly rounded on the Irish members whose sympathies were with the Boers, with the words, 'It is wonderful that honourable members who form the Irish Party should find it in their hearts to speak and act as they do in regard to a war in which so much has been accomplished by the courage, the sacrifices, and, above all, the military capacity of Irishmen.'

If there were those who 'rejoiced in this war', Churchill said, 'and went out with hopes of excitement or the lust of conflict, they have had enough, and more than enough, today'. The war had led to losses which were a cause for regret. He had himself lost 'a good many friends', but he added, 'We have no cause to be ashamed of anything that has passed during the war; nor have we any right to be doleful or lugubrious.'

Churchill ended his speech with a reference to his father, thanking the House for its kindness and patience in hearing him, 'which has been extended to me, I well know, not on my own account, but because of a certain splendid memory which many honourable members still preserve'.

Few, if any, maiden speeches have been so widely reported in the Press. The *Daily Express* called it 'spell-binding'. The *Daily Telegraph* wrote of how, 'Perfectly at home, with lively gestures that pointed his sparkling sentences, he instantly caught the tone and the ear of a House crowded in every part.' *Punch* devoted the whole of its Parliamentary report to it. Although 'nothing', it wrote, either in Churchill's voice or manner, recalled Lord Randolph, 'he has, however, the same command of pointed phrase; the same self-possession verging, perhaps, on self-assurance; the same gift of viewing familiar objects from a new standpoint; the same shrewd, confident judgment'. The *Daily Chronicle* noted 'an unfortunate lisp in his voice' but praised his 'inherited qualities, candour and independence'.

One phrase in Churchill's speech, 'if I were a Boer I hope I should be fighting in the field', offended many Conservatives. After reading the letters of protest in the Press, he wrote in his defence to the *Westminster Gazette*: 'Neither side has a monopoly of right or reason'; whatever the balance of moral right, it was 'rarely sufficient' to outweigh patriotic considerations. 'From this I argue that while the Boer cause is certainly wrong, the Boer who fights for it is certainly right. Much more so then, is the Boer who fights bravely for it.' If, he added, he were 'so unfortunate as to be a Boer, I should certainly prefer to be the best kind of Boer'.

Only two weeks after his maiden speech, Churchill spoke in a debate demanding an enquiry into the dismissal of General Colville, who had been fighting in South Africa. While supporting the Government in resisting an enquiry, Churchill nevertheless declared, 'Perhaps it will not be entirely agreeable to many of my friends on this side of the House if I say that I have noticed in the last three wars in which we have been engaged a tendency – arising partly from good nature towards their comrades, partly from dislike of public scrutiny – to hush everything up, to make everything look as fair as possible, to tell what is called the official truth, to present a version of the truth which contains about seventy-five per cent of the actual article.'

Nor was that all. 'So long as a force gets a victory somehow,' Churchill continued, 'all the ugly facts are smoothed and varnished over, rotten reputations are propped up, and officers known as incapable are allowed to hang on and linger in their commands in the hope that at the end of the war they may be shunted into private life without a scandal.' The Liberal Opposition cheered. Although Churchill went on to support the Government, by insisting that 'the right to select, to promote and dismiss' must be left to the military authorities, he had shown again that he would not mould or curb his views to suit his Party. Yet his defence of the Government had been well-argued and effective. 'There is no doubt,' he told his mother, 'that the speech turned votes and shifted opinion at the time when the current was running very strongly against the Government.'

'May I say you will never make a better speech than you made tonight,' the Secretary of State for War, St John Brodrick, wrote to him. 'Of course you will speak on better subjects – but you filled the House & held it – & got the debate back on to big lines. It was a great success and universally recognised.' Recognition, and advice, came from as far away as India. 'There is no more difficult position,' wrote Lord Curzon, 'than being on the benches behind a Government. It is so hard to strike the mean between independence & loyalty. The great thing is to impress the House with earnestness. They will forgive anything but flippancy.'

Churchill's correspondence and commitments had grown at an extraordinary pace. 'I have more than 100 letters unanswered,' he told his mother in mid-March; '30 or 40 I have not even had time to read.' He was lecturing twice that day at Hastings, the fifth and sixth of fifteen lectures on the Boer War which he gave between March and May. To lessen the burden of writing out every letter by hand, as he had done hitherto, Churchill decided to employ a secretary. Unless he did, he told his mother, 'I shall be pressed into my grave with all sorts of ridiculous things.' He did not even have a cabinet for his correspondence: 'There is a pile on my table now which quite stifles me.' His first secretary, Miss Anning, took down letters at his dictation, and then wrote them out in longhand for him to sign. She also prepared the folders in which his correspondence was kept.

That spring Churchill returned to Europe, travelling first to Paris, then on to Madrid and Gibraltar. On his return to England he lectured to senior Army officers on the role of the cavalry in South Africa. He also entered into a controversy which was greatly to anger the Conservative leaders. St John Brodrick, who had welcomed his support in the Colville debate, now proposed a fifteen per cent increase in military expenditure. Churchill was convinced that this extra expenditure was unnecessary. It would, he argued, be ineffective. It would not make the Army stronger. It was bad value for money. If more public money was to be spent, it should be on the Navy, not the Army.

Churchill launched these criticisms against his own Government's policy in a speech to the Liverpool Conservative Association on April 23. 'Any danger that comes to Britain,' he insisted, 'would not be on land; it would come on the sea.' Two days later he repeated his arguments at Oxford. Having been criticized in *The Times* by both the vice-president and the secretary of the Army League, he wrote in reply: 'A better army does not necessarily mean a bigger army. There ought to be ways of reforming a business, other than by merely putting more money into it. There are more ways of killing a cat, &c.' His letter ended, provocatively, 'I wonder that this has not occurred either to the vice-president or to the secretary of the Army League.'

Not everyone approved of the tone of such ripostes, then or later. But this was Churchill's style; outspoken, vigorous, with the written equivalent of a mischievous grin. This made him enemies, as did his method of coming back to the charge again and again, reinforcing old arguments and presenting new ones. On May 3 *The Times* published his second letter in three days, in which he cited one of his own earlier opinions to show that he was consistent. It was his telegram to the *Morning Post* immediately after the relief of

Ladysmith, in which he had written that once the war was over 'the people of England must devote themselves to stimulating and sustaining the spirit of the people by measures of social improvement and reform'.

On May 10, as Churchill was preparing to present his criticisms of increased Army expenditure to Parliament, an Australian journalist interviewed him for the *Melbourne Argus*. Commenting on the Boer description of Churchill, 'walks with a bend forward', the journalist wrote, 'You see this bend forward not merely when he walks, but when he is seated,' even in the House of Commons 'listening eagerly, and with hot assent or ardent dissent, to everything that is going on.' It gave him the appearance 'of a young panther ready at any moment to make a desperate spring'. Yet although this posture was 'indicative of a nature full of impatience, ardour and ambition' one must also notice, the journalist added, 'the fine self-restraint which enables Mr Churchill to conquer his evidently fierce desire to be in the rage of battle, and to bide his time'.

On May 13, having tabled an amendment to Brodrick's Army scheme, Churchill set out his criticisms of the scheme in the presence of an apprehensive Front Bench. 'I took six weeks to prepare this speech,' he later recalled, 'and learned it so thoroughly off by heart that it hardly mattered where I began it or how I turned it.' It was a speech of considerable power, skill and courage. In it he pointed out that in 1894 the annual cost of the Army had been £17 million. In 1901 it had risen to nearly £30 million. He then referred to his father's stand against increased military expenditure, 'if I might be allowed to revive a half-forgotten episode'. As a result of it, he reminded the House, his father had 'gone down for ever, and with him it seems there also fell the cause of retrenchment and economy, so that the very memory thereof seems to have perished, and the words themselves have a curiously old-fashioned ring about them'.

Churchill then opened a book from which to read his father's letter of resignation to Lord Salisbury of 1886. He had learned the letter by heart, and in a dramatic gesture, closed the book when half way through the reading, at Lord Randolph's sentence, 'I decline to be a party to encouraging the military and militant circle of the War Office and Admiralty to join in the high and desperate stakes which other nations seem to be forced to risk.'

'Wise words, Sir, stand the test of time,' the twenty-six-year-old MP continued, 'and I am very glad the House has allowed me, after an interval of fifteen years, to lift again the tattered flag of retrenchment and economy.' The time had come for a voice to be raised from the Conservative benches to plead the cause of economy. 'If such a one was to stand forward in such a cause, then I say it humbly, but with I hope becoming pride, no one has a better right than I have, for this is a cause I have inherited, and a cause for which the late Lord Randolph Churchill made the greatest sacrifice of any Minister of modern times.'

Churchill then set out his criticism of Brodrick's proposal to set up three Army corps. One such corps, he said, 'is quite enough to fight savages, and three are not enough even to begin to fight Europeans'. The existing system should be adapted without extra expenditure to deal smoothly with minor emergencies and colonial wars. 'But we must not expect,' Churchill warned, 'to meet the great civilised powers in this easy fashion.' It was this European aspect he wished to stress. In a passage which showed just how far his thoughts had gone in understanding what warfare could, and would, become, in the new century, he declared, 'A European war cannot be anything but a cruel, heart-rending struggle, which, if we are ever to enjoy the bitter fruits of victory, must demand, perhaps for several years, the whole manhood of the nation, the entire suspension of peaceful industries, and the concentration to one end of every vital energy in the community.'

'I have frequently been astonished since I have been in this House,' Churchill went on, 'to hear with what composure and how glibly Members, and even Ministers, talk of a European war.' He would not 'expatiate on the horrors of war', but there had been a 'great change which the House should not omit to notice', and he then set out his reasons for believing that, as far as warfare was concerned, that era was at an end. In days when wars had arisen from the policy of a Minister or the passion of a King, when they were fought by small regular armies of professional soldiers, when the fighting itself was often suspended for the winter, 'it was possible to limit the liabilities of the combatants'. But now, 'when mighty populations are impelled on each other, each individual severally embittered and inflamed, when the resources of science and civilisation sweep away everything that might mitigate their fury, a European war can only end in the ruin of the vanquished and the scarcely less fatal commercial dislocation and exhaustion of the conquerors. Democracy is more vindictive than Cabinets. The wars of peoples will be more terrible than the wars of kings.'

'We do not know what war is,' Churchill insisted. 'We have had a glimpse of it in South Africa. Even in miniature it is hideous and appalling,' and he went on to argue that it was upon a strong economy – 'the economic command of markets' – and a strong Navy, that Britain's power and prosperity depended. But there was a 'higher reason' still, he said, for not spending more on the Army. It was known, both by the peoples and the rulers, that 'on the whole British influence is healthy and kindly, and makes for the general happiness and welfare of mankind'. Members of Parliament would make 'a fatal bargain' if they allowed 'the moral force which this country has so long exerted to become diminished, or perhaps even destroyed, for the sake of the costly, trumpery, dangerous military playthings on which the Secretary of War has set his heart'.

The Conservative Front Bench were shocked by this attack from one of their newest back-benchers. Replying, Brodrick accused Churchill of harbouring 'a hereditary desire to run imperialism on the cheap'. Other MPs, particularly Liberals and Radicals, praised not only his sentiments but his courage in expressing them. His father's friend Lord James of Hereford, a member of Salisbury's Cabinet, wrote, 'Although I cannot agree with the views expressed in your speech, I must sincerely congratulate you upon its merits.'

That summer Churchill found himself part of a group of young Conservative MPs who were dissatisfied with Party policy. Calling themselves the 'Hooligans', or 'Hughligans', after one of their leading members, Lord Salisbury's son Lord Hugh Cecil, they dined every Thursday in the House of Commons, inviting a distinguished guest to dine with them. Churchill was already on terms of close personal friendship with several leading Liberals. On July 23 he dined with Lord Rosebery at Durdans, his home near Epsom. His letter of thanks revealed another step forward in Churchill's life. 'I am afraid I disturbed your horses with my motor car yesterday,' he wrote. 'I am learning to drive at present, so this is rather a dangerous period.'

Rosebery had been one of the first of the Hooligans' guests, and he invited the young rebels to spend a Sunday with him at Durdans. Churchill went down earlier, on the Saturday night, to dine and sleep. 'My dear Winston,' Rosebery wrote when the weekend was over, 'I cannot tell you how much I enjoyed the Hooligan visit. It rejuvenated me. If they or any of them wish for moral repose while Parliament sits they will find it here.' Ten days later, another leading Liberal, the future Foreign Secretary Sir Edward Grey, invited Churchill, and the one other Hooligan not then on holiday, to dine with him and Asquith.

In Scotland that summer, Churchill stayed with his uncle Lord Tweedmouth, a former Liberal Minister, at Guisachan. 'I have seen a lot of the Liberal Imperialists lately,' Churchill wrote to Rosebery at the end of September. 'Haldane and Edward Grey were at Guisachan, where I spent a pleasant week.' Richard Haldane was to be Secretary of State for War in a future Liberal Government. In Scotland that September, Asquith took the chair for Churchill when he gave one of his Boer War lectures at St Andrews. These Liberal Imperialists shared many of the views that were maturing in Churchill's mind; they wanted Britain to be strong, but they also wanted a social policy that would benefit the mass of the people, and reduce the extremes of poverty and deprivation.

Not only did Churchill meet the Liberal politicians, but also several senior civil servants who, while ostensibly non-political, were in favour of many Liberal aspirations. On September 4, while staying with his kinsman Lord Londonderry at Stockton-on-Tees, he met Sir Francis Mowatt, who for the past seven years had been Permanent Secretary to the Treasury and Head of the Civil Service. Thirty years later Churchill wrote of how, at this time, 'although I enjoyed the privilege of meeting in pleasant circles most of the Conservative leaders, and was always treated with extraordinary kindness and good nature by Mr Balfour; although I often saw Mr Chamberlain and heard him discuss affairs with the greatest freedom, I drifted steadily to the left.'

Churchill's drift away from the Conservative Party was hastened by Conservative attitudes to the Boer War. Some of the ammunition for his speeches in which he expressed his unease came from inside the Civil Service: 'Old Mowatt' – Mowatt was then sixty-four – 'said a word to me now and then and put me in touch with some younger officials, afterwards themselves eminent, with whom it was very helpful to talk – not secrets, for these were never divulged, but published facts set in their true proportion and with their proper emphasis.'

That autumn Churchill protested publicly against the execution of a Boer commandant by the British military authorities in South Africa and worked behind the scenes to avert the execution of another commandant; 'I was in revolt against "jingoism" ' he explained thirty years later. At Saddleworth in Yorkshire on October 4 he appealed for a 'supreme effort' to end the war in South Africa. Until it was ended 'the gulf of hatred between Boer and Briton grows wider; and every day devastation and ruin rule over larger areas'. How many were there in his audience, he asked, 'who may look in the newspaper tomorrow morning to find, as I found last week, some familiar name, and learn that some bright eye – known and trusted – is closed for ever'.

During his speech at Saddleworth, Churchill spoke of two of his Party leaders, Balfour and Chamberlain, 'I warn these two distinguished men,' they could not devolve upon others 'the weight and burden' of the war. To Chamberlain he wrote direct, on October 14: 'It is not enough for the Government to say, "We have handed the war over to the military: they must settle it all: all we can do is to supply them as they require!" I protest against the view. Nothing can relieve the Government of their responsibility.' A month later, in a speech at Hanley, he rejoiced that Kitchener's powers as Commander-in-Chief in India had at last been curtailed and spoke scathingly of how, only a few weeks earlier, he had himself been 'ridiculed' by a Government Minister for suggesting they should be.

On November 30 Churchill was twenty-seven. Two years earlier he had been a prisoner. Now he was an active and controversial Member of Parliament.

In mid-December 1901, two weeks after his twenty-seventh birthday, Churchill dined with John Morley, Gladstone's biographer and a leading Liberal reformer. During the evening Morley recommended him a book by Seebohm Rowntree, *Poverty: A Study of Town Life*. The moment he read it, Churchill's sense of mission was heightened and enhanced. Rowntree had examined the plight of the poor in York. It was a grim story. 'Who has not considered,' Churchill wrote in his review of the book, 'how he would spend vast wealth? But from the ugly things of life, from its darker facts and hideous possibilities, imagination recoils or is deliberately recalled. It is pleasurable to dwell upon the extremes of wealth. We do not wish to contemplate the extreme of poverty.' The imagination was not stirred by 'the slum, the garret and the gutter'.

Churchill then set out a summary of the harsh life of the working man, and in particular the disasters which befell his family as a result of unemployment, sickness or death. The evil housing conditions was another theme which Rowntree examined, and by which Churchill was shocked. 'Consider the peculiar case of these poor and the consequences,' he wrote. 'Although the British Empire is so large, they cannot find room to live in it; although it is so magnificent, they would have had a better chance of happiness if they had been born cannibal islanders of the Southern seas; although its science is so profound, they would have been more healthy if they had been subjects of Hardicanute.'

Ending his review with bitter irony, Churchill wrote that it would be 'impudent' to urge such arguments upon a Parliament 'busy with matters so many thousands of miles from home'. There was a 'more important consideration' to be borne in mind in urging the relief of poverty: 'Not the duty of man to man, nor the doctrines that honest effort in a wealthy community should involve certain minimum rights, nor that this festering life at home makes world-wide power a mockery, and defaces the image of God upon earth. It is a serious hindrance to recruiting.'

The impact on Churchill of Rowntree's book was immediately apparent. 'For my own part,' he wrote to a leading Birmingham Conservative on December 23, 'I see little glory in an Empire which can rule the waves and is unable to flush its sewers.' In this letter Churchill also referred to the rioters in Birmingham who had set upon the radical Liberal politician, David Lloyd George, and nearly lynched him because of his 'pro-Boer' opinions;. 'I hope the Conservative Party have kept their hands clean.' Having learned that the Conservatives had been actively involved in the riot, Churchill wrote privately that though personally he thought Lloyd George 'a vulgar, chattering little cad', every man had 'a perfect right' to express his opinions; that these opinions should be shouted down 'because they are odious to the majority in the district is a very dangerous, fatal doctrine for the Conservative Party'.

Churchill's disillusionment with the Conservative Party was growing daily. What was wanted, he wrote in his letter of December 23, was a 'well-balanced' policy that would 'co-ordinate development and expansion with the progress of social comfort and health'. It was with 'all the wretched, unorganised middle-thinkers' that he now wished to associate. Yet where was Churchill to go? Was he to respond to the growing overtures from the Liberal Imperialist camp, and from 'the Imperialist' himself, Lord Rosebery? 'As we agreed at Blenheim,' Hugh Cecil wrote to him just after Christmas, 'it is wise to play a waiting game & not to respond to the Imperialist's invitations until he has built himself a house to entertain you in. Now he has only a share in a dilapidated umbrella.'

Churchill did not want to wait; in the third week of December he drew up a list of twelve Conservative MPs, most of them young, who shared his frustration at what they saw as a jingoistic and backward-looking Government and Party. In the second week of January 1902, to a Conservative audience in Blackpool, he spoke about poverty in Britain. It was 'a terrible thing', he said, that there were people, as in York, 'who have only the workhouse or prison as the only avenues to change from their present situation'. 'The Tory Party,' he wrote to Rosebery twelve days later, 'are in a very brutal and bloody frame of mind.' His own mind was now made up. He would take a lead in attacking, not only the Government's military spending, but the whole failure, as he saw it, to use the taxpayer's money in the most effective and beneficial way.

On April 14, during the Budget debate, Churchill denounced the 'shocking lack of Cabinet control' over expenditure. He also made a remarkable prophecy, warning, a year before the issue was to be broached by Chamberlain and to tear at the fabric of British politics, of the perils of a campaign to curb Free Trade and to introduce Protection. 'I wonder, Sir,' he asked, 'what will happen to this country if the Fair-trade issue is boldly raised by some responsible person of eminence and authority? We shall find ourselves once again on an old battlefield. Around will be the broken weapons, the grass-grown trenches and neglected graves – reviving former memories, and party bitterness, such as this generation has not known. How is it going to split existing political organisations, now so artificially serene? These are the questions of the future.'

On April 20 Churchill received encouragement in his search for a policy of economic retrenchment from a distinguished civil servant, Sir Edward

Hamilton, the Permanent Financial Secretary to the Treasury and a former private secretary and confidant of Gladstone, who not only congratulated him on his Budget debate speech, but wrote: 'Please remember that the doors of the Treasury are always open to you. I shall be delighted at all times to render you any assistance, for your father's sake as well as your own.'

Hamilton was twenty-five years Churchill's senior. Like others of an older generation he was attracted by Churchill's zeal, intelligence and eagerness to learn. Churchill now pressed Balfour on the issue of excessive Government spending, asking him on April 24 to appoint a Select Committee of the House 'to report and consider whether national expenditure cannot be diminished without injury to the public service, and whether the money voted cannot be apportioned to better advantage than at present'.

Balfour declined to accept the 'ambitious' terms of reference which Churchill proposed. Unwilling to let the matter drop, Churchill accused the Government, during a debate on May 12, of allowing national expenditure to 'get beyond the point of prudence and reason'. Almost immediately, he received an invitation from Balfour to serve on a select committee being set up to examine Parliamentary control over expenditure. He accepted, becoming a regular participant in its deliberations. But his divergences of opinion with his Party leaders continued to widen. He later recalled, 'I found that Rosebery, Asquith and Grey and above all John Morley seemed to understand my own point of view far better than my own chiefs.'

That spring, a Boer journalist who had completed a twelve-month prison sentence in South Africa for a libel on Kitchener was refused permission by the British military authorities there to go to England on a private visit. It was John Morley who raised the issue in the Commons. He was supported by Churchill, who accused the military authorities of having abused their powers under martial law. Where else, he asked, could the dissemination of anti-British views do less harm than in Britain itself? At the end of the debate, Churchill and seven other Conservatives, including all the available Hooligans, voted against the Government. That night the Hooligans entertained Chamberlain to dinner. 'What is the use,' he asked them, 'of supporting your own Government only when it is right? It is just when it is in this sort of pickle that you ought to come to our aid.'

As the evening drew to a close, and Chamberlain was saying goodnight to his young hosts, he suddenly raised an issue that had not been touched upon all evening. It was the very issue which Churchill had broached in the House of Commons a month earlier. 'You young gentlemen,' Chamberlain told them, 'have entertained me royally, and in return I will give you a priceless secret. Tariffs! They are the politics of the future, and of the near future. Study them closely and make yourselves masters of them, and you will not regret your hospitality to me.'

That summer the Boer leaders accepted defeat and agreed to give up their tenacious guerrilla campaign. Churchill spoke out at once in favour of giving them 'every kind of encouragement' to associate with Britain. His desire to conciliate and unify, and even to see the Boers protect themselves from what he called the 'tender mercy' of the South African loyalists, set him apart from many Conservatives. To his constituents at Oldham he wrote that summer that 'we have passed from war – dragging, draining, dangerous war – to victorious peace'; a settlement had been reached 'based not entirely upon the exhaustion and despair of a brave enemy, but rather on an honourable agreement between fighting races who have learned in the hardest schools to respect each other's qualities'. It was a settlement that had secured for Britain 'all that right and prudence demanded' and had given the Boers 'all that generosity required'.

No month now passed without a further breach between Churchill and his Party leaders. 'I cannot make speeches in the country with any satisfaction now,' he wrote to Rosebery that summer. 'I cannot work up the least enthusiasm on the Government's behalf: and yet popular audiences seem to gape for party clap-trap.' In July, Churchill took up a non-political matter, the case of twenty-nine Sandhurst cadets who had been punished collectively, and arbitrarily, for a series of fires started in the college by an unknown incendiarist. The punishments, he wrote to *The Times* on July 8, violated 'three cardinal principles of equity'. These principles were 'that suspicion is not evidence; that accused persons should be heard in their own defence; and that it is for the accuser to prove his charge, not for the defendant to prove his innocence'.

All twenty-nine cadets had been sent down from the college. None had been charged with any offence. 'Nothing having the remotest semblance to a judicial enquiry has been held.' Even poor parents were having to pay for a term in which their sons were not allowed to be in college, and which would not count towards their time there. 'All the cadets I have seen strenuously deny any complicity with the offence.' Churchill's letter was answered by the headmaster of Sherborne School, the Reverend Frederick Westcott. Soldiers had to learn the lessons of corporate punishment, he wrote. 'The innocent, doubtless, suffer with the guilty; but then they always do. The world has been so arranged.'

'Has it indeed?' Churchill asked in his reply on July 8. No doubt Westcott had taken care 'that the little world over which he presides is arranged on that admirable plan, but it is necessary to tell him that elsewhere the punishment of innocent people is regarded as a crime, or as a calamity to be prevented by unstinting exertion'. So long as the 'delinquencies of a schoolmaster' were within the law, Churchill added, 'the House of Commons has no right to intervene; but when a Commander-in-Chief and a Secretary of State are encouraged to imitate him, it is time to take notice.' His letter ended, provocatively: 'Does Mr Westcott flog his boys in their corporate capacity?'

Churchill wanted to discuss the Sandhurst punishments in the Commons. But Balfour, who had just succeeded his uncle, the ailing Lord Salisbury, as Prime Minister, refused to allow time for any such debate. Churchill encouraged Rosebery to intervene in the matter when it was raised in the Lords. During the debate there, the Commander-in-Chief, Lord Roberts, agreed that each individual case would be investigated and that no innocent cadet would lose a term of study. Commenting on this outcome, *The Times* praised Churchill's efforts, calling him 'an effective advocate'.

Churchill now decided to embark upon an ambitious project which he had long had in mind, a biography of his father. Not content with his father's archive, he sought material far and wide, appealing in *The Times* on September 16 for letters and documents. Five days later he wrote to the former Prime Minister, Lord Salisbury, who had accepted his father's resignation in 1886: 'I write personally to ask you for the loan of any letters of my father which you may have. I also desire to publish some extracts from your letters to him; but all these I will of course submit to you at a later date.'

That September, Churchill was invited by Edward VII to Balmoral. 'I have been very kindly treated here by the King, who has gone out of his way to be nice to me,' he wrote to his mother. 'It has been most pleasant & easy-going & today the stalking was excellent, tho' I missed my stags.' From Balmoral he went to Dalmeny to stay with Rosebery, to whom he outlined his plan for a continued assault on Brodrick's Army scheme by means of joint action by a small but vocal group of Conservative and Liberal Unionist members willing to act and vote together against excessive military spending.

From Dalmeny, Churchill went south to Oldham to address his constituents. During his visit he had a long talk with Samuel Smethurst, a leading local Conservative who shared many of his concerns. 'It is curious and encouraging,' he wrote to Smethurst a few days later, 'that in your reflections you should have produced an idea always in my mind but which I did not perhaps make plain.' This idea, which Churchill set out in his letter for the first time, was 'the gradual creation by an evolutionary process of a Democratic or Progressive wing to the Conservative Party which could either join a central coalition or infuse vitality into the parent body'. Both these possibilities, Churchill told Smethurst, 'are present in my mind as they were in my father's all his life: & the more I turn things over the more I understand a remark which Lord Salisbury once made to my father after his resignation, "that his turn (& the turn of Tory Democracy) would come after Mr Gladstone's death".'

Churchill hastened to assure Smethurst that he need not be afraid 'of any "rash action"; for I am if anything too cautious'. One day perhaps, but not during the present year, would he run the 'risk & peril' of such a course. It was Rosebery, he wrote, who 'realises more nearly than anyone else in public life my ideals of Tory Democracy', but until he was at the head of a definite party with an 'enlarged and detailed' policy, the question of supporting him was premature 'and its discussion very dangerous'. Even should the question of such a new Democratic grouping become 'ripe for decision' at some future time, 'I should have a difficult and perilous choice to make and my own feelings would be divided on every aspect of the problem; personally because of my friendship with Mr Chamberlain & Mr Balfour, politically because of my attachment to the Unionist Party with the making of which my poor father was so intimately concerned.'

On the day that he wrote this letter Churchill was at Canford Manor near Bournemouth, staying with his father's sister Lady Wimborne, studying her collection of family letters and Press cuttings, as part of the preparation of his father's biography, which he hoped to complete within two or three years. In his letter to Smethurst, Churchill set out his own political philosophy, 'broad, tolerant, moderate views – a longing for compromise and agreement – a disdain of cant of all kinds – a hatred of extremists whether they be Jingos or Pro-Boers; and I confess that the idea of a central party, fresher, freer, more efficient, yet, above all, loyal and patriotic, is very pleasing to my heart'. Sooner or later, he believed, the rest of the Liberals would have to join such a Central Party 'to fight with us against a great cosmopolitan Labour movement, anti-national & irreligious and perhaps communistic. I believe a Central Party might postpone that day.'

Churchill was excited to find that his idea of a central party had the support of one of the most influential of the Oldham Conservatives. During his visit to Oldham, he told Rosebery on October 6, 'I was caressed by both parties with a cordiality most satisfactory & even surprising – for I have not been with them for six months.' He had already broached to Rosebery his plan for a possible first move, joint Liberal and Conservative Parliamentary action to curtail the Government's military spending. It was a plan, he wrote, 'which under certain contingencies it might be desirable to follow', and he had already broached it to two of his friends on the Conservative side.

On October 10 Churchill sent Rosebery a copy of the letter he had sent to Smethurst, supporting the evolution of a middle force linking Conservatives and Liberals. 'If by an "evolutionary process" we could create a wing of the Tory Party which could either infuse vigour into the parent body or join a central coalition,' he told Rosebery, 'my plan would become most important as an incident in, or possibly as a herald of, the movement.' But, he warned, the 'risk and peril of it would be very great, & it would carry consequences for me which I cannot foresee; & only the conviction that you are upholding the flag for which my father fought so long & disastrously would nerve me to the plunge'.

Churchill's letter of October 10 continued: 'The Government of the Middle – the party which shall be free at once from the sordid selfishness & callousness of Toryism on the one hand & the blind appetites of the Radical masses on the other – may be an ideal which we perhaps shall never attain, which could in any case only be possessed for a time, but which is nevertheless worth working for: & I, for my part, see no reason to despair of that "good state " '. His aim was a 'Tory-Liberal' central coalition. 'The one difficulty I have to encounter is the suspicion that I am moved by mere restless ambition: & if some definite issue – such as Tariff – were to arise – that difficulty would disappear.'

Churchill had mentioned the very issue which, during the following nine months, was to cause his break with the Conservative Party, a break that was to last for twenty years. It arose almost at once. At the end of October an article in the *Oldham Chronicle* accused him of inconsistency in supporting at one and the same time the recent Conservative corn tax and sugar tax, and the principles of Free Trade. Both taxes, he countered, were for revenue purposes alone. They had been emergency measures imposed in time of war 'when it was absolutely vital to find the necessary money'. They were not intended to protect colonial produce against foreign competition.

'Therefore there is no inconsistency whatever,' Churchill wrote, 'between the vote which I gave in support of this taxation and the principles of Free Trade, of which I must confess myself a sober admirer.' Free Trade was still the policy of the Conservative Party; fifty years earlier Disraeli had declared, 'Protection is not only dead but damned'. Both Balfour and his Chancellor of the Exchequer were Free Traders. But those Conservatives who had begun to campaign for tariffs were determined to win the Party to their cause.

On public platforms all over Britain, Churchill defended the economic merits of Free Trade and open competition in the commercial markets of the world. Cheap food and cheap raw materials were best secured, he argued, by the Free Trade system. The protective tariffs of one country led inevitably to the erection of tariff walls world-wide. Protection would raise prices and cause growing international tension, not only economic but political. 'It would seem to me a fantastic policy,' he wrote to a constituent on November 14, 'to endeavour to shut the British Empire up in a ringed fence.' Why should Britain deny itself 'the good and varied merchandise which the varied traffic of the world offers, more especially since the more we trade with others, the more they must trade with us'. The planet was 'not a very big one compared with the other celestial bodies, and I see no particular reason why we should endeavour to make inside our planet a smaller planet called the British Empire, cut off by impossible space from everything else'.

On November 20 Churchill left England for Egypt, invited by Sir Ernest Cassel to witness the opening of the new Nile dam at Aswan. Travelling up the Nile by boat, he spent each morning writing the biography of his father. He also visited the temples and ruins of ancient Egypt. While in Egypt he celebrated his twenty-eighth birthday. Reaching Aswan, he commented in a letter to his mother on the most recent Trade Union dispute in Britain. There was 'much reason' in the Trade Union case, he wrote, 'yet they make unreasonable demands. These demands the Conservatives meet with flat refusal. I want to see them grapple with the difficulties & remove the force from the demand by conceding all that is just in it. But middle courses are proverbially unpopular.'

Returning to England, Churchill spoke in the Commons on 24 February 1903 against the Government's proposed increase in military spending. 'I am so glad you were there & approved,' he wrote to Rosebery. 'I think it is the most successful speech I have yet made – and the House of Commons purred like an amiable cat.' When the voting came, eighteen Conservatives, including Churchill, joined the Liberal Opposition in voting against the Government. Another fifteen abstained. 'Our advance-guard action has really been most successful,' he told Rosebery. 'Our friends are all extremely well satisfied and more full of fight than ever.' During the debate, both Brodrick and Balfour had indicated that the policy might change. 'My only fear,' Churchill wrote, 'is that we might succeed too soon.'

Churchill continued the campaign against Brodrick, publishing his speeches against the Army scheme in a small booklet, *Mr Brodrick's Army*. A month later, after a last-minute agreement between the Conservative and Liberal front benches not to force a division on the Army scheme, Churchill protested to Campbell-Bannerman. 'Some of my friends were very much perplexed,' he wrote. They had intended 'to persuade as many Unionists to vote against the Government as possible'. Nor was his opposition to the Government's spending limited to the Army scheme. 'Army expenditure does not stand alone,' he wrote to a constituent, 'It is the keystone of an arch of extravagance.'

In this letter Churchill set out his wider frustrations at the nature of parliamentary politics. 'It is of course utterly impossible,' he wrote, 'for any private member acting alone to influence in the slightest degree the policy of a powerful government. He may make speeches; but that is all. Hardly any question is ever decided on its merits. Divisions are taken on strict Party lines and Ministers have at their disposal a monopoly of expert opinion for and against every conceivable course, a battalion of drilled supporters, and the last word in all debates.'

Churchill had encouraged Conservative members to risk the ire of their Party by voting with the Liberals, in order to change the Government's policy on military spending. But his dream was not merely to weaken the monolith of a single Party; what he had always in his mind, he wrote to his constituent, was 'that grand ideal of a National party of which Lord Randolph dreamed and for which he toiled'. This letter was written on April 24. Three weeks later, on May 15, Chamberlain raised the banner of Tariff Reform. Speaking in Birmingham, he challenged the policy and threatened the unity of the Conservative Party, demanding that the existing Free Trade system should be set aside, and that the economic power of Britain and her Colonies be strengthened by Imperial Preference. Colonial goods would be allowed in at their existing prices; the same European goods would have a tariff imposed on them at the ports, making them more expensive and less desirable.

In the national debate which now began, Churchill emerged at once as one of the most vociferous Conservative supporters of Free Trade. As during the debates over Army expenditure, so now during the Free Trade debates, he was helped by the head of the Treasury, Sir Francis Mowatt, who, he later wrote, 'armed me with facts and arguments of a general character, very necessary to a young man who, at twenty-eight, is called upon to take a prominent part in a national controversy'.

It was just over a year earlier that Churchill and his fellow 'Hooligans' had been told by Chamberlain that tariffs were the 'politics of the future'. He and Chamberlain were now on opposite sides of the national debate, and in the struggle for the soul of the Conservative Party. On May 20, five days after Chamberlain's speech, Churchill answered him at Hoxton. He also took the lead in trying to persuade Balfour to dissociate himself from Chamberlain. 'I am utterly opposed,' Churchill wrote to Balfour on May 25, 'to anything which will alter the Free Trade character of this country.' An attempt by Balfour to preserve 'the Free Trade policy & character of the Tory party would command my absolute loyalty'. But if Balfour had made up his mind for tariffs, 'I must reconsider my position in politics.'

Balfour had not made up his mind. The issue was 'one of difficulty', he replied 'and requires the most wary walking'. Then, in the Commons three days later, on May 28, Chamberlain defended his call for tariffs. Churchill was disappointed that the leading Liberal speaker on financial matters, Asquith, was not in the Chamber to answer him. It was Churchill who therefore spoke immediately after Chamberlain, warning that if Chamberlain's policies were carried out it would lead to the Conservative Party becoming a new kind of Party altogether, based on tariffs. It was an 'economic absurdity', Churchill told the House, 'to say that Protection means a greater development of wealth; and to say that it means a fairer distribution of wealth is a "downright lie"'. Once Protection was adopted, he warned, 'the old Conservative Party, with its religious convictions and constitutional principles, will disappear, and a new party will arise, rich, materialistic and secular, whose opinions will turn on tariffs and who will cause the lobbies to be crowded with the touts of protected industries.'

'What a pity your lieutenants were not in their place yesterday!' Churchill wrote to Rosebery. 'Asquith would have had an opportunity after Chamberlain sat down which may not recur. The whole burden of protest was left to us.' Sir Edward Grey had also been elsewhere during the debate of May 28. Meeting him two days later, Churchill rebuked him for his absence. He had been at York, 'I said that was no answer'. Churchill realized how dependent he was upon Liberal parliamentary strategy and skill not to do anything that might strengthen the Government's Protectionist wing. In a letter to Campbell-Bannerman on May 29 he tried to persuade the Liberal Leader to separate his criticism of tariffs from a general attack on the Budget, which Churchill would want to defend. 'You will of course understand,' Churchill wrote, 'that the position of those Conservatives who are unalterably opposed to the impending fiscal change is one of great difficulty and danger; and I earnestly hope you will consider us in the course you take.'

Churchill now plunged into the formation of a Free Food League made up of like-minded Conservative MPs, determined to keep their Party committed to Free Trade. 'Unless you act now,' he wrote to one potential supporter, 'we are going to be withered up and will find no branch or turf on which to rest the soles of our feet. But determined action now may largely destroy Chamberlainism and preserve the Free Trade character of the Tory Party.'

On May 30 Churchill was able to inform Hugh Cecil of twelve 'certain', eleven 'probable' and six 'possible' members of their League. 'Our two main cards,' he told Cecil on June 3, 'are (1) debating & speaking ability in the House of Commons, (2) the anti-food tax cry in the country.' As for newspaper support, he commented, 'The Press will fight while there is a chance of victory, but they melt in the hour of defeat.' When the League was launched on July 13, sixty Conservative MPs had joined. They called themselves Unionist Free Traders. Three days after their formation, Churchill wrote to *The Times* to protest against the activities of Chamberlain's supporters in using the Party machinery 'to disseminate protectionist propaganda'.

As Churchill fought within the Conservative Party for Free Trade, his cousin Sunny, to whom Balfour had offered a position in the Government, wrote of how 'grieved' he was that Churchill was 'going to take such an aggressive part' in opposition to the Government's, and Chamberlain's, fiscal proposals. 'It will mean your ultimate severance from the Tory Party,' the Duke forecast, 'and your identification with Rosebery and his followers.'

'As regards electoral prospects and the Party situation,' Churchill wrote to a fellow Unionist Free Trader on the following day, 'let me say in the strictest confidence that my idea is, and has always been, of some sort of central government being formed.' At a new General Election the Unionist Free Traders would make an electoral pact with the Liberals not to fight against each other. 'Of course,' Churchill wrote, 'this is all very vague and at present chiefly confined to my own cranium. But the Conservative Party will not like the idea of a general election under these conditions and numerous forces will be at work to prolong the supremacy of Conservative forces.'

To a correspondent who insisted that the taxation of imported goods was the key to national prosperity, Churchill replied, 'I would look to improvements in scientific and technical education, to light taxation, to pacific policy and to a stable and orderly state of society as the best means of stimulating the commercial prosperity of our country.'

Bitterness was growing; at the end of July the Edinburgh Conservatives cancelled a meeting which they had asked Churchill to address, because of his opposition to Protection. 'I am sorry to learn,' he replied, 'that there is so much intolerance and prejudice among Conservatives in Edinburgh upon this question of fiscal policy that they cannot even contemplate its free discussion,' and he went on to warn the Edinburgh Conservatives that the Party might not always enjoy 'the support of a great majority'. It might in the future have 'to fight hard for many causes that have long been unchallenged'. If the 'spirit of intolerance' being shown towards people like himself 'were to result in driving from their ranks those who adhere to Free Trade principles – a contingency I earnestly hope may be avoided – there may be cause for regret in the years that are to come'.

That summer Chamberlain sent Churchill a private letter, to assure him that 'I bear no malice for political opposition'. The letter went on to give a perceptive account of Churchill's political position. 'I have felt for a long time,' Chamberlain wrote, 'in fact from your first confidences to me, that you would never settle down in the position of what is called a "loyal supporter". I do not think there is much room in politics for a dissentient Tory, but Heaven knows that the other side stands much in need of new talent, and I expect you will drift there before very long.'

'Is it really necessary,' Chamberlain asked in a postscript, 'to be quite as personal in your speeches?'

Angered by Balfour's failure to declare himself in favour of tariffs, on September 16 Chamberlain resigned from the Cabinet. By persuading him to withhold the news for two days, Balfour, in an extraordinary political sleight of hand, also procured the resignation of the three leading Free Trade Ministers, including the Chancellor of the Exchequer. When the news of all four resignations was known on September 18, it was clear that Balfour had rid himself both of the Tariff and Free Trade wings of his Cabinet. No one knew which way he would reconstruct his administration. Would it, Churchill asked his mother on September 18, 'be a protectionist reconstruction of a Cabinet which does not contain the Free Trade Ministers, or a Free Trade reconstruction of a Cabinet from which JC has resigned? All these things are possible.'

The answer was not long in coming. On October 2, in a speech at Sheffield, Balfour announced that the Conservative Party would embark upon Protectionist legislation. There would clearly be no place for Churchill in the new Government. His Free Trade views were too extreme; they were also proving too extreme for his constituents, more and more of whom were declaring themselves for Chamberlain.

Churchill set out his Free Trade arguments in detail in a letter to his constituents on October 9; three days later the letter was published in *The Times*. In it Churchill wrote that Chamberlain 'cares less about lowering the tariffs of foreign countries than of building up a tariff round our own'. Tariffs on all kinds of food were 'quack remedies'. Labouring men 'must view with unalterable suspicion a scheme for reducing the cost of living by taxing every mouthful they eat'. Britain's colonies would 'reject proposals to cramp their economic development like the Chinese women tie up their children's feet'.

Churchill's constituents were not convinced. Indeed, his local Conservative association was turning against him. 'You would look foolish', his constituency chairman, one of his few remaining supporters, wrote on October 11, 'if when the election came the majority of your own side decided not to run you as their candidate.' His defence of his views had caused deep offence. On October 14 a formal resolution was passed that 'this meeting regrets the tone of Mr Churchill's letter'. 'My letter,' Churchill told Morley two days later, 'has unsealed volcanoes in Oldham; and such fury was never seen. The whole Tory electorate is mad for Protection.'

Churchill's Aunt Cornelia, his father's sister, hoped that her nephew would now join the Liberal ranks. 'I thought your letter quite excellent,' she wrote to him, '& it reminded me of your father's way of going straight to the point. Of one thing I think there is no doubt, & that is that Balfour & Chamberlain are one, and that there is no future for Free Traders in the Conservative Party. Why tarry?' Churchill had come almost to the same conclusion. 'I am an English Liberal,' he wrote to Hugh Cecil on October 24. 'I hate the Tory party, their men, their words & their methods. I feel no sort of sympathy with them – except to my own people at Oldham.'

It was his intention, Churchill told Cecil, that before Parliament met 'my separation from the Tory Party & the Government shall be complete & irrevocable; & during the next session I propose to act consistently with the Liberal Party'. Free Trade was 'so essentially Liberal in its sympathies & tendencies that those who fight for it must become Liberals'. The duty of those like himself who meant to maintain Free Trade was 'not to remain a snarling band on the flank of a government who mean to betray it, but boldly & honestly to range themselves in the ranks of that great party without whose instrumentality it cannot be preserved'.

Churchill held back this letter. Yet it was becoming clear that if the Unionist Free Traders intended to maintain themselves in Parliament as a separate political entity they could expect no help from the Liberals. The Liberals were unwilling, for example, to allow the Unionist Free Traders to be unopposed by Liberal candidates at any future election. 'I am anxious,' Churchill had appealed to Morley a week earlier, 'that you should from your commanding position urge the Liberal Party to look beyond the mere Party advantage of capturing a few seats by destroying men who could perhaps do something for Liberalism in the future.' Not only did Churchill want to 'do something for Liberalism', he also wanted, he had explained to Cecil, 'to help to preserve a reconstituted Liberal Party against the twin assaults of Capital & Labour'.

Churchill was still trying to persuade the Liberals to let the Unionist Free Traders stand unopposed. But on November 2, during a talk with his uncle Lord Tweedmouth, a leading Liberal, he reported to Cecil that 'we should only obtain official Liberal support if we came forward as fair and square Liberal candidates'. Tweedmouth was 'anxious to help', Churchill added, 'but their Liberal machine seems to be just as stupid and brutalised as ours'.

On November 11 Churchill and Cecil were the main speakers at a Free Trade meeting in Birmingham. This was to be a final attempt to sway

Conservative opinion away from Protection, and to do so where pro-Chamberlain feeling was highest. 'I have carefully revised my speech,' Churchill told Cecil a few days before the meeting, 'so as to avoid provocative terms of phraseology and I think I shall have no difficulty in getting the audience to listen to it.' The Birmingham meeting went off without incident, with Churchill making a spirited defence of Free Trade. After he had spoken, one Liberal in the audience commented: 'That man may call himself what he likes but he's no more a Tory than I am.' Three weeks later the Birmingham Liberal Association invited him to stand at the next General Election for Birmingham Central, where his father had once fought.

Churchill had not yet made up his mind to join the Liberal Party. Meanwhile, he spoke that December in support of Free Trade in Chelsea and at Cardiff. He also went to Oldham to put his position before the heads of the local Conservative Association. 'It is unlikely,' he told them, 'that I shall stand for Oldham as the Conservative candidate at the next election.' But first he wished to see if he could influence the working men of the borough by his speeches. 'I might make a real impression upon them & obtain a personal following quite independent of the executive or any existing party organisation.'

That December, Churchill was asked by Lord Tweedmouth if he would like to stand as a Liberal for Sunderland: 'It is open & should be a very good chance.' He was still not ready to take the plunge, but, two days later, still describing himself as a Unionist Free Trader, he sent a letter of support for the Liberal candidate who was challenging a Conservative at a by-election in Ludlow. Free Traders of all parties, he wrote, 'should form one long line of battle against a common foe'. The time had come for 'united action'.

Cecil was outraged by Churchill's appeal for an anti-Conservative vote. 'You have given away the "life" you had as a member of the Party for nothing,' he wrote. Hitherto the Unionist Free Traders had agreed to fight the battle against Protection from inside the Conservative Party. 'But now in one of your thousand foolish passing moods you wholly abandon this line & fling yourself into the arms of the Liberals.' This 'instability', Cecil wrote, 'makes you quite impossible to work with; & will unless you can cure it be a fatal danger to your career'. Cecil would fulfil his promise to speak with Churchill at Worcester and Aberdeen, but after that 'we must be separated'.

Churchill's message of support for the Liberals at Ludlow had also angered his Oldham constituents. Their anger was increased by a speech he made at Halifax on December 21, at which he had said, 'Thank God we have an Opposition,' and which his constituency chairman thought 'foreshadowed your adherence to the Liberal Party'.

'My language does not compromise you,' Churchill sought to assure Cecil, both about his Ludlow message and his Halifax speech, '& you are free to repudiate it if you think worthwhile. Neither does it separate me formally from the Conservative Party: though that is a step which cannot be long delayed.'

Two days after Churchill's Halifax speech, the Oldham Conservative Association's General Purposes Committee passed a resolution informing him that he had 'forfeited their confidence in him as Unionist member for Oldham, and in the event of an election taking place he must no longer rely on the Conservative Organisation being used on his behalf'. Undeterred, he set about trying to form a local Unionist Free Trade organisation at Oldham which would support him in a by-election. His idea was to resign the seat, then stand 'on the Free Trade issue'. To this end he gave an assurance to the local Labour Party that if it did not oppose him in the by-election he would not stand for Oldham at the General Election. Four days later the Conservative Association Executive confirmed the resolution of the General Purposes Committee; he would not receive official Conservative support at the next General Election.

On the last day of 1903 Churchill lunched with Lloyd George; his aim was to find common ground between the Unionist Free Traders and the Liberals, in the event of Liberals agreeing not to stand against Free Traders in certain constituencies. He was pleasantly surprised to find how 'tolerantly' Lloyd George stated his views. Lloyd George spoke to Churchill about the need for the Unionist Free Traders to adopt a 'positive programme', especially towards working men. 'I cannot pretend to have been shocked,' Churchill wrote to Cecil. 'Altogether it was a very pleasant and instructive talk.' But Cecil, sharing the deep Conservative hostility to Lloyd George's radicalism, was angered by Churchill's meeting: 'I do not myself contemplate negotiating with him,' he wrote. He had also decided not to go with Churchill to speak at Aberdeen.

Which way would Churchill turn? Would he resign at Oldham, then hold the seat after a by-election, as a Unionist Free Trader? Or would he, as he had earlier written to Cecil in his unsent letter, leave the Conservatives altogether and join the Liberals? 'The difficulties of the political situation depress me,' he wrote to Cecil on New Year's Day 1904, 'and it seems to me that whatever we may do at this next election, the Tory Party will become permanently capitalist and Protectionist in character, and the Liberal Party will be smashed to pieces between organised capital on the one hand and organised labour on the other.'

It still seemed that the Unionist Free Traders might be able to survive electorally as an independent group; on January 5 Tweedmouth informed Churchill that Asquith and Herbert Gladstone, the son of the former Prime Minister, had been authorised 'to confer with two of your Party as to seats & possible conditions of an understanding'. But the 'first condition' of such an understanding, Tweedmouth warned, was that Churchill's group would vote for a Free Trade amendment the moment Parliament reconvened.

Churchill accepted the Liberal condition and persuaded his fellow Unionist Free Traders to do likewise. But there was now considerable Conservative anger at his leading role in the Unionist Free Trade struggle. One Conservative MP declared that he had 'reached the lowest depths of political ignominy'. His close Conservative friends understood the strength of his convictions. 'It is a great regret to me that your views on this question are what they are,' Lord Dudley wrote to him on January 9, 'but holding them so strongly you are of course right to fight it through to the end.'

On March 2, in his first speech to the new session of Parliament, Churchill attacked the Government's adherence to the Brussels Sugar Convention, which gave West Indian sugar a protected price against all other non-colonial markets. In congratulating him on a 'brilliant speech', the Liberal leader Campbell-Bannerman wrote that its first part 'was the most sustained piece of irony I have ever heard in the House of Commons'.

It was, however, irony at the expense of a Party which was no longer in any mood to forgive or forget. Nor did the Conservative Party particularly want to be given a lesson in government, yet this was what Churchill did. 'It was always found in the past,' he said, 'to be a misfortune to a country when it was governed from one particular point of view, or in the interests of any particular class, whether it was the Court, or the Church, or the Army, or the mercantile or labouring classes. Every country ought to be governed from some central point of view, where all classes and all interests are proportionately represented; and I venture to think that even in modern days that principle to some extent applies to our Government.' As to the Sugar Convention itself, he told the Commons: 'We have dearer food, not as a statement in a leaflet, not as a Parliamentary device of the Opposition, not merely as a menace for the future, but as an accomplished fact, avowed and admitted, and which is vaunted as the achievement of the legislation we are now asked to pass.'

A week after Churchill spoke thus against Protection, his fellow Unionist Free Traders put forward an amendment expressing the Government's opposition to Protection. Initially, in the hope of avoiding a conflict, Balfour gave the amendment his approval, but when the Protectionist

Tories objected he withdrew Party support and the amendment was defeated. 'I think the Government is quite rotten,' Churchill wrote to Samuel Smethurst. 'They are always quarrelling among themselves and are unable to come to any decisive action. An awful slide is in store for the Conservative Party.'

Churchill had begun to vote regularly against the Conservatives. That March he supported a Liberal vote of censure against the Government's use of indentured Chinese labour in South Africa. He also voted in favour of Liberal Bills to restore legal rights to the Trade Unions, and to tax land sales when land was bought cheaply and then sold at a higher price as building land.

The Liberal Association of North-West Manchester now asked Churchill if he would be their candidate at the next election. He could stand if he liked, not as a Liberal, but as a 'special candidate' of the Free Food League. He was tempted to accept, telling Cecil on March 26 that the constituency had wanted someone to reply 'from day to day' during the election to the speeches that Balfour would be making, 'and when you consider that there is no Free Trade politician of the smallest eminence in Lancashire, you will see for yourself the possibilities it offers'.

The Manchester Liberals were convinced, Churchill told Cecil, 'that the effect of my campaign would be felt in all the nine seats of Manchester and in the dozen constituencies which cluster round it'. He now proposed 'to have a go' at Balfour in the Commons, and to ask him 'a quantity of tiresome questions on his fiscal views'. He would also 'ridicule' Balfour's most recent economic proposals. 'Don't be too violent on Tuesday,' Cecil replied. 'Take a reasonable position & argue it persistently.'

The Tuesday debate was that of March 29. As Churchill began to speak, stating that the public had a right to know what public men thought on public questions, Balfour rose from his seat and left the Chamber. Churchill immediately protested to the Speaker that Balfour's exit showed 'lack of deference and respect' to the House. At this, all the front bench Ministers rose and left, followed almost at once by the Conservative backbenchers, some of whom lingered at the door to jeer at Churchill, who stood almost alone, with a few Unionist Free Traders at his side. He continued his speech, but with some difficulty, as it had been largely devised as a series of questions to the now absent Balfour.

'I took your advice as to my speech,' Churchill told Cecil on the following day, 'and couched it in a moderate and sorrowful vein, but as you have probably seen, I was the object of a very unpleasant and disconcerting demonstration. I would far rather have been rudely interrupted, for I might have placated that kind of opposition, or at the worst, laughed at it. But the feeling of the whole audience melting behind one, and being left with crowded Liberal benches and an absolutely empty Government side was most disquieting, and it was only by a considerable effort that I forced myself to proceed to the end of my remarks.'

When Churchill sat down he had been loudly cheered by the Liberals, several of whom later wrote to him to say how shocked they had been by the demonstration. Sir John Gorst, one of Lord Randolph's political allies, and a Unionist Free Trader, criticised his fellow-Conservatives for 'the most marked discourtesy I think I have ever seen'.

On the day of the Conservative walk-out, an episode took place half way around the world which stirred Churchill's anger. This was the killing, at the village of Guru in Tibet, of six hundred Tibetans; 'poor wretched peasants', the British commander, Colonel Younghusband, described them, 'mowed down by our rifles and Maxims'. There had been no British deaths. 'Surely it is very wicked to do such things,' Churchill wrote to Cecil. 'Absolute contempt for the rights of others must be wrong. Are there any people in the world so mean-spirited as not to resist under the circumstances to which these poor Tibetans have been subjected. It has been their land for centuries, and although they are only Asiatic, "liberty" & "home" mean something to them.' That the defeat of the Tibetans should have been greeted 'with a howl of ferocious triumph by Press & Party', Churchill added, 'must be an evil portent'.

On April 18 Churchill accepted the invitation from the Liberals of North-West Manchester to stand as a Free Trade candidate, with full Liberal support. In his letter of acceptance he wrote that what Britain required was 'a decided change from the costly, gaudy trappings of martial ambition to a more sober garb, a closer recurrence to first principles, a higher regard for the rights of others, a firmer reliance upon those moral forces of liberty and justice that have made her renowned'. He was now a Liberal in all but name. On April 22 he spoke for three-quarters of an hour during the debate on the Trade Union and Trade Disputes Bill, upholding the rights of the Trade Unions and urging a constructive policy towards them. The Conservative *Daily Mail* characterised the speech as 'Radicalism of the reddest type'.

Towards the end of his speech Churchill had begun a sentence with the words, 'It lies with the Government to satisfy the working classes that there is no justification.....' At this point he hesitated, seeming to search for words in his memory. He then stopped speaking, appeared confused, fumbled through his notes, and sat down. As he did so, he covered his face with his hands and muttered, 'I thank honourable Members for having listened to me.' A few of the younger Conservative MPs were tempted to jeer at the fall of their opponent. But there were many older Members present who recalled the last, painful, halting, and eventually incoherent speeches of Lord Randolph, and were aghast at the thought that his son had begun to suffer the same terrible collapse.

The collapse was not a serious one; 'I expect he has overdone his nervous system', one medical expert wrote. The loss of memory had been the result of 'defective cerebration: it comes to the readiest at times. Luckily it hardly ever recurs'. Nor did it recur with Churchill. In future. however, he would not rely as hitherto on memorising his speeches, but would supplement his copious memory with full, almost verbatim notes, to guide him.

Churchill had not yet joined himself 'formally' to the Liberal Party, he explained to a friend on May 2. 'That circumstance has not yet occurred. Whether it will occur or not depends on the future course of politics.' Eleven days later he made his fiercest attack yet on Protection. Speaking on May 13 to the Liberal Federation in Manchester, with Morley at his side, he described 'what to expect' if the Conservative Party were to be returned to power under its new Protectionist flag. It would be 'a party of great vested interests', he declared, 'banded together in a formidable federation; corruption at home, aggression to cover it up abroad; the trickery of tariff juggles, the tyranny of a party machine; sentiment by the bucketful, patriotism by the imperial pint; the open hand at the public exchequer; the open door at the public house; dear food for the million, cheap labour for the millionaire'.

Churchill ended his speech with a declaration of faith in Liberalism. 'Our movement,' he declared, 'is towards a better, fairer organization of society; and our faith is strong and high that the time will surely come – and come the sooner for our efforts – when the dull, grey clouds under which millions of our countrymen are monotonously toiling, will break and melt and vanish for ever in the sunshine of a new and a noble age.'

Only one stumbling-block now remained to Churchill joining the Liberal Party, his opposition to Irish Home Rule. He had inherited this opposition from his father; it was integral to Conservative and Unionist thought and policy. In mid-January he had been given some 'notes on Ireland' by Sir Francis Mowatt, the head of the Civil Service. In the third week of May, after talking to one of the Irish Nationalist MPs, he decided to bridge the last remaining gap between himself and the Liberals, and put forward a specific plan for greater Irish control of their own affairs.

Churchill set out his plan in a letter to Morley on May 17. There would be no separate Irish Parliament. Control of the police would remain at Westminster. But Provincial Councils would be set up for education, licensing, rating, drainage and railways. These matters would be entrusted 'absolutely to the Irish people to manage or mis-manage as they choose'.

The new policy 'would constitute a definite step forward from the policy of Local Government & might be boldly described as "Administrative Home Rule". It could be defended by Unionist Free Traders as removing all that was just in the demand for legislative Home Rule, & by Home Rulers as being the penultimate step.'

Such was Churchill's own first step on his road to Home Rule. Two weeks later, on May 30, in a letter to the Jewish leaders in North-West Manchester, he publicly criticized the most controversial of all the new legislation before Parliament, the Government's Aliens Bill. This measure, which had been introduced to Parliament two months earlier, was designed to curb drastically Jewish immigration from Russia to Britain. In his letter Churchill announced that he would actively oppose the Bill. He was against departing 'from the old tolerant and generous practice of free entry and asylum to which this country has so long adhered and from which it has so greatly gained'. He went on to warn of the danger of the proposed legislation in the hand 'of an intolerant or anti-Semitic' Home Secretary. He was concerned, he said, with the effect of the Bill on the 'simple immigrant, the political refugee, the helpless and the poor' who, under the Bill, would not have 'the smallest right of appeal to the broad justice of the English courts'.

Attacking those who were still his own leaders, Churchill described the Aliens Bill as an attempt by the Government 'to gratify a small but noisy section of their supporters and to purchase a little popularity in the constituencies by dealing harshly with a number of unfortunate aliens who have no votes'. The Bill would commend itself 'to those who like patriotism at other peoples' expense and admire Imperialism on the Russian model. It is expected to appeal to insular prejudice against foreigners, to racial prejudice against Jews, and to labour prejudice against competition.'

Churchill's attack on the Aliens Bill was published in the *Manchester Guardian* on May 31. It was the first Parliamentary day after the Whitsun recess. That day the twenty-nine-year-old Member of Parliament entered the Chamber of the House of Commons, stood for a moment at the Bar of the House, looked briefly at both the Government and Opposition benches, strode up the aisle, bowed to the Speaker, turned sharply and emphatically to his right, to the Liberal benches, and sat down next to Lloyd George. He had joined the Liberals. The seat he chose was the one his father had sat in during his years in Opposition, and from which in 1885 he had stood waving his handkerchief to cheer the fall of Gladstone. Lord Randolph's 'dissentient' son now stood alongside Gladstone's Liberal heirs, determined to enhance their ranks, and to help them to electoral victory.

9

Revolt and Responsibilities

From the moment Churchill went to sit on the Liberal Opposition benches in the House of Commons on 31 May 1904 he was at the forefront of Liberal efforts to discredit the Conservatives, and to persuade the public of the merits of Liberalism. In the Commons his attacks on the Government set him at odds with the Conservative world of his family and class. 'I could not help thinking last night,' he wrote to Hugh Cecil on June 2, 'what a wrench it is to me to break with all that glittering hierarchy & how carefully one must organize one's system of thought to be utterly independent of it.' The 'worst of it', he added, 'is that as the Free Trade issue subsides it leaves my personal ambitions naked & stranded on the beach – & they are an ugly & unsatisfactory spectacle by themselves, though nothing but an advantage when borne forward with the flood of a great outside cause'.

On June 4, only four days after his formal adherence to the Liberals, Churchill attacked Balfour's Protectionist policies in a public speech in Manchester. Four days later, in the Commons, he was one of three Liberal speakers who denounced the Aliens Bill; the other two were the Liberal Party leader Campbell-Bannerman, and Asquith. It was Churchill's first speech from the Opposition benches. Then, for the next month, he led the attack on the Bill clause by clause. 'You have infused a new spirit into the younger men of the Opposition – as last night witnesseth!' the Master of Elibank, a Liberal MP since 1900, wrote to him on July 1.

The Aliens Bill was so effectively smothered with amendments, on each of which Churchill spoke against the Government, that on July 7 it was withdrawn. A leading Manchester Jew, Nathan Laski, wrote to thank Churchill 'for the splendid victory you have won for freedom & religious tolerance'. Laski also encouraged Churchill with regard to his new constituency. 'I have had over twenty years' experience in elections in Manchester,' he wrote, '& without flattery I tell you candidly – there has not been a single man able to arouse the interest that you have already done – thus I am sure of your future success.' Other local Liberal leaders echoed this sentiment. 'The people are willing to regard you not only as the Free Trade candidate for North-West Manchester,' one of them wrote to him that summer, 'but as the fighting head of the Free Trade party, and as one of the Liberal leaders in the near future.'

At the end of July, Churchill told Lord Tweedmouth of his talks with Lloyd George on the need to stimulate the Liberal leadership. From Tweedmouth came words of advice, 'Be vigorous but avoid much bitterness or sarcasm at the expense of our own molluscs on the Front Bench; be a cheering voice and a spur to them rather than a whip.' Further advice came from his aunt Lady Tweedmouth, his father's sister, who was dying. 'She begs you not to be too rampageous and aggressive & to remember there is truth in the old maxim *suaviter in modo, fortiter in re.*'

Churchill was prepared to spare the Liberal front bench, but not the Tory. 'It is because these Ministers are uplifted, guarded, served, praised,' he explained to Cecil that July, 'that they excite my attacks.' On August 2, in a sustained onslaught on Balfour's conduct of Government business, Churchill declared: 'There is one thing on which we may congratulate the Prime Minister. After all, we are nearly at the end of the session, and here is the Prime Minister still! The procedure of the House of Commons has been mutilated. Never mind! A great quantity of money has been expended. Never mind! No legislation of any value has been passed. Never mind! But here is the Prime Minister, at the end of the session, a great deal more than many people could have expected or hoped for. I offer to the right honourable gentleman, most sincerely, my most humble congratulations on his achievement.'

While Churchill's barbed style made him many enemies, he himself had been hurt by the private criticism against him in family circles when he had crossed to the Liberal benches. 'Had everyone adopted a tolerant line,' he wrote to his cousin Lady Londonderry, 'the present situation would be vastly different.' As for her own recent expressions of regret at his leaving the Conservatives, 'I appreciate your attitude all the more,' he wrote, 'because I had gathered from tales told that sometimes in the last few months you had commented upon my actions rather more severely than I had reason to expect from one who had known me all my life.'

That summer, as the political storm blew around him, Churchill went with his mother to a dance given by Lady Crewe, the wife of a leading Liberal. At the ball he was introduced by his mother to Clementine Hozier, a beautiful nineteen-year-old girl whose mother had been a friend of Lady Randolph's for many years. The introduction having been made,

Clementine expected Churchill to ask her to dance. He did not do so. 'Winston just stared,' she later recalled. 'He never uttered one word and was very gauche – he never asked me for a dance, he never asked me to have supper with him.' She had of course heard much about this controversial figure, 'nothing but ill. I had been told he was stuck-up, objectionable etcetera. And on this occasion he just stood and stared.'

Clementine had arranged to be rescued if necessary. 'A beau of hers was standing nearby,' her daughter Mary later wrote, 'and, obeying a discreet signal, he came up and asked her to dance with him.' During the course of the dance the young man asked his partner what she was doing talking to 'that frightful fellow Winston Churchill'. Nearly four years were to pass before he was to meet Clementine Hozier again.

That autumn Churchill withdrew from the political fray to try to complete his biography of his father. For three weeks he stayed at Sir Ernest Cassel's villa at Moerel, in the Swiss mountains. There he wrote his book each morning, walked each afternoon and played bridge each evening. 'I sleep like a top & have not ever felt in better health,' he told his mother. Back in England, he went to see Chamberlain to talk about his father. 'We dined alone,' he later recalled. 'With the dessert a bottle of '34 port was opened. Only the briefest reference was made to current controversies.' Chamberlain told Churchill: 'I think you are quite right, feeling as you do, to join the Liberals. You must expect to have the same sort of abuse hurled at you as I have endured. But if a man is sure of himself, it only sharpens him and makes him more effective.' Apart from this one reference to the disputes of the day, their talk, Churchill later wrote, 'lay in the controversies and personalities of twenty years before'. At one moment, Churchill told his mother, 'he got out the cup which my father gave him on his third marriage and made a great fuss about it'.

'You will laugh,' Churchill wrote to a Unionist Free Trader friend, 'when I tell you (secret) that I spent a very pleasant night at Highbury and had five or six hours very interesting and friendly conversation with the great Joe,' and he added: 'My prognostication is that he and the Prime Minister will cut their own throats and bring their party to utter destruction between them, that the Liberals will gain a gigantic victory at the Election – far greater than anything even they imagine – and that they will break into fragments almost immediately afterwards.'

Politically, Churchill had begun to make common cause with the radical wing of the Liberal Party, led by Lloyd George. At Carnarvon on October 18 he shared a platform with the 'Welsh wizard', and at Edinburgh on November 10 he declared that he was more afraid of the 'Independent Capitalist Party' than of the Independent Labour Party, telling his Scottish audience: 'No one seems to care anything but about money today. Nothing is held of account except the bank accounts. Quality, education, civic distinction, public virtue seem each year to be valued less and less. Riches unadorned seem each year to be valued more and more.'

In a sustained attack on the misuse of capital, Churchill told the citizens of Edinburgh: 'We have in London an important section of people who go about preaching the gospel of Mammon, advocating the ten per cent commandments – who raise each day the inspiring prayer "Give cash in our time, O Lord!" ' The last Liberal Government had made it a rule not to allow Ministers to be directors of public companies. He calculated that thirty-one out of the present fifty-five Conservative Ministers were directors, holding sixty-eight directorships between them, 'That laxity of principle is a sign of the degeneration of the day.' So too was the recent sale of a Free Trade newspaper, the *Standard*, to a protectionist proprietor. 'What shall we say', Churchill asked, 'of those who use vast wealth to poison the fountains of public information?'

When Churchill finished speaking the whole audience stood up and applauded. 'I was pleased with that meeting which was in its way a triumph!' he wrote to Lord Rosebery. 'Oh but what a labour & a battle to overturn this government, with our divided & undisciplined army!'

Former Conservative friends continued to have misgivings about Churchill's fierce onslaughts against his old Party. 'I readily admit that my conduct is open to criticism,' he wrote to one of them in November 1904, shortly before his thirtieth birthday, 'not – thank heaven – on the score of sincerity, but from the point of view of taste,' and he went on to explain: 'I had to choose between fighting & standing aside. No doubt the latter was the more decorous. But I wanted to fight – I felt I could fight with my whole heart and soul – so there it is.' Politics was, of course, 'a form of tournament in which mud-slinging & invective are recognised weapons. But taking part in such an ugly brawl does not in my mind prejudice personal relations.'

In the Commons, still pursuing his father's cause of economy in the Army, on 1 March 1905 Churchill criticised the new Secretary of State for War, Hugh Arnold-Forster, for the high expenditure on the General Staff, by which, he explained, he meant 'those gilded and gorgeous functionaries with brass hats and ornamental duties who multiplied so luxuriously on the plains of Aldershot and Salisbury'. Commented King Edward VII when he read this criticism, 'What good words for a recent subaltern of Hussars!'

A week later Churchill introduced his own motion against tariffs. In a powerfully argued speech – 'the best you have ever made' wrote Lewis Harcourt, a future Liberal Colonial Secretary – Churchill told the House: 'We do not want to see the British Empire degenerate into a sullen confederacy, walled off, like a medieval town, from the surrounding country; victualled for a siege, and containing within the circle of its battlements all that is necessary for war. We want this country and the States associated with us to take their parts freely and fairly in the general intercourse of commercial nations.'

The more effectively and strongly Churchill spoke against the Conservatives, the more deeply they resented his criticisms. In April 1905 he felt obliged to leave the Carlton Club, of which, as a Conservative MP, he had been a member for the past five years. He was, he wrote to Lord Londonderry, 'in such constant conflict with the Conservative Party at all points that my membership of their club cannot be justified any longer & has become disagreeable to me'. Churchill added, 'Old friendships have been snapped & on the other hand new obligations have been contracted.'

Two months later Churchill was blackballed for the Hurlingham Club. 'This is almost without precedent in the history of the Club – as polo players are always welcomed,' he wrote to the Master of Elibank, and he added, 'I do not think you & your Liberal friends realize the intense political bitterness which is felt against me on the other side.' Churchill hit back fiercely at those he saw as his enemies, so much so that friends like Elibank became alarmed at the scathing tone of his references to the Government Ministers, and to Balfour in particular. 'You are the sole politician,' Elibank explained, 'who has moved and attracted me' during ten years in Parliament. 'I speak from the point of view of "leading".' The feeling among those 'who inevitably must rank among your backers in order ultimately to carry you and your policy to success in the country' was that continual belittling of Balfour 'conceivably may detract, in the public estimation, from the weight and general effect produced by the high level of your speeches on current problems'.

Churchill also learned, from Ian Hamilton, that at a country house weekend that summer, during which all those present 'male and female, in the smart company there assembled, were prepared to rend you to pieces', it was Balfour who 'spoke so exceedingly nicely about you, and expressed such generous hopes about your future, that no one raised a finger'.

Churchill briefly put current politics behind him in order to finish writing his father's life. 'At present,' he told Rosebery, 'the Statesman is in abeyance, and the Literary gent & the polo player are to the fore.' For the first two weeks of October, at Blenheim, he corrected the printer's proofs of his life of his father. He was also, he told his mother, 'trying to get a great deal of money for my book'. In this task he was extraordinarily successful, receiving £8,000, the highest amount yet paid in Britain for a political biography, and £350,000 in the money values of 1990.

Even as Churchill was finishing his life of his father, a Liberal writer, Alexander MacCallum Scott, published the first biography of Churchill himself. In it Scott wrote approvingly that Churchill was determined 'that capital shall be made the servant and not the master of the State', and that 'the true happiness of nations is to be secured by industrial development and social reform at home, rather than by territorial expansion and military adventures abroad'. Scott also drew attention to the fact that Churchill disagreed with Chamberlain's assertion that the future rested with the great territorial empires; if the British Empire held together, he quoted Churchill as saying, it would not be because of its size or its Army, but 'because it is based upon the assent of free peoples, united with each other by noble and progressive principles; because it is animated by respect for right and justice'.

Scott, who fifteen years later was to be Churchill's Parliamentary Private Secretary at the War Office, commented that after Chamberlain, Churchill was 'probably the best-hated man in English politics', but added: 'He will ever be a leader, whether of a forlorn hope or of a great Party. Already in the House of Commons he leads by a natural right which no man can dispute. He does the inevitable act which no one had thought of before; he thinks the original thought which is so simple and obvious once it has been uttered; he coins the happy phrase which expresses what all men have longed to say, and which thereafter comes so aptly to every man's tongue.'

Scott was certain that Churchill would 'rally in his own person the dispersed forces of Free Trade in one long line of battle'. It was 'a bold and ambitious idea, and the struggle will be a highly dramatic one. Will he win? Is he the destined man to bring back to Lancashire the political hegemony of the provinces? He plays for high stakes, but his nerve is steady and his eye is clear. He will at any rate make a fight for it, and the fight will be something to have lived for and to have seen.'

Free Trade was not the only issue agitating the public mind; at a meeting in North-West Manchester on October 13, Churchill and his fellow-speaker, Sir Edward Grey, were both repeatedly interrupted by two leading suffragettes, Christabel Pankhurst and Annie Kenny. Escorted from the hall by police, the two women were fined fifteen shillings for creating a disturbance, refused to pay, and were sentenced to a week in prison. On hearing this, Churchill offered to pay the fines. The two women preferred the martyrdom of prison.

To a Liberal who was angered at what seemed to have been an over-harsh reaction by the police, Churchill wrote, 'To throw great public meetings into confusion and to disregard the chairman, cannot be defended on democratic grounds.' His letter continued: 'The power of conducting orderly discussions in very large gatherings is one of the most valuable possessions of the British people. With men who disturb such meetings it is easy to deal; but it is repugnant to anyone that any degree of physical force should ever be applied to women. But if sex confers protection, it should also enjoin restraint.' He could not believe that the interruptions would 'materially advance the cause of which these ladies are such earnest and courageous advocates'. Grey, he pointed out, was 'a life-long and active supporter' of votes for women.

On the last day of October, Churchill dined with Edward VII. It was the King's intention, he told his mother, 'to bring home to me the error of my ways'. It was the first time in three years, he told Rosebery, that the King had agreed to meet him. 'He spoke most severely & even vehemently to me about my attacks on A. Balfour. I accepted it all with meekness. In the end he became most gracious & we talked one hour.' Two weeks later Churchill was taken ill. There were rumours that he had suffered a nervous collapse; the King was among those who expressed concern. At the end of the month he cancelled all his meetings for the week and went to Camborne Manor, his Aunt Cornelia's house in Dorset. There he sought to recuperate with the help of a 'wonderful' masseuse who, he told his mother, had 'almost miraculous virtues & I am very comfortable & peaceful'.

November 30 was Churchill's birthday. 'Thirty-one is very old,' he wrote to his mother from Dorset. That week a letter of good wishes for his recovery reached him from an unexpected quarter; from Hugh Arnold-Forster, of whose Army expenditure he was a foremost critic. 'I am truly sorry to hear you are ill,' Arnold-Forster wrote from the War Office. 'Do take care of yourself. You know I don't agree with your politics but you are the only man on your side of the House who seems to me really to understand the Army problem. So from a purely selfish point of view I want you to be well again. May I add that from a personal view I entertain the same view and cherish the same life very strongly.'

On December 1, while still in Dorset, Churchill reported to his mother that the American masseuse had pointed out that his tongue was 're-strained by a ligament which nobody else has'. That, he commented, 'is the true explanation of my speaking through my nose'. He therefore travelled up to London to ask Sir Felix Semon to cut the ligament. Semon refused to do so, with the result, Churchill told his mother on December 4, that his tongue was still 'tied'.

That very day, December 4, Balfour resigned as Prime Minister, calculating that he would leave the Liberals in quarrelsome disarray, and that the Conservatives would in the end emerge all the stronger. The King sent for Campbell-Bannerman, who began at once to form a Government. The

prospect of power united the divergent wings of the Liberal Party: Liberal
Radicals and Liberal Imperialists alike, with the exception of Rosebery,
agreed to serve under the new Prime Minister. Churchill was offered a
junior Ministerial post, as Financial Secretary to the Treasury, under the
new Chancellor of the Exchequer, Asquith. But he preferred a department where he could show his administrative skills under a less brilliant
master, and with more independence than he would have with his chief in
the House of Commons.

The post for which Churchill asked was that of Under-Secretary of State
at the Colonial Office. The Secretary of State, Lord Elgin, would be in the
House of Lords, leaving Churchill to conduct the department's business
in the Commons. His request was accepted. 'I am arranging for the
Colonial Office, so that is all right,' Campbell-Bannerman telegraphed to
him on December 9. 'I had some difficulty in securing my wish,' Churchill
told Cecil, 'as it involved considerable alteration in other minor offices.'
Ten days after his thirty-first birthday, Churchill was a Junior Minister.
'How things have marched since we pitched our tent in the triangle of the
railway station at Estcourt!' wrote his Boer War journalist colleague, John
Atkins.

On his first evening as a member of the Government, Churchill was at
a party in London where he was introduced to Edward Marsh, a Colonial
Office clerk two years his senior.

'How do you do?' asked Marsh. 'Which I must now say with great
respect.'

'Why "with great respect"?' Churchill asked.

'Because you're coming to rule over me at the Colonial Office,' Marsh
replied.

Intrigued, Churchill made enquiries. Then, on the following morning,
his first full day in office, he invited Marsh to his room and asked if he
would be his Private Secretary. Marsh accepted. That night the two men
dined alone at Churchill's flat in Mount Street. 'He was most perfectly
charming to me,' Marsh wrote to Churchill's Aunt Leonie, 'but made it
quite clear what he would expect in the way of help and I almost know I
can't do it.' Marsh was to remain Churchill's Private Secretary in each of
Churchill's Ministerial offices during the next quarter of a century. 'The
first time you meet Winston,' Pamela Plowden told him, 'you see all his
faults, and the rest of your life you spend in discovering his virtues.'

The new Liberal Government called a General Election, determined to
secure a working majority in the Commons. Churchill issued his election
manifesto on 1 January 1906, describing himself as the 'enemy' of any
form of tariff system. He was also in favour of 'a reduction of expenditure
upon armaments', and the taxation of land values. As for Ireland, while

he would oppose any form of separation of Ireland from the United Kingdom, 'I would gladly see the Irish people accorded the power to manage their own expenditure, their own education, and their own public works according to Irish ideas.'

On January 2, as the election campaign began, Churchill's book *Lord Randolph Churchill* was published. It was described by *The Times Literary Supplement* as 'certainly among the two or three most exciting political biographies in the language'. From Lord Rosebery came a private letter of praise about the book, 'Good humoured, impartial, vivid, sympathetic, and written in an admirable style, with little refreshing ironies to flavour the whole composition, it is a book difficult to lay down.' In the book, Churchill referred, in a clear reference to his own thinking, to an England 'of wise men who gaze without self-deception at the failings and follies of both political parties; of brave and earnest men who find in neither faction fair scope for the effort that is in them; of "poor men" who increasingly doubt the sincerity of party philosophy.' It was to that England, he wrote, 'that Lord Randolph Churchill appealed; it was that England he so nearly won; it is by that England he will be justly judged'.

Accompanied by Edward Marsh, Churchill went on January 4 by train to Manchester to launch his first election campaign as a Liberal. During the first day's campaigning the two men walked through the slum areas of the constituency. 'Winston looked about him,' Marsh later recalled, 'and his sympathetic imagination was stirred. "Fancy", he said, "living in one of these streets – never seeing anything beautiful – never eating anything savoury – *never saying anything clever!*" (the italics were his – it would be impossible to give a better rendering of italics in the spoken word).'

Churchill campaigned for eight days. At one meeting he told a heckler who quoted something he had said while a Conservative, 'I said a lot of stupid things when I was in the Conservative Party, and I left them because I did not want to go on saying stupid things.' As to the charge of being a political turncoat: 'I admit I have changed my Party. I don't deny it. I am proud of it. When I think of all the labours Lord Randolph Churchill gave to the fortunes of the Conservative Party and the ungrateful way he was treated by them when they obtained the power they would never have had but for him, I am delighted that circumstances have enabled me to break with them while I am still young, and still have the best energies of my life to give to the popular cause.'

Polling took place on January 13. The results were announced that evening. Churchill had been elected by a majority of 1,241 in an electorate of 10,000. Just as in 1900 his campaign had helped his fellow-Conservative candidates elsewhere, so now his fellow-Liberal campaigners became the beneficiaries of his electoral skill and zeal. His efforts in and around Manchester helped six other Liberal candidates to overturn Conservative seats. 'Bravo!' his cousin Ivor Guest wrote to him. 'You have given the pendulum such a swing as will be felt throughout the whole country.' The Liberal victory was a political triumph and a landslide. The Liberals won 377 seats, their Labour Party allies 53, the Irish Nationalists 83; a 'Ministerialist' total of 513. Against this formidable array were only 157 Tories, eleven of whom were Churchill's former associates, the Unionist Free Traders.

Churchill was now a Junior Minister in a Government furnished with far greater authority than it had expected. He was also the author of a much-acclaimed biography. 'There is such an obvious opening just now for a Dizzy or a Randolph,' William Moneypenny, the biographer of Disraeli, wrote in congratulating him both on his book and on the beginning of his official career, 'that I am half inclined to regret you are immured in Downing Street.' But Churchill was 'immured' nowhere; neither his proximity to power nor his Ministerial responsibilities were to prevent that same independence of action and ideas that had characterised his father, and Disraeli, in the previous century.

At his desk in the Colonial Office, with Edward Marsh at his side, and the guidance of civil servants some of whom were twice his age, Churchill's first work as a Junior Minister was to help draft a constitution for the Transvaal. Since the surrender of the Boers more than five years earlier he had been a strong advocate of conciliation with the two defeated Republics. For more than a year he had supported the grant of self-government to Boer and Briton alike, to culminate in a single confederation. This was now his own Ministerial responsibility. On 2 January 1906, in the first State Paper of his career, he urged the Cabinet to abandon the former Conservative government's plan for the retention of controls, and to grant the Transvaal responsible government.

'Sooner or later', Churchill pointed out, any powers retained by London would be demanded by the Transvaal. By then, however, 'the control of events will have largely passed from our hands. We may not be able, without the employment of force, to prescribe the electoral basis of the new constitution or even to reserve the functions necessary to the maintenance of public order and the King's authority. What we might have given with courage and distinction, both at home and in South Africa, upon our own terms, in the hour of our strength, will be jerked and twisted from our hands – without grace of any kind – not perhaps without humiliation – at a time when the Government may be greatly weakened, and upon terms in the settlement of which we shall have only a nominal influence.'

The Cabinet accepted Churchill's reasoning and instructed him to prepare the detailed drafts needed for a Constitutional settlement. In doing so he sought to create an equality of rights between the defeated Boer and the victorious Briton. 'Do not let us do anything,' he wrote in a note for the Cabinet on January 30, 'which makes us the champions of one race, and consequently deprives us for ever of the confidence of the other.' Churchill now participated in several meetings of a Cabinet Committee set up to decide on whether responsible government was possible. Within a month the Cabinet decided to grant self-government to the Transvaal at an early date. It was Churchill who would have to explain the reasons, and the details, to Parliament.

Another South African issue claimed much of Churchill's time during 1906; as a main part of their attack on the Conservatives during the election campaign, Liberal candidates had denounced as 'slavery' the use of indentured Chinese labour in South Africa. On coming to power, the Liberal Government was pledged to halt the recruitment of Chinese labour and to allow those labourers already in South Africa to go home. Churchill abhorred the conditions under which the Chinese were working, and wanted to press for the most rapid repatriation possible. When the Cabinet, of which he was not a member, wavered in pushing forward a measure which might alienate many South African leaders, Churchill warned Lord Elgin of the inevitable indignation of the House of Commons at the continued use by the mine owners of 'armed compulsion to maintain an immoral contract'.

The Liberal Cabinet felt bound not to go back on the final set of contracts approved by the Conservative Government in its very last months. While agreeing not to allow any further recruitment of labourers, and to encourage repatriation to China, it nevertheless decided, primarily in an attempt not to disrupt the South African economy, against any sudden ending of the indentured labour system. In a note to Elgin, Churchill proposed setting a maximum period of six years for the total elimination of Chinese labour. 'If anything can be done to let the Banks of South Africa down gently and to make them let their clients down gently, I should rejoice,' he wrote. 'Any suggestions to stop a sudden crash should be carefully considered. But crash or no crash, the policy will have to go forward, and the sooner this is realised, the better for all concerned.'

It fell to Churchill to defend in the Commons the decision to wind down indentured labour. The Chinese labour system, he said, was an 'evil inheritance'; it had been a 'sordid experiment'. The Liberal Government's aim was the 'gradual withdrawal' of the system. As to the Liberal Party's election charges of 'slavery', he told the Commons in a passage which provoked derisive jeers from the Conservative benches: 'A labour contract into which men enter voluntarily for a limited and for a brief period, under which they are paid wages which they consider adequate, under which they are not bought or sold, and under which they can obtain relief, may not be a desirable contract, may not be a healthy or proper contract, but it cannot in the opinion of His Majesty's Government be classified as slavery in the extreme acceptance of the word without some risk of terminological inexactitude.'

The Conservative Opposition protested with vigour at the word 'slavery' being called a 'terminological inexactitude'. It was after all the Liberals who, during the election campaign, had made so much political capital out of the accusation of 'slavery'. Coolly, Churchill offered to withdraw the words 'terminological inexactitude'. The very coolness of his offer outraged the Conservatives even more. Then, on February 27, Lord Milner admitted in the House of Lords that while he was British High Commissioner in South Africa he had sanctioned the flogging of Chinese labourers even though they had not been convicted by a magistrate. This, Milner admitted, had been in breach of his own laws; such punishments were indeed unjust.

Churchill now spoke in the Commons of Milner's 'grave dereliction of public duty' and 'undoubted infringement of the law'. A week after this charge, a Radical MP introduced a motion censuring Milner and initiated a debate. In an effort at conciliation, Churchill, while expressing sympathy with the motion, argued that, in the interest of a settlement in South Africa, members should refrain from passing censure upon individuals. He therefore introduced an amendment of his own, condemning the flogging of the Chinese coolies, but not naming Milner.

In introducing his amendment, Churchill was careful not to refer to Milner's part in allowing the floggings. But everything he said angered the Conservatives who heard him. Milner, he told the House, had 'played a part which will leave its imprint, for good or ill, extensively upon the pages of history'. The words 'or ill' were not well chosen.

Churchill then spoke several sentences which he had intended to be moderate and judicious, but which, as he spoke them, enraged the Opposition as much as if they had been a direct attack on Milner. 'Lord Milner has gone from South Africa, probably for ever,' he said. 'The public service knows him no more. Having exercised great authority he now exerts none. Having held high employment, he now has no employment. Having disposed of events which have shaped the course of history, he is now unable to deflect in the smallest degree the policy of the day. Having been for many years, at any rate for many months, the arbiter of the fortune of men who are "rich beyond the dreams of avarice", he is today poor, and I will add honourably poor. After twenty years of exhausting service under the Crown he is today a retired Civil Servant, without pension or gratuity of any kind whatever. It is not worth while to pursue him any further.'

Newly elected Liberal MPs, Churchill continued, must not overlook or underrate 'the vexation and mortification which must be experienced by any vehement and earnest man who sees the ideals, the principles, the policies for which he has toiled, utterly discredited by the people of Great Britain, and who knows that many of the arrangements in which he has consumed all the energies of his life are about to be reversed or dissolved'. Lord Milner, he added, 'has ceased to be a factor in public events'.

'Utterly discredited', 'has ceased to be a factor'; these were harsh phrases, however true.

Churchill ended his speech by appealing to the Liberals not to vote for the censure of Milner, and to defuse the passions of Party politics for the sake of a settlement. The House of Commons, he said, 'can send a message to South Africa which cannot be perverted, misrepresented or misunderstood, a message of comfort to a troubled people, a message of tolerance and conciliation to warring races, a message indeed of good hope to the Cape'. This appeal for comfort, conciliation and hope was well-intended. Indeed, as a result of Churchill's intervention, the Radical motion condemning Milner by name was withdrawn. But his references to Milner excited the passions of his enemies, and were to be referred to over many years as proof of his mischievousness and lack of balance. Balfour, speaking immediately after Churchill, asked that both Churchill's amendment and the original censure motion be rejected with 'equal contempt'.

'Pompous and impertinent' was the view of one Conservative MP, Sir William Anson, Warden of All Souls' College, Oxford. 'Simply scandalous' was the comment of the King, who protested at Churchill's 'violent and objectionable language'. In the immediate aftermath of the Milner debate a Conservative MP brought in a motion to reduce Churchill's salary as a protest against his 'bitter and empoisoned language' in insulting Milner, 'a man whom so many of us esteem, honour and love'. The motion was unsuccessful.

Churchill was certain that he had done and said the right thing. 'After all,' he wrote to Milner's successor as High Commissioner, Lord Selborne, 'no other course but the one adopted by me would have prevented Lord Milner from being censured formally by the House of Commons.' Yet the causes of censure remained. When Selborne reported that the mine owners were continuing to flog their Chinese labourers, Churchill wrote to Elgin, 'What are we to do with people so reckless of their own interests as to continue these floggings and malpractices after all that has happened?' His answer was to continue with the repatriation scheme; it was announced by Churchill on May 3.

On July 31 Churchill announced the establishment of responsible government for the Transvaal. It was expected that a British majority would emerge at the elections and hold the balance of power. In the event, victory was secured by the Boers, and Britain's former adversary, General Botha, became Prime Minister. In his speech on July 31 Churchill asked the Opposition to support responsible government, which abandoned the Imperial controls that the Conservatives had wanted to set. 'We can only make it the gift of a Party,' he said. 'They can make it the gift of England.'

Churchill's appeal, a fellow-Liberal noted, 'struck the right note and moved this strange audience to emotion'. In defending the Transvaal settlement to the King, Churchill wrote: 'Any intelligent community will much rather govern itself ill, than be well governed by some other community: & we, whatever our intentions, have not the knowledge of their problems to enable us to give even good government.' Churchill went on to point out that all the South African business in the Commons had been left 'entirely' in his hands. He had had to speak more often than any other Minister except the President of the Board of Education '& to answer something like 500 questions, besides a great number of supplementary questions put & answered on the spur of the moment'.

Churchill told the King: 'I have had no previous experience in this kind of work. I have had a new & unfathomed House of Commons to deal with in respect of subjects upon which it is strangely excited; & at least four perfectly separate currents of opinion to consider. If therefore I have from time to time turned phrases awkwardly, or not judged quite the right time or tone, I feel certain that Your Majesty will have put the most favourable construction upon my words & will have credited me throughout with loyal & grave intentions.'

'If the dead are in any way conscious of our doings,' Churchill's former schoolmaster, C.H.P. Mayo, wrote to him that autumn, 'your father must visit the scene of his triumph with no less sense of triumph now.'

In August 1906, Churchill left England for a prolonged holiday. At Deauville, on the Channel coast of France, he lived on the yacht of his friend Baron de Forest, and played several polo matches at nearby Trouville. 'I have been very idle here & very dissipated,' he wrote to Marsh, 'gambling every night till five in the morning. I have made a little money – had made a lot.' To his brother Jack, he later reported: 'I took away £260 from the Deauville casino, some of which I spent in Paris on more beautiful French editions – which you might arrange provisionally in the French shelf near the window – & some of which I spent in other directions.' His gambling success at Deauville won him the equivalent of £10,000 in the money values of 1990. He was always to enjoy visiting the tables, often coming away the gainer.

From Paris, Churchill travelled by train to Switzerland, to stay once more at Cassel's mountain villa. There, he told the King, he and Cassel 'propose long walks over the glacier & mountains'. The two men climbed the 9,625-foot Eggishorn, 'a very long pull', Churchill told his mother, '& I should never have got home without the aid of a mule. Le vieillard' – Cassel was then fifty-four – 'tramped it all out like a bird. Rather discreditable to me, I think'. From Switzerland, Churchill went to Berlin, then on to Silesia as the guest of the Kaiser, King Edward's nephew, at German Army manoeuvres. Campbell-Bannerman sent Churchill a word of caution; he had spoken to the King, who 'asked me to warn you against being too communicative and frank with his nephew'. Churchill wrote to his mother, 'I expect I will have to mind my Ps and Qs, so as to appear entirely candid & yet say nothing either platitudinous or indiscreet.'

During the manoeuvres Churchill spoke for twenty minutes with the Kaiser, who told him of the fighting qualities of the Herero tribe in German South-West Africa; the Germans were then ruthlessly suppressing the Herero revolt. 'I said in reply,' Churchill told Elgin, 'that in Natal on the contrary our chief difficulty had not been to kill the rebellious natives, but to prevent our Colonists (who so thoroughly understood native war) from killing too many of them.' Churchill added, 'There is a massive simplicity & force about German military arrangements which grows upon the observer; and although I do not think they have appreciated the terrible power of the weapons they hold & modern fire conditions, and have in that & in minor respects much to learn from our Army, yet numbers, quality, discipline & organisation are four good roads to victory.'

From Silesia, Churchill went to by train to Venice, staying there a week before embarking on a sightseeing trip through Italy, travelling in Lionel Rothschild's motor car with Lionel Rothschild himself, Muriel Wilson and Lady Helen Vincent, at 'forty miles an hour', he told his mother. 'Such a lot of churches we have seen and saints and pictures "galore".' Nothing could exceed the 'tranquil *banalité*' of his relations with Miss Wilson. Then, driving back to Venice 'in one fell swoop of 330 kilometres' he took the night train to Vienna, and continued into the Moravian province of Austria-Hungary, where he was the guest of Baron de Forest at Eichhorn. All three of his hosts that summer, Cassel, Rothschild and de Forest, were Jews, reviving a jibe that used to be made against his father, that he 'only had Jewish friends'.

Churchill returned to London after nearly two months abroad. To the Kaiser, who had sent him signed photographs of the manoeuvres, he wrote of how they would remind him 'of the magnificent & formidable army whose operations I was enabled by Your Majesty's kindness to study so pleasantly, & of that beautiful Silesia which was well worth coming to see for its own sake – & so well worth fighting for'. Thirty-eight years later, at the end of the second of Britain's two wars with Germany, Churchill was to approve the transfer of Silesia to Poland, and its detachment from Germany.

In the autumn of 1906 the Orange Free State was granted responsible government on the same lines as the Transvaal. In announcing this to the Commons on December 17, Churchill spoke about the wider social implications of the settlement. 'The cause of the poor and the weak all over the world,' he said, 'will have been sustained; and everywhere small peoples will get more room to breathe; and everywhere great empires will be encouraged by our example to step forward into the sunshine of a more gentle and a more generous age.'

Churchill's work on the South African settlement prompted 'a special line of congratulation and recognition of the large part you have had in our success' from the Prime Minister, Campbell-Bannerman, who added that the creation of self-governing States in the Transvaal and the Orange Free State was not only the 'greatest achievement' of his Government but 'the finest & noblest work of the British power in modern times. And you have so identified yourself with this courageous & righteous policy, and so greatly contributed to its successful enforcement, that a large part of the credit of it must always be attributed to you.'

The Transvaal settlement left control of native affairs in the hands of the new and predominantly Boer Government. The wisdom of this was questioned by those who felt that a Liberal Government in England could not abandon responsibility for the black population. 'I should certainly not be forward,' Churchill told a correspondent on this issue, 'in pressing upon the South African colonies views in regard to native franchise which they are at present not ready to accept. But our responsibility to the native races remains a real one, and we cannot divest ourselves of it until at least a Federal South African Government shall have placed the whole treatment of native races upon a broad and secure platform beyond the range of local panics.' Of the native grievances Churchill wrote forcefully to Lord Selborne: 'I think it highly desirable that any restrictions to which they now object would necessarily be modified – if not entirely removed – if we had an august Federal authority to deal with, instead of a group of petty governments pursuing local and selfish aims.'

Throughout his time at the Colonial Office, Churchill endeavoured to instil Liberal principles into Colonial administration. His minutes to Elgin were so outspoken that in several cases Elgin asked him to paste them over so that junior officials would not see them. The principle animating them was clear. 'Our duty,' he wrote to Elgin, 'is to insist that the principles of justice and the safeguards of judicial procedure are rigidly, punctiliously and pedantically followed.' Reading a report on the 'pacification' of the tribes of Northern Nigeria, and of the Governor-General's proposed reprisals against a tribe which had burned down a Niger Company depot, Churchill told Elgin: 'Of course if the peace and order of the Colony depend on a vigorous offensive we must support him with all our hearts. But the chronic bloodshed which stains the West African seasons is odious and disquieting.'

Justice was a central theme of Churchill's interventions. When the Governor of Ceylon pleaded 'inconvenience' as a reason for refusing to respond to an appeal for reinstatement by a former head guard on the Ceylon Government railways, Churchill minuted, 'The inconvenience inseparable from the reparation of injustice or irregularity is one of the safeguards against their recurrence.' Churchill added that the Governor's explanations, 'such a jumble of confused arguments, such indifference to ordinary principles of justice and fair play, are intellectually contemptible if not morally dishonouring'. To Elgin, Churchill wrote privately of this episode, 'Let me say most solemnly that the Liberal Party cares very much for the rights of individuals to just & lawful treatment, & very little for the petty pride of a Colonial Governor.' He was concerned by 'the tone & temper which high officers of the Ceylon Government observe towards the amiable, civilised & cultivated people over whom they are set to govern'.

When Elgin declined to take up the case as Churchill wished, an angry private letter followed. 'In over-ruling me,' Churchill wrote, 'you do not assign any reasons, nor attempt to do justice to the very grave arguments I have so earnestly submitted to you.' This caused him 'the most profound disquiet'. The dismissal of a second railway guard in Ceylon and his second trial on the same charge, led to a further protest from Churchill. 'To try a man again upon the original charge,' he wrote, 'to review without any of the safeguards of justice a case already decided in a court of law, to overthrow the acquittal pronounced by judge and jury, and solidly to assert upon departmental authority that the man is guilty after all, is to commit almost every impropriety possible, and to commit them all in the stupidest way.' The administration of justice in Ceylon was 'the vilest scandal of the colonial service'.

When a Zulu revolt was crushed in Natal, Churchill protested to Elgin about the 'disgusting butchery of the natives'. But it was not only on Colonial matters that Churchill defended Liberal principles. In a speech in Glasgow on 11 October 1906 he set out a broad, humane vision for the future; the 'whole tendency of civilisation', he said, was towards 'the multiplication of the collective functions of society'. The State must play an ever-widening part; it must, for example, 'increasingly and earnestly concern itself with the care of the sick and the aged, and, above all, of the children'.

Churchill also approved the existing determination among many Liberals 'to intercept all future unearned increment which may arise from the increase in the speculative value of land'. He wanted the State to take a lead in afforestation. 'I am sorry,' he said, 'we have not got the railways of this country in our hands.' He wanted the State increasingly to assume 'the position of the reserve employer of labour'. Above all, he declared, 'I look forward to the universal establishment of minimum standards of life and labour, and their progressive elevation as the increased energies of production may permit.'

There was a middle way between capitalism and socialism. 'I do not want to see impaired the vigour of competition,' Churchill told his Glasgow audience, 'but we can do much to mitigate the consequences of failure. We want to draw a line below which we will not allow persons to live and labour, yet above which they may compete with all the strength of their manhood. We want to have free competition upwards; we decline to allow free competition to run downwards. We do not want to pull down the structures of science and civilisation; but to spread a net over the abyss.'

At the end of 1906 Churchill was being considered for promotion to the Cabinet, as President of the Board of Education. 'I have been dreading every post to find the rumours true and that I was to lose your help,' Elgin wrote to him on December 27. 'Of course I should like to come into the Cabinet,' Churchill replied, 'so as to be able to take my proper part in national as opposed to departmental politics. But I can easily imagine that no vacancy that would suit me will be created in the near future, & I shall be quite content & happy to go on working under you in the Colonial Office for another year, if events should so shape themselves.'

Churchill remained with Elgin, writing to him that winter, 'No one could ever have had a more trustful & indulgent chief than I have been most lucky to find on first joining a government; & I have learned a very great deal in the conduct of official business from your instruction and example which I should all my life have remained completely ignorant of, if I had gone elsewhere.' Elgin, with a sick wife, and many local obligations in his native Scotland, was glad despite their disagreements to have someone of such unexpected administrative energies in charge in London.

That winter, Churchill went on holiday to the Isle of Wight. 'Unluckily,' he told Elgin, 'the sea has been dead calm, so that there are no great waves that I could watch for hours.' He was now thirty-two years old. Among those whom he met for the first time that year was the Chancellor of the Exchequer's daughter, Violet Asquith. They were sitting next to each other at dinner. 'For a long time he remained sunk in abstraction,' she later recalled. 'Then he appeared to become suddenly aware of my existence. He turned on me a lowering gaze and asked me abruptly how old I was. I replied that I was nineteen. "And I," he said almost despairingly, "am thirty-two already. Younger than anyone else who counts, though." After a long oration he suddenly ended with the immortal words, "We are all worms, but I do believe I am a glow-worm." '

In March 1907 Churchill went on holiday to Biarritz, to another of the magnificent homes of his friend Baron de Forest, and the Baron's father, Baron de Hirsch. 'The King dines or lunches here daily,' he wrote to Elgin, '& seems very well disposed to us.' Churchill added: 'The weather here is glorious & there are a great many people I have known a long time – all Tories! I get a good deal of chaff & prodding, especially from high quarters, endeavouring always to frame suitable replies.' After their talks together in Biarritz, King Edward wrote to Churchill: 'We have known your parents for many years (even before their marriage), & you and your brother since your childhood. Knowing the great abilities which you possess – I am watching your political career with great interest. My one wish is that the great qualities you possess may be turned to good account & that your services to the State may be appreciated.'

On April 15 the Colonial Prime Ministers met in London; Churchill was closely involved in arranging the visit. The Transvaal Premier, elected less than two months earlier, was General Botha, former commander of the Boer armies, who arrived in London with his nineteen-year-old daughter Helen. 'I hear you are engaged to Miss Botha,' Muriel Wilson wrote to him; she looked forward to the day 'when you I hope – & Miss Botha, & all the little Bothas will come & see me.' It was a false rumour; that autumn, still neither married nor engaged, Churchill left Britain for a prolonged European and African journey, accompanied by his father's former servant, George Scrivings.

In France in the second week of September, Churchill attended French Army manoeuvres near Angoulême, where he was far more impressed by the French military effort than by what he called the 'crude absurdities' of the German 'theatrical display' of the previous year. From France he went to Italy for a second motoring holiday, travelling this time with a new friend, F.E. Smith, a Conservative MP of wit and brilliance who quickly became his closest companion, despite the political divide. From Italy, they drove to de Forest's castle at Eichhorn in Moravia where they shot partridge and hare. Churchill then drove back to Italy, travelling the length of the Peninsula to Syracuse, the Sicilian town in which he was to find solace in 1955, after his final retirement from public life.

From Syracuse, accompanied by Edward Marsh, Churchill went by sea to Malta, where he spent a week visiting the island's prison, dockyard, schools and hospitals. At the end of his visit he wrote to Elgin that the complaint of the Maltese – 'that they were never conquered by England, but that now we spend their money without allowing the Maltese any sort of control – is a very real, & to me at least a very painful one'. From Malta he went by Admiralty cruiser to Cyprus; confronted in Nicosia by a large demonstration demanding union with Greece, he told the demonstrators that he would be more impressed by the sound of argument than by flag-waving. As at Malta, however, he felt that British policy to Cyprus needed changing, telegraphing to Elgin, 'Island has been terribly starved by Treasury, and bears deep mark in moral and material conditions.'

Leaving Cyprus, the cruiser took Churchill across the Eastern Mediterranean, through the Suez Canal, and southward through the Red Sea towards Aden. 'I have two beautiful cabins to myself,' he told his mother, 'one of which is quite a large room with a delightful balcony at the end overlooking the waves.' He was spending 'a good deal of every day, and almost every dawn on the bridge; & am becoming quite a mariner'. From Aden he went to Berbera, to study the affairs of the Somaliland Protectorate 'upon which', he told his mother, 'we spend £76,000 a year with uncommonly little return'.

During this sea voyage Churchill prepared six lengthy memoranda which he sent back to the Colonial Office 'upon things I want to have done', he explained to his mother. These memoranda, closely-argued and emphatic as to what he felt was needed or just, provoked Sir Francis Hopwood, the senior civil servant at the Colonial Office, to write direct to Elgin: 'He is most tiresome to deal with & will I fear give trouble – as his father did – in any position to which he may be called. The restless energy, uncontrollable desire for notoriety & the lack of moral perception make him an anxiety indeed!' Hopwood added, 'Marsh gives a vivid description of fourteen hours work in one day upon these memoranda in the heat & discomfort of the Red Sea.'

Reaching the port of Mombasa at the end of October, Churchill wrote to his mother of 'two days of functions & inspections & speeches'. He then went through the Kenya Protectorate by rail. 'Everything moves on the smoothest of wheels for me – a special train with dining & sleeping cars was at my disposal all the way, wherever I wished to stop, it stopped.' Churchill travelled with his Aunt Sarah's husband, Gordon Wilson, who was later killed in action in France in 1914. The two men enjoyed themselves immensely. Churchill told his mother that as the train travelled through Kenya 'we sat (Gordon & I) on a seat in front of the engine with our rifles, & as soon as we saw anything to shoot at – a wave of the hand brought the train to a standstill & sometimes we tried at antelope without even getting down'.

From the railway, Churchill wrote, 'one can see literally every animal in the Zoo. Zebras, lions, rhinoceros, antelopes of every kind, ostriches, giraffes – all'. At Simba, two hundred miles from the coast, their train stayed in a siding for two days while they made hunting excursions into the countryside. 'The first day,' Churchill told his mother, 'I killed one zebra, one wildebeeste, two hartebeeste, one gazelle, one bustard (a giant bird).' The third day was the 'feast of the rhino'. Churchill, Wilson and Marsh set off full of hopes for a kill. Then, he told his mother, 'On turning round the corner of a hill & coming into a great wide plain of dry grass we saw, almost five hundred yards away, a rhinoceros quietly grazing. I cannot describe to you the impression produced on the mind by the sight of the grim black silhouette of this mighty beast – a survival of prehistoric times – roaming about the plain as he & his forerunners had done since the dawn of the world. It was like being transported back into the stone age.'

While walking forward to attack the rhinoceros, the hunters saw two more 'quite close to us'. Churchill fired at the larger one with his rifle '& hit her plum in the chest. She curved round & came straight for us at that curious brisk trot which is nearly as fast as a horse's gallop, & full of surprising activity. Everybody fired & both the rhinos turned off.' They then followed the smaller one, found him later in the day and killed him. 'I must say I found it exciting and also anxious work,' Churchill told his mother. 'The vitality of these brutes is so tremendous that they will come on like some large engine in spite of five or six heavy bullets thumping into them. You cannot resist a feeling that they are invulnerable & will trample you under foot however well you shoot. However, all's well that ends well.'

As he approached the snow-clad peak of Mount Kenya, Churchill was exhilarated by the vastness and beauty of the landscape. Riding forward to the new British station at Embo, 'opened only last year in a hitherto unpenetrated country', he slept on the floor 'having nothing but what we stood up in and only a banana inside us', and telling his mother: 'What a difference to the fag of a London day. My health bounds up every day I spend in the open air.' At Thika he spent a day hunting lions, but without success, 'only finding three great fierce wart-hogs', he told his mother, 'which we killed – galloping one of them down & shooting him with my revolver'.

That night, November 5, dining in Nairobi with the Governor, Churchill told his host that he could now 'advance further into this country & establish a new station & post at Meru – fifty miles beyond Embo'. This decision, Churchill told his mother, 'will bring 150,000 more natives under our direct control & add several English counties to our administrative area. There will not I think be any bloodshed, as the native chiefs want us to come – & about 100 soldiers will be sufficient. This will operate next month: & we do not propose to consult the Colonial Office till it is an accomplished fact!' Churchill added, 'Thus the Empire grows under radical Administration!'

As Churchill travelled through Africa, his brother Jack sent news of his engagement to Lady Gwendeline Bertie, daughter of the 7th Earl of Abingdon. 'You were in love really once,' Jack wrote, 'and you know what that meant. But you had other things to think of. Your career and your future filled more than half of your life.' Churchill knew and liked Lady Gwendeline, 'Goonie' as she was known. Before he left England she had written to him with advice for his African journey: 'Please don't become converted to Islam; I have noticed in your disposition a tendency to orientalism.'

While in Nairobi, Churchill had begun to send a series of accounts of his journey to the *Strand Magazine*, for a total payment of £1,150; more than £40,000 in the money values of 1990. The articles were later written up in book form as *My African Journey*. Reaching Jinja, where the Nile leaves Lake Victoria and begins its 3,500-mile journey to the sea, Churchill waxed enthusiastic in one of his articles about the possibility of a dam being thrown across the river at the Ripon Falls as a source of electric power. Forty-six years later, at that very spot, Queen Elizabeth II was to open a hydro-electric scheme, and to telegraph to Churchill, then her Prime Minister, 'Your vision has become reality.'

From Jinja, Churchill, Wilson, Marsh and Scrivings continued northward through the Uganda Protectorate, on foot and by canoe for three weeks, through country in which 200,000 people had recently died from sleeping sickness. 'Whole populous islands,' Churchill wrote to the King, 'have been swept clear.' He was also eloquent about the benefits which the railway would bring to the region, and on his return to London was to press for a policy of rapid and extensive railway building.

During the journey northward, Churchill celebrated his thirty-third birthday. Continuing by steamer for ten days down the Nile, on December 22 he wrote to the Liberal journalist J.A. Spender, stressing the need for radical social reform. 'No legislation at present in view interests the democracy,' he maintained. 'All their minds are turning more and more to the social and economic issue. This revolution is irresistible. They will not tolerate the existing system by which wealth is acquired, shared & employed. They may not be able, they may be willing to recognise themselves unable, to devise a new system. I think them very ready & patient beyond conception. But they will set their faces like flint against the money power, the heir of all other powers & tyrannies overthrown.'

However willing the working classes might be 'to remain in passive opposition', Churchill argued, 'they will not continue to bear, & they cannot, the awful uncertainties of their lives. This is why standards of wages & comfort, insurance in some effective form or other against sickness, unemployment, old age, these are the questions, and the only questions, by which Parties are going to live in the future.' On his return, he told Spender, this would be his song, 'Social Bulwarks', 'Security' and 'Standardisation'.

On December 23 Churchill and his companions were at Khartoum. That same day, Scrivings was taken ill with choleric diarrhoea. He died a day later, on Christmas Eve. 'Scrivings' death was a great shock to me', Churchill wrote to Jack, '& has cast a gloom over all the memories of this pleasant & even wonderful journey.' Churchill added, 'We all mu. have eaten the same dish which contained the poison – whether it was a tin of ptomaine-poisoned fish, or rotten asparagus, or what, will never be known.'

That Christmas Day at Khartoum, Churchill made the arrangements for Scrivings' funeral. 'We passed a miserable day,' he told Jack, '& I had him buried in the evening with full military honours, as he had been a Yeoman. The Dublin Fusiliers sent their band & a company of men, & we all walked in procession to the cemetery as mourners, while the sun sank over the desert, & the band played that beautiful funeral march you know so well.' Churchill told his mother: 'I thought as I walked after the coffin at Khartoum – I always follow funerals there – how easily it might have been, might then still be, me. Not nearly so much should I have minded, as you would think. I suppose there is some work for me to do.'

After the funeral Churchill and his companions spent 'rather an uncomfortable 48 hours', he told Jack, 'until the danger period was over' expecting that one or other of them would be struck down; for Scrivings, Churchill told his mother, 'ate our food always'. Churchill added: 'To me who have become so dependent upon this poor good man for all the little intimate comforts of daily life, it has been a most keen and palpable loss. I cannot bear to think of his wife & children looking forward to his return – letters by every post – and then this horrible news to lay them low.'

Before leaving Khartoum, Churchill made arrangements for a monument to be erected on Scrivings' grave and wrote an inscription for it. He also told Jack to tell Mrs Scrivings, who for ten years had been Churchill's cook, 'not to be worried about her future, as so far as my limited means allow I will endeavour to look after her & her children'. The death of his servant was 'all the more melancholy', Churchill added, 'when really all the unhealthy & dangerous part of the journey was over & we had been living for ten days on a comfortable Nile steamer. But Africa always claims its forfeits!'

The British Agent in Egypt provided Churchill with a steamer for his journey from Khartoum to Cairo. The steamer 'stops wherever we want at temples', he told Jack. At Aswan he wrote a memorandum on the need for a railway through Uganda to join Lake Victoria with Lake Albert; the 'Victoria and Albert railway' he called it. To Walter Runciman, the Financial Secretary to the Treasury, he wrote from Aswan: 'I have an elaborate scheme on foot which will enable this railway to be built for about £500,000 (plus ferries) in the course of the next two years. If this be done, and the policy settled soon, I hope to catch the whole Congo trade.' His aim was 'commercial solvency'. He had discussed the railway with senior British officials in the Sudan 'and we are absolutely agreed on policy'. He would explain it all 'with maps & figures' on his return.

Reaching Cairo, Churchill elaborated on the scheme for British social policy which he had already outlined to Spender. In a letter to a senior official at the Board of Trade, enclosing a copy of the scheme, he wrote, 'Will you kindly examine, illuminate, & fortify the following.' Basing himself on the premise, 'The main need of the English working classes is Security,' he proposed the introduction of a system of social reform similar to that in Germany, where 'uniform & symmetrical arrangements exist for insurance of workmen against accidents & sickness, for provisions for old age, and through Labour bureaux etc for employment'. What had attracted him to the German system was that 'it catches everybody. The meshes of our safety net are only adapted to subscribers, & all those who are not found on any of those innumerable lists go smashing down on the pavement.'

It was this very class of people, Churchill explained, 'the residue, the rearguard, call it what you will, for whom no provision exists in our English machinery, who have neither the character nor the resources to make provision for themselves, who require the aid of the State'. What he wished to bring to an end was a situation where minimum standards of life and wages and security were 'going to the Devil through accident, sickness, or weakness of character'. His aim was 'competition upwards but not downwards'.

On 17 January 1908 Churchill returned to London after an absence of five months. On the following day he was the guest of honour at the National Liberal Club. 'I come back into the fighting line,' he told 250 enthusiastic listeners, 'in the best of all possible health, and with a wish to force the fighting up to the closest possible point.' That fight was to be in the social field; speaking at Manchester on January 22, he emphasised the need for 'the producing interests' to avoid, through their search for profits, 'a further impoverishment of the great left-out labour interest'. On the following day, at Birmingham, he advocated 'the organisation by the State of the proper training and apprenticeship of any persons, even though it involves large new expenditure'.

Churchill also argued at Birmingham for several other interventions by the State, including the need to promote 'proper methods of technical instruction', to 'mitigate the sorrows of old age', to open the land 'more freely to the millions', and to adjust 'more fairly the burden of taxation upon earned and unearned increment'.

On March 7 Churchill set out these radical themes in an article in *The Nation* entitled 'The Untrodden Field in Politics'. Political freedom, he wrote, 'however precious, is utterly incomplete without a measure at least of social and economic independence'. The State must come to the help of the individual, by technical training, by developing certain national industries and utilities – he mentioned the railways, canals and forests – by solving the 'riddles' of employment and under-employment, and by establishing a 'National Minimum' below which competition would not be allowed to create worse poverty and deprivation, but above which competition 'may continue healthy and free, to vivify and fertilise the world'.

That March, at a dinner party in London, Churchill once more met Clementine Hozier, the girl with whom he had neither danced nor dined at Lady Crewe's dance in 1904. Unknown to him, she had been secretly engaged twice since then, to a thirty-four-year-old banker, Sidney Peel, the son of the 1st Viscount Peel; but she had twice broken off the engagement. Churchill sat next to her at dinner and devoted all his attention to her, to the distress of the lady on his other side.

Had she read his life of Lord Randolph, he asked Clementine.

'No,' she replied.

'If I send you the book tomorrow, will you read it?'

Clementine agreed to read the book, but he did not send it. 'That made a bad impression upon me,' she later recalled. But it was not to be the end of the story.

10

The Social Field

After a long period of ill-health, on 3 March 1908 Campbell-Bannerman advised the King to send for Asquith in the event of his resignation. That same day, the King saw Asquith, who wrote of the audience to his wife: 'He had heard gossip that Winston was anxious to get into the Cabinet keeping his present office as Under-Secretary.' The King opposed any such promotion for an Under-Secretary. But Asquith told the King that Churchill had 'every claim to Cabinet rank' and had behaved 'very well' when twice passed over in the previous year by men 'both of whom had inferior claims'. Asquith noted that the King agreed, and 'was quite warm in his praise of Winston, but felt he must wait till some real Cabinet Office fell vacant'.

Nine days after Asquith's discussion with the King, he asked to see Churchill. His own hope, Churchill told the future Prime Minister, was to succeed Elgin as Colonial Secretary. 'Practically all the constructive action and all the parliamentary exposition has been mine,' he explained to Asquith in a letter two days later. 'I have many threads in hand and many plans in movement.' There was also the possibility of going to the Admiralty, but he felt a personal difficulty in discussing this as his ailing uncle, Lord Tweedmouth, was still First Lord.

At their talk Asquith had suggested that Churchill enter the Cabinet as President of the Local Government Board. This did not appeal. 'There is no place in the Government,' he explained, 'more laborious, more anxious, more thankless, more choked with petty & even squalid detail, more full of hopeless and insoluble difficulties.' As far as the 'peace & comfort' of his life were concerned, he would rather continue as Under-Secretary at the Colonial Office without a seat in the Cabinet.

Churchill told Asquith that since his return from Africa he had been examining a broad social canvas: 'Dimly across gulfs of ignorance I see the outline of a policy which I call the Minimum Standard. It is national rather than departmental.' But if he tried to put it into effect, he reflected, 'I expect before long I should find myself in collision with some of my best friends – like for instance John Morley, who at the end of a lifetime of study and thought has come to the conclusion that nothing can be done.'

Churchill was convinced that much could be done to establish minimum standards of life, labour and leisure. In his letter to Asquith he wrote of the need to end the exploitation of boy labour, to regulate the hours of labour, and to create Labour Exchanges in order to 'de-casualise' employment. Above all, he wrote, underneath 'the immense disjointed fabric of safeguards & insurances which has grown up by itself in England, there must be spread – at a lower level – a sort of Germanised network of State intervention and regulation'.

Asquith, who became Prime Minister on April 8, was impressed; knowing Churchill's energies and abilities he offered him the Presidency of the Board of Trade, a Cabinet post in which he could embark upon social reform. Churchill accepted. He was now in the Cabinet, at the age of thirty-three. He took his place at the Cabinet table on April 9, sitting next to Morley, now Secretary of State for India, who doubted whether the State could play the leading part in social reform that Churchill had mapped out for it.

As a Minister of the Crown, Churchill had to go to Buckingham Palace to 'kiss hands' on his appointment. On the weekend before he did so, he went to stay with his mother at her home in the country. There, he again met Clementine Hozier. 'I liked our long talk on Sunday,' he wrote to her from London on April 16, 'and what a comfort & pleasure it was to me to meet a girl with so much intellectual quality & such strong reserves of noble sentiment. I hope we shall meet again and come to know each other better and like each other more: and I see no reason why this should not be so.' In her thank you letter to Lady Randolph, Clementine referred to Churchill's 'dominating charm and brilliancy'.

Having entered the Cabinet, Churchill had, according to the rules of the time, to seek re-election to Parliament. He knew that it would be a far greater struggle than before to win in Manchester. More than a year earlier he had seen his Jewish constituents, almost a third of the total electorate, turn against him because the Liberal Government had brought in a version of the Aliens Act, despite earlier denunciations in which Churchill had played a predominant part. 'I was concerned,' Churchill had written to a fellow Liberal two years earlier, 'to find the other day how very bitter and disappointed the Jewish community had become in consequence of the continuance of this very harsh & quite indefensible measure.' An even more serious danger was the threatened last-minute defection of many Catholic voters, angry that he would not commit himself to the introduction of Home Rule for Ireland.

Churchill was nevertheless in an optimistic mood. 'Even with the risk that a contrary result may be proclaimed before this letter overtakes you,' he wrote to Miss Hozier on April 16, 'I must say I feel confident of a substantial success.' His letter continued, on a personal note, 'I will let you know from time to time how I am getting on here in the storm; and we may lay the foundations of a frank & clear-eyed friendship which I certainly should value and cherish with many serious feelings of respect.'

The North-West Manchester by-election was held on April 24. It was a close contest, but Churchill lost; his Conservative opponent emerged the victor with the narrow majority of 429 votes. 'It was a very hard contest,' he wrote to Miss Hozier three days later, '& but for those sulky Irish Catholics changing sides at the last moment under priestly pressure, the result would have been different.' Churchill's letter continued: 'The Liberal Party is I must say a good Party to fight with. Such loyalty & kindness in misfortune I never saw. I might have won them a great victory from the way they treat me. Eight or nine safe seats have been placed at my disposal already.' For this reason, he explained, the defeat might prove to be a 'blessing in disguise', as it was 'an awful hindrance', he told Miss Hozier in his letter of April 27, 'to anyone in my position to be always forced to fight for his life & always having to make his opinions on national politics conform to local exigencies'. He would look for a seat to make him 'secure' for many years. 'Still, I don't pretend not to be vexed. Defeat, however consoled, explained or discounted, is odious.'

Churchill was soon found another constituency, Dundee. Thither he hurried and there, on May 9, he stood for Parliament. He polled 7,079 votes. His Conservative and Labour opponents between them received more votes than he did, 8,384 in all, but split the vote almost equally. It was, Churchill told his mother, 'a life seat'.

Returning from Dundee to London, Churchill embarked on his first act of industrial conciliation, seeking to settle a shipbuilding dispute on the Tyne in which 14,000 engineers were on strike. After the shipbuilders declared a lock-out, the strike spread to the Clyde and the Mersey. For three weeks Churchill sought a compromise between the strikers and the employers. After he had seen representatives of both the masters and the men, the strikers accepted a reduction in wages in return for Churchill's offer of a 'permanent machinery' of arbitration for the future. It was a close-run thing, with a ballot among the shipbuilding workers obtaining 24,745 votes in favour of Churchill's proposal, and 22,110 against.

Not content with this agreement, Churchill sought to increase the prosperity of the shipyards by the placing of Government orders, asking Lloyd George for his help in dealing with the matter 'in a Napoleonic spirit'. Shipbuilding orders, placed in the regions where there was high unemployment, would 'have a decisive effect on the voting and would relieve Government unemployment funds in other directions'. Churchill went on to ask: 'Can nothing be done to place a few Admiralty orders on the North-East coast and the Clyde in anticipation of the inevitable programme for next year, if not big ships, surely a few cruisers may be begun so as to carry the engineers and shipbuilders through the winter trade which promises to be exceptionally stringent. It does seem to me clumsy to let these people starve and have their homes broken up all winter, and then some time in June or July when things are beginning to revive to crack on a lot of new construction and have everybody working overtime. These ought to be the sort of situations you and I are capable of handling.'

On July 6 Churchill introduced the second reading of the Mines Eight Hours Bill, the aim of which was to reduce the hours of work in the coal mines. He had worked hard on the Bill, using a method he was later to follow on other occasions, full consultation with those who had the greatest grievance. In 1948 he was to tell a Labour critic in the House of Commons, 'Forty years have passed since I moved the Second Reading of the Mines Eight Hours Bill. In comradeship with Mr Bob Smillie – I do not know if the hon. Member has ever heard of him, he was a much admired leader in those days – I introduced baths at the pitheads.'

During his speech on the Bill, Churchill set out this vision of the future working life of Britain: 'The general march of industrial democracy is not towards inadequate hours of work, but towards sufficient hours of leisure.' Working people did not want their lives to remain 'mere alternations' between bed and factory: 'They demand time to look about them, time to see their homes by daylight, to see their children, time to think and read and cultivate their gardens – time, in short, to live.' No one was to be pitied for having to work hard. Nature gave 'a special reward' to such a person, 'an extra relish, which enables him to gather in a brief space, from simple pleasures, a satisfaction in search of which the social idler wanders vainly through the twenty-four hours'. But the reward of hard work, 'so precious in itself, is snatched away from the man who has won it, if the hours of his labour be too severe to leave any time for him to enjoy what he has won'.

That summer, Churchill worked to establish a system of Labour Exchanges, through which those who were out of work could find employment, and where employers who needed labourers could find them. 'Scarcity of labour in one district,' he explained in a Cabinet memorandum, 'may be coincident with a surplus of similar labour in other districts.' Labour Exchanges would help to remedy this lack of balance. They would also 'show the need or the absence of need, at any given time, for emergency measures of relief'.

Churchill sent his plan to Sidney Webb, who found it 'a quite admirable statement'. At Webb's suggestion Churchill made contact with a young university lecturer, William Beveridge, who was immersed in plans for social reform, and through whom Churchill tested many of his own ideas and was introduced to new ones. With the senior civil servant at the Board, Sir Hubert Llewellyn Smith, he discussed whether legislation to curb sweated labour should be introduced by private Members of Parliament, or by the Government. Churchill favoured Government action.

To help him in the day to day work, Churchill secured the secondment of Edward Marsh from the Colonial Office. 'Few people have been so lucky as me,' he wrote to Marsh that August, 'as to find in the dull and grimy recesses of the Colonial Office a friend whom I shall cherish and hold on to all my life.' On August 6 Churchill and Marsh were at Burley-on-the-Hill in Rutland, a house rented for the summer by Churchill's cousin Frederick Guest. That night there was a fire which raged through the building. Churchill, in pyjamas, overcoat and fireman's helmet, helped to direct the firemen in tackling the blaze, and in saving valuable tapestries and paintings.

Reading of the fire, Clementine Hozier sent Churchill a telegram expressing concern for his safety. He replied, 'I was delighted to get your telegram this morning & to find that you had not forgotten me.' The fire had been 'great fun & we all enjoyed it thoroughly. It is a pity such jolly entertainments are so costly. Alas for the archives. They roared to glory in about ten minutes.' It was very strange, he added, 'to be locked in deadly grapple with that cruel element. I had no conception – except from reading – of the power & majesty of a great conflagration. Whole rooms sprang into flames as if by enchantment. Chairs and tables burnt up like matches. Floors collapsed & windows crashed down. The roof descended in a molten shower. Every window spouted fire, & from the centre of the house a volcano roared skyward in a whirlwind of sparks.'

In this letter, sent on August 7, Churchill told Clementine that his brother Jack had been married that day to Lady Gwendeline Bertie, in a register office at Abingdon. The whole Churchill family had 'swooped down in motor cars', he wrote, 'for all the world as if it were an elopement – with irate parents panting on the path'. In this letter, Churchill invited Clementine to Blenheim. 'I want so much to show you that beautiful place & in its gardens we shall find lots of places to talk in, & lots of things to talk about.' A second letter followed swiftly after the first; she should take the train from Southampton to Oxford via Didcot. 'I will meet you at Oxford in a motor car if you will telegraph to me here what time you will arrive.'

In this second letter, Churchill made reference to 'those strange mysterious eyes of yours, whose secret I have been trying so hard to learn'. As to women, he wrote, 'I am stupid & clumsy in that relation, and naturally quite self-reliant and self-contained.' By that path, he admitted sadly, he had managed to 'arrive at loneliness'.

Clementine went to Blenheim; on her first and second day there Churchill was too shy to ask her to marry him. On the third morning his cousin Sunny went into his bedroom, where he was still in bed, and urged him to get up and not to miss the chance, possibly for ever. Churchill took his cousin's advice, inviting Clementine to walk with him in the garden. As they walked it began to rain. They sheltered in the small ornamental Temple of Diana. There, Churchill plucked up the courage to ask if she would be his wife. She accepted.

The couple decided to keep the news of their engagement secret until Churchill had written to Clementine's mother in London. But as they walked back to the Palace he saw his friend F.E. Smith and blurted out the news. Back at the Palace he wrote to Clementine's mother, 'I am not rich nor powerfully established, but your daughter loves me & with that love I feel strong enough to assume this great & sacred responsibility; & I think I can make her happy & give her a station & career worthy of her beauty & her virtues.'

Churchill asked Clementine to take the letter with her when she returned that day by train to London; but at the last moment he decided to accompany her, and then to bring both mother and daughter back with him to Blenheim. He therefore took the train to London with her, and then returned to Blenheim with mother and daughter in a special train. 'He is so like Lord Randolph,' Clementine's mother wrote to a friend, 'he has some of his faults, and all his qualities. He is gentle and tender, and affectionate to those he loves, much hated by those who have not come under his personal charm.'

The news of Churchill's engagement was made public on August 15. 'I trust that your new alliance will bring you all sorts of new strength,' wrote Morley, 'and smooth the path of high and arduous ascent that is yours.' Two days later Churchill was in Swansea, where, in a major speech on Anglo-German relations he criticised those 'who try to spread the belief in this country that war between Great Britain and Germany is inevitable'. The naval policy of any Party that was likely to be in power, he said, would be based upon 'reasonable measures of naval defence'. This would secure Britain's peaceful development and at the same time 'free us from the curses of continental militarism'. There was 'no collision of primary interests – big, important interests', between Britain and Germany in any quarter of the globe. 'Why, they are among our very best customers, and if anything were to happen to them, I don't know what we should do in this country for a market.'

As for those who argued that Germany was a threat, a rival and a danger, 'these two great peoples', Churchill said, 'have nothing to fight about, have no prize to fight for, and have no place to fight in'. It was only some fifteen thousand 'mischief-makers, snappers and snarlers' in Britain and in Germany who spoke of the danger of war and who wanted war. 'What about the rest of us? What about the hundred millions of people who dwell in these islands and Germany. Are we all such sheep? Is democracy in the twentieth century so powerless to effect its will? Are we all become such puppets and marionettes to be wire-pulled against our interests into such hideous convulsions?'

Churchill was confident the alarmists would not win the day. 'I have a high and prevailing faith in the essential goodness of great people,' he said. 'I believe that working classes all over the world are recognising they have common interests and not divergent interests. I believe that what is called "the international solidarity of labour" has an immense boon to confer on all the peoples of the world.'

That August Churchill reflected on the arbitration procedure which involved him intervening in each industrial and trade dispute as it worsened. What was needed, he suggested at the beginning of September, was 'a more formal and permanent machinery'. To establish this, he proposed a Standing Court of Arbitration, made up of two representatives for labour, two for the employers and a chairman appointed by the Board of Trade. The Court would convene whenever both parties to a dispute requested it. The Cabinet approved Churchill's plan, which was put into effect at once. Within twelve months seven industrial disputes had been settled by the Court.

Churchill and his fiancée planned to get married in the middle of September. Yet even during the short engagement, Clementine hesitated. 'She saw the face of the only real rival she was to know in all the fifty-seven years of marriage that lay ahead,' her daughter Mary later wrote, 'and for a brief moment she quailed.' That rival was public life, which, in their daughter's words, 'laid constant claim to both his time and interest'. As Clementine wavered, her brother Bill wrote to remind her that she had already broken off two engagements, and that she could not make an exhibition of herself and humiliate a public personage such as Churchill. 'But more than Bill's brotherly admonition,' Mary has written, 'it was the warmth of Winston's swift re-assurance, and the force of his own supreme confidence in their future together, which swept away the doubts which had beset her.'

A week before his wedding day, Churchill was asked by one of the electrical workers' trade unions to preside over a second industrial arbitration. He agreed to do so. At a meeting of both sides on September 9, those threatened with lock-out agreed to his compromise proposal to accept wage reductions in return for a promise from the employers of no further reductions for at least six months. The voting was again close, with 4,606 accepting and 3,739 rejecting the plan; but it established Churchill's reputation as a conciliator, a task he was often to undertake in his career.

Three days after this act of arbitration, Churchill was married. The wedding ceremony took place at St Margaret's, Westminster, the parish church of the House of Commons. Churchill was thirty-three, his bride ten years younger. Most of his Cabinet colleagues were on holiday, five of them, including the Prime Minister, were in Scotland. It was Churchill's former headmaster, Dr Welldon, who gave the wedding address. Also present at the ceremony were his mathematics master at Harrow, C.P.H. Mayo, and Lloyd George, who signed the register. Among the wedding gifts was one from Edward VII, a gold-headed walking stick which Churchill was to use for the rest of his life.

'What a relief to have got that ceremony over! & so happily,' Churchill wrote to his mother from Blenheim on the first day of his honeymoon. Everything was 'very comfortable & satisfactory in every way down here, & Clemmie very happy & beautiful'. The weather, however, was 'a little austere with gleams of sunshine; we shall long for warm Italian sun'. Briefly, he and his bride returned to London, to a house he had taken at 12 Bolton Street. Then they went to Italy, first to the village of Baveno on Lake Maggiore, then to Venice. 'We have only loitered & loved,' Churchill told his mother. 'A good & serious occupation for which the histories furnish respectable precedents.'

From Venice, Churchill took his bride to Baron de Forest's castle at Eichhorn in Moravia. Returning to Britain, he introduced her to his constituents in Dundee, where he spoke of the opportunities opening up for State intervention in the social field. Asquith and Lloyd George had just introduced Government-financed pensions for those over seventy. This measure, Churchill declared at Dundee on October 10, marked 'the assertion into our social system of an entirely new principle in regard to poverty, and that principle once asserted cannot possibly be confined within its existing limits'. There was also the need for direct Government intervention in the questions of unemployment, unskilled labour and boy labour. The 'cruel abyss of poverty' could be seen by all. Although many eminent men wanted to 'slam the door' on the sight of poverty, many more 'are prepared to descend into the abyss, and grapple with its evils – as sometimes you see after an explosion at a coal mine a rescue party advancing undaunted into the smoke and steam'.

On November 30, Churchill was thirty-four; his aim was to devise an unemployment insurance scheme to which the State would make a financial contribution. At that very moment, however, while he was preparing the outlines of his scheme, his Cabinet colleague Reginald McKenna, the First Lord of the Admiralty, was pressing for an increase in naval ship-building, and asked the Cabinet to agree to build six Dreadnought battle-ships in 1909, a costly addition to the budget. Churchill and Lloyd George wanted the money needed for at least two of the proposed battleships to be spent instead on social reform. The Conservative Party rejected this, mounting the cry for yet two more battleships, 'We want eight, we won't wait.' As the Dreadnought controversy raged, Churchill was again the target of Conservative scorn. 'What are Winston's reasons for acting as he does in this matter?' one Royal courtier asked another. 'Of course it cannot be from conviction or principle. The very idea of his having either is enough to make one laugh.'

Churchill was second to none in his insistence that Britain must retain naval supremacy. But he was convinced this could be done with only four extra battleships in the coming financial year, leaving funds available for a comprehensive unemployment insurance scheme. That scheme was now ready to be presented to the Cabinet; Churchill set it out on December 11. Three million working men, mostly in shipbuilding and engineering, were to be the immediate beneficiaries of his proposal. For a total contribution of 4d a week, the worker would be insured against sickness, accident or infirmity for fifteen weeks after being taken ill. Of the 4d, the working man would have 2d deducted from his wages, the employer would pay a quarter, and the State a quarter. On re-examining the financial details, he was to amend this to 2d a week from the employers and workmen respectively, and a penny halfpenny from the State.

Determined not to let unemployment insurance be destroyed by the counter-claims of a 'big navy', Churchill supported Lloyd George's criticisms of McKenna with a wealth of statistics which he put forward in Cabinet with vigour. 'I am a Celt,' Lloyd George wrote to him after the Cabinet meeting, '& you will forgive me for telling you that the whole time you were raking McK's squadron I had a vivid idea in my mind that your father looked on with pride at the skilful & plucky way in which his brilliant son was achieving victory in a cause for which he had sacrificed his career & his life.'

At first, Asquith supported the call for six new battleships in 1909. Angrily he wrote to his wife Margot that Churchill and Lloyd George 'by their combined machinations have got the bulk of the Liberal press in the same camp'. They were both going about 'darkly hinting at resignation (which is a bluff)'. There were moments 'when I am disposed summarily to cashier them both'. The dispute rumbled on for the next four months, when it was Asquith himself who proposed, as Churchill and Lloyd George had wished, that only four new battleships should be laid down in 1909. But he appeased the 'big navy' supporters by agreeing that a further four should be laid down in 1910.

The Royal Navy was not to suffer by this decision, which Churchill accepted. But the battle of the Dreadnoughts gave his Conservative enemies yet more ammunition in their battle to undermine his credibility and blacken his character. Nor could these critics know of his constructive suggestion at a meeting of a sub-committee of the Committee of Imperial Defence on 25 February 1909, when the subject of aerial navigation was first discussed. One of the pioneers of aircraft design, C.S.Rolls, was asked for facilities to experiment with a Wright aeroplane on Government land. Churchill wanted to go further. As the secret minutes of the meeting recorded: 'Mr Churchill thought that there was a danger of these proposals being considered too amateurish. The problem of the use of aeroplanes was a most important one, and we should place ourselves in communication with Mr Wright and avail ourselves of his knowledge.' Henceforth, Churchill was to take a close interest in all aerial developments, attending the annual Hendon air shows, befriending the aviators, and encouraging them in their experiments and endeavours.

Social reform continued to dominate Churchill's thinking; in a letter to Asquith immediately after Christmas 1908 he explained that because of difficulties which had arisen about including long-term infirmity in the provisions of unemployment insurance, he would go ahead first with the setting up of Labour Exchanges. He also wanted to see 'some form of State control' of the railways which, he explained, would 'secure the interest of the trading public'. Above all, he wrote, 'we must look ahead and make bold concerted plans for the next two years'. There was 'an impressive social policy to be unfolded' which would pass through both Houses of Parliament and 'leave an abiding mark on national history'. Among the Bills which he was preparing was one to eliminate the abuses of sweated labour. 'I care personally,' he told Asquith, 'and I think the country cares far more about these issues than about mere political change; & anyhow I am confident that there is a great work to be done & that we are the men to do it.'

In a second letter to Asquith, three days before the New Year, Churchill insisted that it was possible to 'underpin' the existing voluntary agencies of social amelioration by a comprehensive system of State action. 'The expenditure of less than ten millions a year,' he argued, 'not upon relief, but upon machinery, & thrift stimuli would make England a different country for the poor.' One area for which he hoped to provide amelioration was that of the bankruptcy of small businesses. That winter he held a conference at the Board of Trade to examine and learn from French bankruptcy legislation, which had advanced further than that of Britain. One of those present, John Bigham, a leading barrister, later expressed his amazement at Churchill's knowledge of the subject. Nor was it only his knowledge that impressed. 'His vigour and versatility were qualifications that would have made him a first class advocate at the Bar.'

That winter Churchill urged Asquith to proceed with legislation for Unemployment Insurance and National Infirmity Insurance. To his disappointment, Asquith decided that the National Insurance Bill would have to be postponed to another parliamentary session because of the complications involved in long-term invalidity. Because of the postponement, it was Lloyd George who was to introduce, and get the credit for, the unemployment insurance scheme on which Churchill had worked so hard. Despite this setback, that spring, he completed two comprehensive Bills, a Trade Boards Bill to eliminate the widespread use of sweated labour, and a Labour Exchanges Bill. Running through both Bills, he told Asquith on January 12, was 'the same idea which the Germans call "paritätisch" – joint & equal representation of masters & men, plus the skilled permanent impartial element' – arbitration.

On the day after he sent this letter, Churchill told the Birmingham Liberal Club, 'Wherever the reformer casts his eye, he is confronted with a mass of largely preventable and even curable suffering.' While the 'vanguard' of the British people 'enjoys all the delights of all the ages, our rearguard struggles out into conditions which are crueller than barbarism'.

The 'main aspirations' of the British people, Churchill told his Birmingham audience, were social rather than political. 'They see around them, on every side and almost every day, spectacles of confusion and misery, which they cannot reconcile with any conception of humanity or justice.' People wondered 'why so little has been done here. They demand that more shall be done'. Churchill repeated this call for social change when he spoke at Newcastle on February 5. The aim of the new social programme was, he said, 'to bring the people into the Government, to open all careers freely to the talent of every class, to associate ever larger numbers with offices of authority'. A month later he presented the Cabinet with his Trade Boards Bill. The new Boards, working through special inspectors, would have powers to prosecute any employer who was exploiting his work force. Exploitation would be defined either as exceptionally low wages, those below the minimum rates to be prescribed by the Board of Trade, or 'conditions prejudicial to physical and social welfare'.

In a single Bill, Churchill established both the principle of a minimum wage for the low paid, and the right to a break for meals and refreshment. The Bill had its second reading in the Commons on April 28. It had,

Churchill told Clementine in a letter written on the Front Bench, 'been beautifully received & will be passed without a Division'. Balfour had been 'most friendly' to it '& all opposition has faded away'. The Bill passed with a large majority. Then, on May 19, he introduced his Labour Exchanges Bill. Modern transport and communications, he told the House, 'knit the country together as no other country has ever been knitted before. Only labour has not profited by this improved organisation.' The Bill would dispose of the need 'of wandering in search of work'. More than two hundred Labour Exchanges would provide information about where work was available, and in which regions, and for which trades, men were needed. The Labour Exchanges now being set up, and the Unemployment Insurance scheme yet to be introduced, were 'man and wife, mutually supported and sustained by each other'.

A leading Labour member called Churchill's proposal 'one of the most far-reaching statements which has been delivered during the time I have been associated with Parliament'. That summer, in a series of meetings with Trade Union leaders and employers, he explained that the role of the Board of Trade under these proposals would be that of arbiter and conciliator between capital and labour. The Labour Exchanges would not be used to provide employers with blackleg labour during a strike. They would make it easier for workmen to find work, and easier for employers to build up a pool of labour.

Amid the work of explaining his Bills to the public and to Parliament, Churchill found time to supervise the preparation of a new London home, 33 Eccleston Square. Clementine, who was expecting their first child, spent much time amid the tranquillity of Blenheim. Even the smallest details of the new London house engaged her husband's attention. 'The marble basin has arrived,' he wrote to her. 'Your window is up – a great improvement. All the bookcases are in position (I have ordered two more for the side windows of the alcove). The dining room gleams in creamy white. The big room is papered, the bathroom well advanced.'

On May 1 Churchill's sister-in-law Lady Gwendeline gave birth to a son, John George. Clementine's child was expected within the next two months. 'My dear Bird,' Churchill wrote to her, 'this happy event will be a great help to you & will encourage you. I rather shrink from it – because I don't like your having to bear pain & face this ordeal. But we are in the grip of circumstances, and out of pain joy will spring, & from passing weakness new strengths arise.'

As a Major in the Queen's Own Oxfordshire Hussars, Churchill was taking part that week in the annual camp of the Oxfordshire Yeomanry. On the day after the Field Day he wrote to his wife, 'These military men very often fail altogether to see the simple truths underlying the relationships of all armed forces, & how the levers of power can be used upon them.' Reflecting on the 'soldiers & pseudo-soldiers galloping about', as eight Yeomanry regiments did mock battle, he told Clementine: 'Do you know I would greatly like to have some practice in the handling of large forces. I have much confidence in my judgment on things when I see clearly, but on nothing do I seem to feel the truth more than in tactical combinations. It is a vain & foolish thing to say – but you will not laugh at it. I am sure I have the root of the matter in me – but never I fear in this state of existence will it have a chance of flowering – in bright red blossom.'

War of a different kind was on Churchill's mind that summer, 'the war against poverty' he called it in a letter to Lloyd George on June 20. Reflecting on the various pieces of current social legislation, including his own, he had come to the conclusion 'that we should reproduce for the defence of this country against poverty and unemployment, the sort of machinery that we have in existence in the Committee of Imperial Defence to protect us against foreign aggression'. He proposed a Committee of National Organisation, over which the Chancellor of the Exchequer should preside. This was 'the only way', he believed, to secure 'the easy, smooth, speedy transaction of a succession of questions', each of which involved three or four Government departments, to prevent 'over-lapping, waste, friction and omission', and to have a 'continuous policy' of social reform.

Churchill set aside all thought of politics and Parliaments when, on July 11, Clementine gave birth to a daughter, Diana. Childbirth had been a considerable strain for Clementine, bringing in its wake great tiredness. Churchill did his utmost to arrange for peace and quiet for her, finding somewhere for her to recuperate far from the hustle and bustle of London life and politics. Within three weeks of his daughter's birth, Churchill himself was again at the centre of an industrial arbitration, this time in the coal industry, where a strike threatened to paralyse coal production. 'We had twenty hours of negotiation in the last two days,' he told his mother on August 4, 'and I do not think a satisfactory result would have been obtained unless I had personally played my part effectually.'

'As far as I can judge,' Sir Edward Grey wrote to Churchill when the dispute was ended, 'it needed your own firmness, trust & insight to bring about a settlement.' Grey considered it 'a real public service of the very best kind'. Asquith and Edward VII likewise sent their congratulations. 'It was a great coup,' Churchill told his mother, 'most useful and timely.' But at that moment of achievement a new crisis loomed, threatening all Churchill's social reform plans, and the reforms of every Government department; the Conservative Peers announced their intention of rejecting Lloyd George's budget, which had already passed by the Commons with a large majority.

At first Churchill did not take the opposition of the Lords too tragically. 'I never saw people make such fools of themselves as all these Dukes and Duchesses are doing,' he told his mother. 'One after another they come up threatening to cut down charities and pensions, sack old labourers and retainers, and howling and whining because they are asked to pay their share, as if they were being ruined.' The latest recruit was the Duke of Portland. Every line of what he was saying 'is worth a hundred votes in the country to us'.

As well as the possible defeat of the budget, there was another threat to Churchill's reform plans; the prospect of overseas entanglement. At the end of August he had a long talk with the German Ambassador in London, Count Metternich, telling the Ambassador that the prospect of a substantial increase in the German naval construction 'had been the cause of the deep disquiet which had spread among all classes and all Parties'. It was 'no good shutting one's eyes to facts', Churchill added; however hard Governments and individuals worked 'to make a spirit of real trust and confidence between the two countries', they would make very little headway while there was a 'continually booming naval policy in Germany'.

That autumn Clementine continued her recuperation at Southwater near Brighton from the strains of childbirth. Throughout her life she was to suffer from bouts of tiredness, accompanied by nervous stress. Her husband always encouraged her to rest, to take her time recuperating, and to free herself from the cares of daily life. He also sent her regular handwritten accounts of his doings, and those of their family. Diana was 'very well', he wrote at the end of August from Eccleston Square, 'but the nurse is rather inclined to glower at me as if I was a tiresome interloper'. He had missed that morning's bath, 'But tomorrow I propose to officiate!'

On September 6, while Clementine was still at Southwater, Churchill spoke at Leicester against the intention of the House of Lords to vote against the Budget. He also spoke of the dangers of class warfare should the Budget proposals, and all they stood for, be rejected. 'If we carry on in the old happy-go-lucky way, the richer classes ever growing in wealth and in number, the very poor remaining plunged or plunging ever deeper into helpless, hopeless misery,' he warned, 'then I think there is nothing before us but the savage strife between class and class, and an increasing disorganisation, with the increasing waste of human strength and human virtue.'

So angry was the King at these words, that his Private Secretary wrote to *The Times* in protest, an act without apparent precedent. 'He & the King must really have gone mad,' was Churchill's comment.

From Leicester, Churchill went to Swindon to attend British Army manoeuvres. During his journey he sent his wife words of encouragement: 'Dearest Clemmie, do try to gather your strength. Don't spend it as it comes. Let it accumulate. Remember my two rules – No walk of more than half a mile; no risk of catching cold. There will be so much to do in the autumn & if there is an Election – you will have to play a great part.' Churchill understood the strain which his political life was putting, and would continue to put, on their relationship. 'I am so much centred in my politics,' he told her, 'that I often feel I must be a dull companion, to anyone who is not in the trade too. It gives me so much joy to make you happy – I often wish I were more varied in my topics. Still the best is to be true to oneself – unless you happen to have a very tiresome self!'

Accompanied by Edward Marsh, and his cousin Frederick Guest, in whose car they travelled, Churchill went that autumn to German Army manoeuvres. At Metz he visited the Franco-Prussian War battlefield of Gravelotte where the French had been defeated in August 1870. 'All the graves of the soldiers are dotted about in hundreds just where they fell – all very carefully kept,' he wrote to Clementine, 'so that one can follow the phases of the battle by the movements of the fallen.'

Driving across the Vosges mountains to Strasbourg, the capital city of the German Province of Alsace, Churchill wrote to Clementine on September 12: 'A year today my lovely white pussy cat came to me, & I hope & pray she may find on this September morning no cause – however vague or secret – for regrets. The bells of the old city are ringing now & they recall to my mind the chimes which saluted our wedding & the crowds of cheering people. A year has gone by – & if it has not brought you all the glowing & perfect joy which fancy paints, still it has brought a clear bright light of happiness & some great things. My precious & beloved Clemmie my earnest desire is to enter still more completely into your dear heart & nature & to curl myself up in your darling arms. I feel so safe with you & I do not keep the slightest disguise.'

In this letter Churchill mused about their daughter. 'I wonder what she will grow into, & whether she will be lucky or unlucky to have been dragged out of chaos. She ought to have some rare qualities both of mind & body. But these do not always mean happiness or peace. Still I think a bright star shines for her.' These were tragically prescient words. Many bright stars were to shine for Diana, but happiness and peace were to elude her.

From Strasbourg, Churchill motored to Frankfurt, 'a very long drive of 220 kilometres, the last three hours of which were in darkness & rain', he told Clementine. 'It is queer that one should like this sort of thing, yet there is such a sense of independence about motoring that I should never think of going by train, if the choice offered.' During the drive across Germany he had been impressed by the innumerable small farms and lack of park walls and country estates. 'All this picture makes one feel what a dreadful blight & burden our poor people have to put up with – with parks & palaces of country families almost touching one another & smothering the villages & the industry.' In Frankfurt he was shown the local Labour Exchanges. 'There is no doubt,' he told her, 'that I have got hold of a tremendous thing in these Exchanges. The honour of introducing them into England would be in itself a rich reward.'

Reaching Würzburg on the evening of September 14, Churchill spent the following day at German Army manoeuvres, watching five Army Corps and three cavalry divisions in action. 'I have a very nice horse from the Emperor's stable,' he told Clementine, '& am able to ride about wherever I choose with a suitable retinue. During September 15 he had a few minutes' conversation with the Emperor, 'who chaffed about "Socialists" in a good-humoured way'. That night at dinner he conversed 'formally & fitfully in broken French' with a Prussian General and the Bavarian Minister of War. As to the German Army, he told Clementine, 'it is a terrible engine. It marches sometimes thirty-five miles in a day. It is in number as the sands of the sea – & with all the modern conveniences. There is a complete divorce between the two sides of German life – the imperialists & the Socialists. Nothing unites them. They are two different nations.'

With the British there were 'so many shades' of colour, Churchill wrote. 'Here it is all black & white (the Prussian colours).' He remained an optimist: 'I think another fifty years will see a wiser & a gentler world. But we shall not be spectators of it.' Their daughter would 'glitter in a happier scene'. Then, echoing a sentiment he had first expressed ten years earlier, during the Boer War, he told his wife, 'How easily men could make things better than they are – if only they tried together!' One day at manoeuvres had confirmed his deepest instincts. 'Much as war attracts me & fascinates my mind with its tremendous situations,' he wrote, 'I feel more deeply every year – & can measure the feeling here in the midst of arms – what vile & wicked folly & barbarism it all is.'

On the last day of the manoeuvres Churchill again saw the Emperor. 'He was very friendly – "My dear Winston" & so on – but I saw nothing of him', only a two-minute talk. He had a longer talk with the Turkish representative at the manoeuvres, Enver Pasha, 'the Young Turk who made the revolution. A charming fellow, very good looking & thoroughly capable. We made friends at once.' Five years later Churchill was to appeal direct to Enver, then Turkish Minister of War, not to commit Turkey to Germany's side in the war, but in vain.

While Churchill was in Germany, Clementine had accompanied Asquith to a political meeting in Birmingham. 'We came out by a side door,' she reported to her husband on the following day. 'A steward said to the crowd, "There's Mrs Churchill" and they all cheered the Pug. Two boys leant into the carriage and said, "Give him our love". Those poor people love and trust you absolutely. I felt so proud.'

From Würzburg, Churchill drove to the battlefield of Blenheim, scene of his ancestor's triumph over the French in 1704. On his return to Britain he was at the forefront of the Liberal struggle against the House of Lords. On October 16 he was at Dundee, speaking to his constituents, telling Clementine, 'I find everyone here in high sprits & full of fight.' The drawbacks of being on the stomp were many: 'Yesterday morning I had half eaten a kipper when a huge maggot crept out & flashed his teeth at me! Today I could find nothing nourishing for lunch but pancakes. Such are the trials which great & good men endure in the service of their country!' His own health was not bad: 'I slept in the train without any veronal like a top. Really that must be considered a good sign of nerves & health.' As to his wife's continuing recuperation: 'My sweet cat – devote yourself to the accumulation of health. Dullness is salutary in certain circumstances. I wish you were here, but I am sure you will not afterwards regret this period of repose.'

Clementine was spending a few weeks resting at a hotel in Sussex, at Crowborough. 'I wish you were not tied all this week by the leg to Crowboro,' Churchill wrote to her on October 25. 'I would like so much to take you to my arms all cold & gleaming from your bath.' He was busy with a new book, a collection of twenty-one of the speeches he had made on social policy over the previous three years. It was published a month later with the title *Liberalism and the Social Problem*, followed within three weeks by a further collection of speeches, *The People's Rights*.

On November 3, with his German visit much in mind, Churchill set down for the Cabinet his thoughts on German naval intentions. There were 'practically no checks upon German naval expansion', he wrote, 'except those imposed by the difficulties of getting money'. Those difficulties were considerable, with an economic crisis so severe that the 'period of severe internal tension' which it was creating was itself a cause for alarm. 'Will the tension be relieved by moderation,' he asked, 'or snapped by calculated violence? Will the policy of the German Government be to soothe the internal situation or to find an escape from it in external adventure? There is no doubt that both courses are open.' Whatever the German Government were to decide, one of the two courses must be taken soon. 'If it be pacific, it must soon become markedly pacific, and conversely.'

With Asquith's encouragement, Churchill prepared a speech to be given at Bristol on November 14, a week before the Lords were to debate the Budget. Clementine went to Bristol with him. As they stepped down from the train a young suffragette, Theresa Garnett, ran forward and tried to hit Churchill in the face with a dog whip. To protect his face, he seized her by the wrists. She then began to push him towards the edge of the platform. At that moment the train began slowly to draw out of the station. Scrambling over a pile of suitcases, Clementine managed to seize her husband's coat and pull him back from the edge. The suffragette was caught hold of by some of the reception committee and at once arrested. As detectives led her away she called out to Churchill, 'You brute, why don't you treat British women properly?'

Shaken by this incident, Churchill nevertheless made a powerful speech that day against the pretensions of the House of Lords. The Conservative Peers, he declared, were 'a proud Tory faction' who thought that they were 'the only persons fit to serve the Crown'. They regarded the Government 'as merely an adjunct to their wealth and titles'. They could not bear to see a Government 'resting on the middle and working classes'. All they could achieve, 'if they go mad', was 'to put a stone on the track and throw the train of State off the line, and that is what we are told they are going to do'.

Churchill was answered by his old adversary Lord Milner, who declared that the duty of the Lords was to vote against the budget, 'and damn the consequences'. Milner's call was heeded; on November 30, Churchill's thirty-fifth birthday, the Lords rejected the budget by 350 votes to 75. Four days later Asquith prorogued Parliament and the General Election campaign began. Its war-cry for all Liberals, including the grandson of a Duke of Marlborough, was 'The Peers versus the People'.

11

Home Secretary

Throughout the General Election campaign Churchill led the Liberal onslaught against the House of Lords. In a speech at Leven in Scotland on 9 January 1910 he described the former Foreign Secretary, Lord Lansdowne, as 'the representative of a played out, obsolete, anachronistic Assembly, a survival of a feudal arrangement utterly passed out of its original meaning, a force long since passed away, which only now requires a smashing blow from the electors to finish it off for ever'. Campaigning throughout Lancashire, he put the Liberal view with enormous skill and energy. 'Your speeches from first to last,' Asquith wrote in the third week of the campaign, 'have reached high-water mark, and will live in history.'

The election results were announced on 15 February 1910. The Liberals had retained power but by the narrowest of majorities; 275 seats as against 273 won by the Conservatives. With 84 seats, the Irish Nationalists again held the balance of political power. The Labour Party's 42 seats made it once more the smallest Party in the Commons. Churchill held his seat at Dundee with the same majority as before, just over nine thousand.

On the day the election results were announced Churchill accepted the senior Secretaryship of State, that of Home Secretary, with responsibility for the police, prisons, and prisoners. Only Robert Peel, the founder of the police force, had held the office at an earlier age, thirty-three. The prospects of the new office filled him 'with excitement and exhilaration', Violet Asquith later recalled. 'He was always eager to move on and break new ground and he was already busily exploring the possibilities of his new kingdom. He would have a fine Army to command, the Police Force, but he was mainly pre-occupied with the fate of their quarry, the criminals. His own experience of captivity had made him the Prisoner's Friend, and his mind was seething with plans for lightening their lot by earned remissions of sentence while "in durance vile", by libraries and entertainment.

"They must have food for thought – plenty of books – that's what I missed most – except of course the chance of breaking bounds and getting out of the damned place – and I suppose I mustn't give them *that*!" '

From his first days as Home Secretary, Churchill embarked upon a comprehensive programme of prison reform. On February 21, six days after becoming Home Secretary, he went to the opening night of John Galsworthy's play *Justice* at the Duke of York's Theatre. With him he took Sir Evelyn Ruggles-Brise, the Chairman of the Prison Commissioners appointed by Asquith fifteen years earlier, and a supporter of solitary confinement. The play was a powerful indictment of solitary confinement and Churchill was much moved by it. Yet, he explained on March 7 to his Permanent Under-Secretary of State, Sir Edward Troup, he was also impressed 'with the importance of making the first period of prison life a severe disciplinary course, of interposing a hiatus between the world which the convict has left and the public works gang which he is to join'.

Two months later Churchill announced that solitary confinement would be reduced to one month for first offenders and those in the intermediate class, and to three months for recidivists. When the new rules were announced Galsworthy wrote to Churchill's Aunt Leonie: 'I have always admired his pluck and his capacity, and a vein of imagination somewhat rare amongst politicians. I now perceive him to have a heart, and to be very human. I think he will go very far, and the further if he succeeds in keeping the fighting elements in him at white rather than red heat.'

That March, Churchill created a distinction, hitherto unknown, between criminal and political prisoners. This move was of immediate benefit to many imprisoned suffragettes. Prison rules which were 'suitable for criminals jailed for dishonesty or cruelty or other crimes implying moral turpitude', he explained to the Commons, 'should not be applied inflexibly to those whose general character is good and whose offences, however reprehensible, do not involve personal dishonour'.

As he had indicated to Violet Asquith, Churchill also tried to set up libraries for prisoners; the committee which he appointed to examine this question recommended that the catalogue of 'a well-managed public library' should be the guide to a prisoners' book list. But his main assault on the existing system concerned those prison sentences which he consi-dered excessive. On this he carried on a vigorous correspondence within his department, and having studied individual cases in detail, frequently expressed his dissatisfaction with individual judges. Commenting on a sentence of ten years' penal servitude for sodomy, he minuted to his officials: 'The prisoner has already received two frightful sentences of seven years' penal servitude, one for stealing lime juice and one for stealing apples. It is not impossible that he contracted his unnatural habits in prison.'

It seemed to Churchill that an upper limit was needed in sentencing. 'Only circumstances of rare and peculiar aggravation,' he minuted, 'would, in my opinion, be sufficient to justify a sentence of over ten years' penal servitude for a single offence unaccompanied by danger to life. Where wealth is deliberately employed to the systematic corruption of minors; where force is used with such brutality as to produce permanent injury; where there is vile treachery, as in the case of a schoolmaster, or where there is evidence of habitual concentration of a man's main activities upon criminal intercourse of this character, then that limit may be exceeded. But for isolated acts of bestiality, even when accompanied by violence amounting to rape, and where the full offence is committed, seven years' penal servitude would appear to me the standard sentence which should be borne in mind.'

On July 3, while preparing reforms intended to reduce the number of offenders being sent to Borstal, Churchill wrote to his advisers, 'I should certainly not consent to be responsible for any system which can be shown to aggravate the severity of the Penal Code.' On July 20 he presented his reforms to the Commons. One of his intentions was to abolish automatic imprisonment for non-payment of fines. 'Let the House see what an injurious operation that is,' he explained. 'The State loses its fine. The man goes to prison, perhaps for the first time – a shocking event. He goes through all the formalities for a four or five day sentence that would apply if he were sentenced to a long term of penal servitude. He is photographed, taken off in a Black Maria, and has his fingerprints taken. All these painful processes are gone through just as in the case of a long sentence.'

The principle Churchill wished to establish was 'time to pay'. In the year before he became Home Secretary, 95,686 people had been sent to prison for four or five days each, through not being able to pay a fine imposed by the courts. Only on account of the congestion of the Parliamentary time-table was his reform delayed until 1914. Within five years of the new rule, the number of those imprisoned for failure to pay fines had dropped to just over five thousand. The majority of those imprisoned were those who had been fined for drunkenness; their numbers dropped from 62,822 in 1908–9 to less than two thousand in 1919.

Churchill's next reform was to reduce the number of young people in prison. Each year more than five thousand between the ages of sixteen and twenty-one were imprisoned. All this was to change. Henceforth no young person could be sent to prison 'unless he is incorrigible or has committed a serious offence'. The imprisonment of young people, Churchill told the

King in one of the regular letters in which he followed the tradition of a Home Secretary sending the Sovereign a full account of proceedings in Parliament, was 'pure waste'. What was needed was a system of 'defaulters' drills', based upon physical exercises, 'very healthy, very disagreeable', done possibly at Police stations. 'No lad between 16 & 21 ought to be sent to prison for mere punishment,' Churchill told his Sovereign. 'Every sentence should be conceived with the object of pulling him together & bracing him for the world: it should be in fact disciplinary and educative rather than penal.'

In the Commons, Churchill defended his cutting back on the imprisonment of young offenders by drawing Members' attention to the fact that 'the evil only falls on the sons of the working classes. The sons of other classes commit many of the same offences. In their boisterous and exuberant spirits in their days at Oxford and Cambridge they commit offences – for which scores of the sons of the working class are committed to prison – without any injury being inflicted on them.' There had been 12,376 boys under twenty-one in prison when Churchill became Home Secretary. By 1919 this number had fallen below four thousand. But Churchill's plan for defaulters' drill, though favoured by the Police and the Lord Chief Justice, did not survive the scrutiny of his officials; the principle which he tried to establish had to wait until the Criminal Justice Bill of 1948 for its implementation.

Underlying Churchill's prison reforms was a real understanding of the nature of imprisonment from the perspective of the prisoner. In the course of his speech on July 10 he referred, in moving terms, to this aspect. 'We must not forget,' he said, 'that when every material improvement has been effected in prisons, when the temperature has been adjusted, when the proper food to maintain health and strength has been given, when the doctors, chaplains, and prison visitors have come and gone, the convict stands deprived over everything that a free man calls life. We must not forget that all these improvements, which are sometimes salves to our consciences, do not change that position.'

Churchill then spoke of the considerations which he believed should guide the penal system of any progressive country, telling the House: 'The mood and temper of the public in regard to the treatment of crime and criminals is one of the most unfailing tests of the civilisation of any country. A calm and dispassionate recognition of the rights of the accused against the State, and even of convicted criminals against the State, a constant heart-searching by all charged with the duty of punishment, a desire and eagerness to rehabilitate in the world of industry all those who have paid their dues in the hard coinage of punishment, tireless efforts towards the discovery of curative and regenerating processes, and an unfaltering faith

that there is a treasure, if you can only find it, in the heart of every man –
these are the symbols which in the treatment of crime and criminals mark
and measure the stored-up strength of a nation, and are the sign and proof
of the living virtue in it.'

That summer Churchill advocated several further pioneering changes
which were to come into effect while he was still at the Home Office. One
innovation was that of entertainment in prison; henceforth a lecture or a
concert would be given four times a year in every prison. 'These wretched
people,' he told the King, 'must have something to think about, & break
the long monotony.' Special concessions would also be made for aged and
weak-minded convicts.

As well as reforms inside prison walls, Churchill abolished police supervision of ex-convicts and replaced it with a Central Agency for the care of
convict prisoners after their release. Former prisoners would no longer be
supervised solely by the Police, but by a separate body made up of specially
nominated official members and representatives of the various existing
Prisoners' Aid Societies.

In explaining this reform to a Liberal colleague while it was still in its
planning stage, Churchill had pointed out that of every four convicts
discharged between 1903 and 1905, three were already back in penal
servitude. 'It is this terrible proportion of recidivism that I am anxious to
break in upon.' Police supervision and aid-on-discharge 'fail altogether to
enable or encourage a convict to resume his place in honest industry. A
supervision more individualised, more intimate, more carefully considered, more philanthropically inspired, is necessary.' Hence the weaving
together of all existing Prisoners' Aid Societies 'into one strong confederacy, to sustain them with funds on a larger scale than they have hitherto
had at their disposal, to place them in contact with individual convicts long
before these are again thrown upon the world, and only to use the ordinary
methods of police supervision in cases which are utterly refractory'.
Churchill's efforts were appreciated by prison reformers. 'These changes,'
Galsworthy wrote to *The Times* on July 23, 'are one and all inspired by
imagination, without which reform is deadly, and by common sense,
without which it is dangerous.'

That summer, in pursuit of the Home Secretary's right to recommend
reprieve in capital murder cases, Churchill studied the documents of a
particular case in which the death penalty had been given, writing out a
detailed ten-point memorandum in which he tried to test the evidence
against arguments and possibilities other than those that had been put
forward in the condemned man's defence. After examining the conten-
tious points carefully, he did not feel able to recommend a reprieve.

A year after leaving the Home Office, Churchill told a friend that 'it had become a nightmare' to him having to exercise his power of life and death in the case of convicted criminals, and in a debate on capital punishment in 1948 he told the House of Commons: 'I found it very distressing nearly forty years ago to be at the Home Office. There is no post that I have occupied in Government which I was more glad to leave. It was not so much taking the decisions in capital cases that oppressed me, although that was a painful duty. I used to read the letters of appeal written by convicts undergoing long or life sentences begging to be let out. This was for me an even more harassing task.'

Churchill continued: 'I remember one capital case in particular. This was the case of a soldier of about forty-five years of age, who in a fit of rage killed his wife or the woman with whom he had long lived. After the crime he walked downstairs where a number of little children to whom he used to give sweets awaited him. He took all his money out of his pocket and gave it to them saying, "I shall not want this any more". He then walked to the police station and gave himself up. I was moved by the whole story and by many features in the character of this unhappy man. The judge who tried the case advised that the sentence should be carried out. The officials at the Home Office, with their very great experience, suggested no interference with the course of the law. But I had my own view, and I was unfettered in action in this respect.'

Churchill recommended a reprieve. Shortly afterwards the soldier committed suicide. Though shaken that the reprieved man had considered 'a life sentence is worse than a death sentence', Churchill was proud of the fact, as he told the Commons in 1948, that 'at every point in our system of criminal justice the benefit of the doubt is given to the accused. At every point in the subsequent consideration of a capital sentence, when it has been passed, the same bias is shown in favour of the convicted person. But when justice and the law have done their best within their limits, when precedents have been searched and weighed, mercy still roams around the prison seeking for some chink by which she can creep in.'

Confronted by the continuing challenge of the Lords against Liberal social reforms, Asquith thought of resignation, to be followed by a second election on the basis of the power of the Lords. Churchill was among those in the Cabinet who opposed any such course, arguing that the Government should fight on, despite its precarious majority. Asquith accepted this advice, announcing on March 18 that the Lords must be rebuilt on a democratic basis. At Manchester on the previous day, to the alarm of the King, Churchill had publicly advocated 'the Crown and the Commons acting together against the encroachments of the Lords'.

Government proposals to curb the powers of the Lords were introduced in the Commons on March 31. Churchill was the main Government speaker. Of the Conservative Peers who never came to the Lords except to vote against the budget, he declared: 'Nothing is more curious than the way in which they let themselves be led by the nose. Here are all these noblemen, placed in an independent station, enjoying easy and full education, and enlightened society, and well guarded and secured in all the affairs of this world, and so far from showing a spirit of independence, they allow themselves to be kept under a very strict discipline; they allow themselves to be led about and driven about, I will not say like a flock of sheep, because that would not be respectful, but like a regiment of soldiers, this way and that way.'

Churchill ended his speech: 'We have reached a fateful period in British history. The time for words is past, the time for action has arrived. Since the House of Lords, upon an evil and unpatriotic instigation – as I must judge it – have used their Veto to affront the Prerogative of the Crown and to invade the rights of the Commons, it has now become necessary that the Crown and the Commons, acting together, should restore the balance of the Constitution and restrict for ever the Veto of the House of Lords.'

'You made a most admirable speech: one of your best,' wrote Asquith. 'The only thing I regret is the last sentence – associating "the Crown" & the people: which I hope may be ignored.'

On April 28 the Lords was presented with the budget. Shirking a constitutional confrontation, it passed it without a division. Not wanting to risk further interference by the Lords in financial measures, Asquith decided to go forward with the Parliament Bill, even if it meant asking the King to create up to five hundred new Liberal peers to ensure the Bill's passage. But on May 6, as controversy raged over the possibility of the creation of so many new peers, Edward VII died.

In view of the inexperience of the new King, George V, a six-month truce was called in the constitutional struggle. Not only did Churchill support this, but called for the setting up of a National Government in which both Liberals and Conservatives, freed from the pressures and demands of their respective extremists, would work together to resolve the constitutional question, to devise a federal system for Ireland, to push forward with a general social welfare programme, and, if the European situation demanded, to introduce compulsory military service, something the Conservatives had been advocating for some time.

That summer Churchill left England with Clementine for a two-month holiday on board Baron de Forest's yacht *Honor*. The cruise took them through the Mediterranean and the Aegean, along the coast of

Asia Minor to Constantinople. Edward Marsh, who had gone from the Board of Trade to the Home Office with Churchill, sent his master several 'pouches' of work as it accumulated; the first was waiting for him when he reached Athens. A month later Churchill wrote to Sir Edward Grey from Crete, 'I have received three substantial mails with departmental work & have chewed up a good many tough bits I had put aside for leisure days.'

At the Turkish port of Smyrna, accompanied by 'a proper escort against brigands', Churchill went on a special train the whole length of the British-built railway to Aidin, 'with a seat fitted up on the cow-catcher', a journey of 260 miles. There was 'no better way', he told Grey, 'of seeing a country in a flash'. Reflecting on his travels through Greece and Turkey, he told the Foreign Secretary, 'The only view I have formed about this part of the world of ruined civilisations & harshly jumbled races is this – why can't England & Germany come together in strong action & for general advantage?'

On his return to England, Churchill was the guest of the Commander-in-Chief, Sir John French, at British Army manoeuvres. 'I am thinking of you galloping about on Salisbury Plain in this delicious crisp weather,' Clementine wrote to him, '& wishing you were Commander-in-Chief on the eve of war instead of Home Secretary on the brink of an Autumn Session.' The holiday was not yet over; travelling to Wales, Churchill and Clementine were Lloyd George's guests at Criccieth, playing golf, motoring through the Welsh countryside, and deep-sea fishing.

'My wife and I will always remember your kindness and hospitality, and Wales in sunshine, shadow and sunset did the honours by sea and land not less agreeably,' Churchill wrote to Lloyd George from his final holiday stop, in Inverness-shire. In Scotland 'I have spent my days walking after horned beasts, and my nights in recovering from the effects of such exertions.' As to their political discussions at Criccieth, 'if we stood together', Churchill told Lloyd George, 'we ought to be strong enough either to impart a progressive character to policy, or by withdrawal to terminate an administration which had failed in its purpose'.

During his Mediterranean cruise Churchill had written a memorandum for Asquith, setting out those areas of prison administration and punishment which he felt still needed to be reformed. He was anxious to bring an end to the existing committal procedure whereby half of all prison committals were for two weeks or even less. Nearly half of these had been sent to prison for the first time, 'a terrible and purposeless waste of public money and human character'. No first-time offender should be sent to prison for a short sentence. 'There are two types of petty offender,' he explained to Asquith, 'the occasional and the habitual. No occasional offender ought to be sent to prison for a single trivial offence.'

Another proposal put forward by Churchill while he was at the Home Office was for curative institutions to be created for habitual drunkards, 'habitual brawlers' and petty offenders who had committed a specified number of offences within a single year. He also proposed uniformity of sentences for similar crimes, and to this end devised a classification of crimes into degrees of seriousness. Offences of the first degree were those against life; offences of the second degree, those against the person; offences of the third degree, those against property; and offences of the fourth degree, those against morals. Within each category, offences were to be distinguished according to their gravity, and appropriate penalties were suggested. A separate scheme of penalties was provided for petty crimes; occasional criminals should not be imprisoned unless the offence was serious enough to justify at least a month's imprisonment. For the habitual petty offender, he proposed a system whereby, after a certain number of unpunished offences, there would be 'disciplinary detention in a suitable institution for not less than one and not more than two years'.

Churchill wished to create a scale of offences which related to the social harm each offence created, and to attach to them an appropriate scale of penalties. He made no headway; as his Civil Servants pointed out, his proposals could be construed as an attempt to dictate sentences to the judges. A draft letter explaining his ideas to the Lord Chief Justice was still in the file when he left the Home Office; his successor, when asked if he would like to take up the matter, replied curtly, 'I cannot undertake to deal with the question at present.' The subject was dropped.

In the first week of November a coal strike broke out in the Rhondda Valley. Within a few days of the outbreak of the strike there were incidents of window-breaking in two of the villages near the pits. The Chief Constable of Glamorgan, with 1,400 county policemen at his disposal, fearing further riots and looting, appealed direct to the Army, asking the General Officer commanding Southern Command to send 400 soldiers, both cavalry and infantry, by train to South Wales. The soldiers started early the following morning, November 7.

It was not until eleven o'clock that morning that Churchill was told troops were on their way to Wales. He at once telephoned the Chief Constable and, after hearing his report, 'definitely decided', he told the King, 'to employ police instead of military to deal with the disorder'. The infantry, still on their journey, were ordered to halt at Swindon. The cavalry were halted at Cardiff. In place of the soldiers Churchill directed reinforcements of London policemen – 200 constables and 70 mounted policemen – to be sent to South Wales. As the Chief Constable awaited their arrival, strikers made a number of attacks on one of the collieries, but the local police drove them off. 'When the Metropolitan Police arrived,' Churchill told the King, 'the rioters had already been beaten from the collieries without the aid of any reinforcements either of London police or military.'

Foiled in their attack on the colliery, the strikers moved into the nearby village of Tonypandy, wrecking many shops. This action, Churchill told the King, 'was not foreseen by anyone on the spot, and would not have been prevented by the presence of soldiers at the colliery itself'. Five hundred additional police were on their way from London. There appeared to be 'no reason at present why the policy of keeping the military out of direct contact with the rioters should be departed from'.

That night, the rioting appeared to be getting out of control. In response to a further appeal from the Chief Constable, Churchill allowed one squadron of cavalry to be moved to the junction of the two disturbed valleys, but no further, telling the King that he was still confident that the policemen already in the valleys would be able 'not merely to prevent attacks upon the collieries but to control the whole district and to deal promptly with any sign of a disorderly gathering large or small. No need for the employment of the military is likely to occur. They will be kept as far as possible out of touch with the population, while sufficiently near to the scene to be available if necessary.'

On November 8, in a conciliatory message, Churchill offered the strikers an interview with the senior government industrial arbitrator. On the following day he was violently attacked by the Conservative newspapers, particularly by *The Times*, for his conciliatory message, and for not having allowed troops to be sent to Tonypandy. If 'loss of life' occurred as a result of the riots, *The Times* declared, 'the responsibility will lie with the Home Secretary', who should have supported the Chief Constable's call for troops. 'Mr Churchill hardly seems to understand that an acute crisis has arisen, which needs decisive handling. The rosewater of conciliation is all very well in its place, but its place is not in the face of a wild mob drunk with the desire of destruction.'

In contrast to *The Times*, the *Manchester Guardian* defended Churchill's action in withholding the troops, an action, it wrote, 'which in all probability saved many lives'. It was true, the *Manchester Guardian* added, that the disorders at one moment seemed so serious 'that Mr Churchill decided to allow the troops to move up into the district so as to be in readiness for anything that might happen. But he never wavered in his determination not to employ the troops unless the disorders passed beyond the control of the police.'

The strikers accepted Churchill's offer of talks; the arbitrator met them in Cardiff on November 11. But ten days later riots broke out again in

Tonypandy. Again, troops were not used. 'The police were quite strong enough,' Churchill told the King, 'to scatter the rioters & beat them out of the town. The military were at hand but did not have to fire.' Six policemen had been seriously injured. Rioting continued on the following day, but was contained. 'The rioters have had a good dusting from the police,' Churchill told the King, '& it has still been possible to keep the military out of direct collision with the crowds.' As to the merits of the case, 'the owners are very unreasonable as well as the men,' Churchill wrote, '& both sides are fighting one another regardless of human interests or the public welfare.'

On November 25, in the Commons, Churchill defended his action in withholding the troops. 'It must be an object of public policy,' he declared, 'to avoid collisions between troops and people engaged in industrial disputes.' The Conservatives accepted this argument; the Liberals welcomed the statement of principle. But, for the Labour Party, Keir Hardie protested against the 'impropriety' of sending the troops at all and the 'harsh methods' of the police. It was this charge, not the original Conservative criticism of lack of ruthlessness, which created the Labour myth that Churchill had been, not the conciliator withholding troops and offering arbitration, but the belligerent sending troops and seeking confrontation. For Liberals, Tonypandy represented the success of moderation. For Labour it became part of a myth of Churchill's aggressiveness.

On November 22, at the height of the Tonypandy dispute, Churchill had been caught up in another battle in London itself. During the Cabinet meeting that day, suffragettes and their male supporters gathered in Downing Street to demand votes for women. As Ministers left the meeting there was a scuffle. Asquith had to be hustled into a taxi and another Minister was badly hurt. Churchill, watching as the police tried to cope with the scuffling, called out as they struggled with Mrs Cobden-Sanderson, 'Take that woman away; she is obviously one of the ringleaders.'

Four days later, while speaking at Bradford, Churchill was constantly interrupted by Hugh Franklin, a supporter of the suffragettes, who had overheard his remark to the police in Downing Street, and had himself been arrested. After the Bradford meeting, Franklin followed Churchill to the station and boarded the evening train to London. As Churchill made his way to the dining-car, Franklin attacked him with a whip, shouting as he did so, 'Take that, you dirty cur.' He was sentenced to six weeks' imprisonment for assault.

The suffragettes were convinced that Churchill was an out-and-out opponent of giving women the vote. This was not so; the 'sex disqualification', he told his constituents on December 2, 'was not a true or a logical disqualification', and he was therefore 'in favour of the principle of women being enfranchised'. But he was unwilling to vote for a Bill which

would give 'an undoubted preponderance to the property vote', or for one
which did not have behind it the 'genuine majority' of the electors. In the
past, he said, whatever support for votes for women he had admitted 'in
friendly discussion' on the subject, 'he had always found it was only the
excuse for renewed abuse and insult'. Every step taken 'in friendship'
towards the suffragettes 'had only met grosser insults and more outrageous action'. In the Commons vote in 1917, Churchill voted in favour
of votes for women.

Parliament had been dissolved on November 18 and a General Election
called, the second within twelve months. 'The Tory Party,' Churchill wrote
in his election manifesto, 'regard themselves as the ruling caste, exercising
by right a Divine superior authority over the whole nation.' And he told
an audience in Birmingham that the veto of the House of Lords was 'harsh
and cruel'; the powers of the Lords needed to be 'shattered into fragments
so that they were dust upon the ground'.

On November 30, his thirty-sixth birthday, Churchill told an election
meeting at Sheffield that once the veto power of the Lords was broken he
looked forward to working with the Conservatives in harmony, to create
through reconciliation and unity 'a better, a fairer, a juster, a more
scientific organisation of the social life of the people, a due correction of
the abuses of wealth and monopoly, religious equality and industrial
progress', as well as prison reform and 'the training of our youth'.

Electioneering over, Churchill went shooting at the home of Lord
Nunburnholme, Warter Priory, near York, with his uncle Lord
Tweedmouth, and several other Liberal Peers. 'Tomorrow pheasants in
thousands,' he wrote to Clementine on December 19, 'the very best wot
ever was seen. Tonight Poker – I lost a little – but the play was low,' and
he added: 'On the whole, survey how much more power and great business
are to me, than this kind of thing, pleasant tho it seems by contrast to our
humble mode of entertainment. I expect I will have a headache tomorrow
night after firing so many cartridges. All the glitter of the world appeals
to me, but not thank God in comparison with serious things.'

The election results were announced in the last week of December. The
Liberal Government remained in power, but with no change in the existing stalemate. The Liberals lost three seats and the Conservatives lost two.
Labour and the Irish Nationalists each gained two, holding the balance
once more and sustaining the Liberal Government with their votes and
demands.

Churchill still favoured a compromise with the Conservatives in order to
work together both on social and imperial policy. But in a letter on 3 January
1911 he told Asquith that the veto of the Lords 'must be restricted as an

indispensable preliminary to any co-operation'. The Parliament Bill should therefore go ahead and sufficient new peers be created to ensure its passage through the Lords. The Lords must not be allowed to delay matters through 'dilatory vapourings'. Until the veto was 'out of the way there can be no peace between parties and no demonstration of national unity. The quicker and more firmly the business is put through, the better for all'. After the veto had been restricted 'I hope we may be able to pursue *une politique d'apaisement*' – a policy of appeasement. This would include 'a liberal grant of honours' to the leading Conservatives, the Order of Merit for Chamberlain, 'a proportion of Tory peers and baronets', and 'something for the Tory Press'.

The Liberal Government should then offer, Churchill wrote, to 'confer' with the Conservatives on Ireland, the Poor Law, boy labour, Insurance and the Navy; Balfour should be given 'full access to all Admiralty information'. As part of the compromise economic proposals, death duties ought not to fall on landed estates 'more than once in 25 years'. In framing their future plans, the Liberals should seek 'a national and not a sectional policy'. All this, he added, 'may lead us further still'.

Churchill was writing this letter at his London home, 33 Eccleston Square, when a messenger arrived from the Home Office with urgent news. During a burglary on the previous night, three men, Fritz Svaars, 'Joseph', and a Russian anarchist known as 'Peter the Painter', had shot and killed three of the six policemen trying to arrest them; now they had been tracked down to a house in Sidney Street in the East End of London. The three men were armed; as their Mauser weapons had a greater range than the police revolvers, a senior police officer had already summoned from the Tower of London a detachment of twenty Scots Guards armed with rifles. The burglars were shooting from the house and a policeman had been killed.

Churchill went immediately to the Home Office, where, after consulting his advisers, he gave his retrospective authority for the earlier despatch of the troops. It was a quarter past eleven in the morning. Unable to learn more than that a 'continuous fusillade' was going on, he later wrote, 'I thought it my duty to go and see for myself what was happening.' Driving to the scene of the siege, he arrived a few minutes before midday. 'It was a striking scene in a London street,' he told Asquith in his interrupted letter, 'firing from every window, bullets chipping the brickwork, police and Scots Guards armed with loaded weapons, artillery brought up etc.'

Churchill was subsequently accused of having taken charge of the siege, and of having given orders which ought to have been given by the police. ydney Holland, a director of the Underground Railway, who was with nim throughout, wrote to him nine days later, 'The only possible excuse for anyone saying you gave orders is that you did once and very rightly go forward and wave back the crowd at the end of the road.' If the burglars had emerged from the house while the crowd was in the road 'there would have been a lot of people shot by the soldiers'. Holland added, 'And you did also give orders that you and I were not to be shot in our hindquarters by a policeman who was standing with a 12-bore behind you!'

At no point did Churchill direct the siege. 'I made it my business however,' he noted a week later, 'after seeing what was going on in front, to go round the back of the premises and satisfy myself that there was no chance of the criminals effecting their escape through the intricate area of walls and small houses at the back.' Returning from this reconnaissance, Churchill found that the house had caught fire. At that moment a junior fire brigade officer came up to him and said that the fire brigade had arrived. He understood that he was not to put out the fire at present.

'Was that right?' the officer asked.

'Quite right,' Churchill replied. 'I accept full responsibility.'

From what he saw at that moment, Churchill later told the Coroner, 'it would have meant loss of life and limb to any fire brigade officer who had gone within effective range of the building'. In agreeing that the fire brigade should stand back, he was acting 'as a covering authority' for the police in charge, in what was clearly a situation of 'unusual' difficulty. 'I thought it better to let the house burn down,' he explained to Asquith, 'rather than spend good British lives in rescuing those ferocious rascals.' At one moment a Maxim gun was brought up, followed by the arrival of a troop of Royal Horse Artillery. Both were later said to have been brought at Churchill's instigation and to have been directed by him. 'I never directed anyone to send for a Maxim gun,' he told the inquest, 'nor did I send at any time for any further military force. The artillery came up as I was driving away.'

The fire eventually burnt itself out. On entering the building the police found two bodies; one man had been shot and the other asphyxiated. The third, Peter the Painter, was never found. Churchill's presence at the siege of Sidney Street was rapidly to become part of the Conservative mockery of his actions. 'He was, I understand,' Balfour told the Commons, 'in a military phrase, in what is known as the zone of fire – he and a photographer were both risking valuable lives. I understand what the photographer was doing, but what was the right honourable gentleman doing?'

The Conservatives laughed at Balfour's wit. In a letter to the King, Churchill called it 'their meed of merriment'. Newsreel film showed Churchill peering from behind a wall at what was quickly known as 'The Battle of Stepney'. At the Palace Theatre, London, this film was shown night after night. Marsh, who had accompanied his master to the scene, wrote to a friend, 'I make the most gratifying appearance as almost the central figure of "Mr Churchill directing the operations" at the Palace which is nightly received with unanimous boos and shouts of "shoot him" from the gallery.' Marsh went on to ask, 'Why are the London music-hall audiences so bigoted and uniformly Tory?' Churchill himself, in a letter published in *The Times* on January 12, protested at the 'sensational accounts' of the siege that had appeared in the newspapers and at 'the spiteful comments based upon them'.

Throughout his period as Home Secretary, Churchill took up cases where he felt the sentence had been too severe. After a visit to Pentonville prison, he used his powers as Home Secretary to recommend the King to commute the prison sentences on seven young offenders. Conservative MPs, led by Lord Winterton, attacked his action in the Commons. 'I must confess,' he replied, 'I was very glad of the opportunity of recommending the use of the prerogative in these cases, because I wanted to draw the attention of the country, by means of cases perfectly legitimate in themselves, to the evil by which 7,000 lads of the poorer classes are sent to gaol every year for offences for which, if the noble Lord had committed them at College, he would not have been subjected to the slightest degree of inconvenience.'

Within the Home Office, Churchill voiced strong criticism of individual judges, and even of the Director of Public Prosecutions, whenever he felt they were imposing, or seeking to impose, penalties that were too harsh. The recently-created system of preventive detention roused his deepest unease. 'I have serious misgivings,' he wrote in a departmental minute, 'lest the institution of preventative detention should lead to a reversion to the ferocious sentences of the last generation. After all preventative detention is penal servitude in all essentials, but it soothes the conscience of judges and of public and there is a very grave danger that the administration of the law should under softer names assume in fact a more severe character.'

Within the Home Office, Churchill's tenure was recognised as constructive and remarkable; he brought the business of the department to the notice of Parliament in a way that few Home Secretaries had done before, or were to do after him. His most senior official, Sir Edward Troup, later recalled, 'Once a week or oftener, Mr Churchill came into the Office bringing with him some adventurous or impossible projects; but after half an hour's discussion something was evolved which was still adventurous, but not impossible.'

In continuing the tradition whereby the Home Secretary sent letters to the King on the debates in Parliament, Churchill angered the new King considerably when, after reporting on a proposal to send 'tramps and wastrels' to special Labour Colonies so that they might realise 'their duty to the State', he commented, 'It must not however be forgotten that there are idlers and wastrels at both ends of the social scale.' Such a comment, the King protested, was 'very socialistic'. Churchill apologised, telling the King, 'In writing these daily letters and trying to make them interesting and reliable it is always possible that some sentiment or opinion may occur which has not received the severe and deliberate scrutiny and reconsideration which should attach to a State Paper.'

In March 1911 Churchill introduced the second reading of the Coal Mines Bill, creating stricter safety standards, building pit-head baths, and lessening cruelty to pit ponies. Less successful was his effort to improve the life of shop-workers. His Shops Bill was intended to reduce the hours of work in shops from eighty to sixty a week, to set aside intervals for the meals of shop assistants, to regulate the hours of overtime, to strengthen the existing regulations on sanitation and ventilation, and to establish one early-closing day each week. Shopkeepers strenuously opposed these measures, which in the committee stage of the Bill were taken out or emasculated one by one, becoming, Churchill complained to the Committee, 'waste paper'.

When the Bill eventually passed, all that Churchill was able to secure was the provision for one early-closing day a week, and compulsory intervals for shop-assistants' meals. By this latter section of the Act, Churchill enshrined the British tea-break into law. But nine more years had to pass before the full Act reached the statute book.

On April 4 Lloyd George introduced the Government's comprehensive unemployment insurance scheme. Although it was subsequently to be associated entirely with his name, many of its principles, as well as its details, had originated with Churchill and been worked out by his Department. 'Lloyd George has practically taken unemployment insurance to his own bosom,' Churchill told Clementine, '& I am I think effectively elbowed out of this large field in which I consumed so much thought & effort. Never mind! There are many good fish in the sea.'

As the Parliament Bill debates continued, Churchill was called upon more and more by the Prime Minister; on one night Asquith was too much affected by drink to continue the behind-the-scenes negotiations with Balfour. As a result, Churchill conducted the negotiations in his stead. 'On Thursday night the PM was very bad,' Churchill told Clementine, '& I squirmed with embarrassment. He could hardly speak & many people noticed his condition. He continues most friendly & benevolent, & entrusts me with everything after dinner.' Up till dinner, Churchill explained, 'he is at his best – but thereafter! It is an awful pity, & only the persistent free-masonry of the House of Commons prevents a scandal. I like the old boy & admire both his intellect & his character. But what risks to run!'

The Parliament Bill proved less controversial than the Liberals had feared. Opposition to the Bill 'reached its lowest ebb last night', Churchill told the King on May 10. 'At one moment only seven Conservative members were in their places to stem the tide of revolution, & of these, two were deep in the pages of the Insurance Bill.' Eight days later, in a private room at the Savoy Hotel, Churchill was present at the inaugural dinner of a new Club, of which he and F.E. Smith were the founding members. Called the Other Club, its aim was to bring round a single dining-table, once a fortnight while Parliament was in session, up to twenty-eight MPs of both Parties, and a similar number of Peers, distinguished soldiers, lawyers, writers, artists, businessmen and journalists. One item in the rules of the Other Club stated that 'Nothing in the rules or intercourse of the Club shall interfere with the rancour or asperity of Party politics'. But its aim was to assuage the bitterness that the past year's politics had created; among the members was his most recent critic, Lord Winterton.

Clementine was now expecting her second child. Learning that she might be unable to be present in Westminster Abbey for the Coronation, the King offered her a ticket for his own box in the Abbey, so that she could watch the pageantry in comfort. On May 28, less than a month before the Coronation, her child was born; a son, he was named Randolph after Churchill's father.

Two days after his son's birth Churchill made a fierce attack in the Commons on those judges whom he believed had been unfair in Trade Union cases. It was his intention, Churchill said, 'to relieve Trade Unions from the harassing litigation to which they have been exposed and set them free to develop and do their work without the perpetual check and uncertainty of frequent trials and without being brought constantly into contact with the courts'. In the past few years Trade Unions had been 'enmeshed, harassed, worried, and checked at every step and at every turn by all kinds of legal decisions, which came with the utmost surprise to the greatest lawyers in the country'.

Where 'class issues' were involved, Churchill continued, 'and where party issues are involved, it is impossible to pretend that the courts command the same degree of general confidence' as in criminal cases. 'On the contrary, they do not, and a very large number of our population have been led to the opinion that they are, unconsciously no doubt, biased.'

There were immediate cries of 'No! No!' and 'Withdraw!' from the Conservative benches. Nor did Churchill's political enemies allow his accusation to be forgotten; on June 3 the *Spectator* described it as 'deeply deplorable' and 'mischievous'. Churchill, meanwhile, was basking in the pleasures of parenthood. 'Many congratulations are offered me upon the son,' he wrote to Clementine from the Oxfordshire Hussars camp at Blenheim on June 2. 'With that lack of jealousy which ennobles my nature, I lay them all at your feet.'

Before Randolph was born, he had been known in his parents' private language as the 'chumbolly'. 'My precious pussy cat,' Churchill wrote in his letter of June 2, 'I do trust & hope that you are being good, & not sitting up or fussing yourself. Just get well & strong & enjoy the richness which this new event will I know have brought into your life. The chumbolly must do his duty and help you with your milk, you are to tell him so from me. At his age greediness & even swinishness at table are virtues.'

The Coronation of King George V and Queen Mary took place on June 22. Churchill and Clementine rode in the procession together. 'Everyone admired the cat, the carriage, the horses and the tiger,' he wrote to her when it was over. He was sure she would 'long look back' to their drive and tell the story of the day to their son and daughter, 'so it will become a tradition in the family & they will hand it on to others whom we shall not see'. Clementine had gone to the seaside to rest from the exertions of the day. Churchill had remained in London; on June 28 he gave a dinner to Lloyd George at the Café Royal. 'He was full of your praises,' Churchill told Clementine, 'said you were my "salvation" & that your beauty was the least thing about you. We renewed treaties of alliance for another seven years.'

On June 29 Churchill drove in procession with the King to the City of London and back through North London. 'Of course,' he told Clementine, 'all the whole route I was cheered and in places booed vigorously.' Riding in his carriage were the Duchess of Devonshire and the Countess of Minto: 'It was rather embarrassing for these two Tory dames. They got awfully depressed when the cheering was very loud, but bucked up a little around the Mansion House where there were hostile demonstrations. They were very civil but rather fussed. I did not acknowledge any cheering & paid no attention at all to the crowds.'

That evening Churchill dined at the Other Club, where Kitchener, who was about to go to Egypt as Agent General, was an invited guest. 'My precious one,' his letter to Clementine, written from 33 Eccleston Square, continued, 'I will come down to you on Saturday, motoring from Walton Heath and arriving for dinner. I will inspect the infantry the next day. Let them all be drawn up in line of Brigade masses. It will be so nice to see you all again. This house is very silent without you; & I am reverting to my bachelor type with melancholy rapidity.'

Within four days of the Coronation, Conservative hostility to Churchill had again surfaced in the Commons, when Alfred Lyttelton, a former Colonial Secretary, said of him that he was 'certainly not free from that which is, well, not characteristic of the Home Office, and which, I think, is generally disliked by Englishmen – I mean certain appeals to the gallery'. The cause of Lyttelton's anger was Churchill's earlier decision to release seven youthful offenders from prison. Referring to other cases where Churchill had criticised the severity of the sentences on young offenders and then reduced them, Lyttelton declared: 'All these cases go to show that the habit has grown up under the Home Secretary of altering, mitigating, and even cancelling sentences without first consulting the justices who imposed them. It is done under a claim of right by the Home Secretary, who, I think I have shown by the plainest possible evidence, has not taken the trouble to make himself acquainted with the law in the cases in which he has taken it upon himself to reverse the penalty.'

Lyttelton then raised the question of the photographer who had taken the pictures of Churchill at Sidney Street, five months earlier. Churchill replied: 'I am sure he does not suppose there is a branch of the Home Office to organise the movements of photographers. It is the misfortune of a good many Members to encounter in our daily walks an increasing number of persons armed with cameras to take pictures for the illustrated Press which is so rapidly developing. I would remind the right hon. Gentleman that his own Leader (Mr A. J. Balfour), when he risked his valuable life in a flying machine was the victim of similar publicity, but I certainly should not go so far as to imitate the right hon. Gentleman (Mr. Lyttelton) by suggesting that he was himself concerned in procuring the attendance of a photographer to witness his daring feat in the way of aerial experience.'

Lyttelton had a further charge to make, criticising Churchill for the way in which 'the military were stopped from going to Tonypandy'. As a result of Churchill's action, he said, 'much suffering was caused and a heavy loss of property brought about'. Even as Churchill defended his action in replacing troops by policemen, further industrial unrest broke out in ports and dockyards throughout England. A strike of dockers at Hull led him to despatch police from London; they were involved in a series of confrontations with the strikers. 'It is impossible to deny that violence has played its part in this,' he wrote to Clementine on the following day, 'but that was not my fault. The House supported me warmly today on the sending of the police.'

Extra police and also troops had been sent that week to the Manchester docks, but by July 10 the strike there was settled. 'The men have received large and justifiable concessions in regard to their wages,' Churchill told the King.

That night, before joining his wife and their two children at the seaside, Churchill went out to buy the two-year-old Diana some toys, writing to Clementine on July 11: 'She is so little it is very difficult to know what will amuse her. Be careful not to let her suck the paint off the Noah's Ark animals. I hovered long on the verge of buying plain white wood animals – but decided at last to risk the coloured ones. They are so much more interesting. The shopman expressed himself hopefully about the nourishing qualities of the paint & of the numbers sold – and presumably sucked without misadventure. But do not trust to this.'

Churchill's letter also contained a reference to his own varying moods. His cousin Ivor Guest's wife Alice, with whom he had dined on the previous night, 'interested me a great deal by her talk about her doctor in Germany, who completely cured her depression. I think this man might be useful to me – if my black dog returns. He seems quite away from me now – it is such a relief. All the colours come back into the picture. Brightest of all your dear face – my darling.'

That July the constitutional crisis reached its climax. In his letters to the King, Churchill gave a vivid picture of the mood of both sides, reporting on July 24 that Asquith had been subjected to 'prolonged organised insult & interruption' for nearly half an hour from a section of the Conservative Party. Churchill's own instinct was for conciliation; the Government would accept several Conservative amendments 'that are not vital', he explained to the King on August 8, 'so as to make the submission of conscientious & honourable men as little galling as possible'. The 'squalid, frigid organised attempt to insult the Prime Minister & prevent debate' came only from a section of the Conservative Party. 'Extremely good relations are maintained by persons most strongly opposed to one another,' Churchill told the King. 'Everything points to a characteristically British solution of this great crisis.'

In agreeing on August 10 to a Government resolution affirming the principle of the payment of Members of Parliament, the Lords accepted that they could not veto money bills. It was a 'memorable and dramatic' moment, Churchill told the King. The 'long drawn out & anxious constitutional crisis' was over. No new peers would have to be created. It was to be hoped 'that a period of co-operation between the two branches of the legislature may now set in & that the settlement of several out of date quarrels may lead to a truer sense of national unity'.

On the previous day the dock strike had spread to London. The Board of Trade was attempting to arbitrate, using procedures established by Churchill two years earlier. If these negotiations were 'abortive', he told the King, 'extraordinary measures will have to be taken to secure the food supply of London, which must at all costs be maintained'. Twenty-five thousand soldiers were being held in readiness '& can be in the capital in six hours from the order being given'.

The London dock negotiations continued throughout August 12. But Churchill reported to the King that day that the situation in Liverpool was 'less satisfactory & it is possible that the military force available will have to be strengthened'. Two days later rioters rampaged through the streets of Liverpool. 'You need not attach any great importance to the rioting of last night,' the Chief Constable telegraphed to Churchill on August 15. 'It took place in an area where disorder is a chronic feature, ready to break out when any abnormal excitement is in force. The object of the riot was purely and simply attack on the police, whom they tempted into side streets where barricades of sanitary dustbins and wire entanglements were placed.'

In all, 250 soldiers, all infantrymen, had been called in to assist the police. Six of the soldiers and two policemen had been injured. There was no civilian loss of life. 'It is necessary in times like the present,' Churchill told the King, 'to make it clear that the police will be supported effectually & to warn persons in crowds not to take liberties with the soldiers.' Three days later he authorised the despatch to Liverpool of a cavalry regiment and an infantry battalion, but also of 250 London policemen, with instructions to the General in charge not to use the military 'until & unless all other means have been exhausted'.

Churchill's sympathies were again with the strikers; it was 'greatly to be hoped,' he told the King, that the Board of Trade arbitrators, who were then in Liverpool, would arrive at a settlement. 'The strikers are very poor,' he explained, 'miserably paid & now nearly starving.'

On August 17 Churchill informed the King that, in the Port of London, the shipowners had been 'dissuaded from provocative action' and that the men's leaders were urging the remaining strikers to return to work. The London docks were calm, but an infantry battalion had been sent to Sheffield, where disorder had broken out. 'Although a spirit of unusual unrest is stirring the whole Labour world,' Churchill told the King, 'due mainly to the fact that wages have not in late years kept pace with the increased cost of living, there is no ground for apprehension.' The forces at the disposal of the Government were 'ample to secure the ascendancy of the Law'. The difficulty was not to maintain order 'but to maintain order without loss of life'.

On August 18 a nationwide railway strike was called. Asquith offered the railwaymen a Royal Commission but they refused on the grounds that it would be too slow. The Government made plans to deliver food, fuel and other essential supplies under police and military escort. 'They will do this,' Churchill told the Commons, 'not because they are on the side of the employers or of the workmen but because they are bound at all costs to protect the public from the dangers and miseries which famine and a general arrest of industry would entail.' Churchill's task as Home Secretary was to protect the railways and to maintain supplies. That night he was able to report to the King that, with less than half the railwaymen having responded to the strike call, all necessary services had been maintained over the whole system. In the London docks a settlement had been reached that day 'on honourable terms for the men'. Their wages would be increased considerably.

The London dockers, Churchill told the King, had 'a real grievance, and the large addition to their wages which they have secured must promote the health & contentment of an unduly strained class of workers, charged as has been realised with vital functions in our civilisation'. The intention of the Government 'to use very large bodies of troops to maintain order & the food supply if the strike was not settled promptly,' he added, 'had a potent influence on the men's decision. They knew that they had reached the psychological moment to make their bargain, & that to go on was to risk all that they had within their grasp.'

At Churchill's urging, special civilian constables were now enrolled to augment the police forces wherever rail or dock strikes continued. At Llanelli in South Wales, rioters had taken advantage of the strike to loot and rampage. On the afternoon of August 19 they attacked a train which was passing through the station under military protection. The train was held up and the engine-driver roughly handled. Troops arrived and were pelted by stones; one soldier was wounded in the head. Shots were fired, and two civilians were killed.

When, shortly after the attack on the train, rioters burned down the business premises of the local magistrate, looted railway trucks, and damaged many small shops in the dock area, the troops took no action, leaving the police to restore order, which they did by charging the rioters with their truncheons. Later that evening a police station was attacked. Troops arrived and the attackers were driven off without loss of life. 'Much regret unfortunate incident at Llanelli,' the King telegraphed to Churchill. 'Feel convinced that prompt measures taken by you prevented loss of life in different parts of the country.'

Throughout August 19 negotiations were being conducted in London by Lloyd George, intended, Churchill told the King, 'to procure a peaceful settlement'. By nightfall the strike was over. 'The Chancellor of the Exchequer is principally responsible for the happy result,' Churchill telegraphed to the King just before midnight. Troops were already being withdrawn from the railway stations and would return to their barracks. 'Publish the fact that peace is made,' Churchill telegraphed to the Mayor of Birkenhead at 1 a.m. on August 20, 'and be specially careful to avoid collisions with those who do not know this yet.' These conciliatory instructions reflected Churchill's instinct throughout the crisis and his understanding of the strength of the workers' grievances. He had also been determined, and it was part of his Ministerial responsibility, to ensure that violence did not spread. It was 'obvious and certain', he told the Commons in the aftermath of the strikes, 'that any Government must, with the whole force of the State, exert itself to prevent such a catastrophe, and because it was certain that in taking such action they would be supported by the good sense and resolution of the whole mass of the people.'

On many occasions during the disturbances Churchill had initiated or supported prompt and forceful action, aimed at halting destructive violence. But those who wanted to use everything he did for their own political advantage, or to revenge his betrayal of the Conservative Party a mere five years earlier, and who had only just adopted two new slogans, 'Tonypandy' and 'Sidney Street', had no difficulty in adding the unrest at Liverpool and Llanelli to the list.

During the summer of 1911 a crisis erupted in North Africa which threatened Europe with war. In an attempt to secure a naval base on the Atlantic Ocean, the German Government sent a gunboat, the *Panther*, to the Moroccan port of Agadir. France, which under the Anglo-French Entente of 1904 had a predominant sphere of influence in Morocco, asked Britain to challenge the German action by sending a British gunboat.

'This would be a serious step,' Churchill wrote to Clementine from the Home Office on 3 July 1911, 'on which we should not engage without being ready to go to all lengths if necessary.' Being Home Secretary, his departmental concerns were elsewhere; but his understanding of European rivalries had always been considerable; his presence at German Army manoeuvres had served only to enhance it. When the Cabinet met on July 4 it was decided, he reported to Clementine, 'to use pretty plain language to Germany and to tell her that if she thinks Morocco can be divided up without John Bull, she is jolly well mistaken'.

In a letter to Lloyd George, Churchill agreed that Germany had 'some (minor) claims about Morocco which if amicably stated we should be glad to see adjusted either there or elsewhere – subject to Britain being safeguarded'. But the German action at Agadir 'has put her in the wrong & forced us to consider her claims in the light of her policy & methods'. If Germany made war on France in the course of the negotiations, he argued, or unless Britain felt that France had chosen unjustifiable ground for any deadlock, 'we should join with France'. Nor should Britain's intended course of action be kept secret. Indeed he advised Lloyd George that 'Germany should be told this now'.

Lloyd George did in fact warn Germany openly. Peace at the price of surrender, he declared at the Mansion House on July 21, 'would be a humiliation intolerable for a great country like ours to endure'. The Germans reacted by denouncing Lloyd George's words as 'a warning bordering on menace'. Suddenly it seemed that war might come at any moment.

In strictest secrecy, using his authority as Home Secretary, Churchill now issued a warrant to the secret service for the 'inspection of correspondence'. The letters of anyone suspected of receiving instructions from Germany were opened. The intercepted letters, he told Grey four months later, showed 'that we are the subject of a minute and scientific study by the German naval and military authorities, and that no other nation in the world pays us such attention'.

In a letter to Grey on July 25, Churchill proposed a British effort to detach Spain from her pro-German stance, 'to make good friends with her', and to promote good relations between Spain and France. 'It is not I think too late yet.' Two days later Churchill told the King that he had been impressed in the Commons by the widespread agreement among MPs that Germany must be prevented from having her way by the threat of force. Asquith had made a statement 'careful & friendly in form & feeling, but strong & firm in substance'. Balfour had supported it, as had the Labour Party leader Ramsay MacDonald, 'restrained, sombre but perfectly correct'. No one else had spoken. 'It may be,' Churchill concluded, 'that this episode, following upon the speech of the Chancellor of the Exchequer, will have exercised a decisive effect upon the peace of Europe. It is certain that it redounds to the credit of British public life.'

At a garden party at 10 Downing Street four days later, while talking to the Chief Commissioner of Police, Churchill learned that as Home Secretary he was technically responsible for the safety of all the reserves of naval cordite in Britain. Three of them were stored in London. Returning to the Home Office, he telephoned the Admiralty to ask that a detachment of Royal Marines be sent to guard these vital munitions. The Admiral in charge declined to act. Shocked by this attitude on the part of the Admiral, Churchill telephoned the War Office and persuaded the Secretary of State for War, Lord Haldane, to send troops to the three magazines.

Churchill himself informed the King that midnight that 'Mr Churchill has felt it his duty to take more effective measures to ensure the safety of the great naval magazines, now under the guard of the Metropolitan Police. Chattenden & Lodge Hill alone hold $3/5$ths of the cordite ammu-

1. Winston Leonard Spencer Churchill:
a photograph taken in Dublin when he was five years old

2. Churchill's father,
Lord Randolph Churchill

3. Churchill's mother, Lady Randolph
Churchill: 'She shone for me
like the Evening Star'

4. Churchill's nanny, Mrs Everest:
he called her 'Oom', 'Woom'
and 'Woomany'

5. In a sailor suit, aged seven

6. Jack, Lady Randolph and Winston in 1889, when Churchill was fifteen

7. Second-Lieutenant, commissioned in the Cavalry on 20 February 1895

8. Cavalry officer in India, after serving with the Malakand Field Force, with which he first saw action on 16 September 1897

9. Conservative candidate at a Parliamentary by-election. He was narrowly defeated on 6 July 1899

10. Journalist, on the way to South Africa, on board the *Dunottar Castle*, which left Southampton on 14 October 1899

11. With fellow journalists on board the *Dunottar Castle*. His friend John Atkins is standing behind him

12. Prisoner of the Boers: in captivity at Pretoria, 18 November 1899

13. Escaped prisoner, arriving at Durban on 23 December 1899

14. Lieutenant, South African Light Horse, revisiting on 24 December 1899 the scene of the armoured train ambush of six weeks earlier

HOW I ESCAPED
FROM PRETORIA.

By Winston Churchill.

THE *Morning Post* has received the following telegram from Mr. Winston Spencer Churchill, its war correspondent, who was taken prisoner by the Boers and escaped from Pretoria:

LOURENCO MARQUES, December 21st, 10 p.m.

I was concealed in a railway truck under great sacks.

I had a small store of good water with me.

I remained hidden, chancing discovery.

The Boers searched the train at Komati Poort, but did not search deep enough, so after sixty hours of misery I came safely here.

I am very weak, but I am free.

I have lost many pounds weight, but I am lighter in heart.

I shall also avail myself of every opportunity from this moment to urge with earnestness an unflinching and uncompromising prosecution of the war.

On the afternoon of the 12th the Transvaal Government's Secretary for War informed me that there was little chance of my release.

I therefore resolved to escape the same night, and left the State Schools Prison at Pretoria by climbing the wall when the sentries' backs were turned momentarily.

I walked through the streets of the town without any disguise, meeting many burghers, but I was not challenged in the crowd.

I got through the pickets of the Town Guard, and struck the Delagoa Bay Railroad.

I walked along it, evading the watchers at the bridges and culverts.

I waited for a train beyond the first station.

The out 11.10 goods train from Pretoria arrived, and before it had reached full speed I boarded with great difficulty, and hid myself under coal sacks.

I jumped from the train before dawn, and sheltered during the day in a small wood, in company with a huge vulture, who displayed a lively interest in me.

I walked on at dusk.

There were no more trains that night.

The danger of meeting the guards of the railway line continued; but I was obliged to follow it, as I had no compass or map.

I had to make wide *détours* to avoid the bridges, stations, and huts.

My progress was very slow, and chocolate is not a satisfying food.

The outlook was gloomy, but I persevered, with God's help, for five days.

The food I had to have was very precarious.

I was lying up at daylight, and walking on at night time, and, meanwhile, my escape had been discovered and my description telegraphed everywhere.

All the trains were searched.

Everyone was on the watch for me.

Four wrong people were arrested.

But on the sixth day I managed to board a train beyond Middleburg, whence there is a direct service to Delagoa.

15. His first article about his escape, published on 30 December 1899

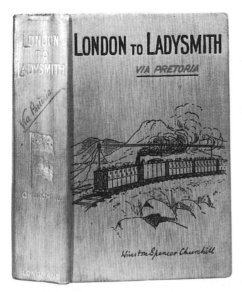

16. *London to Ladysmith via Pretoria*, published on 5 April 1900

17. On active service in South Africa, with moustache

18. Member of Parliament: he was elected on 1 October 1900

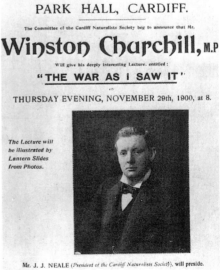

19. Lecture poster, for a lecture on 29 November 1900, the day before his twenty-sixth birthday

20. Young Conservative MP, with his Liberal uncle by marriage,
Lord Tweedmouth, pondering a motor-car problem at Guisachan,
Scotland, 1901. In 1905 Tweedmouth became First Lord of the
Admiralty, a post to which his nephew was appointed six years later

21. Under-Secretary of State for the Colonies, his first Government
post: with the Colonial Premiers and British Cabinet Ministers,
London, 8 May 1907. Seated in front of Churchill (far left), is the
Chancellor of the Exchequer, H. H. Asquith. The Colonial Secretary,
Lord Elgin, is in the centre of the group (with white beard) and the
President of the Board of Trade, David Lloyd George, far right (seated)

22. With his Private Secretary,
Eddie Marsh, Malta, October 1907

23. Revisiting the Mahdi's tomb,
Khartoum, December 1907. The tomb
was still shell-scarred after the
bombardment by Lord Kitchener in
1898, an action which Churchill had
criticized at the time

24. Campaigning as a Liberal,
Manchester, 24 April 1908

25. Arriving at a Levée at St James's
Palace in Privy Councillor's uniform,
6 July 1908, with Lord Morley,
one of his Liberal mentors

26. Clementine Hozier at the time of her engagement

27. Arriving at St Margaret's, Westminster, for his wedding,
12 September 1908. With him is his best man, and former
Conservative fellow rebel, Lord Hugh Cecil

28. A German illustrated newspaper celebrates the wedding of Winston and Clementine

29. President of the Board of Trade, 1908

30. With the Kaiser at German Army manoeuvres, Würzburg, 17 September 1909

31. With Clementine, a photograph published in *Black and White* magazine, 11 December 1909

32. President of the Board of Trade, visiting a Labour Exchange on 1 February 1910, with the Prime Minister, H. H. Asquith (left, also in top hat), and Clementine

33. Home Secretary, at the siege of Sidney Street, 3 January 1911

34. First Lord of the Admiralty, with his wife and one-year-old son
Randolph, summer 1912

35. Cruising on *Enchantress*, summer 1913, with the Prime Minister,
H. H. Asquith, and his daughter Violet
(later Violet Bonham Carter)

36. With Admiral of the Fleet Lord Fisher, leaving a meeting
of the Committee of Imperial Defence, 1913

37. Returning after piloting a flying boat, Portsmouth harbour,
23 February 1914

BRAVO WINSTON!

The Rapid Naval Mobilisation and Purchase of the Two Foreign Dreadnoughts Spoke Volumes for your Work and Wisdom.

MR. WINSTON CHURCHILL, FIRST LORD OF THE ADMIRALTY

AND (INSET) HIS CHARMING AND BEAUTIFUL WIFE

If you listen to the opinion of the navy in general upon Mr. Churchill you will be thankful that such a man has been in control of our navy in the immediate past. Mrs. Churchill must be a proud woman. Mr. Churchill has fought and overcome the Little Navyites in the past so that our fleet may fight and overcome our foes in the future

38. On the eve of war, with an inset photograph of Clementine, published in the *Tatler* on 12 August 1914, eight days after the outbreak of war

39. A family portrait taken at Admiralty House three months after the
outbreak of the First World War. Left to right: Winston Churchill,
his daughter Diana, his wife Clementine, his son Randolph,
his mother Lady Randolph, his nephew Peregrine, his sister-in-law
Lady Gwendeline, his nephew Johnny and his brother Jack.
On Clementine's lap, Sarah, born on 7 October 1914

40. Listening to Lord Kitchener speaking at the Guildhall, 9 July 1915.
Clementine is on her husband's left

nition of the Fleet.' He had arranged for a company of infantry to be sent to each magazine, writing to Clementine two days later that he had 'sent plenty of soldiers to both points I told you of, and all is safe now'. As for the news about Agadir, it seemed that 'the bully is climbing down, & it looks as if all will come out smooth and triumphant'. There was no doubt, he told her four days later, that the Germans were going to settle with the French 'on a friendly basis', and he added, 'They sent their *Panther* to Agadir & we sent our panther to the Mansion House: with the best results.'

In preparation for a meeting of the Committee of Imperial Defence on August 23, Churchill set out his thoughts on the dangers facing France should Germany launch a military attack, and the part that Britain would have to play to help avert a French defeat. The German Army, he forecast, would break through the line of the River Meuse on the twentieth day of war. The French would then fall back towards Paris. 'All plans based on the opposite assumption ask too much of fortune.' The impetus of the German advance would slowly weaken, the more it was extended. From the thirtieth day the Russian army would begin to exercise pressure on the Eastern Front. The British army would be in place in Flanders. By the fortieth day the German forces in the West 'should be extended at full strain both internally and on her war fronts'. This strain would become daily 'more severe' and without a victory 'ultimately overwhelming'. It was then that 'opportunities for the decisive trial of strength may occur'.

Balfour was a member of the Committee of Imperial Defence when Churchill's memorandum was submitted. When he read it again in 1914, on the thirty-fifth day of the war, he commented, 'It is a triumph of prophecy!' Five days later the German forces were halted on the Marne, and thrown back.

On August 30, as the Moroccan negotiations continued, Churchill suggested to Grey that if the negotiations failed, Britain should propose a triple alliance of herself, France and Russia, to safeguard the independence of Belgium, Holland and Denmark. Britain should also 'tell Belgium that, if her neutrality is violated, we are prepared to come to her aid', and to take 'whatever military steps will be most effective for that purpose'. Similar guarantees should be offered to Holland and Denmark, subject to all three States 'making the utmost exertions' of their own once war had begun. To defend Belgium, Britain would be prepared to feed Antwerp and any army based upon it; also to put 'extreme pressure' on the Dutch to keep open the River Scheldt, Antwerp's supply line. If the Dutch were to close the Scheldt, 'we should retaliate by a blockade of the Rhine'.

The Admiralty had proposed joining France in a naval blockade of the Moroccan coast. Churchill opposed this. If French warships went to

Morocco, he wrote to Grey on August 30, 'I am of the opinion that we should (for our part) move our main fleet to the north of Scotland into its war stations. Our interests are European, and not Moroccan.'

Churchill now examined in detail how Britain could best help France to resist a German attack. On August 31 he discussed his ideas with General Henry Wilson, the recently appointed Director of Military Operations at the War Office, who agreed that 'great strategic advantages' would be immediately derived if Britain were able to move her army into a friendly Belgium, 'and from our being able to threaten the German flank in conjunction with the Belgium Army'. In reporting on this conversation to Lloyd George, Churchill set out a principle which was to govern his thinking on foreign affairs before two world wars: 'It is not for Morocco, nor indeed for Belgium, that I would take part in this terrible business. One cause alone could justify our participation – to prevent France from being trampled down & looted by the Prussian junkers – a disaster ruinous to the world, & swiftly fatal to our country.'

On September 2 Churchill received a letter marked 'Secret: destroy' from the Secretary of the Committee of Imperial Defence, Sir Charles Ottley. It contained details of the imminent concentration of the German High Sea Fleet at Kiel. 'We should not relax our vigilance for a moment,' Ottley warned. Churchill sent Ottley's letter to Lloyd George with the comment, 'I hope that McKenna is not as full of cocksureness, as his Admiral is deficient in imagination.' The Admiral was the First Sea Lord, Sir Arthur Wilson.

Scrutinising the Admiralty's dispositions in the North Sea, Churchill was deeply dissatisfied. 'Are you sure that the ships we have at Cromarty are strong enough to defeat the whole German High Sea Fleet?' he asked Asquith on September 13. 'If not they should be reinforced without delay.' The fleet concentrated in the North Sea should be strong enough 'without further aid' to fight a decisive battle with the German Navy. 'And something must be allowed for losses through a torpedo surprise.'

Churchill was angered by the Admiralty attitudes, asking Asquith: 'Are you sure that the Admiralty realise the serious situation of Europe? I am told they are nearly all on leave at the present time.' He was confident, however, that good leadership would be enough, telling Asquith: 'The Admiralty have ample strength at their disposal. They have only to be ready & employ it wisely. But one lapse, as stupid as that revealed at our meeting, & it will be the defence of England rather than that of France which will engage us.'

Admiral Wilson was about to leave the Admiralty for a holiday, telling the War Office on the night of September 13 that everything was ready for any naval emergency: all that was necessary was to 'press the button', which could as well be done by a clerk as anyone else. In reporting this to Lloyd George, Churchill commented, 'I can only say I hope this may be so.'

The Agadir crisis had given Churchill a sense of Britain's naval strengths and weaknesses. He was convinced that he had the energy and foresight, and could quickly acquire the knowledge, to make Britain invulnerable at sea. Determined to succeed McKenna at the Admiralty, he was particularly anxious to create a Naval War Staff, on the Army model, to plan for all possible war contingencies. The question of who should become First Lord was being much discussed that autumn. 'On the whole,' Asquith wrote to Lord Crewe on October 7, 'I am satisfied that Churchill is the right man, and he would like to go.'

12

At the Admiralty

When Parliament reassembled on 24 October 1911, five weeks before Churchill's thirty-seventh birthday, it was announced that he was to be First Lord of the Admiralty. 'I do hope you think well of the change,' he wrote to Morley . 'It is a great responsibility & I now appreciate more than I did three years ago the importance of the office, in its bearings both upon domestic & international politics. I have always been specially attracted to naval & military subjects. I have read much more about war than about anything – I had almost written – all other things. I am I trust a sincere economist.The times are also good – Estimates at a maximum, the fleet enormously strong, the Cabinet very much united. I may reap rightly where another has wrongly sown. We were absolutely right in all that we said at the scare-time. Not a fact then cited by us, but has been verified by events!' Churchill added confidently, 'I think I will be able to find my path along the causeway.'

Within four days of his appointment Churchill completed a memorandum for the Cabinet advocating the establishment of a Naval War Staff. 'Adequate preparation for war is the only guarantee for the preservation of the wealth, natural resources, and territory of the State,' he wrote, 'and it can only be based upon an understanding, firstly, of the probable dangers that may arise; secondly, of the best general method of meeting them as taught by the principles to be deduced from the events of history; and, thirdly, of the most efficient application of the war material of the era.' Now was the time to prepare. In time of peace, preparation provided 'the only field wherein immediate and sustained action of a useful nature is possible'.

For the next two and a half years Churchill made naval preparation his task, visiting naval stations and dockyards, seeking to master the intricacies of naval gunnery and tactics, scrutinising the development of German naval construction, and working to improve naval morale. Typical of his

vigilance was a note to Asquith, written within two weeks of his appointment, 'I have come across one disconcerting fact: there is a shortage of 120
21-inch torpedoes, meaning that thirty of our best destroyers would have
to go to sea without reserves of any kind other than the two they carry.'
This deficiency, he added, 'cannot be fully repaired till April or May at the
earliest'. But repaired it would be: 'It is essential that by the time all vessels
are completed for service,' he wrote to the Fourth Sea Lord ten days later,
'their full reserves of ammunition and torpedoes should be simultaneously
at hand.'

Every deficiency would have to be made good, every gap filled, every
contingency anticipated. Churchill's letter to Asquith of November 5 was
written during his first day on board the Admiralty yacht *Enchantress*,
which, with a complement of 196 officers and ratings, was to be his home
and office for more than two hundred days during the next two and a half
years. On this first journey, setting off from Cowes, he inspected the
dockyard and submarine depot at Portsmouth. On his second voyage
three days later he joined the naval vessels escorting the King and Queen
out of Portsmouth harbour on their way to India for the Delhi Durbar. On
his third voyage, beginning on November 17, he launched the battleship
Centurion at Devonport. On his fourth voyage he inspected the torpedo-
boat destroyer *Falcon*. And on December 9, during his fifth journey in
under six weeks, he inspected the Royal Naval Barracks at Portsmouth and
visited the submarine school.

There was an even more recent branch of war science that Churchill
studied during his first months at the Admiralty; war in the air. That
December he insisted that terms and conditions for a naval air service
'must be devised to make aviation for war purposes the most honourable,
as it is the most dangerous profession a young Englishman can adopt'. No
regard to seniority 'should prevent the really young & capable men who
have already done so much for the new arm being placed effectively at the
head of the corps of airmen'. The Army envisaged its air service as
primarily one of reconnaissance, avoiding, wherever possible, any actual
air battles. Churchill wanted the Navy to use aircraft more aggressively;
both bomb-dropping and machine-gunnery became part of the experi-
mentation and training of the Royal Naval Air Service.

Churchill continued to nourish cross-Party friendships. When Andrew
Bonar Law, one of the founder-members of the Other Club, was elected
leader of the Conservative Party, Churchill wrote to him that his election
'makes me sure that if ever a national emergency makes Party interests
fade, we shall find in the Leader of the Opposition one who in no fictitious
sense places the country and the Empire first'. He hoped the Other Club

would continue. 'Great tact' would be needed, however, in fixing its meetings and in the avoidance of 'bad moments'. But no one could say that 'so far as public things are concerned' fortune had not followed the footsteps of many of its members, 'or that the chance of including in its lists a Prime Minister has become less good since our beginnings'. There were in fact already three future Prime Ministers in the Club, Lloyd George, Bonar Law and Churchill.

From a former Prime Minister came encouragement to Churchill in his new post. 'I am glad you have gone to the Admiralty,' Balfour wrote. 'A fresh eye at this moment is all important.' From a former First Sea Lord, Admiral of the Fleet Sir John Fisher, came a visit, followed by constant letters of exhortation and encouragement, to which Churchill responded with enthusiasm. 'I wish you could have seen the model of the new ships for this year,' Churchill wrote to him on December 3. 'It conforms to almost every requisite which we discussed together.'

Fisher encouraged Churchill to develop the 15-inch gun for battleships, to create a Fast Division of warships capable of a speed of twenty-five knots, and to build warships powered not by coal as hitherto but by oil, making possible a speed of twenty-five knots. Some observers were shocked that Churchill should turn for advice to a retired officer noted for controversy and outspokenness. But the two men, one aged seventy, the other thirty-eight, found an instant affinity of zeal and purpose. Recalling Fisher's advocacy of the 15-inch gun, Churchill later wrote: 'No one who has not experienced it has any idea of the passion and eloquence of this old lion when thoroughly roused on a technical question. He was steadfast and even violent. So I hardened my heart and took the plunge. The whole outfit of guns was ordered forthwith.'

Churchill's concern over German naval developments grew in December; in a letter to a correspondent just before Christmas 1911 he pointed to the 'very rapid growth' of the German Navy in the past few years. The union of that enlarged Navy with the existing large German Army, he warned, 'will be a most sinister and disquieting fact', especially as 'these gigantic engines of destruction' would not be wielded by a democratic Government but by a 'military and bureaucratic oligarchy supported by a powerful Junker landlord class'. It was up to Germany, Churchill added, 'without endangering her own security or liberty at all, to terminate at once the distressing tension which now exists'. Any step she might take to reduce the pace of naval construction 'we will instantly respond to, not only by words and sentiments, but by action'.

Perhaps as a result of Britain's firmness during the Agadir crisis, Churchill wrote, and in particular Lloyd George's Mansion House speech, the 'evil day' had only been postponed; that in itself was surely 'a great deal', particularly, Churchill wrote, as 'I do not believe in the theory of inevitable wars. All the world is changing at once, and it may be that in a few years' time the democratic forces in Germany will again have greater control of their own Government, and that the landlord ascendancy which now exists will be replaced by more pacific and less formidable elements.' Meanwhile, as Russia recovered from her defeat in Manchuria in 1905 at the hands of Japan, she was 'a great corrective to aggressive action on the part of Germany'.

At the beginning of January 1912 Churchill spoke to Sir Ernest Cassel, who was on his way to Germany to see the Kaiser. Until Germany 'dropped the naval challenge', he told Cassel, her policy would be continually viewed in Britain 'with deepening suspicion & apprehension'. Any slackening on Germany's part would produce 'an immediate détente with much good will from England'. Failing any slackening, 'I see little in prospect but politeness & preparation'.

That preparation went steadily ahead. Three days after Churchill's letter to Cassel, he wrote to Fisher to inform him that flights of aeroplanes would soon be regularly attached to the battle squadrons. There would be an increase in the number of submarines under construction. The cruisers being built in 1912 would be as much as two knots faster than their predecessors.

Replying to those Conservatives who believed that Churchill was not doing enough, and who wanted British naval units more widely dispersed throughout the Empire, he was emphatic that such dispersal would be unwise. 'It should not be supposed that mastery of the seas depends upon the simultaneous occupation of every sea,' he wrote. 'On the contrary it depends upon the ability to defeat the strongest battle fleet or combination which can be brought to bear. This ability cannot be maintained by a policy of dispersion.' Napoleon's 'supreme strategic principle' of the concentration of superior forces in the decisive theatre must govern all naval dispositions. 'Dispersion of strength, frittering away of money, empty parades of foolish little ships "displaying the flag" in unfrequented seas, are the certain features of a policy leading through extravagance to defeat.'

On January 31 Sir Ernest Cassel, having returned from Berlin, breakfasted with Churchill and Lloyd George. The news he brought back from his meeting with the Kaiser was that a major German naval expansion was imminent; instead of the twelve battleships hitherto planned, there would be an accelerated six-year building programme, to include fifteen new battleships. When the Germans announced their new programme, Churchill told Grey later that day, Britain would make 'an immediate & effective reply'. Then, if the Germans cared to slow down the tempo of their expansion, so that their new plans were accomplished in twelve rather than six years, 'friendly relations would ensue' between the two countries, and Britain could 'slow down too'.

Cassel had persuaded the Kaiser to show Churchill the new German Navy Law in advance. As soon as he read it, Churchill realised that it contained a further element of danger for Britain, the deepening of the Kiel Canal between the Baltic and the North Sea. At present, he pointed out to Grey, those German battleships which were on the 'wrong' side of the Kiel Canal could only reach the North Sea by a long detour. 'The deepening of the canal by 1915 will extinguish this safety signal.' Once all twenty-five German battleships could be sent rapidly to the North Sea at Germany's 'selected moment' for hostilities, Britain would need to keep 'not less than forty available within twenty-four hours'.

On February 14 Churchill circulated the new German Navy Law to the Cabinet. It was clear that a substantial increase in British naval construction would be needed. Against the previously planned seventeen extra battleships, four extra battle-cruisers and twelve extra small cruisers, Germany now planned to build twenty-five, twelve and eighteen of each type. More than fifty new submarines were to be built. A further 15,000 officers and men were to be added to the existing 86,500. Of Germany's five battle squadrons, two would consist entirely, by April 1914, of the most modern battleships and cruisers. It was not merely the new German construction, Churchill explained, but the increase of personnel, and of vessels of all classes 'maintained in full commission', that was the danger. It practically amounted 'to putting about four-fifths of the German Navy permanently on a war footing'.

Once the new German Navy Law was carried out, Churchill informed the Cabinet on March 9, Germany would have 'at all seasons of the year' at least twenty-five battleships available in the North Sea, as against twenty-two British battleships, 'even counting the Atlantic Fleet'. He therefore proposed that for every German battleship built under the new law, assuming that law were put into effect, Britain would build two. 'Two keels to one on all increases above the existing German Navy Law'; Churchill announced this in the Commons on March 18. At the same time, seeking a way of averting the naval arms race, he proposed a 'Naval Holiday' whereby naval construction would be suspended for a year by both countries, telling the House: 'Any retardation or reduction in German construction will, within certain limits, be promptly followed here, as soon as it is apparent, by large and fully proportioned reductions. For instance, if Germany elected to drop out any one, or even any two, of these annual quotas and to put her money into her pocket for the enjoyment of her people and the development of her own prosperity, we will at once, in the absence of any dangerous development elsewhere not now foreseen, blot out our corresponding quota, and the slowing down by Germany will be accompanied naturally on a larger scale by us.'

Churchill's unexpected, and dramatic offer, continued: 'Take, as an instance of this proposition which I am putting forward for general consideration, the year 1913. In that year, as I apprehend, Germany will build three capital ships, and it will be necessary for us to build five in consequence. Supposing we were both to take a holiday for that year. Supposing we both introduced a blank page in the book of misunde.- standing; supposing that Germany were to build no ships in that year, she would save herself between £6,000,000 and £7,000,000 sterling. But that is not all. We should not in ordinary circumstances begin our ships until she has started hers. The three ships that she did not build would therefore automatically wipe out no fewer than five British potential super "Dreadnoughts", and that is more than I expect them to hope to do in a brilliant naval action. As to the indirect results, even from a single year, they simply cannot be measured, not only between our two great brother nations, but to all the world. They are results immeasurable in their hope and brightness.'

While awaiting the German reply to his offer of a 'Naval Holiday' Churchill returned to the *Enchantress* and to his inspection of naval dock-yards and warships. With him was a new shorthand writer, Harry Beckenham, who was to remain with him throughout his time at the Admiralty. At the end of March, having spent six days at Portland, Churchill wrote to Clementine, 'I have got on the track of a lot of waste of money in refitting & repairing ships unnecessarily – just in order to make work for the dockyards. Probe, Prune, Prepare – one cannot do too much of it.' He was confident of success: 'We shall be much stronger in a year. I wish I had nine lives like a cat, so that I could go into each branch thoroughly. As it is I have to trust so much to others – when I am pretty confident I could do it better myself.' He was also proud of the men under his Ministerial command: 'There are some very nice fellows here – good, hard-working, smart officers of quality & conduct.' There were eleven battleships at Portland and 'seven or eight' other large warships. 'Unluckily there are no Germans to be found. Tiresome people – but their turn will come.'

Churchill now sent his Cabinet colleagues copies of the original German Navy Law, in which, he told Morley on April 7, 'the policy so resolutely and eagerly pursued and developed during the last fourteen years is set forth in all its sinister candour. It is lucky for us we have the situation so well in hand. Since the original Law there have been four successive cumulative increases.'

Still Churchill awaited a positive reply to his offer of a Naval Holiday, writing to Cassel on April 14, in a letter intended for the Kaiser's eye, 'Certainly it must be almost impossible for Germany with her splendid armies and warlike population capable of holding their native soil against all comers, and situated inland with road & railway communications on every side, to appreciate the sentiments with which an island State like Britain views the steady & remorseless development of a rival naval power of the very highest efficiency.' But all was not lost: 'Patience, however, and good temper accomplish much, & as the years pass many difficulties and dangers seem to settle themselves peacefully.'

The Germans had still not announced their new naval programme. At the Royal Academy banquet in London on May 4, Churchill stated that the sole aim of British naval policy, and the only means of averting defeat in the event of a naval war, was the development of the maximum war power 'at a given moment, and at a particular point'. Everything in the naval world was directed 'to the manifestation at a particular place, during the compass of a few minutes, of a shattering, blasting, overbearing force'.

Churchill also ventured a prophecy that day, 'If any two great and highly scientific nations go to war with one another, they will become heartily sick of it before they come to the end of it.' A month had passed since his proposal for a Naval Holiday, but it had not been taken up. On May 9 and 10 he was at Weymouth for the King's inspection of the Fleet, when two major advances were demonstrated to the assembled onlookers; aeroplanes were used to detect submarines beneath the surface, and explosive bombs were dropped from aeroplanes on to targets below. During the review Churchill took Balfour and Morley into a gun turret on the battleship *Orion*. Commented one newspaper, 'Mr Churchill, quite a naval enthusiast, seems to instil into his guests some of his own keen appreciation of naval men and material.'

Speaking in London on May 15, Churchill stressed the horrors which would ensue if war broke out, but concluded, 'It is much more likely, I say it with sincere conviction, that war will never come in our time – and perhaps will have passed from the world, at any rate for the period which our most adventurous imagination enables us to foresee.'

This prophecy was in vain. On May 21 the German Navy Law was passed by the Reichstag. Henceforth Churchill's energies were to be focused on preparing the Royal Navy for conflict with Germany. Within six weeks he had presented the Cabinet with an outline of his proposals for 'an extraordinary increase in the striking force of ships of all classes'. He was confident that he could inspire his subordinates and enhance the power of the Navy. When, in June, he visited a submarine at Portsmouth, the *Daily Express* wrote: 'He had a yarn with nearly all the lower deck men of the ship's company, asking why, wherefore and how everything was done. All the sailors "go a bundle" on him, because he makes no fuss and takes them by surprise. He is here, there, and everywhere.'

In June and July Churchill sailed on *Enchantress* to the Irish ports and to Spithead; among his guests was Austen Chamberlain, Joe's son, a Party adversary, but a personal friend. During the voyage, Clementine's continuing illnesses were much on his mind. 'My dear darling,' he wrote to her on July 9, 'I am so distressed to think of you in pain & discouragement. Hope deferred makes the heart sick. Always to be expecting that you are going to get well & then one thing after another. It is a cruel trial for you. But you will bear it bravely – my own darling & emerge triumphant into the sunlight.'

On July 22, with the German Navy Law now public knowledge, Churchill introduced supplementary Navy Estimates to Parliament. It was a grave moment in his career, and in Britain and Europe's history. Speaking for more than two hours, he explained in detail both the new German Navy Law and Britain's response. Britain would build such warships as were needed to retain her security at sea. 'The state of Europe and of the world would seem to contain many more germs of danger than the period through which we have been passing in our lifetime.' He wished to assert two general principles, 'First that we must have an ample margin of strength instantly ready; and, secondly, that there must be a steady and systematic development of our naval forces untiringly pursued over a number of years.'

On August 1 Churchill wrote to Clementine, who was at the seaside, 'My work has been *incessant* & seems to mount and mount day after day.' He hurried to be with her. 'I have made no plans for Sunday except to come down quietly & see you. We ought really to find a good sandy beach where I can cut the sand into a nicely bevelled fortress – or best of all with a little stream running down. You might explore & report,' and he added, 'My darling one I have much felt the need of kissing your dear face & stroking your soft skin in these solitary days.'

During August and September, Churchill sailed to naval stations all round Britain, watching firing-practice, witnessing tactical exercises, attending launchings, inspecting dockyards, shore installations, armaments works, and examining the latest technical developments. 'This afternoon I studied the torpedo again under my young officer,' he wrote in one of his letters to Clementine. 'It is a tangle of complications, & the 2nd lesson opens up all sorts of vistas of which I never dreamed. I could write ten pages on the "Valve group".'

That autumn Churchill also discussed with the French Ministry of Marine how best to strengthen France as a Mediterranean naval power, thereby allowing Britain to concentrate her own naval strength in the North Sea. He was reluctant, however, to see Britain join the French system of alliances, particularly the alliance with Russia, telling Asquith and Grey that he opposed any agreement which would result in 'tying us up too tightly with France, and depriving us of that liberty of choice on which our power to stop a war might well depend'. No military or naval arrangements ought to be made, he warned, which might expose Britain to the charge of bad faith 'if when the time comes we decide to stand out'.

The supplementary Navy Estimates would ensure that the Royal Navy was numerically strong; Churchill also wanted the sailors to be contented. To this end he pressed for increases in pay for the lower deck, and for facilities for recreation on shore. After a visit to Harwich he sought funds for a football ground, a canteen with a reading room, billiard tables, bowling-alleys, and sleeping accommodation in the town 'so that the men have proper places to go when spending the night ashore'.

No aspect of the naval scene escaped him; warning Lloyd George in October that a further increase in British naval spending would soon be needed, he pointed out that the German battle-cruiser *Seydlitz*, the latest German ship of which the Admiralty had details, was 'superior in armour, only slightly inferior in gun power, and at least equal in every other particular to our latest comparable vessel, the *Tiger*'.

Churchill had repeatedly to fight for his Department with the Chancellor of the Exchequer. When, four days after his letter about the *Seydlitz*, he asked in Cabinet for the extra funds to increase sailors' pay, Lloyd George protested at his 'having looked out for opportunities to squander money'. Two weeks after Lloyd George's rebuke, Churchill learned that Austria-Hungary might be about to build three extra battleships, he wrote at once: 'Look at this. Do you realise what it means if it is true? It is no use being vexed with me and reproaching me. I can no more control these facts than you can.' Should the Austrians build these extra ships 'beyond anything yet foreseen or provided against' by Britain, Churchill warned, 'we shall have to take further measures'.

Churchill had no intention of spending money without full cause; as he prepared the Navy Estimates for 1913-14, he promised the Cabinet 'an unshakeable foundation for every item put forward'. Writing to Lloyd George on December 9 he stated with confidence, 'I am sure the Government have only to put their case plainly and boldly to the House of Commons to receive from one source or another, without any serious difficulty, the sums which are necessary for the safety of the State.'

The pressures on Churchill had begun to affect his private life. 'I was stupid last night,' he wrote to his wife from the *Enchantress* at the start of a seven-day separation, 'but you know what a prey I am to nerves & prepossessions.' He was sorry she was not with him. 'I should like to kiss your dear face and stroke your baby cheeks and make you purr softly in my arms.' And he added: 'Don't be disloyal to me in your thoughts. I have no one but you to break the loneliness of a bustling and bustled existence.'

At the beginning of 1913, after a visit on *Enchantress* to the naval air station at Eastchurch, on the Isle of Sheppey, Churchill asked the young naval pilots there to teach him to fly. It was a dangerous undertaking. In 1912 there had been one death in every 5,000 flights. It was also rare for a civilian to fly, or for anyone over the age of thirty-two to take up flying. His first instructor was the twenty-three-year-old Spenser Grey, a descendant of Earl Grey of the Reform Bill, and a pioneer of sea-plane experiments, which he had carried out in his own plane the previous year. The pilots were amazed and excited that the First Lord should wish to learn their dangerous craft. His enthusiasm was a tonic. One of them, Ivon Courtney, later recalled how, before their first flight together, Churchill said to him: 'We are in the Stephenson age of flying. Now our machines are frail. One day they will be robust, and of value to our country.'

Churchill's relatives and friends deprecated his new activity, particularly when they read of accidents among the pilots; Spenser Grey was himself severely injured when his plane got into a spin and crashed. 'I do not suppose I shall get the chance of writing you many more letters if you continue your journeys in the Air,' Churchill's cousin Sunny wrote to him in March 1913. 'Really I consider that you owe it to your wife, family and friends to desist from a practice or pastime – whatever you call it – which is fraught with so much danger to life. It is really wrong of you.'

Right or wrong, Churchill continued his flying instruction at every opportunity, spending many weekends at Eastchurch. 'Churchill and I would go up perhaps ten times in one day,' Courtney later recalled. 'He was far more keen than most learners to "go up again". He couldn't bear to make mistakes. He always wanted to correct them at once. I remember the time when, on landing, he bent an undercarriage. I imagined he would want to stop flying that day. But the shock did not deter him one bit. It made him more eager. So up we went again.'

Throughout 1913 the *Enchantress* was Churchill's second home; at the Admiralty, the First Sea Lord, Prince Louis of Battenberg, and the other members of the Admiralty Board, followed up the requests emanating from their First Lord. On April 6 Churchill wrote to Clementine from Portsmouth: 'I stay placidly in my nice cabin working all the morning, walk round the dockyard in the afternoon & then home to tea & a couple of hours more work before dinner. The papers in files & bags & boxes come rolling in. One never seems to do more than keep abreast of them.'

Among those whom Churchill met that year was Prince Louis' elder son Dickie, who later recalled: 'Although I was only a thirteen-year-old Naval Cadet he always spoke to me as though I were a fully fledged Naval Officer. No wonder I quickly fell under his spell.' In 1942 Churchill was to appoint that Naval Cadet, then Admiral Lord Louis Mountbatten, as Chief of Combined Operations.

In London, Clementine was preparing to move from their home in Eccleston Square to the First Lord's official residence at Admiralty House, overlooking both Horse Guards Parade and Whitehall. 'I like the idea of these spacious rooms,' Churchill wrote to her in the same letter. 'I am sure you will take to it when you get there. I am afraid it all means very hard work for you – poor lamb. But remember I am going to turn over a new leaf! That I promise. The only mystery is "What is written on the other side?" It may only be "ditto, ditto"!'

As often as possible Clementine joined her husband on *Enchantress*. When she left he would write affectionately of their separation. 'I mewed at the departure of the Catling,' he wrote in June from Portland, 'but I must admit it would be but a poor show for her here. Wind, rain & sea = crowds of men talking shop = cold & sleet = more shop. But it amuses me – I am a fool who should not have been born.' Despite his wife's unease, he had continued with his flying practice. On June 28 he was at London Aerodrome, Hendon, at a flying meeting. 'I have been naughty today about flying,' he confessed to her on the following day. 'Down here with twenty machines in the air at once and thousands of flights made without mishap, it is not possible to look upon it as a very serious risk. Do not be vexed with me. I shall be back tomorrow between 11 and 12.'

That summer Clementine joined her husband for a prolonged and pleasurable journey. Asquith, his wife Margot, and his daughter Violet, went with them. Travelling by train to Venice, they joined *Enchantress* and sailed through the Adriatic to the Mediterranean, visiting Malta, Sicily and Corsica. At Malta, Churchill met Kitchener, had several hours talk with him about the defence of the Mediterranean, and sought, not without some success, to close the gap of age and distrust.

Returning to Britain, Churchill was closely involved in an attempt to resolve the Irish impasse. Early the previous year, at Belfast, where in 1886 his father had warned that the Protestants of Ulster might use unconstitutional methods to prevent Home Rule, he had extolled the virtues of Home Rule and urged the six counties of Ulster to accept it. In reply, Sir Edward Carson had declared Ulster's total opposition to Home Rule and was supported by Bonar Law. The Home Rule Bill was introduced in April 1912; in a speech during the ensuing debate Churchill had appealed to Ulstermen to help sweep the Irish question 'out of life and into history, and free the British realm of the canker which has poisoned its heart for generations'. If they refused, he said, 'if they take to the boats, all we say is they shall not obstruct the work of salvage, and we shall go forward – at any rate – to the end'.

During the debates of 1912 Churchill had called Bonar Law's opposition to Home Rule 'almost treasonable activity'. That autumn, an Ulster MP, Ronald O'Neill, had thrown a book at Churchill across the Chamber, hitting him on the head and drawing blood. There was talk of an Ulster rebellion, fuelled by extremist speeches by both Protestants and Catholics. On his return from the Mediterranean in the summer of 1913, Churchill took a lead in trying to defuse these passions.

At Balmoral in the third week of September, while the guest of the King, Churchill met Bonar Law and spoke to him of a solution based on some special rights for Ulster, possibly outside the framework of Home Rule. 'History teaches us that in such cases British common sense generally triumphs,' he told the Conservative Leader. 'If Ireland has the right to claim separate Government from England, Ulster cannot be refused similar exemption from Government by an Irish Parliament.' But Ireland could not be expected 'to stand by & see the cup, almost at her lips, dashed to the ground'.

The Home Rule Bill would go ahead. But 'some sort of bargain', Asquith confirmed after Churchill's Balmoral talks, could be made about Ulster. All talk of civil war must cease, however; threats of organized disorder were, in Asquith's words, 'almost puerile in their crudity'. Churchill now worked through his friend F.E. Smith, and in the convivial cross-Party atmosphere of the Other Club, to try to effect a compromise whereby Ulster could have a special status, at least in the early stages of the evolution of a self-governing Ireland. No settlement, he told an audience at Manchester on October 18, must be destructive of the unity of Ireland.

During his Manchester speech Churchill repeated his call to Germany for a moratorium on naval shipbuilding. 'If the Germans refuse,' he wrote to Clementine on the following day, 'I shall have made my case for action. If they accept, it will be a big event in the world's affairs.' But, he added, 'they won't accept – they will just butt on the water as in the air!'

In an effort to reduce naval expenditure wherever possible, Churchill now decided to cancel the annual Grand Manoeuvres for 1914. These were estimated to cost £230,000; eight million pounds in the money values of 1990. In their place he proposed a less expensive mobilisation of the Third Fleet. The monetary saving would be £180,000, most of it on fuel.

The result of this decision was that the Third Fleet, instead of being dispersed in the Atlantic on manoeuvres in July 1914, was to be concentrated in the North Sea, fully mobilised.

As well as saving money, Churchill was concerned, he explained to Prince Louis of Battenberg on October 19, to have 'a thorough overhaul of the mobilisation arrangements'. Nothing should be left to chance or custom. As well as mobilising the Third Fleet, he wished to have a test mobilisation of the Royal Fleet Reserve and the Reserve officers, telling Prince Louis, 'Such a step is urgently needed.' Amid these plans for test mobilisation, and while awaiting some German response to his second call for a Naval Holiday, Churchill remained the champion not only of the lower deck but of the men who worked in the dockyards. 'As for the dockyard workmen,' he wrote to Fisher that November, 'it is socially just that men who work all their lives faithfully for the State should have permanency and pension guaranteed, just like Admirals!'

That autumn Churchill resumed his flying instruction. Among his instructors were Eugene Gerrard and Richard Bell Davies, who was to win the Victoria Cross at the Dardanelles. As well as continuing to learn to fly, notching up the hours that would enable him to get his pilot's licence, Churchill kept a close eye on all aspects of aerial warfare and training. In August he had authorised the direct entry of civilian flyers into the naval air wing, and had raised the age of entry from twenty-two to twenty-four. In September he made plans for a war establishment of a hundred seaplanes; indeed, it was he who coined the word 'seaplane', a fact of which, in later years, he was most proud.

In October, from Sheerness, Churchill flew in an airship above Chatham and the Medway. 'She is a very satisfactory vessel,' he wrote to Clementine, 'and so easy to manage that they let me steer her for a whole hour myself.' Also that day he flew in a seaplane and inspected the Sheerness dockyard. 'It has been as good as one of those old days in the South African war, & I have lived entirely in the moment, with no care for all those tiresome party politics & searching newspapers, & awkward by-elections, & sulky Orangemen, & obnoxious Cecils & smug little Runcimans.'

His day at Sheerness encouraged Churchill enormously. 'It is very satisfactory to find such signs of progress in every branch of the naval air service,' he told Clementine. 'In another year – if I am spared ministerially – there will be a great development. When I have pumped in another million the thing will be alive & on the wing.' On November 3 he wrote to her again on the air theme: 'These flying people's affairs are very odd & very criss-cross – & today much difficulty has arisen about their ranks, & their rows & their uniforms & their prospects.' He did his best to create for the airmen a sense of independence of rank and dress and promotion. But Clementine's unhappiness at his continued flying led him to write to her: 'You know so much about me, & with your intuition have measured the good & bad in my nature. Alas I have no very good opinion of myself. At times I think I could conquer everything – & then again I know I am only a weak vain fool. But your love for me is the greatest glory and recognition that has or will ever befall me & the attachment which I feel towards you is not capable of being altered by the sort of things that happen in this world. I only wish I were more worthy of you, & more able to meet the inner needs of your soul.'

Churchill's fascination with, and belief in the future of, aviation, was total; in mid-November he pushed forward with the building of seaplane bases along the south and east coasts, and prepared for seaplane exercises to be held the following summer. He also told his advisers that 'a band should be provided and everything done to foster cohesion, unity and esprit de corps in this new service'. At the end of November he returned to Eastchurch for further flying. On this occasion his co-pilot was Captain Gilbert Lushington. 'I started Winston off on his instruction about 12.15,' Lushington wrote to his fiancée, Airlie Hynes, '& he got so bitten with it, I could hardly get him out of the machine, in fact except for about 3/4 hour for lunch we were in the machine till about 3.30. He showed great promise, & is coming down again for further instruction & practice.'

At lunch Churchill went to Lushington's cabin to wash his hands. In the cabin he saw the photographs of Miss Hynes, whom Lushington said he intended to marry. 'He asked me when it was coming off, & I said when I had saved some money.' That night at dinner, fortified by oysters flown specially for him from Whitstable, Churchill was, in Lushington's words, 'absolutely full out and talked hard about what he was going to do'. November 30 was Churchill's thirty-ninth birthday. In a letter to Lushington that day he asked if he could 'clear up the question of the steering control and let me know what was the real difficulty I had in making the rudder act. Probably the explanation is that I was pushing against myself, though I am not quite sure about this. It may be that they are very stiff and hard to work.'

Churchill asked Lushington to go up with another flying officer and 'sitting yourself in the back seat, see whether there is great stiffness and difficulty in steering, or whether it was all my clumsiness'. He also asked his principal air adviser at the Admiralty to fit one of the Eastchurch biplanes with dual controls 'of exact equality'. Such a machine, he noted, 'would be useful for long distance flying and enable one pilot to relieve the other'. Lushington went up as Churchill asked, flying in the passenger seat. 'I believe you fell into a very common error of beginners, & even of experienced pilots too,' he wrote on December 2, 'of pushing against yourself. I ought to have warned you of the possibility of your doing so, before taking you up. These faults rectify themselves in time.'

Shortly after writing this letter Lushington went up again in the plane in which he and Churchill had flown. On coming in to land the plane sideslipped and crashed. Lushington was killed. His letter to Churchill reached the Admiralty a few days later. 'I think you ought to have it,' Churchill wrote to Airlie Hynes, 'and may I ask you to accept my deepest sympathy in the blow which has fallen upon you. To be killed instantly without pain or fear in the necessary service of the country, when one is quite happy and life is full of success & hope, cannot be reckoned the worst of fortune. But to some who are left behind the loss is terrible.'

Following Lushington's death, many newspapers urged Churchill to give up flying. So did his closest friends. 'Why do you do such a thing as fly repeatedly? F.E. Smith wrote on December 6. 'Surely it is unfair to your family, your career & your friends.' But Churchill did not intend to give up the skill which he was beginning to master.

Churchill had begun to prepare the Navy Estimates for 1914-15. One blow to his search for economy was the refusal of the Canadian Government to pay for the construction of three of the battleships in Britain's future programme. Another was the continuing German refusal to contemplate a moratorium on naval construction, as well as Churchill's decision that merchant ships bringing food to Britain should be armed, enabling them to fire back at any enemy warship that attacked them. Thirty had already been armed; he wanted to arm a further forty in the coming year. This was in addition to the merchant ships being taken over by the Navy and converted into auxiliary cruisers, to protect Britain's food lifelines.

Extra expenditure was also inevitable in three main areas of modernisation; the continuing change from coal-fired to oil-burning ships and the need to build up oil-storage depots; the expansion of the Royal Naval Air Service and the need to build naval air stations and facilities; and the spread of wireless telegraphy as the chief means of secret communication both at sea and in the air. The Cabinet was divided on whether or not to give Churchill £3 million above the previous year's total of £50 million. Some Ministers still felt that Liberalism and increased naval armaments were incompatible. At first Lloyd George supported Churchill. Then he joined those who were demanding a 'substantial reduction' in the Navy Estimates, including the postponement of the construction of at least one of the four battleships to be laid down in 1914-15. In the last week of December, Churchill threatened resignation if his proposal for four new battleships to be laid down in 1914-15 were rejected. 'I am inflexible – thank God – on some things,' he wrote to Grey on Christmas Day 1913.

Churchill prepared charts and statistical tables to show that his proposals were the minimum needed to meet the current German naval expansion. 'I am absolutely fixed, & can do nothing more,' he wrote to Morley on January 13. 'The four ships are vital & no compromise of any sort is possible.' 'While I am responsible,' he wrote to Lloyd George two weeks later, 'what is necessary will have to be provided.' The Navy Estimates of 1914-15 had been prepared 'with the strictest economy'. For all the expenditure incurred or proposed there was 'full warrant & good reason'.

As the crisis continued, Lloyd George offered to accept the estimates for 1914-15 in return for a promise of a definite reduction in the spending for 1915-16. Churchill rejected this. 'I cannot buy a year of office by a bargain under duress,' he replied. In the first week of February, Asquith asked Churchill to 'throw a baby or two out of the sledge' in order to effect a compromise with those whom he called 'the critical pack (who know well that they have behind them a large body of Party opinion)'. Churchill replied: 'I do not love this naval expenditure & am grieved to be found in the position of taskmaster. But I am myself the slave of facts & forces which are uncontrollable unless naval efficiency is frankly abandoned. The result of all this pressure & controversy leaves me anxious chiefly lest the necessary services have been cut too low. The sledge is bare of babies, & though the pack may crunch the driver's bones, the winter will not be ended.'

A week later Churchill agreed to two small cutbacks, in the cruiser programme and recruitment. The Cabinet then accepted his Navy Estimates for the coming year. Had there been any other Chancellor of the Exchequer, the Estimates would have been cut 'by millions', commented one Labour Party critic. 'There would also have been another First Lord of the Admiralty!' was Churchill's comment. 'And who can say,' he told Lloyd George, 'if such gaps were opened, that there would not have been another Government – which does not necessarily mean lower Estimates'.

Three days before he was to introduce his Navy Estimates to Parliament, Churchill was to speak at Bradford, where in 1886 his father had defended his policy of retrenchment and no foreign entanglements. Two days before going to Bradford he was present at a Cabinet meeting which was given alarming news from Ulster. The Protestant leaders had rejected the Government's Home Rule compromise, whereby each of the six Ulster counties would be able to decide by plebiscite in favour of exclusion for six years from the enactment of Home Rule. For the Ulster Unionists this was not enough. They wanted total exclusion from the supremacy of the predominantly Catholic Dublin Parliament which the Home Rule Bill would establish. Ulster Volunteers were preparing to take the law into their own hands, threatening to challenge the police by force should any effort be made to disarm them.

The Cabinet of March 12 were told, as Asquith reported to the King, of the latest series of police reports indicating 'the possibility of attempts on the part of the "volunteers" to seize, by *coups de main*, police and military barracks, and depots of arms and ammunition'. There were only 9,000 British regular troops in Ulster; the bulk of the force, 23,000 men, were stationed in southern Ireland, mostly at the Curragh, outside Dublin. The Cabinet were agreed that it might be necessary to send these troops against the Volunteers, but decided that before any such action was taken a senior Government Minister should issue a public warning to the Unionists. Churchill was the one chosen to issue it. 'You are the only member of the Cabinet who can make such a speech,' Lloyd George told him. 'You are known to have been in favour of conciliation for Ulster. Now you can say that having secured a compromise, Ulstermen will have to accept it or take the consequences.'

At the request of the Cabinet, when Churchill spoke at Bradford on March 14 he challenged in the strongest terms his father's dictum 'Ulster will fight, Ulster will be right', and did so in forceful language which Asquith had approved beforehand. The 'Tory mind', he declared, denounces 'all violence except their own. They uphold all law except the law they choose to break. They are to select from the Statute Book the laws they will obey and the laws they will resist.' This was the political doctrine 'they salute the twentieth century with'. But the Government would not allow the realm of Great Britain to 'sink to the condition of the Republic of Mexico'. If all the 'loose, wanton and reckless chatter we have been forced to listen to these months is in the end to disclose a sinister revolutionary purpose, then I can only say to you, "Let us go forward together and put these grave matters to the proof" '.

Returning to London that evening, Churchill worked to complete his speech on the Navy Estimates in three days' time, March 17. The speech lasted two and a half hours, 'the longest and perhaps also the most weighty and eloquent speech', wrote the *Daily Telegraph*, 'to which the House of Commons have listened during the present generation'. In it, Churchill defended the increase in Britain's naval expenditure by pointing to the upsurge in German and also Austro-Hungarian naval construction. He also drew a distinction between their needs and those of Britain. None of the Great Powers needed navies to defend 'their actual independence or safety', he said. 'They build them so as to play a part in the world's affairs. It is sport to them. It is life and death to us.'

It was not suggested, Churchill told the Commons, that 'the whole world will turn upon us, or that our preparations should contemplate such a monstrous contingency. By a sober and modest conduct, by a skilful diplomacy, we can in part disarm and in part divide the elements of danger.' But Britain's diplomacy, whereby this amelioration would be made, depended 'in great part for its effectiveness upon our naval position'. Britain's naval strength was 'the one great balancing force which we can contribute to our own safety and the peace of the world'. Twenty years later, in the face of a second German threat, Churchill was to insist that Britain's air strength was similarly vital for the preservation of peace.

Churchill won his Navy Estimates battle. But it was now Ireland that dominated the centre of the political stage. There was no way in which the Liberal Government could convince Ulster that its interests were not to be sacrificed to Dublin. Asquith's compromise of a six-year exclusion was unacceptable to the Protestants of Ulster, who believed that they should never come under the rule of Dublin, but could rule Ulster themselves, pushing aside the forces of law and order, if necessary by violence.

On March 15 Churchill was appointed to a Cabinet Committee which reported three days later that the four main depots of arms and ammunition in Ulster were in danger of being 'rushed' by the Volunteers. The War Office had instructed General Paget, commanding the forces in Ireland, to have these depots adequately guarded. Paget declined, fearing that the movement of troops from the Curragh to Ulster would 'possibly precipitate a crisis'. Churchill prepared to use the Royal Navy to defend the Government's policy. The forthcoming practice manoeuvres of the Third Battle Squadron, he told the Cabinet of March 18, would take place at Lamlash, on the Scottish coast, only seventy miles from Belfast. If the railway company declined to help, naval vessels could carry troops by sea, from southern Ireland to Ulster. The Cabinet approved this course of action.

The Third Battle Squadron was then on the Atlantic coast of France. 'Proceed at once at ordinary speed to Lamlash,' Churchill signalled to its commanding Admiral on March 19. That same day he ordered three destroyers direct to a port in southern Ireland, where they were instructed to take a company of infantrymen to near Belfast, where they were to be landed 'at once'. Two more destroyers were ordered to take 550 infantrymen from the South to the North. One destroyer Captain was ordered to land at Bangor, on Belfast Lough, 'in plain clothes', to co-operate with the Army units there. Another was to arrange for the guarding of military stores and ammunition at Carrickfergus. 'The place is to be defended against attack by every means,' Churchill signalled, 'and if co-operation of Navy is necessary, by guns and searchlights from the ship.'

The news from Ulster was of continuing determination on the part of the Ulster Volunteers to seize arms and ammunition. But General Paget's hands were dramatically tied when the commander of the 3rd Cavalry Brigade, General Gough, and fifty-seven of his seventy officers, resigned rather than be sent from their camp at the Curragh to Ulster. Following this 'Curragh mutiny' Paget was more dependent than before on the Navy. On March 21, at his request, four field guns were embarked on the flagship of the Third Battle Squadron, then at Devonport.

In the event, the troops already available in Ulster proved sufficient to guard the stores, and no attacks were made upon them. The Third Battle Squadron remained at Lamlash. The Navy was not required to confront the Ulster Volunteers. But Churchill's naval preparations, despite having full Cabinet sanction, became the object of virulent attack from the Conservative benches; he was accused of wishing to institute an 'Ulster Pogrom'. When he told the House that the Navy's movements had been 'purely precautionary measures', he was accused of having wanted those movements to lead 'to fighting and bloodshed'. This, he retorted, was a 'hellish insinuation'. But it was widely made and widely believed.

Hostility to Churchill reached a peak at a rally in Hyde Park on April 4, when Edward Carson, the Parliamentary leader of the Ulster Unionists, denounced 'Lord Randolph's renegade son, who wanted to be handed down to posterity as the Belfast butcher who threatened to shoot down those who followed his father's advice'. For his part, Churchill still believed that a compromise was possible in Ireland, and worked to secure it. 'The Federal and conciliation movements are both going forward well,' he told Clementine on April 23, 'and there is a tremendous undercurrent on both sides towards a settlement.'

On the night of April 24 hopes of a settlement seemed to be brought abruptly to an end when the Ulster Volunteers, with Carson's connivance, landed some 30,000 rifles and 3 million cartridges at Larne, quickly distributing them. This was the most serious challenge yet by the Ulstermen. But 'from a Parliamentary point of view', Churchill assured Clementine two days later, the situation had been 'much altered in our favour by the gun-running escapade of the Ulstermen. They have put themselves entirely in the wrong.'

At the very moment when Liberal opinion was most incensed against Ulster, Churchill decided to take a personal initiative towards a settlement. The occasion was one of great tension, a Conservative vote of censure on the Government for its alleged hostility to the needs of Ulster. Churchill began by rebuking the censure motion itself. It was, he said, 'uncommonly like a vote of censure by the criminal classes on the police'.

Having defended the Government's actions in Ulster, Churchill ended with a remarkable appeal for conciliation to Carson himself: 'Today I believe most firmly, in spite of all the antagonism and partisanship of our politics and our conflicting Party interests, that Peace with Honour is not beyond the reach of all. Tomorrow it may be gone for ever. I am going to run some little risk on my own account by what I will now say. Why cannot the right hon and learned Gentleman say boldly, "Give me the Amendments to this Home Rule Bill which I ask for, to safeguard the dignity and the interests of Protestant Ulster, and I in return will use all my influence and goodwill to make Ireland an integral unit in a federal system." If the right hon Gentleman used language of that kind in the spirit of sincerity with which everybody will instantly credit him, it would go far to transform the political situation and every man would be bound to reconsider his own position in relation to these great controversies.'

Many Liberals were outraged that Churchill had even broached, let alone offered Carson, the Federal scheme, which for the Irish Nationalists seemed a device to blanket and stifle Home Rule. 'It is absolutely vital,' one Cabinet Minister wrote, 'that you should realise the extent of the fury – for no milder term will fit the facts – which has been aroused in the Irish Party and among large numbers of our Liberal colleagues by the offer to Carson with which you concluded your speech.'

Despite Liberal and Irish Nationalist fury, Churchill's offer cooled the passions of Ulster, enabling negotiations to continue through the summer. 'As you will see,' he wrote to Clementine on April 29, 'I yesterday at the end of my speech, greatly daring, and on my own account, threw a sentence across the floor of the House of Commons to Carson which has revolutionised the situation, and we are all back again in full conciliation.'

In May, Churchill sought to pursue conciliation of another sort, with Germany. He had been invited by the Kaiser to visit Kiel during the naval regatta at the end of June. The father of the German Navy, Grand Admiral Tirpitz, had also expressed a wish to see him. Churchill was willing to go, hoping that such 'direct personal discussion' with Tirpitz might prove the prelude to a wider agreement. He would, he told Asquith and Grey, explain to the Grand Admiral the genuineness of his Naval Holiday proposal for a mutual reduction in the numbers of warships 'in case circumstances should ever render it admissible'.

Churchill also wanted to take up a suggestion made earlier by Tirpitz for a limitation in the size of the largest warships. 'Even if numbers could not be touched,' he felt, 'a limitation in the size would be a great saving, and is on every ground to be desired.' He would even go so far as to propose 'the abandonment of secrecy in regard to the numbers and general characteristics (apart from special inventions) of the ships, built and building, in British and German dockyards'. Naval attachés from both navies could visit each others' dockyards 'and see what was going on'. This,

Churchill argued, 'would go a long way to stopping the espionage on both sides which is a continued cause of suspicion and ill-feeling'.

At the end of June, two British naval squadrons would be in the Baltic, invited by both the Russian and German navies. Churchill proposed joining them, sailing on *Enchantress* first to the Imperial Russian naval base at Kronstadt, and then to Kiel. There would be nothing about his visit to offend the French, he pointed out, as he had already been a guest at the French naval base at Toulon. The Foreign Secretary, Sir Edward Grey, hesitated to sanction Churchill's journey. Hitherto, he wrote, Tirpitz had 'resented' all efforts to discuss naval expenditure. As to the visits to Kronstadt and Kiel, 'I am most reluctant to stand in the way, but they will make a terrible splash in the European Press and give a significance to the cruise of our squadrons that is out of all proportion to anything that was contemplated when the cruises were planned.' The 'wildest reports' would be circulated, and Britain would be involved 'in constant explanations to ambassadors at the Foreign Office, and denials in the Press of the things that will be attributed to us'.

Grey advised that the Kaiser be informed of Churchill's 'inability' to go to Kiel. This should not be 'construed in any way as wanting in respect to the Emperor'. But it effectively ended Churchill's hopes of ameliorating the naval rivalry. Instead of planning a voyage to the Baltic he spent the first week of June on *Enchantress*, first at Plymouth and then at Cherbourg. He also visited the naval cadets at Dartmouth. 'The boys do not seem to be hustled as they used to be,' he wrote to Clementine on June 1, '& all my suggestions have been in the direction of "easing up".'

What Churchill did not tell his wife was that, before his week on *Enchantress*, he had continued with his flying lessons, spending two days at the Central Flying School. He knew that she did not approve, he explained to her on May 29, 'so I did not write you from there as I know you would be vexed'. Now that he was on board *Enchantress*, on his way from Portsmouth to Portland, 'I hasten to tell you how much & how often you & the babies were in my thoughts during these happy & interesting days.' He had flown on one occasion to a Yeomanry camp eleven miles from the school. 'We had a great reception – the men all running out in a mob, as if they had never seen an aeroplane before.'

Churchill's flying instructor on this occasion was a twenty-seven-year-old Royal Marine, Lieutenant Thomas Creswell. Six days after he had flown with Churchill, he and a co-pilot, Lieutenant-Commander Arthur Rice, were killed when their seaplane, the same one which Churchill had flown, broke up and crashed into the sea. Learning of this, Clementine, who was expecting her third child in October, begged her husband to give up flying. He deferred to her plea, writing from *Enchantress* on June 6:

My darling one,

   *I will not fly any more until at any rate you have recovered from your
kitten: & by then or perhaps later the risks may have been greatly reduced.*

   *This is a wrench, because I was on the verge of taking my pilot's
certificate. It only needed a couple of calm mornings; & I am confident of
my ability to achieve it very respectably. I should greatly have liked to
reach this point which would have made a suitable moment for breaking
off. But I admit that the numerous fatalities of this year would justify you
in complaining if I continued to share the risks – as I am proud to do – of
these good fellows. So I give it up decidedly for many months & perhaps for
ever. This is a gift – so stupidly am I made – which costs me more than
anything which could be bought with money. So I am very glad to lay it at
your feet, because I know it will rejoice & relieve your heart.*

   *Anyhow I can feel I know a good deal about this fascinating new art. I
can manage a machine with ease in the air, even with high winds, & only a
little more practice in landings would have enabled me to go up with
reasonable safety alone. I have been up nearly 140 times, with many pilots,
& all kinds of machines, so I know the difficulties, the dangers & the joys
of the air – well enough to appreciate them, & to understand all the
questions of policy which will arise in the near future.*

   *It is curious that while I have been lucky, accidents have happened to
others who have flown with me out of the natural proportion. This poor
Lieutenant whose loss has disturbed your anxieties again, took me up only
last week in this very machine!*

   *You will give me some kisses and forgive me for past distresses – I am
sure. Though I had no need & perhaps no right to do it – it was an
important part of my life during the last seven months, & I am sure my
nerve, my spirit & my virtue were all improved by it. But at your expense
my poor pussy cat! I am sorry.*

Churchill stopped flying. But he intensified his efforts to ensure that the
Royal Naval Air Service was well trained and properly equipped. On
June 9 he approved the entry of two hundred civilians into the service,
and the development of five naval air stations, three less than he had
hoped, because of his Navy Estimate economies. He also continued his
vigilance in regard to social conditions throughout the Navy, pressing for
the introduction of widows' pensions for sailors dying in the service. More
than a decade was to pass, however, and four years of war, before, as
Chancellor of the Exchequer, it fell to Churchill himself to introduce
pensions for all war widows, and also war orphans.

On June 17, in one of his most important initiatives as First Lord,
Churchill asked the House of Commons to authorise a revolutionary

business transaction that he had negotiated: the purchase by the British Government of a fifty-one per cent share in the profits of all oil produced by the Anglo-Persian Oil Company, as well as the first use of all the oil produced at the company's wells. By this purchase, he explained, for the cost of just over £2 million, the Royal Navy would secure all the oil it needed to maintain its warships, without depending on any private company or any foreign government.

Two years before he brought the details of his plan to Parliament, Churchill had appointed Fisher to examine the Navy's oil requiremcnts, one of which was that the Navy 'control an oil-field somewhere'. When Fisher advised the Anglo-Persian oil field as the one to be controlled, Churchill at once began negotiations to acquire it; assisted by a young Treasury official, Richard Hopkins, he had carried these out with his mastery of detail and his ability to reconcile the competing interests of different Government departments. 'What we want now,' he told the Commons on June 17, 'is a proved proposition, a going concern, an immediate supply, and a definite prospect with potentialities of development over which we can ourselves preside. These we find in Persia.'

The House of Commons approved Britain's purchase of a majority shareholding in the Anglo-Persian Oil Company by 254 votes to eighteen. The Admiralty now had control of the oil it needed, in a region within Britain's sphere of influence since the Anglo-Russian Convention of 1906, and with a prospect of considerable profit; over the next fifty years the interest alone of Britain's fifty-one per cent share of the oil profits was to pay for the cost of all battleships built after 1914.

On June 28, eleven days after Churchill's success in acquiring the oil needed by the Navy, an event took place in the Balkans which was to shatter the fabric of Europe: the assassination in the Bosnian city of Sarajevo of the Archduke Ferdinand, heir to the throne of Austria-Hungary, and his wife. There had been an immediate outcry in Austria-Hungary against the assassin, a Serb nationalist, and against Serbia.

It seemed certain that Austria would make demands on Serbia for redress, possibly even make war on her. Russia's sympathies would be with the Serbs, fellow-Slavs struggling to maintain their nationhood. According to both sentiment and alliance, Germany might side with Austria-Hungary, and France with Russia. All this, however, was in the realm of speculation. On July 9, eleven days after the assassination, the Permanent Under-Secretary of State at the British Foreign Office told Sir Edward Grey, 'I have my doubts as to whether Austria will take any action of a serious character and I expect the storm will blow over.'

On board *Enchantress*, Churchill's thoughts were far from the possibility of a wider conflict. On July 9 he wrote to King Alfonso of Spain of his hope 'that I shall have the honour of seeing Your Majesty during your visit in September in the seclusion of the polo world'. But there was to be no 'seclusion', and no 'polo world', in September 1914.

13

The Coming of War in 1914

On 13 July 1914 Churchill wrote to Clementine with various items of news; the Parliamentary session would continue until the end of August, and a new session begin in December. Asquith was 'keen to come on Monday to the yacht,' he told her. 'You must try & make the effort. I am sure it will repay the exertion. I will make a really good plan for you: and all fog or bores will be forbidden.' He made no mention of the tensions in Europe following the assassination of the Archduke Ferdinand more than two weeks earlier. In London, the dominant issue throughout the third week of July was the imminent conference on Ireland which opened at Buckingham Palace on July 21.

That night Sir Edward Grey told Churchill he doubted whether a course could be devised acceptable both to the Irish Nationalists and the Ulster Unionists. The dispute centred on boundaries, in particular those of County Tyrone. 'Failing an Irish agreement,' Churchill wrote to Grey on July 22, 'there ought to be a British decision.' Of course the contending Irish parties 'may think it worth a war, & from their point of view it may be worth a war. But that is hardly the position of the forty millions who dwell in Great Britain; and their interests must when all said & done be our chief & final care.'

Churchill then gave Grey an analogy based on the European situation. It was his first reference to the European crisis; and it contained a hopeful scenario. 'In foreign affairs you would proceed by two stages,' Churchill explained. 'First you would labour to stop Austria & Russia going to war: second, if that failed, you would try to prevent England, France, Germany and Russia being drawn in.' Exactly what Grey would do in Europe, Churchill added, was right in the 'domestic danger', with the difference that in Europe the second step 'would only hope to limit & localise the conflict; whereas at home the second step, if practicable & adopted, would prevent the local conflict'.

That night it was the imminent breakdown of the Irish negotiations that dominated Churchill's letter to Clementine: 'The conference is *in extremis*. We are preparing a partition of Tyrone with reluctant Nationalist acquiescence. Carson absolutely refuses.' The Buckingham Palace conference had broken down. But Carson was to get his wish two days later, when the Cabinet decided to allow any Ulster county to vote itself out of the Home Rule area, and to abolish the six-year time-limit for such exclusion. Ulster could now remove itself from the rule of Dublin.

One question remained to be resolved: the precise borders of the counties of Fermanagh and Tyrone that could vote for exclusion. It was clear that the overwhelmingly Catholic parts of both counties, contiguous as they were to southern Ireland, must be allowed to adhere to Dublin. On July 25, in the wake of the failure of the Buckingham Palace Conference, the Cabinet met again. 'And so,' Churchill later wrote, 'turning this way and that in search of an exit from the deadlock, the Cabinet toiled around the muddy byways of Fermanagh and Tyrone. One had hoped that the events of April at the Curragh and in Belfast would have shocked British public opinion, and formed a unity sufficient to impose a settlement on the Irish factions. Apparently they had been insufficient. Apparently the conflict would be carried one stage further by both sides with incalculable consequences for both sides.'

For more than an hour the Ministers talked. 'The discussion had reached its inconclusive end,' Churchill later wrote, 'and the Cabinet was about to separate, when the grave, quiet tones of Sir Edward Grey's voice were heard reading a document which had just been brought to him from the Foreign Office.' It was the Austrian ultimatum to Serbia, delivered almost a month after the assassination of the Archduke.

Grey had been reading the document, or speaking about it, 'for several minutes', Churchill recalled, 'before I could disengage my mind from the tedious and bewildering debate which had just closed. We were all very tired, but gradually as the phrases and sentences followed one another, impressions of a wholly different character began to form in my mind. As the reading proceeded it seemed absolutely impossible that any State in the world could accept it, or that any acceptance, however abject, would satisfy the aggressor. The parishes of Fermanagh and Tyrone faded into the mists and squalls of Ireland, and a strange light began immediately, but by perceptible gradations, to fall and grow upon the map of Europe.'

Returning to the Admiralty, Churchill wrote to Clementine, who was on holiday with Diana and Randolph at Cromer: 'Europe is trembling on the verge of a general war, the Austrian ultimatum to Serbia being the most insolent document of its kind ever devised. Side by side with this, the Provisional Government in Ulster which is now imminent appears comparatively a humdrum affair.' That night Churchill dined with German ship-ping magnate Alfred Ballin, a confidant of the Kaiser. Ballin spoke gloomily of a sequence of events that could lead to war between Britain and Germany. 'If Russia marches against Austria we must march,' Ballin warned, 'and if we march France must march, and what would England do?'

Churchill replied that he did not know; that it would be up to the Cabinet to decide; but that it would be a mistake for Germany to assume that Britain would do nothing in the event of a Franco-German war. The British Government, he told Ballin, 'would judge events as they arose'. The two men said goodnight, Churchill, with tears in his eyes, imploring Ballin not to let Germany go to war with France.

The Serbian Government, hoping to avoid war with Austria, sent a conciliatory reply to the ultimatum, agreeing to suppress all subversive anti-Austrian movements on Serbian soil, and to bring to justice anyone concerned with the murder of the Archduke. Although Serbia would not agree to any Austrian representative participating in the judicial process, she was willing to submit the whole issue either to the International Tribunal at the Hague, or to the Great Powers in concert. The German Kaiser was impressed. 'A great moral victory for Vienna,' he wrote, 'but with it every reason for war disappears.' Nevertheless, in the Kaiser's view, 'as a visible *satisfaction d'honneur* for Austria, the Austrian Army should temporarily occupy Belgrade as a pledge'. Such an action need not neces-sarily involve Britain. 'Happily there seems to be no reason why we should be anything more than spectators,' Asquith told the King on July 25.

Serbia's conciliatory reply to Austria was sent from Belgrade to Vienna on July 25. That morning Churchill and Prince Louis discussed whether to disperse the ships of Third Fleet, already mobilised, and together, as a result of the test mobilisation plans of the previous year. They decided that the situation was not sufficiently serious to warrant keeping the ships together. At midday, having put off an afternoon conference with his advisers, Churchill took the train to Norfolk, to join his family at the seaside.

At nine o'clock on the morning of July 26 Churchill telephoned Prince Louis from the local Post Office in Cromer. The news he was given was not good; Austria-Hungary was apparently dissatisfied with Serbia's con-ciliatory reply to its ultimatum. Churchill went to the beach, where for three hours he played with his son and daughter, damming the rivulets which ran down the low cliffs to the sea. At noon he returned to the Post Office to speak to Prince Louis again. This time he learned even more disturbing news: Austria had entirely rejected the Serbian answer.

Suddenly the possibility drew much nearer of an Austrian invasion of Serbia which would draw Germany, Russia and France into the conflict.

Germany might seek to attack and defeat France at the outset of war, before turning on Russia. In attacking France, Germany would almost certainly advance through Belgium, whose neutrality Britain was pledged to uphold.

Churchill and Prince Louis discussed what should be done. It was difficult, if not impossible, to conduct such sensitive business on the telephone. Churchill believed, as he wrote a year later, that he had specifically asked Prince Louis 'not to let the Fleet disperse'. Prince Louis recalled their conversation differently, insisting that Churchill had not given him any specific instructions, but had 'begged me to take whatever steps I might consider advisable without waiting to consult you over the telephone. I had great difficulty in hearing you. I certainly never heard any reference to keeping the Fleet together.' On his own initiative, Prince Louis later claimed, he went to the Foreign Office and, at five past four, signalled to the commander of the Home Fleets ordering him not to disperse his ships.

Returning to London at ten o'clock that evening, Churchill went first to the Admiralty, then to the Foreign Office, where Grey told him that Austria seemed determined to force its quarrel with Serbia to the point of war. Would it be helpful, Churchill asked, if the Admiralty were to issue a public statement announcing that the dispersal of the Fleet had been halted? Grey said that it would; that an immediate announcement to that effect would serve as a salutary warning both to Austria and to Germany. Back at the Admiralty, Churchill drafted, with Prince Louis, an official communiqué for the Press: 'Orders have been given to the First Fleet, which is concentrated at Portland, not to disperse for manoeuvre leave for the present. All vessels of the Second Fleet are remaining at their home ports in proximity to their balance crews.'

This announcement was published in *The Times* on the morning of July 27. 'It looked innocent enough,' Churchill later wrote, 'but we hoped the German Emperor at any rate would understand.' When the Cabinet met that morning, however, a majority of Ministers were opposed to any British action against Germany in the event of a German invasion of France. It was pointed out that Britain had no formal alliance with France. 'The Cabinet,' Churchill later wrote, 'was absolutely against war and would never have agreed to being committed to war at this moment.'

Churchill's duty as First Lord of the Admiralty was to ensure that if war came Britain would not be caught unprepared against either naval or air attack. That afternoon he went to Downing Street and obtained Asquith's approval for sending armed guards to all ammunition depots and oil tanks. Orders were also sent out from the Admiralty for armed guards to man all coastal lights and guns. The torpedo reserve was completed. Also on July 27, Churchill ordered an end to the continuing naval blockade off Dundalk and Carrickfergus; all vessels engaged in stopping gun-running to Ulster were sent to their war stations.

In view of Austria-Hungary's naval strength in the Mediterranean, and Britain's interests there, especially in Egypt, Churchill signalled to the Commander-in-Chief Mediterranean on July 27: 'European political situation makes war between Triple Alliance and Triple Entente Powers by no means impossible. This is not the warning telegram, but be prepared to shadow possible hostile men-of-war.' The Admiral was also instructed to concentrate his ships at Malta and to load them with stores and coal. 'Measure is purely precautionary,' Churchill stressed. 'The utmost secrecy is to be observed, and no unnecessary person is to be informed.'

By nightfall on July 27 all vulnerable points along the North Sea coast, chief among them oil tanks and ammunition stores, had been protected by anti-aircraft guns. That day all the Patrol flotillas were raised to full strength and, Churchill informed the King on the following day, 'are moving in succession to their war stations'. For the air defence of Britain, 'The aircraft are collected at and around the estuary of the Thames to guard against airship attack.'

On July 28 Churchill lunched with Kitchener, who was in Britain on a short visit from Egypt, to receive an Earldom. Churchill was so impressed by Kitchener's grasp of the likely severity of a German attack on France that he prevailed upon Asquith not to let his former adversary return to Egypt. Asquith decided to make Kitchener Secretary of State for War; it would undermine Conservative criticism of an all-Liberal war leadership. Kitchener, meanwhile, had set off for Dover by train; Churchill sent messages, the train was halted, and brought back to London.

During July 28 the German High Command in Berlin pressed Austria-Hungary to invade Serbia at once and present the world with a *fait accompli*. Grey urged Austria to step back from the brink, but was told by the British Ambassador in Vienna that postponement or prevention of war with Serbia 'would undoubtedly be a great disappointment in this country, which has gone wild with joy at the prospect of war'. That day, continuing with his naval preparations, Churchill ordered minesweepers to be collected. He also took steps to reinforce the small British naval squadron in the Far East to prevent its being outmatched by the superior German naval forces there.

The First Fleet, having been ordered not to disperse, was in the Channel, concentrated off the Isle of Wight. Although in such a position it constituted a formidable fighting force, its war station in the event of war with Germany was not in the Channel but in the North Sea. On the afternoon of July 28, after consulting with Prince Louis, Churchill decided to send the Fleet into the North Sea at once, hoping thereby both to deter the Germans from any sudden attack on the East Coast, and to intimate that Britain was prepared if necessary to enter the European conflict. 'I feared to bring this matter before the Cabinet,' Churchill later wrote, 'lest it should mistakenly be considered a provocative action likely to damage the chance of peace.' He therefore went to Downing Street to see Asquith, explaining his intentions. 'He looked at me with a hard stare,' Churchill later wrote, 'and gave a sort of grunt. I did not require anything else.'

Returning to the Admiralty, Churchill signalled to the Admiral in charge of the First Fleet that he should sail from Portland to the North Sea. 'Destination is to be kept secret except to flag and commanding officers. Course from Portland is to be shaped to southward, then a middle-Channel course to the Straits of Dover. The squadrons are to pass the Straits without lights.' Later that evening the Cabinet learned that Austria-Hungary had declared war on Serbia. At midnight Churchill wrote to his wife from the Admiralty:

My darling one & beautiful,

Everything tends towards catastrophe & collapse. I am interested, geared up & happy. Is it not horrible to be built like that? The preparations have a hideous fascination for me. I pray to God to forgive me for such fearful moods of levity. Yet I would do my best for peace, & nothing would induce me wrongfully to strike the blow.

I cannot feel that we in this island are in any serious degree responsible for the wave of madness which has swept the mind of Christendom. No one can measure the consequences. I wondered whether those stupid Kings & Emperors could not assemble together & revivify kingship by saving the nations from hell but we all drift on in a kind of dull cataleptic trance. As if it was somebody else's operation.

The two black swans on St James's Park lake have a darling cygnet – grey, fluffy, precious & unique. I watched them this evening for some time as a relief from all the plans & schemes. We are putting the whole Navy into fighting trim (bar the reserves). And all seems quite sound & thorough. The sailors are thrilled and confident. Every supply is up to the prescribed standard. Everything is ready as it has never been before. And we are awake to the tip of our fingers. But war is the Unknown & the Unexpected!

God guard us and our long accumulated inheritance. You know how willingly & proudly I would risk – or give – if need be – my period of existence to keep this country great & famous & prosperous & free. But the problems are very difficult. One has to try to measure the indefinite & weigh the imponderable.

I feel sure however that if war comes we shall give them a good drubbing.

Churchill's reference in this letter to the 'Kings & Emperors' was not mere musing; speaking of the possibility of a European war to his Cabinet colleagues on the morning of July 29 he declared that it was 'an appalling calamity for civilised nations to contemplate', and thought that the European sovereigns could possibly 'be brought together for the sake of peace'.

The Cabinet of July 29 agreed with Churchill's request to put into force a series of precautionary defensive measures. All naval harbours were cleared of civilian vessels, armed guards were sent to bridges and viaducts, and watchers were sent to the coast to report on any hostile ship. But opinion in the Cabinet was divided as to what would constitute cause for war; at least half Asquith's Ministers were unwilling to contemplate war with Germany if France was attacked, reiterating that Britain had no alliance with France.

Churchill was convinced that a German invasion of France would constitute a reason for war. Fearing a split Cabinet, indecision, and possibly even the fall of the Liberal Government, he began to make enquires, when the Cabinet meeting was over, through F.E. Smith, of the possibility of a Coalition Government based upon British military support for France. Several of the Conservatives whom Smith approached, including Carson, were favourably disposed to such a Coalition. Bonar Law, however, rejected the idea.

On the morning of July 30, when Churchill and his senior officers were at their daily Staff Meeting, a signal arrived: the First Fleet had reached the North Sea. Churchill was filled with an immediate sense of relief. 'Always in my mind in the years of preparation,' he later wrote, 'had been the episode of the Russian Fleet surprised by a torpedo attack at anchor off Port Arthur. Hostilities before or simultaneous with the declaration of war had been one of our many nightmares.'

During July 30, convinced that in the end Britain would be at war as the ally of France, Churchill instructed the Admiral commanding the British forces in the Mediterranean to be prepared, as his 'first task', to help the passage of French troop transports from North Africa to Metropolitan France 'by covering and if possible by bringing to action individual German ships', in particular the battle-cruiser *Goeben*, which was even then leaving the Adriatic for the Mediterranean. That night Churchill dined with Asquith. 'Serene as ever,' he reported to Clementine. 'But he backs me well in all the necessary measures.'

On the following day, July 31, the Cabinet learned of strong Liberal Party opposition to any British involvement in a European war on behalf of France. 'So long as no treaty obligation or true British interest is involved,' Churchill wrote to a non-interventionist Liberal MP that day, 'I am of your opinion that we should remain neutral. Balkan quarrels are no concern of ours. We have done our best to keep the peace and shall continue to do so. But the march of events is sinister.'

That day the German Government suggested secretly that Britain should remain neutral in return for a German promise not to take French territory or to invade Holland. Germany would wish to acquire French overseas colonies, however, and could not promise not to invade Belgium. Yet Germany was bound by treaty 'not merely to respect but to defend' Belgium, Churchill pointed out to Clementine.

Grey replied to the German proposals by describing them as 'impossible & disgraceful'. Everything pointed therefore to a collision on these two points. 'Still hope is not dead,' Churchill told Clementine. He thought that Germany was realising 'how great are the forces against her & is trying tardily to restrain her idiot ally', Austria-Hungary. For her part, Britain was working 'to soothe Russia'. But, Churchill added, 'everybody is preparing swiftly for war and at any moment the stroke may fall. We are ready.'

Proudly Churchill told Clementine: 'I could not tell you all the things I have done & the responsibilities I have taken in the last few days: but all is working out well; & everyone has responded. The newspapers have observed an admirable reticence.' His friend de Forest, an Austrian Baron and a British MP, had been told his yacht was ordered out of Dover Harbour. Hurriedly he left London for Dover. 'As he journeyed down the line,' Churchill wrote, 'he found every bridge & tunnel guarded & became increasingly terrified. He telegraphed frantically clamouring for debates & questions in Parliament. Not a man moved – not a question nor so far any mention in the papers. The country will be united when the issue is joined. Be sure of it.'

That night Churchill authorised his senior naval advisers to confer with the French Naval Attaché in London on measures which should be taken together should France and Britain find themselves allies in war. He also sent out summonses to all naval reservists, to enable a complete mobilisation of the Fleet to take place the moment the Cabinet gave its authority.

On the morning of August 1, despite the failure of his Coalition suggestion, Churchill received a letter from F.E. Smith with a Conservative assurance that 'on the facts as we understand them & more particularly on the assumption (which we understand to be certain) that Germany contemplates a violation of Belgian neutrality, the Government can rely upon the support of the Unionist Party'. Churchill read out this assurance to the Cabinet, where, he reported back to Smith, 'it produced a profound impression'. His own view that morning was clear. 'I cannot think war will be averted now,' he told Smith. 'Germany must march through Belgium, and I believe that the bulk of both parties will stand firm against that.'

That morning Churchill asked the Cabinet to authorise full naval mobilisation. But Ministers were still divided, Lloyd George giving a lead to those who were reluctant to commit Britain in support of France. In a letter to Clementine's cousin Venetia Stanley, Asquith wrote: 'Lloyd George, all for peace, is more statesmanlike for keeping the position open. Winston very bellicose and demanding immediate mobilisation.' As the Cabinet discussed the crisis, it was clear that many Ministers were unwilling to go to war despite a German threat to France, or even to Belgium. Churchill himself was reluctant to make an immediate commitment that day to go to war with Germany if Belgium were invaded. 'At the present moment,' he told Lloyd George in a note which he pushed across the Cabinet table, 'I would act in such a way as to impress Germany with our intention to preserve the neutrality of Belgium. So much is still unknown as to the definite purpose of Germany that I would not go beyond this.' But Churchill warned that if the Germans invaded Belgium British public opinion 'might veer round at any moment, & we must be ready to meet this opinion'.

Churchill sought to persuade Lloyd George that it might be necessary to go to war. 'I am most profoundly anxious that our long co-operation may not be severed,' he explained in another note passed across the Cabinet table. 'Remember your part at Agadir. I implore you to come and bring your mighty aid to the discharge of our duty. Afterwards by participating in the peace we can regulate the settlement & prevent a renewal of 1870 conditions.' In a further attempt to influence Lloyd George that day, Churchill sent an Army officer, Major Ollivant, to see him. For the previous year Ollivant had been the War Office liaison officer with the Naval War Staff; Germany's 'chief object as far as this country is concerned,' he explained to Lloyd George, 'lies in preventing the arrival of the British expeditionary army. There is reason to suppose that the presence or absence of the British army will determine the action of the Belgian army. It will very probably decide the fate of France.'

Lloyd George could still not make up his mind whether a German attack on Belgium really would constitute an adequate reason for declaring war on Germany. 'All the rest of our lives we shall be opposed,' Churchill warned him, adding, 'I am deeply attached to you & have followed your instinct & guidance for nearly ten years.'

During August 1 Churchill received an assurance from an influential member of the Conservative Party, Lord Robert Cecil, that if the Government were to send an expeditionary force across the Channel, 'they may count on the support of the whole Unionist Party'. Later that day, however, it seemed as if the crisis might be defused. 'The news tonight opens again hope,' he wrote to Cecil. 'There seems to be the prospect of Austria & Russia resuming negotiations on a formula which Germany has proposed: and every exertion will be made to that end. But a collision between the armies may arise at any moment out of an incident or an accident. And I hold that in all the circumstances if we allowed Belgian neutrality to be trampled down by Germany without exerting ourselves to aid France we should be in a very melancholy position both in regard to our interests & our honour.'

That night Churchill dined alone. Shortly after nine o'clock F.E. Smith called to see him. With him was Max Aitken, later Lord Beaverbrook, a Canadian financier, Conservative MP, and confidant of Bonar Law. Churchill repeated to them what he had written to Cecil, that there was now a chance of war being averted. The three men sat together for a while. 'The suspense was becoming intolerable,' Churchill later wrote. 'I was to see the Prime Minister at eleven that night. Meanwhile there was nothing to be done. We sat down at a card table and began a game of bridge. The cards had just been dealt when another red Foreign Office box came in. I opened it and read, "War declared by Germany on Russia".'

Churchill knew that it could not be long before Germany attacked Russia's ally, France. Leaving his two friends he crossed Horse Guards Parade to 10 Downing Street, where he told Asquith that, despite the Cabinet's refusal earlier that day, he wished to issue an immediate order for full naval mobilisation. 'The Prime Minister simply looked at me and said no word,' Churchill later recalled. 'No doubt he felt himself bound by the morning's decision of the Cabinet. I certainly, however, sustained the impression that he would not put out a finger to stop me. I then walked back to the Admiralty across the Parade Ground and gave the order.' It was midnight; 'I am sorry to say,' he wrote just after midnight to Lord Robert Cecil, 'that since I wrote to you we have learned officially that Germany has declared war on Russia. I cannot think that the rupture with France can be long delayed. And the course of events is likely to be very serious as regards Belgium.'

'Cat dear,' Churchill wrote to Clementine at 1 a.m., 'It is all up. Germany has quenched the last hopes of peace by declaring war on Russia, & the declaration against France is momentarily expected.' On the previous day she had written to him to say that war would be lunacy. 'I profoundly understand your views,' he replied. 'But the world is gone mad – & we must look after ourselves – & our friends.' He hoped she would come up to London for a day or two. 'I miss you much – & your influence when guiding & not contrary is of the utmost use to me.'

The Russian Government now called on France to honour the Franco-Russian Treaty of 1894. At the same moment the Germans prepared to knock France out of the war first, then turn against Russia. The German plan of attack on France was based on an initial drive through Belgium. It was on the basis of that plan that Churchill had predicted, in 1911, that the decisive battle would be fought on the fortieth day, and assessed the likely events leading up to that fortieth day.

Shortly after midday on August 2 the British Government informed Germany that it 'would not allow the passage of German ships through the English Channel or the North Sea in order to attack the coast or shipping of France'. In sending the text of this note to naval commanders in the Channel and North Sea, the Admiralty added, 'Be prepared to meet surprise attacks.'

Lloyd George was gradually accepting the view that Britain must come to the aid of Belgium, but had still not committed himself. To encourage him to do so, Churchill passed him another note during the Cabinet meeting on the evening of August 2 about the opportunities which war would open up in the social field: 'Together we can carry a wide social policy – on the conference basis, your idea – which you taught me. The naval war will be cheap – not more than 25 millions a year.' Churchill added, with an appeal to Lloyd George's qualities which he so admired, and to his vanity, 'You alone can take the measures which will assure food being kept abundant & cheap to the people.'

Still the German armies made no move to cross the Belgian frontier, though their troops were moving towards it and had already occupied the Grand Duchy of Luxemburg. On the morning of August 3 the Cabinet learned that Germany had sent an ultimatum to Belgium, demanding the right of passage of German troops across Belgium. It was agreed that Britain must now intervene to insist that Belgian neutrality be maintained. Devastated by the very thought of a British involvement in a European war, Lord Morley told Churchill that he would resign. Churchill answered, he later recalled, that if Morley would wait for two or three days more, 'everything would be clear, and we should be in full agreement. The Germans would make everyone easy in his conscience. They would accept all responsibilities and sweep away all doubts. Already their vanguards pouring through Luxemburg approached the Belgian frontier. Nothing could recall or deflect them.'

Morley was not convinced. Churchill offered to illustrate the German military movements on a map, but Morley's mind was made up. 'If we have to fight,' he said, 'we must fight with single-hearted conviction. There is no place for me in such affairs.' Morley resigned, as did two other Cabinet Ministers. The rest of the Cabinet began to discuss not the rights and wrongs of becoming involved in the European quarrel, but how most effectively to participate in it. 'I am so glad that you are turning your mind to the vital question of safeguarding the credit & food supply of this country,' Churchill wrote to Lloyd George in yet another note pushed across the Cabinet table.

That afternoon, German troops crossed the Belgian frontier. Speaking in the House of Commons, Grey warned that this act, a violation of Britain's Treaty of 1839, might force Britain to go to war. After his speech he left the Chamber with Churchill.

'What happens now?' Churchill asked.

'Now,' replied Grey, 'we shall send them an ultimatum to stop the invasion of Belgium within twenty-four hours.'

Returning to his room at the Admiralty, Churchill sent a message to Asquith and Grey, asking them to give their immediate authorisation 'to put into force the combined Anglo-French dispositions for the defence of the Channel'. Unless he was expressly forbidden to do this, Churchill added, 'I shall act accordingly'. This joint action, he assured Asquith and Grey, while essential for security against a German naval attack in the Channel, 'implies no offensive action & no warlike action unless we are attacked'. The extent of Churchill's preparations was well known and not unappreciated. On the morning of August 4 *The Times* described him as the one Minister 'whose grasp of the situation and whose efforts to meet it have been above all praise'.

The British ultimatum to Germany, demanding the maintenance of Belgian neutrality, was to expire at midnight Berlin time on August 4. Throughout that day the Cabinet waited in tense expectation. Churchill was particularly worried about how quickly British naval forces could be ordered into action. During the day the German battle cruiser *Goeben* bombarded the French North African port of Philippeville, while the light cruiser *Breslau* bombarded Bône. As a result of Churchill's earlier order, British warships were shadowing both vessels, but as Britain was not yet at war, they could take no action. During the day Churchill begged Asquith and Grey to allow him to order the ships to open fire. 'It would be a great misfortune to lose these vessels as is possible in the dark hours.'

Anticipating another favourable, if equally unspoken, response from Asquith, Churchill telegraphed to the British Admiral, 'If *Goeben* attacks French transports you should at once engage her.' But Asquith now wanted the matter put to the Cabinet, writing at noon that day to Venetia Stanley, 'Winston, who has got on all his war paint, is longing for a sea fight in the early hours of the morning to result in the sinking of the *Goeben*.' The Cabinet listened to Churchill's explanation of why the German battle cruiser should be hunted down. The German Navy's ability to prevent French reinforcements getting from North Africa to France was considerable. Only British warships had the necessary power to stop her. The

Cabinet was insistent, however, that no British act of war should take place before the ultimatum expired an hour before midnight.

Returning to the Admiralty at two o'clock that afternoon, Churchill telegraphed to all ships, 'No acts of war should be committed before that hour.' In the signal to the Admiral shadowing the two German warships in the Mediterranean, he added that this signal 'cancels the authorisation' to engage the *Goeben*.

The Germans made no reply to the British ultimatum. That afternoon their troops drove deeper into Belgium. On the evening of August 4, Churchill dined at Admiralty House with his mother, his brother and Geoffrey Robinson, the editor of *The Times*. When dinner was over he held a conference with a delegation of French Admirals, who asked if they could have the use of a British naval base in the Mediterranean, from which to protect their trade and troop transports. Churchill responded with alacrity: 'Use Malta as if it were Toulon.'

Still no reply to the British ultimatum reached London, only the news of a continued German advance into Belgium. At eleven o'clock that night the ultimatum expired. Churchill at once authorised a signal to be sent from the Admiralty to all ships and naval establishments, 'Commence hostilities against Germany.' Britain and Germany were at war; at a quarter past eleven he once more crossed Horse Guards Parade to 10 Downing Street, where he told Asquith that the signal had been sent. Lloyd George, who was already with the Prime Minister, later told a friend: 'Winston dashed into the room, radiant, his face bright, his manner keen, one word pouring out on another how he was going to send telegrams to the Mediterranean, the North Sea, and God knows where. You could see he was a really happy man.'

14

War

Churchill was not yet forty. The many responsibilities of naval warfare were on his shoulders. To come to the aid of Belgium, British troops had to be transported across the Channel. At the Council of War held on the afternoon of 5 August 1914, he reported that the Dover Strait was completely sealed against any German naval intrusion. The troops could cross unhindered. Three days later, the first ships sailed; within two weeks, 120,000 men had been transported across the Channel without the loss of a single ship or life.

'The Expeditionary Force about which you are so inquisitive is on its road & will be on the spot in time,' Churchill wrote to Clementine on August 9. Aware, however, of the hazards of war, he was worried about his wife and children remaining by the North Sea. Clementine was seven months pregnant. 'It is 100 to 1 against a raid,' he wrote to her, 'but there is still a chance: & Cromer has a good landing place near. I wish you would get the motor repaired & keep it so that you can whisk away, at the first sign of trouble.'

On August 6 the light cruiser *Amphion* sank a German minelayer and took her crew captive. A short while later, *Amphion* herself was sunk by a mine which the minelayer had laid; 150 British sailors were drowned, as were the captured Germans. Churchill decided to give the Commons full details of what had happened. It was an important decision and precedent, prompting the *Manchester Guardian* to comment, 'We much admired Mr Churchill's frankness in giving the account of the loss of the *Amphion* at once to the public.'

Unwilling to see Britain's naval role as a passive one, on August 9 Churchill urged Prince Louis to 'sustain and relieve' defensive actions at sea by 'active minor operations'. He suggested a naval assault on Ameland, one of the Dutch Frisian Islands, which should then be fortified and used as a naval base to hem in the German Fleet, and as an air base from which to bomb the Kiel Canal or vessels in it. Dutch neutrality need be no obstacle. What mattered was that such an initiative would 'maintain in lively vigour the spirit of enterprise & attack, which, when excluded from warlike operations, means that you are only waiting, wondering where you will be hit'.

The Naval War Staff judged the Ameland landing to be impracticable, and no plans were made. But Churchill's search for areas of effective action never ceased. When, on August 11, the two German warships *Goeben* and *Breslau*, having evaded their British pursuers in the eastern Mediterranean and Aegean, entered the safety of Turkish waters, Churchill at once instructed the British admiral to 'blockade' the Dardanelles. When it was pointed out to him that Britain was not at war with Turkey, he changed the instruction to 'carefully watch the entrance in case the enemy cruisers come out'.

On August 12, with Cabinet approval, Churchill set up a naval blockade of the German North Sea ports, to prevent supplies or food from reaching them, or leaving them. Four days later, seeking some means of absorbing the large number of men who were volunteering to fight, he set up a Royal Naval Division, whose men were later to fight on the Western Front and at Gallipoli. When things went well they called themselves 'Churchill's Pets', when things went badly they became 'Churchill's Innocent Victims'. Hundreds rushed to volunteer in the first days, some appealing direct to Churchill for a place. Among those for whom he obtained commissions was the poet Rupert Brooke.

Churchill now offered to send British troop transports into the Baltic, to enable the Russian Army to land in force on the German shore of that sea and to march on Berlin. A month later he arranged for several British submarines to be sent into the Baltic to help the Russian Navy against German warships. He also encouraged Kitchener to send to France the last division of professional soldiers then in England. The Admiralty was confident, he assured Kitchener on August 22, of its ability to secure Britain against invasion.

Two days later, while Churchill was working in the early morning in his bedroom at the Admiralty, the door opened and he saw Kitchener standing in the doorway. 'Though his manner was quite calm,' Churchill later wrote, 'his face was different. I had the subconscious feeling that it was distorted and discoloured as if it had been punched with a fist. His eyes rolled more than ever.' Kitchener had brought the news that the Belgian fortress of Namur had fallen to the Germans. Such forts were hitherto thought to be almost impregnable obstacles to any advancing army. Now Namur was in German hands and the road to the Channel Coast open.

Deeply perturbed by the news, Churchill went to see Lloyd George at the Treasury. It was their first private conversation since the outbreak of war. 'I felt intensely the need of contact with him,' Churchill later wrote, 'and I wanted to know how it would strike him and how he would face it.' Lloyd George gave Churchill the confidence he sought. Returning to the Admiralty he signalled to the new naval Commander-in-Chief, Admiral Jellicoe: 'We have not entered this business without resolve to see it through, and you may rest assured that our action will be proportioned to the gravity of the need. I have absolute confidence in final result.' A day later, as the British and French armies continued to fall back before the German thrust, Churchill wrote to his brother: 'No one can tell how far this great adventure may carry us all. Unless we win, I do not want to live any more. But win we will.'

Churchill's initiatives were unceasing. On August 26 he obtained Cabinet approval to send the Marine Brigade to the Belgian port of Ostend, to force the Germans to deflect troops from their main thrust further south. The stratagem was a success.

Clementine had returned from Cromer to London. She was with her husband when the news arrived of Britain's first naval victory, the sinking of three German cruisers in the Heligoland Bight. No British ships were sunk. Lord Haldane wrote to Churchill: 'The victory of the Fleet is worthy of the inspiring spirit of their First Lord. The British public & our allies will grow a cubit in confidence when they read the news tomorrow.' The victory excited the public; at the Guildhall on September 4, after Asquith and Bonar Law had spoken, the audience called for Churchill to speak. His words were met with rousing cheers. 'Sure I am of this,' he said, 'that you have only to endure to conquer. You have only to persevere to save yourselves, and to save all those who rely upon you. You have only to go right on, and at the end of the road, be it short or long, victory and honour will be found.'

After thirty days of war the British and French Armies were in retreat. A mood of depression had fallen on the public. In his remarks at the Guildhall, Churchill had shown that he had the ability to lift the depression. Seeking to raise the morale of his Cabinet colleagues, he circulated his 1911 memorandum to them on September 2. 'Asquith said to me this afternoon that you were the equivalent of a large force in the field & this is true,' Haldane wrote to him on September 3. 'You inspire us all by your courage & resolution.'

On September 3 Kitchener asked Churchill to take over from the War Office the full responsibility for the aerial defence of Britain. He agreed to do so; one of his first acts was to establish a special air squadron at Hendon, in telephone communication with air stations near the coast 'for the purpose of attacking enemy aircraft which may attempt to molest London'.

That same day, in France, a Royal Naval Air Service pilot, based on Dunkirk, flew to the battle zone and dropped a bomb on a German military unit near the front. It was the first warlike act of what became known as Churchill's 'Dunkirk Circus', soon to be reinforced with armoured cars, mostly Rolls Royce cars with armour plating, to enable aeroplane bases to be established as far as fifty miles inland. Three squadrons of aircraft, twenty-four machines in all, were sent over. Each squadron was commanded by one of the pilots who had earlier taught Churchill to fly: Eugene Gerrard, Spenser Grey and Richard Bell Davies.

After a month of war, the newspapers were full of stories of the continuing retreat. On August 30, during the retreat from Mons, *The Times* had written of 'the broken bits of many regiments' and of British soldiers 'battered with marching'. When Churchill protested about such 'panic-stricken stuff' appearing, Asquith asked him to issue, anonymously, a Press communiqué with more stuffing in it. Churchill did so. 'There is no doubt that our men have established a personal ascendancy over the Germans,' it read, 'and that they are conscious of the fact that, with anything like even numbers, the result would not be doubtful.' Churchill's communiqué was published on September 5. 'I am going to ask Winston to repeat his feat of last Sunday,' Asquith told Venetia, 'and to dish up for them with all his best journalistic condiments the military history of the week.'

Churchill's 1911 memorandum had forecast that the German advance into France would be halted on the fortieth day. On September 8, thirty-eight days after the German thrust had begun, French and British forces began to move forward across the River Marne, driving the Germans back. Paris was saved. That day Churchill spoke to Balfour about his plans. 'He talks airily of a British Army of a million men,' Balfour reported to Asquith, 'and tells me he is making siege mortars at Woolwich as big as, or bigger, than the German ones, in order to crush the Rhine fortresses.'

On September 10, telling only Asquith, Churchill crossed over to France, the first Cabinet Minister to do so in the war. For twenty-four hours he examined the fortifications of Dunkirk and inspected the air bases and armoured cars there. He also discussed the defence of the port with the French Governor, who, in the words of the British Consul, was 'very much encouraged' by Churchill's visit, which had a 'most wholesome effect' on the city's morale. A few days later, at Kitchener's request, Churchill sent the Marine Brigade to Dunkirk, to distract the German forces then moving cavalry units towards the Channel Coast.

Returning to London, Churchill was the Liberal Party speaker at an all-Party 'Call to Arms' at the Royal Opera House. Other than his brief remarks at the Guildhall a week earlier, it was his first public speech of the war. The effect was electrifying, the *Manchester Guardian* calling it 'a speech of tremendous voltage and carrying power'. As did so many of his speeches, it contained not only determination and confidence, but striking phrases which caught the public imagination. Speaking of the British bulldog, Churchill told the audience, 'The nose of the bulldog has been turned backwards so that he can breathe without letting go.' His speech did not gloss over the dangers; the war would be 'long and sombre', he warned. It would have 'many reverses of fortune, and many hopes falsified by subsequent events'.

There were those who felt that Churchill had a lust for battle. 'I am inclined almost to shiver,' Asquith wrote to Venetia on September 14, 'when I hear Winston say that the last thing he would pray for is Peace.' On the day after this comment, having presided at a conference at the Admiralty to accelerate aircraft production, Churchill returned, at Kitchener's request, to France. His mission was to explain to the Commander-in-Chief, Sir John French, why the British Expeditionary Force should take up its position along the Channel Coast, in contact with the Royal Navy, for the protection of the Channel ports.

At French's headquarters Churchill dined with Hugh Dawnay, a fellow colleague-in-arms at Omdurman and in South Africa. He also watched from a haystack the French artillery in action near Soissons. 'I saw for the first time,' he later recalled, 'what then seemed the prodigy of a British aeroplane threading its way among the smoke puffs of searching shells. I saw the big black German shells, the "Coal Boxes" and "Jack Johnsons" as they were then called, bursting in Paissy village. When darkness fell I saw the horizon lighted with the quick flashing of the cannonade. Such scenes were afterwards to become commonplace: but their first aspect was thrilling.'

Back in Britain, Churchill spoke on September 21 at another all-Party recruiting rally, in Liverpool. If the German Fleet did not come out and fight, he said, they would be 'dug out like rats in a hole'. Such a remark, commented the King, 'was hardly dignified for a Cabinet Minister'. It seemed all the more unfortunate when, on the following day, the Germans sank three British cruisers, with the loss of 1,459 officers and men. The three ships were on patrol that day near the Dogger Bank, despite Churchill's written instruction four days earlier that they 'ought not to continue on this beat' because of the risks. His instruction was unknown to the public, and subsequently kept secret by the Government. As a result, he was blamed for the loss of the ships and their men.

On the day of the Dogger Bank disaster Churchill was again in France, his third visit within two weeks. His aim was to encourage both the Royal

Marines and the airmen based at Dunkirk to attack the German lines of communication. German troops, already in occupation of Brussels, were driving towards the Belgian coast. Five days after his return to England he decided to cross over to France yet again. Clementine sought to dissuade him, or at least to persuade him to consult Kitchener in advance. 'It makes me grieve,' she wrote, 'to see you gloomy & dissatisfied with the unique position you have reached thro' years of ceaseless industry & foresight. The PM leans on you and listens to you more & more. You are the only young vital person in the Cabinet. It is really wicked of you not to be swelling with pride at being 1st Lord of the Admiralty during the greatest War since the beginning of the World. And there is still much to be done & only you can do it.'

Churchill took his wife's advice and asked Kitchener, who said he could go. Indeed, Kitchener welcomed the visit to Sir John French's headquarters, as it would enable Churchill to 'discountenance any wild talk' of a breach between Kitchener and French. It also enabled Churchill to tell the commander of the Royal Marines, who was then moving his men up from Dunkirk to Cassel, 'Select your point and hit hard.'

By October 2 the German forces advancing towards the Channel had reached Ypres and were poised to cut off the Belgian fortress and port city of Antwerp from the Allied armies. Asquith saw the fall of Antwerp as even more disastrous than that of Namur. 'It would leave the whole of Belgium for the moment at the mercy of the Germans,' he told Venetia. That day Churchill left London for his fifth visit to France, intending to gauge for himself the state of morale of the Royal Marines, airmen and armoured car operators who had been forced to pull back to Dunkirk from Cassel, and to discuss their future employment with the Commander-in-Chief. No sooner had he reached Victoria Station, however, than he was handed a message from Kitchener and Grey, asking him to abandon his journey and go immediately to Kitchener's house. There he found Grey and Prince Louis already with Kitchener. The cause of their concern was the news that the Belgian Government was about to abandon Antwerp.

For several hours the four men discussed how to get reinforcements to the city. It was clear that if the Belgian Government were to leave it, all armed resistance would collapse. Kitchener feared that if Antwerp could not hold out for at least another week, the Germans would win the race to the sea, and that Dunkirk and even Calais might be overrun, endangering Britain itself. To avert this, he wished to send a British relief force to the city, and to encourage the French to do likewise. As more and more telegrams were brought in, it was clear that the situation at Antwerp was obscure and the danger immediate. It was not even certain that the outer ring of forts was still intact. Churchill, who had been intending to spend that night at Dunkirk, now offered to go instead to Antwerp, to report back to Kitchener on the military situation, and if possible persuade the Belgians, if necessary with Anglo-French help, to hold the city, at least until the Allied forces could get back to the Belgian Coast ana regroup.

Churchill returned to Victoria Station; shortly after midnight a special train took him to Dover, where he embarked on a destroyer for Ostend. From Ostend he drove to Antwerp. It was hoped, Grey telegraphed to the British Ambassador to Belgium, that when Churchill arrived at Antwerp he could have an audience with King Albert of the Belgians 'before a final decision as to the departure of the Government is taken'. The 'intrepid' Winston, Asquith told Venetia on the morning of October 3, 'will go straightway & beard the King & Ministers, & try to infuse into their backbone the necessary quantity of starch'. He and Kitchener were both waiting for Churchill's report. 'I don't know how fluent he is in French,' Asquith added, 'but if he was able to do himself justice in a foreign tongue, the Belges will have listened to a discourse the like of which they have never heard before. I cannot but think that he will stiffen them up to the sticking point.'

Later it was to become fashionable, even for Asquith, to mock Churchill's mission to Antwerp. On the morning of October 3, however, much seemed to depend upon it. When he reached Antwerp shortly after midday, the Belgian Government was still in the city, having decided not to leave before hearing what Churchill had to say, and to offer. The outer ring of forts was intact.

At the outset of his discussions, Churchill was told by Charles de Broqueville, the Belgian Prime Minister, that the Belgians were willing to try to hold the city for the next ten days at least. But he would not do so beyond the fourth day unless British reinforcements could be promised now. Intent on averting the nightmare posed by Kitchener, of a German advance to Calais, Churchill offered the Belgians not only the Marine Brigade then at Dunkirk, but the two brigades of the Royal Naval Division which he had set up in August, and which was still in training. In telegraphing to Kitchener, asking him to authorise the immediate despatch of all three brigades to help the Belgians, Churchill wrote, 'I must impress on you the necessity of making these worn and weary men throw their souls into it, or the whole thing will go with a run.'

The first two thousand Royal Marines would arrive in Antwerp on the following morning. Churchill decided to stay in the city until then in order to ensure their harmonious working with the Belgians. During October 4 he visited the forts, telegraphing to Kitchener that he had found their Belgian defenders 'weary and disheartened'. That day, as the Royal Marines arrived in Antwerp, a telegram from Kitchener told Churchill that the newly formed Naval Brigades could go to the city immediately.

Feeling that his presence could help to animate the defence, and integrate these two sets of British reinforcements, Churchill then took an extraordinary step, telegraphing Asquith early on the morning of October 5 with an offer to resign as First Lord 'and undertake command of relieving and defensive forces assigned to Antwerp'. He had one condition, that he be given 'necessary rank and authority, and full powers of a commander of a detached force in the Field'. He felt it his duty to offer his services in this way 'because I am sure this arrangement will afford the best prospect of a victorious result to an enterprise in which I am deeply involved'.

Asquith declined Churchill's offer. But he was impressed by his efforts so far, writing to Venetia, 'Winston succeeded in bucking up the Belges, who gave up their panicky idea of retreating to Ostend, and are now holding Antwerp for as long as they can, trusting upon our coming to their final deliverance.' In Cabinet that morning several Ministers pressed Asquith to tell them when Churchill would return. He then read out Churchill's telegram. 'I regret to say it was received with a Homeric laugh,' he told Venetia. 'W is an ex-Lieutenant of Hussars and would if his proposal had been accepted have been in command of two distinguished Major Generals, not to mention Brigadiers, Colonels etc, while the Navy was only contributing its little brigades.'

Aware that the Navy's 'little brigades' were the sole British forces then available for the defence of Antwerp, and knowing Churchill's close involvement with modern warfare in the decade and a half since he had been a Lieutenant, Kitchener told Asquith that he was quite prepared to commission him as a Lieutenant-General. But Asquith insisted that Churchill return to Britain as soon as possible. A British General, Henry Rawlinson, was ordered to go to Antwerp with his Division. But Rawlinson informed Kitchener that he could not reach the city for at least three days, possibly four. Meanwhile the German bombardment of the forts intensified. 'In view of the situation and developing German attack,' Churchill telegraphed to Kitchener on the afternoon of October 5, 'it is my duty to remain here and continue my direction of affairs unless relieved by some person of consequence. If we can hold out for next three days, prospects will not be unfavourable. But Belgians require to be braced to their task, and my presence is necessary.'

That evening Churchill went to Marine Brigade headquarters near one of the forts. An Italian war correspondent saw him there, 'He was tranquilly smoking a large cigar and looking at the progress of the battle under a rain of shrapnel, which I can only call fearful.' The two Naval Brigades were expected in Antwerp within twelve hours. Churchill reported this to the Belgian Council of War, which was much relieved. 'I have met Ministers in Council, who resolved to fight it out here, whatever happens,' he informed Kitchener that night.

When the Naval Brigades arrived on the morning of October 6, Churchill saw at once that they were far too tired to take the offensive. He therefore arranged with the Belgians that they should take up defensive positions between the front line and the city. Inadvertently, one unit of the new arrivals was sent forward almost immediately. Driving past them on his way back from the front, Churchill ordered them to return to trenches further back.

By midday on October 6 there were eight thousand British troops in the city. 'Under Winston's stimulus the Belgians are making a resolute stand,' Asquith told Venetia that day. 'He has done good service by way of starching and ironing the Belges.' Asquith added that although General Rawlinson was expected in the city that day, 'Winston persists in remaining there, which leaves the Admiralty here without a head, and I have had to tell them (not being, *entre nous*, very trustful of the capacity of Prince Louis & his Board) to submit all decisions to me.'

That afternoon Rawlinson reached Antwerp. He and Churchill then went together to a Belgian Council of War. Although they were able to convince the Belgians that more reinforcements were on their way, including Rawlinson's 40,000 men, who were even then disembarking at Ostend, the Belgians now decided the city must be abandoned. German heavy howitzers would soon be close enough to bombard the centre. In a telegram to Kitchener, Churchill warned of the 'complete exhaustion and imminent demoralisation' of the Belgian Army.

That evening Churchill made a final visit to the front-line positions. Then, leaving Rawlinson in charge, he returned overnight through Ostend and Dover to London. As he reached Dover on the morning of October 7, his wife gave birth to their third child, Sarah. After visiting mother and child, Churchill went immediately to the Cabinet to report on his three and a half days at Antwerp. 'Winston is in great form & I think has thoroughly enjoyed his adventure,' Asquith told Venetia. 'He is certainly one of the people one would choose to go tiger-hunting with, tho' as you very truly say he ought to have been born in the centuries before specialism. He was quite ready to take over in Belgium, and did so in fact for a couple of days – the army, the navy & the civil government.'

Writing to Clementine from the Cabinet room that morning, Sir Edward Grey told her that he was sitting next to her husband and 'feel a glow imparted by the thought that I am sitting next to a hero. I can't tell you how much I admire his courage & gallant spirit & genius for war.'

Later that day Churchill went to see Asquith and, Asquith told Venetia, 'became suddenly very confidential, and implored me not to take a "conventional view" of his future. Having, as he says, "tasted blood" these last few days he is beginning like a tiger to raven for more, and begs that sooner or later, & the sooner the better, he may be relieved of his present office & put in some kind of military command'. Churchill asked Asquith whether Kitchener's new armies, these 'glittering commands' he called them, were to be 'entrusted to "dug-out trash" bred on the obsolete tactics of twenty-five years earlier'. A political career was 'nothing to him in comparison with military glory'. He was, Asquith concluded, 'quite three parts serious'.

By October 8 the situation in Antwerp had so worsened that the 40,000 British reinforcements then on their way to the city were held back, and the British commander of the Royal Marines and Royal Naval Division sought permission to withdraw. Churchill at once telephoned the commander and urged him 'to hold on, even by his eye-brows'. That evening, however, with Antwerp itself in flames from the German bombardment, Churchill agreed that the British troops should pull out. 'Poor Winston is very depressed,' Asquith told Venetia, 'as he feels that his mission has been in vain.'

In fact, the extra six days' resistance of Antwerp since Churchill had persuaded the Belgians not to evacuate the city enabled the British Army to return safely to the Channel Coast, and to reform in Flanders. Antwerp surrendered to the Germans on the night of October 10. 'This last week,' Asquith told Venetia, 'which has delayed the fall of Antwerp by at least seven days, and has prevented the Germans from linking up their forces – has not been thrown away, and may with Sir J. French all the time coming round have even been of vital value.'

Churchill's dash to Antwerp, and his three and a half days there, quickly became a butt of Conservative derision. In a private letter, Bonar Law, who knew nothing of the background to Churchill's visit or its effect on prolonging Antwerp's resistance, wrote that the episode was 'an utterly stupid business' and that Churchill 'seemed to have an entirely unbalanced mind which is a real danger at a time like this'. The *Morning Post* called the despatch of British troops to Antwerp 'a costly blunder, for which Mr W Churchill must be held responsible'. The *Daily Mail* called it 'a gross example of mal-organisation which has cost valuable lives'.

During the fighting around Antwerp, fifty-seven of the British defenders had been killed. The phrase 'Antwerp blunder', as many called it, was now linked inexorably to Churchill's name. Disconsolately he spoke to his closest friends of resignation. Haldane sought to dissuade him. 'You are unique & invaluable to the nation, full of courage and resource,' he wrote. 'Do not pay the least attention to the fools who write & talk in the Press. It is the real thing that counts, & the nation thoroughly believes in you.' Churchill felt that the outburst of criticism had weakened his position. 'Antwerp was a blow,' he wrote to Sir John French, 'and some aspects of it have given a handle to my enemies, and perhaps for a time reduced my power to be useful.'

On October 8, at the height of the struggle for Antwerp, Churchill authorised one of his former flying instructors, Spenser Grey, to lead a flight of four aeroplanes to Cologne; they dropped their sixteen bombs on a military railway station. On the following day a Royal Naval Air Service pilot dropped his two bombs on a Zeppelin shed at Düsseldorf, destroying the airship inside. According to a report from Germany which reached Churchill later that month, 'The occurrence produced great consternation in Berlin as they did not believe such a raid was possible for a British aviator.'

German forces now reached Ostend and began to move westward. In response to an appeal from the French Army, Churchill ordered a naval bombardment of the German-held coast to begin on October 17. He also ordered a small Marine and Yeomanry force, in which his brother was serving, to make a series of sorties from Dunkirk towards Ostend, to keep the German line as far east as possible. 'My heart marched with you down the road from Dunkirk,' he wrote to his brother. And he added, 'I heard the crack of their shells for four days at Antwerp, & I could be quite content, I can assure you, to ride along in my place with you all.'

The combined Naval and Marine Yeomanry action was effective in helping to halt the German advance along the North Sea coast, leaving a small strip of the Belgian coastline in Allied hands for the rest of the war. But Churchill was frustrated at the lack of opportunities for action. He and Asquith found Prince Louis a negative influence as far as proposals for action were concerned; towards the end of October, Asquith told Venetia that he and Churchill had 'both enlarged on the want of initiative & constructive thought of the present naval advisers'. For example, Asquith told her, nothing had been done to produce protective devices against the submarine; Prince Louis, he added, 'must go'.

Churchill wanted the seventy-four-year-old Lord Fisher as his new First Sea Lord. 'Contact with you is like breathing ozone to me,' he had written to Fisher on New Year's Day 1914. Despite Fisher's irascibility, Churchill was confident that his energy would revitalise the Navy and help drive it to victory. At an audience at Buckingham Palace, however, the King told Churchill that he opposed Fisher's appointment, arguing that the Admiral was too old and too divisive. Fisher later told a friend: 'When the King said to Winston and the Prime Minister (to dissuade them!) that the job would kill me, Winston instantly replied, "Sir, I cannot imagine a more glorious death." !!! Wasn't that lovely?'

According to a note made by the King's Private Secretary, Churchill answered the King's criticisms of Fisher's age with a hint of his own resignation, telling the King he would 'not be sorry to leave the Admiralty as its work was very uncongenial to him: he wanted to go to the war & fight and be a soldier'. After consulting Asquith, the King accepted Fisher as First Sea Lord. Churchill now felt that he had a partner in zeal. *The Times* welcomed the change on the grounds that Fisher would exercise a restraining influence on Churchill. When the King warned Asquith that Fisher 'would be almost certain to get on badly with Winston', Asquith commented to Venetia that on this point, 'I have some misgivings of my own.'

Fisher returned to the Admiralty as First Sea Lord on October 29. That same day the *Goeben* and the *Breslau*, which had earlier been transferred by the Germans to Turkish control, bombarded the Russian Black Sea ports of Odessa, Nikolaev and Sevastopol. The British Government at once sent an ultimatum to the Turks, ordering them to dismiss the German military and naval missions at Constantinople and remove all German personnel from the two warships. The Turks refused to do so. Learning this, Churchill asked Fisher to look into the possibility of bombarding the outer forts of the Dardanelles, telling him, 'It is a good thing to give a prompt blow.'

Churchill wanted to be ready to take immediate action. 'We ought to have a means of striking them ready prepared,' he told Fisher on October 31. The British ultimatum expired at noon that day. Two days later, having obtained Fisher's approval, Churchill signalled Vice-Admiral Carden, who was in command of all British naval forces in the Eastern Mediterranean, to bombard the outer forts at the Dardanelles. 'Retirements should be made before fire from the forts becomes effective,' Churchill told Carden. On the following day the bombardment was carried out. It lasted for ten minutes. One shell, hitting the magazine at the main fort of Sedd-el-Bahr, destroyed almost all its heavy guns. The damage was never repaired.

Fisher's return to the Admiralty coincided with the worst British naval disaster of the war, the sinking of two British cruisers off Coronel, on the Pacific coast of Chile, by a German naval squadron under Count von Spee. The British Admiral, Sir Christopher Cradock, had one battleship, *Canopus*, which, although slower than the rest of his force, had the firepower to keep the German ships at bay. For this reason the Admiralty had earlier instructed him not to separate *Canopus* from the rest of his force. Cradock had discarded this advice, risking, and meeting, defeat, his own death, and the loss of 1,500 men.

Not knowing the facts, there were those who hastened to blame Churchill for this defeat. But the main call was for revenge. Asquith wrote to Venetia: 'If the Admiral had followed his instructions he would never have met them with an inferior force. As I told Winston last night (and he is not in the least to blame) it is time that he bagged something & broke some crockery.' With Fisher's dynamism as a spur, Churchill ordered a formidable force to be concentrated against the victorious von Spee. Within six weeks his squadron was tracked down and destroyed at the Battle of the Falkland Islands. Like Cradock off Coronel, von Spee went down with his ship.

The tragedies of the war now began to impinge upon Churchill. At the end of October he learned that his twenty-eight-year-old cousin Norman Leslie had been killed at Armentières. 'My heart bleeds for you,' he wrote to Norman's mother, his Aunt Leonie. 'We must at all costs win. Victory is a better boon than life and without it life will be unendurable. The British Army has in a few weeks of war revived before the whole world the glories of Agincourt and Blenheim and Waterloo, and in this Norman has played his part. It rests with us to make sure that these sacrifices are not made in vain.'

On November 6 Churchill's friend Hugh Dawnay was killed in the Ypres salient. 'What would happen I wonder,' Churchill wrote to Clementine later that month, 'if the armies suddenly & simultaneously went on strike and said some other method must be found of settling the dispute! Meanwhile however new avalanches of men are preparing to mingle in the conflict and it widens every hour.'

The British Army now struggled to hold a line in Flanders beyond which the Germans would not pass. With the establishment of this Western Front, and its fortification by trenches, barbed wire and machine-gun posts, almost no week now passed without one or more of Churchill's friends being killed. 'My dear I am always anxious about you,' he wrote in November to his brother, who was then at Ypres. 'It would take the edge off much if I could be with you. I expect I should be very frightened but I would dissemble.'

On November 30, Churchill was forty years old. That week, in an attempt to confine the discussion of war policy to as few people as possible, Asquith created a War Council consisting of himself, Grey, Lloyd George, Kitchener and Churchill. At its meeting on December 1, with Fisher's approval, Churchill proposed a British assault on the German North Sea island of Sylt. This would then become a British air base, monitoring any German preparations for the invasion of Britain, keeping the movements of the German Fleet under constant observation, and enabling British pilots to 'drop bombs every few days' on Germany.

The Admiralty was authorised to examine the plan in detail. 'But,' Churchill complained to Fisher three weeks later, 'I cannot find anyone to make such a plan alive & dominant.' Britain's situation, Churchill added, 'is as I have told you, & as you justly say, that of waiting to be kicked, & wondering when & where.'

Churchill's thoughts that winter were not only on the North Sea. 'His volatile mind is at present set on Turkey & Bulgaria,' Asquith told Venetia on December 5, '& he wants to organise a heroic adventure against Gallipoli and the Dardanelles: to which I am altogether opposed.' In the hope of persuading Greece, then neutral, to join the Entente Powers and go to the aid of Serbia, Churchill suggested offering her Constantinople. As a first step to Greece winning this long-desired prize, he envisaged a Greek Army joining with the Royal Navy in a combined naval and military attack on the Gallipoli Peninsula.

On December 14 the Serbian Army drove the Austrians from Belgrade. For the time being there was no need to go to Serbia's aid. But a new sphere of possible military operations quickly emerged, disclosed to the War Council in a telegram from Russia on December 21. This telegram warned that the Russian Army was desperately short of ammunition and urgently needed some diversion against Germany from the West. Churchill suggested a British naval initiative, an incursion into the Baltic and the seizure of the Danish island of Bornholm. Denmark was a neutral state; Churchill hoped to persuade her to join the Entente. Under his plan, Bornholm would become a combined Anglo-Russian base, enabling British troops to cross the Baltic and land at Kiel, and Russian troops to land on the German Baltic coast, whence they could march overland to Berlin. 'The Baltic is the only theatre in which naval action can appreciably shorten the war,' he told Fisher on December 22. 'Denmark must come in, & the Russians be let loose on Berlin.'

Churchill worked tirelessly to devise some plan of campaign that might hasten the end of the war, assisted by his Admiralty Secretary, James Masterton-Smith and by Edward Marsh. On December 22 Asquith told Venetia, 'I am writing in the Cabinet room at the beginning of twilight, and thro' the opposite window across the Parade I see the Admiralty flag flying & the lights "beginning to twinkle" from the rooms where Winston and his two familiars (Eddie and Masterton) are beating out their plans.'

One of these plans came to fruition on Christmas Day, a raid by seven naval seaplanes on the German warships lying in the Schillig Roads off Cuxhaven; all but one of the pilots returned safely. Four days later, in a letter to Asquith, Churchill reiterated his Baltic plan, arguing that no further progress could now be made on the Western Front, where the trench lines were being dug and fortified from the North Sea to the Swiss border. 'Are there not other alternatives than sending our armies to chew barbed wire in Flanders?' he asked. 'Furthermore, cannot the power of the Navy be brought more directly to bear upon the enemy?' Once British ships had seized control of Bornholm, he pointed out, the Russian Army could be landed 'within ninety miles of Berlin'.

Lloyd George was also searching for an alternate war-zone to the Western Front. His plan, which he likewise put to Asquith at the end of December, was for a British landing at the Greek port of Salonica, to link up with the Serbian Army. He also wanted to strike at Turkey by landing 100,000 men on the Syrian coast. This, he explained, would have the effect of relieving the Turkish pressure then being exerted against Russia in the Caucasus.

The Secretary to the War Council, Maurice Hankey, a former Royal Marine Colonel, suggested that same week that Germany 'can perhaps be struck most effectively and with the most lasting results for the peace of the world through her allies, and particularly through Turkey'. A combination of three British Army Corps, plus Greek and Bulgarian troops ought, he wrote, 'to be sufficient to capture Constantinople'. Fisher was so impressed by Hankey's suggestion that he sent Churchill an eight-point plan for the defeat of both Turkey and Austria-Hungary. This included the landing of 75,000 British soldiers at Besika Bay just south of the Dardanelles, a Greek military landing on the Gallipoli Peninsula, and a British naval attack to force the Dardanelles with old battleships. 'I consider the attack on Turkey holds the field,' Fisher wrote to Churchill on 3 January 1915. 'But only if it's immediate.'

The day before Fisher's letter, the Turkish option unexpectedly gained in both attractiveness and urgency when Grey received a telegram from the British Ambassador to Russia, who reported that the Russian Army, hard pressed by the Turks in the Caucasus, wanted Britain to carry out 'a demonstration of some kind against Turks elsewhere, either naval or military', to force the Turks to withdraw some of their forces in the Caucasus. Grey sent this appeal to Kitchener, who wrote at once to Churchill, 'Do you think any naval actions would be possible to prevent Turks sending more men into the Caucasus & thus denuding Constantinople.'

Before Churchill could answer, Kitchener came to see him at the Admiralty. 'Could we not, for instance, make a demonstration at the Dardanelles?' he asked. Churchill replied that a naval attack alone would be ineffectual. A combined military and naval assault might be another matter. Kitchener went back to the War Office to consult with his advisers, but they were adamant that no spare troops were available for such an action. 'We shall not be ready for anything big for some months,' Kitchener told Churchill, but he went on to express his conviction that the 'only place' where a demonstration might 'have some effect in stopping reinforcements going East would be the Dardanelles', particularly if reports could be spread at the same time that Constantinople was threatened.

Churchill summoned his advisers to discuss a possible naval demonstration at the Dardanelles. There was general scepticism, which he shared, about the efficacy of a purely naval attack. Any such attack would in any case have to make use of old battleships not needed in the North Sea. Churchill then telegraphed to Admiral Carden, whose ships were even then blockading the Dardanelles: 'Do you consider the forcing of the Dardanelles by ships alone a practicable operation. It is assumed older battleships fitted with mine bumpers would be used, preceded by colliers or other merchant craft as bumpers and sweepers. Importance of result would justify severe loss. Let me know your views.'

Churchill felt, however, as he had done a month earlier, that the Navy's main contribution to victory would be to seize a German island off the North Sea coast: he had then suggested Sylt; he now suggested Borkum. On January 3, while awaiting Carden's reply from the Dardanelles, he proposed March or April as the date for action, writing privately to Fisher: 'Borkum is the key to all northern possibilities, whether defensive against raid or invasion, or offensive to block the enemy in, or to invade either Oldenburg or Schleswig-Holstein.' An infantry division should now be assigned by the War Office to the capture of Borkum. As to Fisher's plan for invasion of Turkey, 'I would not grudge 100,000 men,' Churchill wrote, 'because of the great political effect in the Balkan Peninsula: but Germany is the foe & it is bad war to seek cheaper victories & easier antagonists.'

Fisher tried to enlist Balfour's support for the Turkish plan. 'The naval advantages of the possession of Constantinople and the getting of wheat from the Black Sea are so overwhelming,' he wrote on January 4, 'that I consider Colonel Hankey's plan for Turkish operations vital and imperative and very pressing.' On the following day Admiral Carden replied to the question about a possible naval attack on the Dardanelles. To the surprise of all at the Admiralty, he did not dismiss the idea. His reply was brief and positive. 'With reference to your telegram of the 3rd inst,' he wrote, 'I do not consider Dardanelles can be rushed. They might be forced by extended operations with large numbers of ships.'

The War Council met that afternoon. Churchill was still eager to push ahead with his North Sea plan, and to get a timetable for it. After the Council, Asquith sent Venetia a summary of the plans that had been proposed: Churchill had advocated the seizure of Borkum and a British military landing near the Kiel Canal. Lloyd George had argued for a landing at Salonica, or on the Dalmatian Coast of Austria-Hungary, F.E.

Smith had sent the Council a plan to land a British force on the Turkish coast near Smyrna; Kitchener had argued for 'Gallipoli & Constantinople.'

In support of the Russian appeal, Kitchener pressed his War Council colleagues for a demonstration at the Dardanelles. Churchill then read out to them Carden's telegram, which seemed to offer the possibility of forcing the Dardanelles by ships alone, and thus enable British warships to reach Constantinople. Returning to the Admiralty, he found that his principal naval advisers shared Carden's view that a systematic naval bombardment of the Turkish forts could be effective. The earlier bombardment of November 3 had impressed them. 'Your view is agreed with by high authorities here,' Churchill telegraphed to Carden on January 6. 'Please telegraph in detail what you think could be done by extended operations, what force would be needed, and how you would consider it should be used.'

The naval attack on the Dardanelles now became a matter of planning and detail. But Churchill still saw his North Sea plan as the one potentially effective naval initiative, and at the War Council on January 7 he set it out in detail. Fisher supported him, telling the Council that the Navy would be ready to seize Borkum within three months. Kitchener agreed to spare a division of troops to take part in the landing. 'W pressed his scheme for acquiring a base at Borkum,' Asquith told Venetia, 'a big business, as it is heavily fortified, and the necessary preparations will take till near the end of March. We gave him authority for this.'

On the Western Front, the conditions of trench warfare worsened with the continuation of winter. Reading a proposal by Hankey for a trench-crossing machine, Churchill's imagination was stirred. On January 5 he wrote to Asquith: 'It would be quite easy in a short time to fit up a number of steam tractors with small armoured shelters, in which men and machine guns could be placed, which would be bullet-proof. Used at night, they would not be affected by artillery fire to any extent. The caterpillar system would enable trenches to be crossed quite easily, and the weight of the machine would destroy all wire entanglements. Forty or fifty of these engines, prepared secretly and brought into positions at nightfall, could advance quite certainly into the enemy's trenches, smashing away all the obstructions, and sweeping the trenches with their machine-gun fire, and with grenades thrown out of the top. They would then make so many *points d'appuis* for the British supporting infantry to rush forward and rally on them. They can then move forward to attack the second line of trenches.'

Churchill wanted Asquith to authorise the necessary expenditure to prepare a prototype. 'The cost would be small,' he wrote. 'If the experiment did not answer, what harm would be done? An obvious measure of prudence would have been to have started something like this two months ago. It should certainly be done now.' Asquith sent Churchill's letter to

Kitchener, who set in motion a certain amount of design work at the War Office. This did not satisfy Churchill, who felt that the military authorities were not really convinced either that the machine could be made, or that it would be of much value once it was completed.

The stalemate and heavy casualties of trench warfare continued. On January 7, two days after his proposal for what would in due course become a new weapon of war, the tank, Churchill again wrote to Asquith about the Western Front. 'Ought we not to get into a more comfortable, dry, habitable line, even if we have to retire a few miles?' he asked. 'Our troops are rotting.' At the War Council on the following day, Lloyd George pressed for military landings on the Adriatic Coast of Austria-Hungary. Kitchener opposed this, stressing again that 'the most suitable objective' of any new military action was at the Dardanelles, 'as an attack here could be made in co-operation with the Fleet'. If successful, he said, 'it would re-establish communication with Russia; settle the Near Eastern question; draw in Greece, and perhaps Bulgaria and Rumania; and release wheat and shipping now locked up in the Black Sea'.

Kitchener's suggestion of a military as well as naval assault on the Dardanelles was supported by Hankey. Success at the Dardanelles, he said, 'would give us the Danube as a line of communication for an army penetrating into the heart of Austria, and bring our sea power to bear in the middle of Europe'. Churchill, while willing to 'study' these suggested operations, spoke forcefully for his Baltic concept, emphasising that it might persuade the Dutch to enter the war on the side of the Entente, thus providing a British naval base in the North Sea 'without fighting for it'; this would enable the British armies to advance from Dutch territory into the German industrial heartland. It was not until 'the Northern possibilities are exhausted', he wrote on January 11 to Sir John French, 'that I would look to the South of Europe for the profitable employment of our expanding military forces'.

Admiral Fisher, however, Churchill's senior naval adviser, was more and more struck by the possibilities of the Turkish theatre of war. 'If the Greeks land 100,000 men on the Gallipoli Peninsula in concert with a British naval attack on the Dardanelles,' Fisher wrote to a friend, 'I think we could count on an easy and quick arrival at Constantinople.'

Amid these crucial daily debates, Churchill found little time for relaxation. On January 10 and 11 he and Clementine were the guests of a Liberal Peer, Lord Beauchamp, at Walmer Castle on the Kent coast, where the Asquiths were also staying. Talking about the war, Churchill said, according to Margot Asquith's account in her diary: 'My God! This is living History. Everything we are doing and saying is thrilling – it will be read by a thousand generations, think of that! Why I would not be out of this glorious delicious war for anything the world could give me (eyes glowing but with a slight anxiety lest the word "delicious" should jar on me). I say, don't repeat the word "delicious" – you know what I mean.'

The Asquith family were fascinated with Churchill, sometimes his sternest critics, at others his warmest admirers; two months earlier Asquith had sent Venetia a thumbnail sketch of him, 'Winston, whom most people would call ugly, but whose eyes, when he is really interested, have the glow of genius'. On another occasion, in reflecting on Churchill's character and qualities, he quoted Edward Grey's description of genius, 'a zig-zag streak of lightning through the brain'.

On January 12 Churchill's Admiralty War Group, headed by Fisher, received another telegram from Carden, not only giving in detail his plan to force the Dardanelles, but suggesting that it might be done in about a month. Carden listed his needs; all of them were surplus to Britain's naval needs elsewhere, including four battleships launched before 1906 and no longer of value in the North Sea. Fisher was so enthusiastic at the thought of forcing the Dardanelles by ships alone that he proposed to add the most modern of all Britain's battleships, the *Queen Elizabeth*, whose 15-inch guns had not yet even been fired. They were about to be tested in the sea off Gibraltar. Far better, Fisher suggested, that they should be fired at the Dardanelles forts.

Churchill was suddenly caught up by the thought of the *Queen Elizabeth* in action at the Dardanelles. For the first time he saw the full prospects opened up once so powerful a warship was in the Sea of Marmara. The *Goeben* and *Breslau* would be out-gunned; Constantinople would be at Britain's mercy; Enver Pasha, now Minister of War, whom Churchill had met before the war both at German Army manoeuvres at Würzburg, and at Constantinople, would abandon the German cause. Churchill explained all this to the War Council on the evening of January 13. According to the minutes of the meeting, Lloyd George 'liked the plan', as did Kitchener. Asquith listened while other ideas were also put forward; Grey wanted a landing at Cattaro, on the Adriatic, to persuade Italy to join the Anglo-French Entente. Lloyd George then reverted to the idea of a landing at Salonica. Churchill again raised his plan for what the minutes of the meeting called 'action in Holland'.

'I maintained an unbroken silence to the end,' Asquith told Venetia, 'when I intervened with my conclusions.' These were twofold; that the Admiralty should consider 'promptly' the possibility of naval action at Cattaro or elsewhere in the Adriatic 'with the view (inter alia) of bringing pressure on Italy', and that the Admiralty 'should also prepare for a naval expedition in February to bombard and take the Gallipoli Peninsula, with Constantinople as its objective'.

Planning for the 'naval expedition' went ahead at once. The vessels Carden had asked for were put under orders; Malta dockyard would fit them with mine-bumpers. A landing place for aeroplanes would be established on the nearby Greek island of Tenedos. At Fisher's request, Churchill persuaded Asquith to give up the Adriatic plan. The naval attack on the Dardanelles, he explained, 'will require practically our whole available margin'. Success, according to Fisher, 'will produce results which will undoubtedly influence every Mediterranean power'.

Fisher now began to waver from his enthusiasm and constructive support of the previous day. He wanted the destroyer flotilla already under Carden's command to be replaced by French ships. When an Australian submarine reached the Dardanelles and joined Carden's fleet, he called it 'inexcusable to waste her on the Turks'. He wrote to Jellicoe of the need for 200,000 troops to act 'in conjunction with the Fleet'; otherwise, he declared, 'I just abominate the Dardanelles'. Churchill had brought in Fisher to strengthen the war-making initiatives of the Admiralty. He now found Fisher's conduct bizarre and disruptive. Others saw clearly the danger which Fisher posed. 'He is old & worn out & nervous,' Captain Richmond, the Assistant Director of Operations at the Admiralty, wrote in his diary on January 19. 'It is ill to have the destinies of an empire in the hands of a failing old man, anxious for popularity, afraid of any local mishap which may be put down to his dispositions.'

On January 25, in a letter to Churchill, Fisher offered to resign. He had already done so once before, in protest against the Government's refusal to shoot German prisoners-of-war as reprisal for Zeppelin attacks on Britain. Now it was the despatch of old battleships to the Dardanelles that had provoked him, 'for they cannot be lost without losing men, and they form the only reserve behind the Grand Fleet'. Churchill replied by pointing out that surplus ships would always be used in ancillary operations, and that 'with care and skill losses may be reduced to a minimum'. His letter ended, 'You & I are so much stronger together.'

Fisher wanted his protest and Churchill's reply to be circulated to the War Council, but Asquith would not allow it. Meanwhile, the ships Carden wanted were on their way to him, from South America, St Helena, Ceylon and Egypt. In all, he was to be sent thirteen battleships, including not only *Queen Elizabeth*, which Fisher had suggested earlier, but two more which he suggested now, despite his letter of protest, *Lord Nelson* and *Agamemnon*.

On January 26, Churchill secured the French Government's agreement to participate in the Dardanelles bombardment. Then, a few hours before the War Council was to meet to give its final approval, Fisher wrote to Asquith that he was against the plan unless there was 'military co-operation'. He would not attend the War Council. Churchill persuaded

Fisher to go with him to see Asquith twenty minutes before the War Council. At this meeting, Asquith was emphatic that 'the Dardanelles should go forward'. But at the War Council, which he agreed to attend, Fisher suddenly got up and tried to leave the room. Kitchener, seeing him leaving, followed him to the door and asked what he intended to do. Fisher replied, as he himself later recorded in the third person, 'that he would not return to the Council table, and would resign his office as First Sea Lord'. Kitchener then pointed out that Fisher was 'the only dissentient, and that the Dardanelles operation had been decided upon by the Prime Minister'.

Fisher agreed to return to the Council table, in time to hear Asquith ask what importance the members attached to the Dardanelles operation. Kitchener, who spoke first, said he considered the naval attack 'to be vitally important'. If successful 'its effect would be equivalent to that of a successful campaign fought with the new armies'. Balfour, invited as a former Prime Minister to give his view, then told the Council that a successful attack would not only 'put Constantinople under our control' but would also 'open a passage to the Danube'. Balfour added: 'It was difficult to imagine a more helpful operation.' Grey was equally enthusiastic, telling the War Council that success at the Dardanelles 'would also finally settle the attitude of Bulgaria and the whole of the Balkans'. The Turks, Grey said, would be 'paralysed with fear when they heard that the forts were being destroyed one by one'.

Fisher now changed his mind again, telling Churchill when the meeting was over that he would support the naval attack. 'When I finally decided to come in,' he told a commission of enquiry two years later, 'I went the whole hog, *totus porcus*.' It was hoped to begin the bombardment of the Dardanelles in mid-February, but delay in the arrival of the minesweepers led to a postponement. At that very moment Churchill's advisers began to argue that a military force was needed, to follow up the naval success by landing on the Gallipoli Peninsula. This had been Churchill's original idea. Asquith now favoured it, as did Hankey.

But where would troops be found? The one spare division of regular troops, the 29th, had already been earmarked for despatch to Salonica, to go to the aid of Serbia. At an emergency meeting of the War Council on February 16, it was learned that King Constantine of Greece, a relation of the Kaiser, refused to allow British troops to land on Greek soil. The 29th Division was therefore free to land at Gallipoli. The War Council approved this plan with alacrity.

The War Council of February 16 also agreed that the Australian and New Zealand troops then in Egypt, on their way to France, should be sent instead to the island of Lemnos, for service at Gallipoli. Churchill was instructed to arrange their transport. The Dardanelles was now a joint naval and military operation. 'You get through,' Kitchener told Churchill, 'I will find the men.' If the naval operations at the Dardanelles 'prosper', Churchill wrote to Kitchener, 'immense advantages may be offered which cannot be gathered without military aid'. At least 50,000 men should be within reach at three days' notice, 'either to seize the Gallipoli Peninsula when it has been evacuated, or to occupy Constantinople if a revolution takes place. We should never forgive ourselves if the naval operations succeeded & the fruits were lost through the army being absent.'

All seemed agreed; three days later, on the morning of February 19, Admiral Carden began the naval bombardment of the outer forts of the Dardanelles, the essential preliminary to forcing the Straits. That afternoon the War Council met to confirm the despatch of the 29th Division to the Eastern Mediterranean. But Kitchener now said that, with the news just arrived of a Russian setback in East Prussia, the 29th Division might soon be needed in France. The 30,000 Australian and New Zealand troops then in Egypt would be enough to support the naval attack at the Dardanelles.

Lloyd George, Asquith and Grey each argued with Kitchener that the 29th Division should be sent to the Eastern Mediterranean. No firm decision was reached. On the following morning Carden reported from the Dardanelles that although there had been no direct hits on the Turkish guns on February 19, the magazines of two of the forts had been blown up. Then gales and low visibility made firing impossible for four days.

At a dinner in the third week of February, following up the ideas he had expressed to Asquith at the start of the year, Churchill was impressed by a proposal put to him by Major Thomas Hetherington, who was attached to the Royal Naval Air Division at the Admiralty for experimental work, for a large cross-country armoured-car that would not only carry guns, but would surmount obstacles, trenches and barbed wire. Churchill had at once asked the Director of Naval Construction at the Admiralty, Captain Eustace Tennyson D'Eyncourt, to try to design such a 'land ship'. To mystify those who might accidentally see the designs, they were called 'water-carriers for Russia', but when it was pointed out that this might be abbreviated to 'WCs for Russia' the name was changed to 'water-tanks', then to 'tanks'.

On February 20 Churchill summoned an Admiralty conference to discuss the best methods of proceeding with the tank. As he was suffering from a bad attack of influenza, it was held in his bedroom. As a result of this meeting a Land Ship Committee was formed with D'Eyncourt as chairman. It held its first meeting two days later and submitted its proposals to Churchill, who accepted them with the comment, 'As proposed &

with all despatch.' An order for the first tank was placed with a firm of agricultural engineers, who suggested using a tractor as the model for the new machine. Having obtained Asquith's approval for his experimental activities, Churchill gave the Committee £70,000 from Admiralty funds to pursue its developments with as much speed as possible.

When the first designs were submitted to him on March 9, Churchill minuted, 'Press on.' Twelve days later D'Eyncourt asked if he could construct eighteen separate prototypes. Churchill approved: 'Most urgent,' he minuted, 'Special report to me in case of delay.' In its report after the war, the Royal Commission on War Inventions told Parliament that 'it was primarily due to the receptivity, courage and driving force' of Churchill that the idea of using the tank as an instrument of war 'was converted into a practical shape'.

With the Turkish option still dominating the War Council's discussions in the third week of February, Churchill continued to press Kitchener to send troops from Egypt to the Aegean. 'The operations at the Dardanelles may go much more rapidly than has been expected,' he wrote on February 20. In that case it would be 'vital' to have enough men to seal off the Peninsula at its narrowest point, the lines of Bulair. Four days later, however, Kitchener told the War Council that if the Fleet succeeded in silencing the forts at the Dardanelles, the Turkish garrison at Gallipoli 'would probably be withdrawn' rather than run the risk of being cut off.

Once more Churchill asked for the 29th Division to be sent to the Dardanelles. With a comparatively small number of troops, the 18,000 men of the 29th Division, 30,000 Australians then in Egypt, 8,500 men of the Royal Naval Division then on their way to the Eastern Mediterranean, and 18,000 French troops, 'we might,' he said, 'be in Constantinople by the end of March'. At the same time, if the naval attack was 'temporarily held up by mines', troops would be needed for 'some local military operation' on the Peninsula itself. But Kitchener had so low an opinion of Turkish troops that he told the War Council of February 24 that no troops at all would be needed; even before the Straits had been forced, indeed, as soon as it became clear that the forts at the Dardanelles were being 'silenced one by one', the Turkish garrison on the Peninsula would flee to Asia, while the garrison at Constantinople, the Sultan, and even the Turkish Army in Thrace 'would also decamp to the Asiatic shore'. Kitchener was adamant; the surrender of Turkey-in-Europe would be achieved by British naval guns alone. Troops were not needed.

So convinced was Kitchener that the Turks would abandon the Gallipoli Peninsula under the impact of naval gunnery alone that when Asquith asked him whether Australian and New Zealand troops 'were good enough' for such an important operation of war, he replied that 'they were quite good enough if a cruise in the Sea of Marmara was all that was contemplated'. Asquith tried in vain to persuade him to allow the 18,000 men of the 29th Division to be sent to the Dardanelles. 'One must take a lot of risks in war,' he explained to Venetia as soon as the War Council was over, '& I am strongly of the opinion that the chance of forcing the Dardanelles, & occupying Constantinople, & cutting Turkey in half, and arousing on our side the whole Balkan Peninsula, presents such a unique opportunity that we ought to hazard a lot elsewhere rather than forgo it.'

Despite Asquith's urging, Kitchener refused to release the 29th Division for the Dardanelles. Disappointed, Churchill returned to the Admiralty and telegraphed to Carden to confirm that he must force the Dardanelles 'without military assistance'. If the operation were successful, Churchill added, an ample military force would be available 'to reap the fruits'.

The naval bombardment was resumed on February 25, when all four outer forts were silenced. As Carden made plans to clear the minefields and destroy the intermediate forts early in March, a further appeal by Churchill, again for troops, was in vain; Kitchener told the War Council on February 26 that he would not release the 29th Division; the Turks were not a serious enemy; 'the whole situation in Constantinople would change the moment the Fleet had secured a passage through the Dardanelles'.

Kitchener's confidence in Turkish weakness was the decisive factor in all that followed. Once more, a bitter argument ensued. Hankey supported Churchill, insisting that troops would be needed 'to clear the Gallipoli Peninsula'. Lloyd George also supported Churchill, telling the War Council that he doubted whether victory would come as easily as Kitchener imagined. But Balfour and Grey supported Kitchener, Grey being particularly scathing about the Turks. Angrily, Churchill told the War Council, as its minutes recorded: 'The 29th Division would not make the difference between failure and success in France, but might well make the difference in the east. He wished it to be placed on record that he dissented altogether from the retention of the 29th Division in this country. If a disaster occurred in Turkey owing to the insufficiency of troops, he must disclaim all responsibility.'

Churchill's plea was in vain. 'We accepted K's view as to the immediate situation, to Winston's immense and unconcealed dudgeon,' Asquith wrote to Venetia. He also told her that he had been so angered by Churchill's mood at the War Council, which he described as 'noisy, rhetorical, tactless and temperless – or full', that he had taken the unusual step of calling him into his study to talk to him a little 'for his soul's good'. Realising that his sense of urgency was not widely shared, Churchill wrote that evening to his brother, who was serving in France: 'The capacity to run risks is at famine prices. All play for safety. The war is certainly settling on to a grim basis, & it is evident that long vistas of pain & struggle lie ahead. The limited fund of life & energy which I possess is not much use to influence these tremendous moments. I toil away.'

On February 28 Churchill learned from the Russian Commander-in-Chief, the Grand Duke Nicholas, that as soon as Carden's fleet had forced the Dardanelles, Russia would send 47,000 men to attack Constantinople from the Black Sea. Churchill's confidence revived. 'Should we get through the Dardanelles, as is now likely,' he told Grey, 'we cannot be content with anything less than the surrender of everything Turkish in Europe,' and he added: 'Remember Constantinople is only a means to an end – & the only end is the march of the Balkan States against the Central Powers.'

On March 1 there was further cause for British optimism when the Greeks offered to send 60,000 troops against Turkey. Suddenly the 29th Division did not seem so essential. 'Winston is breast high about the Dardanelles,' Asquith told Venetia. That day, in the wake of the naval bombardment, a small party of Royal Marines landed at the entrance to the Dardanelles and destroyed thirty Turkish artillery pieces, four machine-guns and two searchlights; they then returned safely to their ship. When, on March 3, the War Council discussed the capture of Constantinople and the future of Turkey, it was as if Carden had already reached the Sea of Marmara. There was general excitement at the thought of the Balkan States, in return for Turkish territory, turning their armies against Austria-Hungary. Churchill went so far as to suggest that Britain should 'hire the Turkish armies as mercenaries'.

Churchill had another reason for welcoming the military participation of the Balkan States, and even Turkish soldiers, against Austria. This would then free Britain's forces for what he believed was the true line of advance to victory. 'He was still of the opinion,' the War Council minutes recorded, 'that our proper line of strategy was an advance in the north through Holland and the Baltic.' The operations in the East 'should be regarded merely as an interlude'.

Churchill waited on tenterhooks for the naval attack. As he waited, the Russians, desperate to acquire Constantinople, announced that they would not allow Greek military participation in the campaign, in case the Greeks took over Constantinople. This was a blow, as was the news from Carden that Turkish mobile howitzers on the shore of the Dardanelles had forced the *Queen Elizabeth* to lengthen the range from which she was bombarding the intermediate forts. Nor had aerial reconnaissance been effective; engine trouble had prevented the seaplanes from flying high enough to spot the howitzers from the air.

The first attempt to force the Dardanelles would take place on March 18. Eight days earlier, to the amazement of everyone else at the War Council, Kitchener, two weeks after he had refused to release the 29th Division for the Dardanelles, announced that the situation on the Eastern Front was no longer dangerous and that the Division could go. Carden, however, had reported that he was confident, once he had finished his destruction of the Turkish shore batteries, that clearing the minefields 'would only take a few hours'. He would then steam into the Sea of Marmara. Churchill told the War Council of March 10 that the Admiralty believed that this was possible 'by ships alone'. No troops would be needed. The naval attack could therefore go ahead without waiting for the 29th Division.

The prospect of success infected the War Council of March 10 so much that various territorial gains were discussed. Russia would be given Constantinople; Britain would take Alexandretta. Lloyd George wanted Britain to acquire Palestine. There was even talk of a defeated Germany being made to give up her African and Pacific possessions. Balfour spoke of neutralising the Kiel Canal. Kitchener wanted Britain to 'inflict an indemnity' on Germany to be paid 'over a long term of years'.

Since the outbreak of war, the Conservative Party leaders had been excluded from all war direction. Churchill, despite his long-standing quarrels with the Conservatives, and in particular with its leaders, felt that an all-Party coalition could help the evolution of war policy. At his suggestion, Bonar Law and Lansdowne had been invited to join the War Council discussion of March 10. 'The unexpected successful destruction of the outer forts of the Dardanelles,' Churchill later recalled, 'gave me a momentary ascendancy. I immediately returned to the Coalition plan; & persuaded the PM to invite the leaders of the opposition into council – ostensibly on the future destination of Constantinople, but really to broach the idea of bringing them into the circle.' But the meeting had not been a success in this regard. 'The opposition leaders sat silent & hungry & Mr Asquith did not press forward.'

On the morning of March 11, intercepted German wireless messages from the German officers attached to the Turkish Army revealed that the forts at the Dardanelles were seriously short of ammunition. New supplies would have to come from Germany, but could not arrive for some weeks. Learning this, Fisher was convinced that the moment had come to press home the attack on the Narrows without further delay. He even offered to leave London at once for the Dardanelles, and personally take command of the naval forces in Carden's place. He was persuaded to stay at his post.

With Fisher's approval Churchill now told Carden that whereas his original instructions 'laid stress on caution and deliberate methods', they wanted him now to feel 'quite free to press the attack vigorously', as Carden had himself suggested. The forts at the Narrows were to be his immediate objective. 'The turning of the corner at Chanak,' Churchill wrote, 'may decide the whole operation and produce consequences of a decisive character upon the war.'

On March 12 the newly-appointed commander of the military forces at the Dardanelles, General Sir Ian Hamilton, left London for the Eastern Mediterranean. Churchill, Hamilton's friend from South African days, arranged for him to travel by a fast cruiser from Marseilles. Before leaving Hamilton saw Maurice Hankey, who wrote in his diary: 'He is in an embarrassing position, as Churchill wants him to rush the Straits by a *coup de main* with such troops as are available in the Levant (30,000 Australians & 10,000 Naval Division). Lord K on the other hand wants him to go slow, to make the Navy continue pounding the Straits, & to wait for the 29th Division.'

Churchill wrote direct to Kitchener that day to ask if Hamilton could land as soon as possible on the Gallipoli Peninsula, to follow up any naval success and to protect the Navy from further Turkish shore fire. But Kitchener said no; the 29th Division must first arrive and be ready 'to take part in what is likely to prove a difficult undertaking in which severe fighting must be anticipated'. Suddenly, for Kitchener, the Turks were no longer the despised and easy adversary. 'I don't see how these concealed howitzers are to be tackled without storming the plateau,' Hamilton wrote to Churchill on March 14, on his way across France by train.

The decisive moment was imminent, yet still the information reaching Churchill made him uneasy. A signal from Carden told of 'unsatisfactory' minesweeping operations 'owing to heavy fire'. Carden added that there had been no casualties. 'I do not understand why minesweeping should be interfered with by fire which causes no casualties,' Churchill replied. 'Two or three hundred casualties would be a moderate price to pay for sweeping up as far as the Narrows.' It was known from intercepted radio messages that the Turks were running out of ammunition, and that the Germans were so worried about the situation that they were contemplating sending out a submarine. 'All this makes it clear that the operations should now be pressed forward methodically and resolutely by night and day, the unavoidable losses being accepted. The enemy is harassed and anxious now. Time is precious as the interference of submarines would be a serious complication.'

As an earnest of the Admiralty's keenness and sense of urgency, Fisher ordered two further battleships to the Dardanelles. On March 15 he and

Hankey discussed how to make the minesweeping less hazardous by some form of smokescreen. It appeared from Carden's latest telegrams that the minesweepers were unable to carry out their task owing to fire from Turkish light guns which could not be located. It might be necessary to put naval units ashore to find and destroy these guns. Churchill appreciated the danger, telling Carden to act in concert with Hamilton 'in any military operations on a large scale which you consider necessary'. No time was to be lost 'but there should be no undue haste'. He did not want Carden to 'push the passage' prematurely. It might be found, he warned, 'that a naval rush would be costly, without decisive military action to take Kilid Bahr plateau'.

Carden decided not to wait for the Army. He would attack on March 18. Then, two days before the attack was due, he informed Churchill that he had been compelled to go on the sick list, and was giving up his command. He was succeeded by his second-in-command, Rear-Admiral John de Robeck. Churchill at once telegraphed to de Robeck, asking him if he was satisfied with the existing plans, 'If not, do not hesitate to say so.' In reply, de Robeck said that he was indeed satisfied, and would carry out Carden's plan to attack in two days' time.

At 10.45 on the morning of March 18 de Robeck launched the naval attack at the Dardanelles. With the aim of pushing past the Narrows and entering the Sea of Marmara, six British and four French battleships entered the Straits and pounded the intermediate forts. By 1.45 not one of the forts under attack was able to return fire. The time had come to withdraw the battleships and send in the minesweepers. As the French battleship *Bouvet* was leaving the Straits it hit a mine, in an area away from the main minefield, and sank. More than six hundred sailors were drowned.

De Robeck continued the action. Orders were given to sweep the minefields in Kephez Bay, and to move forward before dusk to Chanak itself. But the mines had not yet finished their work of destruction. Shortly after four o'clock the British battleship *Inflexible* struck a mine, then a second battleship, *Irresistible,* began to list, and could not move. De Robeck ordered an immediate halt to the action. Then, while covering the rescue of men from *Irresistible,* a third battleship, *Ocean,* struck a mine.

Despite the loss of three battleships, the British casualties had been light; fifty sailors killed and twenty-three wounded during the day's action. But the minefields had not been swept, and the Turkish mobile guns had kept up their fire from both shores. Churchill and Fisher learned of the setback on the morning of March 19. Both were convinced that de Robeck would make a second attack soon; 'De Robeck really

better than Carden,' Fisher wrote to Churchill later that day, 'so Providence is with us.' An enthusiast for action, Fisher now ordered two more
battleships to reinforce de Robeck's squadron. A loss of up to twelve
battleships would have to be expected, he told the War Council that day.
The Council authorised de Robeck to continue the naval attack 'if
he thought fit'. Ministers then discussed the partition of the Ottoman
Empire. Grey wanted to see independent Arab States set up in Syria,
Arabia and Mesopotamia. Kitchener wanted Mecca, the centre of the
Islamic world, to be under British control.

On March 19 de Robeck telegraphed to Churchill that his squadron
was ready 'for immediate action', but means must first be found to deal
with the floating mines. He expected them to be 'easily dealt with'. But
on March 20 the weather was bad, making impossible the necessary
practice 'essential to ensure success'. Then de Robeck changed his mind,
telling Hamilton on March 22 that before he could try again to send his
ships through the Narrows, the Army must go ashore and demolish the
forts. Hamilton was delighted to be asked to help, but pointed out that
his orders from Kitchener were to await the arrival of the 29th Division
from England. That would not be for another three to four weeks.

De Robeck's telegram announcing that he was suspending the naval
attack reached London on the morning of March 23. 'It appears better
to prepare a decisive effort about the middle of April,' he wrote, 'rather
than risk a great deal for what may possibly be only a partial solution.'
Churchill at once drafted a telegram urging de Robeck to try once more
with ships alone 'at the first favourable opportunity'. He should 'dominate the forts at the Narrows and sweep the minefield and then batter
the forts at close range, taking your time, using your aeroplanes and all
your improved methods of guarding against mines'. Intending his telegram to come from all five members of his Admiralty War Group,
Churchill ended it with the words, 'We do not think that the time has yet
come to give up the plan of forcing Dardanelles by a purely naval
operation.' He then went to Downing Street to show the telegram to the
Cabinet. Both Asquith and Kitchener thought de Robeck should press
on. 'The Admiral seems to be in rather a funk,' Asquith told Venetia. 'I
agree with Winston & K that the Navy ought to make another big push,
as soon as the weather clears.'

Churchill returned to the Admiralty, where he found that of the five
members of the War Group, the three most senior, Fisher and the other
two Admirals on the Group, not only supported de Robeck's wish to renew
the attack only in conjunction with the Army, but wanted the telegram to
be held back. Churchill returned to Downing Street, to obtain Asquith's
authority for the telegram to be sent. But despite his personal agreement

with the telegram and support for a renewed naval attack, Asquith was unwilling to overrule Churchill's three most senior advisers.

Momentarily, Churchill contemplated resignation. 'If by resigning I could have procured the decision,' he later wrote, 'I would have done so without a moment's hesitation.' Instead, he sent a personal and secret telegram to de Robeck, asking him to think again, but leaving the decision entirely to the Admiral. It seemed 'very probable', Churchill argued, 'that as soon as it is apparent that the fortresses at the Narrows are not going to stop the Fleet, a general evacuation of the peninsula will take place; but anyhow all troops remaining upon it would be doomed to starvation or surrender. Besides this, there is the political effect of the arrival of the Fleet before Constantinople which is incalculable, and may well be absolutely decisive.' De Robeck would not change his mind. 'To attack Narrows now with fleet would be a mistake,' he replied, 'as it would jeopardise the execution of a better and bigger scheme.' A combined naval and military operation was 'essential' to success.

That night Churchill dined with Asquith. 'The Prime Minister seemed disappointed last night,' he told Fisher on the following morning, 'that we had not sent de Robeck a definite order to go on with his attack at the first opportunity.' But from his brother Jack, who had left the Western Front to join Sir Ian Hamilton's staff, came confirmation that the attack by ships alone would not be renewed. 'The sailors are now inclined to acknowledge that they cannot get through without the co-operation of troops,' Jack wrote on March 25. 'Long range fire on forts is no good unless infantry occupy the forts afterwards and maintain themselves there. Stronger minesweepers are needed against the current. Half the targets are concealed and the ships have the greatest difficulty in locating and firing at the mobile guns.' The aeroplane spotting was 'very bad', as the spotters had little experience.

De Robeck now waited until the assembled Army was ready to attack, when he would help it with his supporting fire. During the military landings which Kitchener planned for April, and during the subsequent nine months of fighting on the Gallipoli Peninsula, the Navy never attempted either to sweep the minefields or to push through the Narrows. Every decision for action subsequently taken at Gallipoli was taken by Kitchener, or by Hamilton and his commanders.

Churchill had become a spectator of events which he had once hoped to dominate and control. Without there having been a naval disaster, without any of the harsh slaughter that had become commonplace on the Western Front, without any conclusive sign that a naval success was impossible, he had been forced to abandon a project that could have knocked Turkey out of the war, rallied the Balkan States against the Central

Powers, given Russia a supply lifeline whereby to renew her own offensive in the East, and ended the stalemate in France and Flanders.

15

Isolation and Escape

More than thirty years after the setback of March 1915 at the Dardanelles, in a phrase which he deleted at the last moment from his Second World War memoirs, Churchill wrote, of his time at the Admiralty from 1911 to 1915, 'It had been my golden age'. Although he remained First Lord, that 'golden age' was over. He was never again to be at the centre of war policy in Asquith's Government. He remained on the War Council and spoke his mind when opportunity arose. But during the final three weeks of detailed planning for the landings on the Gallipoli Peninsula, no War Council was convened, nor did Kitchener send him any of the plans which he was evolving, either for comment or information.

As the time for the Gallipoli landings drew near, Churchill tried to assuage the doubts of others. To Balfour, who on April 8 suggested delaying the landings until the Turkish Army in Syria had been destroyed by a landing at Haifa and an advance to Damascus, Churchill wrote: 'No other operation in this part of the world could ever cloak the defeat of abandoning the effort at the Dardanelles. I think there is nothing for it but to go through with the business, & I do not at all regret that this should be so. No one can count with certainty upon the issue of a battle. But here we have the chances in our favour, & play for vital gains with non-vital stakes.' To his brother Jack, Churchill wrote six days before the Gallipoli landings: 'This is the hour in the world's history for a fine feat of arms, and the results of victory will amply justify the price. I wish I were with you. It would be easier than waiting here.'

In Conservative circles, and in Parliament, voices were being raised that Churchill had been responsible, through lack of foresight, for the failure of the naval attack on March 18. These criticisms were the start of what was to become a widespread public belief that Churchill had neglected basic safeguards, overruled his advisers and bullied the Admirals at the Dardanelles. The first specific charge was that he had failed to foresee the danger of the floating mines. On April 24, in his defence, he circulated to the Cabinet the Admiralty orders to Carden of February 5, in which a specific warning was given about these mines, and suggestions made to counter them. But throughout the Dardanelles debate, beginning during the campaign itself and continuing for more than half a century, memoranda and documents were never to have the power of rumour and malice, or of the need for a scapegoat.

On April 22 an Intelligence report reached London, originating in the Austro-Hungarian Embassy in Constantinople, that the Turks did not have enough ammunition at the Dardanelles to repulse two further naval attacks similar to that of March 18. Encouraged by this, and after consulting with Fisher, Churchill sent de Robeck a telegram suggesting that even now a renewed assault on the Narrows might well be successful. 'Of course you are free to act as you think fit,' Churchill assured him. 'So I mark this telegram personal, as intention of all we say is merely to be helpful and a guide, and not a hard and fast instruction.'

De Robeck had no desire to go back on his decision of a month earlier not to try to force the Dardanelles by ships alone. He saw his sole task now as helping the Army to get ashore and to that task he was steadfastly bound. The 29th Division had at last arrived, and on April 25 the assault on the Gallipoli Peninsula began. More than 30,000 men were put ashore on the first day. Many of them, pinned down on the beaches by Turkish machine-gun fire, fought bravely to reach the cliff-tops. This they did, but were unable to push inland to their first day's objective, the high ground overlooking the Turkish forts on the European shore. There were two sets of landings, one at Cape Helles on the southern tip of the Peninsula, the other at Gaba Tepe further north. Because of an error of navigation the Gaba Tepe force landed not at the lowest, and shortest, crossing-point of the Peninsula, where there were no cliffs to climb, but further north, below a high ridge that barred its way forward, and led only to higher obstacles further inland.

At one of the beaches at Cape Helles, Y Beach, the soldiers landing there, who were more in number than the Turkish force then in the whole Cape Helles area, after landing unopposed, reached the cliff-top above the beach without incident. There they found no Turks at all in front of them, but their message asking what to do next was never answered. Instead of moving inland, unopposed, they waited. Then, after twelve hours, Turkish troops arrived. The British drove them off, nor were the Turks able to return. But then, still without orders from their senior officers, the British soldiers panicked, fearful of the unknown, and within three hours all of them had walked back down to the beach and returned to their ship.

On the morning of April 26, readers of *The Times* not only read the first, highly romanticised, accounts of the battle, but also an obituary of the poet Rupert Brooke, who had died of blood poisoning while still in reserve on one of the Greek Islands in the Aegean. The obituary was written by Churchill, who had met Brooke at the time of his application to join the Royal Naval Division, then on its way to Antwerp. 'Rupert Brooke is dead,' the obituary began. 'A telegram from the Admiral at Lemnos tells us that his life has closed at the moment when it seemed to have reached its springtime. A voice had become audible, a note had been struck, more true, more thrilling, more able to do justice to the nobility of our youth in arms engaged in this present war, than any other – more able to express their thoughts of self-surrender, and with a power to carry comfort to those who watched them so intently from afar. The voice has been swiftly stilled. Only the echoes and the memory remain; but they will linger.'

After five days of muddle, confusion and often intense fighting at Gallipoli, the beachheads and cliff-tops had been secured, but little more. At Cape Helles the 29th and Royal Naval Divisions were never to reach their first day's objective, or to overlook the Narrows. At Gaba Tepe, the Australian and New Zealand troops were likewise never to reach their first day's objective, overlooking the Sea of Marmara. A vast army was ashore, but it was not in the positions needed to help the Navy advance through the Narrows. The Turkish forts were many miles from the men ashore, in no danger of being attacked from the rear.

The Navy, however, did not feel that it had done badly during the landings; Jack Churchill, who had watched the battle from on board ship, reported to his brother: 'The Navy has never had such a time. They dug great chunks out of the hills with their lyddite. Things are going very well, and I hope ships will be in the Sea of Marmara in a fortnight.' Jack added, 'I think de Robeck will have a try to get through as soon as possible.' He was right; de Robeck had not given up his aim of renewing the naval action. 'The Fleet are all ready to have another attack on the Chanak defences,' he wrote to Churchill on April 28, '& only await the right moment.' Meanwhile, minesweeping was continuing.

When a second naval attack might be possible, de Robeck did not say. Nor was the Army's news encouraging. On April 29 de Robeck wrote to Churchill of the 'exhausted condition of troops who have been fighting continuously since dawn on 25th'. On May 2 he reported that the Indian Brigade which had landed at Helles was 'digging in'. A Turkish night attack at Helles was driven off, as was a second night attack on May 3. The British were on the defensive. On the night of May 4, after a panic among black French troops from Senegal caused a gap in the line, a battalion of the Royal Naval Division had been hurriedly moved forward to fill the gap.

Allied stores and landing places were still being shelled by the Turks. 'The Turk can bring his men from Asia Minor etc.,' Jack Churchill told his brother on May 5, 'for nothing threatens him, and most important of all, he can release the divisions from Constantinople and send them down here to crush us.' In an attempt to try to reach the first day's objectives, on May 6 Hamilton launched a renewed attack. It failed to make serious headway. On the following day, when French troops had tried to advance at Helles, Jack Churchill watched in horror as the Turks 'poured in a terrible fire of heavy guns – I suspect "Jack Johnsons" as in France – they did not spare their own men, and Turk & French were blown to bits together'. Jack added, in his letter written on May 9: 'In this war the wounded are very prominent. As you land you have to step over stretchers on the little improvised jetty, and there seem to be blood and bandages all over the beach.'

Churchill was in France on the day Jack wrote this letter. He had gone there three days earlier to help negotiate an Anglo-Italian Naval Convention, part of the agreement whereby Italy would enter the war on the side of the Entente. On May 9 he spent the day in the battle zone, watching the massive, unsuccessful British attack at Aubers Ridge. He too was later to recall the 'hideous spectacle' of the wounded: 'More than a thousand suffering from every form of horrible injury, seared, torn, pierced, choking, dying, were being sorted according to their miseries into the different parts of the convent at Merville. At the entrance, the arrival and departure of the motor ambulances, each with its four or five shattered and tortured beings, was incessant: from the back door corpses were being carried out at brief intervals to a burying party constantly at work.' Everywhere Churchill looked was 'blood and bloody rags. Outside in the quadrangle the drumming thunder of the cannonade proclaimed that the process of death and mutilation was still at its height'.

Churchill returned to London on May 10. Awaiting him was a telegram from de Robeck, asking whether 'by forcing the Dardanelles' the Navy could 'ensure the success' of the military operations now at a stalemate. De Robeck's fear, however, was that on land the Army would not be able to take advantage of a naval success and reach its April 25 objectives, while at sea the Turks would be able to 'close' the Straits behind the Fleet.

Unwilling to endanger the Army by a naval advance beyond the Narrows, after which the fleet would be unable to return to help the Army, Churchill decided on May 11 that all he could do was to encourage de Robeck to try to clear the minefields and then to advance as far as the Narrows, destroying the forts there. Fisher, however, refused to agree even to this limited action. Angered by Churchill's very request, he told him that he would resign if any naval action was taken at the Dardanelles 'until the shores have been effectively occupied'.

Fisher also gave Hankey a verbal message for Asquith, saying that he would resign if there were any action by ships alone. Asquith told Hankey that he thought it 'a very foolish message', but, seeking to calm him, sent a message back that no separate naval action would be taken without Fisher's 'concurrence'. Churchill also tried to deflect Fisher from resignation, writing to him that same day, 'You will never receive from me any proposition to "rush" the Dardanelles,' and appealing to him in strong and emotional language:

> We are now in a very difficult position. Whether it is my fault for trying or my misfortune for not having the power to carry through is immaterial. We are now committed to one of the greatest amphibious enterprises of history. You are absolutely committed. Comradeship, resource, firmness, patience, all in the highest degree will be needed to carry the matter through to victory.
>
> A great army hanging on by its eyelids to a rocky beach, and confronted by the armed power of the Turkish Empire under German military guidance: the whole surplus fleet of Britain – every scrap that can be spared – bound to that army and its fortunes as long as the struggle may drag out: the apparition of the long-feared submarine – our many needs and obligations – the measureless advantages, probably decisive on the whole war, to be gained by success.
>
> Surely here is a combination & a situation which requires from us every conceivable exertion & contrivance which we can think of. I beg you to lend your whole aid & goodwill, & ultimately then success is certain.

Fisher seemed set on resignation. Meeting a senior Admiralty official in the street on May 12 he told him, 'I have resigned and I am off.' Churchill still tried to persuade Fisher to stay, agreeing that afternoon that the *Queen Elizabeth* should leave the Dardanelles at once. Churchill knew that it was the presence of this powerful battleship at the Dardanelles, although originally sent there at Fisher's own suggestion, that most worried the Admiral, particularly in view of the possible arival of German submarines. That evening, in Fisher's presence, Churchill told Kitchener that the *Queen Elizabeth* was coming home. Kitchener was furious, losing his temper and describing the ship's recall as 'desertion of the army at its most critical moment'. Now Fisher erupted. Either the *Queen Elizabeth* would come home at once, would come home that very night, or he would walk out of the Admiralty then and there. Churchill bowed to Fisher's threat, telegraphing to de Robeck that evening, '*Queen Elizabeth* is to sail for home at once with all despatch.'

During May 12 there had been Conservative criticism of Churchill's most recent visit to France. He had been in Paris 'on Admiralty business', Asquith told the Commons. Asked to confirm that Churchill had not performed any official duties while at the Front, Asquith replied, 'No, none,' whereupon there were gleeful, angry cries of 'Joy ride!' from the Conservative benches. 'I am sorry such a question should be asked,' Asquith continued, and in defence of his colleague went on to say that Churchill had not been absent from the Admiralty 'more than fourteen days during the whole of these nine months'.

On the night of May 12 a Turkish torpedo boat managed to leave Chanak stern first and, skilfully slipping down the Straits to the British naval positions off Sedd-el-Bahr, torpedoed the battleship *Goliath*; 570 sailors were drowned. Fisher at once insisted that orders be sent to de Robeck, deprecating any further naval initiative. But Churchill was emphatic that if de Robeck wished to advance as far as the Narrows in conjunction with the Army, he must be allowed to do so. He could not leave the Army in the lurch.

On May 13 Fisher asked Churchill to order de Robeck not to take any independent action. Churchill refused, telling Fisher, 'I cannot agree to send a telegram which might have the effect of paralysing necessary naval action as judged necessary by the responsible Admiral on the spot.' He did agree, however, to telegraph to de Robeck, 'We think the moment for an independent naval attempt to force the Narrows has passed, and will not arise again under present conditions.' De Robeck's task now was to support the Army already ashore by protecting the landing beaches and bombarding the Turkish defences.

Seeking to assuage Fisher's anxieties once and for all, Churchill spent several hours with him on the evening of May 14. Together they scrutinised a list of reinforcements Churchill believed were needed by de Robeck to support the Army. Fisher made no complaint. As Churchill left the room, Fisher's Naval Secretary heard him say to the Admiral: 'Well, good night, Fisher. We have settled everything, and you must go home and have a good night's rest. Things will look brighter in the morning and we'll pull the thing through together.'

Fisher went home to bed. Churchill remained at the Admiralty working. Among the telegrams from de Robeck was a request for more submarines. Five new submarines were to be ready in England by the end of the month. Churchill added two of them to the list of reinforcements on which he and Fisher had just agreed. He then sent a copy of the list to Fisher with a covering note, explaining that the list would not be sent to the Admiralty

War Group before Fisher had a chance to see it again, 'in order that if any point arises we can discuss it'. Churchill added, in conciliatory vein, 'I hope you will agree.'

It was well past midnight. Churchill went to bed. On the following morning, May 15, he went to the Foreign Office to discuss final details of Italy's entry into the war. As he returned across Horse Guards Parade to the Admiralty, his Private Secretary, James Masterton-Smith, rushed up to him with the words, 'Fisher has resigned, and I think he means it this time.' Masterton-Smith handed Churchill a letter from Fisher which began, 'I am unable to remain any longer as your colleague.' He would not go into details, but declared, 'I find it increasingly difficult to adjust myself to the increasing daily requirements of the Dardanelles to meet your views.' Though Fisher did not say so, the two submarines for de Robeck had apparently been the breaking point. His letter ended, 'I am off to Scotland at once so as to avoid all questionings.'

Churchill could not believe that the executive head of the Navy had simply walked away from his post. Returning to the Admiralty building, he looked everywhere for him, confident that he could once again set his mind at ease about the reinforcements for de Robeck on which they had agreed the previous evening, and about the two extra submarines. But Fisher was nowhere to be found. Recrossing Horse Guards Parade, Churchill went to Downing Street to tell Asquith what had happened. The Prime Minister saw at once the political danger of Fisher's disappearance; once known, it could lead to a Conservative call for explanations, even for resignations. Taking a sheet of Downing Street notepaper, Asquith wrote in his own hand, 'Lord Fisher, In the King's name, I order you at once to return to your post, H.H. Asquith, 15 May 1915.'

A search was made for Fisher, who was tracked down at the Charing Cross Hotel, five minute' walk from the Admiralty. He agreed to see Asquith and went to Downing Street, where he found Lloyd George also waiting for the Prime Minister, who was at a wedding. 'I have resigned,' was Fisher's greeting. When Lloyd George asked him why, he replied that he would take no further part in the Dardanelles 'foolishness'. He was off to Scotland that night. Lloyd George begged Fisher to remain at his post, at least until the next War Council meeting in two days' time. But Fisher 'declined to wait another hour'. At that moment Asquith arrived, but could persuade Fisher neither to withdraw his resignation nor to return to the Admiralty building. All that Fisher would agree to was not to leave London for Scotland.

A political crisis was imminent. Asquith asked Churchill to write Fisher a letter, to placate him. Churchill did so. 'The only thing to think of now,' he wrote, 'is what is best for the country and for the brave men who are fighting. Anything which does injury to those interests will be very harshly judged by history on whose stage we are now.' As to the specific cause which had led Fisher to resign, he did not understand it. 'If I did I might cure it. When we parted last night I thought we were in agreement.' The proposals for reinforcements for de Robeck 'were I thought in general accord with your views; & in any case were for discussion between us'.

Fisher remained in hiding throughout May 15. When Churchill asked for a personal interview, he refused it. That same day he sent an old newspaper cutting to Bonar Law, underlining the sentence, 'Lord Fisher was received in audience of the King and remained there about an hour.' Fisher had not gone to see the King recently, but the hint was an obvious one; Fisher had resigned. Although there was no letter or covering note with the cutting, the envelope was addressed in Fisher's well-known handwriting. The Conservatives had been alerted to the crisis.

During May 16, assuming that Fisher's resignation was indeed final, Churchill asked the other members of the Admiralty Board if they would stay on. They agreed to do so, the Second Sea Lord being willing to step into Fisher's place. Driving to Sutton Courtenay, where Asquith was spending the Sunday, Churchill told him that this time Fisher had really resigned. Churchill then told the Prime Minister, 'My office is at your disposal if you require to make a change,' to which Asquith replied, 'No, I have thought of that. I do not wish it, but can you get a Board?'

Churchill assured Asquith that he already had a Board of Admiralty willing to serve, under a new First Sea Lord. But it was too late. Bonar Law had decided to exploit to the full the information which Fisher had sent him. Calling on Lloyd George at 11 Downing Street on the morning of May 17, he asked if it was true that Fisher had resigned. On being told that it was, he told Lloyd George that the Opposition could no longer adhere to the Party truce: 'There was a growing discontent among Conservatives at this attitude of unqualified support.'

'He was especially emphatic,' Lloyd George later recalled, 'as to the impossibility of allowing Mr Churchill to remain at the Admiralty if Lord Fisher persisted in his resignation.' On this point he 'made it clear that the Opposition meant at all hazards to force a Parliamentary challenge'. Asking Bonar Law to wait, Lloyd George went along the corridor to No. 10, where he told Asquith that in order to forestall a Conservative onslaught and the collapse of national unity, a Coalition was essential. Asquith agreed. 'This decision,' Lloyd George later recalled, 'took an incredibly short time.'

Unknown either to Lloyd George or to Churchill, Asquith was in the midst of an intense personal crisis. Two days earlier, Venetia Stanley had told him that she was to be married. He had pleaded with her to go on writing to him, but she had refused to do so. Alone for a moment after Lloyd George had left, he wrote to her, 'Never since the war began had I such an accumulation (no longer shared!) of anxieties,' and he added: 'One of the most hellish bits of these most hellish days was that you alone of all the world – to whom I have always gone in every moment of trial & trouble, & from whom I have always come back solaced, healed & inspired – were the one person who could do nothing, & from whom I could ask nothing. To my dying day, that will be the most bitter memory of my life.'

Asquith had now to decide whether or not to bring the Conservatives into his government, ending nearly a decade of Liberal dominance of British political life, and bringing about a sharing of war-making power. 'I am on the eve of the most astounding & world-shaking decisions – such as I would never have taken without your counsel & consent,' he told Venetia. 'It seems so strange & empty & unnatural.'

Churchill saw no need to bow to Conservative pressure. He had a new Board of Admiralty, and had written a speech to deliver to Parliament that evening, describing and defending every aspect of his conduct of Admiralty business, at the Dardanelles and elsewhere, and explaining his relations with Fisher, and why Fisher had resigned. Hurrying to Asquith's room in the Commons, he begged to be allowed to defend himself, and the Government, and to trounce the Opposition. Churchill then read out the names of the members of his new Board. But no sooner had he done so than Asquith told him: 'No, this will not do. I have decided to form a National Government by a coalition with the Unionists, and a very much larger reconstruction will be required.'

Churchill was aghast, all the more so when Asquith went on to ask, 'What are we to do for you?' Suddenly he realised that his days as First Lord were over. Asquith was determined to avoid a Parliamentary crisis. Lloyd George was also keen to take the maximum advantage of the Conservative desire to enter the Government. There were too many issues on which the Opposition could, if it wished, make serious trouble, including a widely publicised account three days earlier of the shortage of artillery shells in France.

To avert a challenge to his Premiership, Asquith had decided to invite the Conservatives not only to join his administration but to enter the War Council. The Conservative leaders were delighted to be offered, at last, some part in the political and strategic conduct of the war. They no longer had any incentive to challenge publicly any aspect of Liberal war policy. But they did have one condition: Churchill must leave the Admiralty. A decade of Conservative hostility was about to be satisfied; the man who had trounced Brodrick in 1901, belittled Balfour in 1904, abused Milner in 1906, mocked at Lansdowne in 1910, and denounced Carson in 1914, would be forced out of his position of authority and influence.

Asquith now asked Churchill whether he would like to take some other office in the new government or would 'prefer a command in France'. Before Churchill could answer, Lloyd George entered the room. 'Why do you not send him to the Colonial Office?' he asked. 'There is great work to be done there.' Churchill was indignant; he wanted a department which would enable him to have some say in the conduct of the war. To be offered the Colonial Office, which in peacetime was one of the great offices of State, was now both a demotion and an insult.

Churchill remained at the Admiralty for ten more days, in charge of Admiralty business. In a series of letters, first to Asquith and then to the Conservative leaders, he pleaded for some position of influence and authority. At first his tone was tough. 'I will not take any office except a military department,' he wrote to Asquith on May 17, '& if that is not convenient I hope I may be found employment in the field.'

On the morning of May 18 *The Times* singled out Churchill for criticism, referring to 'his disquieting personal adventures on the Continent'. As a civilian Minister in charge of a fighting department, he had sought 'to grasp power which should not pass into his unguided hands'. Churchill recognised the force of the warning, writing that day to Asquith, 'If an office like the Colonies which was suggested were open to me, I should not be right to refuse it.' For him to leave for the trenches 'unless you wish it' would be 'to throw unmerited discredit upon the work I have done here'.

It was his work at the Admiralty of which Churchill was most proud, telling Asquith: 'Above all things I should like to stay here and complete my work, the most difficult part of which is ended. Everything has been provided for and the naval situation is in every respect assured. After four years administration and nine months war I am entitled to say this.' That night Churchill invited Max Aitken and F.E. Smith to Admiralty House. Churchill talked with his two friends into the early hours. 'That Tuesday night,' Aitken later recalled, 'he was clinging to the desire of retaining the Admiralty as if the salvation of England depended upon it.'

On the following morning, unknown to Churchill, Fisher wrote to Asquith setting out six conditions under which he could 'guarantee the successful termination of the war'. The first was that Churchill should not be in the Cabinet 'always circumventing me'. Nor would he serve under Balfour. His main condition was that he should be given 'complete professional charge of the war at sea, together with the absolute sole disposition of the Fleet, and the appointment of all officers of all ranks whatsoever, and absolutely untrammelled sole command of all sea forces whatsoever'.

'Lord Fisher madder than ever,' was Hankey's comment. Asquith's view was the same; he told the King that Fisher's letter 'indicates signs of mental aberration!' There was general agreement that, as Churchill wrote to Kitchener four days later, 'Fisher went mad.'

Churchill now tried to persuade the Conservative leaders as to the wisdom of his conduct of Admiralty business. On May 19 he sent Bonar Law the telegrams relating to two episodes from the early months of the war, writing in his covering note, 'I have borne in silence all these anxious months the charge that I am to blame by my interference with the naval experts for the loss of the three cruisers & the faulty dispositions which led to the action off Coronel.' Also on May 19 Churchill went to see Grey and Lloyd George, to ask them if he could publish in the Press a statement he had just written about the evolution of the Dardanelles. They dissuaded him, arguing that it would alarm the public to realise that success there was in doubt.

On May 20 the newspaper proprietor Sir George Riddell, who called to see Churchill at the Admiralty, recorded his anguished conversation in his diary:

'I am the victim of a political intrigue. I am finished!'

'Not finished at forty, with your remarkable powers!'

'Yes. Finished in respect of all I care for – the waging of war; the defeat of the Germans. I have had a high place offered to me, a position which has been occupied by many distinguished men, and which carries with it a high salary. But all that goes for nothing. This is what I live for. I have prepared a statement of my case but cannot use it.'

Churchill then read Riddell the statement which Lloyd George and Grey had dissuaded him from issuing to the Press, to the effect, Riddell noted, 'that every disposition of ships and the decision on every question of policy had been sanctioned by Fisher, and that the naval attempt to force the Dardanelles had been advised by Admiral Carden and confirmed by Admiral de Robeck'.

That night Churchill went to see Bonar Law to show him the same statement and plead to be allowed to stay at the Admiralty. He also gave the Conservative leader a letter in which he wrote, 'I present to you an absolutely secure naval position; a fleet constantly and rapidly growing in strength, and abundantly supplied with munitions of every kind; an organisation working with perfect smoothness and efficiency, and the seas upon which no enemy's flag is flown.'

Bonar Law promised to speak with his Conservative colleagues, but warned that they would not want him to remain at the Admiralty. While waiting for the final Conservative response, Asquith received a letter which spoke up for Churchill, a 'letter of a maniac' was how he described it in one of his own last letters to Venetia. It was from Venetia's cousin Clementine. 'If you throw Winston overboard,' she wrote, 'you will be committing an act of weakness and your Coalition Government will not be as formidable a War machine as your present Government. Winston may in your eyes & in those with whom he has to work have faults, but he has the supreme quality which I venture to say very few of your present or future Cabinet possess, the power, the imagination, the deadliness to fight Germany. If you send him to another place he will no longer be fighting. If you waste this valuable war material you will be doing an injury to this country.'

Asquith made no reply. Nor did he repeat to Churchill his offer of the Colonial Office. On May 21 Churchill made a final appeal to Asquith, to let him remain at the Admiralty: 'Let me stand or fall by the Dardanelles – but do not take it from my hands.' To this letter Churchill added a postscript, 'I have not come to see you though I should like to; but it would be kind of you to send for me some time today.' Asquith did not do so. Instead he wrote to say that Churchill must 'take it as settled' that he was not to remain at the Admiralty. Bonar Law also wrote that day, dashing any hopes of a Conservative softening. 'Believe me,' he wrote, 'what I said to you last night is inevitable.'

Crushed and humiliated, Churchill wrote to Asquith that afternoon, 'I will accept any office – the lowest if you like – that you care to offer me, & will continue to serve in it in this time of war until the affairs in which I am deeply concerned are settled satisfactorily, as I think they will be.'

'Count on me absolutely – if I am of any use,' Churchill wrote to Asquith in a second letter that day. 'If not, some employment in the field.' Two days later Asquith offered to make him Chancellor of the Duchy of Lancaster, a non-departmental post of an entirely ornamental nature, but retaining his seat at the War Council. Churchill accepted.

For two more days Churchill remained at the Admiralty. One of those who called on him was Kitchener; he was in sympathetic mood and spoke for a while about the work he and Churchill had done together. Then, as he got up to leave, he turned to Churchill with the words, 'Well, there is one thing at any rate they cannot take from you. The Fleet was ready.'

Churchill's days as First Lord of the Admiralty were over. Most commentators assumed that his career was likewise over. But the Editor of the *Observer*, J.L. Garvin, wrote of him with confidence: 'He is young. He has lion-hearted courage. No number of enemies can fight down his ability and force. His hour of triumph will come.' Leaving Admiralty House, Churchill moved with Clementine and their three children into his brother's home at 41 Cromwell Road, opposite the Natural History

Museum. His brother was at the Dardanelles; his wife Lady Gwendeline and their two sons found room for the newcomers and made them welcome. But Churchill was devastated by the failure of the Dardanelles plan. 'He always believed in it,' Clementine later recalled. 'When he left the Admiralty he thought he was finished. I thought he would never get over the Dardanelles. I thought he would die of grief.'

Churchill now had plenty of time for reflection and for trying to work out what had gone wrong. 'If I have erred,' he wrote to Hankey that June, 'it has been in seeking to attempt an initiative without being sure that all the means & powers to make it successful were at my disposal.' From the Antwerp expedition to the Dardanelles, 'nowhere has there been design & decision'. Now, at the Dardanelles, 'without decision & design a very terrible catastrophe may ensue'.

Throughout the summer, Kitchener was making plans for a renewed land-attack on the Gallipoli Peninsula. Balfour, Churchill's successor at the Admiralty, gave naval support for the land army as Churchill had done; one of his first acts was to agree to the despatch of two extra submarines, the specific reinforcements which had led Fisher to resign. Churchill often spoke at the War Council, now renamed the Dardanelles Committee, about his ideas for resuming the land offensive and reaching the forts, so that the Navy could then try once more to get through the Narrows. But his views had no force; he had no War Staff to examine or elaborate them; he had no great Department of State with its budget and its personnel.

Repeatedly, Churchill felt obliged to defend his past work as First Lord. Speaking at Dundee on June 5 he told his constituents: 'The archives of the Admiralty will show in the utmost detail the part I have played in all the great transactions that have taken place. It is to them that I look for my defence.' He also demanded 'a greater element of leadership and design in the rulers'; he himself was so clearly an outsider now. In return for the sacrifices which all were prepared to make, the need was for action: 'Action, not hesitation; action, not words; action, not agitation. The nation awaits its orders. The duty lies upon the Government to declare what should be done.'

In his peroration, Churchill returned to the optimism and vision which had been a noted feature of his speeches after the outbreak of war: 'Look forward, do not look backward. Gather afresh in heart and spirit all the energies of your being, bend anew together for a supreme effort. The times are harsh, the need is dire, the agony of Europe is infinite; but the might of Britain hurled united into the conflict will be irresistible. We are the grand reserve of the Allied cause, and that grand reserve must now march forward as one man.'

Churchill's appeal was widely praised. 'I am now the master of myself & at peace,' he wrote to a friend, '& yesterday I was conscious that I was not powerless.' He was, however, powerless to influence the course of events at the Dardanelles, watching and fretting and warning his colleagues, but without the executive authority to act. In the second week of June he learned of heavy Royal Naval Division losses on Cape Helles during an unsuccessful attempt to seize the objective of the very first day's landing nearly two months earlier.

With more than six hundred men having been killed, two of the five battalions had to be disbanded. 'Poor Naval Division,' Churchill wrote to his brother on June 12. 'Alas the slaughter has been cruel. All are gone whom I knew. It makes me wish to be with you. But for the present my duty is here where I can influence the course of events.' It was a vain hope. Churchill's influence was virtually non-existent, his warnings to his colleagues seldom heeded. Again and again he spoke at the Dardanelles Committee against attacking the Turks with insufficient troops. Better by far the offensives should be postponed until superiority had been attained. 'I have been having a hard battle all these weeks,' he told his brother on June 19, '& have been fighting every inch of the road.' A new offensive was being planned for early August. 'My anxiety is lest you have not enough men to carry it through.'

Churchill had a deeper anxiety still, telling his brother that 'the certainty' that the war would not end that year 'fills my mind with melancholy thoughts. The youth of Europe – almost a whole generation – will be shorn away.'

As a weekend retreat, Churchill had found a house in the country: Hoe Farm near Godalming, a converted Tudor farmhouse in a secluded hollow. 'It really is a delightful valley,' he wrote to his brother, 'and the garden gleams with summer jewellery. We live very simply – but with all the essentials of life well understood & well provided for – hot baths, cold champagne, new peas, & old brandy'. One weekend, his sister-in-law Lady Gwendeline set up her easel at Hoe Farm. He was intrigued, and she, seeing him watching her, wondered if it might be possible to lessen his gloom by encouraging him to take up painting. She suggested that he use her young sons' watercolour paints and showed him the first steps. As he concentrated on the canvas his cares seemed to evaporate. He had found a release for his tension and depression.

A week later Churchill invited Hazel Lavery to Hoe Farm. The wife of the painter Sir John Lavery, she was a painter in her own right and an enthusiast. When she arrived that day Churchill was already at his easel; he had bought it that week together with oil paints, palette, turpentine and brushes. He was intending to paint the scene in front of the house: the drive, the pond, the bushes beyond, the trees and the sky. Later he recalled how his visitor stepped from her car and exclaimed, as she saw him at his easel, 'Painting! But what are you hesitating about. Let me have a brush – the big one.' Then, Churchill recalled, 'Splash into the turpentine, wallop into the blue and white, frantic flourish on the palette – clean no longer – then several large, fierce strokes and slashes of blue on the absolutely cowering canvas. Anyone could see that it could not hit back. No evil fate avenged the jaunty violence.'

Lady Lavery had done her work well. 'The canvas grinned in helplessness before me,' Churchill wrote. 'The spell was broken. The sickly inhibitions rolled away. I seized the largest brush and fell upon my victim with berserk fury. I have never felt in awe of a canvas since.'

Edward Marsh, who was still with Churchill at the Duchy of Lancaster as he had been since their Colonial Office days almost a decade earlier, was present during these first experiments in painting. The 'new enthusiasm', he later wrote, 'was a distraction and a sedative that brought a measure of ease to his frustrated spirit'. The Treasury had given Churchill a room at 19 Abingdon Street, opposite the House of Lords; he had been allowed to retain Marsh's services and also those of his Admiralty shorthand-writer, Harry Beckenham. But his frustration was acute, accentuated at the beginning of July, when he asked Asquith if he could accompany the Prime Minister to the forthcoming Ministerial discussion on inter-Allied strategy at Calais. Asquith said no.

A week later there seemed an upsurge in Churchill's fortunes; Kitchener asked him if he would visit the Dardanelles, to give a Ministerial opinion on conditions and prospects before the coming August offensive. Both Asquith and Balfour gave their approval. In making preparations for the journey, Churchill promised his insurance broker that he would not take an 'active part in the fighting'. But he was aware that 'my mission may in certain circumstances be extended, and that I may have to visit the Balkan States.' Realising that he would be at risk from Turkish shell-fire while on the Gallipoli Peninsula, Churchill wrote out a letter to be given to Clementine 'in the event of his death'. After explaining that his insurance policies would protect her financially, and that his stocks and shares would pay his bills and overdraft, he wrote in the letter: 'I am anxious that you should get hold of all my papers, especially those which refer to my Admiralty administration.' He had appointed her his literary executor. Masterton-Smith would help her 'to secure all that is necessary for a complete record'. His letter continued:

*There is no hurry; but some day I should like the truth to be known.
Randolph will carry on the lamp.*

*Do not grieve for me too much. I am a spirit confident of my rights.
Death is only an incident, & not the most important which happens to us
in this state of being. On the whole, especially since I met you, my darling
one, I have been happy, & you have taught me how noble a woman's heart
can be.*

*If there is anywhere else, I shall be on the look out for you. Meanwhile
look forward, feel free, rejoice in life, cherish the children, guard my
memory. God bless you.*

Churchill spent Sunday June 18 at Hoe Farm, saying goodbye to his
family. On the following day at Downing Street he stayed for a few minutes
in the Cabinet room after the Cabinet had ended, to say goodbye to
Asquith, Kitchener and Grey. As they were shaking his hand and wishing
him luck, Curzon, one of the new Conservative Ministers, unexpectedly
returned. Where, he asked, was Churchill going, that he needed to be
wished good luck?

Curzon was told; he gave the visit his blessing and hurried away to tell
his fellow Conservative Ministers about it. They were aghast. Bonar Law,
whose veto had effectively driven Churchill from the Admiralty two
months earlier, at once informed Asquith that he and his friends feared a
political crisis if Churchill were sent on such a mission. Knowing the
strength of Conservative hostility, Churchill at once wrote to Asquith to
say that he would not go. 'I am extremely sorry,' Asquith replied, 'believing, as I do, that you would have been able to render a very real service to
the Government & the country.'

In the following weeks Churchill asked several times at the Dardanelles
Committee about munition supplies at Gallipoli and the long-term aim of
the August attack. He received no replies, and was at no time brought into
the military or naval discussions. An appeal to Balfour to consider using
British air power to bomb munition factories at Constantinople received
no answer. Nor did anything come of Churchill's hope that summer that
he might be appointed Minister of a special Air Department, independent
of the Army and Navy. Such a 'British Air Service', he told Asquith, could
by the end of the year be made 'indisputably the largest, most efficient and
most enterprising of any belligerent power'.

On July 15 Churchill confided to a young Liberal friend, Sir Archibald
Sinclair, with whom before the war he had shared an enthusiasm for
flying, and who was now serving as an infantry officer on the Western
Front, 'I do not want office, but only war direction.' But he did not see that
he would ever get it. 'Everything else – not that. At least so I feel in my evil

moments,' and he went on to tell Sinclair: 'I am profoundly unsettled: &
cannot use my gift. Of that last I have no doubts. I do not feel that my
judgments have been falsified, or that the determined pursuance of my
policy through all the necessary risks was wrong. I would do it all again if
the circumstances were repeated. But I am faced with the problem of
living through days of twenty-four hours each day: & averting my mind
from the intricate business which I had in my hand – which was my life.'

New military landings and a renewed offensive on the Gallipoli Peninsula were planned for August 6. Three days earlier Churchill wrote to his
brother: 'There are so many "able men" in this Cabinet that it is very
difficult to get anything settled. The parties hold each other in equipoise.
The tendency to the negative is very pronounced. Never mind. They are
in the Dardanelles up to their necks now, & you have only to go forward.'
He was 'soberly hopeful' that the new attack would succeed, but had no
illusions as to the cost. 'The losses will no doubt be cruel: but better there,
where victory will be fruitful, than in the profitless slaughter pit of Ypres.'

The new Gallipoli landings took place at Suvla Bay. 'Now is the moment
I would have loved you to be here,' Hamilton wrote to Churchill on the
eve of the attack. 'I am sure you would have done everyone good going
down the trenches and cheering up the men.' To Kenneth Dundas, with
whom he had gone big-game hunting in East Africa in 1908, and who was
to take part in the new assault with the Royal Naval Division, Churchill
wrote on August 6, 'I trust and earnestly hope that by the time this letter
reaches you the situation will have altered materially in our favour.' His
letter was later returned to him, its envelope marked with the additional
word 'Killed'. Dundas had died in action on August 7, leaving a four-year-
old son.

The objectives of August 6 were never reached. Despite almost no
Turkish opposition at Suvla Bay on the day of the landings, the British
officers hesitated to lead their men forward. Chunuk Bair, the ridge they
had been sent to capture, was not yet manned by the Turks, but while the
British troops halted in the wide plain, the ridge was quickly manned, and
then tenaciously defended. After four days of fierce hand-to-hand fighting, all hope of pressing beyond it to the Narrows, and of enabling the
Fleet at long last to push through into the Sea of Marmara, had come to
nothing.

Churchill received a full account of the battle from his brother. On the
plain at Suvla, Jack had come across the general in command of one of the
two divisions specially sent out for the new landings. 'He seemed apathetic.
I understood that the Brigadiers had said that they could not do any more
and so on. Everybody seemed to have "turned it down". The apathy of the
senior officers had spread to the men.' As to those men, Jack told his

brother: 'From reading all the stories of the war they have learned to regard an advance of 100 yards as a matter of the greatest importance. They landed and advanced a mile & thought they had done something wonderful. They had no standard to go by – no other troops were there to show them what was right. They seemed not to know what they should do.'

Churchill pressed for one further military effort at Gallipoli, but not, he insisted, before at least 20,000 fresh troops had been brought to the Peninsula from Egypt. At the same time he warned against any attempt to renew the offensive on the Western Front, where the German defences had been 'continually strengthened' but where heavy guns and ammunition had not been 'correspondingly accumulated by the Allies'. His views were ignored. On August 21, at Gallipoli, using as Kitchener wished only those troops who had taken part in the earlier attack, Hamilton launched a further assault towards the summit of Chunuk Bair. It was a failure. Churchill now proposed a renewed naval attack, but Balfour turned the idea down. He also declined a request by Churchill to circulate to the Cabinet a note of the provisions that should be made to deal with coming winter weather at the Dardanelles.

Early in September, Sir John French suggested that Churchill might take command of a Brigade on the Western Front. Churchill was relieved, asking Asquith if he could leave the Government and go to France. Aware of the extent to which Churchill's counsel now went unheeded, Asquith was sympathetic. Kitchener, however, vetoed the plan. He had not minded Churchill taking temporary charge at Antwerp, or going on a brief mission to the Dardanelles, but he did not want him in permanent command. Disappointed, Churchill wrote to Asquith, 'I was too much influenced by French who is always so kind to me; & I saw – for a moment – an escape from a situation which on various grounds, public & private, I dislike increasingly as the days pass by.'

Since his removal from the Admiralty, Churchill had been tormented by verbal and newspaper attacks. It was as if all the errors of the naval war from August 1914 until May 1915, as well as the military campaign on the Gallipoli Peninsula, should be ascribed to him. Two days after learning that he could not take a military command in France, he asked Asquith to give Parliament the documents relating to each of the controversial episodes. 'I am repeatedly made the object of very serious charges in all these matters,' he wrote, 'which have never been contradicted, & seem in some way to be confirmed by my leaving the Admiralty.' Sometimes the charges appeared in print, 'but much more are they kept alive by conversation, or by constant references in newspaper articles; & there is no doubt whatever that the belief is widespread that I personally acted in these events wrongfully & foolishly.'

Asquith declined to present the facts to Parliament. Churchill then decided to circulate to his Cabinet colleagues three bulky sets of telegrams relating to those episodes, including Coronel, Antwerp and the Dardanelles, 'with regard to which misconception exists'. Churchill had faith in the ability of documents to convince his critics. Later these same documents were to form the basis of the first two volumes of his memoirs of the First World War. But already he was being taunted at public meetings by the cry 'What about the Dardanelles?' No amount of historical documentation, however accurate, detailed or convincing, was to make that cry go away, or end the suspicions that lay behind it.

On September 21, as the first Ministerial discussions began about withdrawing troops from the Dardanelles, Churchill wrote to a friend, 'It is odious to me to remain here watching sloth & folly, with full knowledge & no occupation.' That day, he proposed landing sufficient troops on the Asiatic shore of the Straits, in order to make 'a dash on Chanak'. Nine days later, on learning of the terrible losses incurred on the Western Front during the renewed offensive which he had earlier opposed, he told a friend, 'With one quarter of the military effort which has been needed to take the village of Loos, we should have been able to get through the Narrows.' A day later Churchill wrote to Lloyd George, 'The same effort and expenditure which had given us the village of Loos would have given us Constantinople and command of the Eastern world.'

Among those killed at Loos was Captain William Sheridan, the husband of Churchill's cousin Clare; their son had been born five days before his father's death.

Throughout October the Dardanelles Committee discussed whether or not to evacuate the Gallipoli Peninsula. The failure to reach a decision angered Churchill considerably. 'The soldiers who are ordered to their deaths have a right to a plan, as well as to a cause,' he wrote in a memorandum which, in the end, he decided not to circulate. On October 20 he sent his colleagues a proposal to use mustard gas in a final attempt to break through the Turkish defences. Given the massacre of Armenians by Turks, as well as the killing of many British soldiers after they had tried to surrender, he hoped 'that the unreasonable prejudice against the use by us of gas upon the Turks will cease'. Large installations of gas should be sent to Gallipoli 'without delay'. The winter season at the Dardanelles was frequently marked by south-westerly gales 'which would afford a perfect opportunity for the employment of gas by us'.

Churchill's suggestion was ignored. So too were his call for compulsory military service and his suggestion, made privately to Asquith, that, in order to secure a more effective prosecution of the war, Kitchener should be replaced at the War Office by Lloyd George. At the end of October, amid public criticisms of Government inefficiency of the sort Churchill had repeatedly voiced in the secrecy of the Cabinet, Asquith announced that he would replace the Dardanelles Committee by a small policy-making body of three; himself, Kitchener and Balfour. Without a Government department to lead, Churchill would have no secret forum in which even to offer his counsel. Hankey suggested to Asquith that he be sent on a mission to Russia, 'to buck up communications of Archangel & Vladivostok for importation of rifles and munitions' but nothing came of this. Later that week Churchill again raised the possibility of a department involving aerial warfare. This too came to nothing, and on October 30 he offered his resignation, telling Asquith that the change in the system of war direction 'deprives me of rendering useful service'.

Hoping that Asquith would defend his part in the Dardanelles operation when he made a statement about the history of the operation to the Commons on November 2, Churchill provided him with a dossier of documentary material. But while defending the operation in general terms, Asquith neither used the materials Churchill had provided nor defended him from the main charge levelled against him, of overruling his naval advisers.

Churchill had become the scapegoat for the failure at the Dardanelles, even for the period after his departure from the Admiralty, during which he was no longer responsible for the Navy, and even for the land war which was Kitchener's domain. He no longer wished to remain in England. On November 6 he asked Asquith to make him Governor-General of British East Africa, and Commander-in-Chief of the forces there. Surprisingly, Bonar Law supported Churchill's request, telling Asquith that 'we are suffering from the want of brains in the higher commands'. But Asquith declined. On November 11 a new inner Cabinet was created. It would have five members, not three, but Churchill was not to be included. That day he sent Asquith a second and final letter of resignation. He did not feel able in times like these 'to remain in well-paid inactivity'. He had a clear conscience which enabled him to bear his responsibility for past events with composure. 'Time will vindicate my administration of the Admiralty, and assign my due share in the vast series of preparations and operations which have secured us the command of the seas.'

After nearly ten years of Ministerial responsibility Churchill was without a place in the Government. A decade of life centred upon Whitehall and Downing Street, spent in Cabinet meetings and with civil servants, was over. He was still a Member of Parliament, but knew how ineffectual Parliament had become in time of war. In a personal statement on November 15, he told the House of his desire that all the documents of his naval administration should be published, and said, in connection with the

Dardanelles, that if Fisher had not approved the operation 'it was his duty to refuse consent'. He had not received from Fisher 'either the clear guidance before the event, or the firm support after, which I was entitled to expect'.

Throughout the past year, Churchill said, 'I have offered the same counsel to the Government – undertake no operation in the West which is more costly to us in life than to the enemy; in the East, take Constantinople; take it by ships if you can; take it by soldiers if you must; take it by whatever plan, military or naval, commends itself to your military experts, but take it, and take it soon, and take it while time remains.' Churchill was confident about the eventual outcome of the war: 'We are passing through a bad time now and it will probably be worse before it is better, but that it will be better – if only we endure and persevere – I have no doubt whatever.'

The fall of Churchill, for such it was, led Bonar Law to tell the Commons, 'He has the defects of his qualities, and as his qualities are large, the shadow which they throw is fairly large also; but I say deliberately, in my judgment, in mental power and vital force he is one of the foremost men in our country.'

Churchill had decided to join his Regiment in France. Before going he gave a small farewell luncheon party at 41 Cromwell Road. Asquith's daughter Violet, who was among those present, later recalled, 'Clemmie was admirably calm and brave, poor Eddie blinking back his tears, the rest of us trying to "play up" and hide our leaden hearts. Winston alone was at his gayest and his best.'

On the morning of November 18, in the uniform of a Major in the Queen's Own Oxfordshire Hussars, Churchill left London for the Western Front. Clementine had given him a little pillow to make his nights more comfortable. That evening Masterton-Smith wrote to her from the Admiralty, 'With those of us who shared his life here he has left an inspiring memory of high courage and tireless industry, and he carries with him to Flanders all that we have to give him – our good wishes.'

'I did not go because I wished to disinterest myself in the great situation,' Churchill wrote to Curzon three weeks later, having learned of the decision to evacuate the Dardanelles, 'or because I feared the burden or the blow: but because I was and am sure that for the time being my usefulness was exhausted & that I could only recover it by a definite & perhaps prolonged withdrawal. Had I seen the slightest prospect of being able to govern the event I would have stayed.'

16

In the Trenches

On crossing to France on 18 November 1915, Churchill had intended to join his regiment at Bléquin, twenty miles from Boulogne, but when he reached the quayside he found a car waiting for him; it had been sent by Sir John French, with orders to bring him to French's headquarters at St Omer. He managed to go with it first to Bléquin, where he spent a few hours with his friends from his Oxfordshire Yeomanry days, before continuing to St Omer, where he spent his first night as a soldier at the headquarters of the Commander-in-Chief; 'a fine château', he wrote to Clementine, 'with hot baths, beds, champagne & all the conveniences'.

During the evening, French suggested that Churchill should either join his staff as an Aide-de-Camp, or take command of a Brigade at the front, with the rank of Brigadier-General. Churchill opted for the Brigade, but asked if he could first have some experience of trench warfare. 'I have made up my mind not to return to any Government during the war,' he wrote to his brother on his first full day in France, 'except with plenary & effective executive power: & this is a condition not likely to be satisfied. So I propose to do my utmost to win my way in the Army which is my old profession & where as you know my heart has long been.'

Churchill was to go for his training to the Guards Division. On his first full day in France he visited the Division's headquarters at La Gorgue. 'To my surprise,' he wrote to Clementine, 'they have only about 15 killed & wounded each day out of 8,000 men exposed! It will make me very sulky if I think you are allowing yourself to be made anxious by any risk like that.' After only a day in France the frustrations of his previous existence seemed to have vanished. 'I am very happy here,' he told Clementine. 'I did not know what release from care meant. How I ever could have wasted so many months in impotent misery, which might have been spent in war, I cannot tell.'

On November 20 Churchill joined the 2nd Battalion, Grenadier Guards, as it went up the line for a twelve-day spell in the trenches; forty-eight hours in the front line itself and forty-eight hours in reserve. His first night was spent just north of Neuve Chapelle, at the battalion's front-line headquarters, 'a pulverised ruin called Ebenezer Farm'. That evening, he later recalled, 'a dead Grenadier was brought in and laid out in the ruined farmhouse for burial the next day'.

The suspicions of the officers at their new arrival was considerable, but quickly evaporated. The conditions of battalion life, he told his wife, 'though hard are not unhealthy, & there is certainly nothing to complain about in them – except for cold feet'. The little pillow she had given him was 'a boon & a pet'. On his second day in the line he moved from Ebenezer Farm to a dugout in one of the forward trenches. This dugout was not more dangerous than battalion headquarters, he hastened to assure her, 'because frequent walks to and from the trenches over an area where stray bullets are skimming are avoided'.

Churchill's first forty-eight-hour spell in the trenches introduced him to a world whose discomforts and perils he was to share for nearly six months. 'Filth & rubbish everywhere,' he wrote to Clementine during his second night, 'graves built into the defences & scattered about promiscuously, feet & clothing breaking through the soil, water & muck on all sides; & about this scene in the dazzling moonlight troops of enormous bats creep & glide, to the unceasing accompaniment of rifles & machine guns & the venomous whining & whirring of the bullets which pass overhead.' Amid these surroundings, Churchill reflected, 'I have found happiness & content such as I have not known for many months.'

In London, the Government had decided to evacuate the Gallipoli Peninsula. Hankey, who like Churchill had been a persistent supporter of seeing the enterprise through, wrote in his diary that he believed the decision to be 'an entirely wrong one', and he added, 'Since Churchill left the Cabinet and the War Council we have lacked courage more than ever.'

To his mother, Churchill wrote on November 24, while in reserve billets for forty-eight hours, 'Do you know I am quite young again.' Two days later, back in his dugout in the front line, he was annoyed to receive an order to go to a point some way behind the line, where he would be collected by a car and driven to a meeting with the Corps Commander. Churchill was now a serving officer and must obey. As he set off, the Germans began shelling the front-line trenches. 'I just missed a whole bunch of shells which fell on the track a hundred yards behind me,' he told Clementine. Then, after an hour walking away from the front 'across sopping fields on which stray bullets are always falling, along tracks periodically shelled', he reached the crossroads at which the Corps

Commander's car was to collect him. But it had been 'driven off ' by shells, and a Staff Officer who arrived to tell Churchill this informed him that the General had only wanted a chat 'and that another day would do equally well'.

Angry at a wasted journey, Churchill made his way back to his dugout, a further hour walking 'across the sopping fields now plunged in darkness'. 'You may imagine,' he told Clementine, 'how I abused to myself the complacency of this General – though no doubt kindly meant – dragging me about in wind & rain for nothing.' Then, reaching the front-line trenches, he learned that a quarter of an hour after he had left them 'the dugout in which I was living had been struck by a shell which burst a few feet from where I would have been sitting', smashing the structure and killing one of the three men who were inside. 'When I saw the ruin I was not so angry with the General after all.'

Churchill's near escape from death prompted him to tell Clementine: 'Now see from this how vain it is to worry about things. It is all chance, and our wayward footsteps are best planted without too much calculation. One must yield oneself simply & naturally to the mood of the game and trust in God, which is another way of saying the same thing.' Such near escapes, he reflected, were 'commonplace experiences out here'. They 'do not excite wonder or even interest'. He himself was lucky in that the approach of a shell did not 'quicken my pulse or try my nerves or make me bob as so many do'. It was 'satisfactory', he added, 'to find that so many years of luxury have in no way impaired the tone of my system. At this game I hope I shall be as good as any.'

Churchill remained with the Guards for five days in all, spending a further forty-eight hours in the front-line trenches. 'I keep watch during part of the night so that others may sleep,' he told Clementine. 'Last night I found a sentry asleep at his post. I frightened him dreadfully but did not charge him with the crime. He is only a lad & I am not an officer of the regiment. The penalty is death or at least two years.'

It was a period of raw, cold winds; of rain, sleet and snow. During less than a week in the line, two men had been killed, two died of their wounds and eight were injured. 'If my destiny has not already been accomplished,' Churchill wrote to Clementine from reserve billets on November 28, 'I shall be guarded surely. If it has, there is nothing that Randolph will need to be ashamed of in what I have done for the country.'

Churchill returned to his front-line dugout. It was only 2 feet 6 inches high. The Company commander whose dugout it was wrote in a letter home of how Churchill had accepted the wet mud floor and constricted space 'with great cheerfulness and we had a good time. He has forgotten his political legacy from Lord Randolph and thinks much more, I am sure, of the military instincts which have descended to him from the great Duke of Marlborough. The result is that he is strictly amenable to discipline, and salutes the Commanding Officer as smartly as any of us when he comes round. It's a funny world.'

It was in the dugout that Churchill spent much of his forty-first birthday. 'We had a good deal of shelling,' he told Clementine, '& for about three hours the trenches were under bombardment at about two shells a minute. I had a splendid view of the whole entertainment. Splinters & debris came very close – inches – but we only had two men hurt in the Company. They were all very glad to be relieved however, & on our return celebrated my birthday with a most cheery dinner.'

Churchill spent the next eight days with the battalion out of the line, at Merville, beyond the range of German artillery. On December 1 he returned to French's headquarters at St Omer, where he amused those present by referring to himself as 'the escaped scapegoat'. Learning that Gallipoli was likely to be evacuated, he declared that if this was decided upon he would go back to the House of Commons and denounce his former colleagues. Speaking of his position on the Dardanelles Committee between May and November, he said, 'I was one of His Majesty's Servants, but not one of his upper servants.' Noted one onlooker, 'He has lost nothing by being in the trenches, not even his brilliant conversational powers.'

Churchill's inventiveness was also undimmed. It was focused now on the stalemate and cruelties of trench warfare. While at St Omer on December 1, he returned to his idea of a wire-crossing device, suggesting, in a memorandum F.E. Smith agreed to circulate to the Cabinet, that in order to avoid attacks other than by the 'bare breasts of men', there be devised a metal collective shield, 'pushed along either on a wheel or better still on a Caterpillar', which would be 'capable of traversing an ordinary obstacle, ditch, breastwork or trench'. Each shield could carry two or three Maxim guns and be fitted with flame apparatus. The strength of the metal would be such that it would crush the barbed wire in front of it, while nothing but a direct hit from a field gun could stop its advance. Caterpillar shields could also be designed with armoured machine-guns mounted on top of them.

Both Clementine and Lady Randolph feared for Churchill's life at the front. 'If you were killed & had over-exposed yourself,' Clementine wrote in his birthday letter, 'the world might think you had sought death out of grief for your share in the Dardanelles. It is your duty to your country to try & live (consistent with your honour as a soldier).' From Lady Randolph came the warning: 'Please be sensible. I think you ought to take the trenches in small doses after ten years of a more or less sedentary life. But I am sure you won't "play the fool". Remember you are destined for greater things than even in the past.'

Despite the political blows which had fallen upon him, and the dramatically altered circumstances of his life, Churchill did not take the change tragically. 'Here I am,' he wrote to Clementine from French's headquarters at St Omer on December 1, 'after a glorious hot bath, between the sheets in this abode of comfort resting before dinner.' He had sent her an 'all well' telegram 'which should for a while put an end to your anxieties'. His departure from the Grenadiers had been very different from his arrival. 'Then the Colonel thought it necessary to remark "we don't want to be inhospitable, but I think it only right to say that your coming was not a matter in which we were given any choice". But today all smiles & hand waves & pressing invitations to return whenever I liked & stay as long as I liked etc. I took of course a great deal of pains & was on my best behaviour, but certainly I succeeded & I felt almost like leaving a place where I had been for months. Our total casualties in the battalion were 35 out of 700 in six days doing nothing.'

The next part of Churchill's letter concerned the hampers which Clementine was arranging to be sent to him from Fortnum and Mason: 'My dear, where are the bi-weekly food boxes? They can be my only contribution to the messes where I live. We eat our rations & the officers have parcels of extras from home. So there are no mess bills. But I want to put something into the common pot. So do send me some useful & practical additions to our fare. Peach Brandy seems to me to be a hopeful feature in the liquor department.' As to his military future, he had lunched for the second time with Lord Cavan, the Commander of the Guards Division, '& had a long talk with him. He strongly advised me to take a battalion before a Brigade: & this is what I think I shall do, if it is open to me. He spoke of my having high command as if it were the natural thing, but urged the importance of going up step by step.'

Churchill ended his letter with advice on morale and finances while Clementine was living with her sister-in-law and her mother-in-law at 41 Cromwell Road: 'Keep a good table. Keep sufficient servants & your maid: entertain with discrimination, have a little amusement from time to time. I don't see any reason for undue skimping.'

While at St Omer, awaiting news of which Brigade he was to command, Churchill befriended a young Captain, Louis Spears. On December 5 he and Spears visited the French front line near Arras. 'The Germans as usual considerately refrained from shelling,' Churchill wrote to Clementine. The French General whose sector it was gave him a French steel helmet, the superior virtues of which he recognised at once. He would continue to wear it 'as it looks so nice & will perhaps protect my valuable cranium'. Two days after this visit to the front, Churchill drove with Spears to the Belgian coast at La Panne, the extreme flank of the Allied trench line, where he saw the point where the trenches ran down to the sea.

On the return journey Churchill spoke to Spears of his plans to shorten the war by attacking Germany through Holland, or via Borkum. Ever inventive, he also spoke 'of torpedoes fired from seaplanes'. Returning to St Omer he found a letter from Curzon, enclosing a report from Admiral Wemyss, de Robeck's successor at the Dardanelles, of which Curzon seemed strongly to approve, urging a renewed naval attack. Churchill's reaction was to try to support the idea. 'Said things were moving fast,' Spears noted in his diary that night, 'and he might have to return to London.'

But by the cold light of morning Churchill realised that return was impossible. 'It would not have been any good my joining in these discussions,' he wrote to Clementine. 'A fresh uncompromised champion like Curzon had a better chance than I could ever have had.' But Curzon's letter and enclosure had revived 'distressing thoughts'. If evacuation took place amid disaster the facts would be 'incredible to the world. The reckoning will be heavy & I shall make sure it is exacted'. In the event, the evacuation of the Gallipoli Peninsula took place without a single casualty.

To Curzon himself, Churchill wrote cheerfully that to have let 'that melancholy situation of our affairs all over the world slide from one's mind after having fixed it so long in mental gaze, has felt exactly like laying down a physical load', and he added, 'Also as one may be killed at any moment – tho' I hope not – worries great & small recede to remote & shadowy distances.'

On December 8 Clementine returned to the Admiralty building where, helped by Masterton-Smith, she was put through by telephone to her husband at St Omer. Churchill was thrilled to hear her voice, but explained in his next letter that, as a Staff Officer had stayed in the room, 'I could not say much & even feared you might think I was abrupt.'

'There is so much I want to say to you, which cannot be shouted into an unsympathetic receiver,' Clementine wrote on the following day. It was six months since she had last been at the Admiralty. While she was there Hankey came out of Churchill's old room. He said to her, 'In these moments of anxiety & difficulty I miss your husband's courage & power to take a decision.'

Most of Churchill's decisions were now made for him. On December 9 he was told that he was to command the 56th Brigade, with the rank of Brigadier-General. 'Altogether it is a very satisfactory arrangement,' he told Clementine. Before joining his Brigade he was to spend a few more days with the Guards Division, then in reserve at Laventie, studying the supply system. 'I am to follow the course of a biscuit from the base to the trenches etc.' He had spent an evening with his old Company, singing songs 'some of a very sultry character'. From Clementine he had received 'the most divine & glorious sleeping bag'; he had spent the night in it 'in one long purr'. His French helmet was 'the cause of much envy. I look most martial in it – like a Cromwellian. I always intend to wear it under fire – but chiefly for appearance.' Opinion among the Grenadiers, he reported, was that after his Brigade he would be appointed to command a Division.

Clementine was in torment. 'I live from day to day in suspense and anguish,' she wrote. 'At night when I lie down I say to myself "Thank God he is still alive". The four weeks of your absence seem like four years. If only my dear you had no military ambitions. If only you would stay with the Oxfordshire Hussars in their billets.'

Churchill's hope of commanding a Brigade, and in due course a Division, was suddenly put in jeopardy when Asquith informed French that the Commander-in-Chief was himself to be replaced. 'A Brigade or a company in the Guards,' Churchill wrote to Marsh when he heard the news, 'is the same or almost the same to me – during the present interlude. I have fallen back reposefully into the arms of fate, but with an underlying instinct that all will be well and that my greatest work is to hand.' That same evening he wrote to Clementine, 'Believe me I am superior to anything that can happen out here. My conviction that the greatest of my work is still to come is strong within me; & I ride reposefully along the gale.' But his thoughts were still on a return to London in the not too distant future: 'I expect it will be my duty in the early months of next year – if I am all right – to stand up in my place in Parliament and endeavour to procure the dismissal of Asquith & Kitchener: & when I am sure that the hour has come I shall not flinch from any exertion or strife. I feel a great assurance of my powers: & now – naked – nothing can assail me.'

Churchill needed the strength of purpose which this letter proclaimed. A few moments after he had sealed it, Sir John French, who was in London, telephoned to St Omer to speak to him. French had just received a letter from Asquith vetoing his command of a Brigade. 'Perhaps you might give him a battalion,' Asquith had added; a demotion from Brigadier-General to Lieutenant-Colonel, and a reduction in command from more than five thousand to less than a thousand men. Asquith knew that on the following day he was going to be questioned in the Commons by a Conservative MP as to whether Churchill had been promised an infantry brigade, if he had ever commanded even a battalion of infantry, and for how many weeks 'he had served at the front as an infantry officer'? Asquith was determined to dodge this particular attack.

Churchill reopened the letter to Clementine and wrote a postscript, 'You will cancel the order for the tunic!' Then he added: 'Do not allow the PM to discuss my affairs with you. Be very cool & detached and avoid any sign of acquiescence in anything he may say.' The suggestion that he might take a battalion riled him. There was no use in doing so, he told Clementine, except under a Commander-in-Chief 'who believes in me & means in a few weeks to promote me'. The 'risks & labour' of commanding a battalion were considerable. He would be in a situation 'of much anxiety and no real scope'.

On December 18, Sir John French's last day as Commander-in-Chief, he and Churchill had a picnic lunch together in the nearby countryside, then returned to St Omer. There, French told his successor as Commander-in-Chief, Sir Douglas Haig, that he was anxious that Churchill, having been vetoed for a brigade, should at least have a battalion. Haig wrote in his diary: 'I replied that I had no objection because Winston had done good work in the trenches, and we were short of Battalion COs. I then said goodbye.'

Haig then asked to see Churchill. The two men had known each other when Churchill was a young MP and Haig a Major. The meeting went well. 'He treated me with the utmost kindness of manner & consideration,' Churchill told Clementine, 'assured me that nothing would give him greater pleasure than to give me a Brigade, that his only wish was that able men should come to the front, & that I might count on his sympathy in every way.'

It was 'quite clear', Churchill added, that Haig would give him 'a fair chance'. In those circumstances he had consented to take a battalion. On the following morning French prepared to leave St Omer for the last time. After saying goodbye to a succession of generals he opened his door and said to Churchill, who was waiting in the ante-room, 'Winston, it is fitting that my last quarter of an hour should be spent here with you.' They talked together for a while, then, Churchill reported to his wife, 'off he went with a guard of honour, saluting officers, cheering soldiers & townsfolk – stepping swiftly from the stage of history into the dull humdrum of ordinary life.'

Churchill did not think French's dismissal was necessary or right. 'But,' he told Clementine, 'Asquith will throw anyone to the wolves to keep himself in office.' His own mind was set on his battalion, though he did not yet know which one it would be. 'I hope to come to these men like a breeze. I hope they will rejoice to be led by me, & fall back with real confidence into my hands. I shall give them my very best.' As to his inner feelings: 'I think of all the things that are being left undone & of my own energies & capacities to do them & drive them along all wasted – without any real pain.

I watch, as far as I can, the weak, irresolute & incompetent drift of Government policy, and turn over what ought to be done in my mind, & then let it all slide away without a wrench.'

To F.E. Smith, who had entered the Government as Attorney-General in June, Churchill wrote on December 18, 'I find myself treated here with good will and I think respect on all sides: tho' I am usually urged to go home and smash the bloody Government.' Briefly, over Christmas, as no battalion had yet been allocated to him, Churchill returned to London. While there, he dined with Lloyd George, whom he found isolated from Asquith and the true centre of political power. He also lunched with the editor of the *Observer*, J.L. Garvin, Fisher's friend, who pressed for the reconciliation of the two men. 'He is willing to bury the hatchet,' Garvin reported eagerly to Fisher, 'and is out and out for your wonder-ship. Why not reopen the old firm on an agreed programme to the accompaniment of throwing up of hats throughout the country? There would be glory enough there for two and to spare.'

Was this mere fantasy? Churchill was excited during his four days in London at the talk of an imminent crisis on conscription. Returning to France on December 27, he told Captain Spears, who recorded his remarks in his pocket diary, that while in London he had seen Lloyd George, 'who is going to try & smash the Government, when either Bonar Law or LG will be PM, & Churchill get Munitions or Admiralty'. Writing that day to Lloyd George, Churchill exhorted him: 'Don't miss your opportunity. The time has come.'

While waiting at St Omer for news of his battalion, Churchill moved from General Headquarters to the house of Max Aitken, who then held the post of Canadian Eye-Witness at the Front. Their friendship blossomed. Aitken encouraged Churchill to think of a return to office and authority. It was a time when he desperately needed such encouragement; he was never to forget Aitken's faith in him at this low ebb in his fortunes. While Churchill was with Aitken at St Omer, Lloyd George was lunching with Clementine at 41 Cromwell Road. 'We must get Winston back,' he told her, and asked if he would be willing to come back to England to take charge of the heavy-gun department of the Munitions Office. A hundred heavy guns due in March would not now be delivered until later 'owing to want of drive of the man in charge'.

Nothing came of Lloyd George's suggestion. On the Western Front, Churchill now visited two parts of the line he had not yet seen. On December 28 he was at Neuve Chapelle: 'The Germans obligingly stopped shelling it as we arrived & I was able without much risk to see this part of the line, which fills in a gap in my now extensive examination of the front.' On the following day he went with Spears to the farthest part of the British front line, on Vimy Ridge, where the French line began. 'The lines are in places only a few yards apart,' he wrote to Clementine of the trenches on the ridge itself, 'but a much less spiteful temper prevails than on the part of the Guards. There you cannot show a whisker without grave risk of death. Here the sentries looked at each other over the top of the parapet: & while we were in the trench the Germans passed the word to the French to take cover as their officer was going to order some shelling.' Luckily the shells were directed on the communication trench along which he and Spears had arrived 'and not on that by which we were returning'.

On New Year's Day 1916 Churchill learned that he was to command the 6th Royal Scots Fusiliers, a battalion in the Ninth Division. That night, at Merris, he dined with the officers of the Ninth. 'Most of the Staff', he told his wife, had met him 'soldiering somewhere or other & we had a pleasant evening'. Of the twelve Colonels commanding other battalions in the Ninth Division, one had been with him at Harrow and Sandhurst, several others on the various campaigns of his Army days. The commander of the Royal Engineers section of the Ninth Division, Major Hearn, had served with him at the Malakand; in a letter to Clementine from France, he described Hearn as 'an Indian acquaintance of mine – fat, shrewd, placid, sensible'.

As to his own battalion, Churchill told Clementine, it had lost so heavily at the battle of Loos that only one of its officers was a regular soldier; he, an eighteen-year-old, had only joined the battalion a few months earlier. The rest of the officers were volunteers, men who had been in professional life in Scotland before the war, and mostly without experience of trench warfare since enlisting. He would have just two weeks 'to pull them together and get them into my hand'. Helping him in this task would be his young Liberal friend, Archibald Sinclair, whom he had managed to secure as his second-in-command.

Churchill looked forward to his new duties with enthusiasm, asking Clementine to send him a one-volume edition of Burns. 'I will soothe & cheer their spirits by quotations from it,' he explained. 'I shall have to be careful not to drop into a mimicry of their accent! You know I am a great admirer of that race. A wife, a constituency & now a regiment attest to the sincerity of that choice!' His first political thoughts in 1916 were of Asquith. 'I have found him a weak and disloyal chief,' he told Clementine on January 2. 'I hope I shall not have to serve under him again. After the "Perhaps he might have a battalion" letter I cannot feel the slightest regard for him any more.' As for the Dardanelles, Asquith had been 'a co-adventurer, approving & agreeing at every stage. And he had the power to put things right with me as regards my policy & myself. But his slothfulness &

procrastination ruined the policy, & his political nippiness squandered the credit.'

Learning that week that his idea of a trench-crossing caterpillar shield was still not being properly followed up, and that Asquith was still avoiding the introduction of conscription, Churchill exclaimed to his wife, 'God for a month of power & a good shorthand writer.'

On January 4 Churchill was formally appointed to his new duties, with the rank of Lieutenant-Colonel. 'I am very glad to have some work to do, after this long appalling waste of my energies,' he wrote from St Omer, 'tho' perhaps some more appropriate outlet could have been found.' On the following day he left St Omer for the village of Moolenacker, ten miles behind the front line, where his battalion was in its reserve billets. The news of his imminent arrival caused 'a mutinous spirit', one young officer later recalled. Could not the fallen politician have gone to some other battalion? When he arrived, another officer recalled the battalion's 'amazement' at the sight of 'a curious contraption' Churchill had brought with him, 'a long bath and a boiler for heating the water'.

That afternoon Churchill gathered his officers together and addressed them with the words, 'Gentlemen, we are going to make war – on the lice.' He then gave, one officer later recalled, 'such a discourse on *pulex Europaeus*, its origin, growth, and nature, its habitat and its importance as a factor in wars ancient and modern, as left one agape with wonder at the erudition and force of its author'. The lecture was only the start; when it was over Churchill set up a committee of company commanders to concert measures 'for the utter extermination of all the lice in the battalion'. Unlike the Dardanelles Committee on which he had so recently served, Churchill's new committee worked with a single purpose to a clearly-defined goal. The French liaison officer with the Division was summoned to help. Unused brewery vats were found at Bailleul and brought to Moolenacker for a collective delousing. 'It was a terrific moment, and by God it worked,' one officer recalled. The Frenchman, Émile Herzog, was also impressed; later, under the pen name André Maurois, he was to become a distinguished novelist and historian.

Churchill's inner peace was briefly disturbed on January 7, when he read in *The Times* of the previous day of a new political crisis centred upon Asquith's refusal to introduce conscription. 'I must confess it excites & disturbs my mind,' he told Clementine. 'I try however not to look back too much, having not only put my hand, but fettered it, to the plough.' He would yield himself to the work of his battalion 'with suppleness & placidity. But peace out here & crisis at home are disturbing combinations to my mind.'

That same day, in a letter to his mother, Churchill again wrote bitterly of Asquith. 'My feeling against him,' he explained, 'is due to the fact that knowing my work, & having been a co-adventurer in my enterprises (not merely an approver), he threw me over without the slightest effort even to state the true facts on my behalf; & still more that thereafter in all the plenitude of his power he never found for me a useful sphere of acting which would have given scope to my energies & knowledge.' Churchill added: 'If I am killed at the humble duties I have found for myself he will no doubt be sorry, & shocked. But the fact will remain that he has treated me with injustice, & has wasted qualities which might have been used in many ways to the public advantage in this time of war.'

For two weeks, helped by the officers of his headquarters staff, Churchill trained his men for their return to the trenches; only a week had passed since they had been taken out of the trenches at Ypres. During his first full day at Moolenacker he wrote to Clementine that the officers were 'all middle-class Scotsmen – very brave & willing & intelligent: but of course all quite new to soldiering. All the seniors & all the professionals have fallen.' The men were 'full of strength & life & I believe I shall be a help to them'. His determination was effective. 'After a very brief period,' one young officer, Jock MacDavid, later recalled, 'he had accelerated the morale of officers and men to an almost unbelievable degree. It was sheer personality. We laughed at lots of things he did, but there were other things we did not laugh at for we knew they were sound.' No detail of the soldier's life was too small for Churchill to notice. Their discipline and their comfort concerned him equally. 'Instead of a quick glance at what was being done, he would stop and talk with everyone and probe to the bottom of every activity.'

'I have never known an officer take such pains to inspire confidence or to gain confidence,' recalled MacDavid, who was to serve on the Western Front until August 1918. 'Indeed he inspired confidence in gaining it.' But Churchill's own peace of mind was continually shaken by his daily reading of the newspapers. News from home stirred angry reflections. 'Whenever my mind is not occupied by work,' he wrote to Clementine on January 10, 'I feel deeply the injustices with which my work at the Admiralty has been treated. I cannot help it – tho' I try. Then the damnable mismanagement which has ruined the Dardanelles enterprise & squandered vainly so much life & opportunity cries aloud for retribution: & if I survive, the day will come when I will claim it publicly.'

'I so long to be able to comfort you,' Clementine replied. 'Later on when you are in danger in the trenches you will be equable & contented, while I who am comparatively at ease will be in mortal anxiety. Try not to brood too much; I would be so unhappy if your naturally open & unsuspicious nature became embittered. Patience is the only grace you need.' She was confident about his political future. 'If you are not killed, as sure as day follows night you will come into your own again.'

Reading in *The Times* of the successful final evacuation of the Gallipoli Peninsula, and of Carson's speech in the Commons criticising 'the hesitancy, the doubts, the failing to make up your mind' at Gallipoli as a 'blot upon the mangement of this war', Churchill wrote to Clementine on January 14: 'Gradually people will see what I saw so vividly this time last year, but alas too late forever. Thank God they all got off safe. If things never turn out as well as you expect them, it is also true they never turn out as badly. There is no culminating catastrophe: only a cruel tale of wasted effort, life & treasure, & opportunity – priceless & unique – gone forever.'

After a week of marches, drills and inspections, trench discipline, gas-helmet training, and rifle and grenade practice at Moolenacker Farm, Churchill learned that there was to be an extra week in reserve. 'I am sorry there is this further delay,' he wrote to his wife, 'for a war without action is really a dreary affair. But these boys were evidently delighted.' The men were also delighted at Churchill's attitude to discipline. Ascertaining by his first question that one troublemaker up before him had fought at Loos, Churchill dismissed the charge against him. The officers were uneasy at this leniency, but Robert Fox, a twenty-year-old machine-gunner who had likewise fought at Loos, later recalled that 'Churchill was scrupulously fair to any man before him on a charge.' He had heard Churchill cross-examine a sergeant who had brought a man up before him 'with all the skill of a counsel at the Bar. The evidence did not satisfy him, so he dismissed the charge.'

'I have reduced punishment both in quantity & method,' Churchill told Clementine on January 16. He was also concerned, as he had been when Home Secretary, with the entertainment of those whose lives were restricted or confined. That evening he organised a combined sports day and concert for his men. 'I think they want nursing & encouraging more than drill-sergeanting.' Mule-races, pillow-fights, obstacle-races, all were provided, followed by a concert. 'Such singing you never heard. People sang with the greatest courage who had no idea either of words or tune.' The concert was followed by a banquet, during which the men gave a special cheer for Clementine. 'Poor fellows,' he told her, 'nothing like this had ever been done for them before. They do not get much to brighten their lives – short though they may be.'

Churchill had a further reminder of his political plight on January 17, when he saw German aircraft in combat all morning in the sky above his billets. 'There is no excuse for our not having command of the air,' he told

Clementine. 'If they had given me control of this service when I left the Admiralty, we should have supremacy today. Asquith wanted this, but in contact with the slightest difficulty & resistance, he as usual shut up.' Two days later Churchill wrote with passion: 'My mind is now filling up with ideas & opinions in many military & war matters. But I have no means of expression. I am impotent to give what there is to be given – of truth & value & urgency. I must wait in silence the sombre movement of events. Still it is better to be gagged than give unheeded counsel.'

He was writing this letter at six o'clock in the evening, Churchill told Clementine, 'a bad hour for me, I feel the need of power as an outlet worst then; & the energy of mind & body is strong within me'. In this letter he asked her to keep in touch with the nascent political opposition world, including Lloyd George, Carson and Bonar Law, as well as those journalists critical of Asquith's conduct of the war. 'Don't neglect these matters,' he wrote on January 19. 'I have no one but you to act for me.' His political instructions were mixed with requests for home comforts and supplies: brandy, cigars, tinned cheese, new boots, a periscope, a new tunic 'with less baggy pockets'.

On January 23, the battalion's last day at Moolenacker, Churchill entertained his officers to dinner at the station hotel at Hazebrouck. On the following day they moved forward for two days to the village of La Crèche. 'Soon we are going to go close up to the Germans,' Churchill wrote to his four-year-old son Randolph, 'and then we shall shoot back at them and try to kill them. This is because they have done wrong and caused all this war and sorrow.'

Churchill was at La Crèche on the anniversary of Lord Randolph's death. 'I thought much of my father on January 24,' he wrote to his mother, '& wondered what he would think of it all. I am sure I am doing right.' From London came tantalising news of the possible establishment of an Air Ministry. 'Do you think there is a chance even now?' Clementine asked him. 'Of course I would take an Air Ministry if it were offered to me,' Churchill replied, 'provided it carried with it a seat on the War Council. But the PM will never face the minor difficulties of such a departure, & I am sure he knows that his interests are best served by my political or other extinction.'

He was thinking over 'a great many plans', Churchill told Clementine, 'but it is better to go on simply here for a while'. Yet not a single day passed without his mind being switched back to political thoughts. On January 25 he sent a long, personal letter to Lloyd George, noting that Asquith was 'stronger than ever'. The alliance Lloyd George had made with those who supported conscription, Churchill wrote, 'brings to the fore untractable forces & personalities who do not view the world as you do. The Tory

dream & intention is a Tory Government. You get the unpopularity of
conscription with such elements as oppose it. Others get the credit.'

'Will last year's tragedy repeat itself magnified this year?' Churchill
asked Lloyd George. 'Will a half-measure campaign in the Balkans be the
counterpart on a vaster scale of Gallipoli: will the next grand offensive cost
us 500,000 instead of only a quarter of a million men? And all this to the
tune of Islam triumphant in Asia, and at a cost of five millions a day.' Lloyd
George made no reply. He knew Churchill's anguish, but could not yet
help.

The 6th Royal Scots Fusiliers were to hold a one-thousand-yard sector of
the front, at the Belgian village of Ploegsteert, known in British soldiers'
parlance as 'Plug Street'. As infantrymen they would spend six days in the
front-line trenches and six in immediate reserve. On reaching his new
reserve headquarters, a Hospice in the village itself, belonging to the
Sisters of Zion, Churchill was delighted, he told Clementine on January
26, to have been met by the nuns, who said that 'we had saved this little
piece of Belgium from the Germans'. Behind the Hospice 'a British field
piece barks like a spaniel at frequent intervals. But the women & children
still inhabit the little town & laugh at the shells which occasionally buff into
the old church.' That night he persuaded the nuns 'to make their excellent
soup for us – so we are free for the moment from "Maggi" & the rest of
the tabloid class.'

Shortly before daylight on January 27 Churchill was to take over his
sector of the trenches. 'Rest assured there will be no part of the line from
the Alps to the sea better guarded,' he told Clementine. 'It will be watched
with the vigilance that mobilised the Fleet.' Calling his officers from the
farms in which they were billeted, he gave them his code of conduct: 'Don't
be careless about yourselves – on the other hand not too careful. Keep a
special pair of boots to sleep in & only get them muddy in a real emergency.
Use alcohol in moderation but don't have a great parade of bottles in your
dugouts. Live well but do not flaunt it. Laugh a little & teach your men to
laugh – great good humour under fire – war is a game that is played with
a smile. If you can't smile, grin. If you can't grin, keep out of the way till
you can.'

Churchill's front-line headquarters was a small shell-battered farm half
way between the Hospice and the trenches. He had a room in it to himself.
There was also a sandbagged barn in which to shelter when shelling began.
Laurence Farm, as it was known, was to be his home for each six-day spell
at the front. On that first day he spent three hours in the trenches 'deciding
all the improvements I am going to make in them'. In the evening he sent
his wife a list of his culinary requirements: 'large slabs of corned beef:

Stilton cheeses: cream: hams: sardines – dried fruits: you might also try a big beefsteak pie, but not tinned things or grouse. The simpler the better, & substantial too; for our ration meat is tough & tasteless.'

During Churchill's three and a half months at the front, no British or German offensive threatened the line. But the German shell-fire was continuous, and machine-gun and rifle fire a constant hazard. The first two-day spell at Laurence Farm, and each subsequent six-day spell, contained the risk of death or injury. Each six-day reserve at the Hospice brought relative safety, despite frequent shelling of a British gun battery a few hundred yards away. 'The artilleryman – particularly the Boche artilleryman, is a creature of habit,' Churchill told Clementine, '& sticks to the target he sets his fancy on. The guns are so accurate that even a hundred yards away one is safe – or almost so.'

Churchill's portable bath and hot-water tank were still with him, providing him with 'that first of comforts'. In search of decent food, he sent Émile Herzog 'to forage for fresh mutton (I am tired of tough frozen beef)', as well as for vegetables and dairy produce. He had also 'seduced the nuns (don't be frightened) into culinary pursuits'. But the comforts could be rudely interrupted. 'I had just had a splendid hot bath,' he wrote to Clementine after his return to the Hospice on January 29, 'the best for a month, & was feeling quite deliciously clean, when suddenly a tremendous bang overhead, & I am covered with soot blown down the chimney by the concussion of a shell these careless Boches have fired too short & which exploded above our roof, smashing our windows & dirtying me! Well, it is an odd world, & I have seen a great deal of it.' To his mother, he wrote that day that he only fretted when he thought 'of the many things that ought to be done, & my real powers lying unused at this great time'. But she should remember, 'we have only to persevere to conquer'. As for him, 'In great or small station, in Cabinet or in the firing line, alive or dead, my policy is "Fight on".' Meanwhile, she should keep in touch with his friends.

Three of Churchill's friends and former political associates were about to visit France. On the afternoon of January 31 he met them at Max Aitken's headquarters in St Omer: Lloyd George, Bonar Law and F.E. Smith. A young officer who had accompanied Churchill to St Omer later recalled that there had been 'full and complete agreement that Asquith had to be got rid of at all cost'. Lloyd George made it clear that he wanted to be Secretary of State for War. 'I hope he will get it,' Churchill wrote to Clementine. The group he wanted to work with, '& form into an effective governing instrument' was Lloyd George, F.E. Smith, Bonar Law, Carson and Curzon. 'Keep it steadily in mind,' he told her. It was the 'alternative Government' when Asquith's days were over.

Churchill was in no hurry. 'If I come through all right,' he wrote to Clementine from the Hospice on his return from St Omer, 'my strength will be much greater than it ever was. I would much rather go back to the trenches tonight, than go home in any position of mediocre authority. But I should like to see my beloved pussy cat.'

In February Churchill spent three six-day periods at Laurence Farm in the front-line trenches. After dark he would go through the barbed wire into no-man's-land to visit the battalion's forward posts, situated in shell craters between the two armies. One night, as he and his officers approached one of the craters, a German machine-gunner opened fire. 'We all made a dive for the shelter of the shell crater, which was now somewhat overcrowded,' one of the officers later recalled, 'and consequently we had to keep in a crouching position. Suddenly a blinding glare of light appeared from the depths of the hole and with it the Commanding Officer's muffled request to "Put out that bloody light!" It was only a matter of seconds before he realised his crouching posture was responsible for pressure on the contact switch of his own flash-lamp, and corrective action swiftly followed.'

Sometimes shells landed in the courtyard of Laurence Farm. On one occasion, just after lunch, Churchill and his officers were sitting round their table 'at coffee & port wine' when shelling began. One shell landed quite near, 'making the window jump'. They at once began to discuss whether they should go into the shelter of the barn, when, he told Clementine, 'there was a tremendous crash, dust & splinters came flying through the room, plates were smashed, chairs broken.' Everyone was covered with debris and the adjutant, Jock MacDavid – 'he is only eighteen' – was hit on the finger.

What Churchill did not tell Clementine was his own good fortune on that occasion. 'Winston had been toying about with his lamp,' MacDavid later recalled. 'He was sitting playing with this thing when the shell came along. A piece of shrapnel almost split the battery holder in two, it lodged in the metal of the battery holder. It was less than two inches from his right wrist. If it had been any nearer it would certainly have taken off his wrist.'

MacDavid went home on sick leave. On his way through London he called on Clementine and gave her the nose of the shell that had caused such havoc. He also brought her the 'exciting news' that her husband was, temporarily, an acting Brigadier, with his headquarters at nearby London Support Farm, and with the ultimate responsibility for four thousand men. But it was only for forty-eight hours, while the Brigadier himself was briefly elsewhere.

On the first of his two days at Brigade headquarters Churchill received an unexpected guest, Lord Curzon. 'I took him out to my shattered farm,' he told Clementine, '& along my own trenches; & he told me all the news & his view of men & politics in his usual sprightly style.' Fortunately 'we successfully avoided the shells & the machine gun bullets, both of which came discreetly & tactfully in the places which we had left or in those which we had not yet reached.'

On his second day at London Support Farm Churchill was visited by Hugh Tudor, a friend from Bangalore days, who was now a General in the Artillery and had fought at Loos. 'My dear,' Churchill told Clementine, 'what mistakes they made at Loos! You simply cannot believe them possible.' Both men were also critical of the telephone system at the front. 'If we had been content at the Admiralty to paddle along at that feeble pace, we should never have mastered the German submarine. Then of course there ought to be ten times (at least) as many light railways on the front. This war is one of mechanics & brains – & mere sacrifice of brave & devoted infantry is no substitute & never will be. By God, I would make them skip if I had the power – even for a month.'

In reserve again, on February 10 from a new and more comfortable billet, Soyer Farm, Churchill watched Ploegsteert being bombarded. 'The shells hitting the church made enormous clouds of red brick dust which mingled gaily with their white smoke. Other black and white shrapnel burst over the street & struck the houses. Three of our men who were strolling in the town were hit – one fatally – & another sustained a shock from being near a shell from which he immediately died.' In his battalion's first forty-eight hours in reserve it had lost eight men, more than it had lost in six days in the front line. 'I am now reduced to under 600 men instead of 1,000,' Churchill told Clementine. 'There are many other battalions like this.'

Shelling had become the daily danger and normality. On a visit that day with Hugh Tudor to British positions in Ploegsteert Wood, Churchill watched as Tudor's artillery opened fire on the German trenches. Then the Germans retaliated. 'This was the first really sharp artillery fire I have been under, & certainly it seemed very dangerous,' he told Clementine. As well as the shells, the Germans fired trench mortars. 'These you can see in the air; & after they fall there is an appreciable interval in which to decide what you will do. I liked these best of all. I found my nerves in excellent order & I do not think my pulse quickened at any time. But after it was over I felt strangely tired: as if I had done a hard day's work at a speech or article.'

Forty years later Churchill wrote to Tudor, who had reminded him of this episode: 'It was in fact the only specimen of representative front-line bombardment that I had the chance to see. I do not think I should have enjoyed it if it had gone on for eight hours instead of one. However, it stopped when you stopped, with agreeable punctuality.'

Churchill returned to Laurence Farm on February 13. 'It almost seems to me,' he wrote that day to Clementine, 'as if my life in the great world was a dream, & I have been moving slowly forward in the army all these years from subaltern to colonel.' On the following night he went into no-man's-land again '& prowled about looking at our wire & visiting our listening posts. This is always exciting.' Returning to Laurence Farm, he got little sleep. There was an artillery duel going on north of Ypres and he could hear the cannonade 'splintering & snarling away all through the night'. Political thoughts could not be banished by the bombardment. Learning on the following day that Curzon was likely to be appointed Air Minister he wrote: 'I must confess it riles me to see how ungrateful they are. But for my personal struggles we should not have had half the air service we have today.'

On the morning of February 16, Laurence Farm was shelled again, receiving several direct hits. Two men were injured, including one of the five officers of Churchill's headquarters staff. 'We hastily seized our eggs & bacon, bread & marmalade & took refuge in our dugout,' he told Clementine. 'Here we remained while perhaps twenty shells were devoted to our farm & its curtilage.' Breakfast continued: 'It was odd gobbling bacon & marmalade in the dugout, while the doctor bandaged the great raw wounds of our poor officer a foot or two away!' Before being sent on sick-leave, the wounded officer was given as a souvenir the nose-piece of the shell which had wounded him. 'He kissed it!' Churchill reported. 'His joy at leaving almost triumphed over the severe pain of his wounds.'

That day Churchill received an account of the first experimental trials of the tank, of which he had been so early and persistent an advocate. 'You see this idea is bearing fruit,' he wrote to Clementine on February 17. 'But what a toil to get anything done! And how powerless I am! Are they not fools not to use my mind – or knaves to wait for its destruction by some flying splinter? I do not fear death or wounds, & I like the daily life out here; but their impudence & complacence makes me quite spiteful sometimes.'

While at Laurence Farm, Churchill amazed his young officers by setting up an easel and starting to paint. His subjects were the battered farmyard with its shell-holes, and shells exploding over Ploegsteert village. Painting absorbed the mental energies which would otherwise brood on politics. He recognised painting's value to him: 'I think it will be a great pleasure & resource to me if I come through all right,' he told his wife on February 22. But he also reflected that day on the contrast between the Admiralty when he had been First Lord and its mood now, under Balfour. 'How easy to destroy. How hard to build. How easy to evacuate, how hard to capture. How easy to do nothing. How hard to achieve anything. War is action, energy & hazard. These sheep only want to browse among the daisies.'

Churchill had no intention of browsing; while in the front line, the safety of his own trenches was his constant concern; he was emphatic that the parapets must be thick enough to stop a bullet, and the dugouts properly sandbagged. 'I find that everyone has heard of the improvements you have effected in your battalion,' Clementine wrote in the third week of February. 'Soldiers back from the front on leave talk about it.' That week a Colonel whom she knew wrote to her from France, about her husband, 'He is awfully well, better than I have seen him for ages, & full of vigour & vitality & had made his battalion from a moderate one into a d – good one.'

The shelling of Ploegsteert and the reserve billets was now continuous. Even behind the village, near Soyer Farm: 'shells came in pursuit, & riding across the ploughed fields shrapnel kept pace with us in the air', Churchill told Clementine. 'One lives calmly on the brink of the abyss. But I can understand how tired people get of it if it goes on month after month. All the excitement dies away & there is only dull resentment.'

On the previous evening a shell had finally brought down the church steeple. 'So this evening we are smashing up one of their steeples & they are retaliating by scattering their shells in twos & threes.' As the shelling continued, German aeroplanes 'sail about unmolested overhead, watching the shooting, & scorning our anti-aircraft guns. There is no doubt who is master of this air!'

On February 26 Churchill returned for the third time to Laurence Farm and the trenches. Snow covered the ground but inside his heavily sandbagged room was 'a glowing brazier', so that he slept 'warm and peaceful'. On the next day two of his men were killed by British artillery shells falling short. The following day three men were killed by German shells. A sixth man was killed by a German shell on the last day in the line.

Churchill now had seven days' leave. Early on March 2, after his battalion had returned to its reserve billets in Ploegsteert, he hurried to Boulogne, where a destroyer took him to Dover. By nightfall he was at home. He had intended only to relax, see friends, dine at his mother's, go twice to the theatre with Clementine, and, his only public engagement, unveil his portrait at the National Liberal Club, where, he had told Clementine, 'I might make a speech'. Otherwise he envisaged no public event. But on reaching 41 Cromwell Road he learned to his surprise that Balfour was to introduce the Navy Estimates in five days' time. He decided to speak in the debate, to denounce what he saw as the Government's failure to take any initiative at sea, and to set out his own ideas for an effective policy in the air.

Throughout March 3, having set aside his earlier plans for leisure, Churchill worked on his speech. That night his mother gave a dinner for him, to which she invited several of those, including J.L. Garvin, who had been actively trying to repair the breach between Churchill and Fisher. Also invited was one of those most active in urging Fisher's return to the Admiralty, C.P. Scott, editor of the *Manchester Guardian*, who had been summoned from Manchester by telegram.

On the following day, to Clementine's horror, her husband invited Fisher to lunch at Cromwell Road. 'Keep your hands off my husband,' she burst out during the lunch. 'You have all but ruined him once. Let him alone now.' But Churchill was still mesmerised by Fisher, wanted to work with him again, and knew that he was still popular in the country. A month earlier, at the start of a Press campaign to bring back Fisher, Churchill had written to Clementine, 'Fisher without me to manage him would be disastrous.' Now he saw a chance to call for Fisher's return, as well as his own.

On the evening of March 5, Churchill and Fisher met again. Churchill read out the speech he intended to make in two days' time. Not only would he attack Balfour's conduct of Admiralty business and defend his own, but he would end his speech by calling for Fisher's return. At four o'clock on the following morning Fisher wrote to Churchill: 'I've slept over what you said to me last night. It's the epoch of your life! I am going to be the humble instrument! So magnificent a proof of your sole object being the war will have (justly) an immense effect on your popularity. Ride in on the crest of that popularity!'

Clementine was alarmed at her husband associating with Fisher in any way: she regarded his desertion of his post in May 1915 as the treacherous act which had led to her husband's downfall, and feared he would again prove a force for ill. Throughout March 6 she pressed Churchill not to speak in the debate, and to return to his battalion. But he was determined to speak, and was urged to do so during the day by C.P. Scott, whom Fisher had persuaded to see him again. 'I urged that on political grounds there could be no question that he would be more useful in Parliament,' Scott recorded in his diary. 'That as regards the Navy there was not a day to be lost in making good the great and acknowledged deficiencies, and the whole movement for that and also for vitalising the Army – as to which he had strong views – would collapse if he left.'

That night Asquith and his wife dined with the Churchills at Cromwell Road. When Margot Asquith told Churchill she was sorry he was going to speak in the debate, he replied 'with a glare in his eye', Margot told her daughter Violet, that he had 'a great deal of importance to say about the

Navy'. Margot also told her daughter that she was convinced that Churchill was 'dreaming of an amazing Opposition that he was going to lead'. Asquith also tried to dissuade Churchill from speaking, but failed. On the morning of the debate, C.P. Scott called again to see Churchill, who told him that making this speech 'needed more courage than the war of the trenches'. As Churchill put the finishing touches to his speech, Fisher wrote again, fearful that Asquith had persuaded Churchill not to speak. 'Am I already too late?' he asked. 'Providence has placed the plum bang in your mouth. Certain Prime Minister! You have no rival as Leader of the opposition.'

The aim of Churchill's speech on March 7 was to rouse MPs to a sense of impending danger. The Navy lacked drive and foresight; the goals which he and Fisher had established a year and a half earlier had not been met. Germany's ability to make war, and to maintain herself at war, had not been matched. MPs were deeply attentive as he told them: 'We see our own great expansion, but remember, everything else around us is expanding and developing at the same time. You cannot afford to indulge even for the shortest period of time in resting on your oars. You must continually drive the vast machine forward at its utmost speed. To lose momentum is not merely to stop, but to fall.' The country was recovering from the shortage of munitions in the Army, he pointed out. 'At a hideous cost in life and treasure we have regained control, and ascendancy lies before us at no great distance.' A shortage in naval material, 'if it were to occur from any cause, would give no chance of future recovery. Blood and money, however lavishly poured out, would never repair the consequences of what might have been even an unconscious relaxation of effort.'

Churchill then spoke about the danger from submarines, and the need for greater efforts against the growing attacks by Zeppelins. A 'purely negative policy' for the Navy, he warned, 'by no means necessarily implies that the path of greatest prudence is being followed.' Then, with a reference to Fisher as well as to himself, he declared, 'I wish to place on record that the late Board would certainly not have been content with an attitude of pure passivity during the whole of 1916.' In the Air, the Admiralty now had resources 'far greater than those which Lord Fisher and I ever possessed'. But it had not been found possible to carry on the policy of raiding Zeppelin sheds 'which, in the early days even, carried a handful of naval pilots to Cologne, Düsseldorf, and Friedrichshafen, and even to Cuxhaven itself.'

Churchill then came to his conclusion, without which, he said, 'I would not have spoken today'. Nor would he have used words of warning 'without being sure first that they are spoken in time to be fruitful, and secondly, without having a definite and practical proposal to make'. There was 'no doubt whatever' in his mind as to what he should say. 'There was a time when I did not think that I could have brought myself to say it, but I have been away for some months and my mind is clear. The times are crucial. The issues are momentous. The Great War deepens and widens and expands around us. The existence of our country and of our cause depends upon the Fleet. We cannot afford to deprive ourselves or the Navy of the strongest and most vigorous forces that are available. No personal consideration must stand between the country and those who can serve her best.'

What was it that Churchill would propose, Lloyd George whispered to Bonar Law. 'He is going to suggest the recall of Fisher,' Bonar Law replied. 'I could not believe it,' Lloyd George told a friend on the following day. But Bonar Law was right.

'I urge the First Lord of the Admiralty without delay,' Churchill continued, 'to fortify himself, to vitalise and animate his Board of Admiralty, by recalling Lord Fisher to his post as First Lord.' The House was amazed and aghast. Ridicule of Churchill followed at once: 'I do not know how many posts he has had in his short and brilliant career,' one Conservative MP, Admiral Sir Hedworth Meux, declared. 'He has succeeded in them all. He might have done better had he stuck to them, but he never has, and I believe what I say now will be approved of by a very large number of Members in this House. We all wish him a great deal of success in France, and we hope he will stay there.'

Churchill was shattered by the hostile, mocking reaction to his proposal. He nevertheless decided not to return to France. Instead, he would speak in a week's time in the Army Estimates debate, convinced that the failings and shortcomings of the War Office needed to be made public. On the morning of March 8, Fisher called at Cromwell Road to urge him to stay in London and continue his Parliamentary criticisms. During his visit he clashed with Clementine, who doubted whether, as a result of his 'Fisher' speech, her husband could possibly win any support at all in Parliament.

In the Commons that afternoon Balfour reminded MPs, in scathing tones, of Churchill's own statement in November 1915 that Fisher had neither supported nor guided him at the critical moment during the Dardanelles crisis. Churchill spoke briefly in his own defence. Balfour ought not 'to be unduly offended or vexed,' he said, 'at the speech which I made, because, after all, a speech is a very small thing, and a failure of any kind in this matter is a vital thing'. It was right that a note of warning should be sounded 'and sounded in time'. As for his call for Fisher's return, which had provided Balfour with all his 'rhetorical and devastating retorts', the 'real fact is that if we could associate in some way or another the driving power and energy of Lord Fisher with the carrying out of Lord Fisher's programme at the highest possible speed, there is no reason to suppose that great public advantage would not result from that.'

Believing he could still raise real issues of military, naval and air deficiencies, and no longer interested in obtaining a Brigade or a Division, on March 9 Churchill asked Kitchener to relieve him of his military command 'as soon as this can be done without disadvantage to the service'. In the meantime he wanted his leave extended, otherwise he would have to return to France the next day. Kitchener showed the letter to Asquith, who approved. Asquith also saw Churchill that day, reminding him of how his father had committed political suicide through 'one impulsive action'. Churchill replied that he had many 'ardent supporters' who looked to him for leadership. 'At the moment you have none who count at all,' Asquith told him.

When they parted Churchill had tears in his eyes. Asquith was convinced that he would return to France. But on the following day the Government candidate at a by-election in East Hertfordshire was defeated by an independent candidate, Noel Pemberton Billing, a Squadron-Commander in the Royal Naval Air Service who had contested the seat in the interests of a strong air policy. Fisher and Garvin hurried to Cromwell Road to encourage Churchill to stay and fight in Parliament. To their delight they found that he had already prepared a speech for the Army Estimates. He read it to them; Fisher later called it 'incomparable', writing to C.P. Scott, 'I believe the Government will soon be cleared out if our friend remains as he should do, and discourses on the Army Estimates next Tuesday.'

Fisher saw Churchill again on the evening of March 10. Churchill had begun to doubt the wisdom of speaking in the Army debate. On the following morning, reverting to the language which had earlier helped cause their breach, Fisher wrote to Churchill that if 'any specious twaddle about honour or Asquithian jugglery persuades you not to rise from the corner of the Front Opposition Bench next Tuesday to brand the government with the massacre of our troops and the utter ineptitude of the conduct of the war, then I say that you become the "murderer" because you are the only man who can prevent it and voice the removal of Kitchener'.

On the evening of March 11 Churchill and Fisher met again. Churchill had still not made up his mind what to do. Max Aitken tried to persuade him to stay in London and speak in the Army debate, but on reflection he decided to return to France. 'I did not feel able after all to take your advice,' he wrote to Aitken when he was back at Ploegsteert, 'for though my instinct agreed with yours, I had small but insistent obligations here which could not be hastily discarded for the sake of a personal opportunity.' Nor did he feel 'the virtue necessary for the tremendous tasks you indicated. My interests were too evident & one cannot tell how much they sway one's judgment.' What was the 'tremendous task': was it to lead an opposition of disaffected Liberals and Conservatives, seeking Kitchener's and even Asquith's overthrow?

Pressed to do so by Clementine, Churchill agreed to return to France. But he still had it in mind, he told one of Asquith's leading Liberal critics, to come back before the Army debate was over. 'I daresay in about a week I shall be able to return to the House of Commons,' he wrote, and asked if there was any chance of the Army Estimates 'running over into the next Parliamentary week. If so, send me a line and I will once again adjust my mind to the topic I mentioned to you.'

Churchill returned to the Western Front on March 13. On his way to Dover with Clementine he rehearsed the arguments in favour of taking his place with the Parliamentary opposition. Clementine, who four months earlier had been so frightened of what might happen to him in the trenches and so unwilling to see him leave for the Western Front, was now sceptical of his political chances were he to return to London, and afraid of the charges of inconsistency and opportunism that would be brought against him if he were to abandon his battalion a mere two months after joining it. Churchill was not convinced; during the journey to Dover he wrote out a letter to Asquith asking to be relieved of his command. He then gave the letter to Clementine, together with a statement which he asked her to give to the Press Association.

Disconsolate, Clementine went to see Carson at Rottingdean, on the south coast. His advice was to avoid a precipitate return. Churchill crossed to Boulogne, then hurried eastward to Ploegsteert. His men were back in their front-line trenches. During the journey he decided that Clementine had been right. Even if he returned for the last days of the Army Debate, it would seem absurdly opportunist and abrupt. He therefore telegraphed that same night to Asquith, withdrawing his letter. Asquith sent his Private Secretary to the Cromwell Road to retrieve the Press Association statement. Clementine, who had just reached London from Rottingdean, was much relieved.

The withdrawal of the letter was only a temporary respite. Churchill was determined to re-enter the political arena. The only question in his mind was when. 'You have seen me very weak & foolish & mentally infirm this week,' he wrote to Clementine on his first night back in his dugout. 'Dual obligations, both honourable, both weighty, have rent me. But I am sure my true war station is in the House of Commons.' Three days later, back in reserve at Soyer Farm, he asked her to keep in touch with Garvin, Scott and others: 'Don't let them drift off or think I have resigned the game.' Reading, a day later, an account of the Army debate in which he had hoped to take a lead, he wrote to her: 'How different I could have made it! My conviction strengthens & deepens each day that my place is there, & that I could fill it with credit & public advantage.'

On his return to his battalion, Churchill found that he had been rebuked by the Brigadier for 'undue leniency' in punishments. He at once prepared statistics to show that since he took over the battalion, offences as well as punishments had diminished. On the evening after his return he 'took a stroll' up the lines of the adjoining battalions, telling Clementine: 'The same conditions & features reproduce themselves in every section – shattered buildings, sandbag habitations, trenches heavily wired, shell holes, frequent graveyards with thickets of little crosses, rank wild-growing grass, muddy roads, khaki soldiers – & so on for hundreds & hundreds of miles – on both sides. Miserable Europe. Only a few rifle shots & the occasional bang of a gun broke the stillness of the evening. One wondered whether the nations were getting their money's worth out of the brooding armies.'

Could he help to a 'victorious peace' more in the Commons than in the trenches, he asked Clementine. 'That is the sole question. Believe me if my life could materially aid our fortunes, I would not grudge it.'

One more military flutter briefly disturbed Churchill's equanimity: the departure of his Brigadier. Suddenly the promotion he had hoped for since January was a possibility, and in his own Brigade. But the position went to someone else, a Grenadier Guards officer three years younger. This shows, he wrote to his wife, 'that I have no prospects'. He no longer minded, he told her. He now knew what he 'ought to do'. Parliament was his place. 'Do not I beg you suppose that I am incapable of facing the perplexities & risks of the Front Opposition Bench,' he wrote to Garvin from Laurence Farm on March 20, 'or that I shall shrink from decision. But I am naturally reluctant to quit this scene (the more so oddly enough that I can do so any moment) and especially am I 'anxious, when I do return, to do so in circumstances which will be most favourable to my usefulness.'

Clementine hoped that her husband would soon settle back to the routine and challenge of his front-line duties. But he no longer had peace of mind at the front, writing to her a day later, 'Do nothing to discourage friends who wish for my return.' She did what she could to set his mind at rest. 'With patience and waiting for a right opportunity,' she replied, 'the future is yours'. She still wanted him to get a Brigade, and remain in France. 'That is what I hope,' she wrote.

Clementine's letter stirred up in Churchill a fierce sense of the injustice of his exclusion from war-direction. He had resigned his office and given up a salary of £4,300 a year 'rather than hold a sinecure at this time'. He would have served five months at the front 'discharging arduous, difficult duties to the full satisfaction of my superiors & to the advantage of my officers & men'. He had a 'recognised position' in British public life acquired by 'years of public work', enabling him 'to command the attention (at any rate) of my fellow countrymen in a manner not exceeded by more than three or four living men'. The period of Britain's national fortunes was 'critical & grave: and almost every question both affecting war & peace conditions, with which I have always been foremostly connected, is now raised'. He could not exclude himself from those discussions or divest himself of responsibilities concerning them. 'Surely,' he asked Clementine, 'these facts may stand by themselves as an answer to sneers & cavillings?'

Churchill was being eaten up by the anger and frustration of almost a whole year's exclusion from lack of decisive influence or power. But his confidence in his abilities, and in his popularity, was undimmed. 'Do not my darling one underrate the contribution I have made to the common cause,' he wrote to Clementine on March 22, 'or the solidarity of a political position acquired by so many years of work & power. Gusts of ill-feeling & newspaper attack sweep by. But public men who really are known by the mass of the nation do not lose their place in public counsels except for something which touches their private character & honour.'

Clementine mustered the arguments against her husband's 'premature return', and sent them to him in each of her almost daily letters. He was not impressed. 'Have a good confidence,' he wrote, '& do not easily lend yourself to the estimate formed by those who will never be satisfied till the breath is out of my body.' Nothing would now turn him from his intention. 'The more I feel myself cool & indifferent in danger here, the more I feel strong for the work that lies before me.' But Carson also discouraged Churchill from returning. C.P. Scott, however, wanted him back, telling him, 'Your place is here, not there.'

Clementine was buffeted by so much contradictory advice. 'These grave public anxieties are very wearing,' she wrote in the last week of March. 'When next I see you I hope there will be a little time for us both alone. We are still young, but Time flies, stealing love away and leaving only friendship which is very peaceful but not very stimulating or warming.' Churchill was shaken by this sad confession:

Oh my darling do not write of 'friendship' to me – I love you more each month that passes and feel the need of you & all your beauty. My precious charming Clemmie – I too feel sometimes the longing for rest & peace. So much effort, so many years of ceaseless fighting & worry, so much excitement & now this rough fierce life here under the hammer of Thor, makes my older mind turn – for the first time I think – to other things than action.

Is it 'Forty & finished' as the old devil's Duchess wrote? But would it not be delicious to go for a few weeks to some lovely spot in Italy or Spain & just paint & wander about together in bright warm sunlight far from the clash of arms or bray of Parliaments? We know each other so well now & could play better than we ever could.

Sometimes also I think I would not mind stopping living very much – I am so devoured by egoism that I would like to have another soul in another world & meet you in another setting, & pay you all the love & honour of the great romances.

Churchill went on to tell Clementine how, two days earlier, on March 26, he and Sinclair had been walking up to the trenches, when they heard several shells on his left, each shot coming nearer 'as the gun travelled round searching for prey'. They could calculate more or less where the next shell would fall. Their road led past a ruined convent, and Churchill said, 'The next shell will hit the convent.' As he and Sinclair drew abreast of the convent, sure enough, he told Clementine,

The shell arrived with a screech and a roar & tremendous bang & showers of bricks & clouds of smoke, & all the soldiers jumped & scurried, & peeped up out of their holes & corners. It did not make me jump a bit – not a pulse quickened. I do not mind noise as some very brave people do. But I felt – 20 yards more to the left & no more tangles to unravel, no more anxieties to face, no more hatreds & injustices to encounter: joy of all my foes, relief of that old rogue, a good ending to a chequered life, a final gift – unvalued – to an ungrateful country – an impoverishment of the war-making power of Britain which no one would ever know or measure or mourn.

But I am not going to give in or tire at all. I am going on fighting to the very end in any station open to me from which I can most effectively drive on this war to victory. If I were somehow persuaded that I was not fit for a wider scope, I should be quite content here – whatever happened. If I am equally persuaded that my worth lies elsewhere I will not be turned from it by any blast of malice or criticism.

Churchill made one last effort to persuade his wife that it was wise for him to come back as soon as possible. If, as she had suggested, he were to wait until there were a Ministerial crisis, 'would it not look as if I had come back like a Sultan hastening unbidden to a feast? Whereas in spite of all crabbing abuse – which has always beset me – I could undoubtedly from the box at Westminster exercise an influence and command attention to matters of vital urgency & import, which would in itself justify retrospectively the step I have taken.'

Clementine remained convinced that any premature return would weaken still further her husband's reputation. His constituency chairman warned that this was also the opinion in Dundee, where it was felt that if he were to oppose Asquith publicly it would put a weapon into the hands of his enemies 'who would hurl the charge of instability at you and use it for all it was worth to thwart your advancement'. Garvin was of the same opinion. Reluctantly Churchill remained at the front, brooding on what he might have done in the past, and what he still might do. 'To be great,' Clementine wrote to him, 'one's actions must be able to be understood by simple people. Your motive for going to the Front was easy to understand. Your motive for coming back requires explanation. That is why your Fisher speech was not a success – people could not understand it. It required another speech to make it clear.'

While Churchill was at Ploegsteert the Germans tried, and failed, to overrun the French defences at Verdun, launching a massive artillery bombardment, unprecendented in war, and wave after wave of infantry assaults. On April 6 he wrote to F.E. Smith, 'I am in the dark completely about the great situation; but Verdun seems to vindicate all I have ever said and written about the offensive by either side in the west.'

That April there was yet another attempt by Asquith's critics to demand conscription. In a letter to F.E. Smith on April 8, Churchill commented that Bonar Law and Lloyd George had 'the supreme chance now' to form a Government together and create 'an effective war organisation'. Whichever became Prime Minister 'the Party of the future might be formed'. The 'easiest opening' for him would be Munitions, though 'of course you know my wishes if they are attainable': a reference almost certainly to the Admiralty but perhaps to the Air Ministry.

'I think Asquith will probably give way at the last moment,' Churchill wrote to Lloyd George on April 10. 'But if not, the moment for you to act has come.' Five days later, not knowing which way Asquith would turn or whether Lloyd George would resign, Churchill wrote to Clementine from Laurence Farm, 'When I am not consumed with inward fury at the damnable twists which I have been served with, and chewing black charcoal with all my might, I am buoyant and lively.'

As Churchill expected, Asquith did make a concession to the demand for conscription, agreeing to extend the existing scheme, but still refusing to accept the need for full compulsory service. He also called a secret session of the House of Commons to explain his policy without the Press or public being present, or being allowed to know anything of the course of the debate. Churchill asked for leave to attend; this was granted on condition he return to his battalion the moment the session was over. 'Good luck to you, Samson,' Sinclair wrote from Ploegsteert as Churchill was on his way to London, 'and if you find your strength has returned, stay where you can most effectively contribute to the defeat of the Philistine.'

Churchill spoke during the secret session, but no record of what he said was made public. 'If only your speech had been reported, I feel the Press would urge your recall,' Clementine wrote to him three days later, when he was back with his battalion. Immediately after the debate he had tried to stay in London, knowing that those, led by Carson, who wanted full conscription, would soon be making an open challenge to Asquith. He wanted to be a part of that challenge. Haig had no objection to his remaining in London, and even sent a message wishing him luck 'for the Cause'. But the Divisional General intervened, sending him a telegram demanding his immediate return, as his battalion was again in the trenches. The crucial debate on conscription took place in Churchill's absence. Asquith introduced the partial measure. So effective was Carson in opposing it that Asquith agreed to withdraw it, and bring in without delay a Bill for full compulsory service.

Carson had triumphed; Churchill had been excluded altogether from the drama. Then, on May 3, his battalion left Ploegsteert for the last time. So weak had most of the infantry battalions become as a result of daily losses through shell-fire that considerable amalgamations were taking place. The 6th Royal Scots Fusiliers was to become part of the 15th Division. Churchill sought no new command. Instead, he asked to be allowed 'to attend to my Parliamentary & public duties which have become urgent'. His request was granted. Before leaving he tried to find good postings for his young officers. 'He took endless trouble,' one of them recalled. 'He borrowed motor cars and scoured France, interviewing Staff Officers great and small in an effort to do something to help those who had served under him.'

On May 6, three days after leaving Ploegsteert for the last time, Churchill gave his officers a farewell lunch at Armentières. On the following day he said goodbye to his men, telling them that he had come to regard the Scot as a most 'formidable fighting animal'. As he rose to shake their hands, one of them recalled, 'I believe every man in the room felt Winston Churchill's leaving us a real personal loss.'

17

'Deep and Ceaseless Torment'

Churchill returned to London on 7 May 1916. He was never to serve in the trenches again. But his return brought with it no prospect of Government employment. Two days after reaching London he spoke in the Commons on the need for more men, and argued that Ireland, hitherto excluded from the conscription bill on political grounds, should be included. 'This is a time for trying to overcome difficulties,' he said, 'and not for being discouraged or too readily deterred by them.' As he spoke these words an Irish Nationalist MP cried out in anger, 'What about the Dardanelles?'

This cry was to haunt Churchill for many years. In an attempt to clear his name of the stigma which was now attached to it, he pressed Asquith to publish the facts about the Dardanelles. When Asquith agreed, he began collecting the documents which showed most clearly his part in the evolution of the enterprise. It was twelve months since his departure from the Admiralty and his loss of authority and influence. 'This accursed year has now come to an end,' he wrote to Fisher on May 14, '& please God there will be better luck for you & me in the next, & some chance of helping our country to save itself & all dependent on it. Don't lose heart. I am convinced destiny has not done with you.'

Churchill's conviction was misplaced. Fisher was never to be invited back to any position of authority. Nor was Churchill offered the post he sought, as Air Minister. Speaking in the Air Board debate on May 17, Churchill described his part in the air defence of Britain immediately after the outbreak of war, and the establishment of air bases in France and Flanders, and defended the early air raids on Zeppelin sheds on the North Sea and the Rhine. Among the distortions of his record that had sprung up and stuck, it was now alleged, he said, that he had 'mismanaged and neglected' the air defence of Britain in the late autumn of 1914. He denied this, giving examples of the success of his efforts.

An Air Board had just been set up by Asquith; as it was without departmental powers, Churchill said, it would be ineffective. Britain had lost the aerial superiority which she had possessed at the outbreak of the war. 'But you can recover it. There is nothing to prevent you recovering it. Nothing stands in the way of our obtaining the aerial supremacy in the war but yourselves.'

Six days after this speech, and six weeks before the opening of the Battle of the Somme, Churchill spoke in the Army Estimate debate, pleading for an understanding of the unfair burden put upon the men in the trenches, when so many soldiers, even those already serving in France, never went anywhere near the front line. It was 'one of the grimmest class distinctions ever drawn in this world'. The House should know something of the burdens put on those who actually went to the front-line trenches. 'I say to myself every day, What is going on while we sit here, while we go away to dinner or home to bed? Nearly 1,000 men – Englishmen, Britishers, men of our race – are knocked into bundles of bloody rags every twenty-four hours, and carried away to hasty graves or to field ambulances.'

Insisting that there should be no further futile offensives, Churchill told the House: 'Do not let us be drawn into any course of action not justified by purely military considerations. The argument which is used that "it is our turn now" has no place in military thought.' What was needed to defeat Germany and Austria-Hungary was 'a real, substantial preponderance of strength'. Then the attacks could be made and the advantage of their interior communications 'swamped and overweighed'. Then 'the hour of decisive victory' would be at hand. 'This hour is bound to come if patience is combined with energy, and if all the resources at the disposal of the Allies are remorselessly developed to their supreme capacity.'

Churchill wanted so desperately to be allowed to pursue these dictates of war in a position of Ministerial authority. But there was no place for him, and he remained an anguished voice in the Commons. When the War Office vote was put to the House on May 31, even Carson and his recently-created pressure group, the Unionist War Committee had no plans to force a division. Churchill alone spoke of shortcomings and lack of drive, of a failure to use the country's resources, including its manpower, in the most effective way. 'We are trying our best,' he said, 'but are we at present developing the full results of the great effort made by the nation? I cannot think so.'

As soon as the Army debate was over Churchill wrote to Fisher about the Navy, 'The dead hand lies heavy on our noble fleets & they even kiss it.'

Reading Churchill's two Army speeches, several soldiers' wives wrote to him with examples of the waste of military manpower. The speeches were even published as a penny pamphlet, *The Fighting Line*. But there was virtually no work for Churchill to do. Curzon invited him once to attend a meeting of the Air Board, to give his view of how to secure aerial supremacy. That same month, following widespread public depression caused by the Admiralty's communiqué after the Battle of Jutland, which laid stress on the losses, Balfour asked him to write a rousing communiqué, to revive public confidence. That was the limit of what he was asked to do.

On June 5 Kitchener left Britain by sea for Northern Russia. On the following day, as part of his preparation of evidence for the Royal Commission on the Dardanelles, Churchill and Sir Ian Hamilton were poring over Kitchener's telegrams to Hamilton, to ensure that no important document would be omitted with regard to Kitchener's hesitations, changes of mind, and neglect of the Army once it was ashore. As they worked in Churchill's study at 41 Cromwell Road they heard a noise in the street below. 'We jumped up,' Hamilton later wrote, 'and Winston threw the window open.' A news-vendor was passing by. 'He had his bundle of newspapers under his arm and as we opened the window was crying out, "Kitchener drowned! No survivors!"'

Kitchener was dead. 'The fact that he should have vanished at the very moment Winston and I were making out an unanswerable case against him,' Hamilton wrote, 'was one of those coups with which his career was crowded – he was not going to answer.' It was widely expected that Lloyd George would succeed Kitchener as Secretary of State for War. Churchill thought that he might be given Lloyd George's post as Minister of Munitions. But the shadow of the Dardanelles still hung over him. 'You will readily understand my wish that the truth should be known,' he wrote to Asquith two days after Kitchener's death.

Asquith did not want full publication of documents in which he himself appeared as a leading supporter of action at the Dardanelles, and decided not to allow any War Council minutes at all to be included among the documents being prepared for publication. Churchill learned of this blow to his hopes on June 19. On the following day he learned that the Admiralty objected to the publication of many of the crucial naval telegrams. 'A considerable period must elapse,' Asquith told the Commons on June 26, 'before these papers are likely to be ready.' There was a further blow to Churchill's hopes of full disclosure four weeks later, when Asquith wrote to him to say that the Government had decided not to publish the Dardanelles documents at all.

On July 7 Lloyd George became Secretary of State for War; Churchill at once appealed to him for publication. 'The personal aspect of this matter is not very important,' he wrote, 'except in so far as it affects the behaviour of colleagues to one another. But the public aspect is serious. The nation

& the Dominions whose blood has been poured out vainly have a right to know the truth. The government had decided of their own accord that the truth could be told & had given a formal promise to Parliament: & now as the time draws nearer they shrink from the task.'

The Government had no wish to rake over the embers of the past. Too many of those still in high positions had taken their part in supporting, or in hampering, the enterprise. Angered but powerless, Churchill went with his family to Blenheim. 'Is it not damnable,' he wrote to his brother Jack, then on the Western Front, in mid-July, 'that I should be denied all real scope to serve this country, in this tremendous hour?' He still hoped for 'a situation favourable to me'. Lloyd George, though he had made only a 'half-hearted fight' to have him made Minister of Munitions, was 'very friendly according to the accounts I get'. Meanwhile, 'Asquith reigns supine, sodden and supreme'.

Churchill had decided not to return to France. 'Tho' my life is full of comfort and prosperity,' he told his brother, 'I writhe hourly not to be able to get my teeth effectively into the Boche. But to plunge as a battalion commander unless ordered – into the mistaken welter – when a turn of the wheel may enable me to do 10,000 times as much would not be the path of patriotism or sense. There will be time enough for such courses. Jack my dear I am learning to hate.'

That summer Churchill sat for his portrait by Orpen. Many years later Lloyd George's secretary, Frances Stevenson, wrote in her diary: 'Orpen described to me a scene in his studio while he was painting Winston just after he had lost office. W came to Orpen for a sitting, but all he did was to sit in a chair before the fire with his head bowed in his hands, uttering no word. Orpen went out to lunch without disturbing him & found Winston in the same position when he returned. At four o'clock W got up & asked Orpen to call him a taxi, & departed without further speech.'

On July 1 British and Empire forces attacked the German trenches on the Somme. Churchill had long been an opponent of such frontal attacks made without any clear superiority of men or tanks. That summer he wrote four articles for the *Sunday Pictorial*, in the last of which he described the changing national attitude to the war as a result of the battles of attrition from Loos to the Somme. 'The faculty of wonder has been dulled,' he wrote, 'emotion and enthusiasm have given way to endurance; excitement is bankrupt, death is familiar and sorrow numb. The world is in twilight; and from beyond dim flickering horizons comes tirelessly the thudding of the guns.'

On July 24, during the supplementary vote of credit for the prosecution of the war, Churchill again spoke in the Commons as the soldiers' friend, asking for a fairer system of front-line service, quicker promotion for those who were at the Front, and a wider recognition of bravery. 'I do not believe that people in this country have any comprehension,' he said, 'of what the men in the trenches and those who are engaged in battle are doing or what their suffering and achievements are.' He also appealed for greater effort to improve the security of the trenches, for trench lights that would be at least as good as those used by the Germans, and for steel helmets of the sort the French used, and that he had worn throughout his time in the trenches: 'Many men might have been alive today who have perished, and many men would have had slight injuries who today are gravely wounded, had this proposal not been put aside in the early stages of the war.' The Admiralty too, he said, should press on 'night and day' with every form of new construction, 'that is, the construction which saves the lives of our men, and does not expose them to needless and hopeless peril'.

On August 1, in a memorandum which F.E. Smith circulated to the Cabinet for him, Churchill argued that with each new offensive on the Western Front the pent up energies of the Army were being 'dissipated', with the result that Germany would be able to release men from the West to fight off Russia's recent advances in the East.

Recognising just how much Churchill had to give, of ideas and practical suggestions, Lloyd George invited him to the War Office to hear his views and discuss them with his advisers. After several further invitations the protests began. 'I know your feelings about him,' the Director-General of Recruiting, Lord Derby, wrote to Lloyd George that August, 'and I appreciate very much that feeling which makes you wish not to hit a man when he is down, but Winston is never down, or rather will never allow that he is down, and I assure you that his coming to the War Office as he does is – not to put it too strongly – most distasteful to everybody in that office.'

Derby was emphatic that the Conservative Party would not work with Churchill, nor would Derby support 'any Government' of which Churchill was a member. 'I like him personally,' Derby wrote. 'He has got a very attractive personality, but he is absolutely untrustworthy as was his father before him, and he has got to learn that just as his father had to disappear from politics so must he, or at all events from official life.'

Churchill refused to 'disappear'; early in September, when he learned that tanks, the 'caterpillars' he had pressed so hard to develop in 1915, were about to be used in battle for the first time, on the Somme, he went at once to see Asquith, to ask that none be used until they could appear in large numbers, thereby adding to their technical effectiveness the element of surprise. Asquith listened so attentively that Churchill was convinced that the tank would be held back until it could be used with maximum, perhaps decisive, effect, probably early in 1917. When, therefore, on September 16, he learned that tanks had been used on the Somme, only fifteen of them, he was deeply disappointed. 'My poor "land battleships" have been let off prematurely & on a petty scale,' he wrote that day to Fisher. 'In that idea resided one real victory.'

Throughout August and September Churchill prepared his case for the Dardanelles Commission of Enquiry. As Asquith still refused to allow him to use the War Council minutes, his presentation lacked one of its chief sources and justification. His hope that he would be able to be present when others gave evidence was dashed when the Chairman, Lord Cromer, informed him that all meetings would be held in secret, and that no one other than the day's witness would be admitted to them. On September 28 he appeared before the Commission, submitting documents and arguments to illustrate what he called five distinct truths concerning the naval attack at the Dardanelles, 'That there was full authority; that there was a reasonable prospect of success; that greater interests were not compromised; that all possible care and forethought were exercised in the preparation; and that vigour and determination were shown in the execution.'

The evidence that Churchill brought to substantiate these claims was voluminous. His desire was that when the Commission's work was over, his evidence would be published. He had also embarked upon a series of three articles in the monthly *London Magazine*, entitled 'The War by Land and Sea'. To Clementine's brother William, who had served at the Dardanelles and was now commanding the cruiser *Edgar*, he wrote two days after appearing before the Commission:

> *Of course I am miserable not to find any means of bringing my mind and knowledge to bear upon the war directly. I have a good deal of influence here, & in Parliament I can get things done. But I long to have power to use against the enemy. A turn of the wheel may give it me again. But meanwhile I languish in hateful ease. It is much the hardest time I have ever had in my life. If the war were not my sole thought, I would not care about political office. But to see things so little comprehended & to be impotent to guide them – at this great time is a deep & ceaseless torment to me.*
>
> *I should have been able to make myself useful to the Army if French had remained: for then I could get my ideas, which are right, considered & brought into action. But his departure left me with no outlook beyond that of the regimental officer, and although the 5 months I served in the trenches was a striking and not unpleasant experience, it cut me off of course absolutely from either information or real activity. So when my*

battalion was broken up I came back here: & here for the present I remain. I write and make large sums of money very easily; & to judge by the way I have lifted the circulation of the Sunday Pictorial & the London Magazine I have a good following in the country.

The success of the Caterpillar has been a great joy to me: it was the last of my projects that was still moving forward. They have not been used in the right way, nor in sufficient numbers; but there is no doubt of their merits and of their relation to the true conception of this war. An official statement about their origin is I believe soon to be published.

Well I expect you have had a dull time. Still you have done your duty, & after 2½ years of Armageddon the breath is still in your body. Voilà déjà quelquechose. How many have gone? How many more to go? The Admiralty is fast asleep and lethargy & inertia are the order of the day. However everybody seems delighted – so there is nothing to be said. No plans, no enterprise, no struggle to aid the general cause. Just sit still on the spacious throne and snooze.

The Dardanelles Committee occupies a good deal of my time, & I am hopeful of a favourable result. Later on I may find an opening in France, if political affairs allow. Nellie has presented us with a son to replace casualties. I often think of you my dear Billie. You know you can always count upon me as your affectionate friend.

Esmond, the baby son of Clementine's sister Nellie, was to be killed in action in 1942, when a Pilot Officer in the Canadian Air Force.

Conservative newspapers clung tenaciously to the old charges; when, that October, the *Daily Mail* referred to 'the contemptible fiasco of Antwerp and the ghastly blunder of Gallipoli', Churchill wrote at once to the Dardanelles Commission to protest that the article 'shows very clearly the kind of attack to which I am exposed and from which I have every right to defend myself before the Commission'. Throughout October he submitted further evidence in answer to what others had told the Commission, which he had been allowed to read as a special concession. He also gave evidence a second time.

Churchill knew that any hope of his return to Government depended on the publication of his evidence. But when the Commission's work was done the Government agreed to publish only a general report. The documents, the submissions and the cross-examinations were not made public. Churchill had been cheated once again. On November 20 he told C.P. Scott he was 'the best abused man in the country'. Almost the only weapon left to him was his pen; on November 26 he published a full account of the Antwerp expedition in the *Sunday Pictorial*.

On November 30 Churchill was forty-two. At that very moment Lloyd George and Bonar Law were challenging Asquith's power. Churchill had no place in their struggle. Meeting him on December 2 as the crisis was at its height, Aitken later recalled that he was 'almost wistfully eager for news'. Three days later Lloyd George, Bonar Law and Curzon resigned from the Government. That same evening Asquith tendered his resignation.

The King asked Bonar Law to form a Government. That night Lloyd George and Aitken were to dine with F.E. Smith. Churchill had not been invited. Before dinner he was with 'FE' at the Turkish Baths of the Royal Automobile Club. While still at the Club, Smith telephoned Lloyd George to remind him about the dinner, and mentioned that Churchill was with him. Lloyd George at once proposed that Churchill join them. 'This suggestion,' Aitken later reflected, 'probably quite carelessly made, produced on Churchill's mind the natural impression that he was regarded as one of the new set of war administrators who were about to grasp the helm. Surely Lloyd George would not ask him to be included in a dinner party on that night of all others if he did not mean to offer him a real post – and a real post to Churchill meant nothing but war-service.'

During the dinner much of the talk was about the new administration. All those present including Churchill took part in it, in Aitken's words, 'on terms of equality'. During dinner Lloyd George had to leave, to see Bonar Law. He asked Aitken to drive with him. On the drive he explained that enormous pressures were being brought on him and Bonar Law to exclude Churchill from any new government. He himself, if he emerged as Prime Minister, would not be able to offer Churchill a Cabinet position. Lloyd George then asked Aitken to return to the dinner party and 'convey a hint of this kind' to Churchill.

Aitken himself expected office in the new Government. Returning to the dinner party, 'I smiled on Churchill,' he later wrote, 'as a senior colleague might on an aspiring junior. I still, so to speak, walked warily, but I walked. Churchill also had every reason to suppose that he was sure of high office. We discussed as allies and equals the personnel of the new Government. Churchill suggested that I might be made Postmaster-General – a task suitable to my abilities. Then I conveyed to him the hint Lloyd George had given me.'

The words Aitken used were these: 'The new Government will be very well disposed towards you. All your friends will be there. You will have a great field of common action with them.' Aitken's account continued: 'Something in the very restraint of my language carried conviction to Churchill's mind. He suddenly felt he had been duped by his ıvitation to the dinner, and he blazed into righteous anger.' Aitken had never known

Churchill address F.E. Smith in any other way than 'Fred' or 'FE', or refer to him as anything but 'Max'. Now he turned on him with the words, 'Smith, this man knows that I am not to be included in the new Government.' Then he walked out into the street.

That evening, Bonar Law asked Asquith if he would serve under him. When Asquith refused, Bonar Law realised that he would not be able to call upon full Liberal support, and advised the King to send for Lloyd George, who became Prime Minister.

While Cabinet-making on December 6, Lloyd George noted in the margin of one list of possible Ministers, '?Air Winston.' In fact, no Air Ministry was established. Nor, as Aitken had intimated on the previous evening, was Churchill offered any place in the new Cabinet. This, he told Sinclair, was 'the downfall of all my hopes and desires. These have not been unworthy, for I had an impulse & gift to give to the war energies of the country. But my treasure is rejected.' He was unlucky, too, that the publication of the Dardanelles Commission report had been delayed because of the political crisis, 'for I am still hopeful', he told Sinclair, 'that it will give a turn to public opinion. But everything has turned out ill for me since the war began. Perhaps we are now at the nadir.'

On December 11, as a gesture of friendship, Lloyd George sent a mutual friend to see Churchill, to tell him that he had no intention of keeping him out of office, and would try to appoint him Chairman of the Air Board. But the Dardanelles Commission Report would have to be published first. Churchill replied that although the position was not in the War Cabinet, and had no department of State behind it, he had no reproaches to make: 'I will take any position which will enable me to serve my country. My only purpose is to help defeat the Hun, and I will subordinate my own feelings so that I may be able to render some assistance.'

Unknown to Churchill, the new First Lord of the Admiralty, Edward Carson, wrote to Bonar Law on December 20, 'I should greatly fear friction if the appointment is made.' Churchill's long battle with the Conservative Party was far from ended. 'When I am absolutely sure there is no prospect of regaining control or part of it here,' he wrote to Sinclair, who had asked if he would come out to the trenches, 'I shall turn again to that resort & refuge.' Had he stayed at the Duchy of Lancaster 'and shut my mouth & drawn my salary, I should today be one of the principal personages in direction of affairs'. Ploegsteert had been a 'costly excursion'. There was no respect in Parliament for those who wore uniform. 'Not one of those gallant MPs who has fought through the Somme at the heads of their battalions stands a chance against less clever men who have stopped & chattered at home. This is to me the most curious phenomenon of all. It is quite inexplicable to me.'

Churchill spent Christmas and New Year at Blenheim with Clementine, Diana, Randolph and Sarah. A month later, shortly after Fisher's seventy-sixth birthday, Churchill wrote to him, 'Our common enemies are all-powerful today & friendship counts for nothing. I am simply existing.'

Speaking on the Army Estimates on 5 March 1917 Churchill made a forceful plea for greater energy and inventiveness in the creation of life-saving and victory-enhancing mechanical devices. 'Machines save life,' he said. 'Machine-power is a substitute for man-power. Brains will save blood, manoeuvre is a great diluting agent to slaughter.' Unless new devices were developed, 'I do not see how we are to avoid being thrown back on those dismal processes of waste and slaughter which are called attrition,' and he begged the Government not to launch in 1917 an offensive similar to that of the Somme in 1916 'unless they are certain that the fair weather months at their disposal, and the reserves they command relatively to the enemy, are such as to give an indisputable result'. Preparations should be made now for the campaign of 1918. It was then that the Allies would be strong enough in manpower and weaponry to ensure a military victory.

By mid-March the Dardanelles Commission was at last ready to publish its report. As a gesture of friendship Lloyd George lent Churchill a draft copy of its Admiralty section. No blame was put on Churchill; indeed the report showed that when the naval attack was called off by de Robeck on March 18, the Turks had only three rounds of ammunition left in their fortress guns. But although the report made clear that Asquith had been as keen to attack Turkey as any of his colleagues, and that it was Kitchener who had failed to give the War Council sufficient details of his military plans, it did not, to Churchill's mind, answer many of the specific charges that had been made against him personally. Nor did it include any of the documents he had wanted published. Worse still, he told Lloyd George, 'quotations from the evidence included in the body of the report do not in numerous cases represent the evidence given before the Commission'.

In his final submission Churchill told the Commissioners that their report failed to set the Dardanelles in the context of the wider war, and especially of the trench stalemate on the Western Front. 'A fifth of the resources, the effort, the loyalty, the resolution, the perseverance vainly employed in the battle of the Somme to gain a few shattered villages and a few square miles of devastated ground, would,' he wrote, 'in the Gallipoli Peninsula, used in time, have united the Balkans on our side, joined hands with Russia, and cut Turkey out of the war.'

A 'good Press sedulously manipulated', Churchill wrote, had repre-sented the battle of the Somme as a series of victories. In a few years' time, however, it would be seen 'that in the ill-supported armies struggling on the Gallipoli Peninsula, whose efforts are now viewed with so much prejudice and repugnance, were in fact within an ace of succeeding in an enterprise which would have abridged the miseries of the World and proved the salvation of our cause. It will then seem incredible that a dozen old ships, half a dozen divisions, or a few hundred thousand shells were allowed to stand between them and success. Contemporaries have condemned the men who tried to force the Dardanelles. History will condemn those who did not aid them.'

Lunching with Churchill on March 20, C.P. Scott asked him if he would be willing to join Lloyd George's Government.

'Not in any subordinate capacity – only in one of the chief posts,' Churchill replied.

Would he be willing to be Secretary of State for War, Scott asked.

'Yes, that would do very well,' said Churchill.

But the post was not on offer. Later that day, two years and two days after the naval attack on the Narrows, the Commons debated the Royal Commission's report on the Dardanelles. Churchill defended his own part with vigour, and was pleased with the reception of his speech and with the debate that followed, telling Sinclair that it had been 'very successful to me personally'. The report having shown that both Asquith and Kitchener had approved the operation, all those who cared for Kitchener's memory, 'and they are many', and all who adhered to 'orthodox Liberalism' had joined to defend the operation. 'I thus have strong bodies of public opinion between me & the malevolence of the Tory Press. This is likely to govern my affairs.'

In an article in the *Sunday Pictorial* on April 8, Churchill reiterated his Parliamentary opposition to a renewed offensive in 1917. But on the following day the British Army launched its spring offensive east of Arras. After three days the Germans had been driven back four miles but their line had held, ending Haig's hope of a breakthrough which could be exploited by the cavalry riding forward deep into German-held territory. 'Cavalry has no role on the Western Front,' Churchill wrote to Sinclair on April 11. 'There will be no galloping through.'

Six days after Churchill's letter, Lloyd George spoke in the Commons in defence of the suppression of a series of articles in the *Nation* which asserted that British troops on a sector of the Western Front had been outwitted by a German tactical withdrawal. After Lloyd George defended the suppression, Churchill rose to speak. At that very moment, Lloyd George left the Chamber, a fact on which Churchill commented with much sarcasm. The suppression itself, he said, betrayed 'an undue love of the assertion of arbitrary power'.

When Churchill went on to say that the House was deeply concerned, Bonar Law interjected, 'We will judge that by the Division.' Churchill was stung to anger: 'Do not look for quarrels,' he said; 'do not make them;

make it easy for every Party, every force in this country, to give you its aid and support, and remove barriers and obstructions and misunderstandings that tend to cause superficial and apparent divergences among men whose aim is all directed to our common object of victory, on which all our futures depend.'

That spring, in search of somewhere in the country where he could relax with his family, Churchill bought Lullenden, a Tudor farmhouse in Sussex. Hidden in its hundred acres of woodland was a small lake on the steep bank of which he loved to paint. His son Randolph was not quite five when his father bought Lullenden; a favourite game, he later recalled, was to chase his father through the dense wood. 'Once he disturbed a nest of bees, or perhaps wasps, and passed through unscathed. All of us children, however, in hot pursuit, were badly stung.'

That April, at Lloyd George's suggestion, Churchill twice met the Minister of Munitions, Dr Christopher Addison, to discuss some part for him in munitions production. On April 27 Addison suggested to Lloyd George that Churchill be made chairman of a Committee within his Ministry, to examine the development of the tank and other mechanical aids to war. Lloyd George declined Addison's suggestion, but he did take up a suggestion by Churchill early in May for a secret session of the House, in order to avoid a combined public and Parliamentary assault on his war policy by disaffected Liberals led by Asquith, and Labour and Irish Nationalist MPs.

The secret session took place on May 10. Asquith had made no plans for a full-scale attack nor did he put up anyone to open the debate. That task fell to Churchill, who once more argued against premature offensives in France. The United States had entered the war at the beginning of April. Her troops would not be ready for action until 1918. 'Is it not obvious,' he asked, 'that we ought not to squander the remaining armies of France and Britain in precipitate offensives before the American power begins to be felt on the battlefield?'

Numerical superiority and artillery preponderance were both necessary for a successful offensive. Britain had neither. Nor had she yet established superiority in the air. 'We have discovered neither the mechanical nor the tactical methods of piercing an indefinite succession of fortified lines defended by German troops.' Further offensives in 1917 would be nothing but 'fresh, bloody and disastrous adventures'. The Allied armies should be trained and increased, and their methods perfected, 'for a decisive effort in a later year'.

Lloyd George refused to commit himself to such a delay, nor did he reveal the extent to which he was already committed to a major offensive later in 1917. But when, after his speech, he and Churchill met by chance behind the Speaker's chair, 'he assured me,' Churchill later recalled, 'of his determination to have me at his side. From that day, although holding no office, I became to a large extent his colleague. He repeatedly discussed with me every aspect of the war and many of his secret hopes and fears.' After Churchill had lunched with Lloyd George on May 19, Frances Stevenson asked the Prime Minister why he was drawing closer to Churchill. 'He says he wants someone in who will cheer him up and help & encourage him, & who will not be continually coming to him with a long face and telling him that everything is going wrong,' she wrote in her diary. 'At present he has to carry the whole of his colleagues on his back.'

The first fruits of the new co-operation came on May 26, when, with Lloyd George's blessing, Churchill crossed over to France with a letter from the Prime Minister to the French Minister of War, asking him to give Churchill 'every facility' for visiting the French sector of the Front. This was Churchill's first official, or semi-official, mission to France for more than two years; he was entertained by the French High Command, taken to see the battlefields of 1916, and lunched in Paris with the French Minister of War. 'It has all been very pleasant,' he wrote to Clementine on May 29, 'but never for the moment does the thought of this carnage and ruin escape my mind.'

On all those whom he met in France he urged the wisdom of postponing the Allied offensive for almost a year, until at least May 1918 and even August 1918, when the vast American reinforcements would have arrived. Sir Henry Wilson, then commanding the Fourth Corps, who lunched with him in Paris, noted in his diary that Churchill was also 'very keen (& rightly so) that the Navy should fight instead of doing nothing, & he has great plans for bringing on fights by laying minefields close up against enemy ports'. Churchill's spirits were reviving: 'I am much stimulated by the change and movement, & new discussions with new people, & I am very full of ideas,' he told Clementine.

From Paris, Churchill went to the British front, where he spent the whole of June 1. Then, on June 2, he lunched with Haig at St Omer, again expressing his conviction that the 1917 offensive should be postponed. Haig noted in his diary that during their discussion Churchill had been 'most humble'. But even as Churchill felt a new strength and purpose, his enemies were at work trying to prevent his return to public office. The *Sunday Times* of June 3, after reporting a rumour that Churchill was to become Chairman of the Air Board, declared that his appointment to any Cabinet post would be 'a grave danger to the Administration and to the Empire as a whole'. His record proved he did not possess 'those qualities of balanced judgement and shrewd far-sightedness which are essential to the sound administrator'.

It was not only the Conservative newspapers that raised their voice against Churchill. In the first week of June, Lord Curzon wrote to Bonar Law to remind him that he had entered Lloyd George's Government only on condition that Churchill was excluded. Lord Derby went to see Lloyd George on June 8 to make the same point in person. That evening Curzon wrote direct to Lloyd George, about Churchill, 'He is a potential danger in opposition. In the opinion of us all he will as a member of the Government be an active danger in our midst.'

Lloyd George had wanted to give Churchill the Air Board, but the ferocity of the response was too great. On June 30, however, as a sign of confidence in Churchill, he went to Dundee to receive the freedom of the city. Two weeks later, on July 16, Lloyd George invited Churchill to join his Government, and asked him what post he would like. Churchill answered at once, Munitions. The existing Minister, Dr Addison, long an admirer of Churchill's qualities, had already told Lloyd George he would step down for Churchill; indeed it was Addison's idea that Churchill should succeed him. The appointment was made public on July 18. For several days there was a storm of Conservative and newspaper protest. The *Morning Post* pointed to Antwerp and the Dardanelles as proof of an 'overwhelming conceit', which had led Churchill to imagine 'he was a Nelson at sea and a Napoleon on land'.

Lord Derby was incensed because the first he knew of Churchill's inclusion in the Cabinet was when he read about it in the newspapers; he went at once to protest to Lloyd George. Anticipating Derby's threat of resignation, Lloyd George stated that if he were to be denied the assistance of those 'whom he thought likely to help him' he himself would resign at once. Among those who congratulated Churchill was his Aunt Cornelia, Lord Randolph's sister. She also had words of caution, 'My advice is to stick to Munitions, and don't try to run the Government.'

18

Minister of Munitions

Churchill spent his first weekend as Minister of Munitions at Lullenden. On the Sunday, 22 July 1917, Maurice Hankey, who lived at Limpsfield, five miles away, was his guest for tea. 'I had an interesting walk & talk with him,' Hankey wrote in his diary, 'rambling round his wild & beautiful property. Lloyd George had given him my war policy report & he was already well up in the whole situation and knew exactly what our military plans were, which I thought quite wrong. He had breakfasted with Lloyd George that morning.'

That evening, Churchill wrote to Lloyd George to reiterate his opposition to a renewed offensive that year in France, and to 'limit the consequences' of any attack that might already have been decided upon, 'I deplore with you the necessity for giving way to the military wish for a renewed offensive in the West.' Churchill also suggested that the time had come to prepare a further amphibious landing against Turkey-in-Europe, making use of the five or six divisions then idle at Salonica which 'would be crouched instead of sprawled'. Once the Turkish Army in Europe were forced to surrender, the Allied troops in Palestine would be 'free by the spring of next year for action in Italy or France'. Churchill ended with a plea to Lloyd George, who was on his way to France, 'Don't get torpedoed; for if I am left alone your colleagues will eat me.'

The headquarters of the Ministry of Munitions was in Northumberland Avenue, at the Hotel Metropole. The hotel, taken over by the Government, was just off Trafalgar Square, only a few minutes' walk from Admiralty House, Churchill's Ministerial home from 1911 to 1915. From what his predecessor, Dr Addison, could learn, the members of the Munitions secretariat 'were not very friendly to the idea of Winston's coming'. Addison introduced him on July 24; a senior departmental officer, Harold Bellman, later recalled how they had expected 'a stormy scene' and that Churchill was received 'rather coldly'. Indeed, Bellman recalled, he opened his remarks by stating 'that he perceived that he "started at scratch in the popularity stakes". He went on boldly to indicate his policy for an even swifter production of munitions. As he elaborated his plans the atmosphere changed perceptibly. This was not an apology. It was a challenge. Those who came to curse remained to cheer.'

Hostility to Churchill's appointment continued; on August 3 the *Morning Post* announced: 'That dangerous and uncertain quantity, Mr Winston Churchill – a floating kidney in the body politic – is back again at Whitehall. We do not know in the least what he may be up to, but from past experience we venture to suggest that it will be everything but his own business.' Four days later Churchill faced his first test as Minister of Munitions, a year-and-a-half-old industrial dispute which had brought Sir William Beardmore's munitions works, and other munitions factories on the Clyde, to a halt. Several of the strike leaders had not only been dismissed from Beardmore's, but arrested and forbidden to reside in Glasgow. Three successive Ministers, Lloyd George, Edwin Montagu and Addison, all Liberals, had upheld the exclusion order.

In an attempt to resolve the dispute, Churchill invited the leader of the 'Clyde deportees', David Kirkwood, a man of his own age, to meet him at the Ministry. In his memoirs Kirkwood recalled how he had expected 'arrogance, military precision, abruptness', but the moment Churchill appeared, 'I knew I was wrong. He came in, his fresh face all smiles, and greeted me simply, without a trace of side or trappings. I felt I had found a friend.' As their talk began, Churchill rang a bell and said, 'Let's have a cup of tea and a bit of cake together.' Kirkwood was amazed: 'Here was the man supposed never to think of trifles, suggesting tea and cakes – a sort of bread and salt of friendship. It was magnificent. We debated over the teacups.'

Kirkwood demanded reinstatement for the 'deportees', in return for a pledge that they would agree to resume working. Churchill recognised Kirkwood's patriotism and accepted the pledge, putting immediate pressure on Beardmore to reinstate them. Three days later the strike was over. Kirkwood himself was offered the job of manager at Beardmore's Mile End Shell factory in London. 'The incurable itch to do something striking,' wrote the *Morning Post* in denouncing the settlement, 'has already been too much for Mr Churchill. He has already celebrated his tenure of office by extending the hand of fellowship to the Clyde deportees, a gang of as dangerous and desperate agitators as ever fomented trouble in the labour world.' Within six weeks of his reinstatement Kirkwood had devised a workers' bonus scheme which made production at Mile End the highest in Britain.

On August 15 Churchill presented his Munitions of War Bill to the Commons. The aim of the Bill, he explained, was 'output on the one hand

and industrial peace on the other'. Special wage awards would be made to skilled men. No worker would be penalised for belonging to a trade union or taking part in a trade dispute. Although in some respects this could be prejudicial to output, 'it removes any suspicion of want of good faith or want of sympathy'. The war could not be won 'unless we are supported by the great masses of the labouring classes of this country'. Unless they gave their support 'with a loyal and spontaneous determination, we must expect disastrous results'.

Churchill was not a member of the War Cabinet, but attended those meetings at which munitions were discussed. When, on August 15, he gave, unasked, his views about the allocation of British field guns to Russia, Derby protested to Lloyd George and persuaded the Chief of the Imperial General Staff, Sir William Robertson, to do likewise. At a second War Cabinet that day, Churchill spoke in favour of a possible transfer of naval guns from the Navy to the Army. It was Churchill's task to produce Britain's munitions of war, and to try to satisfy the competing claims to them; he therefore felt that he must point out what he believed to be the best use of them. There were 'very large reserves' of guns being discarded by the Admiralty, he pointed out, which the War Office could use on land. The First Lord of the Admiralty, Sir Eric Geddes, was not at the meeting, but as soon as he learned Churchill had spoken, he too protested; indeed, he and Derby threatened to resign if Churchill's interventions were not curtailed.

Three days after this dispute Churchill announced the new structure of his Ministry. It was a masterpiece of streamlining, intended, he said, 'by more economical processes, by closer organisation, and by thrifty and harmonious methods, to glean and gather a further reinforcement of war power'. In place of fifty semi-autonomous departments he set up a Munitions Council of eleven members, each of whom would be in charge of several related aspects of munitions production. A Council Secretariat would co-ordinate the purchase of raw materials and supervise production methods. Churchill appointed his former Admiralty Secretary, James Masterton-Smith, to take charge of it, and brought Edward Marsh back to his Private Office.

The Munitions Council met once a week. Specific issues were delegated to Council Committees, seventy-five of which were set up in the following fifteen months. Dozens of businessmen and industrialists participated in the Ministry's efforts, working side by side with the civil servants. Churchill read the Committees' reports and approved them. 'I think I have hardly ever altered a word,' he noted four months later. On September 4 he addressed the Munitions Council on the question of air power. For too long, he said, the Air Force had been 'the drudge of the other services'.

Now, however, there were 'only two ways of winning the war, and they both begin with A. One is aeroplanes and the other is America. That is all that is left. Everything else is swept away.'

Churchill was in his element; work and a clear plan. 'If you know your war plan it is easy to parcel out your material,' he told his Council that day. Five days later he wrote to Lloyd George: 'This is a very heavy department, almost as interesting as the Admiralty, with the enormous advantage that one has neither got to fight Admirals nor Huns! I am delighted with all these clever business people who are helping me to their utmost. It is very pleasant to work with competent people.'

On September 12 Churchill made his first munitions visit to France. From Calais, he and Marsh drove to the war zone. As Messines was reported to be 'unhealthy' they went instead to Wytschaete Ridge, which had been taken two months earlier by Irish and Ulster regiments fighting side by side. No sooner had they reached the ridge than German shells began to burst sixty yards away, hurling fragments to within five or six yards. 'Winston soon began to think it was silly to stay there,' Marsh wrote to a friend, 'and we began picking our way back through the stumps and round the shell-holes of Wytschaete wood.' Leaving Wytschaete, Churchill drove to St Omer for two days of talks with Haig and his staff.

Haig had ordered a major offensive to begin in a week's time, determined to break through the German trenches in the Ypres salient. His objective was to attack through the village of Passchendaele and on to Bruges, even to Zeebrugge, thus ending the stalemate of trench warfare. On September 13, the first full day of his talks with Churchill, he noted in his diary, 'Winston admitted that Lloyd George and he were doubtful about being able to beat the Germans on the Western Front.'

From St Omer, Churchill drove to Poperinghe for tea with his brother, then serving on the staff of the Australian and New Zealand Division. On the way back to St Omer he passed large numbers of troops moving forward to the trenches. 'Many of them recognised Winston and cheered and waved their hands,' Marsh wrote. 'He was as pleased as Punch.'

On the evening of September 16 Churchill presided over a munitions conference at Arras, before driving eastward towards the front. 'Winston was attracted by the sight of shells bursting in the distance – irresistible!' Marsh wrote to his friend. 'Out we got, put on our steel helmets, hung our gas-masks round our necks, and walked for half-an-hour towards the firing. There was a great noise, shells whistling over our heads, and some fine bursts in the distance – but we seemed to get no nearer and the firing died down, so we went back after another hour's delay. Winston's disregard of time, when there's anything he wants to do, is sublime – he firmly believes that it waits for him.'

That night Churchill reached Paris at midnight; rooms awaited him at the Ritz. On September 17 he met his French opposite number, Louis Loucheur, who advocated the establishment of an Inter-Allied Munitions Council. Churchill agreed. His main concern was to present to the Americans 'the joint agreed proposals' of Britain and France. On the following day he held discussions outside Paris with French artillery experts, to ensure the more efficient transport of heavy guns on the congested railway lines. That evening he dined at Amiens, then drove to the coast, where a destroyer took him back to Dover.

Haig's new offensive opened on September 20. Thirteen days later, on October 3, he sent Churchill an urgent appeal for 6-inch howitzer ammunition. Any reduction of supply, he warned, would hamper his present advance. Churchill instructed the British Mission in Washington to put the request to the American War Industries Board. The Commissioner on the Board in charge of raw materials, Bernard Baruch, agreed to provide the shells required. Henceforth Baruch and Churchill were to be in direct telegraphic contact, sometimes daily. They had never met, but through their telegraphic exchanges emerged a close working partnership.

On October 12 Haig's armies opened their assault against the village of Passchendaele, the last high ground before the expected sweep forward. But after twelve days of intense, often hand-to-hand, fighting, over an area less than half a mile in depth, the advance was halted. That day, in Italy, the Italian Army was defeated at Caporetto by a combined German and Austrian Army, and more than a million Italians were in retreat. When news of the extent of that disaster reached the War Office, Churchill was at Lullenden. Lloyd George, who was at Walton Heath, telephoned and asked him to drive over, a distance of twenty miles. 'He showed me the telegrams, which even in their guarded form revealed a defeat of the first magnitude,' Churchill later recalled.

Churchill gave Lloyd George the courage he sought. British and French troops would be sent to Italy to hold the line. Lloyd George himself would go to Italy. Churchill would do everything possible to ensure that the increased call for guns and munitions was met. This was a formidable task; Britain's factories, even working to capacity, had been unable that October to match their September output. 'We should be careful,' Churchill told his Munitions Council on November 7, 'not to dissipate our strength or melt it down to the average level of exhausted nations. It will be better used with design by us, than weakly dispersed.'

That same day, Churchill held his first meeting with the Women's Trade Union Advisory Committee. Almost a million women came within his Ministerial responsibility. Eight months earlier he had voted in favour of the extension of the franchise which, for the first time in British history, gave votes to women; six million women gained the vote as a result of the new Act. Now it was the demand for a fairer wage that dominated the discussion; during the meeting the women's case was put by a thirty-six-year-old Trade Union leader, Ernest Bevin, who, twenty-three years later, was to be a member of Churchill's War Cabinet.

Churchill was sympathetic to the women's demands, telling the meeting that he believed women's labour should be more than 'an incident of the war'. At the end of the meeting he took up a point that had been raised by Bevin: 'If you think that I have an idea that this is to be a mere sham and that we have called you together to keep the women quiet, you make a very great mistake. That is the last thing we have in view. The times are much too serious for games like that. This is really an earnest attempt to face the problem of women in industrial life and in munitions life during the war.'

Two days after his meeting with the women, Churchill told the War Council that the current wage demands by munitions workers were not in any way in excess either of the increases in the cost of living 'or in the degree of effort which has been forthcoming'. That effort was continuous; among Churchill's intiatives in the first two weeks of November were to stop the cut-back in the production of bombing aircraft, and to increase the production of aeroplane engines. Then, on November 18, he returned to Paris to co-ordinate Italian munitions needs with the French and Italians; after three days of talks, the Italian needs were met.

On November 20, while Churchill was in Paris, the British launched the first tank offensive of the war, at Cambrai. Within two weeks the trench lines were overrun and more than forty-two square miles of German-held territory regained. On the first day of the battle Churchill went to the Chamber of Deputies to hear France's new Prime Minister and Minister of War, the seventy-six-year-old Georges Clemenceau, declare, 'No more pacifist campaigns, no more German intrigues, neither treason nor half treason – war, nothing but war.' It was a remarkable performance. 'He ranged from one side of the tribune to the other,' Churchill later recalled, 'without a note or book of reference or scrap of paper, barking out sharp, staccato sentences as the thought broke upon his mind.' It was not a matter of actual words or reasoning: 'Language, eloquence, arguments were not needed to express the situation. With snarls and growls, the ferocious, aged, dauntless beast of prey went into action.'

Churchill was still in France on his forty-third birthday; he remained there until December 4. During his visit he finalised plans to set up a British gun factory at Creil, north of Paris, so that heavy guns could be repaired and modified without needing to be sent back to Britain. He also undertook, at Bernard Baruch's request, to find and buy for the United States those war materials which American troops would need when they reached Europe. Churchill acquired these materials in France, Spain and even Canada; they included 452 aeroplanes.

While in Paris, Churchill was able to persuade Loucheur to allow him to establish an Anglo-American tank factory at Bordeaux, which would assemble parts sent over from Britain and the United States, and would turn out 1,500 large tanks a month from July 1918. It was with these tanks, he believed, that victory would be won. Tanks should be used, he told the War Cabinet on his return to London, not only as a substitute for artillery bombardment but as an 'indispensable adjunct to infantry'. To support his argument, he pointed out that in the battle of Cambrai, which had ended two days earlier, the forty-two square miles which had been gained had cost fewer than 10,000 men killed or wounded, at a cost in munitions of £6,600,000, whereas in Flanders, from August to November that year, the fifty-four square miles gained had cost 300,000 in killed and wounded, and £84 million in ammunition. The first thing to be done, he told the War Cabinet, was to release the thirty to forty thousand 'admirable cavalrymen', most of them already being found other employment, for service in tanks.

Churchill was relieved that the third battle of Ypres was over. 'Thank God our offensives are at an end,' he wrote to Sinclair. 'Let them make the pockets. Let them traipse across the crater fields. Let them rejoice in the occasional capture of placeless names & sterile ridges: & let us dart here & there armed with science & surprise & backed at all points by a superior artillery. That is the way to break their hearts & leave them bankrupt in resources at the end of the 1918 campaign.'

As 1917 came to an end, Churchill's energies focused on that 1918 campaign. But now a new danger loomed: in Russia, a Bolshevik Government, coming to power at the beginning of November, declared that it would make peace with Germany. Once this happened, the Germans would be able to transfer vast numbers of troops from the Eastern to the Western Front, giving them a marked superiority in numbers. Greatly alarmed, on 19 January 1918 Churchill sent Lloyd George an appeal, begging him to ensure that the army was brought to 'full strength' at once. The Navy still had priority in recruitment, Churchill pointed out, and he went on to protest:

> To me this is incomprehensible. The imminent danger is on the Western front; & the crisis will come before June. A defeat here will be _fatal._
>
> Please don't let vexation against past military blunders (which I share with you to the full) lead you to underrate the gravity of the impending campaign, or to keep the army short of what is needed. You know how highly I rate the modern defensive compared with offensive. But I do _not_

like the situation now developing and do not think all that is possible is
being done to meet it.

   Fancy if there was a bad break!

   Look what happened to Italy. One night may efface an army – men at
once – at all costs, from Navy, from Munitions, from Home Army, from
Civil Life. Stint food and commerical imports to increase shells, aeroplanes
& tanks.

   Wire and <u>concrete</u> on the largest possible scale.

   A good plan for counter blows all worked out beforehand to relieve
pressure at the points of attack when they manifest themselves.

   If this went wrong everything would go wrong. I do not feel sure about
it. The Germans are a terrible foe, & their generals are better than ours.
Ponder & then <u>act.</u>

Churchill's actions matched his sense of danger. At the end of January he
pressed the Air Minister not to allow orders to fall below four thousand
aircraft engines a month. If it was 'considered worthwhile', he wrote, the
Ministry of Munitions would support an increase to five or even six
thousand. Crossing to France for the day on February 18, he discussed
with the British Army commanders their needs in ammunition, tanks and
mustard gas, determined to fulfil those needs. He returned to France
three days later to continue those discussions, and to see the trenches near
Vimy, 'walking in mud for five hours', he told Clementine.

   Two days later Churchill visited his own former trenches at Ploegsteert.
'Everything has been torn to pieces,' he told Clementine, '& the shelling is
at all times severe. The British line has moved forward about a mile, but
all my old farms are mere heaps of bricks & mouldering sandbags.' The
strong dugout he had built at Laurence Farm, however, 'has stood out the
whole two years of battering, & is still in use. So also are the cellars of the
convent which I drained & called the "conning tower". Otherwise utter
ruin.'

   From Ploegsteert, Churchill went northwards to Ypres, where, on the
Menin Road, 'the Huns began to fire. The spot is a favourite one – & is
called "Hellfire Corner". Big shells whined overhead & burst with very
loud bangs behind us. Nobody paid the slightest attention.' From Hellfire
Corner, he walked over the duckboards to Glencorse Wood and Polygon
Wood, scenes of fierce fighting during the September and October battle.

   At one point Churchill walked to within five hundred yards of a German
fortified position, Polderhoek Château. 'The view of the battlefield is
remarkable,' he told Clementine. 'Desolation reigns on every side. Litter,
mud, rusty wire & the pockmarked ground. Very few soldiers to be seen,
mostly in "pill boxes" captured from the industrious Hun. Overhead

aeroplanes constantly fired at. The Passchendaele ridge was too far for us to reach but the whole immense arena of slaughter was visible. Nearly 800,000 of our British men have shed their blood or lost their lives here during 3½ years of unceasing conflict. Many of our friends & my contemporaries all perished here. Death seems as commonplace & as little alarming as the undertaker. Quite a natural ordinary event, which may happen to anyone at any moment, as it happened to all these scores of thousands who lie together in this vast cemetery, ennobled & rendered for ever glorious by their brave memory.'

Churchill was amazed at how soldiers now moved about the battle zone. 'It was like walking along a street – not a scrap of cover or even camouflage. Still people kept coming & going & not a shot was fired. In my days at Plugstreet it would have been certain death. But I suppose they are all so bored with the war that they cannot be bothered to kill a few passers-by. We on the other hand shoot every man we can see.' On the way back to his car, he commented, 'we passed the lunatic asylum blown to pieces by the sane folk outside!'

On February 26 and 27, Churchill was in Paris on munitions business. Then he returned to London. In a memorandum on March 5, he asked the War Cabinet to think in terms of a new offensive strategy for 1919, dominated by aircraft and tanks, a type of war 'proceeding by design through crisis to decision – not mere waste and slaughter sagging slowly downwards into general collapse'. Three days later he explained to Lloyd George his wish to see tanks used in large numbers as an integral part of the battle. Sir Henry Wilson, the new Chief of the Imperial General Staff, who was also present, expressed concern that minefields would act as a barrier to a tank advance. Eight days later, Churchill circulated a memorandum in which he suggested various counter-measures, and pressed for work to be done to enable tanks to cross minefields safely. His proposals included a 'large steel hammer' extending twenty feet in front of each tank; a special tank in each group with an undercarriage strong enough to resist the explosions, clearing the way for the others; and a heavy roller or series of rollers pushed in front of a tank to explode the mines. These were, he said, 'crude ideas only intended to excite the scientific mind and lead to the production of definite solutions'.

Within his Ministry, Churchill now set up a Tank Board. The target he gave it was 4,459 tanks by April 1919 and double that number by September 1919. He also wanted to double Britain's air strength, believing, as he had written in his memorandum of March 5, that the results of the war would be decisive if either side had the power to drop 'not five tons but five hundred tons of bombs each night on the cities and manufacturing establishments of its opponents'.

On March 18 Churchill again crossed over to France, his fifth visit since becoming Minister of Munitions eight months earlier. Reaching St Omer he learned that a major German offensive was believed to be imminent. North of the River Oise, British troops were outnumbered two to one. On the following morning he was at British tank headquarters at Montreuil. His next official meeting in France was not for another two days; rather that return to Britain, he decided to visit his friend General Tudor, who was now commanding the Ninth Division. Churchill spent the night of March 19 at Tudor's headquarters at Nurlu. On the following day the two men inspected every part of the Division's defences, from the artillery position at Havrincourt to the South African trenches in Gauche Wood.

That night Churchill slept at Nurlu. He awoke early on March 21, just after four o'clock. For half an hour he lay in bed; then, at twenty minutes to five, he heard six or seven loud explosions several miles away. He thought they were British guns firing. They were in fact German mines exploding under the British trenches. 'And then,' he later recalled, 'exactly as a pianist runs his hands across the keyboard from treble to bass, there rose in less than one minute the most tremendous cannonade I shall ever hear.'

The German offensive had begun. Churchill quickly dressed and hurried to see Tudor, who told him that the British guns were about to open fire. Churchill did not hear them. 'The crash of the German shells bursting on our trench lines eight thousand yards away was so over-powering,' he later wrote, 'that the accession to the tumult of nearly two hundred guns firing from much nearer could not be even distinguished.' Shortly after six o'clock the German infantry began its advance. The South African positions at Gauche Wood were overrun. Churchill wanted to remain with the Division but Tudor persuaded him to leave. Driving to Peronne, he made his way northward to St Omer. By nightfall the road from Nurlu to Peronne was impassable.

Churchill remained at St Omer for the rest of the day. On March 22 he attended the gas conference there. Then, on March 23, as Nurlu itself was overrun, he left for London. At Downing Street, Lloyd George took him aside to ask how it would be possible to hold any positions on the battlefront now that the carefully fortified lines had been taken: 'I answered that every offensive lost its force as it proceeded. It was like throwing a bucket of water over the floor. It first rushed forward, then soaked forward, and finally stopped altogether until another bucket could be brought.' After thirty or forty miles there would be a breathing space and the front could be reconstituted, 'if every effort were made'.

That night Lloyd George and Henry Wilson dined with Churchill at his home at 33 Eccleston Square. In his diary Wilson described Churchill

as 'a real gem in a crisis'. At the War Cabinet on the following day
Churchill announced that all munitions workers would be asked to give
up their Easter holidays. He would also release munitions workers for
the front. On March 26 he worked through the night at the Ministry of
Munitions building, to ensure that the maximum number of artillery
pieces were moved to France in the shortest possible time. He again slept
at the Ministry on the night of March 27. When he awoke on the morning
of March 28 German forces had overrun the whole battlefield of the
Somme, captured from them at such a terrible cost in 1916, and now
threatened to drive a wedge between the French and British armies.
Haig had moved his headquarters from St Omer to Montreuil, near the
Channel Coast.

Lloyd George wanted first-hand evidence that the French and British
armies had the stamina and means to halt the German onslaught. To get
that evidence he decided to send Churchill to the Front. He also needed
to know for certain if the French, hitherto relatively little engaged in the
new battle, would be willing to make a 'vigorous attack' from the south, to
relieve the pressure on the British line. It was up to Churchill to find out;
that morning Lloyd George telegraphed to Clemenceau in Paris to inform
him that Churchill was on his way to French Army headquarters.

Churchill's critics at once raised the alarm. Even as he was on his way to
Folkestone, Bonar Law and Henry Wilson went to see Lloyd George to say
that it was quite wrong for him to be sent on a military mission to French
headquarters. Lloyd George bowed to the protest, sending a telephone
message from Downing Street to await Churchill at Folkestone, telling him
that 'he had better stay in Paris & not at French headquarters. He had
better therefore go straight to Clemenceau, ascertain the position, &
report here.'

At midday Churchill was at Folkestone. No message had arrived from
Lloyd George. Proceeding by destroyer to Boulogne, he drove to Haig's
new headquarters, where he found 'an utter absence of excitement or
bustle'; indeed, the Commander-in-Chief 'was taking his afternoon ride.'
While at Montreuil he was told that in the past week the British Army had
lost more than 100,000 men killed or captured, and over a thousand guns.
Most dangerous of all, the Germans were moving troops towards the as
yet unattacked northern sector of the British line. Suddenly there was a
danger that the British forces would be driven back to the Channel Coast.
A French advance from the south was all the more urgent. But at Haig's
headquarters no one knew what the French intention was, or what forces
they had available to come to Britain's rescue.

Churchill drove south from Montreuil to Amiens, which was already
under German bombardment. At midnight he reached Paris, and, as he

later recalled, 'the luxuries of an almost empty Ritz'. On reaching the Ritz he was handed Lloyd George's message.

March 29 was Good Friday; in Paris that morning a German shell hit a crowded church, killing eighty of the congregation. 'I do hope that when the long range guns start firing you take cover,' Clementine wrote. That morning Churchill received a message that Clemenceau would not only see him but would 'take him tomorrow to the battle and we will visit all the Commanders of Corps and Armies engaged'. At six that evening the two men met for the first time. 'There is a clear bold policy being pushed to the utmost limit with all available resources,' Churchill telegraphed to Lloyd George. 'They are in good confidence here. Clemenceau of course a tower of strength and courage.'

Lloyd George read out Churchill's report to the War Cabinet on the morning of March 30. The Minister without Portfolio, Lord Milner, Churchill's adversary of a previous decade, protested that his mission, even if 'limited' to a visit to Clemenceau, was a 'direct snub' to himself as the Minister who normally conducted talks with the French. Lloyd George knew, however, that Churchill's reports were crucial to his understanding of whether France really would hold out, and help Britain's forces where needed.

At eight o'clock on the morning of March 30, Churchill presented himself at Clemenceau's headquarters. 'We shall show you everything,' Clemenceau told him. 'We shall go together everywhere and see everything for ourselves.' Within two hours they reached Beauvais, where Marshal Foch was waiting for them at the Town Hall. Churchill later recalled how, in his room, 'Foch seized a large pencil as if it were a weapon, and without the slightest preliminary advanced upon the map and proceeded to describe the situation.' With animated gestures and loud cries, Foch traced the German advance during its first massive onrush on March 21. He then described the gradual slowing down of the German advance with each successive day. As he did so 'his whole attitude and manner flowed out in pity for this poor, weak, miserable little zone of invasion which was all that had been achieved by the enemy on the last day. One felt what a wretched, petty compass it was compared to the mighty strides of the opening days. The hostile effort was exhausted.'

The stabilisation of the line, Foch then told his visitors, was 'sure, certain, soon. And afterwards. Ah, afterwards. That is my affair.' The visitors left, driving north to Drury, where General Rawlinson was commanding the Fourth Army. Would the line hold, Churchill asked him. 'No one can tell,' Rawlinson replied. 'We have hardly anything between us and the enemy except utterly exhausted, disorganised troops.' The men of the Fifth Army, who had borne the brunt of the attack, were 'dead from want of sleep and rest. Nearly all the formations are mixed or dissolved. The men are just crawling slowly backwards: they are completely worn out.'

Haig arrived at Drury and asked the French for support. Clemenceau at once gave orders for two divisions of French troops to cross the River Ancre in support of the British. 'If your men are tired,' he said in English, 'and we have fresh men, our men shall come up at once and help you.' This offer, Churchill telegraphed to Lloyd George, afforded immediate relief to soldiers who were 'worn out and deadened by what they have gone through'. Instead of a separate French push further south, there would now be direct French assistance where the British line was weakest.

Clemenceau spoke again: 'I claim my reward. I wish to pass the river and see the battle.' Rawlinson protested that the situation beyond the River Luce could not be established. 'Very well,' Clemenceau replied, 'we will establish it. After coming all this way and sending you two divisions, I shall not go back without crossing the river.' Summoning Churchill to follow, Clemenceau entered his car. As they drove forward, Churchill told Clementine, they passed British soldiers walking away from the battle zone 'as if they were in a dream'. Most of them took no notice of the brightly flagged cars. A few, recognising Churchill, 'gave me a wave or a grin as they would no doubt have done to George Robey or Harry Lauder, or any other well known figure which carried their minds back to vanished England and the dear days of peace and party politics.'

At last they reached the river. The artillery fire was quite close. 'Now, Mr Winston Churchill, we are in the British lines,' said Clemenceau. 'Will you take charge of us? We will do what you say.'

'How far do you want to go?' Churchill asked.

'As far as possible,' Clemenceau answered. 'But you shall judge.'

Map in hand, Churchill ordered his car to lead the convoy. It crossed the bridge. 'The projectiles whined to and fro overhead,' Churchill later recalled. The convoy came to within three or four hundred yards of the last high ground in British hands. 'Rifle fire was now audible in the woods, and shells began to burst in front of us on the road and in the sopping meadows on either side.'

Churchill thought they had gone far enough. Clemenceau agreed to stop, got down from his car and climbed a small rise by the roadside. He remained there for about a quarter of an hour 'questioning the stragglers and admiring the scene'. They were 'in the highest spirits,' Churchill recalled, 'and as irresponsible as schoolboys on holiday. But the French staff officers were increasingly concerned for the safety of their Prime Minister. They urged me to persuade him to withdraw.' Clemenceau agreed to go back. Then, as they reached the road, 'a shell burst among a group of led horses at no great distance. The group was scattered. A wounded and riderless horse came in a staggering trot along the road towards us. The poor animal was streaming with blood.'

Clemenceau, aged seventy-six, advanced towards the wounded horse 'and with great quickness seized its bridle, bringing it to a standstill. The blood accumulated upon the road. A French General expostulated with him, and he turned reluctantly towards his car. As he did so, he gave me a sidelong glance and observed in an undertone, "Quel moment délicieux!" '

The convoy returned to Drury, then went northward through Amiens. Churchill was impressed when the French General in the line on Rawlinson's right expressed confidence that he could hold his own sector for twenty-four hours, when reinforcements would arrive. At eight in the evening the convoy reached Beauvais, where General Pétain, the French Commander-in-Chief, welcomed them on board his train, 'this sumptuous military palace' Churchill called it.

'We had already,' Churchill later wrote, 'been exactly twelve hours either touring along the roads at frantic speeds, or in constant exciting conversation with persons of high consequence. Personally I was quite tired. But the iron frame of "The Tiger" appeared immune from fatigue of any kind or in any form.' Pétain described the situation as he saw it. He was confident that the German offensive would fail, explaining that the current phase was the 'phase of men', during which a new front was being formed. Then would come the 'phase of guns'. A strengthened artillery organisation would be ready within forty-eight hours. Ammunition would arrive within four days.

After dining with Pétain in his train, the visitors returned to Paris reaching the city at one in the morning. Before going to bed Churchill telegraphed to Lloyd George, advising him that as many men as possible ought to be sent to France at once: 'You ought to scour your whole military organisation and also the Navy in order to diminish the superiority of the enemy.' Clemenceau was 'splendid in his resolution and buoyancy'. That Sunday, Churchill wrote also to Clementine about the Tiger: 'His spirit & energy indomitable. Fifteen hours yesterday over rough roads at high speed in motor cars, I was tired out – & he is 76! He makes the same impression on me as Fisher: but much more efficient, & just as ready to turn round & bite!'

Lloyd George wanted the Americans to send substantial drafts of men to France without delay, ideally 120,000 men a month. On the morning of March 31 Churchill went, at Lloyd George's request, to put this idea to Clemenceau. Together they drafted a telegram to President Wilson, putting the urgency to him. Basing himself on all he had learned during the previous day's journey, Clemenceau wrote, with Churchill's guidance, 'I am now able to inform you that, whatever happens, we shall contest the ground step by step, and that from today onward we are certain of stopping the enemy.'

President Wilson agreed to expedite the men in the numbers asked. After another day at the front, Churchill returned to Paris, where he telegraphed to Lloyd George at midnight, 'French are now well established and solidly backed with guns.' The German southward thrust 'does not now cause anxiety'.

Churchill saw Clemenceau again that night; then he telegraphed to Lloyd George, urging him to cross to France at once and settle with Clemenceau the details of the high command structure. 'You and he together can make a good settlement and no one else can.' Lloyd George crossed to Boulogne on the morning of April 3, together with Henry Wilson. Churchill met them at Boulogne and drove with them to Montreuil. But at Sir Henry's insistence he was excluded from the military discussion which took place that morning at Beauvais, at which it was agreed that Foch should become Generalissimo of all Allied forces in France, including the British and American.

Excluded from these discussions, Churchill spent the rest of April 3 in northern France on munitions business, then joined Lloyd George in the evening for the journey from Boulogne to Folkestone and back to London, which they reached at two-thirty in the morning.

On the Eastern Front, the Bolsheviks had made their peace with Germany. Churchill cast about for some means of persuading them to re-enter the war, and re-activate the Eastern Front. If the Bolsheviks could be 'induced' to make common cause with Roumania, he wrote to the War Cabinet, and jointly attack Germany, that would be the moment to send to Moscow 'representatives of the Allies, of sufficient weight to give the Bolshevik Government a new element of stability and a means of reaching a working arrangement with other classes of Russian society'.

Churchill felt that if the former American President, Theodore Roosevelt, who was then in Paris, or the former French Minister of War, Albert Thomas, 'were with Trotsky at the inevitable moment when war is again declared between Germany and Russia, a rallying point might be created sufficiently prominent for all Russians to fix their gaze upon. Some general formula such as "safeguarding the permanent fruits of the Revolution" might be devised which would render common action possible having regard to the cruel and increasing pressure of the Germans.' The Entente representative might become 'an integral part of the Russian Government'.

Churchill was convinced that Britain and the Bolsheviks could make common cause. 'Let us never forget that Lenin and Trotsky are fighting with ropes round their necks. They will leave office for the grave. Show them any real chance of consolidating their power, of getting some kind of protection against the vengeance of a counter-revolution, and they would be non-human not to embrace it. They must, however, be forced by events and aided by foreigners. Without external aid and countenance they can do nothing. Hitherto they have had other hopes but these have utterly failed, and self-preservation will force them to tread a path which is also ours if they can be helped to gain it.'

'In the main,' Churchill wrote in a second memorandum for the Cabinet that April, 'the intellect of Russia, including the Bolsheviks, must, whatever happens in the long run, be hostile to Prussian militarism and therefore drawn towards the Allied parliamentary democracies.'

Churchill sought every possible means of bringing pressure to bear on the German forces. A day before his suggestion of a deal with Lenin, he had written to Loucheur about the need to continue the manufacture of mustard-gas shells, telling him he was 'in favour of the greatest possible development of gas warfare, and of the fullest utilisation of winds, which favour us so much more than the enemy'. Within a month, more than a third of the shells fired by the British Army were mustard-gas shells. But the first gas success that year was achieved by the Germans, when shortly after midnight on April 7 they attacked the northern sector of the British line at Armentières. Three days later, Armentières was overrun.

All the gains of the Third Battle of Ypres had been lost; the woods in the Ypres salient which Churchill had explored in February were again in German hands. Churchill now warned Lloyd George of the danger of the Germans driving a wedge between the British and French forces by reaching the English Channel at Abbeville. 'Is not the sound rule,' he asked Lloyd George on April 18, 'to stand together, retire together, turn together and strike together, as we did after the Marne?'

Following his return from France, Churchill had redoubled his efforts to manufacture munitions. By April 21 he had been able to send Haig twice as many guns as had been lost or destroyed since the start of the German offensive a month earlier. The same was true of aircraft. He had also been able to replace every tank lost by one of a newer and better pattern. In order to find out from Haig the exact needs in heavy gun ammunition, Churchill crossed back to France on April 27. That evening Haig wrote in his diary, 'He has certainly improved the output of the munitions factories very greatly, and is full of energy in trying to release men for the army, and replace them by substitutes.'

On his return from France, Churchill found an appeal from the United States for the two hundred heavy guns which he had promised the Americans five months earlier. They were now urgently needed by the new armies soon to arrive in France. Despite the British losses after March 21, and the despatch of stocks to the armies in Italy, he was able to make good his promise. But his main work that summer was the munitions needs for 1919, the first year in which it was assumed victory would be possible. To expedite these efforts Churchill now lived permanently, and slept, at the Ministry building. This had 'many conveniences from the point of view of getting work done', he told a friend. 'It enables me to work to the last moment before dinner, to get papers when I come back after dinner, and to begin with shorthand assistance as early as I choose in the morning.'

That summer Churchill also instituted the first regular cross-Channel air service, for Ministers and officials who needed to go regularly back and forth to France. Churchill made the first of these flights on May 18, from Le Bourget airport north-east of Paris, in order to return as quickly as possible to London from an Inter-Allied munitions conference.

On June 1 there was a personal interlude, the marriage of Churchill's mother to a member of the Nigerian Civil Service, Montagu Porch. Her second husband, George Cornwallis-West, had left her in 1913 to marry the actress Mrs Patrick Campbell. Porch was twenty-three years younger than Lady Randolph and three years younger than Churchill himself. 'Winston says he hopes marriage won't become the vogue among ladies of his mother's age,' a family friend noted in his diary. Lady Randolph was sixty-four. Churchill and his wife were among those who signed the register; Clementine was four months pregnant.

Two days after his mother's wedding, Churchill flew back to France. Clementine saw him off. 'I had a touching vision of you & your two kittens growing rapidly smaller, and the aerodrome & its sheds dwindling into distant perspective as I whirled away,' he wrote to her from France. 'It was a very beautiful & wonderful journey.'

The Germans, cheated of their victory in March, had launched another offensive, breaking through the French lines between the Aisne and the Marne. There was concern in Paris that the capital itself might be threatened. Churchill landed at Hesdin, then drove to Paris. 'An air raid is in progress,' he wrote to Clementine from Paris on the night of June 6, '& I am due & overdue for bed.' As to the military situation, 'On the whole I am hopeful. But the fate of the capital hangs in the balance – only 45 miles away. Next time I come (if there is a "next time") you must really try to accompany me.'

On June 8 Churchill visited the French front line north of Compiègne. The two French Generals he met there were both 'soberly confident & hoped that they would be attacked', he told Clementine. 'The day had been quiet,' he later recalled, 'and the sweetness of the summer evening was undisturbed even by a cannon shot. Very calm and gallant, and even gay, were the French soldiers who awaited the new stroke of fate. By the next evening all the ground over which they had led me was in German hands, and most of those with whom I had talked were dead or prisoners'. In all, the German Army took 60,000 prisoners during their sweep forward.

Back in Paris, Churchill reported to his wife on the afternoon of June 9 that the battle then raging between Montdidier and Noyon was 'very critical and deadly'. If the French could not hold the Germans back on that sector 'it is not easy to see what the next step on our part should be'. He was, however, hopeful; the line was 'strongly held with troops & good reserves at hand'. That day, in Paris, two German long-range shells fell within 150 yards of where Churchill was in conference.

The Germans failed to reach Compiègne. On June 11 the French began their counter-attack. Churchill flew back to England on the following day. During the flight something went wrong with the engine. 'I very nearly finished an eventful though disappointing life in the salt waters of the Channel,' he told Sinclair. 'We just fluttered back to shore.'

Churchill was angered that month when, at the insistence of Lord Milner, recently appointed Secretary of State for War, the War Cabinet decided to continue to take men from the munitions factories for the front, even though this had begun to lead to a sharp drop in tank production. He was now worried about Britain's ability to win the war in 1919. 'Do the means of beating the German armies in the West in 1919 exist?' he asked the War Cabinet in a memorandum on June 22. 'Can the men be procured? If so, the mechanisms can be prepared. We still have the time. Have we the will-power and the command to look ahead and regulate action accordingly?' When the War Cabinet announced publicly that no British air raids would take place over Germany on Corpus Christi Day, Churchill wrote angrily to Lloyd George, 'Do put your foot down on this. It is abject.'

A further threat to munitions production for 1919 came at the end of June, when strikes broke out in many factories, fuelled by the refusal of the owners to discuss wage increases with the unions. In the most serious case, at the Alliance Aeroplane Works, the strike began with the sacking of a shop steward. Aircraft production was halted. Churchill took drastic action, taking over the works for the Government. He then reinstated the sacked shop steward and allowed the shop committee to continue its activities, defending his action by upholding the workers' claim that the firm 'had opposed the legitimate development of the shop steward and shop committee movement'.

A week later strikes broke out in several tank factories in protest against the transfer of men against their will from one factory to another. This had become necessary because of the continued transfer of men to the front, as insisted upon by the War Cabinet. Confronted by a virtual collapse in tank production, Churchill wanted to force the strikers back to work by withdrawing their exemption from military service. At a meeting with Churchill on July 25, Bonar Law opposed this, not wanting to use the Military Service Act 'as an agent in an industrial dispute'. On the following day 300,000 munitions workers in Leeds threatened to strike from July 29; Lloyd George at once intervened, supporting Churchill's proposal and issuing a statement from Downing Street that all strikers would be liable to be sent to the front. The strike collapsed and tank production resumed. The hopes for a military victory in 1919 were intact.

On August 8 the British Fourth Army, commanded by General Rawlinson, launched a new offensive; British, Canadian and Australian troops all took part. The battle was remarkable because seventy-two tanks, all built as a result of Churchill's ministerial efforts and exhortations, took part in the battle. Wanting to be in France while the tanks were in action, Churchill flew that afternoon to Hesdin. From there he was driven to the Château Verchocq, which Haig had put at his disposal for his future visits to France.

By nightfall on August 8 the tank attack had broken through the German front-line trenches; 400 German guns and nearly 22,000 soldiers were captured. 'I am so glad that it has all come right,' Churchill telegraphed to Haig, who replied, 'I shall always remember with gratitude the energy and foresight which you displayed as Minister of Munitions, and so rendered our success possible.' Churchill sent Haig's telegram to Clementine with the covering note: 'It is certainly very satisfactory to have succeeded in gaining the confidence and good-will of the extremely difficult and to some extent prejudiced authorities out here. There is no doubt that they have felt themselves abundantly supplied.'

On August 9 Churchill went to see Rawlinson at his headquarters at Flixecourt; then he drove with his brother Jack to the front line. 'On our way to the front,' he told Clementine, 'we passed nearly 5,000 German prisoners, penned up in cages or resting under escort in long columns along the roadside.' Among them were more than 200 officers. 'I went into the cages and looked at them carefully. They looked a fairly sturdy lot, though some of them were very young. I could not help feeling sorry for them in their miserable plight and dejection, having marched all those miles from the battlefield without food or rest, and having been through all the horrors of the fight before that. Still, I was very glad to see them where they were.'

Together with his brother, Churchill reached the front near the village of Lamotte, which on the previous morning had been five thousand yards inside the German lines. 'The tracks of the tanks were everywhere apparent,' he told Clementine with pride.

By August 10 the British Army had made further advances, taking another 10,000 prisoners. 'The tide has turned,' Churchill wrote to Clementine that day. 'It is our victory, won chiefly by our troops under a British Commander, and largely through the invincible tank which British brains have invented and developed.' Still focusing on the battles of 1919, he wrote that night to Lloyd George of the need for 100,000 men by the following June if the tanks were not to 'fail in their full effect'. On August 11 he returned to the battle zone. 'The Germans were hardly firing at all,' he told Clementine, 'while our batteries thundered away. There were more German dead lying about than in the other sector which I visited, & all our dead cavalry horses dotted the countryside & disfigured the scene.' He saw a British observation balloon shot down in flames, 'the observers just skipping out in their parachutes in time'.

'I do hope we shall be careful not to waste our men in pushing now that the spurt is finished,' Clementine wrote to her husband on August 13. 'Your remark about not throwing away our men', he replied, 'shows you to be a very wise & sagacious military pussy cat.' On the day of her letter he had driven from Verchocq to Paris to preside at the Inter-Allied Munitions Council. Its task was to fix the munitions programme for 1919. He also called on Clemenceau, who expressed unease at Britain's manpower plans. 'I am also disquieted by what I know,' Churchill wrote to Clementine, '& think we are not making sufficient provision.'

While still in Paris on August 16, Churchill and Loucheur agreed to provide the tank engines and guns needed by the American Third Army. Two days later he pressed Loucheur to help him in the design and manufacture of long-distance bombing planes which could 'discharge the maximum quantity of bombs upon the enemy'. This was the moment, he explained, 'to carry the war into his own country, to make him feel in his own towns and in his own person something of the havoc he has wrought in France and Belgium. This is the moment, just before the winter begins, to affect his morale, and to harry his hungry and dispirited cities without pause or stay.'

Churchill returned to Verchocq for three days. Then on August 19 he flew for the day to Haig's advance headquarters at Frévent. 'He is most anxious to help us in every way,' Haig wrote in his diary, 'and is hurrying up the supply of "10 calibre-head" shells, gas, tanks etc. His schemes are all timed for "completion in next June"! I told him we ought to get a decision this autumn.' Returning at dusk to the airfield near Verchocq, Churchill spoke to a group of young pilots who were waiting to take off on a night bombing raid on Germany. 'You know,' he told his own pilot, 'the people at home have no idea what these lads are going through.'

Churchill remained at Verchocq for another week. By August 24 British troops on the Somme had recaptured almost all the ground overrun by the Germans in March. 'It is very jolly moving about so freely with the armies,' he wrote that day to Clementine, '& yet being able to do my work regularly.' On the following day he flew back to England, going straight from the airfield at Kenley, to Lullenden, less than twelves miles away, to be with his family.

While Churchill was in London on August 31, Bolshevik troops forced their way into the British Embassy in Petrograd. Among the British officers in the building was the Naval Attaché, Captain Francis Cromie, who shot three of the Bolshevik soldiers dead, and was then killed. As soon as Churchill heard this, he dictated a memorandum for the War Cabinet, in which he wrote that Cromie was 'a very gifted man, of exceptionally high professional attainments' whom he had known personally before 1914. He continued: 'I earnestly hope that the Government, in spite of its many pre-occupations, will pursue the perpetrators of this crime with tireless perseverance. Reprisals upon various Bolshevik nonentities who happen to be in our hands are of no real use, though they should be by no means excluded. The only policy which is likely to be effective, either for the past or the future, is to mark down the personalities of the Bolshevik Government as the objects upon whom justice will be executed, however long it takes, and to make them feel that their punishment will become an important object of British policy to be held steadily in view through all the phases of the war and of the settlement.'

Churchill drew a wider moral from the shooting: 'The exertions which a nation is prepared to make to protect its individual representatives or citizens from outrage,' he wrote, 'is one of the truest measures of its greatness as an organised State. The fact that men are dying in thousands in fair war must not deaden us to the entirely different character of an act of this kind.' At its meeting on September 4 the War Cabinet decided to send a telegram to the Soviet Government 'threatening reprisals' against Trotsky, Lenin, and 'the leaders of that Government' if the lives of British subjects were not henceforth safeguarded.

Having negotiated that August with the Chilean Government for the purchase by the Allies of the whole of Chile's nitrate production, an essential component in munitions manufacture, on September 7 Churchill telegraphed to Bernard Baruch in Washington, asking him what the monthly munitions requirements of the United States would be in 1919, so that Allied production plans could be worked out in harmony, to maximum effect. That afternoon he joined his wife and children at St Margaret's Bay near Dover for a brief seaside excursion. Then, at dusk, he drove to Lympne and flew back to Verchocq.

Clementine realised the need for her husband's long absences, but she was unhappy about the increase in the amount of flying he was doing. He begged her not to worry. 'It gives me a feeling of tremendous conquest over space,' he wrote, '& I know you would love it yourself.' On the following day he flew from Verchocq to Haig's headquarters at Montreuil, where he found a confident mood that victory would come before the end of 1918. 'One must always discount the sanguine opinions of the Army,' he told Clementine. 'Still there is an end to every task, & some day the optimists will be right.'

With each British advance Churchill went to the scene to see how his shells, mustard gas and tanks had been used, or misused. On September 9 he visited the newly captured German positions at Drocourt, east of Vimy. 'The ruin of the countryside was complete,' he wrote to Clementine. 'Everywhere pain & litter & squalor & the abomination of desolation. Everywhere too the enemy flung shells at random – now here, now there, to which the working, sleeping, eating, bathing, loitering, marching soldiers paid not the slightest attention.' Most of the British dead in the battle had already been buried, 'but a number of German blue and grey bundles still lie around'.

Churchill did not tell his wife of the full situation at Drocourt. But he did tell Lloyd George, for it illustrated what happened when the advancing infantry no longer had tank support. Each successive fortified German line had been overrun, he wrote to the Prime Minister on September 10, but at the point where the Germans only had left 'a few little pits and holes' from which to fire their machine guns, the advancing troops had 'got beyond the support of the tanks'; in one small space about 380 yards wide 'nearly 400 Canadian dead had just been buried and only a few score Germans'. Churchill added: 'You would have been shocked to see the tragic spectacle of the ground where our attack for the time being withered away. It was just like a line of seaweed and jetsam which is left by a great wave as it recoils.'

Churchill went on to warn Lloyd George that as a result of the heavy expenditure of ammunition on the Western Front since the start of the August offensive, there was grave danger of severe shortages in 1919. In view of what had happened at Drocourt he wanted a substantial increase in the number of tanks for 1919, involving a similar increase in the number of crews. Indeed, he wrote, many more crews would be needed than tanks as the 'permanent wastage of the personnel is high, whereas the tank in any victorious battle recovers very quickly from his wounds and hardly ever dies beyond the hope of resurrection. A few months sojourn in the grave is nearly always followed by a reincarnation.' As well as restoring damaged tanks, Churchill wanted to press ahead with the design of larger, stronger and faster tanks, and to make sure that they too were ready by the summer of 1919.

Haig was alarmed at Churchill's repeated emphasis on the campaigns of 1919. On the evening of September 10 he sent a mutual friend to tell him that 'we ought to aim at finishing the war now and not to delay the provision of tanks until experiments showed we had the perfect design'. But in one area Haig and Churchill were in agreement. On September 12 he wrote to Clementine from Paris, 'I am trying also to give the Germans a good first dose of the mustard gas, before the end of the month. Haig is very keen on it & we shall I think have enough to produce a decided effect.' Churchill added, 'Their whining in defeat is very gratifying to hear.'

This was the first time Churchill had written in a letter of Germany's imminent defeat. It was his tenth wedding anniversary:

> Ten years ago my dearest one we were sliding down to Blenheim in our special train. Do you remember? It is a long stage on life's road. Do you think we have been less happy or more happy than the average married couple?
>
> I reproach myself very much for not having been more to you. But at any rate in these ten years the sun has never yet gone down on our wrath. Never once have we closed our eyes in slumber with an unappeased difference.
>
> My dearest sweet I hope & pray that future years may bring you serene & smiling days, & full & fruitful occupation. I think that you will find real scope in the new world opening out to women, & find interests which will enrich your life. And always at your side in true & tender friendship as long as he breathes will be your ever devoted, if only partially satisfactory   W

From Paris, Churchill returned to Verchocq. He had begun to fulfil a 2,000-gun order from the United States, with which, he told Clementine on September 15, 'they will be able to arm perhaps fifteen additional divisions or nearly half a million men, in time for the crisis of next year'. He was also buying from the United States 2,000 to 3,000 aircraft engines 'for the bombing of Germany' by British pilots in 1919. 'My days here have been fruitful in business,' he told her, '& I have got lots of things moving which were otherwise stuck. The hamper of mustard gas is on its way. This hellish poison will I trust be discharged on the Huns to the extent of nearly

1,000 tons by the end of this month.' He no longer chafed 'at adverse political combinations, or at not being able to direct general policy. I am content to be associated with the splendid machines of the British Army, & to feel how many ways there are open to me to serve them.'

Churchill returned to England on September 17. Nine days later, in the first phase of the battle for the Hindenburg Line, British artillery began a three-day gas bombardment on the German positions with devastating effect. Churchill was back in Paris on September 27 when the Bulgarian Army surrendered unconditionally. The first of the allies of Germany and Austria-Hungary was out of the war. The Balkans, which three years earlier Churchill had hoped to turn against Austria and Germany, were now the Achilles' heel of the Central Powers.

On the Western Front, Haig's armies had captured another 10,000 German prisoners and 200 guns. But, while speaking to munitions workers at Glasgow on October 7, Churchill warned against the current talk 'of the speedy termination of the conflict'. It might be that the course of the battle 'will be better than we have any right to hope for now, but we must not count or build upon too favourable a development of events. We have started out to put this business through, and we must continue to develop to the utmost every resource that can make certain that, whatever the course of the war in 1918, the year 1919 will see our foe unable to resist our legitimate and rightful claims.'

This was too cautious a forecast; on October 15, exhausted by the blood-letting, faced with widespread starvation as a result of the Allied sea blockade, and fearing a total collapse of the Balkan front, the Germans asked for an armistice. President Wilson, who had already set out the Allied conditions for an end to the war, including the return of Alsace and Lorraine to France, turned down the German request. Speaking that day at Manchester, Churchill praised Wilson's 'stern and formidable answer'.

Wilson had made it clear that the war must go on until Germany surrendered; that week the British bombing of German factories, supply dumps and aerodromes intensified. On October 17, as British forces entered Lille, which had been under German occupation for four years, Churchill was again at Verchocq. Clementine, who for more than three years had worked to organise canteens for women munitions workers, wrote to him on October 18:

> Do come home and look after what is to be done with the munition
> workers when the fighting really does stop. Even if the fighting is not over
> yet, your share of it must be & I would like you to be praised as a
> reconstructive genius, as well as for a Mustard Gas fiend, a Tank

*juggernaut & a flying Terror. Besides the credit for all these Bogey parts
will be given to subordinates.*

*Can't the men munition workers build lovely garden cities & pull down
slums in places like Bethnal Green, Newcastle, Glasgow, Leeds, etc. &
can't the women munition workers make all the lovely furniture for them,
babies' cradles, cupboards etc.*

Do come home and arrange all this.

On October 20, in an attempt to win favour with the Allies, the Germans
announced the end of their submarine campaign against merchant ships.
Five days later, accompanied by Marsh, Churchill was again in France,
visiting the newly-liberated areas. On October 26 he toured the battlefield
of Le Câteau, the scene in September 1914 of one of the earliest German
victories, now won back after more than four years. But his attempt to
drive to the front line was frustrated by a fallen railway bridge which the
Germans had blown up. On October 27 he drove to Lille, where he spent
the night; on the following day he was asked to be present on the saluting
stand at a march-past of British troops. Also on the stand was a young
British officer, Major Bernard Montgomery. Before the march-past
ended Churchill had to leave, as he had been invited to lunch with his
friend General Tudor at his headquarters at Harlebeke, across the Belgian
border.

After their lunch Churchill and Tudor drove towards the front line,
reaching a church tower from which they could survey the scene. As they
looked over the German lines there was a heavy shell attack. Then,
recorded Marsh, who was with them, 'the General smelt mustard gas, and
made us stuff handkerchiefs into our mouths till we got back to the motor'.
Mustard gas was being used by both sides.

Churchill spent the night of October 28 at Tudor's headquarters. During dinner, Marsh noted, 'a Hun plane dropped a fairly large bomb in the
street fairly near the house, but this was the only one dropped.' On the
following day Churchill and Marsh set off by car for Bruges. Their drive
nearly ended in disaster. As they entered the village of Desselghem,
looking for a bridge over the River Lys, 'I was puzzled,' Churchill wrote a
week later to Tudor, 'to see a peasant suddenly throw himself down behind
the wall of a house, and something seemed to be very odd about his
gesture. Still, so strong was my impression that we were nearly 10,000
yards from the line that I did not draw any true conclusions from the
incident.'

Unknown to Churchill, the village was less than two thousand yards
from the nearest German positions, and about to be subjected to a severe
bombardment. Hardly had the peasant thrown himself to the ground when

a shell burst fifty yards ahead of the car. Thinking that he was nowhere near the front, Churchill assumed it was a bomb dropped from an aeroplane. Two or three seconds later there was 'a whole series of explosions around us'. Still thinking it was an aeroplane, he contemplated not driving on into the open country, in case his 'large and flaunting car' became a target. 'Very luckily, however, I let the car run on, for the very spot where I had thought of pulling up to make enquiries was struck by another shell almost immediately.'

It was now clear that Desselghem was being struck by artillery shells, not bombs. As the car drove on, Churchill still did not realise how near he had been to the front. 'I continued to speculate stupidly upon the odd habits of the Huns in firing such a very long-range battery upon an obscure village 10,000 yards behind the lines.' Then 'we had another rapid series of shells to enliven our journey'. It was only when he reached Bruges that Churchill learned how close he had been to the Germans. The car had been travelling at forty miles an hour, he told Tudor, and could easily have run straight into the German lines. 'What mugs we should have been!'

From Bruges, Churchill drove south, through recently liberated Belgian villages to Passchendaele, which he reached from what had been the German side, crossing into the former Allied lines and revisiting Hellfire Corner on his way into Ypres. There, after looking at the ruined buildings in the centre of the town, he told Marsh that he wanted to turn them into a war cemetery 'with lawns and flowers among the ruins, and the names of innumerable dead'.

That night Churchill slept at Verchocq. On the following day, as he flew back to England, Turkey surrendered to the Allied Powers. The surrender of Austria-Hungary was expected any day; 'a drizzle of empires falling through the air', Churchill described it to Marsh.

Austria-Hungary surrendered on November 3. In London, Churchill tried to ensure that once the war was over there would be a place for him at the centre of policy-making. At lunch with Lloyd George on November 6 he spoke of 'the degradation of being a Minister without responsibility for policy'. Lloyd George assured him that all Ministers with wartime departments would have places in a peacetime Cabinet.

On November 7 a German delegation crossed into the French lines and asked for an armistice; for three days it discussed the Allied conditions. On November 10 Lloyd George invited Churchill to a special Cabinet meeting to discuss the course of those negotiations. During the meeting a message was brought in that the Kaiser had fled to Holland. At five o'clock the next morning the Germans accepted the Allied terms. Fighting would cease at eleven o'clock that morning. Within fourteen days German troops would evacuate France, Belgium, Luxemburg, Alsace and Lorraine. All

German troops would withdraw from the Rhineland. Allied and American troops would occupy Germany west of the Rhine.

The future of the German Army was also discussed at the Cabinet of November 10. There was general agreement that it should be demobilised as soon as possible. Churchill, however, struck a note of caution. 'We might have to build up the German army,' he warned, as it was 'important to get Germany on her legs again for fear of the spread of Bolshevism.'

On the morning of November 11 Churchill and his advisers discussed the sale of Britain's surplus munitions stock, and the problems of factories then at the height of their daily output, whose shells, guns and tanks would no longer be needed, certainly not in the enormous quantities now being produced. Then, as the eleven o'clock deadline for the ceasefire approached, Churchill stood alone at the window of his room in the Hotel Metropole, overlooking Northumberland Avenue. 'Victory had come after all the hazards and heartbreaks in an absolute and unlimited form,' he later wrote. 'All the Kings and Emperors with whom we had warred were in flight or exile. All their armies and fleets were destroyed or subdued. In this Britain had borne a notable part, and done her best from first to last.'

Churchill's musings continued. 'The material purposes on which one's work had been centred, every process of thought on which one had lived, crumbled into nothing. The whole vast business of supply, the growing outputs, the careful hoards, the secret future plans – but yesterday the whole duty of life – all at a stroke vanished like a nightmare dream, leaving a void behind.' His mind ranged over the problems of demobilisation; what would his three million workers make now? 'How would the factories be converted? How in fact are swords beaten into ploughshares?'

The first stroke of eleven o'clock rang out. 'I looked again at the broad street beneath me. It was deserted. From the portals of one of the large hotels absorbed by Government departments darted the slight figure of a girl clerk, distractedly gesticulating while another stroke of Big Ben resounded. Then from all sides men and women came scurrying into the street. Streams of people poured out of the buildings.' Northumberland Avenue was now full of people. In the Hotel Metropole 'disorder had broken out'. Doors banged. Feet clattered down corridors. 'Everyone rose from the desk and cast aside pen and paper.'

Churchill looked towards Trafalgar Square. It was swarming with people. 'Flags appeared as if by magic.' Clementine, who was expecting the birth of her fourth child that very week, arrived at the Hotel Metropole to be with her husband. They decided to drive together to Downing Street to congratulate Lloyd George. As they entered their car about twenty people jumped excitedly upon it. Surrounded by a wildly cheering crowd, it eventually reached Downing Street.

That evening, Lloyd George invited Churchill to dine with him. The only other guests were F.E. Smith and Sir Henry Wilson. 'LG wants to shoot the Kaiser,' Wilson noted in his diary, 'Winston does not.' The struggles of war were over; the conflicts of peace had begun.

19

At the War Office

On 15 November 1918, four days after the armistice, Churchill's fourth child was born. She was christened Marigold Frances, but known to her parents as 'the Duckadilly'. It had been a difficult birth, and Churchill wished to spend as much time as possible with Clementine. But ten days after Marigold's birth he had to hurry north, to Dundee, to speak to his constituents; Lloyd George had called a sudden General Election.

Lloyd George was determined to keep his Coalition Government together in peace as in war. But many Liberals wished to return to the Party politics of 1914, and to Asquith's leadership. Lloyd George called a General Election for early December; it was up to each Liberal to decide whether to support Asquith or stay with Lloyd George. Churchill emerged in the election campaign as a leading Liberal advocate of maintaining the Coalition. He was also one of the few Coalition politicians who opposed a harsh peace with Germany.

In an attempt to preserve as many Liberal concepts as possible in the new Government's policies, Churchill urged Lloyd George to consider a heavy tax on all war profits. 'Why should anybody make a great fortune out of the war?' he asked him on November 21, ten days after Germany's surrender. 'While everybody has been serving the country, profiteers & contractors & shipping speculators have gained fortunes of a gigantic character.' His proposal was that the Government should 'reclaim everything above, say, £10,000 (to let the small fry off)', and thus substantially reduce Britain's war debt from the coffers of the war profiteers.

On November 26, in a speech to his constituents at Dundee, Churchill warned of the dangers of Bolshevism: 'Civilisation is being completely extinguished over gigantic areas, while Bolsheviks hop and caper like troops of ferocious baboons amid the ruins of cities and the corpses of their victims.' Churchill's listeners cheered; but they heckled loudly when, in the same speech, he advocated a moderate peace. To a former Liberal MP who protested at this call for leniency he wrote on December 4, 'I do not consider that we should be justified in enforcing any demand which had the effect of reducing for an indefinite period the mass of the working class population of Germany to a condition of sweated labour and servitude.'

Returning twice to Dundee, Churchill called for radical measures at home; for the nationalisation of the railways, for the control of monopolies 'in the general interest', and for taxation levied 'in proportion to the ability to pay'. He also supported the idea of 'a permanent League of Nations to render future wars impossible'. The main task of such a League would be to prevent secret armaments. 'Altogether I think the chances of a great majority are very good,' he wrote to Clementine on December 13, 'and it is not impossible that it may be the greatest majority ever yet recorded at a British election.'

Polling day was December 14. The results were not announced for two weeks, to enable the soldiers' votes to be counted. 'I hope,' Churchill wrote to Lloyd George two days before the results were known, 'you will endeavour to gather together all forces of strength & influence in the country & lead them along the paths of science & organisation to the rescue of the weak & poor.'

The election result was a triumph for Lloyd George, whose Coalition Liberals won 133 seats. The Coalition Conservatives won 335 and the Coalition Labour ten; a total of 478 seats for Lloyd George, the majority of them his former Conservative foes. The Asquith Liberals were reduced to twenty-eight and Asquith himself defeated at East Fife. Labour won sixty-three, and Sinn Fein, a new feature of Westminster politics, seventy-three. The Sinn Fein MPs wanted immediate independence for Ireland; in protest at the continuation of British rule they refused to take their seats at Westminster, and formed their own assembly in Dublin. Churchill was returned with what the main Dundee newspaper called 'an immense majority' of 15,365, though it was not as he had hoped the largest ever recorded, or anywhere near it.

Lloyd George wanted Churchill to go to the War Office to take charge of the massive task of demobilisation. At the Ministry of Munitions he had been responsible for three million workers. The number of soldiers to be brought home was nearly three and a half million. Churchill hesitated; he wanted to be First Lord again. 'My heart is in the Admiralty,' he wrote to Lloyd George on December 29. 'There I have long experience, & any claim I may be granted in public goodwill will always rest on the fact that "The Fleet was ready".' He would also like the Air Force to be put with his Admiralty responsibilities. 'Though aeroplanes will never be a substitute for armies,' he argued, 'they will be a substitute for many classes of warship.'

Lloyd George insisted that Churchill go to the War Office, where another urgent and difficult task awaited him. Four months had passed since the murder of Captain Cromie in Petrograd. Bolshevik rule had been consolidated throughout central Russia. But by the end of December there were more than 180,000 non-Russian troops within the frontiers of the former Tsarist Empire, among them British, American, Japanese, French, Czech, Serb, Greek and Italian. Several anti-Bolshevik armies, amounting to more than 300,000 men, looked to these troops for military and moral support, and depended on their governments for money and guns. The Bolsheviks were everywhere being pressed back towards Moscow.

The arms which Britain had sent to Russia in 1917 and 1918, to be used against Germany, had been handed over to the anti-Bolshevik forces for use against the usually poorly-armed Bolsheviks. British troops, sent originally to guard those arms, had become involved in the civil war not only as advisers but as participants. Churchill had not been responsible in any way for these decisions. It was not until the last day of 1918 that he found himself involved in Britain's policy towards Russia; on that day Lloyd George invited him to attend a meeting of the Imperial War Cabinet called specially to formulate British policy against the Bolsheviks.

He was 'all for negotiation' with the Bolsheviks, Churchill told the meeting, 'but he considered there was no chance of securing such a settlement unless it was known we had the power and the will to enforce our views'. If the Bolshevik and anti-Bolshevik Russians 'were ready to come together we should help them'. Otherwise Britain should use force 'to restore the situation and set up a democratic government'. Bolshevism represented only a fraction of the Russian people. It would be 'exposed and swept away' by a General Election held under Allied auspices.

Lloyd George wished to limit Britain's involvement to helping those former Tsarist territories in the Baltic and the Caucasus that were 'struggling to be independent from Russia,' telling the meeting that he was 'definitely opposed' to British military intervention inside Russia itself. But with the approval of Balfour and Milner, British troops had not only been sent to the Caucasus and Baltic regions many months earlier, but were already helping three Russian anti-Bolshevik armies inside Russia; in North Russia, in Siberia, and in South Russia. There were in fact already seven British Generals holding military commands on Russian soil, with 14,000 British troops under their scattered commands.

In sending Churchill to the War Office, Lloyd George agreed that he should also be in charge of Britain's air policy, so that his formal appointment, made on 9 January 1919, was that of Secretary of State for War and Air. He had already entered into his duties, at a moment of extreme tension; the Army for which he was now responsible was deeply discontented. In the week before his arrival at the War Office there had been widespread demonstrations demanding immediate demobilisation. On January 8, for the second day running, angry troops reached Whitehall. At one o'clock they tried to see Lloyd George at Downing Street but were diverted to Horse Guards Parade, where they were met by the commanding officer of the London District, General Feilding. The war was over, they shouted. Why should they return to France? Others were refusing to go to Russia.

It was the day before Churchill's formal appointment as Secretary of State for War. He went at once to Horse Guards Parade.

'How many troops have we to deal with them? he asked Feilding.

'A battalion of Guards and three squadrons of Household Cavalry,' was the reply.

'Are they loyal?' asked Churchill.

'We hope they are.'·

'Can you arrest the mutineers?'

'We are not certain.'

'Have you any other suggestions?'

There were no other suggestions.

'Then arrest the mutineers.'

Churchill, watching from a window, expected firing to break out at any moment. But the soldiers allowed themselves to be surrounded and then gave themselves up. Determined to defuse a tense and volatile situation, Churchill sought a scheme that would be fair, and seen as fair. Hitherto only those men who already had offers of work in Britain were being demobilised. A soldier who had served for only four months, but had an industrial job awaiting him, could go home at once. A soldier who had served for four years, but had no job to go home to, must stay in uniform.

On January 12, four days after the Whitehall mutiny and three days after his appointment, Churchill announced his new scheme. Those who had served in France longest would be released first. All men who had enlisted before 1916 would be demobilised at once. All men over forty, however recent their enlistment, would be allowed home at once. All those who had served for two years or less would have to wait until those who had served longer had been released. In the demobilisation of those who joined in 1916 or after, priority would be given to those who had been wounded. 'It was one of the best things I did,' Churchill told a friend thirty-five years later.

The fairness of Churchill's scheme was at once acclaimed, but he had also to ensure that Britain would have enough men to establish an Army of Occupation on the Rhine. To do this, he proposed retaining conscription for the million men needed in Germany. Lloyd George, who was in Paris for the first stage of the Peace Conference, protested at the retention of any form of conscription, and at the size of the proposed occupation force. As the German Army was to be demobilised, he told Churchill in a telephone message on January 21, 'it is absurd to retain so big an army.'

Churchill crossed to France to explain to Lloyd George the reason why so many men would be needed. During luncheon he told Lloyd George that the Army of Occupation must be strong enough to 'extract' from the Germans 'the just terms which the Allies demand'. Such an army must be 'strong, compact, contented, well-disciplined' if Britain were not to be 'tricked of what we have rightfully won'. Henry Wilson, who was present, noted in his diary, 'Churchill put the case with tact, and clearly.' Before the lunch was over, Lloyd George had agreed to what Churchill proposed. A million men were to be conscripted in time of peace.

Meanwhile Churchill's demobilisation plan was proceeding smoothly. By January 31 more than 950,000 officers and men had returned home. That day, however, Churchill learned that a mutiny had broken out in Calais, among five thousand troops who had earlier been sent back to France from England under the original scheme. They were demanding to be sent back again to England and to be demobilised. Haig, having surrounded their camp with machine-guns and arrested three ringleaders, informed Churchill that it was essential for the ringleaders to be shot.

Churchill acted at once to stop Haig carrying out the executions. 'Unless there was serious violence attended by bloodshed and actual loss of life,' he telegraphed, 'I do not consider that the infliction of the death penalty would be justifiable.' Public opinion would only support the death penalty, Churchill added, 'when other men's lives are endangered by criminal or cowardly conduct'.

There was another urgent problem on Churchill's desk on January 31, a request from Henry Wilson for an immediate decision about the British troops in Russia . The 13,000 British troops in North Russia and the 1,000 in Siberia were isolated and ill-equipped. Wilson wanted them reinforced at once. Other British troops, at Batum on the Black Sea, were already being reinforced. But there was no Cabinet policy, and no guidance from Lloyd George, who was at that very moment proposing to open negotiations with the Bolsheviks on Heybeli Island in the Sea of Marmara.

Churchill opposed these negotiations. During his first week at the War Office he had telegraphed to the two senior British officers in North Russia, General Maynard and General Ironside: 'It would be better to risk a few thousand men (though there would be no risk if the railway could be put right) than to allow the whole fabric of Russo-Siberian resistance to

Bolshevism to crumble. What sort of a Peace (!) should we have if all Europe & Asia from Warsaw to Vladivostok were under the sway of Lenin?'

Lloyd George still favoured conciliation rather than intervention. While in Paris he had obtained the support of Woodrow Wilson for the invitation to the Bolsheviks to peace talks on Heybeli Island. Churchill had learned of this decision when he reached Paris on January 23, hoping to obtain Lloyd George's support for his demobilisation scheme. On the following morning he told Lloyd George that one might as well legalise sodomy as recognise the Bolsheviks'.

Responsible now for maintaining in Russia the British forces sent there by his predecessors, Churchill wanted a clear decision one way or another. 'It seems to me most urgent,' he wrote to Lloyd George on January 27, 'for us to frame and declare our policy. "Evacuate at once at all costs" is a policy. It is not a very pleasant one from the point of view of history. "Reinforce and put the job through" is a policy; but unhappily we have not the power – our orders would not be obeyed, I regret to say.'

Churchill was under no illusions as to the difficulty of fighting in Russia, or the cost of maintaining a large force there, or the possibility of British troops becoming influenced by Bolshevik ideas. He therefore advised Lloyd George, in his letter of January 27, to end all direct British military intervention, and to begin the withdrawal of all British forces. Churchill wanted those at Murmansk and Archangel to be withdrawn as soon as the ice had melted in July. With regard to Siberia and South Russia, he wanted Britain to tell the anti-Bolshevik forces there 'that they have got to shift for themselves, that we wish them well, but that all we can do is to give them moral support', in the form of such British volunteers 'who are ready to serve in these theatres', and material support, in the form of money, arms and supplies.

Churchill also advised Lloyd George that no British regular or conscript troops should be sent to Russia. With regard to arms and supplies, a quota should be fixed 'now'. With regard to British volunteers, the Government should give 'no guarantee' of their numbers. If the anti-Bolshevik forces were defeated by the Bolsheviks 'or throw up the sponge, we should of course withdraw and disinterest ourselves in all that may follow'.

Churchill meant what he said about withdrawing British troops from Omsk. 'Our policy in Siberia is too nebulous,' he wrote to Henry Wilson on January 29, '& our prospects too gloomy.' Even when, on February 6, two of his most senior military advisers urged him to send arms and equipment to the anti-Bolshevik armies, he cautioned them: 'It is highly important to know what the Russians can & will do for themselves. If they put up a real fight, we ought in my view to back them in every way possible. But without them it is no good our trying.'

On February 12 Churchill pointed out to the Cabinet that the Bolsheviks were getting stronger every day. In South Russia, General Denikin's army 'had greatly deteriorated'. The anti-Bolshevik leader on the Don, General Krasnoff, and the ruler of Siberia, Admiral Kolchak, were both discouraged; indeed, 'there was complete disheartenment everywhere.' If Britain were going to withdraw her troops 'it should be done at once'. If she were going to intervene, then she should 'send larger forces there'. His personal belief was that 'we ought to intervene'. But he awaited the Cabinet's decision, and would carry it out.

Lloyd George told the Cabinet that half a million men would be needed to make intervention effective. It was necessary to consult President Wilson, whose troops were also in Siberia and North Russia, and who was due to leave Paris in three days' time. If, Churchill told a second Cabinet on February 12, the President's decision was to declare war on the Bolsheviks, then British forces could play their part. But he still felt that the 'only chance of making headway against the Bolsheviks' was by the Russian armies themselves. If Britain could not support them 'it would be far better to take a decision now to quit and face the consequences, and tell these people to make the best terms they could with the Bolsheviks'.

Britain, Churchill said, was trying 'to animate the wavering hands of the Russian forces', but he had no illusions as to how wavering those hands were or how small were the prospects of victory for the half a million anti-Bolshevik Russian troops. On the morning of February 14 he left London for Paris, as the Cabinet's emissary to ask President Wilson and Clemenceau what policy the Paris Peace Conference powers wished to pursue with regard to Russia. The journey was inauspicious; during the drive from Dieppe to Paris with Henry Wilson, their car was in an accident which smashed the windscreen. The two men reached Paris cold and wet at three in the afternoon. Four hours later they were present at a meeting of the Council of Ten called specially by Clemenceau to decide on Russian policy.

For three days Churchill was at the centre of the discussions. Hankey, who was present, referred to the way in which he opened the proceedings 'with great moderation'. Woodrow Wilson wanted all foreign troops in Russia, including his own, to be withdrawn. When Churchill suggested that volunteers should be allowed to go, and that arms, tanks, aeroplanes and munitions should be sent to the Russian anti-Bolsheviks, Wilson doubted if volunteers would go, and said that in some areas the supplies would be 'assisting reactionaries'. He then sailed for home, leaving Colonel House to represent him. On February 15 Churchill proposed that the Council should at least examine what the military problems of intervention might be. He was supported by the Italian and Japanese Foreign Ministers, but no decision was reached, even about a mere enquiry. On the following day he telegraphed to Lloyd George that when the Council met the next day he would ask it to set up a commission 'to prepare, out of the resources that are available, a war plan against the Bolsheviks'.

Lloyd George was enraged. The only plan to be considered, he replied by telegram, was that of sending equipment and arms to the anti-Bolshevik forces, who must do all their fighting themselves. 'An expensive war against Russia,' he warned, 'is a way to strengthen Bolshevism in Russia and create it at home.' If Britain were committed to war 'against a continent like Russia, it is the road to bankruptcy and Bolshevism in these islands'. Not only did Lloyd George send this telegram to Churchill; he arranged for a copy to go to Colonel House.

By 'planning war against the Bolsheviks', Churchill replied to Lloyd George, he did not mean making war, but only assembling 'in a comprehensive form, possible means and resources for action', and submitting them in a report to the Council. When the Council met on February 17 it did indeed agree to this; a report would be prepared. But Colonel House insisted that the report must be informal and unofficial. There was to be no Allied policy decision, either on intervention, or on withdrawal. All that was decided was that each country must seek the views of its own military advisers.

Churchill returned to London that night. On reaching Downing Street shortly after midday on February 18, he found that while Lloyd George would in no way countenance direct British military intervention in Russia, he was 'quite willing', Churchill told Henry Wilson 'to help the Russian armies, provided it is not too costly'. Indeed, Churchill added, the Prime Minister was 'entirely in opposition to the cutting off of supplies from Kolchak, Denikin & Co as he considered that since we called them into the field for our own purposes in the German War we were bound to help them in this way'.

Lloyd George told Churchill that no more British troops would be sent to Russia. Those troops already in Russia would be withdrawn. Volunteers already in South Russia could stay. Aid to the Siberian and South Russian anti-Bolshevik forces would continue, but must not be too expensive. Two days after his return from Paris, Churchill was the principal guest at the Mansion House. In his speech he declared: 'If Russia is to be saved, as I pray she may be saved, she must be saved by Russians. It must be by Russian manhood and Russian courage and Russian virtue that the rescue and regeneration of this once mighty nation and famous branch of the European family can alone be achieved.' The aid which Britain could give to the Russian armies, 'who are now engaged in fighting the foul baboonery of Bolshevism', could be given by arms, munitions, equipment, and 'technical services raised upon a voluntary basis'. There would be no British military intervention. 'Russia must be saved by Russian exertions, and it must be from the heart of the Russian people and with their strong arm that the conflict against Bolshevism in Russia must mainly be waged.'

Churchill's task now was to withdraw the 14,000 British troops from Russia, and to sustain the anti-Bolshevik forces with supplies and volunteers; up to 2,000 technical assistants and instructors who specifically volunteered for service in Russia. When, on February 21 Lloyd George rebuked him for the expense that would be incurred by what he called 'your Russian policy', Churchill wrote such an angry reply that he decided in the end not to send it. In it he wrote: 'You speak of my "Russian policy". I have no Russian policy. I know of no Russian policy. I went to Paris to look for a Russian policy. I deplore the lack of a Russian policy, which lack may well keep the world at war for an indefinite period and involve the Peace Conference and the League of Nations in a common failure. All I am doing is carrying on from day to day, guided by such indications as I receive from the War Cabinet, for whose decisions I naturally have no responsibility beyond my departmental duty.'

All the British troops in Russia, Churchill pointed out, had been sent before his appointment to the War Office. 'So far I am not responsible for sending a single man to Russia.' This was true; but in the public eye, Churchill, an outspoken public critic of Bolshevism and its excesses, was already being seen as the leader of an anti-Bolshevik crusade. In March, after a Communist seizure of power in Budapest, a member of the Cabinet Secretariat, Dr Thomas Jones, noted, 'Churchill grew very hot and prophesied vast and immediate disaster as a result of the dilatoriness of the Peace Conference.'

To ensure that the troops in North Russia could leave safely, for they were exhausted, ill-equipped and constantly being attacked, Churchill persuaded Lloyd George to authorise a small 'Rescue Force' to go to their assistance. He was keen that this force should take with it, and use, a new poison gas that had been developed in the last months of the war. 'I should very much like the Bolsheviks to have it,' he told his advisers. When, in April, the last French forces left Odessa, he was angry at what he saw as a premature abandonment of Denikin in South Russia. 'Winston says he will seriously consider resignation before submitting to ignominious withdrawal,' one Cabinet Minister noted. Churchill's own comment was acerbic, 'After conquering all the Huns – tigers of the world – I will not submit to be beaten by the baboons!'

Churchill had no doubt that of 'all the tyrannies in history', he told an audience in London that April, 'the Bolshevik tyranny is the worst, the most destructive, the most degrading'. The atrocities committed under

Lenin and Trotsky were 'incomparably more hideous, on a larger scale, and more numerous than any for which the Kaiser is responsible'. That same month he was scandalised when the Government decided to send back to Russia half a million soldiers who had been taken prisoners-of-war by the Germans and were now in Allied custody. Angrily he wrote to his military advisers: 'Whereas we could have made out of these an army of loyal men who would have been available to sustain the defences of Archangel and Murmansk or to aid General Denikin and Kolchak, we are now I presume simply sending a reinforcement of 500,000 trained men to join the armies of Lenin and Trotsky. This appears to me to be one of the capital blunders in the history of the world.'

Fearful of Communism triumphant in Eastern Europe and Asia, Churchill pressed the Government to help put Germany back on its feet by food and a lenient attitude to reparations, writing to Lloyd George on April 9 that his policy, though in all probability too late to be implemented, could be easily expressed, 'Feed Germany; fight Bolshevism; make Germany fight Bolshevism'. When Asquith's daughter Violet asked him what his Russian policy was, he replied even more succinctly, 'Kill the Bolshie, Kiss the Hun.'

By the last week of April the Russian anti-Bolshevik forces in North Russia and Siberia had made such considerable advances that there was even a possibility of their linking up. Churchill at once proposed that the 14,000 British troops in North Russia, whose evacuation through the still-frozen Arctic would not be possible for at least another two months, should, together with the 3,500 men who had recently volunteered to join them, help the local anti-Bolsheviks to 'make a good punch' towards Kolchak's Siberian army. The point of contact could be the town of Kotlas. The local British commanders, General Knox in Siberia and General Maynard at Murmansk, were keen to take part and confident of success. The War Office General Staff proposed a detailed scheme.

Lloyd George agreed to the British forces in North Russia advancing. But on May 18 the local Russian soldiers who would have had to take part in the advance on Kotlas mutinied. The senior British officer at Archangel, General Ironside, shot fifteen of them in order to end the mutiny.

On May 29 Churchill gave the Commons an account of the efforts being made to help the anti-Bolsheviks in North Russia and Siberia. In North Russia, British volunteers were arriving at Archangel and a British naval flotilla was moving southward on the River Dvina 'well armed with guns'. In Siberia, Kolchak's forces were fighting 'with British ammunition and rifles'.

After Churchill's speech a Conservative MP, Samuel Hoare, wrote to congratulate him on 'all you have done in the matter of Russia'. The

Labour *Daily Herald* took another view, denouncing the 'gambler of Gallipoli' for having made a second throw of the dice, 'the new war in Russia'. Churchill cast about for every means to help the anti-Bolsheviks, pressing Lloyd George to recognise Kolchak's government in Siberia, as a gesture of moral support. But the Cabinet rejected his proposal. The Kotlas plan remained; on June 6 Ironside was making plans to advance along the Dvina to Kotlas in a month's time. Bolshevik morale was bad, he reported, 'A strong push will upset everything.' On June 10 Henry Wilson explained Ironside's plan to Lloyd George, who made 'no objection'. On June 11 the War Cabinet approved it.

When, six days later, disturbing news came from Siberia that Kolchak's most westerly army had been defeated, Curzon, Milner and Austen Chamberlain at once called an emergency War Cabinet, at which Churchill urged that the advance to Kotlas should still be tried 'even though the plan for joining hands with Admiral Kolchak was no longer feasible'. No decision was reached. Nine days later Ironside began his advance, capturing 300 Bolshevik soldiers on the first day. Then another mutiny broke out among a battalion of Russian troops forming part of his reserve. Three British and four Russian officers were murdered.

When the War Cabinet met on July 9 it was not the armies, however, but nature, that decided the outcome. The River Dvina, no longer swollen by the melting snows or spring rains, had fallen below the level needed by the Royal Navy flotilla to remain in operation. The flotilla withdrew to Archangel to avoid being stranded. The Kotlas expedition could not continue. Later, when Lloyd George mockingly told Churchill that the attempt to link up with the anti-Bolsheviks at Kotlas had 'failed', Churchill replied bitterly, 'It was never attempted.'

Churchill was Secretary of State for Air as well as for War; Clementine was uneasy at her husband holding the two offices. 'Darling,' she had written that March, 'really don't you think it would be better to give up the Air & continue concentrating on what you are doing at the War Office? It would be a sign of real strength to do so, & people would admire it very much. It is weak to hang on to two offices – you really are only doing the one. Or again, if you swallow the two you will have violent indigestion.'

It would be a '*tour de force*' to do the two jobs, Clementine continued, 'like keeping a lot of balls in the air at the same time. After all, you want to be a Statesman, not a juggler.' Churchill had no intention of giving up his Air portfolio. At the same time, he had taken up flying again, despite a crash-landing in June when the aeroplane he was piloting had to make an emergency landing at Buc aerodrome near Paris. His new flying instructor was the Commandant of the Central Flying School, Colonel Jack Scott, an air ace who had shot down thirteen German aircraft in the war, despite having damaged his legs so badly in a flying accident that he had to be lifted into his cockpit each time he flew.

On July 18, after a full day working at the War Office, Churchill and Scott drove to Croydon aerodrome for one of their routine training flights. The aeroplane had dual controls. As usual Churchill took the machine off the ground himself, but when he had risen to seventy or eighty feet the aeroplane began to lose speed, and to fall. Scott took over the controls but could do nothing. 'We were scarcely ninety foot above the ground,' Churchill later recalled, 'just the normal height for the usual side-slip fatal accident, the commonest of all'. The aeroplane fell swiftly downward. 'I saw the sunlit aerodrome close beneath me, and the impression flashed through my mind that it was bathed in a baleful yellowish glare. Then in another flash a definite thought formed in my brain, "This is very likely Death". And swift upon that I felt again in imagination the exact sensation of my smash on the Buc aerodrome a month before. Something like that was going to happen NOW!'

The aeroplane struck the ground. Churchill was thrown forward but his safety belt held him; it broke only when the force of the crash was over. Streams of petrol vapour rushed past him from the engine, but in the few seconds before the aeroplane hit the ground, Scott had managed to switch off the engine, preventing an explosion. Churchill was safe but bruised. Scott, knocked unconscious, soon recovered. Churchill's friends and relatives were shaken and angered by the risk he had taken. 'I feel dreadfully for Clemmy,' his cousin Lady Londonderry wrote to him. 'I really think it rather evil of you – but I do hope you have not been hurt.'

Churchill again agreed to give up flying. Although he would never obtain a pilot's licence, Clementine would have peace of mind.

Three days after Churchill's air crash, the Russian regiment holding General Maynard's Onega front in North Russia mutinied, handing over its front line positions to the Bolsheviks. When the War Cabinet met on July 25 it was decided that the British troops in North Russia, Siberia and the Caucasus must be withdrawn. Except for the advisers with Denikin in South Russia, the intervention was over. Bitterly Churchill told his colleagues, 'The anti-Bolsheviks might collapse within the next few months, and then the Lenin or Trotsky empire would be complete.'

On July 28 the last 700 American troops left Archangel. That day Churchill was with Lloyd George at Chequers. Henry Wilson was also there. 'Winston very excited & talked of resigning,' he wrote in his diary. At the Cabinet on the following day Churchill asked that Denikin should continue to receive food and munitions for the next six months, as well as up to 2,000 volunteers to supervise his stores and transport, and pilots to teach his aviators to fly. The Cabinet agreed that he should be sent 'one more packet' of supplies.

On August 16 Churchill left England with Clementine for a five-day visit to Cologne, and to the British Army on the Rhine. On his second day in Germany, he learned that the situation in Russia was changing again, and changing dramatically; the anti-Bolshevik Russia armies were once more advancing. Along the Black Sea coast, Denikin had driven the Bolsheviks from Nikolaiev and Kherson, and was poised to enter Odessa; the anti-Bolsheviks were in command of the Black Sea. Along the Baltic coast, General Yudenitch was advancing rapidly on Petrograd. Returning to London, Churchill asked for enough munitions to be sent to Denikin to enable him to wrest all of South Russia from the Bolsheviks. Lloyd George said no, pointing out that the Cabinet had agreed that once Denikin had been sent 'one more packet', Britain would let the Russians 'fight out their own quarrels' at their own expense.

A day after Lloyd George's rebuff to Churchill, Denikin entered Kiev, the capital of the Ukraine, of which he was now the master. Realising that this vast territory was probably the limit of what the anti-Bolshevik forces could conquer and hold, Churchill proposed a negotiated peace; the Bolsheviks would be asked to accept a non-Bolshevik South Russia with Kiev as its capital, and Denikin would be asked to accept Bolshevik rule centred on Moscow. Once an agreed dividing line was reached between the two forces, Britain would sponsor negotiations between Denikin and Lenin. To this end, Churchill cautioned restraint on the part of the British forces in South Russia, telegraphing on September 20 to the senior British officer with Denikin's forces, General Holman, 'I think it inadvisable that British airmen should be used in present circumstances to bomb Moscow.'

Learning that same day that Denikin's troops had entered Kursk, only three hundred miles south of Moscow, Churchill wrote at once to Lloyd George, urging that Britain support Denikin now 'by all means in our power', and to encourage the Baltic Germans to participate in Yudenitch's attack on Petrograd. 'Nothing can preserve either the Bolshevik system or the Bolshevik regime,' he told Lloyd George. 'By mistakes on our part the agony of the Russian people may be prolonged. But their relief is sure. The only question is whether we shall desert them in the crisis of their fate.'

Lloyd George begged Churchill to 'let Russia be for at least 48 hours' and to devote his energies to preparing the Army Estimates, as cuts in expenditure were essential. 'I have found your mind so obsessed by Russia,' he wrote on September 22, 'that I felt I had good grounds for the apprehension that your great abilities, energy and courage were not devoted to the reduction of expenditure.' He added, 'I wonder if it is any use my making one last effort to induce you to throw off this obsession which, if you will forgive me for saying so, is upsetting your balance.'

In his reply that same day, Churchill wrote: 'I may get rid of my "obsession" or you may get rid of me: but you will not get rid of Russia: nor of the consequences of a policy which for nearly a year it has been impossible to define. I must confess I cannot feel a sense of detachment from the tragical scene.' Churchill's obsession was his belief that the whole fate of Russia was in the balance, and that it was possible with a clear plan to topple tyranny. But on the day of his letter to Lloyd George, 400 Polish troops were evacuated from Archangel, and all remaining British troops were withdrawn into the inner defences of the city, preparatory to embarking for home.

On September 24 Britain recognised the independence of Lithuania, but on the following day the War Cabinet rejected any further British commitment to the Baltic States, and urged them to make peace with the Bolsheviks. 'Winston doesn't like that,' one Cabinet Minister wrote in his diary, 'and argues that the Front is one.' The plan Churchill now favoured, he wrote that day to the War Cabinet, was 'to make war upon the Bolshevists by every means in our power, with a coherent plan on all fronts at once', until either the Bolsheviks were defeated or a 'general peace' was negotiated between the warring parties.

On October 4 Denikin's armies began to advance towards Moscow on a broad front; Yudenitch was within fifty miles of Petrograd; in Siberia, Kolchak had begun to move westward again. Learning this, Churchill pressed the War Cabinet to do everything in Britain's power to help these forces at their moment of renewed advance and vigour. 'The Bolsheviks are falling and perhaps the end is not distant. Not only their system but their regime is doomed. Their military effort is collapsing at almost every point on the whole immense circle of their front, while communications, food, fuel, and popular support are all failing within that circle.'

Churchill now wanted Britain to press Poland to attack the Bolsheviks from the West, and to ask the Baltic States to delay as long as possible making their peace with Lenin. The War Cabinet had no intention of following such a course. On October 6 Denikin's troops entered Voronezh, only 300 miles from Moscow, but two days later the War Cabinet insisted that the final 'packet' of munitions and supplies to Denikin must not exceed £14,500,000, and must come wherever possible out of existing War Office stocks. This packet was being sent, Churchill had to inform Denikin, 'on the condition that it would be the last'. That day the last British troops left Murmansk, followed a week later by those at Archangel. The remaining 550 British troops in Siberia were under orders to leave by mid-November. The 144 British military personnel in the Baltic would leave by the end of the year.

At the moment of potential triumph for the anti-Bolshevik forces, British involvement in their fate was coming to an end.

On October 13 Denikin entered Orel, 250 miles south of Moscow. That same day Yudenitch cut the Petrograd-Moscow railway and advanced to within thirty-five miles of Petrograd. 'The Bolshevik system was from the beginning doomed to perish in consequence of its antagonism to the fundamental principles of civilised society,' Churchill wrote to the War Cabinet a day later. The system and the regime would perish 'beneath the vengeance of the Russian nation'. Had it been possible earlier to establish peaceful relations with the Bolsheviks, 'we should have been building on a perishing foundation'.

As Denikin began his final assault on Moscow on October 15, Churchill told Lloyd George that he wanted to leave London for Russia. Once in Russia, he was prepared to 'help Denikin mould the new Russian Constitution'. Lloyd George was not against the idea. 'Winston would go out as a sort of Ambassador,' Henry Wilson noted in his diary.

On October 17 Churchill informed Yudenitch that the War Office was sending him tanks, aeroplanes, rifles, and equipment for 20,000 men. Four hundred Russian officers who had been under training in Britain would leave at once on a British steamship, which would also carry most of the supplies. If Petrograd were captured, Churchill told Curzon that day, it would be 'with British munitions and the aid of the British Fleet'.

Churchill's confidence was complete. 'There are now good reasons for believing that the tyranny of Bolshevism will soon be overthrown by the Russian nation,' he told his constituency chairman on October 18. Britain would use her influence to build up 'a New Russia on the broad foundation of democracy and Parliamentary institutions'. On the following day Churchill discussed with his advisers sending a British General to Yudenitch 'for the entry into Petrograd'; the General would leave Britain on October 23 'to prevent excesses in the event of victory'. But that very day, launching a counter-attack, Trotsky drove Yudenitch from his point closest to the city.

As rapidly as they had risen, the fortunes of the anti-Bolsheviks waned. In South Russia, Denikin's forces came to a halt, their bases suddenly and unexpectedly attacked by an anarchist army led by Nestor Makhno. Taking advantage of Makhno's activities, the Bolsheviks recaptured Orel. Denikin was in retreat. In Siberia, Kolchak fell back eastward again, to Omsk. Churchill's hopes of going to Russia as an emissary of democracy were ended; but he had no intention of abandoning the anti-Bolsheviks. On October 31 the Cabinet discussed the death of more than a hundred British sailors on a British warship bombarding Bolshevik positions in the Gulf of Finland. A Cabinet Minister noted, 'Winston pleads that it may go on bombarding until the ice. PM against.'

On November 3 Yudenitch gave up his attempt to capture Petrograd and retreated to Estonia. Three days later Churchill spoke in the Commons of Lenin's 'demoniacal ability to tear to pieces every institution on which the Russian State and nation depended'. After his speech Balfour went up to him and said, 'I admire the exaggerated way you tell the truth.'

As Denikin's forces gave up the advance on Moscow, Churchill asked the Cabinet in vain for them to be sent further supplies. His plan to finance a special Russian Army Corps for Yudenitch was likewise unsuccessful. His sole Ministerial authority with regard to Russia remained what it had been all year; to organise the British withdrawal. On November 1 the last British troops had sailed from Vladivostok. A month later Kolchak's army collapsed and the Admiral fled yet further eastward, leaving behind a million rounds of mostly British ammunition for the Bolsheviks to use against him. On November 30 Churchill celebrated his forty-fifth birthday amid the collapse of all his hopes for a Russian democratic revival.

By the end of November Denikin had abandoned half of South Russia to the Bolsheviks. The Poles, whom he despised, far from helping him restore his line, advanced deep into the Ukraine. 'The last chances of saving the situation are slipping away,' Churchill wrote to Lloyd George on December 3. 'No action whatever is being taken by us to induce Poland to make her weight tell on the Front, or to arrange matters beteen Denikin and Poland. Very soon there will be nothing left but Lenin and Trotsky, our vanished 100 millions, and mutual reproaches.'

Churchill now begged Denikin to come to a peaceful arrangement with Poland. 'Believe me my friend I understand your difficulties,' he telegraphed on December 11, 'and I pursue only one object, namely, the destruction of the Bolshevik tyrannies which menace the ignorant, thoughtless and tired out nations.' On the following day, as the Bolsheviks entered Kharkov, Denikin's forces fled southward in disarray towards the Black Sea.

'It is a delusion to suppose that all this year we have been fighting the battles of the anti-Bolshevik Russians,' Churchill wrote to the War Cabinet on December 15. 'On the contrary, they have been fighting ours; and this truth will become painfully apparent from the moment they are exterminated and the Bolshevik armies are supreme over the whole vast territories of the Russian Empire.' That day the Bolsheviks entered Kiev. Nine days later, in Siberia, they were in possession of most of Irkutsk, to which Kolchak had fled. On December 26 General Knox sailed from Vladivostok. That same day General Holman telegraphed from South Russia for help in evacuating 800 of the 2,000 members of the British mission to Denikin. On December 31 Churchill ordered the evacuation of the British forces at Batum, on the Black Sea.

Churchill had lost his long rearguard struggle to help the anti-Bolsheviks overthrow the Moscow regime. To many in Britain, particularly to the Labour Party, his 'private war on Russia' was a repetition of previous excesses. In the London evening *Star*, a young New Zealand cartoonist, David Low, portrayed him as a big-game hunter, gun in hand, with six dead cats at his feet. The title was 'Winston's Bag'. Four of the dead cats were labelled: 'Sidney St.', 'Antwerp Blunder', 'Gallipoli Mistake' and 'Russian Bungle'. The two remaining cats had no name. 'Winston hunts lions and brings back cats' was the caption.

Over the New Year holiday, Churchill was a guest at Sir Philip Sassoon's house at Lympne, on the south coast, a luxurious retreat. Lloyd George was also among the guests, as was the newspaper proprietor Lord Riddell. Churchill was at work that weekend, as so many others, on his war memoirs; he had just learned that he was to receive £5,000 from *The Times* for the serial rights, the 1990 equivalent of £75,000, and was soon to receive more than double this for serialisation in the United States. For the past year he had been dictating chapters to his shorthand writer Harry Beckenham.

'I had a long talk with Winston about his book,' Riddell wrote in his diary. 'He says he has written a great part of the first volume. He proposed to dictate 300,000 words, and then cut down the matter and polish it up. He added that it was very exhilarating to feel that one was writing for half a crown a word! He went upstairs to put in two or three hours' work on the book. When he came down, I said to LG, with whom I had been talking, "It is a horrible thought that while we have been frittering away our time, Winston has been piling up words at half a crown each." This much amused LG.'

In mid-January, while Lloyd George was in Paris for the Supreme Allied Council, working on the final terms of the Treaty of Versailles, he summoned the Cabinet to meet in Paris. The Peace Conference had decided to invite the Bolsheviks to discuss trade between Russia and Western Europe. Churchill was still determined to obtain support for Denikin's rapidly retreating armies. 'At times he became almost like a madman,' Frances Stevenson wrote in her diary on January 17. That afternoon Henry Wilson found Churchill in a 'very uncertain mood', talking about whether or not to resign.

'My sweet Clemmie,' Churchill wrote two days later to his wife, 'I would so much rather have spent these days in the basket instead of loafing around here.' Back in London, on January 25 he published an article in the *Illustrated Sunday Herald* in which he wrote of Lenin's 'diabolical' purpose. 'All tyrants are the enemies of the human race,' he declared. 'All tyrannies should be overthrown.' Nine days later, however, on learning that Denikin was likely to be driven into the sea if he went on fighting, he urged the anti-Bolshevik leader to give up the fight, to seek a place of refuge for his soldiers and followers, and to open negotiations with the Bolsheviks for a small territorial area in which his followers might settle.

'Great changes are taking place in the character and organisation of the Bolshevik government,' Churchill told Denikin. 'In spite of the hellish wickedness in which it was founded and has been developed, it nevertheless represents a force of order.' Those at the helm 'are no longer mere revolutionaries but persons who, having seized power, are anxious to retain it and enjoy it for a time. They are believed earnestly to desire peace, fearing no doubt if war continues to be devoured later by their own armies.' A period of peace, coupled with commercial reorganisation, 'may well prepare the way for the unity of Russia through a political evolution.'

Churchill's call for compromise fell on deaf ears. To Denikin, the violence and divisions of civil war made the concept of Bolshevik 'evolution' sound bizarre. Four days after Churchill advocated negotiations between Denikin and the Bolsheviks, the Bolsheviks entered Odessa. Thousands of Denikin's followers were shot. The remnant escaped by sea to the Crimea. That same day, in Siberia, Kolchak was taken by the Bolsheviks from his prison cell and shot.

The last standard-bearers of the intervention were being withdrawn; on March 5 Churchill authorised General Holman to quit Denikin's side and leave Russia altogether. Churchill now favoured a *cordon sanitaire* of which Germany would be part, writing to one of his military advisers on March 10, 'In my view the objective which we should pursue at the present time is the building up of a strong but peaceful Germany which will not attack our French allies, but which will at the same time act as a moral bulwark against the Bolshevism of Russia.'

Of the anti-Bolshevik forces who had stayed on in North Russia after the British withdrew, Churchill wrote on March 23, 'I think that they did all that men could do, holding on month after month with no hope in the world, and everybody wishing to make their peace with the Bolsheviks.' On the following day he left England for a two-week holiday in France. He too now saw a negotiated peace as the only way forward, writing, as he was crossing the Channel, to Lloyd George, 'I should be prepared to make peace with Soviet Russia on the best terms available to appease the general situation, while safeguarding us from being poisoned by them.' He added: 'I do not of course believe that any real harmony is possible between Bolshevism & present civilisation. But in view of existing facts a cessation of arms & a promotion of material prosperity are inevitable: & we must

trust for better or worse to peaceful influences to bring about the disappearance of this awful tyranny and peril.'

On March 27 the last of Denikin's troops evacuated their main supply
base, the port of Novorossiisk. When the Bolsheviks entered the town later
that day they found a vast quantity of British stores; most of Britain's 'final
packet' to the anti-Bolsheviks had become the property, and arsenal, of
those whose defeat it had been intended to secure. Denikin reached the
Crimea with 35,000 troops, his anti-Bolshevik campaign over. Learning
on March 29 that General Holman's mission had been safely evacuated,
Henry Wilson wrote in his diary: 'So ends in practical disaster another of
Winston's military attempts. Antwerp, Dardanelles, Denikin. His judgement is always at fault, & he is hopeless when in power.' But as at the
Dardanelles, effective power had in fact been denied Churchill in his
efforts to use the changing military position in Russia to Britain's advantage.

At Mimizan, on the French Atlantic coast, Churchill was staying at a villa
belonging to his friend the Duke of Westminster, where he hunted wild
boar and painted, with General Rawlinson as his companion. It was four
and a half years since Rawlinson had taken over from him at Antwerp;
exactly two years since he had visited Rawlinson's headquarters at the
height of the German break-through in 1918. 'The General and I,' he wrote
to Clementine on March 29, 'discuss the various battles of the war without
cessation in the intervals of painting and riding. I have not done a scrap
of work. This is the first time such a thing has happened to me. I am
evidently "growing up" at last.'

On March 31 the War Cabinet decided 'to invite General Denikin to give
up the struggle'. One Cabinet Minister noted, 'Winston fortunately
abroad.' But Churchill refused to allow these matters to vex him, writing
from Mimizan to Lloyd George, 'I am having a complete holiday and
trying to forget about all the disagreeable things that are going on.' In the
second week of May, the Polish Army drove the Bolsheviks from Kiev. In
the Crimea, Denikin's successor General Wrangel was holding off a strong
Bolshevik attack.

Churchill wanted a British initiative, not as a participant in the struggle,
but as a mediator, telling a Conference of Ministers on May 28, 'The
British Government should offer to the Soviet Government their whole-
hearted co-operation in concerting a peace between the Soviet Government on the one hand and General Wrangel and the Polish Government
on the other.' The Crimea would become a temporary asylum for the
anti-Bolsheviks 'for at least a year'. Those refugees who wished would be
allowed to return to Russia under an amnesty. The Bolsheviks would agree
to cease interference and agitation in Afghanistan, Persia and the

Caucasus, as well as Bolshevik propaganda in Central Europe and Britain. In return, Britain would recognise Bolshevik Russia.

Even as Churchill set out his plan for a negotiated peace, Wrangel advanced from the Crimea to attack the Bolsheviks in South Russia. Churchill shared the Cabinet's view that the General had forfeited any claim to further British assistance.

Lloyd George now sought Churchill's help over a newly emerging peril, the growing challenge to British rule in Ireland by force and terror. Following the death of sixteen Catholics and Protestants during a violent sectarian clash on June 16, he asked Churchill to join a Cabinet Committee charged with the 'suppression of crime and disorder' in Ireland. His own view, Churchill told Henry Wilson on June 25, was that the situation in Ireland would not be made better 'by the kind of methods the Prussians adopted in Belgium'.

Churchill was quickly repelled by Sinn Fein's acts of terror. On July 1 he suggested to his advisers at the War Office that if a large number of Sinn Feiners were drilling, with or without arms, and could be located and identified from the air, 'I see no objection from a military point of view, and subject of course to the discretion of the Irish Government and of the authorities on the spot, to aeroplanes being despatched with definite orders in each particular case to disperse them by machine-gun fire or bombs, using of course no more force than is necessary to scatter and stampede them.'

It was not only in Ireland that air power was being used to maintain control. Six days after this Irish proposal, Churchill informed the Cabinet that in an uprising in distant Mesopotamia, 'the enemy were bombed and machine-gunned with effect by aeroplanes which co-operated with the troops'. Churchill had strongly deprecated the use of troops, however, by General Dyer in India, when 300 unarmed Indians had been shot during a riot at Amritsar. Churchill insisted on Dyer receiving no further military employment, and in the Commons on July 8 he defended the condemnation passed on Dyer by a War Office commission. The shooting was 'a monstrous event'. There was 'one general prohibition' which could be made when dealing with riots and civil strife. 'I mean a prohibition against what is called "frightfulness". What I mean by frightfulness is the inflicting of great slaughter or massacre upon a particular crowd of people, with the intention of terrorising not merely the rest of the crowd, but the whole district or the whole country. We cannot admit this doctrine in any form. Frightfulness is not a remedy known to the British pharmacopoeia.'

In Ireland, as the Sinn Fein murders continued, Lloyd George asked Churchill's friend General Tudor to set up what Henry Wilson called 'a counter-murder association'; a force later known, because of the colour of its uniform, as the Black and Tans. Churchill 'evidently had some lingering hope of our rough handling of the Sinn Feins', Wilson wrote in his diary on July 12. Two days later, Churchill's concerns swung sharply away from Ireland as Bolshevik troops, having pushed the Poles out of Kiev and the Western Ukraine crossed into the predominantly Polish-speaking regions of Galicia and White Russia, forcing the Poles to evacuate Vilna, a city with more than 80,000 Polish inhabitants. Churchill wanted immediate action againt this onrush of Bolshevik power, writing to Bonar Law: 'All my experience goes to show the advantage of attacking these people. They become very dangerous the moment they think you fear them. It is like taming a tiger – or rather a mangy hyena!'

While awaiting a Cabinet decision on what could, or should, be done to help Poland, Churchill prepared a list of resources which he wanted to send to the Poles, among them aeroplanes, guns and technical advisers. On July 26 the United States announced that it would equip and maintain ten Polish divisions for the duration of the war. Two days later, in an article in the *Evening News* entitled 'The Poison Peril from the East', Churchill described Poland as the 'lynch-pin' of the Treaty of Versailles. It was 'from the point of view of securing and preserving our world peace that the case of Poland must be considered'. But he understood that no British troops could go to Poland's aid; after five years of war the British people did not want any more war, they had learned 'too much of its iron slavery, its squalor, its mocking disappointments, its ever-dwelling sense of loss'.

It was for Germany, Churchill wrote, 'to build a dyke of peaceful, lawful, patient strength and virtue against the flood of red barbarism flowing from the East'. *The Times* immediately protested at the 'unconstitutional impropriety' of such an appeal, pointing out that Germany was the defeated nation about to pay reparations, and having lost considerable territory at Poland's expense. Lord Derby wrote to Lloyd George from Paris, 'Winston's hint of an alliance with Germany to fight the Bolshevists has made the French mad!' But Churchill had not suggested British or German military intervention.

On August 4 the Red Army advanced to within a hundred miles of Warsaw. Churchill hurried to see the Prime Minister as soon as he learned of the threat to the Polish capital. Lloyd George was in the Cabinet Room with two emissaries from Lenin, sent to negotiate a trade agreement, Leonid Krassin and Lev Kamenev. As Churchill waited outside the Cabinet Room, Lloyd George sent him a note, 'I told Kamenev & Krassin that the British fleet would start for the Baltic in three days unless they stopped their advance.' This British ultimatum was delivered on the sixth anniversary of Britain's declaration of war on Germany. When the Cabinet met half an hour later it accepted what Lloyd George had done. But it was clear that no army could be sent to help Poland. 'Again it was August 4,' Churchill later recalled, 'and this time we were impotent. Public opinion in England and France was prostrate. All forms of military intervention were impossible. There was nothing left but words and gestures.'

The Red Army continued to advance on Warsaw. On August 6 the head of the British Mission there, who had earlier been sent to Warsaw to persuade the Poles to negotiate with the Bolsheviks, telegraphed to London for the immediate despatch of 20,000 French and British troops, excluding any who might be affected 'by Bolshevik or Sinn Fein propaganda'. But two days later the French leaders came to London to tell Lloyd George that they were unwilling to send troops. It was agreed that France would send arms and munitions to Poland. Britain's contribution would be 'boots, clothes, saddlery'.

On August 13 the Red Army was only twelve miles from Warsaw. The British Government had abandoned any intention to support Poland, or to be involved in its fate. That day Churchill left London for Rugby, where he played polo. While he was at Rugby he drafted a long appeal to Lloyd George to do everything possible to prevent Poland being 're-absorbed in the Russian system'. As he was writing his appeal he learned that the Poles, having taken the military initiative, were driving the Russians back, and had already captured 63,000 Russian prisoners, 200 guns and a thousand machine-guns. Churchill wrote on top of his appeal for British action, 'Happily superseded by events.' Then, echoing Pitt at the Guildhall in 1805, he added, 'Poland has saved herself by her exertions & will I trust save Europe by her example.'

On August 13, the day the Red Army was only twelve miles from Warsaw, five British officials were murdered in Iraq, where Churchill, as Secretary of State for War, was responsible for civil as well as military control. For two weeks the Cabinet discussed what should be done; Churchill saw no reason to retain control in Iraq if the result was to be military entanglement, but he was overruled. 'Now that the Cabinet have definitely decided that we are to plough through in that dismal country,' he wrote to Lloyd George on August 26, 'every effort must be made to procure vigorous action and decisive results.' His friend General Haldane, the Commander-in-Chief in Iraq, was confident of being able to quell the revolt within three months.

Pursuing the Cabinet's policy to stay in Iraq, despite the growing rebellion, Churchill had already arranged for two air squadrons to join the two already there. On August 29 he suggested they should be equipped with mustard-gas bombs 'which would inflict punishment upon recalcitrant natives without inflicting grave injury upon them'. But extra troops were not readily available. 'We are at our wits' end to find a single soldier,' he wrote to Lloyd George on August 31, and he added: 'There is something very sinister to my mind in this Mesopotamian entanglement, coming as it does when Ireland is so great a menace. It seems to me so gratuitous that after all the struggles of the war, just when we want to get together our slender military resources and re-establish our finances and have a little in hand in case of danger here or there, we should be compelled to go on pouring armies and treasures into these thankless deserts.'

On September 1 Churchill left London with Clementine for Mimizan, where he had spent his holiday the previous March. 'I am here having a little sunshine and change,' he wrote to his constituency chairman a week later, 'which I badly needed after all these years of increasing racket and worry, and after the chilling July and August which we suffered in England.' Churchill always loved the sun: 'In a properly constituted existence like yours (and mine),' he had written to Lloyd George a month earlier, 'each day brings its own diversions, provided only there is sunshine.'

After two and a half weeks in France, Churchill returned for six days to London, where he was warned by Henry Wilson that the Black and Tans in Ireland were carrying out 'indiscriminate reprisals'. Churchill's sympathy was on the side of those who were trying to maintain the peace. 'Naturally everything will be done to prevent violent, harsh or inhumane action by the troops,' he told Wilson on September 18, 'but the greatest help in this respect will be given by the Irish population of towns where troops are quartered if they not only abstain from murdering the soldiers and officers by treacherous means, but also render the assistance which is easily in their power to give, for the detection of the actual criminals.'

On September 22, at three towns in Southern Ireland, the local police, Wilson wrote in his diary, 'marked down certain Sinn Feiners as actual murderers or instigators & then coolly went & shot them without question or trial. Winston saw very little harm in this.' Two days later a member of Tudor's staff, Captain Shore, travelled from Dublin to tell Churchill that reprisals were taking place as a matter of Army policy. Churchill took Shore to see Lloyd George at Downing Street, where he again explained the reprisal policy. Lloyd George gave it his approval; the murder of policemen, he told Churchill, Bonar Law and Fisher, 'can only be met by reprisals'.

That night Churchill left England for Italy, to paint at Amalfi. From there he travelled to Cassis, in the South of France, again to paint. While he was away he wrote to his cousin Shane Leslie, whose home was on the Ulster border, to remind him that when Leslie had asked what advice Churchill would give to Sinn Fein, his reply had been, 'Quit murdering and start arguing.' The moment the murders ceased, Churchill wrote to Leslie on October 2, the Irish question 'will enter upon a new phase, and I shall not be behindhand in doing my utmost to secure a good settlement'. On October 11 Churchill returned to London. Five days later, in a speech to his constituents at Dundee, he denounced the Bolsheviks and Sinn Fein in equal measure.

In the third week of November, Churchill saw copies of several dozen intercepted telegrams, sent from the Soviet Foreign Ministry in Moscow to the Bolshevik negotiators in London. One of the main instructions in the telegrams was the spending of money to stimulate industrial unrest in Britain. Churchill decided to insist that until the Bolsheviks cancelled this instruction, no trade agreement should be signed. Lloyd George pointed out that an end to such propaganda was part of the agreement; once the agreement was signed the incitements would stop.

On November 17 Churchill asked the Cabinet to break off the talks with the Bolsheviks until the incitement ceased. If no such decision were reached on the following day, he would resign. His friend F.E. Smith, recently ennobled as Lord Birkenhead, urged him not to. 'You would cut yourself adrift,' he warned, 'perhaps permanently, certainly for a very long time, from the Coalition, which on every other point you support'; nobody else would resign from the Cabinet and the public would not regard it as a vital point of principle.

Churchill accepted his friend's advice. The negotiations continued, as did the secret instructions for subversion. Churchill remained in the Cabinet, having secured a specific note in the Minutes on November 18 'that no Cabinet Minister was fettered as regards anti-Bolshevik speeches'. That night he went to Oxford, where he denounced the evils of Communism: 'My view has been that all the harm and misery in Russia have arisen out of the wickedness and folly of the Bolshevists, and that there will be no recovery of any kind in Russia or in Eastern Europe while these wicked men, this vile group of cosmopolitan fanatics, hold the Russian nation by the hair of its head and tyrannise over its great population. The policy I will always advocate is the overthrow and destruction of that criminal regime.'

At the beginning of November, studying the reports from Ireland on the reprisal policy of the Black and Tans, Churchill wrote to the Cabinet that some of the reprisals were 'discreditable' even when the provocation was great. 'Many foolish and wrong things' were likely to be done which the authorities would not be able to ignore. But he did not feel that it was right to punish the troops when, 'goaded in the most brutal manner and finding no redress, they take action on their own account'. To help suppress Sinn

41. With Lord Lansdowne and
Lord Curzon, Horse Guards Parade,
July 1915

42. With A. J. Balfour in Whitehall,
July 1915

43. With the officers of his battalion, the 6th Royal Scots
Fusiliers, Ploegsteert, Belgium, March 1916: on Churchill's right
is his second-in-command, Sir Archibald Sinclair, later Leader
of the Liberal Party and Secretary of State for Air in Churchill's
wartime Coalition (1940-45)

44. Minister of Munitions, visiting a Munitions factory
in Glasgow, 7 October 1918

45. At Lille, 28 October 1918, watching a march-past.
Behind him, in bowler hat, is Eddie Marsh; in front of him is
Major (later Field Marshal) Bernard Montgomery

46. The French Minister of Munitions, Louis Loucheur, Churchill, Lloyd George, and the head of the American War Industries Board, Bernard Baruch, Paris, March 1919

47. Secretary of State for War, inspecting British troops, Cologne, August 1919

48. Cartoon by Strube, *Daily Express*, 8 September 1919

49. Cartoon by Low, published in the *Evening Standard* on 21 January 1920, entitled: 'Winston's Bag, He hunts lions and brings home decayed cats'

50. 'Strenuous Lives, Winston's at 9 a.m.' by David Wilson, published in *Passing Show* on 14 February 1920

51. Clementine Churchill and her husband; Gertrude Bell; and T. E. Lawrence ('Lawrence of Arabia') at the Pyramids, 20 March 1921

52. The Cairo Conference, March 1921: on Churchill's right, Sir Herbert Samuel; on his left Sir Percy Cox. T. E. Lawrence is immediately behind Sir Percy Cox. On Cox's left are General Haldane and General Ironside. The lion cub in the foreground was on its way from the Sudan to the London Zoo

53. Leaving 10 Downing Street with Lloyd George and
Lord Birkenhead, 10 February 1922

54. In Dundee, 12 November 1922, for the General Election,
recovering from appendicitis, with two supporters: the one on the
right is his detective, Sergeant W. H. Thompson. Clementine follows
close behind

55. Dictating to his secretary Lettice Fisher, at his home in
Sussex Square, at the start of the Westminster by-election campaign,
6 March 1924

56. The loser doffs his hat, Westminster, 20 March 1924.
Clementine turns to look at the camera

57. Being driven to Buckingham Palace to receive the seals of office as Chancellor of the Exchequer, 7 November 1924

58. The Chancellor of the Exchequer driving himself to the House of Commons in his own two-seater car, 1925

59. Austen Chamberlain (Foreign Secretary), Stanley Baldwin (Prime Minister) and Churchill (Chancellor of the Exchequer), 1925

60. At 10 Downing Street on 3 May 1926, during the General Strike

61. Hunting wild boar in the forest of Eu, near Paris, 31 January 1927

62. Walking from 11 Downing Street to the House of Commons on 24 April 1928, to deliver his fourth Budget. With him is his daughter Diana; his Parliamentary Private Secretary, Robert Boothby (also in top hat); and, on Churchill's left, his detective W. H. Thompson

63. Bricklaying with his daughters Sarah and Mary, building a cottage in the grounds of Chartwell, 3 September 1928

64. On board the *Empress of Australia*, on his way to Canada and the
United States. With him in this picture are his brother Jack,
and the ship's captain. The ship sailed from Southampton on
3 August 1929

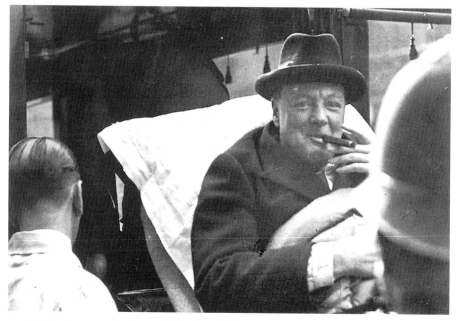

65. Leaving a nursing home in London, 10 October 1932, after a
recurrence of paratyphoid

66. Leaving London with Clementine by air for Paris, 25 September 1934, on the first stage of a cruise in the Eastern Mediterranean

67. With Lloyd George, during a dinner in aid of the Printers Pension Fund, London, 20 November 1934: at that time Lloyd George had been out of office for twelve years, Churchill for five. Churchill was just sixty, Lloyd George seventy-one

68. Cartoon of Churchill's 'bee in his bonnet', 28 November 1934. Churchill had repeatedly warned that the Germans were building an air force that would eventually be larger and more powerful than Britain's

69. Walking with the Foreign
Secretary, Lord Halifax, to the House
of Commons, 29 March 1938, after the
German annexation of Austria

70. Leaving 10 Downing Street during
the Czech crisis, 10 September 1938

71. With the writer and photo-journalist Stefan Lorant at Chartwell,
3 February 1939, preparing for the main feature article in *Picture Post*

72. At Chartwell: a photograph taken on 3 February 1939
and published in *Picture Post* three weeks later

73. At his desk in his study at Chartwell, 3 February 1939: one of a
sequence of photographs published in *Picture Post* on 25 February 1939

74. In his study at Chartwell, 3 February 1939

75. Working at his upright desk, Chartwell, 3 February 1939

76. Co-pilot, leaving a plane at Kenley, 16 April 1939, having visited
No. 615 Squadron, of which he was Honorary Air Commodore

Fein acts of terror he wanted every male in Ireland to carry an identity card. 'Sweeps and roundings up in large areas' would then be more effective.

On November 9 the Director of Intelligence at Scotland Yard told Churchill that a Sinn Fein cell in Glasgow had decided there should be kidnapping reprisals in Britain for the reprisals in Ireland; among those to be kidnapped were Churchill and Lloyd George. Churchill was warned not to go to Scotland 'for the next few days or weeks'. He was also provided with a personal armed bodyguard, Detective Sergeant Walter Thompson.

In Ireland, violence intensified. On November 15 four British officers were seized by armed men while on a train, taken away, and never seen again. Two days later the Black and Tans carried out a reprisal raid in Cork, killing three men. In retaliation, Sinn Feiners raided several Dublin hotels and houses in the early morning of November 21, killing fourteen men, including six British officers, some of whom were pulled out of bed and shot dead in front of their wives. Later that day, in a reprisal for the Dublin killings, soldiers opened fire at a football crowd which contained several gunmen, and nine people were killed.

On November 25 Churchill was at Westminster Abbey with Lloyd George at a memorial service for the six officers murdered in Dublin. Three days later seventeen Black and Tan officers were ambushed near Macroom; sixteen were killed. At the Cabinet on December 1, Churchill warned that there were insufficient troops to control the whole of Ireland, and advised that 'we should select areas and concentrate our forces there.' Eight days later the Cabinet agreed to declare martial law in four counties in Southern Ireland. Anyone found with arms in the martial law areas, Lloyd George told the Commons, would be tried by Court Martial. The penalty for carrying arms would be death.

On December 10, after a soldier of the Black and Tans had been killed in Cork, much of the commercial centre of the city was burned down as a reprisal. At an emergency Cabinet that evening Churchill suggested that if the Sinn Fein MPs were to meet in Dublin, where they had set up their own Parliament in 1919, and were to show 'an attitude bent on peace', then Britain should offer a month's truce. On December 15 he appealed in the Commons for an end to violence: 'Let murder stop, let constitutional dominion begin, let the Irish people carry the debate from the squalid conditions in which it is now being pushed forward by the Irish murder gang.'

'And by the Government,' called out one of the few remaining Irish Nationalist MPs at Westminster.

'Let them carry this debate into the field of fair discussion,' Churchill continued. Parliament was the place to do this. Then 'they will instantly find that there will be a relief of all those harsh and lamentable conditions which are bringing misery upon Ireland'.

At a special Cabinet meeting on December 29 Lloyd George proposed a one or two months' truce. Churchill supported him. As Secretary of State for War he realised the mounting financial burden of Britain's military involvement in Ireland and Iraq. There were also British garrisons on the Rhine, and in Turkey at both Constantinople and Chanak. He had already proposed that Britain come to terms with the Turkish national leader Mustafa Kemal 'and arrive at a good peace with Turkey'. This would not only ease Britain's position in the Middle East, where Turkey was in a position to stir up anti-British feeling, but would 'recreate that Turkish barrier to Russian ambitions which has always been of the utmost importance to us'.

On December 4 Churchill had again urged Lloyd George to come to terms with Turkey. 'The desire you have to retain Mosul, & indeed Mesopotamia, is directly frustrated by this vendetta against the Turks,' he wrote. An anti-Turkish policy was perpetuating 'terrible waste & expense' in the Middle East, making 'cheaper solutions' impossible. Nine days later he had suggested in Cabinet that Britain should withdraw altogether from Northern and Central Iraq 'to a line covering only Basra and the Persian oilfields on the Karun River', relinquishing control over Mosul and Baghdad, and returning them to Turkey. The Cabinet rejected his proposal.

Churchill was losing his enthusiasm for the War Office, where he had become responsible for commitments in which he did not believe, such as in Iraq, and for policies of military suppression, such as in Ireland, where his part had become limited to that of the provider of men and arms, and where his appeals for an end to the killing and the start of negotiations had fallen on deaf ears. He wanted a change; that autumn there had been talk of sending him to India as Viceroy.

Still seeking economies in Iraq and Palestine, on December 31 Churchill suggested, and the Cabinet agreed to, setting up a Middle East Department, to bring the administration of what Churchill had called 'these thankless deserts' under a single authority. Hitherto four departments of state had overlapped in duties and policy; the India Office, the Foreign Office, the War Office and the Colonial Office. The new department would be under the Colonial Office; Lord Milner, as Secretary of State for the Colonies, would be its chief.

That New Year's Eve, Churchill and Lloyd George were again among the guests at Philip Sassoon's house at Lympne. Lord Riddell, who was present, commented on Churchill's 'wonderful verbal memory' as, 'with much gusto', he 'regaled us by reciting numerous music-hall songs and other verses, which he remembered with little effort, although he had not heard many of them for years'. It was not only singing that took place that weekend; Lloyd George needed Churchill's administrative skills to reduce British military expenditure in the Middle East. On the morning of 1 January 1921 he asked Churchill if he would be willing to succeed Milner as Colonial Secretary, and also take charge of the new Middle East Department, with responsibility for Iraq and Palestine.

Churchill's views on Zionism were well-known. A year earlier, in an article in the *Illustrated Sunday Herald*, denouncing those Russian Jews who had taken a leading part in the imposition of Communist rule on Russia, he had called Zionism an 'inspiring movement', telling his readers, 'If, as may well happen there should be created in our own lifetime, by the banks of the Jordan, a Jewish State under the protection of the British Crown, which might comprise three or four millions of Jews, an event will have ocurred in the history of the world which would from every point of view be beneficial; and would be especially in harmony with the truest interests of the British Empire.'

Churchill asked for a week to think over the offer of the Colonial Office. Returning to Lympne on January 7, he accepted. That same day he embarked on his seventh Cabinet post. He was forty-six years old.

20

Colonial Secretary

On 8 January 1921, a month before formally receiving his seals of office as Secretary of State for the Colonies, Churchill began the search for a system of Government for the Middle East which would substantially reduce the cost of ruling the region. In 1920 Palestine, Iraq and Arabia had cost the British taxpayer £37 million; the equivalent in 1990 of £500 million. Churchill's administrative task was to cut this sum by half. Unless Iraq were governed much more cheaply, he telegraphed to the High Commissioner of Iraq, Sir Percy Cox, and to the Commander-in-Chief, General Haldane, his former fellow prisoner-of-war in Pretoria, 'retirement and contraction to the coastal plain is inevitable'.

To cut expenditure, Churchill proposed setting up 'an Arab Government' at Baghdad which would develop the country without making 'undue demands' on Britain. Law and order would be maintained, not by British troops, but by a specially recruited British police force 'of exceptional individual quality' and by Indian troops brought from India. Under the League of Nations Mandate, Britain was pledged to create in Iraq 'an independent nation subject to the rendering of administrative advice and assistance by a mandatory until such time as she is able to stand alone'.

Cox had already proposed an Arabian prince, the Emir Feisal, one of the sons of King Hussein of the Hejaz, to rule Iraq under the Mandate. 'Can you make sure he is chosen locally?' Churchill asked Cox on January 10, adding that Western political methods 'are not necessarily applicable to the East, and basis of election should be framed'.

Churchill planned to visit Iraq in March. But first he went on holiday to the South of France, passing through Paris to see an exhibition of paintings by an artist who had not exhibited before, 'Charles Morin'. It was in fact the first public exhibition of Churchill's own paintings. While in Paris he saw the French Prime Minister, Alexandre Millerand, to whom he stressed that Britain and France had a common interest in 'the appeasement' of the Middle East. 'I pointed out the absolute need from both British and French points of view,' Churchill reported to Lloyd George, 'of appeasing Arab sentiment and arriving at good arrangements with them. Otherwise we should certainly be forced by expense of the garrisons to evacuate the territories which each country had gained in war.'

Millerand warned Churchill that one cause of disturbance in the Arab world was Zionism, which had been much encouraged by Balfour's wartime declaration in favour of a Jewish National Home in Palestine. Churchill pointed out that the British High Commissioner in Palestine, Sir Herbert Samuel, was 'holding the balance' between Arab and Jew and 'restraining his own people, as perhaps only a Jewish administrator could do'.

Churchill believed he could encourage Jewish settlement in Palestine and at the same time allay the fears of the 500,000 Arabs there that they would be dominated by the Jews, then a minority of 80,000. As his adviser on Arabian Affairs, he had appointed Colonel T.E. Lawrence – 'Lawrence of Arabia'. While in the South of France he learned from Lawrence that the Emir Feisal, in talks with Lawrence in London, had agreed 'to abandon all claims of his father to Palestine' in return for the throne of Iraq for himself, and the throne of Transjordan for his brother Abdullah. These agreements, Lawrence explained, 'tend towards cheapness & speed of settlement'. They also provided a clear demarcation line, the River Jordan, between the area in which the Jews would continue to settle, west of the river, and the Arab sovereign state, Transjordan, to the east.

Confident that Feisal and Abdullah would be willing, in return for their kingdoms, to promise not to attack the French in Syria, Churchill instructed Haldane to make plans for the total evacuation of British troops from Iraq by the end of the year, 'so that by December 31st we shall be responsible for nothing outside Basra'.

On Sunday February 6 Churchill was Lloyd George's guest at Chequers, the country house which, a month earlier, had been given by Lord Lee of Fareham as a permanent gift to the Prime Minister of the day. 'You would like to see this place,' Churchill wrote to Clementine that day. 'Perhaps you will some day!' With him at Chequers was their daughter Marigold, who was recovering from a bad cold. She was two and a quarter years old, and 'marched into my room this morning, apparently in blooming health. It was a formal visit & she had no special communication to make. But the feeling was good.'

Churchill now decided not to visit Iraq, but to go instead to Cairo and ask the British officials in Iraq to meet him there. 'I am strongly encouraging this idea,' Lord Milner wrote to Herbert Samuel. 'He is very keen, able & broad-minded & I am sure, if he will only give himself time to thoroughly understand the situation, he will take sound views & you will find him a powerful backer.' Milner warned that Churchill had one weakness: he was 'too apt to make up his mind without sufficient knowledge'. Seeking that knowledge, as was his habit of a Ministerial career spanning fifteen years, Churchill consulted at length, and corresponded in detail with, the experts of his Middle East Department, trying out his ideas on them, and seeking their guidance.

As Churchill began his preparations for the conference in Cairo, Clementine was at St Jean Cap Ferrat in the South of France, recuperating from another bout of tiredness. The topics filling her husband's mind, she wrote to him, made 'this little peninsula seem a pin point in the sea, while you are soaring in an aeroplane above the great Corniche of life'. His own most recent effort, he told her, had been a speech to the English Speaking Union: 'It was uphill work to make an enthusiastic speech about the United States at a time when so many hard things are said about us over there and when they are wringing the last penny out of their unfortunate allies. All the same there is only one road for us to tread, and that is to keep as friendly with them as possible, to be overwhelmingly patient, and to wait for the growth of better feelings.'

The principal cause of tension with the United States was Ireland. Churchill supported the Government's commitment to Irish Home Rule and was seeking a means to implement it. 'I am feeling my way for a plan,' he told Clementine on February 14. He also reported that little Marigold 'pays me a visit every morning and takes great interest in everything that is said to her or shown to her'. That evening he received the seals of his new office; on the following day, in preparation for the Cairo Conference, he continued his attempt to reduce the £20 million annual expenditure in Iraq to £7 million. 'I am determined to save you millions in this field,' he wrote to the Chancellor of the Exchequer, Austen Chamberlain.

Clementine was keen to travel to Egypt with her husband and would join him at Marseilles. 'I am so looking forward to seeing your dear face again,' he wrote, '& I pray that I may read in it a real consolidation of health.' He also reported that their children were well; he had given Diana, Sarah and Marigold 'the choice of Randolph or the Zoo. They screamed for Randolph in most loyal and gallant fashion. So we arranged for the Zoo too.' Randolph was now a boarder at a preparatory school; his father had been down once to see him 'and found him very sprightly'. All four children 'were very loving & ate enormously'.

Before leaving for Cairo, Churchill again urged Lloyd George to make peace with Turkey, thus securing the northern border of Iraq against hostile incursions. But Lloyd George had thrown his support behind the Greeks, who were even then planning a major military offensive from the Aegean shore of Anatolia into the Turkish hinterland. Churchill contemplated resigning if Lloyd George continued to encourage the Greeks, but held back his threat. Then, on March 2, he left London for Marseilles, where he was joined by Clementine; together they took ship for Egypt, reaching Alexandria six days later. There, Churchill visited Aboukir Bay, the scene of Nelson's naval victory over the French in 1798, before continuing by train to Cairo.

The conference began on March 12. Among the experts were Lawrence, Cox and Gertrude Bell; for ten days they passed in review every aspect of the future of the Middle East. Economy was the goal, political stability the means. One proposal which Churchill put forward was for autonomy for the Kurds in northern Iraq. He favoured this because he feared an Iraqi ruler who would 'ignore Kurdish sentiment and oppress the Kurdish minority', but his advisers dismissed these fears, believing that Britain would always be able to exert a moderating influence in Baghdad.

During a one-day break in the conference, Churchill set up his easel at the Pyramids and began to paint. Two days later he rode on a camel around the Sphinx, with Clementine, Lawrence and Gertrude Bell. While riding, Churchill was thrown by his camel and grazed his hand, but he insisted on continuing, a local newspaper reported, 'made several sketches at Sakkara, and accompanied by Colonel Lawrence camelled back to Mena House'.

By the time the conference ended, it was agreed to install the Emir Feisal in Iraq and the Emir Abdullah in Transjordan; to support Abdullah by money in order 'to guarantee there would be no anti-Zionist disturbances'; to reduce the garrison in Iraq by two-thirds and to defend all outlying areas by Royal Air Force units, thereby cutting military expenditure by two-thirds within three to four years; and to set up a civil air route from Cairo to Karachi, thus completing the air link from England to India.

At midnight on March 23 Churchill left Cairo by train for Jerusalem. During a brief stop at Gaza early the following morning he was greeted by a vast Arab crowd crying 'Cheers for the Minister', 'Cheers for Great Britain' and, with even greater enthusiasm, 'Down with the Jews' and 'Cut their throats'. Unaware of what was being shouted, Churchill was delighted by the frenzy. The train continued to Jerusalem, where he stayed at the Augusta Victoria Hospice, once the Kaiser's most impressive building in the Levant, now serving as Government House.

On the day after Churchill's arrival in Jerusalem there were Arab riots in Haifa demanding an end to any further Jewish immigration. When the police opened fire to disperse the mob a thirteen-year-old Christian Arab boy and a Muslim Arab woman were killed. On the following day, March 27, Churchill went to the British Military Cemetery on Mount Scopus, overlooking Jerusalem, where he attended a service of dedication for the two thousand British soldiers buried there. That evening, at dinner with the Emir Abdullah, he explained Britain's desire to see the Emir installed at Amman as ruler of Transjordan, pledged not to indulge in any anti-French or anti-Zionist activity. As for Palestine, Churchill told Abdullah, while Jews would be allowed to enter, 'the rights of the existing non-Jewish population would be strictly preserved'. Abdullah accepted these assurances, but the local Arabs did not; in a petition to Churchill they warned that if Britain did not heed their cry for an end to Jewish immigration, 'then perhaps Russia will take up their call some day, or perhaps even Germany'. The aim of the Zionists, the Arabs warned, was to establish a Jewish kingdom in Palestine 'and gradually control the world'.

The Arabs asked Churchill to abolish the principle of a National Home for the Jews, to set up a National Government 'elected by the Palestinian people', and to end Jewish immigration until a Palestinian Government was set up. Churchill told them it was neither in his power to grant their request, 'nor, were it in my power, would it be my wish', and he added: 'Moreover, it is manifestly right that the Jews, who are scattered all over the world, should have a national centre and a National Home where some of them may be reunited. And where else could that be but in this land of Palestine, with which for more than three thousand years they have been intimately and profoundly associated?' Palestine could support 'a larger number of people than at present'; the Jews would bring prosperity which would benefit all the inhabitants; no Arabs would be dispossessed. Full self-government, with the possibility of a Jewish majority, would take time. 'All of us here will have passed away from the earth and also our children and our children's children before it is fully achieved.'

To the Jews of Palestine, whose deputation he saw immediately after the Arabs, Churchill spoke of Zionism as 'a great event in the world's destiny' and wished it success in overcoming the 'serious difficulties' in its path. 'If I did not believe that you were animated by the very highest spirit of justice and idealism,' he said, 'and that your work would in fact confer blessings on the whole country, I should not have the high hopes I have that eventually your work will be accomplished.'

On March 29 Churchill planted a tree at the site of the future Hebrew University on Mount Scopus. 'The hope of your race for so many centuries will be gradually realised here,' he said, 'not only for your own good but for the good of all the world.' But the non-Jewish inhabitants must not suffer. 'Every step you take should therefore be also for moral and material benefit of all Palestinians,' Jew and Arab alike. 'If you do this,

Palestine will be happy and prosperous, and peace and concord will always reign; it will turn into a paradise,' becoming a land of milk and honey 'in which sufferers of all races and religions will find a rest from their sufferings'.

Churchill had intended to travel north from Jerusalem to the Arab town of Nablus and then on to the Jewish settlements in Galilee. But a week earlier, while he was in Cairo, he had received the news that ill-health had forced Bonar Law to resign as Lord Privy Seal and Leader of the House. His place was taken by Austen Chamberlain, leaving the Chancellorship of the Exchequer vacant. 'Poor Winston, it is bad luck for him being in Cairo at this moment!' Henry Wilson had written in his diary. It was expected in London that Churchill would hurry home from Cairo, but he had continued to Jerusalem. There, however, he made plans to give up his northern journey and return to Alexandria as quickly as possible; he had learned that an Italian ship was leaving for Genoa on March 31 and was determined to catch it. After less than three months at the Colonial Office he was eager to go to the Treasury, his father's last, foreshortened, Cabinet post.

Leaving Jerusalem, Churchill returned to the coast by car, visiting the Jewish town of Tel Aviv, which had been founded in 1909, and then the Jewish agricultural colony of Rishon-le-Zion. At the colony, the 'first in Zion', founded in the 1880s, he was impressed, first by the fifty young Jews, all on horseback, who met him at the entrance, then by the 'white clothed damsels' who awaited him at the centre, and finally by the vine-yards and orange groves. 'I defy anybody,' he told the House of Commons on his return, 'after seeing work of this kind, achieved by so much labour, effort and skill, to say that the British Government, having taken up the position it has, could cast it all aside and leave it to be rudely and brutally overturned by the incursion of a fanatical attack by the Arab population from outside.'

Churchill reached Alexandria in time to catch the boat to Genoa. What he did not know was that the President of the Board of Trade, the Conservative MP Sir Robert Horne, who had been in the South of France when Bonar Law resigned, had already got back to London and was about to be appointed Chancellor. 'Winston still very vexed with the PM,' wrote Frances Stevenson two weeks after Churchill's return. 'It was the joke of the moment his being away when all the changes were made.'

Churchill stayed in the South of France, at the Cap d'Ail. To Austen Chamberlain, who became Leader of the House of Commons, and for whose maiden speech in 1892 Churchill had been present in the Commons' gallery, he wrote in congratulations, 'When I look back on the projects which your father & mine cherished in the eighties of a national party, it is pleasant to reflect that we are both now taking part in its realisation.' Churchill added: 'I shall be back at the end of the week, but after five weeks of continuous racket and travel I must have a few days grace. I am bringing you back 5½ millions this year & I hope 20 off the expenses next year.'

Churchill's hopes of economy in Palestine were not to be fulfilled. Continuing Arab protests about Jewish immigration led at the beginning of May to riots in Jaffa in which thirty Jews and ten Arabs were killed. Samuel's response was to call a temporary halt to Jewish immigration. Churchill supported the High Commissioner's decision, instructing him to announce 'that until immigrants now in the country are absorbed, immigration will not be reopened'. Samuel told Churchill of a hard core of Jewish Communists who had provoked the Arabs to riot. It was Samuel's responsibility, Churchill replied, to 'purge the Jewish Colonies and new-comers of Communist elements, and without hesitation or delay have all those who are guilty of subversive agitation expelled from the country'. He was even more angered by the Arab attempt to use violence through-out Palestine 'in the hope of frightening us out of our Zionist policy'; Britain must firmly maintain law and order, he told Samuel, 'and make concessions on their merits and not under duress'.

Hoping to appease Arab hostility, however, Samuel decided not to collect the fines which had been levied on the Arab rioters. Churchill opposed this decision. 'It is in my opinion essential,' he told Samuel, 'that Jaffa as well as villages should be made to realise responsibilities with least possible delay. We cannot allow expediency to govern the administration of justice.' If Samuel found it difficult to enforce the collection of fines, Churchill added, he would be willing to arrange for the despatch of a warship to help uphold his authority.

In Cabinet on May 31, discussing the long-term future of the Palestine Mandate, and Arab demands for the immediate establishment of an elected assembly, Churchill explained that he had decided to suspend the development of representative institutions in Palestine 'owing to the fact that any elected body would undoubtedly prohibit further immigration of Jews'. At the same time, in an attempt to calm Arab fears, he approved a proposal from Samuel that Jewish immigration would henceforth be limited by the 'economic capacity' of Palestine to absorb the newcomers.

Apprehensive that the riots in Palestine would go on, and the cost to Britain mount inexorably, Churchill grasped eagerly at a casual suggestion by Lloyd George during a Cabinet meeting on June 9, that the Palestine and Iraq Mandates should both be transferred to the United States; Churchill wanted to announce this in the Commons when he spoke on the Middle East on June 14. But Lloyd George, who had not even broached the matter in Washington, persuaded him not to do so. In his speech, Churchill defended Britain's Palestine responsibilities, and the policies which he had inaugurated. 'We cannot after what we have said and done,' he told the House, 'leave the Jews in Palestine to be maltreated by the Arabs who have been inflamed against them.' Arab fears of being pushed off the land were 'illusory'. No Jew would be brought in 'beyond the number who can be provided for by the expanding wealth and development of the resources of the country. There is no doubt whatever that at the present time the country is greatly underpopulated.'

Churchill's speech was a personal triumph; 'one of your very best' Lloyd George told him. But in the debate that followed, a Conservative MP warned that once 'you begin to buy land for the purpose of settling Jewish cultivators you will find yourself up against the hereditary antipathy which exists all over the world to the Jewish race'. Churchill was not deterred. Eight days later, when the Canadian Prime Minister asked him if Britain's aim was to give the Jews 'control of the Government' in Palestine, he replied, 'If, in the course of many, many years, they become a majority in the country, they naturally would take it over.'

On May 29 Churchill's mother had fallen downstairs and broken her ankle. Gangrene set in and on June 10 her left leg was amputated above the knee. 'Danger definitely over,' Churchill telegraphed to Montagu Porch, her third husband, on June 23. But three days later he was summoned to her bedside with the news that she had suffered a sudden haemorrhage. When he arrived she was already unconscious. She died a few hours later, without having regained consciousness. 'She suffers no more pain, nor will she ever know old age, decrepitude, loneliness,' Churchill wrote to a friend a week later. 'I wish you could have seen her as she lay at rest – after all the sunshine & storm of life was over. Very beautiful and splendid she looked. Since the morning with its pangs, thirty years had fallen from her brow. She recalled to me the countenance I had admired as a child when she was in her heyday and the old brilliant world of the eighties & nineties seemed to come back.'

Lady Randolph was sixty-seven when she died. On July 2 she was buried in Bladon churchyard next to Lord Randolph. A cousin who was present wrote of how, at the funeral, 'Jack and Winston were like widowers'. Churchill wrote to Curzon: 'I do not feel a sense of tragedy, but only of loss. Her life was a full one. The wine of life was in her veins. Sorrows and storms were conquered by her nature & on the whole it was a life of sunshine.' Churchill added, 'We all keep moving along the road.'

Six days after his mother's funeral, Churchill addressed the Imperial Conference in London, where he set out his vision of the reconciliation of France and Germany, and the emergence of a Europe whose post-war grievances and inequalities would be removed by negotiation and agreement. 'The aim,' he told the Dominion Prime Ministers, 'is to get an appeasement of the fearful hatreds and antagonisms which exist in Europe and to enable the world to settle down.' Britain's role should be that of ' the ally of France and the friend of Germany'. Unless she could act to mitigate 'the frightful rancour and fear and hatred' between the two countries, these hatreds would 'most certainly in a generation or so bring about a renewal of the struggle' which had only just ended.

That summer Churchill again tried to persuade Lloyd George to make peace with Turkey, but the Prime Minister was too exhilarated by recent Greek successes on the battlefield to see the dangers of a hostile Turkey. Even Turkish support for an anti-British rebellion in northern Iraq did not influence him. Clementine urged her husband not to seek quarrels with Lloyd George, writing on July 11, 'I do feel that as long as he is PM it would be better to hunt with him than to lie in the bushes & watch him careering along with jaundiced eye.'

Clementine's letter also contained a warning against embarking upon speculation in stocks and shares: 'Let us beware of risking our newly come fortune in operations which we do not understand & have not the time to learn & to practise when learned. Politics are absolutely engrossing to you really, and *should* be & now you have Painting for your leisure & Polo for excitement and danger.' The 'newly come fortune' was the Garron Towers Estate in northern Ireland, which Churchill had just inherited from a distant cousin. It would bring him £4,000 each year in rents and revenue, the equivalent of more than £50,000 in 1990, ending the financial worries that had beset earlier years.

At the beginning of August, Churchill's two-and-a-half-year-old daughter Marigold fell ill with meningitis. His Cabinet colleagues hastened to wish the little girl a swift recovery. 'The child is a little better than she was,' Churchill wrote to Curzon on August 22, 'but we are still dreadfully anxious about her.' Two days later Marigold died. Her parents were devastated. It seemed 'so pitiful', Churchill wrote to a friend, 'that this little life should have been extinguished just when it was so beautiful & so happy – just when it was beginning'.

Marigold was buried at Kensal Green Cemetery, in West London. In search of solitude, Churchill went to Dunrobin Castle in Scotland, the home of his friend the Duke of Sutherland, whose thirty-one-year-old brother Alastair had died only four months earlier as a result of wounds received on the Western Front. For several days Churchill stayed at Dunrobin, where he painted and reflected. On September 19 he wrote to Clementine, who had stayed in London to be near her daughter's graveside: 'It is another splendid day: and I am off to the river to catch pictures – much better fun than salmon. Many tender thoughts my darling all of you & your sweet kittens. Alas I keep on feeling the hurt of the Duckadilly. I expect you will all have made a pilgrimage yesterday. It is twenty years since I first used to come here. Geordie & Alastair were little boys. Now Alastair is buried near his father's grave overlooking the bay. Another twenty years will bring me to the end of my allotted span even if I have so long. The reflections of middle age are mellow. I will take what comes.'

Churchill's hopes for a reduction of expenditure in the Middle East were in disarray. Continuing violence in both Iraq and Palestine forced the maintenance of forces larger than he had intended. In northern Iraq, Royal Air Force planes bombed tribesmen who continued to attack outlying British garrisons. In Jerusalem, on November 2, the fourth anniversary of the Balfour Declaration, another Arab riot against the Jewish National Home had left four Jews and one Arab dead. Ten days later Churchill told his advisers, 'Do please remember that everything else that happens in the Middle East is secondary to reduction in expense.'

Not economy, but reconciliation, was Churchill's quest as far as Ireland was concerned. In February 1921 Clementine had written to him: 'Do my darling use your influence *now* for some sort of moderation or at any rate justice in Ireland. Put yourself in the place of the Irish. If you were ever leader you would not be cowed by severity & certainly not by reprisals which fall like the rain from Heaven upon the Just & upon the Unjust. It always makes me unhappy & disappointed when I see you *inclined* to take for granted that the rough, iron-fisted "Hunnish" way will prevail.'

Clementine's advice did not fall on stony ground; in May, Churchill had supported the idea of a truce between the Government and Sinn Fein, in the hope that a more moderate mood would emerge among those who had continued to resort to murder in search of their political goal of an independent and united Ireland. In July he urged his colleagues to acknowledge 'the failure of the policy of force'. The truce came into effect in July. In September, at a meeting of Ministers at Gairloch in Scotland, Churchill, who had driven the 123 miles from Dunrobin, where he was staying after Marigold's death, urged Lloyd George to agree to negotiations without prior conditions. He was willing to offer the Irish the full benefits of Dominion Home Rule; when he set out this plan to his constituents at Dundee three days later, *The Times* praised 'the breadth and lucidity of his speech'.

On October 11 Churchill was one of the seven British negotiators who met the Sinn Fein leaders at Downing Street. 'It is important to make it plain,' Lloyd George told his Ministers during a break in the discussions, 'that we do not intend to have political domination.' This was also Churchill's view; two weeks later he went so far as to suggest that the six Ulster counties should be included in the Dublin Parliament 'with autonomy', and that in order to secure agreement with the South, Ulster should hold its autonomy from Dublin, not from Westminster. By that means, he said, Ulster 'gets her own protection, an effective share in the Southern Parliament and protection for the Southern Unionists'.

The Ulster Unionists objected to autonomy in any form; they wished to remain an integral part of the United Kingdom. Lloyd George, despairing of agreement, talked of resignation. Churchill dissuaded him, warning that the Coalition could well be succeeded by 'a reactionary Conservative Government'. On November 12 Churchill proposed giving the South 'the status of an Irish State', with an all-Ireland Parliament, a position in the Imperial Conference, and a place in the League of Nations. Ulster could 'stay out'.

On November 29, the day before his forty-seventh birthday, Churchill was present at Downing Street when the draft Irish Treaty, to which he had contributed much, was handed to the Sinn Fein delegates. They took it to Dublin, then returned two days later for clarification. Churchill was one of four Ministers who discussed with them the outstanding points, winning the respect of the two Sinn Fein negotiators, Arthur Griffith and Michael Collins, for his willingness to seek a way out of even the most difficult impasse. The delegates went back once more to Dublin, then returned a day later to London. Churchill was again chosen as part of the negotiating team. His search for an acceptable formula on the last remaining question, allegiance to the Crown, was continuous throughout Sunday December 4 and on the following day, when, at midnight, Griffith and Collins raised their final points of detail. Then, just before three o'clock in the early hours of December 6, the Treaty was signed.

'As the Irishmen rose to leave,' Churchill later recalled, 'the British Ministers under a strong impulse walked round and for the first time shook hands.' A day later Churchill advised the Cabinet to waive the death penalty for those Sinn Feiners who had been convicted of murder and were still awaiting execution. His advice was accepted. 'We had become allies and associates in a common cause,' Churchill reflected eight years later; that cause was the Irish Treaty and 'peace between two races and two islands'.

Recognising Churchill's skills both as a conciliator and a master of detailed exposition, Lloyd George gave him the task of guiding the Irish Treaty through Parliament. For most Conservatives, the largest single Party in the Commons, the Treaty was a betrayal of Imperial rule and of the Protestants in the South. Churchill needed all his abilities to persuade them that it was an act of wisdom and statecraft to give Southern Ireland the right to govern itself. Under the Treaty, he explained to the Commons on December 15, Britain retained Southern Ireland's allegiance to the Crown, its membership of the Empire, facilities for the Royal Navy in the south-western ports, and a 'complete option' for Ulster. It was now 'high time that the main body of Irish and British opinion asserted its determination to put a stop to these fanatical quarrels' which had driven Pitt from office, had dragged down Gladstone 'in the summit of his career', and had drawn 'us who sit here' almost to the verge of civil war in 1914.

Churchill's speech, Austen Chamberlain reported to the King, had 'a profound effect' upon the House. In Dublin, the President of the Parliament, Eamon de Valera, rejected the Treaty, insisting that Southern Ireland should become an independent republic with no allegiance to the Crown; but four out of his seven Cabinet Ministers voted to accept the Treaty, and with it the establishment of what was to be called the Irish Free State. Churchill was made Chairman of a Cabinet Committee charged with working out the details for the Treaty's implementation. On December 21 he advised setting up law courts in the Free State as soon as possible and urged that the British Army, committed to leave Southern Ireland, should at once begin 'ostentatious preparations to quit'. There was be no 'hanging on' to British military or civil control.

At the end of 1921 Churchill was plunged into a controversy that had been germinating for many months. Throughout the summer several newspapers had clamoured for greater economy in Government spending, mounting an 'anti-waste' campaign which threatened the stability of the Government. At the end of December a Committee headed by Sir Eric Geddes had recommended drastic reductions in Army, Naval and Air Force expenditure. When Churchill protested at these conclusions, Lloyd George appointed him Chairman of a Cabinet Committee on Defence Estimates, whose aim was to see how far Defence expenditure could be cut down without danger to national security.

Churchill's Committee met on 9 January 1922, and again on January 10 and January 12, when he warned that whatever economies were agreed to, the existing strength of the Navy must be maintained 'to enable us to defend ourselves until we were able to bring the whole fighting resources of the Empire to bear against an enemy'. At a further meeting on January 23 he opposed closing down the Halton Air Training Establishment, one of the Geddes proposals. The boys at Halton, he said, 'were trained in the best possible atmosphere in which the spirit of discipline and loyalty, not only to their service, but also to their country, was instilled in them from the very beginning'. At a fifth meeting on January 25 he agreed, reluctantly, that the Navy Estimates could be cut down, despite the unwillingness of the First Sea Lord, Admiral Beatty, to envisage any economies whatsoever.

On January 27, as he travelled by train to Lympne for a third weekend there, Churchill wrote to Clementine: 'This has been a really hard worked week for me. Continual speeches & discussions one grave subject after another. A foretaste perhaps of what will some day come upon me. I have completely succeeded in conveying all my views on the Financial Geddes Report Committee. But the fighting with the Army, Navy & Air on one hand, & against LG & Geddes & the Stunt Press on the other has been very stiff. I don't feel the slightest confidence in LG's judgment or care for our national naval position. Anything that serves the mood of the moment & the chatter of the ignorant & pliant newspapers is good enough for him. But I try – however feebly – to think for England. Then on the other hand I have to turn and squeeze Beatty most cruelly to get rid of naval "fat" as opposed to brain & bone & muscle. It is a very peculiar ordeal & the vulgar have no idea of it at all. You will no doubt have seen the newspaper speculation & current speeches. Everything here is working up to a shindy. That is as it should be. The sooner the election comes the better now that controversy is definitely engaged.'

Churchill added, on a personal note: 'The children are very sweet. Diana is shaping into a very beautiful being. Sarah full of life and human qualities – & with her wonderful hair.'

At the end of December 1921 Churchill had gone on holiday to the South of France. With him he took several boxes of documents relating to his period as First Lord of the Admiralty; his aim was to weave these into a narrative history of the war, both to tell the story and to answer criticisms of his conduct. He had already accepted a cash payment from a British publisher of £9,000 to begin the book, followed by a further £13,000 from the United States; a total sum in 1990 values of more than £330,000. Lloyd George, who travelled with Churchill in the train from Paris to the South of France, read his early efforts. 'He praised the style,' Churchill told Clementine, 'and made several pregnant suggestions which I am embodying. It is a great chance to put my whole case in an agreeable form to an attentive audience. And the pelf will make us feel very comfortable. Therefore when darkness falls behold me in my burrow, writing, dictating & sifting papers like the editor of a ha'penny paper.'

Churchill and Lloyd George did not discuss only literature. On 2 January 1922 Churchill wrote from the South of France to the Prince of Wales about Ireland, 'The PM has handed the business over to me now: and I am to hurry back from this delightful villa (Lady Essex's) where I have had a few sunny days, to bring the Irish Provisional Government into being at the earliest moment.' Churchill returned to London on January 7. On the following day the Irish Parliament in Dublin voted to accept the Treaty, and de Valera resigned. On January 15 Collins became Prime Minister. Dublin Castle, the centre and symbol of British rule, where Churchill had spent his early youth, was handed over to the Free State on January 16.

That day Churchill ordered the evacuation of British troops to begin at once. Five days later he invited the Prime Minister of Northern Ireland, Sir James Craig, to meet Collins on the neutral ground of his own room at the Colonial Office. Craig accepted. 'They both glowered magnificently,' Churchill later wrote, 'but after a short, commonplace talk I slipped away upon some excuse and left them together. What these two Irishmen, separated by such gulfs of religion, sentiment, and conduct, said to each other I cannot tell. But it took a long time, and as I did not wish to disturb them, mutton chops etc were tactfully introduced about one o'clock. At four o'clock the Private Secretary reported signs of movement on the All-Ireland front and I ventured to look in. They announced to me complete agreement reduced to writing. They wanted to help each other in every way.'

Three days after this meeting, the Free State Government ended its economic blockade of Ulster, and, as envisaged by the Treaty, Free Trade began at once between North and South. On January 30, as a further gesture of conciliation to the South, Churchill prevailed upon Lloyd George, against strong War Office objections, to release thirteen Irish soldiers who had mutinied in India in 1920 and been sentenced by court martial to life imprisonment.

As friction broke out over the actual line of the border between North and South, Churchill strove to calm the tempers that flared again into violence. 'I am glad to have this task in my hands,' he wrote to Clementine on February 4, 'and hope to be able to steer a good course between all the storms and rocks.' On February 15, after thirty people had been killed in Belfast in five days by Irish Republican Army extremists who rejected the Treaty, Churchill again saw Collins in London. The two men agreed to a Boundary Commission, made up of two groups, one from the North and the other from the South, to consult together and resolve, from village to village and farm to farm, the precise line of the border.

On the following day Churchill introduced the Irish Free State Bill to Parliament, telling MPs: 'If you wish to see Ireland degenerate into a meaningless welter of lawless chaos and confusion, delay this Bill. If you wish to see increasingly serious bloodshed all along the borders of Ulster, delay this Bill. If you want this House to have on its hands, as it has now, the responsibility for peace and order in Southern Ireland, without the means of enforcing it, if you want to impose those same evil conditions upon the Irish Provisional Government, delay this Bill.' During his speech Churchill recalled the struggle in 1914, when the issue had been narrowed down to parishes in Fermanagh and Tyrone:

> *Then came the Great War. Every institution almost, in the world, was strained. Great Empires have been overturned. The whole map of Europe has been changed. The position of countries has been violently altered. The modes of thought of men, the whole outlook on affairs, the groupings of parties, all have encountered violent and tremendous changes in the deluge of the world.*
>
> *But as the deluge subsides and the waters fall short, we see the dreary steeples of Fermanagh and Tyrone emerging once more. The integrity of their quarrel is one of the few institutions that has been unaltered in the cataclysm which has swept the world. That says a lot for the persistency with which Irish men on the one side or the other are able to pursue their controversies. It says a great deal for the power which Ireland has, both Nationalist and Orange, to lay its hands upon the vital strings of British life and politics, and to hold, dominate and convulse, year after year, generation after generation, the politics of this powerful country.*

'Winston speaks with great brilliance,' Herbert Fisher, the President of the Board of Education, wrote in his diary.

As the debate continued, Austen Chamberlain's half-brother Neville told the House that he had been 'more convinced than ever' by Churchill's speech that the Boundary Commission would deal fairly with Ulster. When the vote was taken, 302 MPs supported the Government and only 60 voted against. In vain, during the third reading of the Bill on March 3, did several dozen Conservative 'Die-Hards' walk out of the Chamber while Churchill was speaking. Later that same afternoon the Bill went through.

As the murders in Ireland flared up again, Churchill was at the centre of the attempts to isolate the extremists on both sides. 'We will do our best,' he told the Commons on March 27, 'but it rests with Irishmen who care for Ireland to try to bring about a better state of things. They alone can do it.' Two days later he invited Collins and Craig back to London, helping them to draw up an agreement between North and South to end the murders. After two intense days of talks, with Churchill as mediator, agreement was reached. The Irish Republican Army would cease all border attacks. In Belfast the police force would consist of equal numbers of Protestants and Catholics. From Churchill himself came a sweetener; half a million pounds of British Government money, the equivalent of £6,500,000 in 1990, would be spent to help the poor throughout Northern Ireland, to be divided as the community was divided, one third for the benefit of Catholics and two thirds for Protestants.

The peace agreement was signed on the evening of March 30. On the following day the Irish Free State Bill passed into law. Churchill's part in the passage of the Bill and in the reconciliation of the two enemies was widely praised. 'I think this exercise of judgment brings him nearer to the leadership of the country than anyone would have supposed possible,' Lord Knollys, former Private Secretary to the King, wrote to a friend. 'It will modify a great many views.'

In Ireland, however, de Valera denounced the settlement and urged his followers to resist it. There was no doubt, Churchill told the Cabinet on April 4, 'that the Irish have a genius for conspiracy rather than for government'. The Free State Government was 'feeble, apologetic, expostulatory; the conspirators active, audacious and utterly shameless'. Collins had promised to control the IRA but was unable to do so. If the Republicans seized power, Churchill wanted Britain to hold Dublin and blockade the Republican-held areas. Hostile concentrations of Republican forces should be 'dealt with from the air'. But he did not despair of an end to violence. 'Two months ago,' he told the Commons on April 12, 'it was too soon to rejoice. It is still too soon to lament.' It was also too soon 'to mock or jeer'.

In an attempt to strengthen the Free State forces, Churchill began in mid-April to provide them with arms and ammunition. When, a month later, Collins proposed an electoral pact with de Valera and the Republicans for the forthcoming Free State elections, he was deeply shocked, fearing a sudden triumph for armed Republicanism and the complete separation of Southern Ireland from England. 'It would not be an election in any sense of the word,' he wrote to Collins on May 15, 'but simply a farce, were a handful of men who possess lethal weapons deliberately to dispose of the political rights of the electors by a deal across the table.' Churchill's appeal was in vain; five days later Collins and de Valera signed an electoral pact whereby the supporters of the treaty would have fifty-eight seats in the new Parliament and its Republican opponents thirty-five. Ministries would be shared five-four.

Collins came to London, where he explained to Churchill that free elections would have been impossible under the threat by Republican armed gangs to seize the ballot boxes and destroy them. But the election would take place and the Treaty would be upheld; such was Collins's assurance. In explaining to the Commons on May 31 the hope that elections could still preserve the Treaty, Churchill asked: 'Will the lesson be learned in time, and will the remedies be applied before it is too late? Or will Ireland, amid the stony indifference of the world – for that is what it would be – have to wander down those chasms which have already engulfed the Russian people?'

The powers of government, Churchill pointed out, and 'the whole revenues of Ireland', had already been transferred to the Provisional Government in Dublin. British troops were being kept in Dublin in case a Republic was declared outside the capital. The holding of Dublin would be 'one of the preliminary and essential steps in military operations'. That day a small force of Republicans crossed the border into Ulster and threatened to occupy the villages of Belleek and Pettigo. Churchill at once saw Collins, who was in London, and warned him that if any troops, whether pro-Treaty or anti-Treaty, invaded Northern Irish soil, Britain would 'throw them out'.

Collins told Churchill, as he was leaving: 'I shall not last long; my life is forfeit, but I shall do my best. After I have gone it will be easier for others. You will find they will be able to do more than I can do.' Seeking to encourage Collins, Churchill replied with his favourite Boer saying, 'All will come right.' On June 1 Churchill made plans, in conjunction with the Royal Navy, to seize all Irish seaside Customs houses should the Republicans take power, thus denying them the Customs revenues. On June 3 he gave orders for two companies of British troops to eject the Republican forces from Pettigo. They did so on the following day. Seven Republicans were killed and fifteen captured. Churchill now wanted to drive the Republicans out of Belleek, but Lloyd George urged him to pause. 'You have conducted these negotiations with such skill and patience,' he wrote on June 8, 'that I beg you not to be tempted into squandering what you have already gained by a precipitous action however alluring the immediate prospect may be.' Britain's business as an Empire was to be 'strictly impartial in our attitude towards all creeds'.

Before Churchill could defer to Lloyd George's request not to drive the Catholic raiders out of the borderlands, the fort at Belleek was occupied by British troops and the Republicans escaped back across the border without loss. 'Our troops will advance no further,' he assured the Prime Minister.

Churchill now worked with Griffith to devise a constitution for the Free State in conformity with the Treaty. The Free State would be a 'co-equal' member of the British Commonwealth. The Parliament in Dublin would control all revenue and have the power to declare war. The rights of the Protestants in the South would be safeguarded. On June 16 the constitution was ready. Churchill's negotiating skills, patience and knowledge of what was needed had been an important element in the successful outcome. On the following day, in the Free State elections, the pro-Treaty Party led by Collins won its fifty-eight seats, de Valera and the Republicans thirty-five.

A week after this vote in Dublin, Sir Henry Wilson, the former Chief of the Imperial General Staff, and an implacable Ulster Unionist, was shot dead in the street by a Republican gunman. The gun used in the murder was brought by the police to the Cabinet room and placed on the table. That night Churchill decided not to sleep in his bedroom at 2 Sussex Square, telling Clementine, who was then six months pregnant, that it would be too obvious a place for an assassin to find him. Retiring to the attic, he placed a metal shield between himself and the door, and with his Army revolver at his side slept soundly.

In Dublin the Republicans had seized the Four Courts, the building in which the law courts and archives of the Free State were located. After much hesitation, Collins decided the Army should drive them out. Battle began on June 28. When on the following day it was clear that Collins's troops might not be able to dislodge the Republicans, and might even be defeated, Churchill proposed the capture of the Four Courts by British troops brought from Ulster. Throughout June 29 Collins continued the battle, using British high-explosive shells. Aeroplanes, Churchill told him, would be available on the following day.

On June 30 the Republicans set fire to the Four Courts and then surrendered; thirty of them had been killed. Elsewhere in Dublin fighting continued for several days. Writing to Collins on July 7, Churchill told him that the action which he had taken 'with so much resolution and coolness was indispensable if Ireland was to be saved from anarchy and the Treaty from destruction'. His own vision, Churchill wrote, was that in due course the North and South would 'join hands in an all-Ireland assembly without prejudice to the existing rights of either'. The prize was 'so great that other things should be subordinated to gaining it'.

In July, Churchill had to interrupt his Irish concerns and answer a fierce attack by a small group of Conservative Peers and MPs on the Government's policy of creating a Jewish National Home in Palestine. On July 4, after this policy was voted down in the Lords, Churchill defended it in the Commons. 'It is hard enough, in all conscience, to make a New Zion,' he said, 'but if, over the portals of the new Jerusalem, you are going to inscribe the legend "No Israelite need apply", then I hope the House will permit me to confine my attention exclusively to Irish matters.' The Lords had been incensed by the Colonial Office decision to grant the Zionists a monopoly on the development of water power in Palestine for electricity and irrigation. 'Was this not a good gift which the Zionists could bring with them,' Churchill asked, 'the consequences of which – spreading as years went by in general easement and amelioration – would impress more than anything else on the Arab population that the Zionists were their friends and helpers, not their expellers and expropriators, and that the earth was a generous mother, that Palestine had before it a bright future, and that there was enough for all?'

Churchill stressed that the Zionists were bringing their own wealth and enterprise to Palestine: 'I have no doubt whatever – and after all do not let us be too ready to doubt people's ideals – that profit-making in the ordinary sense has played no part at all in the driving force on which we must rely to carry through the irrigation scheme in Palestine.' It was 'sentimental and quasi-religious emotions' that had enabled the necessary funds to be raised. As for Britain's expenditure, Churchill pointed out that in 1920 Palestine had cost the British taxpayer £8 million, in 1921 this had fallen to £4 million and in 1922 would fall again to £2 million.

The Commons voted by 292 in favour of the Government's Palestine policy and 35 against, reversing the vote in the Lords. Two and a half weeks later the League of Nations voted to make the Balfour Declaration an integral part of Britain's Palestine Mandate. With Churchill's effective support, the establishment of a Jewish National Home in Palestine had become a reality.

In Ireland that autumn the forces of the Free State were gaining the upper hand over the Republicans. 'Tell Winston we could never have done anything without him,' Collins told a friend; the message was passed on. On August 16 Republican forces occupied Dundalk but were driven out after forty-eight hours. The forces of the Free State appeared to be in the ascendant. But on August 22 Collins was shot dead in an ambush by men of the Irish Republican Army loyal to de Valera and still implacably opposed to the Irish Treaty.

Despite fierce Republican efforts to force a breach with Britain, and virtual civil war between the two Catholic factions, the Free State Provisional Government maintained its adherence to the Treaty and its control of the machinery of government. Churchill extended what help and encouragement he could to Collins's successor as head of the Provisional Government, William Cosgrave. When Cosgrave's uncle was murdered by the Irish Republican Army Churchill telegraphed at once, 'It is indeed a hard service that is now exacted from those who are rebuilding the Irish State and Nation, and defending its authority and freedom.'

Churchill continued to work to soothe the frictions along the Ulster border, and to uphold the autonomy of the Free State. But events in the

South had passed beyond his, or Britain's control. On September 12 he wrote to his friend Pamela Lytton, 'Ireland, about which you praise me, is I think going to save itself. No one else is going to. They are a proud & gifted race & they are up against the grimmest facts. I do not believe they will succumb. But the pangs will be cruel & long.' That very day the Free State police dispersed Republican pickets outside the Post Office in Dublin. Churchill commented, '*Responsibility* is a wonderful agent when thrust upon competent heads.'

Throughout 1921 and the first eight months of 1922 Churchill had repeatedly urged Lloyd George to make peace with Turkey. He had even contemplated resignation if Britain continued to support the Greek Government in its attempt to control the western provinces of Asia Minor. In the last week of August, Turkish forces launched a major attack on the Greeks; within a week they were driving the Greeks back to the sea, to Smyrna on the Aegean and Chanak at the Dardanelles.

At a Cabinet meeting on September 7, Curzon, then Foreign Secretary, proposed the retention by Britain of the Gallipoli Peninsula, which had been occupied by British forces after the surrender of Turkey in 1918. Churchill supported him. 'If the Turks take Gallipoli and Constantinople,' he told the Cabinet, 'we should have lost the whole fruits of our victory.' Lloyd George agreed.

On September 9 Turkish forces entered Smyrna. Greek rule in Asia Minor was over. As the Cabinet had agreed, the 1,000 British troops stationed at Chanak, on the Asiatic shore of the Dardanelles, prepared to withdraw across the water to the Gallipoli Peninsula. Then the local British commander decided to keep them at Chanak; Lloyd George supported his decision, telling the Cabinet on September 15 of his own determination to keep the Turks out of Europe, if necessary by force. Ministers were now unanimous that the Neutral Zone on both sides of the Straits must be held; to prevent the Turkish Army crossing into Turkey-in-Europe, two towns on the Asiatic shore, Chanak at the Dardanelles, and Ismid on the Constantinople-Baghdad railway, would be defended by force. Churchill was instructed to draft a telegram to the Dominion governments seeking their support, and asking for 'the despatch of military reinforcements'. The telegram was sent with Lloyd George's approval, and in his name.

That same day, as war clouds loomed again at the Dardanelles, personal matters intruded briefly and pleasantly into Churchill's life: Clementine gave birth to their fifth child, a daughter whom they christened Mary. Also that day he bought a country house in Kent, Chartwell Manor. It cost him £5,000, scarcely more than one year's income from his newly-acquired

Garron Towers Estate. Although the house would have to be largely rebuilt, he hoped to make it his home and place of work within a year. Forty years later he was still its proud and contented owner.

On September 16 Churchill and Lloyd George drafted a Press communiqué about the urgent need to defend the Dardanelles and the Bosphorus against a 'violent and hostile Turkish aggression'. The communiqué was published in the British and Dominion newspapers on the following morning, before Lloyd George's explanatory telegram to the Dominion Prime Ministers had been decoded in the respective capitals. The Australian and Canadian Governments were furious both at not being consulted before the public appeal to arms against Turkey, and at the appeal itself. 'In a good cause we are prepared to venture our all,' the Australian Prime Minister telegraphed to London; 'in a bad one, not a single man.' The Canadian Prime Minister replied that Canada would send no troops at all.

Lloyd George and Churchill were convinced that a show of force and firmness at Chanak would deter the Turks from seeking to cross the Dardanelles. In Cabinet they continued to look for means of reinforcing the Chanak garrison and resisting any Turkish attempt to advance to the water. They were supported by the Chancellor of the Exchequer, Sir Robert Horne, and the First Lord of the Admiralty, Lord Lee of Fareham. But the omens for action were bad; on September 18 the French and Italians withdrew their troops from Chanak and Ismid; Britain was alone. On the following day Churchill told the Cabinet that the Governments of Newfoundland and New Zealand had telegraphed their support. Austen Chamberlain now joined those Ministers who were determined to hold the Gallipoli Peninsula 'if necessary alone'.

At the Cabinet on September 20, striking a note of caution, Churchill warned of the dangers of trying to hold all three places, Constantinople, Ismid and Chanak. 'All our misfortunes had arisen in the past from trying to do that for which we had not the strength.' The Cabinet decided that Chanak alone should be held, but on the following day the *Daily Mail* reflected growing public unease in its headline injunction to the Government, 'Get out of Chanak.'

Lloyd George had no intention of bowing to Press pressure. On September 22 he appointed Churchill chairman of a Cabinet Committee to exercise day-to-day control over the movement of troops, ships and aircraft to Chanak. On the following day a thousand Turkish soldiers entered the Neutral Zone south of Chanak and advanced across the Zone to within sight of the British fortified positions. No shots were fired.

The balance of forces was much against Britain. By September 27 the Turks had 23,000 men confronting the British force of 3,500; a further 5,000 British troops could not arrive before October 9. That evening Churchill, once more the voice of prudence, suggested evacuating the Chanak garrison to the European shore and concentrating at Gallipoli. But Lloyd George was insistent that Chanak be held. Evacuation of the Asiatic shore, he said, would mean 'the greatest loss of prestige which could possibly be inflicted on the British Empire'. Churchill disagreed; far more disastrous than evacuation, he replied, would be defeat.

Lloyd George was in bellicose mood; on September 29 the senior British officer at Constantinople, General Tim Harington, was instructed by the War Office to tell the Turks that unless they withdrew from the Chanak perimeter at an hour to be decided by the General, the British forces would open fire. Churchill believed that the ultimatum would result in negotiations, not war: and that once negotiations began the Turks should be offered a territorial solution not entirely unfavourable to them. At Constantinople, however, Harington decided to delay sending the ultimatum, whose actual time limit had been left to him. Then, on the morning of September 30, just as the Australians reversed their earlier decision and agreed to send troops to Chanak, the Turks intimated that they would back down; their troops at Chanak were ordered not to provoke 'any incident' and their leader, Mustafa Kemal, offered to withdraw from the immediate area around Chanak if the British agreed to leave the Asiatic shore and cross to the European side.

On the morning of October 1 the Cabinet learned that Harington had decided not to deliver the ultimatum. At noon it was learned that Kemal had agreed to meet Harington for negotiations. As Harington and Kemal's representative, General Ismet – the victor of the recent battle of Inönü against the Greeks – began their talks two days later, the Turkish troops at Chanak pulled back 1,000 yards from the British lines. Still anxious to ensure that the British garrison could repel any Turkish attack, Churchill supervised the continuing build-up of forces. 'A very formidable artillery is now in position at Chanak,' he telegraphed to the Dominion Prime Ministers on October 7, 'and aviation is developing every hour.'

The Turks were not prepared to try to drive the British into the sea. The policy of diplomacy through strength had succeeded without a shot being fired. But in London the crisis had only just begun. The Conservative Party, still smarting over the Irish Treaty, deeply resenting its four-year political impotence within Lloyd George's Coalition, and encouraged by the critical responses of Canada and, in the first phase, Australia, to the Chanak crisis, decided to try to bring the Coalition to an end. On the morning of October 7 *The Times* published a letter from Bonar Law, the former leader of the Party, who had taken no part in politics for a year and a half, declaring that it was wrong for Britain, as the leading Muslim power – there were more than sixty million Muslims in India – 'to show any hostility or unfairness to the Turk'. Without at least the support of France, Bonar Law asserted, all military action should be avoided: 'We cannot act alone as the policeman of the world.'

Now that talks had begun between Harington and the Turks, and were making progress, Bonar Law's letter made little sense. It had been overtaken by events, and by negotiations. But it provided Conservative MPs with a rallying call to break free from the Coalition. Four days after it was published, the Turks agreed to pull back ten miles from Chanak and ten miles from the edge of the Neutral Zone at Ismid. From Constantinople, the British High Commissioner, Sir Horace Rumbold, reported to London on the day of the signature of the agreement, 'Factors which probably determined the Turks to sign were our display of force, and their knowledge that we would use it in the last resort.' The political upheaval in Britain was now such, however, that it could not be calmed by the fact that war with Turkey had been averted, or that British policy had been effective.

On the morning of October 19 it was announced that an independent Conservative had beaten the Coalition candidate at a by-election in Newport. That same morning 273 of the 335 Conservative MPs met at the Carlton Club in London to discuss whether or not to remain in the Coalition. Austen Chamberlain urged them to remain, but another member of Lloyd George's Cabinet, Stanley Baldwin, the President of the Board of Trade, pressed for an end to the association with Lloyd George. He was supported by Bonar Law. Churchill, who had tried a week earlier to persuade Baldwin not to turn against the Coalition, no longer had any means to influence those meeting at the Carlton Club. Three days earlier he had been taken ill with acute pains in his side; it was appendicitis. From his new London home at 24 Sussex Square he was taken to a nearby nursing-home, where he was operated on during the night of October 18.

The Carlton Club meeting took place as Churchill was emerging from the anaesthetic. As he awoke, he is said to have called out: 'Who has got in for Newport? Give me a newspaper.' The doctor told him he could not have it and must keep quiet. When, a short while later, the doctor returned, he found Churchill unconscious again, with four or five newspapers spread about him on the bed.

Despite an appeal by Balfour, who argued that the Coalition should go on, 185 of those present at the Carlton Club voted to withdraw their support from Lloyd George. Only 88 wished the Coalition to continue. That afternoon Lloyd George went to Buckingham Palace, where he tendered his resignation and that of his Government. Churchill, on his sick bed, was no longer a Minister of the Crown. 'In the twinkling of an eye,' he later wrote, 'I found myself without an office, without a seat, without a party and without an appendix.'

Churchill saw the Chanak crisis as a successful example of how to halt aggression, and then embark on successful negotiations, by remaining firm. But 'Chanak' had become the pretext not only for the fall of the Government but for one more, unjustified, charge of his own impetuosity.

21

Return to the Wilderness

On 23 October 1922, having been re-elected Leader of the Conservative Party, Bonar Law became Prime Minister. Parliament was dissolved three days later and the General Election called for November 15. From the London nursing-home, still recovering from his operation, Churchill issued his election manifesto 'as a Liberal and a Free-trader'. But the days of Liberal Party ascendancy were over; although in his manifesto he poured scorn on the large number of Peers in Bonar Law's Government, what in 1908 he had called his 'life seat' looked likely to desert him. Although the local Conservatives agreed not to put up a candidate against him, the Asquithian Liberals did. Also standing against him and his fellow National Liberal candidate, was E.D. Morel, a leading Labour Party figure, and Churchill's former Prohibitionist challenger, Edwin Scrymgeour, now standing as an Independent with Labour sympathies.

Until a week before polling day Churchill was too ill to travel to Scotland; from his sick-bed he dictated a series of election statements to his short-hand-writer Harry Beckenham. Clementine, whose daughter Mary was only seven weeks old, went to Dundee to speak for him; Louis Spears, who was also helping the campaign, later recalled: 'Clemmie appeared with a string of pearls. The women spat on her.'

Churchill now prepared to make the journey north. 'If you bring Sergeant Thompson etc,' Clementine warned, 'tell him to conceal himself tactfully as it would not do if the populace thought you were afraid of them. The papers are so *vile* they would misrepresent it.' She went on: 'I find what the people like best is the settlement of the Irish question. So I trot that out & also your share in giving the Boers self-government. The idea against you seems to be that you are a "War Monger", but I am exhibiting you as a Cherub Peace Maker with little fluffy wings round your chubby face.'

On November 10 Churchill left London by sleeper for Dundee. On the following evening, at a meeting of his supporters, he was too ill to stand, and had to speak sitting on a special platform. Chanak, he said, was 'a new war which they had endeavoured to stop', and by the time Lloyd George left office it was 'definitely stopped'. That was an achievement which to his dying day he would be 'proud to have participated in'. Churchill then stood up to give his peroration, a message of good cheer to 'suffering, struggling, baffled, tortured humanity the wide world o'er'. The effort of standing was extremely painful and left him exhausted. Two days later, before a hostile audience, he was booed, hissed and interrupted so frequently that he could not finish his speech.

'You will be at the bottom of the poll,' one heckler cried.

'If I am going to be at the bottom of the poll,' he answered, 'why don't you allow me my last dying kick?'

Two days later Dundee went to the polls. The two men elected were Scrymgeour, the Prohibitionist who in 1908 had received only 655 votes, and E.D. Morel, the Labour Party candidate, a leading anti-imperialist. Each received more than 30,000 votes. Churchill's fellow National Liberal, a local Scotsman, came third with 22,244 votes. Churchill was fourth, with 20,466 votes; only the Independent Liberal and the Communist polled fewer votes than he did.

Churchill was out of Parliament for the first time in twenty-two years. As he left Dundee by the night train he was seen off by a crowd of friendly students singing lustily 'Churchill Ygorra'. One of them, an Irishman, called out, 'Collins believed in you, we believe in you.' Asked to say a few words from his sleeping-compartment window he told them, as reported by the local newspaper, 'that he had always been a democrat, and had always believed in the right of the people to make their own institutions. He bowed to that now, even though he thought that it was misguided.'

Those who had worked with Churchill in the past hastened to commiserate with him on his defeat. 'Will you acquit me of impertinence if I write to say how profoundly I resent the Dundee result?' asked Humbert Wolfe, one of his former civil servants at the Board of Trade and then the Ministry of Munitions. 'Perhaps you will let me remind you how deep & how permanent is the affection which you inspire in all who have the honour to serve you. We all (I know!) felt what happened as a blow personal to ourselves. It is of course the most transitory of reverses, but as it may cast a momentary shadow you may care to be assured that when you and Mrs Churchill waited for the result & still more when you heard it you were not alone.' From T.E Lawrence came a cry of anger, 'What bloody shits the Dundeans must be,' he wrote. But Churchill took a different view, telling his former Cabinet colleague Herbert Fisher, 'If you saw the kind of lives the Dundee folk have to live, you would admit they have many excuses.'

The Conservatives were in office for the first time since 1905, having won 354 seats. Labour had the second largest number of seats, 142; Lloyd George's National Liberals won only 62 and the Asquith Liberals 54. It was the end of the Liberal dominance of British politics. Churchill had been a leading Liberal Parliamentarian for seventeen years. Now he had to decide just where his place should be in the changing spectrum of British political life. 'I do not doubt that your star will rise again,' his former headmaster Dr Welldon wrote on November 24, 'and will shine even more brightly than before.' Others were not so certain; a newly elected Lloyd George Liberal, Geoffrey Shakespeare, who dined with him that week, later recalled: 'Winston was so down in the dumps he could scarcely speak the whole evening. He thought his world had come to an end – at least his political world. I thought his career was over.'

Two weeks after his electoral defeat, Churchill was forty-eight years old. Three days later he left London with Clementine and their children for a four-month holiday in the South of France. 'The Whips will find me a seat if I wanted one,' he had written to Louis Spears three days after the election, 'but what I want now is a rest.' The haven he chose was the Villa Rêve d'Or near Cannes. There he stayed for six months, painting and writing his memoirs. Twice during the six months he returned alone to England to supervise the rebuilding of Chartwell and to discuss his forth-coming war memoirs with naval experts.

While in London, Churchill stayed at the Ritz Hotel and worked on his memoirs there. 'I am so busy that I hardly ever leave the Ritz except for meals,' he wrote to Clementine on 30 January 1923. Back in the South of France he wrote to a friend, 'The weather here has been indifferent but I am getting much better in myself.' It was now three months since his defeat at Dundee. In April, just before the publication of the first volume of his memoirs, he wrote to his cousin Sunny: 'It has been very pleasant out here & such a relief after all these years not to have a score of big anxieties & puzzles on one's shoulder. The Government moulders placidly away. But I must confess myself more interested in the past than the present.'

Churchill returned briefly to London in March, taking Randolph with him. On the journey back to France, at Cartier's in Paris, he bought Clementine a diamond dagger ornament. 'I seem to remember that my mother was much gratified by the present, which was perhaps the most important he had ever given to her,' Randolph later recalled. It was Clementine's thirty-seventh birthday. For another six weeks Churchill worked at the Villa Rêve d'Or on his war memoirs.

Five volumes were to be published in all, entitled *The World Crisis*. Appearing over a period of ten years, they covered the origins of the war, the war itself, and the post-war era up to Chanak. Copious documentation, humour, irony, narrative excitement, thoughtful reflection and combative self-defence fill a total of 2,150 pages. The first volume appeared on 10 April 1923, while Churchill was still in France. In its review the *New Statesman* commented: 'He has written a book which is remarkably egotistical, but which is honest and which will certainly long survive him.'

'I think your book a great masterpiece,' wrote Asquith's wife Margot, 'written with a warmth of words, an economy of personal laudation, swiftness of current, selection, lucidity & drama unexcelled by Macaulay.' Margot also had political advice: 'Lie low; do nothing in politics, go on writing all the time & painting; do not join your former colleagues who are making prodigious asses of themselves in every possible manner. Keep friends in every port – lose no one. Pirate ships are no use in times of peace. Your man of war is for the moment out of action but if you have the patience of Disraeli, with your fine temper, glowing mind & real kind unvindictive nature you could still command a great future.'

Churchill returned to London in mid-May. 'After seventeen years of rough official work,' he told the Aldwych Club on May 24, 'I can assure you that there are many things worse than private life.' That summer he supervised the final work of rebuilding and decorating Chartwell, renting a nearby house, Hosey Rigge, which he at once renamed 'Cosy Pig'. At the end of August, leaving Clementine to overlook the work that he had put in train, he went on holiday to the Atlantic coast of France, on board the yacht of his friend the Duke of Westminster, taking with him the proofs of the second volume of his war memoirs.

Clementine was uneasy about leaving London for the country; she felt no special attraction to Chartwell and was worried about the expense of so large a house. Churchill wrote to her on September 2: 'My beloved I do beg you not to worry about money, or to feel insecure. On the contrary the policy we are pursuing aims above all at *stability* (like Bonar Law!). Chartwell is to be our *home*.' Three days later he told her, 'I write and work in bed all morning as usual. If the sun shines, I paint.' His only political comment was about the Italian bombardment of the Greek island of Corfu, 'What a swine this Mussolini is.'

Churchill was back in London at the end of October when the second volume of *The World Crisis* was published. From Bonar Law's successor as Prime Minister, Stanley Baldwin, to whom he had sent a copy, came a friendly handwritten note, 'If I could write as you do, I should never bother about making speeches!' The book contained many of the documents that the Dardanelles Commission had refused to publish. Leo Amery, a Harrow contemporary who was now First Lord of the Admiralty, wrote of his admiration 'for the skill of the narrative itself' and of his sympathy for Churchill 'in your struggle against the impregnable wall of pedantry or in the appalling morasses of irresolution.'

In November 1923 Baldwin announced that he was calling a General Election and would reintroduce Protection. Churchill suddenly found his political voice again, denouncing as 'a monstrous fallacy' the policy he had denounced so forcefully two decades earlier. Once more Free Trade became his banner. No less than seven Liberal associations asked Churchill to be their candidate. Speaking at Manchester on November 16 he appealed for the unity of Asquith and Lloyd George Liberals, under Asquith's leadership. Liberalism, he said to stormy applause, was the only 'sure, sober, safe middle course of lucid intelligence and high principle'. Three days later he accepted the invitation of the West Leicester Liberal Association to be their candidate. The local newspaper, the *Leicester Mail*, was hostile, but Cecil Roberts, the editor of a neighbouring newspaper, the *Nottingham Journal*, gave him its support and sent a convoy of trucks to distribute copies in his constituency.

Among those who helped distribute the *Nottingham Journal* was a young man whom Churchill had recently met for the first time, the twenty-two-year-old Brendan Bracken. It was the beginning of a lifelong association and friendship. But the campaign itself went badly. At one meeting, the *Leicester Mail* reported with glee, Churchill and Clementine 'were greeted by groans and hoots, not a single cheer being heard in the building'. Wherever he spoke the cry went up: 'What about the Dardanelles?' To one such heckler he replied: 'What do you know about the Dardanelles? The Dardanelles might have saved millions of lives. Don't imagine I am running away from the Dardanelles. I glory in it.'

On December 3 Churchill spoke at three large election meetings in London; after one of Churchill's speeches a man smashed the window of the car in which he was trying to drive away from the hostile, hooting crowd. As the car departed, it was spat on. Meanwhile, at West Leicester, Clementine had continued to uphold her husband's cause. 'A great many people think he is essentially military,' she said, 'but I know him very well, and I know he is not that at all. In fact one of his greatest talents is the talent of peace-making.'

The election was held on December 6, a week after Churchill's forty-ninth birthday. His attempt to return to Parliament as a Liberal failed. 'We had every disadvantage to contend with,' he wrote to Cecil Roberts a month later; 'no local press; no organisation; universally interrupted meetings.'

Baldwin's call for an election had been a massive miscalculation; the Conservatives lost nearly a hundred seats. Although they were still the largest Party, Labour and the Liberals could, if they combined, defeat them. Churchill wanted the Liberals to support the Conservatives, form a coalition, and keep out Labour. When Asquith announced that he would not do so, Churchill was outraged. A Labour Government, he told Asquith's daughter Violet, would 'undermine the commercial and business activities of the country'. It would, he wrote in a letter to *The Times* on 18 January 1924, cast 'a dark and blighting shadow on every form of national life'.

Three days after Churchill's letter was published in *The Times*, the Liberal and Labour MPs combined in a Commons vote to defeat the Conservatives. Baldwin resigned and the Labour Party leader, Ramsay MacDonald, became Prime Minister, at the head of a Government dependent on Liberal support. Churchill sent MacDonald a letter of good wishes, to which he replied by hand: 'No letter received by me at this time has given me more pleasure than yours. I wish we did not disagree so much! – but there it is. In any event I hope your feelings are like mine. I have always held you personally in much esteem.'

On February 4 Churchill was again asked to stand as a Liberal, this time for Bristol West. He declined, explaining that he was not willing 'to embark upon a by-electoral contest against the Conservatives'. Two weeks later, on holiday at Mimizan near Bordeaux, he wrote to his wife that he had still not made up his mind about his political future: 'I want time to work. A few months, anyhow.'

On February 22, back in London, Churchill had a long talk with Baldwin. 'He evidently wants very much to secure my return & co-operation,' Churchill told Clementine. Baldwin wanted Churchill to give a lead to those Liberal MPs who were uneasy about Liberal Party support for Labour and who wished 'to act with the Conservatives'. Two days after his meeting with Baldwin, in a letter to the Conservative candidate at a by-election at Burnley, Churchill urged the Liberals there, who had no candidate of their own, not to vote Labour. His letter was published in *The Times* on the following day. Commented the *Glasgow Herald*, 'Compelled by his temperament to be in the thick of the fighting, Mr Churchill seems a predestined champion of the individualism which he has served all his political life – under both of its liveries.'

Churchill now came forward as an Independent candidate at a by-election to be held in the Abbey Division of Westminster. It was one of the most prized Conservative seats, but he hoped to persuade Baldwin to let him stand unopposed by any Conservative challenger, to try to win both Conservative and Liberal support. 'My darling one do not stand unless you are reasonably sure of getting in,' Clementine wrote from the South of France. 'The movement inside the Tory Party to try & get you back is only just born & requires nursing & nourishing & educating to bring it to full strength.' A Liberal by upbringing and conviction, Clementine was uneasy at the possibility of her husband's return to Conservatism. But she did not oppose him. 'Do not however let the Tories get you too cheap,' she wrote. 'They have treated you so badly in the past they ought to be made to pay.'

Despite Baldwin's efforts to have Churchill unopposed by the local Conservative Association, the Westminster Conservatives chose their own candidate, Otho Nicholson, a thirty-two-year-old Old Harrovian. Campaigning began on March 5. On the following day *The Times* denounced Churchill as 'an essentially disruptive force'. Clementine hurried back from the South of France to help him. His candidature became the focus of national attention and interest. 'He is being rung up at his house,' the *Evening News* reported, 'as few people ever have been in the history of the telephone.'

In his election address of March 9, Churchill noted that Baldwin had publicly appealed for Liberal co-operation against Labour. 'I support him in the policy of setting country before Party,' Churchill declared. For its part the Labour Party attacked his attempt 'to overthrow Bolshevik Russia' and his 'personal recklessness during the Dardanelles'. Noted the Deputy Secretary to the Cabinet, Thomas Jones, 'The Dardanelles pursues Churchill most unfairly, for it was one of the big conceptions of the war and if put through with vigour might have shortened the war by a couple of years.'

Baldwin was forced to support the official Conservative candidate. But when Balfour wrote a letter expressing his 'strong desire' that Churchill's 'brilliant gifts' should again be used in the Commons, it was Baldwin who agreed that the letter could be made public. Polling took place on March 19. As the last packet of votes was being counted someone turned to Churchill with a shout, 'You're in by a hundred.' The news of his victory was passed to the crowd in the street and telegraphed all over the world. But it was false; he had in fact been defeated. The official Conservative candidate had won by forty-three votes.

Churchill was determined to return to Parliament. On April 2 he went to see Baldwin and offered to act as the leader of fifty Liberal MPs and candidates, who were prepared to work with the Conservatives in the Commons, and against Labour, provided no official Conservative candidate were put up against them. Two weeks later he told Clementine that the Conservatives were trying to fix him up with a constituency in which they would not oppose him.

Churchill was busy preparing Chartwell for his wife's arrival. 'All yesterday & today we have been turfing & levelling the plateau, the motor mower acts as a roller, and we have done everything now except from the yew tree to the kitchen garden end.' His children were helping 'like blacks', as were his detective and his chauffeur. 'I drink champagne at all meals, & buckets of claret & soda in between, & the *cuisine* tho' simple is excellent. In the evenings we play the gramophone (of which we have deprived Mary) & Mah Jongg.'

Travelling to Liverpool on May 7, Churchill told more than 5,000 Conservatives, at the first Conservative meeting he had addressed in twenty years, that there was no longer any place in British politics for the Liberal Party as an independent force. Only the Conservative Party offered a strong enough base 'for the successful defeat of Socialism'. Liberals like himself must therefore join forces with the Conservatives on a 'broad progressive platform'. Two days later the Conservative Association of Ashton-under-Lyne asked him to be their candidate: two more invitations came from other Conservative Associations that same week and a fourth at the end of the month.

Churchill hesitated to rejoin the Conservative fold; much as he feared Labour, he remained anxious to retain the Liberal associations and attitudes he had held throughout his Ministerial career. In mid-June he was considering the possibility of setting up a new political Party of Liberals who, calling themselves Liberal-Conservatives, would stand at the next election as an independent group, supporting the Conservatives. Nothing came of this. Then, in July, he secured Baldwin's agreement that he would stand at the next election as a 'Constitutionalist' candidate, with full official Conservative support. Baldwin also agreed to find him a safe Conservative seat in or near London, so that once the election campaign began he would be free to speak throughout Britain in the Conservative interest, against MacDonald's economic loan to Soviet Russia, and against the perils of Socialism.

That summer Churchill lived at Chartwell, captivated by the comfort and tranquillity of his new home. He was draining a lake below the house and constructing a dam, with the intention of building a swimming-pool. He had laid down a light-railway track on which a digger could move, to clear the bed of the lake. Once more his detective was mobilised. 'Thompson and I have been wallowing in the most filthy black mud you ever saw, with the vilest odour, getting the beastly stuff to drain away,' Churchill told Clementine.

That autumn Churchill tried to build a bridge between the Conservatives and the Lloyd George Liberals. At a secret meeting with Lloyd George at the latter's home at Churt on August 31, he urged Lloyd George to support the Conservatives at the next General Election, on the basis of shared dislike of MacDonald's loan to Russia. Lloyd George was sympathetic. The moment Labour had committed itself to this loan, he told Churchill, 'they had put their fingers in the cog wheels and would be drawn to their ruin'.

On September 11 Churchill accepted nomination for a safe Conservative seat, Epping, north-east of London. Two weeks later, when he spoke at Edinburgh to a mass meeting of Scottish Conservatives, three leading Conservative politicians, his former adversary Lord Carson, Sir Robert Horne and Balfour, were on the platform as his chief supporters. There was, he declared, 'no gulf of principle' between Conservatives and Liberals. It was Socialism that was the threat; MacDonald's economic loan to Soviet Russia, and his desire for an Anglo-Soviet Treaty, must both be resisted. What Labour offered was clear and unacceptable, 'Our bread for the Bolshevik serpent; our aid for the foreigner of every country; our favours for the Socialists all over the world who have no country; but for our own daughter States across the oceans, on whom the future of the British island and nation depends, only the cold stones of indifference, aversion, and neglect.'

Churchill's speech was widely reported, and by Conservatives warmly acclaimed. 'So Winston is on the war path again – after a prolonged holiday that he has enjoyed,' Clementine's mother, Lady Blanche Hozier, wrote to a friend.

In the week of his Edinburgh speech, Churchill published an article in *Nash's Pall Mall*, of which a quarter of a million copies were later circulated in pamphlet form throughout the United States, warning of the perils of future warfare. 'Might not a bomb no bigger than an orange,' he asked, 'be found to possess a secret power to destroy a whole block of buildings – nay to concentrate the force of a thousand tons of cordite and blast a township at a stroke? Could not explosives even of the existing type be guided automatically in flying machines by wireless or other rays, without a human pilot, in ceaseless procession upon a hostile city, arsenal, camp, or dockyard?'

Such a weapon had already been forecast by H.G. Wells, whose writings Churchill knew well. But there was a new influence in his thinking on scientific matters that had begun to supersede Wells; he had befriended a thirty-eight-year-old Oxford Professor, Frederick Lindemann, to whose brilliant mind and rapid wit he was quickly attracted. Lindemann's father had been born in Alsace before its annexation by Germany. He himself had been born in Germany, at the spa of Baden-Baden, where his American mother was taking the cure. After studying in Berlin and Paris, he worked at the Royal Air Force Laboratory at Farnborough from 1915 to

1918, when he had learned to fly in order personally to investigate the aerodynamic effects of aircraft spin.

Lindemann quickly became a close friend; he would often drive from Oxford to Chartwell for the weekend, and would fascinate Churchill by his descriptions of the most recent inventions, and the possibilities for scientific change. Shortly before starting work on his *Nash's Pall Mall* article, Churchill had written to Lindemann: 'I have undertaken to write on the future possibilities of war and how frightful it will be for the human race. On this subject I have a good many ideas, but I should very much like to have another talk with you following on the most interesting one we had when you last lunched here.' He had read that a man claimed to have invented a ray that could kill mice at a certain distance: 'It may all be a hoax, but my experience has been not to take "No" for an answer.'

Churchill also discussed with Lindemann the relative military strengths of France and Germany, and the remote prospect of their renewed conflict. In his article of September 24 he wrote of the intense German search for revenge for the defeat of 1918 and for revision of the Treaty of Versailles. The French hoped to preserve the Treaty and keep Germany weak 'by their technical military-apparatus, by their black troops, and by a system of alliances with the smaller States of Europe; and for the present at any rate overwhelming force is on their side'. But physical force alone, he warned, unsustained by world opinion, 'affords no durable foundation for security'. Germany was 'a far stronger unity than France, and cannot be kept in permanent subjugation'.

A General Election was called for October 29. In his manifesto, Churchill declared, 'I give my whole support to the Conservative Party.' He was standing as a 'Constitutionalist' with full Conservative support, at Epping, the safe Conservative seat that Baldwin had put at his disposal. The one cloud on his election prospects was 'Die-Hard' opposition to the Irish Treaty, but his outspoken criticism of MacDonald's loan to Soviet Russia was applauded by his constituents. On October 29, against both a Liberal and a Labour challenger, he won the seat by a majority of more than 9,000. Once more he was a Member of Parliament, after nearly two years' absence. He had still not formally returned, however, to the Conservative Party.

Nationally, the result was a complete Conservative victory; 419 seats against 151 for Labour, and a mere 40 for the Liberal Party of which only ten months earlier Churchill had been a candidate and a leading figure. 'I think it very likely that I shall not be invited to join the Government,' he wrote to a friend on November 4, 'as owing to the size of its majority it will probably be composed only of impeccable Conservatives.' Churchill was wrong; many posts were being discussed for him in Baldwin's circle, among them the Board of Trade, the Colonial Office, the War Office and the Admiralty, all of which he had held before. Baldwin's own personal suggestion was the India Office. Austen Chamberlain suggested the Ministry of Health. This last had occurred independently to Clementine when, on November 5, Baldwin requested Churchill to see him. Clementine urged her husband to accept the Ministry of Health if offered it, as there was much to be done 'in housing and other social services'.

'Are you willing to help us?' Baldwin asked him.

'Yes, if you really want me,' Churchill replied.

'Will you be Chancellor?' said Baldwin.

'Will the bloody duck swim?' Churchill had wanted to reply. But, he later wrote, 'as it was a formal and important conversation I replied, "This fulfils my ambition. I still have my father's robe as Chancellor. I shall be proud to serve you in this splendid Office." '

Churchill returned to Chartwell. There, he later recalled, 'I had the greatest difficulty in convincing my wife that I was not merely teasing her.' Churchill's friends were thrilled. 'Winston dear boy,' wrote a former chairman of the Parliamentary Liberal Party, George Lambert, 'I have got a fair instinct for politics. I think I shall live to see you Prime Minister.'

22

At the Exchequer

On 30 November 1924, twenty-five days after accepting office as Chancellor of the Exchequer, Churchill celebrated his fiftieth birthday. Then, having announced his return to the Conservative Party, after an absence of twenty years, he addressed himself to his first Ministerial task at the Treasury, devising and financing a substantial extension of national insurance, the social reform he had been instrumental in creating fifteen years earlier, at the height of his Liberal activities. In this he worked closely with the new Minister of Health, Neville Chamberlain. He also sought means to reduce the burden of income tax on 'professional men, small merchants and business men – superior brain workers of every kind'. The schemes he put up to his officials included pensions for widows and orphans, a major extension of old age insurance and the development of cheap housing. The Government itself, he believed, should experiment with new methods of house construction for those 'who cannot afford to pay at the existing prices'.

On November 28 Churchill told the Deputy Secretary of the Cabinet, Thomas Jones: 'I was all for the Liberal measures of social reform in the old days, and I want to push the same sort of measures now. Of course I shall have to give some relief to the tax-payers to balance these measures of reform.'

Churchill now moved into 11 Downing Street, which was to be his London home for the next four and a half years. From there, on December 9, he wrote to a leading Conservative, Lord Salisbury, a son of the former Prime Minister, to explain his view that an 'increasing distinction' between earned and unearned income might be the most effective and fairest way of raising new taxes. He was, however, opposed to any attempt to 'hunt down the "idle rich" ', explaining to Salisbury: 'If they are idle they will cease in a few generations to be rich. Further than that it is not desirable for the legislature to go. The Christian or the moralist alone can pursue an inquisition into what is "service" and what is "idleness".' Churchill added: 'My maturer views of life lead me to deprecate the personal inquisition, except when self-instituted, into actions which are within the law. I think the rich, whether idle or not, are already taxed in this country to the very highest point compatible with the accumulation of capital for future production.'

The 'existing capitalist system is the foundation of civilisation,' Churchill told Salisbury, 'and the only means by which great modern populations can be supplied with vital necessities.' Five days later, on December 14, he set down for his officials at the Treasury his philosophy of wealth, based upon a combination of the taxation of unearned income and the encouragement of profits and productivity: 'The creation of new wealth is beneficial to the whole community. The process of squatting on old wealth though valuable is a far less lively agent. The great bulk of the wealth of the world is created and consumed every year. We shall never shake ourselves clear from the debts of the past, and break into a definitely larger period, except by the energetic creation of new wealth. A premium on effort is the aim, and a penalty on inertia may well be its companion.'

On 6 January 1925 Churchill crossed to Paris, where, during a week of intensive negotiations, he secured a remarkable settlement of the tangle of international war debts. Henceforth Britain's £1,000 million debt to the United States, for which America had been pressing, would be paid by instalments at the same time as Britain received simultaneous and proportionate payments from France, Belgium, Italy and Japan; countries which themselves owed Britain a total of £2,000 million, and which had hitherto been reluctant to agree to a schedule of repayment. Britain's other debtors, Brazil, Czechoslovakia, Roumania and Serbia, also accepted Churchill's scheme.

All the negotiating States paid tribute to Churchill's skill, patience and grasp of detail. 'To uphold the interests of this country,' Edward Grey wrote to him when the conference was over, '& at the same time to secure this recognition from the representatives of other countries is a rare achievement & a great public service.'

To finance his social reform measures Churchill embarked on several months of bitter controversy. While accepting the need for greater Air Force expenditure, and no reduction in the money being spent by the Army, he pressed for a substantial reduction in naval spending. Convinced that the Admiralty's plans were grandiose and wasteful, he plunged into a political battle similar to the one he had fought in 1908, when, as President of the Board of Trade, he had challenged what he regarded as excessive naval spending; and he did so with the same social goal in mind. But he did not intend to jeopardise Britain's ability to confront an aggressor if international harmony were to break down, explaining to the Cabinet on January 29, and drawing on his pre-1914 experience at the Admiralty: 'During a long peace, such as follows in the wake of great wars, there must inevitably develop gaps in our structure of armaments. We have to select the essential elements of war power from admist great quantities of ancillary and subsidiary improvements. These gaps can be gradually and unostentatiously filled up if deep international antagonisms, the invariable precursors of great wars, gradually become apparent in the world.'

On February 13 the Admiralty accepted Churchill's upper limit of just over £60 million for the coming financial year; almost £1,200 million in the money values of 1990. Given Admiralty fears of Japanese naval expansion, Churchill agreed to make an extra £2 million available for an emergency, and to give the Admiralty the same amount of money for the repair of British destroyers as was spent by Japan 'plus 25%'. The crisis passed. 'He is a Chimborazo or Everest,' wrote Asquith to a friend, 'among the sandhills of the Baldwin Cabinet.'

In his determination to help productive enterprise, Churchill was uneasy at the Treasury's decision, made earlier with the support of the Labour Chancellor of the Exchequer, Philip Snowden, to return to the Gold Standard. To go back to Gold, Churchill told his officials on January 29, 'favoured the special interests oꞁ finance at the expense of the interests of production'. On February 22 he tried to influence them once more: 'I would rather see Finance less proud and Industry more content.' To bring to bear the best arguments possible against a return to Gold, on March 17 he gave a dinner for the Cambridge economist J.M. Keynes and his own officials. But Baldwin, with his authority both as Prime Minister and a former Chancellor of the Exchequer, urged Churchill not to rock a boat which was already virtually launched, and to which the Bank of England was committed.

Churchill gave way. Henceforth, he was to defend the decision of which he had at the time been dubious. Twenty-three years later, after listening to criticism from the Labour Prime Minister of the day, he told the Commons: 'Mr Attlee referred to my action in bringing this country back to the Gold Standard in 1925. He says that I acted on advice. Indeed I did, on the advice of a Committee appointed by Lord Snowden, the Chancellor in the Socialist Government in 1924, of which Mr Attlee was himself a member. What did Lord Snowden say about our return to the Gold Standard? On the Second Reading of the Gold Standard Bill he said that while the Government had acted with undue precipitancy he and his Socialist colleagues were in favour of a return to the Gold Standard at the earliest possible moment.'

Churchill went on to point out that in December 1926 Snowden had written an article in the *Financial Times* in which he stated: 'All the facts therefore do not support the impression that the return to gold has been detrimental to industry. The Bank Rate has not been raised; unemployment has not risen; real wages have not fallen; and the price level has been fairly well maintained.' Churchill continued, 'So far from causing what Mr Attlee calls "untold misery" the facts as I have said show that while I was the Conservative Chancellor of the Exchequer the real wages of our workpeople steadily and substantially increased.'

As Churchill worked on his first Budget, Clementine was in the South of France recuperating from nervous exhaustion. He sent her regular reports of family and Ministerial matters. 'Mary is flourishing,' he wrote that March. 'She comes & sits with me in the mornings & is sometimes most gracious. Diana is just back from school & we are all planning to go to see Randolph this afternoon.' As for Clementine herself: 'Do not abridge your holiday if it is doing you good. But of course I feel far safer from worry and depression when you are with me & when I can confide in your sweet soul.'

A week later Churchill wrote again, distressed to learn that Clementine's mother was dying. Lady Hozier was seventy-three. 'My darling I grieve for you. An old & failing life going out on the tide, after the allotted span has been spent & after most joys have faded is not a case for human pity. It is only a part of the immense tragedy of our existence here below against which both hope & faith have rebelled. It is only what we all expect & await – unless cut off untimely. But the loss of a mother severs a chord in the heart and makes life seem lonely & its duration fleeting. I know the sense of amputation from my own experience three years ago.'

Four days after writing this letter Churchill walked in Lord Curzon's funeral cortège, telling Clementine later that day: 'He faced his end with fortitude & philosophy. I am very sorry he is gone. I did not think the tributes were very generous. I would not have been grateful for such stuff. But he did not inspire affection, nor represent great causes.'

The 'great cause' in which Churchill was now immersed was social reform. His concern was the hardship that fell upon a family after the prolonged unemployment, old age, sickness or death of the breadwinner. 'In a few months,' he told his advisers after receiving a delegation of Old Age Pensioners on March 24, 'the result of the years of thrift may be swept away, and the house broken up.' He intended his Budget to avert that catastrophe. All pensions, he told Neville Chamberlain on April 3, should begin at 65, not 70. Widows should receive a pension from the 'very outset' of widowhood.

Churchill introduced his Budget on April 28. Clementine, Randolph and Diana were in the Gallery to hear him. He spoke for two hours and forty minutes, showing, Baldwin told the King, 'that he is not only possessed of consummate ability as a Parliamentarian, but also all the versatility of an actor'. Lucidity, rhetoric, levity and humour, each had its part in his speech, the centrepiece of which was the insurance and pension schemes.

When misfortune descended upon a workman's home, Churchill said, whether unemployment, distress or the loss of the breadwinner, 'it leaves this once happy family in the grip of the greatest calamity. Although the threat of adversity has been active all these years, no effective provision has been made by the great mass of the labouring classes for their widows and families in the event of death. I am not reproaching them, but it is the greatest need at the present time. If I may change to a military metaphor, it is not the sturdy marching troops that need extra reward and indulgence. It is the stragglers, the weak, the wounded, the veterans, the widows and orphans to whom the ambulances of State aid should be directed.'

Widows and orphans would receive pensions from the moment of their bereavement: 200,000 women and 350,000 children would be the immediate beneficiaries. All other pensions would come into force at the age of sixty-five. 'Restrictions, inquisitions and means tests' would be swept away altogether. Once the act was passed it would be 'nobody's business' what any of the pensioners had 'or how they employed their time'. Churchill had a second major change to announce: those in the lowest income groups would receive a 10 per cent reduction of income tax. It was his hope in doing this 'that by liberating the production of new wealth from some of the shackles of taxation the Budget may stimulate enterprise and accelerate industrial revival'.

Neville Chamberlain, whose Ministry of Health had been deeply involved with the pension scheme, was impressed, writing in his diary on May 1, 'We were pledged to something of the kind, but I don't think we should have done it this year if he had not made it part of his Budget scheme, and in my opinion he does deserve personal credit for his initiative and drive.' Two weeks later Churchill told the British Bankers' Association, 'This is our aim – the appeasement of class bitterness, the promotion of a spirit of co-operation, the stabilisation of our national life, the building of the financial and social plans upon a three or four years' basis.'

In foreign policy Churchill also sought appeasement; on March 11 he had persuaded a conference of senior Ministers not to move towards a Treaty with France which could only serve to isolate and embitter Germany still further, but to work instead for an arrangement 'to include Germany'; from this idea emerged the Locarno Treaties, whereby Britain, Germany, France and Italy guaranteed the security of their post-war frontiers. Churchill also urged, in a private conversation with the Polish

Ambassador, that Poland 'should by all means cultivate the friendship of Germany. If Germany were driven back on Russian support, Poland in the end would be crushed between them.'

Churchill's work as a conciliator was seen most effectively at the end of July, when he was at the centre of the Government's efforts to avert a miners' strike by persuading the mine-owners to withdraw dismissal notices against their men. Despite some Conservative unease, Churchill also persuaded his colleagues to grant a Government subsidy to the mining industry, so that wages would not have to be cut. In Cabinet on July 30 Churchill pointed out that the miners had a certain amount of right on their side.

On August 6 Churchill defended the subsidy in the Commons. The decision to give it had been taken, he said, 'because we have not yet abandoned that hope. If we had plunged into a struggle, allowed a stoppage of the mines, had faced a general strike on the railways, had accepted a temporary paralysis of the entire industry of the country, allowed trade to be checked, allowed social reform to be arrested, our finances to be deranged, had postponed pensions, and restored taxation – if we had taken that position, then for us, and so far as this Parliament is concerned, the door would have been closed to an advance to a better state of things. It may yet happen. But that is not a decision that any sane man or Government would take until every other reasonable possibility had been exhausted.'

Churchill concluded: 'Even if it should be our duty, if ever it should be our duty, to take such a position, then the work of this Parliament is absolutely ruined. For the rest of its life it would be simply toiling back to reach the position occupied in 1924 and 1925 – a position which to-day we find much to be discontented with. No chance of improvement! No hope of expansion! No alleviation of the burdens! Just a simple struggle to work back to where we are now. We have refused to accept such a melancholy conclusion.'

'What a brilliant creature he is!' Neville Chamberlain wrote to Baldwin three weeks later. 'But there is somehow a great gulf fixed between him and me which I don't think I shall ever cross. I like him. I like his humour and vitality. I like his courage. I like the way he took that – to me – very unexpected line over the coal crisis in Cabinet. But not for all the joys of Paradise would I be a member of his staff! Mercurial! a much abused word, but it is the literal description of his temperament.'

That autumn Churchill negotiated a comprehensive agreement for the repayment of France's war debt to Britain; there would be sixty-two annual payments of £12,500,000. But if Germany defaulted on her own reparations payments to France, then France would be entitled to ask for reconsideration of the French debt to Britain. As the negotiations continued, Churchill's opposite number, Joseph Caillaux, fell from office. In reply to Churchill's letter of commiseration, Caillaux wrote, of their long and difficult negotiations together, 'You showed me such courtesy throughout and you received me with so much grace, & had such a happy touch in vivifying & brightening our conversations, that they left me with the impression that we were in complete agreement.'

On November 30 Churchill was fifty-one; that week Baldwin asked him to mediate between the Irish Free State and Ulster. The Free State feared that the border was to be altered in Ulster's favour, and was also reluctant to pay its £155 million debt to Britain for unrecoverable revenues and munitions. Churchill opened negotiations on December 1; at the end of three intense days he had evolved an acceptable formula whereby no border changes would take place, and the Free State's debt would be paid over a period of sixty years. Six weeks after this Irish success, Churchill opened negotiations in London for the settlement of Italy's £592 million war debt to Britain. After two weeks of negotiations it was agreed that Italy would repay the full debt, but to defer all payments for four years, then spread them until 1988. The best evidence of the fairness of the settlement, Churchill commented, 'is the fact that it fully satisfies neither party'.

On 31 January 1926 Clementine left England for a prolonged holiday in the South of France. Churchill remained at Chartwell, where at weekends he entertained political friends, among them the Conservative MP Ronald McNeill, now his Financial Secretary, who before the war, at the height of the 'Ulster pogrom', had hurled a book at him across the floor of the Commons, drawing blood. Fruit trees were being planted 'every quarter of an hour', Churchill reported to Clementine on February 7. A week later there was a gathering of colleagues, among them the Secretary of State for Air, Sir Samuel Hoare, who wrote to a friend, 'I had never seen Winston before in the role of landed proprietor. Most of the Sunday morning we inspected the property, and the engineering works upon which he is engaged.' These consisted of making 'a series of ponds in the valley. Winston seems blissfully happy over it all.'

Churchill was also happy in the presence of his children, who found endless entertainment in their new home's hidden corners and rolling fields. On March 20, as he worked at Chartwell on plans for his second Budget, he wrote to Clementine, who was then in Rome: 'All is well here. Mary breakfasted & Sarah dined with me. Diana talked quite intelligently about politics & seemed to have a lot of information derived from the newspapers. They are all very sweet & it is a joy to have them down here.'

Diana was seventeen, Sarah eleven and Mary three. Randolph, then fourteen, was a boarder at Eton.

In search of revenue for his second Budget Churchill drew up plans to introduce a tax on petrol. He also proposed a 5 per cent annual tax on the purchase price of luxury cars, and a tax on heavy lorries based on their weight and 'road-smashing' characteristics. Another of his ideas was a tax on imported American films. 'It would naturally give great pleasure in this country,' he told his advisers, 'if any revenue could be derived from the profits of American film producers.'

Churchill introduced his second Budget on April 27. As in the previous year, Randolph was in the gallery to hear him. The theme for 1926 was thrift and economy. Luxuries were to be taxed, as was betting; a 5 per cent tax on all bets. The economic picture, Churchill told the House, 'is not black; it is not grey; it is piebald, and on the whole the dark patches are less prominent this year than last'. But he warned that the worsening crisis in the coal industry could lead to the need for new taxes on a substantial scale. The day after his speech, the mine-owners, for whom he was still providing a Government subsidy so that they would not cut their miners' wages, told Baldwin that an immediate wage cut was essential, in view of their losses. The miners refused to contemplate any cut in wages. Baldwin then proposed increasing the working day by one hour, to eight hours, but keeping wages the same. On April 28 the owners agreed, but not the miners.

The owners now demanded an immediate cut in wages. When the miners rejected this on May 1, the entire labour force was shut out; the owners had closed the mines. That same day the Trades Union Congress announced that, in support of the miners, a General Strike would begin on May 3, at one minute to midnight.

Negotiations between the Government and the TUC continued throughout May 2. Shortly after eleven o'clock that evening, news reached the Cabinet, which had gathered in Churchill's room in the House of Commons, that printers at the *Daily Mail*, in apparent anticipation of the strike, had suppressed the paper 'because they did not like its leading article'. Ministers were unanimous that this action made further negotiations impossible. An attempt had been made to silence the Press. Negotiations now would be under duress. There must be an immediate and unconditional withdrawal of the strike notices. 'It is a point worth making,' one of Baldwin's closest associates, J.C.C. Davidson, wrote ten days later, 'that there was no discussion on this point. It has often been written that the extremists forced Baldwin's hand, but nothing could be further from the truth.'

On the morning of May 3 a Cabinet strike-breaking committee was set up under the Home Secretary. Churchill was not a member, but was asked by the Committee to prepare a plan for a Government news-sheet. He did so, proposing that it should be devised 'not merely to contain news, but in order to relieve the minds of the people'. One of its tasks would be to 'prevent alarming news from being spread about'. Churchill added, 'I do not contemplate violent partisanship, but fair, strong encouragement to the great mass of loyal people.' The leading articles should also be 'not violently partisan, but agreeable to the great majority of the people on our side'; in a few short phrases he explained what he meant, 'Constitutional, the hope for peace, Parliament, maintain authority in the country, injury to trade and reputation of the country.'

Speaking in the Commons that afternoon, seven hours before the General Strike was to begin, Churchill's tone was conciliatory. He praised the moderation of the Labour MPs who had spoken, including MacDonald, and welcomed the 'efforts for peace' which had been made by the Trades Union negotiators on the previous day. They had done their best, he said, 'to bring about a warding-off of this shocking disaster in our national life'. He would not use 'one single provocative word'. As for the Government, it could not divest itself of responsibility for 'maintaining the life of the nation in essential services and public order'. Once strike notices were withdrawn, however, negotiations on every aspect of the coal crisis could begin again: 'The door is always open. There is no question of there being a gulf across which no negotiator can pass, certainly not. It is our duty to parley.'

The General Strike began that night; Churchill went to the printing presses of the *Morning Post* to supervise the production of the Government news-sheet. With him was Samuel Hoare, who suggested calling the paper the *British Gazette*. As the first issue was being printed, Churchill told Baldwin that its editorial theme would be that the General Strike was a challenge to the Government, with which there could be no compromise, but that the dispute in the coal industry which had provoked it was one on which 'we are prepared to take the utmost pains to reach a settlement in the most conciliatory spirit'.

Volunteers, many of them students, drove copies of the *British Gazette* to towns throughout Southern England. Lindemann collected fourteen Oxford undergraduates and sent them to London; they reported to the Treasury for their distribution tasks. On Hoare's instructions aeroplanes flew the paper to the north of England. When the first issue was ready to be printed Churchill asked the BBC to broadcast the sound of the presses in action, but the BBC refused to do so. Two days later he proposed that the Government should take over the BBC and use it to broadcast official news. The Cabinet rejected this.

By the morning of May 5 more than 230,000 copies of the *British Gazette* had been printed. In an unsigned article, Churchill wrote that without newspapers Britain was reduced 'to the level of African natives dependent only on the rumours which are carried from place to place'. These rumours would in a few days 'poison the air, raise panics and disorders, inflame fears and passions together, and carry us all to depths which no sane man of any party or class would care even to contemplate'.

Each issue of the *British Gazette* was more widely distributed than the previous one. On May 6 the War Office sent a company of troops to protect the paper-mill which was making the actual paper. The Admiralty sent a naval guard to escort the paper by barge up the Thames. Meanwhile, the editor of the *Morning Post,* H.A. Gwynne, one of Churchill's old Conservative enemies from Home Rule and 'Peers versus the People' days, tried to have Churchill kept out of the building. During the first night's production, he complained to Baldwin, Churchill had tried 'to force a scratch staff beyond its capacity' and had 'rattled them badly'.

At his room in the Treasury, Churchill collected material which he felt should have a place in the paper, giving prominence to those aspects of daily life where the strike was proving least effective. He also marked as 'not recommended for publication' details of serious shortages of flour and sugar, of the overturning and stoning of trams that were still running, and of an incident of looting where the police had used their truncheons to clear the street.

In Cabinet on May 6 Churchill urged the maximum protection for food convoys coming into London from the docks. On May 7 Baldwin supported his proposal to incorporate Territorial Army troops, as volunteers, into the existing volunteer police forces. They would have armbands instead of uniforms, and truncheons instead of rifles. When the Home Secretary asked who would pay for this, Churchill retorted: 'The Exchequer will pay. If we start arguing about petty details, we will have a tired-out police force, a dissipated army and bloody revolution.'

In a BBC broadcast on May 8 Baldwin appealed for an end to the General Strike and a start to negotiations with the coal-miners. In his appeal he repeated Churchill's conciliatory theme of five days earlier, 'No door is closed.' Churchill meanwhile was still supervising the *British Gazette.* 'He butts in at the busiest hours,' Gwynne again complained on May 9, 'and insists on changing commas and full stops until the staff is furious.' In the Commons there were complaints about newsprint being requisitioned for the Government paper but denied to the various Labour broadsheets. Paper could not be made available to newspapers 'engaged in imperilling the life of the nation', Churchill replied. As for the Government, it 'cannot be impartial as between the State and any section of its subjects with whom it is contending'.

On the morning of May 11 more than a million copies of the *British Gazette* were distributed. That day there were intimations that the miners wished to open negotiations with the Government. There must be 'a clear interval', Churchill wrote to Baldwin that day, between the calling off of the General Strike and the resumption of the coal negotiations. 'The first tonight – the second tomorrow. But nothing simultaneous and concurrent.' The Government's message should be: 'Tonight surrender. Tomorrow magnanimity.' On the morning of May 12 the General Council of the Trades Union Congress decided that it could no longer support the miners if they remained on strike. At midday the TUC leaders went to see Baldwin at Downing Street to tell him that the General Strike was over. A few moments later Churchill told the Council Chairman, 'Thank God it is over.'

Ten days after the end of the General Strike, the *New Statesman* accused Churchill of having been the leader of a 'war party' on the night of May 2, and of forcing an end to the Government's negotiations with the TUC. It also alleged that Churchill had said that 'a little blood-letting' would be all to the good. The paper weakened this charge by adding, 'Whether he actually used this phrase or not there is no doubt about his tireless efforts to seize the providential opportunity for a fight.'

Churchill wanted to bring an action for libel against the *New Statesman* for its charge that he wanted blood-letting, telling the Attorney-General: 'As you well know, my arguments in Cabinet were all directed to keeping the Military out of the business, and to using, even at great expense, very large numbers of citizens unarmed. I am sure I never used any language not entirely consistent with this.' Churchill added, 'I certainly do not feel inclined to allow such a lie to pass into the general currency of Labour incriminations.' But it did.

Although the General Strike had lasted only nine days, it had divided the nation. Those who supported it were particularly bitter against those who had 'broken' it. It was not Churchill's reputation as a strike-breaker, however, but his qualities as a conciliator, that led Baldwin to ask him, eight days after the General Strike had ended, to take charge of the Government's negotiations with the miners.

Churchill agreed to do so, working to build a bridge between the miners and the owners. When the owners insisted on a reduction in miners' wages, he countered by proposing that any such reduction in wages should be paralleled by a reduction in owners' profits. There was also a limit to reduced wages, he insisted, 'below which on social grounds miners ought not to work'. These were not new sentiments on Churchill's part; during a Cabinet discussion on a strike in the coal mines five years earlier he had argued that if there been a proper understanding of the miners' needs, 'we could have stopped the strike very much more cheaply in advance'.

That autumn, as the coal strike continued with increasing bitterness on both sides, Baldwin, about to set off for his annual holiday in France, again asked Churchill to take charge of negotiations. On August 26, in Cabinet, Churchill spoke approvingly of the miners' desire for a national minimum wage. That same day, in talks with the miners' leaders, he told them, 'I sympathise with you in your task', and asked them for some offer of terms which he could then press the owners to accept. In the Commons on August 31 his remarks about the miners were, Thomas Jones reported to Baldwin, 'dignified, conciliatory and fair'.

On September 1, in an attempt to break the deadlock, Churchill invited MacDonald to Chartwell. The Labour Leader's visit was kept a closely guarded secret. MacDonald offered to ask the miners' leaders to agree to negotiations on the basis of a comprehensive national settlement with a minimum wage. Two days later, after a meeting with MacDonald in London, Churchill met secretly with the miners' leaders and, in strictest secrecy, worked out with them a formula acceptable to them which the Government could then put to the owners in order to bring the strike to an end. The formula which Churchill accepted was based on the miners' demand for a minimum wage which could not be undercut by individual owners. All now depended on the agreement of the owners, whom Churchill undertook to persuade into accepting the formula. He invited them to Chartwell, in the hope that the country-house atmosphere would induce conciliatory thoughts. But the owners would not yield.

Churchill was angered by the owners' attitude; 'recalcitrant' and 'unreasonable' was how he described it to Baldwin. He now sought to have the principle of a minimum wage incorporated in a Government Bill, the aim of which, he told the Cabinet on September 15, was 'to bring pressure to bear on the owners'. But the Cabinet objected to any such pressure being applied, and Baldwin, who returned that day from France, declined to support Churchill's efforts. Nor would the Cabinet endorse another proposal by Churchill, which was also acceptable to the miners, for a compulsory arbitration tribunal.

Learning that Churchill could no longer rely on Cabinet unanimity behind his proposals, the owners persisted in their refusal to consider a minimum wage. They even refused to attend a tripartite meeting with Churchill and the miners. This refusal, Churchill told the Cabinet on September 24, was 'wholly wrong and unreasonable' and without precedent 'in recent times'. The Cabinet refused, however, to order the owners to a meeting, and to Churchill's chagrin decided that the Government should now dissociate itself from the dispute, leaving the owners and the miners to continue their strife until its conclusion.

On September 27, in the Commons, in a last effort to resolve the dispute, Churchill offered, if the miners would agree to return to work without a national minimum wage, to set up an independent National Tribunal 'having the force of law', which would examine each regional wage settlement and secure a fair settlement in each region. The miners, angered by the refusal of the owners to accept a national minimum wage, refused his offer. Churchill now tried to work out a formula which would enable the miners to accept the National Tribunal without loss of face. His Cabinet colleagues again refused to go along with him. 'Most of our Party dislike Government interference,' one of them explained to a friend on September 29, 'and believe that Winston started a new and unnecessary stage of interference, and were not at all cordial to him.'

Churchill's efforts had been in vain. His pressure on the owners had come to nought. His desire to involve the Government as an arbitrator had been rejected by the Cabinet. His attempt to get the miners to settle had been rejected. 'Now I am afraid it must be fought out,' he wrote to his Parliamentary Private Secretary, Robert Boothby, on October 16, after the miners' final rejection of a National Tribunal. 'These people think themselves stronger than the State. But that is a mistake. There is a similar attitude among the owners.'

Both at the Treasury and at Chartwell, Churchill continued with his war memoirs. Harold Bourne, the manager of Thornton Butterworth, the publishers, was frequently summoned to both; he later recalled how cross Churchill could get if the proof chapters were not in order, but how, after every storm, there seemed to be 'an additional glint in his humorous eyes. Humour seldom seemed far away from him.' Churchill was always keen to see every stage of the proofs. On December 12 he sent Bourne a letter in verse:

> Straight away,
> without delay,
> I want the page proofs day by day.
> On January 4,
> I leave this shore,
> nor will you catch me any more!

Humour and philosophic reflection went almost hand in hand; on December 28 Churchill wrote to Beaverbrook: 'There are very great things to be done by those who reach a certain scale of comprehension & of power in their early prime. As long as health & life are ours, we must try to do them – not to be content except with the best & truest solutions.' His own work continued even on holiday. That winter he would play his last game of polo at Malta. 'If I expire on the ground,' he wrote to his host, 'it will at any rate be a worthy end.'

Churchill was fifty-two. He took with him on his travels at the beginning of 1927 the proofs of the third volume of his war memoirs, which Bourne had got to him in time, and on which he finished working while at Genoa. Then, from Malta, after his final polo match, he turned to political matters, writing to Baldwin about the need to include in the forthcoming Trade Union Bill the right of any individual member of a Union to contract out of the Union's hitherto compulsory political levy. In Athens, he gave a newspaper interview expressing his pleasure at the restoration of Parliamentary Government in Greece. In Rome, he had two short meetings with Mussolini, telling a Press conference in the Italian capital that anyone could see that Mussolini 'thought of nothing but the lasting good, as he understood it, of the Italian people'. Churchill added: 'Had I been an Italian, I am sure I would have been wholeheartedly with you from start to finish in your triumphant struggle against the bestial appetites and passions of Leninism. But in England we have not yet had to face this danger in the same deadly form. We have our own way of doing things.'

One further political issue shadowed Churchill during his holiday; the attack by Chinese warlords on British subjects in two Chinese ports. The Cabinet decided to send reinforcements to China. Churchill approved. 'Short of being actually conquered,' he wrote to Baldwin on January 22 from Eze, in the South of France, 'there is no evil worse than submitting to wrong and violence for fear of war. Once you take the position of not being able in any circumstances to defend your rights against the aggression of some particular set of people, there is no end to the demands that will be made or to the humiliations that must be accepted.' This was the essence of Churchill's criticism of appeasement from weakness.

At Eze, Churchill stayed at Consuelo Balsan's château, Lou Seuil; her marriage to his cousin Sunny had been dissolved in 1921. While at Eze, he continued to monitor the Cabinet's action in China. On January 25 he wrote to the Secretary of State for War to urge him to send out 'plenty of tanks to Shanghai'. But on practical grounds he opposed the despatch of gas shells, telling the Secretary of State: 'I was very glad to see that you had carried your point about gas. "Gas for Asia" may be a phrase of great significance. But I believe you will find tanks even more effective, both for street fighting and operations in open country. I hope that firm action and *adequate forces* will lead to a peaceful solution. But if not, I beseech you, at the outset of what may be great responsibilities, to use the right tackle.'

From Eze, Churchill travelled to Paris, where, on January 26, he lunched with Loucheur and several other French politicians, including Vincent Auriol, who in 1947 became the first President of the Fourth Republic. From Paris he went to the Duke of Westminster's château at Eu for three days' boar-hunting, before returning to London. Shortly after his return, the third volume of *The World Crisis* was published. Readers were struck by his vivid, moving descriptions of the battles of the Western Front. J.M. Keynes described the book as 'a tractate against war – more effective than the work of a pacifist could be'.

On April 11 Churchill introduced his third Budget. MPs crowded into the House to hear him speak. 'The scene was quite sufficient,' Baldwin told the King, 'to show that Mr Churchill as a star turn has a power of attraction which nobody in the House of Commons can excel.' He had withstood Cabinet pressure to reduce death duties, and was content to raise money by imposing new taxes on imported motor-car tyres and imported wines, and increasing old taxes on matches and tobacco.

Old enemies were impressed by Churchill the Chancellor. 'The remarkable thing about him,' Lord Winterton, a Conservative MP since 1904, wrote to a friend, 'is the way in which he has suddenly acquired, quite late in Parliamentary life, an immense fund of tact, patience, good humour and banter on almost all occasions; no one used to "suffer fools ungladly" more than Winston, now he is friendly and accessible to everyone, both in the House and in the lobbies, with the result that he has become what he never was before the war, very popular in the House generally – a great accretion to his already formidable Parliamentary power.'

Cartoonists vied in portraying 'Winsome Winston' and 'The Smiling Chancellor'. In reporting on the Budget speech to the King, Baldwin stressed Churchill's 'cheerful and buoyant optimism' and his sense of the dramatic. 'There is in Mr Churchill an undercurrent of buoyant mischievousness which frequently makes its appearance on the surface in some picturesque phrase or playful sally at the expense of his opponents.' Baldwin added, 'His enemies will say that this year's Budget is a mischievous piece of manipulation and juggling with the country's finances, but his friends will say that it is a masterpiece of ingenuity.'

Amery protested to Baldwin that Churchill's Budget contained nothing but a few 'hand-to-mouth dodges'. There was nothing in it to help the productive industries 'from which the revenue after all is derived'. But Churchill was even then at work on a comprehensive scheme to abolish the system of local rates, in order to relieve British industry and Britain's farmers of the burden which rates imposed on them. Rising unemployment and falling trade were his foes. The money to make up for the rates would be replaced by taxes; Churchill envisaged a petrol tax and a profits tax as the two principal replacement sources of revenue.

The derating scheme was to absorb a great deal of Churchill's energies in the coming year, and to focus his mind on the means of raising additional revenue by taxation; the sum needed to abolish the rates altogether was £50 million, the compensation that would have to be paid to the local authorities for their loss of rating revenue. The hoped-for reward was to see the productive sector of the economy flourish. Derating, he told Baldwin on June 6, would constitute a 'large, new constructive measure which, by its importance and scope, by its antagonisms as well as by its appeal, will lift us above the ruck of current affairs', Industry would be stimulated, agriculture placated, 'and the immense mass of the ratepayers would be astonished and gratified'. If the remaining rating assessment was then shifted from property to profits, 'the relief would come with increasing effect to the depressed and struggling industries and factories, with reactions upon our competitive power and upon employment of the utmost benefit'.

Baldwin gave the scheme his approval. But Neville Chamberlain was annoyed that Churchill should once again, as with the insurance schemes of 1925, be picking the finest plums. Encouraged by the enthusiasm of his Treasury officials, Churchill went ahead, working at his scheme during the summer at Chartwell, while at the same time he painted, organised the building of walls, dams and ponds, and began a new literary venture, his autobiography from childhood to his entry into Parliament in 1900.

That summer Clementine Churchill was knocked down by a bus in a London street and badly shaken. While her husband remained at Chartwell, she went for six weeks to recuperate in Venice. Churchill was dictating sections of his autobiography; each night he would turn out the lights and listen to music on the wireless with his brother Jack. He also went to Scotland to hunt stags, and to catch salmon with his friend the Duke of Westminster. In October he joined his wife in Venice, where he painted, swam, and continued work on his autobiography. In London there was much speculation about his future. 'Baldwin seems to be getting very much under the influence of Churchill,' a Labour MP, Josiah Wedgwood, wrote to a friend, 'perhaps because C never despairs of the republic. He is as young as ever, and the country and politics are still his game. They say that Baldwin is so tired and, perhaps, ill, that he will retire before the election and advise the King to send for Churchill.'

Leaving Clementine to continue her recovery in Venice, Churchill returned to England to work on the details of his derating scheme. His attempt to obtain £3 million of the £50 million he needed by cutbacks in naval expenditure failed; Neville Chamberlain sided with the Admiralty at the Cabinet meeting at which only the minimum naval cutbacks were agreed. As Treasury officials worked to perfect the scheme, one of them warned that the revenue raised for derating would be revenue denied towards the paying off of the national debt. Ever the optimist and enthusiast, Churchill replied, 'I must beg you to inscribe hope and confidence in the growing strength of the country upon all your memoranda.' An unexpected ally was a Conservative MP, Harold Macmillan, who proved such an enthusiast about derating that Churchill gave him a room at the Treasury in which to examine the scheme in detail.

On December 17, three weeks after his fifty-third birthday, Churchill's scheme was ready for circulation to the Cabinet. That day he sent the first copy to Baldwin, to whom he called it 'My Best Endeavour'. Seven days later Neville Chamberlain, to whom he had also sent a copy, replied with five pages of comment and a covering note, 'You will see that my attitude, though cautious, is not wholly unfriendly.' Chamberlain's main suggestion was to make the rating relief partial, 'say 50 per cent', rather than total, to avoid the tax on petrol from which Churchill intended to raise £20 million of the £50 million needed. Such a tax, Chamberlain feared, would greatly antagonise the motorists, a growing slice of the electorate. Macmillan also suggested a partial scheme, 66 per cent derating, as he feared that the profits tax, 'forged no doubt honestly for the purpose of financing this great relief to industry', was capable of proving, in the hands of a Socialist Government, 'a horrid engine of fiscal extortion'.

After studying the scheme, Lord Weir, Churchill's former Director-General of Aircraft Production at the Ministry of Munitions, wrote to him on 3 January 1928, 'You will do more for the coal industry by this action than all the coal commission reports put together.' But Chamberlain now suggested retaining a third of the total rate. Reluctantly Churchill accepted this, 'only bowing to the need of obtaining more general agreement', he told Baldwin on January 4, 'and defacing the classical purity of the conception for the sake of an easier passage!' As less money would now have to be found from taxation, Churchill decided to discard the profits tax and make the petrol tax provide most of the money needed.

On January 9 Churchill and his son spent two days in northern France hunting wild boar. At Chartwell, on their return, James Lees-Milne, then an undergraduate at Oxford, was among the guests; he later recalled how after dinner, with the tablecloth removed from the dining-table, 'Mr Churchill spent a blissful two hours demonstrating with decanters and wine-glasses how the Battle of Jutland was fought. It was a thrilling experience. He was fascinating. He got worked up like a schoolboy, making barking noises in imitation of gunfire and blowing cigar smoke across the battle scene in imitation of gun smoke.' On the following morning Churchill paced up and down his vaulted study dictating his autobiography. 'The sound of footfalls on the boards and his familiar voice were clearly audible. And in the afternoons he was waist deep in waders in the lake.'

Churchill presented his derating scheme to the Cabinet on January 20. 'They seemed a little oppressed with the amount of labour which would be involved,' Churchill wrote to Balfour, 'but after all the bulk of this will fall on me – & I am quite ready to undertake it, & pretty sure I can produce a satisfactory result.' On January 31 the Cabinet Policy Committee, chaired by Neville Chamberlain, agreed that partial derating was to be part of the 1928 Budget. Three days later, at Birmingham, Churchill launched the public campaign for derating, describing rates as 'a harassing burden upon productive industry and agriculture', levied, unlike income tax, 'whether there are any profits or not'.

On February 16 the Cabinet gathered in the Cabinet Room as a mark of respect for Asquith, who had died on the previous day. As they came out Churchill defended his derating scheme to the Deputy Secretary to the Cabinet, Thomas Jones, whom he had earlier welcomed at Chartwell as a 'corrective' influence for Randolph against Lindemann's fierce Conservatism. Churchill told Jones that compensating local authorities for their lost rates 'really was the communist principle, from each authority according to its ability, to each authority according to its need'.

In March the derating scheme ran into difficulties. Chamberlain was uneasy at the way it had eclipsed his own plans to do something for the poor and for the necessitous areas. Churchill tried to encourage him to continue with his own scheme, but to no avail. At each meeting of the Cabinet Policy Committee, Chamberlain raised new objections. 'I can make no progress in the face of your opposition,' Churchill wrote to him on March 12.

An acrimonious correspondence followed. 'Up to now I have done all the giving,' Chamberlain wrote on March 14, and he now insisted that the railways be excluded from Churchill's scheme and continue to pay rates. Churchill argued that this would make impossible his intention of cheaper charges for farmers moving food by rail. But Chamberlain, whose influence and interest lay with placating and wooing the local authorities, was adamant. Again Churchill gave way, writing to Chamberlain with some bitterness that he was 'increasingly inclined to think that we had better leave the handling of these thorny matters to another Parliament, and perhaps to other hands'.

In Cabinet on April 4, after two days of intense discussion, all was settled; 'Complete agreement, and at any rate $3/4$ of what I was aiming at,' was how Churchill described it to Clementine. But the loss of a quarter of his scheme, and Chamberlain's animosity, cast a shadow across his enthusiasm. 'Neville most obstinate and, I thought, unreasonable. Pray God these plans bring back a little more prosperity to Poor Old England.'

Churchill delivered his fourth Budget on April 24. 'Every public gallery was crammed,' Baldwin told the King, 'while in the Peers' Gallery their Royal Highnesses the Prince of Wales and the Duke of Gloucester were seen to take their places.' In a speech lasting for three and a half hours, Churchill fascinated and amused the House; announcing an almost 100 per cent rise in children's allowances, he commented, 'Another example of our general policy of helping the producer.' Clearly, patiently and with a wealth of detail, he then set out his derating scheme, and explained how it would be achieved; its aim, he said, was 'to revive industry and create new jobs'.

Baldwin told the King that Churchill's speech was 'almost the most remarkable oratorical achievement' of his career. But the debate that followed had to take place without him; a severe attack of influenza forced him to stay in bed at Chartwell. As soon as he was able, he went to Scotland to recuperate on the Duke of Westminster's Rosehall estate, where he read Beaverbrook's book on the opening months of the war, about those who had been his friends and fellow-politicians in 1914. 'Think of these people,' he wrote to Beaverbrook, 'decent, educated, the story of the past laid out before them. What to avoid, what to do etc. Patriotic, loyal, clean – trying their utmost. What a ghastly muddle they made of it! Unteachable from infancy to tomb – there is the first & main characteristic of mankind.'

Churchill added at the bottom of his letter, 'No more War.' That July, the Committee of Imperial Defence discussed what was known as the 'Ten Year Rule' for defence spending; a rule laid down by the Committee in 1919 whereby the defence expenditure in any one year was to be based on the assumption that there would be no European war in prospect for the next ten years. Churchill took a lead in proposing that the rule should be 'reviewed every year'. Its aim, he pointed out, was not to hamper the development of ideas, but to 'check mass production until the situation demanded it'. The nation's safety would be preserved, but excessive and premature expenditure avoided; it was essential, he argued, to avoid the production of weapons, ships and planes that would be obsolete by the outbreak of war.

Baldwin at first opposed the Ten Year Rule altogether, but was guided by the arguments of Churchill, and above all of Austen Chamberlain, that a European war was not imminent. The Committee then accepted Churchill's proposal that there should be an annual reconsideration of the rule, so that the moment it appeared that the prospect of war was on the horizon, measures could be taken to prepare for war, using the most up-to-date equipment and weaponry.

In the summer of 1928, as pressure mounted within the Consevative Party for a return to Protection, Churchill was again at odds with his colleagues. 'Take care,' Lord Derby wrote to him in July, 'that there is not an attack on Free Trade disguised under a vendetta against you.' Churchill did not allow himself to become distressed, writing to Clementine that August, 'Really I feel quite independent of them all.' It was clear that the Conservative leadership would not pass to him if those then at the centre of the Party maintained their jealousy and mistrust. 'He is a brilliant wayward child,' Neville Chamberlain wrote to a friend, 'who compels admiration but who wears out his guardians with the constant strain he puts upon them.'

Churchill made his 'guardians' work, or made them feel guilty that he was working when they were not. That summer and autumn he spent most of his time at Chartwell finishing the post-war volume of his war memoirs. 'Remember my counsel to you and abide by it!' Baldwin wrote to him on August 5: 'Paint, pens, dams and nought else.' Churchill also helped with the bricklaying for a small cottage for his five-year-old daughter Mary. 'I have had a delightful month,' he wrote to Baldwin on September 2, 'building a cottage and dictating a book: 200 bricks and 2,000 words a day.'

Each day, Ministerial work was brought by car from the Treasury; Churchill devoted several hours to it daily. That month one of his visitors, James Scrymgeour-Wedderburn, noted in his diary after a two-hour talk alone with Churchill: 'When he becomes engrossed in his subject he strides up and down the room with his head thrust forward and his thumbs in the armholes of his waistcoat, as if he were trying to keep pace with his own eloquence. If he shows signs of slowing down, all you have to do is to make some moderately intelligent observation, and off he goes again.'

That autumn there had been considerable international activity, initiated by the United States, to secure the disarmament of the three strongest powers, Britain, France and the United States herself. 'Personally I deprecate all these premature attempts to force agreement on disarmament,' Churchill wrote to one of his Treasury advisers on September 9. Five days later he explained his unease in greater detail: 'We are frequently told that Germany would disarm on the understanding that other nations would disarm too, and that further France in particular is bound morally to disarm. However I do not admit that any moral obligation exists. The Germans were prostrate and yielded themselves virtually at discretion.

Any undertakings about Allied disarmament were not a matter of bargaining but a voluntary declaration on the part of the Allies.'

Churchill pointed out that since 1919 important changes had taken place in the situation of France: 'She gave up the Rhine frontier in return for a promise by the United States together with Great Britain to come to her aid in the event of German aggression. This American promise has been withdrawn and France has not now the security on which she was induced to abandon the Rhine. The only securities for the defence of France are the French Army and the Locarno Treaties. But the Locarno Treaties depend for their efficiency upon the French Army. As long as that army is strong enough to overpower a German invasion no German invasion will be attempted.'

The British undertaking in the Locarno Treaties to protect Germany 'from the misuse of the French Army', Churchill wrote, 'affords Germany full security, and it is unthinkable that France would attack Germany in defiance of England and Germany together. Thus the strength of the French Army protects us against the most probable danger of our being forced to intervene in Europe, and it is not in our interest at all to press for the whittling down of this force below the point of security. Moreover France will never consent to such a whittling down and all expectations that she will are futile.'

At the end of September Churchill was invited by the King to Balmoral for four days' grouse and stag shooting. While there, he met for the first time the two-and-half-year-old Princess Elizabeth, and wrote to Clementine: 'The last is a character. She has an air of authority & reflectiveness astonishing in an infant.'

That November Churchill was fifty-four. 'You are still a child,' Baldwin wrote to him, 'so I may say "many happy returns".' Churchill spent his birthday at Chartwell. Clementine was at a nursing-home convalescing from blood-poisoning. Churchill remained at Chartwell for as much of each week as he could, dictating the final chapters of his war memoirs. At Christmas he was joined by Clementine, now recovering, by his three daughters, and by Randolph, now in his last few months at Eton.

On 7 February 1929 Churchill was in London for an emergency Cabinet. The Germans, hitherto disarmed and militarily weak, were, according to the most recent reports, developing a new battle-cruiser, light, fast and well-armed, which would have a greater radius of action than any British battle-cruiser, and would fire a heavier weight of shell per minute than its nearest British rival. Cruiser design, Churchill warned, 'was passing into a phase which would render obsolete our existing cruisers'. The new German cruiser would have 11-inch guns; these were debarred to Britain under the Washington Naval Disarmament Treaty of 1922. Churchill was again, as at the time of the German Navy Law in 1912, vigilant in his scrutiny of German intentions, and prospective power.

A General Election was to be held in May. Churchill's first pre-election speech, on February 12, portrayed the dangers of a change of Government. If the Labour Party came to power, he said, it would be bound 'to bring back the Russian Bolsheviks, who will immediately get busy in the mines and factories, as well as among the armed forces, planning another General Strike'. Well-meaning and respectable Ministers would be 'moved here and there like marionettes, in accordance with the decision of a small secret international junta'.

This was Churchill's theme throughout the campaign. It was made all the more urgent and strident by his realisation, as Beaverbrook wrote to a friend, that 'he accepts electoral defeat in advance'. Other Conservative Cabinet Ministers assumed that the Party would be re-elected, and in several private gatherings discussed Churchill's future office; Secretary of State for India and Foreign Secretary were two of the posts mentioned most frequently. Indeed, Baldwin himself suggested to Churchill that he should go to the India Office. He 'seemed to feel', Churchill later recalled, 'that as I had carried the Transvaal Constitution through the House in 1906 and the Irish Free State Constitution in 1922, it would be in general harmony with my sentiments and my record to preside over a third great measure of self-government for another part of the Empire'. Churchill, however, was not attracted by this plan. Lord Birkenhead, then Secretary of State for India, had discussed with him many problems on the path to self-government in India, and he shared what he called Birkenhead's 'deep misgivings about that vast sub-continent'.

Neville Chamberlain revealed his growing animosity when he wrote to a friend that if Churchill were to become Foreign Secretary, Baldwin would 'find himself waking up at nights with a cold sweat at the thought of Winston's indiscretions'. Baldwin, however, with greater faith in Churchill's statesmanship, favoured the Foreign Office for him, telling Leo Amery on March 4 that he would have 'a rare chance of spreading himself and giving life and picturesqueness to what Austen has made a deadly dull business'.

On March 7, as political speculation continued, the fourth volume of Churchill's war memoirs was published; called *The World Crisis: The Aftermath*, it was an eloquent plea for a settlement of post-war grievances and inequalities. Within a month, he agreed to write another multi-volume work, a biography of his ancestor John Churchill, Duke of Marlborough. He was also committed to finishing his autobiography, and had in mind a fifth and final volume on the war dealing with the Eastern Front and the Bolshevik revolution. If the General Election in May went against the Conservatives he would not be idle.

On April 15 Churchill delivered his fifth Budget, a count reached previously only by Walpole, Pitt, Peel and Gladstone, each of whom was, or was to become, Prime Minister. When he announced that he was abolishing the duty on tea which had existed since the reign of Queen Elizabeth, the Labour Shadow Chancellor Philip Snowden called it 'election bribery'. Churchill was quick to point out that Snowden himself had earlier described the duty as 'crushing the bent backs of the working class'.

Churchill spoke for nearly three hours. 'I have never heard you speak better, and that's saying a great deal,' Baldwin wrote on the following day. 'I hate the word brilliant: it has been used to death and is too suggestive of brilliantine: but if I may use it in its pristine virginity, so to speak, it is the right one. I congratulate you with both hands.' It was a speech, wrote Neville Chamberlain in his diary, that had 'kept the House fascinated and enthralled by its wit, audacity, adroitness and power'. Two weeks later, as part of the election campaign, Churchill made his first radio broadcast. 'There was a note in it of extraordinary intimacy with his audience,' wrote the *Daily Express*.

During his broadcast Churchill urged his listeners to vote Conservative, telling them, 'Avoid chops and changes of policy; avoid thimble-riggers and three-card-trick men; avoid all needless borrowings; and above all avoid, as you would the smallpox, class warfare and violent political strife.' On May 6 he repeated this theme in Edinburgh and Glasgow. But speeches were in vain; on May 30 the Conservatives were swept from office, and Ramsay MacDonald formed his second Government.

Churchill was re-elected for Epping; although without Cabinet Office, he was still a Member of Parliament, twenty-nine years after he had first entered the House of Commons. 'He's a good fighter,' T.E. Lawrence wrote to Marsh that June, 'and will do better out than in, and will come back in a stronger position than before. I want him to be PM somehow.'

23

Out of Office

Within two weeks of the Conservative defeat at the polls on 30 May 1929, Churchill began work on his four-volume biography of the 1st Duke of Marlborough. A young Oxford historian, Maurice Ashley, travelled to many archives in Britain and Europe to bring him original material. Having set this literary work in train, he spoke in the Commons in favour of Labour's plans to spend money on public works in order to relieve unemployment in mining areas. But his main political effort was to seek some means of reversing the Conservative defeat. A month after the election, he persuaded Baldwin that the Conservatives should seek an alliance with the Liberals.

On June 27, with Baldwin's approval, Churchill met Lloyd George to discuss a possible Conservative-Liberal compact, limited in the first instance to specific issues as they arose in Parliament. 'I am deeply impressed with the critical character of the present situation,' he explained to Baldwin two days later. 'Eight million Tories, eight million Labour, five million Liberals! Where will those five million go?' If the Conservative Party turned to Protection and if its 'anti-Liberal resentments' had their way, 'there will be only one result – very likely final for our life time, namely a Lib-Lab bloc in some form or other and a Conservative Right hopelessly excluded from power.'

Churchill repeated his plea for a Conservative-Liberal rapprochement at the Shadow Cabinet on July 11, but Amery would not give up his quest for a return to Protection and found at least a partial ally in Neville Chamberlain. Meanwhile, with the rise of nationalism in Egypt, MacDonald announced his Government's decision to withdraw British troops from Cairo to the Suez Canal, and at the same time to recall the High Commissioner, Lord Lloyd, a staunch upholder of British influence. Following Lloyd's dismissal, Churchill later recalled: 'I reacted vehemently against this rough and sudden gesture, and hoped the whole

Conservative Party would have the same sentiments. But Mr Baldwin, brought up as a business man and certainly a great measurer of public feeling, did not think that this was good ground for a fight with the Government. It would unite the Liberals with them and leave the Conservatives in a marked minority.'

Lloyd had appealed to Churchill personally 'to do him justice, and I', Churchill wrote, 'declared I would confront the Government on the issue, which was one not only of weak policy but of personal ill-usage. Mr Baldwin deprecated any such championship of the High Commissioner, but I persisted. When I rose in my place on the Front Opposition Bench to interrogate the Government, he sat silent and disapproving. I immediately perceived that the Whips had been set to work the night before to make it clear to the Party that their honoured Leader did not think this was a good point to press. Murmurs and even cries of dissent from the Conservative benches were added to the hostile Government interruptions, and it was evident I was almost alone in the House.'

Churchill's championship of Lloyd was his first breach with the Conservative leadership. 'Never mind,' he wrote to Lloyd on July 28, 'you have done your best, and if Britain alone among modern States chooses to cast away her rights, her interests and her strength, she must learn by bitter experience.' Six days later Churchill left England on a journey to Canada and the United States with his son, his brother, and his nephew Johnny. 'What fun it is to get away from England,' he wrote to Beaverbrook before leaving, 'and to feel one has no responsibility for her exceedingly tiresome and embarrassing affairs.' But to Clementine, who did not feel well enough to undertake such a long journey, he wrote sorrowfully during the Atlantic voyage: 'My darling I have been rather sad at times thinking of you in low spirits at home. Do send me some messages. I love you so much & it grieves me to feel you are lonely.'

Among those on board ship was Amery, who recorded in his diary Churchill's reflections on the Dardanelles: 'Talking of the series of mischances which just prevented our getting through, he said jestingly that his only consolation was that God wished things to be prolonged in order to sicken mankind of war, and that therefore He had interfered with a project which would have brought the war to a speedier conclusion. His other evidence for a Deity was the existence of Lenin and Trotsky – for whom a hell was needed.'

On August 9 the Churchills reached Quebec. On their second afternoon they drove into the Canadian countryside, entranced by the hills, forests and streams. That night, looking out from their hotel window at the paper mills lit up, Churchill told his son, 'Fancy cutting down those beautiful trees we saw this afternoon to make pulp for those bloody newspapers, and calling it civilisation.' Ensconced in the comfort of a private railway car put at their disposal by the American steel king Charles Schwab, who in 1915 had built submarines for Churchill in under six months instead of the usual fourteen, Churchill travelled across Canada to Vancouver. He and Jack had 'large cabins with big double beds and private bathrooms', he told Clementine. There was a parlour, an observation room and a large dining-room 'which I use as the office and in which I am now dictating', as well as a kitchen, refrigerators, fans, quarters for the staff, and a 'splendid wireless installation'.

Churchill made two speeches in Montreal, one in Ottawa and one in Toronto. 'Never in my life have I been welcomed with so much genuine interest & admiration as throughout this vast country,' he wrote to Clementine. 'All Parties and classes have mingled in the welcome. The workmen in the streets, the girls who work the lifts, the ex-service men, the farmers, up to the highest functionaries have shown such unaffected pleasure to see me & shake hands that I am profoundly touched; & I intend to devote my strength to interpreting Canada to our own people & vice versa; & to bringing about an even closer association between us.'

At Calgary Churchill visited the oilfields; after Randolph remarked that the oil magnates were too uncultured to know how to spend their money properly, he retorted, 'Cultured people are merely the glittering scum which floats upon the deep river of production.'

From Banff, on August 27, Churchill told Clementine that if Neville Chamberlain 'or anyone else of that kind' was made Leader of the Conservative Party, 'I clear out of politics, & see if I cannot make you & the kittens a little more comfortable before I die'. His thoughts were on the premiership. 'Only one goal attracts me, & if that were barred I should quit the dreary field for pastures new.'

After touring the Canadian Rockies and setting up his easel at Lake Louise, Churchill reached Vancouver, where he gave two more speeches before travelling south into the United States, to San Francisco, then south again to the splendours of William Randolph Hearst's castle at San Simeon, overlooking the Pacific Ocean. 'A vast income always overspent,' Churchill told Clementine; 'ceaseless building, & collecting not very discriminately works of art; two magnificent establishments, two charming wives' – one was Hearst's wife, the other his mistress, the actress Marion Davies – 'complete indifference to public opinion, a strong liberal and democratic outlook, a 15 million a day circulation, oriental hospitalities, extreme personal courtesy (to us at any rate) & the appearance of a Quaker elder – or perhaps better Mormon elder.'

Hearst asked Churchill to write for his newspapers, an assignment that was to provide him with an important additional source of income for the next decade. His literary earnings were now extraordinary; that month alone the advance for his Marlborough biography, payment for three articles in *Nash's Pall Mall*, and royalties on the last volume of his war memoirs were the equivalent of two and a half years' earnings for a Prime Minister.

On September 20, after dinner in Hollywood with Charlie Chaplin, Churchill promised to write the film script of 'The Young Napoleon' if Chaplin would play in it. 'He is a marvellous comedian,' Churchill told Clementine, 'bolshy in politics & delightful in conversation.' During five days in Los Angeles, he spoke to several groups of American businessmen about how England and the United States 'ought to work together'. A British diplomat reported to London that these talks had produced 'wonderful and immediate results amongst those who, up to recent times, have been antagonistic to us and our interests'.

After driving through the magnificent Yosemite Valley, Churchill rejoined Schwab's train to travel through the Mojave Desert and on to the Grand Canyon. Then, reaching Chicago, he spoke of how the British and American Fleets, if ever used, 'will be together for the preservation of peace'. From Chicago, he travelled in Bernard Baruch's railway car to New York, then spent some time touring the American Civil War battlefields. 'The farm-houses and the churches still show the scars of shot and shell,' he told Clementine. 'The woods are full of trenches and rifle pits; the larger trees are full of bullets.' Nearly seventy years had passed since the Civil War; 'If you could read men's hearts, you would find that they, too, bear the marks.'

From the battlefields, Churchill went by Schwab's train to the headquarters of Bethlehem Steel, where on Tuesday October 29 he was entertained by the company's senior executives and spent three hours touring the giant plant. He then returned to New York; it was the afternoon of 'Black Tuesday', the day the stock market crashed. His own shareholdings plummeted; his losses were in excess of £10,000, more than £200,000 in the money values of 1990. That night he attended a dinner given in his honour at which more than forty businessmen were present. One of them, in proposing Churchill's health, began his remarks with the words, 'Friends and *former* millionaires.'

On the following day, Churchill later wrote, under his bedroom window 'a gentleman cast himself down fifteen storeys and was dashed to pieces, causing a wild commotion and the arrival of the fire brigade'. Walking down Wall Street 'at the worst moment of the panic' he was recognised by a stranger and invited on to the floor of the Stock Exchange. 'I expected to see pandemonium; but the spectacle that met my eyes was one of surprising calm and orderliness.' The members of the Exchange were walking to and fro 'like a slow-motion picture of a disturbed ant heap, offering each other enormous blocks of securities at a third of their old prices', and for many minutes 'finding no one strong enough to pick up the sure fortunes they were compelled to offer'.

Churchill sailed from New York on October 30. He was in a distressed mood; seven days earlier the Conservative Shadow Cabinet, at Baldwin's urging, had agreed to support the Labour Government's plans for India. Churchill, then in New York, had not been consulted. The decision, announced by the Viceroy, Lord Irwin, on October 31, was to grant Dominion Status to India. While retaining a Viceroy appointed from London, and British military control of defence, India would be ruled within a few years by Indians at both the national and provincial levels. Churchill was certain that this was a wrong decision; that the Hindus and Muslims of India were not yet ready to govern themselves at the centre; that several more decades of British rule were needed before the peoples of the sub-continent could take charge of their destiny without division, bloodshed and inequality; and that once Dominion Status were granted, the demand for full independence, which both MacDonald and Baldwin rejected, would follow with renewed force. Only at the Provincial level, Churchill believed, were the Indians ready for self-government.

Churchill reached London from the United States on November 6. On the following day he was in the Commons to hear Baldwin pledge the Conservative Party to Dominion Status. 'Winston had sat through SB's speech glowering and unhappy,' the Chairman of the Conservative Party, J.C.C. Davidson, wrote to Irwin, while Samuel Hoare wrote to Irwin, 'Throughout the debate Winston was almost demented with fury and since the debate has hardly spoken to anyone.' But Churchill did not intend to remain silent. In an article in the *Daily Mail* on November 16 he stressed that British rule had brought peace and prosperity to India. 'Justice has been given – equal between race and race, impartial between man and man. Science, healing or creative, has been harnessed to the service of this immense and, by themselves, helpless population.' But the Hindus, allowed by Britain to observe their own customs, still branded sixty million of their members as Untouchables, whose very approach in the street was considered an affront and whose presence was considered 'a pollution'.

Dominion Status 'can certainly not be obtained', Churchill wrote, by those who treated their 'fellow human beings, toiling at their side', so badly. The grant of Dominion Status would be 'a crime'. As Churchill was certain it would, the Indian National Congress also rejected Dominion Status. Six weeks after he published his first critical article, the new Congress leader, Jawaharlal Nehru, who, like Churchill, had been educated at Harrow, demanded full independence for India. Nehru urged all

Congress members who were serving in the central and provincial legisla-
tures to resign their seats, and he called for an all-India campaign of total
disobedience to British rule. The Congress campaign was supported by
the spiritual leader of Indian nationalism, Mahatma Gandhi; both he and
Nehru were arrested by Irwin and imprisoned.

On November 30 Churchill celebrated his fifty-fifth birthday. Shortly
before Christmas he offered the BBC £100 if he could broadcast a ten-
minute appeal against Dominion Status for India. The BBC refused. In
vain he protested against the policy of 'debarring public men from access
to a public who wish to hear'.

On 30 October 1930, Churchill published his autobiography *My Early Life*.
It was a gentle, witty account of his school and Army days, with many
relections on life and politics. 'I wish I could do anything half as good,'
Baldwin wrote. T.E. Lawrence commented on 'the ripe & merry wisdom,
and the courage and flair and judgement I take rather for granted having
seen you so much in action', but which a wider public could now get to know.
Lawrence added, 'Not many people could have lived 25 years so without
malice.' From MacDonald came a handwritten note of thanks from
Downing Street: 'When I have the hardihood to put mine in the window you
will have a copy in grateful exchange for this. But then there is no chance
of mine ever coming unless some old fishwife turns biographer. You are an
interesting cuss – I, a dull dog. May yours bring you both credit and cash.'

My Early Life was quickly reprinted and translated into many languages.
But Churchill's satisfaction as an author was in contrast to his unhappiness
at his growing political isolation, as the Conservative Party leaders agreed
to participate in a Round Table Conference in London to work out with
the Indian political leaders the details of Dominion Status. He was also
upset that autumn when the Conservative Party turned its back on Free
Trade. This would make impossible the Conservative-Liberal alliance
which he favoured as a basic political force against Labour. He had no
intention, however, of leaving the Party which he had left on this same
Free Trade issue twenty-six years earlier, telling Amery, a leading advocate of Tariffs, 'I propose to stick to you with all the loyalty of a leech.'

A month before Churchill's fifty-sixth birthday, his friend Lord
Birkenhead died suddenly; he was only two years older than Churchill;
for twenty-five years they had been the closest of friends. In an obituary
published in *The Times* on the following day, Churchill wrote: 'He was the
most loyal, faithful, valiant friend any man could have, and a wise, learned,
delightful companion. He would not, I think, have wished to live except
in his full health and vigour. All who knew him well will mourn him and
miss him often. But even more is our country the poorer. These are the

times when he is needed most. His deeply founded sagacity, his keen, courageous mind, his experience and understanding, his massive system of conclusions, his intellectual independence, his knowledge of all grave issues now pending, make his death at this moment a national impoverishment. His happy, brilliant, generous, warm-hearted life is closed. It has closed in years when he might have made his greatest contribution to the fortunes of the England he loved so well.'

A week before Churchill's fifty-sixth birthday, Clementine wrote to Randolph, who was then an undergraduate at Oxford: 'Politics as you say have taken an orientation not favourable to Papa. Sometimes he is gloomy about this, but fortunately not increasingly so. The success and praise which have greeted his book counteract his sad moments.' There was a moment of gladness at the end of November, the engagement of their daughter Diana to John Bailey, the son of the South African mine-owner and millionaire, Sir Abe Bailey whom Churchill had known for many years. But while the wedding was a high point of the social life of London, the marriage did not last; three years later Diana obtained a divorce and married a young Conservative MP, Duncan Sandys, whom she first met when Randolph was campaigning against him at a by-election.

On December 12 Churchill was the principal speaker at the first public meeting of the Indian Empire Society, set up to combat Dominion Status. His speech reflected the considerable Conservative unease at whether the time had yet come to move towards Dominion Status, particularly in the wake of the growing civil disobedience in India. Privately, Neville Chamberlain told a friend that he did not expect the Indians to be ready for self-government for fifty years or more. But Baldwin's support for Dominion Status had become a matter of Party policy, and Irwin, a lifelong Conservative and close friend of the Conservative leaders, served as a bridge between MacDonald's Government and the Shadow Cabinet.

During his speech of December 12 Churchill warned of the dangers to India 'if the British Raj is to be replaced by the Gandhi Raj'. The rulers of the Indian Native States, and the vast Muslim minority, would both have to 'make terms' with the new power. The Untouchables, 'denied by the Hindu religion even the semblance of human rights', would no longer have a protector. The way to avoid political turmoil in India, he argued, was to concentrate on practical steps 'to advance the material condition of the Indian masses', and to treat with swift severity all extremism and all breaches of the law. The Congress at Lahore, at which the Union Jack had been burnt, ought to have been 'broken up forthwith and its leaders deported'. By firmly asserting 'the will to rule' Britain could have avoided the 'immense series of penal measures' which had, in fact, been taken.

Churchill added, 'Even now, at any time, the plain assertion of the resolve of Parliament to govern and to guide the destinies of the Indian people in faithful loyalty to Indian interests would in a few years – it might even be in a few months – bring this period of tantalised turmoil to an end.'

Churchill then proposed a two-tier solution; the Indian Provincial Governments would move towards 'more real, more intimate, more representative organs of self-government', while the central power would remain firmly in British hands. But civil disobedience must be ended. 'The truth is,' he declared, 'that Gandhi-ism and all it stands for will, sooner or later, have to be grappled with and finally crushed. It is no use trying to satisfy a tiger by feeding him with cat's meat. The sooner this is realised, the less trouble and misfortune there will be for all concerned.'

Lord Irwin commented in a letter to a friend, 'What a monstrous speech Winston has just made.' Churchill was convinced that India was not yet ready to rule itself at the centre; Irwin believed that he could reconcile the needs of the Indian Princely States and the Indian Provinces through a Federal scheme. He also believed he should open negotiations with the imprisoned Gandhi and the Congress leaders whose demand for full independence was as unacceptable to MacDonald as it was to Baldwin.

In a letter to his son on 8 January 1931 Churchill wrote: 'I am going to fight this Indian business *à outrance*.' Nor would he join any administration 'saddled with all the burden of whole-hog Protection, plus unlimited doses of Irwinism for India'. On January 25, in an attempt to persuade Congress to negotiate, Irwin released Gandhi from prison. His one fear, Irwin told Baldwin, was that 'Winston should make mischief ' in Parliament during the next day's debate. Irwin advised Baldwin, 'Send him to Epping for the day.'

Churchill did speak in the debate of January 26. It was his first Parliamentary speech against the Conservative Party since he had rejoined it in 1924, and marked a definite breach with the Party leadership. In it he pointed to a weakness in Government policy, to put the promise of self-government before 'the gleaming eyes of excitable millions', with the 'formidable' powers which would in fact be retained under the Irwin scheme. Indian nationalists would never accept such curbs, he believed, and went on to remind the House that there were at that very moment 60,000 Indians in prison for political offences. The restrictions on civil liberty then in force were 'without precedent in India since the Mutiny'. It was a delusion to believe that the Indians would be content with Dominion Status or self-government. The All-India Parliament which Britain proposed to set up would soon be dominated, he warned, 'by forces intent on driving us out of the country as quickly as possible'.

Churchill's speech made a considerable impact on the Conservative backbenchers, who had not been consulted the previous October about their Party's commitment to the Irwin Declaration. A senior Conservative backbencher, Irwin's cousin George Lane-Fox, wrote to Irwin after the debate: 'When Winston began he had not much support behind him. But I, sitting on the back benches, felt the cleverness of his speech, in the gradual growth of approval among our back benches. They began to feel that this represented their own doubts and what they had been thinking, and gradually quite a number first began to purr and then to cheer.'

It was not MacDonald, but Baldwin, who replied to Churchill's speech. If the Conservatives were returned to power, he declared, they would regard the implementation of the proposed Indian Constitution as their 'one duty'. Baldwin's pledge was cheered by the Labour MPs, but, Irwin's cousin reported, 'there was an ominous silence on our own benches'.

Following Baldwin's speech, Churchill felt he had no option but to resign from the Shadow Cabinet; this he did on the day after the debate. Two days later he began a public campaign of seeking to rally Party support against the India policy. His speeches were thorough, full of foreboding, striking chords of support among Conservatives who felt that Baldwin had committed the Party beyond its natural instincts or beliefs. In an attempt to undermine his criticisms, Conservative Central Office, under the guidance of J.C.C. Davidson, worked to destroy Churchill's credibility rather than to rebut his arguments. For his part, Churchill felt an upsurge of support among the Party rank and file, writing to Randolph on February 8, 'At a stroke I have become quite popular in the Party and in great demand upon the platform.'

Five days later Brendan Bracken wrote to Randolph about his father, 'He has untied himself from Baldwin's apron, rallied all the fighters in the Tory Party, re-established himself as a potential leader & put heart into a great multitude here & in India.' Bracken added that by a series of 'brilliant speeches' in the Commons, Churchill had shown the Conservatives 'the quality of his genius & the incredible drabness & futility of SB'.

On February 17 Gandhi met Irwin in Delhi, the first of eight meetings held over the next four weeks. Many Conservatives were outraged that the Viceroy should talk with the man whose aim was still full independence and who refused to call off civil disobedience. 'It is alarming and also nauseating,' Churchill told the West Essex Conservatives on February 23, 'to see Mr Gandhi, a seditious Middle Temple lawyer, now posing as a fakir of a type well known in the East, striding half-naked up the steps of the Viceregal palace, while he is still organising and conducting a campaign of civil disobedience, to parley on equal terms with the representative of the King-Emperor.' Such a spectacle could only encourage 'all the forces which are hostile to British authority'.

Churchill's speech outraged Labour and Liberal opinion. But for very many Conservatives it expressed in graphic language their own deepest concerns. 'There is no doubt that the whole spirit of the Conservative Party is with me,' Churchill wrote to Clementine. This was not at all fanciful; unknown to Churchill, on February 25 the Principal Agent of the Conservative Party, Hugh Topping, wrote to Neville Chamberlain: 'Many of our supporters are worried about the question of India. They lean much more towards the views of Mr Churchill than to those expressed by Mr Baldwin.' One of the leaders of Baldwin's own constituency Party, Sir Richard Brooke, sent him a word of warning on March 2 that the Indian people were being encouraged 'to expect more concessions than they can be given'. Brooke added, 'Mr Churchill expresses the views of very many Conservatives in this Constituency.'

On March 4, as his talks with Irwin continued, Gandhi agreed to call off civil disobedience and to allow Congress representatives to go to a second Round Table conference in London to discuss the future of India. He also accepted British 'safeguards', themselves unspecified, in defence policy, foreign affairs and the interests of minorities. This Gandhi-Irwin Pact, as it became known, was made public on March 5. Baldwin at once announced his support for it, and for the second Round Table conference; in Parliament on March 12 he called the Gandhi-Irwin Pact 'a victory for common sense'. In reply, Churchill argued that, as a result of the Pact, 'expectations, aspirations and appetites have been excited and are mounting'. Pointing to the recent anti-British riots in Bombay, he declared that it was those who tantalised the Indians with the offer of Dominion Status, but were not willing to give them full independence, who were 'bringing bloodshed and confusion ever nearer to the masses of Hindustan'.

Churchill was convinced that his warnings were correct. Speaking at the Albert Hall on March 18 he called the current policy of negotiations with Gandhi and Nehru, with a view to bestowing 'peace and progress' on India, 'a crazy dream with a terrible awakening'. If British authority were destroyed, all the medical, legal and administrative services which Britain had created 'would perish with it', as would the railway service, irrigation, public works and famine prevention. The Hindus would seek to drive out and destroy the Muslims. Profiteering and corruption would flourish. Indian millionaires, grown rich on sweated labour, would become more powerful and even richer. All sorts of 'greedy appetites' had already been excited 'and many itching fingers were stretching and scratching at the vast pillage of a derelict Empire'. Nepotism, graft and curruption would be 'the handmaidens of a Brahmin domination'.

Worst of all in Churchill's view, the Hindus would tyrannise the Untouchables, 'a multitude as big as a nation – men, women and children deprived of hope and of the status of humanity. Their plight is worse than that of slaves, because they have been taught to consent not only to a physical but to a psychic servitude and prostration.' Both for the Untouchables, and for the five million Indian Christians, it would be 'a sorry day when the arm of Britain can no longer offer them the protection of an equal law'.

Churchill then denounced the part which the 'official' Conservatives had played in characterising him, and those who agreed with him, as 'a sort of inferior race, mentally deficient, composed principally of colonels and other undesirables who have fought for Britain'. But, he said 'we do not depend on colonels – though why Conservatives should sneer at an honoured rank in the British army I cannot tell – we depend on facts. We depend on the private soldiers of the British democracy.'

On the day after Churchill's speech, an official Conservative candidate won a hotly contested by-election at Westminster St George's, defeating by 5,000 votes a Conservative challenger to Baldwin's leadership. The clarion call of loyalty had been sounded. Its echoes were more damaging than arguments to Churchill's India campaign. 'We shall I fear be locked in this controversy for several years,' he wrote to Irwin on March 24, 'and I think it will become the dividing line in England. At any rate you will start with the big battalions on your side.'

At the end of March, Hindu-Muslim violence in Cawnpore led to more than a thousand deaths. Churchill was convinced that this pattern of religious strife could only worsen if self-government were proceeded with. Seventy million Muslims were in danger of being 'bled and exploited' by the Hindus, he warned. 'The feud is only at its beginning.' A month later he pointed out that Indian extremists were continuing to murder British officials, despite the imminent departure of Gandhi for the second Round Table conference in London and Irwin's comment that the condition of India was 'sweeter' than hitherto. In the Cawnpore debate on July 9 he declared the 'outbreak of primordial fury and savagery' at Cawnpore was only a foretaste of what would happen throughout India once Britain withdrew 'its governing, guiding and protecting hand'.

Churchill's warnings were in vain; the co-operation between Mac-Donald and Baldwin in seeking a bi-partisan India policy ensured that even with fifty or sixty Conservative MPs willing to speak out against the Party line, he could not alter the direction of Government policy.

That summer Churchill went with Clementine and Randolph on a driving holiday through France. With him was Violet Pearman, a new secretary, 'Mrs P' as she was known in the Churchill household, who was to be his main secretarial help for the next six years. On August 7, in Biarritz, he made the final corrections to *The World Crisis: The Eastern Front.* 'Thank God it is finished,' he wrote to Edward Marsh. 'I am longing to get on to Marlborough, and am most interested to hear what you think of the two jumble chapters in which I broke into the subject.' Churchill ended on a political note, 'Everybody I meet seems vaguely alarmed that something terrible is going to happen financially.'

A week later, severe economic difficulties forced MacDonald and Snowden to propose a 10 per cent cut in unemployment benefits; this was the basic condition for an essential American loan. The Cabinet was divided on whether to accept; there was much talk about a Labour-Conservative coalition to deal with the economic crisis. When Churchill was at Avignon on August 16 he broke off his holiday and his work to return to London, hoping to persuade his fellow-Conservatives to refuse any responsibility for Labour's discomfiture. Four days later, when he returned to France, the Labour Government was still intact. Then, on August 23, while he was painting at Juan-les-Pins, the Labour Cabinet learned that the Trade Unions would not accept the proposed cut in unemployment benefit. After several senior Ministers had expressed their support for the Trade Union view, the Cabinet resigned.

Britain's second Labour Government was at an end. On the following day the King asked MacDonald to remain as Prime Minister at the head of a National Government made up of politicians of all political parties. Baldwin at once agreed to Conservative participation. Lloyd George, an opponent of participation, was unwell and could not therefore prevent his senior Liberal colleagues from joining the new Government. On August 23 Samuel Hoare, who was to become Secretary of State for India in the new Government, wrote to Neville Chamberlain, 'As we have said several times in the last few days, we have had some great good luck in the absence of Winston and LG.'

Churchill was not invited to join the National Government. When he returned from France at the beginning of September he found all Parties united in their excitement at the coming Indian Round Table Conference, and the imminent arrival of Gandhi in London. Churchill's warning in an article in the *Daily Mail* on September 7, that 'nothing but further surrenders of British authority can emerge', fell largely on stony ground. The Round Table Conference opened on the following day, with MacDonald pledging the new Government's continued support for full Dominion Status. In this he was supported by all his Cabinet, which now included Baldwin, Neville Chamberlain and Hoare.

On October 27 the National Government went to the polls. Support for the new all-Party coalition was overwhelming. The Conservatives, committed to serving under MacDonald, won 473 seats. Liberal Nationals won 35 and National Labour 13. Those Liberals who wished to be associated with the National Government, and who formed a part of it, won 33 seats. The Lloyd George Liberals, bitter opponents of the coalition, won a mere four seats. The Labour Party, outraged by what it saw as MacDonald's betrayal, was reduced to 52 seats, a staggering loss of 236. Under MacDonald's banner of national unity, the Conservative Party had achieved Parliamentary ascendancy. Churchill, who almost doubled his majority at Epping, was isolated but unbowed.

On November 2, within a week of polling day, the final volume of Churchill's war memoirs, *The World Crisis: The Eastern Front*, was published; it marked the culmination of a considerable literary effort. Three days later MacDonald announced his new Government. Baldwin was to be Lord President of the Council and Neville Chamberlain Chancellor of the Exchequer. 'I am very sorry to see that you are not in the new Cabinet,' Rear-Admiral Dewar, a former Deputy Director of the Naval Intelligence Division, wrote to Churchill on November 16. 'I had hoped that you might have gone to the Admiralty and done very necessary work for the Navy.'

As for India, only twenty of the 615 MPs were members of the Indian Empire Society which Churchill had helped to launch eleven months earlier. On December 3, in the debate on the need to continue the process towards Dominion Status, MacDonald asked for a united policy. When Churchill insisted on dividing the House, both Austen Chamberlain and Baldwin spoke against him. When the vote came, 43 MPs supported Churchill, while 369 MPs voted for the Government.

Churchill was now fifty-seven. Following his Parliamentary defeat on December 3 he left England with Clementine and Diana for a long-planned visit to the United States. He was determined to recoup his losses in the Wall Street crash by lecturing, and had contracted to give forty lectures for a guaranteed minimum fee of £10,000. In addition the *Daily Mail* was paying him £8,000 for a series of articles on life, travel and politics in the United States; together, these two sums were the equivalent of more than £375,000 in 1990.

On December 11 Churchill reached New York and on the following day lectured at Worcester, Massachusetts. 'It certainly went extremely well,' he later told Randolph. 'The people were almost reverential in their attitude.' On the following evening, after dining with Clementine at their hotel, the Waldorf-Astoria, he took a taxi up Fifth Avenue, where Bernard Baruch had gathered a group of friends to meet him.

The taxi-driver did not know the house, nor Churchill the number. After driving to and fro for an hour, Churchill saw a corner that he thought familiar. He therefore dismissed the taxi, and began to cross the road. Looking left, he saw the headlights of an approaching car some way off. He therefore began to cross. Suddenly he was struck by a car coming from the right; he had failed to remember the American rule of the road. The blow was a severe one, both on his forehead and to his thighs. He lay at the roadside, in great pain, as a crowd gathered. To a policeman who asked him what had happened, he insisted that the accident had been his fault.

Churchill was taken to the Lenox Hill Hospital, where he developed pleurisy and was in great discomfort. According to legend he had been knocked down by a taxi. But although he had left a taxi in order to cross the road, the car that hit him was a private one. Its driver had driven for more than eight years without an accident.

Recovery was slow, first in the hospital for a week and then at the Waldorf-Astoria for two weeks. But the patient was not idle; on December 28 he telegraphed a full account of the accident to the *Daily Mail*. 'I certainly suffered every pang, mental and physical, that a street accident or, I suppose, a shell wound can produce,' he wrote. 'None is unendurable. There is neither the time nor the strength for self-pity. There is no room for remorse or fears. If at any moment in this long series of sensations a grey veil deepening into blackness had descended upon the sanctum, I should have felt or feared nothing additional.'

Syndicated all over the world, Churchill's article brought him thousands of letters and telegrams wishing him a speedy recovery. 'Of course,' wrote his Aunt Leonie, 'you have been spared to still do great things in the future and I mean to live on to see it all!' Lady Leslie died in 1943, at the age of eighty-three, three years after her nephew had become Prime Minister.

In search of further rest, Churchill went from New York to the Bahamas. 'He is terribly depressed at the slowness of his recovery,' Clementine wrote to Randolph on 12 January 1932. Severe pains in the arms and shoulders added to his distress. 'The doctors call it neuritis,' she added, 'but don't seem to know what to do about it.' The previous night Churchill had been 'very sad, and said that he had now in the last two years had three heavy blows. First the loss of all that money in the crash, then the loss of his political position in the Conservative Party, and now this terrible physical injury. He said he did not think he would ever recover completely from the three events.'

Churchill was determined, however, to get back to the lecture circuit. On January 25 he returned by sea to New York; three days later he lectured in Brooklyn. The 'great opposing forces of the future', he said, would be 'the English-speaking peoples and Communism'. It was quite wrong for Englishmen and Americans to go on as they were doing 'gaping at each other in this helpless way', and being ashamed of Anglo-American co-operation 'as if it were a crime'.

Between January 28 and February 21, travelling almost every day, Churchill lectured in nineteen American cities and his total earnings for the three weeks' work exceeded £7,500; as Prime Minister, MacDonald received £5,000 a year. Because it was thought that Indian supporters of Gandhi and Nehru living in Chicago and Detroit might attack him, Churchill was guarded in both cities by groups of armed detectives.

Just as he had earlier advised his Treasury officials to inscribe 'hope and confidence' on their memoranda, so now Churchill inscribed 'hope and confidence' in his speeches; in New York on February 8, at a meeting of bankers and industrialists, he urged them not to add to monetary deflation 'the hideous deflation of panic and despair'. To the Chairman of Associated Newspapers, Esmond Harmsworth, he wrote three weeks later that his lecture tour had made him feel 'at this great distance, the solid, enduring strength of England and her institutions'. Even the National Government he so despised had, he realised, turned Britain into 'a power respected and considered to be revivified'.

On March 11 Churchill sailed from New York for Britain; six days later, eight of his friends were at Paddington Station to welcome him back, and to celebrate his near escape from death with the gift of a luxury Daimler. The 140 donors included friends from every period of his life. Churchill returned to Chartwell; 'I feel I need to rest and not to have to drive myself so hard,' he wrote to one of his publishers on April 1. 'You have no idea what I have been through.' Three weeks later, in the Commons, he spoke during the debate on Neville Chamberlain's first Budget. Much of his speech was in humorous vein, as was his address on April 30 at the Royal Academy dinner, where, in a sustained metaphor of the art world, he admitted that he himself was 'not exhibiting this year' because of 'differences with the committee', but that he still had 'a few things' on his easel. He then contrasted MacDonald's earlier 'lurid sunsets of Empire and capitalist civilisations' with the use of blue 'in his new pictures' not only for atmosphere 'but even as foundation'. Baldwin could be criticised for lacking a little in colour 'and in precise definition of objects in foreground', but one had nevertheless to admit there was something 'very reposeful' in his twilight studies in half-tones.

'There is so much jealousy in the art world,' Baldwin replied, 'that a kind word to the painter from so distinguished an exponent of a far different style shows a breadth of mind as rare as it is delightful.' Touched by Baldwin's letter, Churchill replied: 'I was very glad that my chaff did not vex you. My shafts, though necessarily pointed, are never intentionally poisoned. If they cut, I pray they do not fester in the wound.'

On May 8 Churchill made his first broadcast to the United States. 'They tell me I may be speaking to thirty millions of Americans. I am not at all alarmed. On the contrary I feel quite at home.' In his broadcast he appealed for a joint Anglo-American policy to fight the economic depression. 'Believe me, no one country can combat this evil alone.'

There was another evil, a far greater danger to world stability, Churchill believed, that needed to be faced by international co-operation; this was the danger posed by Germany, now seething with a desire to regain her lost territories, but faced by a Europe committed to a substantial reduction in its level of armaments. At Geneva, the World Disarmament Conference was working towards a general reduction of all armies, navies and air forces. Nor did its work slacken after March 13, when the most vociferous German advocate of treaty revision and rearmament, Adolf Hitler, received eleven million votes in the election for President, as against eighteen million for Field Marshal Hindenburg and five million for the Communist candidate, Ernst Thaelmann.

In a second ballot on April 10, Hitler's share of the vote rose to forty per cent of the votes cast. Yet, one month later, on May 13, the British Foreign Secretary, Sir John Simon, urged upon the House of Commons the need for further rapid and comprehensive disarmament. Only by reducing the level of arms, Simon argued, could the dangers of a future war be averted; nothing could be worse than for a disarmed Germany to have to face a well-armed France.

Simon's appeal for disarmament was widely and enthusiastically supported. Churchill, however, sounded a note of concern, telling the Commons: 'I should very much regret to see any approximation in military strength between Germany and France. Those who speak of that as though it were right, or even a question of fair dealing, altogether underrate the gravity of the European situation. I would say to those who would like to see Germany and France on an equal footing in armaments: "Do you wish for war?" For my part, I earnestly hope that no such approximation will take place during my lifetime or that of my children.'

On May 26, in an article in the *Daily Mail*, Churchill conceded that 'millions of well-meaning English people' hoped that the Disarmament Conference would succeed, and he continued, 'There is such a horror of war in the great nations who passed through Armageddon that any declaration or public speech against armaments, although it consisted only of platitudes and unrealities, has always been applauded; and any speech or assertion which set forth the blunt truths has been incontinently relegated to the category of "warmongering".'

Churchill went on to point out, however, that as the Disarmament Conference proceeded, each State in fact sought security for itself by maintaining its own existing armaments, while urging all other States to disarm down to the lowest level. But was it likely, he asked 'that France with less than forty millions, faced by Germany with sixty millions, and double the number of young men coming to military age every year, is going to deprive herself of the mechanical aids and appliances on which she relies to prevent a fourth invasion in little more than a hundred years'? Likewise, could the new states of northern and eastern Europe like Finland, Latvia, Lithuania and Poland, be expected not to seek the most effective armaments possible 'to protect themselves from being submerged in a ferocious deluge from Russia'.

The cause of disarmament, Churchill wrote, 'will not be attained by mush, slush and gush. It will be advanced steadily by the harassing expense of fleets and armies, and by the growth of confidence in a long peace. It will be achieved only when in a favourable atmosphere half a dozen great men, with as many first class powers at their back, are able to lift world affairs out of their present increasing confusion.'

On May 30, four days after this article was published, Count von Papen replaced Heinrich Brüning as German Chancellor. Although Hitler and his Nazi Party were not invited to join the new Government, Papen hoped that with Hitler's support he could remain in power for several years. On June 19, in the provincial elections at Hesse, the Nazi vote increased from 37 to 44 per cent, making the Nazis the largest single Party in the province.

In India civil disobedience had broken out again, fuelled by the demand for full independence; several British civilian officials had been murdered, and Irwin's successor as Viceroy, Lord Willingdon, had imprisoned Gandhi. In May, more than two hundred Indians were killed in Hindu-Muslim clashes, and 30,000 imprisoned for civil disobedience. In an attempt to lessen Indian hostility to Dominion Status, MacDonald and Baldwin now proposed increasing the Indian franchise from seven million to thirty-six million voters. Churchill thought this an unwise move, telling a private meeting of the Indian Empire Society on May 25: 'Democracy is totally unsuited to India. Instead of conflicting opinions you have bitter theological hatreds.'

On July 1 Churchill learned that the BBC would still not allow him to broadcast, this time to Paris, on British monetary policy. He was furious, writing to the Foreign Secretary, Sir John Simon, 'Surely such a Government containing so many statesmen, and supported by such overwhelming majorities, has no need to fear independent expressions of opinion upon the controversies of the day?' But the ban remained in force.

Confident that the American economy would recover, that summer Churchill bought £12,000 worth of American stocks, the equivalent of what he had lost in the crash two years earlier. 'If the whole world except the United States sank beneath the ocean,' he told his stockbroker, 'that community could get its living. They carved it out of the prairie and the forests. They are going to have a strong national resurgence in the near future.'

Throughout July and August Churchill worked at Chartwell on his life of Marlborough. In Germany that July, Hitler's Nazi Party won 37 per cent of the poll in the General Election. Churchill was making plans to visit Germany, as part of his intention to see the scenes of Marlborough's military victories; on August 27 he set off for Belgium, Holland and Germany. Lindemann went with him. At Brussels they were joined by a military historian, Lieutenant-Colonel Ridley Pakenham-Walsh, who was to be their guide. On the way to the battlefield at Blenheim, they spent three days in Munich, where one of Randolph's acquaintances, Ernst Hanfstaengel, a friend of Hitler, tried to arrange a meeting between Hitler and Churchill in Churchill's hotel.

Churchill said he was willing to meet the Nazi party leader, though Hanfstaengel later recalled how, during dinner beforehand, he 'taxed me about Hitler's anti-Semitic views'. Hitler made no appearance that night. On the following day Hanfstaengel again tried to persuade him to meet Churchill, but in vain. 'In any case,' Hitler asked him, 'what part does Churchill play? He is in opposition and no one pays any attention to him.' Hanfstaengel replied, 'People say the same about you,' but Hitler was not to be persuaded.

Churchill left Munich for the battlefield of Blenheim. 'The battlefields were wonderful,' he wrote to Pakenham-Walsh three weeks later, 'and I was able to re-people them with ghostly but glittering armies.' From Blenheim he had intended to go to Venice for a holiday, but he was taken ill with paratyphoid fever. Too ill to be brought back to England, he spent two weeks in a sanatorium in Salzburg. But after a few days he began dictating from his sick bed twelve articles for the *News of the World*, which had commissioned him to retell 'The World's Great Stories'. Edward Marsh prepared the outlines for him.

On September 25 Churchill returned to Chartwell. 'It was an English bug which I took abroad with me,' he told his cousin Sunny, 'and no blame rests on the otherwise misguided continent of Europe.' That same day he began working again on his Marlborough biography, discussing historical points with Maurice Ashley and dictating the chapters to Violet Pearman. Work continued throughout the following day. But on September 27, as he and Ashley were walking in the grounds, he collapsed. It was a recur-

rence of the paratyphoid. An ambulance was called and he was taken up
to a London nursing home. He had suffered a severe haemorrhage from
a paratyphoid ulcer.

Churchill still hoped to attend the forthcoming Conservative Party
Conference at Blackpool on October 7. His intention was to move a
resolution against the Party's support for the proposed Indian constitution. But although at one point he contemplated going to Blackpool by
ambulance, he was too ill to do so. Hoare was much relieved; he had
thought that Churchill's resolution might be carried. 'We had a substantial
majority,' he wrote to MacDonald when the vote was taken, 'but it is idle
to blink the fact that the sentiment apart from the reasoning of the meeting
was on the other side.'

Returning from the London nursing home to Chartwell, Churchill
continued to work on his book. 'Mr Churchill is steadily improving,' Violet
Pearman wrote to a friend, 'though progress is rather slow, but as usual
nothing can keep him from work, and he busies himself a good many
hours each day and gets through a lot.' But it would be 'some time before
he really gets as strong as before'. By the end of October Churchill had
completed half of the first of his Marlborough volumes. His mind was
already looking ahead to his next literary effort, a four-volume History of
the English-Speaking Peoples. A publisher was soon found willing to pay
him £20,000 for this endeavour. It was a formidable sum of money for any
author, the equivalent in 1990 of £420,000. A quarter was paid to him at
once; the rest would come when the book was finished.

Throughout the summer and early autumn of 1932 von Papen's Government was demanding 'equality of status' for German armaments; this
meant that Germany, having been disarmed in 1918, must now be allowed
to arm up to the same point as her most heavily armed neighbour, France.
The German Minister of Defence, General Kurt von Schleicher, was
insistent that Germany be allowed to rearm. On September 18 the British
Foreign Office issued an official Note, signed by Sir John Simon, stating
that in Britain's view the disarmament clauses of the Treaty of Versailles
were still binding upon Germany. In protest, von Papen withdrew Germany from the Disarmament Conference.

Churchill, who had just returned from Germany, was shocked to find
so many people in Britain critical of the Simon Note, and insisting that a
disarmed Germany was in an unfair position of inferiority compared to
France. In an article published in the *Daily Mail* on October 17 he argued
that Simon's firm stand had 'done more to consolidate peace in Europe
than any words spoken on behalf of Great Britain for some years'. Simon
had 'raised the hand of warning in the interests of peace'. Such firmness

was essential, Churchill wrote, as every right-wing party in Germany was trying to win votes 'by putting up the boldest front against the foreigner'; Hitler had to 'outdo Papen, and Papen has to go one better than Hitler, and Brüning must hurry or he will be left behind'.

Churchill pointed out in his article that General Schleicher had already declared that 'whatever the Powers may settle, Germany will do what she thinks fit in rearmament', and he went on to warn his readers, 'Very grave dangers lie along these paths, and if Great Britain had encouraged Germany in such adventures, we might in an incredibly short space of time have been plunged into a situation of violent peril.'

On November 6, in the second German General Election in five months, the Nazi Party retained its position as the second largest Party in the State, despite a drop in votes from 37 per cent to 33 per cent. Four days after this vote, the House of Commons debated the Government's continuing policy of disarmament, of which Churchill had been so critical. But he was still too weak from the effects of the paratyphoid to make the journey to London. During the debate, Simon stated that, despite his Note, British policy would henceforth take into account 'the fair meeting of Germany's claim to the principle of equality'. Closing the debate, Baldwin told the House, 'I think it well for the man in the street to realise that there is no power on earth that can prevent him from being bombed.'

'You were badly missed yesterday,' Amery wrote to Churchill, 'when the most incredible amount of sloppy nonsense was talked from every quarter of the House about disarmament.' On November 17, in the *Daily Mail*, Churchill expressed his conviction that the disarmament negotiations at Geneva would fail. As soon as this happened, the National Government should propose to Parliament 'measures necessary to place our Air Force in such a condition of power and efficiency that it will not be worth anyone's while to come here and kill our women and children in the hope that they may blackmail us into surrender'.

On November 23 Churchill was well enough to go up to London, and, in a speech of considerable power and foresight, warned MPs that if Britain forced France to disarm, Germany would take advantage of her own numerical superiority to seek revenge for the defeat of 1918. So far, every concession that had already been made to Germany had been followed by fresh German demands. It was not only 'equality of arms with France' that Germany wanted. Not only France, but also Belgium, Poland, Roumania, Czechoslovakia and Yugoslavia were determined to defend their frontiers 'and to defend their rights'.

Churchill had seen the new Germany during his visit to the battlefield of Blenheim that autumn. 'All these bands of sturdy Teutonic youths,' he said, 'marching through the streets and roads of Germany, with the light of desire in their eyes to suffer for the Fatherland, are not looking for status. They are looking for weapons, and, when they have the weapons, believe me they will then ask for the return of lost territories,' and when that demand was made it would 'shake and possibly shatter to their foundations' the countries that he had mentioned. A 'war mentality' was springing up in certain countries; all over Europe there was 'hardly a factory which is not prepared for its alternative war service'. MacDonald's 'noble, if somewhat flocculent eloquence' must be replaced by greater precision. 'I cannot recall any time,' Churchill said, 'when the gap between the kind of words which statesmen used and what was actually happening in many countries was so great as it is now. The habit of saying smooth things and uttering pious platitudes and sentiments to gain applause, without relation to the underlying facts, is more pronounced now than it has ever been in my experience.'

Churchill continued: 'Just as the late Lord Birkenhead used to say about India – I think it the beginning and end of wisdom there – "Tell the truth to India", so I would now say, "Tell the truth to the British people". They are a tough people, a robust people. They may be a bit offended at the moment, but if you have told them exactly what is going on you have insured yourself against complaints and reproaches which are very unpleasant when they come home on the morrow of some disillusion.' As for France's military strength, 'they only wish to keep what they have got'. No initiative in making trouble would come from France. 'I say quite frankly,' Churchill continued, 'though I may shock the House, that I would rather see another ten or twenty years of one-sided peace than see a war between equally well-matched Powers.'

'I am not an alarmist,' Churchill told the House. 'I do not believe in the imminence of war in Europe. I believe that with wisdom and with skill we may never see it in our time. To hold any other view would indeed be to despair,' and he then set out what he believed to be the only way to revive 'the lights of goodwill and reconciliation' in Europe. 'The removal of the just grievances of the vanquished,' he said, 'ought to precede the disarmament of the victors. To bring about anything like equality of armaments if it were in our power to do so, which it happily is not, while those grievances remain unredressed, would be almost to appoint the day for another European war – to fix it as if it were a prize-fight. It would be far safer to reopen questions like those of the Danzig Corridor and Transylvania, with all their delicacy and difficulty, in cold blood and in a calm atmosphere and while the victor nations still have ample superiority, than to wait and drift on, inch by inch and stage by stage, until once again vast combinations, equally matched, confront each other face to face.'

Commenting on Baldwin's remarks, in the debate he had been too ill to attend, that 'the man in the street' should realise that there was 'no power on earth that can prevent him from being bombed', Churchill pointed out that this assertion had been followed by 'no practical conclusion'. It had created anxiety and also perplexity. 'There was a sense of, what shall I say, fatalism, and even perhaps helplessness about it, and I take this opportunity of saying that, as far as this island is concerned, the responsibility of Ministers to guarantee the safety of the country from day to day and from hour to hour is direct and inalienable.'

Churchill's advocacy of Treaty revision while the victors were still strong, and his call for the maintenance of national armed strength in the face of growing German demands and aggressiveness, remained the cornerstone of his warnings to the Government over the years ahead. Far from building up Britain's air strength, however, MacDonald and Baldwin pressed on with a scheme of European disarmament, in which Britain would give a lead by reducing its own Air Force before others did so.

On November 30 Churchill was fifty-eight. That winter he worked at Chartwell on Marlborough. On December 16 Lindemann arrived to keep him company. 'He was part of our Chartwell life,' Churchill's daughter Sarah later recalled. 'It is hard to remember an occasion on which he was not present. His exterior was conventionally forbidding – the domed cranium, the close-cropped iron-grey hair which had receded as if the brain had pushed it away, the iron-grey moustache, the sallow complexion, the little sniff which took the place of what normally would have been a laugh, yet he could still exude a warmth that made scientific thinking unfrightening.'

Lindemann's presence was always a source of pleasure to Churchill, and of education. Sarah recalled: 'Prof had the gift of conveying a most complicated subject in simple form. One day at lunch when coffee and brandy were being served my father decided to have a slight "go" at Prof who had just completed a treatise on the quantum theory. "Prof," he said, "tell us in words of one syllable and in no longer than five minutes what is the quantum theory." My father then placed his large gold watch, known as the "turnip", on the table. When you consider that Prof must have spent many years working on this subject, it was quite a tall order, however without any hesitation, like quicksilver, he explained the principle and held us all spell-bound. When he had finished we all spontaneously burst into applause.'

On 30 January 1933 Hitler became Chancellor of Germany, invited to do so by President Hindenburg in an attempt to harness the extreme opinions of the Nazi Party to the more moderate politicians who were to be part of the new Coalition Government. A week later Hitler promulgated the first of a series of laws that rapidly increased and consolidated his power; this first law enabled him to silence the democratic, Socialist and Communist Press. This was followed by the arrest of several thousand opponents of Nazism, and by public and popular demands for a revision of the Treaty of Versailles and for German rearmament.

On February 15, at this moment of German nationalist resurgence, and an intensification of Japanese aggression against China in the Far East, the British Cabinet discussed Defence deficiencies set out by the Secretaries of State for War and Air, Lord Hailsham and Lord Londonderry. But after listening to a warning from Neville Chamberlain of the 'financial and economic risks' involved in rearmament, the Cabinet agreed to make itself 'responsible for the deficiencies in the Defence Services which are imposed by the difficult financial situation at the present time'. Economic restraints made rearmament impossible.

Churchill's mind was still very much on what he had seen in Germany five months earlier, and on all that had happened since then, including a vote in the Oxford Union supporting, by 275 to 153, the motion 'That this House refuses in any circumstances to fight for King and Country'. Speaking at Oxford on February 17, Churchill contrasted this attitude with the German one: 'I think of Germany with its splendid clear-eyed youth marching forward on all the roads of the Reich singing their ancient songs, demanding to be conscripted into an army; eagerly seeking the most terrible weapons of war; burning to suffer and die for their fatherland.' He could almost 'feel the curl of contempt' on their lips when they read the Oxford Union message.

On March 2 Randolph returned to Oxford to try to reverse the Union vote. But he gained only 138 votes, against 750 upholding the original motion. 'He stood a hard test at the Oxford Union,' Churchill wrote proudly to Hugh Cecil. 'Nothing is so piercing as the hostility of a thousand of your own contemporaries, and he was by no means crushed under it.' Eight days later Churchill himself faced the hostility of his contemporaries when, in the Commons, he opposed the Government's proposal to reduce Air Force spending for the second year in succession, to close down one of the four flying training schools, and to press France to reduce the size of its Air Force. In defending British lack of preparedness in the air, Sir Philip Sassoon, the Under-Secretary of State for Air, told the Commons that pending the outcome of the Disarmament Conference the Government were 'once again prepared to accept the continuance of the serious existing disparity between the strength of the Royal Air Force and that of the air services of the other great nations.'

Churchill argued that to expect France to halve her Air Force 'in the present temper of Europe' was 'in the region of unrealities'. Without sufficient means of defence neutrality could not be preserved. 'Not to have an adequate Air Force in the present state of the world is to compromise the foundations of national freedom and independence.' He 'regretted very much' to hear Sassoon say that the British Government's ten-year air expansion programme was to be suspended for another year in the interests of continuing hopes for world disarmament. Churchill then called on Baldwin to abandon the Ten-Year-Rule for Defence preparation that assumed there would be no war for the next ten years, and to stop encouraging the 'helpless, hopeless mood'. There was no reason to suppose, he argued, that Britain could not have aircraft 'as good as any country's'. Britain's 'talent in air piloting' was as good as that of any country.

These arguments fell on stony ground; two days after Churchill's speech, MacDonald submitted Britain's disarmament proposals to the Geneva Disarmament Conference. Eight months would be the maximum period of military service in Europe; France, Germany, Italy and Poland would be limited to 200,000 troops each; aerial bombardment would be forbidden; military aircraft would be limited to 500 for each country, with the German figure left open; any excess of aircraft would be destroyed, half by 1936, the rest by 1939.

In presenting this scheme to the Commons on March 23, MacDonald said, 'I cannot pretend that I went through the figures myself.' He then reiterated that the Government's aim was 'equality of status' for Germany in the sphere of armaments. Churchill, who had followed closely the reports of Nazi demands and anti-Jewish and anti-democratic action, told the House, 'When we read about Germany, when we watch with surprise and distress the tumultuous insurgence of ferocity and war spirit, the pitiless ill-treatment of minorities, the denial of the normal protections of civilised society to large numbers of individuals solely on the grounds of race – when we see that occurring in one of the most gifted, learned, scientific and formidable nations in Europe, one cannot help feeling glad that the fierce passions that are raging in Germany have not found, as yet, any other outlet than Germans.'

Churchill went on to say that the British Government's failure to redress German grievances while Germany was still weak, and could not therefore demand them by force, while at the same time pressing for France to disarm, 'have brought us nearer to war and have made us weaker, poorer and more defenceless'. From both the Labour and Conservative benches came cries of 'No! No! No!' There was more furious anger when he said that responsibility should be laid at MacDonald's door.

On behalf of the Government, Churchill's speech was anwered by the Under-Secretary of State at the Foreign Office, Anthony Eden, who said it was unfortunate Churchill had chosen so serious a debate to practise his 'quips and jests'. For Churchill to accuse MacDonald of being responsible for the deterioration of international relations, he said, was 'a fantastic absurdity'. The causes of that deterioration 'went back to a time when Mr Churchill himself had a considerable measure of responsibility'. This charge was to become the stock-in-trade of Government attacks on Churchill; in fact, while he had been Chancellor of the Exchequer, Air Force spending had been increased in four of his five budgets. He had also been a leading advocate of mutual guarantees for the the French and German frontiers. In 1925 he had urged an annual review of the Ten-Year-Rule. In 1929 he had alerted the Cabinet to the renewed German naval rearmament. But his continual vigilance in defence matters was of no concern to those who were opposed to the policies he now advocated.

Eden went on to insist that without French disarmament 'they could not secure for Europe that period of appeasement which is needed'. Britain did not wish France to halve her army, as Churchill alleged. 'The reduction was nothing like that', Eden said, 'it was 694,000 to 400,000.' The Commons cheered Eden's pedantic, but effective, rebuke. 'The House was enraged and in an ugly mood – towards Mr Churchill,' reported the *Daily Despatch*. Churchill received only one letter of support, from Admiral Sir Reginald Custance, who wrote on March 24, 'You were really setting forth the fundamental principle of war and were talking over the heads of your audience who for the most part are quite ignorant of that principle.'

Churchill intended to speak again on European affairs on April 13. Before doing so, he consulted with Major Desmond Morton, whom he had first met on the Western Front in 1916 and whom he had brought into Intelligence work at the War Office in 1919. Since 1929 Morton had been head of the Industrial Intelligence Unit of the Committee of Imperial Defence, responsible for monitoring, throughout the world, the import and use of raw materials for armaments manufactured by the European powers. He was a near neighbour of Churchill's in Kent.

Fortified by information Morton had given him from the Government's own secret sources, Churchill contrasted Hitler's quest for rearmament with MacDonald's continuing pursuit of disarmament, reiterating his earlier warning that 'the rise of Germany to anything like military equality with France, or the rise of Germany or some ally or other to anything like military equality with France, Poland or the small states, means a renewal of a general European war.'

Churchill went on to tell the House that there were not only 'martial or pugnacious manifestations' in Germany, but also 'this persecution of the Jews, of which so many hon. Members have spoken, and which appeals to everyone who feels that men and women have a right to live in the world where they are born, and have a right to pursue a livelihood which has hitherto been guaranteed them under the public laws of the land of their birth'. He then warned of the dangers of the 'odious conditions now ruling in Germany' being extended by conquest to Poland, 'and another persecution and pogrom of Jews begun in this new area'.

Commenting on MacDonald's 'extraordinary admission' that he had not gone through the figures himself, but that he took responsibility for them, Churchill told the House: 'It is a very grave responsibility. If ever there was a document upon which its author should have consumed his personal thought and energy it was this immense disarmament proposal.'

The Government now announced that a Joint Select Committee of both Houses of Parliament would examine the Indian constitutional proposals. Hoare explained to MacDonald that moderate Conservatives were delighted by the setting up of this Committee because it 'gives them an answer to Winston's most damaging line of attack, namely that Parliament was going to be edged out of the final settlement'. Sir John Simon had recently returned from India with a new proposal for Indian rule of the Provinces, but not at the centre. This Simon Report recommendation was what Churchill had long been urging as the sensible course. At the same time, he saw the proposed Joint Select Committee as a device to pay lip-service to Simon while introducing a more radical scheme.

Churchill was far from alone in his unease; on February 17 Hoare told the Viceroy, 'We are doing everything that we can to ensure a good Government majority, but there is no gainsaying the fact that the Conservative Party as a whole is very jumpy in both Houses.' When Churchill spoke at Conservative Party meetings beyond the control of the Whips, he won a far larger share of the vote than in Parliament; at a discussion on India at the National Union of Conservative Associations meeting on February 28 he secured 165 votes as against 189.

As Churchill suspected, the Government had no intention of accepting the Simon Report, but was going ahead with the plan for Indian self-government both in the Provinces and at the centre. In seeking to make this full Dominion Status more acceptable to Conservative critics of its India policy, it announced that 'safeguards' would be introduced both for the Muslims of India and for the independent Princely States, in what would be a predominantly Hindu Government. In Cabinet on March 10 Hoare explained that under the safeguards the Viceroy would have 'great powers', including 'complete control' over the Foreign Affairs and Defence Departments; 'there was no great risk of a Congress majority', he said, as the Princely States would have 30 per cent and the Muslims 30 per cent of the votes in the lower chamber of the All-India Federation.

During the Cabinet discussion, Lord Hailsham warned that under the Government's proposals 'India would be run more and more by Indians who were very clever, but not good administrators and often corrupt, as their own religion compelled them to look after their own relations. Justice would be sold, the poor oppressed, and there would be a breakdown in the services.' Hoare admitted that he 'shared many of the doubts of the Secretary of State for War'. Despite these doubts, the Cabinet agreed to make the All-India Federal scheme the basis of the White Paper.

While waiting for composition of the Joint Select Committee to be announced, Churchill attended a meeting of those MPs who had hitherto voted against the Government's India policy. The aim of the meeting, he told Lord Salisbury, was to establish 'a nucleus in the House of Commons'. The group, which called itself the India Defence Committee, consisted of fifty Conservative MPs.

On March 17 the Government issued its India White Paper. Under the proposed constitution, each Indian Province would be granted autonomy. At the centre, the previously strict Viceregal control would be replaced by a Federal Government with substantial Indian participation. The proposals would be discussed by the Joint Select Committee. Speaking in the Commons on March 30, Churchill appealed to the Government not to use the Committee as a means of prejudicing in advance the debate which the full House must hold on the future constitution of India. He was supported in the division lobby by 42 MPs. The Government had 475 supporters.

On the following day Churchill was asked to be a member of the Joint Select Committee, on which there were to be twenty-five supporters of the Government's policy, and nine opponents. On April 1, before making up his mind whether or not to serve on it, he wrote to Hoare: 'I have watched with grief and indignation the process by which during the last two and a half years you and Baldwin have turned the whole official power of the Conservative Party and of the Government of India to paralysing or overcoming the Conservative resistance at home and loyalist resistance in India in order to bring your scheme into effect.' All the loyalty of the Conservative Party to its leaders, 'added to the drift of Liberal and Socialist opinion, make a tide which may well be irresistible. You will probably have your way. But then the consequences will begin both in India and at home.'

After much thought, Churchill decided not to serve on the Joint Select Committee. On April 5 he wrote to Hoare to explain why: 'I observe that at least three-quarters of the Committee of thirty-four consists of persons of distinction who have already declared themselves in favour of the principle of the abdication at this juncture of British responsibility in the Central government of India. To this I am decidedly opposed. I believe that if the scheme of the White Paper is carried out, it can only lead after some years either to the evacuation or to the re-conquest of India. I do not wish to share the burden for such grievous events. I see no advantage therefore in my joining your Committee merely to be voted down by an overwhelming majority of the eminent persons you have selected. It is better that those who believe in the policy of the White Paper should work it out for themselves in the Joint Committee unhampered by the criticism or protest of those from whom they are unbridgeably divided.'

Several of Churchill's friends were surprised by his decision. 'Will you let me say that I deeply deplore your refusal to enter the Joint Select Committee,' Lord Burnham wrote on April 7. 'I shall especially miss your leadership and guidance.' Churchill replied: 'I am so sorry not to be able to help you, but I feel sure my work lies outside. The way in which the Committee has been picked is a scandal.'

On April 10 Hoare laid before Parliament the list of those who had agreed to serve on the Joint Select Committee. A Conservative member then moved an amendment to remove the six members of the Government who had been selected. Although the amendment was defeated by 209 votes to 118, this 118 constituted the largest vote recorded in Parliament against the National Government's India Policy. Churchill at once issued a statement, which was published in the *Evening News*: 'If the House had been given a free vote the Government proposal would probably have been defeated by a majority of the Conservative Party. What the Government is trying to do is to get support for its views and not to have an impartial investigation. The Government is not looking for advice but for advertisement. It is not seeking guidance but a guarantee.' Churchill was now determined to lead a public crusade against the Government's India policy. 'We are in for a hard long fight,' he wrote to a friend on April 14, 'but I do not despair.' Hoare himself was worried both about Churchill's campaign and about the Joint Select Committee. 'Very rightly,' he wrote to the Viceroy on April 28, 'we shall try and keep evidence down to the lowest possible quantity.' As for Churchill, Hoare wrote: 'His chief ally is the ignorance of ninety nine people out of a hundred. The result will be that he will get a formidable backing in Conservative circles and that he will certainly stir up a great deal of suspicion and irritation in the organisations of many constituencies.'

Hoare's fears of a constituency revolt were borne out on April 28, when the annual meeting of the Horsham and Worthing Conservative Association rejected the India White Paper by 161 votes to 17. That week, Lord

Linlithgow, a friend of Churchill's since before the First World War, was appointed Chairman of the Joint Select Committee. Seeking to persuade Churchill to give up his opposition to the Federal scheme for India, Linlithgow told him that something like the White Paper scheme was 'bound to go through', and that the Indian problem 'does not interest the mass of voters in this country'.

It was against the Government's tariff policy, Linlithgow suggested, that Churchill should concentrate his future opposition. Churchill replied: 'I am so sorry to see the line you take about India. Curiously enough your remarks to me three or four years ago of the immense deterioration in the agricultural department which has taken place since the Montagu Reforms was one of the facts which played a part in forming my judgment.' The Montagu reforms had been in 1917.

Churchill continued: 'Many thanks for your suggestion that it would be better tactics for me to attack the Government upon their trade agreements and let India slide. I do not think I should remain in politics, certainly I should take no active part in them, if it were not for India. I am therefore quite indifferent to any effect which my opposition to the White Paper may produce upon my personal situation.'

Linlithgow still tried to convince Churchill that he was mistaken. The Indian Agricultural Service, he wrote on May 4, had been 'marked for 100 per cent Indianisation' since 1924, and the process had been virtually completed without anyone suggesting that it would be reversed. 'If you and those who are with you are able to recreate the India of 1900,' he wrote, 'and – what is a great deal more difficult – fit it with even reasonable success into the world of 1934, I shall be the first to admit my error of judgement, and to rejoice in your strength and wisdom.'

In his letter Linlithgow accused Churchill of being old-fashioned. 'I think we differ principally in this,' Churchill replied, 'that you assume the future is a mere extension of the past whereas I find history full of unexpected turns and retrogressions. The mild and vague Liberalism of the early years of the twentieth century, the surge of fantastic hopes and illusions that followed the armistice of the Great War have already been superseded by a violent reaction against Parliamentary and electioneering procedure and by the establishment of dictatorships real or veiled in almost every country. Moreover the loss of our external connections, the shrinkage in foreign trade and shipping brings the surplus population of Britain within measurable distance of utter ruin. We are entering a period when the struggle for self-preservation is going to present itself with great intenseness to thickly populated industrial countries.'

Churchill added: 'In my view England is now beginning a new period of struggle and fighting for its life, and the crux of it will be not only the retention of India but a much stronger assertion of commercial rights. As long as we are sure that we press no claim on India which is not in their real interest we are justified in using our undoubted power for their welfare and for our own. Your schemes are twenty years behind the times.'

The 'times' were indeed moving rapidly; on April 7 Hitler formally imposed Nazi rule on each of the German States, ending their century-old autonomy. Six days later a law came into effect barring Jews from national, local and municipal office. During a debate in the Commons that day, Churchill warned the Government once more of the dangers involved in a militarised Germany, telling the House: 'One of the things which we were told after the Great War would be a security for us was that Germany would be a democracy with Parliamentary institutions. All that has been swept away. You have dictatorship – most grim dictatorship'.

Churchill again commented on several frightening details of the German dictatorship: militarism, appeals 'to every form of fighting spirit', the reintroduction of duelling in the universities, and the persecution of the Jews. He continued, 'I cannot help rejoicing that the Germans have not got the heavy cannon, the thousands of military aeroplanes and the tanks of various sizes for which they have been pressing in order that their status may be equal to that of other countries.' Ten days later Churchill spoke at the annual meeting of the Royal Society of St George. In his speech, which was broadcast, he declared: 'Nothing can save England if she will not save herself. If we lose faith in ourselves, in our capacity to guide and govern, if we lose our will to live, then indeed our story is told. If, while on all sides foreign nations are every day asserting a more aggressive and militant nationalism by arms and trade, we remain paralysed by our own theoretical doctrines or plunged into the stupor of after-war exhaustion, then indeed all that the croakers predict will come true, and our ruin will be swift and final.'

Churchill's struggle against the Government's India policy was to reach its climax on June 28, when the Conservative Central Council met in London to discuss the proposed introduction of the India Bill to Parliament. All spring and summer the Government had been busy, Hoare explained to the Viceroy, 'trying to get up an effective organisation to meet the Winston propaganda in the country'. Hoare wanted the man he had chosen to lead this organisation, Francis Villiers, to be offered a knighthood, in the hope that it would help 'in getting the most out of him'. Villiers received his knighthood. Three weeks before the meeting *The Times* warned Conservatives not to follow Churchill's lead. Whatever the merits of any particular proposal he might make to amend the Bill, it declared, 'there can be no permanent reversal of the broad lines of policy which it represents', and the paper went on to warn, in openly political language, that if Churchill's view prevailed 'Mr Baldwin might think it necessary to withdraw from the leadership of the Party, and even from public life.'

When Churchill spoke at the meeting his remarks were continually interrupted, making it difficult for him to unfold his arguments. He was being made 'the victim of a personal campaign', he said, and as the hostile cries continued he called out: 'It is no good being angry with me, because I have to put the case. We have an absolute duty to justify on this occasion our true opinions.' His appeal was no use. The hostility had, as he knew, been well drummed-up beforehand. 'It is easy to run propaganda to victimise a particular man,' he said. Yet even this appeal to be listened to was met, one newspaper reported, by 'cries of dissent and laughter'.

Churchill's main argument, that Provincial autonomy should be tried first, and be seen to work, before the Federal autonomy scheme was put into effect at the centre, did not in itself preclude eventual Indian self-government. Yet it too was greeted by cries of derision. The vote, however, produced the largest dissenting voice recorded against the MacDonald-Baldwin policy, 356. But this was swamped by the 838 votes in favour. Although Churchill's India campaign had not ended, it had faltered amid the uncompromising belittling of his motives by Party leaders and stalwarts who were determined not to let him influence either the Party or the future of India.

The Government's disregard of Churchill's concerns about India, and its refusal to abandon disarmament despite the German threat, marked a low point in Churchill's hopes of influencing events. In July, his friend Terence O'Connor, a Conservative MP who was soon to become Solicitor General, wrote to him with words of encouragment: 'You fill a place in many people's lives, and your own fortunes & happiness are the concern of more people than you can guess.'

As the Disarmament Conference continued its work at Geneva, both Britain and Germany rejected a French proposal for regular inspection and supervision of armaments. Before the discussion, the Cabinet had been informed by the three Service departments that they opposed regular inspection because it would 'expose to the world our grave shortage of war supplies, and we should have to spend many millions in correcting the position in this and other respects'.

The Foreign Office received regular Intelligence reports and information on developments in Germany; on June 21 the British Air Attaché in Berlin, Group Captain Justin Herring, wrote a secret memorandum setting out the evidence that Germany had begun to build military aircraft in violation of the Treaty of Versailles. Herring had been told by a high official at the German Air Ministry that 'the German Government were already engaged in building a military air force'. Herring's memorandum was one of several pieces of evidence of German rearmament which the Permanent Under-Secretary of State at the Foreign Office, Sir Robert Vansittart, printed for distribution to the Cabinet on July 14. A month later, on August 12, Churchill told his constituents, 'There is grave reason to believe that Germany is arming herself, or seeking to arm herself, contrary to the solemn treaties extracted from her in her hour of defeat.'

On September 20 Churchill's concerns were echoed within the Cabinet by Lord Hailsham, the Secretary of State for War, who told his colleagues, as the minutes recorded: 'We had already disarmed to a degree that rendered our position most perilous if there were any risk of war within the next few years. Our ports were almost undefended, and our anti-aircraft defences were totally inadequate. He did not think anyone was prepared to allow that state of affairs to continue. Everyone must agree that some increase in expenditure on armaments would be required within the next few years. He thought this probably referred to the Royal Air Force, also.'

Such was the Secretary of State for War's judgment; it was also Churchill's persistent theme, which the Government of which the Secretary of State for War was a member was to deride as alarmist.

On October 6, amid these grave events and warnings, Churchill's first volume of *Marlborough: His Life and Times* was published. On receiving his copy as the author's gift, Baldwin wrote to him: 'You really are an amazing man! This last book would mean years of work even for a man whose sole occupation was writing history. Well, there is the miracle.'

Churchill always took delight in sending out inscribed copies of his books; two days after publication of *Marlborough* he inscribed a copy to the President of the United States, Franklin D. Roosevelt, whose New Deal he so admired. His inscription read, 'With earnest best wishes for the success of the greatest crusade of modern times.'

On the day of the publication of Marlborough, Churchill was at Birmingham, at the Conservative Party Conference, where Baldwin urged the need for a Disarmament Convention and spoke strongly in favour of 'the limitation of armaments as a real limitation'. Speaking after Baldwin, Churchill supported a motion brought in by Lord Lloyd, expressing 'grave anxieties' at the state of Britain's defences. Britain must not 'continue long', he said, 'on the course on which we alone are growing weaker, while every other nation is growing stronger'. The motion was passed unanimously. It was one thing, however, to win the support of Party members, another to influence the actual policy of the Government.

On October 14 Hitler withdrew Germany from the Disarmament Conference. Nine days later, the Cabinet decided to continue to seek 'the limitation and reduction of world armaments', and to encourage the French Minister of War, Edouard Daladier, to begin direct negotiations with Germany on the cutting back of sample weapons, and to make 'some concessions' to Germany. The Cabinet concluded, 'Our policy is still to seek by international co-operation the limitation and reduction of world armaments, as our obligations under the Covenant and as the only means to prevent a race in armaments.'

In a Cabinet memorandum on October 24, Lord Londonderry, the Secretary of State for Air, noted that Britain's air production had been halted in 1932 as a result of 'the Armament Truce' of November 1931. Although this truce had ended in February 1933, 'as a further earnest of His Majesty's Government's desire to promote the work of the Disarmament Conference, the standstill was voluntarily extended to the current year in spite of marked inferiority in air strength as compared with other great powers'. It was therefore necessary, Londonderry explained, to postpone completion of the 1923 programme from 1936 to 1940.

This decision to continue with disarmament was a secret one; it therefore failed to help the Government on the following day, when at a by-election at East Fulham the seat was won by an anti-Government candidate on a disarmament platform.

On November 7, as the Government continued its quest for disarmament, Churchill told the Commons, 'The great dominant fact is that Germany has already begun to rearm.' There had been imports of scrap iron and nickel and other war metals 'quite out of the ordinary'. He believed, however, that there was a sure way to curb the German thrust for revenge, and to avert war. The League of Nations should be used 'not for the purpose of fiercely quarrelling and haggling about the details of disarmament, but in an attempt to redress Germany collectively, so that there may be some redress of the grievances of the German nation, and that that may be effected before this peril of rearmament reaches a point which may endanger the peace of the world'. Meanwhile Britain had already disarmed 'to the verge of risk – nay, well into the gulf of risk'. It was up to the three Defence Ministers to make adequate provision for Britain's safety, and to ensure that Britain had both the power and the time to realise if necessary 'the whole latent strength of our country'.

On November 12, after an election in Germany in which only the Nazi Party was allowed to canvass, the Nazis won 95 per cent of the vote. 'You have heard me described as a warmonger,' Churchill told the Royal Naval Division Association luncheon audience two days later. 'That is a lie. I have laboured for peace before the Great War, and if the Naval Holiday which I advised and suggested had been adopted, the course of history might have been different.' It was the Nazis 'who declare that war is glorious, who inculcate a form of blood-lust in their children without parallel as an education since Barbarian and Pagan times'. It was the Nazis who had laid down the doctrine 'that every frontier must be made the starting point of an invasion'. There was no time to be lost. 'Here is a practical step to take. Wipe up this Disarmament Conference, sweep away the rubbish and litter of the eight years of nagging and folly and hypocrisy and fraud, and let us go to Geneva, to the other part of Geneva – to the League of Nations.'

The Cabinet were still determined to seek a comprehensive disarmament agreement. On November 29 Baldwin told his colleagues, 'If we had no hope of achieving any limitation of armaments we should have every right to feel disquietude as to the situation not only so far as concerns the Air Force, but also the Army and Navy.' Britain was 'using every possible effort to bring about a scheme of disarmament which would include Germany.' If Germany saw the Commons pass an air rearmament motion 'the effect on her would be serious'.

On November 30 Churchill was fifty-nine. That winter he remained as much as possible at Chartwell, working with Maurice Ashley on the second Marlborough volume. On New Year's Eve, Baldwin wrote to him enthusiastically about Volume One: 'It is A1. If I had – which God forbid – to deliver an address on you, I should say, "Read Marlborough and you may then picture yourself listening to Winston as he paced up and down the Cabinet room with a glass of water in his hand and a long cigar in the corner of his mouth." I can hear your chuckles as I read it.'

Churchill replied on 3 January 1934 that he was glad Baldwin still had 'a kindly feeling' towards him. 'India apart – you have my earnest good wishes; and I shall try to say something about it when I broadcast on the 16th. But after all it is the European quarrel that will shape our lives. There indeed you must feel the burden press.'

In his broadcast on January 16 Churchill indeed praised the efforts made by the National Government to procure a slow but steady economic recovery. He also praised President Roosevelt, for 'the spirit with which he grapples with difficulties'. He also reiterated his warnings about the need for arms and alliances to prevent a return of war. Not only with the former Allies of the war, but with neutrals like Holland, Denmark, Norway, Sweden and Switzerland, 'we must bear our share in building up a confederation of nations so strong that in Europe at least no aggressor will dare to challenge them'.

During 1934 Churchill wrote fifty articles for newspapers and magazines and made more than twenty speeches; his views were thus put before the public on average once every five days. The defence of Britain was his main concern. On February 7 he told the Commons, 'I cannot conceive how, in the present state of Europe and our position in Europe, we can delay in establishing the principle of having an air force at least as strong as any power that can get at us,' and he went on to warn that unless Britain was in 'a proper state of security', a diplomatic crisis would arise 'within a measurable time, in the lifetime of those who are here', when threats would be made and pressure applied, and within a few hours 'the crash of bombs exploding in London and cataracts of masonry and fire and smoke will apprise us of any inadequacy which has been permitted in our aerial defences'.

Churchill advised the Government 'to begin the reorganisation of our civil factories so they can be turned over rapidly to war purposes.' Every factory in Europe, he said, was being prepared so that it could be turned over quickly to war production, in order to produce material 'for the deplorable and melancholy business of slaughter'; and he asked: 'What have we done? There is not an hour to lose.' He went on to criticise the Government for arguing that 'they have to wait for public opinion' and that the public did not wish for rearmament: 'The responsibility of His Majesty's Government is grave indeed, and there is this which makes it all the graver; it is a responsibility which they have no difficulty in discharging if they choose. The Government command overwhelming majorities in both branches of the Legislature. Nothing that they ask will be denied to them. They have only to make their proposals, and they will be supported in them. Why take so poor a view of the patriotic support which this nation gives to those who it feels are doing their duty by it?'

In reply, Baldwin commented first on Churchill's position 'of greater freedom and less responsibility'. He then told the House, 'We are trying to get an ordered armament limitation.' If the Disarmament Conference failed, the Government would feel 'that their duty is to look after the interests of this country first and quickly', but he was confident no such emergency would arise. 'I do not think we are at all bound to have a war.'

During his speech, Baldwin described Churchill's remarks as having been 'of great interest, of excellent temper and full of sound sense'. But Herbert Samuel characterised it differently, telling the House that Churchill's policy was 'Long live anarchy, and let us all go rattling down to ruin together.'

On March 4 the Government published its Defence White Paper, which began with a pledge that the Government would not allow the size of the Royal Air Force to fall below that of Germany: 'His Majesty's Government have made their primary object the attainment of air parity in first-line strength between the principal powers.' The reason given for this was 'that a race in air armaments may at all costs be avoided', and the hope was expressed, in the next sentence, that the Government desired to achieve air parity 'by means of a reduction to the British level'; that is, France and Russia would have to disarm considerably.

The 'parity pledge', despite its qualifications, led to a strong protest from the leader of the Labour Party, Clement Attlee, who declared on March 8, in the Commons, 'We deny the need for increased air arms.' For the Liberal Party, Archibald Sinclair denounced 'the folly, danger and wastefulness of this steady accumulation of armaments'. Churchill, speaking without a Party to back him, but with men of all Parties listening to him, warned that the increase was not enough, telling a packed and attentive House, 'I have not been able to convince myself that the policy which the Government have pursued has been in sufficiently direct contact with the harsh realities of the European situation.' It was not enough to shelter behind the facts of French superiority in the air. It was from the air that the new danger would come. It was therefore necessary to 'raise up for ourselves a security in the air above us which will make us as free from serious molestation as did our control of blue water through bygone centuries'. Germany was 'arming fast, and no one is going to stop her'. No one was proposing 'a preventative war' to stop her breaking the Versailles Treaty.

Churchill went on to warn, 'Everyone is well aware that those very gifted people, with their science and with their factories, with what they call their air sports, are capable of developing with great rapidity a most powerful air force for all purposes, offensive and defensive, within a very short period of time'. Germany was ruled by a 'handful of autocrats' who had become 'absolute masters of that mighty, gifted nation', in full control, 'by every means which modern apparatus renders possible', of public opinion. 'I dread the day when the means of threatening the heart of the British Empire should pass into the hands of the present rulers of Germany'. That day 'is not perhaps far distant. It is perhaps only a year, or perhaps eighteen months distant'. There was still time to take 'the necessary measures'. It was not the parity pledge that was wanted, but the achievement of parity. 'It is no good writing that first paragraph and then producing £130,000. We want the measures to achieve parity'.

Turning then to the Lord President of the Council, Stanley Baldwin, Churchill told the House: 'He has only to make up his mind what has to be done in this matter, and Parliament will vote all the supplies and all the sanctions which are necessary, if need be within forty-eight hours. There need be no talk of working up public opinion. You must not go and ask the public what they think about this. Parliament and the Cabinet have to decide, and the nation has to judge whether they have acted rightly as trustees. The Lord President has the power, and if he has the power he has also what always goes with power – he has the responsibility. Perhaps it is a more grievous and direct personal responsibility than has for many years fallen upon a single servant of the Crown. He may not have sought it, but he is to-night the captain of the gate. The nation looks to him to advise it and lead it, to guide it wisely and safely in this dangerous question, and I hope and believe that we shall not look in vain.'

In his reply Baldwin said he was 'not prepared to admit here today that the situation is hopeless', but that if Britain's efforts at disarmament failed, the government would 'see to it that in air strength and air power this country shall no longer be in a position inferior to any country within striking distance of our shores'. It was with these words that Baldwin gave his authority to the parity pledge. Three days later, on March 11, Churchill wrote to Hoare, 'No time should be lost in doubling the Air Force.' But eight days after Churchill's letter, the Cabinet rejected his suggestion, partly on the grounds that Ministers felt that there was still a possibility of European disarmament, partly because of the expense involved in air force expansion on this scale, and partly because it was thought, as the Foreign Secretary Sir John Simon explained, that 'a German menace, if developed, was more likely to be in the east and south than the west'. It was Austria, Danzig and Memel that appeared to be 'principally menaced'.

While welcoming Baldwin's air parity pledge, Churchill warned that the Government's hopes of air disarmament would be 'very dangerous indeed' if they delayed a review of Britain's defences. On March 21, in the Commons, he advocated the creation of a Ministry of Defence, to co-ordinate the supply and planning needs of the Army, Navy and Air Force under a single Minister. The Cabinet rejected his proposal, amid much ribald comment in private about the impossibility of finding a 'superman' for the task.

The Government now delighted in mocking Churchill. A development in the India debate provided more material for derision. Churchill had accused the India Office of having used 'wrongful pressure' a year earlier to tamper with evidence submitted to the Joint Select Committee. This accusation was portrayed by the Government as so absurd as to be proof of mental aberration. It was in fact well-founded; Hoare, who as Secretary of State for India was supposed to be examining evidence impartially, from all interested groups, had managed, through the intervention of Lord Derby, to persuade one group, the Manchester Chamber of Commerce, to withdraw its evidence, which was critical of certain economic aspects of the India Bill as it affected the Lancashire cotton trade, and to replace it with an innocuous submission.

Churchill was given enough details and documents to make his case that the evidence had been tampered with. But his challenge backfired; the charge seemed so improbable, and the involvement of the India Office so patently wrong, that his allegations were denounced as mere trouble-making. But when he raised the issue in the House of Commons on April 16, the corroborative detail of his charges was such that the Government was forced to set up a Committee of Privileges to examine them. Unknown even to Churchill, one piece of crucial evidence, not available to him, which would have clinched his case, was deliberately withheld from the Committee at Hoare's suggestion; that evidence was a request from one of Hoare's senior officials at the India Office that the Manchester evidence should be rewritten.

After considerable Government activity behind the scenes to ensure a favourable response, the Committee of Privileges published its report on June 9. It concluded that the Joint Select Committee had not been a judicial body 'in the ordinary sense'. This being so, the ordinary rules applying to tribunals 'engaged in administering justice' did not apply to its deliberations. There was therefore no legal basis for accusing its members of applying 'wrongful pressure'. In any case, the report added, 'what was called pressure was no more than advice or persuasion'.

Churchill was distressed at what he saw as sophistry and evasion. He was convinced that he was upholding a basic principle of Parliamentary democracy, that the Government must act honestly in its evaluation of information, and draw the correct conclusions from those facts, however embarassing or alarming they might be, rather than twist them to fit the policy. On June 13 he told the House: 'In any other country in the world, I suppose, I should be put in a concentration camp and visited by a party of overgrown schoolboys. But here one has this right, and I would regard it as most dishonourable to have invoked this procedure unless I could offer solid reasons of duty and fact as a justification for taking that course.'

Churchill was also worried about the effect on the future relationship between Ministers, and those who sought to scrutinise their actions, of the Government's claim that the Joint Select Committee was not a judicial body. 'Many here may live to regret,' he said, 'that the custodians of the rights and privileges of the House of Commons have decided to meet a temporary difficulty by taking that course,' and he quoted with approval Hugh Cecil's criticism of witnesses to the Committee of Privileges 'being marshalled as if they were an orchestra under the baton of a conductor'.

Churchill reiterated his charges in the Commons four days later, but was mocked by many for doing so; one Conservative MP called him 'an extraordinary human being, with such power that he constitutes a definite menace to the peaceful solution of the many problems with which this country is confronted at the present time,' and he added, 'The power of that menace is not decreasing; it is increasing.'

Churchill's action in raising the matter of tampering with evidence did not go unappreciated. 'I admire you quite enormously for your action in recent events,' a friend, Lady Lambton, wrote on June 26, 'and I like to think there is a bright spot in England still, which won't bow the knee to insolent might. When I met the stalwarts of the other side last week, I asked has Winston failed in his case, they said "completely". I then asked "under the same circumstances would Hoare and Derby do what they did again". They looked uncomfortable and I knew my point was gained. And so I said how can you say he failed. He has made a standard & upheld a principle which will last longer than a momentary Parliamentary success, & which makes me and all the other lovers of England say "Thank God for Winston".'

At the end of June, Churchill's cousin Sunny, his friend since boyhood days, died of cancer. In an obituary published in *The Times* on July 1, Churchill wrote: 'Sunny did not enquire too closely about the symptoms which daily struck him new blows. He took the best advice, and lived his life without unduly focusing on the future. But he knew quite well that his end was approaching, that he was, as he said, at the end of his tether. He faced this universal ordeal with dignity and simplicity, making neither too much nor too little of it. He always had the most attractive and graceful manners and that easy courtesy we have been taught by the gentlefolk of a bygone age. At a tea party, for some of those who cared about him, on the last night of his life, when strength had almost ebbed away, he was concerned with the entertainment of his guests, and that his conversation had not been wearisome to them. Then came that good gift of the gods to those in such straits, sleep from which in this world there is no awakening.'

'You are surrounded by devoted friends,' wrote Archibald Sinclair, 'but none, I know, can replace the two whom you have so recently lost.' Lord Birkenhead – F. E. Smith – had died four years earlier. Churchill was deeply saddened by their deaths. When he himself began, for the first time, to speak of being old, Lady Lambton wrote to rebuke him '*Please* don't talk of yourself as a very old man. You are letting us *all* down by doing so. To me you are still a promising lad.'

On June 30 Hitler ordered the murder of his senior rivals in the Nazi Party, as well as the killing of a former Chancellor, General Schleicher, and several prominent Catholics. 'I was deeply affected by the episode,' Churchill later recalled, 'and the whole process of German rearmament, of which there was now overwhelming evidence, seemed to me invested with a ruthless, lurid tinge.' On August 2, a month after the murders, President Hindenburg died, at the age of eighty-seven. On the following day Hitler combined the offices of Chancellor and President. That same day the German armed forces swore a personal oath of 'unconditional obedience' to Hitler as their new Commander-in-Chief.

Throughout the summer Churchill spoke of air defence; on July 7, in his constituency, he proposed that the Government first double the size of the Air Force, and then redouble it. Six days later, in the Commons, Herbert Samuel, unaware, as indeed was Churchill, that the Chief of the Air Staff had unsuccessfully urged the Cabinet to embark on precisely such an expansion, called Churchill's proposal 'rather the language of a Malay run amok than of a responsible British statesman'. In reply Churchill said that the situation was in many ways 'more dangerous' than it had been in 1914, when he and Samuel had been Cabinet colleagues. But Anthony Eden, recently appointed Lord Privy Seal, told the House: 'Where I differ, with respect, from my Right hon Friend the Member for Epping, is that he seems to conceive that in order to have an effective world consultative system nations have to be heavily armed. I do not agree.'

Eden added that 'general disarmament must continue to be the ultimate aim'. Later in the debate Attlee questioned the need for any further rearmament at all, telling the House, about Hitler, 'I think we can generally say today that his dictatorship is gradually falling down.'

Within Government circles the debate on British air weaknesses continued. On July 16, in a note for the Cabinet, Maurice Hankey pointed out that the Chief of Staff's Annual Review for 1933 had disclosed 'considerable deficiencies in our Defence Forces', due largely to the Government's policy in connection with the 'disarmament question' since 1929. On the following day, in a private letter to Baldwin, Londonderry warned that a weak air force would be neither a deterrent to aggression, nor an adequate defence. 'In the absence of proper defences,' Londonderry wrote, 'there would be nothing to stop the enemy concentrating his maximum bombing force against London and continuing to bombard it until he had achieved his aim'.

On July 18 the Cabinet accepted a plan whereby, by March 1939, Britain would have 1,465 first-line aeroplanes. There were those who believed that this was not enough; for the debate on air policy on July 30, Desmond Morton gave Churchill a note of the relative air strengths of Britain, Germany and the other main powers, as well as the Air Ministry's own estimate of Germany's aircraft production capacity. On July 30 Churchill told the Commons that 'at the present time we are the fifth or sixth air Power in the world'. At the existing rate of building, Britain would be 'worse off in 1939 relatively than we are now – and it is relativity that counts.'

Churchill went on to note that even for the existing 'tiny, timid, tentative, tardy' increase in air strength for which the Government had asked 'they are to be censured by the whole united forces of the Socialist and Liberal parties'. He wished to set out 'some broad facts' which in his view could not be contradicted, and ought to be countered by immediate British Air Force expansion on a substantial and decisive scale: 'I first assert that Germany has already, in violation of the Treaty, created a military air force which is now nearly two-thirds as strong as our present home defence air force. That is the first statement which I put before the Government for their consideration. The second is that Germany is rapidly increasing this air force, not only by large sums of money which figure in her estimates, but also by public subscriptions – very often almost forced subscriptions – which are in progress and have been in progress for some time all over Germany.'

Churchill continued: 'By the end of 1935 the German air force will be nearly equal in numbers and efficiency – and after all no one must underrate German efficiency, because there could be no more deadly mistake than that – it will be nearly equal, as I say, to our home defence air force at that date even if the Government's present proposals are carried out. The third statement is that if Germany continues this expansion and if we continue to carry out our scheme, then some time in 1936 Germany will be definitely and substantially stronger in the air than Great Britain. Fourthly, and this is the point which is causing anxiety, once they have got that lead we may never be able to overtake them.'

There were other facts which Churchill believed to be of importance. German civil aviation was three times the size of its British counterpart, and at the same time was designed in such a way as to be easily converted for military purposes. Indeed, the whole scheme of conversion 'has been prepared and organised with minute and earnest forethought'. The same was true of civil and amateur pilots; Germany had five hundred qualified glider pilots against fifty in Britain. Even these pilots had 'air sense' and could quickly be trained for military aviation. Weakness in the air, Churchill warned, 'has a very direct bearing on the foreign situation'. Only if Britain were strong could her air force, in conjunction with that of France, act as 'a deterrent' against German aggression.

As the debate proceeded, several speakers poured scorn on Churchill and his arguments. According to Herbert Samuel: 'It would seem as if he were engaged not in giving sound, sane advice to the country but as if he were engaged in a reckless game of bridge, doubling and redoubling and for terribly high stakes. All these formulas are dangerous.' A leading Socialist, Sir Stafford Cripps, remarked, 'As the Right hon Member for Epping stood in his place declaiming, one could picture him as some old baron in the Middle Ages who is laughing at the idea of the possibility of disarmament in the baronies of this country and pointing out that the only way in which he and his feudal followers could maintain their safety and their cows was by having as strong an armament as possible.'

Churchill did not allow mockery to deflect him. On August 6 he told a friend that he intended, in November, to initiate a debate on air defence by moving an amendment to the address. He would continue to assemble the facts, and during the debate would seek to 'extort more vigorous action' from the Government. 'Whether it will be too little or too late,' he added, 'is a matter upon which I am glad not to have the responsibility. I feel a deep and increasing sense of anxiety.'

In August 1934 Churchill spent three weeks in the South of France, at Maxine Elliott's Château de l'Horizon near Cannes. Maxine, an American-born actress, had been a friend of Churchill's mother. Randolph and Lindemann went with him, as did a mass of material for the third Marlborough volume, much of it collected by John Wheldon, a twenty-three-year-old Oxford graduate who had been working at Chartwell since the beginning of the year. Violet Pearman, who went with Churchill to France, took dictation each day for the new volume. Churchill also dictated to her twelve articles for the *News of the World*; they were on incidents in his life since the turn of the century.

On August 28 Churchill, Lindemann and Randolph left Cannes by car, driving to Grenoble along the recently-opened highway which followed the road along which Napoleon had returned to Paris after his escape from Elba in 1815. To Clementine, who had remained at Chartwell, Churchill wrote: 'I really must try to write a Napoleon before I die. But the work piles up ahead & I wonder whether I shall have the time & strength.' During the drive home, he and Lindemann went to see Baldwin at Aix-les-Bains, and discussed with him the need for a more active air defence policy, both in research and production. As a result of their talk Lindemann was made a member of an Air Defence Research Sub-Committee which was being set up, as part of the Committee of Imperial Defence, and where he would be able to put forward his ideas for new scientific methods of air defence.

On September 25 Churchill left Chartwell for the second time that summer, with Clementine, for a cruise in the Mediterranean on board Lord Moyne's yacht *Rosaura*. Reaching Beirut they travelled overland through Lebanon, Syria, Palestine and Transjordan, visiting the ruins of Petra, where they spent the night. Then they flew across the Sinai desert to Cairo, where Churchill spent two days painting at the Pyramids before returning by yacht from Alexandria to Naples, and from there by train to Paris. The final lap of the journey was again by air, from Paris to Croydon, only a short drive to Chartwell. His thoughts were never far from the

German air challenge; on the day after his return he wrote to the Chairman of Imperial Airways, 'I am sure we must do more to support civil aviation in view of the enormous preponderance of German machines and their convertibility for war purposes.'

While Churchill had been away, his second *Marlborough* volume was published. Among those who wrote to congratulate him was William Darling, a leading Conservative member of the Edinburgh Town Council, who had fought at Gallipoli. 'In these confused and confusing days,' he wrote on November 3, 'I doubt if you know how frequently in ordinary experience men seem to turn half expectantly to you.'

On November 16, having been helped in preparing his speech by Orme Sargent, a Foreign Office official who shared his deep fear of German intentions, Churchill broadcast about Germany. The Nazis, he said, were seeking 'the submission of races by terrorising and torturing their civil population'. Yet disarmament was still 'the shrill cry of the hour'. Peace, however, must be founded upon military preponderance. 'There is safety in numbers. If there were five or six on each side there might well be a frightful trial of strength. But if there were eight or ten on one side, and only one or two upon the other, and if the collective armed forces of one side were three or four times as large as those of the other, then there will be no war.'

Britain could not 'detach' itself from Europe. 'I am afraid that if you look intently at what is moving towards Great Britain, you will see that the only choice open is the old grim choice our forebears had to face, namely whether we shall submit or whether we shall prepare. Whether we shall submit to the will of a stronger nation or whether we shall prepare to defend our rights, our liberties and indeed our lives. If we submit, our submission should be timely. If we prepare, our preparations should not be too late. Submission will entail at the very least the passing and distribution of the British Empire and the acceptance by our people of whatever future may be in store for small countries like Norway, Sweden, Denmark, Holland, Belgium and Switzerland, within and under a Teutonic domination of Europe.'

Churchill's broadcast was heard by tens of thousands of people who would never hear his Parliamentary or public speeches. Wrote one listener, Alexander Filson Young, who in 1900 had been a newspaper correspondent with him in South Africa: 'I am simply aching for the day (which if you keep your health will come), when you will have the power to implement your convictions. When that day comes you will have a following that will astound the scaremongers and isolationists. But oh, the wasted days and years!'

24

The Moment of Truth

Throughout the autumn of 1934 Churchill had been preparing a major Parliamentary appeal for accelerated Air Force expansion. On November 25, three days before the debate, Desmond Morton sent him a three-page analysis of German air plans, facts which were equally available to the Government, for whose Intelligence service Morton worked. Churchill sent Baldwin a précis of what he intended to say during the debate, during which he intended to move an amendment critical of the government's air rearmament plans. It appeared, Churchill wrote to Lloyd George on November 24, that his amendment 'has caused much disturbance in Government circles. The facts set out in the précis cannot I think be controverted and the Cabinet have woken up to the fact that they are "caught short" in this very grave matter.'

Ministers were indeed uneasy; on November 25 Hoare told the Cabinet that it was 'most important to show the world that the Government had just as much as, and more information than Mr Churchill'. At Hoare's suggestion it was agreed that Baldwin should accuse Churchill of exaggeration. But at a further Cabinet meeting on November 26 the Air Staff urged that, in order to meet German expansion plans, the new British air programme should be accelerated, so that all the aeroplanes involved in the existing British scheme would be completed by the end of 1936, instead of 1939.

Churchill's speech of November 28 marked a climax in his campaign for a more active Government policy towards air defence. 'To urge preparation of defence,' he began, 'is not to assert the imminence of war. On the contrary, if war was imminent preparations for defence would be too late.' War was neither imminent nor inevitable, but unless Britain took immediate steps to make herself secure 'it will soon be beyond our power to do so'. In violation of the Treaty of Versailles, Germany was building up a powerful, well-equipped army, 'though little is said about it in public', with factory production geared increasingly to war material. German air rearmament posed the greatest danger. 'However calmly surveyed, the danger of an attack from the air must appear most formidable.'

He did not wish to exaggerate, Churchill said, or to accept 'the sweeping claims' being put forward by alarmists. Nevertheless, he believed, in a week or ten days' intensive bombing of London one could hardly expect 'that less than 30,000 or 40,000 people would be killed or maimed', and with the use of incendiary bombs the situation could be even worse.* As a result of 'such a dreadful act of power and terror', in which bombs could go through a series of floors 'igniting each one simultaneously', as he had been assured 'by persons who are acquainted with the science', grave panic would affect the civilian population, three or four million of whom would be 'driven out into the open country'.

Churchill warned that it was not London alone that would be at risk from aerial bombardment; Birmingham, Sheffield and 'the great manu- facturing towns' would likewise be the targets of bombing raids in the event of war. All dockyards and oil storage depots would be at risk. It was therefore essential to devise means to 'mitigate and minimise' the effects of such attacks. Merely to disperse industries would not be enough. 'The flying peril is not a peril from which one can fly. It is necessary to face it where we stand. We cannot possibly retreat. We cannot move London. We cannot move the vast population which is dependent on the estuary of the Thames.'

Churchill begged the Government not to neglect 'the scientific side of defence against aircraft attack'. He had already heard 'many suggestions' that ought to be explored 'with all the force of the Government behind the examination'. He continued, 'I hope that there will be no danger of service routine or prejudices, or anything like that, preventing new ideas from being studied, and that they will not be hampered by long delays such as we suffered in the case of the tanks and other new ideas during the Great War.'

There was another aspect to the question of defence which must not be overlooked. The 'only direct measure of defence on a great scale', Chur- chill argued, was to possess the power to inflict 'simultaneously upon the enemy' as much damage as he himself could inflict. For this reason he thought it necessary to double or even treble the money being spent on air force expansion. Complete air mastery by one power over another would lead to the 'absolute subjugation' of the weaker power, which would have

---

*In the British bombing of Hamburg in 1943, more than 42,000 German civilians were killed, and tens of thousands more injured, the majority in a single air raid lasting forty-three minutes which created an eight-hour fire-storm.

'no opportunity of recovery'. That was 'the odious new factor which has been forced upon our life in this twentieth century of Christian civilisation.'

Churchill again proposed, as he had done in May, 'that we ought to decide now to maintain at all costs in the next ten years an air force substantially stronger than that of Germany, and that it should be considered a high crime against the state, whatever Government is in power, if that force is allowed to fall substantially below, even for a month, the potential force which may be possessed by that country abroad.'

Germany's illegal air force was 'rapidly approaching equality with our own'; that, Churchill pointed out, was the known fact, 'but beyond the known there is also the unknown. We hear from all sides of an air development in Germany far in excess of anything which I have stated today. As to that all I would say is "Beware!" Germany is a country fertile in military surprises.' Churchill then spoke of the crucial element of productive capacity. It sounded 'absurd to talk about 10,000 aeroplanes,' he said, 'but, after all, the resources of mass production are very great, and I remember when the War came to an end the organisation over which I presided at the Ministry of Munitions was actually making aeroplanes at the rate of 24,000 a year, and planning a very much larger programme for 1919. Of course, such numbers of aeroplanes could never be placed in the air at any one moment, nor a tenth of them, but the figures give one an idea of the scale to which manufacture might easily rise if long preparations have been made beforehand and a great programme of production is launched.'

Churchill reminded the House that during the Air debate in March, Baldwin had said, 'If you are not satisfied, you can go to a Division.' But what was the point, Churchill asked, in dividing the House and calling for votes. 'You might walk a majority round and round these lobbies for a year and not alter the facts by which we are confronted.' Although the Government had announced in July that forty-two new squadrons would be added to the Air Force by 1939, the programme was such, Churchill pointed out, that only fifty new machines would be in full service by March 1936. Despite the details of rapidly growing German air strength which had emerged since July, this programme had not been accelerated. Were this 'dilatory process' to continue even for only a few months, it would deprive Britain of the power 'ever to overtake the German air effort'.

When Churchill sat down, Frances Stevenson noted, he had 'almost an ovation'. In his reply, Baldwin told the House that he had not 'given up hope either for the limitation or for the restriction of some kind of arms'. But it was 'extraordinarily difficult' to give accurate figures of German air strength; it was 'a dark continent' from that point of view, but it was 'not the case' that the German Air Force was 'rapidly approaching equality with us'. The German air strength was in fact 'not 50 per cent' of the British. By the end of 1935 Britain would still have 'a margin of nearly 50 per cent' in Europe. There was therefore 'no ground at this moment for undue alarm and still less for panic. There is no immediate menace confronting us or anyone in Europe at this moment – no actual emergency.'

Baldwin then answered Churchill in words that the Cabinet had agreed he should use: 'I cannot look further forward than the next two years. My right hon friend speaks of what may happen in 1937. Such investigations as I have been able to make lead me to believe that his figures are considerably exaggerated.' Baldwin then repeated the parity pledge, telling the House: 'His Majesty's Government are determined in no condition to accept any position of inferiority with regard to what air force may be raised in Germany in the future.'

Accepting Baldwin's pledge at its face value, Churchill withdrew his amendment. The House then divided on the Labour amendment criticising the existing rearmament plans as excessive; this was defeated by 276 votes to 35. On November 29 Morton wrote to Churchill: 'Your magnificent exposition of the situation last night has undoubtedly gone far to achieve the object in view. At any rate we have a declaration from SB that this Government is pledged not to allow the strength of the British Air Force to fall below that of Germany.' But Morton added that the actual figures available to Baldwin showed that he already knew that Britain had lost its fifty per cent superiority. Commenting on the debate in a letter to the Viceroy, Hoare admitted that if the Cabinet had decided to 'let the Departmental Ministers answer him upon technical service questions', Churchill 'would have scored heavily'.

On the night of November 29 Randolph gave his father a dinner dance at the Ritz to celebrate his sixtieth birthday. Churchill's energies were indefatigable; on December 12, in an attempt to get the Government to agree to more time to debate the India Bill on the grounds that self-government 'only means liberty for one set of Indians to exploit another', he was supported by seventy-five Conservative MPs. The Government, however, obtained a majority of 283. In January 1935 he made one last effort to moderate the India Bill, proposing to limit Indian autonomy, for some years to come, to the Provincial Assemblies, on the lines of the Simon Report. But neither a broadcast on 29 January 1935, nor his support for his son's anti-India Bill candidacy at a by-election, were to any avail. Indeed, when Randolph, by splitting the Conservative vote, enabled the Labour Party candidate to win the seat, there was fierce anger in Conservative newspapers at the 'wrecking activities', not of one but now of two Churchills.

On February 11, at the close of the second reading of the India Bill, Churchill warned that to give India self-government at the centre would enable a small group of politically-motivated men to trample on the rights of millions of inarticulate and ill-represented minorities. Those MPs who would speak against the Bill, he said, hoped 'to kill the idea that the British in India are aliens moving out of the country as soon as they have been able to set up any kind of governing organism to take their place'. They wished to establish the idea that the British were in India 'forever', as 'honoured partners with our Indian fellow-subjects whom we invite in all faithfulness to join with us in the highest functions of Government and administration for their lasting benefit and for our own'.

There were cheers at the end of Churchill's speech. But after Baldwin had promised that 'the rule of law and order' which Britain had established would 'go on' under Indian supervision, the Bill passed its second reading by 404 votes to 133. Among those voting against the Government were 84 Conservatives.

On February 25, while the India Bill was still under scrutiny in Committee, the Indian Princes, meeting in Bombay, passed a resolution expressing strong dissatisfaction with the Federal scheme. This caused commotion in Whitehall; the Government had relied on the Princes' co-operation for the Bill to have a smooth passage. On February 26, encouraged by the Princes' decision, Churchill argued that it had become useless to proceed with the Bill; but Hoare insisted that the Princes must accept the scheme as it stood. The issue was put to the vote and Churchill's motion defeated by 283 to 89. This was the largest opposition he and the India Defence League were able to muster in the Commons.

'The India Bill is now in Committee and I am in the House all day long two or three days a week speaking three or four times a day,' Churchill wrote to Clementine on March 2. 'I have been making short speeches of five, ten and fifteen minutes, sometimes half an hour, always without notes, and I have I think got the House fairly subordinate. I am acquiring a freedom and facility I never before possessed, and I seem to be able to hold my own and indeed knock the Government about to almost any extent. The Government supporters are cowed, resentful and sullen. They keep 250 waiting about in the libraries and smoking rooms to vote us down on every amendment, and we have a fighting force of about fifty which holds together with increasing loyalty and conviction. I have led the opposition with considerable success so far as the debates are concerned. The divisions go the other way, but we mock at them for being lackeys and slaves.'

Churchill then told Clementine of his lack of confidence in the Government itself, and in particular of his despair at the behaviour of its leaders:

'The Government stock is very low. They are like a great iceberg which has drifted into warm seas and whose base is being swiftly melted away, so that it must topple over. They are a really bad government in spite of their able members. The reason is there is no head and commanding mind ranging over the whole field of public affairs. You cannot run the British Cabinet system without an effective Prime Minister. The wretched Ramsay is almost a mental case – "he'd be far better off in a Home". Baldwin is crafty, patient and also amazingly lazy, sterile and inefficient where public business is concerned. Almost wherever they put their foot they blunder. Cabinet Ministers can only hold a meeting in any part of the country with elaborate police arrangements and party caucus arrangements to secure them an uninterrupted hearing. It is quite certain that things cannot last. Lloyd George of course would like to come in and join them and reconstitute a kind of War Cabinet Government, in which I daresay I should be offered a place. But I am very disinclined to associate myself with any administration this side of a General Election.'

When the India Bill finally passed, Churchill was visited at Chartwell by G.D. Birla, one of Gandhi's close friends, who wrote to the Mahatma about Churchill's interest and friendliness. 'Tell Mr Gandhi to use the powers that are offered and make the thing a success,' was Churchill's message. He had 'all along felt that there were fifty Indias' and that only Britain was able to hold the balance between them, at least for a long time to come, and he added, with his usual magnanimity, 'But you have got the thing now; make it a success and if you do I will advocate your getting much more.'

On March 4 the Government published a new Defence White Paper, in which it admitted 'serious deficiencies' in the three Defence services. Defence expenditure was to be increased by £10,000,000. Four days later, in a letter to Clementine, Churchill wrote that the Government, 'tardily, timidly and inadequately have at last woken up to the rapidly increasing German peril'. He added: 'The German situation is increasingly sombre. Owing to the Government having said that their increase of ten million in armaments is due to Germany rearming, Hitler flew into a violent rage and refused to receive Simon, who was about to visit him in Berlin. Hitler alleged he had a cold but this was an obvious pretext. This gesture of spurning the British Foreign Secretary from the gates of Berlin is a significant measure of the conviction which Hitler has of the strength of the German Air Force and Army.'

Churchill added: 'Owing to the severity of their counter-espionage (you saw they beheaded two women with mediaeval gruesomeness last week) it is very difficult to know exactly what they have prepared, but that danger

gathers apace is indisputable. All the frightened nations are at last beginning to huddle together. We are sending Anthony Eden to Moscow and I
cannot disapprove. The Russians, like the French and ourselves, want to
be let alone and the nations who want to be let alone to live in peace must
join together for mutual security. There is safety in numbers. There is only
safety in numbers. If the Great War were resumed – for that is what it
would mean in two or three years' time or even earlier – it will be the end
of the world. How I hope and pray we may be spared such senseless
horrors.'

On March 16 Hitler announced the reintroduction of compulsory
military service throughout Germany. As a result of this decision, the
permitted army of 300,000 could be doubled or even trebled without
difficulty. Indeed, Hitler declared, he already had 500,000 men under
arms. On March 19, during the Air debate in the House of Commons,
Philip Sassoon announced a further increase of just over forty squadrons
in the next four years. He also declared, 'A great many inaccurate figures
have been bandied about and an unduly black picture has been painted of
our weakness in the air.' Nevertheless, he added, 'our numerical weakness
is serious and cannot be allowed to continue'.

Of Baldwin's pledge of November 1934, Sassoon stated: 'We thought
we might have at the end of this year, as the Lord President said, a 50 per
cent superiority over Germany. From that point of view the situation has
deteriorated. There has been a great acceleration, as far as we know, in
the manufacture of aircraft in Germany, but still, in spite of that, at the
end of this year we shall have a margin, though I do not say a margin of
50 per cent.'

During the debate, Churchill again raised the question of the relative
air strength of Britain and Germany. Baldwin had stated three and a half
months earlier that Germany's 'real strength' in the air was less than 50
per cent of Britain's. This statement, Churchill pointed out, was now
admitted to have been untrue; Baldwin had been 'misled' in the figures he
had given to the House. The Government's present figures showed the
two Air Forces 'virtually on an equality, neck and neck'. Churchill expressed his grave concern at these admissions, telling the House: 'I am
certain that Germany's preparations are infinitely more far-reaching than
our own. So that you have not only equality at the moment, but the great
output which I have described, and you have behind that this enormous
power to turn over, on the outbreak of war, the whole force of German
industry.'

Churchill was afraid that the time had already passed when relatively
easy steps could have been taken to give Britain a secure margin of air
superiority: 'If the necessary preparations had been made two years ago

when the danger was clear and apparent, the last year would have seen a substantial advance, and this year would have seen a very great advance. Even at this time last year, if a resolve had been taken, as I urged, to double and redouble the British Air Force as soon as possible – Sir Herbert Samuel described me as a Malay run amok because I made such a suggestion – very much better results would have been yielded in 1935, and we should not find ourselves in our present extremely dangerous position.'

Commenting on Sassoon's earlier statement that 151 aircraft would be added to the British front line during the coming year, Churchill pointed out that the Germans were adding at least 100 or 150 a month, machines which 'are being turned into squadrons for which long trained, ardent personnel are already assembled', and aerodromes prepared. 'Therefore, at the end of this year, when we were to have had a 50 per cent superiority over Germany, they will be at least, between three and four times as strong as we.' 'Britain', he added, had 'lost air parity already both in the number of machines and in their quality'. He continued: 'Everyone sees now that we have entered a period of peril. From being the least vulnerable of all nations we have, through developments in the air, become the most vulnerable, and yet, even now, we are not taking the measures which would be in true proportion to our needs.'

Following Churchill's speech a Labour MP, William Cove, spoke scathingly of 'the scaremongering speech of the rt hon Member for Epping who endeavoured to make our flesh creep'. But on March 25, within a week of the Air debate, Hitler told Sir John Simon, who had at last been received in Berlin, and Anthony Eden, that Germany 'had reached parity with Great Britain' as far as their respective Air Forces were concerned. Churchill wrote on the following day to Clementine: 'The political sensation of course is the statement by Hitler that his Air Force is already as strong as ours. This completely stultifies everything that Baldwin has said and incidentally vindicates all the assertions that I have made. I expect in fact he is really much stronger than we are. Certainly they will soon be at least two times greater than we are so that Baldwin's terms that we should not be less than any other country are going to be falsified. Fancy if our Liberal Government had let the country down in this way before the Great War! I hope to press this matter hard in the next month and a good many of those who have opposed me on India now promise support on this.'

Churchill now received help from an unexpected quarter; on April 7 the head of the Central Department at the Foreign Office, Ralph Wigram, came to Chartwell with information showing that the German aircraft factories 'are already practically organised on an emergency war-time footing'. Wigram had been helped in compiling this information by a junior member of his Department, Michael Creswell, who shared his concerns. A week after his visit to Chartwell, Wigram sent Churchill the Government's own most recent, and secret, figures, which showed that the minimum German first-line air strength had reached 800 aircraft, as against Britain's 453. When he had first seen these figures, Wigram had noted in an internal minute, 'These are grave and terrible facts for those who are charged with the defence of this country.'

Churchill later wrote of Wigram: 'He was a charming and fearless man, and his convictions, based upon profound knowledge and study, dominated his being. He saw as clearly as I did, but with more certain information, the awful peril which was closing in upon us. This drew us together. Often we met at his little house in North Street, and he and Mrs Wigram came to stay with us at Chartwell. Like other officials of high rank, he spoke to me with complete confidence.'

On April 13 Churchill wrote to Clementine: 'The only great thing that has happened has been that Germany is now the greatest armed power in Europe. But I think the Allies are all banking up against her, and then I hope she will be kept in her place and not attempt to plunge into a terrible conflict.' He added: 'My statements about the air last November are being proved true, and Baldwin's contradictions are completely falsified. There is no doubt that the Germans are already substantially superior to us in the air, and that they are manufacturing at such a rate that we cannot catch them up. How discreditable for the Government to have been misled, and to have misled Parliament upon a matter involving the safety of the country.'

On May 2, France and the Soviet Union signed a pact of mutual co-operation. It seemed that Churchill's vision of a union of 'the nations who want to be let alone' was coming to pass. 'Never must we despair,' he told the Commons that day, 'never must we give in, but we must face facts and draw true conclusions from them.' On the following day the *Daily Express* apologised to Churchill for having in the past 'ignored' his warnings of German air strength; an apology put in front of its 1,857,939 readers. Then, on May 22, during a Defence debate in the Commons, Baldwin admitted he had been 'completely wrong' the previous November in his estimate of future German air strength.

Churchill's claims of the pace and scale of German air construction, hitherto mocked as alarmist, were vindicated. He at once proposed a Secret Session of the House, as in 1917, for an unfettered discussion of German air strength and British air policy, but Baldwin refused. 'Speech successful,' Churchill telegraphed to Randolph after the debate, 'but Government escaped as usual.' Nine days later, on May 31, he drew the attention of the House of Commons to the Nazi-type movement which had been created among the German-speaking inhabitants of the Sudeten mountain region of Czechoslovakia. As a result of Germany's growing power, he warned, Austria, Hungary, Bulgaria and even Yugoslavia were beginning to look with admiration at Germany. When the debate was over Morton wrote to Churchill, 'You alone seem to have galvanised the House.'

On June 5 Ramsay MacDonald presided over his last Cabinet; he was ill and unable to continue in office. Baldwin succeeded him as Prime Minister; Hoare became Foreign Secretary; Neville Chamberlain remained at the Exchequer.

Churchill's friends and supporters were disappointed that no place had been found for him in the new Baldwin administration. 'I have been hoping that you were going to be Minister of Defence,' wrote his former flying-instructor, Spenser Grey. 'I really thought they were going to have one & could see no one else with the necessary experience.' On the day the new Cabinet was announced, Churchill spoke in the Commons about his dissatisfaction at the slow pace of research into air defence. The recently established Government Air Defence Research Sub-Committee of the Committee of Imperial Defence had only met twice in the past three months. 'Really the whole story is another slow-motion picture.'

On July 11, in his first speech as Foreign Secretary, Samuel Hoare made an extraordinary reference to Churchill when he spoke of those who 'seem to take a morbid delight in alarms and excursions, in a psychology, shall I say, of fear, perhaps even of brutality', and went on, in scathing tone: 'Only yesterday I heard of a small child, a child of one of my friends, who was found surrounded by a number of air balloons, and her nurse said to her, "Why is it that you have so many air balloons?" The child answered, "I like to make myself afraid by popping." That may be a harmless habit in the case of a child, but it is a dangerous habit in the case of the many alarm-mongers and scaremongers who now seem to take this delight in creating crises, and, if there be crises, in making the crises worse than they otherwise would be.'

Two weeks after Hoare's remarks, Baldwin invited Churchill to become, like Lindemann, a member of the Air Defence Research Sub-Committee. Churchill accepted; he attended his first meeting on July 25. There, he learned of the success, on the previous day, of a series of experiments for locating enemy aircraft by radio-location, later known as radar.

The dangers of war seemed to grow with every passing month. In August, Mussolini threatened to invade Abyssinia. In a private talk with Churchill, Hoare found him 'deeply incensed' at the Italian action, and pressing for the immediate reinforcement of Britain's Mediterranean Fleet. Churchill argued that collective action was needed against Italy, including economic sanctions. The League of Nations should be called upon to act. The Navy should be made ready for whatever action might be necessary. 'Where are the fleets?' he asked Hoare. 'Are they in good order? Are they adequate?

Are they capable of rapid and complete concentration? Are they safe? Have they been formally warned to take precautions?'

That September Churchill received words of encouragement from the editor of the *Observer*, J.L. Garvin: 'On India you couldn't have more than 1/4 of the Unionist party with you. On Defence you can have 3/4 of it at least with you for good, and change all – by stating the case as you alone can state it. I see no other hope.'

Churchill was on holiday in the South of France, painting at Maxine Elliott's château near Cannes when Garvin's letter reached him. European affairs were much on his mind; another guest at the château, Vincent Sheean, later recalled Churchill's hope that if the League of Nations could make sanctions against Mussolini's Italy work '& *stop* the Abyssinian subjugation, we should all be stronger and safer for many a long day'. Sheean noted: 'He had a distinction which he tried to bring out in every talk about Ethiopia just then: it seemed to him very important. "It's not the *thing* we object to", he would say, "it's the *kind* of thing". I had not then succumbed as much to his genial charm as I did later, and I could not quite accept this. I mentioned the Red Sea, the route to India, the importance of Aden. Mr Churchill brushed all that aside: "We don't need to worry about the Italians", he said. "It isn't that at all. It isn't the thing. It's the *kind* of thing." '

When a French woman present protested that every nation including Britain had conquered territory as Italy now threatened to do, Churchill remarked with a benevolent smile across the luncheon table, 'Ah, but you see, all that belongs to the unregenerate past, is locked away in the limbo of the old, the wicked days.' The world had progressed. The aim of the League of Nations was 'to make it impossible for nations nowadays to infringe upon each other's rights'. In trying to conquer Abyssinia, 'Mussolini is making a most dangerous and foolhardy attack upon the whole established structure, and the results of such an attack are quite incalculable. Who is to say what will come of it in a year, or two, or three? With Germany arming at breakneck speed, England lost in a pacifist dream, France corrupt and torn by dissension, America remote and indifferent – Madame, my dear lady, do you not tremble for your children?'

On his return to Chartwell at the end of September, Churchill began to correspond with Admiral Chatfield, the First Sea Lord, hoping that a show of British naval strength in the Mediterranean might deter Mussolini. In London he addressed Conservative businessmen on the need to warn Italy against aggression in Abyssinia. He also spoke of the growth of German rearmament, and of Britain's failure to take measures to match it. 'There ought to be a few members of the House of Commons,' he said, 'who are in a sufficiently independent position to confront both Ministers and electors with unpalatable truths. We do not wish our ancient freedom and the decent tolerant civilisation we have preserved in this island to hang upon a rotten thread.'

This speech was widely reported; after it the poet Osbert Sitwell, one of Churchill's public critics at the time of the anti-Bolshevik intervention in 1919, wrote to apologise 'for my stupidity in the past' and to say that he spoke 'for numberless people'. Two days later Churchill saw the Italian Ambassador, Count Grandi, whom he warned about the dangers of invading Abyssinia; from the Foreign Office, Sir Robert Vansittart thanked him for speaking as he had. At dinner with Vansittart and Alfred Duff Cooper, the Financial Secretary to the Treasury, Churchill expressed his willingness to go with them both to Rome, to try to persuade Mussolini not to launch his attack. 'Nothing came of this,' he later wrote, 'and I doubt very much whether we could have enlightened him. He was convinced that Britain was rotten to the core.'

Mussolini launched his attack on Abyssinia on October 4. That day, at the Conservative Party Conference in Bournemouth, Churchill moved an amendment urging the Government to organise British industry 'for speedy conversion to defence purposes' and to make a 'renewed effort' to establish air parity with Germany. His amendment was carried unanimously. Eight days later he offered his services to Conservative Central Office during the General Election which had been called for mid-November. His offer was accepted. In the Commons he continued to press for increased armaments and for the development of a machine-tool industry capable of greater expansion. The Italian attack on Abyssinia was 'a very small matter', he said, compared with the German danger. There could be no anxieties 'comparable to the anxiety caused by German rearmament. We cannot afford to see Nazidom in all its present phase of cruelty and intolerance, with all its hatreds and its gleaming weapons, paramount in Europe.'

The German Government protested against Churchill's speech, as it did about an article on Hitler which he published in the *Strand* magazine, in which he wrote of how, 'side by side with training grounds of the new armies and the great aerodromes, the concentration camps pock-mark the German soil. In these, thousands of Germans are coerced and cowed into submission to the irresistible power of the Totalitarian State'. He also wrote of the 'brutal vigour' of the persecution of the Jews. 'No past services, no proved patriotism, even wounds sustained in war, could procure immunity for persons whose only crime was that their parents had brought them into the world.' Even the 'wretched Jewish children' were persecuted in the national schools. The world still hoped that the worst might be over, 'and that we may yet live to see Hitler a gentler figure in a happier age'. Yet even as Hitler spoke words of reassurance from Berlin, 'the great wheels revolve; the rifles, the cannon, the tanks, the shot and shell, the air-bombs, the poison-gas cylinders, the aeroplanes, the submarines, and now the beginnings of a fleet, flow in ever-broadening streams from the already largely war-mobilised arsenals and factories of Germany.'

Parliament was dissolved on October 25 and the General Election set for November 14. Many believed that after the election Baldwin would bring Churchill into the Cabinet. From the British Naval Attaché in Berlin, Captain Gerald Muirhead-Gould, came the message: 'The Germans fear, and I hope, you *will* be 1st Lord – or Minister of Defence! Please don't give me away.' On October 31 the British Ambassador to Berlin, Sir Eric Phipps, reported that Hitler himself had expressed concern that Churchill might become 'Minister of the British Navy'.

On October 31, as the election campaign gathered momentum, Baldwin declared, 'I give you my word there will be no great armaments.' Churchill, by contrast, in urging greater rearmament, wrote in the *Daily Mail* on November 12, 'I do not feel that people realise at all how near and how grave are the dangers of a world explosion.' Ralph Wigram, his friend in the Foreign Office, had just sent him copies of the secret despatches from the British Ambassador in Berlin, which the Cabinet also saw, forecasting Hitler's future territorial demands.

The General Election was an overwhelming victory for the Conservatives, who secured 432 seats as against 151 for Labour, and a mere 21 for the Liberals. Randolph was defeated. Churchill, who held his own seat with an increased majority, watched the first results on a screen set up in the Albert Hall. To see the rest of the results come in, he went to Stornoway House, Beaverbrook's house in St James's, where, to his consternation, Beaverbrook greeted him with the words: 'Well, you're finished now. Baldwin has so good a majority that he will be able to do without you.'

Churchill had hoped his breach with Baldwin was over, and that the acceptance of his help during the election had been a signal of political reconciliation. For six days he waited at Chartwell for a telephone call from the Prime Minister. None came; when the first list of Ministers was published, Churchill's name was not on it. 'This was to me a pang and, in a way, an insult,' he later wrote. 'There was much mockery in the press. I do not pretend that, thirsting to get on the move, I was not distressed.' Baldwin's entourage were much pleased, Thomas Jones praising his master for having 'kept clear of Winston's enthusiasm for ships and guns'. In a letter to Davidson, Baldwin himself wrote: 'I feel we should not give him a post at this stage. Anything he undertakes he puts his heart and soul into. If there is going to be war – and no one can say that there is not – we must keep him fresh to be our war Prime Minister.'

Bruised and frustrated, Churchill decided on a long working and painting holiday, first in Majorca and then in Morocco. He postponed his departure for three days in order to attend a meeting of the Air Defence Research Sub-Committee, at which he spoke vehemently, and with copious detail, about Britain's inferiority in the air and in anti-aircraft preparations. Then, on December 10, he and Clementine left London by air for Paris. He was sixty-one years old. It was now five and a half years since he had been a Cabinet Minister.

Churchill and Clementine travelled by train from Paris to Barcelona. There, having been joined by Lindemann, they took the boat to Majorca. As they travelled, a startling diplomatic event took place in Paris; Samuel Hoare reached a provisional agreement with the French Foreign Minister, Pierre Laval, whereby Mussolini would be allowed to retain his conquests in Abyssinia, almost 20 per cent of Abyssinian territory, in return for halting the war which his troops were finding it easier and easier to win. At a stroke, the League of Nations had been flouted, collective security abandoned, and sanctions spurned. So great was public indignation in Britain that on December 18, after ten days of outcry, the British Cabinet renounced the 'Hoare-Laval Pact'. Hoare resigned and was succeeded as Foreign Secretary by Eden.

Clementine returned to England to spend Christmas at Blenheim; Churchill spent the festive season at Tangier. 'Eden's appointment does not inspire me with confidence,' he wrote to Clementine on December 26. 'I expect the greatness of his office will find him out.' Churchill ended his letter, 'Your wandering, sun-seeking, rotten, disconsolate W.'

Hoping that some Cabinet post might still be found for him, Churchill also wrote that day to Randolph, who was now a successful journalist: 'It would in my belief be very injurious to me at this juncture if you publish articles attacking the motives & characters of Ministers, especially Baldwin & Eden.' If he were to ignore this advice, 'I shall not be able to feel confidence in your loyalty & affection for me'.

Churchill travelled on to Marrakech, where, on December 30, he spent several hours in the company of an even more disconsolate Lloyd George, who had been out of public office for thirteen years. 'What a fool Baldwin is, with this terrible situation on his hands, not to gather his resources & experience to the public service,' Churchill wrote to Clementine that day. In this letter he also wrote with anguish of 'our defences neglected, our Government less capable a machine for conducting affairs than I have ever seen', and he added, 'The Baldwin-MacDonald regime has hit this country very hard indeed, and may well be the end of its glories.'

Reflecting on the confident spread of dictatorship and the feeble response of the democracies, Churchill wrote to Clementine from Marrakech on 8 January 1936, 'The world seems to be divided between the confident nations who behave harshly, and the nations who have lost confidence in themselves and behave fatuously.' He still hoped that there might be a chance of entering the Cabinet, and was angered when Randolph finally decided to stand at a by-election in Scotland, at Ross and Cromarty, against Ramsay MacDonald's son Malcolm, who was already Secretary of State for Dominion Affairs in Baldwin's Cabinet.

Randolph had decided to stand entirely on his own initiative, but Churchill was worried, he told Clementine, that Baldwin might regard the contest 'as a definite declaration of war by me'. He added, 'I was reading what Marlborough wrote in 1708 – "As I think most things are settled by destiny, when one has done one's best, the only thing is to await the result with patience." '

The by-election was held on February 10. Malcolm MacDonald was elected, and Randolph came third after the Labour candidate. The whole episode, wrote the *Edinburgh Evening News*, 'seems to be regarded as another nail in the political coffin of Mr Winston Churchill, either as a candidate for the Admiralty or Cabinet Minister charged with the Co-ordination of Defence services'.

The Government had become uneasy at Churchill's knowledge of British and German air strengths, and at the accuracy of his forecasts. On January 30 Hankey wrote to him to ask 'whether you are prepared to communicate in confidence any special intelligence on which your information is based'. Churchill replied that the figures he had given were 'the fruits of my judgment' and went on to remind Hankey of November 1934, 'when I drew attention to the secret growth of the German military air force, and made certain statements about its strength relative to our own. These statements were disputed by Mr Baldwin, who I presume after full consideration of all the Intelligence information at the disposal of the Air Ministry, put forward other statements. But only a few months later in the spring Mr Baldwin was forced to confess in the House of Commons that the Government with their official information were wrong, adding "we were all in it". Here then was a case in which an independent outside judgment was proved to be nearer the truth than the estimate from the Government based on all their secret sources.'

'For these reasons,' Churchill added, 'I hope you will not brush aside my minimum estimates, although they have no other foundations than my own judgment.' Unknown to Churchill, the new Secretary of State for Air, Lord Swinton, shared his anxiety that the Royal Air Force was falling behind Germany, pointing out to the Cabinet on February 10 the disadvantages of the existing air programme, and, two weeks later, proposed a new programme, whereby there would be 1,750 first-line aircraft by the year 1939. The Cabinet accepted this.

On February 10 Churchill received from Morton details of German arms production which Morton's own Intelligence unit had prepared. It was clear that Germany had decided to maintain a very high rate of arms production. Yet, unknown to Churchill, four days earlier the Cabinet had rejected the setting up of a Shadow Armaments Industry on the grounds that any interference with normal trade would 'adversely affect the prosperity of the country' and would 'attract Parliamentary criticism'. That month, however, there was a growing demand in Parliament and the newspapers for a Minister of Defence. A motion to this effect was to be put before the Commons on February 14. Three days earlier, the First Commissioner of Works, William Ormsby-Gore, wrote to Baldwin, 'I hope you will not under-rate the very strong feeling there is among many well-informed people that some drastic improvement of the existing organisation is needed.'

After the debate of February 14 Hankey wrote to the head of the Treasury, Sir Warren Fisher, 'I am afraid we have got to make some concession for a Minister of Defence. What I want is something that will work and not upset the psychology of the whole machine.' Hankey and Fisher, the two most senior civil servants, were determined that the new Minister should not be a disruptive influence. 'The Minister should be a disinterested type of man,' Fisher wrote to Neville Chamberlain on February 15, 'with no axe to grind or desire to make a place for himself.' Fisher suggested that Lord Halifax, the former Lord Irwin, would fit the position. Austen Chamberlain, however, wrote to his sister on February 15: 'In my view there is only one man who by his studies & his special abilities & aptitudes is marked out for it, & that man is Winston Churchill! I don't suppose that SB will offer it to him & I don't think that Neville would wish to have him back, but they are both wrong. He is the right man for that post, & these are such dangerous times, that consideration ought to be decisive.'

On February 23 Hoare saw Baldwin. After the meeting he explained to Neville Chamberlain that Baldwin had no intention of making Churchill Minister of Defence. 'On no account,' Hoare explained, 'would he contemplate the possibility of Winston in the Cabinet for several obvious reasons, but chiefly for the risk that would be involved by having him in the Cabinet when the question of his (SB's) successor became imminent.' Baldwin 'evidently desires above all things to avoid bringing me in,' Churchill wrote to Clementine. 'This I must now recognise.' She replied sympathetically, 'My darling, Baldwin must be mad not to ask you to help him.'

On February 29, as the discussion intensified, the magazine *Cavalcade* reported that even 'left-wing Conservatives, who were hostile to Winston over the India question, now take the line that if there must be a Defence Minister Winston Churchill is the man'. Two prominent Conservative back-benchers, Harold Macmillan and Lord Castlereagh, had 'whispered to the Whips that Winston Churchill is the man'.

On March 3 Churchill wrote to Clementine that Neville Chamberlain had recently told a mutual friend, 'Of course if it is a question of military efficiency, Winston is no doubt the man.' Chamberlain himself would not take the post, Churchill explained to her, 'because he sees the PM'ship not far off. Every other possible alternative is being considered & blown upon.' Some candidates were judged unsuitable because they were peers, Hoare because of continuing public hostility to the Hoare-Laval Pact, Kingsley Wood because he hoped to be Chancellor of the Exchequer '& anyhow does not know a Lieutenant-General from a Whitehead torpedo', Sir Robert Horne because he did not wish to give up a lucrative City directorship. 'So at the end it may all come back to your poor –' and here Churchill drew a small pig. He continued: 'I do not mean to break my heart whatever happens. Destiny plays her part. If I get it, I will work faithfully before God & man for *Peace*, & not allow pride or excitement to sway my spirit. If I am not wanted, we have many things to make us happy.'

The Ministry of Defence, Churchill added, 'would be the heaviest burden yet. They are *terribly* behindhand.' On March 3, before any decision had been reached about a Ministry of Defence, the British Government published its Defence White Paper, expanding the Army, Navy and Air Force. But Swinton, in commenting on the Air Ministry's estimate of German air production reaching 1,500 by April 1937 and 2,000 at some later date, minuted on March 4: 'I feel bound to express a personal anxiety which I feel with regard to estimates of this nature, however carefully prepared. German capacity to produce aeroplanes is enormous.'

On March 7 Hitler sent his troops into the Rhineland, the German sovereign territory which had been demilitarised by the victorious Allies in 1919. Two days later, speaking for the Labour Party, Attlee opposed the Government's new defence proposals on the grounds that they were too bellicose. Churchill, in supporting the proposals in the Commons on March 10, set out other measures he felt were needed; industry should be prepared in such a way that it could be turned from peace to war production 'on the pressing of a button'; a skeleton Ministry of Munitions should be created.

Referring to the decision, announced in a sentence in the White Paper, that it was 'not possible' to recondition the Territorial Army, Churchill asked: 'Do you want anything other than this tell-tale sentence to prove that industry has not been organised? And what a discouragement to the Territorial Force, which we must exert ourselves in every way to recruit from the gallant and patriotic youth of this country, who have taken this burden on themselves, when they see that a long interval must elapse, even in times like this, before it will be possible to recondition them.'

During his speech Churchill praised the Defence White Paper as a step, albeit belated, in the right direction, and approved Neville Chamberlain's decision to set up a special financial Committee to make sure that the money was spent wisely. 'When things are left so late as this,' he said, 'no high economy is possible. That is part of the price nations pay for being caught short. All the more must every effort be made to prevent actual waste.' Even under the increased armaments of the new White Paper, Britain was not truly safe because she lacked 'the expansive power of the industrial plant'.

Churchill added: 'There is a general impression that we are overhauling Germany now. We started late but we are making up for lost time, and every month our relative position will improve. That is a delusion. The contrary is true. All this year and probably for many months next year Germany will be outstripping us more and more. Even if our new programmes are punctually executed, we shall be relatively much worse off at the end of this year than we are now, in spite of our utmost exertions. The explanation of this grievous fact lies in the past.'

British diplomacy was already adversely affected by Britain's military weakness; on March 12, at a meeting of the Commons Foreign Affairs Committee, Churchill urged a co-ordinated plan under the League of Nations to help France challenge the German action in the Rhineland. He was answered by Hoare, who said that the nations who might participate in such a plan 'were totally unprepared from a military point of view'. That, noted one observer, 'definitely sobered them down'. On the following day, in an article in the *Evening Standard*, Churchill argued that the only antidote to the weakness of individual states was to re-establish 'a reign of law' in Europe. Only by such action might it be possible to stop 'the horrible, dull, remorseless drift to war in 1937 or 1938'. There was only one way to preserve peace: this was 'the assembly of overwhelming force, moral and physical, in support of international law'.

On March 14 the Government at last announced the establishment of the new Cabinet post, Minister for Co-ordination of Defence. The man chosen was the Attorney-General, Sir Thomas Inskip; Lindemann called the appointment 'the most cynical thing that has been done since Caligula appointed his horse as consul'. Sir William Goodenough, a retired Admiral, wrote to Churchill: 'That, after all the labour, this great mountain should give birth to such a small mouse as announced this morning is deeply disappointing,' and he added, 'I had – we all had – hoped for someone who would carry a torch to lead & light us on our way. The problem is essentially one to be solved by executive action. DAMN.'

In his diary, Chamberlain commented that the militarisation of the Rhineland had 'afforded an excellent reason for discarding both Winston and Sam, since both had European reputations which might make it dangerous to add them to the Cabinet at a critical moment. Inskip would create no jealousies. He would excite no enthusiasm but he would involve us in no fresh perplexities.'

Following the remilitarisation of the Rhineland, Hitler offered negotiations to settle Anglo-German differences. On March 17 the Cabinet debated the future of Britain's relations with Germany. According to the Cabinet minutes, 'our own attitude had been governed by the desire to utilise Herr Hitler's offers in order to obtain a permanent settlement'. Those who were convinced that no such 'permanent settlement' was possible with Nazi Germany turned to Churchill for leadership. Wigram, who shared the view of many in the Foreign Office that Churchill could be an effective voice against the growing German propaganda, brought with him to Chartwell in mid-March a copy of the secret final despatch of Sir Horace Rumbold, the British Ambassador to Berlin at the time Hitler had come to power. It warned of the intensity of Hitler's territorial ambitions.

Would Austria be next on the list of Hitler's advances, Churchill asked the Commons on March 26. And would Britain take the lead in establishing an 'effective union' of those States threatened by Germany? To help such a union forward, he invited the Soviet Ambassador, Ivan Maisky, to lunch with him at the beginning of April, with Sir Robert Vansittart's approval.

On April 6 the Commons debated whether to continue economic sanctions against Italy. Churchill now spoke critically of sanctions; they had failed to save Abyssinia; they had roused the antagonism of Italy, so that in future years Britain would need to maintain larger forces throughout the Mediterranean; and they had involved costly naval expenditure. In his view the policy of sanctions obscured 'a graver matter still', the German threat to Europe. 'Herr Hitler has torn up all the Treaties and garrisoned the Rhineland. His troops are there, and there they are going to stay.' In six months' time the line of new fortifications in the Rhineland would enable the German Army to attack France through Belgium and Holland. Once these two North Sea countries passed 'under German domination', Britain's own security would be at risk.

Once Germany felt strong enough to challenge France, Churchill warned, the position of Poland, Czechoslovakia, Yugoslavia, Roumania,

Austria, and the Baltic States would be 'profoundly altered'. Several of these States would feel obliged to commit themselves to the German system. Others would be incorporated by force. 'Where shall we be then?' he asked, and went on to warn against any attempt by Britain to negotiate with Germany 'on behalf' of Europe. 'We have not the solidarity of conviction, nor the national defences fit for such a dominant role.'

When Hankey lunched at Chartwell on April 19, Churchill stressed the need for a Ministry of Supply or a Ministry of Munitions. 'He went out of his way,' Hankey afterwards wrote to Inskip, 'to explain that he did not want the job for himself.' Churchill also outlined to Hankey a plan, which Hankey regarded as 'fantastic', to send part of the British Fleet into the Baltic, to be based on a Russian port, to ensure permanent British naval superiority over the Germans there. He also wanted Inskip to collect all the evidence he could about Russia's military capacity as an ally.

Two days after Hankey's visit to Chartwell, Churchill was sent a secret and official letter from Reginald Leeper, head of the Information Department of the Foreign Office, asking if he would be willing to speak in public to counter German propaganda, and to explain the urgency of preserving democratic values. This was an extraordinary request from a civil servant to an opponent of the Government's policy of getting on good terms with Germany. Churchill invited Leeper to Chartwell, where Leeper explained that Vansittart felt strongly that Churchill should act as a focus of opinion among the various groups who felt that democracy had to be defended by collective security, adequate armaments, timely preparation and plain speaking.

Churchill agreed to speak for the recently created Anti-Nazi Council, which had the support of several prominent members of the Labour Party and the Trade Union movement who did not accept the Party's opposition to rearmament. He also urged the Government to take the Trade Unions into its confidence in regard to all plans to expand munitions production. To this end he proposed measures against profiteering, telling the House on April 23, 'You will not get the effective co-operation of the working people unless you can make sure that there are not a lot of greedy fingers having a rake-off.' The Government should set up either a Ministry of Supply or a Ministry of Munitions. If the required guns, shells, and 'above all' aeroplane factories could not be created under peacetime conditions, the Government should introduce 'not necessarily war conditions, but conditions which would impinge upon the ordinary daily life and business life of this country'.

Five days later, in the secrecy of the Cabinet, Inskip spoke in support of Churchill's call for a new Ministry, with powers to give priority to Government orders in connection with armaments, but Chamberlain replied that he was unwilling to set up a Ministry of Supply 'until after decisions had been reached on the major policy of the Government'.

The chasm was widening between those who believed that Hitler had no aggressive designs, and those who saw a pattern of aggression in the making. On May 4 Lord Londonderry, who had recently been in Berlin and met Hitler, wrote to Churchill: 'I should like to get out of your mind what appears to be a strong anti-German obsession'. Churchill replied that Londonderry was 'mistaken in supposing that I have an anti-German obsession', and went on to explain: 'British policy for four hundred years has been to oppose the strongest power in Europe by weaving together a combination of other countries strong enough to face the bully. Sometimes it is Spain, sometimes the French monarchy, sometimes the French Empire, sometimes Germany. I have no doubt who it is now. But if France set up to claim the over-lordship of Europe, I should equally endeavour to oppose them. It is thus through the centuries we have kept our liberties and maintained our life and power.'

Churchill went on to warn Londonderry: 'I hope you will not become too prominently identified with the pro-German view. If I read the future aright Hitler's government will confront Europe with a series of outrageous events and ever-growing military might. It is events which will show our dangers, though for some the lesson will come too late.'

Many serving officers shared Churchill's sense of urgency and, at considerable risk should they be found out, approached Churchill direct, to help him build up his arguments. The former head of the Naval Air Division at the Admiralty, Captain Maitland Boucher, sent him a seven-page note on the working of the Fleet Air Arm and its problems. Boucher stressed the lack of training facilities at aerodromes, the disruptive effect of the conflicting systems of naval and air force discipline, the Air Ministry's failure to supply the Fleet Air Arm with adequate aircraft, the poor performance of the aircraft, and the 'dangerously slow' machinery of joint Admiralty and Air Ministry control. 'I do not pose as an expert on these matters,' Churchill told the Commons on May 14, 'but as one who is accustomed to judge the opinion of experts.'

On May 19, as he had been encouraged to do by his friends in the Foreign Office, Churchill spoke at the first of a series of luncheons given by the Anti-Nazi Council. Among those present was Hugh Dalton, Chairman of the National Executive of the Labour Party. Churchill suggested that they ought 'to keep some opportunity to proclaim that there are men of all classes, all sorts and conditions, all grades of human forces, from the humblest workman to the most bellicose Colonel, who occupy a common ground in resisting dangers and aggressive tyranny'. To Asquith's daughter Violet, who asked Churchill what his specific proposal might be, he replied: 'I would marshal all the countries including Soviet Russia, from the Baltic southward right round to the Belgian coast, all agreeing to stand by any victim of unprovoked aggression. I would put combined pressure on every country neighbouring Germany to subscribe to this and to guarantee a quota of armed force for the purpose.' This would ensure 'an overwhelming deterrent against aggression'.

Churchill's arguments were directed to avoiding and averting war; the allegation that he was 'in favour of war' was a 'foul charge', he told the Commons on May 21. 'Is there a man in this House who would not sacrifice his right hand here and now for the assurance that there would be no war in Europe for twenty years?'

As Churchill's influence increased, Baldwin's need to belittle his judgment grew. On May 22 Thomas Jones wrote down Baldwin's comments in his diary: 'One of these days I'll make a few casual remarks about Winston. Not a speech – no oratory – just a few words in passing. I've got it all ready. I am going to say that when Winston was born lots of fairies swooped down on his cradle with gifts – imagination, eloquence, industry, ability – and then came a fairy who said "No one person has a right to so many gifts", picked him up and gave him such a shake and twist that with all these gifts he was denied judgment and wisdom. And that is why while we delight to listen to him in this House we do not take his advice.'

Despite these strictures, Churchill's fears were shared by many of those even within Government circles. That month, Hankey was pressing the Cabinet about the deficiencies, writing to Inskip on May 22: 'I feel constrained to submit to you my concern as to the rate at which our defence programmes are proceeding. An examination of the timetable since the process of reconditioning our Defence Services was first started a year ago is not very flattering to efficiency.' Hankey emphasised that the circumstances were such 'that questions connected with Defence Programmes might, administratively, need to be dealt with on a war basis'.

That night, at Rhodes House, Oxford, Churchill reminded the assembled students and dons that when he had last spoken in Oxford, and had said that Britain must re-arm, 'I was laughed at. I said we must make ourselves safe in our island home, and then the laughter rose. I hope you have learned wisdom now.'

On May 25 a serving officer, the Director of Training at the Air Ministry, Squadron-Leader Charles Torr Anderson, went to see Churchill at Churchill's flat in Victoria, 11 Morpeth Mansions. He brought with him seventeen foolscap pages of notes to illustrate the theme that not enough was being done 'to fit the RAF for war' and a further fourteen pages of statistical information on the lack of preparedness for war as far as pilots and pilot-training were concerned.

That summer, working mostly at Chartwell, Churchill completed the third volume of his Marlborough biography. A young Oxford don, Bill Deakin, agreed to help him organise the enormous amount of historical material. It was a time of formidable concentration. 'I never saw him tired,' Deakin later recalled. 'He was absolutely totally organised, almost like a clock. He knew how to husband his energy, he knew how to expend it. His routine was absolutely dictatorial. He set himself a ruthless timetable every day and would get very agitated and cross if it was broken.'

Churchill would begin the working day in bed, at eight in the morning, reading the proofs of the new volume. Then he would break off to dictate his correspondence. Then he would ask Deakin to look up various facts and details, or ask Deakin to read to him the revised version of a paragraph or section. This work would go on right up until lunch. 'At luncheon he did not come downstairs until the guests were there. He would never greet them at the door.' Lunch itself was a complete break. 'His lunchtime conversation was quite magnificent,' Deakin recalled. 'After lunch, if people were there, he would cut himself off completely from politics, from writing. If he had guests he would take them round the garden. If there were no guests he would potter off into his room.'

No work would be done in the afternoon. At a certain point Churchill would lie down for a few minutes. Then, at five o'clock, he would sign the letters he had dictated in the morning, and clear any further mail that had come during the day. Still no more work would be done on the book, though Deakin might give him a memorandum on some aspect of the work: an historical controversy or suggested method of explaining a topic or factual digest. At about six he might play cards with Clementine or Randolph. At seven he would take a bath: he loved to soak in as hot a bath as possible, then scrub himself vigorously with a brush. Then he would dress for dinner, 'the event of the day' Deakin called it. 'In very good form he could hold forth on any subject – memories of Harrow, or the Western Front – depending on the guests. After the ladies had left he might sit up with his male guests until midnight. He seldom talked about the work he was doing, though he might bring out something that had interested him.'

At midnight, when the guests had left, Deakin recalled, '*then* he would start work', until three or four in the morning. 'One felt so exhilarated. Part of the secret was his phenomenal power to concentrate – the fantastic power of concentrating on what he was doing – which he communicated. You were absolutely a part of it – swept into it.' During the late night work either Violet Pearman, or her deputy Grace Hamblin, who had been at Chartwell since 1932, would be on call to take dictation. The memorandum that Deakin might have given Churchill five or six hours earlier would somehow have been read, absorbed and recast. 'Now he would walk up and down the room dictating. My facts were there, but he had seen them as a politician. My memorandum was a frame. It set him off, it set off his imagination.'

Many of Churchill's correspondents still felt that he ought to be in the Cabinet. 'In the present posture of affairs,' he wrote to one of them on June 3, 'I have no wish whatever for office. If all our fears are groundless, and everything passes off smoothly in the next few years, as pray God indeed it may, obviously there is no need for me. If on the other hand the very dangerous times arise, I may be forced to take a part. Only in these conditions have I any desire to serve.'

That same day, ironically, Inskip wrote to Churchill to ask his advice on how better to carry out his Defence co-ordination task. Churchill replied at once with his thoughts on how Inskip should proceed. 'Your job, like Gaul, seems divided into three parts,' he wrote. '(i) Co-ordinating strategy and settling quarrels between the Services, (ii) Making sure the goods are delivered under the various programmes, and (iii) Creating the structure of War industry and its organisation.' Churchill then set out in detail how a 'powerful machine' could be set up, to grow in scope from month to month, ensuring that the supply needs of the three Services were met. 'It was my experience,' he wrote, recalling 1914, 'that while people oppose all precautions in time of peace, the very same people turn round within a fortnight of war and are furious about every shortcoming. I hope it may not be yours.'

'Personally', Churchill added, 'I sympathise with you very much in your task. I would never have undertaken such a task knowing from experience how fierce opinions become upon these subjects once the nation is alarmed. It is an awful thing to take over masses of loosely defined responsibilities.'

Inskip was indeed finding his task frustrating. At a Cabinet Committee on June 11 he argued in favour of emergency powers to enable him to make various factories turn to war production. He was supported by the Air Minister, Lord Swinton. But both Samuel Hoare, who had returned to the Cabinet as First Lord of the Admiralty, and Neville Chamberlain, argued against emergency powers. 'Germany's next forward step,' said Chamberlain, 'might not necessarily lead us into war.' The disturbance of the economy 'could only be justified by over-powering conditions'.

The desire not to disturb the economy affected all Government thinking; on June 12 the inventor of radar, Robert Watson-Watt, appealed direct to Churchill to help influence what he called 'the Air Ministry's unwillingness to take emergency measures' with regard to his work, which the Ministry had not allowed to be tested 'in conditions at all comparable to war conditions'.

In his public speeches Churchill continued to demand the introduction of greater compulsion for industry, and a more rapid improvement in the equipment and training of troops and airmen. 'I have done my best during the last three years and more,' he told his constituents on June 20, 'to give timely warning of what was happening abroad, and of the dangerous plight into which we were being led or lulled. It has not been a pleasant task. It has certainly been a very thankless task. It has brought me into conflict with many former friends and colleagues. I have been mocked and censured as a scaremonger and even as a warmonger, by those whose complacency and inertia have brought us all nearer to war and war nearer to us all. But I have the comfort of knowing that I have spoken the truth and done my duty, and as long as I have your unflinching support I am content with that. Indeed I am more proud of the long series of speeches which I have made on defence and foreign policy in the last four years than of anything I have ever been able to do, in all my forty years of public life.'

Speaking at Birchington in Kent three weeks later, Churchill quoted a statement by Inskip that Britain had 'reached the planning stage'. He then pointed out that Germany had 'finished her planning stage three years ago, and her whole industry has long been adapted on an unexampled scale for war'. It was his duty 'to keep up a remorseless pressure on the Government to face the realities of the position, and to make exertions appropriate to our needs'. This he certainly did, making full use of fortnightly articles in the *Evening Standard*, with a circulation in London alone of more than three million. In the Commons, however, he warned on July 20 that 'the influence of the Conservative Party machine is being used through a thousand channels' to spread the 'soporific' message that there was no need for alarm, that 'a great deal was being done' and that 'no one could do more'.

Churchill was convinced that more ought to be done; that Hitler's consolidation of power in Germany, his intensification of arms and aircraft production, and his growing pressure upon Austria and Czechoslovakia, meant that 'the whole spirit and atmosphere of our rearmament should be raised to a higher pitch', even though this would mean laying aside 'a good deal of the comfort and smoothness of ordinary life'.

Once more Churchill asked for a Secret Session of the House of Commons, but this was refused. Instead, Baldwin agreed to receive a deputation of senior Conservatives, including Churchill, Austen Chamberlain and Amery, to discuss Defence policy in secret. The meeting took place on July 28; Baldwin had Inskip with him. 'This thought preys upon me,' Churchill told them. 'The months slip rapidly by. If we delay too long in repairing our defences, we may be forbidden by superior power to complete the process.' He then went into great, and carefully worked out detail, basing himself on material brought to him by Anderson, Morton, Wigram and Watson-Watt. First, he spoke about the need to accelerate and improve pilot training, to make greater provision for the defence of London and other cities, to protect Britain's oil supply depots against German air attack, and to pursue more vigorously than was being done the development of radar, the one 'potent discovery'.

Speaking of the relative air strength of Britain and Germany, Churchill stressed the efforts being made in Germany to train pilots and to practise 'night-flying under war conditions', and noted that 'everything turns on the intelligence, daring, the spirit and firmness of character of the Air pilots'. There should be more permanent commissions, and more university candidates should be admitted. To date, only fifty had been allowed to be commissioned each year.

Were all the squadrons in the Air Force list up to full strength, Churchill asked? 'I have heard of one that had only 30 airmen instead of 140,' and he continued, 'When such strict interpretations are put forward of first-line air strength for the purpose of comparison with Germany, it is disconcerting to hear that many of our regular squadrons, not new ones in process of formation, but regular long-formed squadrons, are far below their strength, and have a large proportion, if not the whole, of their reserve aircraft either taken away for service in the flying training schools or unprovided with the necessary equipment or even, in some cases, without engines.'

There were many worries on Churchill's mind, including the gap between the planning of an aircraft and its actual delivery, and the delay in providing spare parts. 'I may emphasise the fact', he said, 'that in this superfine sphere of the air, an aeroplane without everything is for all practical purposes an aeroplane with nothing. It may figure on your lists. It will not be a factor in actual fighting.' His conclusion was a stark one: 'I say there is a state of emergency. We are in danger as we have never been before,' not even at the height of the German submarine campaign of the First World War.

At a second meeting of the Defence deputation on July 29, Churchill spoke of the many items of war supply, including ammunition, tanks, lorries and armoured cars, for which, he argued, 'our industry, which is so comprehensive and variegated', should be made to contribute on a substantial scale. He was worried also about the shortage of machine-guns, bombs, poison-gas, gas-masks, searchlights, trench mortars and grenades. As the Admiralty was also dependent on the War Office for such items, a shortage of any one of them 'would cause grave injury to the Navy'. On the scale Britain was then acting 'even at the end of two years the supply will be petty compared to the needs of a national war, and melancholy compared to what others have already secured in time of peace.'

Complaint was made, Churchill said, 'that the nation is unresponsive to the national needs', and that the Trade Unions were 'unhelpful'. 'We see the Socialists even voting against the Estimates'. As long as the Government assured the public there was no emergency those obstacles would continue, 'but I believe they will all disappear if the true position about foreign armaments is set before the public, and if the true position about our own condition is placed before them, not by words, not by confessions, but by actions which speak louder than words, measures of State ordering this, that and the other, by events, by facts which would make themselves felt when people see this was happening here and that happening there.'

'I do not at all ask that we should proceed to turn ourselves into a country under war conditions,' Churchill ended, 'but I believe that to carry forward our progress of munitions we ought not to hesitate to impinge to a certain percentage – 25 per cent, 30 per cent – upon the ordinary industries of the country, and force them and ourselves to that sacrifice at this time.'

That day, unknown to Churchill, Inskip himself again asked the Cabinet for special powers, explaining to his colleagues that a shortage of building materials was holding up the reconditioning programme of all three Services; but his request was turned down. In replying to the deputation, Baldwin made no reference to Inskip's own appeal for special powers of the sort Churchill was advocating, nor did he answer Churchill's detailed assertions; instead, he spoke of the adverse effect on Britain's trade if the peace-time economy were to be turned even half-way towards war conditions. That was a question, he said, which he had discussed 'mainly' with the Chancellor of the Exchequer, Neville Chamberlain. Both of them felt that to disturb peace-time production 'might throw back the ordinary trade of the country perhaps for many years, and damage it very seriously at a time when we might want all our credit, the credit of the country'.

Baldwin went on to raise doubts about 'the peril itself', and in particular about the possibility of a war between Britain and 'Germany alone'. He asked the deputation if they were really prepared to warn people that Germany 'is arming to fight us', and he added, 'It is not easy when you get on a platform to tell people what the dangers are.' He had tried to get people to 'sit up' to the dangers, but 'I have never quite seen the clear line by which you can approach people to scare them but not scare them into fits.'

Speaking of Hitler, Baldwin told the deputation: 'We all know the German desire, and he has come out with it in his book, to move East, and if he should move East I should not break my heart. I do not believe she wants to move West because West would be a difficult programme for her.'

Baldwin's statement ended: 'I am not going to get this country into a war with anybody for the League of Nations or anybody else or for anything else. There is one danger, of course, which has probably been in all your minds – supposing the Russians and Germans got fighting and the French went in as allies of Russia owing to that appalling pact they made, you would not feel you were obliged to go and help France, would you? If there is any fighting in Europe to be done I should like to see the Bolshies and the Nazis doing it.'

When the meetings were over, Baldwin submitted the transcripts of what had been said to the Air Ministry, the Admiralty and the War Office. One of the Air Ministry's answers began bluntly, 'It is agreed that the potential air output of the British aircraft industry is not equal to the Germans.' The Air Ministry memorandum also confirmed 'the failure of the aircraft industry to keep its delivery programme.' The War Office memorandum agreed with most of Churchill's contentions in the military and industrial sphere, which it described as 'perfectly correct'. Of the problems of Home Defence, the War Office agreed 'that the present situation is unsatisfactory', and on another point it commented: 'Mr Winston Churchill has given his opinion that Germany's enormous war preparation will enable her to launch her first offensive on a 1918 scale; that this may prevent a stalemate of trench warfare; and that, therefore, we shall have no breathing space in which to organise the nation, as we did in 1915. Although no one can say whether or not this prophecy will be fulfilled, the danger that it may be fulfilled is sufficiently great to be taken into serious account.'

That August, Churchill visited the French Maginot Line defences on the border with Germany. 'The officers of the French Army are impressive by their gravity,' he wrote to Clementine. 'One feels the strength of the nation resides in its army.' In mid-September Churchill was back at Chartwell, preparing the speech he was to give in Paris, at the request of his friends at the Foreign Office, to counter German propaganda. It was in Paris, on September 24, that he set out the evils of totalitarianism and the virtues of democracy. 'How could we bear,' he asked, 'to be treated like schoolboys when we are grown-up men; to be turned out on parade by tens of thousands to march and cheer for this slogan or for that; to see philosophers, teachers and authors bullied and toiled to death in concentration camps; to be forced every hour to conceal the natural workings of the human intellect and the pulsations of the human heart? Why, I say that rather than submit to such oppression, there is no length we would not go to.'

Churchill's speech was a clarion call for the maintenance of democratic values. 'Between the doctrines of Comrade Trotsky and Dr Goebbels,' he said, 'there ought to be room for you and me, and a few others, to cultivate opinions of our own.' Aggressive action should be judged, not from the standpoint of Right and Left, but from that of right and wrong. 'We are in the midst of dangers so great and increasing, we are the guardians of causes so precious to the world, that we must, as the Bible says, "Lay aside every impediment" and prepare ourselves night and day to be worthy of the Faith that is in us.'

The Paris speech was widely reported. 'You have never done anything better,' wrote one of Churchill's former Liberal Cabinet colleagues, Herbert Fisher. The London evening newspaper, the *Star*, commented, 'We should like to hear Mr Churchill's defence of democracy reverberate from the sounding board of high office.'

On October 15, at a meeting of the Anti-Nazi Council, Churchill praised the decision of the Trades Union Congress to urge the Labour Party to support whatever rearmament was needed 'in order that free countries should not be trampled down'.

Eight days later, in a break from politics, Churchill celebrated the publication of the third volume of his Marlborough biography by sending out more than seventy inscribed copies. But there was a shadow to the celebration; a month earlier his daughter Sarah had announced her intention to marry an Austrian-born music hall comedian, Vic Oliver, who had been twice married before. There was much ribaldry in certain newspapers that Churchill was against the marriage. But Sarah was determined, and eloped to the United States, where she and Vic Oliver were married. 'I nearly wrote you a line last month and then I hesitated,' Baldwin wrote to Churchill on October 9. 'But I do want you to know that I felt with you from my heart when I read in the papers of certain domestic anxieties that must have caused you pain. I know you well enough to realise how closely these things touch you.'

Churchill, seeing Sarah's distress, gave the couple his blessing; two years later he took steps, through a senior official at the Home Office, Sir Alexander Maxwell, to ensure that his son-in-law's travel documents made it impossible for the Germans to have some claim on him as a Jew when he went with Sarah to New York on a German ship. 'Although in the first instance, as you may have heard,' he wrote to Maxwell, 'I opposed his marriage with my daughter, I have come to like and esteem him greatly.'

At its meeting on October 15 the Anti-Nazi Council had decided to set up a 'Defence of Freedom and Peace' movement whose aim was to uphold 'democratic government and public law', to resist all attacks on this freedom 'by violence at home or attack from abroad', and to join with other threatened nations 'in preserving peace and withstanding armed aggression'. Churchill told those present: 'We will make every effort in our power to rally around that Covenant all the effective aid that we can get from any quarter without respect to party or nation', and he added, 'We have the means of being the spear-point of all this vast mass of opinion which guards our rights.'

The first public meeting of the new organisation was to be held at the Albert Hall, under the public auspices of the League of Nations Union, and was intended to bring together on a single platform all those organisations which favoured collective security and rearmament. Thus the idea put to Churchill by Vansittart and Leeper at the beginning of the year became a reality. On October 21 Churchill explained to A. H. Richards, the Secretary of the Anti-Nazi Council, 'I do not contemplate the building up of a new and rival society, but only a welding together of those organisations and galvanising them into effective use.' Writing about his Labour colleagues on the Council, Churchill told Austen Chamberlain, 'I have been surprised to find the resolution and clarity of thought which has prevailed among them, and the profound sense of approaching danger.'

On November 8 Churchill was again sounding his warnings in the Commons. 'Unless there is a front against potential aggression there will be no settlement,' he said. 'All the nations of Europe will just be driven helter-skelter across the diplomatic chessboard until the limits of retreat are exhausted, and then out of desperation, perhaps in some most unlikely quarter, the explosion of war will take place, probably under conditions not very favourable to those who have been engaged in this long retreat.'

Churchill now prepared to speak in the forthcoming Defence debate. Two weeks before the debate another Air Force officer, who had just returned from a visit to Germany, Squadron Leader Herbert Rowley, went to see him at Morpeth Mansions with details of set-backs in the British aircraft programme. On the day after Rowley's visit, the Commander of the Tank Brigade, Brigadier Percy Hobart, brought him details of deficiencies in the tank programme. The debate itself was opened, on November 11, by Inskip, who stated that Britain now possessed 960 aeroplanes available for Home Defence, and who insisted that all was proceeding well in defence preparations.

On November 12 Churchill moved an amendment stating that Britain's defences, particularly in the air, were no longer adequate for the peace, safety and freedom of the British people. There would be 'a great increase in the adverse factors' in 1937, he warned, and only 'intense efforts' could counteract them. And yet, he said, there were still serious deficiencies in the strength and weapons of many elements in the national defence, including the Territorial Army, the Regular Army and the Royal Air

Force. 'The Army lacks almost every weapon which is required for the latest form of modern war. Where are the anti-tank guns, where are the short-distance wireless sets, where are the field anti-aircraft guns against low-flying armoured planes?'

Speaking from personal experience about the tank as a weapon of war, Churchill told the House: 'This idea which has revolutionised the conditions of modern war, was a British idea forced on the War Office by outsiders. Let me say they would have just as hard work today to force a new idea on it. I speak from what I know. During the war we had almost a monopoly, let alone the leadership, in tank warfare, and for several years afterwards we held the foremost place. To England all eyes were turned. All that has gone now. Nothing has been done in "the years that the locust hath eaten" to equip the Tank Corps with new machines.'

Churchill then warned MPs: 'A very long period must intervene before any effectual flow of munitions can be expected, even for the small forces of which we dispose. Still we are told there is no necessity for a Ministry of Supply, no emergency which should induce us to impinge on the normal course of trade.'

Turning to the Government's arguments for the delays in embarking upon a rearmament programme between 1933 and 1935 Churchill declared: 'I have heard it said that the Government had no mandate for rearmament until the General Election. Such a doctrine is wholly inadmissible. The responsibility of Ministers for the public safety is absolute and requires no mandate. It is in fact the prime object for which Governments come into existence. The Prime Minister had the command of enormous majorities in both Houses of Parliament ready to vote for any necessary measures of defence. The country has never yet failed to do its duty when the true facts have been put before it, and I cannot see where there is a defence for this delay.'

The Government continued to assert the danger of turning Britain 'into one vast munitions camp', Churchill pointed out. He deprecated such exaggeration, telling the House: 'The First Lord of the Admiralty in his speech the other night went even further. He said, "We are always reviewing the position." Everything, he assured us, is entirely fluid. I am sure that that is true. Anyone can see what the position is. The Government simply cannot make up their mind, or they cannot get the Prime Minister to make up his mind. So they go on in strange paradox, decided only to be undecided, resolved to be irresolute, adamant for drift, solid for fluidity, all powerful to be impotent. So we go on preparing more months and years – precious, perhaps vital, to the greatness of Britain – for the locusts to eat. They will say to me, "A Minister of Supply is not necessary, for all is going well." I deny it. "The position is satisfactory." It is not true.'

Churchill ended his criticisms on a personal note, telling his fellow MPs: 'I have been staggered by the failure of the House of Commons to react effectively against those dangers. That, I am bound to say, I never expected. I never would have believed that we should have been allowed to go on getting into this plight, month by month and year by year, and that even the Government's own confessions of error would have produced no concentration of Parliamentary opinion and force capable of lifting our efforts to the level of emergency. I say that unless the House resolves to find out the truth for itself it will have committed an act of abdication of duty without parallel in its long history.'

The Times, so long a hostile critic of Churchill's efforts, called his speech 'brilliant'. It made many MPs increasingly uneasy that the Cabinet was not gripping the situation as it should. 'His style is more considered and slower than usual,' the National Labour MP Harold Nicolson wrote in his diary, 'but he drives his points home with a sledgehammer.'

It was Baldwin himself who replied to Churchill, seeking to explain why he had not rearmed more forcefully between the autumn of 1933 and the General Election in the summer of 1935: 'I put before the whole House my own views with an appalling frankness. You will remember at that time the Disarmament Conference was sitting in Geneva. You will remember at that time there was probably a stronger pacifist feeling running through this country than at any time since the War.' He then recalled the by-election at Fulham in the autumn of 1933, when a National Government seat had been lost to a pacifist candidate. 'My position as the leader of a great party was not altogether a comfortable one.'

Baldwin explained. 'I asked myself what chance was there – when that feeling that was given expression to in Fulham was common throughout the country – what chance was there within the next year or two for that feeling being so changed that the country would give a mandate for rearmament? Supposing I had gone to the country and said that Germany was rearming and that we must rearm, does anybody think that this pacific democracy would have rallied to that cry at that moment? I cannot think of anything that would have made the loss of the election from my point of view more certain.'

The contrast between Churchill's charges and Baldwin's explanation provoked much comment. 'I cannot recall seeing the House as a whole so uneasy,' one young Conservative MP, Patrick Donner, wrote to Churchill. Commenting on Baldwin's speech, Londonderry wrote to Churchill: 'We told him and Neville of the risks, but they were too much frightened of losing by-elections. Neville was really the villain of the piece, because he as Chancellor blocked everything on the grounds of finances.' Another Conservative MP, Sir Archibald Boyd-Carpenter, wrote: 'I must send you a few words of congratulations on your wonderful & inspiring speech yesterday. I said to myself "Thank God someone has courage" & I feel it all the more after the pathetic effort of SB which makes one feel almost ill,' Churchill replied: 'I have never heard such a squalid confession from a public man as Baldwin offered us yesterday.'

Aware of growing support among MPs for Churchill's call for greater vigilance, Baldwin agreed to receive a second Defence deputation.Five days before the meeting, Anderson provided Churchill with the most recent summaries of German Air Force production prepared by the Air Ministry's German Intelligence Section. From this material, acquired by the Secret Service through agents in Germany, it was clear that if war became a possibility in 1937 or 1938, Britain would not have sufficient air defence to resist a sustained attack, or sufficient air power to counter-attack, or to demand a 'hands off' policy.

On the crucial question of comparative strengths, the Air Ministry estimated that the 372 British bombers which would be operational in June 1937 would have to be set against the eight hundred German bombers, quite apart from the question of whether a further eight hundred German reserve bombers could also be counted as first-line. Three days before the deputation, another person with access to classified material, Major G. P. Myers, wrote to Churchill that of eighty-nine Hawker Fury fighters ordered by the Government from General Aircraft Ltd, only twenty-three had been delivered within the contract date.

On November 23 the second Parliamentary deputation called on Baldwin to discuss the state of Britain's defences. Once again, although Inskip was present, none of the three Service Ministers, Hoare, Swinton and Duff Cooper, were at the meeting to hear the criticisms of their departments, or to answer the critics face to face. Baldwin was accompanied by Neville Chamberlain and Lord Halifax; the deputation, as before, was led by Austen Chamberlain and Lord Salisbury. As the discussion continued, it was clear that many of Churchill's fears and assertions had been admitted by the service departments. Nearly two years had passed since the 1935 election, yet the scale of arms production was still not adequate to meet a German threat in 1937 or 1938. Explaining why there could still be no rapid expansion of the Territorials for the defence of London, Inskip told the deputation, 'At present there is undoubtedly a shortage of equipment'.

The discussion of November 23, the record of which filled fifty-eight printed foolscap pages, was dominated by Churchill's continuing questioning. 'I could certainly name the number of a dozen squadrons,' he said, 'which have nothing like their proper outfit of aeroplanes. Others, where there are a great number of pilots but so few aeroplanes for them that the pilots cannot go on with the training.' The fact remained, Churchill said, 'that we have not got eighty effective Metropolitan Squadrons, or anything like that to guard us in the coming year', to which Inskip replied, 'If the emphasis is on "effective", I agree.'

On November 25, five days before his sixty-second birthday, Churchill received a message from his cousin Frederick Guest which told him of a breakthrough in his efforts to rally the widest possible spectrum of opinion. The message read: 'Attlee will support you on any rearmament programme. He admires & likes you. The door is open if you want to talk to him.' Buoyed up by this knowledge, Churchill prepared the major appeal which the Anti-Nazi Council had asked him to make for public unity and 'self-imposed discipline' when he spoke at the Albert Hall on December 3. But his new-found political position was momentarily weakened by a short but tempestuous episode, the Abdication Crisis.

In January 1936 the Prince of Wales had succeeded his father as King. Churchill had known and been friends with the new King since his investiture as Prince of Wales twenty-five years earlier. During Edward VIII's first year on the throne, rumour had linked his name with that of Wallis Simpson, an American woman who was about to divorce her second husband. Churchill knew that Edward wanted above all else to marry Mrs Simpson once her second marriage had been set aside; this had happened at the end of October. Churchill did not at all approve of the King's choice, and supported those who were working hard behind the scenes to try to persuade Mrs Simpson to give him up. But on November 16 the King had informed Baldwin of his intention to marry her.

A constitutional crisis blew up. Baldwin, supported by the Cabinet, gave the King the choice either of giving up Mrs Simpson or abdicating. Desperate to marry, on December 2 he told Baldwin that he was prepared to choose abdication. With Baldwin's approval, Churchill had gone to see him two days later to try to persuade him not to give up the throne hastily. The King asked Churchill to get him more time to make up his mind; he wanted two weeks more 'to weigh the whole matter'. Churchill sent Baldwin a full account of his conversation with the King, and of the King's 'mental exhaustion'. The combination of public and private stresses, he pointed out, 'is the hardest of all to endure. I told the King that if he appealed to you to allow him time to recover himself and to consider now that things have reached this chaos the grave issues constitutional and personal with which you have found it your duty to confront him, you would I was sure not fail in kindness and consideration. It would be most cruel and wrong to extort a decision from him in his present state.'

Confident that Baldwin would allow the King at least a month in which to decide on what course to take, Churchill told the King: 'Your Majesty need not have the slightest fear about time. If you require time there is no force in this country which would or could deny it.' He was wrong; on Sunday December 6 Baldwin told a meeting of senior Ministers, 'This matter must be finished before Christmas.' In Neville Chamberlain's view, to wait even that long, three weeks, was impossible, as the continued uncertainty was, he warned, hurting the Christmas trade.

Unknown to Churchill, the King did not really want more time; he had decided that he would marry Mrs Simpson even if it meant giving up the throne. Churchill, however, after a meeting at Chartwell that Sunday with Archibald Sinclair and Robert Boothby, was still hopeful that the King could remain, provided he agreed publicly to a declaration, which Churchill and his two friends drafted, and sent to the King on December 6: 'The King will not enter into any contract of marriage contrary to the advice of his Ministers.'

Still believing that the King would accept this formula if he were given time to do so, on December 7 Churchill went to the Commons to ask 'that no irrevocable step will be taken before the House has received a full statement'. To his amazement there were immediate and indignant howls of derision. Cries of 'Drop it' and 'Twister' came from all parts of the House. He remained standing, trying to explain his point about giving the King a little more time to make up his mind. But the shouts of derision continued and he could not make himself heard. Walking out of the Chamber he turned angrily to Baldwin with the words, 'You won't be satisfied until you've broken him, will you?'

MPs were convinced that Churchill was trying to discredit Baldwin and lead a revolt against him. It was not so; he was only trying to make it possible for the King to give up Mrs Simpson and thus remain on the throne, thereby averting the constitutional implications of a situation whereby a Prime Minister could put pressure on a King to make so momentous a decision quickly. But the impression that Churchill had decided to use the Abdication crisis to make trouble for the Government was widespread and damaging. *The Times* called the episode in the Commons 'the most striking rebuff of modern Parliamentary history'. Harold Nicolson wrote in his diary that night, 'He has undone in five minutes the patient reconstruction work of two years.' On December 11 the *Spectator* declared, 'He has utterly misjudged the temper of the country and the temper of the House, and the reputation which he was beginning to shake off of a wayward genius unserviceable in council has settled firmly on his shoulders again.'

This was momentarily the public view, which the Government did nothing to discourage. But on the very afternoon of Churchill's humiliation in the Commons, when he spoke at a meeting of Conservative backbenchers about Air Force deficiencies, his speech, so his cousin Frederick Guest told him, was 'admirable, and very well received'. Another MP who was present at the afternoon meeting also wrote, to Inskip, that Churchill's remarks were 'well received'. Fourteen years later, Churchill himself recalled, in a letter to Brendan Bracken, that although he had been 'naturally conscious of the overwhelming opinion of its Members, that afternoon I addressed a very large gathering of the Conservative Committee on military defence, speaking I think for nearly an hour, and was listened to with the utmost attention'.

When Baldwin told the House three days later that the King had signed a Deed of Abdication, Churchill's speech, in which he stressed the danger of any further 'recrimination or controversy', was listened to with respect. 'What has been done, or left undone, belongs to history,' he said, 'and to history, as far as I am concerned, it shall be left.' Amery noted in his diary, 'Winston rose in face of a hostile House and in an admirably phrased little speech executed a strategical retreat.' When Churchill spoke of how the King would be particularly remembered 'in the homes of his poorer subjects', MPs cheered his remarks. 'Dangers gather upon our path,' he said. 'We cannot afford – we have no right – to look back. We must look forward. We must obey the exhortation of the Prime Minister to look forward.' These final words were greeted with what the official Parliamentary record described as 'loud cheers'.

Writing to the Duke of Westminster a week later, Churchill confided, 'It is extraordinary how Baldwin gets stronger every time he knocks out someone or something important to our country.' To Lloyd George, who was on holiday in the West Indies, Churchill wrote on Christmas Day: 'It has been a terrible time here, and I am profoundly grieved at what has happened. I believe the Abdication to have been altogether premature and probably quite unnecessary. However, the vast majority is on the other side. You have done well to be out of it.'

On New Year's Day 1937 Churchill wrote to Bernard Baruch: 'I do not feel that my own political position is much affected by the line I took; but even if it were, I should not wish to have acted otherwise. As you know in politics I always prefer to accept the guidance of my heart to calculations of public feeling.'

25

No Place for Churchill

On 2 January 1937, while spending the New Year at Chartwell, Churchill learned that his Foreign Office friend and informant, Ralph Wigram, who had been ill for some time, had died at the age of forty. He wrote at once to Wigram's widow, Ava: 'I admired so much his courage, integrity of purpose, high comprehending vision. He was one of those – how few – who guard the life of Britain. Now he is gone – and on the eve of this fateful year. Indeed it is a blow to England and to all the best that England means. It is only a week or so that he rang me up to speak about the late King. I can hear his voice in my memory. And you? What must be your loss? But you still will have a right to dwell on all that you did for him. You shielded that bright steady flame that burned in the broken lamp. But for you it would long ago have been extinguished, and its light would not have guided us thus far upon our journey.'

'He adored you so,' Ava Wigram replied, '& always said you were the greatest Englishman alive.' On January 4 Churchill drove from Chartwell to Uckfield for Wigram's funeral. 'The widow was ravaged with grief,' he wrote to Clementine three days later, '& it was a harrowing experience. There appears to be no pension or anything for Foreign Office widows: but she says she can manage on her own resources. Her future seems blank & restricted. A sombre world!'

After the funeral Churchill gave a small luncheon at Chartwell for the mourners, including Sir Robert Vansittart. Clementine, who was on holiday in Switzerland, realised how much Wigram's death had saddened her husband. 'He was a true friend of yours,' she wrote on January 5, '& in his eye you could see the spark which showed an inner light was burning.' Four days later she wrote again: 'I felt Mr Wigram's death would make you unhappy. I'm afraid you will miss him very much.'

Throughout the early months of 1937 Churchill received yet more information of Government slackness in Defence preparations and planning. His new sources included both his former national insurance expert at the Board of Trade, Sir William Beveridge, and his former Director of Naval Construction at the Admiralty, and co-inventor of the tank, Sir Eustace Tennyson d'Eyncourt. But Churchill no longer saw any point in continual public speaking. 'At the present time non-official personages count for very little,' he wrote to a senior Liberal Peer, Lord Davies, on January 13. 'One poor wretch may easily exhaust himself without his even making a ripple upon the current of opinion.'

Churchill did correspond with Ministers privately, seeking to encourage them to greater efforts and vigilance. On January 14 he wrote to Inskip about what he feared was the Government's dilatory policy towards machine tool orders: 'With a proper system of control the whole capacity of British industry could be brought in review, and the Government then, when placing the order abroad, would have warned the British firm producing one vital part, that their services would be required, and they would not then be bespoken by the German Government. You say that it is the Government policy not to interfere with normal trade. It may be Government policy and yet not be right. You are under a misapprehension when you suggest that I wish you to ask the machine tool industry "to abandon _all_ their ordinary trade". I should be quite content if instead of "all" were written "all the Government requires".'

He had been assured that the British armament programme was falling 'ever more into arrears', Churchill told Inskip, and that Britain's relative weakness in the air, compared to Germany, was 'marked and deplorable'. His letter ended on a personal note: 'I postponed writing this letter to you until I was delighted to hear you were rapidly recovering from your influenza. I am telling your secretary not to show it to you till you are quite restored. Grave as are the times, I hope you will make sure you have the necessary period of convalescence. All my household has been down with this minor scourge, and a certain number of days of complete relief from work of any kind is absolutely necessary for perfect recovery. So far I have survived and if I escape altogether I shall attribute it to a good conscience as well as a good constitution.'

Speaking in the Air debate on January 27, Inskip defended the current air programme. At least 120 of the promised 124 squadrons would be completed by July 1938, he said, 'though not all brought up to their complement'. Speaking after Inskip, Churchill stressed the fact that of the 124 squadrons promised by March 31, only a hundred would actually be ready. But even of these hundred, twenty-two were 'not in a condition to take part in fighting'. This left only seventy-eight squadrons instead of the promised 124, a shortage of forty-six. 'Therefore', Churchill told the House, 'I say that we have not got the parity which we were promised. We have not nearly got it, we have not nearly approached it. Nor shall we get it during the whole of 1937, and I doubt whether we shall have it or anything approaching it during 1938.'

Two days after Churchill's speech, he received through Anderson an eight-page memorandum written by Group Captain Lachlan MacLean, Senior Air Staff Officer at the headquarters of No.3 Bomber Group. The memorandum was critical of many aspects of Air Force development, including long-distance navigation, maintenance work and pilot training. MacLean did not know that Anderson had sent his memorandum to Churchill; the first he heard of it was when Churchill asked to see him at Morpeth Mansions.

On February 2 Churchill sent Clementine, who was then on a holiday cruise in the West Indies, the news that Baldwin was likely to give up the premiership in May, immediately after the Coronation of George VI, and that Neville Chamberlain, who was 'already in fact doing the work, will without any doubt or question succeed him'. It would, Churchill wrote, 'be a great relief and simplifiction of our affairs to have all uncertainty cleared up at that date one way or the other. I really do not care very much which'.

Churchill, still troubled by money worries following the collapse of his shares in the American stock market crash, now thought of selling Chartwell. 'If we do not get a good price we can quite well carry on for a year or two more,' he told Clementine. 'But no good offer should be refused, having regard to the fact that our children are almost all flown, and my life is probably in its closing decade.'

During the Defence debate on March 4, Churchill welcomed the Government's recently announced increases in defence spending over the coming five years, but went on to ask, 'When a whole continent is feverishly arming, when mighty nations are laying aside every form of ease and comfort, when scores of millions of men and weapons are being prepared for war, when whole populations are being led forward or driven forward under conditions of exceptional overstrain, when the finances of the proudest dictators are in the most desperate condition, can you be sure that all your programmes so tardily adopted will, in fact, be executed in time?'

Churchill ended his speech by appealing for a genuine British commitment both to the military potential of the League of Nations, and to the moral forces which it embodied. Of those moral forces he declared: 'Do not let us mock at them for they are surely on our side. Do not mock at them, for this may well be a time when the highest idealism is not divorced from strategic prudence. Do not mock at them, for these may be years, strange as it may seem, when Right may walk hand in hand with Might.'

On March 16 Austen Chamberlain died; his friendship with Churchill dated back to the turn of the century. In the four years since Hitler had come to power their views of the German danger had been closely linked. On March 18 Churchill wrote to Chamberlain's widow of how 'shocked and shaken to the depths' he had been when he had gone to the Foreign Office and learned the news. His letter continued: 'I pray indeed that you may find the resources in your spirit to enable you to bear this supreme stroke. Nothing can soften the loneliness or fill the void. Great happiness long enjoyed casts its own shadow. All his friends of whom I am proud to be one will miss him painfully. In this last year I have seen more of him & worked more closely with him than at any time in a political & personal association of very nearly forty years. I feel that almost the one remaining link with the old days indeed the great days has been snapped.'

'I know that you loved Austen,' Lady Chamberlain replied on March 20, '& will feel his loss greatly. He always had a great affection & admiration for you even when you did not agree!'

Towards the end of March, Churchill returned to France for a nine-day holiday at Cap Martin. 'I paint all day,' he wrote to the former King, now Duke of Windsor, 'and as far as my means go, gamble after dark.' He also wrote privately to Inskip about Britain's first-line strength in the air. On March 22, a week before Churchill left for France, Inskip had told the Commons that as from April 1 there would be 103 squadrons based in the United Kingdom. But to Churchill he wrote privately to explain that ten of those squadrons would be under strength in aircraft 'pending the delivery of further machines' and that some of the recently formed Auxiliary Air Squadrons would likewise 'not be up to establishment'. Inskip added, 'I feel justified in giving you, as a Privy Councillor, this further confidential information, especially as you have already had so much secret information in this connection.'

In his reply to Inskip, Churchill accepted that there must be 'a great deal of reorganisation and weakness during a period of rapid expansion'. He also sent him 'in personal confidence' a memorandum on air squadron deficiencies by someone whom he described as 'a Staff Officer of the Air Force', but did not name. The memorandum had been written by Group Captain Lachlan MacLean; returning it to Churchill on April 8, Inskip noted, 'It is undesirable that it should be among my papers in view of your wish that I should treat it as very confidential.'

In sending Inskip this memorandum, Churchill set out his own views on how the deficiencies which MacLean had detailed should be tackled: 'I wonder you do not get a list made out of everything that a regular Air Squadron should have – pilots, machines, spare engines, spare parts, machine guns, bombing sights etc together with the reserves of all kinds which should be kept at the station. And then, armed with this, go down accompanied by three or four competent persons to visit, quite by chance, some Air Squadron by surprise. If then during the course of a whole day your people went through the list while you cross-examined the officers, you should have some information on which you could rest with some security.'

'The reason why I am not dwelling upon these matters in public,' Churchill told Inskip, 'is because of the fear I have of exposing our weakness even more than is already known abroad.' After reading his letter to Inskip, Morton wrote to Churchill, 'As often before, I am astonished at your knowledge of detail on Defence matters.'

The Labour Party now brought a motion condemning the Royal Navy's refusal to support British ships trying to take food to the Republicans in Spain, pointing out that while Britain and France adhered to the non-intervention agreement, Germany and Italy ignored it. To cries of dissent from the Labour benches, Churchill spoke in support of the Government's contention that non-intervention must continue. 'Is it not an encouraging fact,' he asked, 'that German, French, Russian, Italian and British naval officers are officially acting together, however crankily, in something which represents, albeit feebly, the Concert of Europe, and affords, if it is only a pale, misshapen shadow, some idea of those conceptions of the reign of law and of collective authority which many of us regard as of vital importance?'

Churchill urged Britain's continued neutrality towards Spain. 'I refuse to become the partisan of either side,' he declared. 'I will not pretend that, if I had to choose between Communism and Nazism, I would choose Communism. I hope not to be called upon to survive in the world under a Government of either of these dispensations. I cannot feel any enthusiasm for these rival creeds. I feel unbounded sorrow and sympathy for the victims.'

Appealing for one final effort by all the outside powers to abandon conflict and seek reconciliation, Churchill told the House: 'We seem to be moving, drifting, steadily, against our will, against the will of every race and every people and every class, towards some hideous catastrophe. Everybody wishes to stop it, but they do not know how. We have talks of Eastern and Western Pacts, but they make no greater security. Armaments and counter-armaments proceed apace, and we must find something new.'

Churchill's critics recognised the quality of his mind; one Conservative MP, Henry Channon, though against Churchill being in the Government, wrote in his diary: 'Winston Churchill made a terrific speech, brilliant, convincing, unanswerable and his "stock" has soared, and today people are buying "Churchills", and saying once more that he ought to be in the government, and that it is too bad to keep so brilliant a man out of office; but were he to be given office, what would it mean? An explosion of foolishness after a short time? War with Germany? A seat for Randolph?'

Writing from the Foreign Office on April 16, Eden thanked Churchill for his words of support during the debate: 'I can assure you they were appreciated by the occupant of this anxious office. May I also say how very good I thought your speech as a whole; indeed I heard many opinions that the speech must be ranked among your very best. It was difficult to make with the House in that tempestuous and unreasoning mood, and you contrived to sober them and cause them to reflect.'

That April, Baldwin announced that he would retire from the premiership by the end of May. In declining an invitation from the Duke of Windsor to visit him in France during May, Churchill explained that he did not think it 'wise' to leave England then. 'The Government will all be in the process of reconstruction, and although I am not very keen upon office, I should like to help in Defence.' As he once more waited for the call, Churchill found a way of making his views more widely known in Europe. A thirty-three-year-old Hungarian Jew, Emery Reves, had set up a press service in Paris, dedicated to international understanding and democratic values. Reves placed Churchill's fortnightly *Evening Standard* articles in newspapers throughout Europe, including those in Warsaw, Prague, Belgrade, Bucharest and Helsinki; twenty-six cities in all.

In these articles Churchill urged all threatened states to band together to prevent German incursions. But while Churchill continued to advocate collective security, Geoffrey Dawson, the Editor of *The Times*, had other views, writing to a friend on May 23: 'I should like to get going with the Germans. I simply cannot understand why they should apparently be so much annoyed with *The Times* at this moment. I spend my nights in taking out anything which I think will hurt their susceptibilities and in dropping in little things which are intended to soothe them.'

Three days after this clear characterisation of appeasement by Dawson, Neville Chamberlain succeeded Baldwin as Prime Minister. Like Dawson, he was determined to find some basis for conciliation with Germany, hoping to draw Europe away from the brink of war, not by collective security and rearmament, but by a negotiated settlement of German grievances. There was to be no place for Churchill in Chamberlain's scheme of things. For ten years they had disagreed on almost every issue of substance with which they had been confronted, from derating in 1927 to the Abdication, and above all about the priority of armaments, and the need to be able to confront Germany; deep differences on policy were exacerbated by a clash of personalities.

On the day Chamberlain became Prime Minister, Lord Derby asked Churchill if he would second a motion, at a Conservative Party meeting in Caxton Hall, nominating Chamberlain as Leader. As the senior Conservative Privy Councillor in the Commons, the task would naturally fall to Churchill. While preparing his speech, he read the new Cabinet appointments. 'Heartiest congratulations on your great promotion,' he telegraphed to Duff Cooper, who had been made First Lord of the Admiralty. Inskip remained Minister for the Coordination of Defence. Hoare went to the Home Office. Leslie Hore-Belisha became Secretary of State for War.

One young back-bencher who joined the new Government was Robert Bernays; since the 1935 election he had sat near Churchill below the gangway. 'Many congratulations', Churchill telegraphed on learning of his appointment as Parliamentary Secretary at the Ministry of Health. 'I have only one regret,' Bernays replied, 'and that is that I am now removed too far to hear your whispered and pungent comments on the passing Parliamentary scene – which were always so exhilarating. I shall always be grateful – as must be every young man in the house to-day – for the way in which you continually demonstrate to what heights the art of Parliamentary debate can be made to attain.'

No post was offered to Churchill, who on May 31 spoke, as he had offered to do, at the Caxton Hall meeting. After recalling Chamberlain's 'memorable achievement' as Chancellor of the Exchequer in restoring Britain's financial credit and stimulating foreign trade, he reminded the meeting that the leadership of the party had never been interpreted 'in a dictatorial or despotic sense', and he appealed for the continued recognition of the rights of those who disagreed with party policy: 'The House of Commons,' he said, 'still survives as the arena of free debate. We feel sure that the leader we are about to choose will, as a distinguished Parliamentarian and a House of Commons man, not resent honest differences of opinion arising between those who mean the same thing, and that party opinion will not be denied its subordinate but still rightful place in his mind.'

In his diary Channon described Churchill's speech as 'an able, fiery speech not untouched by bitterness'. Chamberlain would not need to call a general election until 1940.

Speaking during the Budget debate on June 1, Churchill began with a good-humoured welcome to Chamberlain that set the House laughing. 'I take a friendly interest in this new Government,' he said. 'I do not quite know why I do. I cannot go so far as to call it a paternal interest, because, speaking candidly, it is not quite the sort of Government I should have bred myself. If it is not paternal, at any rate I think I may call it an avuncular interest.'

Churchill then set out his objections to the method Chamberlain had proposed for raising a new tax, the National Defence Contribution, by a special levy on industry. This levy, he believed, would be 'a check to enterprise' and not help the revenue. Instead, 'it would be opening up a whole vista of doubtful, superfluous and troublesome new matter'. He knew from his experience as Minister of Munitions 'that if the Government cannot maintain a mental and moral relationship with those who are producing arms they may be confronted with the gravest difficulties'. After a detailed presentation of the obstacles, Churchill urged Chamberlain to show 'the flexibility and resilience of mind, and the necessary detachment from personal and departmental aspects', to drop the scheme. His speech was successful. 'One of your best ever,' a former Liberal MP, Lord Melchett wrote on June 2, 'and I believe it was due to the facts you presented, to the tactful manner in which you handled the Prime Minister – grave and gay – that you gave him the courage to abandon NDC.'

Melchett added, 'You are a *very* great man, and God knows why you are not in the Cabinet to guide this old country in the difficult times we are going through.' Churchill knew how deep was the gulf between him and Chamberlain. 'I am not anxious to join the Government unless there is some real task they want me to do,' he replied. 'They are very pleased with themselves at present.'

That summer, Churchill's sources of information widened, giving him even greater knowledge of the gap between the war supplies being manufactured and the needs of the three services. In June he was sent information by Colonel Henry Hill, the former commander of the London Air Defence Brigade, and by Admiral Bertram Ramsay, the former Chief of Staff, Home Fleet, both of whom went to see him at Morpeth Mansions. On June 14 he gave another luncheon to the Anti-Nazi Council. A Jewish refugee from Germany, Eugen Spier, who was present, later recalled Churchill's warning that Britain's safety was being 'fatally imperilled' both by its lack of arms, and by the Government fostering in the Germans 'the dangerous belief that they need not fear interference by us whatever they do'.

Two weeks after Churchill spoke these words, the Supply Committee of the Committee of Imperial Defence discussed Britain's defence preparedness. Unknown to Churchill, its conclusions completely bore out his fears. During the discussion, the Committee's Chairman, Sir Arthur Robinson, pointed out that the absence of firm War Office orders meant that 'the supply work as a whole could not proceed effectively towards a conclusion'. The Air Ministry, Robinson added, had also disclosed 'a huge gap' between the supplies being manufactured 'and the needed war potential'. On present lines, his Committee concluded, 'it will not be possible for supply preparations to be completed by November 1939'.

Amid his preoccupations about defence, Churchill continued work on his final *Marlborough* volume. Deakin was frequently at Chartwell to help him. Violet Pearman and Grace Hamblin took turns in working the late-night shifts. 'My Senior and myself worked alternately with him long into the night,' Miss Hamblin later recalled. 'He would come from the dining room at about 10 o'clock – refreshed and often jovial. It was very obvious that this was his best time for working and that he enjoyed these hours. He would become entirely immersed, and would dictate until 2 or 3 in the morning: sometimes very slowly, and always weighing every word, and murmuring sentences to himself until he was satisfied with them – then bringing them forth, often with tremendous force, and glaring at the poor secretary when driving home a point. Often one of his "young men" – a literary assistant – or sometimes a friend – Professor Lindemann or Mr Bracken – would be present during these sessions, and I am sure he liked to have human company at these times – if there were two of us so much the better.'

Grace Hamblin added: 'There is no doubt he was a very hard taskmaster. He drove us. And he rarely gave praise. But he had subtle ways of showing his approval, and we would not have had it otherwise. He worked so hard himself and was so absolutely dedicated to the task in hand that he expected the same from others. He accepted it as his right. And in time we who worked for him realised that in full return for the stress and strain, we had the rare privilege of getting to know the beauty of his dynamic, but gentle character.'

On July 6, as pressure of correspondence and literary work grew, Churchill appointed a residential secretary, Kathleen Hill, to join Violet Pearman and Grace Hamblin. When her boss was away from Chartwell, Mrs Hill later recalled, 'it was as still as a mouse. When he was there it was vibrating,' and she added, 'He was a disappointed man, waiting for the call to serve his country.'

With Swinton's approval, on July 9 Churchill visited the Royal Air Force station at Biggin Hill to watch an interception exercise. Shortly after his visit, Anderson sent him a letter from MacLean; it told of a high casualty rate among pilots. Anderson took MacLean to Chartwell, writing to Churchill after their visit: 'In all sincerity I was very impressed by that incident in the life of the Duke of Marlborough which you read, and by your conclusion as to the power of personal example and inspiration. It is just that influence which is so disastrously absent from the Air Force at this moment. We are, as a Service, peculiarly dependent on, and susceptible to, the genuine inspiration of leadership, far more so than either the Navy or the Army, since in war, work is mainly done as indivduals and not in groups or companies.'

On September 17 Churchill appealed to Hitler, in an article in the *Evening Standard*, to abandon the persecution of Jews, Protestants and Catholics. Given Nazi persecution, he wrote, there could be no return of Germany's pre-war colonies and no British financial help. But he ended on a note of conciliation. 'One may dislike Hitler's system and yet admire his patriotic achievement,' he wrote. 'If our country were defeated I hope we should find a champion as indomitable to restore our courage and lead us back to our place among the nations.' He had appealed before 'that the Führer of Germany should now become the Hitler of peace', and he went on to explain: 'When a man is fighting in a desperate conflict he may have to grind his teeth and flash his eyes. Anger and hatred nerve the arm of strife. But success should bring a mellow, genial air and, by altering the mood to suit the new circumstances, preserve and consolidate in tolerance and goodwill what has been gained by conflict.'

Churchill's private correspondence revealed how unlikely he thought it that Hitler would mellow, and how serious he believed the situation to be. Writing from Chartwell on September 23, he told Lord Linlithgow that the year 1938 'will see Germany relatively stronger to the British Air Force and the French Army than now.' Churchill ended his letter with a forecast: 'I do not believe in a major war this year, because the French Army at present is as large as that of Germany and far more mature. But next year and the year after may carry these Dictator-ridden countries to the climax of their armament and of their domestic embarrassments. We shall certainly need to be ready by then'. As for himself, 'I have been living a perfectly placid life here painting and working at Marlborough, in fact I have hardly moved outside the garden since Parliament rose.'

On October 3 Churchill invited Eden to lunch at the Savoy with his Freedom and Peace group. Many of the group's supporters were influential in Labour and Liberal circles, 'but of course,' Churchill wrote teasingly, 'we always have a proportion of live Conservatives as well'. Without the support of the Trade Unions, Churchill wrote, 'our munition programme cannot be properly executed. This aspect is of real public importance. It may well be in the future that the Trade Unionists will detach themselves from particular political parties.' This, Churchill believed, 'would be an enormous gain to our political life'.

On October 4 a collection of Churchill's magazine articles was published as a book, entitled *Great Contemporaries*. It spanned his whole life, and contained penetrating and amusing essays, including those on Rosebery, Balfour, Asquith and the ex-Kaiser. At the request of the Foreign Office the essay on Hitler, originally printed in the *Strand* magazine, had been made less sharp. But neither the toned-down essay nor the conciliatory article in the *Evening Standard* marked any change in Churchill's attitude; on October 23 he wrote to Londonderry, who insisted that friendship with Germany was still possible: 'You cannot expect English people to be attracted by the brutal intolerances of Nazidom, though these may fade with time. On the other hand, we all wish to live on friendly terms with Germany. We know that the best Germans are ashamed of the Nazi excesses, and recoil from the paganism on which they are based.'

'We certainly do not wish to pursue a policy inimical to the legitimate interests of Germany,' Churchill told his friend of forty years, 'but you must surely be aware that when the German Government speaks of friendship with England, what they mean is that we shall give them back their former Colonies, and also agree to their having a free hand so far as we are concerned in Central and Southern Europe. This means that they would devour Austria and Czechoslovakia as a preliminary to making a gigantic middle-Europe bloc. It would certainly not be in our interest to connive at such policies of aggression. It would be wrong and cynical in the last degree to buy immunity for ouselves at the expense of the smaller countries of Central Europe. It would be contrary to the whole tide of British and United States opinion for us to facilitate the spread of Nazi tyranny over countries which now have a considerable measure of democratic freedom'.

At present, Churchill told Londonderry, Germany seemed intent upon a policy which would lead her 'to invade her smaller neighbours, slay them and take their farms and houses for themselves'. This was not an idea he had been 'brought up to admire'. All that Germany had to do in order to win British goodwill was 'not to commit crimes'. Churchill added, 'One must hope that in the passage of years these Dictators will disappear like other ugly creatures of the aftermath.'

On October 12, at a dinner in London, Churchill privately expressed his unease at the general lack of air preparedness. Hankey, who was at the dinner, wrote to Inskip, 'From some views which I heard Mr Winston Churchill declaiming to a group at the Trinity House Dinner, I should judge that he has a pretty shrewd knowledge of the situation, though he told me afterwards that he could not use his information in Parliament in the present dangerous world situation'.

That very day, Churchill had received a letter from Group Captain MacLean about the forthcoming visit to Britain of a German Air Mission, to be led by the German Air Minister, General Milch. MacLean sent Churchill the official notes of what Milch was to be shown, together with the comment by Air Chief Marshal Edgar Ludlow-Hewitt 'that we should have to comb the country in order to produce sufficient aircraft to get up any sort of show'. The Air Ministry had decided to allow the German mission to inspect on the ground one example of each modern aeroplane; as none of them were as yet completely equipped either with blind-flying panels or gun turrets, arrangements were being made by the Air Ministry, first to provide one fully-equipped example of each type, and then to train special pilots to carry out a simple formation fly-past. MacLean noted, 'This is a fair commentary on the state of equipment *and* the state of training!!!' Encouraged by Hankey's apparent interest at the dinner, Churchill sent him a copy of MacLean's letter, describing MacLean as 'a high Staff Officer of the RAF', but not naming him. Marking his letter to Hankey 'Secret and Personal', Churchill wrote: 'As one small instalment of the alarming accounts I have received of the state of the RAF, I send you the enclosed. It is for your own personal information, and I trust to our friendship and your honour that its origin is not probed. But look at the facts! We have invited the German Mission over – why I cannot tell. Highly competent men are coming. A desperate effort is now being made to present a sham-show. A power driven turret is to be shown, as if it was the kind of thing we are doing in the regular way. Ought it to be shown at all?'

Churchill's letter continued: 'You will see that a special telegram has to be sent to fetch one of the only men acquainted with this turret to give a demonstration. You will also see the feelings of some of the high officers concerned. You will also see from the statement, made by the Air Officer Commanding-in-Chief Bomber Command (paper C marked in red), Ludlow-Hewitt, how he is forced to address himself to the task of making a show; and what exertions are necessary to put little more than a hundred bombers in the air – the great majority of which (as the Germans will readily see) can barely reach the coast of Germany with a bomb load.'

In appealing to Hankey to take action, Churchill wrote: 'I remember how you played an essential part in saving the country over the convoy system, and how when young officers came to you and told you the truth, against Service rules, you saw that the seed did not fall on stony ground. If I had opportunity I could unfold a most shocking state of affairs in the Air Force, and no one would be more pleased than I if I could be refuted categorically. But you have a great responsibility – perhaps on the whole second to none – and therefore I leave the matter for the moment in your hands.'

Churchill ended his letter: 'Please send me the stuff back when you have done with it, for I am much inclined to make a Memorial to the Prime

Minister upon the whole position. Obviously it cannot be dealt with in public.'

Hankey had been concerned for some time about deficiencies in the rearmament programme. But he was angered that secret information had been given to Churchill. His reply was an eight-page rebuke; he would not 'on the present occasion' probe the origin of Churchill's information, he wrote, but he could not conceal 'that I am a good deal troubled by the fact of your receiving so many confidences of this kind'. Hankey added: 'You and I are very old friends who have hunted together in circumstances of supreme danger and difficulty. I have always valued your friendship. The frequent commendation of one for whom I have an immense admiration has been, and remains, a tremendous encouragement, especially in the parlous times through which we are passing. I feel, therefore, that I can open my mind quite frankly to you on the subject. It shocks me not a little that high Officers in disciplined Forces should be in direct communication with a leading Statesman who, though notoriously patriotic beyond criticism, is nevertheless in popular estimation regarded as a critic of the Departments under whom these Officers serve.'

'Backstairs' information, Hankey added, could only breed distrust and have 'a disintegrating effect on the discipline of the Services'. He advised Churchill to give his informants 'friendly counsel', in the interest first of the Service and second of their own 'careers and reputations', that they should speak, not to him but to 'their Commanding Officers' or to a 'friend' in the Air Department. Stung by Hankey's rebuke, Churchill's reply was curt: 'My dear Maurice, I certainly did not expect to receive from you a lengthy lecture when I went out of my way to give you, in strict confidence, information in the public interest. I thank you for sending me the papers back, and you may be sure I shall not trouble you again in such matters. Yours very sincerely, Winston S. Churchill'.

Churchill sent his reply to Hankey on October 21. Nine days earlier a secret document, of which he knew nothing, showed panic and conflict within Government circles about Britain's air preparedness. The document, an Air Staff memorandum circulated to the Cabinet by Swinton, stated that by December 1939 Germany would have a total first-line strength of 3,240 as against Britain's total of only 1,736. Swinton also pointed out that Britain's anti-aircraft artillery and searchlight defences 'will admittedly not even be within sight of completion to the approved scale until 1941'. Yet according to the Cabinet's Home Defence sub-committee, even the approved scale did not provide 'sufficient security'. Swinton's covering memorandum concluded, 'It is clear, therefore, that while we are to-day in a position of grave inferiority to Germany in effective air strength, the completion of our present programme will not provide an adequate remedy, and that by 1939 we shall still have failed to achieve that equality in air striking power with Germany which represents the policy of His Majesty's Government and the subject of Mr Baldwin's pledge to the country.'

Aware that Britain could not catch up with Germany in the air race, Churchill now focused his energy on the need to form a united front against Nazism. By means of the Freedom and Peace luncheons he extended the range of his contacts both inside the Labour movement and among his fellow-Conservatives. On November 2 he brought together as his guests at the Savoy Hotel, the Foreign Secretary, Anthony Eden, and the Socialist Mayor of Manchester, Joseph Toole. 'We have a small "focus",' Churchill explained to Lord Derby, 'which aims at gathering support from all Parties, especially those of the "left", for British rearmament, for the association of the two Western democracies (France and Britain), and for the maintenance of peace through British strength.' Derby too, an old adversary, agreed to attend.

In a letter to Lord Linlithgow on November 3, Churchill wrote bitterly, 'The deadly years of our policy were 1934 and 1935, "The year that the locusts have eaten". I expect we shall experience the consequences of these years in the near future.' But he did not intend to give way to despair, telling Linlithgow: 'our people are united and healthy. The spirit of Britain is reviving. The working people are ready to defend the cause of Liberty with their lives. The United States signals encouragement to us, for what that is worth. We must all fight our corners as well as we can, each in his station great or small.'

'Of course', Churchill told Linlithgow, 'my ideal is narrow and limited. I want to see the British Empire preserved for a few more generations in its strength and splendour,' and he added, 'Only the most prodigious exertions of British genius will achieve this result.'

At the end of November, Lord Halifax visited Hitler; his visit marked a turning point in the Government's policy of active appeasement. Reporting to the Cabinet on November 24, Halifax said 'he had encountered friendliness and a desire for good relations', although he admitted that his judgment might be wrong. The Germans, he added, 'had no policy of immediate adventure', and all would be well with Czechoslovakia if she treated 'the Germans living within her borders well'. In conclusion, Halifax told his colleagues that he would expect 'a beaver-like persistence' on the part of Germany 'in pressing their aims in Central Europe, but not in a form to give others cause – or probably occasion – to interfere'. Halifax also pointed out that Hitler 'had suggested an advance towards disarmament' and that he had also 'strongly criticised widespread talk of an imminent catastrophe and did not consider that the world was in a dangerous state'.

Chamberlain supported Halifax, telling the Cabinet that, with regard to the League of Nations, he 'took the same view as Herr Hitler. At present it was largely a sham, owing more particularly to the idea that it could impose its view by force'.

Preoccupied by the worsening balance of power, Churchill pointed out to General Ironside, who drove down to Chartwell to see him on December 5, that whereas the French Army was 'an incomparable machine at the moment', and would remain so in 1938 and 1939, by 1940 'the annual contingent in Germany would be double that of France'. Churchill and Ironside agreed that 1940 would be 'a very bad time for us'.

Ironside was impressed by Churchill. 'He ought to be the Minister of Supply if we are in for a crisis', he wrote in his diary. 'His energy and fiery brain seem unimpaired with age. He is certainly not dismayed by our difficulties. He says that our rulers are now beginning to get frightened. He said that sometimes he couldn't sleep at night thinking of our dangers, how all this wonderful Empire which had been built up so slowly and so steadily might all be dissipated in a minute.'

Halifax's visit to Hitler was discussed in the Commons on December 21, when Chamberlain expressed his regret that the debate was taking place at all. 'It is so difficult to say anything that can do good and so easy to say much that might do harm,' he said. During the debate, Churchill spoke of the persecution of the Jews in Germany. 'It is a horrible thing,' he said, 'that a race of people should be attempted to be blotted out of the society in which they have been born,' and he went on to express his unease about Halifax's visit to Berlin: 'We must remember how very sharp the European situation is at the present time. If it were thought that we were making terms for ourselves at the expense either of small nations or of large conceptions which are dear, not only to many nations, but to millions of people in every nation, a knell of despair would resound through many parts of Europe. It is for this reason that Lord Halifax's journey caused widespread commotion, as everyone saw, in all sorts of countries to whom we have no commitments other than the commitments involved in the Covenant of the League.'

It would be wrong, Churchill told the House, for any nation to give up 'a scrap of territory to keep the Nazi kettle boiling', and he went on to reiterate his theme of close relations with France as the keystone to British security. 'The relations,' he said, 'are founded upon the power of the French Army and the power of the British fleet.' Britain and France together, he believed 'with all their world-wide connections, in spite of their tardiness in making air preparations, constitute so vast and formidable a body that they will very likely be left alone undisturbed, at any rate for some time to come'. Towards the end of his speech Churchill argued that it would be wrong to ignore 'the moral forces involved' in public opinion: 'For five years I have been asking the House and the Government to make armaments – guns, aeroplanes, munitions – but I am quite sure that British armaments alone will never protect us in the times through which we may have to pass.'

Chamberlain's Government was now pursuing a policy diametrically opposed to that which Churchill advocated. On December 22 Inskip explained to the Cabinet the dangers inherent in increased defence expenditure, insisting that it was of vital importance to maintain Britain's credit facilities and 'general balance of trade'. Seen 'in its true perspective', the maintenance of British economic stability 'could properly be regarded as a fourth arm in defence, alongside the three Defence Services without which purely military effort would be of no avail'. Another reason for not increasing defence expenditure, Inskip explained, was that Britain's 'long term' foreign policy aimed at 'changing the present assumption as to our potential enemies'. Far from working with France, as Churchill wished, this would involve planning and expenditure on the basis of 'no continental role' for the Army, whose main task would be home and imperial defence. In addition, Inskip wrote, 'Germany has guaranteed the inviolability and integrity of Belgian territory, and there seems no good reason for thinking it would be in Germany's interest not to honour this agreement.'

Chamberlain supported Inskip, stating that he did not accept that air parity with Germany was still essential, and explaining to his Cabinet that 'no pledge can last for ever'. Baldwin's pledge, after having been long neglected, was thus officially, but secretly, abandoned. After Sir John Simon had spoken against putting any money into an 'exaggerated production of reserves', Halifax drew the logical conclusion, telling his colleagues that as as result of their discussion 'it was of great importance to make further progress in improving relations with Germany'.

Churchill was now sixty-three. On 2 January 1938 he left England for another holiday at Maxine Elliot's Château de l'Horizon. There he dictated the last chapters of the fourth and final volume of his biography of Marlborough, working so hard, Violet Pearman wrote to a friend, that he did not even have time to paint. He had been very tired when he set off on his journey, but seemed to regain strength through working. 'Mr Churchill looks better even for this short change,' Mrs Pearman wrote to

Lindemann. 'He has not lost a single thing on his journeyings alone, and is very pleased.'

On his return to Chartwell at the beginning of February, Churchill found information awaiting him about training problems in Bomber Command; the information came from MacLean, whom he invited back to Chartwell to discuss the matter in detail. Wigram's friend Michael Creswell, who had just spent two and a half years at the Berlin Embassy as Third Secretary, also asked to see him to discuss the most recent information on the strength of the German Army.

At the end of January, Group Captain Frank Don, who had just spent three and a half years in Berlin as Air Attaché, arranged, without informing the Air Ministry, to give Churchill the latest details of German air preparations. The Cabinet also had these details, but rejected a new Air Staff scheme put forward by Swinton, designed to go as far towards meeting them as peace-time financing would allow. Swinton warned his colleagues that the scheme that was agreed, 'to speak quite frankly, was inadequate *vis-à-vis* Germany'.

On January 27, as the first phase of a 'general appeasement' of European tensions, Chamberlain proposed, at the Cabinet Foreign Policy Committee, 'an entirely new chapter' in the history of African colonial development', whereby Germany 'would be brought into the arrangement by becoming one of the African Colonial Powers'. Under Chamberlain's plan, Hitler's Germany would be given 'certain territories to administer' in Africa.

Chamberlain also hoped to win Mussolini's friendship. At a Cabinet meeting on February 16 it became clear that Eden, in his insistence on a firmer attitude towards Italy, did not have Chamberlain's support. The disagreement, which was known to many MPs, came to a climax on February 17 at the meeting of the back-bench Foreign Affairs Committee, at which Churchill was present, and spoke in support of Eden. Eden later wrote that Churchill had urged the Committee 'to rally behind me at a difficult time' and had told his fellow MPs, 'if we were weak now, the risk of war would inevitably be greater in the future'.

Not to be deflected in his search for Italian friendship, Chamberlain decided to open negotiations with Mussolini. Isolated in Cabinet, Eden resigned. Churchill was at Chartwell talking to Group Captain Don when the news of Eden's resignation was brought in. 'I must confess,' he later wrote, 'that my heart sank, and for a while the dark waters of despair overwhelmed me.' Eden, whom he had earlier feared was a lightweight, had now become the 'one strong young figure standing up against long, dismal, drawling tides of drift and surrender, of wrong measurements and feeble impulses.' That night Churchill was unable to sleep: 'From midnight till dawn I lay in my bed consumed by emotions of sorrow and fear. I watched the daylight slowly creep in through the windows, and saw before me in mental gaze the vision of Death.'

Hankey felt otherwise, telling a friend that he had woken up that morning 'with a strange feeling of relief', and he went on to explain that Chamberlain was 'determined to improve relations with Italy and if possible with Germany'. During the Eden resignation debate on February 21, Churchill spoke both of the appeasement of Italy, and of Hitler's action on February 16 in forcing the Austrian Government to give the Ministry of the Interior to an Austrian Nazi. 'This has been a good week for Dictators,' he said. 'It is one of the best they have ever had. The German Dictator has laid his heavy hand upon a small but historic country, and the Italian Dictator has carried his vendetta to a victorious conclusion against my right Hon friend the late Foreign Secretary. The conflict between the Italian Dictator and my right Hon friend has been a long one. There can be no doubt, however, who has won. Signor Mussolini has won. All the might, majesty, dominion and power of the British Empire was no protection to my right Hon friend. Signor Mussolini has got his scalp.'

Churchill warned the House that Chamberlain had acted 'in the hope that by great and far-reaching acts of submission, not merely in sentiment and pride, but in material matters, peace may be preserved,' and he went on to ask: 'What price shall we all have to pay for this? No one can compute it. Small countries in Europe will take their cue to move to the side of power and resolution.' His concluding words sent a chill down the spine of many of those who heard him: 'I predict that the day will come when, at some point or other, you will have to make a stand, and I pray to God, when that day comes, that we may not find, through an unwise policy, that we have to make that stand alone.'

The *Yorkshire Post* described Churchill as having voiced 'as on many other occasions, the widespread sentiments of anxiety and perplexity in the country'. The *Evening Standard*, however, not only opposed Churchill's call for collective action to deter Germany from aggression, but cancelled his contract for fortnightly articles. The *Daily Telegraph*, a paper opposed to the Government's appeasement policy, and owned by Churchill's friend Lord Camrose, agreed to serve as his fortnightly journalistic outlet.

On February 26 Chamberlain appointed Halifax to succeed Eden as Foreign Secretary. Hitler was even then putting renewed pressure on Austria to become part of the German Reich. In response to this pressure, the Austrian Prime Minister, Kurt von Schuschnigg, called a plebiscite; Austrians would be asked to vote for or against preserving their independence. On the afternoon of March 11 Halifax telegraphed to Schuschnigg that Britain could not 'take the responsibility' of advising him to take any action 'which might expose his country to dangers against which His Majesty's Government are unable to guarantee protection'. That same afternoon, after Italy announced it would do nothing to help preserve Austrian independence, Schuschnigg resigned. At ten o'clock in the evening German troops crossed into Austria. Within twenty-four hours thousands of those hostile to the new Nazi regime were arrested and sent to concentration camps. Hundreds were shot. Tens of thousands of liberals, democrats, socialists and Jews sought to flee.

During the Austria debate in the Commons on March 14, Chamberlain promised a 'fresh review' of Britain's Defence programmes. Churchill welcomed this promise, but warned that if action were delayed too long a point might well be reached 'where continued resistance and true collective security would become impossible'. He continued, 'The gravity of the events of the 11th of March cannot be exaggerated. Europe is confronted with a programme of aggression, nicely calculated and timed, unfolding stage by stage, and there is only one choice open, not only to us, but to other countries who are unfortunately concerned – either to submit, like Austria, or else to take effective measures while time remains to ward off the danger and, if it cannot be warded off, to cope with it.'

Churchill then spoke of Czechoslovakia, the country which was likely to be threatened next and which, he pointed out, manufactured the munitions on which both Roumania and Yugoslavia depended for their defence. She had been isolated politically and economically as a result of Hitler's annexation of Austria. Surrounded now on three sides by Germany, her communications and her trade were both now in jeopardy. 'To English ears,' he said, 'the name of Czechoslovakia sounds outlandish. No doubt they are only a small democratic State, no doubt they have an army only two or three times as large as ours, no doubt they have a munitions supply only three times as great as that of Italy, but still they are a virile people; they have their treaty rights, they have a line of fortresses, and they have a strongly manifested will to live freely.'

Churchill feared that Chamberlain's promise to accelerate rearmament would not, in itself, be enough to preserve peace. The small states of Europe had to be brought into a system of collective defence; had to feel that they could rely upon Britain's word, and he continued, addressing the Conservative benches: 'I know that some of my hon Friends on this side of the House will laugh when I offer them this advice. I say, "Laugh, but listen". I affirm that the Government should express in the strongest terms our adherence to the Covenant of the League of Nations and our resolve to procure by international action the reign of law in Europe.'

Churchill advocated 'a solemn treaty for mutual defence against aggression', organised by Britain and France 'in what you may call a Grand Alliance', and explained, 'If they had their Staff arrangements concerted; if all this rested, as it can honourably rest, upon the Covenant of the . League of Nations, in pursuance of all the purposes and ideals of the League of Nations; if that were sustained, as it would be, by the moral sense of the world; and if it were done in the year 1938 – and believe me, it may be the last chance there will be for doing it – then I say that you might even now arrest this approaching war.' He then told the House, 'Before we cast away this hope, this cause and this plan, which I do not at all disguise has an element of risk, let those who wish to reject it ponder well and earnestly upon what will happen to us if, when all else has been thrown to the wolves, we are left to face our fate alone.'

'Winston makes the speech of his life in favour of the League,' Harold Nicolson noted in his diary that night. On March 15 the *Star* declared, in its leading article, 'We are grateful that one man spoke out in Parliament last night, and made a speech which fitted the hour.' But at the very moment of Germany's annexation of Austria, the Government publicly abandoned Baldwin's air parity pledge of 1934. Of the promise to have 1,500 first-line machines by March 1937 Inskip told the Commons: 'That promise was not accompanied by another promise that they would be modern machines. It was well known to everybody that they would be to a large extent of obsolescent types.'

Inskip also revealed the Cabinet's decision not to define air parity as equal first-line strength, telling the House, 'I think the Prime Minister is only doing what most men of common sense would do in saying that if you attempt to take first-line strength as the one yard stick in determining parity, you are proceeding on a wholly deceitful basis'. Staggered by this new definitition, Churchill recalled that three and a half years earlier the Government had based its parity promise on a calculation of British first-line strength, and he added: 'I think it is very unsatisfactory that now, this having been deliberately adopted as the standard by the Government, we should be invited to adopt an entirely new and vague standard. I am quite certain that we should not have been invited to adopt that standard unless it was impossible for the Government to show that they had maintained their pledge upon the standard which they formerly prescribed to the House.'

On March 18, in his final *Evening Standard* article, Churchill pressed the Government to join the recent French declaration to aid Czechoslovakia if she were the victim of unprovoked aggression. But the British Government had quite different plans; at the Cabinet's Foreign Policy Committee that day, Inskip described Czechoslovakia as 'an unstable unit in Central Europe' and told his colleagues he saw no reason why Britain 'should take any steps to maintain such a unit in being'. Commenting on the French declaration upholding the integrity of Czechoslovakia, Chamberlain 'wondered', the minutes recorded, 'whether it would not be possible to make some arrangement which would prove more acceptable to Germany'.

Czechoslovakia would be asked to make some territorial concession to Germany with regard to its German-speaking border areas, the Sudetenland mountains. Yet these mountains constituted Czechoslovakia's natural defence line and contained much of its raw material and industrial wealth.

Despite the deep divisions over policy between Churchill and Chamberlain, there were those in Whitehall who felt that Churchill ought now to be given a Ministerial task. There was talk of making him Air Minister. Among those who were attracted to this was Thomas Jones, the former Deputy Secretary to the Cabinet, who wrote to a friend on March 20 that 'his driving power would soon be felt throughout the Department down to the typists and messengers'. But on 'policy', Jones added, 'he would have to be kept in chains'.

Chamberlain had no intention of bringing Churchill in. He and Halifax both rejected Churchill's call for a Grand Alliance. On March 21 Halifax told the Cabinet Committee on Foreign policy 'that the great majority of responsible people in the country would be opposed to any new commitments'. This was also Chamberlain's conclusion. But with Hitler now master of Austria, and beginning a barrage of propaganda against the Czechs, Churchill was convinced that peace in Europe would only be preserved, he told the Commons on March 24, by means of an 'accumulation of deterrents against the aggressor'. Commenting on a statement by Chamberlain earlier in the debate, that France and Britain would work together for their mutual defence, he asked whether it was an actual alliance. If so, 'Why not say so? Why not make it effective by a military convention of the most detailed character? Are we, once again, to have all the disadvantages of an alliance without its advantages, and to have commitments without full security?'

Churchill believed that an Anglo-French arrangement for mutual defence constituted 'the great security' for both Britain and France, and he exhorted the Government: 'Treat the defensive problems of the two countries as if they were one. Then you will have a real deterrent against unprovoked aggression, and if the deterrent fails to deter, you will have a highly organised method of coping with the aggressor. The present rulers of Germany will hesitate long before they attack the British Empire and the French Republic if those are woven together for defence purposes into one very powerful unit'. Churchill then spoke of Czechoslovakia. Unless German pressure were countered, he declared, 'Czechoslovakia will be forced to make continuous surrenders, far beyond the bounds of what any impartial tribunal would consider just or right, until finally her sovereignty, her independence, her integrity, have been destroyed'.

Churchill told the Commons, 'Now the victors are the vanquished, and those who threw down their arms in the field and sued for an armistice are striding on to world mastery.' Halifax disagreed; a week earlier he had told his Cabinet colleagues that he 'distinguished in his own mind between Germany's racial efforts, which no one could question, and a lust for conquest on a Napoleonic scale which he himself did not credit'.

On the day after his speech of March 24 Churchill flew to Paris, where to Halifax's annoyance he stressed, with all the leading French politicians whom he met, the need for a binding Alliance between their two countries, to serve as a rallying point for the States of Central Europe and the Balkans. 'If France broke,' he wrote on April 14 in the first of his *Daily Telegraph* articles, 'everything would break, and the Nazi domination of Europe, and potentially of a large part of the world, would seem to be inevitable.' A month later, at Morpeth Mansions, Churchill met Konrad Henlein, the leader of the Sudeten Germans. Henlein told Churchill that he was prepared to accept autonomy for the Sudeten Germans within Czechoslovakia's existing borders. By this means the territorial integrity of Czechoslovakia would be preserved. Speaking at Bristol three days later, Churchill said that he saw no reason why the Sudeten Germans should not become 'trusted and honoured partners in what was after all the most progressive and democratic of the new States of Europe'.

That May, despite continual pressure from Swinton and support from Duff Cooper, the Cabinet turned down an accelerated Air Ministry expansion scheme; a scheme, Swinton warned, that was itself 'below what the Air Staff regard as the minimum insurance'. On May 16, having failed to persuade Chamberlain to adopt the minimum air scheme, and beset by criticisms of Air Ministry incompetence, Swinton resigned. Two weeks later Churchill told an audience at Sheffield: 'It is now admitted that there has been a lamentable breakdown and inadequacy in the most vital sphere of all, namely our Air Force and our Air Defences. The Air Minister, Lord Swinton, has been forced to resign, but I will tell you that in my opinion he is one of the least blameworthy among those responsible. He worked night and day. He accomplished a great deal, and his contribution to rearmament was far greater than that of some others who now hold high office of State.'

On August 19, at Chartwell, Churchill received a German Army officer, Major Ewald von Kleist, who belonged to an anti-Nazi group of officers opposed to a German attack on Czecholsovakia. Von Kleist asked Churchill for a letter that he could show his fellow-officers. 'I am sure that the crossing of the frontier of Czechoslovakia by German armies or aviation in force will bring about a renewal of the world war,' Churchill wrote. 'I am as certain as I was at the end of July 1914 that Britain will march with France, and certainly the United States is now strongly anti-Nazi. Such a war, once started, would be fought out like the last to the bitter end, and one must consider not what might happen in the first few months, but where we should all be at the end of the third or fourth year.'

As to the spectre of air bombardment, which four years earlier had influenced Baldwin against British rearmament, Churchill told Kleist: 'It would be a great mistake to imagine that the slaughter of the civil population following upon air-raids would prevent the British Empire from developing its full war power. Though, of course, we should suffer more at the beginning than we did last time. But the submarine is practically mastered by scientific methods, and we shall have the freedom of the seas and the support of the greater part of the world. The worse the air-slaughter at the beginning, the more inexpiable would be the war. Evidently all the great Nations engaged in the struggle, once started would fight on for victory or death'.

Throughout the summer of 1938 Churchill worked at Chartwell to finish his fourth and final *Marlborough* volume. He also completed the first chapter of his History of the English-Speaking Peoples, writing to Lord Halifax on August 20 that he was 'horribly entangled with the Ancient Britons, the Romans, the Angles, Saxons and Jutes all of whom I thought I had escaped for ever when I left school!'

A week later, as negotiations between the Czechs and the Sudeten Germans continued, Chamberlain wrote to Churchill, 'Our latest information from Prague is rather more encouraging.' Churchill did not share Chamberlain's optimism. 'The fabricated stories of a Marxist plot in Czechoslovakia,' he told his constituents on August 27, 'and the orders to the Sudeten Deutsch to arm and defend themselves, were disquieting signs, similar to those which preceded the seizure of Austria.' If left to their own devices, Churchill believed, Henlein and the Czech President, Edouard Beneš, could settle their differences without any transfer of territory to Germany. A British negotiator, Churchill's former Liberal colleague Lord Runciman, was even then in Prague, seeking to bring the two sides together. It was possible, however, Churchill warned, that 'outside forces, larger and fiercer ambitions, might prevent that settlement'.

Were that to happen, and the Germans then invaded Czechoslovakia, it would be 'an outrage against civilisation and freedom of the whole world'. Every country would ask itself, 'Whose turn will it be next?'

On August 30 Halifax told the Cabinet that he had discussed the Czech situation with Churchill, who had referred 'to the possibility of a joint note to Berlin from a number of Powers'. Halifax deprecated any such joint policy, warning his colleagues that 'if we were to invite countries to sign a joint note, they would probably ask embarrassing questions as to our attitude in the event of Germany invading Czechoslovakia'. Chamberlain supported Halifax, telling the Cabinet that the policy 'of an immediate declaration or threat might well result in disunity, in this country, and in the Empire'. He did not think that war was a prospect 'which the Defence Ministers would view with great confidence'.

Inskip then told the Cabinet, 'On the question whether we were ready to go to war, in a sense this country would never be ready owing to its vulnerable position.' Britain had not yet reached 'our maximum preparedness and should not do so for another year or more.' Nor could she put an army into the field 'for many months after the outbreak of war'.

The fourth volume of Churchill's book *Marlborough, His Life and Times* was published on September 2. That same day Germany mobilised, and Hitler declared that the Sudeten Germans needed to be protected against their Czech rulers. Churchill wrote to the journalist Richard Freund, 'I have very strongly the feeling that the veto of France, Britain and Russia would certainly prevent the disaster of war.' That afternoon the Soviet Ambassador, Ivan Maisky, drove down to Chartwell, where he told Churchill that the Soviet Government wished to invoke Article II of the League of Nations Covenant, under which the League Powers were obliged to consult together if war was imminent.

According to Maisky, the Soviet Union was anxious to examine with Britain and France various means of defending Czechoslovakia against a German attack. On September 3 Churchill sent Halifax an account of this conversation, but in his reply two days later, Halifax doubted whether action under Article II 'would be helpful'. Despite encouragement from Churchill, the Government did not wish to become involved with Russia.

On September 7, to Churchill's amazement and anger, *The Times* expressed its support for the separation of the Sudetenland from Czechoslovakia. Two days later, as German troops massed on the Czech frontier, Chamberlain decided to seek negotiations with Hitler, and to exclude the Czechs from those negotiations. Unaware of this decision, Churchill went that day to Downing Street. 'He had come,' Hoare later recalled, 'to demand an immediate ultimatum to Hitler. He was convinced it was our last chance of stopping a landslide, and according to his information, which was directly contrary to our own, both the French and the Russians were ready for an offensive against Germany.'

That night Churchill telephoned Halifax, to reiterate his call for an ultimatum. He could not know that Halifax, that very evening, had warned the French Government that Britain would not be willing 'automatically to find ourselves at war with Germany because France might be involved in discharge of obligations which Great Britain did not share and which a large section of opinion in this country had always disliked'. Churchill wanted the Franco-Russian Pact to serve as a cornerstone of tripartite action. Halifax was determined to separate Britain from it.

On September 11 Churchill went back to Downing Street, where he told Chamberlain and Halifax that Britain should inform Germany 'that if she set foot in Czechoslovakia we should at once be at war with her'. He was convinced that such a declaration would deter Hitler from action. Halifax and Chamberlain disagreed. In line with the leader in *The Times* four days earlier, they were prepared to accept a plebiscite in the Sudetenland, on the understanding that if a majority voted to separate from Czechoslovakia they should be allowed to do so. Returning to Morpeth Mansions, Churchill wrote to Lord Moyne: 'Owing to the neglect of our defences and the mishandling of the German problem in the last five years, we seem to be very near the bleak choice between War and Shame. My feeling is that we shall choose Shame, and then have War thrown in a little later, on even more adverse terms than at present.'

Chamberlain believed that war could be averted if the Czechoslovak Government would accept the loss of the Sudetenland. On September 15 he flew to Hitler's mountain retreat at Berchtesgaden in the Bavarian Alps, where he told Hitler that in principle he had nothing against the separation of the Sudetenland from Czechoslovakia, and would support a plebiscite to determine the views of the inhabitants. 'If as I fear the Government is going to let Czechoslovakia be cut to pieces,' Churchill wrote to A.H. Richards, on September 17, after Chamberlain's return from Berchtesgaden, 'it seems to me that a period of very hard work lies before us all.'

Unknown to Churchill, Chamberlain told the Cabinet that very morning that he wanted neither publicity nor debate about the fact that for the past five days the Sudeten leaders, who had earlier wanted to accept autonomy, were receiving 'their orders' from Berlin. 'As regards Parliament,' Chamberlain told the Cabinet, his own view was 'that a discussion would result in wrecking very delicate negotiations.' Those negotiations were not about the principle of transfer, which Chamberlain had conceded at Berchtesgaden, but about the details of a plebiscite and the timetable of the transfer of territory. On September 21, in strictest secrecy, the British and French Governments urged Beneš to agree to the transfer of the Sudetenland to Germany. If he refused, they told him, it would create a situation 'for which France and Britain could take no responsibility'.

Unaware of this message, Churchill was certain that if Beneš resisted a German invasion, Britain and France would support him. That same day he contemplated sending him a telegram, 'Fire your cannon, and all will be well.' In the end he did not send it, feeling, he later wrote, 'that I should be grasping responsibilities which I had no right to seek, and no power to bear'.

That night Churchill issued a statement to the Press. The collapse of Czechoslovakia, he warned, would place Britain and France in an ever weaker and more dangerous situation. 'The mere neutralisation of Czechoslovakia means the liberation of twenty-five German divisions, which will threaten the Western front; in addition to which it will open up for the triumphant Nazis the road to the Black Sea. It is not Czechoslovakia alone which is menaced, but also the freedom and the democracy of all nations. The belief that security can be obtained by throwing a small State to the wolves is a fatal delusion. The war potential of Germany will increase in a short time more rapidly than it will be possible for France and Great Britain to complete the measures necessary for their defence.'

Chamberlain flew back to Germany on September 22, to Bad Godesberg on the Rhine, where he told Hitler of an Anglo-French Plan, worked out in London, for a plebiscite, to be followed, if the plebiscite favoured it, by the transfer of the Sudetenland to Germany. Churchill was given details of the plan when he went to Downing Street that afternoon. He then called a meeting at Morpeth Mansions of several friends, all of them Peers or MPs, among them Lord Lloyd, Archibald Sinclair, Brendan Bracken and Harold Nicolson, who feared that Czechoslovakia was going to be abandoned. 'While I wait for the lift to ascend,' Nicolson noted in his diary, 'Winston appears from a taxi. We go up together. "This", I say, "is hell". To which Winston remarked, "It is the end of the British Empire." '

During the meeting of Churchill's friends at Morpeth Mansions, Clement Attlee telephoned to say that the Opposition were prepared, Nicolson noted, 'to come in with us if we like'. Nicolson added: 'We continue the conversation. It boils down to this. Either Chamberlain comes back with peace with honour or he breaks it off. In either case we shall support him. But if he comes back with peace with dishonour, we shall go out against him. "Let us form the focus", says Winston.'

At Godesberg, Hitler demanded the immediate cession of the Sudetenland. Chamberlain tried to argue in favour of a plebiscite first. On the second day of the meeting he acceded to Hitler's demand that there should be no plebiscite at all in areas with more than 50 per cent German-speaking inhabitants. He also agreed that all Czech fortifications and war materials in the area should be transferred to Germany.

Assuring Hitler that he would urge the Czech Government to accept these terms, Chamberlain returned to England, where he told senior members of his Cabinet that he 'thought he had established some degree of personal influence over Herr Hitler' and that he was 'satisfied that Herr Hitler would not go back on his word once he had given it to him'. Hitler had assured Chamberlain that he wanted 'no Czechs' inside Germany.

On September 26 Churchill went again to see Chamberlain and Halifax at Downing Street, to ask for a declaration by Britain, France and Russia, that Hitler would not be allowed to invade Czechoslovakia. But Chamberlain was even then pressing the Czechs to agree to Hitler's demands; on the morning of September 28, when the Czechs refused them, Chamberlain telegraphed to Hitler, asking for a further conference.

That afternoon Chamberlain gave the Commons an account of the crisis so far; as he was speaking he was handed a message. He interrupted his speech to say that the message was from Hitler, inviting him to a Four-Power Conference of Germany, Italy, France and Britain, to take place in Munich. Amid much excitement and applause he declared that he would accept the invitation and fly to Munich. Most MPs rose in their seats and waved their order papers with enthusiasm. Churchill, Eden, Amery and Nicolson remained seated. Those MPs near Churchill called out, 'Get up! Get up!' Then, as Chamberlain rose to leave the Chamber, Churchill rose to shake his hand and wished him 'God Speed'.

Chamberlain flew back to Germany on September 29, reaching Munich at noon. He at once asked Hitler if a Czech delegation which had also arrived in Munich could be a party to the discussions. Hitler refused; instead, the Czechs were kept waiting in a separate room while their fate was decided. For twelve hours Hitler, Chamberlain, Daladier and Mussolini discussed the details and timetable of the transfer of the Sudetenland to Germany. Shortly after midnight their agreement was presented to the Czechs, who were given the choice of accepting or rejecting them. There could be no further negotiations on the terms themselves.

The German occupation of the predominantly German-speaking areas was to begin on the following day; without a plebiscite and without delay. Where the linguistic majority was uncertain, there would be a plebiscite. In the transferred areas Germany would acquire all fortifications, arms and industrial installations.

That night, before the details of the Munich Agreement reached London, Churchill was at the Savoy Hotel dining at the Other Club. Among those dining there was the First Lord of the Admiralty, Duff Cooper. The first details of the Munich terms reached the Savoy in the early hours of the morning. As soon as he heard them, Duff Cooper left the room, determined to resign from the Government. When Churchill left the hotel he paused in the doorway of one of the restaurants, from which emerged the sounds of laughter and enjoyment. Then, as he turned away, he muttered to a friend, 'Those poor people! They little know what they will have to face.'

Three days later the House of Commons debated the Munich Agreement. Having resigned from the Cabinet, Duff Cooper spoke first, telling the House in his resignation speech: 'The Prime Minister has believed in addressing Herr Hitler through the language of sweet reasonableness. I have believed that he was more given to the language of the mailed fist.' Chamberlain replied: 'Ever since I assumed my present office my main purpose has been to work for the pacification of Europe, for the removal of those suspicions and those animosities which have so long poisoned the air. The path which leads to appeasement is long and bristles with obstacles. The question of Czechoslovakia is the latest and perhaps the most dangerous. Now that we have got past it, I feel that it may be possible to make further progress along the road to sanity.'

Not all MPs saw 'Munich' as a triumph; the Labour Party leader, Clement Attlee, described it as both a 'humiliation' and a 'victory for brute force'. The Liberal leader, Archibald Sinclair, said that a policy 'which imposes injustice on a small and weak nation, and tyranny on free men and women, can never be the foundation for lasting peace'. More than thirty Conservatives also spoke against the agreement, including Eden, Amery, and Bonar Law's son Richard.

When Churchill rose to speak on October 5 he knew that he was expressing the unease of many ordinary men and women. 'All is over,' he began. 'Silent, mournful, abandoned, broken, Czechoslovakia recedes into the darkness. She has suffered in every respect by her association with the Western democracies and with the League of Nations, of which she has always been an obedient servant.' The Munich Agreement was 'a total and unmitigated defeat'. In a period of time 'which may be measured by years, but which may be measured only by months, Czechoslovakia will be engulfed in the Nazi regime'. When Hitler chose 'to look westward', Britain and France would bitterly regret the loss of the Czech fortress line. Many people, 'no doubt honestly', believed that they were 'only giving away the interests of Czechoslovakia, whereas I fear we shall find that we have deeply compromised, and perhaps fatally endangered, the safety and even the independence of Great Britain and France'.

Churchill refused to accept the view that the Munich agreement was a triumph for British diplomacy, or that it would open the way, as

Chamberlain believed, to a reduction of European tension, and to even closer relations between Britain and Germany. Starkly, he declared: 'We are in the presence of a disaster of the first magnitude which has befallen Great Britain and France. Do not let us blind ourselves to that. It must now be accepted that all the countries of Central and Eastern Europe will make the best terms they can with the triumphant Nazi Power. The system of alliances in Central Europe upon which France has relied for her safety has been swept away, and I can see no means by which it can be reconstituted. The road down the Danube to the Black Sea, the resources of corn and oil, the road which leads as far as Turkey, has been opened.'

Hitler need not fire 'a single shot', Churchill said, to extend his power into the Danube basin. 'You will see, day after day, week after week, the entire alienation of those regions. Many of those countries, in fear of the rise of the Nazi Power, have already got politicians, Ministers, Governments, who were pro-German, but there was always an enormous popular movement in Poland, Roumania, Bulgaria and Yugoslavia which looked to the Western democracies and loathed the idea of having this arbitrary rule of the totalitarian system thrust upon them, and hoped that a stand would be made. All that has gone by the board.'

Turning to what he was convinced was the fatal flaw in the policy of appeasement, Churchill told the House: 'The Prime Minister desires to see cordial relations between this country and Germany. There is no difficulty at all in having cordial relations with the German people. Our hearts go out to them. But they have no power. You must have diplomatic and correct relations, but there can never be friendship between the British democracy and the Nazi Power, that Power which spurns Christian ethics, which cheers its onward course by a barbarous paganism, which vaunts the spirit of aggression and conquest, which derives strength and perverted pleasure from persecution, and uses, as we have seen, with pitiless brutality the threat of murderous force. That Power cannot ever be the trusted friend of the British democracy. What I find unendurable is the sense of our country falling into the power, into the orbit and influence of Nazi Germany and of our existence becoming dependent upon their good will or pleasure.'

It was to prevent that, Churchill continued, that 'I have tried my best to urge the maintenance of every bulwark of defence — first the timely creation of an Air Force superior to anything within striking distance of our shores; secondly the gathering together of the collective strength of many nations; and thirdly, the making of alliances and military conventions, all within the Covenant, in order to gather together forces at any rate to restrain the onward movement of this Power. It has all been in vain.

Every position has been successively undermined and abandoned on specious and plausible excuses.'

In the five days since Chamberlain's return from Munich there had been great public rejoicing, most visible in the enthusiasm of the crowds which welcomed Chamberlain back from Munich. Churchill ended his speech by referring to this jubilation:

> I do not grudge our loyal, brave people, who were ready to do their duty no matter what the cost, who never flinched under the strain of last week – I do not grudge them the natural, spontaneous outburst of joy and relief when they learned that the hard ordeal would no longer be required of them at the moment; but they should know the truth.
>
> They should know that there has been gross neglect and deficiency in our defences; they should know that we have sustained a defeat without a war, the consequences of which will travel far with us along our road; they should know that we have passed an awful milestone in our history, when the whole equilibrium of Europe has been deranged, and that the terrible words have for the time being been pronounced against the Western democracies:
>
> 'Thou art weighed in the balance and found wanting.'
>
> And do not suppose that this is the end. This is only the beginning of the reckoning. This is only the first sip, the first foretaste of a bitter cup which will be proffered to us year by year unless by a supreme recovery of moral health and martial vigour, we arise again and take our stand for freedom as in the olden time.

One of Chamberlain's Ministers, Malcolm MacDonald, later recalled how his own palms were sweating as Churchill spoke these words. When the vote was taken at the end of the debate, thirty Conservative MPs abstained. Thirteen of them, including Churchill, remained defiantly in their seats.

Triumphant at the annexation of the Sudetenland, Hitler now attacked Churchill publicly, telling an audience at Munich on the fifteenth anniversary of his first attempt to seize power: 'Mr Churchill may have an electorate of 15,000 or 20,000. I have one of 40,000,000. Once and for all we request to be spared from being spanked like a pupil by a governess'.

Returning to Chartwell, Churchill was momentarily defeated. To Paul Reynaud, who had resigned as Minister of Justice from the French Cabinet, in protest at Munich, he wrote: 'You have been infected by our weakness without being fortified by our strength. The politicians have broken the spirit of both countries successively,' and he went on to ask: 'Can we make head against the Nazi domination, or ought we severally to make the best terms possible with it – while trying to rearm? Or is a common effort still possible?'

Churchill did not have the answer. 'I do not know on what to rest today,' he admitted to Reynaud, and on October 11 he wrote to a Canadian acquaintance: 'I am now greatly distressed and for the time being staggered by the situation. Hitherto the peace-loving powers have been definitely stronger than the Dictators, but next year we must expect a different balance.'

26

From Munich to War

Churchill's opposition to the Munich Agreement marked his complete breach with Conservative Central Office. On 29 October 1938 he wrote to a Conservative Party stalwart, Sir Henry Page Croft: 'It may be possible to fight within the ranks of the Conservative Party, but will there be any rally of the strong forces of the Conservative Party to defend our rights and possessions, and to make the necessary sacrifices and exertions required for our safety, or is it all to go down the drain as it did in the India business, through the influence of the Central Office and the Government Whips? If so, I know my duty.'

Among those who were critical of Churchill's Munich speech was a senior Conservative member of his constituency, Sir Harry Goschen, who wrote to the constituency chairman: 'I cannot help thinking it was rather a pity that he broke up the harmony of the House by the speech he made. Of course he was not like a small ranting member, and his words were telegraphed all over the Continent and to America, and I think it would have been a great deal better if he had kept quiet and not made a speech at all.'

Another of Churchill's former constituency supporters, Colin Thornton-Kemsley, who had been active during the Munich debate drumming up an anti-Churchill lobby, later recalled, 'We wanted him to support the Conservative administration, not to discredit them.'

Despite vociferous local criticism, which Conservative Central Office encouraged, and which culminated in a public meeting at Winchester House in the City of London, Churchill's constituents gave him a vote of confidence on November 4. But Churchill sensed a mood of restraint among many MPs who might have been his allies; when, on November 12, the Secretary of the Anti-Nazi Council, A.H. Richards, suggested inviting Eden to one of its luncheons, Churchill replied, 'I doubt if Mr Eden would come. He is very shy at present.'

To the editor of the *Sunday Referee*, R.J. Minney, who had written to Churchill urging him to embark on a national speaking campaign to rouse public opinion from its 'state of apathy', he replied pessimistically on November 12: 'I am afraid that making speeches in the country no longer has the old effect. In the first place they are not reported or replied to as they used to be before the War. I did five or six meetings in March and April, in order to warn the country of what was coming this autumn, and everywhere had very large meetings in the best halls and platforms representative of all three parties, but while the labour entailed was enormous, it did not seem to produce the slightest result.'

Speaking at Weimar on November 6, Hitler warned the democracies of the 'dangers' of free speech, especially 'freedom for war-mongering'. Referring to Churchill's appeals to the opponents of Nazism inside Germany to make their voices heard, he declared, 'If Mr Churchill had less to do with traitors and more with Germans, he would see how mad his talk is, for I can assure this man, who seems to live on the moon, that there are no forces in Germany opposed to the régime – only the force of the National-Socialist movement, its leaders and its followers in arms.'

That same evening Churchill issued a reply to Hitler, who had gone on to abuse the other 'gentry' in British politics who had criticised him. 'I am surprised that the head of a great State should set himself to attack British Members of Parliament who hold no official position and who are not even the leaders of parties,' Churchill avowed. 'Such action on his part can only enhance any influence they may have, because their fellow-countrymen have long been able to form their own opinions about them, and really do not need foreign guidance.'

On November 17, a week after *Kristallnacht*, the night of anti-Jewish violence throughout Germany, Austria and the Sudetenland, Churchill asked the Commons, 'Is not this the moment when all should hear the deep, repeated strokes of the alarm bell, and when all should resolve that it shall be a call to action, and not the knell of our race and fame?' He went on to urge support for a Liberal amendment calling for the setting up of a Ministry of Supply. Chamberlain decided to use sarcasm to try to lessen the impact of Churchill's call. 'I have the greatest admiration for my right hon. Friend's many brilliant qualities,' he said. 'He shines in every direction. I remember once asking a Dominion statesman, who held high office for a number of years, what in his opinion was the most valuable quality a statesman could possess. His answer was, judgment. If I were asked whether judgment is the first of my right hon. Friend's many admirable qualities I should have to ask the House of Commons not to press me too far.'

Churchill did not know that in Cabinet on October 31 Chamberlain had told the Cabinet: 'A good deal of false emphasis had been placed on rearmament, as though one result of the Munich Agreement had been that it would be necessary for us to add to our rearmament programmes. Acceleration of existing programmes was one thing, but increases in the scope of our programme which would lead to a new arms race was a different proposition.' Chamberlain's proposition was not to abandon the Munich policies, but to continue with them, 'aimed', as he told his colleagues, 'at securing better relations'.

Nor did Churchill know that in a secret memorandum for the Cabinet, circulated on October 25, the new Secretary of State for Air, Sir Kingsley Wood had told his colleagues, 'It is clear that in our previous programmes of expansion we have not taken a sufficiently long-range view and have underestimated both the capacity and intentions of Germany.'

In advocating a Ministry of Supply on November 17, Churchill called upon the Conservative back-benchers to join him in supporting the Liberal amendment. 'Hon Gentlemen above the gangway,' he said, 'pledged, loyal, faithful supporters on all occasions of His Majesty's Government – must not imagine that they can throw their burden wholly on the Ministers of the Crown. Much power has rested with them. One healthy growl from those benches three years ago – and how different to-day would be the whole lay-out of our armaments production! Alas, that service was not forthcoming.' To vote for a Ministry of Supply would not affect the life of the Government, he said, but it would make the Government act. 'It would make a forward movement of real energy.' It was not a Party question, it had 'nothing to do with Party'; it was 'entirely an issue affecting the broad safety of the nation'.

Churchill's call was a complete failure. Not fifty, but only two, MPs went into the Lobby with him: Brendan Bracken and Harold Macmillan. Bitterly, Churchill wrote to Duff Cooper five days later: 'Chamberlain has now got away with everything. Munich is dead, the unpreparedness forgotten, and there is to be no real, earnest, new effort to arm the nation. Even the breathing space, purchased at hideous cost, is to be wasted.'

On December 1, the day after his sixty-fourth birthday, Churchill finished the first volume of his history of the English-Speaking Peoples. Four days later he was in the Commons to criticise the state of London's anti-aircraft defences. Then, still stung by Chamberlain's rebuke in the Ministry of Supply debate, he told his constituents on December 9:

> The Prime Minister said in the House of Commons the other day that where I failed, for all my brilliant gifts, was in the faculty of judging. I will gladly submit my judgment about foreign affairs and national defence during the last five years, in comparison with his own.

In February the Prime Minister said that tension in Europe had greatly relaxed. A few weeks later Nazi Germany seized Austria. I predicted that he would repeat this statement as soon as the shock of the rape of Austria passed away. He did so in the very same words at the end of July. By the middle of August Germany was mobilising for those bogus manoeuvres which, after bringing us all to the verge of a world war, ended in the complete destruction and absorption of the Republic of Czechoslovakia.

At the Lord Mayor's banquet in November at the Guildhall, he told us that Europe was settling down to a more peaceful state. The words were hardly out of his mouth before the Nazi atrocities on the Jewish population resounded throughout the civilised world.

Churchill also spoke of Chamberlain's predecessor:

In 1934 I warned Mr Baldwin that the Germans had a secret Air Force and were rapidly overhauling ours. I gave definite figures and forecasts. Of course, it was all denied with all the weight of official authority. I was depicted a scaremonger. Less than six months after Mr Baldwin had to come down to the House and admit he was wrong and he said, 'We are all to blame' and everybody said, 'How very honest of him to admit his mistake.'

He got more applause for making this mistake, which may prove fatal to the British Empire and to British freedom, than ordinary people would do after they rendered some great service which added to its security and power. Well, Mr Chamberlain was, next to Mr Baldwin, the most powerful Member of that Government. He was Chancellor of the Exchequer. He knew all the facts. His judgment failed just like that of Mr Baldwin and we are suffering from the consequences of it today.

Next Churchill referred to Lord Samuel, his colleague in the Liberal Government before the First World War. 'Four years ago,' he reminded his listeners, 'when I asked that the Air Force should be doubled and redoubled – more than that is being done now – Lord Samuel thought my judgment so defective that he likened me to a Malay running amok. It would have been well for him and his persecuted race if my advice had been taken. They would not be where they are now and we should not be where we are now.'

'It is on the background of these proved errors of judgment in the past,' Churchill ended, 'that I draw your attention to some of the judgments which have been passed upon the future, the results of which have not yet been proved.'

Four days after Churchill's speech, A.H. Richards wrote to him: 'I feel that for you, it has been a year of great exertion, but not a labour in vain. There are indications that around you are gathering resolute and dynamic forces in your valiant and unsparing efforts for the preservation of our precious heritage, freedom.' Eight days later Richards wrote again, telling Churchill that fifteen different towns had written to ask if Churchill could speak in their main halls. Richards added, 'In moving among people of all classes I find more than ever that the general feeling is that had we heeded in time your very wise counsel in the matter of Rearmament and the Covenant – so oft and so resolutely repeated during the past five years, we should not have drifted into such dire peril.'

To Clementine, who was on a cruise in the West Indies, Churchill wrote on December 22, 'Everything goes to show that our interests are declining throughout Europe, and that Hitler will be on the move again in February or March, probably against Poland.' On Christmas Day, Halifax's Principal Private Secretary, Oliver Harvey, wrote in his diary that the Government, in particular Inskip, was not pressing on with rearmament 'fundamentally, as the situation demands'. Harvey added: 'A much more vigorous and imaginative personality should be there. Winston is the obvious man, but I believe the PM would rather die than have him.'

Remaining at Chartwell, Churchill wrote about the Wars of the Roses and Joan of Arc. One morning, reading of the death, at the age of sixty-eight, of the man who had fallen in love with Clementine in 1903, he wrote to her: 'My dearest Clemmie, you will be saddened to know that Sidney Peel has died. I do not know the cause. Many are dying now that I knew when we were young. It is quite astonishing to reach the end of life & feel just as you did fifty years before. One must always hope for a sudden end, before faculties decay. But that is a lugubrious ending to my letter. I love to think of you in your sunshine. But I hope & pray that some solid gains are being made in your poise & strength.'

A week later, Churchill's first granddaughter, Edwina, was born, the daughter of Diana and Duncan Sandys. She came 'most unexpectedly,' Churchill wrote to Clementine, 'was less than eight months old and weighed just over four and a half pounds. She was perfectly well in the afternoon, sitting up and could see me. The baby is tiny but perfect, and by my latest news, thriving.'

On 7 January 1939 Churchill flew to Paris, where he lunched with Reynaud, saw the former Prime Minister Léon Blum, and took the night train to the South of France, for two and a half weeks with Maxine Elliott at the Château de l'Horizon. From there he wrote to Clementine about his talks with French politicians in Paris: 'They all confirm the fact that the

Germans had hardly any soldiers at all on the French frontier during the crisis. And Blum told me, (secret) that he had it from Daladier himself that both Generals Gamelin and Georges were confident that they could have broken through the weak unfinished German line, almost unguarded as it was, by the fifteenth day at the latest, and that if the Czechs could have held out only for that short fortnight, the German armies would have had to go back to face invasion. On the other side there is their great preponderance in the air, and it depends what you put on that how you judge the matter.'

Churchill added, 'I have no doubt that a firm attitude by England and France would have prevented war, and I believe that history will incline to the view that if the worst had come to the worst, we should have been far better off than we may be at some future date.'

Of his Cabinet prospects, Churchill wrote to Clementine, 'I do not think it would be much fun to take these burdens and neglects upon my shoulders, certainly not without powers such as they have not dreamed of according.' And in a reflection prompted by a silver cup sent to him by the former Prime Minister of Northern Ireland, Sir James Craig, with quotations on it from his father, himself and his son, he wrote: 'I wish some of these dirty Tory hacks, who would like to drive me out of the Party, could see this trophy.' Life on the Riviera was a mixture of work and play. 'Just as at Chartwell I divided my days between building and dictating,' he told Clementine on January 18, 'so now it is between dictating and gambling. I have been playing very long, but not foolishly, and up to date I have a substantial advantage.'

Churchill returned to England in the last week of January. 'Never have I seen you in such good form,' Maxine Elliot wrote after he had gone, 'and we rocked with laughter continually. Your *joie de vivre* is a wonderful gift and on a par with your other amazing gifts – in fact you are the most enormously gifted creature in the whole world and it is like sunshine leaving when you go away.'

Within Churchill's constituency, despite the vote of confidence in November, critical voices had continued to denounce his hostile attitude towards Munich. Unless the 'mood of intolerance in some Party circles at the present time' were firmly resisted, he warned his constituents on January 25, it would 'destroy the quality of the House of Commons'. Much remained to be done before the country was secure; both with regard to Air Raid Precautions, and the setting up of a compulsory register of those liable for military service in war-time, he feared there was still insufficient 'clarity of thought or vigour of execution', and he went on to tell his constituents: 'Nearly five months have passed since the trenches in the parks were dug; yet there has not been found the mental and moral grip either to fill them in, or make them permanent. They gape, a discreditable advertisement of administrative infirmity, and I am afraid that they are not the only instance which could be cited in this sphere.'

Churchill reminded his constituents that at the time of the Munich Agreement there were those who had hoped that Britain had purchased 'even at a great price, a lasting peace', while others felt that at least a 'breathing space' had been gained. 'Let us make sure that this breathing space is not improvidently cast away.' But the 'breathing space' was being lost; on January 26, in rejecting Hore-Belisha's proposed Army increases for the coming year, Chamberlain told the Cabinet: 'Finances could not be ignored since our financial strength was one of our strongest weapons in any war which was not over in a short time'. As a former Chancellor of the Exchequer, the financial position looked to him 'extremely dangerous.'

This cautious attitude to defence spending revealed itself in several ways. On 1 January 1939 an Advisory Panel of Industrialists, set up in the previous month to report on delays and problems in the rearmament programme, stressed in its report to Chamberlain that industry was still 'operating, it must be remembered, on a peace-time basis'. In suggesting that this phrase should be omitted from the final report, the head of the Civil Service, Chamberlain's confidant Sir Horace Wilson, minuted on January 27: 'There are previous references to the peace-time basis and I do not see any point in rubbing it in quite so much. Repetition rather invites the comment that it might be a good thing to put the country on a war footing and we do not want to do that just yet.'

'How indescribably bloody everything is,' Churchill wrote to his sister-in-law Lady Gwendeline on January 30. That week, Inskip left the Ministry for Co-ordination of Defence and went to the Dominions Office. Churchill was widely canvassed for the vacant post, but it went elsewhere, to Lord Chatfield, the former First Sea Lord.

Chamberlain was still confident that Munich had been a step, not on the path of rearmament and preparation for war, but of conciliation and negotiation for peace. On February 19 he wrote to his sister: 'I myself, am going about with a lighter heart than I have had for many a long day. All the information I get seems to point in the direction of peace & I repeat once more that I believe we have at last got on top of the dictators. Of course that doesn't mean that I want to bully them as they have tried to bully us; on the contrary I think they have had good cause to ask for consideration of their grievances, & if they had asked nicely after I appeared on the scene they might already have got some satisfaction. Now it will take some time before the atmosphere is right but things are moving in the direction I want. I think we ought to be able to establish excellent relations with Franco who seems well disposed to us, & then, if the Italians are not in too bad a temper we might get Franco-Italian conversations going & if they were reasonably amicable we might advance towards disarmament. At any rate that's how I see things working round, & if I were given three or four more years, I believe I really might retire with a quiet mind.'

On February 18 the British Ambassador to Berlin, Sir Nevile Henderson, had informed the Foreign Office that Marshal Goering, head of the German Air Force, had asked him, 'What guarantee had Germany that Mr Chamberlain would remain in office and that he would not be succeeded by "a Mr Churchill or a Mr Eden" Government?' This question, Goering added, 'was Germany's main preoccupation'. On February 22, during a debate in which Churchill again called for a Ministry of Supply, Chamberlain referred to him as 'Bogey No.1 in some parts of Europe'. The hint was quickly taken up by some of Churchill's constituents, who now tried to have him replaced by someone more enthusiastic about appeasement.

In a speech to his constituents on March 10, Churchill defended both his record, and his belief that any attempt to do a deal with Hitler would fail. 'I am carrying on no factious opposition,' he said. 'I have no axe to grind in the matter. I am simply engaged in trying to get this country strongly armed, properly defended, and to have a foreign policy that will arrive at peace with honour.'

It was no use sending Members to Parliament 'to say the popular things of the moment', Churchill told his constituents in a second meeting four days later. 'What is the value of our Parliamentary institutions, and how can our Parliamentary doctrines survive, if constituencies tried to return only tame, docile, and subservient members who tried to stamp out every form of independent judgment? I have been out of office now for ten years, but I am more contented with the work I have done in these last five years as an Independent Conservative than of any other part of my public life. I know it has gained for me a greater measure of goodwill from my fellow countrymen than I have ever previously enjoyed.'

One of Churchill's constituency critics, Colin Thornton-Kemsley, expressed the view of Conservative Central Office, telling the meeting, 'I think that unless Mr Churchill is prepared to work with the Conservative Party, National Government, and our great Prime Minister, he ought no longer to shelter under the goodwill and name which attaches to a great Party'. But Churchill's constituents rallied to his support.

On March 9 Chamberlain told a meeting of Lobby Correspondents that 'the international situation now seems to give less cause for anxiety than for some time past.' On the following day Hoare told the Chelsea Conservative Association that 'confidence, almost suffocated in the late autumn by defeatism, had returned; hope had taken the place of fear', and if the three dictators were to work with the Prime Ministers of Britain and France 'with a singleness of purpose', Europe might be at the dawn of a new 'Golden Age'. Four days later the Germans began troop movements towards the borders of the already truncated Czech State as a prelude to further annexation. 'The Czechoslovakian Republic is being broken up before our eyes,' Churchill told his constituents that day.

On the following morning German troops crossed into Czechoslovakia. That night Hitler slept in the Presidential Palace in Prague, and on the following morning proclaimed a Protectorate over Bohemia and Moravia. Czechoslovakia had ceased to exist, its Slovak region proclaiming full independence and total support for Nazi Germany. 'It seems to me,' Churchill wrote on March 19 to the former British Ambassador to Berlin, Sir Horace Rumbold, 'Hitler will not stop short of the Black Sea unless arrested by the threat of a general war, or actual hostilities.'

On March 21 Churchill was visited by a senior Home Office official, Forbes Leith Fraser, the Chief Intelligence Officer of the Air Raid Precautions Department, who gave him details of deficiencies in his department. Churchill wrote at once to Chamberlain, urging an immediate state of 'full preparedness' for Britain's anti-aircraft defences, and explained why he believed action was essential: 'Such a step could not be deemed aggressive, yet it would emphasise the seriousness of the action HMG are taking on the Continent. The bringing together of these officers and men would improve their efficiency with every day of their embodiment. The effect at home would be one of confidence rather than alarm.'

In wanting Britain's anti-aircraft defences manned at once, and publicly, 'it was of Hitler I am thinking mostly,' Churchill explained to Chamberlain. 'He must be under intense strain at this moment. He knows we are endeavouring to form a coalition to restrain his further aggression. With such a man anything is possible. The temptation to make a surprise attack on London or on the aircraft factories about which I am even more anxious would be removed if it was known that all was ready. There could, in fact, be no surprise, and therefore, the incentive to the extremes of violence would be removed and more prudent counsels might prevail. In August 1914 I persuaded Mr Asquith to let me send the Fleet to the North Sea so that it could pass the Straits of Dover and the narrow seas *before* the diplomatic situation had become hopeless. It seems to me that manning the anti-aircraft defences now stands in a very similar position, and I hope you will not mind my putting this before you.'

'My dear Winston', Chamberlain replied that same day, 'Thanks for your note. I have been spending a lot of time on the subject you mention but it is not so simple as it seems.' Ten days later, shocked by the German occupation of Prague, Chamberlain gave a British guarantee to Poland. Did the guarantee include the predominantly German-speaking Polish Corridor, which had been detached from Germany in 1919? On April 1 a leading article in *The Times* stated: 'The new obligation which this country yesterday assumed does not bind Great Britain to defend every inch of the present frontiers of Poland. The key word in that statement is not integrity but "independence".'

Churchill was alarmed. 'There was a sinister passage in *The Times* leading article on Saturday,' he told the Commons on April 3, 'similar to that which foreshadowed the ruin of Czechoslovakia, which sought to explain that there was no guarantee for the integrity of Poland, but only for its independence.' His suspicion was well-founded; that same day Chamberlain explained to his sister that the British guarantee to Poland was 'unprovocative in tone, but firm, clear but stressing the important point (perceived alone by *The Times*) that what we are concerned with is not the boundaries of states, but attacks on their independence. And it is we who will judge whether this independence is threatened or not.'

On April 7, Good Friday, Italian troops invaded Albania. That day Churchill was at Chartwell, where Harold Macmillan was one of the guests. He later recalled Churchill's search for maps and the frequent telephone calls to find out the location of all British warships in the Mediterranean. 'I shall always have a picture of that spring day,' Macmillan later wrote, 'and the sense of power and energy, the great flow of action, which came from Churchill, although he held no public office. He alone seemed to be in command, when everyone else was dazed and hesitating.' On the following day Churchill telephoned Chamberlain several times to urge the summoning of Parliament for the next day, a Sunday. He also urged Chamberlain to order a British naval occupation of the Greek island of Corfu, to indicate to Mussolini, thus far and no farther. 'Hours now count,' he said, 'to recover the initiative in diplomacy.'

Chamberlain took no such action. In the Commons on April 13 Churchill criticised the Government for what he considered its mistaken attitude to the situation in Europe and the Mediterranean. 'How was it that on the eve of the Bohemian outrage Ministers were indulging in what was called "sunshine talk", and predicting the dawn of a golden age? How was it that last week's holiday routine was observed at a time when, quite clearly, something of a very exceptional character, the consequences of which could not be measured, was imminent? I do not know. I know very well the patriotism and sincere desire to act which animates Ministers of the Crown, but I wonder whether there is not some hand which intervenes or filters down or withholds Intelligence from Ministers.' Many of Churchill's listeners believed that this was a reference to Sir Horace Wilson.

A similar process of 'sifting and colouring and reducing' had taken place, Churchill said, in 1934, with the figures of German air strength. 'The facts were not allowed to reach high Ministers of the Crown until they had been so modified that they did not present an alarming impression.' There was a 'tremendous risk' if Ministers only attached importance to those pieces of information 'which accord with their earnest and honourable desire that the peace of the world shall remain unbroken.' He had two practical suggestions to make; the first was the 'full inclusion' of the Soviet Union in a defensive bloc with Britain, France and Poland; and second was the promotion of a 'self-protective union' in the Balkans, including Roumania, to which Britain had just given a guarantee similar to that given earlier to Poland. 'The danger is now very near. A great part of Europe is to a very large extent mobilised. Millions of men are being prepared for war. Everywhere the frontier defences are manned.'

When the debate was over, Churchill went to see the Chief Whip, David Margesson. He did not go to complain about naval dispositions or preparedness, but, Margesson told Chamberlain, to express a 'strong desire' to enter the Cabinet. This suggestion, Chamberlain told his sister, 'caught me at a moment when I was certainly feeling the need of help, but I wanted to do nothing too quickly. The question is whether Winston, who would certainly help on the Treasury Bench in the Commons, would help or hinder in Cabinet or in Council. Last Saturday for instance he was on the telephone all day urging that Parliament should be summoned for Sunday & that the Fleet should go and seize Corfu that night! Would he wear me out resisting rash suggestions of that kind?'

On April 18, pressed to do so by the Advisory Panel of Industrialists, Chamberlain at last agreed to establish a Ministry of Supply. 'Winston has won his long fight,' Brendan Bracken wrote to a friend. 'Our Government are now adopting the policy he advised three years ago. No public man in our time has shown more foresight, and I believe that his long, lonely struggle to expose the dangers of the dictatorships will prove to be the best chapter in his crowded life.'

The new Minister of Supply was the former Minister of Transport, Leslie Burgin, who had entered Parliament in 1929, almost thirty years after Churchill. His appointment led to a demand in many newspapers for Churchill's inclusion in the Cabinet. On April 22 the *Evening News* suggested that Churchill should be appointed either First Lord of the Admiralty or Secretary of State for Air. On April 26 Percy Cudlipp, editor of the *Sunday Pictorial*, wrote to tell him that 'only 73 out of the growing total of 2,400 letters are against you joining the Cabinet'. Some of those who objected were cranks, 'The more serious objectors blame you for Gallipoli.'

On April 27 Churchill criticized in the Commons Chamberlain's reluctance to introduce compulsory military service, something Hore-Belisha had unsuccessfully pressed in Cabinet. The national service register then being introduced, whereby people indicated their willingness to serve when the Government eventually decided to institute a call-up, was not enough: 'A gesture was not sufficient; we wanted an army and might want it soon.' Even the register ought to have been introduced immediately after Munich. The impulse to resist the Nazi principles, Churchill declared, 'comes from the mass of the people'. *The Times* called Churchill's speech 'one of the finest of his Parliamentary performances', to which MPs had flocked.

On May 10 the *News Chronicle* published a survey in which 56 per cent of those questioned said that they wanted Churchill in the Cabinet, 26 per cent were against, and 18 per cent did not know. Four days earlier Emery Reves had told him that his fortnightly articles were no longer allowed to appear in Poland, Roumania or Greece 'through fear of Germany'. Nor was he confident that appeasement was over; the Government's recent decision to curtail Jewish immigration into Palestine seemed to him an indication of a similar mood, and in the Commons on May 22, speaking of the proposed Arab veto on all Jewish immigration after 1944, he declared, 'Now, there is the breach; there is the violation of the pledge; there is the abandonment of the Balfour Declaration; there is the end of the vision, of the hope, of the dream.'

His fear, Churchill told the House, was that this 'violation' of the pledge to the Jews might now embolden Britain's potential enemies in Europe 'to take some irrevocable action and then find out, only after it is all too late, that it is not this Government, with its tired Ministers and flagging purpose, that they have to face, but the might of Britain and all that Britain means.' Turning to the Government Ministers on the front bench, Churchill warned: 'Never was the need for fidelity and firmness more urgent than now. You are not going to found and forge the fabric of a grand alliance to resist aggression, except by showing continued examples of your firmness in carrying out, even under difficulties, and in the teeth of difficulties, the obligations into which you have entered.'

That summer Churchill was among the leading advocates, with Eden and Lloyd George, of bringing the Soviet Union into a binding alliance with Britain and France. Chamberlain not only had doubts, however, about the Soviet military capacity, but, he told his sister, 'worse than that was my feeling that the Alliance would definitely be a lining up of opposing blocs & an association which would make any negotiation with the Totalitarians difficult if not impossible'.

Negotiations with the Soviet Union were begun but with no sense of urgency; not Halifax, but a senior diplomat, was sent to Moscow to lead the talks. The Russians, suspicious of Western intentions, and concerned to acquire a protective band of Baltic and Polish territory, began secret negotiations with Germany. As the summer progressed, Churchill became increasingly worried about the sense of defeatism and despair which he began to feel around him. On June 11 Halifax spoke in the Lords about Anglo-German relations. At one point in his speech he referred to 'the really dangerous element in the present situation, which is that the German people as a whole should drift to the conclusion that Great Britain had abandoned all desire to reach an understanding with Germany and that any further attempt at such a thing must be written off'.

Churchill wrote to Halifax that same day to explain why he had been 'a little disturbed' by this speech: 'I am sure you realise that to talk about giving back colonies, or *lebensraum*, or any concession, while nine million Czechs are still in bondage, would cause great division among us. Very bad reports are coming from Bohemia and Moravia about the oppression and terrorism of the Nazi regime upon these conquered people, and similar conditions are developing in Slovakia. At any moment bloody episodes may occur, and it is even said that many executions by the Gestapo have already taken place. Therefore, it seems to me quite impossible even to enter into discussions with Hitler at the present time.'

At dinner two days later, sitting next to the American columnist Walter Lippmann, Churchill was shocked to learn from Lippmann that the United States Ambassador, Joseph Kennedy, was telling his friends that when war came Britain, facing defeat, would surrender to Hitler. Harold Nicolson who was present at the dinner recalled that the moment Churchill heard the word 'surrender' he turned to Lippmann and declared: 'No, the Ambassador should not have spoken so, Mr Lippmann; he should not have said that dreadful word. Yet supposing (as I do not for one moment suppose) that Mr Kennedy were correct in his tragic utterance, then I for one would willingly lay down my life in combat, rather than, in fear of defeat, surrender to the menaces of these most sinister men. It will then be for you, the Americans, to preserve and to maintain the great heritage of the English-Speaking peoples.'

On June 22 Churchill wrote in the *Daily Telegraph* that the Germans were intensifying their demands on Poland, and that their demand for the Free City of Danzig and the Polish Corridor would cut Poland off from the sea. Five days later his collected newspaper articles for 1938 and 1939 were published in book form, entitled *Step by Step*. 'It must be a melancholy satisfaction to see how right you were,' Clement Attlee wrote to him, and from Eden came the comment, 'The reading of it is somewhat painful, but no doubt salutary.'

There was now an intensification of calls for Churchill's inclusion in the Cabinet. On June 21 Halifax spoke privately of the need 'for having Churchill in'. Malcolm MacDonald later recalled that several Junior Ministers urged Chamberlain to make Churchill 'a war minister, or war-to-be minister, but Neville was reluctant'. According to the *Star*, the Chief Whip, David Margesson, had been told by many back-benchers that bringing Churchill in 'to one of the key posts in the Cabinet would create fresh confidence'. On July 2 the *Sunday Graphic* reported speculation that he would soon be made First Lord of the Admiralty. In the *Observer*, J.L. Garvin commented, 'That one who has so firm a grasp of European politics should not be included in the Government must be as bewildering to foreigners as it is regrettable to most of his own countrymen.'

Chamberlain was not convinced, telling Lord Camrose, one of the newspaper proprietors pressing hardest for Churchill's inclusion, that he did not feel he would 'gain sufficiently from Winston's ideas and advice to counterbalance the irritation and disturbance which would necessarily be caused'. During his talk with Camrose, Chamberlain also expressed the view that if Hitler were to ask for Danzig 'in the normal way' then 'it might be possible to arrange things'. On July 2 Chamberlain told his sister that he could not believe Hitler really wanted war, or that he would be sorry to compromise 'if he could do so without what he would feel to be humiliation'.

On the far left, Stafford Cripps now joined those urging Churchill's inclusion in the Cabinet, but Chamberlain would not yield. 'If Winston got into the Government,' he told his sister on July 8, 'it would not be long before we were at war.'

Two days before Chamberlain wrote this letter, the Foreign Office had heard from the British Military Attaché in Berlin that Hitler's Finance Minister, Count Lutz Schwerin von Krosigk, had advised a visiting British General: 'Take Winston Churchill into the Cabinet. Churchill is the only Englishman Hitler is afraid of. He does not take the PM or Halifax seriously, but he places Churchill in the same category as Roosevelt. The mere fact of giving him a leading Ministerial post would convince Hitler that we really meant to stand up to him.'

Chamberlain still hoped that Poland might agree to let Hitler acquire Danzig, and that this would satisfy him until more wide-ranging talks could begin. He was also convinced that the 'Bring Back Churchill' campaign had petered out. But it continued to gain momentum; on July 13 a Liberal candidate, T.L. Horabin, won a by-election in North Cornwall largely on a 'Bring Back Churchill' platform, defeating the Conservative candidate.

Churchill remained at Chartwell, working on his history of the English-Speaking Peoples. 'It has been a comfort in this anxious year to retire into past centuries,' he wrote to his publisher, Sir Newman Flower. When Ironside visited him on July 24, Churchill told the General that it was now 'too late for any appeasement. The deed was signed, and Hitler is going to make war.' Three days later Ironside wrote in his diary: 'I keep thinking of Winston Churchill down at Westerham, full of patriotism and ideas for saving the Empire. A man who knows you must act to win. You cannot remain supine and allow yourself to be hit indefinitely. Winston must be chafing at the inaction. I keep thinking of him walking up and down the room.'

It was now announced that Parliament would be adjourned from August 4 until October 3. During an angry debate on August 2, Attlee, Sinclair, Eden, Macmillan and Churchill were among those who protested against such a long break, and asked for Parliament to reassemble in the third week of August. 'This is an odd moment,' Churchill said, 'for the House to declare that it will go on a two months' holiday. It is only an accident that our summer holidays coincide with the danger months in Europe, when the harvests have been gathered, and when the powers of evil are at their strongest.'

Churchill continued: 'At this moment in its long history, it would be disastrous, it would be pathetic, it would be shameful for the House of Commons to write itself off as an effective and potent factor in the situation, or reduce whatever strength it can offer to the firm front which the nation will make against aggression. It is a very hard thing, and I hope it will not be said, for the Government to say to the House, "Begone! Run off and play. Take your masks with you. Do not worry about public affairs. Leave them to the gifted and experienced Ministers" – who, after all, so far as our defences are concerned, landed us where we were landed in September last year, and who, after all – I make all allowances for the many difficulties – have brought us in foreign policy at this moment to the point where we have guaranteed Poland and Roumania, after having lost Czechoslovakia, and not having gained Russia.'

Not only did Chamberlain reject the appeal for a shorter break, he said that the vote would be treated as a vote of confidence. As a result, the Government had its way. After the vote a young Conservative MP, Ronald Cartland, who within a year was to be killed in action during the retreat to Dunkirk, said to Churchill, 'Well, we can do no more,' to which Churchill replied: 'Do no more, my boy? There is a lot more we can do. This is the time to fight – to speak – to attack!'

On August 8, as Parliament prepared for a two-month adjournment, Churchill made a fifteen-minute broadcast to the United States. 'Holiday time, ladies and gentlemen!' he began. 'Holiday time, my friends across the Atlantic! Holiday time, when the summer calls the toilers of all countries for an all too brief spell from the offices and mills and stiff routine of daily life and bread-winning, and sends them to seek if not rest at least change in new surroundings, to return refreshed and keep the myriad wheels of civilised society on the move. Let me look back – let me see. How did we spend our summer holidays twenty-five years ago? Why, those were the very days when the German advance guards were breaking into Belgium and trampling down its people on their march towards Paris! Those were the days when Prussian militarism was – to quote its own phrase – "hacking its way through the small, weak, neighbour country" whose neutrality and independence they had sworn not merely to respect but to defend.'

All over Europe, Churchill told his American listeners, there was a hush. 'It is the hush of suspense, and in many lands, it is the hush of fear.' One could also hear the tramp of armies; the armies of Germany and Italy. 'After all, the dictators must train their soldiers. They could scarcely do less in common prudence, when the Danes, the Dutch, the Swiss, the Albanians – and of course the Jews – may leap out upon them at any moment and rob them of their living space.'

Two days after this broadcast, Churchill visited the Royal Air Force station at Biggin Hill, not far from Chartwell, where, at Kingsley Wood's invitation, he watched Fighter exercises. Then, on August 14, he flew to Paris, before going to the Maginot Line, where, in a gesture of confidence by the French military authorities, he was shown sections no other foreign politician had been allowed to see, including underground railways in the sector facing the Siegfried Line.

When he asked what was the nature of the French defences from the point where the Maginot Line came to an end, to the coast at Dunkirk, Churchill was told by General Georges that there were 'field works' guarding the two-hundred-mile gap. Churchill's face 'had ceased smiling', Louis Spears, who accompanied him, later recalled, 'and the shake of his head was ominous when he observed that he hoped these field works were strong, that it would be very unwise to think the Ardennes were impassable to strong forces. 'Remember,' Churchill said, 'that we are faced with a new weapon, armour in great strength, on which the Germans are no doubt concentrating, and that forests will be particularly tempting to such forces since they will offer concealment from the air.'

Three days later Churchill was back in Paris. On August 17 he went to Dreux to paint once more at the Château St Georges Motel. That day *The Times* published an appeal signed by 375 members of the staffs of British universities, urging his inclusion in the Government. In the Strand, a large poster had appeared, bearing the three words,

'WHAT PRICE CHURCHILL?'

77. Speaking outside the Mansion House as part
of a Territorial Army recruitment drive, 24 April 1939

THE MASTER BUILDER

ANTI AGGRESSION WALL

78. The Press campaign for Churchill's inclusion in
the Government begins: a cartoon in the *Star* on 5 July 1939

79. 'Calling Mr Churchill', a cartoon by Strube in the *Daily Express*, 6 July 1939. Beaverbrook is calling 'Mr Winston Please!'

80. 'The Old Sea-Dog', 'Any telegram for me?': a cartoon by E. H. Shepard published in *Punch* on 12 July 1939

81. 'What price Churchill?': a poster which confronted passers-by in the Strand on 24 July 1939

82. Painting at the Château St Georges Motel, west of Paris,
20 August 1939

83. Walking with Anthony Eden
to the House of Commons,
29 August 1939

84. First Lord of the Admiralty:
leaving Morpeth Mansions on the
morning of 4 September 1939, with his
secretary Kathleen Hill, on the way to
the Admiralty

85. First wartime broadcast, 1 October 1939

86. A German wartime cartoon, sent to Churchill in October 1939

87. At the Supreme War Council, Paris, 5 February 1940.
From left to right in foreground: Lord Halifax (Foreign Secretary),
Edouard Daladier (Prime Minister of France), Sir Alexander Cadogan
(Permanent Under-Secretary of State, Foreign Office), Neville
Chamberlain (Prime Minister), Churchill (First Lord of the Admiralty)
and Sir Kingsley Wood (Secretary of State for Air)

88. Midday, 10 May 1940, with Sir Kingsley Wood and Anthony Eden at the 'garden gate' of 10 Downing Street. Churchill's detective is in the doorway, behind Eden. Six hours after this photograph was taken, Churchill was Prime Minister

89. Cartoon by Low, *Evening Standard*, 14 May 1940, 'All behind you Winston': a contrast to Low's cartoon of twenty years earlier (illustration No. 49). Next to Churchill are three leading members of the Labour Party: Clement Attlee (Lord Privy Seal), Ernest Bevin (Minister of Labour and National Service) and Herbert Morrison (Minister of Supply). Immediately behind Churchill is Neville Chamberlain (Lord President of the Council)

90. Supreme War Council, Paris, 31 May 1940. Next to Churchill is
General Dill (Chief of the Imperial General Staff). Also on the step are
Attlee (with watch chain) and the French Prime Minister, Paul
Reynaud (with handkerchief in breast pocket)

91. During an inspection of harbour defences at Dover,
28 August 1940. Detective-Inspector Thompson is carrying
Churchill's gas mask as well as his own

92. With Clementine, during their journey down the Thames on 25 September 1940, to inspect the damage done to the London docks during a German bombing raid on the previous night

93. Viewing the bomb damage, 25 September 1940

94. Welcoming Roosevelt's emissary, Harry Hopkins, to London, 10 January 1941. Brendan Bracken stands behind them

95. At Bristol after the air raid of 12 April 1941

96. Talking to a woman whose home had been destroyed during the air raid on Bristol

97. Watching the first Flying Fortress arrive from the United States,
6 June 1941

98. At work on the train, England, June 1941: his secretary's silent
typewriter is in front of him as he dictates

99. Hymn-singing with Roosevelt on board the *Prince of Wales*,
Placentia Bay, Newfoundland, 10 August 1941

100. Entertained to tea by pilots of 615 Squadron, Manston aerodrome,
25 September 1941

101. Addressing Congress, 26 December 1941

102. At the controls, returning from Bermuda to Britain by flying boat,
14 January 1942

103. Listening to the Soviet national anthem on the tarmac at Moscow airport, 13 August 1942

104. With Stalin in the Kremlin, 16 August 1942. Stalin has signed (top left) and dated this photograph

105. On board the *Queen Mary*, approaching the United States: with close-range weapons crews, 11 May 1943

106. Reaching the United States: sailors on the *Queen Mary* respond to the V-sign, 11 May 1943

107. In the Roman Amphitheatre at Carthage, 1 June 1943

108. Eisenhower's headquarters, St George's Hotel, Algiers,
3 June 1943: seated, Anthony Eden, General Brooke (Chief of the
Imperial General Staff), Churchill, General Marshall (Chief of Staff of
the American Army) and General Eisenhower (Supreme Allied
Commander in Europe). Behind Churchill are Air Marshal Tedder
(Eisenhower's Army and Air Force deputy), Admiral King
(United States Chief of Naval Operation) and General Alexander
(Supreme Allied Commander, Mediterranean). General Montgomery
(Commander of the Eighth Army) looks on, far right

109. With Clementine at Quebec, August 1943. Churchill is wearing slippers monogrammed with his initials, 'WSC'

110. Amid the bomb damage, Malta, 19 November 1943

For four days Churchill painted at St Georges Motel. To the artist Paul Maze, who worked alongside him, he remarked, 'This is the last picture we shall paint in peace for a very long time.' Talking of the size and quality of the German Army, he told Maze, 'They are strong, I tell you, they are strong.' Then, Maze recalled, 'his jaw would clench his large cigar, and I felt the determination of his will. "Ah," he would say, "with it all, we shall have him".'

On August 23 Churchill returned to London, where he learned of an impending agreement between Russia and Germany. On the following day Chamberlain recalled Parliament, and the Fleet was ordered to its war stations. On August 25 Britain signed a formal Treaty of Alliance with Poland.

For five days, Hitler hesitated. Churchill worked at Chartwell on his history of the English-Speaking Peoples. 'I am, as you know, concentrating every minute of my spare life and strength upon completing our contract,' he told Newman Flower. He had still not 'cleared away the Queen Elizabeth block', he wrote to the historian G.M. Young on August 31, but he added proudly that he already had 530,000 words in print: 'It is a relief in times like these to be able to escape into other centuries. Happily there are good hopes that Chamberlain will stand firm.'

That night Hitler's armies invaded Poland. At 8.30 on the following morning, September 1, the Polish Ambassador, Count Raczynski, telephoned Churchill to give him the news. The House of Commons was summoned for six o'clock that evening. Churchill drove up to London; at Chamberlain's request he went first to Downing Street, where Chamberlain invited him to join the War Cabinet. 'I agreed to his proposal without comment,' Churchill later recalled, 'and on this basis we had a long talk about men and measures.'

Chamberlain and Churchill agreed that there should be a small War Cabinet of six members, from which the three Service Ministers would be excluded. Churchill would join this War Cabinet as Minister without Portfolio. But no such appointment was made. Nor was any ultimatum sent to Germany, despite Britain's new Treaty of Alliance with Poland. When Chamberlain spoke in the Commons that evening, he explained that Britain had not sent an ultimatum, but a note seeking 'satisfactory assurances' that the German Government had 'suspended all aggressive action against Poland' and was prepared promptly to withdraw its forces from Poland.

The Germans did not reply. Shortly after midnight Churchill wrote to Chamberlain from Morpeth Mansions, 'I remain here at your disposal.' He waited at Morpeth Mansions throughout the next morning, September 2, expecting to be asked to go to Downing Street to join the

War Cabinet. No such message came; Kathleen Hill later recalled how he was 'pacing up and down like a lion in a cage. He was expecting a call, but the call never came.' During the morning Maurice Hankey, who had also been invited to join the Cabinet, went to see Churchill. 'As far as I can make out,' he wrote the next day to his wife, 'my main job is to keep an eye on Winston! I spent 1½ hours with him yesterday morning. He was brimful of ideas, some good, others not so good, but rather heartening and big. I only wish he didn't give one the impression that he does himself too well!'

The Cabinet met that afternoon without Churchill. Its members were unanimous that an ultimatum should be sent to Germany, to expire at midnight. But when Chamberlain spoke in the Commons that evening, it was not to announce any ultimatum, for none had been sent, but to speak of a compromise formula whereby a British declaration of war might be avoided. 'If the German Government should agree to withdraw their forces,' the formula read, 'then His Majesty's Government would be willing to regard the position as being the same as it was before the German forces crossed the Polish frontier.'

The House was 'aghast', Amery later recalled: 'For two whole days the wretched Poles had been bombed and massacred, and we were still considering within what timetable Hitler should be invited to tell us whether he felt like relinquishing his prey!' Churchill later recalled: 'There was no doubt that the temper of the House was for war. I deemed it even more resolute and united than in the similar scene on August 3, 1914, in which I had also taken part.'

Five members of Chamberlain's Cabinet, Simon, Hore-Belisha, Sir John Anderson, Walter Elliot and Earl De La Warr, went immediately to a room in the Commons, where they agreed that, unless their earlier decision for a midnight ultimatum were adhered to, they would resign. Meanwhile, a number of MPs, including Duff Cooper, Eden and Bracken, went to see Churchill at Morpeth Mansions to express, Churchill later recalled, 'their deep anxiety lest we should fail in our obligations to Poland'. 'We were all in a state of bewildered rage,' Duff Cooper wrote in his diary. Churchill told his visitors that he had agreed the previous evening to join the War Cabinet, but that since then he had not heard a word from Chamberlain. Had he not felt himself already 'almost a member of the Government', he said, he would have spoken out in the Commons after Chamberlain had read out the formula for a possible compromise.

Churchill discussed the crisis with his visitors until after midnight, their talk punctuated by the thunder-claps of a fierce autumnal storm. Then, with their approval, he wrote to Chamberlain: 'It seems to me that entirely different ideas have ruled from those which you expressed to me when you said "the die was cast".' He felt entitled to ask the Prime Minister to let him know 'how we stand, both publicly and privately' before the debate began at noon the next day. 'It seems to me,' he continued, 'that if the Labour Party, and as I gather the Liberal Party, are estranged, it will be difficult to form an effective War Government.'

Conveying the unease not only of his friends, but of almost all those who had heard Chamberlain's statement announcing further delay, Churchill went on, 'There was a feeling tonight in the House that injury had been done to the spirit of national unity by the apparent weakening of our resolve.' He therefore asked Chamberlain to make no announcement of the composition of the War Cabinet, or of his own place in it, 'until we have had a further talk'. This was not a threat to pull out. 'As I wrote to you yesterday morning, I hold myself entirely at your disposal, with every desire to aid you in your task.'

Unknown to Churchill, that very midnight Chamberlain had been visited by the group of Cabinet Ministers who had agreed among themselves to demand that the British ultimatum be sent to Germany without further delay. He bowed to their demand, having had no answer from Hitler that the British condition for starting negotiations, a withdrawal of German troops to the frontier, was acceptable. The British ultimatum was sent to Berlin at nine in the morning of September 3, giving the Germans two hours to halt their advance into Poland. No reply came by eleven. Britain and Germany were at war.

27

Return to the Admiralty

At 11.15 on the morning of 3 September 1939, Churchill was at his Morpeth Mansions flat, listening to Chamberlain announce over the radio that Britain was at war with Germany. No sooner had Chamberlain finished speaking than an air-raid siren sounded. Churchill went up to the roof to see what was going on and was impressed to see thirty or forty barrage balloons in the sky. Then, he later recalled, 'armed with a bottle of brandy and other appropriate medical comforts', he went with Clementine to a basement shelter along the street. 'Everyone was cheerful and jocular, as is the English manner when about to encounter the unknown.'

The air-raid warning was a false alarm; when the all-clear sounded Churchill went to the House of Commons. On reaching his seat he was handed a note from Chamberlain asking him to come to see him when the debate was over. Chamberlain then spoke, followed by Arthur Greenwood for the Labour Party. Such was Churchill's stature that, although out of office for more than ten years, he was asked to speak next. 'This is not a question of fighting for Danzig or fighting for Poland,' he said. 'We are fighting to save the whole world from the pestilence of Nazi tyranny and in defence of all that is most sacred to man. This is no war of domination or imperial aggrandisement or material gain; no war to shut any country out of its sunlight and means of progress. It is a war, viewed in its inherent quality, to establish, on impregnable rocks, the rights of the individual, and it is a war to establish and revive the stature of man.'

In his diary that day Amery wrote, 'I think I see Winston emerging as PM out of it all by the end of the year.' Churchill as yet held no Cabinet position. After the debate he went to Chamberlain's room, where Chamberlain offered him the post he had held from 1911 to 1915, First Lord of the Admiralty, together with a place in the War Cabinet. He accepted, then sent a message to the Admiralty that he would arrive later that afternoon to take up his duties. The Board of Admiralty signalled at once to all ships, 'Winston is back.'

Churchill attended the War Cabinet at five that afternoon. Then he went to Admiralty House with Kathleen Hill, who later recalled how he entered the First Lord's Room and went up to a cupboard in the panelling. 'I held my breath. He flung the door open with a dramatic gesture – there behind the panelling was a large map showing the disposition of all German ships on the day he had left the Admiralty in 1915.' That evening Churchill met his Board. 'He surveyed critically each one of us in turn,' one of them later recalled, 'and then, adding that he would see us personally later on, he adjourned the meeting. "Gentlemen," he said, "to your tasks and duties".' Churchill later wrote, of his first encounter with the First Sea Lord, Sir Dudley Pound, 'We eyed each other doubtfully. But from the earliest days our friendship and mutual confidence ripened.'

Within two weeks of the outbreak of war, Churchill received a letter from Colin Thornton-Kemsley, who six months earlier had tried to remove him from his constituency. 'You warned us repeatedly about the German danger & you were right,' Thornton-Kemsley wrote from his Army camp. 'A grasshopper under a fern is not proud now that he made the field ring with his importunate chink. Please don't think of replying – you are in all conscience busy enough in an office we are all glad you hold in this time of Britain's danger.'

Churchill did reply, telling his former opponent, 'I certainly think that Englishmen ought to start fair with one another from the outset in so grievous a struggle, and as far as I am concerned the past is dead.'

At the War Cabinet on the morning of September 4, hoping to relieve some of the enormous German military pressure on the Polish front, Churchill proposed a joint attack by the French Army and the British Air Force on the Siegfried Line, forcing the Germans to defend their western front. No such action was taken. But this was to be Churchill's constant purpose: to seek every possible area of action, to speed up every measure; not to be content with routine or delay. Each day, he dictated a dozen or more notes to his subordinates with suggestions for action, or with queries. On the night of September 4 he told his advisers, 'The First Lord submits these notes to his naval colleagues for consideration, *for criticism and correction*, and hopes to receive proposals for action in the sense desired.' When the matter was urgent, Churchill would glue to his minute a bright red label on which were printed the three words, 'ACTION THIS DAY'.

At sea, German submarines had begun the systematic sinking of British merchant ships. One proposal Churchill made that week, to which he attached 'the highest importance', was that the Admiralty news bulletin 'should maintain its reputation for truthfulness'. His responsibilities quickly went beyond the war at sea. On September 6 Chamberlain appointed him to a War Cabinet Committee to determine the size of Britain's land forces and the rate at which their equipment should be completed, a decision repeatedly delayed and postponed by the pre-war Government. 'We must take our place in the Line,' Churchill told his committee on September 8, 'if we are to hold the Alliance together and win the war.' His aim was to have twenty British divisions ready for fighting alongside the French by March 1940, and fifty-five divisions equipped and ready for action by the end of 1941. But the accelerated pace Churchill proposed for preparing new Army divisions was opposed by the Air Ministry on the grounds that it might adversely affect the pace of aircraft production; the mobilisation of the factories which Churchill had urged repeatedly in his wilderness years had been too tardy to enable Britain's war needs to be met when most needed.

Churchill continued to press for the building of shadow factories which, if not set up in advance, could not suddenly be created when the need became urgent. To Kingsley Wood, who did not believe that a fifty-five division Army could be created within two years without detriment to the Air Force, Churchill wrote on September 9, 'Pardon me if I put my experience and knowledge, which were bought not taught, at your disposal.' Churchill now knew the worst as regards the effect of pre-war shortages and delays, but his outward mood was one of confidence. Learning that the British Ambassador to Rome, Sir Percy Loraine, had spoken of a possible negotiated peace once Poland was defeated, Churchill minuted, 'Loraine does not seem to understand our resolve. Surely he could be rallied to a more robust mood.'

On September 9, in strictest secrecy, the first troops of the British Expeditionary Force sailed to France without loss. Churchill, whose warships escorted them, thus repeated one of his proudest achievements of August 1914. Twice in twenty-five years he had been responsible for the safe passage of a British Army to France.

That day, to help him study the mass of technical material that was reaching him each day, and to pursue research and development of new scientific ideas, Churchill appointed Lindemann 'Personal Adviser to the First Lord in Scientific Matters'. A month later he made him head of a special Statistical Department in his Private Office, with instructions to provide 'a weekly picture of the progress of all new construction, showing delays from contract dates'. Lindemann and the team that worked under him also provided weekly reports on ammunition, torpedo and oil deliveries, and production. Within a short time, Lindemann's charts had become a feature of the conduct of Admiralty business, scrutinised by

Churchill each morning to find any area of weakness, or potential danger, and to act upon it.

As in August 1914, Churchill's first offensive plan was for a British naval incursion into the Baltic; he now proposed a naval expedition led by two 15-inch-gun battleships, to threaten the German Baltic coast. He put this idea to his advisers on September 12, with March 1940 as its envisaged starting date. 'I commend these ideas to your study,' he wrote, 'hoping that the intention will be to solve the difficulties.' Two days later he pressed the War Cabinet to make full use of the offensive power of the Air Force by attacking those German synthetic-oil plants which were 'isolated from the civilian population'. But in reply, Kingsley Wood spoke of the need to keep Britain's 'small and inferior Air Force' untouched until Britain's own existence was threatened; the position would be 'immeasurably better' by March 1940, he said.

On September 15 Churchill was able to tell Chamberlain of the discovery of 'the mass of wartime artillery which I stored in 1919'. The guns and ammunition which, as Minister of Munitions, he had sent into storage then, would now constitute 'the heavy artillery, not of our small Expeditionary Force, but of a great army.' That night Churchill left London by train for the naval base at Scapa Flow, where he learned once again of the slow pace of pre-war preparations; the defences of Scapa would not be completed until the spring of 1940. He also learned that the Navy did not have sufficient destroyers to provide even a single destroyer-escort for each battleship.

Worried by the ability of the Germans to move their essential iron-ore supplies from the mines in Sweden by rail to the Norwegian port of Narvik, and then southward by ship through Norwegian territorial waters to Germany, on September 19 Churchill suggested to the War Cabinet that the Navy lay mines inside Norwegian waters, forcing the iron-ore ships out into the open sea where they could be sunk. No decision was reached, but, in a discussion on a possible British air offensive against Germany, Samuel Hoare told his colleagues: 'A considerable time would elapse under our present programme before we even achieved parity with the Germans.' Five years earlier, Hoare was among those who had most belittled Churchill's judgment when he warned that Britain was losing air parity with Germany.

In the East, Russia now activated her August pact with Germany, advancing rapidly into Poland and cutting off any chance of continued Polish resistance from the eastern provinces. Trapped between a superior German military machine and the Russian advance, the Poles had no choice but to contemplate defeat and partition. With Russia and Germany actively allied, Churchill abandoned his plan to send a British Fleet into the Baltic. 'But,' he told Pound, 'the search for a naval offensive must be incessant.'

On September 26 Churchill spoke in the Commons, giving a short survey of the war at sea. The convoy system was already in place, he said, but one had to remember that 'war is full of unpleasant surprises'. His theme was that of his Mansion House speech in October 1914, 'We have only to persevere to conquer.' After the speech, Harold Nicolson wrote in his diary: 'In those 20 minutes Churchill brought himself nearer the post of Prime Minister than he has ever been before. In the lobbies afterwards even Chamberlainites were saying "we have now found our leader". Old Parliamentary hands have confessed that never in their experience had they seen a single speech so change the temper of the House.'

Former critics now saw Churchill's qualities. 'Winston is the only Cabinet Minister who can put things across in an arresting way to our people,' Thomas Jones wrote to a friend on September 30. 'The PM is costive and dull and talks of endurance and victory in the most defeatist tones.'

On October 1 Churchill made his first wartime radio broadcast. Of Poland in defeat he said, 'She will rise again like a rock, which may for a spell be submerged by a tidal wave, but which remains a rock.' As for the Royal Navy, it was now taking the offensive against German submarines, 'hunting them day and night – I will not say without mercy, because God forbid we should ever part company with that – but at any rate with zeal, and not altogether without relish.' The war might last for at least three years, but Britain would fight to the end, 'convinced that we are the defenders of civilisation and freedom'.

'Heard Winston Churchill's inspiring speech on the wireless,' Jock Colville, Chamberlain's Junior Private Secretary, wrote in his diary. 'He certainly gives one confidence and will, I suspect, be Prime Minister before the war is over.' Five days later, after Hitler spoke in Berlin of his willingness to negotiate peace with Britain and France in return for 'effective hegemony' over Czechoslovakia and Poland, Churchill advised his colleagues to reject any negotiations until reparations had been offered 'to the States and peoples who have been so wrongfully conquered' and until their 'effective life and sovereignty' had been unmistakably restored. He also advised them to try to find some way, while Italy remained neutral, to wean Mussolini away from Hitler.

There was a short break for Churchill from the concerns of war on October 4, when he went to St John's, Smith Square, for the wedding of his son Randolph to the nineteen-year-old Pamela Digby. To those who said the couple did not have enough money to be wed, Churchill commented, 'What do they need? – cigars, champagne and a double bed.'

On October 8 Churchill proposed setting up what he called a 'Home Guard' of half a million men over forty, men 'who are full of vigour and experience', many of whom had served in the last war but who were now being told that they were not wanted. They could guard domestic installations and liberate younger men for service in units preparing to go overseas.

In naval matters, reflecting on his visit to Scapa Flow, he advised that the Fleet there should not be 'tethered', as he had seen it. 'These next few days are full of danger.' His warning was timely, but not acted upon in time. Two days later, on October 14, a German submarine penetrated the Scapa Flow defences and sank the battleship *Royal Oak*, then at anchor; more than eight hundred officers and men were drowned. 'When I brought the news to Churchill,' one of his Private Secretaries, John Higham, later recalled, 'tears sprang to his eyes and he muttered, "Poor fellows, poor fellows, trapped in those black depths." '

Churchill went back to Scapa on October 31. His first instruction there was to order the camouflaging of the existing oil tanks, and the creation of dummy oil tanks which the Germans could see more easily and waste their bombs on. Two days later, having returned to London, he crossed the Channel by destroyer for France, his first wartime visit, to offer the French Navy a complete supply of Britain's revolutionary new submarine-detection device, and training in the use of it. The French Minister of Marine, Admiral Darlan, to whom he made the offer, was visibly moved by it. In Paris, Churchill saw the Prime Minister, Daladier, to whom he said that Britain wished 'to go better than our word' in the number of troops being sent to France.

Returning to London, Churchill spoke in the Commons on November 7 of the loss of the *Royal Oak* and the continuing German sinking of British merchant ships. Striking that balance between realism and confidence that was to become the hallmark of all his wartime speeches, he said: 'There will not be in this war any period when the seas will be completely safe; but neither will there be, I believe and trust, any period when the full necessary traffic of the Allies cannot be carried on. We shall suffer and we shall suffer continually, but by perseverance, and by taking measures on the largest scale, I feel no doubt that in the end we shall break their hearts.'

In a broadcast on November 12, by which time diplomatic and agents' reports had revealed German preparedness to attack in the West, he again spoke with confidence in the outcome of the war. 'Violent and dire events' might well occur. There would be 'very rough weather ahead'. But 'it may well be that the final extinction of a baleful domination will pave the way to a broader solidarity of all the men in all the lands than we could ever have planned if we had not marched together through the fire.'

Since the beginning of November, British shipping losses had increased in the North Sea, mainly through the German use of magnetic mines, to which no countermeasures were known. Admiralty experts worked day and night to try to find the secret of the new mine. On the night of November 22 the search took a turn towards a solution. 'A number of magnetic mines had now been located,' Churchill told the War Cabinet two days later, 'one of which had fallen on the mud near Shoeburyness, where it was uncovered at low tide.'

Naval officers were examining the mine. Two protuberances, which it was assumed were detonators, were detached, and taken away, with the mine, for detailed examination. At eleven o'clock on the night of November 23 Lieutenant-Commander Roger Lewis, one of the four men who had recovered the mine, reported to the Admiralty building. 'I gathered together eighty or a hundred officers and officials in our largest room,' Churchill later recalled, 'and a thrilled audience listened to the tale, deeply conscious of all that was at stake.'

When Lewis ended his account, Churchill commented, 'To sum up, you have dissected this monster, divided it into pieces and now you can examine it at leisure! You will be able to find out all the life history of this animal!' It was midnight. 'We have got our prize', Churchill told the assembled sailors, 'as good a ship as ever sailed the seas, and we owe a great deal to the public spirit of Lieutenant-Commander Lewis and his colleague Lieutenant-Commander Ouvry who have been up against it today'. One result of the recovery of the mine was the award, at Churchill's instigation, of the first five naval decorations of the war, two DSOs, one DSC and two DSMs, bestowed personally by King George VI.

On November 30 Churchill was sixty-five. From Asquith's daughter Violet came a word of greeting, 'You need no blood-transfusions, unlike some of our colleagues!' A week later he gave the Commons a further account of the war at sea. 'When estimating our naval tonnage,' Harold Nicolson noted, 'he adds in the ships operating on the Canadian Lakes. But he is vigorous and eloquent.'

That week Churchill was angered by Air Ministry objections to his plan to drop several thousand mines in the Rhine, with a view to disrupting one of Germany's main raw material and munitions supply routes. When the Air Ministry wrote that the scheme was 'unprofitable', Churchill commented in the margin, 'Don't irritate them, dear!' and in a letter to Kingsley Wood, seeking his support for the mining, he wrote: 'The offensive is three or four times as hard as passively enduring from day to day. It therefore requires all possible help in early stages. Nothing is easier than to smother it in the cradle. Yet here perhaps lies safety.'

On November 30 the Soviet Union had invaded Finland. Many Englishmen wished to go to the aid of the Finns. Churchill was not one of them; for him Germany was the enemy against whom all effort had to be focused. 'I still hope war with Russia may be avoided, & it is my policy to try to avoid it,' he wrote to Dudley Pound as the war in Finland intensified. The bases which Russia would acquire from Finland, he pointed out, 'are only needed against Germany'. His chief concern was not the Baltic, but the Atlantic coast of Norway. In one week, seven German iron-ore ships had made use of Norwegian territorial waters. 'We must now make our case for action,' he wrote to Pound on December 7. A message from Washington indicated that President Roosevelt's reactions to the mining of Norwegian waters 'were more favourable than he had hoped', he told the War Cabinet on December 11.

Churchill now asked the War Cabinet for a decision as a matter of urgency. As well as mining Norwegian waters, he proposed a military landing at Narvik and an advance overland into Sweden to occupy the ore fields themselves. He proposed December 29 as the first day for action. But the War Cabinet, while agreeing to his plan in principle, refused to set a date, and asked that further enquiries be made, especially of the harmful effect the overland advance through Sweden might have on neutral opinion.

In the South Atlantic, the German pocket battleship *Graf Spee* was sinking merchant ships almost daily. On December 13, in the first dramatic naval success of the war, she was tracked down by three British cruisers, hit more than fifty times, and forced to find refuge in Uruguayan territorial waters. 'It had been most exciting to follow the drama of this brilliant action from the Admiralty War Room,' Churchill later recalled.

Four days later the *Graf Spee* blew herself up. In a broadcast that night, Churchill gave details of the action to the nation, confident, that 'in the end the difficulties will be surmounted, the problems solved and duty done'. Wrote one Conservative MP, Vyvyan Adams, 'I wish you could talk to us every night!' and he added, 'You are right, if I may say so, to emphasise the hardness of the struggle ahead.' To David Margesson, whose sister had just died, Churchill wrote that month, 'The world grows more ugly as we march through it.'

Shortly before Christmas, spurred by Churchill's encouragement, those working under him found a means to demagnetise ships, so that they could pass over the lethal magnetic mines without harm. 'We think we have got hold of its tail,' he telegraphed to President Roosevelt on December 24.

On Christmas Day Churchill reiterated to Chamberlain that all his naval advisers were 'dead set' on capturing the Swedish iron-ore fields 'and think it may be the shortest and surest road to the end'. Two days later he told the War Cabinet that the Admiralty were ready to send a naval force to stop the ore ships moving southward as soon as the War Cabinet authorised it. Once more, however, the only decision was to postpone a decision. On December 29, the day Churchill had originally proposed for action, he noted for the War Cabinet that eighteen iron-ore trains a day, instead of the ten hitherto, were being despatched from the mines to Narvik. 'Thus the German ore is flowing down and the British grievance is getting cold.'

Churchill now proposed a new timetable for action, with the seizure of German ore-bearing ships to begin in six days' time, on 4 January 1940. While warning that if there were too long a delay the Germans 'might attempt to forestall us', the Chiefs of Staff nevertheless favoured a larger operation against Sweden in March, rather than the coastal action against Norway in January. Churchill was cast down: 'I fear the effect will lead to purely negative conclusions, and that nothing will be done.'

On January 6 Churchill left London for France, crossing from Dover in the destroyer *Codrington*. With him were 'Prof' Lindemann, whom he described to the Commander-in-Chief of the British Expeditionary Force, Lord Gort, as 'in all my secrets'; his son Randolph; his secretary Kathleen Hill; his naval aide-de-camp Lieutenant-Commander 'Tommy' Thompson, who was to travel with him throughout the war; two police inspectors, and his former Detective, Walter Thompson, now back at his side, who was also to remain with him until the war was ended. That morning Churchill drove to Vincennes, to discuss with General Gamelin and Admiral Darlan the dropping of mines in the Rhine; Darlan was keen to act as soon as possible.

Churchill then drove to the Maginot Line, and finally to the headquarters of the French Army Staff at La Ferté, where he spent the night in a nearby hotel. On the following day he visited the headquarters of the British Advanced Air Striking Force, near Rheims, where he inspected gun positions and aerodromes, and stayed the night. On January 8 he went to Arras, where he lunched with Lord Gort and visited various military units. 'Anyone at home who feels a bit gloomy or fretful,' he said in a statement to the Press on the following day, 'would benefit very much by spending a few days with the British and French Armies. They would find it at once a tonic and a sedative. Unhappily the Admiralty cannot guarantee to find transport for all of them.'

Back in London on January 9, Churchill pressed for an improvement in the quality of the anti-aircraft guns in the British sector. He had also been disturbed, as in August 1939, by the two-hundred-mile gap between the northern end of the Maginot Line and the North Sea. This gap ran through Belgium. But despite pressure from both Chamberlain and Churchill, the Belgian King refused to allow British troops to move forward to fill it; he wanted the onus for the breaking of Belgian neutrality to be left to the Germans.

This was not the only negative decision that upset Churchill that week. On January 12 the War Cabinet decided, despite his urging to the contrary, that 'no action should be taken' to interrupt the German iron-ore traffic from Narvik. His frustration was intense. In a letter to Halifax on January 15 he wrote of 'the awful difficulties which our machinery of war-conduct presents to positive action. I see such immense walls of prevention, all built and building, that I wonder whether any plan will have a chance of climbing over them.' He had one or two projects moving forward, among them mining the Rhine and mining Norwegian waters, 'but all I fear will succumb before the tremendous array of negative arguments and forces'. One thing was 'absolutely certain, namely, that victory will never be found in taking the line of least resistance'.

At the War Cabinet on January 18 Churchill was angered to learn that the Ministry of Supply committee whose task was to co-ordinate munitions manufacture in the Birmingham area was only being inaugurated on the following day, that it would be solely advisory, and that it would have no powers to place actual orders for munitions. He had first advocated a Ministry of Supply with real powers on 23 April 1936. The Ministry had not been set up until 14 July 1939. Now he was learning that it still had no power to compel a manufacturer to fit in with the needs of the armed forces.

On January 20, in his fourth radio broadcast of the war, Churchill spoke of the Finns, who were still fighting stubbornly to resist the Russian Army. 'Only Finland,' he said, 'superb, nay, sublime – in the jaws of peril – Finland shows what free men can do.' He was scathing of the neutral States: 'Each one hopes that if it feeds the crocodile enough, the crocodile will eat him last.' They all hoped that the storm would pass 'before their turn comes to be devoured. But I fear – I greatly fear – the storm will not pass. It will rage and it will roar, ever more loudly, ever more widely. It will spread to the South; it will spread to the North.' There was no chance of a 'speedy end' to the war except through united action. If at any time Britain and France, 'wearying of the struggle, were to make a shameful peace, nothing would remain for the smaller States of Europe, with their shipping and their possessions, but to be divided between the opposite, though similar, barbarisms of Nazidom and Bolshevism'.

Churchill ended, however, on a note of confidence: 'Let the great cities of Warsaw, of Prague, of Vienna, banish despair even in the midst of their agony. Their liberation is sure. The day will come when the joybells will ring again throughout Europe, and when victorious nations, masters not only of their foes but of themselves, will plan and build in justice, in tradition, and in freedom a house of many mansions where there will be room for all.' The decisive factor in the victory would not be numbers but 'a cause which rouses the spontaneous surgings of the human spirit in millions of hearts'. If it had been otherwise, 'how would the race of men have risen above the apes; how otherwise would they have conquered and extirpated the dragons and monsters; how would they ever have evolved the moral theme?'

Millions of listeners were inspired by Churchill's words, which were listened to not only in Britain and France, but on clandestine radios throughout the conquered lands. However, four neutral states, Norway, Holland, Denmark and Switzerland, protested at his call for them to join the Allies. Halifax passed on these protests to Churchill, who replied: 'What the neutrals say is very different from what they feel: or from what is going to happen. This however touches upon prophecy.' Halifax did not tell Churchill that the French Government considered his call to the neutrals 'timely and carefully phrased', and had praised the speech itself for its 'realism and resolution'.

'Asking me not to make a speech,' Churchill added, 'is like asking a centipede to get along and not put a foot on the ground'.

A week later Churchill broadcast again, describing some of the atrocities which the Nazis were perpetrating in Poland, where thousands of civilians had been murdered in savage, indiscriminate butchery. From these 'shameful records', he said, 'we may judge what our own fate may be if we fall into their clutches'. Yet from these same records 'we may draw the force and inspiration to carry us forward upon our journey and not to pause or rest till liberation is done and justice achieved'.

More than three months had passed since Poland had been overrun. Since then Britain had remained on the defensive. Churchill was convinced that action should still be taken against the German iron-ore ships moving without interruption from Narvik to Germany. At the Supreme War Council in Paris on February 5, which he attended, it was finally decided to take control of the Swedish iron-ore fields.

At the Council that day it was also agreed to help Finland against Russia by sending more than 30,000 British and French troops to Scandinavia. The British Chiefs of Staff set March 20 as the date for a landing at Narvik.

Shortly after Churchill returned from France, a German supply ship, the *Altmark*, was sighted in Norwegian territorial waters. Locked below deck were 299 British prisoners, most of them the merchant seamen whom the *Graf Spee* had captured after sinking their ships in the South Atlantic. They were now being transferred to Germany to be interned. A British destroyer, the *Cossack*, had followed the *Altmark* into Norwegian waters. On February 16 Churchill personally wrote out the order to the commander of the destroyer, Captain Philip Vian, 'You should board *Altmark*, liberate the prisoners and take possession of the ship.' If the Norwegian torpedo-boat which was then alongside the *Altmark* should open fire, Churchill added, 'you should defend yourself using no more force than is necessary, and ceasing fire when she desists'.

Churchill waited anxiously that night to learn what had happened. A boarding party from the *Cossack* had gone on board the *Altmark*. In the ensuing fight, four Germans were killed; the rest surrendered or fled ashore. All the British prisoners were liberated. 'Winston deserves much credit,' wrote Lord Lloyd in a private letter on February 18. Five days later Churchill spoke at the Guildhall, to welcome back the crews of the warships which had ended the depredations of the *Graf Spee*. Theirs had been a brilliant sea fight, he said. 'In a dark, cold winter it warmed the cockles of the British heart.'

'Winston overbidding the market in his speeches,' was Hoare's comment. But for the British public there was something special in Churchill's language, tone and mood which made, and was to continue to make, his speeches a tonic. On February 27 he spoke again, introducing the Navy Estimates to Parliament for the first time since 1914. In his speech he gave details of 'outrages' committed by the Germans upon fishing fleets, small unarmed merchant-vessels, and lightships. Fishing-craft and small vessels were therefore being armed 'because it was found that nothing gives better results in respect to one of these raiders than to fire upon it at once'.

From Churchill's pre-war secretary Violet Pearman came a letter of thanks for his 'heartening' speech. 'I think the country relies on you more than any other member of the Cabinet to express national feeling in the only way that Germany understands, standing up to the bully and proving him the coward that he is.'

In his diary Halifax, a critic of more than a decade, noted on February 28: 'What an extraordinary creature he is, but I must say the more I see of him the more I like him. It is the combination of simplicity, energy and intellectual agility that is so entertaining.'

The Chiefs of Staff had set March 20 as the date for the Narvik landing and a military advance on the Swedish iron-ore fields. Churchill therefore went ahead with plans to mine Norwegian territorial waters as the preliminary to a landing. But on February 29 Chamberlain told the War Cabinet that the Labour Party leaders, Clement Attlee and Arthur Greenwood, had taken the view that Britain 'would not be justified in taking action that would injure a third party'. The United States might also object, Chamberlain felt, to the laying of mines in neutral waters. At present therefore the operation should be postponed. Churchill was outraged. The plan should have been carried out 'three months ago', he said. It was still not too late. It would 'do more to hasten the defeat of Germany than any other single measure within our power at the present time'.

Churchill was helpless in the face of Chamberlain's opposition, and the unwillingness of the War Cabinet to stick to a clear plan or fix a definite timetable. It was only on March 12 that the War Cabinet agreed to go ahead with a landing at Narvik, to be followed by a second landing further south. But on the following day the Finns signed a treaty with the Soviet Union, giving up large tracts of territory and fortifications. That night Chamberlain gave a 'standstill' order on the Narvik expedition.

Greatly vexed, Churchill wrote to Halifax that night: 'Considering the discomfort & sacrifice imposed upon the nation, public men charged with the conduct of the war should live in a continual stress of soul. Faithful discharge of duty is no excuse to Ministers: we have to contrive & compel victory.' Britain had sustained a 'major disaster' by not acting in the North, '& this had put the Germans more at their ease than they have ever been. Whether they have some positive plan of their own which will open upon us, I cannot tell. It would seem to me astonishing if they have not.' The Germans must have also have been thinking what to do. 'Surely they have a plan. We have none.'

On March 26 the Chiefs of Staff, of whom Pound was one, renewed their request for action against the Swedish iron-ore shipments to Germany. When the Supreme War Council met in London two days later, it agreed with Chamberlain's request to 'take all possible steps' to prevent Germany getting Swedish ore. Thus Churchill's proposal, first made on September 19, was finally being pushed forward as Allied policy. It was agreed that minefields would be laid in Norwegian waters on April 8, followed by naval control of the coastline and a military landing at Narvik. Churchill was relieved; a Cabinet Office interpreter, Captain Berkeley, noted in his diary that when the conclusions were reached 'Winston chortled loudly'. At last his energies could be put into a clear plan with a set timetable. In a broadcast on March 30 he forecast 'an intensification of the struggle', adding, 'We are certainly by no means inclined to shrink from it.'

Confidently, on April 2 Chamberlain declared in a public speech that Hitler had 'missed the bus'. But as Churchill had forecast in his letter to Halifax, the Germans also had a plan; it was to cast into jeopardy and confusion all that the War Cabinet had so belatedly agreed to do. Indeed, the nature and timing of the German plan were such that, at the very moment on April 8 that British naval forces were laying their mines in the fiord leading to Narvik, German military forces were being transported by sea to six points on the Norwegian coast, including Oslo. On the following morning a German force also landed at Narvik.

The British Government had delayed too long; despite Churchill's repeated calls for action. Within forty-eight hours the Germans had occupied Oslo. Denmark was occupied unopposed. On the evening of April 10, the British general who had earlier been appointed commander designate of a British Field Force, Major-General Mackesy, was instructed, while still in London, 'to eject the Germans from Narvik and establish control of Narvik itself'. His troops would not be ready to leave Britain for at least thirty-six hours.

It was too late; in the battle in northern Norway, as in the south, the Germans had the ascendancy, and air superiority. 'It is not the slightest use blaming the Allies,' Churchill told the Commons on April 11, 'for not being able to give substantial help and protection to neutral countries, if they are held at arm's length by the neutral countries until those countries are actually attacked on a scientifically prepared plan by Germany.' He made no public reference to his own quest for a plan and for action more than six months earlier, or to the War Cabinet's subsequent changes of plan, cancellations, hesitations and delays.

On April 13 seven German warships were sunk off Narvik, but the town itself remained in German hands. Further south there were successful British landings north and south of Trondheim, as part of a pincer attack on which Halifax was particularly keen, even though it diverted troops from the intended assault on Narvik. Off Narvik, General Mackesy decided that a direct assault on the town would not be 'practicable'. He did, however, land at three other points, the nearest thirty miles north of the town, and waited for a favourable moment to attack. By mid-April that favourable moment had not come; deep snow and night-time temperatures of zero degrees Fahrenheit led Mackesy to propose on April 17 a delay in any assault until the end of the month.

It looked as if a new word, 'Narvik', was going to be added to the earlier list of Churchill's failures. But the public no longer looked at individual episodes. It wanted leadership. Men and women of all political parties, and all walks of life, believed that Churchill could provide that leadership. His position in the country was 'unassailable', Colville noted on April 26. Three days later, as German troops forced the British to abandon the pincer assault on Trondheim and withdraw from their two coastal footholds, a deputation of senior Members of Parliament went to see Halifax to protest about the 'want of initiative' shown by the Government in almost every sphere of war policy.

Among many Conservatives in the House of Commons, so long loyal to Chamberlain, the failure in Norway was creating a mood of anger, even pressure for a change of Prime Minister. Henry Channon, a Chamberlain loyalist, noted in his diary on April 30 the view of many MPs 'that Winston should be Prime Minister as he has more vigour and the country is behind him'.

Between April 19 and mid-May more than a thousand top-secret German radio messages, orders, instructions, reports and routine returns, transmitted by radio in the Enigma cypher used by the German Air Force and Army in Norway for their most urgent and sensitive communications, were decrypted and read every day by the Government Code and Cypher School at Bletchley, north of London. The ability to decrypt these top-secret radio messages was a triumph of British Intelligence; a direct eavesdropping on the enemy. But so sudden and unexpected was the ability to decrypt these signals as they were picked up, that no secure system had yet been devised to convey the precious information to the British commanders in the field.

Despite repeated urging by Churchill, on May 5 General Mackesy again refused to attack the port. Churchill had no authority to overrule him, and no means to explain to him that the exhortations being sent to him were based on a precise knowledge of enemy strength and intentions.

The public had become restless at the continuing withdrawals and failures in Norway. There was growing mockery at Chamberlain's statement two months earlier that Hitler had 'missed the bus'. Many in both the Labour and Liberal Oppositions wanted Churchill to lead a Parliamentary revolt against Chamberlain. This he refused to do. He was a loyal member of the War Cabinet and would work as part of a team, without conspiracy. His task was to find some means of capturing Narvik; to this end he was devoting his time to the intricacies of military and naval planning.

Despite continued urging by Churchill, who knew from Enigma the German plans and weaknesses, the British admiral in command off Norway, Lord Cork, hesitated to try to drive the Germans from Narvik. On May 1, in the hope of giving a greater impetus to the war direction, Chamberlain appointed Churchill to be chairman of the Military Co-ordination Committee, consisting of the three service Ministers and now vested with enhanced authority to give 'guidance and direction' to the Chiefs of Staff. But the change came too late. On May 3 the Chief of the Imperial General Staff, General Ironside, wrote in his diary: 'I hear that there is a first class row commencing in the House, and of a strong movement to get rid of the PM. Naturally the only man who can succeed is Winston and he is too unstable, though he has the genius to bring the war to an end.'

In Cabinet on May 6, Halifax took an initiative when, he later noted, 'I suggested one way to gain time was to delude the Germans with peace talk'.

Churchill flared up in anger, accusing Halifax of treason, whereupon Halifax passed him a note: 'You are really very unjust to my irresponsible ideas. They may be silly, are certainly dangerous, but are not high treason.' Churchill gave the note back to Halifax with an apology: 'Dear Edward, I had a spasm of fear. I am sorry if I offended. It was a very deadly thought in the present atmosphere of frustration. You could not foresee this. Forgive me, W'.

Chamberlain now made another mistake, telling the Commons that in the battle for Norway 'the balance of advantage' rested with Britain. This was clearly untrue. In a mood of anger and uncertainty, people even spoke of bringing Lloyd George back to power, at the age seventy-seven. Parliament was to debate the Norwegian battle on May 7. That morning Lord Cork telegraphed to Churchill that he could, after all, attack Narvik with what he called 'a good chance' of success. His telegram did not reach London until the evening; Parliament meanwhile, in angry mood, had begun its Norwegian debate.

As the Minister responsible for the Royal Navy, Churchill was one of the main targets of criticism on May 7. Loyally he prepared to defend the Government's actions, even those which he had opposed in the secrecy of the Cabinet. His task would be to wind up the debate; for much of its stormy course he therefore sat silent. When Chamberlain entered the House to defend the Norwegian campaign he was greeted by cries of 'Missed the bus!' When, incredibly, he made a reference to the complacency of the British people, there were loud and ironic cries from all sections of the House.

A few moments later Amery spoke. A former Conservative Minister, and Chamberlain's friend and political colleague for two decades, he turned towards the Prime Minister and quoted the words Cromwell had spoken to the Long Parliament nearly three hundred years earlier: 'You have sat too long for any good you have been doing. Depart, I say, and let us have done with you. In the name of God, go!'

The debate was to continue on May 8. That night Channon noted in his diary: 'The atmosphere was intense, and everywhere one heard whispers: "What will Winston do?" '

The second day of the Norway debate was as stormy as the first. There was fear that a feeble Government was inviting military disaster, even defeat. When the Labour Opposition called for the debate to end with a Vote of Censure on the Government, Chamberlain retorted that he had 'friends' in the House. His remark was greeted with cries of derision. 'It is not a question of who are the Prime Minister's friends,' retorted Lloyd

George. 'It is a far bigger issue,' and he went on to demand Chamberlain's resignation.

Lloyd George also told the House that Churchill should not be blamed for all that had gone wrong in Norway. Churchill at once rose from his seat to declare, 'I take complete responsibility for everything that has been done at the Admiralty, and I take my full share of the burden.' Lloyd George then electrified the crowded Chamber by warning Churchill that he 'must not allow himself to be converted into an air-raid shelter to keep the splinters from hitting his colleagues'.

Churchill had soon to speak. Before doing so he talked briefly to Harold Macmillan. 'I wished him luck,' Macmillan later recalled, 'but added that I hoped his speech would not be too convincing.'

'Why not?' Churchill asked.

'Because we must have a new Prime Minister, and it must be you.'

Churchill understood his friend's concern. 'He answered gruffly,' Macmillan recalled, 'that he had signed on for the voyage and would stick to the ship.'

When Churchill spoke, he not only defended the Navy's conduct off Norway but also, as Lloyd George and Macmillan had feared, defended the Government's aim to try to drive the Germans from the Norwegian coast. 'One saw at once,' Channon wrote in his diary, 'that he was in bellicose mood, alive and enjoying himself, relishing the ironical position in which he found himself: i.e. that of defending his enemies, and a cause in which he did not believe.' In fact, Churchill was hopeful that the position in Norway could be improved. He knew, though he could not say so, that Lord Cork was now willing to try to seize Narvik, and was even then making plans to do so.

Commenting on Chamberlain's remark that he had 'friends' in the House, Churchill said: 'He thought he had some friends, and I hope he has some friends. He certainly had a good many when things were going well.' In a normal vote, Chamberlain and the Conservatives could count on a majority of more than two hundred. That night they secured a majority of only eighty-one. It was a hollow victory. As the vote was announced, many members, in a hostile demonstration against the Prime Minister, began to sing 'Rule Britannia'. But even this unprecedented demonstration was drowned in cries of 'Go! Go! Go! Go!' as Chamberlain left the Chamber. David Margesson even feared for his master's physical safety as he walked out with him.

Chamberlain was devastated. That evening he went to Buckingham Palace to see the King, not to resign but to tell him he would try to form an all-Party Government, bringing in Labour and the Liberals. The hatreds which now existed between Chamberlain and the Opposition parties were too deep, however, to be bridged. For them, he was the embodiment of sloth and failure. On the following morning, May 9, he told one of his closest confidants, Sir Kingsley Wood, that if Labour would not agree to serve under him, he would resign. That day Churchill lunched with Kingsley Wood, who not only urged him to make clear his willingness to succeed Chamberlain, but warned that Chamberlain wanted Halifax to succeed him. Kingsley Wood's advice to Churchill was emphatic, 'Don't agree.'

That afternoon Chamberlain summoned Churchill and Halifax to Downing Street. The 'main thing', he told them, was to preserve national unity. Labour must therefore come into the Government. If Labour would not agree to serve under him, he was 'quite ready to resign'. He then asked the Labour Party leaders, Attlee and Greenwood, to come to Downing Street. Would they be willing, he asked them in front of Halifax and Churchill, to enter a Government of which he, Chamberlain, was Prime Minister? Or, if they would not serve under him, would they be willing to serve under another Conservative figure?

The Labour leaders explained that the answer to either question would depend upon the views of the Labour Party. They could quite quickly find out these views, as the Party was even then holding its annual conference, at Bournemouth. They thought, however, that the answer was likely to be 'no' to serving under Chamberlain, and 'yes' to serving under someone else. With that, they left Downing Street for the south coast, leaving Chamberlain, Churchill and Halifax alone. It was clear that either Churchill or Halifax would soon be Prime Minister. It was also clear that Chamberlain definitely preferred Halifax, his colleague of the past decade, to Churchill.

Chamberlain told the two contenders that Halifax was the one being 'mentioned as most acceptable'. Halifax explained, however, that he was reluctant to try to guide the fortunes of war from the House of Lords. He would be held responsible for everything, he said, but would not have 'the power to guide the assembly upon whose confidence the life of every Government depended'. Not being able to lead in the Commons, Halifax said, 'I should be a cypher'. Churchill made no comment. Halifax then said that he thought 'Winston would be a better choice'. Churchill did not demur. He was, Halifax noted a few hours later, 'very kind and polite, but showed that he thought this was the right solution'.

Churchill assured Chamberlain and Halifax that until he was asked by the King to form a Government, he would have no communication with either the Labour or Liberal leaders. With that, the meeting ended. Chamberlain's hopes of avoiding a Churchill premiership seemed to be fading. Now the Government Chief Whip, David Margesson,

Chamberlain's eyes and ears in the House of Commons, told him that Parliamentary opinion had been 'veering towards Churchill'.

That evening Churchill had dinner with several close political friends, among them Sinclair and Eden. He was in confident mood, telling his guests that he thought it plain that Chamberlain would advise the King to send for him, as Halifax 'did not wish to succeed'. There was even some talk over the dinner-table about the composition of his new Cabinet, assuming he were asked to form one; Churchill said he would want to keep Chamberlain in the Cabinet, make Eden Secretary of State for War, and make himself Minister of Defence as well as Prime Minister.

That night Churchill received a telephone call from Randolph, who was in his Army camp in northern England. What, asked Randolph, was the latest news? 'I think I shall be Prime Minister tomorrow,' his father replied.

In the early hours of the morning of May 10, Hitler's forces struck at Holland, Belgium and France. Chamberlain, learning this when he woke up, at once decided that such a moment of crisis was not the time for a change of Prime Minister. He must stay on; his place was at the helm.

Churchill's first meeting that morning began at six o'clock. Together with Oliver Stanley, the Secretary of State for War, and Hoare, the Secretary of State for Air, he discussed the immediate military, naval and air measures needed in the light of the German offensive. 'Churchill,' recalled Hoare, 'whose spirit, so far from being shaken by failure or disaster, gathered strength in a crisis, was ready as always with his confident advice.' Churchill, Hoare and Stanley had breakfast together. 'We had had little or no sleep,' Hoare later wrote, 'and the news could not have been worse. Yet there he was, smoking his large cigar and eating fried eggs and bacon, as if he had just returned from an early morning ride.'

At seven o'clock that morning Randolph telephoned his father again. He had just heard on the wireless the news of the German offensive. 'What's happening?' he asked. 'Well,' replied his father, 'the German hordes are pouring into the Low Countries.'

'What about what you told me last night,' Randolph asked, 'about you becoming Prime Minister today?'

'Oh, I don't know about that,' Churchill replied. 'Nothing matters now except beating the enemy.'

This was also Chamberlain's view; at eight o'clock that morning, when the War Cabinet met at Downing Street, he was in the chair as usual. When Hoare went to see him an hour later he found that Chamberlain's inclination 'was to withhold his resignation until the French battle was finished'. Slowly during the morning Conservative MPs learned that Chamberlain was staying on. Many of them were angry, even outraged. A senior

Conservative, Lord Salisbury, on being asked his opinion, told the discontented members, as one of them noted, 'that we must maintain our point of view, namely that Winston should be made Prime Minister during the course of the day'.

Shortly before ten o'clock, Kingsley Wood went to see Chamberlain at Downing Street. The Prime Minister told his colleague and friend of many years 'that he was inclined to feel that the great battle which had broken upon us made it necessary for him to remain at his post'. Wood was emphatic, however, that, as he told Chamberlain, 'the new crisis made it all the more necessary to have a National Government, which alone could confront it'.

A second War Cabinet had been summoned for eleven o'clock that morning. It met, with Chamberlain presiding, to discuss the German advance. At Churchill's suggestion, Sir Roger Keyes, one of Chamberlain's fiercest critics during the Norwegian debate two days earlier, was sent to Belgium to try to stiffen the resolve of the Belgian King. At half past four that afternoon the War Cabinet met again. It was reported that German paratroops had seized the airfield at Rotterdam, and that Holland was in danger of being rapidly overrun. A messenger from the War Office handed a note to Ironside, who read it out; German paratroops had landed behind the lines in Belgium. There was a discussion about the need to warn troops in Britain about what action to take against parachutists attempting to land.

Another messenger came in with a note for Chamberlain. The Prime Minister took it but said nothing, letting the discussion continue for a while. Then he interrupted it. He had now received, he said, from Bournemouth, the Labour party's answer to his two questions of the previous afternoon. Their message was emphatic; no members of the Labour Party were prepared to serve 'under the present Prime Minister'. The Labour leaders were prepared, however, to serve under a new Prime Minister. With this brief but stark communication Chamberlain's premiership was effectively over. Within an hour he was at Buckingham Palace tendering his resignation to the King. That night the King wrote in his diary, 'I asked Chamberlain his advice, & he told me Winston was the man to send for.'

In the early evening of May 10, Churchill went to Buckingham Palace. 'I suppose you don't know why I have sent for you?' the King asked with a smile.

'Sir, I simply couldn't imagine why,' was Churchill's reply.

The King laughed, then said to Churchill, 'I want to ask you to form a Government.'

Churchill's eight and a half months of frustration were over. His life's ambition had been fulfilled. Before leaving Buckingham Palace he gave the King the names of some of those he hoped to have in his Government; among them four senior Labour men, Clement Attlee, Arthur Green-wood, Ernest Bevin and Herbert Morrison. It would be an all-Party Government, or, as he liked to call it, a 'Grand Coalition'.

While Churchill was talking to the King, his son Randolph, in his Army camp, was given a message asking him to telephone Admiralty House. He was put through to one of his father's Private Secretaries, whose message was brief, 'Only to say that your father has gone to the Palace and when he comes back he will be Prime Minister.'

28

Prime Minister

By nightfall on 10 May 1940 Churchill was Prime Minister. He later wrote of how, when he went to bed that night, he was conscious 'of a profound sense of relief. At last I had authority to give directions over the whole scene. I felt as if I were walking with destiny, and that all my past life had been but a preparation for this hour and for this trial.' Yet there was still some Conservative opposition to his emergence as Prime Minister; on May 11 Lord Davidson wrote to Stanley Baldwin: 'The Tories don't trust Winston. After the first clash of war is over it may well be that a sounder Government may emerge.'

Family, friends, and a wide circle of supporters rejoiced at Churchill's premiership. 'All your life I have known you would become PM, ever since the Hansom Cab days,' wrote Pamela Lytton, his girl-friend of forty years earlier. 'Yet, now that you are, the news sets one's heart beating like a sudden surprise. Your task is stupendous.' And from his son Randolph came a letter of filial encouragement: 'At last you have the power and authority out of which the caucus have cheated you and England for nine long years! I cannot tell you how proud and happy I am. I only hope that it is not too late. It is certainly a tremendous moment at which to take over. I send you all my deepest wishes for good fortune in the anxious days ahead.'

From the outset of Churchill's premiership, daily dangers threatened the survival of Britain. To help make up the deficiencies in aircraft, Churchill appointed Lord Beaverbrook to be Minister of Aircraft Production; Eden went to the War Office and Sinclair to the Air Ministry. These were friends on whom he knew he could count to get on with their jobs without the need for constant prodding. His offer to Lloyd George of the Ministry of Agriculture was turned down; Lloyd George no longer felt confident in victory. Attlee became Churchill's deputy in the War Cabinet. Ernest Bevin became Minister of Labour and National Service, and Herbert Morrison Minister of Supply. Churchill relied on these Labour men to sustain the enormous effort needed to increase war production and maintain the unity of the nation.

On the afternoon of May 13 Churchill summoned all his Ministers to Admiralty House and told them, 'I have nothing to offer but blood, toil, tears and *sweat*.' He repeated these words a few hours later in the Commons, when he declared:

> *You ask, what is our policy? I will say: It is to wage war, by sea, land and air, with all our might and with all the strength that God can give us; to wage war against a monstrous tyranny, never surpassed in the dark, lamentable catalogue of human crime. That is our policy.*
>
> *You ask, what is our aim? I can answer in one word: victory, victory at all costs, victory in spite of all terror, victory, however long and hard the road may be; for without victory there is no survival. Let that be realised; no survival for the British Empire, no survival for all that the British Empire has stood for, no survival for the urge and impulse of the ages, that mankind will move forward towards its goal.*
>
> *But I take up my task with buoyancy and hope. I feel sure that our cause will not be suffered to fail among men. At this time I feel entitled to claim the aid of all, and I say, 'Come then, let us go forward together with our united strength.'*

Returning to Downing Street, Churchill learned that Hitler's armies were driving deeper and deeper into Holland, Belgium and France. He wanted to take an immediate initiative, bombing Germany, but the neglect of Britain's air power before the war was one reason why the War Cabinet decided, on May 13, that this could not be done; Lord Halifax put it bluntly when he called Britain 'the nation in the weaker position'. Two days later, with Italy still neutral, Halifax suggested that 'it might be of value' if Churchill sent a personal message to Mussolini.

Churchill agreed to do so. In the message, which was sent on the following day, he asked, 'Is it too late to stop a river of blood from flowing between the British and Italian peoples?' Whatever the course of the battle in France, 'England will go on to the end, even quite alone, as we have done before, and I believe with some assurance that we shall be aided in increasing measure by the United States, and indeed by all the Americas.' This was also Churchill's theme when he telegraphed to Roosevelt that day, May 15, his telegram also containing words of foreboding: 'If necessary, we shall continue the war alone, and we are not afraid of that. But I trust you realise, Mr President, that the voice and force of the United States may count for nothing if they are withheld too long. You may have a completely subjugated Nazified Europe established with astonishing swiftness, and the weight may be more than we can bear.'

On the morning of May 16, as German troops broke through the Maginot Line, news reached London of an imminent French withdrawal which would expose Britain's Expeditionary Force to danger. Determined to exert whatever personal influence he could to prevent a withdrawal, Churchill flew to Paris; there he found the French High Command without any plan of counter-attack. That evening he sent a telegram to the War Cabinet in London to ask if the French requests for extra British fighter and bomber help could be met: 'It would not be good historically if their requests were denied and their ruin resulted.' The War Cabinet agreed.

On the morning of May 17 Churchill flew back to London. 'Winston is depressed,' noted his Junior Private Secretary, Jock Colville. 'He says the French are crumpling up as completely as did the Poles, and that our forces in Belgium will inevitably have to be withdrawn in order to maintain contact with the French.' At the War Cabinet on May 18 Neville Chamberlain, whom Churchill had appointed Lord President of the Council, suggested that Churchill himself broadcast to the nation on the following night, to indicate 'that we were in a fix and that no personal considerations must be allowed to stand in the way of measures necessary for victory'.

Churchill accepted Chamberlain's suggestion; it was his first broadcast as Prime Minister since taking office nine days earlier. 'Is this not the appointed time for all to make the utmost exertions in their power?' he asked, and went on to speak of the 'groups of shattered States and bludgeoned races; the Czechs, the Poles, the Norwegians, the Danes, the Dutch, the Belgians – upon all of whom the long night of barbarism will descend, unbroken even by a star of hope, unless we conquer, as conquer we must; as conquer we shall.'

The nation was inspired by Churchill's broadcast. 'I listened to your well-known voice last night,' Baldwin wrote from his home in Worcestershire, 'and I should have liked to have shaken your hand for a brief moment and to tell you that from the bottom of my heart I wish you all that is good – health and strength of mind and body – for the intolerable burden that now lies on you.' Captain Berkeley, who ten days earlier had written in his diary that 'Winston has no judgment', wrote on May 20: 'The PM gave a magnificent broadcast address last night. He is being "sublime" at every stage and after narrowly averting a serious collapse in Paris four days ago has been galvanising everybody here.'

The burdens on Churchill that evening were as great as any he had faced. They were highlighted immediately after the broadcast by his decision, taken after anguished consultation with Air Chief Marshal Sir

Edgar Ludlow-Hewitt, Commander-in-Chief of Bomber Command, not to send any more bombers to fight in the air above France, despite urgent French appeals for more; every bomber in Britain might soon be needed to try to beat off a German invasion of Britain itself. That same night, anticipating that it might be necessary to try to extricate the British forces from France as they were driven back towards the sea, Churchill asked the Admiralty to assemble 'a large number of small vessels in readiness to proceed to ports and inlets on the French coast'.

One avenue of potential and immediate supplies was the United States; Churchill remained determined to acquire the use of the fifty First World War destroyers that were lying idle in American naval yards. But Roosevelt would not agree to send them; his advisers feared Britain would be defeated and that the destroyers would then fall into German hands. Learning on May 20 that Roosevelt had even been told by Joseph Kennedy, his Ambassador in London, that the British might seek a negotiated peace with Hitler, Churchill telegraphed to the President: 'Our intention is, whatever happens, to fight on to the end in this Island, and provided we can get the help for which we ask, we hope to run them very close in the air battles in view of individual superiority.'

Churchill added: 'Members of the present Administration would likely go down during this process should it result adversely, but in no conceivable circumstances will we consent to surrender. If members of the present Administration were finished and others came in to parley amid the ruins, you must not be blind to the fact that the sole remaining bargaining counter with Germany would be the Fleet, and, if this country was left by the United States to its fate, no one would have the right to blame those then responsible if they made the best terms they could for the surviving inhabitants. Excuse me, Mr President, putting this nightmare bluntly. Evidently I could not answer for my successors, who in utter despair and helplessness might well have to accommodate themselves to the German will.'

The defeat of the British forces in France might lead Hitler to seek a quick victory in Britain itself; that night, in anticipation of a possible imminent German invasion, Churchill ordered all vulnerable airfields, that is, those with no defence forces available, to be guarded with local volunteers, and all soldiers in infantry depots who had not yet taken a musketry course to be exercised 'in firing a few rounds of ball ammunition'. Even as Churchill issued these instructions, advance units of the German Army, reaching Abbeville, drove a wedge between the British and French forces in northern France; in the summer of 1918 Churchill had warned Lloyd George that this precise move was a possibility; he had specifically named Abbeville as the point at which the Germans would reach the sea and divide the Allied armies.

The German troops at Abbeville now struck northward along the Channel Coast. Twenty-four hours later they were approaching Boulogne. Churchill decided to return to France to see if he could persuade the French to try to link up with the now isolated British force. Reaching Paris shortly before midday on May 22, he asked the new French Commander-in-Chief, General Weygand, if French troops would participate in a strategic plan whereby the British and French forces, attacking from both north and south against the German wedge, would cut off the Germans on the coast and enable the separated Allied armies to link up. 'I will try,' was Weygand's reply. Returning to London that afternoon Churchill was 'almost in buoyant spirits', General Ironside noted; but within a few hours reports began to reach him that the French fighting spirit was 'bad'.

Weygand made no northward move. On May 24 the British were forced to evacuate Boulogne. The British troops in Calais were being shelled. Churchill was upset by what he saw as a lack of energy on the part of the local British commander, in not going to the aid of the men at Calais, writing angrily to the head of his Defence Office, Major-General Sir Hastings Ismay, 'Of course if one side fights and the other does not, the war is apt to become somewhat unequal.' Later he learned that action had in fact been taken to send a relief force to Calais, but that the main need was now to keep Dunkirk open for troops and shipping, as the Germans drew their net tighter and tighter round the Channel ports.

That week, in utmost secrecy, the code-breakers at Bletchley, their extraordinary success in Norway having been to no avail, succeeded in breaking the Enigma machine cypher used by the German Air Force in France. This was a more complicated cypher than the one used in Norway, and one in which as many as a thousand top-secret messages were passing each day between German Air Force headquarters and units in France and Flanders. These messages threw considerable light on German Army operations as well as Air Force activities. But it was from German documents captured in the field that the British learned on May 24 of a German plan to cut the British forces off from the sea. Seeking an immediate counter-measure, that night Churchill ordered 'an advance north to the ports and the beaches'.

The Army was to be extricated, if possible, and brought home; the Navy was to prepare 'all possible means for re-embarkation, not only at the ports but on the beaches'. Once the Army was brought back from France, Churchill told his Ministers, 'he thought we could hold out in this country'. Two days later Reynaud flew to London, calling on Churchill at Admiralty House to tell him that he could 'hold out no hope that France had sufficient power of resistance'. Captain Berkeley noted: 'Reynaud was not impressive. The PM was terrific, hurling himself about, getting his staff into hopeless tangles by dashing across to Downing Street without a word of warning, shouting that we would never give in etc.'

That evening the order was issued for the evacuation by sea of as many soldiers as could be taken off from the quaysides, jetties and beaches of . Dunkirk. To prevent the Germans reaching Dunkirk from the West, the British troops at Calais were ordered to hold out; they would not be evacuated. Having approved what Ismay called this 'grim' decision, Churchill was ' unusually silent' during dinner at Admiralty House 'and he ate and drank with evident distaste'. As he rose from the table, Churchill told Eden that he felt 'physically sick'; two months later, in Parliament, he was to call the men who held out at Calais 'the bit of grit that saved us'.

On May 27 the United States asked to lease British airfields in Newfoundland, Bermuda and Trinidad. Churchill, still denied the destroyers that he believed to be vital for Britain's survival, refused. The United States had given Britain 'practically no help in the war', he told the War Cabinet that day, 'and now they saw how great was the danger, their attitude was that they wanted to keep everything that would help us for their own defence'. On the eastern flank of the Dunkirk perimeter, he was told, a Belgian battalion holding a crucial sector 'had been wiped out by a wave of sixty enemy bombers'. That evening the Belgian King called for an armistice, with effect from midnight.

In distant Scandinavia, the long-awaited yet now almost forgotten Norwegian campaign reached a climax on the night of May 27 with the successful occupation of Narvik by British, French and Polish troops. What the victorious troops there did not know was that, because of the urgent need for troops to defend Britain, their commanders were already under orders to withdraw from Narvik within a week. That same night, at Dunkirk, 11,400 British troops had been rescued; 200,000 were still encircled, together with 160,000 French troops.

In the Commons, Churchill spoke on May 28 of how the Belgian Army 'has fought very bravely and has both suffered and inflicted heavy losses'. Nevertheless, its surrender had added 'appreciably' to the peril of the troops at Dunkirk, whose situation was 'extremely grave'. The House should prepare itself for 'hard and heavy tidings'. Nothing that might happen at Dunkirk, however, 'can in any way relieve us of our duty to defend the world cause to which we have vowed ourselves; nor should it destroy our confidence in our power to make our way – as on former occasions in our history – through disaster and through grief to the ultimate defeat of our enemies'.

As he waited that day for further news from the beaches, Churchill listened in the secrecy of his five-member War Cabinet to Halifax's suggestion that Britain should take up an offer from Mussolini to negotiate a general peace. Chamberlain seemed to support Halifax, telling his colleagues that 'while we would fight to the end to preserve our independence, we were ready to consider decent terms if such were offered to us'. Churchill was dismayed and angered. It was a thousand to one against any such 'decent terms' being offered. 'Nations which went down fighting rose again, but those who surrendered tamely were finished.' He was supported by the two Labour members of the War Cabinet, Attlee and Greenwood. Fortified by their toughness, when he spoke a few moments later to the full Cabinet, twenty-five Ministers in all, he reiterated his belief that Britain would rather go down fighting than negotiate peace. 'He was quite magnificent,' Hugh Dalton, newly appointed Minister of Economic Warfare, wrote in his diary. 'The man, and the only man we have for this task.'

Churchill told the full Cabinet that he had thought carefully over the past two days 'whether it was part of my duty to consider entering into negotiations with That Man'. The Germans would demand Britain's fleet, her naval bases, and much else. Britain would become a 'slave state' with a puppet Government 'under Mosley or some such person'. Yet Britain still had 'immense reserves and advantages', and, he concluded: 'I am convinced that every man of you would rise up and tear me down from my place if I were for one moment to contemplate parley or surrender. If this long island story of ours is to end at last, let it end only when each one of us lies choking in his own blood upon the ground.'

There were immediate cries of approval all round the table; Churchill's Ministers were united, and inspired. 'Quite a number,' he later wrote, 'seemed to jump up from the table and come running to my chair, shouting and patting me on the back.' There was no doubt, he added, 'that had I at this juncture faltered at all in leading the nation I should have been hurled out of office. I am sure that every Minister was ready to be killed quite soon, and have all his family and possessions destroyed, rather than give in.' When the members of the War Cabinet met again a few moments later, Churchill told them that he did not remember having 'ever heard before a gathering of persons occupying high places in political life express themselves so emphatically'.

Churchill's ability to believe that every Minister was ready to be killed, and have his family killed, rather than give in, and his ability to convince others that it was so, was a potent factor enabling the nation to face the terrifying prospect of invasion, and the cruel reality of aerial bombardment. But there were still those in the War Cabinet who wished to continue their discussion of a possible negotiated peace. Chamberlain, however, having veered away from his earlier opinion, suggested that evening that

Britain should persuade Reynaud 'that it was worth his while to go on fighting'. Halifax, however, was not convinced; he again proposed that negotiations take place through the Italians. He also wanted a public declaration of British war aims, if only, he explained, to win American support. What was really needed to impress the Americans, Churchill retorted, was 'a bold stand against Germany'.

Later that evening, seeking an extra counter to Halifax's waverings, Churchill offered Lloyd George a place in the War Cabinet. But the former Prime Minister, whose tenacity Churchill had so admired in the First World War, declined. 'Several of the architects of this catastrophe are still leading members of your Government,' he told Churchill, 'and two of them are in the Cabinet that directs the war.'

This was true; but Churchill did not dare to break the sense of national unity by removing Chamberlain and Halifax from the War Cabinet. He was confident that he could create so strong an atmosphere of determination throughout the country, that the doubts of the waverers would not weaken the national resolve.

By midnight on May 28 a further 25,000 troops had been taken off from the beaches of Dunkirk. On the following day as many as 2,000 troops an hour were being got away safely. A vast armada of boats large and small, including paddle-steamers and pleasure craft from dozens of coastal holiday resorts, was crossing and recrossing the North Sea to rescue them. Many were sunk, and hundreds of soldiers and rescuers killed, by the unceasing German air attacks. That night, in an attempt to encourage the resolve of his own Ministers and senior civil servants, Churchill issued a single page exhortation which read: 'In these dark days the Prime Minister would be grateful if all his colleagues in the Government, as well as high officials, would maintain a high morale in their circles; not minimising the gravity of events, but showing confidence in our ability and inflexible resolve to continue the war till we have broken the will of the enemy to bring all Europe under his domination. No tolerance should be given to the idea that France will make a separate peace; but whatever may happen on the Continent, we cannot doubt our duty and we shall certainly use all our power to defend the Island, the Empire and our Cause.'

This message, signed 'WSC', was circulated to all thirty-five War Cabinet and other Ministers, all thirty-nine Junior Ministers, forty-six 'High Officials', and the six Dominion representatives.

On the morning of May 30 Churchill gave orders for the French troops on the Dunkirk beach-head to be allowed to share the available shipping. Even though it must reduce the number of British troops embarked, he said, 'for the common good this must be accepted'. By midday, more than 100,000 troops had been taken off and had reached Britain safely since the start of the evacuation, despite the continual German air attacks. More than 860 vessels were now involved in the evacuation, and as many as four thousand troops being taken off each hour. As Churchill monitored these movements he remained emphatic that French troops must be taken off as well. If not, he said, 'irreparable harm' might be done to Britain's relations with France.

How much longer the evacuation could continue was unclear. On the afternoon of May 30 Churchill informed the Commander-in-Chief of the Expeditionary Force, Lord Gort, that once no further organised resistance was possible, he was authorised 'to capitulate formally and to avoid useless slaughter'. Fearing that a German invasion might follow immediately after the evacuation, and the capture by the Germans of vast quantities of British military equipment, Churchill told the War Cabinet that Britain 'should not hesitate to contaminate our beaches with gas' if this could be done to advantage. That day, in the hope, even at the eleventh hour, of stimulating French resistance, Churchill again flew to Paris, together with Attlee, General Dill and Ismay. The presence of German fighters in the skies north of the city forced a substantial detour, first to Weymouth to pick up an escort of nine Hurricanes, then across the Channel to Jersey, then crossing the French coast west of St Malo, then due east to Villacoublay near Versailles, where, for a while, the plane was virtually lost at the wrong end of the vast aerodrome.

In Paris, Churchill and Attlee faced Reynaud and Pétain; the latter, in civilian clothes, looking 'senile, uninspiring and defeatist', Ismay later recalled. 'No sort of good spirit on the French side' was Berkeley's comment.

Churchill told the French leaders that the evacuation of Narvik would begin in forty-eight hours; the 16,000 French and Polish troops being evacuated would be transferred to France to defend Paris. Further British troops would be sent to Western France, together with Canadians, to build up a land force there, also for the defence of Paris. There were already two British divisions in Western France, and only three ready for action in Britain itself. No more help could be spared. The fourteen further divisions in Britain were undergoing training equipped only with rifles 'and therefore totally unfit for modern warfare'. Ten British air squadrons were fighting in France; the remaining twenty-nine squadrons were desperately needed to deal with any German air attack on Britain's aircraft factories: if these were put out of action 'the situation would then become hopeless'.

Britain and France must remain in the closest accord, Churchill said. For this reason he would give orders to get French troops 'off first from now on' at Dunkirk. He was 'absolutely convinced' that the two countries

had only ' to carry on the fight to conquer'. Even if one of them should be
struck down, the other must not abandon the struggle. 'The partner that
survives will go on.' If, through some disaster, Britain were laid waste, the
Government was prepared 'to wage war from the New World'. If either
ally were defeated, Germany 'would give no quarter: they would be
reduced to the status of vassals and slaves forever'.

Reynaud was visibly moved by Churchill's words, but not so Pétain.
Listening to Churchill saying goodbye to them, Louis Spears later recalled how he knew from Churchill's tone 'that he realised in his heart
that the French were beaten, and that they knew it, and were resigned
to defeat'. After a night disturbed by a German air raid, a 'petty raid'
Churchill later called it, the Englishmen prepared to return to London.
'Winston was ebullient as ever,' Berkeley noted. 'When we started back
he insisted on pacing round the aerodrome to review our nine Hurricanes, tramping through the tall grass in the flurry of propellers with
his cigar like a pennant.'

. Reaching London without incident, Churchill was shown a proposal
that, in the event of invasion, the Royal Family and the Government should
be evacuated to Canada. He replied that 'no such discussion' was to be
permitted. The Germans were not to have the pleasure of any such
evacuation: 'I believe we shall make them rue the day they try to invade
our island.' That evening he was told that the Germans were about to
overrun the Dunkirk beaches. Six ships had been sunk that morning and
many soldiers drowned. His first response was to continue the evacuation
for one more day, but he accepted the arguments of the Chiefs of Staff
that any further evacuation would be impossible.

Churchill and his advisers were certain that the moment the Dunkirk
evacuation ended, and Germany was in control of the Channel Coast of
France, Hitler would launch his invasion of Britain. Yet even as the last
Allied troops were taken off the Dunkirk beaches, and German forces
prepared to take prisoner those who had not been able to get away,
Churchill was able to breathe more freely. On June 1 War Office Intelligence interpreted the Enigma decrypts as meaning that the Germans were
likely to complete the overrunning of France before turning against the
United Kingdom. Thanks to this triumph of signals intelligence, Churchill
knew that Britain had its first breathing-space, however short. When, that
same day, the Director of the National Gallery proposed sending the most
valuable paintings to Canada, he answered: 'No, bury them in caves and
cellars. None must go. We are going to beat them.'

By first light on June 3 the Dunkirk evacuation came to an end; 224,318
British and 111,172 French troops had been taken off. Seventy-one heavy
guns and 595 vehicles had also been saved at Dunkirk, though the Ger-

mans captured a mass of war material. Of the 222 Royal Navy vessels involved in the evacuation, thirty had been sunk, including six destroyers. But with the danger of immediate invasion known by Churchill and his Chiefs of Staff to be over, it was agreed to send two British divisions to Western France, with a third to follow. At the same time, British bombers would give priority to French-nominated targets.

Churchill was in fighting mood, telling Colville on June 3 that he was 'tired of always being on the defensive' and was contemplating 'raids on enemy territory'. This mood was reflected on the following day in a minute to Ismay: 'How wonderful it would be if the Germans could be made to wonder where they were going to be struck next, instead of trying to force us to wall in the Island and roof it over. An effort must be made to shake off the mental and moral prostration to the will and initiative of the enemy from which we suffer.' After visiting his father that day, Randolph wrote to him on return to his Army camp, 'I cannot tell you how stimulating & reassuring it was to see you again & to find you so full of courage & determination.' Churchill was also alert to any apparent slackening of effort, writing that day to Lindemann: 'You are not presenting me as I should like every few days, or every week, with a short clear statement of the falling off or improvement in munitions production. I am not able to form a clear view unless you do this.'

That week the war in the air was Churchill's main cause for concern; in the three previous weeks, during the battle over France and Flanders, 453 aircraft had been manufactured, but 436 shot down. Nevertheless, the battle in the skies above France had been the first British air victory of the war, with 394 German planes destroyed above the Dunkirk beaches for the cost of 114 British aircraft. Given an almost three-to-one German superiority in numbers of aircraft, these British losses were hard to bear, but on June 4 Beaverbrook was able to assure Churchill that fighters were now being manufactured at a rate of thirty-five a day, with a weekly production rate of more than two hundred aircraft. That same day Churchill learned from Arthur Purvis, his chief arms negotiator in Washington, that half a million American rifles and five hundred field-guns were ready for shipment. But destroyers could not be spared; that was Roosevelt's decision, conveyed with 'regret'.

Speaking on June 4 in the House of Commons, Churchill admitted that when the date of his speech had been fixed a week earlier, 'I feared it would be my lot to announce the greatest military disaster in our long history'. He had not expected more than 20,000 or 30,000 men to have been got safely away from Dunkirk. What had happened was 'a miracle of deliverance', but, he warned, 'we must be very careful not to assign to this deliverance the attributes of a victory. Wars are not won by evacuations.'

In his peroration, which, he explained to Roosevelt, was addressed 'primarily to Germany and Italy', Churchill declared:

> *Even though large tracts of Europe and many old and famous States have fallen or may fall into the grip of the Gestapo and all the odious apparatus of Nazi rule, we shall not flag or fail.*
>
> *We shall go on to the end. We shall fight in France, we shall fight on the seas and oceans, we shall fight with growing confidence and growing strength in the air, we shall defend our island, whatever the cost may be.*
>
> *We shall fight on the beaches, we shall fight on the landing grounds, we shall fight in the fields and in the streets, we shall fight in the hills; we shall never surrender.*
>
> *And even if, which I do not for a moment believe, this island or a large part of it were subjugated and starving, then our Empire beyond the seas, armed and guarded by the British Fleet, would carry on the struggle, until, in God's good time, the New World, with all its power and might, steps forth to the rescue and the liberation of the Old.*

The House of Commons was deeply moved; 'That was worth 1,000 guns, & the speeches of 1,000 years,' wrote the Labour MP Josiah Wedgwood. 'Even repeated by the announcer,' Vita Sackville-West wrote to her husband, 'it sent shivers (not of fear) down my spine. I think one of the reasons why one is stirred by his Elizabethan phrases is that one feels the whole massive backing of power and resolve behind them, like a great fortress: they are never words for words' sake.'

Churchill had no illusions as to the severity of the task ahead. Even though the Germans had decided not to turn on Britain until France was defeated, the defeat of France could not be far off. That night he wrote to Baldwin, in reply to his letter of good wishes: 'We are going through very hard times & I expect worse to come: but I feel quite sure better days will come: though whether we shall live to see them is more doubtful.' Churchill ended his letter, 'I do not feel the burden weigh too heavily, but I cannot say that I have enjoyed being Prime Minister very much so far.'

On June 5, only twenty-six days after having crossed into France, the German Army began its offensive towards Paris. That day, seeking every possible means to help the French, Churchill proposed a series of 'butcher and bolt' raids on the German-held coast, with tanks being carried across the Channel in flat-bottomed boats 'out of which they can crawl ashore, do a deep raid inland, cutting vital communications, and then back, leaving a trail of German corpses behind them'. While the best German troops were attacking Paris, only 'ordinary German troops of the line' would be left in many towns. 'The lives of these must be made an intense torment.'

The German advance was so swift, however, that there was no time to prepare any such hit-and-run raids. The division of British troops in northern France, commanded by General Fortune, was being forced back to the Channel Coast with heavy losses. Off Narvik, on the last day of the evacuation, three British warships were sunk and 1,500 sailors and evacuees drowned. Frustrated at the daily reports of withdrawal and delay, Churchill wrote to Pound on June 6: 'We seem quite incapable of *action.*' To Eden he wrote that same day, about the delays in bringing troops back to Britain from Palestine and India: 'We are indeed the victims of a feeble and weary departmentalism.' He was also annoyed by Reynaud's continual demands for greater British air support, reminding him on June 7 that 144 British fighters had operated over France on the previous day, but agreeing to send twenty-four barrage balloons, with crews, from Britain to Paris, for the defence of the French capital.

That was the end of the help Britain could give; on the evening of June 8 Churchill, Sinclair and Beaverbrook decided that no more fighters could be sent to France without the danger, Reynaud was told, 'of ruining the capacity of this country to continue the war'. On the following day Reynaud sent his newly appointed Under-Secretary for National Defence, General Charles de Gaulle, to London, to ask that the whole of Britain's Air Force be engaged in the Battle for France. Churchill explained to de Gaulle that once these aircraft were destroyed, there would be no means of protecting Britain from the air assault that must precede any German invasion. De Gaulle understood the British dilemma and priority. 'Speaking for himself, he agreed with our policy,' Churchill reported to the War Cabinet as de Gaulle flew back to France, and he added that the young general had given 'a more favourable impression of French morale and determination'.

It was too late. Even the launching on June 9 of Churchill's earlier Admiralty scheme for dropping mines in the Rhine, though seriously disrupting the Rhine traffic, could no longer influence the battle in France. That day the British forces under General Fortune were driven to the sea at St Valery-en-Caux. Fog prevented their evacuation. Then, as German troops began their assault on Paris, Italy declared war on both Britain and France. 'People who go to Italy to look at ruins,' Churchill commented that night, 'won't have to go as far as Naples and Pompeii again.'

On June 10 Churchill decided to fly once more to France, to encourage the French to defend Paris. As he prepared to leave he learned that the French Government was evacuating its capital. 'What the hell,' was his immediate comment. 'It seemed,' wrote Colville, 'that there was no perch on which he could alight.' The French Cabinet had gone southward to the River Loire. There, on June 11, at the Château de Muguet, not far from the town of Briare, he was confronted by the French leaders in disarray. Reynaud and de Gaulle were all for trying to continue the fight, possibly from Western France. Weygand and Pétain were convinced that the fight was already lost. Churchill spoke of the coming British help, if the French could hold out over the 'lean weeks'. A Canadian Division was landing in France that night. One of the British divisions withdrawn from Dunkirk would arrive in about nine days' time. The troops withdrawn from Narvik were on their way. A third British division was available if the French could provide the artillery for it. If France could hold out for nine months, until the following spring, the British would have trained and equipped as many as twenty-five divisions 'to place at the disposal of the French command, to employ anywhere'.

Spring 1941 was much too far off for Weygand and Pétain; almost too far for Reynaud and de Gaulle. But it was an offer seriously meant, and made in order to instill confidence. When Weygand spoke, it was to hold out no hope, either for Paris or for any large town to the south: 'I have no reserves. There are no reserves.' Churchill again urged the French to hold on 'for another three or four weeks', when the British and Canadian forces building up in Western France could attack the German flank. Weygand replied that it was 'a question of hours', not days or weeks. Churchill then spoke of defending Paris so fiercely that, refusing to accept defeat, it would absorb immense armies. 'The French perceptibly froze at this,' noted Spears. 'To make Paris a city of ruins will not affect the issue,' said Marshal Pétain. Nor would Pétain allow himself to be influenced by Churchill's reference to the Marshal's courage in adversity in March 1918, when Churchill and Clemenceau had visited him at Beauvais and found him a tower of strength.

Churchill then suggested that if a 'co-ordinated defence' failed, Britain could help France to maintain 'guerilla warfare on a gigantic scale'. With intense and visible wrath, Pétain told Churchill that this would mean 'the destruction of the country'. Nor did Reynaud dissent. Churchill then tried to paint a long-term picture of hope. 'It is possible the Nazis may dominate Europe,' he said, 'but it will be a Europe in revolt, and in the end it is certain that a regime whose victories are in the main due to its machines will collapse. Machines will beat machines.' Hearing this, Eden later recalled, Pétain was 'mockingly incredulous'. Nor did the French, other than de Gaulle, respond to Churchill's final suggestion that they hold out in Brittany, to which British reinforcements could then be sent, as well as French troops from North Africa. That evening Reynaud told Churchill that Pétain had already informed him 'that it would be necessary to seek an armistice'.

Churchill slept at the Château de Muguet; then, on the morning of June 12 he flew back to Britain, seeing from 8,000 feet the port of Le Havre in flames. That day General Fortune was forced by superior German air and artillery power to surrender his 'division at St Valery-en-Caux. In the evening, Reynaud telephoned Churchill to tell him that the French Government had left Briare for Tours, and to ask if Churchill would return to France. He agreed to do so, driving to Hendon airport on the morning of June 13 with a member of his Defence Secretariat, Colonel Leslie Hollis. 'I remember the morning well,' Hollis later wrote. 'It was a warm day with the sun shining. I marvelled at the calmness and serenity everywhere, and then realised with a shock that hardly anyone in the crowds of people out in the sunshine – the clerks, the typists in their summer frocks, the shoppers – realised what fearful danger faced Britain. I was already so used to living near calamity that I had imagined others felt as I did.'

On reaching Hendon at eleven o'clock, Churchill learned that bad weather was forecast for later that day. Because of this, the Air Staff advised that the flight be postponed. 'To hell with that,' Churchill told Hollis. 'I'm going, whatever happens! This is too serious a situation to bother about the *weather*!' Awaiting Churchill at Hendon were Beaverbrook, Ismay, Halifax, Halifax's senior adviser, Alexander Cadogan, and the Supreme War Council's interpreter, Captain Berkeley. Flying in two aircraft, the British mission crossed the Channel from Weymouth to the Channel Islands, and then on to Tours. 'Thunderstorm and rain as we arrived on pock-marked aerodrome,' Cadogan noted in his diary. Ismay later recalled how Tours airfield 'had been heavily bombed the night before; but we landed safely and taxied around the craters in search of someone to help us. There was no sign of life, except for groups of French airmen lounging about by the hangars. They did not know who we were, and cared less. The Prime Minister got out and introduced himself. He said, in his best French, that his name was Churchill, that he was Prime Minister of Great Britain, and that he would be grateful for a "*voiture*".'

A car was found and Churchill drove into Tours, to the Préfecture. As Reynaud had not yet arrived, the British group lunched at the Grand Hotel; while they did so, the Secretary of the French War Cabinet, Paul Baudouin, arrived, and began at once to talk, Churchill later recalled, 'in his soft silky manner about the hopelessness of French resistance'. Baudouin's pessimistic talk was an ill-omen, and yet, Hollis later recalled: 'Churchill paid no attention to this Niagara of doom; he might have been hearing an actor declaiming the decline of hope in some stage tragedy. His mind was made up; the defeatism of others could not change his intention.'

The luncheon ended, and the British group returned to the Préfecture. Reynaud had still not arrived nor did anyone seem to know where he was. Churchill waited, his time at Tours limited; as the airfield had no lights, the pock-marked condition of the runway made a take-off after dark impossible. Eventually Reynaud arrived, as did two more Englishmen, Sir Ronald Campbell, the Ambassador, and General Spears. As the group went up the stairs to the meeting, Churchill hung back, until he could ask Spears about Baudouin. 'I told him', Spears later recalled, 'that he was now doing his damnedest to persuade Reynaud to throw in the sponge.' He was 'working on behalf of Weygand and Pétain'. Churchill then 'growled' that he had gathered as much.

The British and French representatives were shown into a room on the first floor; there was no table, but a desk at which sat Georges Mandel, the Minister of the Interior. General Ismay later wrote to Churchill about this meeting with Mandel: 'When we found him in his office at the Préfecture after our lunch at the hotel, he was energy and defiance personified. His lunch, uneaten, was on a tray in front of him, and he had a telephone in each hand and was snapping out decisive orders in every direction. He was the only ray of sunshine – except when you inspired Reynaud to courage – that we ever saw on the French side.'

Churchill was pleased to see and hear Mandel, a friend from the inter-war years. But Mandel, who was later to be murdered by pro-Nazi Frenchmen, was not a member of the Supreme War Council, and had to withdraw almost at once. Reynaud then took Mandel's place at the desk, telling Churchill, in grave tones, that the French Government would soon have to plead for an armistice. Britain would be asked to release France from her earlier pledge not to make a separate peace with Germany. A former French Prime Minister, Edouard Herriot, who was at the Préfecture that afternoon, later learned that as Reynaud made this request 'tears streamed down Mr Churchill's face'.

Churchill urged Reynaud to delay the decision to seek an armistice. 'Was another week possible, or less?' he asked. Reynaud made no reply. He did agree, however, that there would be 'no separate peace' at least until Roosevelt had been asked to take 'a further step forward'. Churchill promised to telegraph to Roosevelt at once. Given 'immediate help' from America, 'perhaps even a declaration of war', he told Reynaud, victory was 'not so far off'. These were fighting words, and effective ones. 'The meeting finished in a much more confident mood on the part of Reynaud than had appeared possible,' Captain Berkeley noted in his diary. 'He is obviously fighting a desperate battle against the majority of his Cabinet, Weygand, and countless other occult forces, and Winston's brave assurances comforted him.'

On the drive to the airfield Churchill begged Reynaud: '*Don't* give in, don't go over to the enemy. Fight on!' That day the Germans entered Paris, the sixth European capital to fall to their forces in nine months; Warsaw, Copenhagen, Oslo, The Hague, and Brussels already lay under Nazi domination.

There were now more than 150,000 British and Canadian troops in Western France, and more were landing that day at Cherbourg. They could join the French in holding Brittany, or even move forward towards the German flank west of Paris. But on the afternoon of June 14 it was learned in London that Weygand had rejected any resistance in Brittany. Churchill at once ordered a halt to any further disembarkation of British troops, while still hoping that those already in Western France might move forward. That evening he spoke on the telephone to their commander, General Alan Brooke, to whom he put his ideas for an offensive. But after nearly half an hour of the strongest possible advocacy for action, Churchill accepted Brooke's judgment that all British forces must be brought back to Britain.

In the early hours of June 15 Churchill learned that the United States would not come to France's aid. Later that morning, with Chamberlain's full support, he telegraphed to Roosevelt urging him to think again. A declaration by the United States that 'it will if necessary enter the war' might, Churchill said, 'save France'. Failing any such declaration 'in a few days French resistance may have crumpled and we shall be left alone'. Churchill added, 'If we go down you may have a United States of Europe under Nazi command far more numerous, far stronger, far better armed than the New World.'

Despite a second forceful telegram to Roosevelt later that day, Churchill was unable to get any American declaration of war. During June 15 he considered flying back to France, to Bordeaux, to which the French Government had now withdrawn, to make arrangements for the transfer of the French Fleet to Britain in the event of a French surrender. He did not go, however, fearing that his advocacy that France continue the fight at this late stage would be resented. Seven months later, however, he told Roosevelt's emissary Harry Hopkins that if he had gone to Bordeaux 'in those last fateful days' he might have been able 'to tip the balance in favour of further resistance overseas'.

On the morning of June 16 Churchill learned that France was about to ask for an armistice. At the War Cabinet that morning it was agreed to release France from her earlier pledge not to enter into a separate negotiation with Germany 'provided, but only provided, that the French Fleet is sailed forthwith to British harbours'. Churchill and his advisers were fearful that the Germans would use the many fine warships of the French

Fleet to help launch an invasion of Britain, but they had no way of enforcing any such proviso, and the French Fleet remained in its ports.

Could nothing be done to prevent a French surrender? In London, a member of the French economic Mission to Britain, René Pléven, who many years later was to be a peacetime Prime Minister, suggested the political union of Britain and France. Their sovereignty would be merged and their defensive capabilities united. There would no longer be two states fighting separately to survive, and being knocked out one by one. Even if the new Union were defeated by the Germans in France, it would continue the fight in Britain. There could thus be no separate surrender; the 250,000 French troops then in western France, far from laying down their arms, would be evacuated to Britain to fight as an integral part of the new Union. The French Fleet would sail to British ports as part of the Union's fleet.

On first hearing of the idea of an Anglo-French Union, Churchill was dismissive of it. But so many of his advisers liked it that during June 16 he thought again. Perhaps, even at the eleventh hour, it would enable Reynaud to stand up to Pétain and Weygand. Chamberlain was keen, as was General de Gaulle, who had come to London on the previous day to authorise a shipment of arms, then on its way from the United States to France, to be landed in Britain instead. 'Some very dramatic move was essential,' he told Churchill, who agreed to give the idea of Union his support. A Declaration of Union was at once prepared; it was ready at 4.30 that afternoon. De Gaulle wanted Churchill to fly with it to Bordeaux on the following morning and give it to Reynaud, believing that it would enable Reynaud to keep France in the war. The War Cabinet suggested that Churchill, Attlee and Sinclair should all go to France, as representatives of the three main British political parties, to discuss the Declaration with Reynaud.

A train was at once organised, to leave London for Southampton at 9.30 that evening. A cruiser was alerted at Southampton to take Churchill to Concarneau, on the Brittany coast, to meet Reynaud at noon the next day. Just as he was leaving Downing Street, accompanied by Clementine, who wanted to see him off at the station, a telegram arrived, 'Meeting cancelled, message follows.' Captain Berkeley noted in his diary: 'Winston refused to be put off, and drove down to Waterloo, and stuck there for half an hour while Ismay and Pound in turn begged him to be reasonable. Finally he went back to Downing Street to await further news.' The news came shortly before midnight: at a crisis meeting of the French Government at Bordeaux all Reynaud's skills at seeking to postpone an armistice had been in vain. Pétain and Weygand had won the day. The Declaration of Union could no longer be a factor in the fate of France; it was not even made public.

That night Reynaud resigned; Pétain formed a Government and within a few hours asked the Germans for an armistice. Britain was alone. 'We have become the sole champions now in arms to defend the world cause,' Churchill declared in a two-minute broadcast that afternoon. 'We shall do our best to be worthy of this high honour. We shall defend our Island home, and with the British Empire we shall fight on unconquerable until the curse of Hitler is lifted from the brows of mankind. We are sure that in the end all will come right.'

Throughout June 17 British troops were being taken back from France; when the liner *Lancastria* was bombed at St Nazaire, nearly three thousand troops and civilians on board were drowned. Churchill forbade publication of the news of Britain's worst maritime loss of the war, telling his advisers, 'The newspapers have got quite enough disaster for today at least.' That same day the deposed Reynaud wrote to Churchill from Bordeaux: 'The project of Franco-British Union is worthy of your imagination and your daring. It is there that the future lies for our two countries.' That evening, de Gaulle, a strong advocate of Union, was flown back to Britain. To ensure that he would become a focus of French resistance, Churchill approved a proposal by Desmond Morton to spend British Government money on a public relations expert to promote his name and cause.

Churchill had now to raise the morale of the nation and to sustain it; as part of this task he made every effort to stop the growing call for scapegoats for the pre-war neglect of Britain's defences, telling the House on June 18: 'There are many who would hold an inquest in the House of Commons on the conduct of the Governments – and of the Parliaments, for they are in it, too – during the years which led up to this catastrophe. They seek to indict those who were responsible for our affairs. This also would be a foolish and pernicious process. There are too many in it. Let each man search his conscience and search his speeches. I frequently search mine.' Churchill went on to warn, 'Of this I am certain, that if we open a quarrel between the past and the present, we shall find that we have lost the future.'

In this same speech, Churchill told the House that under Beaverbrook's energetic direction the number of aircraft being manufactured in Britain had risen from 245 to 363 a week. Now it was the pilots, Churchill said, who would have 'the glory of saving their native land, their island home, and all they love, from the most deadly of all attacks'. What Weygand had called the 'Battle of France' was over. 'I expect that the Battle of Britain is about to begin. Upon this battle depends the survival of Christian civilisation. Upon it depends our own British life and the long continuity of our institutions and our Empire. The whole fury and might of the enemy must very soon be turned on us. Hitler knows that he will have to break us in this island or lose the war. If we can stand up to him, all Europe may be free, and the life of the world may move forward into broad, sunlit uplands; but if we fail, then the whole world, including the United States, and all that we have known and cared for, will sink into the abyss of a new dark age made more sinister, and perhaps more protracted, by the lights of a perverted science. Let us therefore brace ourselves to our duty and so bear ourselves that if the British Empire and its Commonwealth last for a thousand years men will still say, "This was their finest hour".'

Churchill repeated this speech over the radio four hours later. He was tired, and to those who had heard it earlier in the Commons it sounded much less convincing in its broadcast form; but to those who heard it for the first time as they sat around their wireless sets, it was an inspiration. These were 'only words', he later reflected. Foreigners, who did not understand 'the temper of the British race all over the globe when its blood is up, might have supposed that they were only a bold front, set up as a good prelude for peace negotiations'. He knew that 'Rhetoric was no guarantee of survival'. Peace terms might have been offered for which many 'plausible excuses' could have been presented. Many might have asked why Britain should not join the 'spectators' in neutral Japan, the United States, Sweden and Spain, to watch with detached interest, 'or even relish a mutually destructive struggle between the Nazi and Communist Empires?'

That night 120 German bombers attacked eastern England; nine civilians were killed. A new phase of the war had begun. 'Let us get used to it,' Churchill told the House of Commons in a Secret Session on June 20. 'Eels get used to skinning.' Steady and at times intense bombing must become a 'regular condition' of British life. The outcome of the battle would depend upon 'the courage of the ordinary man and woman'.

From western France more than 111,000 British troops had been evacuated; about 16,000 had been taken prisoner. 'It may well be,' Churchill told the Secret Session, 'our fine Armies have not said goodbye to the Continent of Europe.' Britain was already making plans 'for 1941 and 1942'. Would she be able to hold out that long? At Chequers that weekend, the slow pace of United States supplies, grave anxiety about the future of France, and secret knowledge of the extent of Britain's own weakness should Germany invade, caused almost unbearable concern. The strain on everyone who knew the full extent of the dangers was considerable; it was greatest on Churchill, whose responsibilities, so recently acquired, were formidable, yet whose power, so long denied, might still prove insufficient to avert defeat. His own mood reflected the grimness of the hour, affecting even his personal behaviour, so much so that one of his friends complained that weekend to Clementine, who wrote to her husband:

> My Darling,
> I hope you will forgive me if I tell you something that I feel you ought to know.
> One of the men in your entourage (a devoted friend) has been to me & told me that there is a danger of your being generally disliked by your colleagues & subordinates because of your rough sarcastic & overbearing manner – It seems your Private Secretaries have agreed to behave like school boys & 'take what's coming to them' & then escape out of your presence shrugging their shoulders. Higher up, if an idea is suggested (say at a conference) you are supposed to be so contemptuous that presently no ideas, good or bad, will be forthcoming.
> I was astonished & upset because in all these years I have been accustomed to all those who have worked with & under you, loving you – I said this & I was told 'No doubt it's the strain'.
> My Darling Winston – I must confess that I have noticed a deterioration in your manner; & you are not so kind as you used to be. It is for you to give the Orders & if they are bungled – except for the King, the Archbishop of Canterbury & the Speaker you can sack anyone & everyone. Therefore with this terrific power you must combine urbanity, kindness & if possible Olympic calm.
> You used to quote: – 'On ne règne sur les âmes que par le calme' – I cannot bear that those who serve the country & yourself should not love you as well as admire and respect you. Besides you won't get the best results by irascibility & rudeness. They will breed either dislike or a slave mentality – (Rebellion in War Time being out of the question!)
> Please forgive your loving devoted & watchful
> Clemmie

Clementine ended this letter with a sketch of a cat. Then she tore the letter up. Four days later she pieced it together and gave it to her husband. The stresses on Churchill were widely understood. 'You must indeed have had a terrible time during the last fortnight,' Samuel Hoare wrote from Madrid a week later.

On June 21 Churchill learned that as a result of decrypts from the German Air Force's most secret radio communications, a system of intersecting beams had been uncovered along which German bombers were flying by night on to a precise target, on which their bombs would then drop automatically. Knowing that Britain's night-fighters were then almost powerless, the news of the beams was, he later recalled, 'one of the blackest moments of the war'. But the young scientist who had uncovered them, R.V. Jones, also had the answer to them; the beams could be bent, throwing the raider off course, whereby he would drop his bombs in the open countryside.

Each day during the last week of June and the first week of July, Churchill discussed anti-invasion plans with his advisers, suggesting areas of urgent research and immediate preparation, visiting the beaches on which the Germans might land, and meeting the divisional commanders whose task would be to repel the invader. He was much impressed when one of these commanders, General Montgomery, carried out a mock attack on a coastal airfield which was presumed to have been captured. At dinner that evening in Brighton, as the two men watched through the window a platoon of soldiers preparing a machine-gun post in a kiosk on the pier, Churchill told Montgomery that when he was at school near there in the 1880s he used to go and see the performing fleas in that very kiosk.

As part of the German armistice terms, Hitler had insisted, as Churchill feared, on the surrender of the French Fleet. Those French warships which were then at Alexandria could easily be seized by the British naval forces in Egypt. Those at Toulon and Dakar were beyond Britain's reach. But those at the French naval base of Mers el-Kebir, at Oran, including two battle-cruisers and four cruisers, were within range of British naval forces in the Mediterranean. Churchill and the Chiefs of Staff were determined to deny these warships to the Germans, even if it meant opening fire on Britain's ally of two weeks earlier. But first they planned to send Admiral Phillips and Lord Lloyd direct to Oran, to appeal to the French naval authorities there not to allow the ships to fall into German hands; then they gave the French naval commander there, Admiral Gensoul, three options: to sail his ships to a British port and join the Royal Navy as an ally against Germany; to sail his ships to a British port and hand them over to British crews; or to sail to a French West Indies port and accept demilitarisation, with immediate repatriation of the crews to France if they so desired. A fourth option was added when the first three proved unacceptable; to scuttle his ships in the harbour at Mers el-Kebir.

Despite long negotiations throughout the morning and afternoon of July 3, Admiral Gensoul refused to go back on the terms of the Franco-German Armistice. He would accept none of the British options, not even the last. In this he was supported by the former French Chief of the Naval Staff, Admiral Darlan, who was now Minister of Marine. Darlan, loyal to Pétain's Government, which had been established with German approval at Vichy, insisted that the armistice terms be implemented; Gensoul and his men should pay 'no attention' to British demands, he telegraphed, and should 'show themselves worthy of being Frenchmen'.

Darlan's instruction was communicated by radio signal to Gensoul; a similar instruction communicated to the French Admiral at Dakar was known to the British. The War Cabinet realised that the instruction sent to Dakar must be the same as that sent to Oran. Gensoul had lost all freedom of action; at 5.55 the British Admiral off Oran, Sir James Somerville, gave the order for his ships to open fire. When Somerville called a cease-fire five minutes later, one of the two French battle-cruisers had been beached, a cruiser blown up, and 1,200 French sailors killed. The second battle-cruiser had managed to slip out of harbour and reach Toulon unharmed under cover of darkness. 'I need hardly say,' Churchill told the Commons on the following day, 'that the French ships fought, albeit in this unnatural cause, with the characteristic courage of the French Navy.' More bitterly he confided to Dudley Pound, 'The French were now fighting with all their vigour for the first time since the war broke out.'

Within a few days 'Oran' had become a symbol of British ruthlessness and determination. Six months later Churchill told Roosevelt's emissary, Harry Hopkins, that Oran had been 'the turning point in our fortunes, it made the world realise that we were in earnest in our intentions to carry on.' This was no moment, he told the Commons on July 4, for 'doubt or weakness; it is the supreme hour to which we have been called'. Invasion was probably imminent, he warned, and the Government was making every possible preparation: 'I feel that we are entitled to the confidence of the House and that we shall not fail in our duty, however painful.' Despite German propaganda that Britain was ready to enter negotiations for a compromise peace, the war would be prosecuted 'with the utmost vigour by all the means that are open to us until the righteous purposes for which we entered upon it have been fulfilled.'

Churchill had spoken for just under half an hour. When he sat down the whole House rose and cheered. As they did so his eyes filled with tears. 'Up till that moment,' he later recalled, 'the Conservative Party had treated me with some reserve, and it was from the Labour benches that I received the warmest welcome when I entered the House or rose on serious occasions. But now all joined in solemn stentorian accord.'

Anti-invasion preparations now dominated Churchill's waking hours. Unlike Paris, he assured Josiah Wedgwood, London would be defended street by street and suburb by suburb; it 'would devour an invading army, assuming one ever got so far. We hope however to drown the bulk of them in the salt sea.' Churchill also gave orders for the destruction of oil-storage tanks on the East Coast once the invading forces were approaching them. Most of these were the same oil depots he had been responsible for defending in 1914. A month later, in drafting instructions for policemen, soldiers and members of the Home Guard who might be in towns overrun by the Germans, he wrote: 'They may surrender and submit with the rest of the inhabitants, but must not in those circumstances give any aid to the enemy in maintaining order, or in any other way. They may however assist the civil population as far as possible.'

Seeking some means of taking the war to Germany, on July 8 Churchill told Beaverbrook that the 'one sure path' to a British victory was a bomber offensive against Germany. If Hitler were repulsed on the beaches of Britain, or did not try to invade at all, he would 'recoil eastward'. Although Britain could do nothing to stop him going east, 'there is one thing that will bring him back and bring him down, and that is an absolutely devastating, exterminating attack by very heavy bombers from this country upon the Nazi homeland.' That week Churchill commented to Colville: 'Even if That Man reached the Caspian, he would return to find a fire in his backyard. It would avail him nothing if he reached the Great Wall of China.'

That July the bombing initiative lay with Germany; on July 9 dockyards in South Wales were bombed. That week eighty-eight civilians were killed, but, as a result of a War Cabinet decision, the figures were kept secret. 'I never hated the Hun in the last war,' Churchill told one of the South Coast Generals on July 11, 'but now I hate them like an earwig.' If the Germans were to invade, he commented on the following day, the Home Guard must be armed to face them, and even women must be 'allowed to fight'.

As German bombers intensified their attacks over Britain, the fighter pilots of the Royal Air Force fought them with skill and courage. In a broadcast on July 14 Churchill told the nation: 'We await undismayed the impending assault. Perhaps it will come tonight. Perhaps it will come next week. Perhaps it will never come. We must show ourselves equally capable of meeting a sudden violent shock or – which is perhaps a harder test – a prolonged vigil. But be the ordeal sharp or long, or both, we shall seek no terms, we shall tolerate no parley; we may show mercy – we shall ask for none.' Not only in Britain but in every land there were vast numbers of people 'who will render faithful service in this war, but whose names will never be recorded. This is a War of the Unknown Warrior; but let all strive without failing in faith or in duty, and the dark curse of Hitler will be lifted from our age.'

That night Churchill warned Ismay that 'everybody should be made to look to their gas masks now'. Many masks would require overhauling. Action should be taken at once. On the following day, determined not to allow Hitler's occupation forces to be unmolested, he invited Hugh Dalton to take charge of 'a new instrument of war', the Special Operations

Executive, soon known by its initials as SOE, to co-ordinate all subversion and sabotage against the Germans overseas. 'And now,' Churchill told Dalton, 'set Europe ablaze.' It was to prove a difficult, dangerous and often disheartening task, in which the Germans had many successes in disruption and deception; but within three years a formidable array of networks and agents had penetrated almost every region of German-occupied Europe, organising escape routes for Allied aircrew and soldiers, carrying out rescue and Intelligence-gathering tasks in co-operation with local patriots, setting up and arming local sabotage groups, and preparing local Resistance forces for the day when the Allied armies would land, whether in Italy or northern Europe, or in due course Burma, Malaya and the Dutch East Indies, and would need active local participation behind the lines.

On July 24 an agreement was signed in Washington whereby the United States would manufacture 14,375 aircraft for Britain in the coming twenty-one months. Similar agreements were being negotiated for the manufacture of rifles, field-guns, anti-tank guns and their ammunition. These agreements, which were kept strictly secret, gave Churchill renewed confidence in the long-term prospects of waging an offensive war. So also did the arrival that month of the first twenty-six of 238 reconnaissance aircraft built for Britain in the United States. But still the Americans held back on sending destroyers. To encourage them, Churchill reluctantly agreed to a full exchange of technical secrets, giving the Americans Britain's radar knowledge, and her latest developments in air-to-air and ground-to-air communication.

Churchill also sent Roosevelt a personal appeal on July 31 for 'fifty or sixty of your oldest destroyers', ending his telegram: 'Mr President, with great respect I must tell you that in the long history of the world this is a thing to do *now*. Large construction is coming to me in 1941, but this crisis will be reached long before 1941. I know you will do all in your power, but I feel entitled and bound to put the gravity and urgency of the position before you. I am sure that with your comprehension of the sea affair, you will not let the crux of the battle go wrong for want of these destroyers.'

Still Roosevelt hesitated, fearing that a British defeat would give Germany not only the Royal Navy, but also any American vessels which might be transferred to Britain as Churchill wished. German command of the Atlantic would be America's danger. But naval reinforcements were badly needed, as shipping losses mounted; on August 7 Churchill was distressed to learn that the *Mohamed Ali el-Kebir*, with 732 British military and naval personnel on board, had been sunk by a German submarine in the North Atlantic. Only when he was told that six hundred of those on board had been rescued did he recover his equanimity. But it made his quest for the

American destroyers all the more urgent; he therefore proposed offering America the use of Britain's naval bases in the West Indies in return for leasing the destroyers. At the same time, in an exercise in confidence and ingenuity that amazed those who heard it, he told his weekend guests at Chequers that within a year he hoped to be able to launch a series of 'formidable' raids on German-held Europe, landing forces of 10,000 men to seize the Cherbourg Peninsula, to invade Italy, or to land in Holland for a 'destructive' strike into the Ruhr.

The reading of Germany's top-secret Enigma signals on August 10 made it clear that no preparations for invasion had been made for at least the next month. This gave Churchill, the Chiefs of Staff and their advisers a further month to make their preparations; and to concentrate on the growing war in the air. For the previous three days German bombers had not attacked. 'The swine had needed three days in which to lick their wounds before they came again,' was Churchill's comment. When the next raid came, on August 11, sixty-two of the raiders were shot down, for the loss of twenty-five British planes. Those of the German aircrews who were not killed were taken captive; the British pilots who survived being shot down over Britain could, and did fight again, some within a matter of hours. But 526 British pilots had been killed in action in June and July. At Chequers that night Churchill told his guests that the life of Britain now depended on the intrepid spirit of the airmen. He added, his voice trembling with emotion, 'What a slender thread the greatest of things can hang by.'

During renewed German daylight bombing raids on August 14, despite much damage to factories and dockyards, seventy-eight German aircraft were shot down over Britain, for the loss of only three British pilots. That evening Churchill was given further good news; Roosevelt had accepted the destroyers-for-bases deal, in return for Newfoundland, Bermuda and the Bahamas being added to the West Indies bases which Churchill had offered to lease to America for ninety-nine years. When Colville remarked that Roosevelt's reply 'rather smacks of Russian demands on Finland', Churchill told him, 'The worth of every destroyer is measured in rubies.' But at the same time Churchill told the British Ambassador in Washington that any public announcement of the conditions would have a 'disastrous effect' on British morale. The illusion of a self-reliant Britain had to be maintained.

The Blitz was at its height. On August 15 a hundred German bombers struck at dockyards, factories and airfields in the North-East. At the same time, as part of what was to become known as the Battle of Britain, eight hundred German aircraft tried to pin down Britain's fighters in the South and destroy their landing grounds. In the North-East, thirty of the hundred German bombers were shot down for the cost of only two British pilots injured. In the South, forty-six German aircraft were shot down, for the loss of twenty-four British fighters, and the death of only eight pilots. That evening, at Downing Street, Churchill was 'consumed with excitement' as news of the successful struggle was brought in to him, so much so that he drove to Fighter Command headquarters at Stanmore to watch the course of the battle from its nerve-centre. By the end of the day, seventy-six German aircraft had been shot down; Churchill telephoned Chamberlain, then gravely ill in the country, to tell him the good news.

On August 16 Churchill followed the battle from the operations room of 11 Group, Fighter Command, at Uxbridge. Almost all Britain's fighter squadrons were in the air that day, in combat, but forty-seven British aircraft were destroyed by the Germans while still on the ground. As he was driven away from the operations room, Churchill turned to Ismay with the words, 'Don't speak to me; I have never been so moved.' After about five minutes he leaned forward to Ismay with the words, 'Never in the field of human conflict has so much been owed by so many to so few.' He repeated these words four days later when he gave the House of Commons a survey of the war; they were words that would 'live as long as words are spoken and remembered', Asquith's daughter Violet wrote to him, and she added: 'Nothing so simple, so majestic & so true has been said in so great a moment of human history. You have beaten your old enemies "the Classics" into a cocked hat! Even my father would have admitted that. How he would have loved it!'

There was another sequence of sentences in Churchill's speech of August 20 that expressed the public mood of defiance and confidence. Revealing the destroyers-for-bases deal with the United States, which meant that the two countries would in the coming years have to be 'somewhat mixed up together in some of their affairs for mutual and general advantage', Churchill said that it was a process he could not stop even if he wished: 'No one can stop it. Like the Mississippi, it just keeps rolling along. Let it roll. Let it roll on full flood, inexorable, irresistible, benignant, to broader lands and better days.'

Churchill followed up his words with deeds. A month earlier Roosevelt had agreed, under conditions of the strictest secrecy, to send a high-level mission to London to hold discussions on possible areas of joint Anglo-American strategic co-operation. The mission's true purpose was hidden under the title 'Standardisation of Arms Committee'. To welcome its three members to Britain, Churchill gave them a dinner at 10 Downing Street on August 22, two days after his 'Mississippi' remarks. His personal inspiration was itself an element in Britain's war-making powers; when General Pakenham-Walsh had been sent on a mission to the United States a month earlier, the Permanent Under-Secretary of State for War asked Churchill to see him first, 'in order that he may have the glow of Mount Sinai on him when he reaches Washington'. Churchill kept his private thoughts to his inner circle, telling them at the end of August that the United States was 'very good in applauding the valiant deeds done by others'.

The time had come to regularise the system of war policy-making that had worked since May under the pressure of violent and uncertain events. On becoming Prime Minister, Churchill had also appointed himself Minister of Defence, with Ismay as head of his Defence Office. It was as Minister of Defence that he presided at the Chiefs of Staff Committee; the three Chiefs of Staff, Admiral of the Fleet Sir Dudley Pound, General Sir John Dill and Air Chief Marshal Sir Cyril Newall, met daily to make the decisions for immediate action, as well as future operations. When Churchill did not attend, he was represented by Ismay.

The relationship between Churchill and the Chiefs of Staff was one of mutual respect, fortified by the need to work closely together for a common purpose against a ruthless enemy. Each decision of war policy had to be approved by the three Chiefs of Staff; if they did not agree with one of Churchill's proposals for action, then that proposal could not go ahead. But the issues on which he and the Chiefs of Staff were in agreement far outnumbered those over which they were in dispute. In the main, their relationship was close, constructive and far-seeing, forged in the crucible of danger and the need for survival.

Even at the level of the Chiefs of Staff, Churchill's leadership was remarkable; 'He provided the flow of ideas, the stimulus and drive, and the political guidance,' a member of the Defence Secretariat, Colonel Ian Jacob, later wrote. 'They turned all this into a consistent military policy and saw to it that plans were matched by resources.' One of Churchill's Private Secretaries, John Peck, later recalled 'their deep respect, even on the frequent occasions when they disagreed with him, for his *military* talents if not genius'. There were even times, Peck added, when the Chiefs of Staff turned to Churchill for military guidance. Those who saw Churchill and the Chiefs of Staff at work agreed that they made, in Jacob's words, 'a formidable combination'.

On August 24 Churchill prepared a note on what should be the relationship of the various war-policy groups that now existed. A Joint Planning Committee of senior Service officers and Intelligence chiefs would suggest plans for military, naval and air operations. The Joint Planning Committee would also 'work out details of such plans as are communicated to them by the Minister of Defence', that is, by Churchill himself. All these plans would then be referred to the Chiefs of Staff Committee, and, if approved, would go ahead without further consultation. If, however, the Chiefs of Staff Committee had any 'doubts and differences', the plans would then go to a newly established Defence Committee of the War Cabinet, consisting of Churchill, Attlee, Beaverbrook, and the three Service Ministers, Eden, Sinclair and A.V. Alexander. During the discussions of the Defence Committee, the Chiefs of Staff would be present, as would Ismay.

In explaining the purpose of the Defence Committee, Churchill told Eden that he felt 'sure' that he could count upon the three Service Ministers on it 'to help me in giving a vigorous and positive direction in the conduct of the war, and in overcoming the dead weight of inertia and delay which has so far led us to being forestalled on every occasion by the enemy.' The Defence Committee quickly became the arbiter of all war operations. The War Cabinet was the arbiter of all decisions outside the sphere of operations. The Cabinet itself became the principal instrument for carrying out the policies decided upon by the Defence Committee and the War Cabinet; each Minister not on the Committee was entrusted with wide areas of responsibility and was expected to fulfil his tasks without interference, and with energy.

The co-ordination of these efforts was entrusted to the Cabinet Office, under the supervision of the Cabinet Secretary, Sir Edward Bridges, who was also Secretary to the War Cabinet. 'His advice was honest and fearless,' John Martin, one of Churchill's Private Office later recalled, 'and he was ready to stand up to Churchill if he disagreed with him. In return the Prime Minister came to place great reliance on his judgment and turned to him to ensure the execution of his policies.' Among Bridges' tasks was to ensure that the highest degree of secrecy was maintained throughout the administration; this he did with skill and tact.

A remarkable war-making instrument was in place; Churchill, with his forceful energy, his long experience and his unswerving faith in a victorious outcome, provided it with the impetus and the fire.

Also on August 24 Churchill asked for Major Jefferis, whom he had first met at the Admiralty while planning to drop mines into the Rhine, to be promoted to Lieutenant-Colonel. Jefferis, who had much impressed Churchill by his inventiveness and energy, was in charge of the Army's experimental establishment at Whitchurch, only ten miles from Chequers; it was later brought under Churchill's direct control at the Ministry of Defence, and was visited by Lindemann every two weeks. Sometimes examples of the latest bombs, mines and explosives were brought over to Chequers to be demonstrated to the Prime Minister.

It was on August 24 that German bombs first fell in daytime in central London. On the following day, as retaliation, eighty British bombers struck at Berlin. On August 26 Churchill saw an Air Ministry note that the next target was Leipzig. He did not approve. 'Now that they have begun to molest the capital,' he told the Chiefs of Staff, 'I want you to hit them hard, and Berlin is the place to hit them.'

For the next twelve days, no less than six hundred German bombers struck each day at British cities and airfields. Churchill often watched the raiders from the roof of one of the Government buildings in Whitehall. But he was aware of how little any one man could do to affect the battle in the skies, the battle of pilot against pilot. 'Each night,' he told Colville on August 27, 'I try myself by Court Martial to see if I have done anything effective during the day. I don't mean just pawing the ground, anyone can go through the motions, but something really effective.'

On August 28, Churchill visited the coastal defences at Dover and Ramsgate, where, having seen the effect of German bombing, he gave orders that all civilians whose houses had been damaged or destroyed 'should receive full compensation'. He also gave orders for the more rapid filling of bomb craters on the coastal airfields. His mood was robust, but not brusque or sour; a member of the American mission whom he had taken with him to the coast thanked him not only for the trip, 'but because a man loaded with responsibility can at the same time be the genial host that you were'.

That weekend at Chequers, Churchill again discussed possible offensive action with the Joint Planning Committee. One idea he put forward was the capture of Oslo, thereby undoing 'Hitler's first great achievement'. Another was the seizure of some North German territory, 'so that the enemy might be made to experience war in his own land'. These ideas, he added, were *'just* to study'. Churchill had all his life been a believer in the Classical adage 'Neglect no means'. But he recognised how dependent he was on the energy and initiative of others. 'Very fine arguments are always given for doing nothing', he minuted on September 5.

When Churchill spoke in the Commons on September 5 he withheld details of the most recent British losses. These had been heavy; fifty fighter pilots killed in a single week, and 469 civilians, many of them workers in aircraft factories. There was also a major success which had to remain secret, the sending through to Malta, which was then under Italian air bombardment, of four warships from Gibraltar carrying anti-aircraft guns and other essential supplies. The Admiralty had resisted this operation, and was still reluctant to do the same for the longer run to Egypt. 'Naturally,' Churchill minuted on the following day, 'they all stand together like doctors in a case which has gone wrong. The fact remains that an exaggerated fear of Italian aircraft has been allowed to hamper operations.'

Nearer home, misinterpreted Intelligence indications led on September 6 to the fear of a German invasion on the following day. At seven minutes past eight on the evening of September 7 the code-word 'Cromwell' was sent to all British forces in the United Kingdom, alerting them to 'immediate action'. It was a false alarm; Hitler had not even set a date for the invasion of Britain. The real activity planned for that night was the launching of the whole of Germany's bomber strength against Britain. That night two hundred bombers struck at London, and three hundred Londoners were killed. When on the following morning Churchill visited the ruins of an air-raid shelter in which forty people had been killed, the survivors and the relatives of the dead almost overwhelmed him as he got out of his car, calling out: 'We thought you'd come. We can take it. Give it 'em back.'

Ismay, who was with Churchill, later wrote to him, recalling the incident, 'You broke down completely.' As he tried to get Churchill back to his car through the throng, a woman called out: 'You see, he really cares, he's crying.' Returning to Downing Street, Churchill was told of an Enigma decrypt which made clear that the German invasion plans were so ill-advanced that even the training was not complete, and that there had been no 'hard and fast decision to take action in any particular direction'. Relieved, but not lulled into complacency, he at once suggested bombing raids on German port facilities at Calais, Boulogne and other ports in which final invasion preparations would have to be made, to 'affect the morale' of German troops being assembled there, and to make unusable as many as possible of the 1,700 self-propelled barges and two hundred sea-going ships that had been spotted there by photographic reconnaissance.

As the Blitz continued, London's weekly death toll rose to almost a thousand. On September 11 Churchill broadcast words of stern defiance, telling his listeners:

> These cruel, wanton, indiscriminate bombings of London are, of course, a part of Hitler's invasion plans. He hopes, by killing large numbers of civilians, and women and children, that he will terrorise and cow the people of this mighty imperial city, and make them a burden and anxiety to the Government and thus distract our attention unduly from the ferocious onslaught he is preparing. Little does he know the spirit of the British nation, or the tough fibre of the Londoners, whose forebears played a leading part in the establishment of Parliamentary institutions and who have been bred to value freedom far above their lives.
>
> This wicked man, the repository and embodiment of many forms of soul-destroying hatreds, this monstrous product of former wrongs and shame, has now resolved to try to break our famous Island race by a process of indiscriminate slaughter and destruction. What he has done is to kindle

a fire in British hearts, here and all over the world, which will glow long
after all traces of the conflagration he has caused in London have been
removed. He has lighted a fire which will burn with a steady and
consuming flame until the last vestiges of Nazi tyranny have been burnt
out of Europe, and until the Old World – and the New – can join hands to
rebuild the temples of man's freedom and man's honour, upon foundations
which will not soon or easily be overthrown.

On September 13, as the German bombing of London intensified, the War
Cabinet and the Defence Committee met in specially fortified rooms below
ground level. Known then as the Central War Rooms, later as the Cabinet
War Rooms, they were situated under the old Board of Trade building
opposite St James's Park, a substantial structure built just before the First
World War. That such a sanctuary was needed became clear two days later,
September 15, when, during the course of the day, a total of 230 bombers
and 700 fighters crossed the coast and made for London.

It was a Sunday; by mid-morning, as the first wave of incoming aircraft
was reported, it was clear that a major aerial assault had begun. Shortly
before midday Churchill drove from Chequers with Clementine and his
daughter-in-law Pamela to the headquarters of No. 11 Group at Uxbridge,
to follow the course of the air battle. The Group Controller in the underground operations room when he arrived was Wing Commander Eric
Douglas-Jones. It was the moment of crisis; at one point Churchill said to
Douglas-Jones: 'Good Lord, man, all your forces are in the air. What do
we do now?' Had one more wave of German bombers and fighters crossed
the coast, there would have been no reserves to challenge them. Douglas-
Jones gave a confident reply, 'Well, Sir, we can just hope that the squadrons will refuel as quickly as possible and get up again.'

Another wave of German bombers and fighters crossed the coast. Every
light bulb on Douglas-Jones' panel showed red: every available fighter was
in the air engaging the enemy. Turning to Air Vice-Marshal Park, Churchill asked, 'What other reserves have we?'

'There are none,' Park replied.

The all-clear sounded at 3.50. As he left the operations room, Churchill
patted the Controller on the shoulder and said, 'Well done, Douglas-
Jones.' Pamela Churchill later recalled how, as they drove back to Chequers, 'He was absolutely – totally – exhausted. It was as if he had
personally repulsed the German bombers.' Reaching Chequers half an
hour later, Churchill put on the black satin eye-band that he used when in
need of a nap, and fell asleep.

By eight o'clock that evening, when Churchill woke, it was clear, not only
that the Germans had failed to overwhelm the British fighter defences,

but that their losses had been so high, with fifty-nine of their bombers destroyed, that any further air battles on that scale would cripple them. The Battle of Britain, whose 'day' is now celebrated on September 15, had been won. The German bombing continued, but henceforth the British defenders gained each day in confidence and strength.

As 10 Downing Street itself was now reported to be unsafe, Churchill, his wife and his staff moved on September 16 to a set of rooms in the Board of Trade building. These rooms were not underground, as were the Central War Rooms, but above ground level, overlooking St James's Park; they had been fortified inside with steel girders and outside with steel shutters to be closed whenever an air raid began. Known as 'No.10 Annexe', this set of rooms, one of which Churchill turned into a map room, became his working headquarters for the rest of the war. There he ate and there he slept; he is known to have gone underground to sleep on only three nights.

'We have now through the dark hours a tremendous firing of guns of all types,' Captain Berkeley wrote in his diary on September 17. 'For this we have to thank the PM, who stamped and shouted a week ago that something must be done or morale would crack. The searchlights had proved quite useless and people were getting desperate listening to the buzzing of the Boche wandering unopposed in the London sky. So the guns were brought in.'

On September 17, a day after moving into No.10 Annexe, Churchill told the Commons, 'I feel as sure as the sun will rise tomorrow that we shall be victorious.' No military or civilian setback was to shake Churchill's confidence. But each day's news continued to be severe; that day in North Africa, Italian troops crossed the Libyan border and advanced sixty miles into Egypt. At sea, seventy-seven children being evacuated to Canada and seventy-two of the adults and crew accompanying them had been drowned when their ship, the *City of Benares*, was torpedoed.

Over London, on the night of September 16, the Germans had begun a vicious form of indiscriminate bombing, dropping mines by parachute. These mines drifted to the ground without any possibility of being directed on to a military or strategic target. More parachute mines were dropped on the night of September 18; on the following day Colville noted in his diary that Churchill was 'becoming less and less benevolent towards the Germans, having been much moved by the examples of their frightfulness in Wandsworth which he has been to see, and talks about castrating the lot!'

For two months the first British offensive of Churchill's premiership had been under preparation: an attack, on behalf of General de Gaulle and his

Free French Movement, against the French West African port of Dakar. Churchill's hope was that the French authorities at Dakar would abandon their loyalty to Vichy and switch to de Gaulle, giving the Free French their first overseas success. 'General de Gaulle's preparations for installing himself in West Africa must be aided in every way,' Churchill had told the Chiefs of Staff, who agreed with him, after some initial hesitation, that British troops should lead the assault. On September 15, learning that Vichy warships had reinforced the garrison at Dakar, Churchill called off the enterprise, but at the War Cabinet two days later both Chamberlain and Eden were emphatic that the attack should go ahead. As with so many wartime enterprises, Churchill was later to be accused of a lack of caution which was the opposite of his actual view at the time.

The attack, launched on September 23, was a failure. The Vichy forces resisted tenaciously, their gunners hitting the British battleship *Resolution* and the cruiser *Cumberland*. The expedition was called off. Churchill, though dismayed, was unbowed; that night, after ordering a hundred heavy bombers to attack Berlin, and a further fifty to strike at German barges and other installations in the Channel ports, he told Colville: 'Let 'em have it. Remember this. Never maltreat the enemy by halves.'

29

Britain at Bay

At the end of September 1940, Churchill learned that 6,954 civilians had been killed that month by German bombs. Under his vigilant eye, anti-invasion preparations were continuous, as was the search for more effective anti-aircraft measures. He also sought to encourage those inside German-occupied Europe. To the people of Czechoslovakia he broadcast on September 30: 'Be of good cheer. The hour of your deliverance will come. The soul of freedom is deathless; it cannot, and will not, perish.'

In the first week of October a further 2,000 people were killed in London and several other cities by German bombing. But in a speech in the Commons on October 8 Churchill pointed out that at the existing rate of destruction it would take ten years for half of the houses of the capital to be destroyed. But 'quite a lot of things are going to happen to Herr Hitler and the Nazi regime before ten years are up'. As to the homes that had been destroyed, 'we will rebuild them more to our credit than some of them were before. London, Liverpool, Manchester and Birmingham 'may have much more to suffer, but they will rise from their ruins, more healthy, and, I hope, more beautiful'.

On the day of this speech by Churchill, his son Randolph entered Parliament as a Conservative MP, after an uncontested by-election. He arrived at Westminster at an historic moment in his father's political career. Neville Chamberlain having left the War Cabinet because of his rapidly deteriorating health, Churchill was asked to become Leader of the Conservative Party, the Party for which he had first entered Parliament forty years earlier, during the reign of Queen Victoria, but which after four years he had then left for the next two decades.

Clementine wanted her husband to decline the Party Leadership. Her argument, their daughter Mary has recalled, was 'that he was called by the voice of the whole nation, irrespective of Party', and that by accepting nomination he would 'affront a large body of opinion'. But Churchill needed Party colleagues for his work and was to feel 'sustained through some tough times', his daughter wrote, 'by the assurance of their solid support'. On October 9 he accepted the Leadership. On the following day his grandson Winston, Randolph's son, was born; his mother Pamela being then at Chequers. Churchill commented during his next visit there that if the Germans were to bomb Chequers that weekend they could kill 'three generations at one swoop. Probably they don't think I am so foolish as to come here.' Noted Colville, 'He does not object to chance, but feels it a mistake to be a victim of design.' Churchill therefore decided to spend the weekends nearest to the full moon, when Chequers would be most easily visible from the air, at a house further from London, and one better protected by trees, Ditchley Park, north-west of Oxford.

Churchill's comments to his guests at the weekend were lively and informal. On October 13 he told them, 'A Hun alive is a war in prospect.' He also commented 'that this was the sort of war which would suit the English people once they got used to it. They would prefer all to be in the front line taking part in the battle of London than to look on hopelessly at mass slaughters like Passchendaele.' He had arranged, when shells were in short supply, for anti-aircraft guns to fire loud blank-charges, 'to avoid discouraging silence for the population'. The blanks would also confuse the Germans 'by the flashing on the ground' and at the same time make them 'less aware of our attacking fighters'.

The German air raids continued; on October 14, when Churchill was dining in a small room specially shuttered at the back of 10 Downing Street, a bomb fell on the Horse Guards Parade. He at once ordered his butler, cook and servants to put the whole meal in the dining room, leave their kitchen and go into the basement shelter. Three minutes later a second bomb, falling fifty yards away in the yard on the Treasury side of the building, destroyed the kitchen altogether. Churchill's staff had been saved by his foresight. Two days later another bomb fell in the yard, killing four people sheltering in a Treasury basement. On October 17, as the civilian death-toll in London alone reached ten thousand, in the smoking-room of the Commons an MP pressed Churchill to institute reprisals. He replied: 'This is a military and not a civilian war. You and others may desire to kill women and children. We desire (and have succeeded in our desire) to destroy German military objectives. I quite appreciate your point. But my motto is "Business before Pleasure".'

On October 21 Churchill learned that the 500th British merchant ship had been sunk, a total of more than two million tons of lost shipping. 'This preys on the PM's mind greatly,' Colville noted. That day, in the Atlantic, German aircraft attacked two merchant-shipping convoys coming from Canada, sinking seventeen ships in one and fourteen in the other. That night, as bombs fell on London, Churchill broadcast to France from the underground Central War Rooms, telling his listeners that, in London, 'we are waiting for the long-promised invasion. So are the fishes.'

As for France, Churchill declared, 'never will I believe that her place among the greatest nations of the world is lost for *ever*'. Frenchmen must rearm their spirits before it was too late: 'Presently you will be able to weight the arm that strikes *for* you.' Britain sought one thing only, 'to beat the life and soul out of Hitler and Hitlerism. That alone, that all the time, that to the end. We do not covet anything from any nation except their respect.' His broadcast ended: 'Good night, then; *sleep* to gather strength for the morning. For the morning will come. Brightly will it shine on the brave and true, kindly on all who suffer for the cause, glorious upon the tombs of heroes. Thus will shine the dawn. *Vive la France!* Long live the forward march of the common people in all the lands towards their just and true inheritance, and towards the broader and fuller age.'

Throughout that week and the next, the German bombing of Britain was severe. In the last week of October, more than eight hundred civilians were killed in Britain, including fifty Londoners sheltering under a railway arch which received a direct hit, bringing the month's death toll to more than six thousand. The greatest danger lay in a German invasion being launched at this moment of continuous and destructive bombardment. On October 27, however, a German top-secret radio message, sent by Enigma to the German forces gathered at the Channel Ports for the invasion of Britain, instructed them 'to continue their training according to plan'. The message was immediately picked up by a radio listening-post in Britain and decrypted at Bletchley within hours. Those who then interpreted the message concluded that invasion could hardly be imminent if 'training' was still to continue.

On October 28, photographic reconnaissance, an essential arm of Intelligence, detected a considerable movement of German shipping eastward, away from Britain. This, combined with the previous day's message, was decisive. Hitler had no plan to invade Britain that month, nor, with winter weather imminent, could he possibly have any such plan for the next four to five months at least. At Chequers on November 2, Colville, who did not know the reason, noted in his diary that Churchill 'now thinks invasion is off'.

Churchill's relief was considerable; but on October 28, the day of the second encouraging clue that Hitler had no immediate plans to invade Britain, Mussolini's forces invaded Greece, and Italian aircraft bombed Athens. 'Then we must bomb Rome,' was Churchill's immediate response, in a note to the new Chief of the Air Staff, Sir Charles Portal. In fact, it was military targets in Naples that were bombed three days later, when

Berlin was also attacked. 'The discharge of bombs on Germany is pitifully small,' was Churchill's comment.

With the threat of invasion no longer imminent, Churchill did his utmost to find men, aircraft, arms and ammunition for Greece, to which Britain had given a guarantee in March 1939. Eden emphasised the danger of sending too much from Egypt, lest the Italians tried to advance even closer to Cairo. But on November 3, the day on which the first British troops landed in Greece, Churchill exhorted him to 'grasp the situation firmly, abandoning negative and passive policies and seizing the opportunity which has come into our hands'. Churchill added, ' "Safety First" is the road to ruin in war, even if you had the safety, which you have not.' On the following day Churchill warned the War Cabinet, 'If Greece was overwhelmed it would be said that in spite of our guarantees we had allowed one more small ally to be swallowed up.'

The Joint Planners and the Chiefs of Staff both approved 'leaving Egypt thin for a period' in order to help Greece. Like Churchill, they recognised that the many shortages in war supplies could not be allowed to halt measures judged essential for war policy. But there were hopeful pointers, military and political, as well as harsh ones. On November 3, for the first time in nearly two months, no German bombers flew over London. 'Evidently they do not like the reception they got here,' Churchill commented on the following day, 'or the retaliation on Berlin.' On November 5 Roosevelt was elected President for a further four-year term. Then, on the morning of November 6, the headquarters of the German 16th Army sent top-secret instructions to the relevant commander that part of the apparatus for equipping invasion barges in Belgium and Northern France 'should be returned to store', leaving behind only what was needed for 'exercises'. This instruction was picked up and decrypted at Bletchley Park; Churchill was handed a copy of it in the locked box, to which he alone had the key, on the evening of November 6. Hitler would be turning elsewhere for his next conquest.

There was further good news for Churchill on November 7; military supplies for Egypt were carried by five British warships the whole length of the Mediterranean, as he had been urging for some time. A day later he learned that the Commander-in-Chief, Middle East, General Wavell, had completed a plan to drive the Italian Army out of Egypt. 'I purred like six cats,' Churchill later recalled. 'At long last,' he told his advisers, 'we are going to throw off the intolerable shackles of the defensive. Wars are won by superior will-power. Now we will wrest the initiative from the enemy and impose our will on him.' Henceforth Churchill had to seek a delicate balance between the war supplies needed for Egypt and those needed for Greece; there were not enough for both, yet both had to be defended. He had also to make sure that Britain's cities had adequate anti-aircraft defence; on November 8, alerted to a shortage of anti-aircraft guns in Coventry, where the city's munitions factories had already been bombed sixteen times, he gave instructions to strengthen Coventry's anti-aircraft defences. These instructions were carried out at once; he had affixed one of his special bright red 'ACTION THIS DAY' labels to them.

On November 11 the public was elated when British naval air forces launched an attack with aerial torpedoes on the Italian Fleet at anchor at Taranto; three of Italy's six battleships were sunk. It was Britain's first naval victory of Churchill's premiership. He at once sent an account of it to Roosevelt, whose Secretary of the Navy, Frank Knox, suggested taking immediate precautionary measures to protect Pearl Harbor, where he considered that 'the greatest danger will come from aerial torpedoes'. Knox was right: the Japanese also learned the lesson of Taranto. A year later their torpedo bombers were to find a fleet at anchor when they struck at that same Pearl Harbor.

On the night of Britain's victory at Taranto, Churchill was preparing a Parliamentary obituary of Neville Chamberlain, who had died on the previous day. His speech was a moving attempt to understand all Chamberlain had striven for. 'It is very good,' Kathleen Hill told him after he had dictated it to her, to which he replied, 'Well, of course I could have done it the other way round.'

Churchill told the House that it had fallen to Chamberlain, in one of the supreme crises of the world, 'to be contradicted by events, to be disappointed in his hopes, and to be deceived and cheated by a wicked man. But what were these hopes in which he was disappointed? What were these wishes in which he was frustrated? What was that faith that was abused? They were surely among the most noble and benevolent instincts of the human heart – the love of peace, the toil for peace, the strife for peace, the pursuit of peace, even at great peril and certainly to the utter disdain of popularity or clamour.'

On November 14 Churchill was one of the pall-bearers at Chamberlain's funeral in Westminster Abbey. Returning to Downing Street, and to the war, he telegraphed to Wavell, 'Now is the time to take risks and strike the Italians by land, sea and air.' Then, having finished lunch, he set off by car for his second weekend at Ditchley Park. The car had not been on its way for five minutes when Churchill, working his way through the urgent material which one of his Private Secretaries had given him on his departure, read the most recent Air Intelligence estimate of forthcoming German bomber targets. It seemed almost certain that a heavy raid was in prospect that very night. Its target was not yet known; but several earlier reports had suggested that the next big raid would be on London. Churchill at once told his driver to turn round and take him back to Downing Street. He was not going to spend the night 'peacefully in the country', he told the Private Secretary, 'while the metropolis was under heavy attack.'

Not London, in fact, but Coventry was the target for that night. Had this been known, every possible effort would have been made, according to the established pattern, to send fire-fighting appliances and civil defence help to the threatened city. No attempt was ever made, as was alleged many years later, to protect any source of Intelligence regarding the air raids by denying the target-city whatever defences and help could be sent to it. But for some days there had been conflicting indications about the target of the next big raid. Not only London, but also the Thames Valley, the Kent or Essex coasts, Coventry, and Birmingham, had each been mentioned as the possible target. The Air Ministry Intelligence estimate in which Churchill was told that the raid was definitely to be that night also noted that the target was 'probably in the vicinity of London'. Added to this estimate was a note that if later information were to indicate 'Coventry, Birmingham or elsewhere' it was hoped that instructions for counter-measures would still be got out in time.

On returning to Downing Street to await the raid on London, Churchill gave instructions for the women members of his staff to be sent home. Later he sent two of his duty Private Secretaries to a deep air-raid shelter in Piccadilly with the words 'You are too young to die'. He then waited impatiently for the raid to begin, first in the underground Central War Rooms and then on the Air Ministry roof.

At ten minutes to four that afternoon, Air Intelligence was informed that the beams for that night's bombing had been detected; they were pointing at Coventry. British bombers were at once sent off to bomb the airfields from which the attack would come, while a continuous fighter patrol, at times of a hundred fighters, was maintained over Coventry itself. Three and a half hours later three hundred German bombers struck. It was the heaviest raid yet on a munitions centre. The city's anti-aircraft defences, so recently strengthened as a result of Churchill's initiative, and alerted now by the Air Ministry's warning, kept the attacking aircraft very high. The fire density of the anti-aircraft barrage, likewise alerted, was greater than that yet put up on any one night over London. But as well as the damage done to the munitions factories, a fire-storm was created in the city centre, 568 civilians were killed, and the Cathedral destroyed.

The renewed German bombing offensive continued for a week, with 484 civilians being killed in London and 228 in Birmingham. Thanks to the success of Signals Intelligence, the beams were identified on each occasion, and defensive measures taken in advance, as indeed had been done at Coventry. But the weight of bombs dropped was heavy; in London seven hospitals were among the buildings hit. Retaliation was swift; Berlin was bombed on November 16 and Hamburg two days later, when 233 German civilians were killed.

'Winston flogs on, wildly but with the same genius,' Captain Berkeley had written in his diary on November 12. 'He is virtually a dictator and it is only seldom some brave Minister rebels. The Chiefs of Staff, at any rate, are quite subservient and wholly engaged in ways and means.' Two weeks later, Churchill told Eden that never in his life had he felt more equal to his work. On November 30 he celebrated his sixty-sixth birthday. 'Very few men in history have had to bear such a burden as you have carried in the last six months,' Eden wrote to him that day. 'It is really wonderful that at the end of it you are fitter & more vigorous, and better able than ever to guide & inspire us all.'

Much inspiration and guidance were still needed; on December 8, in a raid which killed eighty-five civilians, German bombers destroyed part of the House of Commons. But two days later Churchill was able to announce the success of Wavell's offensive in the Western Desert; more than five hundred Italian soldiers had been taken prisoner. Within twenty-four hours the number of prisoners had risen to seven thousand, three Generals among them. 'One has a growing feeling,' Churchill telegraphed to Field Marshal Smuts, 'that wickedness is not going to reign.'

On December 16 Churchill exhorted Wavell to do his utmost 'to maul the Italian Army and rip them off the African shore to the utmost possible extent.' On the following night, after discussing Churchill's 'qualities and defects' with two other Civil Servants, Captain Berkeley wrote in his diary: 'If only there were just a few more anything like him! Even the spectacularly successful campaign in Egypt would probably never have been launched if he had not ceaselessly urged Wavell on. Thank heavens he has been proved right.'

On December 18, on a visit to his old school at Harrow, Churchill wept as the boys sang their rousing patriotic songs. To Eden he spoke on the following night of the dark days of the summer: 'Normally I wake up buoyant to face the new day. Then I awoke with dread in my heart.' Although the months of desperation were now over, a long and difficult struggle lay ahead.

Churchill was ever searching for ways of influencing events. On December 23 he sent a private message to Pétain and Weygand at Vichy, urging them to forsake their German yoke and set up the standard of French revolt in North Africa, with British military support, and offering to enter into secret Staff talks. That same night he broadcast to the Italian people, telling them of his faith that the day would come 'when the Italian nation will once more take a hand in shaping its own fortunes'.

On the following day, December 24, after wishing his staff 'a *busy* Christmas and a *frantic* New Year', Churchill left for Chequers to spend Christmas with his family; while there he followed his own injunction to his staff, dictating several minutes; but eventually he lent himself to the festive atmosphere. After dinner, noted Colville, 'the shorthand writer was dismissed and we had a sort of sing-song until after midnight. The PM sang lustily, if not always in tune.' When Sarah's husband Vic Oliver, now billed as 'England's Favourite American Comedian', played Viennese waltzes, Churchill 'danced a remarkably frisky measure of his own in the middle of the room'.

Returning to London on December 28, Churchill at once pressed the Chiefs of Staff to examine the possible capture of the Italian island of Pantelleria, between the Tunisian coast of Africa and Sicily. Its capture 'would be electrifying', he wrote, 'and would greatly increase our strategic hold upon the Central Mediterranean. It is also a most important step to opening the Narrows to the passage of trade and troop convoys, whereby so great an easement to our shipping could be obtained.' The Joint Planning Committee examined the idea, as did the Chiefs of Staff, but only to dismiss it; it would be easy to seize the island, but too costly to hold and supply it afterwards. Churchill deferred to their reasoning.

On the night of December 29 German bombers made a heavy incendiary-bomb raid on London's docks and railway stations. Eight Wren churches were among the hundreds of buildings destroyed. 'They burned a large part of the City of London last night,' Churchill telegraphed to Roosevelt on the following evening, 'and the scenes of widespread destruction here and in our provincial centres are shocking; but when I visited the still-burning ruins today the spirit of the Londoners was as high as in the first days of the indiscriminate bombing in September, four months ago.' On the advice of the British Embassy in Washington, this paragraph was not sent to the President, for fear, the Embassy explained, 'that it might revive the defeatist impression of some months ago'.

Relations with Roosevelt had reached a difficult point, almost a breaking point. Many of Churchill's most urgent requests for war supplies had failed to win the President's approval. Britain's inability to pay was proving a serious stumbling-block. Arms purchases for December, January and February amounted to $1,000 million; but her gold reserves and dollar balances had been so depleted by a year of war expenditure as to total only $574 million. The Americans had offered to provide the equipment for ten British divisions, but, Churchill told his War Cabinet colleagues, wanted $257 million paid in advance out of these rapidly dwindling gold reserves. Roosevelt had gone so far as to send an American warship to the Simonstown naval base near Cape Town to collect the $50 million of Britain's gold reserves held in South Africa.

Churchill's first instinct was to protest vehemently. Such a move, he wrote in a draft letter to Roosevelt which in the end he held back, 'would wear the aspect of a sheriff collecting the last assets of a helpless debtor'. It was 'not fitting that any nation should put itself wholly in the hands of another'. The message as finally sent on the last day of 1940 was firm but conciliatory. Britain needed to know how America would want to be paid, and to know soon. Two days after sending this appeal, Churchill learned that a ship with seven and a half million American cartridges had sunk after a collision with another ship in its convoy. This 'grievous blow', as Churchill called it, almost offset the relief and pleasure at another victory by Wavell, the capture on January 4 of the Libyan port of Bardia, taking 45,000 prisoners and capturing 462 heavy guns. Two days later Wavell reached the outskirts of Tobruk.

As the public learned of a victory, Churchill learned of danger; a top-secret German Air Force message decrypted and shown to him on January 9 suggested that preparations were being made for a German invasion of Greece. So far, the Greeks had managed to halt the Italian attack, and to drive the invader back across the Albanian border. But once Germany were to intervene the whole balance of power in the Balkans, the Aegean and the Eastern Mediterranean would change. Even neutral Turkey might throw in its lot with Germany, as it was being pressed to do. Once more Britain would have to move resources from Wavell's victorious army, which would then be in jeopardy, to the defence of an ally; 'the prosecution of the campaign in Libya must now take second place' was how Churchill expressed it to his colleagues. Eden agreed.

All Britain's war plans now depended upon the attitude of the United States towards payment for arms supplies. On January 8 Roosevelt's emissary Harry Hopkins reached Britain; two days later Churchill spent three hours alone with him at Downing Street. A friendship began that day which was to grow rapidly, with incalculable benefits for Britain. From the outset Churchill was as frank with Hopkins as he was with his closest advisers. 'He thinks Greece is lost,' Hopkins reported to Roosevelt, 'although he is now reinforcing the Greeks – and weakening his African Army.' Hopkins added that Churchill was in 'close touch' with Pétain, with a view to encouraging a Vichy French move against the Germans in North Africa.

Churchill took Hopkins to Ditchley for the weekend, where the two men discussed Britain's needs. One of Churchill's advisers told Hopkins that anything less than twenty-four million tons of war supplies and sixteen million tons of food 'would definitely have a deleterious effect on our war effort'. Even as Churchill and Hopkins talked, Roosevelt was announcing the financial solution; the United States would build what Britain needed and then lease it to her, on a rental basis, with payment to be delayed until after the war. But before this Lend-Lease arrangement came into force, Britain must pay all the debts she could in gold, and by the sale of British commercial assets in the United States. It was a hard bargain, depriving Britain of what was left of her economic strength, but it constituted an American commitment to the long-term provision of Britain's war needs. Congress would still have to approve, and that would take time, but the principle of help had been laid down. Roosevelt had been in earnest when he had declared in his annual end of the year radio broadcast, 'We must be the great arsenal of democracy.'

Travelling with Churchill in Scotland, on January 17 Hopkins heard him tell a Glasgow audience, 'My one aim is to extirpate Hitlerism from Europe.' That evening, at dinner, Hopkins told the assembled company, 'I suppose you wish to know what I am going to say to President Roosevelt on my return?' He would, he said, be quoting a verse from the Bible, 'Whither thou goest, I will go; and where thou lodgest, I will lodge; thy people shall be my people, and thy God my God.' Hopkins paused, then added quietly, 'Even to the end.' Churchill wept; the American emissary's words, wrote one of those present, 'seemed like a rope thrown to a drowning man'.

Churchill took Hopkins to Dover, to see the gun batteries there and to look across the Channel to the cliffs of German-occupied France. If he had to make a speech after German forces had landed in Britain, Churchill told his guest, he would end with the words, 'The hour has come; kill the Hun.' But in fact a German top-secret radio signal sent by Enigma machine, and decrypted at Bletchley on January 12, had confirmed that invasion was no longer a German design; this particular message was an instruction to the German wireless stations which would have been needed to organise the movement of equipment for any invasion, that they were not to be manned after January 10.

On January 22 Churchill gave the Commons details of a Production Executive which had been created to 'ginger up' production, and an Import Executive to streamline the distribution of Britain's imports. 'This great nation is getting into its war stride,' he said. 'It is accomplishing the transition from the days of peace and comfort to those of supreme, organised, indomitable exertion.' That same day Australian and British forces under Wavell entered Tobruk, capturing 25,000 Italian soldiers. Churchill's mood was benign; at Chequers five days later Colville noted in his diary, 'The PM has throughout been at his most entertaining and shown the sunniest side of his disposition.' At dinner on the previous evening he had told his guests, including Hopkins, that 'he hated nobody and didn't feel he had any enemies – except the Huns, and that was professional!'

In all, Hopkins spent twelve evenings with Churchill; in his report to Roosevelt he stressed that Churchill was not only Prime Minister, 'he is the directing force behind the strategy and the conduct of the war in all its essentials. He has an amazing hold on the British people of all classes and groups. He has particular strengths both with the military establishment and the working people'. From Chequers, Hopkins went to London, where he concluded two agreements, one whereby American aircraft-carriers would transport aircraft to Britain 'in case of urgent need', and one for the pooling of British and American Intelligence in 'enemy-occupied countries'. That same day, January 27, a Staff Conference opened in Washington to determine 'the best methods' whereby the British and American armed forces could defeat Germany, 'should the United States be compelled to resort to war'. The aim of the talks was to secure 'unity of field command' in the event both of strategic and tactical joint operations. Their conclusion was emphatic: even in the event of war breaking out in the Pacific, the Atlantic-European theatre would still be the decisive one, once Germany and the United States were at war.

As Hopkins prepared to return to Washington, the Americans sent Britain the Japanese equivalent of the German Enigma machine, a Purple machine on which tens of thousands of top-secret Japanese diplomatic, consular, naval and merchant-shipping radio signals, received by listening posts in Britain and overseas, could be decrypted. This machine, accompanied by two American Signals Intelligence experts, was taken to Bletchley. Henceforth two nations, one at war and the other at peace, were to act in concert as if they were both at war.

During a final weekend at Chequers, Hopkins produced a large box of gramophone records, 'all American tunes or ones with an Anglo-American significance', Churchill's Principal Private Secretary, Eric Seal, wrote home. 'We had these until well after midnight, the PM walking about, sometimes dancing a pas-seul, in time with the music. We all got a bit sentimental & Anglo-American, under the influence of the good dinner & the music. The PM kept on stopping in his walk, & commenting on the situation – what a remarkable thing that the two nations should be drawing so much together at this critical time, how much we had in common etc.'

In the Western Desert the westward advance continued. At the battle of Beda Fomm in the first week of February, 130,000 Italians were taken prisoner. By February 8 all of Cyrenaica was in British hands. That same day the Lend-Lease Bill was passed in the House of Representatives by 260 to 165 votes. Only the Senate vote remained. In a radio broadcast on February 9, his first for five months, Churchill spoke of a 'mighty tide' of American sympathy, goodwill and effective aid that had 'begun to flow' across the Atlantic. His message to Roosevelt, he said, was 'Put your confidence in us. Give us your faith and your blessing and, under Providence, all will be well. We shall not fail or falter; we shall not weaken or tire. Neither the sudden shock of battle, nor the long-drawn trials of vigilance and exertion will wear us down. Give us the tools, and we will *finish* the job.'

From Field Marshal Smuts in South Africa came the message, 'Every broadcast is a battle.' Churchill now planned, he wrote to the Chiefs of Staff Committee on February 11, to turn Cyrenaica into 'the beginning of a Free Italy', ruled by Britain under a Free-Italian flag and serving as the starting point of 'a real split in Italy and anti-Mussolini propaganda'. Four or five thousand Italian troops could be trained and based there, 'sworn to the liberation of Italy from the German and Mussolini yoke'. The day after Churchill set down this plan for discussion with the Chiefs of Staff, a German General, Erwin Rommel, arrived in Tripoli with instructions to drive the British out of Cyrenaica.

The German plan to conquer Greece was also advancing; many of its operational orders were sent by top-secret cypher and decrypted at Bletchley. For Churchill and his closest advisers, the priority of the despatch of British military help to Greece was hard to decide. The needs of the Western Desert could not easily be set aside. But Eden wanted to send help to Greece, and was supported both by Wavell, with whom he visited Athens at the end of February, and by the Chief of the Imperial General Staff, General Dill. Churchill was inclined to caution. 'Do not consider yourself obligated to a Greek enterprise if in your hearts you feel it will only be another Norwegian fiasco,' he telegraphed to Eden and Wavell on February 20. 'If no good plan can be made please say so. But of course you know how valuable success would be.'

At the War Cabinet on February 24 Churchill asked all six Ministers, Attlee, Bevin, Greenwood, Kingsley Wood, Beaverbrook and Sir John Anderson, to express their views. All six were in favour of sending military assistance to Greece. 'While being under no illusions,' Churchill telegraphed to Eden, 'we all send you the order "Full Steam Ahead".'

Even more than Greece and the land battle, the German submarine successes in the Atlantic were becoming a cause of deep concern; it was the Battle of the Atlantic that threatened to close Britain's food and supply life-line. One of Churchill's staff, reporting a particular convoy disaster on

February 26, called it 'distressing'. Churchill replied: 'Distressing! It is terrifying. If it goes on it will be the end of us.' In the three months beginning in March, half a million tons of Allied shipping were sunk by German air attack. Every day Churchill was presented with the most recent statistics of these sinkings; what cargoes had gone down, what escorts had been lost, what was still on its way. 'How willingly would I have exchanged a full-scale invasion,' he later wrote, 'for this shapeless, measureless peril, expressed in charts, curves, and statistics. This mortal danger to our life-line gnawed my bowels.'

At Chequers on March 1 Churchill told the Australian Prime Minister, Robert Menzies, that the German sinking of merchant ships was 'the supreme menace' of the war. 'The PM in conversation will steep himself (and you) in gloom,' Menzies wrote in his diary. But on the following night he noted: 'Churchill's course is set. There is no defeat in his heart.'

On March 3, as an unexpected reminder that the British position in North Africa might not be as secure as was thought, German aircraft dropped mines into the Suez Canal, closing it completely for a week. A day after the mines had been dropped, the first British troops left Egypt for Greece. Under a plan devised by Eden, Wavell and Dill, Australian and New Zealand troops would follow, to take up a defensive position on the Aliakmon Line. To Eden's consternation, the Greek Commander-in-Chief changed this plan, announcing that the British and Commonwealth troops would be sent to the northern frontier. Despite the dangers posed by this, Eden told Churchill, in a personal message, that he did not see 'any alternative to doing our best to seeing it through'.

Churchill thought otherwise; if Germany were to send an ultimatum to Greece, he told the War Cabinet on March 5, the Greeks would find it 'impossible to carry on the struggle' and there would be 'little or nothing which we could do to assist them in time'. The War Cabinet agreed, but, still in Athens, Eden and Dill were determined to live up to Britain's promise of support, as was Wavell in Cairo. As if to underline this determination, the Greeks now agreed to allow all Allied forces to be sent as originally planned to the Aliakmon Line, less exposed than at the frontier. A final War Cabinet decision was to be taken on March 7. In front of the Ministers was a telegram from Eden, then in Cairo, which stated: 'To have fought and suffered in Greece would be less damaging to us than to have left Greece to her fate.' Wavell agreed with him, said Eden, as did Smuts, who had just arrived in Cairo from South Africa.

The combined advocacy of Eden, Dill, Wavell and Smuts was decisive. At the War Cabinet on March 7 the first Minister to speak was Ernest Bevin, who supported military assistance to Greece. Churchill then said that in his view 'we should go forward with a good heart'. Robert Menzies, who was present, agreed with Churchill; it was a far cry from Australia's rejection of the Chanak commitment in 1922. There was no dissent; more than 60,000 British, Australian and New Zealand troops were put under orders to sail from Egypt to Greece. That night Colville noted in his diary: 'The PM much happier. His mind is relieved now that a great decision has been irrevocably taken.' Churchill was also relieved to learn that night that in Washington, Hopkins told him over the telephone, the Senate had passed the Lend-Lease Bill by 60 votes to 31. 'Thank God for your news,' Churchill telegraphed to Hopkins on the following day, and to Roosevelt he wrote, 'Our blessings from the whole British Empire go out to you and the American nation for this very present help in time of troubles.'

For the period ending in six months' time, Britain had been 'appropriated' $4,736 million to continue 'resisting aggression'. This was the amount already owed by Britain for the arms, munitions, aircraft and shipping being produced in the United States for that period. Even so, Churchill pointed out privately to his colleagues, the forced sale of Britain's assets in the United States meant that 'we are not only to be skinned, but flayed to the bone', while at the same time the ship-building aspect of the American programme was 'less than half of what we need'. The German Navy's top-secret radio signals were at this time being sent by an Enigma key that could not be broken at Bletchley, with the result that the Germans had a crucial advantage in the Battle of the Atlantic.

'The sinkings are bad and the strain is increasing at sea,' Churchill explained to Roosevelt on March 10. A week later a special envoy, sent by Roosevelt to London, Averell Harriman, was invited to Chequers. Like Hopkins, he was in Roosevelt's confidence; like Hopkins, he was determined to ensure that Britain's needs were met. 'We accept you as a friend,' Churchill told him. 'Nothing will be kept from you.' Within three weeks of Harriman's arrival, Roosevelt agreed to put ten United States naval cutters at Britain's disposal for convoy duties.

On March 19 Churchill was Harriman's host at dinner at 10 Downing Street. During dinner there was a heavy air raid on London; Churchill took Harriman on to the Air Ministry roof to see it. 'A fantastic climb it was,' wrote Eric Seal, 'up ladders, a long circular stairway, & a tiny manhole right at the top of a tower.' That night more than five hundred Londoners were killed.

The Germans now made their final plans to invade Greece, and to make an alliance with Yugoslavia. On March 22 Churchill sent Dr Cvetković, the Yugoslav Prime Minister a long and impassioned appeal to remain neutral, and thus to preserve Yugoslavia's true independence. 'There are only

65,000,000 malignant Huns,' Churchill told him, 'most of whom are already engaged in holding down Austrians, Czechs, Poles, and many other ancient races they now bully and pillage. The peoples of the British Empire and the United States number nearly 200,000,000 in their home-lands and British Dominions alone.' This appeal failed; two days later Dr Cvetković travelled to Berlin and signed a pact with Hitler. Churchill at once approved the efforts of Special Operations Executive to rally anti-German opinion in Belgrade, and instructed the British Embassy there to do all in its power to warn the pro-German elements of the folly of their path. 'Continue to pester, nag and bite,' he told the Ambassador, Sir Ronald Campbell, on March 26. 'Demand audiences. Don't take NO for an answer. Cling on to them, pointing out Germans are already taking the subjugation of the country for granted.' That night the anti-Germans seized power in Belgrade. 'Yugoslavia has found its soul' was Churchill's comment.

Setbacks and successes crowded in upon one another: that March there was a sharp increase in German air raids over Britain, with 4,259 civilians killed. But in the last week of March, guided by the comprehensive reading of the Italian Army's top-secret radio messages, British forces defeated the Italians in both Eritrea and Southern Ethiopia. That same week, also guided by the successful decrypting of high-grade Italian cypher mes-sages, and helped by the British air forces recently arrived in Greece, the Royal Navy sank three Italian heavy-cruisers and two destroyers off Matapan. But in a single week 60,000 tons of Allied merchant shipping was sunk in the Atlantic; at the end of the month the cruiser *York* was sunk in the Mediterranean, though with the loss of only two of her crew of more than six hundred.

During the last week of March, as a result of Britain's ability to read the Japanese top-secret diplomatic telegrams, Churchill was able to follow the travels and talks of the Japanese Foreign Minister, Yosuke Matsuoka, in Rome, Berlin and Moscow. While in Berlin, Matsuoka was pressed, on Hitler's authority, to agree to a Japanese attack on British possessions in the Far East as soon as possible. An attack on Singapore, he was told, would be a decisive factor in the 'speedy overthrow of England'. Reading Matsuoka's own top-secret account of this German pressure, Churchill decided to send him a message, which Matsuoka could read during his return journey to Japan through Moscow on the Trans-Siberian railway. The message contained eight questions designed to make Japan pause before committing its fleets and armies against Britain; questions, Chur-chill wrote to Matsuoka, which seemed to 'deserve the attention' of the Japanese Government and people. The questions read:

1. Will Germany, without the command of the sea or the command of the British daylight air, be able to invade and conquer Great Britain in the spring, summer or autumn of 1941? Will Germany try to do so? Would it not be in the interests of Japan to wait until these questions have answered themselves?

2. Will the German attack on British shipping be strong enough to prevent American aid from reaching British shores, with Great Britain and the United States transforming their whole industry to war purposes?

3. Did Japan's accession to the Triple Pact make it more likely or less likely that the United States would come into the present war?

4. If the United States entered the war at the side of Great Britain, and Japan ranged herself with the Axis Powers, would not the naval superiority of the two English-speaking nations enable them to dispose of the Axis Powers in Europe before turning their united strength upon Japan?

5. Is Italy a strength or a burden to Germany? Is the Italian Fleet as good at sea as on paper? Is it as good on paper as it used to be?

6. Will the British Air Force be stronger than the German Air Force before the end of 1941 and far stronger before the end of 1942?

7. Will the many countries which are being held down by the German Army and Gestapo learn to like the Germans more or will they like them less as the years pass by?

8. Is it true that the production of steel in the United States during 1941 will be 75 million tons, and in Great Britain about 12$^1/_2$, making a total of nearly 90 million tons? If Germany should happen to be defeated, as she was last time, would not the 7 million tons steel production of Japan be inadequate for a single-handed war?

'From the answers to these questions,' Churchill added, 'may spring the avoidance by Japan of a serious catastrophe, and a marked improvement in the relations between Japan and the two great sea Powers of the West.' As an added inducement to caution, Sir Charles Portal had already given instructions, he told Churchill, 'that a heavy attack should be made on Berlin on the night that we expect Matsuoka to be there'.

Churchill was under no illusions about Japanese intentions. 'Let me have a report,' he minuted to Ismay a month later, 'on the efficiency of the gunners and personnel managing the 15-inch batteries and searchlights at Singapore.' Were they, he asked, fitted with radar? The defences at Singapore were to be made efficient, but no new forces were to be sent out, and no fighter aircraft could be spared. This was made clear by the Defence Committee in answer to an Australian request for the immediate despatch of British naval and air reinforcements to Singapore. But in the

event of a 'serious, major attack' by Japan on Australia, Churchill remarked, 'we would abandon everything to come to their help'; that,
however, 'did not mean that we would give up our great interests in the
Middle East on account of a few raids by Japanese cruisers'. The painstak-
ing build-up of Britain's military strength in the Middle East could not be
jeopardised.

For several months the German Army had been building up its forces
along the German-Soviet border. To coerce Yugoslavia into concluding
its pact with Germany, some of these forces had been moved into the
Balkans. When the pact was signed, an order was given for these forces to
return to the Soviet border. After the overthrow of the pro-German
Government in Belgrade, Hitler, cheated of an acquiescent Yugoslavia,
made plans to invade; as part of his plan he countermanded an earlier
order to transfer three Panzer divisions to the Soviet border. This counter-
mand was sent by a top-secret radio message; Churchill read it as soon as
it was decrypted at Bletchley. As it showed clearly that the Germans had
been engaged in a build-up of their forces on the Soviet border, he decided
to send the information to Stalin. 'Your Excellency will readily appreciate
the significance of these facts,' Churchill commented. To disguise their
most secret source, he pretended that they came from a 'trusted agent'.

Churchill knew that once Hitler conquered the wheatfields of the
Ukraine and overran the oilfields of the Caucasus he could devote all his
resources to the invasion of Britain; Russia's ability to resist and to survive
a German attack was clearly a crucial British interest. He therefore arranged for Stalin to be sent any further indications of German troop
concentrations in the East. Meanwhile, starting on April 2, it was in the
Western Desert that the Germans were taking the initiative, with Rommel
driving Wavell's forces back towards the Egyptian border. Also reaching
Churchill from April 2, a series of decrypts of German top-secret messages
made it clear that a German invasion of Greece and Yugoslavia was
imminent. Reading decrypts of these messages, Churchill at once informed the new Yugoslav Prime Minister, General Simovic, disguising his
source by describing it as 'our agents' in France and 'our African Army
Intelligence'. On April 5 further decrypts revealed that the attack was
timed for the following day. This information was also passed on to the
Yugoslav leaders.

On April 6, Palm Sunday, German bombers struck at Belgrade; several
thousand civilians were killed in one of the most ferocious bombing raids
of the war. The Greek port of Piraeus was also bombed; six ships with
British military supplies were sunk before a seventh ship, with two hundred tons of high explosives on board, received a direct hit and blew up,
devastating the port. An eighth ship, bringing essential supplies for a

Greek explosives factory, was sunk at sea. When Churchill spoke in the Commons on April 9 he was greeted by cheers, but his news was bad; German forces had entered Salonica that morning.

Churchill wanted alertness maintained throughout Britain; on April 8 he instructed Bridges to ensure that there was no 'serious break' in Ministerial work over Easter. Ministers were responsible, he wrote, for being on the telephone 'at the shortest notice' and should take their holidays in rotation: 'I am told that Easter is a very good time for invasion.' German bombing raids over Britain had continued since the beginning of the year; on April 9 it was officially announced that nearly 30,000 British civilians had been killed in air raids since the start of the war. On April 11 another raid on Coventry led to serious setbacks in aircraft production. On the following night Churchill travelled by train to Bristol with Clementine, Mary, Averell Harriman, Ismay and Colville, for an honorary degree ceremony; he had been Chancellor of the University for the past fifteen years. In a railway-siding just outside the city, he and his entourage slept in the train, waiting for the dawn. While it was still dark they were woken up by the noise of a massive air raid on Bristol itself.

That morning Churchill visited the scenes of devastation; he was shocked and moved. Although the people in the bombed parts of the city looked 'bewildered', Colville noted in his diary, they were 'thrilled at the sight of Winston who drove about sitting on the hood of an open car waving his hat'. Ismay wrote after the war, in a letter to Churchill: 'At one of the rest centres at which you called there was a poor old woman who had lost all her belongings, sobbing her heart out. But as you entered, she took her handkerchief from her eyes and waved it madly about shouting "Hooray, hooray".' Back at Chequers that evening, Churchill learned that Roosevelt was prepared to extend American naval patrols in the Atlantic to the 25th meridian, and report to Britain the location of any 'aggressor ships or planes' that the patrols located. Thus the grim sights of the morning were offset that same night by a feeling of growing American involvement.

On April 13 German forces occupied Belgrade; in Greece, German troops began their attack on the Aliakmon Line; in distant Iraq, the pro-German Rashid Ali, who had seized power in Baghdad ten days earlier, besieged the Royal Air Force base at Habbaniya, and threatened Britain's Middle Eastern oil supplies. In Libya, Rommel's forces were approaching Tobruk. On April 16 the Belfast dockyards were bombed, and considerable damage done to the city itself, 675 civilians being killed. On the following night 450 German bombers struck at London; it was one of the heaviest raids on the capital; 1,180 people were killed and more than two thousand seriously injured.

On April 17, after eleven days of struggle against overwhelming odds, the Yugoslav Army surrendered to the Germans. On the following day, in Athens, the Greek Prime Minister committed suicide. The British War Cabinet had already agreed that once its troops in Greece could no longer hold the Aliakmon Line they should be withdrawn from Greece altogether, and go to Crete, thus creating a fifth war zone in the Eastern Mediterranean and Middle East. Asked by the Air Force commander, Middle East, which of the five war zones should be given priority for his fighter forces, Churchill replied, with the approval of the Chiefs of Staff, 'Libya counts first, evacuation of troops from Greece second, Tobruk shipping unless indispensable to victory must be fitted in as convenient, Iraq can be ignored, and Crete worked up later.'

The evacuation of British forces from Greece began on April 24. For seven days German dive-bombers struck at the troop transports. Several thousand troops were killed, 650 on board two destroyers that had previously rescued them from the sea. In all, 50,000 men were evacuated, but a further 11,500 were taken prisoner. 'I am afraid you have been having a very worrying time lately,' the fifteen-year-old Princess Elizabeth wrote to Churchill on April 23, 'but I am sure things will begin to look up again soon.' Four days later, at this bleakest of times for Britain since the previous summer, Churchill broadcast from Chequers with confidence in the final outcome. 'No prudent and far-seeing man can doubt,' he said, 'that the eventual and total defeat of Hitler and Mussolini is certain, in view of the respective declared resolves of the British and American democracies.' The British Empire and the United States had 'more wealth, more technical resources, and they make more steel, than the whole of the rest of the world put together'. They were determined 'that the cause of freedom shall not be trampled down, nor the tide of world progress turned backwards, by the criminal Dictators.' That night at dinner when the Director of Military Operations at the War Office, General Kennedy, suggested that Britain might have to evacuate Egypt, Churchill was so 'infuriated', another of those present noted, that 'we had some trouble calming him down'.

Churchill realised that Egypt might well be lost, though he expected the troops there to fight to the last man. 'Anyone who can kill a Hun or even an Italian has rendered a good service,' he wrote in a Directive for the Defence of Egypt on April 28. Four days later he warned Roosevelt that if Egypt were lost, to continue the war against a Germany triumphant in Europe and the greater part of Asia and Africa would be 'a hard, long and bleak proposition'. Churchill pressed Roosevelt for an immediate American declaration of war. 'You alone can forestall the Germans in Morocco,' he wrote. The situation for Egypt was hazardous. 'Personally I think we shall win, in spite of the physical difficulties of reinforcing by tanks and air. But I adjure you, Mr President, not to underrate the gravity of the consequences which may follow from a Middle Eastern collapse. In this war every post is a winning post, and how many more are we going to lose?'.

The German bombing of Britain had continued with undiminished ferocity; on May 2 Churchill visited the bombed areas of Plymouth. In five days of raids on Liverpool twenty merchant ships were sunk. Yet in public Churchill maintained his mood of confidence, telling the Commons on May 7 that when he looked back over the perils that had been overcome, and remembered all that had gone wrong and also all that had gone right: 'I feel sure we have no need to fear the tempest. Let it roar, let it rage. We shall come through.'

On May 10, in the heaviest German air raid of the Blitz of 1941, more than 1,400 civilians were killed, most of them in London. Among the buildings destroyed was the Chamber of the House of Commons. 'The Huns obligingly chose a time when none of us was there,' Churchill told Randolph, who was then serving in Cairo as an Official Spokesman at General Headquarters. To his chauffeur, who drove him from the An-nexe to see the burnt-out Chamber, Churchill remarked, 'I shall never live to sit in the Commons Chamber again.'

For three nights the glow of fires lit the London sky. But on the night of this devastating raid Churchill learned that the United States would make available to Britain a third of its pilot-training facilities. A week later the Italian forces in Italian East Africa surrendered, and Rommel's troops were pushed back thirty miles. But Churchill and his closest advisers knew from the German's own top-secret radio signals that it was against Crete that the main German effort was now poised. The attack on Crete began on May 20. As the battle there raged, in the North Atlantic the *Prince of Wales* and the *Hood* joined in the pursuit of the *Bismarck* and the *Prinz Eugen.*

Churchill awaited at Chequers the news of both the island and the ocean battles. It was there, in the early hours of May 24, that he learned of the sinking of the *Hood*, with the loss of 1,500 men. Three days later, a few moments after he had finished speaking to the House of Commons, meeting at nearby Church House because the Chamber had been bombed to rubble, he was handed a piece of paper and rose again, to tell the House: 'I have just received news that the *Bismarck* is sunk.' Nearly two thousand German sailors had perished.

That same day, Wavell ordered the evacuation of Crete. Despite a brilliant and tenacious Allied defence, German air power, based in Greece, had proved the decisive factor in the outcome of the battle, during the course of which more than four thousand of the defenders had been killed, many blown to pieces by German 500-lb bombs. During the four days of evacuation, 16,500 men were taken off, but as German air attacks on the embarkation ports intensified, five thousand men had no option but to surrender. In the battle at sea, more than two thousand officers and men of the Royal Navy were killed; other Allied naval forces also suffered heavy losses.

In search of solitude Churchill spent the evening of June 1 at Chartwell. He quickly recovered his buoyancy, and was relieved to learn that Roosevelt had agreed both to the American occupation of Iceland, thereby liberating the British troops there for service in the Middle East, and to the despatch of British war supplies to Egypt on ships flying the American flag. These supplies included 200 tanks from American Army production, 24 anti-aircraft guns, 700 ten-ton trucks, ammunition, and water-supply equipment.

On June 6, at an airfield in Southern England, Churchill was further cheered as he watched the first Flying Fortress from the United States make a safe and welcome landing. There was also good news two days later, when Allied forces advanced into Vichy-held Syria. 'I feel more sure than ever,' he wrote that day to his son, 'that we shall beat the life out of Hitler and his Nazi gang.' The fighting on Crete, he told the Commons on June 10, had attained 'a severity and fierceness which the Germans have not previously encountered in their walk through Europe'.

That day Churchill was shown an Intelligence study of the most recent top-secret German radio signals, giving the exact dispositions of a considerable number of German units now massed along the Soviet border. He decided to send the information to Stalin; it was transmitted on June 11. On the following day Churchill told the Dominion and Allied representatives in London: 'We shall break up and derange every effort which Hitler makes to systematise and consolidate his subjugation. He will find no peace, no rest, no halting-place, no parley.' Though he could not say so, his transmission of German military secrets to Stalin was part of this plan. 'The stars in their courses proclaim the deliverance of mankind,' he told the American people in a broadcast on June 12. 'Not so easily shall the onward progress of the peoples be barred. Not so easily shall the lights of freedom die.' Even if Hitler invaded Britain, he had told the Dominion and Allied representatives on the previous day, 'we shall not flinch from the supreme trial.'

On June 15 Wavell launched a new offensive against Rommel in the Western Desert, but after an initial success, was forced to withdraw for the loss of a hundred tanks. Once more, for the second time in three weeks, Churchill went to Chartwell to be alone. In the previous two months, half a million tons of merchant shipping had been sunk, and there had been virtually no successes. Yet on June 18, after Churchill's return from Chartwell, Colville found him in 'good spirits'; he was 'now busy considering where next we could take the offensive'. Seeking a 'fresh eye' in the Middle East he decided to replace Wavell, who had wanted to remain on the defensive in Cyrenaica. His choice of successor was Auchinleck, who had attracted his favourable attention by his prompt and efficient action in sending troops from India to Basra at the time of Rashid Ali's revolt in Iraq. It was Auchinleck who would devise the next plan of attack in the Western Desert. 'I think you are wise to make change,' Wavell telegraphed to Churchill on June 22, 'and get new ideas and action on many problems in Middle East, and am sure Auchinleck will be successful choice.'

That weekend Churchill was at Chequers. Diligent monitoring of the Germans' own Enigma messages had made it clear, to those in Churchill's secret circle, where the next blow would fall. 'The PM says a German attack on Russia is certain,' Colville noted in his diary on June 21, 'and Russia will assuredly be defeated.' That night, as Churchill slept, German troops crossed the Soviet border.

30

The Widening War

Churchill was told of Germany's invasion of Russia at eight o'clock on the morning of 22 June 1941. His first comment was, 'Tell the BBC I will broadcast at nine tonight.' Throughout the day he prepared his broadcast, consulting with many of his colleagues. There was a widespread feeling that the Russians would be quickly defeated; both Sir John Dill and the American Ambassador John G. Winant, who were at Chequers during the day, expressed the view that Russia could not last six weeks. Others present, including Eden and Sir Stafford Cripps, were of similar mind. Churchill listened to their arguments, then closed the discussion with the words, 'I will bet you a Monkey to a Mousetrap that the Russians are still fighting, and fighting victoriously, two years from now.'

The Prime Minister was offering odds of 500:1 in favour of Russia fighting on; a Monkey was racing parlance for 500, a Mousetrap was a sovereign. 'I recorded your words in writing at the time,' Colville wrote to him nine years later, 'because I thought they were such a daring prophecy, and because it was such an entirely different point of view from that which everybody else had expressed.' That Russia would be defeated had also been Churchill's view on the previous day.

Churchill had no doubt what Britain's response to the German attack on Russia must be. 'No one has been a more consistent opponent of Communism for the last twenty-five years,' he said in his broadcast that night. 'I will unsay no word I have spoken about it. But all this fades away before the spectacle which is now unfolding. The past, with its crimes, its follies, its tragedies, flashes away.' Hitler hoped to defeat Russia before the winter came and then turn his forces against Britain 'before the Fleet and air-power of the United States may intervene'. The Russian danger 'is therefore our danger, and the danger of the United States, just as the cause of any Russian fighting for his hearth and home is the cause of free men and free peoples in every quarter of the globe'. Any man or State 'who fights on against Nazism will have our aid'. It followed therefore 'that we shall give whatever help we can to Russia'.

Churchill was true to his word. On June 23, to take as much pressure as possible off the Russian front, he authorised a series of intensified bombing raids on German military and naval installations in northern France. This activity, said the Soviet Ambassador, Ivan Maisky, had given 'satisfaction' to the Russians. 'WSC has acted with great rapidity to forestall any two-mindedness in Cabinet and in Parliament,' Captain Berkeley noted in his diary.

On June 27 the cryptographers at Bletchley broke the Enigma key being used by the German Army on the Eastern Front. Within twenty-four hours Churchill gave instructions that Stalin was to be shown the fruits of this precious military Intelligence; this was done in disguised form so as not to reveal, and thus possibly endanger, its source. The information thus conveyed to Stalin was of the greatest value in enabling his commanders to anticipate, then and in the coming months, some of the most threatening German moves.

As the Germans drove eastward across Russia, Churchill also made plans to try to resist two possible German moves if Russia were defeated. The first danger was what he called an 'extraordinary assault' on Britain itself. 'I am having everything brought to concert pitch by September 1,' he told Robert Menzies on June 29. The second was the possibility of a German advance through the Caucasus, Turkey and Syria, to Palestine and the Suez Canal. To maximise the defence capacity of the forces in the Middle East, Churchill appointed a Minister of State in Cairo, and sent out Roosevelt's emissary, Averell Harriman, to examine the best methods of bringing war supplies direct from America to Egypt.

On June 30, with a possible Russian defeat at the forefront of his mind, Churchill gave orders for 'stern individual resistance' throughout Britain in the event of a German paratroop landing. He envisaged as many as a quarter of a million German parachute troops being sent in. 'Everyone in uniform,' he wrote, 'and anyone else who likes, must fall upon these whenever they find them and attack them with the utmost alacrity.' The spirit to be 'inculcated ceaselessly' into all ranks, particularly training schools and depots, was,

Let every one,
Kill a Hun.

In a further attempt to try to force German aircraft back from the Russian front, on July 3 the first of a series of British night-bomber raids was launched against the Ruhr and Rhineland. On July 4 Churchill offered to bomb the Russian oilfields in the Caucasus in order 'to deny oil to the enemy'. The danger of a Russian defeat seemed acute. On July 6 he warned Auchinleck that a Russian collapse might soon alter the balance of forces in the Western Desert 'to your detriment' without in any way diminishing the 'invasion menace' to Britain itself. In a telegram to Stalin on July 7 he promised, 'We shall do everything to help you that time, geography, and our growing resources allow.' On the previous day 400 air sorties had been made against northern France, he told Stalin, while on the same night 250 heavy bombers had struck against Germany: 'This will go on. Thus we hope to force Hitler to bring back some of his air power to the West and gradually take some of the strain off you.' Churchill's telegram ended with an assertion of his conviction, familiar to the British and Americans, 'We have only to go on fighting to beat the life out of these villains.'

On July 10, in proposing a British naval force to work alongside the Russian Navy in the Arctic, Churchill told his colleagues: 'The advantage we should reap if the Russians could keep in the field and go on with the war, at any rate until the winter closes in, is measureless. A premature peace by Russia would be a terrible disappointment to great masses of people in our country. As long as they go on, it does not matter so much where the front lies. These people have shown themselves worth backing and we must make sacrifices and take risks, even at inconvenience, which I realise, to maintain their morale.' Two days later, in Moscow, an Anglo-Soviet agreement was signed, pledging mutual assistance against Germany and no separate peace.

The German bombing raids on Britain continued. So too, in an attempt to derange the German war effort against Russia, did the British bombing of Germany; Frankfurt was bombed on the night of July 7, Wilhelmshaven on July 11, and Hanover on July 14. Speaking at the Mansion House that evening, Churchill declared, 'We will mete out to the Germans the measure, and more than the measure, they have meted out to us.' His words were interrupted by loud and prolonged cheering. He continued, with a direct challenge to Hitler, 'You do your worst, and we will do our best.' Two nights later, Hamburg was bombed.

On July 19, as German forces reached the half-way point between the German-Soviet frontier and Moscow, Stalin asked Churchill to consider two possible British military landings to take pressure off Russia, one in Norway and the other in northern France. Churchill put both plans to the Chiefs of Staff, but they rejected them as far too risky. Churchill had no doubt that his advisers were right. To attempt a landing in force in northern France, he told Stalin on July 20, 'would be to encounter a bloody repulse', while petty raids 'would only lead to fiascos doing more harm than good to both of us. It would all be over without their having to move, or before they could move, a single unit from your front.' Churchill added, 'You must remember that we have been fighting alone for more than a year, and that, though our resources are growing, and will grow fast from now on, we are at the utmost strain both at home and in the Middle East.' The Battle of the Atlantic, 'on which our life depends', as well as the movement of convoys under constant submarine and air attack, 'strains our naval resources, great though they be, to the utmost limit'.

What could be done was already being done, Churchill told Stalin. British submarines, and a minelayer, were on their way to the Arctic. A British fighter squadron would also soon be on its way. Five days later the War Cabinet agreed to send Russia two hundred fighter aircraft, sixty of which would have to come from British war supplies being manufactured in the United States. These fighters would be sent, Churchill told Stalin, in spite of the fact that it would 'seriously deplete our fighter aircraft resources'. As Stalin had requested, between three and four million pairs of boots would also be sent, as well as large quantities of rubber, tin, wool, cloth, jute and lead. Where Britain had inadequate stocks, Churchill explained, she would ask the United States to provide. Aid to Russia added an extra dimension of work; the continuing possibility of a Russian defeat brought an extra dimension of worry. The British Minister Resident in the Middle East, Oliver Lyttelton, warned Churchill on July 21 that 'if Russia collapses soon' the British might be driven out of Egypt altogether, and forced to fight a defensive battle in Palestine or even Syria.

The last week of July was the hundredth week of the war; despite a slackening of German bomber attacks, five hundred British civilians had been killed that month. To his secretary Elizabeth Layton, Churchill commented during late-night dictation on July 28, 'We must go on and on, like the gun-horses, till we drop.' But as August began there was one dramatic lightening of the dangers: as a result of prodigious effort at Bletchley in breaking the German Naval Enigma, it became possible to read all German submarine instructions with few gaps and little delay. Henceforth, trans-Atlantic convoys could be routed away from the submarine packs. In May more than ninety merchant ships had been sunk; in August the figure fell below thirty.

On August 2 Churchill asked Auchinleck, who had been summoned specially to Chequers, if the next offensive in the Middle East could be carried out in September or October. When Auchinleck explained that November was the earliest that his forces would have the necessary two-to-one superiority, Churchill deferred to his commander's judgement. Then, on August 3, he left Chequers for his first journey outside Britain since the fall of France more than a year earlier. At Thurso, in Scotland, he went on board the *Prince of Wales*. 'It is twenty-seven years ago today that Huns began their last war,' he telegraphed to Roosevelt from on board ship on August 4. 'We must make good job of it this time.'

Churchill's destination was Newfoundland, his purpose to meet Roosevelt. On August 7 Clementine wrote to her husband, while he was still on board ship: 'I do hope my Darling that this momentous journey besides being an impulse to American resolve will rest & refresh you.' Two days later, reaching Placentia Bay, Churchill left the *Prince of Wales* to join Roosevelt on board the heavy cruiser *Augusta*. On the following day Roosevelt attended Divine Service on the *Prince of Wales*; Churchill had chosen the hymns. That afternoon, for the British, there was a brief expedition ashore, Colonel Jacob noting in his diary, 'We clambered over some rocks, the PM like a schoolboy, getting a great kick out of rolling boulders down a cliff.' On August 11 three sets of talks began: between the diplomats present, the Chiefs of Staff, and the President and Prime Minister.

The United States made five main pledges at Placentia Bay. She would give aid to Russia 'on a gigantic scale' and would co-ordinate that aid with Britain; she would allocate considerably more merchant ships to take bombers and tanks across the Atlantic to Britain; she would provide a five-destroyer escort for every North Atlantic convoy to Britain, together with a cruiser or other capital ship; she would deliver bombers both to Britain and West Africa using American pilots, many of whom would then stay on to give war training; and she would take over all naval patrol duties as far east as Iceland. There were also two important Anglo-American agreements: both countries would 'respect the rights of all peoples to choose the form of government under which they live' – the document in which this pledge appeared became known as the Atlantic Charter; and Japan would be asked to remove her troops from French Indo-China and stop any further encroachment in the South-West Pacific.

Churchill had drafted a specific warning to be sent to Japan, that if she continued her encroachments, 'the United States Government would be compelled to take counter-measures, even though these might lead to war between the United States and Japan.' At Placentia Bay Roosevelt agreed to this, but on his return to Washington decided against any threat of war.

The British team was to some extent disappointed in the results of the discussions. One 'most distressing revelation', they told Churchill, was a reduction in heavy-bomber allocations to Britain, owing to American shortages and production difficulties. In addition, one of Churchill's military staff, Colonel Jacob, wrote in his diary that not a single American Army officer had shown 'the slightest keenness to be in the war on our side'. But the American naval officers present, Churchill told the War

Cabinet on his return, 'had not concealed their keenness to enter the war'. Even more important, he said, 'I have established warm and deep personal relations with our great friend.' That friend had gone so far as to tell Churchill that all American convoy escort vessels had been ordered to attack any German submarine which showed itself, even if it was '200 or 300 miles away from the convoy'. Roosevelt had 'made it clear', Churchill added, 'that he would look for an "incident" which would justify him in opening hostilities'.

While Churchill had been crossing the Atlantic to see Roosevelt, Hitler had flown as far east as Borisov, half way between his East Prussian headquarters and Moscow, to inspect his victorious troops. Might Russia be overrun while the United States was still neutral? On August 25 the War Cabinet minutes recorded Churchill's fear: 'He sometimes wondered whether the President realised the risk which the United States was running by keeping out of the war. If Germany beat Russia to a standstill and the United States made no further advance towards entry into the war, there was a great danger that the war might take a turn against us. While no doubt we could hope to keep going, this was a very different matter from imposing our will on Nazi Germany.'

Returning from Placentia Bay, Roosevelt had hastened to assure the American people that the United States was no nearer to war than before the meeting. 'I ought to tell you,' Churchill telegraphed to Hopkins, 'there has been a wave of depression through Cabinet and other informed circles here about President's many assurances about no commitments and no closer to war etc'. And to Randolph, who was still in Cairo, Churchill wrote on August 29, 'One is deeply perplexed to know how the deadlock is to be broken and the United States brought boldly and honorably into the war.' Without an American declaration of war, Churchill told his guests at Chequers on August 30, 'though we cannot now be defeated, the war might drag on for another four or five years, and civilisation and culture would be wiped out'. If America came in now, the war might end in 1943. Even coming into the war next March might be too late.

There was one initiative Churchill could take: at the end of August, to secure a safe route whereby American war supplies could get to Russia quickly, British and Soviet forces entered Persia. Russia occupied the northern half of the country, including the capital, Teheran, and Britain the southern half, including the oilfields which Churchill had acquired for Britain in 1914. But might the acquisition of this supply route have come too late? By September 1 German troops were less than two hundred miles from Moscow. In a message to Stalin on September 6, Churchill promised to send, from Britain's own production, one half of the aircraft and tanks for which Russia had asked. He would seek the other half from the United

States. Meanwhile, he told Stalin, 'we shall continue to batter Germany from the air with increasing severity and to keep the seas open and ourselves alive'.

There was a phrase in Churchill's telegram to Stalin which might have seemed wishful thinking, or mere morale-boosting. The information 'at my disposal', he said, 'gives me the impression that the culminating violence of the German invasion is already over and that winter will give your heroic armies a breathing space'. Churchill added that this 'was a personal opinion'. But it was not: it derived from a careful scrutiny of the decrypts of Germany's own top secret radio signals between Berlin and the Eastern Front, which showed that the German Air Force was suffering considerable supply and maintenance difficulties. These decrypts also confirmed other reports that Germany was anxious about the continuing Russian resistance, and that there would be no victory before the winter.

On September 6, having sent his telegram to Stalin, Churchill visited Bletchley, where he told the staff how much they were worth to the war effort. When he learned six weeks later that a shortage of typists there was holding up the work, he minuted, 'Make sure they have all they want as extreme priority and report to me that this has been done.' Churchill called the staff at Bletchley 'the geese that laid the golden eggs – and never cackled'. In his messages to Roosevelt and others, he referred to their tens of thousands of decrypts as his 'Boniface', giving them the name of a supposed British agent in the field.

Realising from his most secret source that the Germans were now less certain of defeating Russia before the onset of winter, when conditions would worsen considerably, Churchill pressed ahead with the maximum aid to Russia in the shortest time possible. Beginning on September 20, Russia was sent the whole of Britain's tank production for the coming week. On the following day Churchill learned from Roosevelt that in the coming nine months the United States would send Britain at least six thousand tanks. 'Your cheering cable about tanks,' Churchill replied on the following day, 'arrived when we were feeling very blue about all we have to give up to Russia. The prospect of nearly doubling the previous figures encouraged everyone.'

If Germany could not defeat Russia before winter, the much-dreaded German invasion of Britain would be impossible that year. Three weeks had already passed since the September 1 deadline for maximum British preparedness. Churchill now offered, if Stalin requested it, to send a substantial British military force to the Caucasus, commanded by Wavell, to help the Russians stave off any German attempt to reach the oil-wells of the Caspian Sea. In the last week of October, however, the Germans' most secret signals showed that it was not the Caucasus but Moscow that had become their winter objective. In the four days beginning on October 21 Churchill authorised nine separate warnings to be sent to Stalin, based on decrypted German orders giving precise details of German dispositions and intentions on the Moscow front. Stalin had no other source for such crucial facts.

On October 2, having read further German messages brought to him in his locked box, giving details of the gathering of German military and air forces on the Moscow front, Churchill wrote to Colonel Menzies, the head of the British Secret Service: 'Are you warning the Russians of the developing concentration? Show me the last five messages you have sent to our Missions on the subject.' In London, Clementine Churchill prepared to launch an Aid to Russia Appeal, which in its first twelve days raised a mass of medical aid, including a million doses of phenacetin, the most effective painkiller then in use. In Moscow, Beaverbrook and Harriman were negotiating a formidable package of military aid, including 1,800 British fighters, 900 American fighters and 900 American bombers over the coming nine months, as well as naval guns, submarine-detection sets, anti-aircraft guns and armoured cars. More than a million metres of Army cloth were to be supplied each month. To get these supplies to Russia, not only the trans-Persian route, but the much quicker and much more dangerous Arctic route would be used.

'We intend to run a continuous cycle of convoys, leaving every ten days,' Churchill told Stalin on October 4. The first of these convoys, with twenty heavy tanks and 193 fighters, would reach Archangel on October 12. It did so; eight days later, with German troops only sixty-five miles from Moscow, instructions were given with Churchill's approval that every tank shipped to Russia should be furnished with three months' spares 'whatever sacrifice this might entail'.

To help Russia, and to see British troops in action, Churchill now pressed for two amphibious operations, one against Norway as soon as possible, and the other against Sicily, to follow the hoped-for success of Auchinleck's imminent offensive in the Western Desert, now planned for mid-November. In both cases the Chiefs of Staff turned the operations down. On October 27, when the Sicily plan was rejected, a senior diplomat, Sir Alexander Cadogan, noted in his diary, 'Poor Winston very depressed.' Four days later Churchill wrote to Randolph: 'The Admirals, Generals and Air Marshals chant their stately hymn of "Safety First".' As for himself: 'I have to restrain my natural pugnacity by sitting on my own head. How bloody!'

Seeking someone who would share his instinct for the maximum possible offensive action, on November 16 Churchill asked General Alan Brooke if he would be willing to succeed Dill as Chief of the Imperial

General Staff, and the Army's representative on the Chiefs of Staff Committee. Brooke accepted. Forty-five years earlier his brother Victor, who was killed in action in 1914 during the retreat from Mons, had been one of Churchill's close Army friends. His brother Ronald, who died prematurely in 1925, had ridden with Churchill into Ladysmith on the night the siege was lifted in 1900. Now a third brother was to be Churchill's daily companion, adviser, foil and colleague for three and a half years. It was to be an onerous responsibility, but a constructive partnership. 'I did not expect that you would be grateful or overjoyed at the hard anxious task to which I summoned you,' Churchill wrote to Brooke on November 18. 'But I feel that my old friendship for Ronnie and Victor, the companions of gay subaltern days and early wars, is a personal bond between us, to which will soon be added the comradeship of action in fateful events.'

That very morning Auchinleck launched his offensive in the Western Desert against Rommel's army. By nightfall he had made advances of up to fifty miles towards the British forces besieged in Tobruk. Rommel's top-secret messages told of serious fuel and tank shortages: not only did Churchill read the decrypts of these messages as sent to him from Bletchley but arranged for summaries of them to be sent daily by secret cypher to Auchinleck. This knowledge enabled Auchinleck to press the offensive even when his own tank resources were badly stretched. On the fifth day of the battle, a German top-secret signal gave details of the sailing of two ships with vital aviation fuel for the German and Italian forces. Twenty-four hours later both ships had been sunk and the fuel supplies of Rommel's air support drastically curtailed.

On November 29 Auchinleck's forces reached Tobruk; the siege was over. That same day, at the mouth of the river Don, Russian forces drove the Germans back along the northern shore of the Sea of Azov. There could be no German breakthrough to the Caucasus that winter. The Russian Southern Front had held. On the following day Churchill was sixty-seven; among more than a hundred telegrams and letters which he acknowledged personally was one from Stalin. Four days later, as the front in the Western Desert began to stabilise, he contemplated sending three divisions, 12,000 men in all, to the Russian Southern Front, 'wherever it may rest', provided Stalin preferred troops to supplies. The Defence Committee were unwilling, however, to take any troops away from the Western Desert, preferring to press on with the offensive there; Churchill had no option but to defer to their collective will, which the War Cabinet then endorsed. 'The only thing that matters,' he telegraphed to Auchinleck on December 4, 'is to beat the life out of Rommel & Co.'

That week two naval losses in the Mediterranean caused Churchill much distress: the sinking of the *Barham*, with the loss of more than five hundred men, and the sinking of the *Neptune*, with only one survivor out of a crew of seven hundred. The loss of *Neptune* was particularly cruel; she had been struck by a mine at the very moment when, as a result of an Enigma decrypt, she was about to intercept a supremely important supply convoy on its way to Rommel. With these supplies, Rommel was able to avoid the prospect of further retreat. On December 5, however, Churchill learned from another Enigma decrypt that a German Air Corps had been ordered from Russia to the Mediterranean, to give Rommel the extra air support he had so strongly requested. Britain's battle in the Western Desert had forced the Germans to withdraw essential units from the East.

This encouraging news with regard to Russia was offset by a flurry of speculation that Japan planned some military action in the Far East. British, Dutch and Siamese territory were all within range of her sea and air forces. Churchill had begged Roosevelt on November 30 to 'prevent a melancholy extension of the war' by warning the Japanese that any aggression on British, Dutch or Siamese territory would lead to an American declaration of war. In reply, Roosevelt explained that for constitutional reasons he could not give guarantees to other states, but he urged Churchill to issue a British guarantee on behalf of Siam. Such a guarantee would be 'whole-heartedly supported by the United States,' he said, but did not explain what that support would be. British policy, Churchill told the War Cabinet on December 2, 'is not to take forward action in advance of the United States'.

No public declaration of support for Siam was made, either in London or Washington. But on the morning of Sunday December 7, while at Chequers, Churchill agreed that in the event of a Japanese invasion force approaching Siam, as now seemed likely, British naval and air units would attack the Japanese troop transports. Later that morning he learned that Roosevelt intended to announce in three days' time, on December 10, that if Japan invaded British, Dutch or Siamese territory, the United States would definitely regard it as a 'hostile act' against America. 'This is an immense relief,' Churchill telegraphed at once to Auchinleck, 'as I had long dreaded being at war with Japan without or before the United States.'

It was the 'strong American Fleet at Hawaii', the British War Cabinet had been told six weeks earlier, that would 'restrain' the Japanese from any 'major venture' into the Gulf of Siam. Even so, with substantial Japanese forces now clearly on the move, Churchill telegraphed just after midday to the Siamese Prime Minister: 'There is a possibility of imminent Japanese invasion of your country. If you are attacked, defend yourself. The preservation of the full independence and sovereignty of Siam is a British interest and we shall regard an attack on you as an attack on ourselves.'

At Chequers that evening Churchill's dinner guests were Averell Harriman and Gilbert Winant, the American Ambassador to Britain. As they dined, Japanese aircraft struck at the American Fleet at anchor at Pearl Harbor. For an hour and a half the attackers wheeled over the dockyards, hurling their torpedoes and bombs, and leaving in their wake four battleships destroyed and two thousand Americans dead. At nine o'clock in the evening, British time, Churchill turned on a small wireless set to hear the news. It began with items from the Russian and Libyan fronts, followed, he later recalled, by some few sentences 'regarding an attack by Japanese on American shipping at Hawaii, and also Japanese attacks on British vessels in the Dutch East Indies'.

A telephone call was put through to Roosevelt. 'Mr President,' Churchill asked, 'what's this about Japan?'

'It's quite true,' Roosevelt replied. 'They have attacked us at Pearl Harbor. We are all in the same boat now.'

A short while later, news reached Chequers from the Admiralty that Japanese forces were attempting to land in Malaya. Britain and the United States had been attacked by the same enemy, and at the same time. The Dutch East Indies and Siam were likewise invaded that day. 'The enemy has attacked with an audacity which may spring from recklessness,' Churchill told the Commons on December 8, 'but which may also spring from a conviction of strength.' Later that same day the United States Congress voted to declare war on Japan: 'Today all of us are in the same boat with you and the people of the Empire, and it is a ship which will not and cannot be sunk,' Roosevelt telegraphed to Churchill as soon as the vote was known.

Fearing that the demands of war in the Pacific would lead to a falling off of American help to Britain, and of America's hitherto ever-widening participation in the Atlantic convoys, Churchill made plans on December 8 to leave for the United States in two days' time. Britain would have to be 'careful', he told the King, 'that our share of munitions and other aid which we are receiving from the United States does not suffer more than is, I fear, inevitable'. But Roosevelt was unable to see him for at least a month, and the visit was postponed. Disappointed, Churchill told Roosevelt: 'I never felt so sure about final victory, but only concerted action will achieve it.'

With the destruction of so many American warships at Pearl Harbor, the Anglo-American naval ascendancy in the Far East had been wiped out. Even with the recent arrival at Singapore of two British warships, the *Prince of Wales* and the *Repulse*, sent there by Churchill before Pearl Harbor in the hope of deterring the Japanese from an adventure southward, the balance of naval power had swung from an eleven-to-ten Anglo-

American superiority to an inferiority of four-to-ten. On the evening of December 9 Churchill and his advisers discussed what the two British warships, now so substantial a part of the Allied naval strength, should do. Churchill made two suggestions: either they should 'vanish into the ocean wastes and exercise a vague menace', behaving as 'rogue elephants', or they should cross the Pacific and join the remnants of the American Fleet at Pearl Harbor.

No final decision was reached: only to 'reconsider the problem in the morning light'. By morning light, however, the ships themselves had taken the fateful decision, deciding to intercept a Japanese force that was reported to be landing on the Malayan coast. The report was a false one, but it led the two ships under the flight path of Japanese torpedo-bombers returning from an attack on Singapore harbour. In London, it was the morning of December 10, Churchill was in bed working on official papers when the telephone rang at his bedside. It was Dudley Pound. Churchill later recalled: 'His voice sounded odd. He gave a sort of cough and gulp, and at first I could not hear quite clearly. "Prime Minister, I have to report to you that the *Prince of Wales* and the *Repulse* have both been sunk by the Japanese – we think by aircraft. Tom Phillips is drowned." "Are you sure it's true?" "There is no doubt at all." So I put the telephone down. I was thankful to be alone. In all the war I never received a more direct shock.'

Churchill was not alone. Kathleen Hill was in the room when Pound's telephone call came. 'I sat in the corner of the room silently and unobtrusively', she later recalled. 'When he was upset I used to try to be invisible. When the two ships went down, I was there. That was a terrible moment. "Poor Tom Phillips" he said.'

The loss of the *Prince of Wales* and the *Repulse* was a severe blow to Britain; six hundred officers and men had been drowned, and the waters of the Far East opened to an even greater Japanese naval superiority than before. But the impact of the sinkings was offset on the following day when, without any provocation, first Italy and then Germany declared war on the United States. Roosevelt, absorbed by war in the Pacific, had no plans to declare war on Hitler, nor had he done so in the four days following Pearl Harbor. Now it was Hitler himself who brought Germany into a state of war with the United States. Britain no longer had to fear that the bulk of America's war effort would be directed against Japan, with far less war material available for Britain.

As a result of Hitler's arrogant declaration, America suddenly became a European belligerent, after more than two years of neutrality. 'I am enormously relieved at the turn world events have taken,' Churchill telegraphed to Roosevelt on December 11. To Eden, who was on his way to Moscow, Churchill signalled that same day, 'The accession of the United

States makes amends for all, and with time and patience will give certain victory.'

With America now at war with both Germany and Italy, Roosevelt agreed to see Churchill as soon as possible; on December 12 he left London by night train for the Clyde, where he boarded the *Duke of York* for the journey across the Atlantic. While on board, amid violent gales, he learned each day of successful Russian counter-attacks near Leningrad, Moscow, and the Sea of Azov. 'It is impossible to describe the relief with which I have heard each successive day of the wonderful victories on the Russian front,' he telegraphed to Stalin on December 15. 'I never felt so sure of the outcome of the war.' Part of Churchill's relief was the realisation that Hitler was now so tied down in Russia, his armies fighting so far east amid horrific winter conditions, and suffering such enormous casualties, that any plans to invade Britain in 1942 must finally have been set aside.

During Churchill's storm-tossed journey westward, Japanese forces attacked Hong Kong. 'We must expect to suffer heavily in this war with Japan,' he wrote to Clementine on December 21, 'and it is no use the critics saying "Why were we not prepared?" when everything we had was already fully engaged. The entry of the United States into the war is worth all the losses sustained in the East many times over. Still these losses are very painful to endure and will be very hard to repair.' To the Chiefs of Staff, who were on board with him, Churchill commented bitterly that the Americans were more likely to be prepared to land in Europe in 1944 than 1943. 'The negative in our counsels in the present time is as 10:1. There is therefore no need to fear any excess of venturesome action for 1943 at this stage.' As for night-bombing, the method favoured by the Chiefs of Staff as the principal means of bringing Germany to its knees, in Churchill's view it would not by itself be decisive: 'The force of events will compel a much more complex strategy upon us.'

On December 22, after ten days on board ship, Churchill reached Hampton Roads, then flew to Washington. 'There was the President waiting in his car,' he later recalled. 'I clasped his strong hand with comfort and pleasure.' For three weeks Churchill was to be Roosevelt's guest at the White House. Their talks began on the first day, with agreement to make plans for a joint Anglo-American landing in French North Africa, 'with or without invitation' from Vichy. That same day the British Chiefs of Staff and their American counterparts, the Joint Chiefs, agreed, as a result of considerable persuasion by Pound, Brooke and Portal, and to Churchill's enormous relief, that the Atlantic-European theatre was the decisive one, that 'Germany is still the key to victory' as it had been described during the American-British Staff Conversations in February 1941, and that the defeat of Germany should precede the defeat of Japan.

On December 22, as the discussions between Churchill and Roosevelt continued, Japanese forces landed on the Philippines, driving the American defenders before them. Three days later, after a seventeen-day siege, the British, Canadian and Indian defenders of Hong Kong surrendered to the Japanese. Meanwhile, in Washington, Churchill and Roosevelt continued to plan their joint war strategy: American bombers would operate against Germany from bases in the United Kingdom; American troops would be based in Northern Ireland, liberating the British troops there for service in the Middle East; should the Philippines fall, American troops would be diverted to Singapore; and substantial American forces would be sent to defend Australia. On December 26, with these decisions worked out and agreed to, Churchill addressed both Houses of Congress. 'I cannot help reflecting,' he told them, 'that if my father had been American and my mother British, instead of the other way round, I might have got here on my own. In that case, this would not have been the first time you would have heard my voice.'

That afternoon Churchill and Roosevelt discussed the shipping needs which their decisions had created. In the evening Churchill told the British Chiefs of Staff that he was contemplating an agreement whereby the general direction of the Pacific war would be from Washington, and operations in the Atlantic, Europe and North Africa from London. That night, as he lay in bed in the White House, the room was so hot that he decided to open the bedroom window. 'It was very stiff,' he told his doctor, Charles Wilson, on the following day. 'I had to use considerable force and I noticed all at once that I was short of breath. I had a dull pain over my heart. It went down my left arm.'

Churchill had suffered a mild heart attack. The 'textbook treatment', Wilson, later Lord Moran, wrote in his diary, 'is at least six weeks in bed. That would mean publishing to the world, and the American newspapers would see to this, that the PM was an invalid with a crippled heart and a doubtful future.' The doctor therefore decided to tell no one, not even his patient. 'Your circulation is a bit sluggish,' was all he told him. 'It is nothing serious. You needn't rest in the sense of lying up, but you musn't do more than you can help in the way of exertion for a little while.'

The Conference continued. On the morning of December 27 Churchill discussed with General Marshall, the United States Army Chief of Staff, the question of an Allied Supreme Commander in the Far East. Marshall favoured Wavell. That evening Churchill discussed the same problem with his own Chiefs of Staff. It was agreed that Wavell should be given the job, with an American Deputy. The American action, Churchill telegraphed to his War Cabinet, was 'broad-minded and selfless'. But one member of

Churchill's negotiating team pointed out privately that the Americans had been 'very bitter at times in blaming the British when things went wrong'.

From Washington, despite feeling unwell, Churchill travelled by train to Ottawa, where on December 30 he addressed the Canadian Parliament. Recalling the comment of Weygand in 1940 that Britain would soon have its neck wrung like a chicken, he commented, to the delight of his listeners: 'Some chicken!' When their laughter had died down he added, 'Some neck!'

Returning to Washington by train, Churchill agreed on New Year's Day 1942 to a declaration, prepared by Roosevelt, to be issued by the 'United Nations', those twenty-six states which were either fighting Germany and Japan, or were under German and Japanese occupation, expressing their determination to secure complete victory over Germany and Japan. 'The declaration could not by itself win battles,' Churchill later wrote, 'but it set forth who we were, and what we were fighting for.' On the following day Churchill and Roosevelt presided jointly over a meeting to determine the scale of United States war production in 1942 and 1943. Then, on January 5, Churchill flew from Washington to Florida, to recuperate by the sea in a secluded bungalow at Pompano, north of Miami. On his third day at Pompano, Churchill telegraphed to the War Cabinet, 'Am resting in south on Charles Wilson's advice for a few days after rather a strenuous time.'

Churchill spent five days in Florida, swimming in the warm sea, and dictating memoranda on war policy, including his opposition to a request by Stalin that the Baltic States be reincorporated in the Soviet Union after the war. Returning to Washington, he and Roosevelt agreed that they should each provide 90,000 troops for a landing in French North Africa, and that in the event of a Japanese advance towards Australia, Roosevelt would send 50,000 American troops to Australia's defence. The two leaders also set up a Combined Chiefs of Staff Committee to determine the broad programme of requirements based on strategic policy, a Combined Raw Materials Board to form a 'common pool' of all available munitions, and an Anglo-American Shipping Adjustment Board whose work would be based on the assumption that their shipping resources were henceforth pooled.

The Conference ended on January 12. Roosevelt's last words to Churchill were, 'Trust me to the bitter end.' When two weeks later Churchill congratulated the President on his sixtieth birthday, Roosevelt replied, 'It is fun to be in the same decade with you.' Their ally Stalin was also in the same decade; he had just celebrated his sixty-second birthday.

On January 14 Churchill left Washington by flying boat to Bermuda, a four-hour flight, during which he took control of the plane for some twenty minutes. During this time, the pilot later wrote, 'the Prime

Minister asked if he could make a couple of slightly banked turns, which he did with considerable success'. From Bermuda he had intended to go on by sea, but because of the worsening situation in Malaya it was decided to continue by flying boat, a further distance of 3,365 miles and a flight of just under eighteen hours. As the plane approached its destination it was found to be somewhat off-course, approaching within five or six minutes' flying time of the German anti-aircraft batteries at Brest. 'We are going to turn north at once,' Churchill was told as soon as the error was discovered. As the plane approached Plymouth, British radar reported a 'hostile bomber' flying in from the direction of Brest. Six fighters were ordered into the air to shoot it down. Their error was discovered just in time, and Churchill returned to Britain safely. He had been away for more than a month.

Two days after Churchill's return he learned from Wavell, for the first time, that no major defence works had ever been constructed on the northern, landward, side of Singapore Island. All the main defences had been located so as to deal with an attack from the open sea. The Japanese, however, were now advancing overland, approaching the island from the north. Churchill was nevertheless determined that there should be a vigorous defence. The 'entire male population', he told the Chiefs of Staff on January 19, should be utilised to build earthworks which could then be fortified. The city of Singapore should be converted into a citadel 'and defended to the death'. There must be no surrender. 'Commanders, Staffs, and principal officers are expected to perish at their posts.'

Wavell was no longer under British direction, however. As a result of the Washington agreements, his command came under the control of the United States. Churchill could send only 'suggestions', as he explained to Wavell in a telegram on January 20, and he added, 'I want to make it absolutely clear that I expect every inch of ground to be defended, every scrap of material or defences to be blown to pieces to prevent capture by the enemy, and no question of surrender to be entertained until after protracted fighting among the ruins of Singapore City.'

On January 27, in the Commons, Churchill demanded a Vote of Confidence 'because', he told the House, 'things have gone badly and worse is to come'. The debate lasted for three days; on the third day he told the House: 'In no way have I mitigated the sense of danger and impending misfortunes – of a minor character and of a severe character – which still hang over us. But at the same time I avow my confidence, never stronger than at this moment, that we shall bring this conflict to an end in a manner agreeable to the interests of our country, and in a manner agreeable to the future of the world.' Churchill won his Vote of Confidence by 464 to one.

As the vote was being taken, it was announced that the Japanese were within eighteen miles of Singapore.

'Worse is to come'; these had been Churchill's words. Four days after he had spoken them, the German Submarine Command, as part of an internal security drive, altered its Enigma machine in such a way that the messages sent on it were once again to prove unreadable to British Intelligence, and were to remain unreadable for the rest of the year. When he did learn, at the very moment of Singapore's distress, of the loss of this precious Intelligence, he could share the dismal knowledge only with a tiny handful of colleagues; less than twenty-five of those working in Whitehall knew the secret of Enigma. What neither Churchill nor they knew was that, to compound the danger, German Naval Intelligence had at that very moment broken the British cyphers carrying most of the Allied signals about the North Atlantic convoys. The Battle of the Atlantic, which the previous autumn seemed to have been won by Britain after considerable earlier losses and hardship, was once again a battle filled with anxiety and danger.

On February 5, as the Japanese forces approached Singapore, even the ability of Burma to resist was cast into doubt. Searching for new alliances and commitments, Churchill proposed flying at once to India, to meet the Chinese Nationalist leader Chiang Kai-shek and work out an Anglo-Chinese strategy on Burma's northern border; and to offer India an Assembly to discuss a new constitution, with a view to complete independence after the war. 'What a decision to take, and how gallant of the old boy himself!' wrote Eden's Private Secretary, Oliver Harvey. The episode in Washington led Churchill's doctor to advise against any such journey. 'But for his heart,' Eden told Harvey, 'there could be no question he was the right one to go.' Not danger to his heart, however, but a feeling that he must be in Britain when Singapore fell persuaded Churchill not to make the journey.

On the morning of February 14 Wavell informed Churchill that, in the view of their commander, General Percival, the troops in Singapore were 'incapable of further counter-attack'. Churchill at once gave Wavell authority to instruct Percival to surrender; this took place on the following day. Among those taken prisoner by the Japanese were 16,000 British, 14,000 Australian and 32,000 Indian soldiers. 'Here is the moment,' Churchill broadcast that night from Chequers, 'to display that calm and poise, combined with grim determination, which not so long ago brought us out of the very jaws of death. Here is another reason to show – as so often in our long story – that we can meet reverses with dignity and with renewed accessions of strength. We must remember that we are no longer alone. Three-quarters of the human race are now moving with us. The whole future of mankind may depend upon our action and upon our conduct. So far we have not failed. We shall not fail now. Let us move forward steadfastly together into the storm – and through the storm.'

Colville, who was then in South Africa, serving with the Royal Air Force, commented, 'All the majesty of his oratory was there, but also a new note of appeal, lacking the usual confidence of support.' Wrote Harold Nicolson: 'His broadcast last night was not liked. The country is too nervous and irritable to be fobbed off with fine phrases. Yet what else could he have said?' What Churchill could not say was that Wavell had told him of the troops fighting not only in Malaya but also in Burma, 'Neither British, Australians or Indians have shown any real toughness of mind or body.' This perturbed Churchill immensely, but could no more be conveyed outside his secret circle than could news of the loss of the German submarine codes.

Despite Churchill's success in the Vote of Confidence, public criticism of the inner direction of the war was growing. To the King, Churchill compared his task to 'hunting the tiger with angry wasps about him'. The real worries had to be borne almost alone. 'He said he was tired of it all,' Captain Richard Pim, the head of Churchill's Map Room, noted on February 18, 'and hinted that he was very seriously thinking of handing over his responsibilities to other shoulders.' On the following day Churchill made Attlee Deputy Prime Minister, but to those who had demanded that he give up his own second post as Minister of Defence, he said, in the Commons on February 24, 'However tempting it might be to some, when much trouble lies ahead, to step aside adroitly and put someone else up to take the blows – the heavy and repeated blows – which are coming, I do not intend to adopt that cowardly course.' Two weeks later Clementine wrote to Churchill's cousin Oswald Frewen: 'He is so brave. The attacks themselves would not do it, but combined with the grief and tragedy of Singapore, I hope his stout heart will not be broken.'

In public, Churchill's pugnacity had returned. But his family saw his inner distress. 'Papa is at a very low ebb,' Mary wrote in her diary on February 27. 'He is not too well physically, and he is worn down by the continuous crushing pressure of events.' There was not much consolation that day, when a successful British commando raid on a German radar station on the Channel Coast revealed, as a result of the successful capture of radar components, that in some respects German radar was more advanced than British. The British public rejoiced in the success of the raid; Churchill knew its dark side, as he knew of so many dangers of which the public had no inkling.

On February 28 Japanese forces invaded Java. In the ensuing naval battle, British losses were heavy. 'These are as you say days of anguish for Winston, so full of strength & yet so impotent to stem this terrible tide in the Far East,' Clementine wrote to a cousin that day. Mary noted in her diary that her father was 'saddened – appalled by events' and 'desperately taxed'. It was almost three months since Pearl Harbor. 'When I reflect how I have longed and prayed for the entry of the United States into the war,' Churchill telegraphed to Roosevelt on March 5, 'I find it difficult to realise how gravely our British affairs have deteriorated since December 7.'

On the day Churchill sent this telegram, the senior British officer in Burma, General Sir Harold Alexander, who had been the senior officer at the Dunkirk evacuation, gave orders for Rangoon to be abandoned. Three days later the Dutch on Java surrendered and more than 10,000 British and Australian troops were taken prisoner. To help try to redress the growing negative aspects of the war, Churchill asked General Brooke to become Chairman of the Chiefs of Staff Committee. He also appointed as Chief of Combined Operations a naval officer, Lord Louis Mountbatten, a great-great-grandson of Queen Victoria, and the son of Prince Louis of Battenberg, Churchill's First Sea Lord in 1914. Churchill also proposed that week to fly to see Stalin, either at Teheran, or at the Soviet city of Astrakhan on the Caspian Sea, in order to complete the negotiations for an Anglo-Soviet Treaty. 'And this,' wrote Oliver Harvey, 'from a man afflicted with a heart who may collapse at any minute. What courage and what gallantry, but is it the way to do things?'

Nothing came of the proposed visit to Russia. Nor could Churchill offer Stalin the prospect of something for which Stalin had begun to press with vigour: the launching later that year of an Allied amphibious landing in northern Europe that would draw German troops away from the eastern Front, a 'second front'. Indeed, on March 8 Churchill received a survey of America's amphibious-landing potential from Roosevelt, in which the President mentioned June 1944 as the date by which the 'troop-carrying capacity' of United States vessels would reach the necessary 400,000 men. By June 1943 it would only be 130,000, insufficient for a major amphibious landing of the sort required in northern Europe, if a thrust was then to be made into Germany itself. For a landing in September 1942, as desired by Stalin, America could provide only forty per cent of the landing craft and 700 of the 5,700 combat aircraft needed. Little wonder that, a month later, Clementine described her husband as 'bearing not only the burden of his own country but for the moment of an unprepared America'.

American lack of preparedness was the decisive factor, as Roosevelt himself had made clear, in the inability of the Allies to mount an amphibious attack against northern Europe in 1942. In its place, the bombing of German cities and industry would continue to be the main offensive action against Germany from the West; 'It is not decisive,' Churchill told Portal on March 13, 'but better than doing nothing, and indeed a formidable method of injuring the enemy.' Enigma decrypts had begun to give details of a new German offensive against Russia planned for the summer. Churchill at once proposed 'taking the weight off Russia' by the heaviest British air offensive against Germany 'which can be produced'. The Chiefs of Staff agreed; but they rejected Churchill's request that a British air contingent should be sent to Russia to fight 'side by side' with the Soviet Air Force when the new German attack began. Fighter aircraft could not be spared from the Middle East, Brooke explained, in case of a renewed German offensive there.

The fall of Singapore was a cause of distress for Churchill; in a speech on March 26 he called it 'the greatest disaster to British arms which our history records'. But the pace of the Japanese advance was too swift, and Japanese air power too strong, to be halted. On April 3 the Burmese city of Mandalay was bombed and two thousand civilians killed. On April 4, four British warships were sunk and more than five hundred men drowned in a Japanese air attack on Ceylon. On April 6, Japanese forces landed on the Solomon Islands, one of Australia's Pacific Ocean Mandates. Answering renewed criticism that there had not been sufficient foresight in planning, Churchill told the Commons on April 13, 'An immense amount of discussion and planning preceded these lamentable events, but study and discussion are not in themselves sufficient to prepare against attack by a superior force of the enemy.' Four days earlier the American forces on the Bataan Peninsula in the Philippines surrendered, and 35,000 American troops were taken prisoner; a disaster on the Singapore scale. 'The best that can be hoped for,' Churchill told the Commons in Secret Session on April 23, 'is that the retreat will be as slow as possible.'

Each day brought news of fresh disasters, to confront which Churchill sought at least an hour or two of solitude. 'I went to Chartwell last week,' he wrote to Randolph on May 2, 'and found Spring there in all its beauty. The goose I called the naval aide-de-camp and the male swan have both fallen victims to the fox. The Yellow Cat, however, made me sensible of his continuing friendship, although I have not been there for eight months.'

Throughout April the British convoys to Russia had suffered severe losses, being repeatedly attacked by German bombers based in northern Norway. In one convoy that month only eight of the twenty-three ships reached Russia. One was sunk and the rest forced to abandon their voyage. On May 2, after Roosevelt asked for an increase in the number of convoys, to make up the losses, Churchill replied, 'I beg you not to press us beyond our judgment in this operation, which we have studied most intently, and of which we have not yet been able to measure the full strain.'

The 'full strain' was everywhere being revealed; in Burma, Mandalay surrendered on May 3 and the whole rich country, which Churchill's father had annexed to the British Empire in 1886, fell under Japanese control. In the Mediterranean, Malta was under severe aerial bombardment. In the Philippines, the American forces on Corregidor Island surrendered on May 6; eight hundred men had been killed during a tenacious defence. On the following day, after a two-day battle, British naval and military forces which had landed on Vichy-controlled Madagascar, to deny the island to the Japanese, entered Diego Suarez, the principal port, forcing the surrender of the Vichy-loyal garrison. These operations, Churchill told the Commons that day, 'which were not without risks of various kinds, have been carried with great dash and vigour'.

On May 15, speaking at Leeds, Churchill told the vast crowd that had come to hear him: 'We have reached a period in the war when it would be premature to say that we have topped the ridge, but now we see the ridge ahead.' One of his secretaries, Elizabeth Layton, who was with him, wrote the next day to her parents: 'There is no doubt about it at all; people regard him, one and all, as *their* PM.' He appealed to the masses, 'as well as to the brains and the "elite". And he surely deserves it; he is just as warm-hearted, and one might even say lovable, as he could possibly be.'

That summer Churchill was constantly scrutinising the plans being made for an eventual landing in northern Europe, with the aim of defeating Germany on land. On May 26 he set out his thoughts on the floating piers that would be needed to unload the landing-ships once they had crossed the Channel. 'They must float up and down with the tide,' he wrote. 'The anchor problem must be mastered. Let me have the best solution worked out. Don't argue the matter. The difficulties will argue for themselves.'

The task was put to the construction engineers Taylor Woodrow. Two concrete harbours, each the size of Dover Harbour, had to be constructed in such a way that they could be towed across the English Channel. But no substantial cross-Channel assault could be contemplated while the German Army was still undefeated in North Africa, and while the German power to take the initiative there remained. On the very night of Churchill's note, Rommel launched an offensive against the British forces in the Western Desert. 'Retreat would be fatal,' Churchill telegraphed to Auchinleck. 'This is a business not only of armour but of will power. God bless you all.'

As the armies of Rommel and Auchinleck battled in the Western Desert, British bombers struck on May 30 at Cologne. It was the first thousand-bomber raid of the war. Much damage was done to German industrial installations, but thirty-nine of the bombers were shot down. There was also an engagement that week of even greater impact on the outcome of the war: in the Pacific, as a result of a joint Anglo-American effort at decrypting Japanese top-secret radio signals, a Japanese invasion fleet on its way to Midway Island, the stepping-stone to Pearl Harbor, was brought to battle on June 4; all four Japanese aircraft carriers were destroyed. With so many war zones, so many captive nations, and so many possible war plans, Churchill decided to cross the Atlantic for a second meeting with Roosevelt.

In the Western Desert, Rommel was pressing forward to Tobruk. The garrison there, Churchill telegraphed to Auchinleck on June 15, should contain as many troops 'as are necessary to hold the place for certain'. Two days later he left London by train for Stranraer in Scotland; there he boarded the same flying boat he had returned to England in five months earlier.

'PM in tremendous form,' Brooke wrote in his diary during the flight across the Atlantic, 'and enjoying himself like a schoolboy.' After twenty-six hours in the air, and a refuelling stop in Newfoundland, the flying boat landed at Anacostia Naval Air Base, less than three miles from the White House. After a night at the British Embassy in Washington, he flew by United States Navy plane to New Hackensack, the nearest airfield to Hyde Park, Roosevelt's home on the Hudson river. Roosevelt awaited him at the airfield and, Churchill later wrote, 'saw us make the roughest bump landing I have ever experienced'.

Roosevelt then drove Churchill to see his estate overlooking the Hudson. 'In this drive I had some thoughtful moments,' Churchill later wrote. 'Mr Roosevelt's infirmity prevented him from using his feet on the brake, clutch, or accelerator. An ingenious arrangement enabled him to do everything with his arms, which were amazingly strong and muscular. He invited me to feel his biceps, saying that a famous prize-fighter had envied them. This was reassuring; but I confess that when on several occasions the car poised and backed on the grass verges of the precipices over the Hudson I hoped the mechanical devices and brakes would show no defects. All the time we talked business, and though I was careful not to take his attention off the driving we made more progress than we might have done in formal conference.'

During his talks with Roosevelt at Hyde Park on June 20, Churchill stressed that as 'no responsible British military authority' could see any chance of success for a cross-Channel landing in September 1942, the new war zone that autumn should be the Atlantic and Mediterranean coasts of French North Africa. Roosevelt agreed; it was the American inability to provide sufficient combat aircraft and landing-craft that made a full-scale assault impossible. Looking even further ahead, the two men also reached an agreement, of the utmost secrecy, whereby the United States and Britain would share 'as equal partners' their respective researches into the creation and manufacture of an atom bomb.

That night Churchill and Roosevelt went by Presidential train to Washington, where Churchill was Roosevelt's guest at the White House. On the following morning, as he and Roosevelt were talking in the President's study, a pink slip of paper was brought in and handed to the President, who read it, said nothing, then passed it to Churchill. The message read, 'Tobruk has surrendered, with 25,000 men taken prisoner.' Churchill did not believe it, and asked Ismay to telephone London. But before Ismay could do so, a second message arrived, from the commander of the British naval forces in the Mediterranean, whose message began, 'Tobruk has fallen.'

There could be no further cause for disbelief. 'Defeat is one thing,' Churchill later wrote, 'disgrace is another.' For a few moments no one spoke. Then Roosevelt turned to Churchill with the words 'What can we do to help?'

As the details emerged during the day it became clear that the number of prisoners taken was closer to 33,000. It was also clear that Rommel was continuing his advance towards the Egyptian border, and might even cross into Egypt. That night Roosevelt offered to send an American armoured division round the Cape to Egypt. To Auchinleck, Churchill telegraphed, 'Whatever views I may have about how the battle was fought, or whether it should have been fought a good deal earlier, you have my entire confidence, and I share your responsibilities to the full.'

For the second time within two years, Egypt would have to be defended. 'You are in the same kind of situation,' Churchill telegraphed to Auchinleck, 'as we should be if England were invaded, and the same intense drastic spirit should reign.' That day he learned that American shipping difficulties made it impossible for the promised armoured division to be sent to Cairo, which was itself now endangered by Rommel's success in crossing the Egyptian frontier. Instead, the Americans now offered 300 tanks and 100 self-propelled howitzers; they would be sent out in two cargo ships specially requisitioned from the Havana sugar traffic.

On the evening of June 23, Churchill left Washington by train for Camp Jackson in South Carolina. There, on the morning of June 24, he watched a battalion of American troops doing a parachute drop. 'I had never seen a thousand men leap into the air at once,' he later recalled. That afternoon he watched a brigade of soldiers at a field firing exercise, using live ammunition. He then returned by air to Washington. Then, shortly before midnight on June 25, he boarded his flying boat at Baltimore, telling Hopkins as he shook his hand, 'Now for England, home, and – a beautiful row.' He had just learned that there was to be a Vote of Censure against him in the House of Commons. The debate began on July 1, the day on which German forces reached El Alamein, 250 miles inside Egypt and less than 200 miles from Cairo. According to one of Churchill's severest Labour critics, Aneurin Bevan: 'The Prime Minister wins debate after debate and loses battle after battle. The country is beginning to say that he fights debates like a war and the war like a debate.'

In his defence, Churchill pointed out that he had to carry the War Cabinet with him 'in all major decisions' and that the Chiefs of Staff exercised 'direct operational control' over the fighting forces. He asked for 'no favours'. He had undertaken the office of Prime Minister after defending his predecessor, Chamberlain, 'to the best of my ability' at a time when the life of the Empire 'hung upon a thread'. Churchill added: 'I am your servant, and you have the right to dismiss me when you please. What you have no right to do is to ask me to bear responsibilities without the power of effective action.' If the Vote of Censure were defeated, Churchill told the House, 'a cheer will go up from every friend of Britain and every faithful servant of our cause, and the knell of disappointment will ring in the ears of the tyrants we are striving to overthrow.'

The Vote of Censure failed by 475 votes to 25. Churchill returned to 10 Downing Street where, that same afternoon, he saw Amery's son Julian, who had just returned from the Western Desert and who urged him to visit the troops there, to improve their morale.

'Your presence in the battle area would be enough,' Amery told him.

'You mean just go round and talk to them?' Churchill asked.

'Yes, to the officers and the men,' Amery replied.

Churchill liked the idea of going to the battle zone; but Eden said he felt the Prime Minister would be 'in the way'.

'You mean like a great blue-bottle buzzing over a huge cowpat?' Churchill asked him.

Cairo it would be; as plans were being made for the journey, another Arctic convoy on its way to Russia was savagely mauled. Of its thirty-four merchant vessels, twenty-three were sunk; only eleven reached Russia. Of nearly six hundred tanks being carried by the convoy to Russia, five hundred were lost. The August and September convoys would have to be abandoned. On July 14 Churchill learned that nearly 400,000 tons of shipping had been sunk in the Arctic and Atlantic in a single week, 'a rate unexampled in either this war or the last', he told Roosevelt, 'and, if maintained, beyond all existing replacement plans.'

Churchill faced these setbacks without panic. Major-General John Kennedy, Director of Military Operations at the War Office, noted in his diary on July 17: 'Winston certainly inspires confidence. I do admire the unhurried way in which he gets through such a colossal amount of work, and yet never seems otherwise than at leisure. He was particularly genial and good-humoured today. I can well understand how those around him become devoted to him – and dominated by him. I remember Dudley Pound once saying, "You cannot help loving that man", and I can see the truth of this sentiment.'

President Roosevelt, hoping for some form of limited cross-Channel landing in September 1942, possibly on the Cherbourg Peninsula, sent Hopkins to London in the last week of July with two of the American Joint Chiefs of Staff, General Marshall and Admiral King. But Churchill and the British Chiefs of Staff were emphatic that the Cherbourg plan was too small to help Russia and too weak to succeed in holding on to the Peninsula. After three intensive days of discussion, the Americans agreed to abandon the Cherbourg operation, to give the North African landings the priority for 1942, and to try to prepare for a major cross-Channel landing in 1943.

Churchill told Stalin by telegram both about the suspension of the Arctic convoys and the postponement of the cross-Channel landing. Stalin was indignant, all the more so because in South Russia Hitler's armies had broken through to the Caucasus and were threatening Russia's principal oil-wells. The British Ambassador in Moscow, Sir Archibald Clark Kerr, stressed the 'immense advantages' of an early meeting between Churchill and Stalin, so that Churchill could explain not only the reasons for the changes, but also the plans being made for effective action and help. Churchill decided to fly on from Cairo to Russia. 'We could then survey the war together and take decisions hand in hand,' he telegraphed to Stalin on July 31.

For the first time in his life Churchill would be flying in an un-pressurised cabin at 15,000 feet, in an American Liberator bomber. To get used to the experience he went to Farnborough late on the evening of July 31 for a special oxygen mask test, asking the expert who would accompany him if the mask could be adapted so that he could smoke his cigar while wearing it. The mask was duly adapted, and on the following night, accompanied by General Brooke and Charles Wilson, Churchill flew from Lyneham airport to Cairo. 'I think much of you my darling,' Clementine wrote to him three days later, '& pray that you may be able to penetrate & then solve the problem of the Middle East stultifications and frustrations or what is it? This first part of your journey is less dramatic & sensational than your visit to the Ogre in his Den; but I should imagine it may be more fruitful in results.'

As soon as he reached Cairo, Churchill sensed the weariness and lack of drive that had crept into all military planning. He was urged by General Brooke to replace Auchinleck, but hesitated to do so. 'The PM hates the idea of removing one of his commanders,' Charles Wilson noted in his diary on August 4. But Churchill finally made up his mind that Auchinleck must go. 'Exactly what I have always told him from the start,' was Brooke's comment. Auchinleck's command of the Eighth Army would go to General Gott, and his post as Commander-in-Chief, Middle East to General Alexander. It was Alexander who had brilliantly extracted the British Expeditionary Force from Dunkirk in May 1940, and the British and Imperial forces from Burma in May 1942. Like Churchill he was an Old Harrovian; Churchill felt confidence in what he described to Clementine as 'his grand capacities for war'. General Gott, however, so Brooke warned Churchill, was said to be 'tired out'. To test this, Churchill flew to the Eighth Army positions at El Alamein to inspect the positions there and spend time with Gott. 'He inspired me at once with a feeling of confidence,' Churchill wrote three weeks later.

Having flown back to Cairo, Churchill informed the War Cabinet of the proposed changes in command. Then, on the evening of August 7, he learned that Gott had been killed in a plane crash: shot down by German fighters while on the same route back to Cairo that Churchill had taken two days earlier. Gott was replaced by General Montgomery, whose aggressive zeal on the eve of the expected invasion of Britain had impressed Churchill in June 1940. Montgomery's noted abrasiveness was not necessarily a negative factor. 'If he is disagreeable to those about him,' Churchill wrote to Clementine on August 9, 'he is also disagreeable to the enemy.'

During his nine days in Cairo, Churchill visited all the Eighth Army units and addressed them. 'At one place,' he told his wife, 'they nearly all came from Oldham', his constituency of forty-two years earlier. 'They showed the greatest enthusiasm.' Everywhere he was cheered with vigour and listened to with attention, as he spoke of the American tank reinforcements on their way, and the prospects of victory. 'The more I study the situation on the spot,' he told Clementine, 'the more I am sure that a decisive victory can be won if only the leadershp is equal to the opportunity.' On August 10, the day after writing this letter, he sent Alexander a directive, formally dated five days later, setting out the nature of the victory that was required: 'Your prime and main duty will be to take or destroy at the earliest opportunity the German-Italian Army commanded by Field Marshal Rommel, together with all its supplies and establishments in Egypt and Libya.' To Ismay he wrote on August 10, 'I am sure that simplicity of task and singleness of aim are imperative now.'

Shortly after midnight on August 10 Churchill flew eastward from Cairo to Teheran, a journey of 1,300 miles, taking six hours. Once more oxygen masks were needed, as the Liberator flew over the mountains of western Persia. From Teheran he flew northward on August 12 to

Moscow, his plane escorted by ten American-built Aircobra fighters that were part of Britain's Lend-Lease purchases. Late that afternoon, after a ten-and-a-half-hour-flight from Teheran, Churchill landed at Moscow. From the airport he was driven to a villa outside the city, where a hot bath and lavish refreshments were waiting, 'far beyond our mood or consuming powers', he later recalled. Two hours later he was driven into Moscow, and to the Kremlin.

The Soviet leader was in sombre mood, telling Churchill at the outset of their talk that the Germans were making a 'tremendous effort' to get to Stalingrad on the Volga, and to Baku on the Caspian. In the south, the Red Army had been 'unable to stop the German offensive'. Churchill then explained to Stalin that there could be no cross-Channel landing in 1942; that only two and a half American divisions had yet arrived in Britain; that the twenty-seven divisions which would form the American component of any cross-Channel force could not arrive before December; that the Anglo-American plan was to launch the invasion in 1943; but that in 1943 it might be found that the Germans would 'have a stronger army in the West than they have now'. At this point, the official British record noted, 'Stalin's face crumpled into a frown'.

Churchill told Stalin that if throwing 200,000 men ashore would draw back 'appreciable German forces' from the Russian front, 'he would not shrink from this course on the grounds of loss'. But if it 'drew no men away and spoiled the prospects for 1943, it would be a great error'. Stalin was contemptuous, telling Churchill, 'A man who was not prepared to take risks could not win a war', and he went on to ask why the British were 'so afraid of the Germans.' In reply, Churchill spoke of 1940, when Hitler, he said, had been afraid of invading Britain. Had Hitler not been afraid, he Churchill 'would not be here to tell the tale'.

Stalin was both angry and glum: angry that no cross-Channel landing was in prospect that September, and glum because it looked as if there would be no action whatsoever by Britain and the United States to draw off German troops or aircraft from the swiftly crumbling Eastern Front. Churchill now spoke of the British bombing of Germany. This was already considerable, he said, and would increase. Britain looked upon the morale of the German civilian population 'as a military target. We sought no mercy and we would show no mercy.' Britain hoped to 'shatter' twenty German cities, as several had already been shattered: 'If need be, as the war went on, we hoped to shatter almost every dwelling in almost every German city.'

At this point, the record of the meeting noted, 'Stalin smiled and said that would not be bad'. Churchill's promise of the massive bombing of German cities 'had a very stimulating effect upon the meeting, and thenceforward the atmosphere became progressively more cordial'. Churchill then told Stalin that there was another operation being prepared at that very moment, an amphibious landing, details of which he was authorised by Roosevelt to impart. At this, the record noted, 'Stalin sat up and grinned'. Churchill then gave an account of the North African landings. The 'second front' for 1942 would be in North Africa. It could be carried out by seven American and five British divisions, a quarter of those needed to cross the English Channel.

Stalin was pleased and impressed: 'May God help this enterprise to succeed,' he said. But on the following day he was again in angry mood, telling Churchill, 'You British are afraid of fighting. You should not think the Germans are supermen. You will have to fight sooner or later. You cannot win a war without fighting.' In his reply, Churchill told Attlee on the following day, 'I repulsed all his contentions squarely but without taunts of any kind.' When Stalin repeated that the British were not prepared to operate on the Continent because they were afraid of fighting the Germans, Churchill replied, 'I pardon that remark only on account of the bravery of the Russian troops.'

Churchill sought some means of improving the hostile atmosphere. 'I then exclaimed,' he reported to Attlee, 'there was no ring of comradeship in his attitude. I had travelled far to establish good working relations. We had done our utmost to help Russia and would continue to do so. We had been left entirely alone for a year against Germany and Italy. Now that the three great Nations were allied, victory was certain provided we did not fall apart, and so forth. I was somewhat animated in this passage and before it could be translated he made the remark that he liked the temperament (or spirit?) of my utterance. Thereafter the talk began again in a somewhat less tense atmosphere.'

Churchill and Stalin now discussed war supplies and production. When Churchill asked about the Caucasus front, Stalin called for a relief model and explained on it the Russian defensive plan. That night Stalin gave a banquet for Churchill, who was in a somewhat depressed mood, having just learned of the loss of three warships, eight merchant ships and six aircraft, on a Mediterranean convoy taking supplies from Gibraltar to Malta. 'The Prime Minister perked up a bit,' one observer noted, 'when photographs were taken of him sitting with Stalin on sofas.' Stalin then invited Churchill to watch a film, but he was tired, and asked to be excused. 'After a cordial handshake,' he told Attlee, 'I then took my departure and got some way down the crowded room but he hurried after me and accompanied me an immense distance through corridors and staircases to the front door where we again shook hands.' Stalin's gesture was appreciated. 'This long walk,' reported the British Ambassador, 'or rather trot, for he had to be brisk in order to keep pace with Mr Churchill, is, I understand, without precedent in the history of the Soviet Kremlin in so far as we have impinged upon it.'

Churchill had a final talk with Stalin on August 15, when he told the Soviet leader that, in order to make Germany 'more anxious about an attack across the Channel' that summer, there would soon be a 'serious raid' by some eight thousand men with fifty tanks, who would stay a night 'and kill as many Germans as possible' and then withdraw: 'a reconnaissance in force' which could be compared, Churchill explained, 'to a bath in which you feel with your hand to see if the water is hot'. This was to be the Dieppe raid of August 17.

Stalin then invited Churchill to his apartment in the Kremlin for a farewell drink. The drink turned into a banquet lasting more than six hours. The only tension was during a discussion of the Arctic convoys.

'Has the British Navy no sense of glory?' asked Stalin.

'You must take it from me that what was done was right,' Churchill replied. 'I really do know a lot about the Navy and sea-war.'

'Meaning that I know nothing?' Stalin remarked.

'Russia is a land animal,' Churchill answered. 'The British are sea animals.'

Stalin fell silent, then quickly recovered his good humour. The rest of the evening was spent in wide-ranging and amicable discussion, including Stalin's recollection of his visit to London in 1907 to attend a Bolshevik conference. It was 3.15 in the morning before Churchill got back to his villa. An hour and fifteen minutes later he had to leave for the airport, and at 5.30 he was airborne. As he flew southward, Soviet troops were forced out of the Caucasian oil town of Maikop. But the defence lines Stalin had shown Churchill on the relief map still held.

Reaching Cairo on August 17, Churchill had a long talk with Alexander and Montgomery about their coming offensive. On the following day he drove with Alexander and Brooke 130 miles to Montgomery's headquarters by the sea, at Burg el-Arab. There, after discussing the desert war, he bathed. On the following day there were further discussions as to how to beat Rommel. 'On the way to bed,' Brooke noted in his diary, 'PM took me down to the beach where he was transformed into a small boy wishing to dip his fingers into the sea. In the process he became very wet indeed.' That day, on the Channel Coast, Canadian forces, with some British and a few American troops in support, landed at Dieppe. The raid, Mountbatten reported to Churchill, was a success; the Germans had been 'rattled' by it and ninety-six German aircraft had been shot down. So had ninety-eight British aircraft, but Mountbatten hastened to assure Churchill that 'thirty pilots are safe'. The lessons learned at Dieppe,

Mountbatten told the War Cabinet on August 20, would be 'invaluable' in planning the future cross-Channel invasion.

Churchill remained in the Western Desert throughout August 20, swimming in the morning, and then visiting those areas of Montgomery's defences against which it was known, from the Germans' own top-secret messages, that Rommel planned an assault. 'I saw a great many soldiers that day,' Churchill later recalled, 'who greeted me with grins and cheers. I inspected my own regiment, the 4th Hussars, or as many of them as they dared to bring together – perhaps fifty or sixty – near the field cemetery in which a number of their comrades had been newly buried. All this was moving, but with it all there grew a sense of the reviving ardour of the Army. Everybody said what a change there was since Montgomery had taken command. I could feel the truth of this with joy and comfort.'

Churchill arrived back in England on the evening of August 24. Clementine and Randolph were at Lyneham airport to welcome him. Back in London was a message from General Douglas MacArthur, who had commanded the American forces in the Philippines, and now, in Australia, awaited the moment when he could launch the reconquest of the lost islands. 'If disposal of all the Allied decorations were today placed by Providence in my hands,' MacArthur had told a senior British officer at his headquarters, 'my first act would be to award the Victoria Cross to Winston Churchill. Not one of those who wear it deserves it more than he. A flight of 10,000 miles through hostile and foreign skies may be the duty of young pilots, but for a Statesman burdened with the world's cares it is an act of inspiring gallantry and valour.'

On 28 August 1942, after top-secret German and Italian messages had been decrypted at Bletchley, three Italian fuel ships, bringing vital fuel oil for the German Air Force in the Western Desert, were sunk. Rommel, desperate not to find himself even shorter of fuel if he delayed any longer, launched his attack on Montgomery's defences in the Western Desert on August 30. But his fuel shortages were too serious for him to break through the skilfully defended positions on the Alam Halfa ridge, fifteen miles south-east of El Alamein. At last Cairo and Alexandria were beyond his grasp. The tide of war was turning.

At the beginning of September Churchill agreed to send Stalin that month's Arctic convoy which had earlier been cancelled. Stalin was now willing, for the first time, to provide long-range bomber cover for the convoys once they were east of Bear Island. Another danger was thus diminished.

Each Tuesday Churchill gave a dinner at 10 Downing Street to Generals Eisenhower and Clark, the two Americans who were in charge of the

North African landings. On September 12 they were his weekend guests at Chequers, where discussions continued with the British Chiefs of Staff. Churchill's was the voice of encouragement and confidence; also of exhortation and a concern for detail. He still had to bear the burden of bad news anywhere in the war zones; that day he learned of the loss of thirteen of the forty merchant ships in the September Arctic convoy, even though it had been escorted by seventy-seven warships. The only redeeming features were that forty of the attacking German aircraft had been destroyed by the British naval fighter escort for the loss of only four British fighters, and that only two of the escorts had been sunk.

That week a voice from the past sent Churchill words of encouragement: 'I am all puffed up with pride at your great achievements, yes, puffed out like an old pouter pigeon,' his eighty-three-year-old Aunt Leonie wrote on September 14. Churchill replied: 'It is a great pleasure to me to know that you follow my toils. It seems to me that the tide of destiny is moving steadily in our favour, though our voyage will be long and rough.' A few days earlier he had received a telegram from Wavell with disappointing news: the hoped-for offensive against the Japanese in Burma would not take place that year. A 'heavy sick rate from malaria' and a shortage of British naval escort craft, had combined to curtail Wavell's plans.

As Churchill read the German top-secret messages about shortages and sickness in the Western Desert, he made sure that the most precise textual versions of these messages, rather than the usual paraphrases, were sent to Alexander, who knew their true source, so that he, Montgomery, and their Intelligence Staffs could assess Rommel's weaknesses and the best moment to attack. When he travelled, it was to visit munitions factories and military installations. On October 12 he visited the Home Fleet. 'Your presence with us has been an encouragement and inspiration to all,' the commanding Admiral signalled him.

Pressed that October by Eden to give his view on a post-war organisation based upon the Four Great Powers, Churchill was hesitant. 'It sounds very simple,' he wrote, 'to pick out these four Big Powers' – the United States, Britain, China and the Soviet Union. 'We cannot, however, tell what sort of a Russia and what kind of Russian demands we shall have to face. It would be a measureless disaster if Russian barbarism overlaid the culture and independence of the ancient States of Europe.' His own hope for the post-war world, Churchill told Eden, was for a 'United States of Europe' excluding Russia, in which the barriers between the nations of Europe 'will be greatly minimised and unrestricted travel will be possible'. The new Europe would be guarded by an international police force, one of whose tasks would be keeping Russia at bay. He did not want to spend time on these themes, however, telling Eden, 'Unhappily the war has prior claims on your attention and on mine.'

On October 23, from his positions at El Alamein, Montgomery launched his attack on the German-Italian forces. Four things were in his favour: Rommel was in Germany, his forces commanded by the less charismatic General Stumme; the German-Italian forces had betrayed their location, plans and shortages through their own top-secret signals being regularly decrypted; photo-reconnaissance of the enemy's defensive positions was remarkably effective; and Montgomery's troops, now well-armed, keen, and confident in their commander, were determined to drive the enemy from Egypt.

On the first day of battle General Stumme was killed and Rommel recalled from Germany. Relentlessly the Allied forces advanced westward. Within three days 1,500 Germans and Italians had been taken prisoner. When Rommel attempted to assemble his forces for a counter-attack on October 27, British bombers pulverised his concentration area, dropping eighty tons of bombs in two and a half hours, with the result, Alexander reported to Churchill, that the counter-attack 'was defeated before he could even complete his forming up'.

The fighting had been severe: after ten days of battle more than 1,700 British and Allied troops had been killed. But on November 2 Rommel sent a top-secret signal to Berlin to say that his army was no longer able to prevent a tank breakthrough. Nor could he withdraw in an orderly way in view of his lack of motor vehicles and low stocks of fuel. This signal was decrypted at Bletchley and sent to Churchill that same evening. A copy was also sent to Alexander. The decrypt made clear that the moment had come to launch the assault. Within forty-eight hours the British armoured formations had passed through the German front and, Alexander reported to Churchill on November 4, 'are operating in the enemy's rear areas. Such portions of the enemy's forces as can get away are in full retreat, and are being harassed by our armoured and mobile forces and by our Air Forces.'

Later that day Churchill learned that nine thousand enemy prisoners had been taken, and 260 German and Italian tanks either captured or destroyed. On the following day the King wrote to him by hand, 'When I look back and think of all the many arduous hours of work you have put in, and the many miles you have travelled, to bring this battle to a successful conclusion, you have every right to rejoice; while the rest of our people will one day be very thankful to you for what you have done.'

On November 4 Churchill had told Alexander that he wanted 'to ring the bells all over Britain for the first time this war'. To give such an order he would need to know that Montgomery had taken at least 20,000 prisoners. 'Ring out the bells!' Alexander telegraphed two days later. 'Prisoners estimated at 20,000, tanks 350, guns 400, motor transport *several thousand*'. Churchill was about to give orders for the bells to be rung; two years earlier they would have rung out only if Germany had invaded Britain. But he decided not to do so until the North African landings had taken place on the following day 'in case', he explained to Alexander, 'of some accident which would cause distress'.

Churchill sent this telegram to Alexander on November 7. That same day he sent Stalin a warning, based upon a decrypted German top-secret message, that Hitler, having despaired of capturing the Caspian oil city of Baku, now planned 'to wreck it by air attack'. Churchill added, 'Pray accept this from me.' Stalin did, thanking Churchill for the warning, and taking the necessary measures to combat the danger.

On November 8 British and American troops landed in force at Algiers, Oran and Casablanca. Churchill's son was among them. 'Well, here we are, safe and sound in the anchorage to the west of Algiers,' he wrote to his father that morning. 'Nearly everything has gone according to plan.' Everyone felt that it was 'a real privilege to be taking part in these great events.' In addition, Randolph reported, 'All goes well between us and the Americans.' The naval planner of the British landings was Admiral Bertram Ramsay, who before the war had brought Churchill details of naval deficiencies.

After fierce fighting, in which Vichy French forces tenaciously resisted the Allied effort, all three ports were taken. There was an unexpected bonus in the fact that the Vichy Commander-in-Chief, Admiral Darlan, who was then, by chance, in Algiers visiting his sick son, declared himself for the Allies, and ordered the local Vichy forces to lay down their arms.

Churchill was elated by the success in North Africa. During that night's dictation, Elizabeth Layton noted, 'Once he began to bark, then quickly stopped himself and said "No, no; quite all right, *quite* all right. Tonight you may rejoice. Tonight there is sugar on the cake." '

On November 9 Churchill told the Chiefs of Staff that in view of the success of the North African landings 'an entirely new view must be taken of possibilities of attacking Hitler in 1943'; mainland Europe must be attacked from the Mediterranean. Rather than limit the follow-up there to Sicily or Sardinia, as previously envisaged, he wished to plan for the invasion of Italy itself 'with the object of preparing the way for a very large-scale offensive on the underbelly of the Axis in 1943', or, 'better still, the invasion of Southern France'. To the Director of Movements at the War Office he explained two weeks later: 'I never meant the Anglo-American Army to be stuck in North Africa. It is a springboard and not a sofa.' Speaking at the Mansion House in London on November 10, he told the Lord Mayor's Luncheon, 'Now this is not the end. It is not even the beginning of the end. But it is, perhaps, the end of the beginning.'

During this speech Churchill noted that in the Western Desert Rommel's retreating forces had been subjected to 'blasting attacks' by the Royal Air Force as they tried to flee along the coast in their vehicles. As he read these accounts, Churchill said, 'I could not but remember those roads of France and Flanders, crowded, not with fighting men, but with helpless refugees – women and children – fleeing with their pitiful barrows and household goods, upon whom such merciless havoc was wreaked. I have, I trust, a humane disposition, but I must say I could not help feeling that what was happening, however grievous, was only Justice grimly reclaiming her rights.'

Churchill's speech of November 10 became memorable for one particular sentence in it, 'I have not become the King's First Minister in order to preside over the liquidation of the British Empire.' Seldom quoted is his next remark, that, if such a task were ever prescribed, 'someone else would have to be found' to carry it out. It was a personal declaration of his belief in Empire, not a political statement that the Empire would never be dissolved. As important, if not more so, Churchill had gone on to say that Britain sought no territorial expansion; her only war aim was to 'effect the liberation of the people of Europe from the pit of misery into which they have been cast by their own improvidence and by the brutal violence of the enemy.' As to his own part in the process of war-making, 'I am certainly not one of those who need to be prodded,' he told the House of Commons on November 11. 'In fact, if anything, I am a prod. My difficulties rather lie in finding the patience and self-restraint to wait through many anxious weeks for the results to be achieved.'

On November 11, as the Allies consolidated their hold on French North Africa, Hitler's forces took over the Unoccupied Zone of Vichy France. Two days later, in the Western Desert, Montgomery's forces entered Tobruk, which was never again to fall under German control. On November 15 Churchill ordered church bells to ring throughout England to celebrate the victory in the Western Desert. 'There is still a long road to tread,' he telegraphed to King Abdullah, whom he had installed as ruler in Amman in 1921, 'but the end is sure.'

31

Planning for Victory

On 19 November 1942 the Red Army began to encircle the German forces besieging Stalingrad. 'The operations are developing not badly,' Stalin telegraphed to Churchill on the following day. Three days later the German forces were encircled. Their commander, General von Paulus, proposed abandoning the siege and breaking out of the Russian ring. Hitler ordered him to stay and fight. Von Paulus obeyed, with the result that his army was slowly but relentlessly destroyed. As Churchill had prophesied to Stalin during their meeting in Moscow, the Anglo-American landings in North Africa played their part in this; of five hundred transport aircraft which the Germans rushed to Tunisia to forestall the Allied forces advancing from Algiers, four hundred had to be withdrawn from the Eastern Front, where they had been ferrying essential supplies to the German forces surrounded at Stalingrad.

In the Atlantic, the British inability to read the top-secret German submarine signals continued. In November 721,700 tons of Allied shipping were sunk, the highest figure for any month of the war and a grave worry to those who monitored Britain's supply and food needs. 'You who have so much land,' Churchill telegraphed to Stalin on November 24, 'may find it hard to realise that we can only live and fight in proportion to our sea communications.' On November 30, Churchill's sixty-eighth birthday, the Germans were still masters of the Atlantic; but within two weeks, in a triumph of cryptography, the Enigma key used by the German submarines was at last broken. With occasional gaps and delays, those Germans who directed the submarines to their targets were henceforth to betray their submarines' most secret movements until the end of the war.

German top-secret signals also revealed a massive build-up of German forces in Tunisia; Churchill thus realised that the attempt to capture Tunis would be more long-drawn-out than he had previously thought, and that any exploitation of the capture of Tunis, and the driving of the Germans out of Africa altogether, could delay a cross-Channel landing in 1943. This he did not want to do, nor did he want too great a perfectionism to delay those landings. Reading a report of major changes in designs to landing-craft being considered as a result of the lessons learned at Dieppe, he minuted, 'The maxim "Nothing avails but perfection" may be spelt shorter, "Paralysis".'

Churchill now pressed his advisers to draw up plans for a cross-Channel landing in August or September 1943. All depended upon driving the Germans out of Tunisia by the end of January or early February 1943. Montgomery, confident of being able to defeat Rommel in Libya and advance rapidly westward, made his confidence widely known. 'It might be well,' Churchill told Alexander, 'for you to give a friendly hint from me to General Montgomery about the disadvantages of his making confident statements that he will beat and outwit Rommel before the impending battle has been fought.' The impending battle was at Agheila, west of Tobruk, on the coastal road leading through the Libyan capital, Tripoli, to Tunisia. Would Montgomery not seem 'foolish', Churchill asked, 'if as is possible there is no battle at Agheila and Rommel slips away?' This was indeed what happened: Rommel withdrew from his Agheila positions without serious interference and prepared to defend the Libyan capital.

West of Tunisia, General Eisenhower's forces were worsted in battle on December 12, their subsequent counter-attack being hampered and then brought to a halt by the heavy and continual rain. The battle for Tunisia was going to be a prolonged struggle. Just as Hitler had insisted that his forces trapped at Stalingrad hold out to the end, so now he demanded that Tunisia be held at all cost, in order to continue to tie down huge quantities of Allied shipping in long and wasteful jouneys round the Cape. Churchill still hoped that victory in Tunisia would come in time for the cross-Channel assault to be launched in the autumn of 1943. But at a Staff Conference on December 16, the Chiefs of Staff argued that it could not be done; the rate and scale of the American troop build-up in Britain was inadequate for the task. Because of their 'magnificent' railways, the Germans would be able to bring superior forces by rail to confront the Allied troops brought ashore. It would make more sense militarily during 1943 to 'force Italy out of the war and perhaps enter the Balkans'. The defection of Italy in itself would drive Germany to send troops to hold down the Balkans.

Churchill, supported by Eden, pressed for the cross-Channel landing as the priority for 1943. But the Chiefs of Staff were emphatic that the Americans were no longer planning to have enough troops in Britain for the landings to be possible by then. In strictest secrecy, Mountbatten told Churchill and the Chiefs of Staff that despite an agreement to the contrary, 'the Americans were putting the good engines into their own landing-craft and fitting ours with the unsatisfactory type'; at the same time, many of the landing-craft needed to transport the cross-Channel forces were being diverted by the Americans to the Pacific, which was also absorbing so many naval vessels that even the next Arctic convoy to Russia would lack its American escorts. Churchill's hopes for a 1943 cross-Channel landing had been frustrated by the realities of American policy.

On December 17 a powerful declaration was issued simultaneously from London, Washington and Moscow; Churchill personally approved it. The declaration denounced the systematic mass murder of millions of Jews which, the facts having gradually become known, it called 'this bestial policy of cold-blooded extermination'. It also warned that those committing these crimes would be hunted down after the war and brought to trial; Churchill himself was emphatic that the murderers should not be allowed to escape justice. He was also vigilant in trying to help Jewish refugees from Nazism; learning that week of the successful rescue of 4,500 Jewish children and 500 accompanying adults from the Balkans, a plan which he himself had earlier approved, he minuted, 'Bravo!'

That Christmas, the fourth of the war, Churchill stayed at Chequers with his family. On Christmas Day he learned that Admiral Darlan, the former Vichy Commander-in-Chief who had become High Commissioner in Morocco and Algeria, had been assassinated by a French student in Algiers. 'Darlan's murder,' he later wrote, 'however criminal, relieved the Allies of the embarrassment of working with him, and at the same time left them with all the advantages he had been able to bestow during the vital hours of the Allied landings.' In Darlan's place, Churchill and Roosevelt appointed General Giraud, who had recently escaped from captivity in Germany.

In an attempt to devise an agreed Anglo-American strategy for 1943, Churchill decided to meet Roosevelt again, this time in North Africa. Mary Churchill wrote in her diary on 3 January 1943: 'It appears that he *might* get a coronary thrombosis – & it might be brought on by anything like a long &/or high flight. The question is whether he should be warned or not. Mummie thinks he should not – I agree with her.'

Nine days later Churchill flew to Casablanca with the British Chiefs of Staff, the Joint Planners and Mountbatten. On January 14 this formidable team was joined by Roosevelt and the American Joint Chiefs. Their discussions lasted for eight days, during which several major policy decisions were made, chief of them the priority of the Mediterranean over the cross-Channel assault. In view of the shortage of shipping and escort vessels, it was also decided that, as far as the Mediterranean was concerned, the most realistic amphibious target, once Tunisia were captured, would be Sicily; the troops would not have to be brought across the Atlantic, but could come from North Africa. In order to carry out a cross-Channel assault in 1944, 938,000 American troops would be assembled in Britain by the last day of 1943. But enough would have arrived by mid-1943 to enable a cross-Channel raid to take place 'with the primary object of provoking air battles and causing enemy losses'. If the German loss of morale and resources permitted, a bridgehead would be seized on the Cherbourg Peninsula.

The priority of Hitler's defeat before the defeat of Japan was also re-established. Once Germany had been 'brought to her knees', Churchill assured Roosevelt, Britain would continue to fight Japan with all her resources. In order to resolve any doubts there might be about Britain remaining in the war until the defeat of Japan, Churchill agreed to a public declaration that Britain and the United States would continue the war until they had brought about the 'unconditional surrender' of both Germany and Japan. There would be no armistice, no negotiated peace, no bargaining: only the complete and utter surrender of both armies.

To deceive the Germans that the cross-Channel landings would take place later that same year, and help placate the Russian demand for a second front in 1943, a deception plan was agreed at Casablanca. It had three elements; an American landing on the coast of Brittany, an Anglo-Russian invasion of Norway, and an Anglo-American landing in the Pas-de-Calais area. This latter was to be given extra verisimilitude by British agents and the French Resistance beginning pre-invasion preparations in a manner that would force the Germans to take the threat of a landing seriously; unfortunately, the Germans were not deceived, and four hundred agents were arrested.

On January 23, the last day of the Casablanca conference, the Eighth Army entered Tripoli. 'Rommel is still flying before them,' Churchill told newspaper correspondents on the following day. He then accompanied Roosevelt to Marrakech, a five-hour drive, to show the President his holiday haunt of 1936. That evening the two men watched the glow of the sunset on the snow-capped Atlas mountains; 'the most lovely spot in the world', Churchill murmured as they gazed on it. On the following morning Roosevelt left Marrakech. Churchill remained for one more day, telegraphing to Clementine when Roosevelt had gone, 'Am going to paint a little this afternoon.' A view of the Atlas mountains, it was the only picture he painted during the war.

From Marrakech, Churchill flew eastward to Cairo, where, on January 27, after talks with Colonel Keble, the head of Special Operations

Executive in the Middle East, and with his own former research assistant Bill Deakin, who was also with SOE Cairo, he decided to send a British mission to the Communist partisan leader in Yugoslavia, Josip Broz, known to his followers as Tito. Deakin volunteered to be parachuted in first, with one other officer, Captain William Stuart, and two wireless-operators.

On January 30 Churchill flew from Cairo, along the coast of Palestine and Syria, to the Southern Turkish town of Adana. It was a four-hour flight; at Adana a train was waiting which took him some six miles to a spot where, on a siding, waiting in his own train, was the Turkish President, Ismet Inönü. The two trains were then joined together. During the first day's discussion, held in Inönü's train, Churchill tried to persuade the Turks to accept British and American aid if Turkey were attacked by Germany. Inönü made no commitment, stressing that Turkey was 'at present neutral'.

That night Churchill slept in his train. Only when the 'circumstances were favourable', he told Inönü on the following morning, would it be in Turkey's interest 'to play her part'. It was agreed that British Staff Officers would go to the Turkish capital 'forthwith', to make plans with the Turkish General Staff 'for the movement and subsequent maintenance of British forces into Turkey in the event of Turkey being drawn into the war'. From Adana, Churchill flew to Cyprus, a half-hour flight. There he spent the night, and on the following morning spoke to the officers and men of the 4th Hussars, of which he was Colonel-in-Chief. 'Winston was grand,' their Commanding Officer wrote to his wife. 'He radiated confidence and made a most stirring speech to the troops.' That afternoon Churchill flew back to Cairo, where he learned that the German Army surrounded at Stalingrad had surrendered; 45,000 soldiers were taken prisoner. 'This is indeed a wonderful achievement,' he telegraphed to Stalin.

That evening Churchill dined at the British Embassy in Cairo. Randolph was also present. 'Father and son snapped at each other across me, which was very disconcerting,' Sir Alexander Cadogan noted. 'However, we got Winston on to the Omdurman campaign, on which he held forth, at the dinner table, till 11.30.' On the following morning Churchill flew from Cairo westward to Tripoli, a flight of nearly six hours, across 1,400 miles of desert so recently held by the Germans. There he told the men of the Eighth Army: 'When history is written and all the facts are known, your feats will gleam and glow and will be a source of song and story long after we who are gathered here have passed away.'

That night Churchill slept in one of the three Army trucks which Montgomery had converted into caravans. Then, on February 4, he was driven into Tripoli itself. Tears ran down his cheeks as he took the march past of the 51st Highland Division and other Allied units, 40,000 men in all. His Military Secretary, Colonel Jacob, commented, 'The bitter moment in the White House when Tobruk fell was swallowed up in the joy of the morning in Tripoli.' During a picnic lunch laid on by Montgomery, the puffs of anti-aircraft shells were seen in the sky as a German reconnaissance aircraft was spotted and driven off. In the afternoon Churchill inspected the 8,000 men of the New Zealand Division, telling them: 'The good cause will not be trampled down. Justice and freedom will reign among men.' That afternoon he watched the final repairs being made to Tripoli harbour, before dining with Montgomery, and then sleeping in the bomber that was to fly him to Algiers in the early hours of February 5.

After a five-hour flight Churchill reached Algiers at nine in the morning, then spent the day discussing the problems of the new French administration there, insisting that the Vichy laws against the Algerian Jews, laws which were still in force, be repealed. At midnight he boarded his Liberator bomber to return to England. But magneto failure made it impossible to start the engines. After sitting for two and a half hours on the airfield, he returned in the middle of the night to Algiers, where he spent the whole of February 6. During the morning he saw the two former senior Vichy officials who were now administering Algiers. 'I told them that if they marched with us, we would not concern ourselves with past differences,' he later recalled.

That afternoon Churchill played bezique with Randolph, before returning to the airfield. One of the two Liberators taking the participants back from the Casablanca conference had crashed, and two of the British participants had been killed. As he sat in his Liberator waiting for take-off, Churchill told Jacob: 'It would be a pity to have to go out in the middle of such an interesting drama without seeing the end. But it wouldn't be a bad moment to leave. It is a straight run in now, and even the Cabinet could manage it!'

After an eight-and-a-half-hour flight Churchill reached Lyneham in Wiltshire. It was almost midnight; going on by train to London, which he reached at one o'clock in the morning, he found thirteen of his Cabinet Ministers at the station to greet him. He had been away for nearly four weeks. 'Please let me get into the train before you come out,' Clementine Churchill had written. 'I like to kiss my Bull-finch privately & not be photographed doing it!' From London he and Clementine were driven to Chequers where, that same evening, he gave the War Cabinet an account of his travels. Four days later, on February 11, he told the House of Commons that the 'dominating aim' of Anglo-American policy was 'to make the enemy burn and bleed in every way that is physically and reasonably possible, in the same way as he is being made to burn and bleed along the vast Russian front from the White Sea to the Black Sea'.

That was the policy; but it irked Churchill that there was to be a three-month gap between the capture of Tunisia and the invasion of Sicily, a gap that Eisenhower sought to widen by a further month. 'I think it is an awful thing,' Churchill telegraphed to Hopkins on February 13, 'that in April, May and June, not a single American or British soldier will be killing a single German or Italian soldier, while the Russians are chasing 185 divisions around.'

Since his return from North Africa on February 7, Churchill had not been feeling well. On February 16 it was announced that he had pneumonia. He remained in bed in No.10 Annexe for a week, in fever and discomfort. 'It was miserable having him ill and knowing how he hated it,' Elizabeth Layton wrote to her parents. 'He was so sweet, too, any time one had to go in; seemed quite pleased to see one.' A telegram from Montgomery cheered him up; the Eighth Army had driven the Germans from Ben Gardane, inside the Tunisian frontier, and overrun the airfields at Medenine. He also learned that Tripoli harbour, after a scandalous delay in rehabilitating the port, was now fully working: he at once sent a message to the soldiers working in the docks, 'Tell them they are unloading history.'

In western Tunisia, Eisenhower's troops had again been mauled by the Germans, and 170 tanks lost, setting back by at least a month the possible capture of Tunis, and threatening to delay the date of the invasion of Sicily. From his sickbed, on February 19, Churchill suggested that Britain might try to capture Sicily without the Americans, if Montgomery could take Tunis alone. On February 20 Rommel's forces drove the Americans from the Kasserine Pass. When Mary saw her father on the following day she noted: 'I was shocked when I saw him. He looked so old & tired – lying back in bed.'

Churchill was too ill on February 20 to see any official papers. But two days later, with his temperature at 102°, he did dictate a seven-page letter to the King, in answer to the King's worries about Anglo-American co-operation in Tunisia. He did not feel 'seriously disturbed', Churchill wrote, though he pointed out to the King that during the battle of the Kasserine Pass he had seen a German top-secret signal, decrypted at Bletchley, in which the Germans had ordered a renewed attack 'on account', as the signal had phrased it, 'of the low fighting value of the enemy'. Churchill had confidence, however, in the Americans, telling the King that they were men 'who will not hesitate to learn from defeat, and who will improve themselves by suffering until all their martial qualities have come to the front.'

The Americans regained control of the Kasserine Pass on February 24. By March 3 Churchill was well enough to go to Chequers, where he worked through his mass of telegrams with General Ismay – whom he knew affectionately as 'Pug'. The nurse who accompanied him, Doris Miles, later recalled: 'I was very struck by his immense vigour and enthusiasm, his determination to get over his illness as quickly as possible. He told me that he ate and drank too much (roast beef for breakfast) and took no exercise at all, but was much fitter than "old so-and-so who is two years younger than me". He loved watching films, particularly newsreels, and was delighted if he featured in them "Look Pug, there we are!" He was very kind to me – interested to know that my husband was a Surgeon Lieutenant in a destroyer on the Russian convoys.'

On his third day at Chequers, Churchill wrote to a friend: 'I am much better but am staying in the country for a few days. Of course, I work wherever I am and however I am. That is what does me good.' In a broadcast from Chequers on March 21, his first broadcast in more than a year, Churchill set out his plan for post-war Britain, echoing his own previous goals of 1908 and 1924, and drawing, as he had done in 1908, on the ideas of William Beveridge; it was a report by Beveridge that now served as the blueprint for the new scheme. In his broadcast Churchill spoke of the need to establish a National Health Service on 'broad and solid foundations', to provide national compulsory insurance 'from cradle to grave', and to ensure far wider educational opportunities and 'fair competition' so extended that Britain would draw its leaders 'from every type of school and wearing every kind of tie'. Tradition would still play its part, 'but broader systems must now rule'. State enterprise and free enterprise should 'pull the national wagon side by side'.

As Churchill spoke, a slip of paper was put in front of him. 'I have just received a message from General Montgomery,' he told his listeners, 'that the Eighth Army are on the move and that he is satisfied with their progress. Let us wish them God speed in their struggle, and let us bend all our efforts to the war, and to the ever more vigorous prosecution of our supreme task.' The battle continued for more than a week. The Italian-German forces, now commanded by an Italian, General Messe, defeated Montgomery's frontal attack on their Mareth Line defences, forcing him to adopt an alternative plan, a wide outflanking move. On March 27, as evidence grew that this was succeeding, Churchill telegraphed to Montgomery, 'We have every confidence you will pull it off.'

On the following day Montgomery telegraphed that the enemy resistance was disintegrating. 'Bravo!' Churchill replied. 'I was sure of it. Now the question is the cop.' But the enemy withdrawal was well-conducted, Montgomery was excessively cautious, and the number of prisoners taken was small.

The German and Italian forces were not to give up easily their hold on the Tunisian shore. 'Hitler with his usual obstinacy is sending the Hermann Goering Division and the 999th German Division into Tunisia, chiefly by air transport in which at least a hundred large machines are employed,' Churchill told Stalin in explanation of the delay in driving the Germans and Italians from North Africa. His knowledge of Hitler's moves was still accurate and precise, as a result of his daily scrutiny of the hundreds of decrypted top-secret German signals.

The amount of time and work involved in following these details and exploiting each piece of information was enormous. In the last week of March, after his first dictation to a new secretary, Marian Holmes, Churchill told her: 'You know you must never be frightened of me when I snap. I'm not snapping at you but thinking of the work.' This was said, Miss Holmes wrote in her diary, 'with a cherubic smile'. As he recovered from his pneumonia, Churchill was in reflective mood, telling the editor of *The Times,* Robin Barrington-Ward, who found him 'pink, fresh in colour, hardly a wrinkle, voice firm, all his usual animation and emphasis': 'I shall come out of the war an old man. I shall be seventy. I have nothing more to ask.' Churchill's thoughts were on the future of a Europe dominated by Russia. 'I have wooed Joe Stalin as a man might woo a maid,' he said. He would favour a post-war confederation of the smaller states of Europe, 'I do not want to be left alone in Europe with the bear.'

On April 6 Montgomery attacked again, driving his adversary from the Wadi Akarit. By the evening of April 7 he had taken six thousand prisoners. That evening Churchill learned that United States troops moving forward from Western Tunisia had 'joined hands' with the Eighth Army. All was now set to drive the German and Italian forces into the Tunisian 'tip'. But on the following day he was told that Eisenhower did not wish to follow up a Tunisian success by invading Sicily, because of the presence of two German divisions on the island, in addition to the six Italian divisions that had been expected. All Eisenhower had done was to endorse an assessment made three months earlier by the British Joint Planning Committee and already rejected by Alexander and those who were planning the invasion. But Churchill was outraged: 'I trust the Chiefs of Staff will not accept these pusillanimous and defeatist doctrines from whomever they come,' he minuted. The adoption of such an attitude by the Allied commanders 'would make us the laughing stock of the world'. Eisenhower should be asked 'what happens' if two German divisions 'meet him at any of the other places he may propose'.

Churchill added, 'This is an example of the fatuity of Planning Staffs playing upon each other's fears, each Service presenting its difficulties at the maximum, and Americans and Englishmen vying with each other, in the total absence of one directing mind and commanding willpower.' The Russians had been told that the next Arctic convoys would have to be cancelled because the escort ships were needed for the invasion of Sicily. Now Eisenhower was baulking at Sicily because there would be two German divisions in addition to six Italian. 'What Stalin would think of this when he has 185 German divisions on his front, I cannot imagine.'

The British Chiefs of Staff shared Churchill's sense of anger, as did the United States Joint Chiefs. The landings would go ahead, even with two German divisions to be fought in addition to the Italians. A sense of victory was in the air: on April 11 Churchill told Stalin that Montgomery had now taken 25,000 prisoners in Tunisia, and that the massive bombing of German factories was proceeding without respite. What he did not tell him was that the Chiefs of Staff had decided that the landing-craft needed for Sicily were those also needed for the limited cross-Channel landing. To ensure a successful landing on Sicily, even the limited cross-Channel plans for 1943 had to be given up. Churchill was hopeful, however, that success in Tunisia and Sicily would be such as to show 'substantial results' thereafter.

'The battle in Tunisia is begun,' Churchill telegraphed to Stalin on April 20. 'It is intended to carry matters to a conclusion, if possible by continuous pressure.' But ten days later he learned from Alexander that the battle had been temporarily called off, in view of the strong German artillery concentrations in the coastal sector, and 'the desperate nature of the enemy's resistance'. There were those in Washington who wanted the Pacific, not Sicily, to be the Allied priority that summer, so much so that they were no longer transferring landing-craft essential for Sicily from the Far East.

To prevent the abandonment of Sicily, Churchill decided that he must speak to Roosevelt personally. 'I am conscious of serious divergences beneath the surface,' he telegraphed to Hopkins on May 2, 'which, if not adjusted, will lead to grave difficulties and feeble action in the summer and autumn. These difficulties we must forestall.' Two days later he left London by train for the Clyde, boarding the *Queen Mary* on the following afternoon for his third transatlantic voyage of the war. During the second day out, he learned from Alexander that the battle in Tunisia had been renewed. He was also told that a German submarine, its route revealed to the British by its own top-secret orders, was likely to cross their course about fifteen miles ahead. He at once gave orders for a machine-gun to be put in the lifeboat he would be using should the ship be sunk. Averell Harriman, who was with him, noted Churchill's words: 'I won't be captured. The finest way to die is in the excitement of fighting the enemy. (Then, after a moment's thought) It might not be so nice if one were in the water and they tried to pick me up.'

The submarine made no appearance. All thought of it was eclipsed on the evening of May 7, when a series of signals reaching the *Queen Mary* told of the capture of Tunis, entered by the British First Army; and then of Bizerta, entered by the Americans. On the following day Alexander reported the capture of 20,000 prisoners. 'Overjoyed at your splendid news,' Churchill replied. 'History will admire your handling of these great armies.' Two days later a further 30,000 prisoners had been counted, including nine German Generals. Churchill at once gave orders for the church bells to be rung again.

All North Africa was now in Allied hands, after three years of changing fortunes and bitter war. As the *Queen Mary* reached American waters, Alexander told Churchill in triumph that the number of German and Italian prisoners was likely to exceed 100,000: 'No one has got away, except a mere handful by air.' By the end of the month, it was known that more than 240,000 prisoners had been taken.

That night, Churchill slept in the White House where, starting the following morning, he and Roosevelt worked out their war plans. Despite Eisenhower's hesitations, they agreed that the invasion of Sicily would have immediate priority, followed by the invasion of Italy. If Italy collapsed by August, further operations could take place either in the Balkans or in southern Europe. In November, all Allied resources would be switched to the cross-Channel landing, which would take place 'on the largest scale' by May 1944.

Leaving the Combined Chiefs of Staff to tackle the details, Roosevelt took Churchill to Shangri-La, his mountain retreat in Maryland, now known as Camp David. Returning to Washington on May 14, Churchill pressed for a British landing against the Japanese in Sumatra. He was supported by Wavell, whose responsibility it would be. Roosevelt wanted the attack to be on China, through northern Burma, but Wavell warned that Burma was 'the most malarial country in the world'. Churchill agreed with Wavell, telling Roosevelt that he was 'not prepared to undertake something foolish purely in order to placate the Chinese'. To Churchill's chagrin, no decision was reached. Learning that there had been serious delays in building up Britain's air bases in Assam, from which any assault must come, he telegraphed to Attlee: 'I am disquieted about the way in which our affairs in this theatre have been conducted. The opportunity should be taken of gripping the whole situation and injecting new vim into all proceedings.'

Addressing Congress on May 19, Churchill warned that any 'discord or lassitude' among the Allies would give Germany and Japan the power 'to confront us with new and hideous facts'. His warning continued: 'We have surmounted many serious dangers, but there is one grave danger which will go along with us to the end; that danger is the undue prolongation of the war. No one can tell what new complications and perils might arise in four or five more years of war. And it is in the dragging out of the war at enormous expense, until the democracies are tired or bored or split, that the main hopes of Germany and Japan must now reside.' Clementine was among those who listened to the broadcast of Churchill's speech in England. 'It warmed me to hear your voice so strong, resonant & resolute,' she wrote.

Churchill had now to deal with a matter of the utmost sensitivity. On May 15 he had received a disturbing telegram from Sir John Anderson, the Minister responsible for all matters connected with research into the atom bomb, who was working closely on this with Professor Lindemann, now ennobled as Lord Cherwell, that four months earlier the Americans had stopped the exchange of information on the bomb. Yet this exchange had been agreed by Churchill and Roosevelt at Hyde Park in June 1942. 'That we should each work separately would be a sombre decision,' Churchill had warned Hopkins at the beginning of April, but still the Americans had refused to exchange information. Churchill had therefore decided to go ahead with an independent British atom bomb. It would require a vast diversion of resources and perhaps even a prolongation of the war; but if Britain wished to have such a bomb, she would have to manufacture it herself. What made this decision possible was that the principal components not available in Britain, uranium and heavy water, could be bought from Canada.

It now appeared, however, from Anderson's telegram, that the Canadian Government, without informing Britain, had agreed to sell the United States the entire output of Canada's uranium mines for the next two years, as well as all Canada's production of heavy water. Britain could no longer even contemplate making her own bomb. Churchill would have to raise the issue with Roosevelt and accept whatever conditions the Americans might offer. On the last day of the Washington talks Churchill and Roosevelt agreed that Britain and the United States would work together to manufacture the atom bomb. Exchange of information, suspended earlier in the year, would be resumed, and, Churchill told Anderson, the enterprise would henceforth 'be considered a joint one, to which both countries would contribute their best endeavours'. It was assumed, Churchill added, 'that this weapon may well be developed in time for the present war'.

The Washington discussions ended on May 25. The one point which worried Churchill was an American preference to strike at Sardinia after Sicily, and before the invasion of Italy. Churchill saw this as a time-consuming diversion of forces from the main aim. He therefore decided to fly to North Africa, to raise the issue with Eisenhower and the other senior American officers on whom the carrying out of these assaults would fall.

On May 27 he went by flying boat first to Newfoundland, then to Gibraltar, an airborne journey of seventeen hours. On the Gibraltar leg the flying boat was struck by lightning, causing the pilot some anxiety, but, as Churchill later wrote, 'there were no consequences, which after all are what is important in air journeys'. On May 28 he flew from Gibraltar to Algiers in a specially converted Lancaster bomber. 'Very comfortable,' Brooke wrote in his diary, 'with a special cabin for PM, dining rooms, berths for four besides PM, and lavatory.' It was only a three-hour flight. At dinner that evening in Algiers, Brooke noted that Churchill used all his skills 'trying to impress on Eisenhower what is to be gained in knocking Italy out of the war'. On the following day Eisenhower agreed that if Sicily proved 'an easy proposition' then the next move should be against the Italian mainland.

On June 1 Churchill flew from Algiers to a military aerodrome in the desert, where he attended the briefing of an American squadron that was about to bomb Pantelleria Island, half-way between the Tunisian tip and Sicily. After watching the bombers set off on their mission, he flew on to Tunis, where, in the Roman amphitheatre at Carthage, he addressed a vast number of troops. Flying back to Algiers on the following day in the Lancaster, he took charge of the controls for a while, 'and gave us something of a swaying passage for a bit,' Brooke wrote in his diary.

In Algiers, Churchill learned that the two rivals for leadership of the French forces beyond Vichy control, Generals Giraud and de Gaulle, had agreed to become joint presidents of the newly established French Committee of National Liberation. 'The bride and bridegroom have at last physically embraced,' Churchill telegraphed to Roosevelt on June 4. 'I am entertaining the new Committee at lunch today, but I will not attempt to mar the domestic bliss by any intrusions of my own.'

That afternoon Churchill flew back to Gibraltar in his bomber. Because the weather was bad, he decided not to continue from Gibraltar to England, as originally intended, by flying boat, but to continue in the bomber. That same day, another flying boat, using a similar flight path from Lisbon to Plymouth, was shot down and all its passengers killed; among the dead was the actor Leslie Howard.

Churchill was back in London on the morning of June 5. 'We have been rather anxious about you since they got Leslie Howard,' his daughter Diana wrote in welcoming him back. After giving the War Cabinet an account of his journey, he went that afternoon to Chequers, where he prepared a statement for the Commons which he delivered on June 8. Of the relations between the British and American policy-makers he said: 'All sorts of divergences, all sorts of differences of outlook and all sorts of awkward little jars necessarily occur as we roll ponderously forward together along the rough and broken road of war. But none of these makes the slightest difference to our ever-growing concert and unity. There are none of them that cannot be settled face to face by heart to heart talks and patient argument.'

On June 11 Eisenhower's forces captured Pantelleria. A week earlier, while in Algiers, Churchill had said that there were only three thousand Italians on the island and had offered Eisenhower five centimes for every Italian captured over three thousand. As there were in fact 9,500 Italians, Churchill had to pay up sixty-five francs. On June 13 two more small Italian islands, Lampedusa and Linosa, surrendered. The way was open for the invasion of Sicily. Meanwhile, the bombing of Germany continued, with growing intensity. On June 20, during a raid on the industrial city of Wuppertal, more than three thousand citizens were killed in the firestorm created by the raid. A week later, at Chequers, after watching a film of the bombing of German towns, Churchill suddenly sat bolt upright and said to his neighbour, 'Are we beasts? Are we taking this too far?'

Two days later Churchill was presented with photographic and Intelligence evidence which made it clear that the Germans were developing a new weapon, a rocket which could hurl a bomb from a launch-site on the coast of France to London; the evidence had been brought to him by his son-in-law Duncan Sandys, who, having been badly injured in the Norwegian campaign, had been made responsible for the search for, and discovery of, secret weapons. 'Arrived at conclusion that a definite threat exists,' Brooke noted in his diary, 'and that we should bomb Peenemunde experimental station at earliest possible date.'

On July 3 the Allies began intensive bombing raids on the airfields of Sicily, as a prelude to invasion. 'You know my hope,' Churchill telegraphed to Alexander four days later, 'that you will put your right paw on the mainland as soon as possible. Rome is the bull's-eye.' Throughout July 9 he was at Chequers, awaiting news of the Sicily landings; Admiral Ramsay was again in charge of the naval operation. Clementine was feeling tired that evening and asked her daughter-in-law Pamela to stay up with Churchill in her place.

The landings were expected to begin in the early hours of July 10, 'so we settled down,' Pamela later recalled, 'to play bezique which he loved, and then one of the Private Secretaries came in to say that the winds had got up and they had delayed the landings, they did not know for how long. So we played bezique through the night and every now and again he would put down the cards and he would say, "So many brave young men going to their death tonight. It is a grave responsibility". He was so preoccupied that night with whether it would be a success or a failure, and I'm sure that he related it to Gallipoli and the Dardanelles and was wondering if another fiasco could happen, but then we would go on playing bezique and he'd talk about other things, but he would always then set down the cards and talk about the young people and the sacrifices that they were being asked to make.'

Pamela added: 'It was a very very tense and torturous night for him and he would keep going back to the little operations rooms and he would check out some things and then he would come back again.' When the news of the landings finally came through at four o'clock in the morning, 'he wanted to go straight off to the war room and consult as to how they were going, how many aircraft were being lost and so on. Once the landings had happened he wanted the details'. The first detail Churchill learned was that the port of Syracuse was under Allied control. 'It is a tremendous feat,' he telegraphed at once to Eisenhower, 'to leap on shore with nearly 200,000 men.'

On July 16, as the battle in Sicily entered its sixth day, Churchill decided he must once more discuss with Roosevelt the immediate next stage, invasion of the Italian mainland at the most northerly point of the coast possible. 'I must say the PM doesn't let the grass grow under his feet', was Oliver Harvey's comment in his diary on July 16. 'He is anxious to pin the Americans down before their well-known dislike of European operations except cross-Channel get the better of them again, and they pull out their landing-craft and send off their ships to the Pacific.'

Churchill now made plans for his fourth transatlantic crossing of the war. His aim was to persuade the Americans to follow up the imminent conquest of Sicily by the invasion of Italy at least as far as Rome, and then to assist the Yugoslav, Greek and Albanian partisans in the liberation of the Balkans, by air support, arms, and coastal landings by small Commando units. The Germans already had fifteen divisions tied down in the Balkans: well-orchestrated partisan war would draw in many more. On the evening of July 24, at Chequers, he discussed the war with Guy Gibson and his wife Eve; he was about to send the air ace on a goodwill mission to Canada and the United States. 'We were shown a film, captured from the Germans,' Eve Gibson later wrote, 'depicting the atrocities inflicted on the Jews and the inhabitants of occupied countries. It was quite ghastly and the Prime Minister was very, very moved. He told me that it was shown to every American serviceman in this country.'

While Churchill was watching a film on the following evening a message was brought in: Mussolini had resigned. King Victor Emmanuel had taken over command of the Italian Armed Forces, with Marshal Badoglio as Prime Minister. The Fascist Party was dissolved and the Fascist Grand Council, its instrument of government, abolished. 'Now that Mussolini has gone,' Churchill telegraphed to Roosevelt on July 26, 'I should deal with any non-Fascist Italian government which can deliver the goods.' Those 'goods' were the entry of Allied forces into Italy, and their right, as Roosevelt told Churchill that same day, to use 'all Italian territory and transportation' against the Germans.

Armistice negotiations with Italy began at once. There was great excitement in Britain at the end of Mussolini as a war-leader. But Churchill warned the Commons on July 27 that Britain's 'prime and capital foe is not Italy but Germany'. He was nevertheless in confident mood; in the Atlantic, as a result of Bletchley's final mastery of German top-secret submarine communications, thirty-five German submarines had been sunk in July, making a total of eighty-five sunk in the ninety-one days since May 1.

At midnight on August 4, the twenty-ninth anniversary of Britain's declaration of war in 1914, Churchill left London by night train for Scotland, with Clementine, Mary, and three hundred other British participants, for the Quebec Conference. On the afternoon of August 5 they left the Clyde on board the *Queen Mary*. During the five-day voyage Churchill himself marked on the map in his travelling map room the daily advances in Sicily. Captain Pim, who was in charge of the Map Room, later recalled the Prime Minister coming in one day after breakfast 'in his multi-coloured dressing-gown saying, "Put your finger on Aderno and Paterno" – both towns in Sicily which we had just heard had been captured from the enemy.' Aderno was only fifty miles from the Strait of Messina.

On August 9 Churchill reached the Canadian port of Halifax, where he boarded the train for Quebec. Crowds met the train at every station; rumours that an 'important personage' would be on board were rife. Some said it was the Pope, others that it was Stalin. On reaching Quebec, Churchill found a telegram from Stalin, congratulating him on the continuing victories in Sicily. In return Churchill sent Stalin 'a small stereoscopic machine' together with photographic slides of the damage done by British bombs to German cities. 'They give one a more vivid impression than anything that can be gained from photographs,' Churchill told him. In a bombing raid on Hamburg two weeks earlier, the amazing total of 42,000 Germans had been killed, and a third of the city's residential buildings destroyed.

From Quebec, Churchill went by train to Roosevelt's home at Hyde Park. There, it was agreed that Mountbatten, whom Churchill had earlier described as 'young, enthusiastic and triphibious', should become Supreme Commander in South-East Asia. 'There is no doubt,' Churchill telegraphed to the War Cabinet, 'of the need of a young and vigorous mind in this lethargic and stagnant Indian scene.' It was also agreed, with regard to the atom bomb, that Britain and the United States 'will never use this agency against each other'. After two nights at Hyde Park, Churchill returned by train to Quebec.

It was while he was at Quebec on August 17 that Churchill received a telegram from Alexander announcing that 'the last German soldier was flung out of Sicily and the whole island is now in our hands'. Its conquest had taken thirty-eight days. That night 571 British heavy bombers struck at the German rocket research-station at Peenemunde on the Baltic, setting back production of the new rocket bomb by many months. The Quebec Conference ended two days later, its conclusions having been worked out over five days by the Combined Chiefs of Staff, in accordance with Churchill's general design, and with Roosevelt's approval. The 'primary' Anglo-American effort in 1944 would be the cross-Channel landing. Its aim would be not only to land in northern France but from there 'to strike at the heart of Germany and destroy her military forces'. Any conflict of priorities between operations in the Mediterranean and the Channel would be resolved in favour of the Channel. In deference to considerable pressure from the American Chiefs of Staff, there would also be a landing in the South of France, as a diversion to help the cross-Channel landings; the American Chiefs of Staff felt most strongly that such a landing would force the Germans to draw troops away from the Channel.

To enable supplies to be accumulated for the cross-Channel landing, although the advance in Italy would include the capture of Rome, as Churchill wished, it would go no farther north than the Pisa-Ancona line; it would not seek to drive on to the top of the Adriatic, or into Southern Austria. Operations in the Balkans would be limited to sending air and sea supplies to the partisans, and the use of 'minor Commando forces'.

On August 20 Churchill and Roosevelt went for the day to a log-cabin retreat on the Grand Lac d'Epaule. There they fished, and discussed the relative merits of Sumatra and Burma as the next British objective in the Far East, Roosevelt demonstrating at lunch his preference for Burma by use of wine glasses and salt cellars. Returning to Quebec Roosevelt explained his idea for a post-war international security organisation, to be set up between victory and the signature of the peace treaties. When his Secretary of State, Cordell Hull, rose about midnight to go to bed, Churchill was scandalised. When Hull protested that it was late, Churchill replied, 'Why, man, we are at war!'

At their meeting on August 23 Roosevelt and Churchill agreed with the Combined Chiefs of Staff that plans should be made to defeat Japan within twelve months of the collapse of Germany, but not before. The primacy of the war in Europe was secure. Churchill was worried that the cross-Channel force would not be strong enough to hold its position once it was ashore. General Marshall agreed that the initial assault, which during their discussions in May had been planned for three divisions, would now have four and a half.

The Quebec Conference ended on August 24. Two days later Eden found Churchill looking unwell, and 'a bad colour'. Churchill was still worried that there would be too long a delay between the victory in Sicily a week earlier and the landings on the Italian mainland, as negotiations with the Italians dragged on. There was also a personal worry. Hearing that Eden, Brooke, Portal and Mountbatten were to fly back to England together by flying boat, he told Eden: 'I don't know what I should do if I lost you all. I'd have to cut my throat. It isn't just love, though there is much of that in it, but you are my war machine. Brookie, Portal, you and Dickie, I simply couldn't replace you.'

That day Churchill left Quebec for a holiday at La Cabane de Montmorency, a fishing-camp high in the Laurentian Mountains which had been put at his disposal by a Canadian industrialist, Colonel Frank Clarke. 'When night fell,' Churchill's doctor noted, 'Winston came out on the wooden pier, gazing up at the Aurora Borealis. This quiet life is doing him good, but he feels he is playing truant.' On the following day he fished at the lakeside with Mary. He also worked while at La Cabane on a broadcast he was to make to the Canadian people. Various members of the British delegation, who were at other lakeside cabins, motored over for lunch and dinner. On August 29 one of them noted in his diary: 'Winston in terrific form, singing Dan Leno songs and other favourites of the Halls of forty years ago, together with the latest Noël Coward.' Two days later Churchill returned to Quebec, where he made his broadcast: 'Here at the gateway of Canada, in mighty lands which have never known the totalitarian tyrannies of Hitler and Mussolini, the spirit of freedom has found a safe and abiding home.'

From Quebec, Churchill went by train to Washington. There, on September 1, he learned that the Italian Government had agreed to the Allied terms of surrender. Meanwhile, German troops were pouring into Italy from the north. 'The Italian landing is the biggest risk we have yet run,' Churchill telegraphed to the War Cabinet on September 2, 'though I am fully in favour of running it.' Two days later, on the fourth anniversary of the British declaration of war on Germany, British and Canadian forces crossed the Straits of Messina and landed on the Italian mainland. Churchill immediately focused on the final stage of the war, telegraphing that day to Eden and Attlee that he wished to have a Tripartite Conference to address the question: 'If we win, what are we to do with Germany? Is it to be divided, and if so how?' He would invite Stalin and Roosevelt to London or Edinburgh, or both.

The future of Russian power was henceforth to exercise much of Churchill's thought. 'I think it inevitable,' he telegraphed to Field Marshal Smuts on September 5, 'that Russia will be the greatest land power in the world after this war will have rid her of the two military powers, Germany and Japan, who in our lifetime have inflicted upon her such heavy defeats. I hope, however, that the "fraternal association" of the British Commonwealth and the United States, together with sea and air power, may put us on good terms and in a friendly balance with Russia at least for the period of rebuilding. Further than that I cannot see with mortal eye, and I am not as yet fully informed about the celestial telescopes.'

On the evening of September 5 Churchill went by night train from Washington to Boston, to receive an honorary degree at Harvard. Having made his acceptance speech at noon on September 6, he returned at once by train to Washington, reaching the capital on the following morning. During the journey back, noted Cadogan in his diary, 'Winston enjoyed himself hugely, making the V-sign from the train window at all the engine drivers on the line and at all the passers-by. He quite unnecessarily rushes out on to the rear platform of the car, in a flowered silk dressing gown, to attract and chat with anyone he can find on the platform at stopping places.'

On September 8, in Washington, Churchill learned of the formal surrender of the Italian armed forces to the Allies. That night German troops began to occupy Rome. On the following morning Allied troops landed at Salerno. But Eisenhower's plan to land an airborne division near Rome had to be cancelled: 'We have reason to believe,' Alexander explained in a telegram to Churchill, 'the Germans are in occupation of airfields.' Churchill spent the afternoon of September 9 with Roosevelt: both were agreed that if the Anglo-American forces were quickly successful in Italy, then considerable aid in munitions and supplies should go to the partisan forces in the Balkans. Churchill spoke of the 75,000 and more men of the Polish Army, 'burning to engage the enemy', who might be put ashore on the Dalmatian Coast of Yugoslavia. Certainly the setting up of garrisons in the Balkans 'with a few of our mobile columns' might be of value. Roosevelt agreed, telling Churchill that in the Balkans 'we should be prepared to take advantage of any opportunity that presented itself'.

When Churchill went back to Hyde Park to spend the day with Roosevelt on September 11, it was the news of a setback at Salerno that chiefly concerned them. 'The Prime Minister was most upset,' Ismay later recalled. 'It reminded him of the Suvla Bay landing in the Gallipoli campaign, when the troops got ashore successfully but failed to move inland for two or three days, thus giving the enemy time to concentrate against them.' There was another recollection of Suvla Bay that also troubled

Churchill. The battle there was lost, he telegraphed to Alexander, because Sir Ian Hamilton had been advised by his Chief Staff Officer 'to remain at a remote central point where he would know everything. Had he been on the spot he could have saved the show. At this distance and with time lags I cannot pretend to judge, but I feel it my duty to set before you this experience of mine from the past.' By the time he received Churchill's telegram, Alexander was already on his way to the Salerno beach-head. 'I am sure you will be glad to know that I have already anticipated your wise advice,' he replied.

September 12 was the Churchills' wedding anniversary; at dinner that night Roosevelt proposed their health and then drove them to the station, where they took the train to Halifax, a journey of more than thirty-seven hours. As they were on their way, German parachutists seized Mussolini from a mountain refuge in the Apennines and took him to see Hitler, who then agreed to set him up as head of a Fascist Government in northern Italy.

Churchill reached Halifax on September 14. Boarding the battleship *Renown*, he was, recalled Mary, 'in relaxed and genial form'. That evening in the Admiral's cabin he called for a box of matches and demonstrated the disposition of Kitchener's forces at the battle of Omdurman in 1898. When he noted that he had been under fire on his twenty-first birthday, Mary, whose twenty-first birthday it was the next day, pointed out excitedly that she had beaten her father by just over a year; the Anti-Aircraft Battery in which she served had been in action several times against German bombers over London a year earlier; 'no doubt quite ineffectively', she later commented.

Five days after leaving Halifax, *Renown* reached the Clyde. During the voyage Dudley Pound's health, already poor, had deteriorated; on the train journey to London he gave Churchill his letter of resignation. At Euston Station Churchill was greeted, Captain Pim later recalled, by all his Cabinet colleagues 'and cheering crowds, and was obviously in the best of form'. Also at Euston was an ambulance, which took Pound to the Royal Masonic Hospital.

Three days after reaching London, Churchill answered allegations in the House of Commons that the delay in invading Italy had been due to the prolonged negotiations with Mussolini's successors. The 'sole limiting factor', he explained, had been the preparation of the landing-craft needed, and he went on to tell the House, 'When I hear people talking in an airy way of throwing modern armies ashore here and there as if they were bales of goods to be dumped on a beach and forgotten, I really marvel at the lack of knowledge that still prevails of conditions of modern war.'

There was another worry on Churchill's mind that autumn, the possibility, he explained to John Anderson, 'that the rocket or long-range cannon bombarding will begin at the turn of the year'. London would then again become a target. As for 10 Downing Street itself, 'the building is so old and frail that a near miss by a heavy bomb might bring it all down with a run.' Despite these worries Churchill knew that the power of the Allies was at last in the ascendant; on September 25, Soviet forces entered Smolensk, one of the cities of Western Russia which had been overrun by the Germans in the autumn of 1941. Four days later the German battleship *Tirpitz* was disabled by British midget submarines which attacked her at her Norwegian anchorage, enabling the Arctic convoys to be renewed. On October 1 British troops entered Naples. With almost no fighting, Corsica and Sardinia were occupied by the Allies. But in the Atlantic, German submarines, equipped with a new type of acoustic torpedo, were proving a danger once more to the convoy-escort vessels, even though, knowing their locations through Enigma, the escorts were able to track them down.

On October 7, alert to the possibility of rapid developments in the Mediterranean, Churchill proposed to the Chiefs of Staff, including Pound's newly-appointed successor Admiral Sir Andrew Cunningham, who in 1915 had served at the Dardanelles, that an operation should be launched to capture the Island of Rhodes, in the Aegean Sea. On the previous day the Joint Planning Committee had submitted a plan for such an attack, dependent upon British forces giving up the much smaller, nearby island of Kos. Churchill welcomed the Rhodes plan, and at once ordered his plane to be made ready; he would fly to Tunis to see Eisenhower, and obtain the troops needed. Nor had he given up hope for holding Kos. Cadogan noted in his diary that night: 'He is excited about Kos and wants to lead an expedition into Rhodes!'

Brooke was angered by Churchill's enthusiasm. 'I can control him no more,' he wrote in his diary. 'He has worked himself into a frenzy of excitement about the Rhodes attack, has magnified its importance so that he can no longer see anything else and has set himself on capturing this one island even at the expense of endangering his relations with the President and the Americans and the future of the Italian campaign. He refused to listen to any arguments or to see any dangers.' That night Churchill's dictation was to Marian Holmes, who wrote in her diary: 'The PM said he had had a bad day, a very bad day. In a rather confiding way he said, "The difficulty is not in winning the war; it is in persuading people to let you win it – persuading fools." He seemed distressed and said he felt "almost like chucking it in". He had been trying to persuade the Americans to invade Rhodes.'

On the following morning Churchill received a telegram from Roosevelt, declining absolutely to agree to an operation against Rhodes; there could be no 'diversion of forces or equipment' that might affect either the advance in Italy to the north of Rome, or the cross-Channel assault, codenamed 'Overlord', now planned for May 1944. Churchill replied that the landing-craft to be used in the Rhodes attack would be able to move back to Britain 'nearly six months' before they would be needed for the cross-Channel assault. But Rooosevelt refused to change his mind.

That afternoon Churchill drove to Chequers. On his way he stopped at the Royal Masonic Hospital where, at the request of the King, he handed Dudley Pound the insignia of the Order of Merit. Pound, the victim of two recent strokes, was unable to speak, but recognised Churchill and grasped his hand. Thirteen days later, on Trafalgar Day, he died.

The Russian Government was pressing Britain to recognise the June 1941 frontiers of the Soviet Union, with the Baltic States and Eastern Poland as a part of Russia. Churchill did not disagree, telling Eden on October 6, 'I think we should do everything in our power to persuade the Poles to agree with the Russians about their Eastern Frontier' in return for Poland being given German territory in East Prussia and Silesia as compensation. This was to be the starting point of the conference of the Three Powers, now planned to take place in Teheran. The matter on which Stalin most sought reassurance was the date and scale of the cross-Channel landing.

In early October, however, more than a month before the Teheran Conference was to take place, Churchill had second thoughts about the date of the cross-Channel landings. The decrypting of a top-secret German signal showed that Hitler, hitherto apparently willing to withdraw his forces in Italy northward, not facing a major battle, now insisted that the line be held south of Rome. Italy was to be fought for with the same determination as Tunisia; nothing was to be given up without the toughest fight. It was therefore clear that the more effort the Allies put into the campaign in Italy, the more German divisions would be sent against them, and the more German divisions they would be able to contain and defeat. Even the Russian front would gain from this diversion of German forces deep into Italy.

There were already eleven Allied divisions in Italy, fighting twenty-five German divisions. A further twenty-two Allied divisions were being assembled in Britain for the cross-Channel landing. Churchill felt that these twenty-two would not be enough for northern Europe but that, if moved to Italy, they could force the Germans into larger commitments and greater losses. For this reason, on October 19 he told the Chiefs of Staff that he feared that by a landing in north-west Europe 'we might be giving the enemy the opportunity to concentrate, by reason of his excellent roads and rail communications, an overwhelming force against us and to inflict on us a military disaster greater than that of Dunkirk. Such a disaster would result in the resuscitation of Hitler and the Nazi regime.'

The Chiefs of Staff agreed that as an alternative to 'Overlord' Britain should reinforce the Italian theatre 'to the full'. By focusing the next phase of military operations in the Mediterranean, she could also 'enter the Balkans', and hold the position in the Aegean Islands, where only Leros was now in British hands. Based both in Britain and now in bases in southern Italy, the Anglo-American bomber force would intensify the air attacks on Germany.

To Eden, who was in Moscow, Churchill explained the new plans on October 20, writing of 'the dangers of our being committed to a lawyer's bargain for "Overlord" in May for the sake of which we may have to ruin the Italian and Balkan possibilities', while at the same time having 'insufficient forces' in northern France 'to maintain ourselves after the thirtieth or fortieth day'. Although Eden replied that the Russians would accept no cancellation or even postponement of 'Overlord', Churchill persevered in his advocacy of the Mediterranean plan. On October 22 he pointed out to Roosevelt that even two British divisions in Sicily, which could have joined the battle in Italy, were about to be transferred to Britain as part of the 'Overlord' build-up and would not be in action for more than six months. To General Marshall he telegraphed on October 24: 'I feel in my marrow the withdrawal of our 50th and 51st Divisions, our best, from the edge of the Battle of Rome in the interests of distant "Overlord". We are carrying out our contract, but I pray God it does not cost us dear.'

These two British divisions were not the only ones being withdrawn on American insistence; two more were about to go, as well as four American divisions, the best in the Italian war zone. On October 26 Churchill wrote to Eden that the battle in Italy must be 'nourished and fought until it is won'; then would be the time for the cross-Channel landing. It should be made clear to Stalin that the assurances given about carrying out 'Overlord' in May could well be 'modified by the exigencies of battle in Italy'. Bitterly Churchill commented, 'This is what happens when battles are governed by lawyers' agreements made in all good faith months before, and persisted in without regard to the ever-changing fortunes of war.' Britain would do its 'very best' for 'Overlord', but, he added, 'it is no use planning for defeat in the field in order to give temporary political satisfaction'.

The British Chiefs of Staff agreed with Churchill, and urged the American Joint Chiefs to give Italy the priority until at least the capture of Rome. British and American landing-craft, which could have been used for an amphibious landing on the Italian coast near Rome, were about to leave the Mediterranean for Britain as part of the 'Overlord' preparations. On October 27 Churchill told the War Cabinet he would resign if his request for 'nourishing the battle' in Italy were refused. Brooke also was emphatic that sufficient forces must be sent to Italy to secure success there.

In order to calm Stalin, Churchill telegraphed to Eden on October 29 to stress that 'Overlord' would not be abandoned, but that the retention of landing-craft in the Mediterranean 'in order not to lose the battle of Rome may cause a slight delay, perhaps till July'. Eisenhower now intervened in Churchill's support to say that if the landing-craft were withdrawn from Italy as planned, his advance on Rome would be delayed until January or even February 1944. When Churchill asked Roosevelt to take this view into account, the American Joint Chiefs agreed that the landing-craft due to leave Italy in mid-December could remain there for one more month. But after that they would have to be transferred. 'Overlord' must not be delayed beyond its agreed May date. The 50th and 51st Divisions were to go back to Britain at once, as were two other British and four American divisions.

Churchill and Roosevelt agreed that they must thrash these matters out face to face, before meeting Stalin. On November 11, troubled by a heavy cold and sore throat, and feeling ill as a result of inoculations for cholera and typhoid, Churchill left London by train for Plymouth, where he again boarded the battleship *Renown*, which had brought him across the Atlantic less than two months earlier. Up to that moment, Captain Pim calculated during their first day at sea, Churchill had travelled a total of 111,000 miles by sea and air since September 1939, spending 792 hours at sea and 339 hours in the air. Reaching Gibraltar, Churchill had a long talk on board ship with the Minster-Resident in North-West Africa, the Conservative MP Harold Macmillan, to whom he expressed his concern that the Mediterranean position both in Italy and in the Aegean Sea had not been exploited 'with vigour and flexibility'. That night Macmillan wrote in his diary, 'It is of course infuriating for Winston, who has felt that all through the war he is fighting like a man with his hands tied behind his back, and yet no one but he, and that with extraordinary patience and skill, could have enticed the Americans into the European war at all.'

On November 16 *Renown* reached Algiers. Again Churchill did not disembark, but had long talks with various senior officers who came on board. When someone remarked that the Chiefs of Staff system was a good one, he commented: 'Not at all. It leads to weak and faltering decisions – or rather indecisions. Why, you may take the most gallant sailor, the most intrepid airman, or the most audacious soldier, put them at a table together – what do you get? The sum total of their fears!'

Reaching Malta on November 17, Churchill felt so unwell that he spent most of his two days there in bed. While at Malta, he learned that the Germans had seized the Dodecanese island of Leros, taking five thousand British soldiers prisoner; it was Germany's 'first success since Alamein', he commented. His efforts to have a weightier Allied initiative and more substantial forces in the Dodecanese had been rejected earlier by the Americans. 'Like you,' he told the British commander in the Eastern Mediterranean, General Sir Maitland Wilson, 'I feel this is a serious loss and reverse, and, like you, I have been fighting with my hands tied behind my back.' From Clementine came a letter of sympathy and encouragement: 'Never forget that when History looks back, your vision & your piercing energy, coupled with your patience & your magnanimity, will all be part of your greatness. So don't allow yourself to be made angry – I often think of your saying that the only worse thing than Allies is *not* having Allies!'

On November 21 *Renown* reached Alexandria. Churchill flew at once to Cairo where, on the following day, he greeted Roosevelt at the airport. The Cairo Conference opened on November 23. Discovering that Roosevelt had never seen the Sphinx or the Pyramids, Churchill drove there with Sarah to make sure that the President would be able to get to them without walking, and then went back to drive there with Roosevelt. 'It was a lovely drive,' Sarah wrote to her mother, 'and the President was charming – simple and enthusiastic. I think he enjoyed himself – I think he enjoyed the trouble Papa took.'

At the Conference itself, Churchill continued to urge the Italian campaign as the first priority, without taking any more forces away from it, until the capture of Rome in January; then taking Rhodes, the principal Dodecanese island, in February; sending supplies to the Yugoslav partisans; and, finally, putting the main effort into the cross-Channel landing, postponed from May to July. Eisenhower supported Churchill's plan to make Italy the first priority, but he wanted to go farther north than Rome; indeed, Eisenhower told the Conference that in his view Italy was 'the correct place in which to deploy our main forces and the objective should be the valley of the Po. In no other area could we so well threaten the whole German structure including France, the Balkans and the Reich itself. Here also our air power would be closer to vital objectives in Germany.'

Eisenhower even wanted 'Overlord' postponed, stressing, as the minutes of the meeting of November 26 noted, 'the vital importance of continuing the maximum possible operations in an established theatre, since much time was invariably lost when the scene of action was changed, necessitating, as it did, the arduous task of building up a new base.' No decision was reached, save only to try to resolve it after Churchill and Roosevelt had seen Stalin. On November 27 they flew in separate planes to Teheran, a five-and-a-half hour flight. Churchill was too tired to dine that night, as he had hoped, with Stalin and Roosevelt. And on the following morning he learned that, an hour before the first formal meeting of the conference, Stalin had seen Roosevelt alone. At this meeting Roosevelt distanced himself from Churchill's, and Eisenhower's, view of the primacy of the Italian campaign. Instead, he 'made it clear', Hopkins told Churchill's doctor, 'that he was anxious to relieve the pressure on the Russian front by invading France'.

The first meeting of the Big Three took place on the afternoon of November 28, Churchill telling the three delegations that they represented probably the 'greatest concentration of worldly power that had ever been seen in the history of mankind'. During their discussion that day, Roosevelt spoke of a possible Allied advance through Italy to the northern Adriatic and Istria, and from there north-east to the Danube. Subsequent mythology was to ascribe this idea to Churchill; but Churchill now suggested that the South of France landing should be considered as the next move after victory in Italy, and that it should take place at the same time as the cross-Channel landing. Stalin favoured this: he did not relish Roosevelt's idea of an Anglo-American army on the Danube.

That evening Roosevelt, the host at a dinner for Churchill and Stalin, felt unwell and went to bed early. His two guests then discussed the future of Germany. Churchill said he would 'forbid all aviation, civil and military', but added that he was not against the 'toilers' in Germany, to which Stalin replied that the Russians shot any working-class prisoners-of-war who, when asked why they fought, said they were only obeying orders. Turning to the question of the Polish border, Churchill suggested that 'Poland might move westward, like soldiers taking two steps left close'. Russia would acquire the eastern third of Poland, and Poland would move westward into Germany. 'If Poland trod on some German toes,' Churchill said, 'that could not be helped, but there must be a strong Poland. This instrument was needed in the orchestra of Europe.' Churchill then took three matches and demonstrated what he had in mind; the Polish eastern frontier moving westward to the old Curzon Line, and the Polish western frontier moving westward to the River Oder. Stalin was pleased.

At the next full session of the conference, Stalin spoke strongly against any postponement of the cross-Channel landing beyond May. On the following day Churchill's advisers told him that the only suitable moon periods at that time were the five days after May 8, and the five days after June 10. At a private meeting with Stalin on the morning of November 30, Churchill explained once more his reasons for wanting to persevere in Italy. The removal of the four British divisions from Italy for 'Overlord' had left the troops still in Italy 'somewhat disheartened' and 'we had not been able to take full advantage of Italy's collapse'. But he went on to point out that the removal of those troops 'also proved the earnestness of our preparations for "Overlord" '. At the full session of the conference that afternoon, it was agreed that the May date for 'Overlord' should stand. The Italian campaign had become a side-show, albeit one in which German divisions would be forced to engage in continual battle.

That night Churchill was host at the third dinner of the conference. As it was his sixty-ninth birthday there were toasts from start to finish. In one of them Churchill raised his glass and said, 'I drink to the Proletarian masses', whereupon Stalin raised his glass, 'I drink to the Conservative Party.' Churchill told Stalin, 'England is getting pinker,' to which Stalin replied, 'It is a sign of good health.'

On the following day the conference discussed Russia's post-war frontier and Poland's acquisition of German territory as compensation. Churchill was prepared, he said, to tell the Poles 'that the plan was a good one and the best they were likely to get, and that His Majesty's Government would not argue against the Soviet Government at the peace table'. He was 'not going to break his heart', Churchill said with some emphasis, 'about the cession of parts of Germany to Poland', or about the cession of the city of Lvov, which Stalin claimed, to Russia. Poland would have to accept the Curzon Line, first proposed by Britain in 1920, thereby excluding the eastern third of the country which Poland had acquired in 1921 after defeating the Russian Bolshevik forces. The Poles, Churchill added, 'would be wise to take our advice; they were getting a country 300 miles square', and he was 'not prepared to make a great squawk about Lvov'. Poland could also get part of East Prussia. Whether they would agree to these gains and losses was doubtful; the minutes recorded Churchill's words: 'We should never get the Poles to say they were satisfied. Nothing would satisfy the Poles.' But he would put it to them that they should accept.

As to Germany, all were agreed that she should be broken up into a number of smaller States; Churchill stressed the need for the 'isolation' of Prussia. He also proposed making the States of southern Germany part of a Danubian Confederation centred around Bavaria, Austria and Hungary; 'a broad, peaceful, cow-like confederation', he described it.

By the end of the Teheran Conference Stalin got the Anglo-American cross-Channel landing and the Soviet Union's western frontier exactly as he wished. On December 2 Churchill flew back to Cairo, where he tried to persuade the Turkish President, Ismet Inönü, to enter the war. Once Turkey joined the Allies, Churchill believed that Bulgaria, Roumania and Hungary, each hitherto loyal to Germany, 'might fall into our hands', and the next Big Three conference 'might be held in Budapest!' But Inönü resisted all blandishments; Turkey, like Argentina, was not to enter the war until just before the final defeat of Germany.

On December 9 Churchill was again feeling unwell. 'He was looking very tired,' Brooke noted in his diary, 'and said he felt very flat, tired, and with pains across his loins.' He was so tired that after his bath he did not have the energy to dry himself, but lay on the bed wrapped in his towel. But each day he held several meetings with experts and advisers, discussing aid to the partisans in Yugoslavia, Greece and Albania, and the possibility of regaining control of the Dodecanese. Among those who dined with him was Julian Amery, who had been working behind German lines in Albania. After dinner on December 10, Amery wrote to his father, reporting Churchill's reply to a question about his future travel plans, 'I am the victim of caprice, and travel on the wings of fancy.'

An hour later Churchill was off again, by air to Tunisia, an eight-and-a-half-hour flight, which ended at the wrong airport. 'They took him out of the plane,' Brooke later recalled, 'and he sat on his suit-case in a very cold morning wind, looking like nothing on earth. We were there about an hour before we moved on, and he was chilled through by then.' The correct destination was an airfield forty miles away, near Carthage, where Eisenhower was waiting. Churchill had intended to fly on from there to Italy, to visit British troops. But he was worn out. 'I am afraid I shall have to stay with you longer than I had planned,' he told Eisenhower. 'I am completely at the end of my tether and I cannot go on to the front until I have recovered my strength.'

Churchill remained in bed throughout December 11. On the following morning his temperature was 101. A pathologist was flown from Cairo and a portable X-ray machine from Tunis; Churchill had pneumonia. He remained in bed, but continued to see visitors and to dictate telegrams to his shorthand writer Patrick Kinna. The doctors protested about the volume of work being done, Kinna later recalled, 'but to no avail'.

On the night of December 14 Churchill's heart began to show signs of strain. Lord Moran feared that he was going to die. Churchill himself was philosophical, telling Sarah, 'If I die, don't worry – the war is won.'

32

Illness and Recovery

On 15 December 1943, as Churchill lay ill at Carthage, Brigadier Bedford, a heart specialist, arrived from Cairo. 'He is giving digitalis to calm the heart,' noted Macmillan. Later that day Lieutenant-Colonel Buttle, an expert on the new antibiotic sulphonamide, M & B, was flown in from Italy. 'I had a long talk with him,' Macmillan wrote, 'and begged him to be firm and *forbid* telegrams or visitors.' That evening Churchill summoned Lord Moran and told him: 'I don't feel well. My heart is doing something funny – it feels to be bumping all over the place.' He had suffered a mild heart attack, 'what is called "fibrillation",' Macmillan noted in his diary on the following day. 'It was not very severe but has alarmed them all.' On December 16 Professor John Scadding, a specialist in chest diseases, was flown from Cairo. Churchill's pulse was steadier and his lung clearing. As he lay in bed, weak but cheerful, he asked Sarah to read to him. Their choice was Jane Austen's *Pride and Prejudice*.

On December 17 Clementine arrived at Carthage to be with her husband. That evening they dined alone. It was nearly six weeks since they had last seen each other. After dinner they were joined by Sarah and Randolph. Lord Moran was rather fussed that the talking went on too long, but, Clementine wrote to Mary, 'Papa showed no sign of fatigue, and once or twice when I got up to go to bed, he would not let me go.' During the night, Churchill suffered a second mild heart attack. 'Papa is very upset,' Clementine told Mary on December 18, 'as he is beginning to see that he cannot get well in a few days and that he will have to lead what for him is a dreary monotonous life with no emotions or excitements.'

Churchill continued to receive visitors, though only one at a time. He also discussed by telegram with the Chiefs of Staff the proposed amphibious landing at Anzio, on the Italian coast just south of Rome. On December 23 both Eisenhower and Alexander came to see him, to discuss details of the landing. Its aim was to lead to the capture of Rome, and an advance northward to the Pisa-Rimini line. On December 24 Churchill left his bed for the first time in two weeks, for a Christmas Eve conference with Alexander and several other Generals, Admirals and planners, about how to provide the landing-craft for Anzio in time for the target date of January 20. Even this, he telegraphed to the Chiefs of Staff shortly after midnight, meant a month's delay in sending some of the 'Overlord' landing-craft to Britain. Then, on Christmas Day, five Commanders-in-Chief, summoned by telegram, converged on Carthage to make the final plans for Anzio, the importance of which was stressed at the outset by Eisenhower, who still felt strongly, as he told the gathering, 'that the right course was to press on in Italy, where the Germans were still full of fight'.

Nothing was to be allowed to interfere with the May date for 'Overlord'. But the Anzio landing had now become the next major Allied operation of war, and Churchill's Christmas Day conference, which he attended in his dragon dressing-gown, set the seal on its importance, retrieving what could be retrieved of the Italian campaign. Admiral Sir John Cunningham was confident that he could put the men ashore. A successful landing, all were agreed, would lead not only to the rapid capture of Rome, but to the destruction of a 'substantial part' of the German forces in Italy. 'We cannot afford to go forward leaving a vast unfinished business behind us,' Churchill telegraphed to Roosevelt when the conference ended. 'If this opportunity is not grasped we must expect the ruin of the Mediterranean campaign of 1944.'

Churchill entertained the five Commanders-in-Chief to Christmas luncheon, his first meal out of bed since he had been taken ill. 'The doctors are quite unable to control him,' his Principal Private Secretary, John Martin, wrote home that day, 'and cigars etc have now returned. I was amazed to find him dictating their bulletin.' As well as dictating the doctors' bulletin, Churchill dictated a resumé for the Chiefs of Staff, and for Roosevelt, of all the military decisions taken at the morning's conference. That night he had a long talk with Macmillan about the French National Committee. He was angered that de Gaulle had turned against several former senior Vichy officials who had agreed some time earlier to work with the Allies, and was unwilling even to see him. Macmillan urged him to do so. 'Well, perhaps you are right,' Churchill said. 'But I do not agree with you.' Then, Macmillan noted in his diary, 'He took my hand in his in a most fatherly way and said: "Come and see me again before I leave Africa, and we'll talk it over". He really is a remarkable man. Although he can be so tiresome and pigheaded, there is no one like him. His devotion to work and duty is quite extraordinary.'

On the morning of December 27 Churchill flew from Carthage to Marrakech. Despite his doctors' worries about the danger of his flying above 10,000 feet in order to cross the mountains, and the need to use an oxygen mask for much of the flight, Air Commodore Kelly, the senior Air Force medical officer in North Africa, who especially accompanied Churchill, later recalled that 'the PM was in great form'. By late afternoon he was at the Villa Taylor, which was to be his home for the next eighteen days. Learning from Roosevelt on December 29 that the President approved the Anzio landing, Churchill telegraphed: 'The sun is shining today, but nothing did me the same good as your telegram showing how easily our minds work together on the grimly simple issues of this vast war.' Alexander had told him that the initial landing would be made by one British and one American division. 'I am glad of this,' he told Roosevelt. 'It is fitting that we should share equally in suffering, risk and honour.'

On December 31 Eisenhower and Montgomery reached Marrakech, to discuss the 'Overlord' plans with Churchill. That day he told Clementine, 'I am not strong enough to paint.' For New Year's Eve, wrote Jock Colville, who had returned to Churchill's Private Office after two years in the Royal Air Force, 'Punch was brewed, the PM made a little speech, the clerks, typists and some of the servants appeared, and we formed a circle to sing Auld Lang Syne.'

On New Year's Day 1944 Churchill went into his wife's room more cheerful. 'I am so happy,' he said, 'I feel so much better.' That day he drove with Montgomery to a spot two hours away where they had a picnic lunch, then drove on into the mountains to a viewpoint which Churchill remembered from his holiday in 1936. 'The General was in the highest spirits,' he later recalled. 'He leapt about the rocks like an antelope, and I felt a strong reassurance that all would be well.'

On January 4 Churchill telegraphed to Stalin, whose troops had just driven the Germans back across the 1939 Russo-Polish frontier, congratulating him on this advance, and telling him that everything was now going 'full blast' for 'Overlord'. Montgomery, he added, 'is full of zeal to engage the enemy and of confidence in the result'. That day Churchill learned that there would be a shortage of landing-craft at Anzio once the actual landing had been effected, as all but a third were to be withdrawn for 'Overlord' before the inevitable counter-attack could be repulsed. He at once proposed flying from Marrakech to Malta, to discuss the question with Alexander. Instead, Alexander persuaded him to allow an American and a British senior officer, General Bedell-Smith and General Gale, both of whom knew all the details, to come and see him at Marrakech. They were able to assure him that the withdrawals would be phased in such a way as to avoid danger.

The Anzio commanders and their planning staffs flew to Marrakech on January 7 for a final two-day discussion. 'Everyone is in good heart,' Churchill telegraphed to Roosevelt when the meetings were over, 'and the resources seem sufficient. Every aspect was thrashed out in full detail by sub-committees in the interval between the two conferences.'

Each morning Churchill worked; then, if the weather was good, he went for a lunchtime picnic. On January 12 de Gaulle was his guest; Churchill urged him to try to avoid such actions against former Vichy supporters as would create 'so wide a schism in France that the resultant friction in any territory that might be liberated would hamper our military operations and therefore be a matter of concern to us.' At one moment, when de Gaulle was being obstinate, Churchill said to him: 'Look here! I am the leader of a strong, unbeaten nation. Yet every morning when I wake my first thought is how can I please President Roosevelt, and my second thought is how can I conciliate Marshal Stalin. Your situation is very different. Why then should your first waking thought be how you can snap your fingers at the British and Americans?'

Churchill's friend Louis Spears had earlier remarked that the hardest cross Britain had to bear was the Cross of Lorraine; but all went well enough that day for de Gaulle to invite Churchill to review the French troops of the Marrakech garrison, and on the morning of January 13 the two men stood side by side on the saluting-base. After the parade Churchill drove off for another of his picnics. 'Winston was in a heavenly mood,' one of those present wrote, 'very funny and very happy.'

On the following day Churchill left Marrakech by air for Gibraltar, where he went on board the battleship *King George V*. During the voyage he spent more than an hour in the Gunroom answering questions from the Midshipmen, one of whom wrote to his parents: 'He seemed amazingly well & has terrific personality which seems to radiate from him.' To Colville, who like himself had been at Harrow, Churchill confided that day that the lines in one of the school songs, 'God give us bases to guard and beleaguer', had always inspired him, despite the fact that he 'detested football'.

Shortly before midnight the battleship reached Plymouth. The King had sent his own train to bring the Prime Minister to London. 'Unlike the previous homecomings,' recalled Churchill's Private Secretary, John Peck, 'there were no political, strategic or diplomatic dramas – the atmosphere was one of immense relief that the PM was back alive and well and truly in control of events.' There was to be no relaxation, however, in Churchill's schedule; reaching London on the morning of January 18 he was in the House of Commons two hours later for Prime Minister's Questions, then, at noon, in his room at the Commons, gave the War Cabinet an account of his travels, leaving his room, Colville noted, 'at 1.28, to lunch with the King at 1.30'.

Hoping for a rapid success at Anzio, on January 19 Churchill suggested to the Chiefs of Staff two follow-up operations. One was a 2,000-strong commando force for the Dalmatian Coast, 'to go round and clean up every single island the Germans have occupied, killing or capturing their garrisons'. The other was an advance into northern Italy, forcing the Germans to withdraw behind the Alps, so that it would then be 'open to us to turn left into France, or to pursue the Germans towards Vienna, or to turn right towards the Balkans'.

Such plans depended upon a rapid success at Anzio, where the landings began in the early hours of January 22. When Alexander reported that immediately after the landing he had sent out 'strong-hitting, mobile patrols' to make contact with the Germans, Churchill replied: 'Am very glad you are pegging out claims rather than digging in beach-heads.' But within four days it became clear that the Germans were determined, and able, to trap the landing forces at the beach-head, and that there would be no quick breakthrough, and no early link-up with the mass of the Allied armies to the south. 'The Germans are fighting magnificently,' Churchill told a friend during an evening at the Other Club on January 27. 'Never imagine they are crashing. Their staff work is brilliantly flexible. They improvise units out of unrested remnants and those units fight just as well as the fresh ones.'

By January 28 it was clear that Anzio had failed in its purpose. 'The situation as it now stands,' Churchill telegraphed to Sir John Cunningham, 'bears little relation to the lightning thrust envisaged at Marrakech', and to the Chiefs of Staff he confided on January 29: 'We hoped to land a wild cat that would tear the bowels out of the Boche. Instead we have stranded a vast whale with its tail flopping about in the water.' Two days later, as the two senior American generals involved, Mark Clark and John Lucas, consolidated the bridgehead, Churchill told the War Cabinet that Anzio had now become 'an American operation, with no punch in it'. Nor did he have any means of influencing the American Joint Chiefs, who on February 3 decided to transfer fighter aircraft from the Mediterranean to China, on the assumption that the Allied role in Italy would henceforth be purely defensive.

Churchill was distressed by this; the assumption of the defensive in Italy 'is I think disastrous', he told the Chiefs of Staff on February 3. 'I never imagined that Alexander would not be free to push on to the north and break into the Po Valley.' To bring the armies in Italy to a standstill, he warned, 'would be most short-sighted and would simply enable the enemy to transfer divisions rapidly from North Italy to oppose the "Overlord" landing'.

To help the cross-Channel landing, the largest amphibious enterprise of all time, Churchill now presided over an 'Overlord' Committee of the War Cabinet, whose task was to ensure that nothing was neglected or delayed. His 'fiery energy and undisputed authority dominated the proceedings,' Ismay later recalled. 'The seemingly slothful or obstructive were tongue-lashed; competing differences were reconciled; priorities were settled; difficulties which at first appeared insuperable were overcome; and decisions were translated into immediate action.'

British weapons were to be dropped in Poland; as the Red Army drew ever nearer it was in Britain's interest, Churchill told the Defence Committee on February 3, that Poland should be 'strong and well-supported. Were she weak and overrun by the advancing Soviet armies, the result might hold great dangers in the future for the English-speaking peoples.'

Stalin was a master of deception; on February 5 he assured Churchill that 'of course Poland would be free and independent and he would not attempt to influence the kind of Government they cared to set up after the war'. On the following day Churchill urged the Polish Government in London to accept these assurances, and to cede Eastern Poland to Russia in return for German territory in East Prussia, Silesia and on the Baltic coast of Pomerania. Ten days later, at a meeting on February 16, he told the Polish Government leaders, in the words of the transcript of the discussion: 'The Poles must rejoice at the advance of the Russian armies, dangerous though this might be to them, since it was their only hope of liberation from the Germans. There was no reason to suppose that Russia would repeat the German desire to dominate all Europe. After the war Great Britain and the United States of America would maintain strong forces, and there were good hopes of the world settling down into a peace of thirty or forty years which might then prove much more lasting.' But if Poland rejected the proposed borders and took up a position against the Russians, he 'doubted whether the United States would be ready to go on fighting in Europe for several years to liberate Warsaw. It was no use expecting us to do more than we could.'

Churchill argued in vain; the Polish Government in London was only prepared to consider ceding territory to Russia if it could have an assurance that an all-Party Government would be established in Poland as soon as she was liberated. Stalin would give no such assurance. He already had his own Polish nominees for an all-Communist Government waiting in the wings, ready to be installed in the first town to be liberated.

On February 22 Churchill gave the Commons a survey of the war. In answer to criticisms of the bombing of German cities, he explained that the Anglo-American bombing of Germany was 'our chief offensive effort at the present time'. Since the war began, 38,300 British pilots and aircrew had been killed and more than ten thousand aircraft lost. But in the previous forty-eight hours, nine thousand tons of bombs had been dropped on Germany. 'The air power was the weapon which both marauding States selected as their main tool of conquest,' Churchill told the House. 'This was the sphere in which they were to triumph. This was the method by which the nations were to be subjugated to their rule. I shall not moralise further than to say that there is a strange, stern justice in the long swing of events.'

Air power, as well as Russia's increasingly clear determination to dominate Eastern Europe despite Stalin's recent promises, was on Churchill's mind at Chequers on March 4, when he told his guests that he did not have long to live, but that he had a political testament for after the war, 'Far more important than India or the Colonies or solvency is *the Air*. We live in a world of wolves – and *bears*.' The latest evidence of Stalin's attitude to an independent Poland, Churchill told the War Cabinet two days later, suggested 'he was unlikely to be influenced by argument'. On March 10 Churchill warned Stalin that Russian treatment of Poland 'will prove to be a touchstone and make all sorts of far more important things far more difficult'. And in a covering message to the British Ambassador in Moscow, Sir Archibald Clark Kerr, he commented, 'Appeasement has had a good run.'

It was now less than three months before the cross-Channel landings. As well as presiding over the weekly 'Overlord' Committee of the War Cabinet, Churchill had regular talks with Eisenhower and his Chief of Staff, General Bedell Smith, with whom he examined every aspect of the landings, among them the artificial harbours, the airborne assault, the naval bombardment, and the air support. 'I am satisfied that everything is going on well,' he telegraphed to Marshall on March 11. By a diligent reading of enemy top-secret cypher messages and other Intelligence reports, British staffs had built up a comprehensive picture of the location and size of every German unit in northern France.

By a successful British plan of deception, devised by Colonel John Bevan and his staff at the Central War Rooms, the Germans were led to believe that the main assault would come somewhere between Dieppe and Calais. It was once more the Germans' own top-secret messages that, painstakingly decrypted, revealed that they had fallen for the deception. The true landing-point, the Normandy coast, was kept secret from them. So too was the one condition for the landing laid down by the Chiefs of Staff: if, at the date chosen for the assault, the Germans had twenty mobile divisions in France capable of being sent to reinforce their troops at the beach-head, the whole operation would be called off.

To decide what to do if there were indeed twenty German mobile divisions in France on the date chosen, Churchill proposed flying to Bermuda for a discussion with Roosevelt. But while Lord Moran protested in vain that it was 'all wrong' that the Prime Minister should go, Roosevelt's doctors were successful in persuading the President, who was suffering from a heavy cold, not to risk the journey. Churchill was relieved. 'The PM this morning confessed he was tired,' Cadogan wrote in his diary on March 21. 'He is almost done in.'

In Italy, the Anzio beach-head was still encircled by the Germans; the main Allied forces, then fifty miles to the east, were unable to reach them because of a tenacious German defence at Monte Cassino. There was now no chance of the capture of Rome that spring, or of any exploitation farther north. The only remaining point of pressure on Germany that year, in the west, would be Normandy.

On March 23 Churchill went with Eisenhower on a two-day inspection of the American troops in Britain who would be taking part in the Normandy landings. Returning to Chequers, he worked for two days on his first broadcast for exactly a year. 'The PM seemed very tired but sweet-tempered and solicitous,' Marian Holmes noted in her diary at the end of the first day. In his broadcast, made from Chequers on the evening of March 26, Churchill, who knew how close Germany now was to developing a rocket bomb, spoke of possible new 'forms of attack' from Germany. But, he declared, 'Britain can take it. She has never flinched or failed. And when the signal is given, the whole circle of avenging nations will hurl themselves upon the foe and batter the life out of the cruellest tyranny which has ever sought to bar the progress of mankind.'

Many of those who listened to Churchill's broadcast could sense that he was tired. 'People seem to think that Winston's broadcast last night was that of a worn and petulant old man,' Harold Nicolson noted in his diary. Worn he certainly was; two days later Brooke noted in his diary after a Staff Conference: 'We found him in desperately tired mood. I am afraid that he is losing ground rapidly. He seems quite incapable of concentrating for a few minutes on end, and keeps wandering continuously. He kept yawning and said he was feeling desperately tired.' Exhaustion, too, emerged; on March 29, after the Government had been defeated on a clause in the Education Bill, as a result of a Conservative backbench revolt in favour of equal pay for men and women teachers, Churchill insisted on a vote of confidence. 'He looked tired, wounded and barely audible,' noted Henry Channon. In the smoking-room, Nicolson told him that it had been excessive to insist the rebels swallow their vote. Could not some other method be devised to humble them? 'No. Not at all,' Churchill replied. 'I am not going to tumble round my cage like a wounded canary. You knocked me off my perch. You have now got to put me back on my perch. Otherwise I won't sing.'

The vote was taken on March 31. 'The Government got its majority of over 400,' Colville noted in his diary, 'and the PM was radiant. I thought it was cracking a nut with a sledgehammer.' Churchill was already on the move again, travelling by train overnight to Yorkshire, for a visit to the British troops training for the Normandy landings. One of the demonstrations he was shown was a lorry swimming through water.

On April 7, Good Friday, Churchill spoke to all the senior British and American officers involved in the Normandy plan. Wrote Brooke, 'He was looking old and lacking a great deal of his usual vitality.' Commented the Director of Military Operations at the War Office, General Kennedy: 'Winston spoke without vigour. He did not look up much while he spoke. There was the usual wonderful flow of phrases, but no fire in the delivery. I thought he was going to burst into tears as he stepped down to sit beside Eisenhower and Monty and the Chiefs of Staff while the officers filed out of the room. But I afterwards heard that members of the audience who saw him on that day for the first time were tremendously impressed and inspired.'

Churchill was physically exhausted. 'Struck by how very tired and worn out the PM looks now,' Colville noted in his diary on April 12. Churchill was greatly disappointed that week to learn from Alexander, who had flown back to London, that the Anzio beach-head, although secure, could still not be linked up with the main army in Italy, nor could a new attempt to do so be started for another month. Nevertheless, he was able to ensure that no further troops would be withdrawn from Italy. 'Although the fighting at the bridge-head and on the Cassino front has brought many disappointments,' Churchill told General Marshall on April 12, 'you will I trust recognise that at least eight extra German divisions have been brought into Italy down to the south of Rome and heavily mauled there'. The Enigma decrypts, Churchill pointed out, showed that Hitler had been saying 'that his defeats in South Russia are due to the treacherous Badoglio collapse of Italy which has involved thirty-five divisions'.

'At any rate,' Churchill added, 'I believe that our action in Italy has played a large part in rendering possible the immensely important advances made in South Russia, which as a further benefit are convulsing the Satellites'. Churchill now addressed the question of what the Allied object in Italy should be, telling Marshall, in support of a renewed British plea for landing-craft to be transferred at once from the Pacific to the Mediterranean: 'At the moment my own position is as follows. We should above all defeat the German army south of Rome and join our own armies. Nothing should be grudged for this. We cannot tell how either the Allied or enemy armies will emerge from the battle until the battle has been fought. It may be that the enemy will be thrown into disorder, and that great opportunities of exploitation may be open. Or we may be checked, and the enemy may continue to hold his positions south of Rome against us with his existing forces. On the other hand, he may seek to withdraw some of his divisions to the main battle in France. It seems to me we must have plans and preparations to take advantage of the above possibilities.'

If the advance to Rome were successful, Churchill told Marshall, 'I would not now rule out either a vigorous pursuit northward of the beaten enemy nor an amphibious cat's-claw higher up to detain him or cut him off.' Plans and preparations ought to be contrived 'to render possible' either an amphibious landing north of Rome or the South of France landing 'in one form or another'. If thirty-four German divisions could be kept in the western Mediterranean theatre, he explained, 'the forces there will have made an immense contribution to "Overlord" '. Churchill then told Marshall that he had 'hardened very much upon "Overlord"', and was 'further fortified by the evident confidence of Eisenhower, Brooke and Montgomery'.

As the plans for the cross-Channel attack proceded, Churchill was worried about the scale of French civilian casualties likely to be caused by the planned bombing of railway lines and rail junctions in northern France prior to the attack. Such casualties were estimated at between twenty and forty thousand. 'Considering that they are our friends,' Churchill wrote to Eisenhower, 'this might be held to be an act of very great severity, bringing much hatred on the Allied Air Forces.' Eisenhower agreed to reduce the scale of the bombing, but even so it was severe, and at least five thousand French civilians were killed.

Churchill worked both to ensure the success of the Normandy landings, and to mitigate the severity of the bombing of northern France. Those who worked closest with him were aware of the great strains upon him. 'PM, I fear, is breaking down,' Cadogan noted in his diary after a War Cabinet on April 19. 'He rambles without a pause and we really got nowhere.' Cadogan added: 'I am really fussed about the PM. He is *not* the man he was twelve months ago, and I really don't know if he can carry on.' But carry on he did, and once again with renewed energy. In a debate on April 21, on the British Empire and Commonwealth, in which he looked forward to India being a self-governing Dominion after the war, his speech showed 'more vigour' than of late, Colville noted.

The month of May opened with a British protest to Russia, whose forces had entered Roumania and begun the widespread arrest of anti-Communist as well as Fascist leaders. The Russians at once complained about

British interference, leading Churchill to tell Eden on May 2, 'Never forget that Bolsheviks are crocodiles.' And when further unjustified complaints arrived from Moscow a week later about alleged British interference in Roumania, Churchill told the War Cabinet that these complaints 'led him to despair of the possibility of maintaining good relations with Russia'. In Greece also he feared that a showdown was approaching because of 'Communist intrigues'. 'We ought to watch this movement carefully,' he warned Eden on May 4. 'After all, we lost 40,000 men in Greece and you were very keen on that effort at that time. I do not think we should yield to the Russians any more in Greece.'

Recurring weariness was now a regular feature of Churchill's day. 'He looked very old and tired' was Brooke's comment on May 7. Churchill told Brooke that evening, Brooke noted in his diary, that he could still sleep well, eat well, 'and especially drink well, but that he no longer jumped out of bed the way he used to, and felt as if he would be quite content to spend the whole day in bed'. Brooke added, 'I have never yet heard him admit that he was beginning to fail.' Churchill was sixty-nine. On May 10 he reached the fourth anniversary of his Premiership; more than two hundred weeks of responsibility and worry. Above all was the frightening spectre of the Normandy landings. To an American visitor, John J. McCloy, the Under Secretary for War, Churchill confided, 'If you think I'm dragging my feet, it is not because I can't take casualties, it is because I am afraid of what those casualties will be.' He then told McCloy of the large number of his contemporaries who had been killed in what he called the 'hecatombs' of the First World War. He himself was 'a sort of "sport" in nature's sense as most of his generation lay dead at Passchendaele and the Somme. An entire British generation of potential leaders had been cut off and Britain could not afford the loss of another generation.'

On May 12 Churchill left London for three days of inspection of the assembling troops. To Eisenhower, who came with him for part of the journey, he had already stressed the need for extra vehicles to cater for the Free French Division which had been added to the landing force. In his appeal, Churchill pointed out that at the Anzio beach-head 125,000 men and 23,000 vehicles 'only got twelve miles' before being brought to a halt by the Germans. Churchill's vigilance and drive were a crucial component of the war-making capacity of Britain. 'Whatever may be the PM's shortcomings,' Colville noted on May 13, 'there is no doubt that he does provide guidance and purpose for the Chiefs of Staff and the Foreign Office on matters which, without him, would often be lost in the maze of inter-departmentalism, or frittered away by caution and compromise. Moreover, he has two qualities, imagination and resolution, which are conspicuously lacking among other Ministers and the Chiefs of Staff.' At the final briefing for senior officers on May 15, General Kennedy noted in his diary that Churchill spoke 'in a robust and even humorous style, and concluded with a moving expression of his hopes and good wishes. He looked much better than at the last conference, and spoke with great vigour, urging offensive leadership, and stressing the ardour for battle which he believed the men felt.'

On May 20 Churchill received a clear indication that the Germans would not have the additional twenty divisions in Western Europe which would have meant that the Normandy landings would have to be called off. Helped by British military supplies parachuted to them, Tito's partisans were holding down twenty-five German divisions in Yugoslavia, where Randolph was then serving as one of the British liaison officers with Tito. A further twenty-three German divisions were being engaged in Italy, where Alexander had renewed the offensive on May 14 and finally taken Cassino. Further German divisions were waiting on the Channel Coast near Boulogne for what was believed by the Germans, thanks to successful deception, to be the true target of the cross-Channel assault. The size and location of all these divisions were known through the German top-secret messages being decrypted every day at Bletchley, through agents, and through the ever-vigilant eyes of Air Force reconnaissance aircraft. Churchill's daughter Sarah was then serving with the Photographic Reconnaissance Interpretation Unit at Medmenham, west of London.

When he spoke in the Commons on May 24, Churchill again seemed tired. 'His charm and humour were unabated,' Harold Nicolson wrote to his sons, 'but the voice was not thunderous and three times Members called out to him to "Speak up!".' Five days later, in reply to a request to have his portrait painted, he replied with a wry humour, 'I am afraid I can make no promise in wartime, and will hardly be worth painting unless the war stops soon.'

During May 24 Churchill was told of a shortage of naval pumping equipment needed to raise the concrete caissons of the Mulberry harbour in order to tow them across the Channel. This crucial element in the assault had to be solved at once. It was Churchill who suggested calling upon the pumping resources of the London Fire Brigade.

On the last weekend before the Normandy landings, Churchill was at Chequers. There, he learned that Randolph had just escaped, with Tito, from a German parachute attempt to capture the Partisan headquarters. On May 28 Churchill wrote to Randolph: 'We have a lovely day at where we live from time to time, and all is fair with the first glory of summer. The war is very fierce and terrible, but in these sunlit lawns and buttercup meadows it is hard to conjure up its horrors.' On the following day, reading of the high French civilian deaths as the Allied bombing of French railway junctions intensified, Churchill wrote to the air commander, disagreeing that the 'best targets' had been chosen. 'You are piling up an awful load of hatred,' he wrote.

Alexander now reported that the troops at Anzio had joined with the main army in Italy; all was now ready for the advance to Rome. 'How lucky it was,' Churchill telegraphed to him on May 31, 'that we stood up to our United States Chief of Staff friends and refused to deny you the full exploitation of this battle!' As Alexander prepared for the battle of Rome, Admiral Ramsay was put in command of all naval forces in the Channel. On the following day, June 2, Churchill left London by train to visit troop assembly points in southern England. On June 3 he watched troops at Southampton embarking on their landing-craft; on the following day he visited more troops as they embarked. After he returned to the train, Marian Holmes noted in her diary, 'he looked anxious, but he was amiable'.

On the evening of June 4 Churchill returned to London, to No.10 Annexe. 'Went into PM at 10.30 pm and didn't emerge until 3.45 am,' Marian Holmes wrote in her diary. 'He drives himself too hard and he nearly fell asleep over the papers.' During the night's work Churchill went along the corridor to his Map Room. While he sat there in his chair, looking up at the maps, the news was brought in that Rome had been captured.

It had been hoped to launch the Normandy landings on June 5, but bad weather had forced a postponement of one day. During June 5 it became clear from decrypted German top-secret messages that, because of this bad weather, the Germans no longer expected a cross-Channel attack during the next four or five days. Rommel had even gone on leave that day to Germany. The Allied knowledge that this was the German calculation was a factor in Eisenhower's decision to cross on the following day, despite a poor weather forecast.

Churchill had no visitors on the morning of June 5. As he dictated to his secretaries, he was brought a note from Clementine, who wrote, 'I feel so much for you at this agonising moment – so full of suspense, which prevents one from rejoicing over Rome!' 'Tonight we go,' Churchill telegraphed to Stalin on the afternoon of June 5. 'We are using 5,000 ships, and have available 11,000 aircraft.'

Churchill and Clementine dined alone on the night of June 5. Then he went to the Map Room for a last look at the Allied and German dispositions, the latter revealed largely by Enigma decrypts. Before going to bed, Clementine joined him in the Map Room. His concerns were with those who in a few hours' time would be approaching the beaches of German-occupied France, of Hitler's much-vaunted Fortress Europe. 'Do you realise,' he told her, 'that by the time you wake up in the morning, twenty thousand men may have been killed?'

33

Normandy and Beyond

As Churchill slept in the early hours of 6 June 1944, the first glider-borne troops landed in Normandy. When he woke up, he was told that these landings had been unopposed. He spent most of the morning in his Map Room, the landings being plotted for him as the news came in. At midday he went to the Commons, where he told a hushed and expectant House, 'This vast operation is undoubtedly the most complicated and difficult that has ever taken place.' He returned to the House that evening, to say that all was proceeding 'in a thoroughly satisfactory manner'. By the following morning the last of the German opposition on the beaches had been overcome; in the first twenty-four hours' fighting, three thousand troops had been killed. 'We had expected to lose 10,000 men,' Churchill telegraphed that day to Stalin.

The public was exhilarated by the initial successes, so much so that when Churchill spoke in the Commons on June 8 he felt the need to advise MPs to give 'strong warnings against over-optimism' when they spoke in their constituencies, and to combat the idea 'that these things are going to be settled with a run'. Great dangers lay behind, but 'enormous exertions lie before us'. On June 9 Churchill learned of the extent of those exertions, when he was told that although the British and American forces had linked up their beach-heads, the Americans were already twenty-four hours behind schedule, and that heavy German opposition had been encountered 'along the whole British front'. Indeed the British line had remained virtually static for twenty-four hours, and Caen, the vital objective for that day, was as yet beyond their grasp. Worst of all, insufficient land had been liberated to set up air-strips, with the result that all air support had to come from bases in England. This was a blow, leading Churchill to wonder whether the Allies might not have to be content for some time to come with securing the Cherbourg and Brest Peninsulas, and no more; 'the smaller and larger lunette', he called them.

Despite a tenacious German defence, nearly 400,000 men were ashore by midday on June 10. 'One united heave,' Churchill telegraphed that day to Tito, 'and we may be freed from the agonies of war, and the menace of tyranny.' In Italy, Alexander was driving northwards the remains of twenty-three German divisions. In Russia, Stalin had launched the first phase of his promised summer offensive. On the morning of June 12, Churchill's train took him to Dover, where he crossed the Channel by destroyer, then transferred to the barge of the Admiral commanding the British naval forces at the beach-head, Admiral Vian of *Cossack* fame. On board the barge, he sang a song he had learned during his schooldays at Harrow. It was about the Spanish Armada and in it were the lines,

> *But snug in her hive, the Queen was alive,*
> *And Buzz was the word in the Island.*

The sailors listened, but to Churchill's disappointment, he told the boys of Harrow seven years later, 'not one of them knew the words'. From the barge, he clambered on to an American amphibious army truck which ran him up the beach at Courseulles. Montgomery met him at the beach and drove him by jeep to his headquarters château at Cruelly, five miles inland and about three miles from the front. The château had been heavily bombed the night before. 'I told him,' Churchill later wrote, 'he was taking too much of a risk if he made a habit of such proceedings. Anything can be done once or for a short time, but custom, repetition, prolongation, is always to be avoided when possible in war.' Returning to Courseulles, Churchill saw a German air raid on the harbour. Then he re-embarked in Vian's barge and sailed along the shore, watching landing-craft unloading lorries, tanks and guns. West of Hamel he saw an artificial harbour being prepared, with its caissons, wave-dampeners and floating piers. Close by was a monitor with 14-inch guns, firing inland. 'Winston said he had never been on one of His Majesty's ships engaging the enemy and insisted on going aboard,' Brooke, who was with him, noted in his diary. 'Luckily we could not climb up owing to seaweed on the bilges, as it would have been a very noisy entertainment had we succeeded. Then we returned to our destroyer and went right back to the east end of the beach where several ships were bombarding the Germans.'

As the destroyer was about to turn, Churchill said to Vian, 'Since we are so near, why shouldn't we have a plug at them ourselves before we go home?'

'Certainly,' Vian replied, and within a few moments all his guns were firing on the coast. 'We were of course well within the range of their artillery,' Churchill later wrote, 'and the moment we had fired Vian made the destroyer turn about and depart at the highest speed. We were soon out of danger and passed through the cruiser and battleship lines. This is the only time I have ever been on board a naval vessel when she fired "in anger" – if it can so be called. I admired the Admiral's sporting spirit.'

On the three-hour sea voyage back to Portsmouth, Churchill slept. When he returned to London he was told that 13,000 German soldiers had already been taken prisoner. That evening, however, while Churchill was dining with Clementine and Mary, Captain Pim came in to report that the first German flying bombs were on their way. During the night twenty-seven were despatched across the Channel. Four reached London, and two people were killed. Churchill and the Chiefs of Staff decided to divert aircraft needed for Normandy to bomb the launching-sites, of which sixty-seven had been identified by June 14, but bad weather over the Calais area impeded the counter-attacks. On the following night, fifty flying bombs exploded in the London area. When one of Churchill's Private Secretaries, Christopher Dodds, left the Annexe with John Peck to see if anything was visible, 'we met the PM who had already been out to see for himself'. It was an episode, Dodds later recalled, 'exemplifying the PM's energy and (hair-raising!) disregard for personal danger'. Churchill's comment, in a telegram to Stalin, was, 'We had a noisy night.'

On June 18, sixty-three service personnel and fifty-eight civilians were killed when a flying bomb fell on the Guards Chapel during a church service. That night, at a Staff Conference, and on the following night at a specially convened War Cabinet Committee, Churchill and his advisers discussed the measures needed to prevent public panic. 'He was at his best,' the First Sea Lord, Admiral Cunningham, noted in his diary, 'and said the matter had to be put robustly to the populace, that their tribulations were part of the battle in France, and that they should be very glad to share in the soldiers' dangers.' It was agreed that when the flying bombs came, as they did at every hour of the day and night, the air-raid sirens should be sounded as little as possible. 'The PM said one must have sleep,' Cunningham noted, 'and you either woke well-rested, or in a better land!'

More than half a million Allied soldiers were ashore in Normandy. But still the Germans held Caen. In London, 526 civilians had been killed by the end of the first week of the flying-bomb attacks. Almost permanent conferences were being held in Churchill's Map Room to determine the best means of countering the attacks; of 700 flying bombs sent over in the first week, two hundred had been shot down by anti-aircraft guns and fighters. To reduce the danger of one method of defence impeding the other, Churchill proposed that the fighters should have a 'free run' by day and the anti-aircraft guns by night. The new weapon was an ever-present danger; while dictating a telegram to Roosevelt on June 20, about post-war

Anglo-American oil policy, Churchill broke off his line of argument to tell the President, 'At this moment a flying bomb is approaching this dwelling.' After continuing his dictation a few moments longer he added, 'Bomb has fallen some way off.'

An acrimonious dispute now arose between the British and Americans. It had its origins in the Italian war zone. Four French and three American divisions were about to be taken away from Alexander's army in Italy for the landing in the South of France, planned for August 15. On June 15 the Joint Planning Committee in London, on the basis of the German Army's own top-secret signals, had advised the British Chiefs of Staff that the South of France landing would be a less effective blow to the German forces than renewing the advance in Italy at full strength, and launching an amphibious landing at the head of the Adriatic, to be followed by an advance into northern Yugoslavia. At a Staff Conference on June 22 Churchill supported this recommendation, telling the Chiefs of Staff that, on the basis of the top-secret information available of Germany's own plans, an amphibious landing 'at the head of the Adriatic in the Trieste area' would be more effective than a South of France landing in drawing German divisions away from Normandy. It was clear from the Enigma decrypts that the Germans would not defend the South of France with any real zeal, but they would defend the passes leading from Italy to Austria with tenacity, sending down more and more forces to prevent an Allied breakthrough from the south.

   Alexander was eager to continue his attack northward through Italy. General Maitland Wilson, commanding the British Forces in the Middle East, was keen to carry out an amphibious landing at the head of the Adriatic, and strike eastward, first to Zagreb, then towards Austria and the Danube. Churchill and the British Chiefs of Staff pressed Roosevelt and the American Chiefs for an amphibious landing at the head of the Adriatic. On June 28 their view seemed to be reinforced by a top-secret German naval signal, sent early that day and decrypted at Bletchley the same morning: a directive from Hitler himself which made it clear that he intended to hold the Apennines at all cost. 'And now we have the most marvellous information,' Brooke noted in his diary, 'indicating clearly the importance Hitler attaches to northern Italy.' It would be a 'grave strategic error', Brooke, Portal and Cunningham telegraphed to the American Chiefs of Staff later that day, 'not to take advantage of destroying the German forces at present in Italy and thus drawing further reserves on to this front'.

   That day Churchill telegraphed to Roosevelt to remind him of 'how you spoke to me at Teheran about Istria'. He also sent Roosevelt a copy of the decrypted German naval signal. But on the following day Roosevelt re-jected the Adriatic plan, telling Churchill that for 'purely political considerations' in the United States he would never survive 'even a slight setback' in Normandy if it became known 'that fairly large forces had been diverted to the Balkans'. Churchill hastened to point out that the new plan had nothing to do with the Balkans. At the Teheran Conference 'you emphasised to me the possibilities of a move eastward when Italy was conquered, and specifically mentioned Istria. No one involved in these discussions has ever thought of moving armies into the Balkans; but Istria and Trieste in Italy are strategic and political positions, which you saw yourself very clearly might exercise profound and widespread reactions, especially now after the Russian advances.'

Roosevelt proposed putting the dispute to Stalin. Churchill was against this, pointing out that on a 'long-term political view' Stalin might well prefer the British and Americans to do their fighting in France 'and that East, Middle and southern Europe should fall naturally into his control.'

Churchill decided to go to see Roosevelt to put the Adriatic plan to him in person. On June 30 he gave orders for both his flying boat and his Lancaster bomber to be made ready for a flight across the Atlantic. But Roosevelt had made up his mind; the South of France landing would go ahead, and Alexander's army in Italy must therefore be reduced in strength. 'What can I do Mr President,' Churchill telegraphed on July 1, 'when your Chiefs of Staff insist on casting aside our Italian offensive campaign, with all its dazzling possibilities, relieving Hitler of all his anxieties in the Po basin (*vide* Boniface), and when we are to see the integral life of this campaign drained off into the Rhone Valley in the belief that it will in several months carry effective help to Eisenhower so far away in the north?' Churchill added, 'I am sure that if we could have met, as I so frequently proposed, we should have reached a happy agreement.'

Roosevelt would not change his mind. Churchill and the British Chiefs of Staff, and their two senior military commanders in the Mediterranean, were forced to abandon their preferred strategy. Alexander would not be allowed to exploit a known German weakness, and a classic opportunity. It was a low ebb in the Anglo-American wartime relationship.

By June 28 the number of Allied soldiers killed since the Normandy landings had reached 7,704, of whom 4,868 were American, 2,443 British and 393 Canadian. In London the flying bombs had exacted a heavy toll; in the first sixteen days' bombardment 1,935 civilians had been killed. On June 30 Churchill and his wife spent the day visiting anti-aircraft units active in the battle against the flying bomb. Elizabeth Layton noted, 'It really was rather fun, Master and Mistress sitting amid the corn, cameras snapping on every side, rather anxious Generals rushing about.'

'Is there anything on the cards?' asked Churchill, but no bombs came over. On the following day he learned that Soviet forces, advancing along the whole Eastern Front, had in a single battle near Bobruisk killed 16,000 German soldiers and taken 18,000 prisoners. 'This is the moment,' he telegraphed to Stalin, 'to tell you how immensely we are all here impressed with the magnificent advances of the Russian Armies which seem, as they grow in momentum, to be pulverising the German Armies which stand between you and Warsaw, and afterwards Berlin.' Churchill added that in Normandy more than three-quarters of a million troops were now ashore, and 50,000 Germans had been taken prisoner. 'The enemy is bleeding on every front at once, and I agree with you that this must go on to the end.'

On July 6 the flying-bomb death toll reached 2,752. It was a weapon, Churchill told the Commons that day, 'literally and essentially indiscriminate in its nature, purpose and effect'. That night, because of the danger of flying bombs, the Staff Conference was held in the underground Central War Rooms. 'There is no doubt the PM was in no state to discuss anything,' Andrew Cunningham wrote in his diary, and he added, 'Very tired and too much alcohol.' Eden, who was also present, called it a 'deplorable evening'. When Churchill began to criticise Montgomery, noting that even Eisenhower had called him 'over-cautious', Brooke lost his temper at Churchill's criticism.

When the meeting was over Churchill returned above ground to the Annexe, for his nightly dictation. 'PM in mellow mood and quite chatty for him,' noted Marian Holmes. 'Loads of work and got to bed finally at 3.40 am.' In search for some possible means of retaliation that might force the Germans to call off the flying-bomb attacks, Churchill dictated a minute that night to the Chiefs of Staff about the possible use of gas. 'I should be prepared to do anything,' he wrote, 'that might hit the Germans in a murderous place. I may certainly have to ask you to support me in using poison gas. We could drench the cities of the Ruhr and many other cities in Germany in such a way that most of the population would be requiring constant medical attention. We could stop all work at the flying-bomb starting points.'

Churchill had in mind mustard gas 'from which nearly everyone recovers'. He would use it only if 'it was life or death for us' or if it would 'shorten the war by a year'. To this end it might even be used on the Normandy beach-head. 'It is absurd to consider morality on this topic,' he wrote, 'when everybody used it in the last war without a word of complaint from the moralists or the Church. On the other hand, in the last war the bombing of open cities was regarded as forbidden. Now everybody does it as a matter of course. It is simply a question of fashion changing, as she does between long and short skirts for women.'

It would be several weeks or even months, Churchill added, 'before I shall ask you to drench Germany with poison gas'. In the meantime he wanted the matter studied, he wrote, 'in cold blood by sensible people, and not by that particular set of psalm-singing uniformed defeatists which one runs across, now here, now there'. The enquiries were made. It emerged that the Air Staff had already made plans for one-fifth of Britain's bomber effort to be employed on dropping gas, if such a form of warfare were decided on. But the military experts to whom Churchill remitted the question doubted whether gas, of the essentially non-lethal kind envisaged by Churchill, could have a decisive effect, and no gas raids were made. 'Clearly,' he commented, 'I cannot make headway against the parsons and the warriors at the same time.'

News had just reached London of the mass murder in specially-designed gas chambers of more than two and a half million Jews at Auschwitz, which had hitherto been identified only as a slave-labour camp. In early July it became clear that more than half a million Hungarian Jews were in the process of being deported to their deaths there. When the Zionist leader Dr Chaim Weizmann appealed to Eden for the bombing of the railway lines to the camp, Eden showed his appeal to Churchill, who minuted that same day, July 7, 'Get anything out of the Air Force you can, and invoke me if necessary.' Weizmann also asked for the strongest possible public protest. 'I am entirely in accord with the biggest outcry possible,' was Churchill's immediate response.

The outcry was made at once, in the form of considerable press coverage of the killings, and radio broadcasts from London to the Hungarian railway workers, warning them that they would be considered war criminals if they continued to participate in the deportations. Within forty-eight hours the Hungarian Government forced the German authorities in Hungary to end the deportations. More than a hundred thousand Jews had been saved.

Before news of the halt to the Hungarian deportations was known, Churchill rejected a Gestapo offer to 'negotiate' the release of a million Hungarian Jews in return for trucks, food and money. The offer was a ruse by the Gestapo, intended to give the Jews of Hungary a false hope of rescue, at the very moment when more than 400,000 of them were being deported to their deaths; it was 'a naked piece of blackmail on threats of murder', Churchill told Eden on July 11. As for the murder of Jews by the Nazis, he added: 'There is no doubt that this is probably the greatest and most horrible crime ever committed in the whole history of the world, and it has been done by scientific machinery by nominally civilised men in the name of a great State and one of the leading races of Europe. It is quite clear that all concerned in this crime who may fall into our hands, including the people who only obeyed orders by carrying out the butcheries, should be put to death after their association with the murders has been proved.'

On July 10 Allied forces entered Caen; that day Brooke found Churchill 'in good and affable mood'. But there was distressing news later that day from the Home Front: ten thousand houses had already been destroyed in one month of flying-bomb attacks, Churchill told Stalin, 'as compared with 63,000 during the whole of the 1940/41 blitz'. He was quite prepared, he told the flying-bomb committee of the War Cabinet that evening, to 'threaten the heaviest possible scale of gas attack on Germany if the indiscriminate attack on London was not stopped'. But he was not convinced that the 'present scale' of the attack on London 'justified such a serious step'.

On July 18 Churchill learned from his Intelligence experts that the Germans had developed an even more effective weapon than the flying bomb; a rocket which could carry a bomb weighing more than eleven tons, capable of a speed of 4,000 miles an hour, and able to reach London within four minutes of being launched from northern Europe. The flying bomb, or V-1, with its aeroplane engine and wings, was ten times slower, and much easier to intercept, than this new rocket-propelled bomb, known as the V-2.

As well as the rocket danger, there was an ever-present political worry: as Soviet forces crossed into central Poland, Churchill wanted a meeting with Roosevelt and Stalin, to try to preserve some form of democratic government for Poland. 'I would brave the reporters of Washington or the mosquitos of Alaska!' he told Roosevelt, in trying to persuade the President to agree to a meeting. He also suggested the Scottish port of Invergordon. 'The weather might well be agreeable in Scotland at that time,' he wrote. But Roosevelt, after initial keenness, declined, worried about the coming Presidential election. 'As you know,' he told Churchill, 'domestic problems are unfortunately difficult for three months to come.'

In Normandy, a joint Anglo-American offensive was poised to break out of the bridgehead. Relieved by the prospect of an accelerated advance through northern France, Churchill flew to Cherbourg on July 20, was shown an unfinished flying-bomb site that had been aligned on Bristol, and visited the landing-beaches. While Churchill explored the scenes of victory, Hitler, at his headquarters more than a thousand miles to the east, was injured by a bomb placed under the table on which he was studying a battle map. An Army plot to kill him had failed; terrible retribution was wreaked on all who had taken part in it, or had shown sympathy to those who wished to see him removed from power. Major Ewald von Kleist, who had visited Churchill at Chartwell in 1938, was arrested; the letter which Churchill had written to him, at Kleist's request, was found among his papers. Kleist was executed. Rommel, recovering from an Allied fighter attack on his car in Normandy, and distantly involved in the plot, was given the choice of execution or suicide. He chose suicide.

Continuing his visit to the Normandy beach-head, Churchill slept that night on board the light-cruiser *Enterprise*. On July 21 he called on Montgomery at his headquarters at Blay, visited a field hospital and a field bakery, and, at an artillery battery near Villers Bocage, 'had rounds fired', its regimental history noted, 'until he was satisfied that he understood the gun drill'. The history added, 'He gave great joy to the batmen and cooks and fatigue men of 276 Battery by stopping his car on the way back and having his photograph taken with them.' After Churchill had left, the regiment's commanding officer wrote to him: 'I know how much you enjoy getting near the battle, but I would like to tell you how tremendously pleased, heartened and honoured every soldier was by your visit. It means very much to them that you should wish to come and see them at work in their gun pits.'

Churchill slept that night again aboard the *Enterprise*. Then he returned to shore, lunched with Montgomery, made a tour of the landing-strips in the battle area, and was given a flight in a captured German aircraft. That evening he flew back to Britain, where he learned that Stalin had established a Polish Committee of National Liberation at Lublin, on what was intended to be Polish soil after the war. The Polish Government in London was excluded from this Committee. It was of the 'utmost importance', Churchill telegraphed at once to Roosevelt, 'that we do not desert the orthodox Polish Government'. The 'great hope' was 'fusion of some kind between Poles relying on Russia, and Poles relying on USA and GB'.

On July 31, with Red Army units only fifteen miles from Warsaw, the Poles rose in revolt against the German occupation forces. For many Poles the hope was to establish an independent Polish authority in the capital before the Russians arrived. On August 4, German forces, amounting to a division and a half, began to attack the insurgents, and the Hermann Goering Division was summoned from Italy, together with two SS Divisions. That day, Russian air activity over Warsaw ceased. Churchill, who had just agreed to a Polish request to drop ammunition and supplies into the city, appealed to Stalin to help the Poles. Stalin refused to help, replying derisively about the ability of the Poles to resist. Yet Polish resistance was to continue for more than a month.

On August 4 Eisenhower lunched with Churchill and outlined a proposal for the cancellation of the South of France landing due to begin in eleven days' time, and for switching the forces assembled for it to Brittany. This change of plan would bring substantial Allied forces to the flank of the armies in Normandy. On August 5 Churchill flew to France, intending to put the American plan to Montgomery, whose own offensive would thereby be much enhanced. But as his plane reached the Cherbourg Peninsula it was recalled to Britain; fog on the landing-strip at which he was expected had caused the preceding plane to crash and all its occupants had been killed.

Churchill flew back to southern England, to Eisenhower's 'Advance Command Post' at Portsmouth, where it quickly emerged that Eisenhower had unexpectedly changed his mind, and now wanted the South of France landing to go ahead as planned, but that his Chief of Staff, General Bedell-Smith, still favoured a Brittany landing. Churchill at once appealed to Hopkins to seek Roosevelt's approval for the Brittany plan. On the following morning, while awaiting a reply from Hopkins, he flew back to Normandy, to try once more to put the plan to Montgomery. But on reaching Montgomery's new headquarters in the Forêt de Cerisy, he found that the battle there was at its height, and sensing the tension, cut short his visit after an hour and returned to Britain.

Awaiting Churchill when he reached the Annexe was a telegram from Hopkins. Although he had not yet heard from Roosevelt, he was certain that the President's answer 'will be in the negative'. That afternoon, the British Joint Staff Mission in Washington put the case for the Brittany plan to the American Chiefs of Staff. 'We could not budge them,' they reported back to London. A day later, Roosevelt telegraphed to Churchill that he wanted no change of plan. The Brittany landing was dead; the South of France landing would go ahead as planned.

In Italy, as a result of the build-up for the South of France landing, Alexander's army had been reduced by seven divisions. Yet he still took the offensive, and on August 10 forced the Germans to withdraw from Florence. That night Churchill flew from London to Algiers, on his way to Italy. He wanted to be with Alexander, to see something of the battle, and to discuss the many problems now besetting the Mediterranean operations. 'I do hope you will get a little rest with the brush as well as with the binoculars,' Oliver Lyttelton wrote to him.

While in Algiers, Churchill had a long talk with Randolph, who was still in pain as a result of a plane crash while making a second journey to partisan-held Yugoslavia, and suffering also from the blow of a disintegrating marriage. 'No reference was made by either of us to family matters,' Churchill wrote to Clementine. 'He is a lonely figure by no means recovered as far as walking is concerned. Our talk was about politics,

French and English, about which there was plenty of friendly badinage & argument.' Randolph urged his father to reverse his recent refusal to meet de Gaulle. 'After all,' he wrote a few days later, 'he is a frustrated man representing a defeated country. You as the unchallenged leader of England and the main architect of victory can afford to be magnanimous without fear of being misunderstood.'

From Algiers, Churchill flew to Naples, where he was General Maitland Wilson's guest at the Villa Rivalta, overlooking the Bay. While there he received an appeal from the Poles still fighting in Warsaw, and still denied help by Stalin. 'They implore machine guns and ammunition,' Churchill telegraphed to Stalin from Naples on August 12. 'Can you not give them some further help, as the distance from Italy is so very great?' Stalin declined. That day twenty-eight British and Polish pilots made the fourth 1,400-mile round trip from southern Italy to Warsaw. Three planes were lost. The nearest fully operational Soviet airstrip to Warsaw was less than fifty miles away.

During August 12 Churchill received Tito at the Villa Rivalta, urging him to establish a democratic system in Yugoslavia 'based on the peasants'. In the afternoon he went by Admiral's barge to a small beach where he bathed in the waters of a hot spring. On the return journey he was recognised by two convoys of troops preparing for the South of France landing. As he passed the cheering troops he sent them a message wishing them well. 'They did not know,' he later wrote, 'that if I had had my way they would be sailing in a different direction.'

That night Churchill received an invitation from Roosevelt for a meeting in Quebec in September, without Stalin. Churchill accepted. On the following day he went by boat to Capri, to view the Tiberius rock over which the Roman Emperor had thrown his victims, and to see the Blue Grotto, by whose azure waters he was entranced. Then, guarded by a dozen American military policemen, he undressed on the rocks and swam. During lunch in a restaurant on the island he was 'in holiday mood', wrote one of the Englishmen present, 'and talked about chewing-gum defacing the features, demonstrated how to light a cigar without interrupting his conversation, and enquired about the arrangements for the Capri water supply'. Returning to Naples, he presided over a conference between Tito and his fellow Yugoslav leader Dr Ivan Subasic, the Ban of Croatia, persuading them to accept a 'fusion and cessation' of the civil war.

On August 14 Churchill again swam, this time at a point beyond Cumae in the open sea. After he had made a V-sign, on leaving, to an enthusiastic group of Italians at the pier, Churchill asked one of the Englishmen on board:

'D'you think they like that?'

'Yes, though I believe the sign also has an improper connotation in Mediterranean lands.'

'I know that, but I have superseded that one – V for Victory.'

After returning to Naples for lunch, Churchill flew to Corsica. There, in Ajaccio harbour, he boarded the *Royal Scotsman*, a former merchant ship carrying six assault landing-craft. That night, while he slept on board, eleven Allied divisions landed in Southern France. At eight in the morning of August 15 he transferred to the destroyer *Kimberley*, which steamed towards the coast, where shortly after midday 'we found ourselves in an immense concourse of ships,' Churchill wrote to Clementine, 'all sprawled along twenty miles of coast with poor St Tropez in the centre. It had been expected that the bombardment would continue all day, but the air and the ships had practically silenced the enemy guns by 8 o'clock. This rendered the proceedings rather dull.'

Churchill looked at 'the panorama of the beautiful shore with smoke rising from many fires started by the shelling, and artificial smoke being loosed by the landing troops and the landing-craft drawn up upon the shore'. But it was from 'a long way off', and he was disappointed. Had he known beforehand what the conditions would be, he told Clementine, he would have requested a picket boat and gone 'with perfect safety very much nearer to the actual beaches'.

Opposition in the air was light, at sea there was none, and on land very little and very brief. In terms of what the Americans had expected of these landings, a massive switch of German forces from northern France, they were the greatest failure of the war in the West. Churchill told the King, 'Your Majesty knows my opinion of the strategy, but the perfect execution of the plan was deeply interesting.'

Returning to Naples by sea, on the morning of August 16 Churchill studied a series of German top-secret messages about the imminent German withdrawal from Greece. He at once obtained the approval of the Chiefs of Staff to send a British military force to Athens at the earliest possible moment to forestall the Greek Communists there. Then, after communicating this decision to Roosevelt, he went for another swim, this time off the island of Procida. 'We have had altogether four bathes,' he wrote to Clementine, 'which have done me all the good in the world. I feel greatly refreshed and am much less tired than when I left England.'

On August 17 Churchill drove through the devastated town of Cassino, and then flew over the monastery which, as the main German fortification, had been pulverised by Allied bombardment. Then he flew north to Alexander's headquarters at Siena. As the weather was too bad to visit the front with any chance of seeing anything, for three days he visited the troops in the rear areas. Near Livorno he fired the first shot of a howitzer

that had been set on a German artillery position north of Pisa. On August
20, the weather having improved, Alexander took Churchill to a forward
artillery observation point about two miles from the front line, on the Arno
River. Then he flew back to Naples, where dinner was enlivened by a
German aircraft making repeated low-level attacks on the port before it
was brought down and destroyed by naval gunfire.

Churchill's thoughts were still on the folly of denuding Alexander's
army for the South of France landing. With half of what had been taken
away, he later wrote, the Allies 'could have broken into the Valley of the
Po, with all the gleaming possibilities and prizes which lay open towards
Vienna. That evening Alexander maintained his soldierly cheerfulness,
but it was in a sombre mood that I went to bed. In these great matters,
failing to gain one's way is no escape from the responsibility for an inferior
solution.'

On August 21 Churchill flew from Naples to Rome for a day of discussion about the proposed British military expedition to Greece. 'Winston
in very good heart,' Macmillan noted that night. On the following afternoon the discussion was about the political future of Italy. 'Winston was
like a dog worrying at a bone,' Macmillan wrote. 'But his peculiar method
does succeed in eliciting the truth.' Churchill argued in favour of 'a steady
process of relaxation of control' in Italy, which should no longer be an
occupied enemy state, but a 'friendly co-belligerent'.

'We finally broke up at 7 pm,' Macmillan wrote, 'all but Winston completely exhausted.' That night after dinner Churchill had a long talk with
Brigadier Maurice Lush of the Allied Control Commission, who found the
Prime Minister cheerful, 'for he was, next day, continuing his participation
in the battle with Alex and his men.' Churchill told Lush that he 'hoped so
much to take part in the first stages of an autumnal breakthrough' which
would enable Alexander 'to swing to the right, overcome Austria, and so
alter history'. Then, Lush later recalled, 'he gave me a cheerful "good
night" at 2 am'.

On the following day Churchill telegraphed to the Chiefs of Staff that
if Alexander could break through into the Po Valley, 'I certainly contemplate a move into the Adriatic.' And to Smuts he confided two days later
that he still hoped Alexander's army would reach 'the great city', Vienna.
'Even if the war comes to a sudden end, there is no reason why our armour
should not slip through and reach it as soon as we can.' He had told
Alexander that in the event of the war ending suddenly he should 'be
ready for a dash with armoured cars'; Vienna was the prize.

On August 23 Churchill flew from Rome to Alexander's headquarters
at Siena, where he authorised the establishment of a Jewish Brigade
Group to fight as an integral part of Alexander's army. 'This will give

great satisfaction to the Jews when it is published,' he wrote, 'and surely they of all other races have a right to strike at the Germans as a recognisable body.' On the following day he visited the New Zealand Division. On August 25, as he worked at Alexander's headquarters, de Gaulle entered Paris.

That day Alexander launched a new assault on the German defences, Churchill went with him to a high point overlooking the battle zone. 'The whole front of the Eighth Army offensive was visible,' he later wrote. 'But apart from the smoke puffs of shells bursting seven or eight thousand yards away in scattered fashion, there was nothing to see.' Then, after a picnic, the two men went further forward, to an old castle overlooking a valley. 'Here one certainly could see all that was possible,' Churchill recalled. 'The Germans were firing with rifles and machine guns from thick scrub on the farther side of the valley, about five hundred yards away. Our front line was beneath us. The firing was desultory and intermittent. But this was the nearest I got to the enemy and the time I heard the most bullets in the Second World War.'

On August 27 Churchill flew back to Naples for two days' more talks about the impending British expedition to Greece. He also wrote a message to the Italian people, setting out what he called 'one or two quite simple, practical tests, by which one could answer the question 'What is freedom?' There were in fact seven questions, which were 'the title deeds on which a new Italy could be founded'. The questions were:

> Is there the right to free expression of opinion and of opposition and of criticism of the Government of the day?
> Have the people the right to turn out a Government of which they disapprove, and are constitutional means provided by which they can make their will apparent?
> Are their courts of justice free from violence by the Executive and from threats of mob violence, and free of all association with particular political parties?
> Will these courts administer open and well-established laws which are associated in the human mind with the broad principles of decency and justice?
> Will there be fair play for poor as well as for rich, for private persons as well as Government officials?
> Will the rights of the individual, subject to his duties to the State, be maintained and asserted and exalted?
> Is the ordinary peasant or workman, who is earning a living by daily toil and trying to bring up a family, free from the fear that some grim police organisation under the control of a single Party like the Gestapo,

started by the Nazi and Fasci⁻t Parties, will tap him on the shoulder and pack him off without fair or open trial to bondage or ill-treatment?

These questions, *The Times* commented, contained words 'both of encouragement and warning'. They also contained the essence of Churchill's political philosophy.

That day Churchill left Naples by air for London, having to fly first to Rabat, where, as thunderstorms were reported further north, he spent the night. Then, on the morning of August 29, he flew from Rabat to London. During the flight he was taken ill, his temperature rising to 103. It was pneumonia again. Two nurses were called in, a lung specialist took blood tests and X-rays, and M & B was administered. 'It would be a tragedy if anything were to happen to him now,' Sir Andrew Cunningham, who saw him that night, wrote in his diary. 'With all his faults (& he is the most infuriating man) he has done a great job for the country, & beside there is no one else.'

As Churchill recovered, slowly, in bed at the Annexe, the Germans had lost control of much of northern France, and had been driven back across the Belgian border. 'How wonderful it is to see our people leaping out at last after all their hard struggles,' he telegraphed to Montgomery, recently promoted Field Marshal, on September 2. In Italy that day, Alexander's forces entered Pisa and pierced the Gothic Line defences, but were confronted by eight new German divisions sent hastily to stop any further thrust northward. As an answer to the one question that mattered in the Italian campaign, 'Who is containing whom?', Italy continued to be a drain on German resources.

The Warsaw insurgents were still fighting against impossible odds, and without Soviet help. On September 3 Churchill suggested to Roosevelt that they should both tell Stalin that, if he did not at least allow British and American aircraft to use Soviet air bases near Warsaw to ferry in help to the insurgents, Britain and America 'would take certain drastic action in respect of our own supplies to Russia'. But Roosevelt did not want to upset Stalin, from whom, unknown to Churchill, he was even then asking permission to use Soviet air bases in Siberia as staging-posts for American bombing raids against Japan.

Churchill was so angered by the Soviet refusal to help Warsaw that on September 4, despite a recurrence of fever, he left his sick bed in the above-ground Annexe and descended to the Central War Rooms. The whole War Cabinet shared his anger. But they were reluctant to do anything to break up still further the already fragile working of the alliance, limiting their protest to a collective telegram to Stalin, stating that the Soviet action in denying help to Warsaw 'seems to us at variance with the spirit of Allied co-operation to which you and we attach so much importance both for the present and for the future'.

The Warsaw uprising was being systematically and savagely crushed and thousands of Poles executed. It was to be more than four months before the Russians entered the capital.

On the morning of September 5 Churchill left London by train for Greenock, on the Clyde; that afternoon he boarded the *Queen Mary*. A nurse, Dorothy Pugh, and a penicillin expert, Brigadier Whitby, were both on board. During the voyage Churchill learned that those American servicemen on board, who were going on leave, were having to lose a week's leave because of the week's wait at Greenock for Churchill to come on board. He at once telegraphed to Roosevelt to ask if the week could be made up to them. 'It would be a pleasure to me if this could be announced before the end of the voyage and their anxiety relieved,' Churchill wrote. Roosevelt agreed.

Churchill was not feeling well; as a result of his visit to Italy he had been advised to continue a course of malaria pills for another two weeks, and these pills seemed to upset him. On September 8, after a Staff Conference on board, Brooke wrote of how Churchill 'looked old, unwell and depressed. Evidently found it hard to concentrate and kept holding his head between his hands.' At the conference Churchill warned the Chiefs of Staffs of his concern that their proposal to divert forces from Italy to the Far East, a proposal based on the assumption that a German collapse was likely before the end of 1944, was based on a dangerous assumption, as 'German garrisons were showing stout resistance at most of the ports'. The Americans had failed to take St Nazaire and had been checked at Nancy. The Germans were also putting up a 'stout resistance' in the forts around Antwerp, 'a port we badly needed'.

That day, as the *Queen Mary* continued westward, British forces entered Brussels. But other news bore out Churchill's warning: German forces were holding Boulogne, Calais and Dunkirk, and had retaken Metz. In the east, Stalin's advance knew no such setbacks; on September 9 Soviet forces entered Bulgaria, and on the following day Bulgaria surrendered. Roumania had already abandoned Germany and joined the Allies. The Russians now had the prospect of a rapid advance through the Balkans and into Hungary.

On September 10 the *Queen Mary* reached Halifax. From there a twenty-hour train journey took Churchill to Quebec, where Roosevelt's train was awaiting him on an adjoining track. During their first day in Quebec, September 12, they learned that American forces had crossed the German frontier west of Aachen. But a message from London that day reported, accurately, that 'enemy resistance increases as Allies approach German frontier'.

Roosevelt now agreed that there would be no further withdrawals from Alexander's army. The Americans were even willing to let Alexander have the landing-craft needed for an Istrian landing. Churchill was greatly relieved. 'He had always been attracted by a right-handed movement with the purpose of giving Germany a stab in the Adriatic armpit,' he told the conference. 'Our objective should be Vienna.'

On September 13 Roosevelt's Secretary of the Treasury, Henry Morgenthau, spoke of a post-war Germany that would be allowed no industry at all. The Ruhr would be closed down. The shipyards would be dismantled. At first Churchill was ill at ease with this. 'I'm all for disarming Germany,' he told Morgenthau, 'but we ought not to prevent her living decently. There are bonds between the working classes of all countries, and the English people will not stand for the policy you are advocating. I agree with Burke. You cannot indict a whole nation. What is to be done should be done quickly. Kill the criminals, but don't carry on the business for years.'

In reporting Morgenthau's plan in a telegram to the War Cabinet two days later, however, Churchill wrote, 'I was at first taken aback at this, but I consider that the disarmament argument is decisive and the beneficial consequences to us follow naturally.' Part of the economic benefit to Britain of a 'pastoral' Germany would be that Britain would have to supply Germany with much of its industrial needs, thus stimulating British industry. On September 15 Churchill and Roosevelt signed an agreement 'looking forward to converting Germany into a country primarily agricultural and pastoral in its character'. This agreement was rejected by the State Department in Washington before it could even be discussed by the War Cabinet in London.

On September 17, while Churchill was still in Quebec, three airborne divisions, British and American, including a Polish Parachute Brigade, 35,000 men in all, parachuted behind German lines in Holland, with the object of seizing a bridge over the Rhine at Arnhem. As the battle began, Churchill left Quebec by train for Hyde Park, where he was Roosevelt's guest for two days. Clementine was with him; in a letter to Mary she wrote of how the President 'with all his genius, does not – indeed cannot (partly because of his health and partly because of his make-up) – function round the clock, like your father. I should not think his mind was pinpointed on the war for more than four hours a day, which is not really enough when one is a supreme war lord.'

Churchill and Roosevelt discussed the atom bomb, which, they were told, would 'almost certainly' be ready by August 1945. That week it had taken 2,600 sorties, and the loss of more than a hundred planes, to drop 9,360 tons of high explosive bombs on Germany; one atom bomb, carried in a single plane, would be the equivalent of at least 20,000 tons of high explosive. The two men rejected a suggestion that 'the world should be informed' about the atom bomb with a view to an international agreement regarding its use. They also decided that when the bomb was finally available 'it might perhaps, after mature consideration, be used against the Japanese, who should be warned that this bombardment will be repeated until they surrender'.

Churchill was not certain that the atom bomb would need to be used. During the last day of the discussions at Quebec he had thought it 'quite possible' that the current 'heavy, sustained and ever-increasing' bombing of Japanese cities by the Americans 'might cause Japan to throw up the sponge'. People stood up to heavy bombardment if they thought it would 'sooner or later' come to an end. 'There could be no such hope for Japan.' All they could look forward to was 'an ever-increasing weight of explosives on their centres of population'.

Leaving Hyde Park on September 19, Churchill took the night train to New York, where on the following morning he re-embarked on the *Queen Mary*. 'PM in excellent form,' noted Cunningham, '& most interesting about his time at the Admiralty in the last war.' Much of Churchill's work on the voyage was to prepare the speech he would make on his return. 'Work with a vengeance,' Marian Holmes wrote in her diary on September 24. 'PM dictated a further 2,000 words of speech. I got the best view of his behind that I have ever had. He stepped out of bed still dictating, and oblivious of his all-too-short bed jacket. Anyway, he was in a kind and conciliatory mood, and I felt the waves of his approval.'

On September 26 the *Queen Mary* reached Greenock, where John Peck was waiting with the most recent and urgent telegrams. The worst news was from Arnhem; the attempt to seize and hold a bridge over the Rhine had failed; 1,400 of the 35,000 troops involved had been killed. Travelling south overnight, Churchill's train stopped at Rugby to pick up another urgent pouch; it contained the grave news that the last resistance of the Polish patriots in Warsaw was being overcome, and savage reprisals were being carried out against tens of thousands of Poles in the city.

At ten in the morning the train reached London. An hour and a half later Churchill was in the Commons to answer Prime Minister's questions. The fate of the perpetrators of Nazi atrocities was raised; the Government, he said, were 'resolved to do their utmost to prevent Nazi criminals finding refuge in neutral territory from the consequences of their crimes'. The war in the Far East was also on his mind that day; in a telegram to Stalin he explained that the eventual opening of a Russian front against Japan 'would force them to burn and bleed, especially in the air, in a manner which would vastly accelerate their defeat'.

Churchill now decided to go to see Stalin; that night he asked Portal to prepare a flight schedule to Moscow. He had a number of reasons for being on his travels again so soon. Fearing the financial and physical burden on Britain of a long war against Japan, he wanted to persuade Stalin to declare war on Japan as soon as Germany was defeated. He also wanted to discuss the political future of Yugoslavia and Greece, which he hoped to exclude from Communist control, and of Poland, where he was personally and morally committed to the establishment of a freely-elected Government. 'I cannot conceive that it is not possible,' he had told the Commons that day, 'to make a good solution whereby Russia gets the security which she is entitled to have, and which I have resolved that we shall do our utmost to secure for her, on her Western frontier, and, at the same time, the Polish nation have restored to them that national sovereignty and independence for which, across centuries of oppression and struggle, they have never ceased to strive.'

Before leaving for Moscow, Churchill twice took Clementine to the theatre; on October 3 to Shaw's *Arms and the Man* and on the following night to Shakespeare's *Richard III*, both with Laurence Olivier, Ralph Richardson and Sybil Thorndike. On his return to the Annexe on October 4 he learned that British forces had successfully entered Greece, landing at Patras, on the Gulf of Corinth, from which the Germans had withdrawn. In Poland, however, to Churchill's intense distress, after so many hours trying to help them, the Warsaw insurgents had at last been crushed. 'When the final Allied victory is achieved,' he told the Commons on October 5, 'the epic of Warsaw will not be forgotten. It will remain a deathless memory for the Poles, and for the friends of freedom all over the world.'

Two days later, with the political future of Poland high among his concerns, Churchill left London by air for Naples, where he learned that Alexander's armies were now 'stuck in the Apennines with tired forces' and could not spare any men for an amphibious landing at the head of the Adriatic. After four hours in Naples he flew to Moscow where, shortly after midday on October 9, his plane landed at the wrong aerodrome, took off again, and then landed at the airport where Maisky, Vishinsky and a guard of honour awaited him. He was driven to Molotov's dacha, which had been put at his disposal.

That same evening Churchill was driven from the dacha into Moscow, a forty-five minute drive. In his first talk with Stalin, he reaffirmed his earlier acceptance, at Teheran, of the Curzon Line as Russia's eastern frontier. Churchill promised to 'bring pressure to bear' on the Poles to do likewise. The discussion then turned to Southern Europe and the Balkans. Britain had a 'particular interest' in Greece, Churchill told Stalin, but Roumania was 'very much a Russian affair'. He did not want to use the phrase 'dividing into spheres', Churchill said, 'because the Americans might be shocked', but as long as he and Stalin 'understood each other' he could explain it to the Americans.

Churchill then produced what he described to Stalin as 'a naughty document'. On this were listed the 'proportional interest' of Russia and Britain in five countries. For Roumania, Churchill suggested 90 per cent Russian interest and 10 per cent British. For Greece, he proposed 90 per cent British 'in accord with USA' and 10 per cent Russian. Yugoslavia and Hungary were both listed as fifty-fifty, and Bulgaria as 75 per cent to Russia and 25 per cent to 'the others'.

Stalin studied the list and then, Churchill later recalled, 'took his blue pencil and made a large tick upon it, and passed it back. After this there was a long silence. The pencilled paper lay in the centre of the table.' Eventually Churchill said:

'Might it not be thought rather cynical if it seemed we had disposed of these issues, so fateful to millions of people, in such an off-hand manner? Let us burn the paper.'

'No, you keep it,' was Stalin's reply.

The discussion turned to Turkey, where Churchill told Stalin he was in favour of Russia having free access through the Dardanelles to the Mediterranean 'for her merchant ships and ships of war'. Russia, he said, had a 'right' and also a 'moral claim' to this, which he would support. Churchill then asked Stalin not to encourage Communist participation in the civil war in Greece or to 'stir up' Communism in Italy. Stalin agreed. Speaking of Togliatti, whom Churchill had met in Rome in August, Stalin commented that he was 'a wise man, not an extremist, and would not start an adventure in Italy'.

Churchill did not get back to the dacha until 3.10 in the morning. He had been travelling and working continuously for sixty hours, sleeping only while travelling. 'I gave him some papers,' noted Marian Holmes, who expected dictation, 'but he said he couldn't work.' Sleeping soundly, Churchill woke on the morning of October 10 and stayed in bed, dictating. Then, shortly after midday, he drove back to the Kremlin, where Stalin was host at a luncheon that lasted four hours. At the end of the meal Churchill announced, 'I'm going back to the embassy for my Young Lady'. He was then driven to the British Embassy, asked Elizabeth Layton to join him in his car, and told her as they drove back to the dacha, 'I think I'll dictate in the dark.' Along the twenty-three-mile route, armed guards stood to attention and saluted as they passed.

Churchill wanted to send Stalin a formal note of their discussion about the Balkans. 'These percentages which I have put down,' he explained, 'are no more than a method by which in our thoughts we can see how near we are together, and then decide upon the necessary steps to bring us into full agreement.' If published, the percentages might be considered 'crude, and even callous', but they might serve as a 'good guide for the conduct of our affairs', which, if managed well, might prevent 'several civil wars and much bloodshed' in the countries concerned. Churchill added, 'Our broad principle should be to let every country have the form of Government which its people desire.' No ideology should be imposed on any small State. 'Let them work out their own fortunes during the years that lie ahead.'

Harriman, who was in Moscow as Roosevelt's emissary to the talks, and to whom Churchill showed this letter, said he was certain both Roosevelt and Hull would 'repudiate' it. The letter was therefore never sent, despite its assertion of the principle of self-determination. On October 11 Churchill remembered that Albania had been omitted from the list of percentages. He therefore proposed fifty-fifty, the same division as for Yugoslavia and Hungary. But for Hungary, Molotov had insisted upon a drastic change in Russia's favour, from fifty-fifty to 80-20. To this Eden had agreed.

In a telegram to the War Cabinet, Churchill explained that the percentages were 'only an interim guide for the immediate post-war future', and would be 'surveyed' by the Great Powers, including of course the United States, when they met at the armistice or the peace table to make 'a general settlement of Europe'. In the event, no Peace Conference took place. Except in Greece, the degree of control exercised by Russia was to be determined, not by the percentages in Churchill's 'naughty document', but by the arrival of the Soviet Army and its political commissars. The Russians, Churchill told the War Cabinet, were 'insistent in their ascendancy' in Roumania and Bulgaria, 'both Black Sea countries'.

That evening Churchill entertained Stalin to dinner at the British Embassy, across the Moscow River from the Kremlin. When Churchill remarked that his hostile attitude to the Italian people had changed because of the enthusiastic welcome they had given him on his recent visit, Stalin commented that the same crowd had supported Mussolini. The dinner went on until four in the morning, so late that Churchill slept at a house in the city which Stalin had set aside for him at 6 Ostrovskaya Street. 'I have had very nice talks with the Old Bear,' Churchill wrote to Clementine on October 13. 'I like him the more I see him. *Now* they respect us here & I am sure they wish to work with us.'

In the evening, at the Spiridonovka Palace in central Moscow, Churchill and Stalin had a long talk with the leading members of the Polish Government in London, whom Churchill had urged to fly to Moscow during his visit, and whom he begged to accept the loss of pre-war territory in return for participation in the Communist-dominated National Liberation Committee which Stalin had established at Lublin. The London Poles would not accept the Curzon Line. When Churchill proposed that they accept it subject to the final agreements of a Peace Conference, it was Stalin's turn to refuse; the Poles must accept the new line without conditions. At this point, the minutes of the meeting recorded, Churchill made 'a gesture of disappointment and hopelessness'.

Later that night, as the sky of Moscow was lit with rockets celebrating the entry of Soviet forces into the Latvian capital of Riga, Churchill and Stalin again met the Lublin Polish leaders at the Spiridonovka Palace. Dutifully, they echoed Stalin's sentiments. Two days later Churchill telegraphed to the King: 'The day before yesterday was "all Poles day". Our lot from London are, as your Majesty knows, a decent but feeble lot of fools, but the delegates from Lublin seem to be the greatest villains imaginable.' On October 14 Churchill had a two-hour talk with the London Poles at the British Embassy. When the Prime Minister of the 'London Poles', Stanislaw Mikolajczyk, said that Polish public opinion would not accept the loss of the eastern territories, Churchill replied: 'What is public opinion? The right to be crushed!' Of course nothing could prevent Poland from declaring war on Russia, but by doing so Poland would lose the support of the other powers.

Still Mikolajczyk would not accept the Curzon Line. During a ninety-minute talk that afternoon at the house on Ostrovskaya Street, Churchill could not persuade him to do so. As for Britain, Churchill told him, she was 'powerless in the face of Russia' with regard to the future Polish Government. But he then went to see Stalin in the Kremlin, to propose a compromise formula; the London Poles would accept the Curzon Line, in return for fifty-fifty participation in the future Government of Poland. After an hour of discussion, Stalin agreed. The onus was now on Churchill to persuade the London Poles to concede the frontier.

That night Stalin went with Churchill to the Bolshoi Theatre. They arrived after the start of the evening's programme, the first act of the ballet *Giselle*, had already begun. It was only when the lights went up for the interval that the audience saw Churchill, whereupon, he reported to the King, there was at once a 'prolonged ovation'. Then, when Stalin came into the box and stood at his side, there was 'an almost passionate demonstration'. The interval was followed by two hours' singing and dancing by the Red Army Choir. 'I noticed the PM thoroughly enjoying the songs,' noted Marian Holmes, 'and beating time to them with his hands. Stalin didn't change his personal expression at all.'

From the Bolshoi Theatre, Churchill returned briefly to the town house before going to the Kremlin for a discussion with Stalin on military matters. The Soviet Army did not intend to advance into western Yugoslavia, Stalin said, but would prefer to link up with Alexander in Austria, at which Churchill promised that Alexander would push forward to Vienna 'as soon as possible'.

On the morning of October 15, Churchill woke up in great discomfort, the victim of a violent attack of diarrhoea. That afternoon he again received the London Poles, and asked them to accept the formula to which Stalin had agreed the previous afternoon. But they refused to accept the loss of the city of Lvov, which lay just to the east of the Curzon Line. Churchill lost his temper with them, pacing up and down the room and declaiming; 'I will have nothing more to do with you. I don't care where you go. You only deserve to be in your Pripet Marshes. I shall indict you.' Oliver Harvey noted in his dairy, 'A painful scene to witness, the PM so right and the Poles so foolish – like the Bourbons expecting everything to come back to them.' Before the meeting ended Churchill proposed a compromise. He would go to see Stalin and appeal to him 'in the interests of Anglo-Soviet relations' and for the effect of such gesture upon 'world opinion' towards Russia, to let the Poles keep Lvov; but he would only make this appeal on the condition that, if Stalin rejected it, the Poles would agree to accept the Curzon Line without amendment. The Poles refused.

That afternoon Churchill developed a fever. No more meetings could be held that day. As his temperature rose above 100, two doctors and two nurses were summoned from Cairo. But on the following morning the temperature was back to normal and the summons was countermanded. The fever, Churchill explained to Clementine, 'came from the tummy and not from the chest, and I am now quite well again'. On the afternoon of October 16 he returned to the Kremlin with a Curzon Line formula devised by Eden, and acceptable to the London Poles, that would describe the disputed line not as a 'frontier' but a 'demarcation line'. For two hours Churchill tried to persuade Stalin, but in vain. 'The Prime Minister used all possible arguments,' Eden telegraphed to the War Cabinet, 'but was unable to move him.'

For one more day Churchill shuttled between the London Poles and Stalin, to whom he forcefully put their case. But Stalin now made it clear that whatever formula might be devised about the frontier, as far as the future Polish Government was concerned, it was his Lublin nominees who would have the majority.

On October 17 Churchill and Stalin had a final, six-hour conference, from ten that evening until four in the morning. Still trying to find some basis for an agreement between Stalin and the London Poles, Churchill persuaded Stalin to accept the phrase 'basis for frontier' rather than 'frontier' in describing the Curzon Line. But on the political predominance of the Lublin Communist Poles, Stalin would still not give way. The London Poles could participate, but no longer as equals.

Discussing the future of Germany, Churchill told Stalin that the Ruhr and the Saar should be 'put permanently out of action', and Germany's metallurgical, chemical and electrical industries stopped 'for as long as he had a word to say, and he hoped for a generation at least'. Stalin did not demur. When Churchill then said that Germany should be 'deprived of all her aviation', Stalin agreed that 'neither civil nor military flying should be allowed' and that all training schools for pilots should be forbidden. Churchill also told Stalin that he would like to see Poland, Czechoslovakia and Hungary form a 'separate grouping', a Customs union with no trade or commercial barriers.

On one point, central to Churchill's purpose in going to Moscow, there was hardly any discussion and no dispute; Stalin agreed that, 'on the day the German armies are destroyed', Russia would declare war on Japan. 'We must remember the supreme value of this in shortening the whole struggle,' Churchill telegraphed to Roosevelt shortly before leaving Moscow.

At seven on the evening of October 18 Churchill had one last meeting with the London Poles, but failed to persuade them to accept the final formula to which Stalin had agreed, even though he reported Stalin's willingness to appoint the Prime Minister, Mikolajczyk, as head of a Polish Government of National Unity; but only if the Curzon Line were to be the border, and Lvov were to become a Soviet city. Many hours of negotiation had failed. Henceforth, the London Poles were effectively excluded from the fate of their country.

That night Stalin gave Churchill a farewell dinner in the Kremlin. It lasted six hours, until two in the morning. During dinner news arrived that Soviet forces had entered Czechoslovakia, and Moscow was again illuminated by multi-coloured rockets. That morning, Stalin went to Moscow airport to see Churchill off. As Churchill had not yet arrived, he waited in the rain. Then, in a short farewell ceremony, Churchill informed Stalin's interpreter, Vladimir Pavlov, that he had been awarded an honorary CBE. The new Commander of the Order of the British Empire, for such Pavlov had become, had 'been privy', Churchill explained, 'to the most deadly secrets of State'. His insignia would follow later. Stalin then went on board Churchill's plane, where he was shown the Prime Minister's travelling comforts, then left the aircraft to stand on the tarmac waving his handkerchief as the plane took off.

From Moscow, Churchill flew to the Crimea, a five-hour flight, dined at the airport near Simferopol, and then flew on through the night, for a further six hours, to Cairo. On the following morning he flew to Naples, a seven-hour flight involving a wide westerly detour via Benghazi to avoid flying over Crete, which was still held by the Germans. At Naples he spent the day at the Villa Rivalta; among his requests was that more of the soldiers in Italy be allowed to go to Britain on leave, now that, with the liberation of most of France, it was possible for them to travel by train from Marseilles to Paris and then on to Le Havre.

On the morning of October 22 Churchill flew from Naples to London, arriving in the afternoon after a six-and-a-half-hour flight; his total flying time from Moscow had been more than twenty-four hours. Met at the airport by Clementine, he was driven to Chequers, where Sarah and Diana were among those waiting to welcome him. 'He looks none the worse for his journeys,' John Martin wrote to Randolph, 'and seems to me to have returned from Moscow fitter and in better spirits than he has been for a long time.'

On October 27, in giving an account of his Moscow visit to the Commons, Churchill said, 'I have not hesitated to travel from court to court like a wandering minstrel, always with the same song to sing, or the same set of songs.' His aim was 'the unity of the Allied Powers'. Harold Nicolson, who heard him speak, wrote to his sons later that day: 'A few months ago he seemed ill and tired and he did not find his words as easily as usual. But today he was superb. Cherubic, pink, solid and vociferous.'

Five days later Churchill once more tried to persuade the Polish Government in London to accept the Curzon Line, go to Moscow to tell Stalin, and then participate in the deliberations of the Lublin Poles. When the Poles said that they would want 'assurances' that they could still deal with Polish territories east of the Curzon Line, Churchill told them, 'This is nonsense, a pure utopia!' Cadogan noted in his diary: 'PM knocked them about badly – and rightly. Finally gave them forty-eight hours in which to say "Yes" or "No". Think that's right.'

Twenty-four hours later the Poles said 'No'. Churchill's long search for a compromise had been in vain.

Churchill was now looking towards the coming of peace 'in March, April or May', he told the Commons on October 31. If the Labour Party wished to withdraw from the Coalition once Germany was defeated, although it would be a matter of regret to many people, it would not be one of 'reproach or bitterness'. A General Election would then be called and the country could return to Party politics. He had a 'clear view', Churchill said, that it would be wrong to continue the present Parliament 'beyond the period of the German war', and in a powerful defence of the system of Government he had supported and participated in for half a century, he told the House: 'The foundation of all democracy is that the people have the right to vote. To deprive them of that right is to make a mockery of all the high-sounding phrases which are so often used. At the bottom of all the tributes paid to democracy is the little man, walking into the little booth, with a little pencil, making a little cross on a little bit of paper. No amount of rhetoric or voluminous discussion can possibly palliate the overwhelming importance of that point. The people have the right to choose representatives in accordance with their wishes and feelings.'

That evening Harold Nicolson wrote in his diary, 'I have never admired Winston's moral attitude more than I did this morning.'

34

War and Diplomacy

Among the problems with which Churchill was confronted on his return from Moscow was the future of Palestine. Several months earlier he had refused to implement the decision of the 1939 Palestine White Paper, which envisaged an Arab veto on all Jewish immigration from May 1944; this White Paper had greatly aroused his anger at the time. On 4 November 1944, two weeks after his return from the Crimea and Cairo, he lunched at Chequers with Dr Weizmann, the Zionist leader. During their discussion, Churchill told Weizmann that if the Jews could 'get the whole of Palestine' as their State it would be 'a good thing', but if it came to a choice between no State at all and a Palestine partitioned into two States, one Arab and one Jewish, 'then they should take the partition'.

In his desire to further the cause of Jewish statehood, Churchill advised Weizmann to go at once to Cairo, to discuss the future of Palestine with the new Minister of State in the Middle East, Lord Moyne, one of his closest friends, with whom he had talked in Cairo two weeks earlier, and whose well-known dislike of Zionism, Churchill explained to Weizmann, was now 'a thing of the past'. Moyne had 'changed and developed' in the last two years, Churchill told the Zionist leader. Weizmann at once prepared to leave for Cairo; but was too late. Within twenty-four hours, Moyne was dead; gunned down with his driver by two Jewish terrorists.

Churchill was deeply shocked; but he opposed reprisals. Pressed by the Colonial Secretary to suspend at once all Jewish immigration to Palestine, he refused to do so. He also refused to appoint, as Moyne's successor, either of two suitable nominees, because he knew they were hostile to Zionism. But in the debate on Moyne's murder he told the Commons: 'If our dreams for Zionism are to end in the smoke of assassins' pistols and our labours for its future to produce only a new set of gangsters worthy of Nazi Germany, many like myself will have to reconsider the position we have maintained so consistently and so long in the past. If there is to be any hope of a peaceful and successful future for Zionism, these wicked activities must cease, and those responsible for them must be destroyed root and branch.'

There was, Churchill told the Commons, an avenue of hope: 'I have received a letter from Dr Weizmann, President of the World Zionist Organisation – a very old friend of mine – who has arrived in Palestine, in which he assures me that Palestine Jewry will go to the utmost limit of its power to cut out this evil from its midst.' Weizmann had appealed to the Jewish population 'to render all necessary assistance to the authorities in the prevention of terrorist acts, and in the eradication of the terrorist organisation'.

Moyne's murderers, members of the extremist Stern Gang, were executed in Cairo, the scene of their crime. The Jewish Agency and the British authorities in Palestine joined forces in tracking down other members of the Stern Gang and their caches of arms. Churchill's support for Jewish statehood in Palestine remained firm and uncompromising.

In the weeks immediately following his return from Moscow, Churchill acted to uphold his 'percentages' agreement with Stalin. Learning in the first week of November that the head of the British Military Mission in Roumania had protested about the extent of Russian control there, he wrote to Eden, 'We have only a ten per cent interest in Roumania, and are little more than spectators.' Unless care were taken, 'we shall get retaliation in Greece, which we still hope to save'. Every liberated or 'subverted' country, Churchill explained to Eden a week later, was 'seething with Communism'. All were linked together 'and only our influence with Russia prevents their actively stimulating this movement, deadly as I conceive it to the freedom of mankind'.

On November 10 Churchill was on his travels again, flying to Paris, which he had last seen shortly before its fall in 1940. On November 11, the Armistice Day of the Great War, he drove as General de Gaulle's guest to the Arc de Triomphe, where they laid wreaths at the Tomb of the Unknown Soldier before taking the salute at an hour-long march-past. 'He had a wonderful reception,' Brooke wrote in his diary, 'and the Paris crowd went quite mad over him.' Four days later Churchill telegraphed to Roosevelt that he had re-established 'friendly private relations' with de Gaulle, and that he had 'a considerable feeling of stability' in France 'in spite of Communist threats'. The French politicians he had met had impressed him. 'I hope you will not consider that I am putting on French clothes while I say this.'

To help de Gaulle internally, Churchill instructed Ismay to send two thousand rifles and one hundred Sten guns 'as fast as possible' to the French Ministry of the Interior, 'for the purpose of arming the police'.

From Paris, Churchill went overnight by train, with de Gaulle, to Besançon. From there they drove sixty miles through heavy snow to a French artillery observation-post near the front line. It was snowing too heavily to see anything; indeed the French attack planned for that afternoon had to be put off because of the snow. On the way back to French headquarters for lunch, Churchill's car twice had a puncture, and once stuck in a rut at the side of the road. 'He arrived completely frozen and almost rolled up on himself like a hedgehog,' Brooke later recalled. 'He was placed in a chair with a hot water bottle at his feet and one in the back of his chair; at the same time good brandy was poured down his throat to warm him internally. The results were wonderful, he thawed out rapidly and when the time came produced one of those indescribably funny French speeches which brought the house down.'

That night Churchill returned to Paris on de Gaulle's train. 'Winston was in excellent form,' Brooke wrote in his diary, 'and even de Gaulle unbent a little.' Reaching Paris, Churchill's coaches were detached and sent eastward again, this time to Rheims. There Eisenhower was waiting to take him to his headquarters, where he was told the General's plans to reach the Rhine. Returning to London, he learned that Russia's 'aloofness' in Greece was having a dampening effect on the Greek Communists. 'This "aloofness" of Russia,' he commented to Eden, 'shows the way in which they are keeping to the general lay-out we fixed at Moscow.' Four days later he wrote again, 'This is good, and shows how Stalin is playing the game.'

To at least one member of Churchill's Secretariat, the week following Churchill's return from France was not a good one. 'He has frittered away his time in the last week,' Colville wrote in his diary on November 30, 'and has seemed unable or unwilling or too tired to give his attention to complex matters. He has been reading the first paragraph or so and referring papers to people without seeing what is really required of him. Result: chaos.' When Churchill spoke in the Commons on November 29, however, his speech was well received. He spoke, noted Nicolson, 'of the need of youth – "Youth, youth, youth and renovation, energy, boundless energy" – and as he said these words, he bent his knees and pounded the air like a pugilist – "and of controversy, health-giving controversy. I am not afraid of it in this country," he said, and then took off his glasses and grinned round at the Conservative benches. "We are a decent lot," he said, beaming upon them. Then he swung round and leant forward over the box right in the faces of the Labour people: "All of us," he added, "the whole nation." '

Nicolson commented: 'It read so mildly in the newspapers next morning. Yet in fact it was the perfect illustration of the Parliamentary art.'

On November 30 Churchill celebrated his seventieth birthday at the Annexe with Clementine, his three daughters – Diana, Sarah and Mary – his brother Jack and his son-in-law Duncan Sandys. Three close friends were also present, Eden, Beaverbrook and Bracken. After Beaverbrook. proposed the toast, wrote Mary, 'Papa's reply made me weep. He said we were "the dearest there are" – he said he had been "comforted and supported by our love", and then, very slowly – almost solemnly – he clinked glasses with each one of us.' On the following day he drove from Chequers to Harrow for the school songs. Afterwards there was a sherry party at which, wrote Colville, 'the PM talked long and charmingly to the School Monitors, much as he did to the Midshipmen on the *King George V* last January, enthralling but never patronising'.

That week Churchill's main worry was the apparent breach, in Yugoslavia, of the fifty-fifty October agreement with Stalin. 'Tito has turned very nasty,' he told Smuts, 'and is of course thinking now only of grabbing Trieste, Istria, Fiume etc for a virtually Communised Yugoslavia. I am having great difficulty in getting the right-hand move, to which you know I am attracted, under way in time to influence events. Everything is very ponderous.'

The 'right-hand move' was the advance from the head of the Adriatic through the Ljubljana gap to Zagreb, and then northwards into Austria; the move General Maitland Wilson had first proposed five months earlier.

On December 3 Churchill protested to Tito about his refusal to allow British warships to dock at Split and Sibenik, two of the Dalmatian ports under Partisan control. He also protested when Tito asked for the withdrawal of a British military unit helping the Partisans near Dubrovnik. But even as he was fighting this losing battle to obtain the fifty-fifty division of influence in Yugoslavia, Churchill saw danger looming for Britain's predominant position in Greece, where the Government in Athens was finding it impossible to demobilise the Communist guerilla forces. 'It is important to let it be known,' he told Eden, 'that if there is a civil war in Greece we shall be on the side of the Government we have set up in Athens, and that above all we shall not hesitate to shoot.'

So vehement was Churchill against the growing dominance of the Communist forces in parts of Athens that on the morning of December 4 he provoked a word of caution from Clementine:

My darling Winston,
Please do not before ascertaining full facts repeat to anyone you meet
today what you said to me this morning i.e. that the Communists in
Athens had shown their usual cowardice in putting the women & children
in front to be shot at – because altho' Communists are dangerous, indeed

*perhaps sinister people, they seem in this war on the Continent to have
shown personal courage.*

  *I write this only because I may not see you till tomorrow & I am anxious
(perhaps over-anxious).*

  Your loving & devoted

                                    Clemmie

  *'Tout savoir, c'est tout comprendre; tout comprendre, c'est tout
pardonner.'*

Throughout December 4 Churchill received details of growing Communist violence in the streets of Athens, including the murder of many
policemen, and the seizing of police stations. That night he telegraphed
to the senior British officer in Greece, General Scobie, 'Do not hesitate to
fire at any armed male in Athens who assails the British authority or Greek
authority with which we are working.' In carrying out these orders the
extra authority of the Greek Government would be helpful, but, Churchill
added, 'Do not hesitate to act as if you were in a conquered city where a
local rebellion is in progress.' As for the Greek Communist forces approaching Athens from the surrounding countryside, 'you should surely
be able with your armour to give some of them a lesson which will make
the others unlikely to try.' Churchill's telegram ended, 'It would be a great
thing for you to succeed in this without bloodshed if possible, but also with
bloodshed if necessary.'

Scobie had taken 1,800 Communist prisoners. On the following day
there were protests in the Commons at Britain's action, and a debate which
Churchill demanded should be treated as a Vote of Confidence. 'One must
have some respect for democracy and not use the word too lightly,' he said.
'The last thing that resembles democracy is mob law, with bands of
gangsters, armed with deadly weapons, forcing their way into great cities,
seizing the police stations and key points of government, endeavouring to
introduce a totalitarian regime with an iron hand, and clamouring, as they
can nowadays if they get power, to shoot everyone who is politically
inconvenient.'

'Democracy is no harlot,' Churchill continued, 'to be picked up in the
street by a man with a tommy-gun.' If the vote went against him for his action
in Greece, 'I will gladly accept my dismissal at the hands of the House; but
if I am not so dismissed – make no mistake about it – we shall persist in this
policy of clearing Athens and the Athens region of all who are rebels against
the authority of the constitutional Government of Greece.' When the Vote
of Confidence was taken, 279 MPs voted for the Government and 30 against.
That night Churchill asked Macmillan to join him at the Annexe. 'He
rambled on in a sad and depressed way,' Macmillan wrote in his diary that

night. 'The debate had obviously tired him very much, and I think he realised the dangers inherent in the Greek policy on which we are now embarked. He has won the debate, but not the battle of Athens.'

On December 9 Churchill gave orders for military reinforcements to be sent to Greece from Italy 'without the slightest delay'. That day Scobie telegraphed that he had used machine-guns and tanks against Communist strongpoints inside Athens, killing fourteen 'rebels' and capturing 250. Scobie found 'most worrying' the 'activities' of the Russian Military Mission in Athens, headed by Colonel Grigori Popov. Churchill did not take alarm; Stalin after all had remained silent about Greece. 'Remember the percentages we wrote out on paper?' Churchill asked Eden on December 11. 'I think we have had pretty good treatment from Stalin in Greece, much better in fact than we have had from the Americans.'

On December 9 the Chief of the American Naval Staff had cancelled the order whereby seven American landing-craft were conveying British troops and supplies to Greece. There was also anger in the United States when Churchill's orders to Scobie to act as though he were in a 'conquered city' were published in the *Washington Post*. They had been accidentally leaked during their secret transmission through Italy.

On December 12 Alexander reached Athens from Italy. The situation was 'more serious' than he had previously thought, he telegraphed to Churchill. That day the War Cabinet agreed to support Alexander with whatever measures or reinforcements he thought necessary. At his side, the Greek Government forces, commanded by General Plastiras, were struggling to maintain control. Encouraging news reached Churchill that day from Alexander, who telegraphed, 'I met Colonel Popov of the Russian Military Mission today and walked him down the street in friendly and animated conversation', for the 'benefit', Alexander added, of the Greeks, 'who I hope will be duly impressed'. Stalin was keeping his October bargain.

Macmillan, who was now in Athens, and the British Ambassador there, Reginald Leeper, both recommended the appointment of Archbishop Damaskinos as Regent, and the creation of a Government under him which the Communists could accept. Churchill was at first uneasy about this, being afraid that the Archbishop would establish 'a dictatorship of the Left'. If the 'powers of evil' were to prevail in Greece, he warned on December 22, 'we must look forward to a quasi-Bolshevised Russian-led Balkan Peninsula and this may spread to Hungary and Italy'. In Athens, Macmillan, Leeper and Scobie were trying to persuade the Greek Communists to join a 'broad-based' Cabinet led by the Archbishop.

On the evening of December 22, at the Annexe, Churchill spoke to John Martin and Jock Colville of flying to Athens 'to settle the matter'. But nothing was decided by the early hours of the morning; so long did the discussion go on that it was too late for Churchill to drive down to Chequers that night as planned, and he slept at the Annexe. On the following day, December 23, he worked in bed all day, until five in the afternoon. The news from the battlefield was of a successful German counter-attack into the Ardennes, with American troops driven back and surounded. Then he was driven to Chequers, where his family had already gathered for Christmas. As soon as he arrived, however, he told Clementine he would not be staying for the Christmas celebrations; he would be flying to Athens instead. She was devastated, went to her room, and wept.

That night Churchill asked Colville to make the flying arrangements for the journey to Athens. His only fear, he told Colville, was lest 'the weather bugger us up'. On the morning of December 24 Eden offered to go in his place; after a long talk on the telephone, Eden agreed to go with him. They would leave that very night, Christmas Eve. 'Two of your friends,' Churchill telegraphed to Alexander, 'of whom I am one, hope to be in Athens tomorrow.'

Half an hour before midnight, while the Christmas Eve festivities were at their height throughout Britain, Churchill left Chequers for Northolt. At 1.05 he was airborne; his aircraft, an American C54 Skymaster transport just converted for his use, had completed its trials only the previous day. 'She is the most luxurious craft imaginable,' Marian Holmes and Elizabeth Layton wrote in their joint diary of the unexpected journey. 'There are bunks for eight besides the PM, and a dining saloon' and swivel chairs and satin curtains throughout the aircraft. A snowstorm over France forced the Skymaster to climb to 13,500 feet; Churchill was woken up so that he could put on an oxygen mask.

On the morning of December 25 the Skymaster landed at Naples to refuel. 'Love and many thoughts for you all at luncheon today,' Churchill telegraphed to Clementine. 'I am sorry indeed not to see the tree.' At 10.45 he was airborne again; during the flight he dictated a telegram to Roosevelt: 'Anthony and I are going out to see what we can do to square this Greek entanglement. We cannot abandon those who have taken up arms in our cause, and must if necessary fight it out with them.'

At two in the afternoon on Christmas Day, Churchill's Skymaster landed at Kalamaki airport near Athens. He did not leave the plane; instead, as British soldiers guarded it, he held a conference on board with Alexander, Scobie, Macmillan and Leeper. As the wind howled round the plane, and those inside it got colder and colder, it was decided to invite the Greek Communists to join in a discussion with all the Greek parties, with a view to ending the fighting and setting up an all-Party Government led by the Archbishop. Churchill then prepared a communiqué announcing this invitation. As he dictated it, noted Elizabeth Layton, his cabin in the aircraft 'was bumping up and down in the wind. He looked flushed and uncomfortable, and was wrapped in several coats.' At one moment in the dictation Churchill stopped and said to her, 'That was a cannon – did you hear it?'

At four o'clock that afternoon Churchill left the Skymaster and was driven to the naval base at Phaleron Bay, passing a spot which had been shelled by the Communists that very morning. Reaching the base just after sunset, he was taken by barge to the cruiser *Ajax*, flagship of the Mediterranean Fleet. A few hours later the Archbishop arrived on board; as the Admiral and Colville led him to Churchill's cabin they came face to face with a fancy-dress party which was wending its way along the decks as part of the Christmas Day festivities. The revellers took the Archbishop, in his black robes and tall hat, for the leader of a rival party of revellers, but fortunately the Admiral intervened, 'in time', Colville noted, 'to prevent disaster'.

Churchill was impressed by Damaskinos, whose bitterness over the Communist atrocities had led him to issue an encyclical against them that very day. Would he be willing to preside over a conference of all the Greek political parties, including the Communists, Churchill asked. Damaskinos agreed to do so, and returned to the city.

On the morning of December 26 Churchill went on deck, from where, Colville noted, he could see 'the smoke of battle in the street-fighting west of the Piraeus, and there is a constant noise of shell-fire and machine-guns'. Four British fighters could be seen in the sky, strafing a Communist strongpoint on the side of one of the hills surrounding Athens. Later, while Churchill was dictating to Marian Holmes in his cabin, shells exploded near the battleship. 'There – you bloody well missed us!' he cried. 'Come on – try again!'

As Churchill prepared to leave *Ajax* for the shore, the ship was again straddled by Communist shell fire. Later, a salvo fell close to the Admiral's barge as it approached the shore with Churchill on board. An armoured car and military escort was at the quayside, to take him to the British Embassy, where he made what Colville described as a 'stirring speech' to the secretaries, typists and cypher clerks, thanking them for their excellent work in arduous conditions.

'I addressed all the plucky women on the Embassy staff who have been in continued danger and discomfort for so many weeks, but are in the gayest of moods,' Churchill telegraphed to Clementine. Then, shortly after five o'clock, he left by armoured car for the conference room at the Greek Foreign Ministry. Among those awaiting him there was Colonel Popov, Stalin's representative.

111. At Teheran, with Stalin and Roosevelt, 28 November 1943.
Behind them are Molotov, Harriman, Sir Archibald Clark Kerr (British
Ambassador to Russia), Sarah Churchill and Eden

112. Recuperating at Tunis,
Christmas 1943

113. With Eisenhower, Tunis,
Christmas 1943

114. Inspecting bomb damage to Lord Kitchener's statue, Horse Guards Parade, 21 February 1944

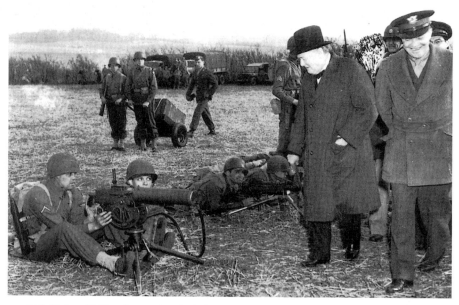

115. Before D-Day: inspecting American troop preparations in Britain with General Eisenhower, 23 March 1944

116. Normandy, 21 July 1944, with Brigadier P. G. Calvert-Jones,
at the Observation Post of C Troop, 121st Medium Regiment, Royal
Artillery, near Audrieu, watching a British artillery concentration fall
on German positions along the Tilly-Villers Bocage road. This was the
first time in the war that Churchill had looked over German positions

117. Normandy, 22 July 1944. Lieutenant-General O'Connor,
Churchill, Field Marshal Smuts, General Montgomery and
General Brooke. A contemporary caption notes that they were
watching British planes 'pass over to bomb the enemy'

118. With British troops, and General Montgomery, Normandy,
22 July 1944

119. With Tito, at the Villa Rivalta, Naples, 12 August 1944

120. With General Alexander in Italy, 26 August 1944, in the town of Croce, near the Metauro River

121. At Yalta with Roosevelt, during a break in the proceedings, 4 February 1945

122. At Yalta with Roosevelt and Stalin, 9 February 1945. Air Chief Marshal Portal is behind Churchill

123. In Athens with the Regent, Archbishop Damaskinos,
14 February 1945

124. At the Fayyum Oasis with Ibn Saud, King of Saudi Arabia,
17 February 1945. Churchill's naval aide-de-camp, Tommy Thompson,
is on the far right.

125. At the Siegfried Line, 4 March 1945, with Field Marshal Brooke, Field Marshal Montgomery and General Simpson (commanding the Ninth American Army)

126. Picnicking on the west bank of the Rhine with Brooke and Montgomery, 26 March 1945

127. Victory-in-Europe Day (VE-Day): attempting to drive along
Whitehall in an open car to the House of Commons, 8 May 1945

128. Electioneering west of London, 23 June 1945

129. Electioneering in his constituency, with Clementine, 26 June 1945

130. Walking over the rubble through the courtyard of Hitler's Chancellery, Berlin, 16 July 1945. Churchill's daughter Mary is on his right

131. With President Truman at Potsdam, leaving Truman's residence, 16 July 1945

132. Victory Parade on the Charlottenburger Strasse, Berlin,
21 July 1945. On Churchill's immediate right, the Labour Party Leader
and Leader of the Opposition, Clement Attlee, who was to return to
London to become Prime Minister in Churchill's place

133. Close-up of the parade. Left to right: Lord Cherwell, Field
Marshal Montgomery, Churchill, General Ismay, Field Marshal
Alexander, Churchill's doctor Lord Moran (paper in hand), Anthony
Eden and Clement Attlee

134. With his son Randolph and daughter Mary at an American military cemetery near Namur, 15 July 1946

135. At Chartwell, working on the proofs of his war memoirs, 29 April 1947

136. Weeping at the ovation given to his speech to the Congress of Europe at The Hague, 7 May 1948. Clapping, from left to right are Dr Kerstens (Holland), Paul Ramadier (France), Dr Retinger (Secretary General of the Congress) and Denis de Rougement (one of the founders of the European Movement)

137. At the Old Surrey and Burstow Hunt, Chartwell Farm, 27 November 1948, three days before his seventy-fourth birthday

138. Election headquarters, October 1951. On 26 October 1951 Churchill became Prime Minister for the second time

139. At Windsor, in his Garter robes, 14 June 1954

140. Churchill and Eden reach Washington, 25 June 1954. They are greeted by John Foster Dulles (Secretary of State) and Richard Nixon (Vice-President)

141. Escorting Queen Elizabeth to her car after a dinner at 10 Downing Street on 4 April 1955, his last night as Prime Minister. Lady Churchill and the Duke of Edinburgh are behind the Queen. Both Churchill and the Queen are wearing the sash of the Order of the Garter

142. Painting in the South of France, at La Pausa, Roquebrune, 1957. Churchill was then eighty-two

The Communist delegates had not yet arrived. Nor could Churchill know if they had any intention of arriving. Shells could be heard still falling in the distance, as could the sound of rocket fire from the British fighters. In a room lit only by a few hurricane lamps, the Archbishop made his opening statement. He would be willing to form a Government, he said, and if necessary to do so without the Communists. Churchill then began to speak; he was half-way through his statement when everyone suddenly heard what Colville called 'noises off, and three shabby desperadoes, who had been searched and almost stripped before being allowed to enter, came into the dimly-lit conference room.' It was the Communist delegates. The proceedings then began all over again.

After the Archbishop had repeated his speech, Churchill told the delegates, 'Mr Eden and I have come all this way, although great battles are raging in Belgium and on the German frontier, to make this effort to rescue Greece from a miserable fate and raise her to a point of great fame and repute.' He and Eden would be available for consultation at any time. He wished them well. Whether Greece remained a monarchy or became a republic 'is a matter for Greeks and Greeks alone to decide'. As he was speaking the sound of gunfire could be heard outside. At one point, Colville noted, 'the roar of descending rockets' fired by the British fighters at a nearby Communist position 'almost drowned his words'.

It was, Churchill told Clementine, 'intensely dramatic, all those haggard Greek faces round the table and the Archbishop with his enormous hat, making him, I should think, seven feet high'. As to the Communist delegates, they 'certainly look a much better lot than the Lublin illegitimates'. When the Greeks began to speak, the discussion became heated, whereupon Churchill rose to his feet and declared: 'I should like to go now. We have begun the work. See that you finish it.' On his way out, he shook the hands of the three Communist delegates. Colonel Popov, who was present throughout, had made no comment or intervention.

The Greek delegates, Churchill told his wife, 'are the very top ones. We have now left them together as it was a Greek show. It may break up at any moment. We shall wait for a day or two if necessary to see. At least we have done our best.' Churchill returned to *Ajax*, which had moved a mile further off shore to avoid the spasmodic Communist mortar fire. That afternoon, while he was briefly on the bridge with the ship's Captain, further shells fell in the sea around them. Should he return fire, the Captain asked, to which Churchill replied, 'I have come to Greece on a mission of peace, Captain. I bear the olive branch between my teeth. But far be it for me to intervene with military necessity. RETURN FIRE!'

That night Churchill again slept aboard *Ajax*. As a precaution against underwater attack, depth charges were exploded throughout the night.

At noon on the following day, December 27, he returned to the British Embassy. As he was about to leave the building with Scobie, to visit British military positions in the city, a burst of machine-gun fire from more than a mile away struck the wall of a house thirty feet above him. 'Several bursts were fired,' Colville noted, 'and a woman in the street was killed.'

Continuing with his visit to the troops,' Churchill then returned to the Embassy for lunch, after which he saw the United States Ambassador and, Colville noted, 'gave him a piece of his mind about the very inadequate support the USA have given us in this whole affair'. He then gave a Press Conference, his words continually interrupted by the roar of mortar shells. 'If no satisfactory and trustworthy democratic foundation' could be agreed upon by the Greeks themselves, he said, 'you may have to have, for the time being, an international trust of some kind or other. We cannot afford to see whole peoples drifting into anarchy.'

Churchill then saw the Archbishop once more, to be told that the Communists were demanding very severe terms for joining the Government. Two of the Communist delegates asked to see him, but the Archbishop was strongly against any such meeting. Churchill hesitated. 'Winston very inclined to see them,' Macmillan noted in his diary, 'but I persuaded him (and Anthony agreed) that if we were going to put our money on the Archbishop, we must let him play the hand as he thought best.' Macmillan added: 'Winston partly wanted to see them as a good journalist, but partly because he has an innocence which is very charming but sometimes dangerous. He believed he could win them over. But I felt he would much more probably be deceived and betrayed.'

Churchill accepted Macmillan's and Eden's advice. Then he wrote to the two Communists to explain to them that as the conference was 'wholly Greek in character', he could not see them. He hoped, however, 'that the discussions that have taken place and contacts which have been made will result in a speedy end to the melancholy conflict proceeding between men of one country'. He made no accusation or recriminations. 'The hatreds between these Greeks are terrible,' he wrote to Clementine.

In the evening Churchill returned to *Ajax*. That night Macmillan found him 'still worrying about his refusal to grant a private interview' with the Communist delegates. But it was too late. His Greek mission was at an end. It would be up to the Archbishop to find a Prime Minister who could form the broadest possible Government, with or without the Communists. Britain would continue to defend that Government's position, at least in Athens itself. That night Churchill telegraphed to the Chiefs of Staff, asking them to agree to a brigade of troops then in Palestine being sent to Athens; they did. He also asked that fifteen of the women on the staff of the British Embassy in Athens should be given the British Empire Medal in the imminent New Year's Honours List. One of the women whose name he sent forward was awarded the MBE for 'tireless devotion to duty under fire'.

Aboard *Ajax* on the morning of December 28, Churchill thought of staying in Athens another day and calling another meeting of the conference. Macmillan wrote in his diary, 'He did not like the idea of going home without a peace, or at least a truce, arranged.' But by midday he had agreed to leave Athens without further meetings. Before setting off for the airport he sent Roosevelt a full account of what had been done, telling the President: 'I do not consider Archbishop is at all Left Wing in Communist sense. On the contrary he seems to be an extremely determined man bent on establishing a small strong executive in Greece to prevent the continuance of civil war.' It was a 'painful sight', Churchill added, 'to see this city with street-fighting raging, now here, now there, and the poor people all pinched and only kept alive by rations we are carrying to them, often at loss of life, at the various depots.' Britain had lost 'over one thousand men'. She was now reinforcing, and the military conflict would go on. 'The vast majority of the people long for a settlement that will free them from the Communist terror.'

As he prepared to leave *Ajax*, Churchill received a telegram from Montgomery to say that the German offensive in the Ardennes, aimed at the recapture of Antwerp, had failed. After addressing the ship's company, he left by barge for Phaleron, and then drove in a procession of jeeps and armoured cars to Kalamaki airport. After a short speech to the Royal Air Force personnel there, he boarded his Skymaster. There was one final hitch. As the plane was taxi-ing for take-off, Churchill called out, 'Stop the aircraft!' He had been reading a draft copy of the final communiqué of his visit, which said that he, Eden, Macmillan and Alexander had left the capital. This, Churchill felt, might give the impression that Britain was abandoning Greece to her fate. The aircraft was stopped and an amended communiqué given to one of the British diplomats still standing on the tarmac.

The Skymaster was finally airborne at 2.30; Churchill hoped to be back in England that evening, but after touch down at Naples there were reports of fog over southern England. He would stay that night at Naples. 'Hope to be with you at dinner tomorrow,' he telegraphed to Clementine. 'I was feeling lonely.'

On the morning of December 29 Churchill flew from Naples to London, flying over liberated France from Toulon to Cherbourg. At 3.30 in the afternoon the plane landed at Bovingdon airbase, where Clementine was waiting to greet him. Two and a half hours later, at Downing Street, he and Eden gave the War Cabinet an account of their journey. Then, at 10.30 that evening, they had a two-hour session with King George II of Greece, who was unwilling to appoint Damaskinos as Regent. At 1.30 a.m. they saw George again. 'I had to tell the King that if he did not agree, the matter would be settled without him, and that we would recognise the new government instead of him,' Churchill told Roosevelt. Finally, at 4 a.m., the Greek King accepted a Damaskinos Regency. Churchill then went to bed, twenty-two hours after he had been awakened at Naples.

In Athens, the Communists continued to put forward terms which Damaskinos was not prepared to accept. In the end, he asked General Plastiras to form a Government, from which the Communists were excluded. In Washington and in London there was strong criticism of Britain's intervention in Greece. 'The bitter misunderstandings which have arisen in the United States and in degenerate circles at home,' Churchill told Clementine, 'are only a foretaste of the furies which will be loosed about every stage of the peace settlement. I am sure in Greece I found one of the best opportunities for wise action that this war has tossed to me from its dark waves.'

Stalin was now threatening to recognise the Lublin Poles as the Government of Poland, and to exclude altogether the London Poles. On learning this, Churchill pressed for the quickest possible meeting of himself, Roosevelt and Stalin, who, however, said his doctors would not let him leave the Soviet Union, and suggested they meet at the Soviet Black Sea resort of Yalta. The ailing Roosevelt would therefore have to travel more than six thousand miles, and the seventy-year-old Churchill nearly four thousand. 'If we had spent ten years on research,' Churchill told Hopkins, 'we could not have found a worse place in the world.' Roosevelt would go by ship as far as Malta, then on by air. Churchill would fly all the way. He and Roosevelt would meet in Malta first. 'I shall be waiting on the quay,' Churchill telegraphed to the President on New Year's Day 1945.

For much of New Year's Day Churchill worked in bed. 'You know I can't give you the excitement of Athens every day,' he told Marian Holmes during the dictation. But on January 3, only five days after his return from Greece, he left England once more, flying from Northolt to Eisenhower's headquarters just outside Paris. On the following evening he took an overnight train to Montgomery's headquarters near Ghent. After spending the morning with Montgomery, he was driven to Brussels and flew back to England. His discussions had given him a clear picture of the plans for the next phase of the battle, the advance to the Rhine. He had found 'no trace of discord' on his visit, Churchill told Roosevelt, but 'there is this brutal fact: we need more fighting troops to make things move'.

In an attempt to put Eisenhower's mind at ease, Churchill telegraphed to Stalin to ask when the next Russian offensive would be, in order, he explained, to give Eisenhower 'the assurance that the German reinforcements will have to be split between both our flaming fronts'. The next Soviet offensive would come not later than 'the second half of January', Stalin informed him. 'I am most grateful to you for your thrilling message,' Churchill replied.

In the political sphere, January 11 saw an agreement signed between Tito and the former Ban of Croatia, Dr Subasic, whereby the future Government of Yugoslavia would be shared between the Communist and non-Communist parties; thus Churchill's fifty-fifty Moscow agreement with Stalin on Yugoslavia seemed secure. 'We should insist as far as is possible,' Churchill explained to Roosevelt, 'on full and fair elections deciding the future régime of the Yugoslav people or peoples.'

On January 12 Churchill was angered when Montgomery, in a public speech, appeared to belittle the American contribution in the Ardennes battle. 'I thought his speech most unfortunate,' Churchill told the Chiefs of Staff. 'It had a patronising tone and completely overlooked the fact that the United States lost perhaps 80,000 men and we but 2,000 or 3,000. Through no fault of ours we have been very little engaged in this battle, which has been a great American struggle with glory as well as disaster.'

Churchill now made his plans to fly to Yalta. The issues to be discussed were mounting. On January 15 he telegraphed to Roosevelt about growing Soviet pressure in Persia, where the Russians hoped, he said, 'to secure what they want by the using of the big stick'. Before leaving he gave the Commons a survey of the war situation; his speech, noted Colville, 'was the best effort I have heard him make since 1941 or even 1940'; Harold Nicolson wrote of its 'immense vivacity, persuasiveness and humour'.

Speaking of the Anglo-American demand for the unconditional surrender of Germany, which had been widely criticised as too severe, Churchill stressed that the Germans knew full well 'how strict are the moral limits within which our action is confined', and he spoke out to them, to Britain's foes: 'We are no extirpators of nations, or butchers of peoples. We make no bargain with you. We accord you nothing as a right. Abandon your resistance unconditionally. We remain bound by our customs and our nature.'

Before Churchill spoke this last sentence, Nicolson noticed that he had taken off his glasses, and, as he spoke, 'struck his breast like an orangoutang'; a powerful and effective gesture. Britain would behave with humanity, even to the defeated tyrants.

On January 20, Hungary signed an armistice with the Allies. That day the Red Army crossed the German borders both in East Prussia and Silesia.

There was a sense of elation in London. But Churchill was angered that day by a letter from Attlee protesting at his lengthy disquisitions in Cabinet on papers which he had not read, and on subjects which he had not taken the trouble to master. Colville commented: 'Greatly as I love and admire the PM I am afraid there is much in what Attlee says, and I rather admire his courage in saying it. Many Conservatives – and officials such as Cadogan and Bridges, feel the same.'

Tersely, Churchill replied to Attlee, 'You may be sure I shall always endeavour to profit by your counsels.' Then he invited his staff to go with him to the Air Ministry to see a film-show, bidding them, Colville noted, to 'cast care aside and "not bother about Atler or Hitlee"', and so all the typists, drivers, servants etc' went off to see a newsreel of the German Air Force attack on British airfields in Holland on New Year's Day, and then *Dark Victory*, a 1939 American film about a society girl who discovers she is dying of a brain tumour, starring Bette Davis, with small parts by both Humphrey Bogart and Ronald Reagan.

On January 29 Churchill left London on the first lap of his journey to Yalta. On reaching Malta, at four in the morning of January 30, he felt so ill that he remained in bed in the aeroplane for six hours, while it sat on the tarmac. Then he felt well enough to leave the aeroplane for the cruiser *Orion*, where he went straight back to bed. At dinner that night he was feeling better, and had what Eden called 'some quite good preliminary talk on our conference problems'.

For the next two days there were more discussions with Eden, and with the Chiefs of Staff. It was also a time of reflection: 'I am free to confess to you,' Churchill wrote to Clementine on February 1, 'that my heart is saddened by the tales of the masses of German women and children flying along the roads everywhere in forty-mile-long columns to the West before the advancing armies. I am clearly convinced that they deserve it; but that does not remove it from one's gaze. The misery of the whole world appals me, and I fear increasingly that new struggles may arise out of those we are successfully ending.'

On the morning of February 2 Roosevelt reached Malta. His frailty was at once apparent, as were his failing powers. At the meetings which he attended he said almost nothing, yet decisions crucial for the future of Europe, and of democracy, were being made. The burden of America's cause, as well as Britain's, fell on Churchill's shoulders. He bore the burden unhesitatingly; when, at a meeting of the Combined Chiefs of Staff that afternoon, he said 'it was essential that we occupy as much of Austria as possible, as it was undesirable that more of Western Europe than necessary should be occupied by the Russians', there was no dissent. That night, on

Orion, Churchill visited the wardroom where, wrote Marian Holmes, 'he stood at the bar and had a drink with all the officers crowding round him. He is simply wonderful at these impromptu chats'. Churchill's last words to the young officers were: 'I hope you've looked after my two young ladies. They go everywhere with me and don't mind putting up with my bad temper.'

Shortly after midnight Churchill, his daughter Sarah and Eden drove to Malta's airport. Three hours later they were airborne. Seven hours later they landed at Saki airport in the Crimea, where they waited for Roosevelt's plane to arrive. The President was a 'tragic figure', Churchill later wrote. 'He could not get out of the open motor car, and I walked at his side while he inspected the guard.' From the airport Churchill was driven for more than seven hours across the southern Crimea and over the Tauride Mountains to Yalta, to the magnificent Vorontsov Villa, overlooking the Black Sea, which was to be his base for the next eight days. Built in the Scottish baronial style by a former Tsarist Ambassador to Britain, it had been given by Hitler as a gift to Field Marshal von Manstein, after his conquest of the Crimea in 1942.

On the afternoon of February 4, Stalin called on Churchill at the Vorontsov Villa. Churchill's first act was to present Stalin's interpreter, Pavlov, with the insignia of the CBE, about which Churchill had told him in Moscow three and a half months earlier. He then informed Stalin of the Anglo-American offensive due to start in four days' time, with the Rhine as its object, and showed him the Map Room in which Captain Pim had displayed the latest information from all the war fronts. An hour after Stalin left, Churchill was driven along the corniche to the Livadia Palace, once the residence of Tsar Nicholas II, where the ailing Roosevelt was staying, and where the Conference itself would take place. The first meeting began at five o'clock. 'We had the world at our feet,' Churchill later reflected. 'Twenty-five million men marching at our orders by land and sea. We seemed to be friends.'

At the first plenary session Churchill proposed Staff discussions on a possible Anglo-American landing at the head of the Adriatic and through the Ljubljana gap 'in order to join up with the Russian left flank'. He also asked for a Soviet attack on Danzig, where the Germans were building a new type of submarine, 'ahead of us in certain technical ways', which had already sunk twelve ships in waters close to the British Isles. Stalin agreed. When, at dinner that night, Roosevelt suddenly agreed with Stalin that peace should be made by the Great Powers and not by the small ones, Churchill remarked, 'The eagle should permit the small birds to sing and care not whereof they sang.'

On February 5, at a meeting of the British, American and Soviet Chiefs of Staff, the Russians, having pointed out that several divisions of German troops were being brought back across Europe to the Eastern Front, asked for a substantial Allied air attack on German communications in the. Berlin-Leipzig-Dresden region, and for the bombing of these three specific cities, as a matter of urgency. This was agreed and instructions given for a series of Anglo-American raids. That same day the Big Three discussed the political future of Germany. Stalin envisaged the dismemberment of Germany into five separate states, as proposed by Roosevelt at Teheran. Listening to this, Churchill commented to Eden, 'The only bond of the victors is their common hate.' To make Britain safe in the future, he added, 'she must become responsible for the safety of a cluster of feeble States'. To Stalin's chagrin, Churchill then advised caution with regard to the too-rapid 'dismemberment' of Germany.

In discussing the Allied occupation of Germany, Churchill pressed successfully for the French to be allowed a Zone, Roosevelt pointing out, to Churchill's alarm, that the American occupation would be 'limited to two years'. In discussing reparations, Churchill opposed too high a demand on Germany, recalling the failure of heavy reparations after the last war and telling Roosevelt and Stalin: 'If you want your horse to pull your wagon, you have to give him some hay.' It was agreed to instruct a Reparations Commission to work out the final sum. That night Churchill said to Sarah, before he went to sleep, 'I do not suppose that at any moment in history has the agony of the world been so great or widespread. Tonight the sun goes down on more suffering than ever in the World.'

On February 6 the Big Three discussed the World Organisation which they were in the process of creating. Its main instrument of decision in international disputes was to be a Security Council in which the Great Powers would exercise control. Churchill insisted, however, that the British Government would not be doing justice to its intentions if 'no provision was made for a full statement of grievances by the many smaller nations of the world'. No Great Power should have the right of veto on a matter in which it was one of the disputants; he instanced the question of China asking the Security Council for the return of Hong Kong. Both sides would state their case, and the Council would decide.

The discussion then turned to Poland, which was to dominate the Yalta Conference. 'Coming from America,' said Roosevelt, he took 'a distant point of view of the Polish question; the five or six million Poles in the United States were mostly of the second generation.' Churchill then spoke of the right of the Poles, within the new and more westerly frontiers on which Stalin had insisted, 'to live freely and to live their own lives in their own way'. Britain had gone to war in order that Poland could be 'free and sovereign'. It was Britain's wish that Poland 'should be mistress in her own house and captain of her own soul'. Poland must have 'full and free elections'. There must be a 'free vote of the Polish people' on their future Constitution and Administration.

When Stalin pressed the claims of the Lublin Poles for primacy in any interim governing instrument, Churchill replied, and reiterated, that the Lublin Government had no right to say that it represented the Polish nation. Somewhat testily, at this point Roosevelt remarked that 'Poland has been a source of trouble for over 500 years', to which Churchill replied, 'We must do what we can to put an end to those troubles.' Over the next five days Churchill was to spend many hours pressing for free elections for Poland and a multiplicity of political parties, urging 'real, substantial and effective representation' of the London Poles in any interim Government, as well as the participation of other independent, Trade Union and Socialist leaders then in Poland whom the Americans wanted included.

On February 7, driving with Sarah from the Vorontsov Villa to the Livadia Palace for the next meeting of the Big Three, Churchill looked out across the sun-sparkling sea, and then remarked, 'The Riviera of Hades.' That day, at the formal session, he supported a proposal by Molotov that the Soviet Union, though a single country, should have three seats at the United Nations Assembly; Russia, Byelorussia and the Ukraine. 'I should like to make a friendly gesture to Russia in this matter,' Churchill telegraphed to the War Cabinet, 'in view of other important concessions by them which are achieved or pending.' Russia received the three seats, which she has retained to this day.

One question raised on February 7 was how far to the west Poland's frontiers should be drawn. Stalin envisaged the German city of Breslau, and a large wedge of territory between the Eastern and Western Neisse rivers, being a part of the new Poland. Churchill thought that this was going too far west; that the Eastern Neisse river should be the limit of Poland's westward expansion, not the Western Neisse, which at certain points was more than a hundred miles further west. 'It would be a great pity,' Churchill said, 'to stuff the Polish goose so full of German food that it died of indigestion.' Stalin countered that there were no Germans left in that region 'as they had all run away'. Once more, Stalin's view was to prevail; his Army was already master of most of the region under discussion.

Physically the conference was not proving as hard as the one at Teheran, Sarah told her mother. 'They do not meet till 4 in the afternoon, when they have a whacking session of 4 to 5 hours and then they part, generally to their separate lairs. We dine quietly here – generally just Papa and Anthony and me – which of course is heaven. The pouch arrives unfortunately at about midnight – which prevents him getting to bed much before two.' Each morning Churchill would rise late, have an early lunch, work at his desk, have an early afternoon sleep, and be ready for the day's plenary session at four.

At the plenary session on February 8, Stalin stressed that only those States which had declared war on Germany could be invited to the first United Nations Conference fixed for April 25. Churchill then asked that Turkey should be invited, 'if she was now ready to make a death-bed confession and declare war'. Stalin agreed. Turkey accepted this offer with alacrity, declaring war on Germany on February 23, with effect from March 1.

The discussion then turned to Poland. As Stalin would not allow the London Poles an equal place in the interim Government of Poland, Churchill proposed another solution: Britain's worries about the Lublin Government would be removed, he said, 'if a free and unfettered general election were held in Poland by ballot and with universal suffrage and free candidatures'. Once such an election had been held, Britain 'would salute the Government that emerged without regard to the Polish Government in London'. He was pressing, Churchill telegraphed that day to the War Cabinet, for a 'free, fair, and unfettered election, which alone can give life and being to a Polish Government'.

To Churchill's surprise, Stalin then promised that free elections would be held. When Roosevelt asked how soon they could be held, Stalin replied disarmingly, 'It should be possible to hold them within a month.' There was nothing that Churchill could do but to accept that promise. When, over the coming weeks, it was slowly, deceptively, and systematically broken, the wartime Anglo-Soviet alliance was broken with it.

Ending the discussion that afternoon with a brief reference to Greece, Stalin told Churchill that he 'did not wish to interfere'. Churchill replied that he was 'much obliged'.

That night Stalin was host to Roosevelt and Churchill at his own residence, the Yusupov Palace. In a short speech, Churchill told the dinner guests that in the past nations that were comrades in arms had drifted apart within five or ten years of war: 'Thus toiling millions have followed a vicious circle, falling into the pit, and then by their sacrifices raising themselves up again. We now have a chance of avoiding the errors of previous generations, and of making a sure peace.'

During the toasts, Churchill raised his glass to the interpreters, to whom he declared, 'Interpreters of the World, Unite! You have nothing to lose but your audiences.' This parody of Karl Marx 'went with a bang', Portal wrote; Stalin was amused.

During the plenary session of February 9, Churchill and Roosevelt obtained assurances from Stalin that British and American observers would be able to monitor the elections in Poland, and that the leader of the London Poles, Stanislaw Mikolajczyk, would be able to take part in them, together with other candidates from his Peasant Party. In this way, Stalin built yet further on the credit of his promise of free and swift elections. He also gave Churchill an assurance on Yugoslavia, that he would use his influence to persuade Tito to carry out the January 11 agreement with Subasic, for an Assembly of National Liberation made up of all the pre-war political Parties, and a freely elected Constituent Assembly which would in due course confirm any legislation decided upon. When Churchill said that he knew he could 'rely on Marshal Stalin's goodwill' in asking Tito to give these assurances, Stalin replied emphatically, the minutes recorded, 'that when he made a statement he would carry it out'.

The last topic that day was the treatment of war criminals. At Teheran, Stalin had proposed taking 50,000 Germans and shooting them without trial. Churchill, who had been so offended by this at the time that he had walked out of the room in protest, now said that a list of war criminals would be drawn up and those on the list brought to trial, though personally he was inclined to feel that 'they should be shot as soon as they were caught and their identity established'. Stalin, hitherto an advocate of summary executions, now claimed to favour the judicial process. Roosevelt commented that it should not be 'too judicial'; journalists and photographers should be kept out 'until the criminals were dead'.

The plenary was over; driving back along the corniche to the Vorontsov Villa, Churchill found a telegram from Montgomery awaiting him: British and Canadian troops had reached, and breached, the Siegfried Line. Seven German towns and villages had been overrun and 1,800 prisoners taken. On the west bank of the Rhine south of Strasbourg, all German resistance had ceased. That night Churchill was in good humour; 'PM seems well,' commented Cadogan, 'though drinking buckets of Caucasian champagne which would undermine the health of any ordinary man.'

On the afternoon of February 10, at a private meeting with Stalin at the Yusupov Palace, Churchill agreed to the repatriation to Russia of those Russians who had been taken prisoner by the British while fighting with German units. Stalin particularly asked that these men should not be 'ill-treated' by the British before they were sent back. Churchill then 'begged' Stalin for good treatment of those British prisoners-of-war whom Soviet forces were liberating from prisoner-of-war camps in the East, telling the Soviet leader, 'Every mother in England is anxious about the fate of her prisoner sons.'

Thus was linked the fate of a hundred thousand Russians, of whom at least ten thousand were to be executed on their enforced return, and a hundred thousand Britons who were to be welcomed home with enthusiasm and love.

At the end of their meeting, Churchill told Stalin he would 'welcome the appearance of Russian ships in the Pacific', and that henceforth Russian warships should be allowed free access and egress at the Dardanelles, despite the clauses of the Montreux Convention of 1936 forbidding this. It was 'intolerable', Churchill said, that Russia should be 'at the mercy of the Turks, not only in war but in peace'. Churchill and Stalin then drove in their separate cars from the Yusupov to the Livadia Palace, for the final plenary meeting, where Churchill again expressed his unease, supported by a telegram from the War Cabinet in London, at pushing the Polish frontier as far west as Russia had proposed. A compromise word was found; Poland would receive 'substantial' territorial accessions in the west, the actual line to be determined later. In fact, the final line existed from the moment the Red Army reached it, exactly where Stalin wanted it.

At this last meeting Stalin agreed to defer to Churchill's view, also backed up by a strong telegram from the War Cabinet in London, not to press for the high scale of reparations he had hoped to extract from Germany. It too was an easy assurance to give; in the next six years Stalin was to take what he wanted from all the defeated and liberated States that lay within his military and political control. One more assurance was given by Stalin at Yalta, in strictest secrecy, and adhered to scrupulously: the Soviet Union would go to war against Japan as soon as possible after the defeat of Germany.

That night Churchill gave a dinner party at the Vorontsov Villa for Stalin and Roosevelt. After dinner he took his guests into his Map Room. There was something on the maps for each guest: Soviet forces were on the east bank of the Oder within thirty-eight miles of Berlin; British and Canadian forces were on the western bank of the Rhine; American forces, having returned to the Philippines, had entered Manila.

While the Big Three were in the Map Room there was one sour moment. During the discussion of the various military advances, Stalin suggested that the British might wish to make an earlier armistice than the Russians. Churchill, extremely hurt, went to a corner of the Map Room and, with his hands in his pockets, began to sing the opening lines of one of his favourite songs, 'Keep right on to the end of the road.' Stalin was puzzled. Then Roosevelt said with a broad grin to the Russian interpreter, Berezhkov, 'Tell your Chief that this singing by the Prime Minister is Britain's secret weapon.'

On the following day, February 11, the Big Three met at noon to sign a Declaration on Liberated Europe, upholding 'the right of all peoples to choose the form of government under which they will live', and pledging themselves to 'the restoration of sovereign rights and self-Government to those peoples who have been forcibly deprived of them by the aggressor nations'. Where necessary, in order to help set up interim Governments 'broadly representative of all democratic elements in the population', the Big Three would 'jointly assist' in the holding of 'free elections'.

It was also confirmed, in a separate communiqué, that elections would be held in Poland for the establishment of a Polish Provisional Government of National Unity. Although on the surface it seemed that Poland had emerged as the main beneficiary of Yalta, and this communiqué confirmed the principle of free elections, it did so according to the formula Churchill had himself proposed to break the deadlock, that the Lublin Government would be the mainspring of the new Government, 'reorganised on a broader democratic basis with the inclusion of democratic leaders from Poland itself and from Poles abroad'.

Despite its pledge to the holding of 'free and unfettered elections as soon as possible on the basis of universal suffrage and secret ballot', the communiqué on Poland made it clear that the London Poles, the Polish Government on behalf of which Britain and Churchill in particular had fought for so long, had been relegated to the status of 'Poles abroad'. Now they did not even have equality of status with the Lublin Poles; the communiqué was as unyielding on this point as Stalin himself had earlier been. In the last formal words exchanged at Yalta, Churchill warned Stalin that he would be 'strongly criticised for it at home on the grounds that we had yielded completely to the Russian view'. Churchill was right; there was to be considerable unease in Britain that the London Poles had been relegated to the sidelines, and that nothing could be done to ensure a democratic and independent Poland. But from the moment Soviet troops stood on the banks of the Oder, as they did that week, or were masters of Warsaw, as they had been for the previous three weeks, no number of communiqués or pledges could affect the outcome.

The Yalta communiqué having been signed, Churchill left the Livadia Palace for the last time, returning along the winding hill-side road to the Vorontsov Villa. It was shortly after five o'clock. He had intended to stay at the Villa that night, but, as his car drove through its magnificent Gothic entrance way he suddenly turned to Sarah with the words, 'Why do we stay here? Why don't we go tonight – I see no reason to stay a minute longer – we're off.'

Churchill then sprang out of the car and, hurrying into the Private Office, announced to his secretariat, 'I don't know about you – but I'm off! I leave in fifty minutes.' Describing the subsequent turn of events, Sarah told her mother: 'After a second's stunned silence, everyone was galvanised into activity. Trunks and large mysterious paper parcels given to us by the Russians – whoopee – filled the hall. Laundry arrived back clean but damp. Naturally fifty minutes gave us time to change our minds six more times.' After endless conflicting suggestions, including going by sea or air, and going to Athens, or Cairo, or Istanbul, 'Papa, genial and sprightly like a boy out of school, his homework done, walked from room to room saying: "Come on, come on!" '

By 5.30 the cavalcade of cars was ready, driving westward along the rugged coast, beneath towering bare cliffs, and then, darkness having fallen, leaving the sea to go inland across a mountain pass to Sebastopol. There Churchill boarded the *Franconia*. 'I thought he looked tired,' the ship's Captain, Harry Grattidge, later wrote, 'but his first question was whether the courier had arrived so that he could get to work.' On the following afternoon Churchill left the *Franconia* and was driven to the Crimean War battlefields. At the small port which had been the British base in those distant days Churchill was struck, he later recalled, by the 'large number of prisoners-of-war, slaves, Roumanians etc who were toiling there, no harder than they could make them'. The Russians were already using the defeated peoples to rebuild their devastated cities. On returning to the *Franconia* Churchill asked Grattidge if he could have his clothes deloused. This, Grattidge noted, 'defeated us'.

With the *Franconia* still anchored off Sebastopol, Churchill worked throughout February 13 in the comfort of his cabin. That night, while he slept, more than eight hundred British bombers struck at the city of Dresden, dropping 1,471 tons of high explosive bombs and 1,175 tons of incendiaries. A few hours later, American bombers dropped another 689 tons of bombs on the burning city. The Russian purpose, explained at Yalta eight days earlier, was achieved: refugees on the roads, fleeing westward from the firestorm, disrupted the movement of German reinforcements seeking to pass through the burning city to the front further east. But the cost, sixty thousand civilian dead, was as high as any single raid during the bombing in Europe.

On February 14 Churchill left the *Franconia* to drive to Saki aerodrome, a journey of three hours. During the drive, he later recalled, 'we saw a colossal heap of locomotives – a thousand or more – which had been pitched into a chasm by the Germans before they quitted. Amazing sight.' After a short speech of farewell to the Russian guard of honour at the airport, in which he spoke of 'the redeemed Crimea, cleansed by Russian valour from the foul taint of the Huns', and of their 'great leader' Stalin, Churchill left Soviet soil for the last time, flying south-west to Athens, where Archbishop Damaskinos was now Regent. The fighting in the capital had ended, and Churchill drove with the Archbishop through streets which echoed not to the sound of mortar fire but to the cheering of enthusiastic bystanders. Then, in Constitution Square, with the Parthenon glowing in the evening light, Churchill addressed the largest crowd he had ever seen; Macmillan, who was present, estimated it at about 40,000. 'Let party hatreds die,' he declaimed. 'Let there be unity. Let there be resolute comradeship.' As Churchill left the square, a Greek band played 'God Save the King'. Churchill failed to recognise their version and continued to walk away, until he noticed that General Scobie had stopped and was standing to attention.

That night the Archbishop called on Churchill, to ask him not to forget the ancient Greek claims to Constantinople. 'Dismiss those dreams from your mind,' was Churchill's reply. Then, shortly before midnight, he left the British Embassy for his Skymaster, where he slept while the plane remained on the tarmac. After dawn on February 15 he flew from Athens to Cairo, where he was driven direct from the airport to Alexandria, and then taken by boat to the American heavy-cruiser *Quincy*. There Roosevelt awaited him. 'I felt he had a slender contact with life,' Churchill later recalled. The two men were not to meet again.

From the *Quincy*, Churchill flew back to Cairo, where he stayed in the Minister Resident's villa. Then, on February 17, he drove into the desert, to Lake Fayyum, where he gave a banquet to the ruler of Saudi Arabia, King Ibn Saud, and asked the King's assistance, in regard to Palestine, 'to promote a definite and lasting settlement between the Jews and Arabs'. What Churchill had in mind was a Middle East Federation, headed by Ibn Saud, in which a Jewish Palestine would be an integral and at the same time independent part.

Churchill later wrote, in some notes for his war memoirs, that before the banquet he had been told that the King could not allow drinking or smoking in his presence. Far from accepting the Arab custom, he took an independent line: 'I was the host and I said that if it was his religion that made him say such things, my religion prescribed as an absolute sacred ritual smoking cigars and drinking alcohol before, after, and if need be during, all meals and the intervals between them. Complete surrender.' The King was not, however, without resources of his own. 'We were given something to drink', Churchill wrote. 'Did not know what it was. It seemed a very nasty cocktail. Found out afterwards it was an aphrodisiac.'

Returning to Cairo, Churchill telegraphed Clementine to tell her of his 'Most interesting interviews with one Emperor, two Kings and one President.' The Emperor was Haile Selassie of Abyssinia, who had shown 'no particular gratitude' for all that Britain had done to restore him to the throne; the Kings were Ibn Saud, and Farouk of Egypt; the President was Shukri Qwatli of Syria.

Churchill spent February 18 in Cairo, 'an idle day', one observer noted in his diary. At midnight he went to the airport and boarded his Skymaster, but it was not yet ready for take-off. 'Sometimes he would burst into a small snatch of song, and go right through the song too,' Elizabeth Layton wrote to her parents. 'He was in a grand mood, rather sleepy and very funny, and I must admit rather lovable.' At two o'clock in the morning the Skymaster was ready and Churchill airborne yet again, this time for a non-stop flight of thirteen hours and forty minutes. He had been away from England for three weeks.

Bad weather over London forced the Skymaster to divert to Lyneham in Wiltshire. Churchill was then driven three hours to Reading, where he waited at the Station Hotel until Clementine could join him. From Reading they drove to London, where the War Cabinet was waiting at 10 Downing Street; Churchill gave them an account of the Yalta Conference. 'He is marvellously well,' Clementine reported that day to Mary, 'much, much better than when he went off for this most trying and difficult of conferences.' That night they dined with the King and Queen at Buckingham Palace.

The issue which confronted Churchill most starkly on his return was the future of Poland. Many Conservatives doubted that Stalin would keep his word about free elections. 'The proof of the pudding is in the eating,' Churchill wrote to the Prime Minister of New Zealand. 'We are only committed on the basis of full execution in good faith of the terms of the published communiqué. Personally in spite of my anti-Communist convictions I have good hopes that Russia, or at any rate Stalin, desires to work in harmony with the Western Democracies. The alternative would be despair about the long future of the world. We shall not flinch however from our duty as we conceive it, to the last scrap of our life and strength.'

If Stalin did not give 'reality' to his undertakings about Polish elections, Churchill told the War Cabinet on February 21, 'our engagement would be altered'. Britain would indeed continue to recognise the Polish Government in London as 'the legitimate Government of Poland' until a Government had been set up in Poland on the basis of the Yalta communiqué: free elections and a secret ballot. At dinner at Chequers two days later, Colville noted that 'the PM was rather depressed, thinking of the possibilities of Russia one day turning against us, saying that Chamberlain had trusted Hitler as he was now trusting Stalin (though he thought in different circumstances) but taking comfort, as far as Russia went, in the German proverb about trees not growing up to the sky.' When Bomber Command had completed its destruction of Germany, Churchill asked, 'What will lie between the white snows of Russia and the white cliffs of Dover?' Perhaps, however, the Russians 'would not want to sweep on to the Atlantic, or something would stop them as the accident of Ghenghis Khan's death had stopped the horsed archers of the Mongols, who retired and never came back'.

On February 24 the exiled President Beneš of Czechoslovakia lunched with Churchill at Chequers, together with his Foreign Minister, Jan Masaryk. Churchill told them that 'a small lion was walking between a huge Russian bear and a great American elephant, but perhaps it would prove to be the lion who knew the way'.

Three days later, during the Yalta debate in the House of Commons, Churchill tried to calm the widespread unease about the future of Poland. He had the impression, he said, that Stalin and the Soviet leaders 'wish to live in honourable friendship and equality with the western democracies. I feel also that their word is their bond.' But times were far different from 1940 and 1941, when Britain's actions had seemed plain and simple. 'If a man is coming across the sea to kill you, you do everything in your power to make sure he dies before finishing the journey. This may be difficult, it may be painful, but at least it is simple.' Four years had passed since then. 'We are now entering a world of imponderables, and at every stage occasions for self-questioning arise. It is a mistake to look too far ahead. Only one link in the chain of destiny can be handled at a time.'

Churchill ended with an appeal that the Great Powers 'must seek to serve and not to rule'. In a peroration which at the last moment he decided not to deliver, he had intended to say: 'No one can guarantee the future of the world. There are some who fear it will tear itself to pieces and that an awful lapse in human history may occur. I do not believe it. There must be hope. The alternative is despair, which is madness. The British race has never yielded to counsels of despair.'

That evening, in the smoking-room, Poland dominated all conversation. After talking to Churchill there, Harold Nicolson wrote: 'He is really sensible. He says he does not see what else we could possibly do.' Not only were the Russians very powerful, 'but they are on the spot; even the massed Majesty of the British Empire would not avail to turn them off that spot'. Colville noted on the following day, 'The PM is trying to persuade himself that all is well, but in his heart I think he is worried about Poland and not convinced of the strength of our moral position.'

Churchill recognised the strength of the feeling that Poland had been betrayed. 'There is a great deal of uneasiness in both parties that we are letting the Poles down,' he telegraphed to Roosevelt on February 28. Churchill also told Roosevelt of many stories 'put about' of the wholesale deportations of Poles by the Russians, and of executions by the Lublin Poles 'of elements they do not like'. He had no means, he said, of verifying or of contradicting these allegations. That night news reached Churchill of massive Russian political intimidation in Roumania, backed by troops, for the establishment of a Communist minority government. The Moscow 'percentages' agreement prevented any British response. But Poland was not a part of that agreement; its democratic future had been guaranteed by the Yalta communiqué. Angered and frustrated by Stalin's obduracy, Churchill told Colville that night, 'I have not the slightest intention of being cheated over Poland, not even if we go to the verge of war with Russia.'

35

'Advance, Britannia!'

On 2 March 1945, eleven days after returning from Yalta, Churchill flew from London to Brussels, lunching with Mary, who was serving in an anti-aircraft battery, and then flying on to Eindhoven in Holland to dine with Montgomery, before going on by car to Geldrop, where he spent the night in Eisenhower's train. Then, on the morning of March 3, he crossed the German border for the first time since 1932, visiting the United States Ninth Army at Jülich and being driven to the Siegfried Line. 'On arriving there,' General Brooke later recalled, 'the column of some twenty or thirty cars halted, we processed solemnly out and lined up along the Line. As the photographers had all rushed up to secure good vantage points, he turned to them and said: "This is one of the operations connected with this great war which must not be reproduced graphically." To give them credit they obeyed their orders and, in doing so, missed a chance of publishing the greatest photographic catch of the war! I shall never forget the childish grin of intense satisfaction that spread all over his face as he looked down at the critical moment.'

Churchill spent that night in Eisenhower's train, before crossing back into Germany on March 4, where he visited the First Canadian Army and then, at the German village of Goch, pulled the lanyard to fire an eight-inch gun. 'Winston fretting because he was not allowed nearer the front,' Brooke noted in his diary. That night he slept in Eisenhower's train as it made its way southward to Rheims, where, at Eisenhower's headquarters just outside the city, he spent the next day watching in the Map Room the course of the battle he had hoped to witness at closer quarters.

He was 'anxious to go full out about Poland', Churchill telegraphed to Eden from Rheims. For this reason he did not want Britain to make any protest about Soviet actions in Roumania, lest, by reference to the Moscow percentages agreement of the previous October, Stalin should reproach Britain 'for breaking our understanding with him about Roumania', at the very moment that strife about Poland came to a head. He had 'every intention', Churchill told Eden in a second telegram that day, 'of working to the utmost for a Poland free to manage its own affairs – and to which Polish soldiers in our service will be glad to return'.

Churchill spent his fourth consecutive night in Eisenhower's train, before flying back to London on the morning of March 6. His first letter that day was to a Conservative MP worried about Poland. 'We are now labouring to make sure that the Yalta agreement about Poland and free elections is carried out in the spirit as well as in the letter,' Churchill wrote. Later that day, however, he learned that only Moscow's nominees would be allowed to be members of the Government of Poland. This made it 'clear', Churchill told his colleagues, 'that the Russians were not going to carry out the conditions on which we had agreed'. With these words the Yalta Agreement on Poland was effectively dead, twenty-three days after it had been made.

On March 7 the news from Poland itself was ominous: two sealed trains, each with two thousand Polish priests, intellectuals and teachers on board, had been sent to Soviet labour camps on the Volga. As many as six thousand Polish officers who had fought against the Germans in units loyal to the Polish Government in London had been arrested. Many had been killed. Reading these details, Churchill asked that they should be sent on to Roosevelt.

That same day, as Cologne was abandoned by its defenders, units of the American Army crossed the Rhine at Remagen. But the excitement of these successes was overshadowed by anger that the Soviet military authorities in Roumania were threatening to remove the former Prime Minister, General Radescu, from the sanctuary he had found at the British Military Mission. That evening Churchill told the War Cabinet that it was the intention of the British Military and Air Missions in Roumania to open fire on the Russians if they tried to remove Radescu by force. The War Cabinet agreed that the Missions should 'open fire if necessary' to guard the fugitive.

Churchill was now fully disillusioned with Stalin, and was no longer willing to allow the Russians a free hand in Roumania in return for their acceptance of a non-Communist Government in Greece. The refusal to allow opposition parties, and the deportations of opponents of Communism, had accelerated in the past weeks, making a mockery, he telegraphed to Roosevelt on March 8, of the Yalta Declaration on Liberated Europe. All parties and all classes, he told the President, had set their hearts against a Soviet domination of Poland. 'Labour men are as keen as Conservatives, and Socialists as keen as Catholics.' Once it was seen 'that we have been deceived and that the well-known Communist technique is being applied behind closed doors in Poland, either directly by the Russians or through their Lublin puppets, a very grave situation in British public opinion would be reached'.

Churchill urged Roosevelt to join with him in 'dogged pressure and persistence' to preserve Polish freedom. But Roosevelt was in no position to answer, or even to read, Churchill's telegram. He was dying, his nearness to death hidden even from his closest ally and partner. On March 18, in a personal appeal to Roosevelt, Churchill expressed his hope that the recent 'rather numerous' telegrams on Poland, Roumania and other topics, eight long telegrams in less than three weeks, 'are not becoming a bore to you', and he added: 'Our friendship is the rock on which I build for the future of the world so long as I am one of the builders.' Peace with Germany and Japan 'will not bring much rest to you and me (if I am still responsible). As I observed last time, when the war of giants is over, the wars of the pygmies will begin. There will be a torn, ragged and hungry world to help to its feet.' What would Stalin or his successor say, Churchill asked the President, 'to the way we should both like to do it?'

On the day that Churchill sent this telegram, he learned that 71,000 American troops had been killed in action since the Normandy landings. In the same period there had been 33,000 British and Canadian deaths. Montgomery was meanwhile preparing a new forward assault. On March 23 Churchill flew in a Dakota to Holland, landing at the bomb-scarred aerodrome at Venlo. Then he drove across the German border to Montgomery's headquarters at Straelen. 'It is hoped to pass the river tonight,' Churchill telegraphed that night to Stalin, 'and tomorrow establish the bridgeheads.'

In the early hours of March 24, from an artillery Observation Point at Ginderich, Churchill watched Montgomery's offensive begin, as airborne troops went in across the Rhine some four miles to the east.

Cadogan noted in his diary, in London: 'Monty attacked last night and it seemed to go well. PM there, of course.' More than two thousand aircraft flew overhead and across the river to Wesel and beyond. But as Churchill watched, he also saw, as he later recalled, 'aircraft in twos and threes coming back askew, asmoke, or even in flames. Also at this time tiny specks came floating to earth. Imagination, built on a good deal of experience, told a hard and painful tale.'

From Ginderich, Churchill drove with Brooke the full length of Montgomery's line, first into Xanten, then through Marienbaum, and finally to high ground just south of Kalkar, from where they could see the crossing-place of the 51st Highland Division. On the following morning Churchill flew from the airstrip at Straelen, for more than a hour and a half, in Montgomery's tiny Messenger aircraft. In all he flew 140 miles, mostly at 500 feet. His pilot, Flight-Lieutenant Trevor Martin, later recalled seeing flashes of British artillery to the west of them as, from the cramped plane, and with no radio with which to contact the ground, they looked down on German defensive positions east of the Rhine. 'I was worried,' Martin wrote, 'that the Americans in particular would not know that it was one of our aeroplanes.'

Returning safely to Straelen, Churchill was driven to Eisenhower's headquarters further south, near Rheinburg. From there, Churchill, Eisenhower and Montgomery drove to Büderich, on the west bank of the Rhine. After Eisenhower had left, and he and Montgomery prepared to leave, Churchill saw a small launch come close by.

'Why don't we go across and have a look at the other side?' Churchill asked.

'Why not?' was Montgomery's unexpectedly brief reply.

Crossing with several senior American officers, the two men reached the eastern side. 'We landed in brilliant sunshine and perfect peace on the German shore,' Churchill later recalled, 'and walked about for half an hour or so unmolested.' Then, after crossing back, they drove to Büderich, where Churchill clambered over the twisted girders and broken masonry of the road bridge. As he did so, German shells began to fall into the river about a mile away. 'Presently they came nearer. Then one salvo came overhead and plunged in the water on our side of the bridge. The shells seemed to explode on impact with the bottom, and raised great fountains of spray about a hundred yards away.' Several other shells fell among the motor cars which were concealed on the bank not far behind them. At that moment General Simpson, whose front it was, came up to Churchill with the words: 'Prime Minister, there are snipers in front of you; they are shelling both sides of the bridge; and now they have started shelling the road behind you. I cannot accept responsibility for your being here and must ask you to come away.'

As Brooke watched, Churchill put his arms round one of the twisted girders of the bridge. 'The look on Winston's face,' he later recalled, 'was just like that of a small boy being called away from his sand castles on the beach by his nurse!' Churchill returned to Montgomery's headquarters at Straelen, where, with his thoughts on the political future of Europe, he told Colville that he 'hardly liked to consider dismembering Germany until his doubts about Russia's intentions had been cleared away.'

On the following day Churchill crossed the Rhine again, this time by pontoon bridge, to the village of Bislich, and spent more than an hour and a half on the eastern side. It was a moment of deep satisfaction after five and a half years of fierce struggles and setbacks, delayed hopes and ceaseless exertions. From Bislich he drove down the east bank of the Rhine for a while, before recrossing the river in a tank-landing vehicle. Then, after picnicking on the west bank of the river with Brooke and Montgomery, he wrote in Montgomery's special message book: 'The Rhine and all its fortress lines lie behind the 21st Group of Armies. A beaten army, not long ago Master of Europe, retreats before its pursuers. The goal is not long to be denied those who have come so far and fought so well under proud and faithful leadership. Forward on all wings of flame to final Victory.'

That afternoon Churchill flew back from Venlo, accompanied by twelve Spitfires. 'The PM worked in the plane, which was alternatively too hot and too cold,' wrote Colville, 'and we landed at Northolt after an exciting weekend, much the better in health and temper.' That night he dined alone with Clementine, who wrote to Montgomery: 'Winston loved his visit to you. He said he felt quite a reformed character & that if in earlier days he had been about with you, I should have had a much easier life – referring I suppose to his chronic unpunctuality & to his habit of changing his mind (in little things!) every minute! I was very much touched & said I had been able to bear it very well as things are. So he then said perhaps he need not bother to improve? But I said "Please improve becos we have not finished our lives yet".'

Two days later, Clementine flew from London in her husband's Skymaster, first to Egypt, and then to Russia, at the start of a strenuous five-week journey to visit the many hospitals throughout the Soviet Union which had been helped by her Red Cross Fund. Churchill went to Northolt to see her off. 'You are ceaselessly in our thoughts,' he wrote after she had gone. That same evening the nature of Soviet intentions, which had been on Churchill's mind while he was visiting the Rhine, was made crystal clear with regard to Poland when fourteen Polish leaders, representing all the non-Communist political parties, were taken under promise of safe conduct to a Soviet Army base near Warsaw, and then arrested.

Returning at midnight from Northolt to the Annexe, Churchill spent the next two hours dictating his Parliamentary tribute to Lloyd George, who had died on the previous day at the age of eighty-two. 'There was no man so gifted, so eloquent, so forceful, who knew the life of the people so well,' he told the Commons on the following day. 'When I first became Lloyd George's friend and active associate, now more than forty years ago, this deep love of the people, the profound knowledge of their lives, and of the undue and needless pressures under which they lived, impressed itself indelibly upon my mind.' As for Lloyd George's assumption of the Premiership in 1916, Churchill quoted Carlyle's verdict on Cromwell, 'He coveted the place; perhaps the place was his.'

Churchill ended his tribute by referring to Lloyd George's social legislation of earlier times and his leadership in a previous war: 'Much of his work abides, some of it will grow greatly in the future, and those who come after us will find the pillars of his life's toil upstanding, massive and indestructible; and we ourselves, gathered here today, may indeed be thankful that he voyaged with us through storm and tumult with so much help and guidance to bestow.'

From Cairo, Clementine wrote to her husband: 'I loved your speech about LG. It recalled forgotten blessings which he showered on the meek and lowly.'

At the end of March, a serious strategic dispute disrupted the harmony of Anglo-American war planning. Eisenhower decided, and informed Montgomery by telegram, that the Anglo-American forces would not advance as hitherto intended direct to Berlin, but in a more southerly direction, through Leipzig, to Dresden. In Eisenhower's view, Berlin was less important as a centre of German industry and resistance than the cities further south, even though his change of plan would leave Berlin as the Russian prize. Eisenhower had even contacted Stalin about this, and had obtained Stalin's approval of the new direction, without previously consulting, or even informing, the Combined Chiefs of Staff.

On March 30 the British Chiefs of Staff protested vehemently at Eisenhower's change of plan. Churchill supported them. 'The idea of neglecting Berlin and leaving it to the Russians to take at a later stage does not appear to me correct,' he wrote on March 31. 'As long as Berlin holds out and withstands a siege in the ruins, as it may easily do, German resistance will be stimulated. The fall of Berlin might cause nearly all Germans to despair.'

Elaborating on his plan, Eisenhower stated that his aim was to join forces with the Russians on the Elbe south of Berlin, but not to cross the Elbe. Churchill was angered by this, telegraphing direct to Eisenhower on March 31, 'Why should we not cross the Elbe and advance as far eastward as possible?' This had 'an important political bearing' as the Russians now seemed certain to be about to enter Vienna. 'If we deliberately leave Berlin to them, even if it should be in our grasp, the double event may strengthen their conviction, already apparent, that they have done everything.'

In a further telegram to Eisenhower on April 2, Churchill urged 'the importance of entering Poland, which may well be open to us', if Eisenhower were to advance east of the Elbe. 'I deem it highly important that we should shake hands with the Russians as far to the East as possible.'

In the midst of his telegraphic exchange with Eisenhower, Churchill learned that the fourteen Polish leaders arrested by the Russians outside Warsaw had disappeared. Churchill protested at once to Stalin, warning him that he would have to raise in Parliament this grave violation of the Yalta Agreement, and reminding the Soviet leader: 'No one has pleaded the cause of Russia with more fervour and conviction than I have tried to do. I was the first to raise my voice on 22nd June 1941. It is more than a year since I proclaimed to a startled world the justice of the Curzon Line for Russia's Western frontier, and this frontier has now been accepted by both the British Parliament and the President of the United States. It is as a sincere friend of Russia that I make my personal appeal to you to come to a good understanding about Poland with the Western Democracies, and not to smite down the hand of comradeship in the future guidance of the world which we now extend.'

Neither Stalin nor Eisenhower were to defer to Churchill's respective appeals. Poland was not to have an independent Government, and the Anglo-American army was neither to cross the Elbe nor enter Berlin. It was 'by no means certain', Churchill told the Dominion representatives on April 3, 'that we could count on Russia as a beneficent influence in Europe, or as a willing partner in maintaining the peace of the world. Yet, at the end of the war, Russia would be left in a position of preponderant power and influence throughout the whole of Europe.'

The end of the war in Europe was clearly close; having crossed the Rhine, Montgomery's forces were taking between 15,000 and 20,000 prisoners every day as they pressed into the Ruhr. In Italy, Alexander's forces launched a renewed assault on April 9. Two days later Eisenhower's forces reached the Elbe. Although they were less than seventy miles from Berlin, they made no move towards the bomb-shattered capital. That same day, as a sign of the new political reality, the Soviet Union signed a treaty of friendship, mutual aid and post-war collaboration with Tito's Yugo-slavia.

On April 12 Churchill learned that two close family friends, Clementine's cousin Tom Mitford, and Basil Dufferin, 4th Marquess of Dufferin and Ava, had been killed in action. That same day Mary was awarded the MBE for her work with an anti-aircraft battery. Churchill sent these items of news to Clementine, who was still in Russia, in a telegram late on April 12. It was midnight. As he continued his work he was told that Roosevelt was dead. 'I feel a very painful personal loss, quite apart from the ties of public action which bound us so closely together,' he telegraphed to Harry Hopkins. 'I had a true affection for Franklin.'

Churchill made immediate plans to fly to Hyde Park for Roosevelt's funeral. He would leave at 8.30 on the evening of April 13. Everything was made ready for his departure, but by 7.45 he had still not decided whether to go. 'PM said he would decide at aerodrome,' noted Cadogan in his diary. At the last moment Churchill decided not to go, explaining to the King that with so many Cabinet Ministers already overseas, with Eden on his way to Washington, and with the need for a Parliamentary tribute to Roosevelt, 'which clearly it is my business to deliver', he ought to remain in Britain.

On April 17 American forces entered Nuremberg, the scene of Hitler's triumphant pre-war rallies. On the following day, in the House of Commons, Churchill delivered his tribute to Roosevelt. When death came upon him, it had been announced, 'he had finished his mail'. Churchill commented: 'That portion of his day's work was done. As the saying goes, he died in harness, and we may well say in battle harness, like his soldiers, sailors, and airmen, who side by side with ours are carrying on their task to the end all over the world. What an enviable death was his. He had brought his country through the worst of its perils and the heaviest of its toils. Victory had cast its sure and steady beam upon him.'

Churchill had now to build up a relationship with Roosevelt's successor, Harry Truman, whom he had never met. Through their telegraphic exchanges, which were daily and voluminous, Churchill formed an impression, as he told Eden on April 20, 'that the new man is not to be bullied by the Soviets'. But the inexorable advance of Soviet power could not be halted or diverted. On April 21, Soviet troops reached the suburbs of Berlin. That same day, the Soviet Government signed a Treaty of Mutual Assistance with the Lublin Government. As far as Poland was concerned, as twelve days earlier with Yugoslavia, the Yalta Agreement was dead.

The imminence of the defeat of Hitler was bitter-sweet. As American forces penetrated deeper and deeper into Germany, they entered concentration camps in which thousands of corpses, and thousands of emaciated, starving and broken survivors, further testified to the horrors of Nazism. As soon as Eisenhower gave Churchill over the telephone details of what had been found, Churchill sent an all-Party Parliamentary delegation to visit the largest of the camps so far discovered, at Buchenwald, and, on April 24, arranged for photographs of the victims to be circulated to the Cabinet. 'Here we are all shocked by the most horrible revelations of German cruelty in the concentration camps,' he wrote to Clementine.

On April 25 Churchill was told that Hitler's principal partner in terror, Heinrich Himmler, wished to open negotiations with the Allies behind Hitler's back. Churchill at once telephoned Truman. It was the first time that they had spoken together. The two men agreed that there could be no 'piecemeal' surrender by any Germans; the surrender must be made simultaneously to Britain, the United States and the Soviet Union. That same afternoon, American and Russian forces linked up on the Elbe. The Third Reich had been cut in half. On the following day, reading an Ambassador's report that efforts were being made by the British forces in Belgium to capture, or at least to detain, the heir to the Habsburgs, Churchill telegraphed direct to the Ambassador that it was no part of British policy to 'hunt down' the Archduke, or to treat the former Austrian monarchy as 'a criminal organisation'.

Churchill's telegram continued: 'Personally, having lived through all these European disturbances and studied carefully their causes, I am of opinion that if the Allies at the peace table at Versailles had not imagined that the sweeping away of long-established dynasties was a form of progress, and if they had allowed a Hohenzollern, a Wittelsbach, and a Habsburg to return to their thrones, there would have been no Hitler.' For the German military classes in post-Versailles Germany, Churchill added, a 'crowned Weimar', as opposed to the Weimar Republic, would have represented in 1919 'a symbolic point on which their loyalties could have centred'.

On April 29 Churchill made one final appeal to Stalin to desist from the unilateral imposition of Soviet will in Poland, and also in Yugoslavia. 'There is not much comfort,' he wrote, 'in looking into a future where you and the countries you dominate, plus the Communist Parties in many other States, are all drawn up on one side, and those who rally to the English-speaking nations and their associates or Dominions are on the other. It is quite obvious that their quarrel would tear the world to pieces, and that all of us leading men on either side who had anything to do with that would be shamed before history. Even embarking on a long period of suspicions, of abuse and counter-abuse, and of opposing policies, would be a disaster hampering the great developments of world prosperity for the masses, which are attainable only by our trinity.'

Churchill hoped that there was nothing in this telegram which would unwittingly give Stalin offence. 'But do not, I beg you, my friend Stalin, underrate the divergencies which are opening about matters which you may think are small to us, but which are symbolic of the way the English-speaking democracies look at life.' That evening Moscow radio announced that, with the entry of Soviet forces into Vienna, a Provisional Austrian Government had been set up. The Western Allies had not been consulted about its composition, and were refused permission to send a delegation to the city. Churchill at once protested, and was joined in his protest by Truman.

That night, after dinner at Chequers, Churchill was watching a film of *The Mikado,* and singing each of the songs, when there was a telephone call from General Alexander. The film was stopped. The German armies in Italy had surrendered unconditionally. The war in Italy was over. In Central Europe, Eisenhower's troops had reached the Danube at Linz. Churchill urged Truman to allow them to continue into Czechoslovakia. 'There can be little doubt,' he telegraphed to the President on April 30, 'that the liberation of Prague and as much as possible of the territory of Western Czechoslovakia by your forces might make the whole difference to the post-war situation of Czechoslovakia and might well influence that in nearby countries. On the other hand, if the Western Allies play no significant part in Czechoslovakia's liberation, that country will go the way of Yugoslavia.'

Churchill's appeal was again too late; Eisenhower had already informed the Soviet High Command that he would advance no further than Linz. The Americans were also committed to withdraw up to 140 miles from their forward positions in Germany, once the war ended, as these positions were inside the area agreed at Yalta as inside the Soviet Zone. In a telegram to Truman on April 30 Churchill tried to have any such withdrawal delayed; he also urged that the Western Allies occupy Istria, which would otherwise fall to Tito's Communist forces. Truman, while unwilling to go back on the agreement about the future Zones of Occupation in Germany, accepted Churchill's suggestion about Istria. The Western Allies would do their utmost to enter Trieste and to hold it: 'There is no need for obtaining prior Russian consent,' Truman told Churchill. But that very day Yugoslav Partisan forces were fighting inside Trieste; the first New Zealand troops were not to arrive for another forty-eight hours. 'No violence should occur except in self-defence,' Churchill telegraphed to Alexander. A quarrel with Tito, he explained, 'would be a matter for the Peace Table and not for the field'.

Even as the last corner of pre-war Italy came under Yugoslav and Anglo-American control, Mussolini, once the senior partner of the Italo-German Axis, was caught by Italian partisans and killed. Two days later, on the evening of May 1, while Churchill was dining at 10 Downing Street, Radio Hamburg announced that Hitler was dead. The news was brought in to Churchill while he dined. 'As you see,' he telegraphed to Clementine, who was still in the Soviet Union, 'both our great enemies are dead.' Hitler had committed suicide.

On the evening of May 2 Churchill dined quietly with two friends of pre-war years, Lady Juliet Duff and Venetia Montagu. The only other guest was Noël Coward, who later recalled how, towards the end of dinner, during which Churchill had been 'at his most benign', he and the two ladies were suddenly struck by how significant it was that they were in the presence of the man who had contributed 'so much foresight, courage and genius' to the winning of the war. 'Emotion submerged us, and without exchanging a word, as simultaneously as though we had carefully rehearsed it, the three of us rose to our feet and drank Mr Churchill's health.'

On the following day Churchill had several causes for satisfaction. During the morning Captain Pim came in to announce that British forces had entered Rangoon. Later that day, Montgomery's forces, urged to do so as a matter of urgency, reached the Baltic Sea at Lübeck, cutting the Russians off from Denmark, which several Intelligence reports had indicated they would occupy as the culmination of their continuing advance along the Baltic. Montgomery had reached Lübeck, Churchill told Eden, 'with twelve hours to spare'. By evening there was even more dramatic news; Admiral von Friedeburg, representing Hitler's successor Admiral Doenitz, had arrived with three other representatives of the German armed forces at Montgomery's headquarters on Lüneburg Heath, just south of Hamburg, to negotiate the German surrender.

The total defeat of Germany was clearly imminent; on May 3 more than half a million German soldiers surrendered to Montgomery. These were followed, Churchill telegraphed to Clementine on May 4, by 'far more than a million today'. In Italy, Alexander had taken a million prisoners-of-war. All German forces in north-west Germany, Holland and Denmark 'are to be surrendered tomorrow morning'. And yet, Churchill added, 'beneath these triumphs lie poisonous politics and deadly international rivalries'. It was clear that a further meeting of the Big Three would be needed, if these rivalries were to be resolved. 'Meanwhile,' Churchill telegraphed to Truman on May 6, 'we should hold firmly to the existing position obtained or being obtained by our armies in Yugoslavia, in Austria, in Czechoslovakia, on the main central United States front and on the British front reaching up to Lübeck including Denmark.'

That night, as Churchill slept, the German Chief of Staff, General Jodl, signed the German instrument of surrender at Eisenhower's headquarters at Rheims. All fighting was to cease at midnight on May 8. Eisenhower himself telephoned this news to Ismay in the small hours; Ismay at once passed it on by telephone to John Martin at 10 Downing Street. Martin decided not to wake Churchill, but to send the news in to him as soon as he awoke. It was Captain Pim who then brought him the news. 'For five years,' Churchill commented, 'you've brought me bad news, sometimes worse than others. Now you've redeemed yourself.'

During May 7 Churchill encouraged Eisenhower to move his troops forward to Prague. Eisenhower did so, with the result that some American units entered the Czech capital before the Russians. They withdrew, however, as soon as the Soviets arrived. That same day, in urging Alexander to advance eastward from Trieste and southward into Istria, Churchill telegraphed, 'Let me know what you are doing in massing forces against this Muscovite tentacle, of which Tito is the crook.'

Throughout Britain, excitement was rising at the imminence of victory. On the afternoon of May 7 Churchill tried to persuade Truman to declare that same evening that Victory in Europe had arrived. Truman was unwilling to do so, Stalin having asked to postpone the rejoicing until May 9, as his troops were still fighting in parts of Czechoslovakia and along the Baltic. At five o'clock on the afternoon of May 7, Churchill, in his second telephone call to Truman's office in an hour, explained 'that crowds celebrating in the streets of London were beyond control', and that he must make an announcement of victory at the latest at noon on May 8. Meanwhile, he worked on a short victory broadcast which he still hoped to make that evening; he finished dictating it just before six o'clock. But then a telephone call from Washington persuaded him to delay at least until the next day.

In a short break from these telegraphic and telephonic exchanges, and dictation, Churchill led the three Chiefs of Staff into the garden at 10 Downing Street for a group photograph. He had already had put out for them a tray of glasses and drinks, and raised his glass to them as 'the architects of victory'. Ismay, who was present, later wrote, 'I hoped that they would raise their glasses to the chief who had been their master-planner; but perhaps they were too moved to trust their voices.'

On the morning of Tuesday May 8 Churchill worked in bed at his victory broadcast. He also sent out an enquiry to ensure that there was no shortage of beer in the capital for the evening's celebrations. At one moment he slipped out of his bedroom and went along the corridor to the Map Room, carrying with him champagne and a large Gruyère cheese, together with a note, 'For Captain Pim and his officers with the Prime Minister's compliments on Victory Day in Europe.' From Clementine, who was in Moscow, came a telegram of congratulations, 'All my thoughts are with you on this supreme day, my darling. It could not have happened without you.'

Shortly after one o'clock Churchill left Downing Street for Buckingham Palace, where he lunched with the King. 'We congratulated each other on the end of the European War,' the King wrote in his diary. 'The day we have been longing for has arrived at last and we can look back with thankfulness to God that our tribulation is over.' Returning to Downing Street, at three o'clock Churchill broadcast to the British people, describing the various surrender negotiations and telling them, 'The German war is therefore at an end.' At one moment in his broadcast Churchill spoke of 'the evil-doers, who are now prostrate before us'. At these words there was a gasp from the crowds gathered in Parliament Square to hear the speech relayed.

Churchill then warned that the war against Japan had yet to be won, 'Japan, with all her treachery and greed, remains unsubdued,' and he ended his speech with the words 'Advance, Britannia!'

Randolph was flying from Belgrade to Caserta at 8,000 feet when he heard his father's words. 'Was greatly moved by your splendid speech,' he telegraphed on reaching Italy. Clementine listened to her husband's broadcast over a wireless in the British Embassy in Moscow. With her was the former French Prime Minister, Edouard Herriot, who had last seen Churchill at Tours in June 1940, tears streaming down his face when he learned that the French Government intended to give up the fight. Now it was Herriot who wept.

His broadcast over, Churchill was driven through a vast and milling crowd to the House of Commons. 'We have all of us made our mistakes,' he told his fellow MPs, 'but the strength of the Parliamentary institutions has been shown to enable it at the same moment to preserve all the title-deeds of democracy while waging war in the most stern and protracted form.' Churchill then recalled how, twenty-six years earlier, he had been in the Commons to hear the announcement of the German surrender terms in November 1918. There had then been a service of thanksgiving at St Margaret's; he now proposed the identical motion for an adjournment, and led MPs across Old Palace Yard to the church. Later that afternoon Churchill went on to the balcony of the Ministry of Health, where he spoke briefly to the vast crowds in Whitehall. 'This is your victory,' he told them, at which they roared back, 'No – it is yours.'

That evening, as the celebrations in the streets of London continued, Churchill returned to the balcony and made another short speech: 'A terrible foe has been cast to the ground, and awaits our judgement and our mercy'. Then he returned to the Annexe, where he worked through a pile of telegrams six inches high, his usual evening's burden of work. One of the telegrams was from the British Chargé d'Affaires in Moscow, Frank Roberts, reporting a petulant Soviet complaint about Britain's concern for the fate of the fourteen Polish politicians arrested outside Warsaw while under pledge of safe conduct. 'We are utterly indifferent to anything the Soviets may say by way of propaganda,' Churchill replied. 'It is no longer desired by us to maintain detailed arguments with the Soviet Government about their views and actions.'

This telegram was sent to Moscow at two hours before midnight on that day of celebration. An hour later a telegram arrived from Eden in San Francisco: 'All my thoughts are with you on this day which is so essentially your day. It is you who have led, uplifted and inspired us through the worst days. Without you this day could not have been.'

36

'An Iron Curtain'

Wednesday 9 May 1945 was the first day of peace in Europe; throughout the morning Churchill worked in bed, then lunched in bed. In the afternoon he went by car with his daughter Mary to the American, French and Russian Embassies, in each of which toasts were drunk to the victory. In Moscow, where May 9 was being celebrated as the Victory Day, Clementine was among those gathered at the British Embassy, from where she sent a telegram to her husband, 'We all assembled here, drinking champagne at twelve o'clock, send you greetings on Victory Day.'

That evening Churchill went as on the previous night to the Ministry of Health balcony overlooking Whitehall, where he told the vast crowd, 'London – like a great rhinoceros, a great hippopotamus, saying "Let them do their worst – London can take it" – London could take anything.' He wished to thank them 'for never having failed in the long, monstrous days and in the long nights black as hell'.

The celebrations that week were overshadowed by events in the East: in a telegram to Eden on May 11, Churchill expressed his fear that Soviet encroachments in Central Europe and the Balkans, of which he was receiving hourly reports, would lead to a 'period of appeasement' followed 'by a third World War'. He was convinced that 'the Russian peril, which I regard as enormous, could be better faced if we remain united', yet he saw no means of halting the intense Soviet pressure, especially amid the euphoria of victory. When told by the Foreign Office that the fourteen Polish negotiators, seized earlier by the Soviets outside Warsaw while under safe conduct, were now in Moscow as prisoners, he commented, 'I do not see what we can do now in this interlude of joymaking.'

Disturbed by newspaper reports of the imminent departure of at least half the American troops in Europe to the Pacific, on May 12 Churchill telegraphed to Truman, to warn him that the Russians would have the power to maintain 'very large armies in the field for a long time'. He felt 'deep anxiety' because of the Russian 'misinterpretation' of the Yalta decisions, their attitude to Poland, their overwhelming influence in the Balkans, 'the combination of Russian power and the territories under their control or occupied, coupled with Communist techniques in so many other countries, and above all their power to maintain very large armies in the field for a long time'. What, he asked, would be the position in Europe after a year or two, when 'the British and American armies have melted and the French have not yet been formed on any major scale, when we may have a handful of divisions, mostly French, and when Russia may choose to keep two or three hundred on active service?'

The new map of Europe gave Churchill cause for alarm about Soviet intentions. 'An iron curtain is drawn down upon their front,' he told Truman. 'We do not know what is going on behind. There seems little doubt that the whole of the region Lübeck-Trieste-Corfu will soon be completely in their hands.' To this would be added the 'enormous area' which the Americans were about to withdraw from in central Germany, between Eisenach and the Elbe. Once this withdrawal was made, 'a broad band of many hundreds of miles of Russian-occupied territory will isolate us from Poland'. Then, as the attention of the Western Allies focused on inflicting 'severe penalties' on Germany, 'it would be open to the Russians in a very short time to advance if they chose, to the waters of the North Sea and the Atlantic'.

Churchill urged Truman to join him in coming to 'an understanding' with Russia 'or see where we are with her', before the Anglo-American forces were substantially withdrawn from Europe. This could be done only by a personal meeting with Stalin. 'This issue of a settlement with Russia before our strength has gone,' Churchill ended, 'seems to me to dwarf all others.' Truman agreed, and plans were made for him and Churchill to meet Stalin at Potsdam in two months' time.

On the evening of May 13 Churchill broadcast to the British people. It was five years ago 'on Thursday last', he said, that the King had commissioned him 'to form a National Government of all parties to carry on our affairs'. Five years was 'a long time in human life, especially when there is no remission for good conduct'. He wished he could say 'that all our toils and troubles were over. Then indeed I could end my five years' service happily, and if you thought you had had enough of me and that I ought to be put out to grass, I tell you I would take it with the best grace.' But there was still 'a lot to do'. On the continent of Europe 'we have yet to make sure that the simple and honourable purposes for which we entered the war are not brushed aside or overlooked in the months following our success, and that the words "freedom", "democracy" and "liberation" are not distorted from their true meaning as we have understood them. There would be 'little use in punishing the Hitlerites for their crimes if law and justice did not rule, and if totalitarian or police governments were to take the place of the German invaders.'

In private Churchill anticipated a 'showdown' with Russia over the sovereignty and independence of Poland, Czechoslovakia, Austria and Yugoslavia. But he also sought to accelerate Russia's entry into the war against Japan now that Germany was defeated. This too had been a decision finalised at Yalta. Returning to Downing Street on May 14, Jock Colville noted in his diary: 'The volume of work is if anything more pressing than when I left. Victory has brought no respite. The PM looks tired and has to fight for the energy to deal with the problems confronting him.'

Churchill still hoped to maintain the Coalition in being until the defeat of Japan. This hope was enhanced on May 18 when Attlee went to see him at the Annexe to tell him that he was 'favourably disposed' to persuading the Labour Party to remain in the Coalition until Japan was defeated. Three other senior Labour men, Bevin, A.V. Alexander and Morrison, each of whom had held high Ministerial Office under Churchill since May 1940, were likewise disposed to continue the Coalition. Churchill proposed a national referendum to ascertain if this was the will of the people. Attlee asked if, in Churchill's formal letter proposing the continuation of the Coalition, a sentence could be added that the Government would do its utmost 'to implement the proposals for social security and full employment contained in the White Paper which we have laid before Parliament'. Churchill agreed; these proposals, a Four-Year Plan of social reform, had been worked out at his request by his assistant of pre-First World War days, William Beveridge.

As in May 1940, so in May 1945, the Labour Party was holding its annual conference at a moment of political decision. In May 1940 it was the refusal of the Labour Party activists, then meeting at Bournemouth, to serve under Chamberlain that had effectively brought Churchill to power. Now it was the Party members' equally strong desire, expressed at Blackpool, to return to the cut and thrust of Party politics, and the possibility of the first Labour Government since 1931, that effectively made sure the Coalition would come to an end. It was ten years since the previous General Election. Many Labour politicians had held Government office under Churchill, had gained great experience, and wished, above all, to put their Socialist ideals into practice. Attlee telephoned Churchill from Blackpool on the evening of May 21 to tell him the news.

Churchill realised that nothing could now save the Coalition. At noon on May 23 he went to Buckingham Palace to tender his resignation to the

King. He had been leader of an all-Party government, the 'Grand Coalition' as he sometimes called it, for five years and thirteen days. The King asked him to form a Caretaker Government until elections could be held and the votes of soldiers overseas counted; this would take at least two months. Churchill agreed to remain as Prime Minister and to form a Conservative administration. 'We must hope for re-union,' he wrote to Bevin, 'when Party passions are less strong.'

On the morning of May 26 Churchill completed the last of his Cabinet appointments. He then drove with Clementine to his constituency, for his first speech in what was now an election campaign. His theme was the need to maintain the Conservative Caretaker Government in power, because 'we shall take very good care of everything that affects the welfare of Britain and all classes of Britain'. Two days later he gave a farewell Party at 10 Downing Street to the outgoing Coalition Cabinet. As he made a short farewell speech, tears coursed down his cheeks. 'The light of history will shine on all your helmets,' he told them.

A final Cabinet photograph was to be taken in the garden. It had begun to rain. As the photographer set up his camera and rearranged the group, Churchill commented, 'We'd better finish this or my political opponents will say that this is a conspiracy on my part to give them all rheumatism!' The photograph taken, Churchill was driven to Buckingham Palace, where he kissed hands on his reappointment as Prime Minister.

The General Election campaign now began in earnest. Churchill's principal theme was the perils inherent in Socialism. Watching with anguish the regimes that were even then being imposed on Eastern Europe by the Soviets, he warned in a broadcast on June 4 that no Labour Government 'could afford to allow free, sharp or violently-worded expressions of public discontent', and he went on to declare: 'They would have to fall back on some form of Gestapo, no doubt very humanely directed in the first instance. And this would nip opinion in the bud; it would stop criticism as it reared its head, and it would gather all the power to the supreme Party and the Party leaders, rising like stately pinnacles above their vast bureaucracies of Civil Servants, no longer servants and no longer civil. And where would the ordinary simple folk – the common people as they like to call them in America – where would they be once this mighty organism had got them in its grip?'

Not only did Churchill warn that a Labour Government would bring in 'some form of Gestapo', he also stated that Socialism was 'inseparably interwoven with Totalitarianism and the abject worship of the State'. Not only property, but liberty 'in all its forms', was struck at by the fundamental conceptions of Socialism.

Widespread criticism met the 'Gestapo speech', as it quickly became known. Sarah wrote approvingly to her father to say that if she were a 'thinking' Labour voter 'it would have started me thinking along completely new lines about socialism', but she went on to say that she was 'not quite sure' that Labour voters would understand why what he said would really be so. 'Socialism as practiced in the war,' she pointed out, 'did no one any harm and quite a lot of people good. The children of this country have never been so well fed or healthy, what milk there was, was shared equally, the rich didn't die because their meat ration was no larger than the poor; and there is no doubt that this common sharing and feeling of sacrifice was one of the strongest bonds that unified us. So why, they say, cannot this common feeling of sacrifice be made to work as effectively in peace?' Sarah added, 'Don't think I am a rebel!'

In a subsequent broadcast on June 13 Churchill stressed the constructive aspects and aims of Conservatism, and at Sarah's suggestion elaborated on the Coalition Government's Four-Year Plan, prepared by Beveridge and made public two years earlier, for social insurance, industrial injuries insurance, and a National Health Service 'to be shaped by Parliament and made to play a dynamic part in the life and security of every family and home'. He also announced that the Conservatives would provide free milk for 'the very poor' and for the under-fives. But he still felt the need to censure 'in the most severe terms' the efforts of the Socialists 'to drag their long-term fads and wavy Utopias across the practical path of need and duty'. He also warned, in an echo of his 'Gestapo speech', that if the Socialist system came into force 'the natural change of parties in office from time to time would necessarily come to an end, and a political police would be required to enforce an absolute and permanent system upon the nation'.

Churchill ended his broadcast of June 13 with a further reference to social policy, suggested to him by Sarah: a housing programme that would use 'war-time expedients' to ensure that homes were built for all. 'Every method,' he said, 'public or private, for houses, permanent or temporary, will be employed, and all obstructions, be they price-rings, monopoly, or any other form of obstacle, will be dealt with by the whole power of Parliament and the nation.' This was a firm and fighting pledge, but the broadcast did not go well. The reference to the political police was found offensive by some, ludicrous by others, on whose votes a Conservative majority would have to rest. In addition, there was a tiredness in both broadcasts which was commented on. 'Neither of the two broadcasts is the true PM,' a member of Churchill's staff, Edith Watson, told Lord Moran, and she added, 'There was no "vim" in them.'

Throughout the election campaign Churchill was thinking about developments in Eastern Europe; on June 14 Radio Moscow announced that the fourteen Polish political leaders arrested near Warsaw would be brought to trial in Moscow. At the same time, despite a personal protest by Churchill to Eisenhower, the Americans began to withdraw their troops from a broad swathe of land in central Germany and Czechoslovakia, to a line agreed upon earlier with Russia, and up to which Soviet forces now took control. Churchill believed that conflict with Russia must be avoided, telling Eden, 'The gulf between Britain and Russia is unbridgeable except by friendly diplomatic relations'. He went on to stress that the 'similarity and unity' which Britain had with the United States would not only grow, but was 'indispensable to our safety'.

Preparations were now being made for the final Big Three conference, to be held at Potsdam in a month's time. On June 14 Churchill told the Commons that he would be taking Attlee with him, in case anyone were to say, 'Why are you committing yourself to something for which you have no authority, when in the ballot box there may be something which strips you of your authority?' At this a Labour MP called out, 'Is the right hon. Gentleman going to take the Gestapo with him?'

Despite the continued reverberations of the Gestapo speech, Churchill's personal popularity was enormous, attested to almost everywhere by the vast crowds which came to cheer him at every point on his election tours. It was as if the leader of the nation during the war years, and the leader of a Party deep in an election struggle, were two quite separate men. 'On the way out to Chequers last night,' John Martin wrote to his wife on June 17, 'the PM's car was slowed down in a traffic jam just outside the White City where crowds were coming away from the greyhound races. Immediately he was surrounded by an extremely enthusiastic mob – smiling and waving and cheering – not a sign of unfriendliness or opposition. It was a remarkable demonstration and these were very much the "common people".'

On June 18 the trial began in Moscow of the fourteen Polish political leaders; once more Churchill's concerns were focused on the tyranny of Communism in the East. But his third election broadcast two days later fared no better than the previous two. 'He is very low, poor darling,' Clementine wrote to Mary. 'He thinks he has lost his "touch" & he grieves about it.' In his broadcast he warned that a Socialist Government 'could not allow itself to be challenged or defeated at any time in any form of Parliament that they might allow'. Churchill's criticisms of Socialism did not deflect him from his own radical views, which he had expressed so forcefully thirty-five years earlier. In a letter to Eden on June 23 he commented, 'There is nothing immoral in nationalisation so long as you pay the people who owned the property originally in a fair way.'

On June 21, as the election campaign reached its climax, news came from Moscow that twelve of the fourteen Polish political leaders had been given prison sentences of up to eight years. For Churchill, who had fought long and hard on behalf of a Polish democratic future, the news was final confirmation of his fears that tyranny would be imposed wherever Communism held sway.

What Churchill feared most in Britain was not a Socialist programme in itself, but that control of the Parliamentary Labour Party would be exercised by the Party's Executive; 'unrepresentative persons', he had called them in his broadcast of June 20, who would 'share the secrets and give the orders to the so-called Ministers of the Crown'. This fear was reinforced by the claim of the Chairman of the Labour Party Executive, Harold Laski, that although Attlee would go to Potsdam with Churchill, the Labour Party would not be committed to any decisions reached there, as these would not have been debated by the Party Executive.

On June 30, in his final election broadcast, Churchill warned that the influence of the Labour Party Executive on Ministers was 'abhorrent to the methods hitherto pursued in British public life' and would 'strike at the root of our parliamentary institutions'. To those who believed that they could somehow vote Labour or Liberal, without losing him as Prime Minister, he declared: 'There is no truth in stories now being put about that you can vote for my political opponents at this election, whether they be Labour or Liberal, without at the same time voting for my dismissal from power. This you should not hesitate to do if you think it right and best for the country. All I ask is that you should do it with your eyes open.'

To his Cabinet colleagues Churchill stressed, in a memorandum on July 3, the need for an 'intensive effort' at house-building, to be handled exactly with the energy that would have been put 'into any of the battles we have won'. He also asked them to prepare legislation both for a National Insurance scheme and a National Health Service. This aspect of his efforts was unknown to the electorate; that evening, at Walthamstow, where Labour was in the ascendant, the booing and heckling were such that he was almost prevented from speaking.

There were to be three hundred Liberal candidates at the election, led by Sir Archibald Sinclair, whom Churchill had encouraged to enter Parliament as a Liberal immediately after the First World War. Another of Churchill's Liberal friends was Horatia Seymour, who had a cottage on the estate at Chartwell. A lifelong Liberal, she would be voting Liberal once more, she wrote to him on July 3, nor could she tell any of the Party's candidates in three-cornered fights to stand down in favour of the Conservative candidate, as Churchill wished. The 'judgment and intelligence' of the Conservative Party had been 'so grievously at fault in the years before 1939', she wrote. 'No one taught me more about that than *you*, dear Winston!'

Polling day was on July 5. To enable the service vote to be counted, there was to be a three-week delay before the results were announced. Churchill had already planned a ten-day holiday, between polling day and the start of the Potsdam Conference. On July 7 he flew to Bordeaux, then drove south to the Château de Bordaberry, near the Spanish border, for a week's relaxation. In the morning he swam in the Atlantic. In the afternoon he painted. 'Winston at first low and tired,' Mary later recalled, 'but the magic of painting soon laid hold of him, absorbing him for hours on end, and banishing disturbing thoughts of either the present or the future.'

Churchill sent only one official telegram from Bordaberry. It was to Field Marshal Montgomery, now the Commander-in-Chief, British Army of Occupation, and it read: 'Please see that no establishments in which research and development has been carried on by the Germans are destroyed. Much of the apparatus there could be used by our own engineers and scientists.' He also sent a single minute, to the Chancellor of the Exchequer Sir John Anderson, asking that there should be a 'ruthless combing' of the armed services, so that, without affecting the front-line effort against Japan, the necessary manpower could be found 'to meet our civilian and export needs'.

On the afternoon of July 15 Churchill flew with Mary from Bordeaux to Berlin, a flight of four and a half hours. His one week respite was over. Waiting to greet him at the villa which was to be his base while at Potsdam, 23 Ringstrasse, were Eden, Attlee, Alexander and Montgomery. 'The PM looks very old,' Montgomery wrote to a friend. 'I was shocked when I saw him; he has put on ten years since I last saw him.'

On the following morning Churchill had his first meeting with Truman, spending two hours at Truman's Berlin residence, four hundred yards from his own. 'He told me he liked the President immensely -- they talk the same language,' wrote Mary to her mother. 'He says he is sure he can work with him.' That afternoon Churchill was shown over the ruins of Hitler's Chancellery. In the square in front of the building a crowd of Germans had gathered. Except for one old man who 'shook his head disapprovingly', Churchill later recalled, 'they all began to cheer. My hate had died with their surrender and I was much moved by their demonstrations, and also by their haggard looks and threadbare clothes.'

On his second day at Potsdam, Churchill lunched at 23 Ringstrasse with Truman and the American Secretary of War, Henry Stimson, who put a piece of paper in front of Churchill with the words: 'Babies satisfactorily born.' He had no idea what this meant. 'It means,' Stimson told him, 'that the experiment in the American desert has come off. The atomic bomb is a reality.'

Stalin was not yet to be told of this dramatic development. At the first plenary session, held after Churchill's lunch with Stimson, Churchill pressed for 'the early holding of free elections in Poland which would truly reflect the wishes of the Polish people', one of the principal decisions of the Yalta Conference. At a private meeting with Stalin after the plenary session, Churchill spoke of the German people. They had always believed 'in a symbol. If a Hohenzollern had been allowed to reign after the last war, there would have been no Hitler.' Although he did not say so, he had first seen a Hohenzollern, the Emperor William II, fifty-four years earlier, at the Crystal Palace in May 1891.

During a moment of small talk, Stalin told Churchill that he had taken to smoking cigars. Churchill commented that if a photograph of a cigar-smoking Stalin could be 'flashed across the world, it would cause an immense sensation'.

On July 18 Truman was Churchill's guest at lunch. For two hours they were alone. During their discussion Churchill asked whether 'unconditional surrender' might not be expressed in 'some other way' as far as Japan was concerned, 'so that we got all the essentials for future peace and security, and yet left the Japanese some show of saving their military honour and some assurance of their national existence, after they had complied with all the safeguards necessary for the conqueror'. Truman commented, as the note of the conversation recorded, 'He did not think the Japanese had any military honour after Pearl Harbor.'

Churchill also told Truman of his hopes for the closest possible post-war co-operation between their two countries. When Truman spoke of the need even for bilateral arrangements to come under the United Nations, Churchill commented that the proposals were meaningless if they were common to everybody; a man might propose marriage to a young lady, but it was 'not much use if he were told that she would always be a sister to him. I wanted, under whatever form or cloak, a continuation of the present war-time system of reciprocal facilities between Britain and the United States in regards to bases and fuelling points in their possession.' Truman seemed 'in full accord with this,' Churchill noted, 'if it could be presented in a suitable fashion, and did not appear to take crudely the form of an alliance à deux.'

At the end of their talk, Truman told Churchill that it was 'the most enjoyable luncheon that he had had for many years'. Truman had replied in 'an encouraging way' to Churchill's proposal that the Combined Chiefs of Staff should be kept in being 'until the world calmed down after the great storm'. That afternoon, however, in regard to the war against Japan, Churchill learned that the United States Chiefs of Staff, while willing to consult with their British opposite numbers on general strategic matters, would only do so on condition that in the event of disagreement 'the final decision on the action to be taken will lie with the United States Chiefs of Staff '. Britain, while making a substantial contribution to the war against Japan, would have to accept American strategic direction, as she had essentially also done in Europe.

The second plenary session took place on the afternoon of July 18. When Churchill pressed Stalin about Poland, the Soviet leader assured him that the Provisional Government had 'never refused to hold free elections'. After an hour and twenty minutes the session was at an end, 'much to the PM's annoyance', Sir Alexander Cadogan wrote home, 'as he wanted to go on talking at random and was most disappointed – just like a child with its toys taken away from it. But Truman closed the proceedings.'

That night Churchill dined alone with Stalin. They were together for five hours. The Russian people, Stalin told Churchill, lacked both education and manners 'and still had a long way to go'. He also forecast a Conservative majority of eighty in the General Election. Turning to global politics, Churchill said that he would 'welcome Russia as a great power on the sea'; at the Dardanelles, in the Pacific, and at the Kiel Canal, 'which should have an international regime like the Suez Canal'. Speaking of the nations of Central Europe, Stalin assured Churchill that he was 'against Sovietisation of any of these countries. They would have free elections.' Like his assurance on Poland earlier that day, this too was a lie.

On the morning of July 21 there was a British Victory Parade in Berlin. On their way to the saluting-base, Churchill and Attlee drove in separate jeeps along a line of cheering troops. Churchill's Private Secretary, John Peck, later reflected, 'It struck me and perhaps others as well, although nothing was said, as decidedly odd that Winston Churchill, the great war leader but for whom we should never have been in Berlin at all, got a markedly less vociferous cheer than Mr Attlee, who – however great his contribution in the Coalition – had not hitherto made any marked personal impact upon the fighting forces.'

That afternoon, at a further plenary session, both Churchill and Attlee protested to Stalin that the new Polish frontier was to be drawn too far westward, including within Poland one quarter of pre-war Germany's arable land. They were supported in their protest by Truman. But Stalin had no intention of returning Silesia to Germany. Nor, at a further plenary dominated by discussion of Poland, would he accept that the cities of Stettin or Breslau should remain in Germany; Poland's new frontier with Germany would be the Oder, and the Western Neisse. The combined efforts of Churchill and Truman could not persuade him to change his mind.

The Americans had now learned more about the nature of the atom-bomb test in the New Mexico desert. On the morning of July 22, Stimson went to see Churchill to give him the details; inside a one-mile circle the devastation had been total. Churchill went at once to see Truman. Here, Churchill felt, was the weapon that, he later recalled, might give the Japanese 'an excuse which would save their honour and release them from their obligation of being killed to the last fighting man'.

On July 23 Churchill gave a banquet for Stalin and Truman. During one of the toasts, Stalin suddenly asked Churchill, who had earlier in the day opposed Stalin's request for a Soviet naval base in the Sea of Marmara or at the Dardanelles, if Russia could have a base on the Aegean Sea instead, at the Greek port of Dedeagatch, just outside the Dardanelles. Churchill was non-committal, merely telling Stalin: 'I will always support Russia in her claim to the freedom of the seas all year round.'

Churchill and Attlee now planned to go back to London on July 25, for the election results. The victor was to return to Potsdam two days later, to continue with the Conference. That night, at his villa, Churchill asked Eden, 'What do the Party say now about the election result?' 'They still think that we will get in with a majority of about seventy,' Eden replied.

On the day before he was due to return to London, Churchill saw eight of the Polish Communist leaders, who had flown specially from Warsaw to Berlin to meet him. In vain he tried to persuade them to allow Germany to retain parts of Silesia. But when he urged them to hold 'free and unfettered' elections in Poland, and to set up an all-Party government as agreed upon at Yalta, their leader, Boleslaw Bierut, assured him that Poland's future political development 'would be based on the principles of Western democracy'. It was a worthless assurance; Bierut was to become the ruler of as strict a Stalinist system as any in Eastern Europe.

At the plenary session on the afternoon of July 24 Churchill rejected Stalin's request for a Soviet naval base on the Sea of Marmara. He also rejected the use of force in the handing over of some 10,000 Ukrainian prisoners-of-war who had served in the German Army, and were now being held by the British, pending repatriation to Russia, as also agreed at Yalta.

Two and a half months had passed since the defeat of Germany. The defeat of Japan now seemed to depend, not upon Soviet participation in the war, but upon the atom bomb. At the end of the plenary session of July 24, Truman took Stalin aside to tell him about the new weapon. Churchill, studying Stalin's reaction as he listened to Truman's account, described it thus: 'A new bomb! Of extraordinary power! Probably decisive on the whole Japanese war! What a bit of luck!' That night Churchill dined alone with Admiral Lord Louis Mountbatten, Commander-in-Chief South-East Asia, whom he invited to Downing Street when he was next in London, to talk about the Admiral's future. 'I have great plans in store,' Churchill told him. Mountbatten, who had so recently been in India with the British troops who had already cast their votes in the election, later wrote, 'It was a mournful and eerie feeling to sit there talking plans with a man who seemed so confident that they would come off, and I felt equally confident that he would be out of office within 24 hours.'

Churchill and Attlee were to leave Potsdam on the afternoon of July 25. That morning Churchill had a second meeting with Boleslaw Bierut, who again assured him that post-war Poland would not emulate the Soviet system. It would indeed seek to follow 'the English model' of democracy: Poland would be 'one of the most democratic countries in Europe'; the 'whole Russian army' was leaving Poland; the Polish elections would be 'even more democratic than those in England'. But Churchill knew that the democratic Poland for which Britain had gone to war in September 1939, and had sought to uphold at Teheran and Yalta, no longer existed.

At a further plenary session that morning, Churchill again pressed Stalin not to push Poland's frontiers so far westward. He was once more supported by Truman. Stalin again rejected their request, but countered with one of his own, that coal mined by the Germans in the Ruhr should be sent to the Russian Zone of Germany and to Poland. Churchill argued that this could only be done in exchange for food for the Germans. Stalin disagreed, telling Churchill, 'There is still a great deal of fat left in Germany.'

No agreement was reached; only to defer the matter 'until a later meeting'. It was now 12.15 p.m. The ninth plenary session of the Potsdam Conference was over. There seemed no need for farewells. Both Stalin and Truman expected Churchill to be back within forty-eight hours, still Prime Minister, and still in charge of Britain's negotiating team. Churchill returned to his villa, from where, a few minutes later, he was driven to Gatow airfield. At 1.23 his aircraft took off for Britain. Two hours and twenty minutes later it landed at Northolt, where he was told that there was considerable gloom at Labour Party headquarters, where it was expected that the Conservatives would win the election with a majority of thirty seats. Although this was forty less than Eden's estimate, it would still provide a working majority.

That evening, at dinner at the Annexe, Churchill learned that his daughter Diana and son-in-law Duncan Sandys 'were gloomy about Duncan's fate' at his South London constituency. That night, just before dawn, Churchill woke up with what he later recalled as 'a sharp stab of almost physical pain', whereupon a hitherto 'subconscious conviction that we were beaten broke forth and dominated my mind'. The power to shape the future would be denied him. 'The knowledge and experience I had gathered, the authority and goodwill I had gained in so many countries, would vanish.'

At ten o'clock that morning, Thursday July 26, Captain Pim received the first election returns; ten Conservative seats had fallen to Labour. He went at once to see Churchill. 'The Prime Minister was in his bath,' he later recalled, 'and certainly appeared surprised, if not shocked. He asked me to get him a towel and in a few minutes, clad in his blue siren suit and with cigar he was in his chair in the Map Room – where he remained all day.' By noon it was clear that there would be a Labour landslide. Randolph Churchill and Duncan Sandys were among the Conservative MPs who lost their seats. 'To my dying day,' one of those present at luncheon that day, David Margesson, wrote to Churchill six years later, 'I shall never forget the courage and forbearance you showed at that most unhappy luncheon after defeat was known. It was a terrific example of how to take it on the chin without flinching.'

'It may well be a blessing in disguise,' Clementine commented.

'At the moment it seems quite effectively disguised,' was Churchill's reply.

With 393 seats in the new Parliament, Labour had a majority of 146 over all other parties. The Conservative seats had fallen, from 585 in the Parliament of 1935, to 213. For the first time in British history more votes had been cast for Labour than for the Conservatives. When Moran spoke of the 'ingratitude' of the British people, Churchill replied: 'I wouldn't call it that. They have had a very hard time.'

Constitutionally, Churchill could have returned to Potsdam as Prime Minister and resigned only when Parliament reassembled a few days later. But he was determined to accept the verdict of the electorate without delay, and at seven o'clock that evening went to Buckingham Palace to tender his resignation to the King. He was now Leader of the Opposition. Two hours later a statement which he had dictated on his return from the Palace was read out over the radio. 'Immense responsibilities abroad and at home fall upon the new Government,' he said, 'and we must all hope they will be successful in bearing them.'

On the following morning, July 27, Attlee flew back to Potsdam as Prime Minister. Churchill, no longer leader of the nation, remained in London. During the morning he said goodbye to the Chiefs of Staff. 'It was a very sad and very moving little meeting at which I found myself unable to say much for fear of breaking down,' Brooke wrote in his diary, and he added, 'He was standing the blow wonderfully well.' Next there were farewells to his Private Secretaries, then a farewell Cabinet. When it was over Churchill called Eden back. 'He was pretty wretched, poor old boy,' Eden wrote in his diary. 'Said he didn't feel any more reconciled this morning, on the contrary it hurt more, like a wound which becomes more painful after the first shock.'

Forty years later, Elizabeth Layton recalled how, on the evening of July 27, 'Mary was in tears, Mrs C went to bed early, and Mr C remained calm.' As he was about to have his bath, Churchill called for Captain Pim. 'He turned quite grey in his bath,' Pim later recalled. 'I thought he would faint. Then he turned to me and said: "They are perfectly entitled to vote as they please. This is democracy. This is what we've been fighting for." '

At Chequers that weekend there were no boxes of telegrams to keep Churchill's mind on the pressures and events of the day. On the evening of July 28 Mary 'saw with near desperation a cloud of black doom descend'. She and Sarah played him his favourite Gilbert and Sullivan records to no avail. But then some French and American marches 'struck a helpful note', and finally 'Run Rabbit, Run' and 'The Wizard of Oz' had 'a cheering effect'. On the following day Churchill wrote from Chequers to Hugh Cecil, his fellow-Conservative rebel of forty years earlier: 'I must confess I found the event of Thursday rather odd and queer, especially after the wonderful welcomes I had from all classes. There was something pent-up in the British people after twenty years which required relief. It is like 1906 all over again. My faith in the flexibility of our Constitution and in the qualities of the British people remains unaltered. We must expect great changes which will be hard for the departing generation to adapt themselves to. The next two years will present administrative difficulties of an unprecedented character, and it may well be that a Labour administration will have a much better chance of solving these than we.'

Churchill was consistent in this view, telling Brendan Bracken that he intended to be 'a support to the "stable men" of the Labour Party so as to curb the "wild men" '. Of the new Secretary of State for War, J.J. Lawson, he wrote to Brooke: 'I am sure you will like your new Secretary of State. He is an absolutely true and decent fellow, but he will need all your help and that of the Department.' And to Attlee he wrote on August 3: 'I shall look forward to talking things over with you when the House opens. We have an immense amount of work to do in common, to which we are both agreed and pledged.' Two days earlier Marian Holmes, who had remained at No. 10 under Attlee, had written in her diary: 'Working for the new PM is very different. He calls us in only when he wants to dictate something. No conversation or pleasantries, wit or capricious behaviour. Just staccato orders. Perfectly polite, and I'm sure he is a good Christian gentleman. But the difference is between champagne and water.'

Churchill was within four months of his seventy-first birthday. Nearly six years had passed since the end of his wilderness decade and his return to the centre of war administration. He had never spared himself, never rested, never accepted defeat or stalemate. The years of war-direction had been exhausting. His wife was afraid that once he laid down his many burdens he might simply fade away. His energies were formidable, however, even after so much effort. Mentally he remained alert and vigilant, but the fact that his power to influence events was over was very hard to bear. At Potsdam, Truman accepted Stalin's insistence that the Western Neisse become Poland's western border. Attlee deferred to the Americans. Churchill commented a year later, 'I would never have agreed to the Western Neisse and was saving it up for a final "show-down".'

On August 6 an atom bomb was dropped on Hiroshima. The effect was devastating; the number of identified victims was 138,690. A year later Churchill told Mountbatten, 'The decision to release the atom bomb was perhaps the only thing which history would have serious questions to ask about', and he added, 'I may even be asked by my Maker why I used it, but I shall defend myself vigorously and shall say, "Why did you release this knowledge to us when mankind was raging in furious battles?"' To George Bernard Shaw he wrote in August 1946: 'Do you think that the atomic bomb means that the architect of the universe has got tired of writing his non-stop scenario? There was a lot to be said for his stopping with the Panda. The release of the bomb seems to be his next turning-point.'

On the day after the Hiroshima bomb, Churchill told a friend that, had he remained Prime Minister, he believed he could have persuaded the Americans to use their new power 'to restrain the Russians'. He would have had 'a show-down with Stalin and told him he had got to behave reasonably and decently in Europe, and would have gone so far as to be brusque and angry with him if needs be'. Truman and his advisers had shown 'weakness in this policy'.

Two days after the Hiroshima bomb, the Soviet Union declared war on Japan. A day later a second atom bomb was dropped, the target being Nagasaki, where 48,857 Japanese were killed. 'It may well be,' Churchill wrote to Attlee on August 10, 'that events will bring the Japanese war to an early close. Indeed I hope this may be so, for it means an immense lightening of the load we expected to carry.' To his secretary, Elizabeth Layton, Churchill commented that day, as they drove from London on the way to Chartwell, through crowds excited by the prospect of victory over Japan, 'You know, not a single decision has been taken since we left office to bring this about.' Not knowing what to say, Miss Layton muttered, was it not better for him now to have a rest. 'No,' he replied, 'I wanted – I wanted to do the Peace too.'

On August 15 Japan surrendered unconditionally to the Allied powers; the Second World War was over. The peacemaking in which Churchill so wished to participate was to be done by others. At times he was 'bitter', Clementine wrote to Mary, at other times 'lion-hearted', about his exclusion. To Averell Harriman he had remarked, a week after the election defeat, 'This has been the longest week of my life, but I am all right now.'

On September 2 Churchill left England by air, flying to Italy in the Prime Minister's plane, which Attlee had put at his disposal. Clementine remained in England, struggling both to make Chartwell habitable after the neglect of the war years, and to prepare their new London house, 28 Hyde Park Gate. Churchill travelled with Sarah. He also took with him, and began reading while still on the plane, a printed set of his war-time minutes to the Chiefs of Staff. His mind was already focused on a task that was to take him more than five years, the preparation of his war memoirs. 'Even during luncheon he went on reading,' Lord Moran wrote of the flight to Italy, 'only taking his eyes from the script to light a cigar.'

Churchill's destination was the Villa delle Rose, on Lake Como, which Alexander had chosen for him as the ideal place for a complete rest, and for painting. Perched above the lake, with a series of gardens leading down to the shore, and a panoramic view of the opposite shore with its villages, woods and mountains, the villa became Churchill's home for seventeen happy days. That first day he was driven over the mountains to Lake Lugano, where he found a spot which caught his painter's eye, and began at once to paint. On the following day, after three hours' painting on the shore of Lake Como, near the villa, he told Sarah, 'I've had a happy day.' Sarah wrote to her mother, 'I haven't heard that for I don't know how long.'

In a letter to Clementine on September 5 Churchill wrote: 'I am much better in myself and am not worrying about anything. We have had no newspapers since I left England, and I no longer feel any keen desire to turn their pages. This is the first time for very many years that I have been completely out of the world. The Japanese War being finished and complete peace and victory achieved, I feel a great sense of relief which grows steadily, others having to face the hideous problems of the aftermath. On their shoulders and consciences weighs the responsibility for what is happening in Europe. It may all indeed be "a blessing in disguise".'

One of the officers who was at the villa, Brigadier Harold Edwards, noted in his diary, 'Churchill has the most fascinating chuckle, and his face, when he is pleased with a thought of his, or a situation conjured up by a remark of someone else, wrinkles up like a baby's – like Puck's.' Edwards wrote, of Churchill's eyes: 'They can be hard as he looks at you – or as tender as a woman's – they can weep easily. I believe now the story of how he cried – of how he wept – as described by M. Herriot, when he realised all was lost in France. He is emotional – not "Irishly" so. I think the right description is that he allows himself to react fully and without restraint and without troubling himself about what impression he makes on the on-looker. He is no actor, no poseur.'

On September 6 Field Marshal Alexander arrived at the villa. For two days he and Churchill painted together, crossing the lake by speedboat to various quiet bays. 'The painting has been a great pleasure to me,' Chur-chill wrote to his wife after Alexander had gone, 'and I have really forgotten all my vexations. It is a wonderful cure, because you cannot really think of anything else.' On the evening of September 8, four days before the anniversary of his marriage in 1908, he had taken over the controls of the speedboat as it drove back across the lake to the villa. 'When I was driving the speed-boat back,' he wrote to Clementine, 'there came into my mind your singing to me "In the Gloaming" years ago. What a sweet song & tune & how beautifully you sang it in all its pathos. My heart fills with love to feel you near me in thought. I feel so tenderly towards you my darling & the more pleasant & agreeable the scenes & days, the more I wish you were here to share them & give me a kiss.'

After a week at the Villa delle Rose, Churchill had painted three pictures and begun a fourth. 'I paint all day & every day,' he wrote to Mary on September 10, '& have banished care & disillusionment to the shades.' But world affairs could not be banished; while he was at Como he was con-sulted by Attlee about the atom bomb, and the need for an international agreement to regulate it. In his reply Churchill wrote of the deterrent effect of the bomb, given 'the supreme resolve of all nations who possess or may possess the weapon to use it at once, unitedly, against any nation that uses it in war'. For this purpose, he wrote, 'the greater the powers of the US and GB in the next few years the better are the hopes. The US therefore should not share their knowledge and advantage except in return for a system of inspection of this and all other weapons-preparations in every country, which they are satisfied after trial is genu-ine.'

On September 19 Churchill left Lake Como for the Villa Pirelli on the Mediterranean, eighteen miles east of Genoa. 'Sunshine is my quest,' he told his wife. On his first day at the Villa Pirelli he swam in the sea. On the following day he went to the nearby village of Recco, where he began to paint the railway viaduct and some bombed houses. The local inhabitants were not amused, and began to boo and shake their fists. 'Without any more ado,' the local British Military Commander, Colonel Wathen, later recalled, 'Mr Churchill packed up and came home. The incident upset him somewhat, but he readily admitted that it was a tactless thing to do, and said that *he* would have been damned annoyed if Hitler had started to paint the bomb damage in London.'

From Genoa, Churchill motored westward along the coast to Monte Carlo, a road he had last traversed with Clementine in 1921, after the Cairo Conference. He spent two days at the Hôtel de Paris at Monte Carlo. 'The food scrumptious, the wines the best. It was like the old days,' he told her; they had last stayed there in 1932. On September 23 he moved further westward to Antibes, where Eisenhower put a fully-staffed villa at his disposal.

Churchill asked Clementine to join him in the South of France, but she felt that the continuing needs of Chartwell and their new London house, 28 Hyde Park Gate, made it impossible for her to do so. On September 24, reading of a Russian demand for naval and air bases in the Mediterranean, in the former Italian colony of Tripolitania, Churchill wrote to her: 'Their wish is a strange one and belongs to a very crude and out-of-date form of Czarist imperialism. In these matters they are about forty years behind the times, and I do not myself see any serious objections to their having these places if they will be reasonable in other directions. All navies, sea-borne commerce and overseas naval and air bases are merely hostages to the stronger sea and air power. However I have no doubt that these demands will cause a great stir. The Bolshevisation of Europe proceeds apace and all the Cabinets of Central, Eastern and Southern Europe are in Soviet control, excepting only Athens. This brand I snatched from the burning on Christmas Day.' Little was known, Churchill told Clementine, as to what was happening 'behind the Russian iron curtain, but evidently the Poles and Czecho-Slovakians are being as badly treated as one could have expected'.

After twenty-five days of sunshine, and having completed fifteen paintings, Churchill returned to London, to the house at Hyde Park Gate. Among the many invitations awaiting him there was one forwarded through President Truman, asking him to give a course of three or four lectures at Westminster College, Fulton, Missouri; 'a wonderful school in my home State' Truman called it. Churchill and Clementine were already planning to stay that winter at Miami Beach.

On October 21 Churchill told his constituents that he had looked forward, on his return from Potsdam, to throwing all his 'personal strength' and that of his colleagues into the demands of peacetime; demobilisation, house-building, the switch-over of industry from war to peacetime production and 'the liberation of the British genius and energy from the long thralldom of war conditions'. But these, he added, were now 'vain repinings'.

Although cut off from the hourly inflow of information from the capitals of the world which had marked his life in office, Churchill followed with avid attention the newspaper reports of Soviet activity in Europe and beyond. The defection in Canada that October of a leading Soviet spy led him, on October 26, to tell the Canadian Prime Minister, Mackenzie King, that there was 'nothing to be gained' by not letting the Russians know 'that we were not afraid of them'. The Russians were 'realist-lizards', all belonging to 'the crocodile family'. They would be 'as pleasant with you as they could, although prepared to destroy you.' What was needed, Churchill told King, 'was a continued alliance between the US and Britain. It must not be written, it must be understood.'

Before leaving for the United States, Churchill held weekly meetings of his Shadow Cabinet, to devise opposition policy and co-ordinate its speaking and parliamentary activities. But he spent as much time as he could at Chartwell, now being slowly returned to its pre-war comfort. German prisoners-of-war were employed to clear first the fish-pool and then the swimming-pool, both of which Churchill had lovingly created twenty years earlier, and which during the neglect of the war years had become clogged and overgrown.

Clementine had never been at ease with the demands of Chartwell. That autumn, Mary has recalled, she suffered 'from depression and nervousness. The build-up of her worries, which her fatigue served to enlarge, made her often impatient and irascible with Winston; and he, for his part, could be demanding and unrealistic. These months saw a series of scenes between them. After any quarrel they both suffered pangs of remorse, and both were always anxious to make it all up. But these were difficult days for them both.'

That November, Churchill made a short visit to Paris and Brussels. Everywhere he was met by cheering, exuberant crowds. 'I have never seen such excitement or enthusiasm,' the British Ambassador to Brussels recalled. 'People broke through the police cordon, dodged the motor-cycle escort which surrounded the car, and threw their bouquets into the car if they were not actually successful in handing them to Mr Churchill. One girl leapt on to the running-board, threw her arms round his neck and kissed him fervently.'

In his speech to a joint meeting of the Belgian Senate and Chamber on November 16 Churchill spoke of the origins of what he called 'The Unnecessary War'. If the Allies had resisted Hitler strongly in his early stages, he said, even up to the German remilitarisation of the Rhineland in 1936, 'he would have been forced to recoil, and a chance would have been given to the elements in German life which were very powerful especially in the High Command to free Germany of the maniacal Government and system into the grip of which she was falling'. The German people had twice voted by a majority against Hitler before 1933, Churchill reminded his listeners, 'but the Allies and the League of Nations acted with such feebleness and lack of clairvoyance that each of Hitler's encroachments became a triumph for him over all moderate and restraining forces until, finally, we resigned ourselves without further protest to the vast process of German rearmament and war preparation which ended in a renewed outbreak of destructive war'.

'Let us profit at least by this terrible lesson,' Churchill declared. 'In vain did I attempt to teach it before the war.' Although he did not say so, he was even then preparing the early chapters of his war memoirs, in which he intended to examine the years between the wars and set out for his readers his inter-war warnings and suggestions. He did call in his Brussels speech for a 'United States of Europe' which would, he explained, 'unify this Continent in a manner never known since the fall of the Roman Empire, and within which all its peoples may dwell together in prosperity, in justice, and in peace'.

Here, three months after the defeat of Japan and six months after the defeat of Germany, were the three themes that were to dominate Churchill's post-war thinking: the close working together of Britain and the United States as a deterrent to Soviet expansion; the mutual banding together of the democracies, under the United Nations, to avert a second drift to war through weakness in the face of tyranny; and the creation of a United Europe. He was convinced that the Second World War could have been avoided. He felt this so strongly that when he was invited to send a message of greeting to Baldwin on his eightieth birthday, he declined to do so. Instead, he wrote to those who had asked for the message, 'I wish Stanley Baldwin no ill, but it would have been better for our country if he had never lived.'

On November 30 Churchill was seventy-one. 'To those that love you,' his daughter Mary wrote on New Year's Day 1946, 'and there are so great a number, it is a grief to see you so set aside – and so saddened. The grief is the greater for the little we can do to help you.' In the New Year's Honours list, Churchill had been awarded the Order of Merit. 'I was so proud and excited,' Mary wrote, 'when I read in the Press this morning of yet another distinction which is yours.'

'The OM comes from the King alone, and is not given on the advice of Ministers,' Churchill explained to one of those who congratulated him. 'This renders it more attractive to me.' On January 8 he went to Buckingham Palace to receive it, and on the following day, from Southampton, sailed with Clementine in the *Queen Elizabeth* for the United

States. One of his wartime secretaries, Jo Sturdee, travelled with him. A new secretary, Elizabeth Gilliatt, remained at Hyde Park Gate to deal with the mass of letters and keep Churchill in touch with events at home. Also he had decided to publish his wartime secret session speeches in volume form; typing out those speeches was Miss Gilliatt's first task.

The voyage had a sad aspect to it; Randolph's marriage had ended in divorce. 'I grieve so much,' Churchill wrote to Pamela Churchill's mother, Lady Digby, two days before before leaving, 'for what had happened which put an end to so many hopes for Randolph and Pamela. The war strode in however through the lives of millions. We must make the best of what is left among the ruins.'

Disembarking in New York on the evening of January 14, Churchill and Clementine went at once by train to Miami Beach where, on their arrival during the morning of January 16, Churchill was asked to give a press conference. It was held on the patio of the house that was to be his home for nearly three weeks, 5905 North Bay Road, which had its own access to the ocean. Asked by a newsreel cameraman to say ten words into the microphone, Churchill replied: 'I have been asked to say just ten words, but haven't been told what ten words they should be. The ten that come to my mind are, "The great pleasure I feel in enjoying the genial sunshine of Miami Beach".'

The local journalists were entranced by their visitor. 'A look of genial impishness' was what one of them noted, and he added: 'The humor that has lubricated his life flashes in his face and sparkles on his tongue. Lubricated his life? Who that has fought as he has fought could live at all except a saving humor balanced him?' In serious vein, Churchill told the journalists why he supported the Labour Government's request for a four-billion-dollar loan from the United States. 'If we're not given the opportunity to get back on our feet again,' he said, 'we may never be able to take our place among other nations.'

Churchill's arrival in the United States generated a vast correspondence, an average of three hundred letters a day. Three secretaries were needed to deal with this; one of them, Lorraine Bonar, who was waiting at the house to welcome her new master, wrote to her mother, 'Well, the great man has arrived and he's just wonderful – he entirely captivated me with his lack of pretentiousness and is really charming to everyone.' He was, she added, 'quite a tease', but there were also times, she later recalled, when he could be 'very difficult and contrary, and even had his little spats with Mrs Churchill when he screamed "Clemmie" at her from across the hall. Once they went for about two days with only the very necessary speaking between them.'

In a letter to his old Army friend General Tudor, Churchill described the difficulties of adjusting after the election defeat six months earlier: 'I found it none too easy to change over so quickly from a life of intense activity and responsibility to one of leisure in which there is nothing to be looked for but anti-climax. However, luckily, I have my painting, into which I have plunged with great vigour, and many other amusements, so that the time passes away pleasantly and rapidly.'

During his first week at Miami Beach, Churchill's temperature rose, and remained high for several days; but then it went down, and Churchill not only painted but swam in the ocean. On January 30 he had a long talk with Emery Reves, who before the war had ensured the wide circulation of his articles throughout Europe, about the publishing aspects of his war memoirs. 'I have not forgotten what you have done for me before the war,' Churchill told Reves, 'and I shall want you to handle it.' Over the next decade, and more, Reves made sure that the memoirs obtained the widest possible circulation, translation, and financial benefit.

On February 1 Churchill and Clementine, accompanied by Sarah, flew from Miami to Havana. It was his first visit to Cuba since 1895. After calling on the Cuban President, he gave a press conference; asked to criticise the Attlee Government, he replied, 'I do not discuss the government of my country when I am away from there'. Asked about the General Election result, he said, 'In my country the people can do as they like, although it often happens that they don't like what they have done.'

After six days' sightseeing, swimming and painting, Churchill returned from Havana to Miami by air on February 8. Two days later he flew to Washington, where he dined with Truman at the White House. There, he tried out the theme of the speech that he was to deliver at Fulton. The Secretary of State, James Byrnes, was also there. Both men, he wrote to Attlee, 'seemed to like it very well', and he added, 'There is much fear of Russia here as a cause of future trouble.' Bevin's attitude at the United Nations in this regard 'has done us a great deal of good'.

On February 12 Churchill gave lunch to Eisenhower at the British Embassy. On the following day he flew back to Miami, where, a week later, in a talk with his American financier friend Bernard Baruch, and with Byrnes, both of whom had flown specially down from Washington to see him, he put the British Government's opinion that the American Loan should be interest-free.

'I am sure your Fulton speech will do good,' Attlee wrote to Churchill on February 25. On the following day, to a gathering of more than 17,000 people in Burdine Stadium, Miami, he drew the conclusion, from his own lack of success in passing examinations at school and his subsequent experience in receiving honorary degrees, 'that no boy or girl should ever be disheartened by lack of success in their youth, but should diligently and faithfully continue to persevere and make up for lost time'.

Churchill left Miami on March 1 by train for Washington, where he first showed his Fulton speech to Admiral Leahy, Truman's senior Service adviser, who was, Churchill informed Attlee and Bevin, 'enthusiastic' about it. Byrnes, to whom he also showed it, was 'excited about it and did not suggest any alterations'. News reaching Washington that day of a Soviet decision not to withdraw its troops from northern Persia, as agreed between Bevin and Molotov six months earlier, seemed to add weight to Churchill's advocacy of Anglo-American firmness.

On March 4 Churchill went from the British Embassy to the White House, where Truman and Leahy joined him for the twenty-four-hour overnight train journey to Missouri. Churchill was impressed to learn from them that, in an effort to show America's determination not to allow Soviet expansion into the Aegean or the Mediterranean, the battleship *Missouri*, on which the Japanese surrender had been signed in Tokyo Bay, would soon be sent to the Mediterranean with a naval task force.

Churchill reported to Attlee and Bevin that, during the train journey westward, Leahy had told him that this task force 'would consist of another battleship of the greatest power, two of the latest and strongest aircraft carriers, several cruisers and about a dozen destroyers'. Both Truman and Leahy 'mentioned the fact that the *Missouri* class carry over 140 anti-aircraft guns'. Churchill commented: 'The above strikes me as a very important act of state and one calculated to make Russia understand that she must come to reasonable terms of discussion with the Western Democracies. From our point of view, I am sure that the arrival and stay of such a powerful American Fleet in the Straits must be entirely beneficial, both as reassuring Turkey and Greece and as placing a demurrer on what Bevin called cutting our life-line through the Mediterranean by the establishment of a Russian naval base at Tripoli.'

Churchill continued to work on his speech during the train journey. Then, as the train steamed beside the broad Missouri river, he showed the speech to Truman. 'He told me he thought it was admirable,' Churchill wrote to Attlee and Bevin, 'and would do nothing but good, though it would make a stir.'

In words which were broadcast throughout the United States, Churchill spoke at Fulton of the 'supreme task and duty' of American democracy, and of the English-speaking world, 'to guard the homes of the common people from the horrors and miseries of another war'. The United Nations must be made to work effectively, to be 'a force for action, and not merely a frothing of words'. Each member state should provide it with an air squadron, to be directed when needed by the United Nations itself; 'I wished to see this done after the First World War, and I devoutly trust it may be done forthwith.' But the secret of the atom bomb should be kept by Britain, Canada and the United States, not shared with the United Nations: 'I do not believe that we should all have slept so soundly had the positions been reversed, and if some Communist or neo-Fascist State monopolised for the time being these dreaded agencies.'

Churchill then spoke of his admiration for the Russian achievement in the war and declared: 'We welcome Russia to her rightful place among the leading nations of the world. We welcome her flag upon the seas. Above all, we welcome constant, frequent and growing contacts between the Russian people and our own people on both sides of the Atlantic. It is my duty, however, for I am sure you would wish me to state the facts as I see them to you, to place before you certain facts about the present position in Europe.' The 'facts' as Churchill saw them were these: 'From Stettin in the Baltic to Trieste in the Adriatic, an iron curtain has descended across the Continent. Behind that line lie all the capitals of the ancient states of Central and Eastern Europe. Warsaw, Berlin, Prague, Vienna, Budapest, Belgrade, Bucharest and Sofia, all these famous cities and the populations around them lie in what I must call the Soviet sphere, and all are subject in one form or another, not only to Soviet influence but to a very high and, in many cases, increasing measure of control from Moscow. Athens alone – Greece with its immortal glories – is free to decide its future at an election under British, American and French observation.'

Churchill then spoke of the 'pre-eminence and power' of the Communist parties of Eastern Europe, far beyond their numbers, and of their attempts to obtain 'totalitarian control'. This, he said, was 'certainly not the Liberated Europe we fought to build up. Nor is it one which contains the essentials of permanent peace.' What was needed now was 'a new unity in Europe', within the structure of the United Nations and its Charter; a unity from which no nations should be 'permanently outcast'. The need for such a unity was urgent; even in countries 'in front of the iron curtain' such as Italy and France, and in places far from the Russian frontier 'throughout the world', Communist Parties or Communist fifth columns 'constitute a growing challenge and peril to Christian civilisation'.

A new war was neither inevitable nor imminent, Churchill said. It was because he believed that 'we hold the power to save our future' that he was speaking in these terms. 'I do not believe that Soviet Russia desires war. What they desire is the fruits of war, and the indefinite expansion of their power and doctrines.' What was needed was 'a settlement' with Russia. The longer this was delayed, the greater the dangers would be. From what he had seen 'of our Russian friends and Allies during the war, I am convinced that there is nothing they admire so much as strength, and there is nothing for which they have less respect than weakness, especially military weakness'. Narrow margins of military superiority were not enough; these offered 'temptations to a trial of strength'. If the Western democracies stood together, no one was likely 'to molest them'. But if 'they become divided or falter in their duty and if these all-important years are allowed to slip away, then indeed catastrophe may overwhelm us all'.

Churchill then recalled the bitter years before the war. 'Last time I saw it coming and cried aloud to my own fellow-countrymen and to the world, but no one paid any attention,' and he went on to explain: 'Up till the year 1933 or even 1935, Germany might have been saved from the awful fate which has overtaken her and we might all have been spared the miseries Hitler let loose upon mankind. There never was a war in all history easier to prevent by timely action than the one which has just desolated such great areas of the globe. It could have been prevented in my belief without the firing of a single shot, and Germany might be powerful, prosperous and honoured to-day; but no one would listen and one by one we were all sucked into the awful whirlpool.' This must not be allowed to happen again; it could be prevented 'by reaching now, in 1946, a good understanding on all points with Russia'.

Churchill urged the Americans not to underestimate the strength of Britain and the British Commonwealth. If, he said, this strength could be added to that of the United States, 'with all that such co-operation implies in the air, on the sea, all over the globe, and in science and industry, and in moral force, there will be no quivering, precarious balance of power to offer its temptation to ambition or adventure'. On the contrary, there would be 'an overwhelming assurance of security'. If all Britain's 'moral and material forces and convictions' were joined with those of the United States 'in fraternal association', then it was his conviction, and vision, that 'the high-roads of the future will be clear not only for us but for all, not only for our time but for a century to come'.

Churchill had originally intended to call his speech 'World Peace'. Now he entitled it 'The Sinews of Peace'. It was a noble vision, but the speech was again dismissed as alarmist, as his speeches from 1932 to 1938 had been. In London, *The Times* described as 'less than happy' his contrast between Western democracy and Communism, stating that the two creeds had 'much to learn from each other, Communism in the working of political institutions and in the establishment of individual rights, western democracy in the development of economic and social planning'. Far from becoming known as 'The Sinews of Peace', Churchill's speech quickly became known as the 'Iron Curtain' speech, as if it had actually created the iron curtain and sought to hold it in place. According to the *Wall Street*

Journal: 'The United States wants no alliance, or anything that resembles an alliance, with any other nation.'

Churchill was 'convinced', as he told Attlee and Bevin on his return to Washington on March 7, 'that some show of strength and resisting power is necessary to a good settlement with Russia', and he added, 'I predict that this will be the prevailing opinion in the United States in the near future.'

On March 8, as the storm grew over Churchill's alleged call for a military alliance against Russia, and at the same time his actual call for a 'good understanding' with Russia was ignored. Truman gave a press conference at which he denied that he had known in advance what Churchill was going to say. That same day, having travelled overnight by train from Washington, Churchill repeated his theme at the University of Virginia. There, in Eisenhower's presence, he told his listeners: 'Peace will not be preserved by pious sentiments expressed in terms of platitudes, or by official grimaces and diplomatic correctitude, however this may be desirable from time to time. It will not be preserved by casting aside, in dangerous years, the panoply of warlike strength. There must be earnest thought. There must also be faithful perseverance and foresight. Greatheart must have his sword and armour to guard the pilgrims on the way. Above all, among the English-speaking peoples there must be the union of hearts based upon convictions and common ideals.'

On March 12, when Churchill was in New York, the Communist Party newspaper *Pravda* published in Moscow an attack on what it called his 'old slanders' concerning Soviet 'expansionist tendencies'. Churchill also learned that day that, on the previous day, two Labour MPs had asked Attlee to 'repudiate' the Fulton speech. When Attlee declined to do so, ninety-three Labour members tabled a motion of censure against Churchill, calling the speech 'inimical to the cause of world peace'. Their objection was to what they called his 'proposals for a military alliance' between the Commonwealth and the United States 'for the purpose of combating the spread of Communism'. Among the signatories was a future Labour Prime Minister, James Callaghan.

Unknown to the Labour malcontents, Churchill had continued to help Attlee and the Labour Government on the matter of the American Loan. At a meeting of the National Press Club in Washington on March 11, and again at a private luncheon with several leading American financiers in New York on March 13, he put the case for a lenient American attitude; Attlee was grateful for this help, sending a special note of 'warm thanks and appreciation'.

Stalin was stung by the Fulton speech; in an unprecedented question-and-answer session printed in *Pravda* on March 14, he described it as 'calculated to sow the seeds of discord between the Allied Governments and make collaboration difficult'. Churchill was 'now in the position of a warmonger'. He had 'many friends not only in England but also in the USA'. Just as Hitler had 'begun the process of unleashing war' by pronouncing his racial theories, so Churchill 'is starting his process of unleashing war also with a racial theory, declaring that only those people who speak English are full-blooded nations, whose vocation it is to control the fate of the whole world'.

Churchill ignored Stalin's charges; but in the final speech of his visit, made in New York on March 15, he answered the main American criticism of his Fulton speech, telling a Civic Reception: 'I have never asked for an Anglo-American military alliance or a Treaty. I have asked for something different, and in a sense I asked for something more. I asked for fraternal association – free, voluntary, fraternal association. I have no doubt that it will come to pass, as surely as the sun will rise tomorrow.'

On March 20 the Churchills sailed from New York on the *Queen Mary*. When the ship was two days out, the battleship *Missouri* sailed from New York for Istanbul. That same day the Soviet Union announced that all Soviet troops would be evacuated from Persia. '*New York Times* attributes changed Russian tactics to your two speeches,' Randolph telegraphed to his father from New York on March 24, and from London came a message of congratulations on the Fulton speech from Asquith's daughter Violet, who wrote, 'Events have powerfully reinforced your words.' In a note of thanks for the trip she had shared with him, his daughter Sarah wrote, 'I know it was far from perfect for you, but you contributed to the World Cause, quite apart from all you did for poor Old England.'

37

Mapping the Past, Guiding the Future

On 29 March 1946, three days after his return to London from the United States, Churchill invited his pre-war literary assistant Bill Deakin to lunch with him at Hyde Park Gate. It was the first step in setting up a research team for the war memoirs and devising a method of work for what were intended to be four or five volumes, and were later extended to six. Deakin was given the responsibility of searching through Churchill's wartime archives, stored in a vault in Whitehall, and extracting Churchill's principal minutes and memoranda. He was also in charge of preparing outlines and drafts of each of the chapters, particularly in their diplomatic and political aspects.

For the military side, Churchill asked a former Chief of Staff to Mountbatten, General Sir Henry Pownall, to be his assistant. Naval aspects were put in the hands of Commodore G.R.G. Allen. Churchill asked General Ismay, the former head of his Defence Office, to keep a watching brief over what was being written; Ismay was always ready to contribute his own recollections of those events which Churchill could not remember in detail. Dozens of other contemporaries sent Churchill diary extracts of particular episodes he wished to describe.

An enormous expenditure of time and energy went into the preparation of the war memoirs. A young barrister, Denis Kelly, was employed to sort out Churchill's own archive at Chartwell. Two new secretaries, Lettice Marston and Chips Gemmell, joined Jo Sturdee and Elizabeth Gilliatt.

Whether at Chartwell, in London, or on his travels, work on the memoirs became a feature of Churchill's daily life. Also, at Attlee's request, on March 31 he set out his views on the importance of a peacetime co-ordinator for the supply needs of the three defence services, drawing Attlee's attention not to his own advocacy of this in 1936 but to a memorandum by his father, dated 21 March 1890, advocating the appointment of someone who 'would as it were set up a great shop from which the military and naval heads could procure most of the supplies they need'. The 'advent of the Air', Churchill commented, had made such a project 'indispensable'.

The underlying theme of the Fulton speech was also something that Churchill found an opportunity to reiterate in Britain. On May 7, on receiving the Freedom of Westminster, he declared, 'The supreme hope and prime endeavour is to reach a good and faithful understanding with Soviet Russia.' In the Commons on June 5 he warned that 'the Sovietising and, in many cases, the Communising' of Central and Eastern Europe, 'against the wishes of the overwhelming majority of the people of many of these regions, will not be achieved in any permanent manner without giving rise to evils and conflicts which are horrible to contemplate'. The crushing of the Hungarian uprising by Soviet forces in 1956 was to take place in Churchill's lifetime; the 'Czech Spring' of 1968, likewise brought to an abrupt end by the Soviets, took place three years after his death.

Churchill now studied the literature of the United States of Europe movement. But when he was told on June 19 that its main object was in fact 'to restrain Russia' he at once wrote to one of those who wished him to join it, 'I think it would be a pity for me to join an organisation which had such a markedly anti-Russian bent.' He planned to set out his own vision of a United Europe during a speech in Zurich. On August 23 he left Chartwell for the Villa Choisi on the shore of Lake Geneva. The villa had been put at his disposal by the local canton of Bursinel. There, in the pleasant seclusion of an idyllic lakeside setting, he worked at his speech, continued with his war memoirs, and painted.

Churchill stayed at the Villa Choisi for four weeks. Clementine and Mary were with him, as were two of his four secretaries, Elizabeth Gilliatt and Lettice Marston. 'We are having a delightful time here with every comfort and the strictest privacy,' Churchill wrote to a friend on August 29. 'I find lots to paint in the garden.'

Speaking at the University of Zurich on September 19, Churchill appealed for 'a kind of United States of Europe'. But where to start, he asked his listeners, and he went on to say that he had a proposal that would 'astonish' them, 'The first step in the re-creation of the European family must be a partnership between France and Germany.' There could be no revival of Europe 'without a spiritually great France and a spiritually great Germany'.

Churchill's appeal for the reconciliation of France and West Germany, as a prelude to a united Europe, was made, he said, in the shadow of an 'awful agency of destruction', the atom bomb. If used by 'several warring nations', the bomb would not only bring to an end 'all that we call civilisation, but may possibly disintegrate the globe itself'. Hence the urgency in ending the long-standing feud between the two great nations of Western Europe. The process 'must begin now'. But he did not limit the process of reconciliation to Europe alone. The work needed 'friends and sponsors', Britain and the Commonwealth, as well as 'mighty America, and I trust Soviet Russia – for then indeed all would be well'.

Once more, Churchill had spoken about Russia, not as a permanent adversary, but as a potential partner. As for his call for Franco-German reconciliation, 'The French are startled, as they were bound to be,' Leo Amery told him, 'but the idea will sink in all the same.'

That autumn Randolph wrote to his father to complain about the possibility of land nationalisation. Churchill replied: 'I am opposed to State-ownership of all the land, but we must not conceal from ourselves that we should be much stronger if the soil of our country were divided up among two or three million people, instead of twenty or thirty thousand. Man is a land animal. Even rabbits are allowed to have warrens, and foxes have earths.'

Churchill's own 'earth' was Chartwell. That autumn, fearing that his income was such that he could no longer afford to maintain it, he spoke gloomily to his friend Lord Camrose about having to put it on the market. When Camrose asked whether he would accept £50,000, he replied with a chuckle that for such a sum, the 1990 equivalent of a million pounds, he would 'throw in the corpse as well'. Camrose at once suggested that a consortium of wealthy men buy it for that amount, allow Churchill to live in it for the rest of his life for a nominal rent of £350 a year, and on his death give it to the National Trust as a permanent memorial. Churchill was delighted. He would leave 'lots of papers and documents in the house', he said, and went on to tell Camrose that he had always thought that he would like to be buried at Chartwell, and that the proposal made his mind 'definite' on that point.

The money was quickly raised, from seventeen benefactors, including Camrose himself. Then, as Churchill worked at Chartwell on his war memoirs, Camrose, who had gone specially to New York, and Emery Reves, negotiated the sale of the memoirs in the United States. Churchill would receive $1,400,000, the 1946 equivalent of £5,600,000 in 1990. His money worries were over, especially in regard to the legacy that he would be able to leave to his grandchildren, in the form of a trust. There was no way to repay this generosity, Mary later wrote to him, 'except by our loving gratitude, which overflows, and trying to show our children and dependents the same largeness of heart and steadfastness of love which you have always shown to yours'.

Seven secretaries were drawn into the memoir-writing task, including Clementine's secretary Grace Hamblin. Bill Deakin became a regular commuter between the vaults under Whitehall and Chartwell. 'Everything was devoted to his memoirs,' Deakin later recalled. 'He concentrated ruthlessly on this. He saw it as his monument.' There was also the persistent call of politics; Churchill had no intention of neglecting his part as Leader of the Opposition. At Blackpool, on October 5, he declared his support for profit-sharing schemes and 'intimate consultation' between employers and employees, intended to make the employee a 'partner'. He also reiterated his call for the creation of a United States of Europe, which ought, he declared in a public statement that October, to stretch 'from the Atlantic to the Black Sea'. Until that could be done, a start should be made in Western Europe. Russia, he told Attlee on October 10, would not march westward to the North Sea or the Atlantic for two reasons: 'The first is their virtue and self-restraint. The second, the possession by the United States of the atomic bomb.'

To a friend who feared that a United Europe would serve only to challenge the Soviet bloc, Churchill wrote on October 19: 'I am not attracted to a Western bloc as a final solution. The ideal should be EUROPE.' To divide Europe into two opposing blocs, east and west, would be a 'vice'. Without the 'resurrection and reconciliation of Europe', he wrote to a Labour MP on November 7, 'there is no hope for the world'. To General de Gaulle, who was then a private citizen but whose support for a United Europe he now sought, Churchill wrote on November 26, 'It is my conviction that if France could take Western Germany by the hand and, with full English co-operation, rally her to the West and to European civilisation, this would indeed be a glorious victory and make amends for all we have gone through, and perhaps save us having to go through a lot more.'

De Gaulle replied that Churchill's call for reconciliation between France and Germany had been 'badly received' in France. Nor would Attlee allow any formal Labour Party association with a small all-Party Handling Group which Churchill had just set up, to win Parliamentary support for a European Federation. But Churchill did not give up. 'Life slips away,' he wrote to Louis Spears, 'but one fights with what strength remains for the things one cares about.'

On November 30 Churchill was seventy-two. Among the things he cared about was the retention of British sovereignty in India, and the creation of a Jewish State in at least some part of Palestine. The Labour Government opposed both courses. It also opposed a compromise suggestion which Churchill made in the Commons that, on both the Indian and Palestine questions, Britain should 'invoke the aid' of the United Nations. That winter Churchill spent much of his time at Chartwell writing his memoirs. 'It is a colossal undertaking and I may well collapse before the load is carried to the top of the hill,' he wrote to Attlee on December 28.

'However, it is a good thing to get a certain amount of material together which, if not history, will still at least be a contribution thereto.'

On 11 February 1947 Churchill and Clementine were at St Margaret's, Westminster, for the marriage of their daughter Mary to Christopher Soames, a Guards Officer whom she had met when he was Assistant Military Attaché in Paris. Henceforth, Soames was to be a boon companion to Churchill, helping him in the management of Chartwell Farm, which he had just acquired together with other land near Chartwell itself, and accompanying him on many of his journeys overseas.

Churchill's joy at the marriage of his youngest daughter was followed by sadness: his brother Jack was dying. On February 20 he spoke to a friend of 'my dear Jack, every day washed nearer the reef, at which he glares with undaunted eyes'. Three days later Jack died. 'I know you loved him dearly,' Sarah wrote to her father, 'and he adored you, with a love untinged by envy of the triumphs, excitements and high destiny of your life.' To Lord Quickswood, his former best man, Lord Hugh Cecil, Churchill wrote in reply to his letter of condolence: 'We have always been attached to one another, & after his house was blown up in the war he lived with me at No. 10 or the Annexe. He had no fear & little pain. Death seems very easy at the end of the road. Do you think we shall be allowed to sleep a long time? I hope so. (Ready to serve if really required). The only thing Jack worried about was England. I told him it would be all right.'

To ensure the adequate defence of England, Churchill gave his support to the Labour Government's National Service Bill, making all men between the ages of 18 and 26 liable for conscription for eighteen months. But he could not resist telling the House, during the debate on March 31, in a reference to Attlee and A.V. Alexander: 'It is certainly an irony of fate that the Prime Minister and the Minister of Defence should be the men to bring a Conscription Bill before the House now, after two years of peace, when all our enemies have surrendered unconditionally. Why, these were the very politicians who, four months before the outbreak of the war, led their followers into the Lobby against the principle of compulsory military service, and then had the face to accuse the Conservative Party of being "guilty men".'

When, under pressure from its left wing, the Labour Government reduced the term of conscription to a year, Churchill told the House: 'The title of Minister of Defence should be changed. He should be called the "Minister for Defence unless attacked". What a lamentable exhibition he has made of himself.' Churchill was even more angered when Attlee announced that Britain would withdraw from its role as protector of

Greece and Turkey, and do so within thirty-eight days. But he was delighted when Truman immediately took up the mantle of defender of 'free people' trying to maintain their independence 'against aggressive movements that seek to impose upon them totalitarian régimes'. This Truman Doctrine, as it became known, came into force on May 22. 'I cannot resist,' Churchill had written to Truman ten days earlier, 'after the year that has passed and all that has happened, writing to tell you how much I admire what you have done for the peace and freedom of the world, since we were together.'

Churchill wrote this letter on the day after his return from Paris, whither he had gone to receive the Médaille Militaire. Clementine had advised him not to attend the ceremony in his wartime Air Commodore's uniform, writing to him before he left:

> I would like to persuade you to wear Civilian clothes during your Paris visit. To me, air-force uniform except when worn by the Air Crews is rather bogus. And it is not as an Air-Commodore that you conquered in the War but in your capacity & power as a Statesman.
>
> All the political vicissitudes during the years of Exile qualified you for un-limited & supreme power when you took command of the Nation. You do not need to wear your medals to show your prowess. I feel the blue uniform is for you fancy-dress, & I am proud of my plain Civilian Pig.

Churchill at first deferred to Clementine's advice, telling his valet, 'I shall wear civilian clothes and take no uniform at all.' But in the event he took his uniform, and wore it at the ceremony at the Cour des Invalides, where he was presented with the medal, and at the Arc de Triomphe, where he laid a wreath at the tomb of the Unknown Warrior.

On May 20 Churchill was asked by Attlee to accept a non-partisan policy towards India. The Labour Government's plan was to divide India into two States, the predominantly Hindu 'India' and the predominantly Muslim 'Pakistan', each to be granted Dominion Status with the right of eventual independence. This plan of partition, which had been insisted upon by the leaders of the Muslim minority, was also acceptable to the leaders of the Indian Congress Party and to the Viceroy, Lord Mountbatten. On May 20 Mountbatten went with Attlee to see Churchill, who accepted the Labour leader's appeal; the Conservative Party would not oppose the legislation needed to grant Dominion Status to India.

Thus, in an act of conciliation, ended Churchill's hope, for which he had earlier fought so hard, to maintain some form of British rule in India, at least at the centre. Churchill was true to his word; when the Indian Independence Bill was presented to the House of Commons on July 4, it was supported by the Conservatives. On August 4, in a further gesture of conciliation, this time towards Communist Eastern Europe, he told a Conservative rally at Blenheim, 'We do not wish the slightest ill to those who dwell on the east of that Iron Curtain, which was never of our making. On the contrary, our prosperity and happiness would rise with theirs,' and he went on to make an appeal that was to be answered only a quarter of a century after his death: 'Let there be sunshine on both sides of the Iron Curtain; and if ever the sunshine should be equal on both sides, the Curtain will be no more. It will vanish away like the mists of morning and melt in the warm light of happy days and cheerful friendship.'

That autumn Churchill took a lead in trying to rally both Conservative and Liberal forces against the Labour Government, which had now proposed the nationalisation of the steel industry. 'It is forty-one years,' he said during a Party Political Broadcast on August 16, 'since, as a young Liberal Minister in Mr Asquith's Government, arguing against this same Socialist fallacy, I said: "The existing organisation of society is driven by one mainspring – competitive selection. It may be a very imperfect organisation of society, but it is all we have got between us and barbarism." I should now have to add totalitarianism, which indeed is only state-organised barbarism.'

Living mainly at Chartwell, Churchill continued to work on the first two volumes of his war memoirs. He was also active in persuading the Conservative Party to oppose the Burma Independence Bill, speaking against the Bill on November 5. Commenting on a recent statement by Attlee about India, whose Independence Bill the Conservatives had not opposed, he spoke of 'the impressive scene, with the quiet little man and his quiet little voice sweeping away our position in India'. India had at least remained in the Commonwealth; the aim of the new Bill 'is to cut Burma out of the Empire altogether, and to make her a foreign Power'. To this he was totally opposed. His fear was that anarchy would follow swiftly upon a British withdrawal. When Arthur Henderson, for the Government, spoke of the need to allow the Burmese to enjoy 'the same democratic freedom that we enjoy ourselves', he retorted with a bitter reference to the civil war between Hindus and Muslims in India: 'What about the deaths of half a million people in India? Enjoying democratic freedom!'

When the House divided at the end of the debate, there were 288 votes cast for Burmese independence, and 114 against; Churchill was angry that so few Members, scarcely half the House, had bothered to be present on what, for Labour MPs, 'must be a joy-day'.

On November 30 Churchill was seventy-three. That night there was a dinner party at Hyde Park Gate. 'Winston was in sombre mood, convinced that this country is destined to suffer the most agonising economic distress,' Colville wrote in his diary. 'He says that the anxiety he suffered during the Battle of the Atlantic was "a mere pup" in comparison. We could only get through if we had the power of the spirit, the unity, and the absence of envy, malice and hatred which are now so conspicuously lacking. Never in his life had he felt such despair, and he blamed it on the Government, whose "insatiable lust for power is only equalled by their incurable impotence in exercising it".' Colville added, 'The phrases and epigrams rolled out in the old way, but I missed the indomitable hope and conviction which characterised the Prime Minister of 1940-41.'

On December 6, when he received the Freedom of the City of Manchester, Churchill spoke openly of his anxieties, warning that Socialism, 'that is to say the substitution of State control by officials for private enterprise', would make it impossible for Britain to sustain its existing population. At least a quarter of the population would have to 'disappear in one way or another' as living standards fell. Emigration, 'even if practised on a scale never before dreamed of, could not operate in time to prevent this melancholy decline'.

Four days after his Manchester speech Churchill left Northolt by air, in search of sun, and determined to make progress on his war memoirs. From Paris he flew to Marrakech, where for a month he painted and worked on his war memoirs. Unease at the future was not easily set aside, however. To Clementine, who had not felt up to the expedition, he wrote on December 12: 'I continue to be depressed about the future. I really do not see how our poor island is going to earn its living when there are so many difficulties around us, and so much ill-will and divisions at home. However I hope to blot all this out of my mind for a few weeks.'

Painting and writing went well, with sets of printer's proofs and historical notes arriving almost daily. But with the onset of a bad cough, Churchill asked Lord Moran to join him. Moran did so, bringing with him Clementine. Both were relieved that it was not another bout of pneumonia, and Churchill, likewise relieved, was quickly out of bed and back at work, and at his easel.

On 4 January 1948 Burma became an independent republic. That day, Lord Cherwell flew out to join Churchill at Marrakech, bringing with him eight chapters of the war memoirs that had been scrutinised by Edward Marsh. Further notes and suggestions arrived that week from the Oxford philosopher Isaiah Berlin. Not all criticism was equally well-received. When Emery Reves wrote that, in his considered opinion, there were too many documents quoted in full in the narrative, and that considerable rewriting was needed to weave them into the text, Churchill was cast down.

It was Sarah who sought to set his mind at rest. 'You are the best historian – the best journalist – the best poet,' she wrote. 'Shut yourself up and only listen to a very few, and even then, write this book from the heart of yourself, from the knowledge you have, and let it stand & fall by that. It will stand – everyone will listen to your story. I hate to see you pale & no longer happily preoccupied.'

Reves could also give welcome advice; on January 14 he opposed the title Churchill had chosen for the first volume, 'Downward Path', as it 'sounds somewhat discouraging'. Churchill then chose another title from a selection that Reves sent him; the book would be called 'The Gathering Storm'.

Churchill left Marrakech on January 18. Four days later he spoke in the Commons during the debate on Foreign Affairs. The only way to avoid a conflict with Russia, he declared, was to 'bring matters to a head with the Soviet Government, and, by formal diplomatic processes, with all their privacy and gravity, to arrive at a lasting settlement'. This was the very word, 'settlement', that he had used in his Fulton speech.

The Soviet Union seemed in no mood for compromise. On February 21 the Czechoslovak Communist Party, on orders from Moscow, seized power in Prague. When four Czech refugees, including General Ingr, the Minister of Defence in the wartime Czech Government-in-Exile, came to Hyde Park Gate to seek his advice, Churchill asked both Bevin and the American Ambassador, Lewis Douglas, to receive them. He also told his former Military Secretary, Ian Jacob, who had recently been appointed head of the BBC's Overseas Service, that one of the Czechs had told him that 'the BBC is listened to now in Czechoslovakia even more than in the war, but that there is a feeling that the best use of this great opportunity is not being made'.

Following the subjugation of Czechoslovakia to Communist rule, Churchill was stirred to a fierce reflection. On April 17 Lewis Douglas reported to Washington, after a talk with Churchill about the Soviet grip on Eastern Germany, 'He believes that now is the time, promptly, to tell the Soviets that if they do not retire from Berlin and abandon Eastern Germany, withdrawing to the Polish frontier, we will raze their cities.'

On April 19 *Life* began the serialisation of the first volume of Churchill's war memoirs. It was the beginning of a massive public readership, enhanced when the volume itself was published, and renewed with the appearance of each of the subsequent five volumes. These formed the first fully-documented account of the war, and the only account written by one of the Big Three. Sales were enormous, both at home and abroad.

The central theme in the first volume was the weakness of the democracies in the face of tyranny before 1939, and of the national hatreds and rancours built up during the inter-war years. On May 7, at the inaugural meeting of the Congress of Europe in The Hague, Churchill made a powerful plea for letting 'national rancours and revenges die'. He also urged 'progressively effacing frontiers and barriers which aggravate and congeal our divisions', and he welcomed the West German delegates to the Congress, describing the 'German problem' as that of restoring the economic life of Germany and reviving 'the ancient fame of the German race without thereby exposing their neighbours and ourselves to any rebuilding or reassertion of their military power, of which we still bear the scars'.

The question to be asked, Churchill told his listeners at The Hague, was: 'Why should so many millions of humble homes in Europe, aye, much of its enlightenment and culture, sit quaking at the dread of the policeman's knock? That is the question we have to answer here. That is the question which perhaps we have the power to answer here. After all, Europe has only to arise and stand in her own majesty, faithfulness and virtue, to confront all forms of tyranny, ancient or modern, Nazi or Communist, with forces which are unconquerable, and which if asserted in good time may never be challenged again.'

Two days later, in Amsterdam, Churchill spoke of how he understood the 'toils and sufferings' of the Germans, the Russians, and the Japanese. 'It is not against any race or nation that we range ourselves. It is against tyranny in all its forms.' To this end, Churchill supported the French proposal, first made at The Hague less than three months after his own speech there, for a European Assembly. He was angered when Attlee told him, in a private letter, that it was Bevin's view that the Foreign Secretary 'could not for the time commit himself' to such an Assembly. In reply, Churchill expressed his hope that the Government would find it possible to 'place themselves more in line with Western European opinion'. But the Labour leaders shied away from a commitment to Europe that was unpopular with their rank and file members.

Twice that summer Churchill was in conflict with the Party which he led. In his memoirs he had castigated Chamberlain's foreign policy and feebleness. In the Commons he demanded that Britain recognise the newly declared State of Israel. On June 2 Henry Channon noted in his diary, after a lunch given in Churchill's honour at the Savoy Hotel: 'His reception was tepid, but not in the least unfriendly – though gone is the rapture of yesteryear. I think that the Party resents both his unimpaired criticism of Munich, recently published, and his alleged pro-Zionist leanings.'

Such sentiments did not deter Churchill from continuing to seek British recognition for Israel, or from criticising in his memoirs those policies with which he had disagreed. But to those who were preparing his draft chapters he wrote that summer, 'Full justice must be done to the other side', and he made frequent efforts to make sure that the views of those to whom he had been opposed were given a place in his narrative. 'You must understand,' he explained to Ismay, 'that it is no part of my plan to be needlessly unkind to the men we chose at the time, who no doubt did their best.' But offence could still be caused: several aggrieved generals sought changes in future editions, which Churchill agreed to. When Volume Two was published, three French generals, together with the son of a fourth, protested. In sending these protests to Churchill, Emery Reves commented: 'It seems that your memoirs have aroused the aggressive spirit of the French generals which was so sadly lacking in 1939. Perhaps it was a mistake not to publish this second volume at the beginning of the war.'

Churchill did not dismiss out of hand the criticisms made by the French generals; indeed, they were much in his mind when, in a special preface for the French edition, he wrote: 'The facts which I testify are that the French army was not given a good chance before the war by the politicians or the Chamber, and secondly that it was ripped apart by the incursion of the German armour on a scale and in a manner which few of us, whether in office or in private station, could foresee. Thus for all the bravery of its soldiers and the skill of its commanders its men never had their chance of fighting it out with the Germans, front to front and face to face.'

Current affairs impinged on Churchill's writing that summer when, on June 24, the Soviet forces in Eastern Germany imposed a total road and rail blockade into and out of Berlin. Ernest Bevin spoke out against the Soviet stranglehold, and a massive air-lift was organised, to fly in vital supplies to Berlin around the clock. Bevin was 'right to speak for a united Britain', Churchill told his constituents on July 10. But he was still uneasy. 'The gravity of events makes me anxious,' he wrote to Montgomery on July 18. 'I trust we are not approaching another "Munich". For such a crime by a British Government there would be no forgiveness.' Nine days later, viewing the crisis from its widest perspective, he wrote to Eisenhower, who had just decided not to stand for the Presidency of the United States, that what was needed to avert a third world war was 'a settlement with Soviet Russia as a result of which they would retire to their own country and dwell there, I trust, in contentment'. It was 'vital for the fut ᵕ , Churchill added, that the moment for such a settlement should be chosen 'when they will realise that the United States and its Allies possess overwhelming force'.

On August 22 Churchill and Clementine left England for Aix-en-Provence, where, at the Hôtel du Roy René, he worked on his war memoirs. He also pondered the resolution of the Berlin blockade, telling a friend who visited him: 'I would have it out with them now. If we do not, war might come. I would say to them, quite politely: "The day we quit Berlin, you will have to quit Moscow." ' To Eden, he suggested that the showdown should be delayed for a year, when the American Air Force 'will have a third more atomic bombs and better, and far more effective, means of delivery, both by airplanes and from the bases they are developing, the largest of which is in East Anglia'. What Churchill did not know was that the Labour Government was already developing Britain's own atom bomb.

From Aix, Churchill moved on September 20 to Beaverbrook's villa, La Capponcina, on the Côte d'Azur. Clementine returned to London. The daily despatch of historical queries from Churchill to his advisers continued until Churchill's return to Chartwell on October 2. From there he made several journeys to speak about the need for 'resistance to tyranny in all its forms', a phrase he used at Biggin Hill, near Chartwell, in a speech to 615 Squadron on October 5, and again four days later at Llandudno, in North Wales, to a Conservative Party rally, where he said, of the Russians: 'Let them release their grip upon the satellite States of Europe. Let them retire to their own country, which is one-sixth of the land surface of the globe. Let them liberate by their departure the eleven ancient capitals of Eastern Europe which they now hold in their clutches.' Churchill added, in an echo of his advice with regard to Germany in 1932, 'The western nations will be far more likely to reach a lasting settlement, without bloodshed, if they formulate their just demands while they have the atomic power, and before the Russians have got it too.'

On November 27, three days before his seventy-fourth birthday, Churchill, so *Time* reported, 'donned jodhpurs, fortified himself with rum punch and galloped off to hounds astride a borrowed horse'. A month later he left England once more for Paris and the South of France, where he again stayed for two weeks at the Hôtel de Paris in Monte Carlo. It was while he was there that he read the statement in an American officer's memoirs that, in 1944, 'a full-scale invasion of the Balkans was no longer contemplated'. Churchill was already the victim of a growing misrepresentation of many aspects of his wartime strategy. Of this statement he replied: 'No one ever contemplated at any time a full scale invasion of the Balkans. This is one of the silly stories that the Americans have propagated. I never myself contemplated anything but commando and partisan assistance.'

Churchill was back in England on 13 January 1949. Six weeks later he returned to Europe, to speak in Brussels in favour of the establishment of a European Court of Human Rights. There must, he said in his speech to the Council of the European Movement on February 26, be some means by which events such as the recent arrest and imprisonment in Hungary of Cardinal Mindszenty 'can be brought to the test of impartial justice'. Nor could the supporters of a United Europe 'rest content', he said, with the division of Europe into 'the free and the unfree': the Europe 'we seek to unite is *all* Europe'.

That March, Churchill planned to visit the United States, having been invited to speak at the Massachusetts Institute of Technology. On the way there, he intended to stay for a while in Jamaica with Lord Beaverbrook. But Clementine opposed this first phase of his journey at what she called, in a note which she sent him on March 5, 'this moment of doubt and discouragement among our followers'. The Conservative rank and file were growing uneasy at the continuing Labour rule. There was also unease at Churchill's leadership, which many Tories felt was not firm or decisive enough. This had become clear at the series of more than thirty luncheons which Clementine had arranged at Hyde Park Gate so that her husband could meet as many Conservative backbenchers as possible. To stay with Beaverbrook, she warned, would 'increase that doubt & discouragement. It would seem cynical and an insult to the Party'.

Clementine's letter continued: 'You often tease me and call me "pink" but believe me I feel it very much. I do not mind if you resign the Leadership when things are good, but I can't bear you to be accepted murmuringly and uneasily. In my humble way I have tried to help, with political lunches here, visits to Woodford, attending to your constituency correspondence. But now & then I have felt chilled & discouraged by the deepening knowledge that you do only just as much as will keep you in Power. But that much is not enough in these hard anxious times.'

Churchill accepted his wife's advice. 'The political situation here is uneasy,' he wrote to Beaverbrook five days later, 'and I do not feel I ought to be away so long.' Then, on March 18, he sailed on the *Queen Elizabeth* for New York. It was almost exactly fifty-five years since he had first crossed the Atlantic, 'which', he wrote to the Cunard White Star Line, 'is a long time as human lives go'. Speaking in New York on March 25, he praised the recently signed Atlantic Pact, the forerunner of the North Atlantic Treaty Organisation, NATO. The American people, he said, were 'in it because there's no way out, but if we pool our luck and share our fortunes I think you will have no reason to regret it'. The Pact was necessary because, he said, 'you have not only to convince the Soviet Government that you have superior force – that they are confronted by superior force – but that you are not restrained by any moral consideration, if the case arose, from using that force with complete material ruthlessness. And that is the greatest chance of peace, the surest road to peace. Then, the Communists will make a bargain.'

Europe would have been 'Communised' some time ago, Churchill said, and London would have been 'under bombardment', but for the deterrent effect of the atom bomb in the hands of the United States. He reiterated this point during a private talk with Truman at the White House a few days later, when he urged the President to make public that the United States was indeed prepared to use the atom bomb to defend democracy. Then, on March 31, after travelling by train to Boston, he gave the speech at the Massachusetts Institute of Technology for which he had come to the States. 'Little did we guess,' he said, recalling the year 1900, 'that what has been called the Century of the Common Man would witness, as its outstanding feature, more common men killing each other with greater facilities than any other five centuries put together in the history of the world.' Communism had now created a 'fundamental schism' with the rest of mankind. But he did not believe that any people could be held in thrall for ever. 'The machinery of propaganda,' he said, 'may pack their minds with falsehood and deny them truth for many generations of time, but the soul of man thus held in trance, or frozen in a long night, can be awakened by a spark coming from God knows where, and in a moment the whole structure of lies and oppression is on trial for its life.'

The 'aim and ideal' today, Churchill went on, were friendship with Russia. If, however, there was to be a war of nerves, 'let us make sure our nerves are strong and are fortified by the deepest convictions of our hearts. If we persevere steadfastly together, and allow no appeasement of tyranny and wrong-doing in any form, it may not be our nerve, or the structure of our civilisation, which will break – and peace will be preserved.'

On April 7, as Churchill was on his way back to Britain on board the *Queen Mary*, Truman made the statement which Churchill had urged him to make. He would 'not hesitate', he said, to use the atom bomb if it were necessary for the welfare of the United States, or if the fate of the democracies of the world were at stake. This statement, Churchill wrote to a friend after his return to Britain, 'will, I have no doubt, be a help to the cause of peace', while to Truman he wrote two months later: 'I was greatly impressed by your statement about not fearing to use the atomic bomb if the need arose. I am sure this will do more than anything else to ward off the catastrophe of a third world war.'

The need for a unity of all democratic forces influenced even Churchill's attitude to India. Less than two years after his acceptance of the Indian Independence Bill, he accepted a further Labour Government proposal, that India could remain in the Commonwealth as an

Independent Republic. 'I have no doubt,' Churchill told a leading Conservative Peer, Lord Salisbury, on April 28, 'that it is our duty to do all we can to make a success of the new system.' And in the House of Commons that day he spoke of how the 'dangers and difficulties' shared in common by all states 'may well make new harmonies with India and, indeed, with large parts of Asia'.

Churchill's decision to welcome the Republic of India into the Commonwealth was accepted by his Party. To Field Marshal Smuts, who objected to it, he wrote a month later, 'When I asked myself the question, "Would I rather have them in, even on these terms, or let them go altogether?" my heart gave the answer, "I want them in." Nehru has certainly shown magnanimity after sixteen years' imprisonment.' Churchill continued, 'The opposition to Communism affords a growing bond of unity.' Even the Burmese, whose Independence he had opposed, might have a place in the new scheme of things. 'It is possible, even, that Burma may take a second-class ticket back,' he wrote to Lord Salisbury. 'This I should welcome. Perhaps you will remember the difficulty I had to get the Party to vote against the Burma Independence Bill. But now, in their tragedy and misery, many Burmese must be turning their minds back to the palmy days of Queen Victoria.' Churchill added: 'These may be but the vain dreams of an aged man. However, I cannot despair.'

That summer Churchill went to Italy, once more accompanied by sufficient secretaries and boxes of papers to enable him to continue work on the fourth volume of his war memoirs. Clementine went with him, as did General Ismay and Bill Deakin. They stayed first at Gardone, on Lake Como, and then at Carezza. The working holiday was broken off in mid-August, when Churchill travelled to Strasbourg, for the inaugural meeting of the Council of Europe, as head of the British Parliamentary Opposition section. Herbert Morrison headed the Government section. One of Churchill's fellow-Conservative delegates, Harold Macmillan, was amazed at how Churchill entered into the spirit of debate and politics. 'He walked about, chatted to each representative, went into the smoking-room, and generally took a lot of trouble to win the sympathetic affection of his new Parliamentary colleagues.' For four days, Churchill entertained French, Belgian, Dutch and Italian delegates at his villa. Then, in his speech on August 17, he called upon the Council of Europe to act as a 'European unit' in the United Nations. Looking round the hall, he asked, in a dramatic outburst, 'Where are the Germans?'

Churchill pressed the Council to invite a West German delegation to join its deliberations as soon as possible. This must be done before the end of the month. The year ahead was 'too precious to lose. If lost, it might be lost for ever. It might not be *a* year. It might be *the* year.' It was only by the 'growth and gathering of the united sentiment of Europeanism, vocal here and listened to all over the world', he said, 'that we shall succeed in taking, not executive decision, but a leading and active part in the revival of the greatest of continents, which has fallen into the worst of misery'. As Churchill had suggested, West Germany was invited to attend the Council of Europe; though the decision was not made until the next session, held in Paris at the beginning of November. Within two years, she had been made a full member with full voting rights.

From Strasbourg, Churchill went south to the French Riviera, where, once more ensconced at La Capponcina, and helped by Denis Kelly, he was to resume work for a few days on his war memoirs before returning to Strasbourg. The film star Merle Oberon was also a guest; on the afternoon of August 23 Churchill, suitably attired, turned somersaults in the sea to amuse her. Kelly later recalled how 'as we sat afterwards drinking dry martinis in our towels, he suddenly put his own weak whisky and soda on the bar, looked at my skinny body and grunted, "Denis, you're a disgrace to the British Empire." '

That evening Churchill played cards with Beaverbrook. When he got up from the table for a moment, he found that his right leg had gone to sleep. He continued playing, but then noticed a 'cramp' in his right arm. That night, not aware that anything serious was wrong, he discussed with Kelly his worries about Beaverbrook's anti-Americanism. 'Those people don't know what it's all about,' he said, as he splashed about in his bath.

In the morning Churchill realised that all was not well. The cramps had persisted, and he found that he could not write very easily. Lord Moran was summoned from London and flew out at once. Churchill had suffered a mild stroke. When he tried to do so he found that he could not sign his name. His return visit to Strasbourg was at once cancelled, as was a plan he had made to go to Switzerland for a short painting holiday. For three days he stopped work altogether, except to practise his signature, asking Elizabeth Gilliatt again and again, 'Is it all right?' On the fourth day he felt well enough to do some dictation.

Worried and irritated that it might be noticed that the stroke, which was kept strictly secret, had slightly impaired his gait, Churchill returned to England by air on August 31, flying to Biggin Hill and being driven straight to Chartwell. On September 3 he went to Epsom, where he saw Colonist II, a racehorse that he had recently bought. But he made no public speech until October 13, when he spoke at the Conservative Trades Union Congress in London, and then, on the following day, to the annual Conservative Conference, also held in London. Six days later he was in Bristol, to deliver the Chancellor's address at the honorary degree ceremony. On October 21 he spoke again, at the annual Alamein Reunion in the Albert Hall.

Whenever possible that autumn, Churchill stayed at Chartwell. There, on September 16, he had executed a seven-year Deed of Covenant in favour of Lord Moran's wife, so that she would receive £500 a year free of tax. This was the second seven-year deed he had signed for her; in the money values of 1990 it was the equivalent of £8,000 a year. Knowing that his doctor was not well-off, he insisted upon helping. 'I hope you will not forbid me to do this,' he wrote.

There had been many other acts of generosity on Churchill's part, both in financial help and moral support. For more than twenty years he had been paying his son's often substantial debts, and when Randolph's first marriage had broken down he made generous provision for Pamela. He had ensured that the two daughters of his secretary Violet Pearman, who had died shortly after the outbreak of war, while in her early forties, would be provided for. In the 1930s and 1940s several Ministers with personal problems, including Eden, had gone to see him and had received his help. In 1937 Ethel Snowden, the widow of one of his most forceful Labour critics, Philip Snowden, wrote to him, on reading his obituary of her husband: 'Your generosity to a political opponent marks you for ever in my eyes the "great gentleman" I have always thought you. Had I been in trouble which I could not control myself, there is none to whom I should have felt I could come with more confidence that I should be gently treated.'

Throughout September and October, work on the war memoirs continued; there was a constant revision of the chapters as Churchill received, from many of the participants in the drama, the criticisms he had sought from them. Dozens of letters with suggestions and answers to queries were scrutinised by Kelly and Deakin, who then worked with their master to amend the chapters accordingly. 'You must admit I have made a prodigious effort,' Churchill said to his publisher, Desmond Flower, when his task was finally done. On November 2, in London, Churchill spoke at the National Book Exhibition. 'Writing a book is an adventure,' he said. 'To begin with, it is a toy and an amusement; then it becomes a mistress, and then it becomes a master, and then a tyrant. The last phase is that just as you are about to be reconciled to your servitude, you kill the monster, and fling him out to the public.'

That month Churchill was seventy-five. The fourth volume of his war memoirs was now on the verge of completion, set back only briefly when a bad cold, in the second week of December, forced him to stay in bed for a week at Hyde Park Gate. On December 19 he was back at Chartwell, 'in grand form', Archibald Sinclair told a friend, 'as lively, and incessant, in his conversation as he was in Cabinet in the old days, eating, drinking and smoking as voraciously as ever.' Sinclair added: 'He took me around the farms, showed me short-horns, and Jerseys and then a huge brick hen-house which he had built himself, "Chickenham Palace". Alongside was a noisome & messy little piece of ground, "Chickenham Palace Gardens". "What kind of hens?" I asked. "Oh, I don't bother about the details," growled Winston.'

On December 29, Churchill left England once more, his fourth over-seas journey that year, for Madeira, which he had last seen fifty years earlier on his way to the Boer War. He had intended to stay for several weeks, in order to complete the fourth volume of his memoirs. To expedite this, Deakin again joined him in the New Year. But within a week of their work having begun, Attlee announced that there would be a General Election on February 23. Churchill had to hurry back to England; he flew back on 12 January 1950 and, beginning the following day, held a series of consultations at Chartwell about the Conservative election manifesto. Churchill wanted two words to be given particular stress, 'incentive' and 'stimulus'.

To Clementine, who had remained in Madeira, Churchill telegraphed on January 16: 'Hope all has been pleasant. Here nothing but toil and moil.' That day he went up to London, where further consultations were held each day at Hyde Park Gate. 'One day we were nine hours in the dining room,' Churchill told his wife on January 19. Two days later he made the first Conservative Party political broadcast of the campaign, telling his listeners that the choice before them was 'whether we should take another plunge into Socialist regimentation, or by a strong effort, regain the freedom, initiative and opportunity of British life'.

On the morning of January 24 Churchill again felt unwell. 'Everything went misty,' he told Lord Moran, who, in assuring him that it was not a stroke, told him, 'You seem to get arterial spasms when you are very tired.' The election campaign had to go on; Churchill enlisted the help of two young men to draft his speeches for him, Reginald Maudling, a future Chancellor of the Exchequer, and George Christ, editor of the Conserva-tive Party's weekly newsletter. They helped him prepare his Constituency speech of January 28, in which he attacked the nationalisation record of the Labour Government; the Bank of England had been nationalised in 1945, Coal, Civil Aviation and Transport in 1946, Electricity in 1947, and Gas in 1948. The Iron and Steel Bill, which had passed its second reading in November 1948, and was awaiting only the Labour victory for its implementation, 'we shall repeal', Churchill declared. He repeated this pledge at Leeds on February 4.

From Leeds, Churchill travelled to Cardiff, where he quoted Lloyd George's warning of twenty-five years earlier that 'Socialism means the community in bonds'. From Cardiff he went to Devonport, to speak in Randolph's election campaign. Then he returned to his constituency, before travelling north to Edinburgh, where on February 14 he spoke of his hope that it might be possible to find some 'more exalted and august foundation for peace' than the atom bomb. He could not help 'coming back', he said, to the idea 'of another talk with Soviet Russia upon the highest level'. Then, using the word 'summit' for the first time in reference to talks between world leaders, he said: 'The idea appeals to me of a supreme effort to bridge the gulf between the two worlds, so that each can live their life, if not in friendship, at least without the hatreds of the cold war. You must be careful to mark my words in these matters because I have not always been proved wrong. It is not easy to see how things could be worsened by a parley at the summit, if such a thing were possible.'

Following this expression of hope for a 'parley at the summit' to end the Cold War, Churchill returned to London, and then on to Chartwell. On the following day, February 16, it was widely reported that he had died. He at once issued a Press statement in which he declared, 'I am informed from many quarters that a rumour has been put about that I died this morning. This is quite untrue.' Then, in an effort to pinpoint the source of the rumour, he added, 'It is however a good sample of the whispering campaign which has been set on foot. It would have been more artistic to keep this one for Polling Day.'

In the final Conservative Party political broadcast, on February 17, Churchill called for 'one heave' of Britain's shoulders to 'shake herself free' from Socialism. He then travelled north to Manchester, for a final speech before polling day. On February 23 he cast his vote in his constituency, returning to Hyde Park Gate to hear the results over the radio during the early hours. By midday on February 24 it was clear that Labour was to remain in power. But if the nine Liberal seats were taken into account, Labour could muster an overall majority of only six.

Both Churchill's sons-in-law, Duncan Sandys and Christopher Soames, had been elected. But Randolph had lost, albeit narrowly; it was his fourth failed attempt to enter Parliament. Churchill remained Leader of the Opposition. A move had begun, in Conservative circles, to have him replaced as Leader by someone younger, almost certainly Anthony Eden. But Churchill was confident that he could lead his Party into victory at the next election, which could not be far off. One unsuccessful candidate, Anthony Barber, who twenty years later became Chancellor of the Exchequer, wrote to him, 'To most of the young candidates like myself it was a great inspiration to have a man of your personality and experience at the helm, and I hope you will not consider it either impertinent or common-place when I say that your leadership since the end of the war has been one of the most vital factors which has brought our Party back to its present position.'

Churchill returned to Chartwell, determined to finish the fourth and fifth volumes of his war memoirs before the next election, and thus leaving only one more volume to be done later. Often working late into the night, he dictated large sections of the narrative to a new secretary, Jane Portal. In Parliament, he continued to speak forcefully against the Attlee Govern-ment, first on March 7, again on March 16. Henry Channon noted in his diary on March 16: 'Winston spoke in the Defence debate for over an hour and seemed in the highest spirits. No extinct volcano he.' On March 28 Churchill spoke in the Commons again, arguing that the time had come for West Germany to take a part in Western defence. 'Britain and France united,' he said, 'should stretch forth hands of friendship to Germany, and thus, if successful, enable Europe to live again.'

On May 16 Churchill was the guest of honour at a luncheon of the Conservative backbench 1922 Committee. He knew that his speech would be a test of their willingness to continue to have him as Party leader. He had prepared it with care, setting out what he saw as the Party's policies at home and abroad; the 'individual right to freedom' at home, no more nationalisation, working with the Liberals against Labour, seeking a United Europe, bringing Germany back into Europe, being strong in the face of Russia. 'The word "appeasement" is not popular,' he said, 'but appeasement has its place in all policy. Make sure you put it in the right place. Appease the weak, defy the strong. It is a terrible thing for a famous nation like Britain to do it the wrong way round.'

Churchill was gratified by the warmth of his reception, telling the backbenchers: 'I hope you will give me as your Leader the confidence and the sympathy which I require. Your welcome here today has removed the barrier which had risen in my mind.' He would come more frequently to their meetings, he said, and hoped also to see their Executive 'at regular intervals'. He would also set up a Committee of the Shadow Cabinet to prepare the Party for the next election. Two days later, in Edinburgh, Churchill made a sustained attack on the Labour Government's policy of high and punitive taxation, and on the 'utter failure' of nationalisation. 'We proclaim the State is the servant and not the master of the people,' he said. As before, he was helped in preparing his speech by George Christ, but he did not always use the draft speech Christ had given him. On one occasion, in thanking Christ for his draft he also apologised. 'The fact that I did not use it,' he wrote, 'in no way detracts from the help you gave me.

It gave me a rope with which to crawl ashore till I could walk on my own feet up the beach.' The amount of speechmaking which Churchill undertook was formidable for a man of seventy-five. 'I have had a tremendous pitch,' he wrote to Randolph on May 21; 'three speeches, and two nights in the train.'

Old age, however, was taking its toll; on May 25 the distinguished neurologist Sir Russell Brain told Churchill that the reason why the 'tightness' over his shoulders had increased was that the cells in his brain which received sensory messages from the shoulder were dead. Within a month a second specialist, Sir Victor Negus, confirmed that Churchill was suffering from increasing deafness, telling him that he would no longer be able to hear 'the twittering of birds and children's piping voices'. But he soldiered on, working throughout June at his war memoirs, with Deakin and Kelly alternating as his weekend helpers. Deakin later recalled his master's 'enormous power of living for the moment, the most intense concentration I have ever known'.

Churchill was back in London on June 26, when, in the House of Commons, he denounced the Labour Government's refusal to participate in a conference in Paris designed to set up a coal and steel pool for Western Europe. Britain's absence, he said, might 'spoil the hopes of a general settlement' and 'derange the balance of Europe'. He went on to explain, 'I am all for a reconciliation between France and Germany, and for receiving Germany back into the European family, but this implies, as I have always insisted, that Britain and France should in the main act together so as to be able to deal on even terms with Germany, which is so much stronger than France alone.' The Labour Government's refusal to participate in the conference revealed, he said, 'a squalid attitude'. In this same speech, he supported the Labour Government's adherence to United Nations action, following a North Korean invasion of South Korea; on July 5 he gave Conservative support for the Government in its motion to send troops to resist the 'unprovoked aggression' by the North.

On July 27 Churchill called for a secret session of the House to discuss the worldwide build-up of Soviet armed forces. Attlee opposed the call and the House divided. Churchill's appeal failed, but by only a single vote, 295 against 296. He now prepared to speak at the opening session of the Consultative Assembly of the Council of Europe in Strasbourg, to urge the creation of a European Army. On August 6 he flew from Biggin Hill to Strasbourg where, for the next four days, he worked on his speech. Macmillan, who was with him, wrote in his diary on August 10, 'One cannot but admire his extraordinary attention to detail and desire to perfect and improve.'

Churchill made his speech on August 11, appealing to all the Western European countries to 'bear their share and do their best' in the military defence of Europe. He was 'very glad', he said, that the Germans, 'amid their own problems, have come here to share our perils and augment our strength'. The freedom and civilisation of Western Europe lay 'under the shadow of Russian Communist aggression', supported by enormous armaments. If the Germans threw in their lot with Western Europe, 'we should hold their safety and freedom as sacred as our own'. A 'real defensive front' had now to be created in Europe. 'Those who serve supreme causes must not consider what they can get but what they can give. Let that be our rivalry in these years that lie before us.'

Churchill's resolution in favour of a European Army was passed by 89 votes to 5, with 27 abstentions, mostly the British Labour Party delegates. The strength of the vote gave Churchill a sense of considerable achievement. The West Germans agreed to make a contribution of five or six divisions to the European Army; France accepted this. 'The ending of the quarrel between France and Germany,' Churchill wrote to Truman on August 13, 'by what is really a sublime act on the part of the French leaders, and a fine manifestation of the confidence which Western Germany has in our, and your, good faith and goodwill, is I feel an immense step forward towards the kind of world for which you and I are striving. It is also the best hope of avoiding a third World War.'

Returning to England, on August 26 Churchill made a Party political broadcast in which he regretted that the Government had ignored his appeal at Edinburgh in February 1949 for a meeting with the Soviet leaders 'at the summit'. The 'only way' to deal with Communist Russia, he said, was by having 'superior strength in one form or another, and then acting with reason and fairness'. In the Commons on September 12 he criticised the Government for allowing the continued sale of machine tools to Russia. It was 'intolerable to think', Churchill told the House, that British troops were being sent into action 'at one end of the world', Korea, 'while we are supplying, or are about to supply, if not the actual weapons of war, the means to make weapons of war, to those who are trying to kill them or get them killed'.

'I should think,' Churchill told the House, 'that the feeling of the great majority of those in this House would be that no more machine-tools of a war-making character and no more machines or engines which could be used for war-making purposes should be sent from this country to Soviet Russia or the Soviet satellite nations while the present tension continues.' Churchill's appeal was successful, and sale of machine tools was halted. But he was unsuccessful a week later in trying to persuade the Government not to bring into force the nationalisation of iron and steel at a time when the nation was so evenly divided on the issue, and 'disturbing the smooth and efficient working of an industry vital to our defence programme'.

On October 1 Churchill celebrated a rare anniversary for any politician, the fiftieth anniversary of his first election to Parliament. Ten days later he flew to Denmark, to receive an honorary degree from the University of Copenhagen. After listening to the fulsome words of introduction about his years as war leader, he replied, 'I was only the servant of my country and had I, at any moment, failed to express the unflinching resolve to fight and conquer, I should at once have been rightly cast aside.' The war was again in Churchill's thoughts at the end of October when the House of Commons at last returned to its pre-war Chamber in the Palace of Westminster, from which it had been bombed out in May 1941.

Speaking after Attlee, Churchill described himself as 'a child of the House of Commons', and added: 'The Prime Minister said – and said quite truly – that the House of Commons was the workshop of democracy. But it has other claims, too. It is the champion of the people against executive oppression. I am not making a Party point; that is quite unfitting on such an occasion. But the House of Commons has ever been the controller and, if need be, the changer of the rulers of the day and of the Ministers appointed by the Crown. It stands forever against oligarchy and one-man power. All these traditions, which have brought us into being over hundreds of years, carrying a large proportion of the commanding thought of the human race with us, all these traditions received new draughts of life as the franchise was extended until it became universal. The House of Commons stands for fredom and law.'

Churchill was touched that Attlee decided to name an un-bombed arch in the Commons the 'Churchill Arch'. A week later, a snap division led to an anti-Government majority of six; 'sugar for the birds', Churchill called it. But as it was not a Vote of Confidence, the Government had no need to resign.

On November 30 Churchill was seventy-six. That day, in a Foreign Affairs debate in the Commons, he again advocated a meeting at the summit, calling it, and even the process leading up to it, 'the best hope of avoiding a third world war, not by appeasement of opponents from weakness, but by wise measures, fair play from strength, and the proof of unconquerable resolve'. Two weeks later, during a debate on the international situation, he praised Attlee's support for close Anglo-American relations, and endorsed Attlee's support for West German rearmament. The decision to accept a rearmed West Germany as an integral part of Western European defence, had been made by Attlee and Bevin against the wishes of most of their Cabinet colleagues; they knew, however, that despite Party, and Foreign Office, hostility, they could rely on Churchill to bring the Conservatives, half the electorate, to support the policy and make it bi-partisan, as Churchill had earlier done on Indian independence.

Three days after his speech in support of Attlee's defence policy, Churchill left London by air for Casablanca, then travelled by car to Marrakech, where he hoped to complete the fifth volume of his war memoirs. 'I have worked as much as eight hours a day in my bed, which is very comfortable,' he reported to Clementine on Christmas Day. As well as the work on the memoirs, he enjoyed almost daily excursions for painting and picnicking. 'I came here to play', he added in a wistful postscript, 'but so far it has only been *work* under physically agreeable conditions.'

On New Year's Day 1951 Churchill set off by car to find 'a sunlit painting paradise'; he found it at Tinerhir, across the High Atlas mountains, and stayed there for two days. On his return to Marrakech, Kelly, who had come out with him, returned to London; but Deakin flew out on January 5, together with Churchill's daughter Diana. Two days later Clementine joined them, in time for a second expedition across the mountains to Tinerhir. Amid these pleasant excursions, not only Volume Five but also Volume Six, the last, made progress towards completion.

On January 20, after more than seven weeks in the sun, Churchill returned from Marrakech to London, where he plunged back into the political struggle, seeking constantly to undermine the precarious Labour majority in the Commons. But a majority of six could not be tripped up, particularly when, as in the vote of No Confidence on February 15, during which Churchill led the Conservative onslaught, six of the nine Liberals voted with the Government. Five days later, on another division, the Government secured a majority of eight. That March, Ernest Bevin was forced by illness to resign. In a Party political broadcast on March 17 Churchill praised 'his steadfast resistance to Communist aggression' and his strengthening of Britain's ties with the United States.

In the Commons and in the country Churchill continued to criticise Labour policies. On May 18, in Glasgow, as Chinese and United Nations forces were battling in Korea, he rebuked the Labour benches for their pro-Chinese and anti-American sentiments, 'although it is the Chinese who are killing our men and the Americans who are helping us'. On June 7 he led the Opposition in a debate that lasted for twenty-one hours. Harold Macmillan commented: 'Conscious that many people feel he is too old to form a Government and that this will probably be used as a cry against him at the election, he has used these days to give a demonstration of energy and vitality. He has voted in every division, made a series of brilliant little speeches; shown all his qualities of humour and sarcasm; and crowned all by a remarkable breakfast (at 7.30 a.m.) of eggs, bacon, sausages and coffee, followed by a large whisky and soda and a huge cigar. This latter feat commanded general admiration. He has been praised every day for all this by Lord Beaverbrook's newspapers; he has driven in and out of Palace Yard among groups of admiring and cheering sightseers, and altogether nothing remains except for Colonist II to win the Ascot Gold Cup this afternoon.'

Clementine did not approve of her husband's new-found racing enthusiasm. 'I do think this is a queer new facet in Winston's variegated life,' she had written to a friend in May, and she added: 'Before he bought the horse (I can't think why) he had hardly been on a racecourse in his life. I must say I don't find it madly amusing.' But for Churchill it was a new pleasure. When, at a race at Hurst Park earlier in the year, Colonist II had come in first, beating Above Board, in the royal colours, he wrote to Princess Elizabeth, 'I wish indeed we could both have been victorious – but that would have been no foundation for the excitement and liveliness of the Turf.'

The summer passed with Labour still in power. On June 27 the Shadow Cabinet discussed the nationalisation of Iranian oil by the new Prime Minister, Dr Mossadeq. The main assets acquired by Mossadeq were the Anglo-Persian Oil Company's oil wells and refinery at Abadan, which Churchill himself had secured for Britain in 1914. Churchill was worried about the ability of the Soviet Union to take advantage of the Iran imbroglio. 'Limitless supplies of oil,' he telegraphed to Truman on June 29, 'would remove the greatest deterrent upon a major Russian aggression.' Churchill showed his telegram to the new Labour Foreign Secretary, Herbert Morrison, who wrote to him in reply, 'I think this message might be very helpful, and I am glad you sent it.'

Speaking in the Commons on July 30, Churchill welcomed Truman's despatch of a mediator to Teheran. He was 'most anxious', he said, 'to encourage the United States Navy to take a leading part in the Mediterranean.' Since the end of the war 'I have always been anxious that the United States should become more interested in what is taking place in Persia and in Egypt'. During his speech he criticised the British Government for not being willing to challenge Egypt's refusal to allow ships bound for Israel to go through the Suez Canal; Britain should have done this 'two years ago, or supported Israel in doing it two years ago', and he went on to ask, 'Why could we not have refused all military exports, and all payments on the ground of sterling balances, until the matter was satisfactorily settled?'

'He was in tremendous form,' Macmillan noted in his diary, adding that by his speech Churchill had 'established a complete ascendancy over the Party and indeed over the House'.

Churchill was in ebullient mood; on August 3 *The Times*, in a leading article, praised his newly published fourth volume and, quoting one of Roosevelt's wartime telegrams to Churchill, 'It's fun to be in the same decade as you', commented, 'Many readers will feel the same sort of exhilaration as they turn the pages of this most graphic and revealing autobiography.' The author, meanwhile, was busy putting the finishing touches to the proofs of his fifth volume, telling Clementine on the day of *The Times* review: 'I am virtually re-writing the early chapters of Volume Five as I deal with them. They take four or five hours apiece, and there are twenty in all. You may imagine I have little time for my other cares – the fish, indoors and out-of-doors, the farm, the robin (who has absconded). Still, I am sleeping a great deal, averaging about nine hours in the twenty-four.'

Clementine was on holiday in France, at Annecy in the Haute Savoie. On August 15 Churchill left England to join her. There, without any of his 'young gentlemen' to help him, he worked for a week on Volume Five, dictating his revisions to Jane Portal. 'He had this premonition,' she later recalled, 'that he would be Prime Minister after the next election; a very strong premonition that he would get back. He talked about it all the time.' After a week at Annecy, bad weather persuaded Churchill to travel further south. He chose Venice, where he was able to bathe in the warm waters of the Lido.

While at Venice, Churchill completed the final revisions of his fifth volume. On September 12 he was back in England. Eight days later he received a short note from Attlee: 'My dear Churchill, I have decided to have a General Election in October. I am announcing it tonight after the nine o'clock news. Yours sincerely, C.R. Attlee.' Churchill began at once to help prepare the Party manifesto. He was 'very conscious', he told several of his senior Conservative colleagues that day, of the difficulties that would face any Conservative administration, both at home and abroad, reflecting with disarming candour that 'he could not add to his reputation; he could only hazard it'.

The General Election campaign of 1951 was the sixteenth time Churchill had gone to the hustings since 1899. On October 2 he made his first speech of the campaign, at Liverpool. On the following day the Conservative Manifesto was published; it contained one surprise item, a promise to introduce an Excess Profits Levy on armaments manufacturers during the period of rearmament. This levy was Churchill's own idea; he remembered his hostility to the high profits made by arms manufacturers in the First World War, and also before 1939, and did not wish this to be repeated during his own administration.

As the General Election campaign gathered in intensity, the *Daily Mirror* coined a phrase which caused Churchill great distress. 'Whose finger do they want on the trigger,' it asked, 'Attlee's or Churchill's?' To this Churchill answered, in a speech in his constituency on October 6, 'I am sure we do not want any fingers upon any trigger. Least of all do we want a fumbling finger.' He did not believe that a third world war was inevitable, but if it came it would not be a British finger pulling the trigger that started it. 'It may be a Russian finger, or an American finger, or a United Nations Organisation finger, but it cannot be a British finger.' Britain's influence in the world was not what it was 'in bygone days'. He could indeed wish it were greater, 'because I am sure it would be used, as it has always been used to the utmost, to prevent a life-and-death struggle between the nations'.

On October 8 Churchill made the first Conservative Party political broadcast of the campaign. The difference between the Conservative and Socialist outlooks, he said, was the difference between the ladder and the queue: 'We are for the ladder. Let all try their best to climb. They are for the queue. Let each wait his place until his turn comes.' Churchill also spoke of 'a profound longing for some breathing space, for some pause amid the frenzy.' Commenting on this broadcast, David Butler, an expert on electioneering, wrote: 'In his moderation and vigour, in his clarity and technical adroitness in delivery, Mr Churchill gave the best Conservative broadcast of the election, perhaps the best broadcast for any Party. It was thought by many to be his finest personal effort since the war.'

Churchill now spoke at Election meetings almost every day: on October 23 he told an audience at Plymouth that if he remained in public life he would strive to make 'an important contribution to the prevention of a third world war, and to bringing the peace that every land fervently desired'. He prayed that he might have this opportunity. 'It is the last prize I seek to win.'

Polling took place on October 25. That morning, in a graphic visual reiteration of its 'finger on the trigger' question of two weeks earlier, the *Daily Mirror* published a photograph of a man with a cigar, in close half-profile, with the caption, 'Whose finger on the trigger?' This accusation, for which Churchill quickly secured a formal apology, did not prevent his return to power. Although the actual number of Labour votes cast was slightly greater than the number of votes cast for the Conservatives, the Conservatives won 321 seats as against 295 for Labour. The Liberal seats fell from nine to six.

Among the Conservative candidates, Randolph was yet again unsuccessful; he was never to stand for Parliament again. On the evening of October

26 his father went to Buckingham Palace, where once again, as in May 1940 and May 1945, he was asked by the King to form a Government. 'I do hope Winston will be able to help the country.' Clementine wrote to a friend. 'It will be up-hill work, but he has a willing eager heart.'

38

Prime Minister in Peacetime

Churchill lost no time in forming his administration. As in May 1940, he appointed himself Minister of Defence. Anthony Eden, who in 1945 had hoped to succeed him as leader of the Party, became Foreign Secretary for the third time in his career; he had first held this high office in 1935. R.A. Butler, who had played a leading part in the revival of the Conservative Party fortunes in the constituencies, was made Chancellor of the Exchequer. Harold Macmillan was summoned to Chartwell and asked to 'build houses for the people'; he became Minister of Housing. 'It was fun to join again in the old scenes which reminded me of the wartime Churchill,' he later recalled. 'Children, friends, Ministers, private secretaries, typists, all in a great flurry but all thoroughly enjoying the return to the centre of the stage.'

The first Cabinet of Churchill's peacetime administration met on 30 October 1951. Its first act was to put in train the denationalisation of iron and steel, an election pledge. It also decided that, in view of the severe economic crisis with which it was confronted, all Ministers would accept an immediate reduction in salary; Churchill proposed to draw £7,000 instead of the Prime Minister's statutory salary of £10,000. At a second Cabinet, on November 1, he endorsed Butler's proposal for a drastic cut in Government spending. Four days later, in his first reference to Foreign Affairs since becoming Prime Minister, he told the House of Commons that he and Eden held to the idea 'of a supreme effort to bridge the gulf between the two worlds, so that each of us can live its life, if not in friendship, at least without the fear, the hatreds, and the frightful waste of the "cold war".'

On November 30 Churchill was seventy-seven. His Duty Private Secretary that day was David Hunt, who later recalled how, after dinner, 'he came down to the Cabinet Room to work just the same, and with his usual thoughtfulness invited me to have a drink with him'. Churchill said to

Hunt, 'You've never seen a Prime Minister of seventy-seven before.' Hunt replied, 'No, but you have.' The last Prime Minister in office at Churchill's age was Gladstone.

Was Churchill too old to embark upon the rigours of the Premiership? Clementine had been most uneasy at the prospect of his returning to office at such an age. Even Churchill realised that the burdens of office would be severe; to Jock Colville, whom he invited to join his Private Office as Joint Principal Private Secretary, he confided that he intended to remain Prime Minister for one year only, and then hand over to Eden. He 'just wanted', he explained, 'to have time to re-establish the intimate relationship with the United States, which had been the keystone of his policy in the war, and to restore at home the liberties that had been eroded by wartime restrictions and postwar Socialist measures'.

In search of the first of these objectives, Churchill informed the Cabinet on December 11 that he intended to visit the United States as soon as possible. He also had a practical aim in mind, to ask for assistance in the form of 'equipment or materials' for Britain's defence programme. Before leaving, he went to Paris with Eden, where, on December 18, at the end of a two-day visit, he assured the French that Britain favoured the establishment of a European Defence Community, even though she could not join it. The British were prepared to associate themselves with it 'as closely as possible in all stages of its political and military development'. In private, Churchill would have preferred what he later called a 'Grand Alliance' of national armies, rather than 'a sludgy amalgam' of forces, but, whatever happened, he declared on December 22 in his first broadcast as Prime Minister, 'we shall stand up with all our strength in defence of the free world against Communist tyranny and aggression', working in 'true comradeship' for a United Europe. The aim was to avert war and enhance peace. 'It may be that this land will have the honour of helping civilisation to climb the hill amid the toils of peace, as we once did in the terrors of war.'

On the last day of 1951 Churchill left London by train for Southampton, where he went on board the *Queen Mary*. New Year's Day 1952 was spent at sea. When, during the voyage, Colville tried to get Churchill to read some preliminary material for the American talks, he was reluctant to do so, commenting that he was going to America 'to re-establish relations, not to transact business'. But the economist Donald MacDougall, who showed him the brief for the economic part of the talks, was delighted when, after Churchill read it, 'he sent me back a masterly summary in true Churchillian prose'.

The *Queen Mary* reached New York on 4 January 1952. From New York, Churchill flew in Truman's plane to Washington. That night he and

Truman dined together on board the Presidential yacht. Churchill was full of praise for the American effort in Korea and for American rearmament. 'Now the free world is not a naked world,' he said, 'but a rearming world.' He hoped that the United States would join Britain in sending forces to guard the freedom of navigation through the Suez Canal. As he prepared to leave the yacht to go to the British Embassy, Churchill turned to Dean Acheson, the American Secretary of State, with the words, 'Did you feel that around the table this evening were gathered the governments of the world – not to dominate it, mind you – but to save it?'

The Washington talks continued for two more days. With regard to NATO, Churchill pledged the British Government to make 'the biggest contribution of which they were capable'. His aim, he told Truman at the first formal session of the conference, was that the 'strength of the West would now reverse Soviet fears of the friendship between Britain and the United States, 'so that they would fear our enmity more than our friendship, and would be led thereby to seek our friendship.' Churchill's sentiments were so deeply felt and strongly expressed, one of the British diplomats present wrote in his diary, that Truman 'was quite abrupt on one or two occasions with poor old Winston and had a tendency, after one of the old man's powerful and emotional declarations of faith in Anglo-American co-operation, to cut it off with a "Thank you, Mr Prime Minister. We might pass that to be worked out by our advisers." A little wounding.'

At the fourth session, Churchill argued in favour of a European Army, as offering 'the only method of integrating German forces in the defence of Western Europe'. But he warned that the current struggle in French Indo-China, where the French were fighting 'like tigers' to protect their Far Eastern Empire, meant that France was not doing her 'full part' towards the European Army. Were it not for this, he said, 'the French would become stronger in Europe, and therefore be willing to permit the Germans to become stronger'.

During their Washington talks, Churchill and Truman reaffirmed, and made public, a secret understanding which Truman had made earlier with Attlee, that the atom bomb would not be used from the American air bases in East Anglia without British consent. In reporting this agreement to the Commons two months later, Churchill also referred to Britain's own atomic bomb. 'I was not aware until I took office,' he said, 'that not only had the Socialist Government made the atomic bomb as a matter of research, but that they had created at the expense of scores of millions of pounds the important plant necessary for its regular production.' This weapon, Churchill added, would be tested during 1952 by agreement with the Australian Government 'at a suitable place in that continent'.

On January 9 Churchill left Washington for New York. Two days later he travelled by night train to Ottawa, where he spoke at a banquet given in his honour by the Government of Canada. Despite the unconditional surrender of Germany and Japan, he said, 'Peace does not sit untroubled. in her vineyard.' Now, the North Atlantic Treaty Organisation, NATO, was 'the surest guarantee not only of the prevention of war, but of victory should our hopes be blasted'.

His speech made, Churchill returned by overnight train from Ottawa to Washington, where for two days he worked at the British Embassy on the speech he was to make to Congress. Much of the work was done in bed; indeed, at 11.20 on the morning of January 17 he was still in bed, forty minutes before he was expected at the Capitol, which, by a superhuman effort and the assistance of a motor-cycle escort, he reached in time. His theme was a hopeful one: 'Under the pressure and menace of Communist aggression,' he said, 'the fraternal association of the United States with Britain and the British Commonwealth, and the new unity growing up in Europe – nowhere more hopeful than between France and Germany – all these harmonies are being brought forward, perhaps by several genera-tions, in the destiny of the world. If this proves true – and it has certainly proved true up to date – the architects in the Kremlin may be found to have built a different and a far better world structure than what they planned.'

Churchill also spoke about the Middle East, telling Congress that it was 'no longer possible' for Britain alone 'to bear the whole burden of main-taining the freedom of the famous waterway of the Suez Canal'. That had become 'an international rather than a national responsibility'. There were more than 80,000 British troops in the Canal Zone. Even 'token forces' of the United States, France and Turkey would create a 'symbol of the unity of purpose which inspires us'. Nor did he believe that it would be an exaggeration to say that such token forces 'would probably bring into harmony all that movement by which the Four-Power policy may be made to play a decisive part by peaceful measures, and bring to an end the wide disorders of the Middle East in which, let me assure you, there lurk dangers not less great than those which the United States has stemmed in Korea'.

Churchill then spoke of an area of the Middle East, where, he said, 'there is still some sunshine as well as shadow', telling Congress: 'From the days of the Balfour Declaration I have desired that the Jews should have a national home, and I have worked for that end. I rejoice to pay my tribute here to the achievements of those who have founded the Israelite State, who have defended themselves with tenacity, and who offer asylum to great numbers of Jewish refugees. I hope that with their aid they may convert deserts into gardens; but if they are to enjoy peace and prosperity they must strive to renew and preserve their friendly relations with the Arab world without which widespread misery might follow for all.'

Turning to Europe, Churchill spoke about the prevention of a third world war by means of a 'united command' of the strongest possible forces; the sooner this was done, 'the sooner, also will our sense of security, and the fact of our security, be seen to reside in valiant, resolute and well-armed manhood, rather than in the awful secrets which science had wrested from nature'. Those secrets, the secrets of the atom bomb, constituted, 'at present', what he called 'the supreme deterrent' against a third world war, and the 'most effective guarantee' of victory should such a war take place.

That afternoon, at the fifth and final session of the Washington Conference, Churchill explained to Truman his reluctance to seek a meeting with the Soviet leaders until such time as they 'indicated that they were prepared to make a genuine effort to reach an understanding with the democracies'. He was afraid that if such a conference took place, and then broke down, people would assume that 'war would be inevitable'. But if the democracies were to make an intensive effort 'by broadcasting, by dropping leaflets, and by all other methods of propaganda that were open to them', to bring to the people behind the Iron Curtain the 'true facts' of the situation, the leaders of the Kremlin, fearing 'such a revelation of the truth to the masses whom they held in their grip', might agree to renew the conference, which, Churchill thought, might then be resumed 'with greater hope of success'.

Churchill's hopes revealed the extent of his determination to find some way out of the impasse of the Cold War. On the following day he went by train from Washington to New York. 'I have just finished what seems to me the most strenuous fortnight I can remember,' he wrote to Clementine from New York on January 20, '& I am staying here for 48 hours to recover. I never had such a whirl of people & problems, and the two speeches were very hard & exacting ordeals.' Two days later he sailed for Southampton, reaching England on January 28.

On February 6 King George VI died. Churchill spoke movingly of his final illness when he broadcast on the following day. 'During these last months,' he said, 'the King walked with death, as if death were a companion, an acquaintance whom he recognised and did not fear. In the end death came as a friend; and after a happy day of sunshine and sport, and after "good night" to those who loved him best, he fell asleep as every man or woman who strives to fear God and nothing else in the world may hope to do.' Of the new Queen, 'the Second Queen Elizabeth', Churchill told his listeners, 'I, whose youth was passed in the august, unchallenged and tranquil glories of the Victorian Era, may well feel a thrill in invoking, once more, the prayer and the Anthem:"God Save the Queen".'

Churchill's own health was not good; on February 21 he suffered a small arterial spasm. Lord Moran feared that it might be followed by a stroke. The pressures of the premiership had to be reduced. Several senior Party members who were consulted suggested that Churchill might resign as soon as the Coronation was over, in May 1953. One thought was he should go to the House of Lords, remaining Prime Minister but giving Eden the management of the Commons. Churchill, meanwhile, had gone down to Chartwell to recuperate. He was also working on his speech in answer to a Labour Motion of Censure accusing him of wanting to make war on China in order to hasten the end of the military stalemate in Korea.

When Churchill spoke in the debate on February 26, his vigour seemed unimpaired; not only did he deny the charge, but, with devastating effect, revealed that the Labour Government had twice, first in May and then in September 1950, agreed with the United States that in certain circumstances and contingencies action would be taken 'not confined to Korea'. Labour MPs were shocked, the Conservatives delighted. Harold Nicolson commented: 'How much better he is in the House than on a platform! How he loves it! He is looking white and fatty, a most unhealthy look, you would say, if he were anyone else, but somehow out of this sickly mountain comes a volcanic flash.'

In Cabinet, Churchill's main concern remained national and imperial defence, and the sending of a clear signal to Russia that Britain was not defenceless. On his initiative, more than 30,000 men were registered for Home Guard duty. At the same time, troops in depots throughout England were organised into five hundred 'mobile columns', capable, he later told the Commons, 'of giving a good account of themselves and imposing a considerable deterrent upon any airborne adventure by being able to kill or capture the ones who land.' Casting his eye far afield, on February 20 he asked the Chiefs of Staff to make sure that the Falkland Islands were properly defended, and that a detachment of Royal Marines be sent in a frigate to the vicinity of the islands.

On March 5 Churchill introduced the Defence Estimates in the Commons, telling MPs that his first impression, on becoming Minister of Defence the previous October, as well as Prime Minister, had been 'a sense of extreme nakedness such as I had never felt before in peace or war – almost as though I was living in a nudist colony'. Now all that was being rectified. But financial considerations would mean that defence spending might have to be slowed down and even reduced, 'We must not mislead the country into expectations beyond what its life energies can fulfil.'

To reduce his workload, Churchill asked Field Marshal Alexander to take over the Ministry of Defence. But Defence issues still dominated his thinking; on March 19, when the Cabinet's Defence Committee discussed an American suggestion to extend the area of conflict in the Korean War by bombing ports and lines of communication in China, he spoke out against such action. 'It would be silly to waste bombs in the vague inchoate mass of China,' he said, 'and wrong to kill thousands of people to no purpose.'

The Labour Opposition now instituted a series of late-night, and even all-night, sessions, hoping to wear the Conservatives down. Churchill was a frequent attender, but it was not a happy time for him. 'Could there be any more nauseating performance,' Channon noted on April 9 in his diary, 'than that of half a dozen hale young Socialists howling at Mr Churchill, jeering at his pronouncements and even at his entrances and exits to the House, taunting him with his advanced age and growing deafness?' A week later Churchill was taken ill; 'a miserable cold has settled on my chest', he told Moran. He recuperated at Chartwell, but returned to London to speak in the Commons on April 25. 'I cannot remember a time,' he said, 'and my experience is a long one – when public difficulty and Party strife have both risen to such heights together.'

On May 3 Churchill broadcast a survey of the first six months of his administration. Three or four years of 'steady, calm, resolute Government' were needed, he said, to redress the balance of the Labour Government's years 'of extravagance and waste, of overspending, and of living upon American money'. He had already put his full support behind Butler's first budget, and would continue to sustain his Chancellor of the Exchequer in his search for economies. At Cabinet on May 7, Churchill strongly supported Butler's plea to reduce the cost of the British forces in Germany, then estimated at £130 million a year. Churchill proposed that a Cabinet Committee be set up to seek ways of cutting this down to £70 million. His proposal was accepted.

Although he attended every Cabinet meeting, and presided over the Cabinet Defence Committee, Churchill found it harder and harder to read the mass of materials submitted or to follow the intricacies of some of the discussions. 'The bright and sparkling intervals still come, and they are still unequalled,' Colville wrote in his diary on May 16, 'but age is beginning to show.' That night Churchill went so far as to speak to Colville about the possibility of a coalition government, to deal with Britain's financial difficulties. 'He would retire in order to make it possible,' Colville noted. 'He might even make the demand for it an excuse for retiring.' As to the merits of a coalition, which Churchill had earlier proposed during the political turmoil of 1910, he now commented, 'Four-fifths of the people of this country were agreed on four-fifths of the things to be done.'

In the debate on transport on May 21 Churchill's mental vigour was unimpaired. At one point he described Herbert Morrison as 'a curious mixture of geniality and venom'; the geniality was natural, he explained, the venom 'has to be adopted for him to keep on sides' with the Labour backbenchers. Speaking of the Conservative Government's decision not to denationalise the railways he said: 'I have never been shocked by the nationalising of the railways, in fact, I believe I proposed it on my own before almost all the members of the House had even thought about going into Parliament. I am by no means sure I have been right. It is no part of my case that I am always right. Anyhow, we have to face facts. The railways are and will remain nationalised.'

Churchill had prepared his remarks beforehand with his usual care. But when he spoke on the evening of May 23 to a Tax Inspectors' dinner in London, his speech was written almost entirely by Colville. This was the first time in more than half a century of public speaking that Churchill had allowed this to happen. Colville commented, 'This is indeed a sign of advancing senility,' and a week later he wrote in his diary, 'Mrs Churchill does not think he will last long as Prime Minister.' But Churchill's stamina was not to be written off; on June 11, as the guest of honour at the annual luncheon of the Press Association, he spoke with vigour of how Britain was now fighting 'not for vainglory or imperial pomp, but for survival as an independent, self-supporting nation'.

Work had still to continue on the final volume of the war memoirs; on June 13 Deakin went down to Chartwell to assure Churchill that all his helpers, including General Pownall, Commodore Allen and Denis Kelly, were making continuous progress. The appendices and maps were now almost completed; Churchill was content that his helpers should take on the full weight of these final aspects. Three days later Colville wrote in his diary: 'The Prime Minister is depressed and bewildered. He said to me this evening: "The zest is diminished." I think that it is more that he cannot see the light at the end of the tunnel. Nor can I. But it is 1.30 a.m., approaching the hour when courage and life are at their lowest ebb.'

Unknown to Churchill, that very day, June 16, four members of his Government met in London and decided to ask him either to resign at once, or to set a date for his resignation. They were the Leader of the House and Lord Privy Seal, Harry Crookshank; the Commonwealth Secretary, Lord Salisbury; the Scottish Secretary, James Stuart; and the Chief Whip, Patrick Buchan-Hepburn. It was Buchan-Hepburn, who had been Churchill's Private Secretary after the election defeat in 1929, who undertook to convey the message; he did so on the evening of June 23, but was not well received. Three days earlier, Churchill had told Lord Moran, 'There is a move to get me out.'

Now Churchill knew the truth, but he could still find the reserves of energy needed to lead his Party and defend his Government. On July 1 the Opposition attacked the Government's failure to have known in advance of the recent American bombing of North Korean hydro-electric plants. These plants, on the Yalu River, lay along the Chinese border. Churchill led the Government's defence with skill and effectiveness. Channon noted in his diary, 'The old lion, coolly dressed in light grey trousers and a short coat, fairly pulverised his attackers; rarely has he been more devastating.' Channon added, 'Perhaps he is aware of the growing Tory discontent.'

The burden of Britain's position weighed heavily on Churchill; to Clementine, who was on holiday in Italy, he explained on July 11: 'It is a very bleak outlook, with all our might, majesty, dominion & power imperilled by having to pay the crashing bills each week. I have never seen things so tangled & tiresome. But we must persevere.' Ten days later Churchill told Clementine that Eden's absence through jaundice added to 'my burdens'. There was also the problem of Lord Salisbury, who, Churchill wrote, had been 'very tiresome', being of 'a defeatist frame of mind' as far as proceeding with the denationalisation of steel was concerned.

In Cabinet, Churchill's suggestions were often decisive. On July 24 he successfully supported Macmillan's plea not to reduce Government spending on housing. Five days later he proposed an amnesty for men who had deserted from the armed forces during the war; he thought it was a 'grievous thing' that so many men were still living in Britain 'as outcasts and outlaws'. His proposal was eventually accepted, and an amnesty declared. In the Commons, too, his authority was considerable; on July 30, in a speech which he had worked on himself, he defended the need to keep Britain's defence spending 'within the limits of our economic strength'. The effort had been considerable. 'Am recovering from speech,' he telegraphed to Clementine the following evening.

On August 14 Churchill and his wife gave a wedding reception at No. 10 for Churchill's niece Clarissa and Anthony Eden. Three days later there was another family celebration, the christening at Westerham Church of Churchill's grandson Jeremy Soames. Then, on September 9, Churchill and Clementine left London for a holiday in the South of France, at Beaverbrook's villa, La Capponcina. 'To be lent a villa sounds the perfect way to spend a few peaceful days,' wrote the Queen, in approving her Prime Minister's departure. His holiday coincided with the publication of Volume Five of his war memoirs. It was also a chance for him to make

further progress with the sixth and final volume; to this end, both Elizabeth Gilliatt and Jane Portal flew out with him. He stayed at La Capponcina
for two weeks, painting, swimming and working on his book. A typical note
was one which he dictated, to be sent to Deakin, which began: 'The death
of President Roosevelt. How did it reach me? How soon did I speak to
Parliament? What did I say?'

On September 25 Churchill returned to England by air. Six days later
he flew north to Scotland, where he was the Queen's guest at Balmoral.
While he was there, news reached No.10, in the early hours of the morning, of the successful explosion of Britain's first atom bomb, at Monte Bello
Island off the north-west coast of Australia. A new Private Secretary,
Anthony Montague Browne, who had arrived at No.10 while Churchill
was in Scotland, was advised to telephone Balmoral and have the Prime
Minister woken up to tell him the news, 'but even at this early stage', he
later recalled, 'I concluded that this would be imprudent!'

The following day Churchill returned to London. In a letter to the
Queen on his return he wrote: 'I was keenly impressed by the development
of Prince Charles as a personality since I last saw him at Windsor. He is
young to think so much.' Prince Charles was then not quite four years old.
A week after his return to London, Churchill travelled north again, to
Scarborough, where on October 11 he addressed the Conservative Party
Conference, speaking of the need for continuing economy in Government
spending. He repeated this theme in the Commons on November 4, and
at the Cabinet Defence Committee the following day. It had been his
father's theme seventy years earlier. That month Churchill wrote to R.A.
Butler, whose own father had just died: 'I know what it was to me to lose
my father, although I had seen him so little. I revered and admired him
from a distance, except for a few glittering occasions.' Churchill added, 'I
have striven to vindicate his memory.'

On November 4 General Eisenhower was elected President of the United
States. Publicly, Churchill welcomed the appointment. Privately, he was far
from happy, telling Colville five days later: 'I am greatly disturbed. I think
this makes war much more probable.' Churchill now felt a new mission and
a renewed sense of purpose: to use his great authority as Prime Minister to
try to bring about a reconciliation between the United States and the Soviet
Union. Would he have the stamina to pursue such a goal? That same day,
Colville noted in his diary: 'He (W) is getting tired and visibly ageing. He
finds it hard work to compose a speech and ideas no longer flow.'

Churchill again referred, as he had done in May, to the possibility of
resignation. On November 28 the Assistant Under-Secretary of State at
the Foreign Office, Evelyn Shuckburgh, a confidant of Eden, noted in his
diary: 'PM has told Clarissa he wants to give up. She says he is looking for

an opportunity and Anthony must be gentle with him. Must let him go to America.' Churchill had spoken that day to Eden himself. He had asked Eden, so Shuckburgh reported, to let him leave office 'as privately as possible. Only one speech.' Two days later Churchill was seventy-eight; but Gladstone had still been Prime Minister at eighty-seven.

Eden pressed Churchill to say when he would resign. At Chequers on December 7 Churchill spoke to Eden of the speeches 'I could make more easily if I were not Prime Minister.' But he would give no promise and set no date. His mind was still set on a visit to Eisenhower. He wanted to fly, but Lord Moran warned about the risk of such a long flight; even with a pressurised cabin, he warned, Churchill's circulation might be impaired. Churchill decided to go by sea, and on the evening of December 30 left Waterloo by boat-train for Southampton, where he once more went on board the *Queen Mary*. While on board ship, on New Year's Day 1953, Churchill told Colville that he, Colville, 'should assuredly live to see Eastern Europe free of Communism'. Colville died in 1987, two years before the tearing down of the Berlin Wall.

The *Queen Mary* reached New York on January 5. As Eisenhower would not be inaugurated President for another two weeks, Churchill had decided to meet him privately in New York. The two spent two hours alone together. While in New York, Churchill visited his mother's birthplace, 426 Henry Street, Brooklyn.

At a second meeting with Eisenhower on January 7, Churchill urged the President-elect to go with him as soon as possible after his inauguration to meet Stalin. Eisenhower declined; Churchill could go to Moscow, he said, but he would prefer meeting the Soviet leader on neutral territory, say in Stockholm. Eisenhower also asked Churchill if he would have any objection to his meeting Stalin alone. 'It would have been objected to strongly during the war when our contribution in forces was about equal,' Churchill replied. 'Now I don't mind. But don't be in a hurry. Get in your reconnaissance first.'

On the morning of January 8 Churchill flew in the President's aircraft to Washington, where Truman, in the last days of his Presidency, received him at the White House and was then his dinner guest at the British Embassy. On January 9 he flew from Washington to Jamaica, where he stayed for nearly three weeks. There, as well as painting and swimming, he continued work on the final volume of his war memoirs. He also reflected on his American visit; at dinner one night he described Eisenhower as 'a real man of limited stature'.

While Churchill was still in Jamaica, Eden confided in Shuckburgh, 'He doesn't think the Old Man will ever go.' On January 29, ignoring his doctor's earlier worries, Churchill returned to England by air. One of his first Cabinet interventions after his return was to argue in favour of the abolition of rationing for chocolate and sweets. The Minister concerned was insistent that if this were done, stocks of sugar would run out. Churchill refused to budge, however, and on February 5 the ration was abolished. Within six months, there was a glut of sugar.

On March 5 it was announced on Radio Moscow that Stalin was dead. Churchill at once saw a chance of starting some form of dialogue with Stalin's successors, to whom he sent a message of 'regret and sympathy' on their leader's death. 'I have a feeling,' he telegraphed to Eisenhower on March 11, 'that we might both of us together or separately be called to account if no attempt was made to turn over a leaf, so that a new page could be started, with something more coherent on it than a series of casual and dangerous incidents at the many points of contact between the two divisions of the world.' But Churchill's telegram crossed with a letter from Eisenhower, in which the new President rejected any meeting at the summit for fear that it would provide the new Soviet Government with 'another propaganda mill'.

Churchill did not allow Eisenhower's attitude to stop him: on March 28 he showed Eden a draft letter which he wanted to send to Molotov, to set up at least a meeting of Foreign Ministers. In his draft, Churchill suggested Vienna as the meeting place. But when he told Eisenhower of this more limited initiative, the President was still sceptical. On April 11 Churchill telegraphed a third time to Eisenhower, to try to convince him that some meeting at the summit should take place. 'Great hope has arisen in the world,' he wrote, 'that there is a change of heart in the vast, mighty masses of Russia – and this can carry them far and fast, and perhaps into revolution.' A day later Churchill telegraphed again: 'A new hope has, I feel, been created in the unhappy, bewildered world. It ought to be possible to proclaim our unflinching determination to resist Communist tyranny and aggression, and at the same time, though separately, to declare how glad we would be if we found there was a real change of heart and not let it be said that we had closed the door upon it.'

Speaking at Glasgow on April 17, to a meeting of Scottish Conservatives, Churchill made his hopes public; 'Is there a new breeze blowing in the tormented world?' he asked. Three days later he was buoyed up by an announcement from Washington that Eisenhower was willing to consider discussions with Russia on points of substance; this was 'a bold and inspiring initiative', he told the Commons that day. At the very moment when opportunities seemed to be opening up in foreign policy, however, Eden was taken gravely ill, the result of an operation that had gone wrong. In a second operation on April 29 he nearly died. In despair, he flew to Boston for a third operation. Churchill decided to take charge of the Foreign Office himself, as he had done during Eden's earlier illness. To the British diplomat, Pierson Dixon, with whom he lunched on May 2, Churchill commented, about the crisis in Laos, that he had been able 'to remain ignorant about these outlandish areas all his life; it was hard that they had come to tease him in his old age'.

That spring, Churchill accepted the Queen's request that he become a Knight of the Garter; henceforth he was 'Sir' Winston. To Pamela Lytton he wrote, in answer to her letter of congratulation: 'I took it because it was the Queen's wish. I think she is splendid.'

On May 5 Churchill informed Eisenhower that if the American President would not go to Moscow, he, Churchill, was quite prepared to go alone. 'I am not afraid of the "solitary pilgrimage" if I am sure in my heart that it may help forward the cause of peace, and even at the worst can only do harm to my reputation'. Churchill added: 'I have a strong belief that Soviet self-interest will be their guide. My hope is that it is their self-interest which will bring about an easier state of affairs.' Of the men now ruling Russia, only Molotov had any contacts outside Russia. 'I am very anxious to know these men,' Churchill told Eisenhower, 'and talk to them, as I think I can, frankly and on the dead level. It is only by going to Moscow that I can meet them all.'

On May 11 Churchill set out in the Commons his reasons for wishing to try to open up talks with Stalin's successors, and to do so 'without long delay'. It might well be, he said, that 'no hard and fast agreements would be reached, but there might be a general feeling among those gathered together that they might do something better than tear the human race, including themselves, to bits'.

Churchill's speech angered the Foreign Office, 'since it was felt', Colville later recalled, 'that a friendly approach to Russia would discourage the European powers working on the theme of western union'. Eden recalled a year and a half later how angry he had been, reading it on his sickbed. The Minister of State at the Foreign Office, Selwyn Lloyd, was, however, 'enthusiastic' about it. The French Prime Minister, René Mayer, anxious not to be excluded from any summit, asked Eisenhower for a pre-summit meeting. On May 20 Eisenhower telephoned Churchill to ask if France could be included in the next high-level meeting of Western leaders. Churchill at once agreed, suggesting Bermuda as a meeting place, but a political crisis in France delayed any decision from Paris for more than three weeks.

Politics and foreign affairs were set aside in the last week of May, as Britain prepared to celebrate the Coronation of Elizabeth II. On May 27

Churchill, resplendent in his Garter robes, gave a pre-Coronation dinner at 10 Downing Street. The Coronation itself took place on June 2. 'He was very tired when the day came, almost reluctant to go,' Jane Portal later recalled. But go he did, riding with Clementine to Westminster Abbey in a closed two-horse carriage. When the ceremony was over, wearied by his exertions, Churchill left the procession as it went back to the Palace, and turned his carriage into Downing Street.

But there was no respite from work. On the afternoon of June 3 he took the Chair at the opening meeting of Commonwealth Prime Ministers at No.10, welcoming them to London and giving them a survey of the world scene. The Soviet leaders must, he said, be deeply worried about the danger of an atomic war, since, once such a war began, 'the mighty ocean-land in Russia and Siberia would quickly become uncontrollable and, once the peoples realised that they were free to do as they liked, and could no longer be controlled by the central machinery of Soviet Government, they might show their preference for living happily by themselves, without allegiance to a unified Soviet State'. It was important to find out what Soviet intentions and policies were. To this end, Churchill told the Commonwealth Prime Ministers, it was his intention to hold 'informal talks' with the Soviet leaders as soon as possible.

On June 5, in Eden's absence, Churchill was host at a Foreign Office banquet for the Queen at Lancaster House. On June 8 and 9 he again presided at the meeting of Commonwealth Prime Ministers. Not until June 12 was he able to go down to Chartwell. But he had still to finalise plans for the Bermuda Conference, at which he hoped to persuade both the Americans and the French to endorse his desire to talk to the new Russian leaders, possibly alone, and if necessary in Moscow. On June 20 he was at Downing Street discussing these plans with Selwyn Lloyd and Pierson Dixon. 'Mentally he is more alert than he was towards the end of the war,' Dixon wrote in his diary. 'As always he did all the work himself in the sense of dictating the telegrams himself after reaching his decision.'

Three days later Churchill was back in London for a dinner at No.10 in honour of the Italian Prime Minister, Alcide de Gasperi. It was to be his last formal engagement before leaving for Bermuda. At the end of the dinner he made a short speech, mainly about Julius Caesar, the Roman conquest of Britain, and the Roman Legions. Then, when the time came for the guests to leave the dining-room, he rose, to lead them into the drawing room. After taking a few steps, he slumped down on the nearest chair.

Churchill had suffered a stroke. Mary was at once brought to him by a guest who had taken alarm at his pallor; later she recalled that her father 'looked unhappy and uncertain and was very incoherent'. On the following morning, to the amazement of those closest to him, he insisted on presiding at the Cabinet 'even though', Colville recalled, 'his mouth was drooping badly and he found it difficult to use his left arm'. The Cabinet met at noon. None of the Ministers noticed that anything was wrong; Butler later commented that Churchill had been 'curiously and unexpectedly silent as he allowed items to go forward without much comment from himself'. Macmillan thought he was 'very white' and 'did not talk very much'.

After the Cabinet, Churchill lunched with Clementine, Mary and Christopher Soames. 'Winston was extremely tired,' Mary later recalled, 'and once more had difficulty in getting up from his chair.' On the following morning his health worsened. To the last moment he hoped to attend that morning's Cabinet, but by noon he wanted only to go down to Chartwell. There, during the evening, Colville noted, 'his physical powers had deteriorated considerably'.

By the following day, June 26, Churchill's left side was partially paralysed, and he had lost the use of his left arm. Lord Moran, who saw his patient that afternoon, doubted whether he could possibly survive the weekend. But he was well enough that evening to dictate a telegram to Eisenhower, postponing the Bermuda meeting. A press statement issued that night by Moran and Sir Russell Brain announced that Churchill was in need of 'a complete rest'. It did not reveal why.

Recovery was clearly going to be a long and arduous process. But it began almost at once, confounding Moran's Friday alarm. By Sunday, Churchill felt well enough to sit at the head of the table for luncheon. Beaverbrook was his main guest; on the question of commercial television, Churchill told him that there ought to be a free vote in the House of Commons. 'Today he is gayer,' Mary wrote in her diary, 'there is a distinct improvement.' Talking on the following day to Colville, Churchill said 'that he thought probably that this must mean his retirement, but that he would see how he went on, and if he had recovered sufficiently well to address the Tory Party at their Annual Meeting in October, he would continue in office.'

Churchill had set himself a target, four months away. This seemed to aid his recovery. On June 30, a week after his stroke, he welcomed the Cabinet Secretary, Sir Norman Brook, to Chartwell. 'He was in a wheelchair,' Brook later recalled. 'After dinner, in the drawing-room, he said that he was going to stand on his feet. Colville and I urged him not to attempt this, and, when he insisted, we came up on either side of him so that we could catch him if he fell. But he waved us away with his stick and told us to stand back. He then lowered his feet to the ground, gripped the arms of his chair, and by a tremendous effort – with sweat pouring down his face – levered himself to his feet and stood upright. Having demonstrated that he could do this, he sat down again and took up his cigar.' Norman Brook reflected, 'He was determined to recover.'

39

Recovery, Last Ambition, Resignation

As Churchill recovered from his stroke, he invited more and more friends and colleagues to visit him at Chartwell. Harold Macmillan, lunching there on 2 July 1953, later recalled his 'astonishment that a man who had suffered such a calamity could show such gaiety and courage'. The atmosphere at dinner, Macmillan wrote, far from being oppressive, was 'almost lively'.

By July 4 Churchill could walk a short distance unaided. Two days later he felt well enough to have a visitor from the Foreign Office, Sir William Strang, with whom he discussed the French desire for a three-power meeting of Foreign Ministers, to win support for the continuing French struggle in Indo-China. 'Today,' he told Strang, 'we should have been at Bermuda.' With the prospect of a meeting with the Russians still very much on his mind, on July 17 Churchill telegraphed to Eisenhower, explaining why he would have preferred any Four-Power meeting of Foreign Ministers to be preceded by a meeting of Heads of State and Prime Ministers. 'Above all,' he explained, 'I thought that you and I might have formed our own impression of Malenkov, who has never seen anybody outside Russia.' It was only after such a meeting that they should 'set our State Secretaries to work along less ambitious, if more hopeful, easier lines'.

Eisenhower was still unwilling to contemplate a meeting at the summit; Churchill was equally unwilling to abandon the idea. Colville, lunching alone with him on July 24, noted in his diary: 'Still very wrapped up with the possibility of bringing something off with the Russians and with the idea of meeting Malenkov face to face. Very disappointed in Eisenhower whom he thinks both weak and stupid.' That afternoon Churchill was well enough to go from Chartwell to Chequers, a three-hour drive.

On July 27 a very frail Anthony Eden, just returned from Boston after his third operation, went to see Churchill at Chequers. That day the Korean War came to an end with the signing of an armistice agreement; a summit seemed even more hopeful. Three days later Elizabeth Gilliatt told Lord Moran that his patient was 'clamouring for work'. During the August Bank Holiday, Eden returned to Chequers. Colville noted in his diary: 'Winston is firmly hoping for talks which might lead to a relaxation of the Cold War and a respite in which science could use its marvels for improving the lot of man and, as he put it, the leisured classes of his youth might give way to the leisured masses of tomorrow. Eden is set on retaining the strength of NATO and the Western Alliance by which, he believes, Russia has already been severely weakened. W is depressed by Eden's attitude (which reflects that of the FO), because he thinks it consigns us to years more of hatred and hostility.' Still more depressing, Colville wrote, was that Lord Salisbury, after a visit to Washington, reported that he found Eisenhower 'violently Russophobe, greatly more so than Dulles, and that he believes the President to be personally responsible for the policy of useless pinpricks and harassing tactics the US is following against Russia in Europe and the Far East'.

On August 8 Churchill was well enough to preside, at Chequers, over a meeting of Ministers to discuss the Soviet reply to a Three-Power note inviting them to a conference of Foreign Ministers. 'Apart from his un-steady walk,' Colville wrote in his diary, 'the appearances left by his stroke have vanished, though he still tires quickly.' Four days later the Russians announced that they had developed an atom bomb. 'The PM still inclining to think we should have another shot at understanding,' Colville wrote. Churchill's words to him were, 'We must not go further on the path to war unless we are sure there is no other path to peace.'

Eight weeks had passed since Churchill's stroke. 'Cheering beyond telling is this marvellous recovery,' Brendan Bracken wrote to Beaver-brook on August 14. Four days later Churchill was driven up to London, where, for the first time since the morning after his stoke, he presided at a Cabinet meeting. On the following morning he saw the British Ambas-sador to Moscow. That same day he laid the foundations of yet another literary effort, the rewriting of his pre-war history of the English-speaking peoples, which had been set up in print on the eve of war but never published. His principal helper, who came to see him in the Cabinet Room that day, was to be Alan Hodge, editor of the monthly magazine *History Today*. 'I've been living on the Second World War,' Churchill told Lord Moran that day. 'Now I shall live on this history. I shall lay an egg a year – a volume every twelve months should not mean much work.'

Returning to Chartwell, Churchill worked to finish the last chapters of the sixth volume of his war memoirs. Commodore Allen and Denis Kelly both came down to help him. Walter Graebner of Time-Life, who went to visit Churchill on a day when he was working on his account of the Battle of Leyte Gulf in the Pacific, later recalled: 'Work began at the luncheon table after the second bottle of champagne was emptied and cigars were lighted. "Now let's get down to it," Churchill said. We were still sitting there at a quarter to five, Churchill having gone over every word in the manuscript to make sure that he understood the full story of the battle and that he had related it clearly and in his best words. In the years that I knew him, his mind was never sharper than on that grey August afternoon in 1953.'

Churchill now felt well enough to travel up to London whenever necessary; he did so on August 25 for an afternoon Cabinet meeting, after which he worked on the proofs of his sixth volume until dinner. On the following day he stayed up until a quarter to two talking to Eden and Macmillan. All was not entirely well, however, as Clementine wrote to Mary on September 5: 'I am sad about Papa; because in spite the brave show he makes, he gets very easily tired & then he gets depressed. He does too much work & has not yet learnt how & when to stop. It just tails off drearily & he won't go to bed. He is making progress, but now it is imperceptible. If no set-back occurs the improvement can continue for 2 years. I expect you have seen from the newspapers the tremendous "*va-et-vient*" of ministers. Papa enjoys it very much. Incidentally they are even more tired than he is by the sitting over the dinner table till after midnight!'

Churchill was back at No. 10 on September 8, for a Cabinet discussion about possible Egyptian action against the British forces on the Suez Canal. There was talk of a military response, but Churchill urged caution. It should 'not be forgotten', he said, that there were economic and financial sanctions that could be applied 'without having recourse to active intervention by British forces'. It was always open to Britain, he pointed out, by blocking Egypt's sterling balances, to 'control the flow of oil to Cairo'.

On September 11, against Clementine's advice, Churchill went north to the races at Doncaster. From there he travelled in the Royal Train to Balmoral. That Sunday he accompanied the Queen to Crathie Kirk, where he had last worshipped with King Edward VII forty-five years earlier, when President of the Board of Trade. 'What an innings he has had!' was Lord Moran's comment. After returning to London for another Cabinet meeting, Churchill left England on September 17 for a two-week holiday in the South of France. Once more, he stayed at Beaverbrook's villa. At first all did not go well. 'The PM has been in the depths of depression,' Jane Portal wrote to R.A. Butler, her uncle, and she went on to explain: 'He broods continually on whether to give up or not. He was exhausted by Balmoral and the Cabinets and the journey. I sometimes feel he would be better engaged on his history of the English-Speaking Peoples which is already very remarkable. He greatly likes your messages telling him all the news and you are in high favour. He is preparing a speech for the Margate conference but wonders how long he can be on his pins to deliver it. He has painted one picture in tempera from his bedroom window.'

Slowly, but only slowly, Churchill's mood improved. 'The kittens are very kind to me,' he wrote to Clementine on September 21, 'but evidently they do not think much of my prospects. I have done the daily work and kept check on the gloomy tangle of the world, and I have dictated about 2,000 words of a possible speech for Margate in order to try & see how I can let it off when it is finished to a select audience. I still ponder on the future and don't want to decide unless I am convinced. Today I went into Monte Carlo and bought a grisly book by the author of *All Quiet on the Western Front*. It is all about concentration camps, but in good readable print, which matters to me. It is like taking refuge from melancholy in horror. It provides a background. I have read almost 3/4 of *Coningsby*, but the print was faint and small. I am glad I did not have to live in that artificial society of dukes & would-be duchesses with their Tadpoles & Tapers.'

The 'grisly book' was *Spark of Life* by Erich Maria Remarque; *Coningsby* was one of the novels of his Conservative predecessor Disraeli, whose death in 1881 had been one of his first political memories.

Colville, who flew out to join Churchill on September 23, later recalled that the Prime Minister 'spent hours painting the rocks and pine trees'. Painting, Churchill wrote to Clementine on September 25, was 'a great distraction and a little perch for a tired bird'. On the following day, having looked again at the pre-war proofs of *A History of the English-Speaking Peoples*, he wrote to Beaverbrook, 'On the whole I think I would rather have lived through our lot of troubles than any of the others, though I must place on record my regret that the human race ever learned to fly.'

Churchill advised Beaverbrook to be 'careful' about his opposition to a German Army. 'Although armies are no longer the instruments by which the fate of nations is decided,' he wrote, 'there is certainly going to be a German army and I hope it will be on our side and not against us. This need in no way prevent, but may on the contrary help, friendly relations with the bear.'

On September 30 Churchill flew back to England. Nine days later he travelled to Margate to make the speech, the reception of which would help him decide his political future. He spoke for fifty minutes, standing throughout, and without losing his place or his concentration. During this speech he reiterated his hopes of May 11 for a meeting at the summit with the Russians. He also told the assembled Conservatives that the NATO alliance existed 'not to play Russia against Germany or Germany against Russia, but to make them both feel they can live in safety with each other, in spite of their grievous problems and differences'. Britain's role was to use her growing influence with both 'to relieve them of any anxiety they may feel about each other'. Personally, he added, he welcomed Germany 'back among the great powers of the world'. The speech was a success. It was also, Jane Portal later recalled, a 'terrific ordeal'. Although news of his stroke had been kept secret, all sorts of rumours had circulated about his ill-health. 'Everyone,' Miss Portal added, 'was watching him for frailty. It was a triumphant achievement to have got through that.'

On October 16 Churchill learned that he had been awarded the Nobel Prize for Literature. It was a fitting tribute to one whose first book had been published more than fifty years earlier, whose five-volume history of the First World War had become a classic, and whose six-volume history of the Second World War was now so nearly completed. Four days later he returned to the House of Commons, for the first time since his stroke, for Prime Minister's Questions. 'He seemed self-confident,' was Channon's comment, 'though a touch deaf in spite of his hearing-aid, but apparently more vigorous than before.' Channon doubted, however, 'whether he can carry on for long'.

There was now renewed pressure on Churchill to retire. Clementine wanted him to hand over to Eden, who was desperate to be summoned to take his place. But on November 3, when he made his first Parliamentary speech since his stroke, Churchill's vigour was such that it gave him confidence that he need not step down. Channon commented on the speech in his diary: 'Brilliant, full of cunning and charm, of wit and thrusts, he poured out his Macaulay-like phrases to a stilled and awed House. It was an Olympian spectacle. A supreme performance which we shall never see again from him or anyone else. In eighteen years in this honourable House I have never heard anything like it.'

Churchill left the Chamber and walked unaided to the smoking-room and then, Channon noted, 'flushed with pride, pleasure, and triumph, sat there for two hours sipping brandy and acknowledging compliments. He beamed like a school-boy.' Neither Channon nor any of those who crowded round the triumphant speaker realised that he was recovering from a stroke; one which had led most of those who knew of it, including his doctors, to conclude that he would never speak in the Commons again. 'That's the last bloody hurdle' were his words to Moran on returning to his room in the Commons, and he added, 'Now, Charles, we can think of Moscow.'

The first stage of any such journey to Moscow would have to be a preparatory meeting with the Americans and the French; within forty-eight hours of his Parliamentary triumph, Churchill once more invited Eisenhower to Bermuda. It was agreed that they would meet there for four days, beginning on December 4, together with the new French Prime Minister, Joseph Laniel. Churchill was determined to try to find a way to renew relations with Russia; at his suggestion, Colville and Soames had gone to the Soviet Embassy for a private talk on the possibilities of détente. But a telegram from the new British Ambassador in Moscow, William Hayter, boded ill for Churchill's hopes. The Soviets viewed co-existence, Hayter reported on November 24, as that 'of the snake and the rabbit'. The new Soviet leader, Malenkov, 'seems to have concluded that Stalin's methods were too rough. Other and more subtle methods of weakening the West are henceforth to be adopted.'

Churchill was not put off by this stark appraisal. On December 1, the day after his seventy-ninth birthday, he left London by air for Bermuda, a long and at times rough flight of seventeen hours. Lord Cherwell was with him as, Churchill had written to Eisenhower, 'I want to talk over with you our "collusion" on atomics etc,' Churchill added: 'Indeed it might strengthen the impression, to which I gathered you were favourable, that our meeting was not simply an incident in the recent correspondence with the Soviets. He can always slip across to Washington after we have had a talk, if you thought it convenient for him to see more of your people.' The atomic aspect had been Cherwell's particular responsibility for more than ten years, since the very first years of the war.

On the day after his arrival in Bermuda, Churchill went to the airport to welcome the French Prime Minister, Laniel, and his Foreign Minister, Georges Bidault. On the following day he returned to the airport to greet Eisenhower and Dulles. During a private talk, Eisenhower told Churchill that if there were a deliberate breach of the Korean armistice by the Communists, the United States 'would expect to strike back with atomic weapons at military targets'. Churchill did not object, telling Eisenhower, as the minutes recorded, that he 'quite accepted this'. Then, Colville later recalled, he walked down to the beach, where he sat 'like King Canute defying the incoming tide (and getting his feet wet in consequence)'.

The first plenary session of the Bermuda Conference opened that afternoon. In discussing the Soviet Union, Bidault doubted that there was really a 'new look'. Churchill replied, 'Let us make sure that we do not too lightly dismiss this possibility'. He would not be 'in too much of a hurry to believe that nothing but evil emanates from this mighty branch of the human family, or that nothing but danger and peril could come out of this vast ocean of land in a single circle so little known and understood'. To Churchill's amazement, Eisenhower then proceeded to describe the new

Russia as a tart; 'despite bath, perfume or lace, it was still the same old girl'. But perhaps they could pull her 'off the main street and put her on a back alley'. He did not want, said Eisenhower, 'to approach this problem on the basis that there had been any change in the Soviet policy of destroying the capitalist free world by all means, by force, by deceit or by lies. This was their long-term purpose. From their writings it was clear there had been no change since Lenin.'

Eisenhower asked Churchill to 'correct him' if he was wrong; he then adjourned the Conference. That evening, in discussion with Churchill and Eden, he again raised the question of future American action in Korea, if the truce was broken. Churchill, much encouraged by Eden, now 'strongly resisted' Eisenhower's suggestion that in the event of hostilities breaking out again America should use the atom bomb.

At a further meeting with Churchill on the following morning, Eisenhower proposed, as part of a speech he was to make at the United Nations, to refer to the 'obsolete Colonial mould' which was now being broken. After lunch that day, Churchill persuaded Eisenhower to remove from his speech what Colville called this 'obnoxious phrase'. More significantly, Churchill persuaded Eisenhower to replace the phrase about the United States being 'free to use the atomic bomb' by one about the United States 'reserving the right to use the atomic bomb'. The central theme of Eisenhower's proposal, the control of atomic energy by an international body, was very much acceptable to Churchill. It seemed a way back from the brink.

Much of the rest of the Conference was taken up discussing the European Defence Community, and by a series of appeals from Churchill to the French, urging them to accept a German military contingent as an integral part of the defence of Western Europe. When Bidault spoke with passion about the current Franco-German dispute over the Saar, on France's eastern border, Churchill, as the minutes of the meeting recorded, 'begged and implored his French friends not to let a few fields in the Saar valley come between the life and death of the flaming spirit of France and the break-up of the great structure on which so many hopes had been founded'. If Germany were left totally disarmed she would be 'at the mercy of Russia at any moment'.

The French were not to be convinced. Nor would the Americans agree to Churchill's request to participate with Britain in the policing of the Suez Canal Zone. As to the purpose of Churchill's visit, a common approach to Russia, with a view to a summit meeting, the Americans were adamant that nothing would come of it but a propaganda victory for the Soviets. When the Conference ended on December 8 Churchill was a disappointed man. He had travelled far, and mastered his illness, but his advocacy had failed.

Churchill left Bermuda by air on the evening of December 10. Eleven days later he explained to a former Labour Minister of Works, Richard Stokes: 'American anxiety about Russian rearmament must be borne in mind. We cannot get through without them.' He was upset, however, early in the New Year, to learn that the Americans were intending to give military aid to Pakistan, and to initiate some form of military collaboration between Pakistan and Turkey; this, he told the Cabinet on 7 January 1954, 'could do nothing for the moment to increase the military strength of the West, and it was bound to be regarded by the Soviet Government as a provocative gesture'.

On January 21 Churchill read in the newspapers of the death of his fellow-soldier of Omdurman days, Richard Molyneux. It was to help heal Molyneux's wound after the battle that Churchill had given some of his own skin for grafting. 'He will take my skin with him, a kind of advance guard, into the next world,' Churchill commented on reading of his friend's death. Churchill's own departure for the next world did not now seem as imminent as some had feared. After Archibald Sinclair had seen him at the Other Club on January 28, and again at No. 10 on the following morning, he wrote to Beaverbrook: 'Neither at night, nor in the middle of his morning's work, was there any trace of tiredness – still less of weakness or lethargy. He still radiates gaiety & power and his authority is unimpaired.'

In Cabinet on February 3 Churchill made his first intervention on a question which had begun to loom on the political horizon, the possibility of legislative restrictions on coloured immigration from the Commonwealth. The 'rapid improvement of communications', he said, was likely to lead 'to a continuing increase in the number of coloured people coming to this country, and their presence here would sooner or later come to be resented by large sections of the British people'. It might well be true, however, he told the Cabinet, that the problem had 'not yet assumed sufficient proportions to enable the Government to take adequate counter-measures'.

That February there were two calls in the Press for Churchill's resignation, one in the *Daily Mirror* and the other in *Punch*. There was also disappointment for Churchill that month when, at the long-awaited Four-Power meeting of Foreign Ministers, held in Berlin, the Russians proved obdurate and unyielding. But when he spoke in the Commons on February 25 he made it clear that he still hoped for détente. 'Patience and perseverance,' he said, 'must never be grudged when the peace of the world is at stake. Even if we had to go through a decade of cold-war bickerings punctuated by vain parleys, that would be preferable to the catalogue of unspeakable and also unimaginable horrors which is the alternative. We must not shrink from continuing to use every channel that is open or that we can open, any more than that we should relax those defensive measures indispensable for our own strength and safety.'

There was 'no contradiction', Churchill said, between the policy of building up the defence strength of the free world against 'potential armed Soviet aggression' and trying at the same time 'to create conditions under which Russia may dwell easily and peacefully side by side with us all'. His appeal ended: 'Peace is our aim, and strength is the only way of getting it. We need not be deterred by the taunt that we are trying to have it both ways at once. Indeed, it is only by having it both ways at once that we shall have a chance of getting anything of it at all.'

Churchill's stamina could still astound those who knew of his stroke. After a five-hour Cabinet meeting on March 4, Lord Moran asked him if he was tired. 'Not at all,' he said. 'Now I am going out to dinner with the American Ambassador.' Moran commented, 'This astonishing creature obeys no laws, recognises no rules.' A week later, however, when Churchill dined with Butler, he told his Chancellor of the Exchequer, 'I feel like an aeroplane at the end of its flight, in the dusk, with the petrol running out, in search of a safe landing.' The only political interest he had left, Churchill confided, was in 'high-level conversations with the Russians'.

Those who wanted Churchill to resign were becoming more vociferous, and more bitter. On March 22, in the privacy of his diary, Harry Crookshank called him 'gaga'. Four days later, however, Jane Portal, who saw him almost every day, described him to Lord Moran as 'quite perky'. He was also increasingly active in trying to win Eisenhower over to one more attempt at a high-level conference with Russia, and to promote greater East-West trade. But in answer to an appeal for an increase in trade with Russia, Eisenhower replied that he did not want the Russians to have the benefits of western consumer goods.

Churchill did not slacken in his efforts to influence the President. With the explosion that month of an American hydrogen bomb, there were many who felt a sense of panic. Churchill still hoped, however, as he told Eisenhower on March 27, 'to promote an easement of relations with Soviet Russia and to encourage and aid any development of Russian life which leads to a wider enjoyment by the Russian masses of the consumer goods of which you speak, and modern popular amenities and diversions which play so large a part in British and American life'. In the climate of the Cold War, such sentiments were far-sighted. But with each telegram sent by Churchill to Eisenhower, Anthony Eden felt that his own authority as Foreign Secretary was being undermined. Tension between the two men grew almost to breaking-point. On March 31 Eden told one of his advisers, in exasperation, 'This simply cannot go on; he is gaga; he cannot finish his sentences.'

That day, the *New York Times* seemed to endorse Eden's judgement. 'For the first time since Parliament reconvened last autumn,' it wrote, 'Sir Winston appeared unsure of himself and tired. This was not the Churchill of two years ago and was only a shadow of the great figure of 1940.' Triumphantly, the *Daily Mirror* printed this comment on its back page with the headline, 'What America says about Churchill now.' A 'shadow' he may have been by comparison with 1940, but the *New York Times* was unaware of Churchill's continuing vigilance in world affairs. On the previous day he had written to his friend Lord Beaverbrook, the proprietor of the *Daily Express:* 'I think the Express took a very sensible line about not trying to forbid the United States to proceed with their hydrogen experiments. A breach with them might well be fatal to world peace and to our survival, for they could quite easily go on alone and we are far worse placed geographically.' Churchill added: 'I grieve that you continue to oppose so violently the rearmament, under proper limits, of Western Germany. It is going to happen anyway and it is better to have them on our side than against us.'

Frail though he was, Churchill was at that very moment preparing a speech on the hydrogen bomb, which he made in the Commons on April 5. Nothing could be more disastrous to the survival of Western Europe and the safety of Britain, he warned, 'than a great dispute between Britain and the United States'. He also spoke, as he had done almost a year earlier, on May 11, of the possibility of a summit meeting; one which would now have a different 'topic' as a result of Eisenhower's United Nations speech proposing a new consultative and co-operative machinery for the industrial atomic sphere.

Churchill told the Commons, 'If Russia, the British Commonwealth, and the United States were gathered round the table talking about the commercial application of atomic energy, and the diversion of some of their uranium stockpile, it would not seem odd if the question of the hydrogen bomb, which might blow all these pretty plans sky-high, cropped up, and what I have hoped for, namely a talk on supreme issues between the Heads of States and Governments concerned, might not seem so impossible as it has hitherto.' There were, he concluded, two main aims of British policy: 'One is to lose no opportunity of convincing the Soviet leaders and, if we can reach them, the Russian people, that the democracies of the West have no aggressive design on them. The other is to ensure that until that purpose has been achieved we have the strength necessary to deter any aggression by them and to ward it off if it should come.'

As Churchill spoke these words, his remarks were punctuated by cries of 'Resign!' from the Labour benches. So loud were the cries that at times they drowned his words. It was not the interruptions, however, but Churchill's lack of reaction to them, that caused the greatest comment. 'The virulence of the attack for once did not stimulate him to combat,' wrote the Parliamentary correspondent of *The Times*. 'It seemed to rob his voice of resonance and left him ploughing doggedly through this section of his speech.'

Churchill's performance on April 5 marked a turning point; it was 'the first time', one of his Private Secretaries, Anthony Montague Browne, later recalled, 'that I realised unmistakably how much his powers had waned. In days gone by he would have put aside his notes and devastated the opposition because he had the strongest case.' There was an 'overwhelming impression', Evelyn Shuckburgh noted in his diary, 'that the PM has made a real bloomer, and exposed his aged feebleness to the House'.

Despite the setback of April 5, Churchill, fearful of a world riven by nuclear conflict, expressed his concerns at the Royal Academy Banquet on April 28, and, two days later, at the Albert Hall. At Chequers on April 26 he had sought to impress on President Eisenhower's representative, Admiral Radford, who was hoping for a British commitment to participate in the war in Indo-China, 'the danger of war on the fringes, where the Russians were strong and could mobilise the enthusiasm of nationalist and oppressed peoples'. His policy was 'quite different', he told the Admiral; 'it was conversations at the centre'. Such conversations should lead neither to appeasement nor to an ultimatum, but should be 'calculated to bring home to the Russians the full implications of Western strength and to impress upon them the folly of war'.

On the day that Admiral Radford was at Chequers, the sixth and final volume of Churchill's war memoirs was published in London. In congratulating him, Brendan Bracken wrote, 'There never was such an animal as WSC.' But Churchill was now mentioning July as a possible date for his retirement; watching as Eden received daily press coverage for his work in Geneva at an international conference on Indo-China. 'He is going through a Valley of Decision, or rather of indecision, about the time when he should relinquish power,' Violet Bonham Carter wrote to a friend after a visit to Churchill at Chartwell, 'and I felt that he was in great agony of mind. I urged him, rightly or wrongly, to stay on. He said to me, "You know you and Beaverbrook are the only two people who really want me to stay." ' Bracken was another who seemed to favour Churchill staying on, writing to Beaverbrook that month, 'Churchill alone has the capacity to hold on to excitable Uncle Sam's coat-tails.'

On May 27 Churchill was to address a Conservative Women's rally at the Albert Hall. 'I do not conceal from you that original composition is a greater toil than it used to be,' he wrote to Clementine two days earlier, 'while I dislike having my speeches made for me by others as much as I ever did.' For more than two days he worked on his speech, then spoke for forty minutes, telling the women that it was his belief 'that we may live to see – or you may – the awful secrets which science has wrung from nature serve mankind instead of destroying it, and put an end to the wars they were called forth to wage'.

Churchill was already planning to fly to Washington, to discuss with Eisenhower an Anglo-American exchange of information on the peaceful use of atomic energy. To that end, he would once more take Lord Cherwell with him. On being told of Churchill's plan, Eden took the opportunity, in a letter to him on June 7, to suggest to him that he should resign as Prime Minister as soon as he was back from the trip. 'My dear Anthony,' Churchill replied, 'I am not able to commit myself to what you suggest,' and he went on to explain, 'I am increasingly impressed by the crisis and tension which is developing in world affairs and I should be failing in my duty if I cast away my trust at such a juncture or failed to use the influence I possess in the causes we both have at heart.' He would not expect, however, to stay on 'beyond the autumn'.

Following Eden's letter, Churchill discussed his resignation with Macmillan, to whom he said he was thinking of going in the autumn. A few days later he received a typewritten letter from Macmillan, saying that in his view it would be better, if a new administration were to be formed that year, 'for Ministers to be installed in their new offices before and not after the summer holidays'. Churchill was not pleased. 'My dear Harold,' he replied on June 20, 'I received your letter yesterday morning. I do not think it ought to have been written except in your own hand. I was well aware of your views, Yours sincerely, Winston S. Churchill.'

Churchill was convinced that he could still influence the Americans to a policy of détente with Russia, on the basis of having first constructed what he described to Eisenhower in a message on June 21 as 'the world front against Communist aggression'. Greece, Turkey, Iraq, Pakistan, and Tito's Yugoslavia, which in 1948 had broken with Moscow, could all be brought into that front. 'I seek as you know,' he added, 'to convince Russia that there is a thoroughly friendly and easy way out for her, in which all her hard-driven peoples may gain a broader, fuller, happier life.'

On the evening of June 24 Churchill, Eden and Cherwell left London by air for Washington. A year had passed since the stroke. The main purpose of the visit, Colville noted during the flight, was 'to convince the President that we must co-operate more fruitfully in the atomic and hydrogen sphere and that we, the Americans and British, must go and talk to the Russians in an effort to avert war, diminish the effects of the Cold War, and procure a ten years' period of "easement" during which we can divert our riches and our scientific knowledge to ends more fruitful than the production of catastrophic weapons.'

At Washington airport Churchill was met by Dulles, and by the Vice-President, Richard Nixon, then driven to the White House, which was to be his home for the duration of the talks. To his surprise, at their very first meeting that morning Eisenhower at last expressed agreement with the idea of a high-level meeting with the Russians. Churchill then proposed a 'reconnaissance in force' to Moscow, possibly by himself, 'to see if anything promising developed'. Eisenhower was prepared to see Churchill go alone to Moscow; he himself would not, however, go to a meeting 'anywhere under the present Soviet rule'. When Churchill suggested that a Churchill-Malenkov-Eisenhower meeting could take place in neutral Stockholm, or in London, Eisenhower agreed. As to Churchill's preliminary 'reconnaissance in force' to Moscow, he told Eisenhower, 'I swear to you that I will not compromise you in the slightest.'

Before Churchill had left for Washington, the Cabinet's Defence Policy Committee, of which he was Chairman, decided that Britain should produce its own hydrogen bomb. This decision was kept secret from the full Cabinet. On June 26, however, Churchill told Eisenhower that Britain would be manufacturing its own bomb, and would do so in Britain. The two men also discussed 'the dangers which now face the world as a result of the portability of the bomb'. A general moratorium on hydrogen bomb experiments was thought, however, to be 'unwise', in the light of what the minutes of the discussion called 'the difficulties of detection', as well as the possibility of the concealment of any explosion.

At a public luncheon on June 26, Churchill addressed thirty leading Senators and Congressmen. Communism was a 'tyrant', he said, but 'meeting jaw to jaw is better than war'. This approach still did not commend itself to Dulles, who, at a private talk with Churchill on the following day, expressed his doubts about any initial meeting between Churchill and the Russians. According to Dulles' note of their conversation, 'I pointed out that if Mr Churchill should make an exploratory mission alone, it would not be looked upon well in this country, and also we might have to make it clear that Mr Churchill was in no sense speaking or acting for the United States. Sir Winston said he fully understood this. On the other hand, he would be going not in any sense as an intermediary between the United States and the Soviet Union, but representing the spirit and purpose of "our side". I urged that the matter be very carefully weighed before any positive decision was made.'

The Washington talks ended on June 29. In a final communiqué that morning, Churchill and Eisenhower announced their agreement that West Germany, which had now become the German Federal Republic, 'should take its place as an equal partner in the community of Western nations where it can make its proper contribution to the defence of the free world.' Thus came to fruition the idea Churchill had first put forward at Zurich eight years earlier. At lunch that day the question of Anglo-American nuclear co-operation was discussed; the conclusions of that discussion remain secret to this day. Churchill then flew from Washington to Ottawa, where he told the Canadian Prime Minister and the Minister of Defence of Britain's decision to manufacture a hydrogen bomb.

At midday on June 30, in Ottawa, Churchill broadcast to the Canadian people, before dining with the Canadian Prime Minister. From the dinner table he was driven to the airport for a flight to New York. Reaching New York after midnight, he was driven straight to the docks, where he boarded the *Queen Elizabeth*. At noon on the following morning he was bound for home. During the voyage he finally decided on what Colville called 'an expedition to Russia, where he would ask for freedom for Austria as an earnest of better relations'.

Eden, who was also on board, pressed Churchill to make a precise commitment to retirement. Churchill agreed to do so, telling Eden on the morning of July 2 that he would go to Moscow in early August, then hand over to Eden on September 21. Later that day Churchill dictated a telegram to Molotov, proposing a meeting between himself and the Soviet leaders, 'which might be the prelude to a wider reunion where much might be settled'. On being sent the text of this telegram, Eisenhower replied, 'You did not let any grass grow under your feet.'

Eden was angered that Churchill intended to despatch the telegram from on board ship, without consulting the Cabinet. 'After a great deal of talk,' Colville noted in his diary, 'Eden was sent for and eventually agreed to a compromise.' Churchill would send the telegram to the Cabinet as Eden wished, 'provided he could say that Eden agreed with it in principle (which of course he does not). Eden weakly gave in.' To Churchill's surprise and satisfaction, when R.A. Butler sent a message to the ship about the proposed telegram, he appeared 'generally satisfied about the main idea'. The telegram was then sent to Moscow. Other than Butler, however, no other Cabinet Minister had seen it.

On July 6 the *Queen Elizabeth* reached Southampton. On the following day Churchill told the Cabinet of the decision to manufacture a British hydrogen bomb. He had no doubt, he said, that the 'best hope of preserving world peace was to make it clear to potential aggressors that they had no hope of shielding themselves from a crushing retaliatory use of atomic power'. That evening Churchill received Molotov's reply to his ship-board telegram. It was entirely favourable to a meeting of the sort he had proposed; in Moscow between himself and Malenkov. All seemed set fair for Churchill's last great act of statesmanship. But when the Cabinet met on July 8, it was soon clear that many Ministers were totally opposed to Churchill's initiative, and deeply resented the fact that it had been taken without consulting them.

Lord Salisbury and Harry Crookshank both spoke against Churchill's telegram to Molotov. Butler then dealt Churchill's initiative a crushing blow. The draft telegram had reached him, he said, during the afternoon of Saturday July 3, when he was in Norfolk. It had been addressed to him personally. 'There was nothing in the telegram to suggest that the views of the Cabinet were being invited.' Indeed, even before he had been able to despatch his own comments, 'a further telegram had been received from the Prime Minister enquiring whether the message had been transmitted to Moscow.' This, Butler said, 'had confirmed his view that he had not been expected to invite the views of other Cabinet colleagues – and it would in any event have been very difficult for him to do so when Ministers were dispersed at the week-end.'

Butler's account shocked Churchill's Ministers. As the discussion continued, it was clear that the majority of them would not support a Moscow visit. Churchill looked for a way out, telling the Cabinet that he would consult first with Eisenhower. This was accepted. All would depend, he told Eisenhower, on whether 'the Cabinet decide to go forward with the project'. But he did not mean to give up his idea of a Three-Power meeting, telling Eisenhower, in a telegram on July 9: 'I do not intend to go to Moscow. We can only meet as equals, and though Stockholm which you mentioned to me before you took office, or Vienna, are both acceptable, Anthony has proposed what I think is the best, namely Berne.' Malenkov could come to Berne once the Geneva Conference was over, with Molotov coming from Geneva, 'and Anthony and I could have a few talks on the dead level'. There could then be a Three- or a Four-power Conference in London in September.

'Of course,' Churchill admitted, 'all this may be moonshine. The Soviets may refuse any meeting place but Moscow. In that case all would be off for the present, or they will give nothing and merely seek, quite vainly, to split Anglo-American unity. I cherish hopes not illusions and after all I am "an expendable" and very ready to be one in so great a cause.'

In Cabinet, Eden intervened forcefully against Churchill's continuing initiative. The dangers of a meeting such as Churchill proposed, he told his colleagues on July 9, were the lack of any fixed agenda and the problem of 'the questions which the Russians were likely to raise'. As an alternative to the creation of a European Defence Community, Eden warned, 'they would probably suggest that a united Germany should be admitted to the NATO, and that NATO should thereafter be widened to include the Soviet Union'. As regards the project for 'a broader meeting', Eden warned, Britain must be prepared for the Russians to press the suggestion that this should be on a Five-Power basis, 'including Communist China'.

Although Churchill still refused to abandon his hopes of a meeting with Malenkov, the weight of Cabinet opinion was clearly against him. On July 16 Macmillan went to see Lady Churchill to tell her that the Cabinet was 'in danger of breaking up' on this issue. There was considerable anger in Cabinet at what several senior Ministers felt was the unconstitutional nature of Churchill's ship-board telegram to Molotov. When the Cabinet met on July 23 there was widespread agreement that Ministers ought to have been consulted in advance on a telegram of such importance. As to the substance of Churchill's proposal, Eden was outspoken, telling the Cabinet emphatically that he did not believe 'that any good would come from a bi-lateral meeting with the Russians at the present time'. He added, however, rather ambivalently, that in view of the fact that Churchill 'with all his long experience' felt so strongly that the attempt was worth making, he was 'ready to acquiesce – so long as the meeting was not held on Russian soil'.

The Cabinet decided to postpone their decision until their next meeting three days later. When they met on July 26 it was clear that the majority opinion was still against any Churchill-Malenkov meeting, wherever it might be held. Churchill therefore withdrew his proposal. But the new factor of the hydrogen bomb convinced him that some effort ought to be made to end the Cold War. When, on July 29, there was criticism in the Commons of the Anglo-Egyptian Agreement, signed two days earlier in Cairo, whereby British troops were to withdraw from the Suez Canal Zone, Churchill begged MPs to see the matter in its wider perspective. 'How utterly out of all proportion to the Suez Canal and the position we held in Egypt,' he said, 'are the appalling developments and the appalling spectacle which imagination raises before us,' and he went on to explain: 'Merely to try to imagine in outline the first few weeks of a war under conditions about which we did not know when this Session commenced, and about which we had not been told – merely to portray that picture and submit it to the House would, I am sure, convince Hon. Gentlemen of the obsolescence of the base and of the sense of proportion which is vitally needed at the present time, not only in military dispositions but in all our attempts to establish human relationships between nation and nation.'

Churchill's appeal was effective. 'Before he sat down,' Moran wrote in his diary, 'he had restored to the House a sense of proportion, so that they were able to measure the importance of Suez against the incredible calamities of a war of annihilation.' But despite this Parliamentary success, during an intervention that lasted a mere four minutes, more and more Ministers now joined the private but determined move to secure his resignation. Had he not first spoken of June, then of July, then of September, as the month in which he would leave? Could he not fix a date now? Churchill was 'a marvel & mystery,' his daughter Mary wrote in her diary on July 29, 'and none of us *really* know what his intentions are – perhaps he doesn't himself!'

Churchill went down to Chartwell. To the consternation of his Cabinet, he now decided not to hand over to Eden in September. Eden asked if the change-over could at least be in October, so that he could go to the Party Conference that month as Prime Minister, or as imminent Prime Minister. But Churchill did not accept this. He wished, he said, to remain at the helm until the early months of 1955. 'I brood much about things,' he wrote to Clementine, who was on holiday in the South of France, on August 10, 'and all my moods are not equally gay.' He was particularly put out when it was announced that Attlee was to visit Moscow. 'There would have been an outburst of joy if I'd seen Malenkov,' he told Moran on August 12. 'Now Attlee has done it.' Churchill clung with tenacity to the hope of a Russian meeting. He set out his arguments, first to Butler and then to Macmillan, who noted them down in his diary on August 24, after a visit to Chartwell: 'He proposed to stay on as long as he could. He had a unique position. He could talk to anybody, on either side of the Iron Curtain, either by personal message or face to face. Having now fully recovered his health, he could not abandon his commission.' Churchill also told Macmillan that a 'fag-end' Government, such as Eden would have to lead if Churchill resigned before an election, 'could never succeed. Such brilliant figures as Lord Rosebery and Arthur Balfour had been swept aside, in spite of their talents and charm, after they had succeeded Gladstone and Salisbury.' Churchill added that, as Macmillan noted, 'he was PM and nothing could drive him out of his office, so long as he could form and control a Government and have the confidence of the House. This continual chatter in the lobbies and the Press about his resignation was intolerable. It arose, of course, from his illness last year. But he was now recovered. Naturally, like any man of nearly eighty, who had had two strokes, he might die at any moment. But he could not undertake to die at any particular moment! Meanwhile, he did not propose to resign.'

Churchill showed Macmillan the letter he was writing to Eden, explaining that he intended to remain Prime Minister until a General Election in November 1955. The letter gave him much anguish, particularly as Clementine was most reluctant to see him remain in office for another year, and more. 'Harold thought I ought to send it,' Churchill wrote to Clementine on the following day. 'It has gone. The responsibility is mine. But I hope you will give me your love.'

On August 27 Eden went to see Churchill. Their talk confirmed that Churchill did not intend to stand down for at least a year. 'You are young,' Churchill told him. 'It will all be yours before you are sixty. Why are you in such a hurry?' Two days later, Churchill announced in Cabinet that he would be staying on. He again looked forward to what he called, in a letter to Bernard Baruch, a 'Top Level' meeting with the Russians. 'You will, I am sure, be glad to hear that I am not thinking of retirement at the present time,' he told Baruch. 'I feel earnestly I still have something to contribute to the cause of "Peace through Strength". I am sure that I shall always get a fair hearing in my Mother's Land. I have seemed to gather vigour as this year has progressed and can do a long and thorough day's work especially if I get a good sleep in the middle of the day.' Churchill added, 'My mind is continually oppressed by the thermo-nuclear problem, though I still believe it is more likely to bring War to an end than mankind.'

On the last day of August Churchill was shocked to learn that the French Assembly had rejected the European Defence Community by 319 votes to 264. He at once wrote to the German Chancellor, Dr Konrad Adenauer, to ask him to agree not to press, in any future defence arrangement, for larger German forces than had been envisaged in the EDC plan. 'This would invest the new Germany with a moral dignity and respect,' he wrote, 'far more worth having than merely claiming the right to create as many divisions as she chose, or as anybody else, and plunging into an endless legalistic argument on the subject.' This advice came, Churchill explained, 'from one who after so many years of strife has few stronger wishes than to see the German nation take her true place in the worldwide family of free nations'.

In a letter to Eisenhower on September 18, Churchill told the President: 'I do hope and pray that you and I will still keep the German contribution as our No. 1 target, and also to get them on our side instead of on the other.'

At Chequers, Graham Sutherland was painting a portrait of Churchill, to be presented to him by both Houses of Parliament on his eightieth birthday. On September 1 Clementine wrote to Mary: 'Mr Graham Sutherland is a "Wow". He is really a most attractive man & one can hardly believe that the savage cruel designs that he exhibits, come from his brush.' Churchill had already given him three sittings, but no one had seen the beginnings of the portrait 'except Papa & he is much struck by the power of the drawing'. As the painting progressed, Sutherland made sure that it was covered up after each sitting. When he finished it, it was taken away, its final state seen neither by Churchill nor Clementine.

On October 9 Churchill spoke at the Conservative Party Conference in Blackpool. He had now been leader of the Conservative Party for fourteen years, he pointed out. He made no reference to standing down. 'At any rate for the moment,' wrote the *Observer*, 'the rank and file seem content that he should go in his own time and how he pleases.' Unknown to the *Observer*, Macmillan had written to Churchill a week earlier, urging him to fix a date for his retirement, and to choose a date sufficiently long enough before the Election to give Eden 'a fair run on his own' before polling day.

Immediately after his return from Blackpool, Churchill invited Macmillan to Chartwell. After their talk, Macmillan noted in his diary that Churchill would remain Prime Minister 'without any commitment written or verbal' as to the date of his resignation. Churchill also offered to appoint Macmillan Minister of Defence; Macmillan accepted. On October 26 Mary wrote in her diary: 'How fantastic it now seems that one actually thought & believed that Papa must retire! He is in full flight now – having reshuffled his government.'

Churchill allowed himself no respite. On November 9 he spoke at the Guildhall, on November 12 at Harrow School, on November 23 at Woodford, and on November 26 at Bristol University, where, Moran noted, the students 'had no feeling that he was an old man; on the contrary, he seemed to be one of themselves, and two thousand young voices shouted their joy and approval. The same puckish humour marked his approach to their seniors.' Among those at Bristol when Churchill spoke was a former British Ambassador to Washington, Sir Oliver Franks, who told Moran he had seen Churchill a few days earlier at Buckingham Palace, 'sitting on the sofa, apparently too weary to listen to anybody; his face was white and like a mask, his body had flopped, he seemed a very old man who had not long to live. But at Bristol he was pink, his expression was full of animation and his eyes twinkled.'

On November 30 Churchill was eighty; no Prime Minister since Gladstone had been in office at that age. No living Member of Parliament other than Churchill had first been elected in the reign of Queen Victoria. That morning, before a vast gathering in Westminster Hall, he was presented with the Sutherland portrait, which he described as 'a remarkable example of modern art. It certainly combines force with candour.' But he had not liked it; it seemed to combine a look of unredeemed ruthlessness with senility. After her husband's death, Clementine gave orders for it to be destroyed.

More acceptable that morning was Attlee's tribute, in which he praised Churchill's 'full share' in the Liberal social reforms before the First World

War, and went on to describe the Dardanelles campaign of 1915 as 'the only imaginative strategic idea of the war'. Attlee added, 'I only wish that you had had full power to carry it to success.' In his reply, Churchill said: 'I am now nearing the end of my journey. I hope I still have some services to render,' and in answer to Eisenhower's congratulations he wrote, on December 7, of his one remaining aspiration, telling the President, 'I still hope we may reach a top level meeting with the new regime in Russia and that you and I may both be present.'

Did Churchill still have the stamina for such activities? In a note written three months later, Colville recalled: 'He was ageing month by month and was reluctant to read any papers except the newspapers or to give his mind to anything that he did not find diverting. More and more time was given to bezique and ever less to public business. The preparation of a Parliamentary question might consume a whole morning; facts would be demanded from the Government departments and not arouse any interest when they arrived (they would be marked "R" and left to moulder in his black box); it was becoming an effort even to sign letters and a positive condescension to read Foreign Office telegrams.' And yet, Colville added, 'on some days the old gleam would be there, wit and good humour would bubble and sparkle, wisdom would roll out in telling sentences and still, occasionally, the sparkle of genius could be seen in a decision, a letter or phrase'.

On December 21 Eden went to see Churchill at Downing Street to ask him to set a date for his resignation. Churchill spoke of 'the end of June or July' as a possible date, but would make no commitment. When a group of senior Cabinet Ministers came to see him on the following day, he told them, as Eden noted in his diary, 'that it was clear we wanted him out'. Nobody contradicted him. Nor did he any more wish to hang on against the obviously unanimous opinion that he must resign, not at some vague moment in the summer, but in time to give Eden a full run-up to the election. Early in 1955 he decided, without informing Eden or Macmillan, to go at the beginning of the Easter Recess; that year the House would rise on April 7. 'His only wish now,' Bracken told Beaverbrook on January 17, 'is to find a small villa in the South of France where he can spend the winter months in the years which remain to him.'

Churchill's decision to resign at the beginning of April remained a close secret. He had still not given up hope for a meeting with the Russians; on January 12 he had told the French Prime Minister, Pierre Mendès-France, that he had 'for some time felt a strong desire to establish a direct personal contact with the new leaders of the Soviet Government such as might lead to a fruitful Four-Power Conference'. There were other ideas which he looked forward to advancing, among them the possible admission of Israel into the Commonwealth. 'Israel is a force in the world,' he wrote to Eden on February 9, '& a link with the USA.' Nine days later, at a luncheon at Buckingham Palace, he raised the question of Israel as a member of the Commonwealth with Evelyn Shuckburgh, telling him: 'Do not put that out of your mind. It would be a wonderful thing. So many people want to leave us, it might be the turning of the tide.' Churchill also wanted to encourage Nehru 'to be able to do what no other human being could,' as he explained to the Indian Prime Minister on February 21, 'in giving India the lead, at least in the realm of thought, throughout Asia, with the freedom and dignity of the individual as the ideal rather than the Communist Party drill book'.

Exactly a month after Bracken told Beaverbrook that Churchill intended to resign that April, Macmillan, who had not been told, noted in his diary: 'I think now he has taken the final decision to go. He is resigned to it and has begun to plan a future and quite agreeable life for himself.' Macmillan had come to this conclusion after a Cabinet meeting at which Churchill had been in a 'very merry mood'. At one point during the discussion, the question had arisen of the future lay-out of Parliament Square, and of its possible redesign and enlargement. This, Churchill told his Ministers, would be 'a good subject for a politician in retreat'. It was the first time, Macmillan wrote, that Churchill had referred in Cabinet to a time when he might no longer be Prime Minister. When Macmillan went to Chartwell on February 26, Churchill told him he had in mind resigning on April 5. He also told his visitor that he wished to hear the next Budget 'as PM'. As the Budget would be introduced on March 28, this in no way conflicted with the resignation date.

Churchill had one more major speech to make. 'He dictated it all himself,' Jane Portal later recalled. Like one of his earliest speeches in Parliament, in 1901, it dealt with the dramatic change in the nature of war. In 1901 it had been the ominous prospect of the use of the whole industrial resources of a nation for war; in 1955 it was the hydrogen bomb, 'What ought we to do?' Churchill asked. 'Which way shall we turn to save our lives and the future of the world? It does not matter so much to old people; they are going to die soon anyway; but I find it poignant to look at youth in all its activity and ardour and, most of all, to watch little children playing their merry games, and wonder what would lie before them if God wearied of mankind.'

The best defence would be 'bona fide disarmament all round'. But the 'long history and tradition of Russia makes it repugnant to the Soviet Government to accept any practical system of international inspection'. The Great Powers must devise 'a balanced and phased system of disarmament'. Until that could be reached, there was only 'one sane policy' for the free world, the policy of defence through deterrents. 'These deterrents may at any time become the parents of disarmament, provided that they deter.'

The hydrogen bomb, 'with its vast range of destruction and the even wider area of contamination, would be effective also against nations whose population, hitherto, has been so widely dispersed over large land areas as to make them feel that they were not in any danger at all.' This was 'well understood' by the leaders on both sides. That is why he had hoped 'for a long time' for a top-level conference 'where these matters could be put plainly and bluntly from one friendly visitor to the conference to another'. Then, Churchill believed, 'it may well be that we shall, by a process of sublime irony, have reached a stage where safety will be the sturdy shield of terror, and survival the twin brother of annihilation'. There was still time and hope, he believed, 'if we combine patience and courage'. In his peroration, the last Churchill was to deliver in the House of Commons, he declared: 'The day may dawn when fair play, love for one's fellow men, respect for justice and freedom, will enable tormented generations to march forth serene and triumphant from the hideous epoch in which we have to dwell. Meanwhile, never flinch, never weary, never despair.'

Churchill had spoken for three-quarters of an hour. His powers, commented the *Sunday Times*, 'as he has so brilliantly demonstrated, are still of the highest order'. What the newspaper did not know was that Churchill had finally decided to relinquish office. But on the second day of the debate, in answer to criticism that in the matter of the hydrogen bomb Britain had followed the dictation of the United States, Churchill astounded the House by making the first public reference to his stroke. 'I was prepared in every way to go over to see the President,' he said, recalling the early months of 1953. 'However, I was struck down by a very sudden illness which paralysed me completely, physically. That is why I had to put it off.'

Six days later, on March 8, during a lunch with Eden at Downing Street, Churchill confirmed that he would resign on April 5, in less than a month. Three days later he was shown a telegram from the British Ambassador in Washington, Sir Roger Makins, reporting a suggestion by Eisenhower that he, Churchill and Adenauer could meet in Paris on May 8, the tenth anniversary of VE Day, to ratify the new defence agreement that was to replace the European Defence Community. Eisenhower had also said, according to the Ambassador, that while he was in Paris he might be prepared to 'lay plans for a meeting with the Soviets in a sustained effort to reduce tensions and the risk of war'.

Churchill did not at first take in the implication of what Eisenhower had proposed. On rereading the Washington telegram, and a somewhat disparaging Foreign Office comment that had been attached to it, he suddenly saw a chance to revive his hopes for a top-level meeting. But May 8 was a month and three days after he had intended to resign. Eisenhower's suggestion, he wrote to Eden on March 12, 'must be regarded as creating a new situation which will affect our personal plans and time-tables'. Churchill thought he saw a light at the end of his long tunnel towards a meeting at the summit. 'The magnitude of the Washington advance towards a top-level Meeting,' he told Eden, 'is the dominant fact now before us, and our reply must not underrate it, or fail to encourage its development.' The Cabinet must be shown the Washington telegram. Meanwhile, 'a cordial interim message should be sent for Makins to deliver'.

Eden was distressed that Churchill wished to take a new diplomatic initiative, let alone to remain at the helm for another month. But when Churchill returned from Chequers to London on the evening of March 13 he told Eden that his offer to go on April 5 was now withdrawn, overtaken by the prospect of a Paris meeting, followed by a London summit.

The Cabinet met at noon at No. 10 to discuss the Makins telegram. Eden was emphatic that it betokened no new development in relations with Russia. Churchill disagreed; he attached 'primary importance,' he said, 'to the President's willingness to come to Europe for the purpose of making plans for a Four-Power meeting with the Russians'. This, he said, was 'a new and significant initiative, and we should welcome it'.

The Cabinet now discussed the possibility that the Paris meeting would be held in May as proposed by Eisenhower, to be followed by a Four-Power meeting in June. Churchill then suggested that perhaps the June meeting, at which the Russians would be present, could be held in London. Was it the mention of June that suddenly made Eden see red? To the mystification of his colleagues, who knew nothing of the April 5 hand-over date, he then asked, slowly and deliberately, 'Does that mean, Prime Minister, that the arrangements you have made with me are at an end?'

Churchill was angered that Eden should raise the resignation issue in this way. He began to reply somewhat indistinctly about 'the national interest' and 'this has been my ambition', whereupon Eden broke in with the words, 'I have been Foreign Minister for ten years. I am not to be trusted?'

'It seems certain facts are not known to all of us,' interrupted Lord Salisbury, who knew nothing of the April 5 date, and who now insisted that the Cabinet be told what was going on between Churchill and Eden.

But Churchill refused. 'I cannot assent to such a discussion,' he said. 'I know my duty and will perform it. If any member of the Cabinet dissents, his way is open.'

Ministers left Downing Street bewildered by what had happened. 'The poor Cabinet, most of whom knew nothing about the inner story, seemed puzzled and worried,' Churchill wrote to Clementine. 'Of course, as you know, only one thing has influenced me, and that is the possibility of arranging with Ike for a top level meeting in the near future with the Soviets. Otherwise I am very ready to hand over responsibility. I thought this Makins message offered a new chance, and that is why I am testing it.'

By an extraordinary irony, and coincidence, immediately after the Cabinet of March 14 Churchill had to put the finishing touches to a speech, in the Commons, in answer to a Labour vote of censure critical of the Government's efforts to secure world peace, and calling for a conference with the Soviet Union. The motion was moved by Attlee. 'I have tried very hard,' Churchill told the House – few statements could have been more true, and none more galling for Eden to listen to – 'to set in motion this process of a conference at the top level and to bring about actual results.' Malenkov had now been replaced by Marshal Bulganin and Nikita Khrushchev. 'Although I do not pretend to measure what the recent changes in the Soviet oligarchy imply,' Churchill told the House, 'I do not feel that they should in any way discourage us from further endeavours.'

Attlee's vote of censure was defeated, and Churchill prepared to make those 'further endeavours' for the Paris meeting and the London summit. But within a few hours of his speech a message was brought to Downing Street from the American Embassy, with the news, as Churchill reported at once to Clementine, 'that Ike was not willing himself to participate in a meeting with Russia.' This was indeed so; on March 16 a telegram from Makins confirmed that neither Eisenhower nor Dulles was contemplating an 'early' Four-Power meeting with the Russians. The London summit was dead. For Churchill the news was a blow; for Eden it was a joy. The hand-over date of April 5 could be reinstated. 'PM seems rather low,' Macmillan wrote in his diary after lunching at No. 10 on March 17, and he added, 'It is now certain that the crisis of indecision is over.'

It was not quite over. On March 27 Churchill learned that Marshal Bulganin had spoken favourably about the prospect of Four-Power talks. Two days later, at an audience at Buckingham Palace, he told the Queen that he thought of putting off his resignation. 'He had asked her if she minded,' Colville noted on the following day, 'and she said no!' A few days later Queen Elizabeth's Private Secretary, Sir Michael Adeane, wrote to Churchill to say that the Queen had 'fully understood' why, on March 29, 'there still seemed to be some uncertainty about the future'. It was an uncertainty that could not, and did not last long. During March 30 it became clear that whatever Bulganin had said, there was no real prospect of a top-level conference in the near future, especially given Eisenhower's hostile attitude to any such meeting. Churchill would resign on April 5 as planned.

At six-thirty on the evening of March 30 Churchill asked Eden and Butler to see him. 'Anthony and I were invited into the Cabinet room,' Butler later recalled. 'Winston made a slip by asking me to sit on his right, but then corrected himself and beckoned to Anthony. We gazed out over Horse Guards Parade. Then Winston said very shortly, "I am going and Anthony will succeed me. We can discuss details later." The ceremonial was over. We found ourselves in the passage, where Anthony and I shook hands.'

On the morning of March 31 Churchill asked Sir Michael Adeane to inform the Queen that he would resign in five days' time. 'Though she recognised your wisdom in taking the decision which you had,' Adeane replied, 'she felt the greatest personal regrets and that she would especially miss the weekly audiences which she has found so instructive and, if one can say so of State matters, so entertaining.'

A lifetime of politics was coming to an end; yet a newspaper strike made it certain that Churchill's resignation would receive little public coverage. On April 4 he and his wife gave a farewell dinner at No.10 to the Queen and the Duke of Edinburgh. At noon on the following day he held his last Cabinet meeting, wishing his colleagues 'all good fortune in the difficult, but hopeful, situation which they had to face'. He next saw the Ministers not in the Cabinet, telling them, 'Man is spirit', and leaving them with one piece of advice, 'Never be separated from the Americans.'

Churchill was then driven to Buckingham Palace, where he submitted his resignation to the Queen. 'She asked me whether I would recommend a successor,' he noted on his return to Downing Street, 'and I said I preferred to leave it to her. She said the case was not a difficult one and that she would summon Sir Anthony Eden. After some further conversation Her Majesty said she believed that I wished to continue in the Commons but that otherwise she would offer me a Dukedom. I said that I would like to go on in the Commons while I felt physically fit but that if I felt the work was too hard I would be very proud if she chose to reconsider her proposal.'

That afternoon, during his last hour at Downing Street, Churchill gave a tea party for the staff at No.10, about a hundred people; secretaries, telephonists, messengers and drivers. Then, cheered by his guests as he walked to the front door, he was driven to Chartwell.

Churchill had no intention of allowing retirement or old age to curb his love of adventure; a week after his resignation he was on his travels again, flying with Clementine to Sicily. As he boarded the plane, he was handed a letter from the Queen, written in her own hand. 'In thanking you for what you have done,' she wrote, 'I must confine myself to my own experience, to the comparatively short time – barely more than three years – during which I have been on the throne and you have been my First Minister. If I do not mention the years before and all their momentous events, in which you took a leading part, it is because you know already of the high value my father set on your achievements, and you are aware that he joined his people and the peoples of the whole free world in acknowledging a debt of deep and sincere thankfulness.'

The Queen's letter continued: 'During the more recent years you have had to face the Cold War and with it threats and dangers which are more awe-inspiring than any which you have had to contend with before, in war or peace. By your foresight and by your shaping of our destiny you have, if it were possible to do so, enhanced the admiration in which you are held, not only here but throughout much of the world and you know that you will take with you into retirement a deep fund of affectionate goodwill. For my part I know that in losing my constitutional adviser, I gain a wise counsellor to whom I shall not look in vain for help and support in the days which lie ahead. May there be many of them.'

For two weeks Churchill stayed at a hotel, the Villa Politi, in Syracuse. It was from there, on April 18, that he replied to the Queen, telling her that from her first days as Queen he had felt 'the impact of a new personality upon our unfolding history', and he went on to explain: 'Our Island no longer holds the same authority or power that it did in the days of Queen Victoria. A vast world towers up around it and after all our victories we could not claim the rank we hold were it not for the respect for our character and good sense and the general admiration not untinged by envy for our institutions and way of life. All this had already grown stronger and more solidly founded during the opening years of the present Reign, and I regard it as the most direct mark of God's favour we have ever received in my long life that the whole structure of our new formed Commonwealth has been linked and illuminated by a sparkling presence at its summit.'

Churchill ended his letter with a reflection on the 'historical atmosphere' of Syracuse: 'Our hotel rises out of the sinister quarries in which six thousand Athenian prisoners of war were toiled and starved to death in 413 BC, and I am trying to paint a picture of a cavern's mouth near the listening gallery whose echoes brought secrets to the ears of

Dionysius. All this is agreeable to the mental and psychological processes of laying down direct responsibility for the guidance of great affairs and falling back upon the comforting reflection, "I have done my best".'

40

Last Years

Churchill had taken with him to Sicily two close friends; one, Lord Cherwell, he had known for thirty-five years, the other, Jock Colville, had been a member of his Private Office for eight of the past fifteen years. One day, in conversation with them, Churchill expressed his regret that he had not taken up, while Prime Minister from 1951 to 1955, the recommendations made by Cherwell and others concerning Britain's failure to produce technologists in sufficient numbers. Cherwell and Colville replied that it was still not too late, and the idea was born of an institution in Britain similar to the Massachusetts Institute of Technology, at which Churchill had spoken in 1949. It was Colville who offered to raise the money; on his return to England he began the often daunting process which led within five years to the establishment of a new college, Churchill College, Cambridge.

Returning to London on 28 April 1955, Churchill watched and welcomed Eden's activities in leading the Conservative Party into the General Election. He also welcomed the announcement that Four-Power talks would after all be held that summer between the British, French, American and Soviet Foreign Ministers. During the election campaign he made several speeches in his constituency, and one at Bedford, for his son-in-law Christopher Soames. He made no attempt to intervene in Conservative politics, or to influence the conduct of the election campaign in any way. 'I have at the moment a great desire to stay put and do nothing,' he wrote to Bernard Baruch on May 26.

The election result was a decisive victory for the Conservatives. On the day the results were known, the Cabinet Secretary, Sir Norman Brook, wrote to Churchill from the Cabinet Office: 'You have been much in my thoughts during this Election, and I should like to send you my sincere congratulations on its result. For it is a most remarkable testimony to the record and achievement of your Government over the past 3 1/2 years. The real issue was whether the people were content with the Government they had had. And it is very evident that they were. The drop in the Labour vote is surely significant. I am sure you must be gratified by the way things have gone.'

Churchill's mood after the Election was benign. On May 29, at Chartwell, Lord Moran recorded Elizabeth Gilliatt's comment: 'He has been so good-tempered. Even when he had three speeches on his hands and we were looking out for storms, there was never a cross word. You know, Lord Moran, how he dislikes a new secretary. Now he has two, and he has been so sweet to them. This morning I was unpunctual, but when I said I was sorry, well, you heard how kind he was.' The new secretaries were Doreen Pugh and Gillian Maturin. It was intended that they should remain until the correspondence generated by the Election had cleared, a matter, it was thought, of three or four weeks. In the event, Miss Maturin stayed for three and a half years and Miss Pugh for nearly ten.

On May 30, in the course of a long and friendly letter, Eden told Churchill that he expected to hold a top-level meeting with the Russians that July. 'I was sorry I could not persuade Ike to test the Malenkov "New Look" in 1953,' Churchill replied on the following day, and he added: 'Khrushchev has the Army in a way that Malenkov did not, so that if there is a "New Look" it may be more fruitful. I do not think the Russian Army wants war. There is no such thing as military glory now. Soldiers would be safer than civilians, though not so comfortable as in time of peace. Surveying the scene from my detached position, I feel the corner will be gradually turned, and that the human race may be subjected to the test of extreme prosperity.'

At Chartwell, Churchill worked on his history of the English-Speaking Peoples, helped by Denis Kelly and Alan Hodge. On June 2 work was halted when he suffered a spasm of an artery, and for several days had some difficulty writing, picking up his coffee cup, or holding his cigar in his mouth. But he felt well enough six days later to go up to London for the opening of Parliament, and was pleased when, on entering the Chamber, he heard an MP cry out 'Churchill', whereupon there was a great clapping of hands in the public gallery, and MPs crowded round him, cheering and waving their order papers with enthusiasm.

Churchill returned to Chartwell, and to work on his history. On June 15 he learned from Macmillan that he could retain the services of one of his former Private Secretaries, Anthony Montague Brown. 'Please make all use of him you can for as long as you wish,' Macmillan wrote. He also wrote to Montague Browne: 'I am lending you to Winston because he needs somebody. In the nature of things it will only be a year or two.' In fact, Montague Browne was to be Churchill's devoted Private Secretary for nearly ten more years. 'From 1955 until my father drew his last breath,' Mary later recalled, 'Anthony was practically never absent from his side,' and she commented: 'The mail poured in. My father's business affairs, and his private life, Anthony really masterminded and managed, advised and helped. His knowledge, his professional know-how, his devotion to my father was one of the major factors in the last ten years of my father's life.'

On June 21 Churchill returned to London to speak at the Guildhall, at the unveiling of his statue. 'I confess,' he said, 'that like Disraeli I am on the side of the optimists. I do not believe that humanity is going to destroy itself. I have for some time thought it would be a good thing if the leaders of the great nations talked privately to one another. I am very glad that this is now going to happen.' The statue which Churchill unveiled was the work of a Yugoslav Jewish refugee, Oscar Nemon.

From the Guildhall, Churchill returned to Chartwell. 'I am getting much older now the stimulus of responsibility & power has fallen from me,' he wrote to Pamela Lytton on June 30, 'and I totter along in the shades of retirement.' On July 18 he wrote to Eisenhower: 'It is a strange and formidable experience laying down responsibility and letting the trappings of power fall in a heap to the ground. A sense not only of psychological but of physical relaxation steals over one to leave a feeling both of relief and denudation. I did not know how tired I was until I stopped working.' To his friend General Tudor he wrote a month later, about his departure from office, 'The worst thing about it is that when you let all these responsibilities drop, you feel your power falls with the thing it held.'

On September 15 Churchill flew with Clementine to the South of France for a prolonged stay at Beaverbrook's villa. It was the start of a new pattern of life for him, spending more and more time in the sun and comfort of the French Riviera. Much of his time was spent in painting. He also dictated the preface to the new book. In October, Hodge and Kelly flew out to help him. Clementine returned to England on October 16. For five short speeches that he had agreed to give on his return, Churchill told her, George Christ had sent him 'a fine set of notes'. In England, Deakin had rejoined the team; he flew out to join Churchill on October 28. Before returning to London, Churchill began to search for what he called his 'Dream Villa', which he hoped to buy. He was never to find it.

Returning to England on November 14, Churchill made his five short speeches; in his Constituency, to the boys of Harrow School, to the Young Conservatives, at the Drapers' Hall, and at the Mansion House. On this latter occasion he was given the Freedoms of Belfast and Londonderry. On November 30 he celebrated his eighty-first birthday. Then, in the second week of January 1956, he flew back to the South of France, not this time to Beaverbrook's villa at the Cap d'Ail, but to La Pausa, at Roquebrune, perched amid olive groves high above the Corniche. This villa, the home of Emery Reves and his wife Wendy, was to become the 'Dream Villa' of Churchill's last years. Named by him 'Pausaland', it provided him with comfort, calm and privacy, as well as magnificent views for painting. 'So far I have not left this luxurious house,' he wrote to Clementine on January 15, '& have passed the time mainly in bed revising the Book.' Two days later he wrote again: 'Reves & Wendy are most obliging. They ask the guests I like and none I don't.'

Churchill's pleasure at his new life was evident in all his letters. To Clementine, who had stayed in London dogged by ill-health, and was planning a long sea voyage to Ceylon, he wrote on January 30: 'I spend the days mostly in bed, & get up for lunch and dinner. I am being taken through a course of Monet, Manet, Cezanne & Co by my hosts who are both versed in modern painting and practise in the studio – now partly an office with Miss Maturin. Also they have a wonderful form of gramophone which plays continuously Mozart and other composers of merit and anything else you like on 10-fold discs. I am in fact having an artistic education with very agreeable tutors.' Churchill's pleasure at his first sojourn at La Pausa was evident from all his letters. '*Except for the book*,' he wrote to Clementine at the beginning of February, 'I am idle & lazy.'

A week later Churchill flew back to London. 'It was very nice having a month under your care,' he wrote to Wendy Reves the day after his return, 'and I am certainly the better for it, although I get older as the days pass.' That month he went to the Commons for the free vote on hanging, where he voted to retain the death penalty. Then, on March 1, he flew back to La Pausa. While he was there the first bound copies of Volume One of *A History of the English-Speaking Peoples* arrived from the printer, entitled 'The Birth of Britain'. He meanwhile was working with Kelly and Hodge on the fourth and final volume. Each morning they came up from their hotel to work with him, as he sat up in bed surrounded by books and papers. One morning the narrative on which they were working dealt with the Congress of Berlin of 1878. Putting his finger on the sentence mentioning 1878, Churchill told Kelly, 'I'm alive now.'

On April 6 Clementine reached Marseilles on her way back by sea from Ceylon. Churchill telephoned the ship to ask her if she would like to join him at La Pausa. 'Cannot sort and re-pack crumpled and inadequate clothes,' she telegraphed in reply, 'so am making straight for home.' Five days later, when Clementine was still at sea, Churchill unexpectedly flew back to England in order to be waiting for her when she arrived. His return coincided with an intensification of the crisis in the Middle East, with Egypt insisting on keeping the Suez Canal closed to ships bound for Israeli ports.

Pressure was being put on Israel not to react. On April 13, two days after his return from France, Churchill referred to this during a short speech to the Primrose League, of which he was Grand Master, at the Albert Hall. If, he said, Israel was to be 'dissuaded from using the life of their race to ward off the Egyptians until the Egyptians have learnt to use the Russian weapons with which they have been supplied, and the Egyptians then attack, it will become not only a matter of prudence but a measure of honour to make sure that they are not the losers by waiting'.

The Middle East was also one of the subjects to which Churchill referred in a letter which he wrote to Eisenhower on April 16. 'I am so glad that you recognise so plainly the importance of oil from the Middle East,' he told the President. 'When I was at the Admiralty in 1913 I acquired control of the Anglo-Persian Company for something like £3,000,000, and turned the large fleet I was then building to that method of propulsion. That was a good bargain if ever there was one.' Turning to the current confrontation between Egypt and Israel, Churchill wrote, 'I am sure that if we act together we shall stave off an actual war between Israel and Egypt,' and he went on to tell Eisenhower: 'I am, of course, a Zionist, and have been ever since the Balfour Declaration. I think it is a wonderful thing that this tiny colony of Jews should have become a refuge to their compatriots in all the lands where they were persecuted so cruelly, and at the same time established themselves as the most effective fighting force in the area. I am sure America would not stand by and see them overwhelmed by Russian weapons, especially if we had persuaded them to hold their hand while their chance remained.'

That April the Soviet leaders, Bulganin and Khrushchev, came to Britain; Eden invited Churchill and his wife to lunch with them at No.10 on April 17. 'I sat next to Khrushchev,' Churchill told Moran. 'The Russians were delighted to see me. Anthony told them I won the war.' The war was much on Churchill's mind three weeks later, when he flew from London to Aachen to receive the Charlemagne Prize. The ceremony took place on May 10, sixteen years to the day since he had become Prime Minister in the war against Germany. His aim in his acceptance speech was twofold; to urge upon the Germans a receptiveness to any possible relaxation in Soviet policy, and at the same time to warn them not to be too hasty in their desire for reunification. With these themes in mind, Montague Browne had drafted the speech, which Churchill then delivered. 'It was his own idea,' Montague Browne later recalled, and he added, 'It struck a chill.'

For the next three days Churchill visited British Army bases and spoke, impromptu, on six occasions. Dinner with the British troops at Celle was 'a tremendous success', Montague Browne remembered. 'The soldiers were so nice to him. It was very much his atmosphere.' On the afternoon of May 13 he flew back to Biggin Hill, escorted by fighters of 615 Squadron. 'Altogether the visit leaves a pleasant memory in my mind,' he wrote to Eisenhower, 'and I was glad to see that in spite of the march of time I can still do four days' continuous toil.'

At the end of May, Churchill returned to La Pausa. Clementine went with him, as did Sarah. In July he flew back to Germany, for a race-meeting at Düsseldorf. Shortly after his return to England, President Nasser of Egypt nationalised the Suez Canal. 'Personally, I think that Britain and France ought to act together with vigour,' Churchill wrote to Clementine on July 30, 'and if necessary with arms, while America watches Russia vigilantly. I do not think the Russians have any intentions of being involved in a major war.'

Eden had begun to prepare for a possible invasion of Egypt, and sent Churchill a considerable number of secret telegrams in order to keep him in touch with events. On July 30 he saw Churchill in the Prime Minister's room in the House of Commons and gave him more details. 'I am pleased with the policy being pursued about Suez,' Churchill wrote to Clementine on August 3. 'We are going to do our utmost. Anthony told me everything, and I even contemplated making a speech, but all went so well in the Thursday debate that this would have been an unnecessary hazard. As I am well informed, I cannot in an unprotected letter tell any secrets, but I feel you may rest assured that there will be no ground of complaints on what we try to do.' When Macmillan dined with Churchill at Chartwell two days later they discussed a possible British invasion of Egypt. 'Surely if we landed,' Macmillan told him, 'we must seek out the Egyptian forces, destroy them and bring down Nasser's Government?' Churchill then 'got out some maps', Macmillan wrote in his diary, 'and got quite excited'.

Anxious to give Eden the benefit of his advice, on August 6 Churchill set off by car from Chartwell for Chequers. Taking Doreen Pugh with him, he dictated as they drove, then stopped in a lay-by so that she could type out what he had dictated: 'The military operation seems very serious. We have a long delay when our intentions are known. The newspapers and foreign correspondents are free to publish what they choose. A censorship should be imposed. In a month it should be possible for at least 1,000 Russian & similar volunteers to take over the cream of the Egyptian aircraft and tanks. This might expose us to much more severe resistance.' Churchill added: 'The more one thinks about taking over the Canal, the less one likes it. The long causeway could be easily obstructed by a succession of mines. We should get much of the blame of stopping work, if it is to be up to the moment of our attack a smooth-running show. Cairo is Nasser's centre of power.'

Churchill had been glad to learn from Eden that armoured divisions would be used, 'properly supported by air'. When he reached Chequers he handed him the note and, after a short talk, returned to Chartwell. To Clementine, who was on holiday in Switzerland, he wrote three days later: 'The unity of Islam is remarkable. There is no doubt that Libya, to whom we have paid £5,000,000 a year, like Jordania, to whom we paid £10,000,000 or more, are whole-heartedly manifesting hostility.'

On September 12 Churchill and Clementine were together at Hyde Park Gate for their forty-eighth wedding anniversary. Five days later Churchill flew to the South of France to return to La Pausa. Clementine remained in London. For company, Lord Cherwell flew out; for work on the last volume of the History. Hodge was there, and a young Oxford don, Maurice Shock, who was helping on the Gladstone and Disraeli section. In mid-October Hodge returned to London with his wife Jane, who wrote to Churchill that when her daughters asked her where she had been, 'I shall tell them I have been visiting the world's kindest great man.'

On October 19 Churchill suffered a black-out, fell down, and lost consciousness for twenty minutes. It was another stroke. Nine days later he was well enough to return to Britain. Two days later, Israeli forces crossed into the Sinai desert, destroying the Egyptian Army and reaching within a few miles of the Suez Canal. Following a twelve-hour Anglo-French ultimatum to Egypt, insisting that an Anglo-French force be allowed to 'move temporarily' to the Suez Canal, British bombers struck at Egyptian airfields, while British troops set sail from Malta towards Port Said at the Canal's northern end.

On November 3, as the British forces were still on their way to Egypt, Churchill issued a public statement giving 'the reasons that lead me to support the Government on the Egyptian issue'. In spite of all the efforts of Britain, France and the United States, he wrote, 'the frontiers of Israel have flickered with murder and armed raids'. Egypt, 'the principal insti-gator of these incidents', had 'rejected restraint'. Israel, 'under the gravest provocation', had 'erupted against Egypt'. Britain intended 'to restore peace and order' to the Middle East, 'and I am convinced that we shall achieve our aim'. He was also 'confident that our American friends will come to realise that, not for the first time, we have acted independently for the common good'.

Churchill's message was published in the newspapers on the morning of November 5, at the very moment when British and French paratroops, in advance of the forces still on their way by sea, landed at the northern end of the Suez Canal, capturing Port Said. 'My dear Winston,' Eden wrote to him that day, 'I cannot thank you enough for your wonderful message.

It has had an enormous effect, and I am sure that in the US it will have maybe an even greater influence.' Eden added, 'These are tough days – but the alternative was a slow bleeding to death.' 'Thank you for your kind words,' Churchill replied, 'I am so glad it was a help.'

On the morning of November 6, the seaborne forces of Britain and France finally reached Port Said, landed, and advanced southward along the Canal. Later that same day, however, after a week of intense American pressure, augmented by the refusal of many Cabinet colleagues to support him, Eden agreed to a ceasefire. On the following day, November 7, Churchill was at a ceremony in Parliament Square, for the unveiling of a statue to Field Marshal Smuts. During the course of his few remarks Churchill declared, with Nasser's triumph much in mind: 'Today, among the many clamours and stresses of the world we are beset by a narrow and sterile form of the vast and sometimes magnificent force of nationalism. To Smuts, great patriot though he was, this shallow creed would have been distasteful and alien. His own qualities transcended nationality.'

On November 20 Jock Colville dined with Churchill at 28 Hyde Park Gate. The eventual withdrawal of the Anglo-French forces had been accepted by Eden as the one condition on which Eisenhower and the United States would continue to support Britain. Speaking of Eden's decision to attack Egypt, Colville asked Churchill:

'If you had been Prime Minister, would you have done this?'

'I would never have dared, and if I had dared, I would never have dared stop,' Churchill replied.

To another friend, Churchill commented with asperity, 'This would never have happened if Eisenhower had been *alive*.'

On 9 January 1957, beset by illness, and stunned by the savagery of the criticism of his actions at Suez, Eden resigned. Coming up from Chartwell to London on the following day, Churchill, then eighty-two, was asked as a matter of courtesy to Buckingham Palace, for his advice as to Eden's successor. He recommended Macmillan, as did the three other Privy Councillors who were consulted. That night Macmillan became Prime Minister; on the following night he dined at Hyde Park Gate with Churchill.

Churchill was once more about to leave England in search of the sun, his destination was again La Pausa. The last volume of his History was now almost done; Kelly, Hodge and Montague Browne were with him to check the final facts. After three weeks, work was completed. Then, on February 13, he flew back to England, for a whirl of engagements, including lunch with Macmillan, dinner at the Other Club and a quiet evening with Randolph, before flying back to La Pausa with Clementine. 'He has aged,'

Macmillan noted in his dairy, 'but is still very well-informed and misses little that goes on.'

Churchill's life at La Pausa revolved around painting; among his visitors was the Greek shipowner, Aristotle Onassis,whose conversation and personality he much enjoyed. 'The conversation centred on politics & oil,' Churchill wrote to Clementine, who had returned to England. 'I reminded him that I had bought the Anglo-Persian for the Admiralty forty or fifty years ago and made a good profit for the British Government, about 3 or 4 hundred millions! He said he knew all about it. All this reminded me of poor Hopkins – but I think we did it together. I enjoy the credit.' Hopkins, a thirty-three-year-old Treasury official in 1913, had died in 1955.

After five weeks at La Pausa, Churchill returned to England. Old age was slowly taking its toll. After dining at Chartwell in April, Macmillan noted in his diary, 'He was in good form though getting very deaf. He does not say much now, for the first time he listens. All this is rather sad – for the fight has gone out of him. He is a very charming, courteous old man.' But he was still able to speak in public on special occasions, and did so at the Primrose League annual gathering at the Albert Hall in May. He was also still keen to spend as much time as possible in the South of France; that summer he stayed for a month at La Pausa, sending his wife regular hand-written letters. He painted almost every day. He dined out. He read novels. He continued his search for a Dream Villa. But more and more often he was in a reflective mood. 'I am weary of a task which is done,' he wrote in one of his letters home that summer, '& I hope I shall not shrink when the aftermath ends. My only wish is to live peacefully out the remaining years – if years they be.'

The passage of Churchill's remaining years was inevitably marked by the sadness of the death of close friends. In July 1957 his closest friend and confidant, Lord Cherwell, died; he was seventy-one years old, the same age as Clementine. Before the war it was with 'Prof' that he had examined the weaknesses and inventions of Britain's Defence policy. It was to him that Churchill had entrusted the secrets of Britain's nuclear policy during both his wartime and peacetime premierships. He went to Oxford for Cherwell's funeral. 'As we came up the aisle of Christ Church Cathedral,' one of the mourners later recalled, 'the congregation rose spontaneously to their feet. After the service he drove to the cemetery. He walked in procession up the cemetery path. He walked beyond the path, advancing over the difficult tufts of grass, with unfaltering but ageing steps, onward to the graveside of his dear old friend.'

In October, the third volume of Churchill's history was published. The fourth volume was finished. 'I have now retired from literature,' Churchill wrote to Bernard Baruch, 'and am endeavouring to find ways of spending pleasantly the remaining years of my life.' That autumn he went with Clementine for three weeks to Beaverbrook's villa at Cap d'Ail. To a guest with whom, one luncheon, he discussed India, Churchill commented, with a twinkle in his eye, 'I am now merely a retired, and tired old reactionary.' To Montague Browne he remarked a few days later: 'I think the earth will soon be destroyed by a cobalt bomb. I think if I were the Almighty I would not recreate it, in case they destroyed Me too next time.'

From La Capponcina, Churchill returned to La Pausa. 'I have started a new picture of flowers painted indoors,' he wrote to Clementine, who had returned to England, 'and am about to get up for the purpose.' That October, while Churchill was still at La Pausa, the Soviet Union launched the first satellite. 'The satellite itself, etc, does not distress me,' he wrote to Clementine. 'The disconcerting thing is the proof of the forwardness of Soviet sciences compared to the Americans. The Prof was as usual vigilant and active. Plenty of warnings were given but we have fallen hopelessly behind in technical education & the tiny bit we have tends to disperse & scatter about America & the Dominions. This is the mechanised age, & where are we? *Quality & of the front rank* indeed we still possess. But numbers are lacking. The necessary breeding ground has failed. We must struggle on; & look to the Union with America.'

A month after returning to England, Churchill was eighty-three. Indomitable, he attended several debates in the Commons, returned in the New Year to La Pausa, painted, read novels, and continued to send Clementine handwritten accounts of his activities. But in February 1958, while at La Pausa, he caught bronchial pneumonia. When he recovered, the House of Commons sent him a message of congratulations. So did Brendan Bracken, who wrote: 'I am pleased and relieved beyond all telling by your rapid recovery. If you were to write a book on "Health without Rules" it would outsell all your other books.'

In March, while still at La Pausa, Churchill suffered two further bouts of fever. After his return to England in April the fever recurred. Two nurses were brought to Hyde Park Gate to look after him; they were to remain his constant helpers, assisted by a male nurse, Roy Howells. Such help was part of the sad reality of old age. But by the end of the month, though now visibly frail, Churchill was well enough to dine at the Other Club, and to take his seat in the Commons.

In July, rebellion in Iraq led to the murder of the King, his family, and his Prime Minister. In the Lebanon, an appeal for American help led to the arrival of American troops in Beirut. In Britain, the Government supported the American action, to which the Labour Opposition, still angered by the Suez intervention, was opposed. Churchill decided to speak on these events in the Commons, in support of the Government's attitude, and, after telling Macmillan that he would intervene in the debate, wrote out in the note form which had been his habit for more than half a century, what he would say:

'*America & Britain* must work together, reach *Unity* of purpose.'

'The complications which the problem presents can be cured if, & only *if*, they are dealt with by united forces & common principles, not merely increase of strength.'

'When we divide we lose.'

'It is not primarily a question of material force.'

'Anthony Eden & Suez. He was *right*. These recent events prove him so. It may be that his actions were *premature*.'

Churchill intended going on to say that it would be 'too easy to mock at the USA' for its action in the Lebanon; this was no time 'for trying to balance a long account' with America because of her opposition to Suez. 'The accounts are balancing themselves. What is really foolish is for two nations like England & USA to search for points of difference.' The Americans were 'in every way justified' in entering the Lebanon. 'They do not need our material or military help. If they did, I am sure they would receive it.'

Having prepared his speech notes, Churchill hesitated. He was too frail and too tired to embark upon a further Parliamentary speech. 'I spent an hour or two thinking what I would say,' he wrote to Macmillan on July 15, 'and came to the conclusion that I had nothing worth saying. I will turn up to support you in the Lobby. Forgive change of plan.'

That summer Churchill returned to La Capponcina, again the guest of Lord Beaverbrook. He had only been there a week when he learned that Brendan Bracken had died. He had known him, as he had Lord Cherwell, since the 1920s, and given him Cabinet Office in the war. He had welcomed his counsel and enjoyed his company. He at once prepared to fly back to England, but then he was told that Bracken had specifically asked for 'no memorials', and so remained in France. 'I know how much you loved Brendan,' Colville wrote, 'and what this breach with the happier past will mean to you.' Meanwhile, Beaverbrook had left La Capponcina for Canada. 'I am very glad that you liked my companionship,' Churchill wrote to him a few days later. 'It has now become very feeble, though none the less warm. The ties we formed so many years ago and strengthened in the days of war have lasted out our lifetime.'

On September 12 Churchill and Clementine celebrated their Golden Wedding at La Capponcina; Randolph and his daughter Arabella flew out to be with them. Ten days later Churchill embarked on a new venture, a cruise on the yacht *Christina*, as the guest of Onassis. The days on board the yacht were a time of tranquility, presided over by a considerate and amusing host. During the day Churchill rested or played bezique. Each evening there was a film. After ten days *Christina* reached Gibraltar, from where Churchill flew back to England. Then, on October 12, he returned by air to La Pausa. He had planned to paint, 'but,' he explained to Clementine, 'I am doubtful, inert & lazy.' Later in his letter he wrote, 'The closing days or years of life are grey and dull, but I am lucky to have you at my side.'

Concern for Clementine's health was a dominant feature of Churchill's thoughts and letters whenever she was away from him. There was concern also for the well-being of three of his children; Diana was frequently depressed and sought the help of the Samaritans; Randolph had a fierce temper and lost many friends; Sarah, like Randolph, was the victim of alcoholism, and was hounded by the press. For Churchill, the plight of his three children, each of whom was talented and affectionate, was a source of pain.

Life at La Pausa provided Churchill with distraction and even excitement; having never flown in a helicopter before, he accepted an invitation from the captain of the American Aircraft carrier *Randolph* to fly out to the carrier and inspect a naval guard of honour. The helicopter ride was 'an exhilarating incident', he told Wendy Reves, who accompanied him. Then, on November 6, he flew to Paris, to be decorated by de Gaulle with the Croix de la Libération, the highest award given to those who had served with the Free French Forces or in the Resistance. He began his speech of thanks, which he made in English, with the words, 'I have often made speeches in French, but that was wartime, and I do not wish to subject you to the ordeals of darker days.'

Back in London, Churchill went almost every day to the Commons, and again contemplated making a speech, but again decided against it. On November 30 he was eighty-four. Five weeks later he left with Clementine for Marrakech, for five weeks in the North African sun which he so enjoyed, after which he and Clementine joined *Christina* for his second cruise, along the Moroccan Coast and to the Canary Islands. Then, in March 1959, he flew back to London for a hectic four days, including a visit to Chartwell and dinner at the Other Club, before flying back to La Pausa.

At La Pausa Churchill painted. Thirty-five years earlier he had written in *Nash's Pall Mall*: 'Painting is a friend who makes no undue demands, excites no exhausting pursuits, keeps faithful pace even with feeble steps, and holds her canvas as a screen between us and the envious eyes of Time or the surly advance of Decrepitude. Happy are the painters, for they shall not be lonely. Light and colour, peace and hope, will keep them company to the end, or almost to the end, of the day.'

While Churchill was at La Pausa, Sarah, then acting in a play in Liverpool, was arrested late one night after losing her way while returning to her hotel; after a brief appearance in court the next morning she was fined £2 for drunkenness and released from custody. Some newspapers revelled in her distress. 'I think they treated her very roughly at Liverpool and roused her fiery spirit,' Churchill wrote to Clementine from La Pausa, and he added: 'I am sorry this burden rests on you & hope that staying with Mary and Christopher will relieve your troubles. Dearest, my thoughts are with you. It all falls on you. "Poor lamb!" With all my love I remain a wreck (but with its flag still flying).'

Churchill returned to London at the beginning of April. A week later he suffered another small stroke, but once more his determination overcame his infirmity; a week after the stroke he went to his constituency to speak at the meeting in which he would be renominated as its candidate. His speech was prepared for him by Montague Browne, but he read it himself, speaking for more than twenty minutes, slowly, and in a voice at times scarcely audible. It was a formidable effort. Then, as he left the platform, he turned to Montague Browne with the words, 'Now for America.'

Nothing could dissuade Churchill from crossing the Atlantic once more. 'He is determined to visit America again, so that is that!' Montague Browne told a friend. Clementine did not feel well enough or strong enough to make the journey. Churchill kept her in touch with his activities, writing on May 5 on White House stationery – he was Eisenhower's guest: 'My dearest Clemmie, Here I am. All goes well & the President is a real friend. We had a most pleasant dinner last night & I caught up my arrears of sleep in 11 (eleven) hours. I am invited to stay in bed all the morning & I am going to see Mr Dulles after luncheon.' When he did see Dulles, he was shocked by the Secretary of State's appearance; Dulles was to die of cancer two weeks later.

In several talks with Eisenhower, Churchill raised various points the Foreign Office had asked him to raise about American discrimination against British contractors. On the way to Washington airport at the end of the visit, he said to the British Ambassador, 'I hope you will give the Prime Minister a good report of my visit; and say that I behaved myself.'

Returning to Britain in mid-May, Churchill soon left again for sunnier climes, joining *Christina* for a cruise in Greek and Turkish waters, and then spending several weeks at La Pausa; for four years it had been a haven of peace and contentment, his beloved 'Pausaland'.

Frail but indomitable, on September 29 Churchill spoke in his constituency at his adoption meeting, and a few days later spoke in the neighbouring constituency of Walthamstow on behalf of the candidate there. At the General Election on October 3 the Conservatives were returned to power with an increased majority. On November 30 Churchill was eighty-five; in search of sun, he went to the Hôtel de Paris in Monte Carlo, where he and Clementine stayed in a penthouse suite with magnificent views over the Corniche and the Mediterranean. Later that year he went on another cruise on board *Christina*, to the West Indies. Returning to England, he remarked to his daughter Diana, 'My life is over, but it is not yet ended.'

A week before his eighty-sixth birthday, Churchill suffered another small stroke. On his birthday he was well enough to get up for lunch with his family. Three months later he was on his travels once more, flying to Gibraltar to rejoin *Christina* for another cruise with 'Ari' Onassis to the West Indies. During the voyage he wrote to Clementine, who had not been well enough to undertake the journey:

> *My darling Clemmie,*
> *Here is a line to keep us posted*
> *in my own handwriting – all done*
> *myself! And to tell you how*
> *much I love you: we have travelled*
> *ceaselessly over endless seas –*
> *quite smoothly for weeks on end*
> *and now here we are – within*
> *a few days of meeting Ari and his*
> *family. This is the moment for me*
> *to show you that I still possess*
> *the gift of writing & continue to use*
> *it. But I will not press it too far*
> > *Ever your devoted*
> > *W*

Christina sailed from the West Indies along the Atlantic Coast of the United States to New York. From there, Churchill flew back to London. Then, after two months at home, he returned to Monte Carlo for the rest of the winter. Painting was no longer possible for him; his pastime now was to read novels, and to be with friends and family; his twenty-one-year-old grandson Winston was among those who flew out to be with him. Churchill still managed to write several times to his wife, by hand. One of these letters read:

My dearest Clemmie,

    All is very pleasant and the days slip by. We are steadily wiping off old friendship's debts with lunches and dinners. I find it very hard to write a good letter and wonder at the rate with which my friends accomplish their daily tasks. It is amazing they can succeed so well.

    But now here I have written what is at least the expression of my love. Darling, when I was young I wrote fairly well, but now that I am played out you have my fondest love,

    Your devoted Winston

PS. I am daily astonished by the developments I see in my namesake. He is a wonderful boy. I am so glad I have got to know him.

Churchill left the South of France at the beginning of September 1961, returning to Chartwell. On October 30 he attended the State Opening of Parliament; a month later he was eighty-seven; that night he dined with Beaverbrook at Hyde Park Gate, then, on the following day, flew once more to Monte Carlo. It was there, at the start of another visit in June 1962, that he fell down, breaking his hip. A French hospital bed was made ready for him, but he told Montague Browne, 'I want to die in England.' When this comment was relayed to Downing Street, Harold Macmillan sent a Royal Air Force Comet to fly him back to London. As he was brought off the aircraft on a stretcher he gave the onlookers a V-sign.

On 1 April 1963 Clementine Churchill was seventy-eight. That day her eighty-eight-year-old husband sent her a handwritten letter:

> *My darling one,*
>   *This is only to give you*
>   *my fondest love and kisses*
>   <u>*a hundred times repeated.*</u>
>   *I am a pretty dull and*
>   *paltry scribbler; but my*
>   *stick as it writes carries my*
>   *heart along with it.*
>   *Your ever & always*
>   *W*

Later that April, Churchill returned to the Hôtel de Paris at Monte Carlo for two weeks. Then he flew back to London. As the result of considerable urging from Clementine he agreed not to stand again for Parliament. In June he returned to Monte Carlo and to *Christina*. The cruise, which was to be his last, took him to Sardinia, Corfu and Athens. Back in London in July he went once more to the House of Commons, where MPs were shocked by his frailty. Two weeks later he suffered another stroke. That October, Diana committed suicide. She was fifty-four years old and had long suffered from depression. 'The lethargy of extreme old age dulls many sensibilities,' Mary has written, 'and my father only took in slowly what I had to tell him, but then he withdrew into a great and distant silence.'

Two days before his eighty-ninth birthday, Churchill went to the House of Commons again; he was brought into the Chamber in a wheelchair. That night he dined at the Other Club. He returned twice more to the Commons, his last visit being on 27 July 1964. In mid-October he left Chartwell for London for the last time. On November 30 he was ninety. Taken to the window at Hyde Park Gate to acknowledge the cheers of the crowd, he raised his hand in the V-sign. On December 8 Bill Deakin came to lunch with him; two days later they went together to the Other Club. 'It had become increasingly difficult to awake the spark, formerly so vital,' one of the members there that evening later recalled, 'and all that could be said was that he knew where he was and was happy to be there.' A month later, on 10 January 1965, Churchill suffered a massive stroke. Two weeks later he died.

The nation mourned, showing its grief at Churchill's lying-in-state in Westminster Hall, when 300,000 people filed past his coffin, and during the State Funeral, the first given to a commoner since the death of the Duke of Wellington more than a century earlier. Men and women wept as the coffin was borne past them on a gun-carriage through the streets of London, followed by members of Churchill's family, led by Clementine and Randolph. The funeral service at St Paul's was attended by six thousand people, including six Sovereigns and fifteen Heads of State. It ended with the sounding of the Last Post and the Reveille by a trumpeter high up in the Whispering Gallery. The coffin was then taken by barge along the Thames to Waterloo Station, and on by train, to the parish church at Bladon, where Churchill was buried next to his parents and his brother Jack, within sight of his birthplace, Blenheim Palace.

In her message to Parliament, the Queen called Churchill 'a national hero'. Attlee, his wartime deputy and post-war successor, described him as 'the greatest Englishman of our time – I think the greatest citizen of the world of our time'. At the next meeting of the Other Club, which Churchill had hoped to attend, and which was the only engagement marked on his February calendar, Macmillan told those present, 'Our finest hour and our greatest moment came from our work with him.' Lord Chandos, the former Oliver Lyttelton, recalled Churchill's qualities as a statesman: 'He enjoyed a conflict of ideas, but not a conflict between people. His powers were those of imagination, experience, and magnanimity. Perhaps not enough has been made of his magnanimity. He saw man as a noble and not as a mean creature. The only people he never forgave were those, who, in the words he so often used, "fell beneath the level of events".'

Each generation will make its own assessment of Churchill's career. 'It is difficult to overtake slander,' he himself had written in February 1942, 'but the truth is very powerful too.' As the years pass and the historical record is studied without malice, Churchill's actions and aims will be seen to have been humane and far-sighted. His patriotism, his sense of fair play, his belief in democracy, and his hopes for the human race, were matched by formidable powers of work and thought, vision and foresight. His path was often beset by controversy, disappointment and abuse, but these never deflected him from his sense of duty and his faith in the British people.

'It is hardly in the nature of things,' Churchill's daughter Mary had written to her father in 1951, 'that your descendants should inherit your genius – but I earnestly hope they may share in some way the qualities of your heart.' Four years later Randolph had written to him: 'Power must pass and vanish. Glory, which is achieved through a just exercise of power – which itself is accumulated by genius, toil, courage and self-sacrifice – alone remains. Your glory is enshrined for ever on the unperishable plinth of your achievement; and can never be destroyed or tarnished. It will flow with the centuries.' Such was a son's encouragement at the time of his father's final resignation. From Mary had come further words of solace nine years later, when his life's great impulses were at last fading. 'In addition to all the feelings a daughter has for a loving, generous father,' she wrote, 'I owe you what every Englishman, woman & child does – Liberty itself.'

MAPS

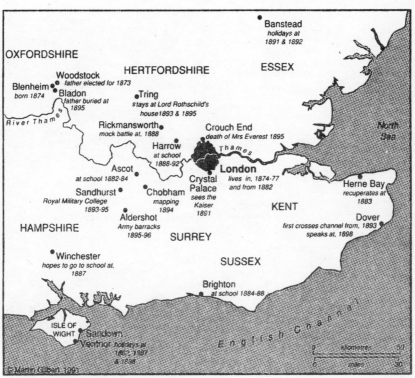

1. Southern England, 1874–97

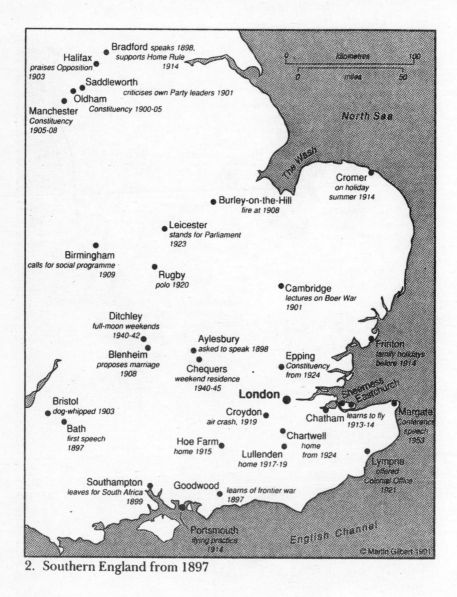

Bradford speaks 1898,
supports Home Rule
1914

Halifax
praises Opposition
1903

Saddleworth
criticises own Party leaders 1901

Oldham
Constituency 1900-05

Manchester
Constituency
1905-08

Kilometres
0   100

miles
0   50

North Sea

The Wash

Cromer
on holiday
summer 1914

Burley-on-the-Hill
fire at 1908

Leicester
stands for Parliament
1923

Birmingham
calls for social programme
1909

Rugby
polo 1920

Cambridge
lectures on Boer War
1901

Ditchley
full-moon weekends
1940-42

Aylesbury
asked to speak 1898

Epping
Constituency
from 1924

Frinton
family holidays
before 1914

Blenheim
proposes marriage
1908

Chequers
weekend residence
1940-45

London

Sheerness
Eastchurch

Bristol
dog-whipped 1903

Croydon
air crash, 1919

Chatham

learns to fly
1913-14

Margate
Conference
speech
1953

Bath
first speech
1897

Hoe Farm
home 1915

Chartwell
home
from 1924

Lullenden
home 1917-19

Lympne
offered
Colonial Office
1921

Southampton
leaves for South Africa
1899

Goodwood

learns of frontier war
1897

Portsmouth
flying practice
1914

English Channel

© Martin Gilbert 1991

2. Southern England from 1897

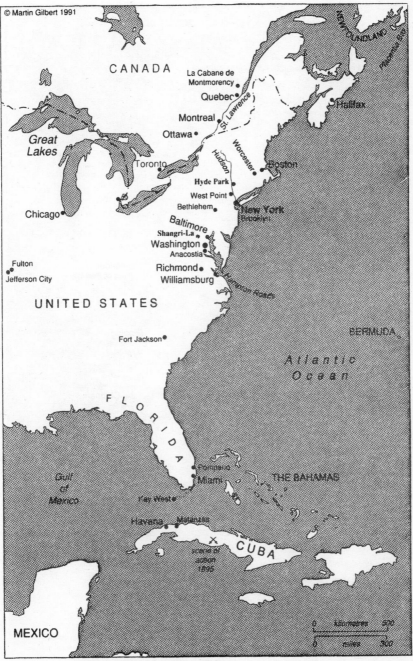

© Martin Gilbert 1991

NEWFOUNDLAND

Placentia Bay

CANADA

La Cabane de
Montmorency

Quebec

Halifax

Montreal

St. Lawrence

Ottawa

Great
Lakes

Worcester

Toronto

Hudson

Boston

Hyde Park

West Point

Bethlehem

Chicago

New York

Brooklyn

Baltimore

Shangri-La

Washington

Anacostia

Fulton

Richmond

Jefferson City

Williamsburg

Hampton Roads

UNITED STATES

Fort Jackson

BERMUDA

Atlantic
Ocean

FLORIDA

Gulf
of
Mexico

Pompano

Miami

THE BAHAMAS

Key West

Havana

Matanzas

scene of
action
1895

CUBA

MEXICO

kilometres   500

miles   300

3. Visits to the New World, 1895–1961

4. Ireland

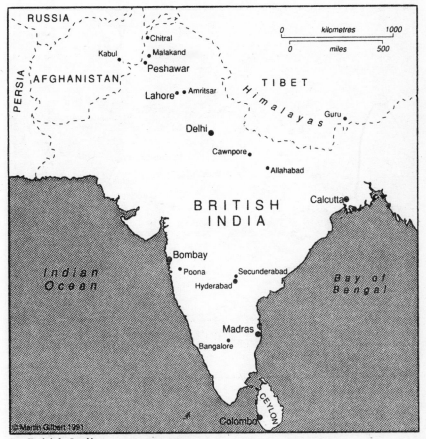

5. British India

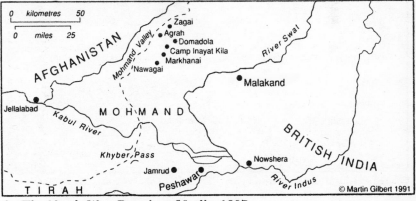

6. The North-West Frontier of India, 1897

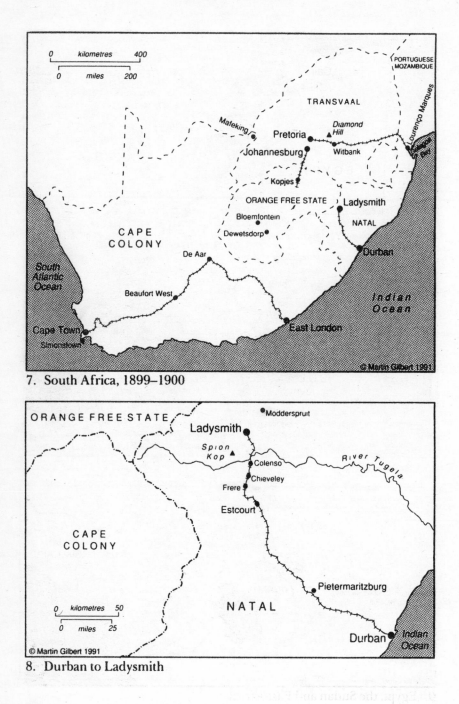

7. South Africa, 1899–1900

8. Durban to Ladysmith

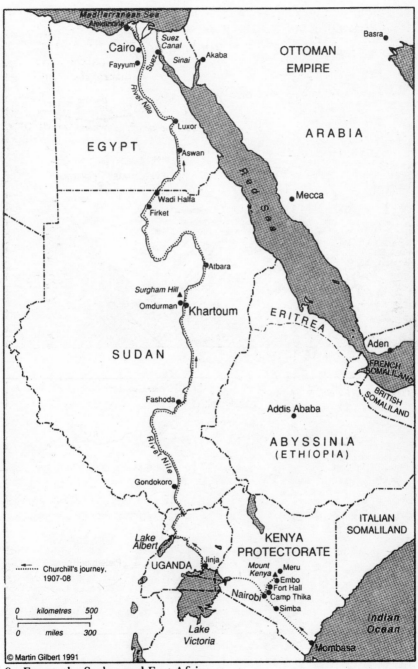

9. **Egypt, the Sudan and East Africa**

10. Europe, 1914–18

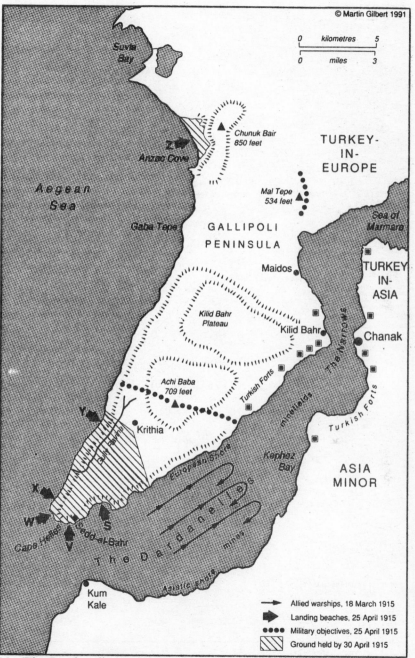

© Martin Gilbert 1991

| 0 | kilometres | 5 |
| 0 | miles | 3 |

Suvla Bay

Chunuk Bair
850 feet

Z
Anzac Cove

TURKEY-
IN-
EUROPE

Aegean
Sea

Mal Tepe
534 feet

Gaba Tepe

GALLIPOLI
PENINSULA

Sea of
Marmara

Maidos

TURKEY
IN-
ASIA

Kilid Bahr
Plateau

Kilid Bahr

Chanak

Turkish Forts

The Narrows

Achi Baba
709 feet

Turkish Forts

Y

Krithia

minefields

Gully Ravine

European Shore

Kepnez
Bay

Turkish Forts

X

ASIA
MINOR

W

S

Cape Helles
Sedd-el-Bahr
V

The Dardanelles

mines

Asiatic Shore

Kum
Kale

→ Allied warships, 18 March 1915
➡ Landing beaches, 25 April 1915
●●●● Military objectives, 25 April 1915
▨ Ground held by 30 April 1915

11. The Dardanelles and Gallipoli, 1915

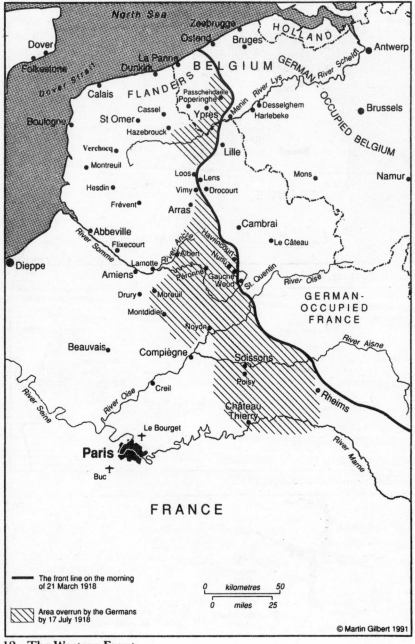

12. The Western Front

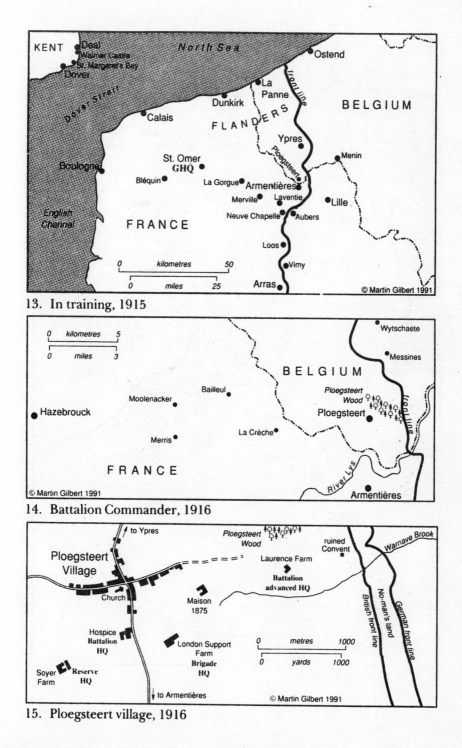

13. In training, 1915

14. Battalion Commander, 1916

15. Ploegsteert village, 1916

16. Russia: the intervention, 1919–20

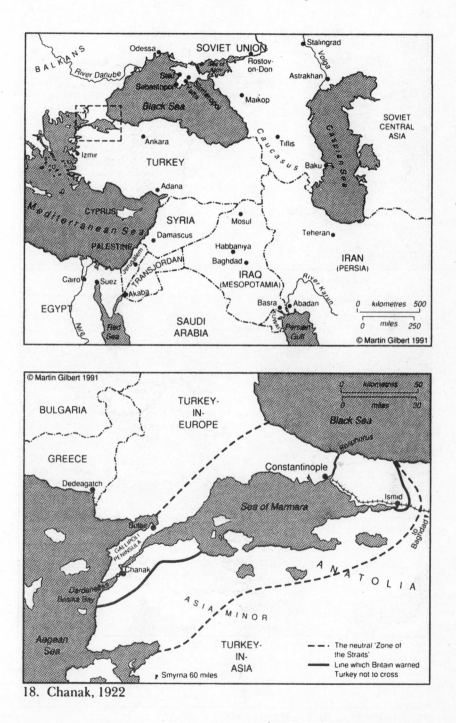

18. Chanak, 1922

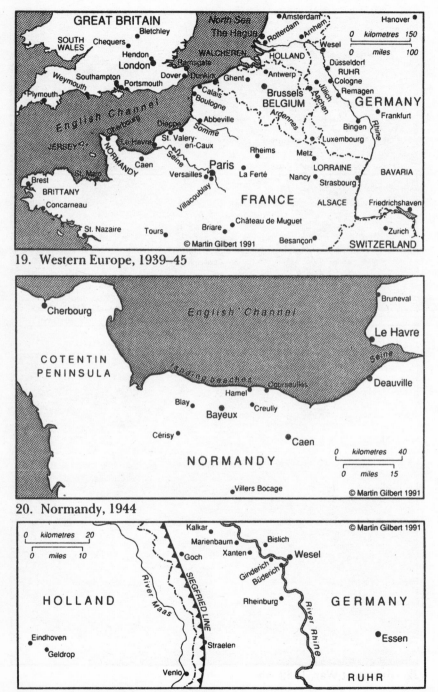

19. Western Europe, 1939–45

20. Normandy, 1944

21. Crossing the Rhine, March 1945

22. Britain at War, 1939–45

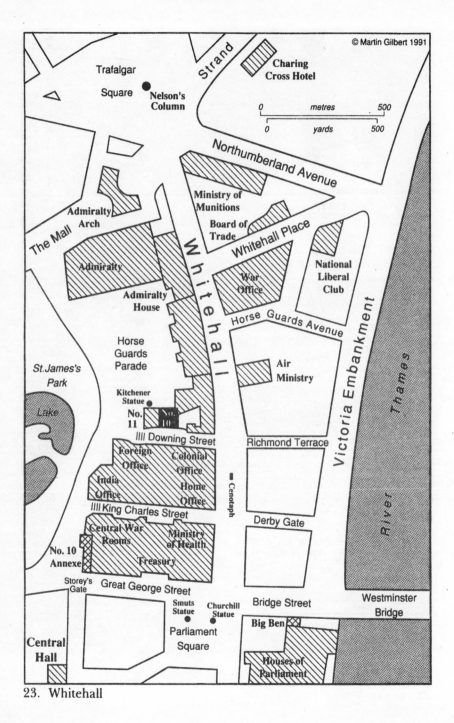

23. Whitehall

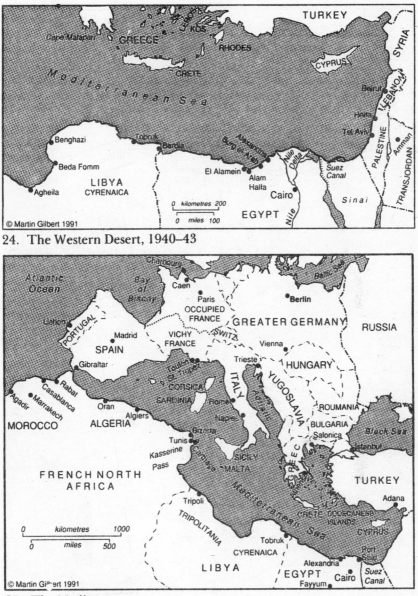

24. The Western Desert, 1940–43

25. The Mediterranean

26. Central and Eastern Europe, and Italy, 1939–45

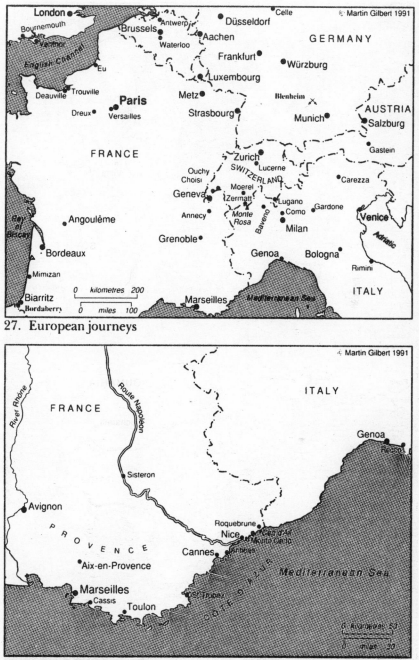

27. **European journeys**

28. **South of France**

Index

Compiled by the author

614; 'has had a good run', 769; of tyranny, 884; 'has its place', 890

Arabia: and the Dardanelles, 305

Arabs: in Palestine, 432, 435, 436, 437; need for 'appeasing' sentiment of, 432; and Zionism, 435; to veto Jewish immigration (after 1944), 614; and Palestine, 803; and a Middle East Federation (1945), 825; and Israel, 903

arbitration: Churchill offers 'permanent machinery' for (1908), 195, 199; Churchill presides over (1908), 199; to be 'permanent' and 'impartial', 203; Churchill active in (1909), 205; Churchill offers, in South Wales (1910), 220; Churchill favours, during Liverpool dock strike (1911), 231

Archangel: a possible Churchill mission to (1915), 328; British troops at 1919), 408; American troops leave (1919), 414; British troops leave (1919), 416; Polish troops evacuated from (1919), 416 British aid reaches (1941), 708

Arctic Ocean: British help to Russia in (1941), 703; convoys to Russia through, 708, 720, 724, 725, 729, 730, 731

Ardennes (Belgium): Churchill's concern for (August 1939), 618; battle in (1944), 809, 811, 813, 815

Argentina: neutral, 761

Aristophanes: Churchill in play by, 15

Armageddon: two and a half years of, 367 and the First World War, 506

Armenians: massacre of, 327

Armentières: Churchill gives his officers a farewell lunch at (1916), 360; a German mustard-gas attack on (1918), 390

armistice: Germany accepts terms of (1918), 400

armoured train: Churchill travels to Colenso on, 108; and Churchill's efforts, under fire, to clear the line, 110; Churchill's second journey on, 110; derailed, 110; becomes 'famous in the story of the war', 126; Churchill passes wreck of (1900), 126;

Arms and the Man (Shaw), 795

Army General Staff: Churchill criticises expenditure on (1905), 170

Army League: criticisms of Churchill by, 141

Arnhem: parachute landing at (1944), 793, 794

Arnold-Forster, Hugh: Churchill criticises, 170; wishes Churchill well, 173

Arras: Churchill visits front-line near (1915), 335; battle of (1917), 371; Churchill in conference at (1917), 378; Churchill visits (1940), 631

Ascot: Churchill boards at, 3

Ascot races: Churchill backs some winners at, 44

Ascroft, Robert: and Churchill's first Parliamentary candidature (1899), 103, 104; dies, 104

Ashley, Maurice: Churchill's research assistant, 491, 508, 524

Ashton-under-Lyne: Conservatives of, asks Churchill to stand for (1924), 462

Asia: submission of 'most ferocious savages' in (1898), 87; Islam 'triumphant' in, 345

Asiatics: and 'liberty', 163

Asquith, H.H.: Churchill meets (1893), 36; Lord Randolph's attack on, 41; at Tring with Churchill, 61; pays 'great attention' to what Churchill says (1899), 104; and Churchill's 'good fight' at Oldham (1899), 105; hears Churchill's maiden speech, 139; Churchill dines with (1901), 144; presides for Churchill (1901), 144; understands Churchill's 'point of view', 148; not in Chamber at crucial moment (1903), 155; and Churchill's move towards the Liberals, 161; becomes Chancellor of the Exchequer, 174; becomes Prime Minister, 193; and the Dreadnought controversy, 201; congratulates Churchill on arbitration, 205; his praise (1910), 211; hopes Churchill's association of Crown and Commons may be ignored, 217; and the Battle of Downing Street (1910), 221; affected by drink, 226; and the constitutional crisis (1911), 230; and Agadir (1911), 234; on *Enchantress* with his wife Margot and daughter Violet, 249; and the Navy Estimates crisis (1914), 254; and the coming of war in 1914, 265, 266, 268, 269, 271, 272; and the opening months of war, 279, 280; 'almost inclined to shiver', 281; 'leans on you',

INDEX   1035

Churchill, 20

Markhanai (North-West Frontier): Churchill in action near (1897), 76

Marlborough, 1st Duke of: Churchill's ancestor, 1; Churchill contemplates writing a biography of (1898), 87; recalled, 334, 579; and destiny, 549

Marlborough, 7th Duke of: Churchill's grandfather, 1; dies, 5

Marlborough, 8th Duke of: dies, 33

Marlborough, 9th Duke of (Sunny): succeeds to Dukedom, 33; Churchill's friendship with, 42, 89; his advice, 91; Churchill rides towards Pretoria with (1900), 127; at marriage of Churchill's mother, 134; rents Churchill a bachelor flat (1901), 135; forecasts Churchill's 'severance from the Tory Party' (1903), 156; urges Churchill to propose to Miss Hozier, 198; urges Churchill to give up learning to fly, 248; dies, 529

Marlborough, Dowager Duchess of (Fanny): Churchill's grandmother, 16, 38, 41, 47, 48; and her grandson 'beginning to be ambitious', 24; advice from, 25; encouragement from, 26; Churchill confides in, 79; dies, 104

Marlborough, Dowager Duchess of (Lily): Churchill's aunt, 35, 36, 37, 51, 52, 72

Marlborough, Duchess of (Consuelo): 'very kind to me', 42; for subsequent index entry see Balsan, Consuelo

Marlborough, His Life and Times (Winston S. Churchill): genesis of, 488; work on, 491, 502, 508, 509, 512, 524, 532, 557, 579, 580, 586, 593; payment for, 494; published (from 1933), 522, 533, 563

Marmara, Sea of: and the Dardanelles, 295, 300; and the Gallipoli landings, 311; and Stalin, 853

Marne, Battle of the (1914), 280

Marrakech: Churchill stays at (1935), 548; Churchill takes Roosevelt to (1943), 738; Churchill recuperates at (1943-44), 765; Churchill's return visits to 878, 894, 954

Marsh, Edward: joins Churchill (1905), 174; accompanies Churchill, 175, 186; joins Churchill at Board of Trade, 197; sends Churchill work, to Athens, 218; with Churchill at the Admiralty, 290; and Churchill's first steps as a

painter, 323; 'blinking back his tears', 329; with Churchill at the Ministry of Munitions (1917-18), 377; with Churchill in France (1917-18), 378, 399; Churchill's continuing friendship with, 502; helps Churchill on his war memoirs (1947), 878

Marshall, General George C.: Churchill's talks with (1941), 714; offers to help (June 1942), 723; and the Cherbourg plan, 725; and Churchill's hopes for the battle in Italy, 771

Marston, Lettice: Churchill's secretary, 871, 872

Martin, (Sir) John: his recollections, 673; with Churchill at Carthage (1943), 764; and the surrender of Germany (1945), 839; and the 'common people', 848

Martin, Flight-Lieutenant Trevor: flies with Churchill near Rhine (March 1945), 832

Martini-Henry rifle: Churchill fires (1888), 19

Martyrdom of Man (Winwood Reade): Churchill reads, 67

Marx, Karl: Churchill's parody of (1945), 820

Mary, Queen: coronation of (1911), 228

Masaryk, Jan Garrigue: Churchill's encouragement to (1945), 827

Massachusetts Institute of Technology (MIT) (Boston): Churchill's speech at (1949), 884

Masterton-Smith, James: with Churchill at the Admiralty, 290; and Fisher's resignation, 315; and Churchill's record at the Admiralty, 323; and Churchill's qualities, 329; with Churchill at Munitions (1917-18), 377

Matabeleland: Churchill seeks action in (1896), 62, 63

Matsuoka, Yosuke: Churchill's message to (1941), 693

Maturin, Gillian: Churchill's secretary, 944, 946

Maudling, Reginald: helps Churchill (1950), 888

Maurois, André: and Churchill's war on lice (1916), 341; Churchill's request to (1916), 346

Maxwell, Sir Alexander: helps Churchill, 563

Mayer, René: and Churchill wish for talks

slander: 'difficult to overtake', 959
slavery: a 'terminological inexactitude', 178
Slovakia: independent (1939), 611
Smethurst, Samuel: Churchill confides in (1902), 150, 151, 162
Smillie, Bob: Churchill's work with, 196
Smith, F.E. (later Earl of Birkenhead): Churchill's friendship with (from 1906), 185, 198, 227, 318, 334, 339, 346, and Ulster, 250; urges Churchill to give up learning to fly, 253; and the coming of war in 1914, 269, 270; and the political crisis of December 1916, 368; with Churchill on armistice night (1918), 402; his friendship, 426; and India, 488; dies (1929), 496; his dictum recalled, 511
Smolensk: Soviet forces liberate (1943), 755
Smuts, General: his encouragement, 690; Churchill confides his fears to (1943), 753
Smyrna: Churchill's expedition from (1910), 218; Greeks driven back to (1922), 450
Snowden, Ethel: and Churchill's character, 887
Snowden, Philip: and the Gold Standard, 469, 470; and 'election bribery', 489; and the financial crisis of 1931, 502
Soames, Christopher: marries Mary Churchill (1947), 875; enters Parliament (1950), 889; and Churchill's continuing search for a summit (1953-55), 920; Churchill speaks for, 943
Soames, Jeremy: christened, 907
social reform: Churchill's appeal for (1900), 124; and the 'true happiness' of nations, 172; Churchill's philosophy of, 183; Churchill stresses need for (1907), 188; Churchill immersed in (1925), 470
social security: plans for (1945), 845
Socialism: and the Conservative Party, 462; Churchill warns of perils of (1945), 846; Churchill's further warnings (1947), 878; 'the community in bonds' (Lloyd George), 889; contrasted with Conservatism, 897
'socialistic': a Churchill comment criticised as, 226
Sofia: 'in the Soviet sphere' (1946), 866

Soissons: Churchill watches artillery in action at (1914), 281
soldiering: 'not my metier', 55
soldiers: and 'pseudo-soldiers', 205
solitary confinement: reform of, 212
Solomon Islands: Japanese land on (1942), 720
Somervell, Robert: an inspiring teacher (1889), 24
Somerville, Admiral: opens fire (1940), 667
Somme: battle of (1916), 362, Members of Parliament serve at, 369; recalled, 370, 773
South Africa: Churchill leaves for (1899), 106; Churchill offers to withdraw altogether from, 114; Churchill leaves, 131; Churchill's search for a settlement in, 176; and the native franchise, 182; Churchill inspects troops from (1918), 384
South Africa Medal, 62
South African Light Horse: Churchill accepts commission in (1900), 121
South African War: many of Churchill's friends killed in, 42
South Russia: British troops in (1919), 405, 410; and the anti-Bolshevik Russians (1919), 408; possible landing at (1943), 733; proposed landing in (1944), 751, 780, landing on (1944), 787
South Wales: troops sent to, then de-trained (1910), 219; bombed (1940), 668
Southampton: Churchill leaves for South Africa from (1899), 106; Churchill returns to (1900), 133; Churchill to sail from (1940), 662; Churchill watches cross-Channel preparations at (1944), 775
Southport: electors of, seek Churchill as their candidate (1900), 122
Soviet Union: Churchill prepared 'to make peace with' (1920), 420; and a British peace initiative (1920), 421; incitement by (1920), 426 Churchill speaks against loan to (1924), 462; fear of a 'ferocious deluge' from, 507; wants to be 'left alone' (1935), 541; to be a 'friend' of a United Europe, pact with France (1935), 543; and collective security, 553, a potential ally, 554; and Czechoslovakia (1938), 594; call for an

Alliance with (1939), 614; negotiations with (1939), 614; not 'gained' for the Allies, 617; advances into Poland (September 1939), 626; invades Finland (November 1939), 630; and Anglo-French help for Finland (1940), 633; signs peace with Finland (March 1940), 635; invaded by Germany (June 1941), 701; British aid to (1941-45), 704; American aid for, 705; occupies northern Persia, 706; battles in (November-December 1941), 709; convoys to, 720; and the post-war world, 731; Churchill's fears of European domination by, 743; convoys to, resumed, 755; political pressure from (1943-45), 756; and the postwar world, 768; and the campaign in Italy (1944), 771; and Roumania, 772; and Greece, 773; and Poland, 784, 785, 837; Churchill's fear of, 826, 832, 835; Britain might go 'to the verge of war with' (1945), 828; and Yugoslavia, 835; Churchill's support for (since 1941), 835; and Denmark (1945), 839; a Victory Day complaint from, 841; a possible 'understanding' with, 844; continued demand for bases by, 860; and an Anglo-American alliance, 861; and the mission of the Missouri (1946), 865; Churchill's words of welcome to (1946), 866; need for a 'settlement' with (1946), 866; leaves Persia, 869; Churchill calls for an understanding with (1946-51), 872, 879, 881, 884; restraints on, 874; Churchill's advice to (1948), 882; peace with, through 'superior force', 883; Churchill critical of machine-tool sales to (1950), 892; and oil, 895; Churchill's call for an understanding with (1946-51), 899; to be told the 'true facts', 903; a warning signal to, 904; Churchill seeks talks with (1952-55), 909, 910, 911, 912, 915, 918, 920, 921, 922, 923, 924, 925, 926, 931, 932, 934, 936, 937; and the prospect of atomic war, 912; possesses atom bomb (1953), 916; discussed at Bermuda (1953), 920; a 'provocative gesture' to (1954), 922; the first postwar summit with (1955), 944; and the Suez Crisis (1956), 948; and the first satellite (1957), 952

Soyer Farm: Churchill's reserve billet at (1916), 348, 350, 355

Spain: and Cuba (1895), 58; and the Agadir crisis (1911), 234; 'spectators' in (1940), 664

Spanish Armada (1688): recalled, 778

Spanish Red Cross (military decoration): Churchill receives (1895), 60

Spanish troops: and the 'art of retreat', 60

Spears, Captain Edward Louis: Churchill befriends (1915), 335; Churchill confides in, 339; campaigns at Dundee (1922), 455; Churchill confides in (1922), 457; accompanies Churchill (August 1939), 618; and the fall of France (1940), 654; with Churchill (1940), 658; at Tours, 660; and de Gaulle, 766

Special Operations Executive S.O.E.: established (1940), 668; in Belgrade (1941), 693

Spectator: finds Churchill's criticism of the judges 'deeply deplorable', 228; and the effect of the Abdication crisis on Churchill, 569

Spencer, 1st Earl: Churchill's ancestor, 1

Spender, J.A.: Churchill stresses need for social reform to, 188

Spier, Eugen: his recollection (of 1937), 578

Spion Kop, battle of (1900): 'terrible' scenes on, 122

Spithead: Churchill visits (1912), 246

Split (Dalmatia): and Tito, 806

St Andrews: Churchill lectures at (1901), 144

St George's School, Ascot (1882-4): Churchill boards at, 3, 5, 6

St Helena, 296

St Margaret's Bay (Kent): a brief respite at (1918), 396

St Margaret's, Westminster: Churchill married at (1908), 200

St Nazaire: *Lancastria* sunk at (1940), 663; Germans hold (September 1944), 792

St Omer: Churchill's visits to (1915-18), 331, 334, 335, 336, 337, 341, 346, 373, 378

St Paul's Cathedral: Churchill's funeral at (1965), 958

St Valery-en-Caux: British driven back to (1940), 657, 659

Stalin, Joseph: Churchill sends secret information to (from April 1941), 695,